www.wadsworth.com

www.wadsworth.com is the World Wide Website for Thomson Wadsworth and is your direct source to dozens of online resources.

At *www.wadsworth.com* you can find out about supplements, demonstration software, and student resources. You can also send e-mail to many of our authors and preview new publications and exciting new technologies.

www.wadsworth.com
Changing the way the world learns®

HUMAN DEVELOPMENT

A Life-Span View

FOURTH EDITION

—

ROBERT V. KAIL
Purdue University

JOHN C. CAVANAUGH
University of West Florida

THOMSON™

WADSWORTH

Australia • Brazil • Canada • Mexico • Singapore • Spain
United Kingdom • United States

THOMSON

WADSWORTH

Human Development: A Life-Span View, **Fourth Edition**
Robert V. Kail, John C. Cavanaugh

Publisher: Vicki Knight
Executive Editor: Michele Sordi
Development Editor: Kristin Makarewycz
Assistant Editor: Jennifer Keever
Senior Editorial Assistant: Jessica Kim
Technology Project Manager: Amanda Kaufmann
Marketing Manager: Dory Schaeffer
Marketing Assistant: Natasha Coats
Marketing Communications Manager: Kelley McAllister
Project Manager, Editorial Production: Mary Noel
Creative Director: Rob Hugel
Art Director: Vernon Boes
Print Buyer: Doreen Suruki

Permissions Editor: Kiely Sisk
Production Service: Gretchen Otto, G & S Book Services
Text Designer: John Walker Design
Photo Researcher: Roman Barnes
Copy Editor: Kay Mikel
Cover Designer: John Walker Design
Cover Images (clockwise from top left): Seiya Kawamoto/ Getty Images; Nancy Honey/Getty Images; Ken Weingart/Getty Images; Getty Images; John Terrence Turner/Getty Images; Tim Hall/ Getty Images
Compositor: G & S Book Services
Printer: Transcontinental Printing/Interglobe

Printed in Canada
2 3 4 5 6 7 09 08 07

For more information about our products, contact us at:
Thomson Learning Academic Resource Center
1-800-423-0563

For permission to use material from this text or product, submit a request online at http://www.thomsonrights.com. Any additional questions about permissions can be submitted by e-mail to thomsonrights@thomson.com.

Thomson Higher Education
10 Davis Drive
Belmont, CA 94002-3098
USA

Library of Congress Control Number: 2005933769

SE ISBN-13: 978-0-495-09304-6
SE ISBN-10: 0-495-09304-1

LL ISBN-13: 978-0-495-13067-3
LL ISBN-10: 0-495-13067-2

ISE ISBN-13: 978-0-495-13057-4
ISE ISBN-10: 0-495-13057-5

Brief Contents

1 The Study of Human Development 1

PART I
PRENATAL DEVELOPMENT, INFANCY, AND EARLY CHILDHOOD

2 Biological Foundations: Heredity, Prenatal Development, and Birth 45

3 Tools for Exploring the World: Physical, Perceptual, and Motor Development 87

4 The Emergence of Thought and Language: Cognitive Development in Infancy and Early Childhood 131

5 Entering the Social World: Socioemotional Development in Infancy and Early Childhood 177

PART II
SCHOOL-AGE CHILDREN AND ADOLESCENTS

6 Off to School: Cognitive and Physical Development in Middle Childhood 219

7 Expanding Social Horizons: Socioemotional Development in Middle Childhood 265

8 Rites of Passage: Physical and Cognitive Development in Adolescence 307

9 Moving Into the Adult Social World: Socioemotional Development in Adolescence 339

PART III
YOUNG AND MIDDLE ADULTHOOD

10 Becoming an Adult: Physical, Cognitive, and Personality Development 377

11 Being With Others: Forming Relationships in Young and Middle Adulthood 415

12 Work and Leisure: Occupational and Lifestyle Issues in Young and Middle Adulthood 451

13 Making It in Midlife: The Unique Challenges of Middle Adulthood 489

PART IV
LATE ADULTHOOD

14 The Personal Context of Later Life: Physical, Cognitive, and Mental Health Issues 535

15 Social Aspects of Later Life: Psychosocial, Retirement, Relationship, and Societal Issues 577

16 The Final Passage: Dying and Bereavement 617

Contents

Preface   xiii
About the Authors   xxiii

CHAPTER **1**

The Study of Human Development   1

1.1 How to Use This Book   2
Learning and Study Aids   2
Terminology   3
Organization   4

1.2 Thinking About Development   5
Recurring Issues in Human Development   5
Basic Forces in Human Development: The
    Biopsychosocial Framework   7

1.3 Developmental Theories   11
Psychodynamic Theory   11
Learning Theory   14
Cognitive-Developmental Theory   15
The Ecological and Systems Approach   18
Life-Span Perspective, Selective Optimization With
    Compensation, and Life Course Perspective   19
■ REAL PEOPLE: APPLYING HUMAN
    DEVELOPMENT: Sarah and Elizabeth
    Delany   23
The Big Picture   24

1.4 Doing Developmental Research   24
Measurement in Human Development Research   25
General Designs for Research   28
Designs for Studying Development   30
■ SPOTLIGHT ON RESEARCH: Stability
    and Change in Life Satisfaction   31
Integrating Findings From Different Studies   34
Conducting Research Ethically   34
Communicating Research Results   35
Applying Research Results: Social Policy   36
■ CURRENT CONTROVERSIES: Stem Cell
    Research   37
Putting It All Together   38
Summary   38
Key Terms   40
Learn More About It   40

PART **I**

PRENATAL DEVELOPMENT, INFANCY, AND EARLY CHILDHOOD

CHAPTER **2**

Biological Foundations   45
Heredity, Prenatal Development, and Birth

**2.1 In the Beginning: 23 Pairs
    of Chromosomes   46**
Mechanisms of Heredity   46
Genetic Disorders   49
Heredity, Environment, and Development   51
■ REAL PEOPLE: APPLYING HUMAN
    DEVELOPMENT: Ben and Matt Pick Their
    Niches   55

2.2 From Conception to Birth   57
Period of the Zygote (Weeks 1–2)   57
■ CURRENT CONTROVERSIES: Conception
    in the 21st Century   57
Period of the Embryo (Weeks 3–8)   59
Period of the Fetus (Weeks 9–38)   61

2.3 Influences on Prenatal Development   63
General Risk Factors   63
Teratogens: Drugs, Diseases, and Environmental
    Hazards   65
■ SPOTLIGHT ON RESEARCH: Impact of Prenatal
    Exposure to PCBs on Cognitive Functioning   68
How Teratogens Influence Prenatal Development   69
Prenatal Diagnosis and Treatment   72

2.4 Labor and Delivery   75
Stages of Labor   75
Approaches to Childbirth   76
Adjusting to Parenthood   77
Birth Complications   78
Infant Mortality   80
Putting It All Together   82
Summary   82
Key Terms   84
Learn More About It   84

CHAPTER 3
Tools for Exploring the World   87
Physical, Perceptual, and Motor Development

3.1   The Newborn   88
The Newborn's Reflexes   88
Assessing the Newborn   89
The Newborn's States   90
Temperament   93

3.2   Physical Development   96
Growth of the Body   96
The Emerging Nervous System   100

3.3   Moving and Grasping—Early Motor Skills   105
Locomotion   106
Fine-Motor Skills   109

3.4   Coming to Know the World: Perception   112
Smell, Taste, and Touch   112
Hearing   113
Seeing   114
■ SPOTLIGHT ON RESEARCH: How Infants Become Face Experts   120
Integrating Sensory Information   121

3.5   Becoming Self-Aware   122
Origins of Self-Concept   123
Theory of Mind   123
■ REAL PEOPLE: APPLYING HUMAN DEVELOPMENT: "Seeing Is Believing . . ." for 3-Year-Olds   125
Putting It All Together   126
Summary   126
Key Terms   128
Learn More About It   128

CHAPTER 4
The Emergence of Thought and Language   131
Cognitive Development in Infancy and Early Childhood

4.1   The Onset of Thinking: Piaget's Account   132
Basic Principles of Cognitive Development   132
Sensorimotor Thinking   134
Preoperational Thinking   135
■ REAL PEOPLE: APPLYING HUMAN DEVELOPMENT: Christine, Egocentrism, and Animism   136
■ SPOTLIGHT ON RESEARCH: Finding Toys in a Shrunken Room   139
Evaluating Piaget's Theory   140
Extending Piaget's Account: Children's Naive Theories   143

4.2   Information Processing During Infancy and Early Childhood   147
General Principles of Information Processing   147
Attention   147
Learning   148
Memory   149
■ CURRENT CONTROVERSIES: Preschoolers on the Witness Stand   151
Learning Number Skills   152

4.3   Mind and Culture: Vygotsky's Theory   154
The Zone of Proximal Development   155
Scaffolding   155
Private Speech   156

4.4   Language   157
The Road to Speech   157
First Words and Many More   161
Speaking in Sentences: Grammatical Development   167
Communicating With Others   169
Putting It All Together   172
Summary   172
Key Terms   174
Learn More About It   175

CHAPTER 5
Entering the Social World   177
Socioemotional Development in Infancy and Early Childhood

5.1   Beginnings: Trust and Attachment   178
Erikson's Stages of Early Psychosocial Development   178
The Growth of Attachment   179
What Determines Quality of Attachment?   183
Attachment, Work, and Alternative Caregiving   184
■ REAL PEOPLE: APPLYING HUMAN DEVELOPMENT: Lois, Bill, and Sarah   186

5.2   Emerging Emotions   187
Experiencing and Expressing Emotions   187
Recognizing and Using Others' Emotions   190
Regulating Emotions   191

5.3   Interacting With Others   193
The Joys of Play   193
Helping Others   197
■ SPOTLIGHT ON RESEARCH: Are Empathic Children More Likely to Help?   198

5.4   Gender Roles and Gender Identity   202
Images of Men and Women: Facts and Fantasy   202
Gender Typing   204
Biological Influences   207
Evolving Gender Roles   208
Putting It All Together   209
Summary   210

Key Terms 212
Learn More About It 212

PART II

SCHOOL-AGE CHILDREN AND ADOLESCENTS

CHAPTER 6

Off to School 219
Cognitive and Physical Development in Middle Childhood

6.1 **Cognitive Development 220**
More Sophisticated Thinking: Piaget's Version 220
■ REAL PEOPLE: APPLYING HUMAN DEVELOPMENT: Combinatorial Reasoning Goes to the Races 221
Information-Processing Strategies for Learning and Remembering 223

6.2 **Aptitudes for School 226**
Theories of Intelligence 226
Binet and the Development of Intelligence Testing 230
Do Tests Work? 231
Hereditary and Environmental Factors 232
The Impact of Ethnicity and Socioeconomic Status 235

6.3 **Special Children, Special Needs 238**
Gifted and Creative Children 238
Children With Mental Retardation 239
Children With Learning Disabilities 240
■ SPOTLIGHT ON RESEARCH: Improving Reading Skill in Children With Reading Disability 241
Attention-Deficit Hyperactivity Disorder 242

6.4 **Academic Skills 244**
Reading 244
Writing 247
Math Skills 249
■ REAL PEOPLE: APPLYING HUMAN DEVELOPMENT: Shin-ying Loves School 250
Effective Schools, Effective Teachers 252
■ CURRENT CONTROVERSIES: Computers in the Classroom 253

6.5 **Physical Development 255**
Growth 256
Development of Motor Skills 257
Physical Fitness 258
Participating in Sports 258
Putting It All Together 259
Summary 260
Key Terms 262
Learn More About It 262

CHAPTER 7

Expanding Social Horizons 265
Socioemotional Development in Middle Childhood

7.1 **Family Relationships 266**
The Family as a System 266
Dimensions and Styles of Parenting 267
Siblings 274
Divorce and Remarriage 276
Parent-Child Relationships Gone Awry: Child Abuse 279

7.2 **Peers 283**
Friendships 283
■ SPOTLIGHT ON RESEARCH: Influence of Best Friends on Sexual Activity 286
Groups 286
Popularity and Rejection 288
Aggressive Children and Their Victims 290

7.3 **Television: Boob Tube or Window on the World? 292**
Influence on Attitudes and Social Behavior 292
Influences on Cognition 295
Criticisms of TV 296

7.4 **Understanding Others 296**
Describing Others 297
■ REAL PEOPLE: APPLYING HUMAN DEVELOPMENT: Tell Me About a Girl That You Like a Lot 297
Understanding What Others Think 298
Prejudice 300
Putting It All Together 302
Summary 302
Key Terms 304
Learn More About It 305

CHAPTER 8

Rites of Passage 307
Physical and Cognitive Development in Adolescence

8.1 **Pubertal Changes 308**
Signs of Physical Maturation 308
Mechanisms of Maturation 310
Psychological Impact of Puberty 311

8.2 **Health 315**
Nutrition 316
Physical Fitness 318
Threats to Adolescent Well-Being 320

8.3 **Information Processing During Adolescence 322**
How Does Information Processing Improve in Adolescence? 322
Limits on Information Processing 324
■ SPOTLIGHT ON RESEARCH: Beliefs Can Interfere With Effective Reasoning 324

8.4   Reasoning About Moral Issues   326
Kohlberg's Theory   326
■ REAL PEOPLE: APPLYING HUMAN
DEVELOPMENT: Schindler's List   328
Cultural Differences in Moral Reasoning   330
Beyond Kohlberg's Theory   331
Promoting Moral Reasoning   333
Putting It All Together   334
Summary   335
Key Terms   336
Learn More About It   336

CHAPTER **9**

Moving Into the Adult Social World   339
Socioemotional Development in Adolescence

9.1   Identity and Self-Esteem   340
The Search for Identity   340
Ethnic Identity   343
Self-Esteem in Adolescence   345
The Myth of Storm and Stress   346

9.2   Romantic Relationships and Sexuality   348
Romantic Relationships   348
Sexual Behavior   348
Sexual Orientation   351
Sexual Coercion   352
■ SPOTLIGHT ON RESEARCH: Why Are Some
Boys More Likely to Perpetrate Dating
Violence?   352

9.3   The World of Work   354
Career Development   354
■ REAL PEOPLE: APPLYING HUMAN
DEVELOPMENT: "The Life of Lynne,"
a Drama in Three Acts   356
Part-Time Employment   358

9.4   The Dark Side   360
Drug Use   360
Depression   363
Delinquency   365
■ CURRENT CONTROVERSIES: When Juveniles
Commit Serious Crimes, Should They Be Tried
as Adults?   367
Putting It All Together   368
Summary   369
Key Terms   370
Learn More About It   370

PART **III**

YOUNG AND MIDDLE ADULTHOOD   375

CHAPTER **10**

Becoming an Adult   377
Physical, Cognitive, and Personality Development

10.1   When Does Adulthood Begin?   378
Role Transitions Marking Adulthood   378
Going to College   380
Psychological Views   381
So When Do People Become Adults?   382
■ REAL PEOPLE: APPLYING HUMAN
DEVELOPMENT: Britney Spears's Transition
to Adulthood   383

10.2   Physical Development and Health   384
Growth, Strength, and Physical Functioning   384
Health Status   384
Lifestyle Factors   385
■ CURRENT CONTROVERSIES: Binge Drinking
on College Campuses   386
Social, Gender, and Ethnic Issues in Health   389

10.3   Cognitive Development   391
How Should We View Intelligence in Adults?   392
What Happens to Intelligence in Adulthood?   392
■ SPOTLIGHT ON RESEARCH: The Seattle
Longitudinal Study   393
Going Beyond Formal Operations: Thinking
in Adulthood   396
The Role of Stereotypes in Thinking   400

**10.4   Who Do You Want to Be? Personality
in Young Adulthood   404**
Creating Scenarios and Life Stories   405
Possible Selves   406
Personal Control Beliefs   408
Putting It All Together   410
Summary   410
Key Terms   412
Learn More About It   412

CHAPTER **11**

Being With Others   415
Forming Relationships in Young and Middle Adulthood

11.1   Relationships   416
Friendships   416
Love Relationships   418
■ SPOTLIGHT ON RESEARCH: Patterns
and Universals of Romantic Attachment Around
the World   421
The Dark Side of Relationships: Violence   422

11.2   Lifestyles   425
Singlehood   426

Cohabitation 427
Gay and Lesbian Couples 429

■ REAL PEOPLE: APPLYING HUMAN DEVELOPMENT: Maggie O'Carroll's Story 429

Marriage 430

11.3 The Family Life Cycle 435
Deciding Whether to Have Children 435
The Parental Role 436

11.4 Divorce and Remarriage 440
Divorce 441

■ CURRENT CONTROVERSIES: "Covenant Marriage," A Way to Keep Couples Together? 443

Remarriage 446

Putting It All Together 447
Summary 447
Key Terms 448
Learn More About It 448

CHAPTER 12

Work and Leisure 451
Occupational and Lifestyle Issues in Young and Middle Adulthood

12.1 Occupational Selection and Development 452
The Meaning of Work 452
Holland's Theory of Occupational Choice Revisited 453
Occupational Development 454
Job Satisfaction 457

■ SPOTLIGHT ON RESEARCH: The Connection Between Job Satisfaction and Employee Turnover 458

12.2 Gender, Ethnicity, and Discrimination Issues 462
Gender Differences in Occupational Selection 462
Women and Occupational Development 463
Ethnicity and Occupational Development 465
Bias and Discrimination 466

■ CURRENT CONTROVERSIES: Is It Sexual Harassment? 469

12.3 Occupational Transitions 470

■ REAL PEOPLE: APPLYING HUMAN DEVELOPMENT: Changing Occupations to Find Satisfying Work 471

Retraining Workers 472
Occupational Insecurity 473
Coping With Unemployment 473

12.4 Work and Family 475
The Dependent Care Dilemma 476
Juggling Multiple Roles 478

12.5 Time to Relax: Leisure Activities 481
Types of Leisure Activities 482
Developmental Changes in Leisure 482

Consequences of Leisure Activities 483

Putting It All Together 484
Summary 485
Key Terms 486
Learn More About It 486

CHAPTER 13

Making It in Midlife 489
The Unique Challenges of Middle Adulthood

13.1 Physical Changes and Health 490
Changes in Appearance 491
Changes in Bones and Joints 491
Reproductive Changes 494

■ CURRENT CONTROVERSIES: Hormone Replacement Therapy 496

Stress and Health 498
Exercise 501

13.2 Cognitive Development 503
Practical Intelligence 503
Becoming an Expert 507
Lifelong Learning 508

13.3 Personality 510
Stability Is the Rule: The Five-Factor Model 510

■ SPOTLIGHT ON RESEARCH: Is Personality in Young and Middle Adulthood Set in Plaster? 512

Change Is the Rule: Changing Priorities in Midlife 512

13.4 Family Dynamics and Middle Age 517
Letting Go: Middle-Aged Adults and Their Children 518
Giving Back: Middle-Aged Adults and Their Aging Parents 520

■ REAL PEOPLE: APPLYING HUMAN DEVELOPMENT: Taking Care of Mom 521

Grandparenthood 523

Putting It All Together 526
Summary 526
Key Terms 528
Learn More About It 528

PART IV

LATE ADULTHOOD 533

CHAPTER 14

The Personal Context of Later Life 535
Physical, Cognitive, and Mental Health Issues

14.1 What Are Older Adults Like? 536
The Demographics of Aging 536
Longevity 539
The Third-Fourth Age Distinction 543
So How Long Will You Live? 543

14.2 Physical Changes and Health 544
Biological Theories of Aging 544
Physiological Changes 546
Health Issues 553

14.3 Cognitive Processes 555
Information Processing 555
■ CURRENT CONTROVERSIES: Information Processing in Everyday Life: Older Drivers 557
Memory 558
Creativity and Wisdom 561

14.4 Mental Health and Intervention 564
Depression 565
Anxiety Disorders 567
Dementia: Alzheimer's Disease 567
■ REAL PEOPLE: APPLYING HUMAN DEVELOPMENT: What's the Matter With Mary? 568
■ SPOTLIGHT ON RESEARCH: Training Persons With Dementia to Be Group Activity Leaders 571
Putting It All Together 572
Summary 573
Key Terms 574
Learn More About It 575

CHAPTER **15**

Social Aspects of Later Life 577
Psychosocial, Retirement, Relationship, and Societal Issues

15.1 Theories of Psychosocial Aging 578
Continuity Theory 578
Competence and Environmental Press 579
■ REAL PEOPLE: APPLYING HUMAN DEVELOPMENT: Still Flying at 91 581

15.2 Personality, Social Cognition, and Spirituality 581
Integrity Versus Despair 582
Well-Being and Social Cognition 583
■ SPOTLIGHT ON RESEARCH: Understanding the Influences on Subjective Well-Being 583
Religiosity and Spiritual Support 586

15.3 I Used to Work at . . . : Living in Retirement 588
What Does Being Retired Mean? 589
Why Do People Retire? 590
Adjustment to Retirement 591
Keeping Busy in Retirement 592

15.4 Friends and Family in Late Life 593
Friends and Siblings 594
Marriage and Gay and Lesbian Partnerships 596
Caring for a Partner 597
Widowhood 598
Great-Grandparenthood 599

15.5 Social Issues and Aging 601
Frail Older Adults 601
Living in Nursing Homes 602
Elder Abuse and Neglect 606
Politics, Social Security, and Medicare 608
■ CURRENT CONTROVERSIES: Saving Social Security 610
Putting It All Together 612
Summary 612
Key Terms 614
Learn More About It 614

CHAPTER **16**

The Final Passage 617
Dying and Bereavement

16.1 Definitions and Ethical Issues 618
Sociocultural Definitions of Death 618
Legal and Medical Definitions 620
Ethical Issues 621
■ CURRENT CONTROVERSIES: The Terri Schiavo Case 624

16.2 Thinking About Death: Personal Aspects 626
A Life Course Approach to Dying 627
Dealing With One's Own Death 627
Death Anxiety 630
Creating a Final Scenario 631
The Hospice Option 632
■ REAL PEOPLE: APPLYING HUMAN DEVELOPMENT: One Family's Experience With Dying 634

16.3 Surviving the Loss: The Grieving Process 636
The Grief Process 636
Normal Grief Reactions 638
Coping With Grief 640
■ SPOTLIGHT ON RESEARCH: Grief Processing and Avoidance in the United States and China 641
Traumatic Grief Reactions 642

16.4 Dying and Bereavement Experiences Across the Life Span 643
Childhood 644
Adolescence 646
Adulthood 646
Late Adulthood 648
Putting It All Together 650
Summary 651
Key Terms 653
Learn More About It 653

Glossary 656
References 667
Name Index 732
Subject Index 743

Preface

"To boldly go where no one has gone before" is a phrase familiar to millions of *Star Trek* fans around the world. The desire to explore the unknown to further our knowledge and understanding is a fundamental characteristic of being human. Boldly going into the unknown is also what each of us does in the course of our development. None of us has been where we are headed; indeed, in a real sense, we create our own destinies.

Human development is both the most fascinating and most complex science there is. *Human Development: A Life-Span View, Fourth Edition* introduces you to the issues, forces, and outcomes that make us who we are.

Contemporary research and theory on human development consistently emphasize the multidisciplinary approach needed to describe and explain how people change (and how they stay the same) over time. Moreover, the great diversity of people requires an appreciation for individual differences in the course of development. *Human Development: A Life-Span View, Fourth Edition* incorporates both and aims to address three specific goals:

- To provide a comprehensive, yet highly readable, account of human development across the life span.
- To provide theoretical and empirical foundations that enable students to become educated and critical interpreters of developmental information.
- To provide a blend of basic and applied research, as well as controversial topics and emergent trends, to demonstrate connections between the laboratory and life and the dynamic science of human development.

ORGANIZATION

A MODIFIED CHRONOLOGICAL APPROACH The great debate among authors and instructors in the field of human development is whether to take a *chronological approach* (focusing on functioning at specific stages of the life span, such as infancy, adolescence, and middle adulthood) or a *topical approach* (following a specific aspect of development, such as personality, throughout the life span). Both approaches have their merits. We have chosen a modified chronological approach that we believe combines the best aspects of both. The overall organization of the text is chronological: We trace development from conception through late life in sequential order and dedicate several chapters to topical issues pertaining to particular points in the life span (such as infancy and early childhood, adolescence, young adulthood, middle adulthood, and late life).

But because the developmental continuity of such topics as social and cognitive development gets lost with narrowly defined, artificial age-stage divisions, we dedicate some chapters to tracing their development over larger segments of the life span. These chapters provide a much more coherent description of important developmental changes, emphasize the fact that development is not easily divided into "slices," and provide students with understandable explications of developmental theories.

BALANCED COVERAGE OF THE ENTIRE LIFE SPAN A primary difference between *Human Development: A Life-Span View, Fourth Edition* and similar texts is that this book provides a much richer and more complete description of adult development and aging. Following the introductory chapter, the remaining fifteen chapters of the text are evenly divided between childhood, adolescence, adulthood, and aging. This balanced treatment reflects not only the rapid emergence of adult development and aging as a major emphasis in the science of human development but also a recognition that roughly three-fourths of most people's lives occurs beyond adolescence.

As a reflection of our modified chronological approach, *Human Development: A Life-Span View, Fourth Edition* is divided into four main parts. After an introduction to the science of human development (Chapter 1), Part 1 includes a discussion of the biological foundations of life (Chapter 2) and development during infancy and early childhood (Chapters 3–5). Part 2 focuses on development during middle childhood and adolescence (Chapters 6–9). Part 3 (Chapters 10–13) focuses on young and middle adulthood. Part 4 examines late adulthood (Chapters 14 and 15), and concludes with a consideration of dying and bereavement (Chapter 16).

CONTENT AND APPROACH

THE BIOPSYCHOSOCIAL EMPHASIS Our text provides comprehensive, up-to-date coverage of research and theory from conception to old age and death. We explicitly adopt the biopsychosocial framework as an organizing theme, describing it in depth in Chapter 1, then integrating it throughout the text—often in combination with other developmental theories.

AN ENGAGING PERSONAL STYLE On several occasions, we communicate our personal involvement with the issues being discussed by providing examples from our own experiences as illustrations of how human development plays itself out in people's lives. Additionally, every major section of a chapter opens with a short vignette, helping to personalize a concept just before it is discussed. Other rich examples are integrated throughout the text narrative and showcased in the *Real People* feature in nearly every chapter.

EMPHASIS ON INCLUSIVENESS In content coverage, in the personalized examples used, and in the photo program, we emphasize diversity—within the United States and around the world—in ethnicity, gender, race, age, ability, and sexual orientation.

MEDIA LINKS At the end of each chapter are links to the interactive CD-ROM, *Life-Span: A Multimedia Introduction to Development,* to help students relate chapter topics to content on the CD. Additionally, within the chapters there are links to interactive on-line exercises related to research discussed in the chapter.

CHANGES IN THE FOURTH EDITION Besides updating the Fourth edition with several hundred new reference citations to works from the past three years, we have made several significant changes. An updated photo program now includes captions so that what they are depicting is clear at a glance, and the figures are now also captioned and numbered to make the information more accessible. To reinforce students' understanding of current research data, new interactive online exercises link the text's *Focus on Research* boxes (indicated with an icon at the end of the box) to online critical thinking exercises, related articles, and websites on the Book Companion Website (http://psychology.wadsworth.com/kail_cavanaugh4e/). Each of the book's four parts now ends with a two-page Visual Summary. These visual overviews help students reinforce their overall understanding of the material covered in each part of the text before they move on to new topics. The *Forces in Action* and *See For Yourself* boxes, which appeared in the Third Edition, have been eliminated to further streamline the material.

Of particular note are these content additions:

■ Chapter 2 includes new discussion of adjusting to parenthood that includes postpartum depression as well as new material on the value of stimulation (i.e., "massage therapy") for low birth-weight babies.

■ Chapter 4 has a new section on individual differences in word learning that includes information about bilingualism.

- Chapter 6 now includes a section on physical development in middle childhood.
- Chapter 7 includes a new section on bullying in middle childhood.
- Chapter 8's material on anorexia and bulimia has been rewritten entirely and now includes information on eating disorders in boys.
- Chapter 11 has a new discussion about global patterns of romantic attachment.
- Chapter 12 contains expanded international information, such as the United Kingdom's effort at eliminating age discrimination in the workplace by December 2006 and regarding occupational aspirations.
- Chapter 14 includes a new section on personal longevity with a link to a life expectancy calculator.
- Chapter 16 includes an extensive discussion of the Terri Schiavo case.

To provide an extensive guide to improvements made throughout the Fourth Edition, we continue with a substantial list of changes by chapter.

CHAPTER 1: THE STUDY OF HUMAN DEVELOPMENT

- New *Current Controversies* feature on stem cell research.
- New *Spotlight on Research* feature on change and stability in life satisfaction.
- Revised discussions of Vygotsky's theory, meta-analysis, and interpreting a correlation.

CHAPTER 2: BIOLOGICAL FOUNDATIONS

- Reorganized content presentation so that material on genetic disorders now precedes material on behavioral genetics.
- Significantly revised section on "heredity, environment, and development," includes two major parts: behavioral genetics and a section called "paths from genes to behavior" that is organized around four major principles by which genetic information is converted into behavior.
- Expanded coverage of the behavioral repertoire of the fetus.
- Substantially revised material on "approaches to childbirth."
- Added a new subsection called "adjusting to parenthood" that includes postpartum depression as well as new material on the value of stimulation (i.e., "massage therapy") for low birth-weight babies.

CHAPTER 3: TOOLS FOR EXPLORING THE WORLD

- Updated description of the BNAS, new information about sleep-related problems (nightmares, sleep walking, bedwetting), new information about incidence and prevention of SIDS in African-American babies, and a much revised description of temperament.
- Added new information about infants' perception of music, a much revised account of infants' depth perception, and new information about infants' perception of faces, including a new *Spotlight on Research* feature.
- Includes new information about infants' understanding of intentionality.

CHAPTER 4: THE EMERGENCE OF THOUGHT AND LANGUAGE

- The description of sensory-motor thinking has been reorganized completely.
- Expanded discussion of autobiographical memory that is organized around Nelson and Fivush's (2004) new theory.
- New subsection on individual differences in word learning that includes information about bilingualism.

CHAPTER 5: ENTERING THE SOCIAL WORLD

- Material on growth of attachment has been revamped completely.
- Significantly revised material on socialization of altruism.
- Added new material on biological influences on gender typing.

CHAPTER 6: OFF TO SCHOOL

- Expanded discussion of monitoring now includes metacognition and self-regulated learning.
- New material on Sternberg's theory of successful intelligence, emotional intelligence, and stereotype threat.
- Added new section devoted to physical development.

CHAPTER 7: EXPANDING SOCIAL HORIZONS

- New material on influence of socioeconomic status of parental styles as well as a new subsection on the influence of the marital system on children's development.
- Revised material on adolescent friendship that includes a new *Spotlight on Research* feature on friends' influence, much revised material on popular and rejected children, and a new section on "Aggressive Children and their Victims."

CHAPTER 8: RITES OF PASSAGE

- Includes much revised material on environmental contributions to onset of puberty and on the impact of rate of maturation.
- Completely rewritten material on anorexia and bulimia and now includes information on eating disorders in boys.

CHAPTER 9: MOVING INTO THE ADULT SOCIAL WORLD

- Extensively revised coverage of influences on adolescents' self-esteem.
- Revised coverage of romantic relationships, new information about STDs, and substantially revised coverage of sexual coercion, including a new *Spotlight on Research*.
- Rewritten presentation of factors contributing to life-course persistent anti-social behavior.

CHAPTER 10: BECOMING AN ADULT

- Updated *Real People* feature on Britney Spears.
- Updated *Current Controversies* feature on college binge drinking.
- Revised discussions of life-style factors, drinking alcohol, nutrition, stereotypes in thinking, the life-story model of personality, and possible selves.

CHAPTER 11: BEING WITH OTHERS

- New *Spotlight on Research* feature on global patterns of romantic attachment.
- Revised discussions of: friendships in adulthood, love relationships, developmental forces and relationships, cohabitation, marriage, single parents, and divorce.

CHAPTER 12: WORK AND LEISURE

- Updated the *Real People* feature on changing occupations to find satisfying work.
- Revised discussions of mentors, alienation and burnout, traditional and nontraditional occupations, women, and occupational development.
- Updated statistics on labor force issues.
- Expanded international information, such as United Kingdom's effort at eliminating age discrimination in the workplace by December 2006 and regarding occupational aspirations.

CHAPTER 13: MAKING IT IN MIDLIFE

- New *Current Controversies* feature on Hormone Replacement Therapy.
- New *Spotlight on Research* feature on whether personality in young and middle adulthood changes.
- New *Real People* feature on taking care of an aging parent.
- Revised discussions of stress, exercise, applications of practical intelligence, personality traits, and grandparenting.

CHAPTER 14: THE PERSONAL CONTEXT OF LATER LIFE

- New section on personal longevity with a link to a life expectancy calculator.
- Extensively revised *Current Controversies* feature on older drivers.
- New *Spotlight on Research* feature on Montessori techniques as an intervention for people with Alzheimer's disease.
- Revised discussions of international population trends, treatment of Parkinson's disease, sleep, nutrition, and updates on Alzheimer's disease.

CHAPTER 15: SOCIAL ASPECTS OF LATER LIFE

- Revised *Current Controversies* feature about Social Security to include current political discussions.
- Revised discussions of spirituality, retirement, relationships, social security, and Medicare.

CHAPTER 16: THE FINAL PASSAGE

- New *Current Controversies* feature on the Terri Schiavo case.
- New *Real People* feature on hospice.
- New *Spotlight on Research* feature on cross-cultural results on dealing with grief over time.
- Revised discussions of: definition of death (whole-brain vs. higher brain), euthanasia, and coping with grief.

SPECIAL FEATURES

Three special features are a significant reason why this textbook is so unique. These features are woven seamlessly into the narrative, signaled by a distinct icon for each—not boxed off from the flow of the chapter. The three features are

SPOTLIGHT ON RESEARCH, which emphasize a fuller understanding of the science and scope of life-span development.

CURRENT CONTROVERSIES, which highlight debates over social and developmental issues.

REAL PEOPLE: APPLYING HUMAN DEVELOPMENT, which illustrate the everyday applications of life-span development issues.

These features are described in the *How to Use This Book* section of Chapter 1, and each one appears in nearly every chapter thereafter.

PEDAGOGICAL FEATURES

Among the most important aspects of *Human Development: A Life-Span View, Fourth Edition* is its exceptional integration of pedagogical features, designed to help students maximize their learning.

- *Integration of Features and Key Terms.* One of the first things you may notice in paging through this text is that the three special features described earlier, which are normally set apart in boxes in other texts (boxes that students often skip!), are integrated directly into the narrative. Continuing with this integrative theme, definitions of key terms are provided in context within the chapter narrative. Key terms themselves are in bold and the definition sentences are in italics. This *unrivaled* integration is meant to help the student stay focused, providing a seamless presentation of human development across the life span.

■ *Section-by-Section Pedagogy.* Each major section (every chapter has four or five) has been carefully crafted: It opens with a set of learning objectives, a vignette, typically includes one or more *Think About It* questions in the margin encouraging critical thinking, and ends with a set of questions called *Test Yourself* that reinforces key elements of the section. For easy assignment and to help readers visually organize the material, major units within each chapter are numbered. To provide better clarity and accessibility, figures are now numbered and figures and photos are captioned.

■ *Chapter-by-Chapter Pedagogy.* Each chapter opens with a table of contents and a brief *Introduction*. A *Putting It All Together* section follows the chapter's final section to tie major chapter themes together (usually referring back to the individuals described in the section vignettes as well), and includes a bulleted, detailed *Summary* (broken down by section), followed by a list of *Key Terms* (with page references), and *Learn About It* (which lists books and websites where students can learn more about human development).

In sum, we believe that our integrated pedagogical system will give the student all the tools she or he needs to comprehend the material and study for tests.

SUPPLEMENTARY MATERIALS

An extensive array of supplemental materials are available to accompany this text. These supplements are designed to make teaching and learning more effective. For more information on any of these resources, please call the Thomson Learning Academic Resource Center at 800-423-0563 or go to www.wadsworth.com.

Instructor Resources

Available to qualified adopters. Please consult your local sales representative for details.

INSTRUCTOR'S RESOURCE MANUAL The *Instructor's Manual* for the Fourth Edition has been revised by Nina Lyon Jenkins of University of Maryland Eastern Shore. It includes a wealth of material, including Chapter Overviews, Chapter Outlines, Learning Objectives, Lecture Expanders, *Spotlight on Research* Activities, *See for Yourself* Activities, and In-Class and Outside of Class Activities including Demonstrations and Role Plays, Writing Assignments, and Student Projects. Critical Thinking Discussion Questions, Internet Activities, InfoTrac® College Edition Articles and Activities, Video Recommendations, and Handouts are also included in this heavily revised Instructor's Resource Manual. Finally, the *Instructor's Resource Manual* includes transition guides to help instructors switch easily from a major competing text to our Fourth Edition. ISBN: 0-495-13054-0

MULTIMEDIA MANAGER INSTRUCTOR'S RESOURCE CD-ROM Authored by Ed Morris of Owensboro Community College, this one-stop lecture and class preparation tool makes it easy for you to assemble, edit, and present customized, media-enhanced lectures for your course using Microsoft PowerPoint. It includes chapter-specific lecture outlines and art from the text (all on ready-made Microsoft PowerPoint slides) as well as video clips and other integrated media. This CD also contains the full Instructor's Manual with Test Bank. ISBN: 0-495-13059-1

TEST BANK Bradley Caskey and Richard Seefeldt, both of the University of Wisconsin at River Falls, have revised the *Test Bank* for the Fourth Edition. The authors have increased the number of questions by 25% for this edition, and have focused on increasing the number of applied-type questions. Each question is identified by learning objective, main text page reference, classification (conceptual, factual, or applied), and level of difficulty. An array of additional questions are provided and identified as those that appear on the book's website, where students can take interactive quizzes with instant feedback. ISBN: 0-495-13055-9

EXAMVIEW® COMPUTERIZED TESTING Create, deliver, and customize tests and study guides (both print and online) in minutes with this easy-to-use assessment and tutorial system. *ExamView* offers both a Quick Test Wizard and an Online Test Wizard that guide you step-by-step through the process of creating tests, while its "what you see is what you get" capability allows you to see the test you are creating on the screen exactly as it will print or display online. You can build tests of up to 250 questions using up to twelve question types. Using *ExamView's* complete word processing capabilities, you can enter an unlimited number of new questions or edit existing questions. ISBN: 0-495-13060-5

JOININ™ ON TURNINGPOINT® Book-specific JoinIn™ content for classroom response systems tailored to this text allows you to transform your classroom and assess your students' progress with instant in-class quizzes and polls. Pose questions and display students' answers seamlessly within the Microsoft® PowerPoint® slides of your own lecture, in conjunction with the "clicker" hardware of your choice. 0-495-13065-6

THOMSONNOW FOR KAIL/CAVANAUGH'S HUMAN DEVELOPMENT This web-based program, by David Ward of Arkansas Tech University, helps your students discover the areas of text where they need to focus their efforts through a series of diagnostic pretests and posttests, personalized study plans with learning modules that parallel the modules in the book, eBook files, and other integrated media elements. While students can use ThomsonNOW without any instructor setup or involvement, an Instructor Gradebook is available for you to monitor student progress. The gradebook can also be easily integrated with a WebCT® or Blackboard® gradebook. ISBN: 0-495-17175-1

BOOK COMPANION WEBSITE As users of this text, you and your students will have access to an extensive selection of additional online tools, quizzes, and activities available on the Book's Companion Website http://psychology.wadsworth.com/kail _cavanaugh4e/ on the Wadsworth Psychology Resource Center. Please see the complete description under *Student Resources*.

WEBTUTOR™ ADVANTAGE ON WEBCT® AND BLACKBOARD® http://webtutor .thomsonlearning.com. Save time building or web-enhancing your course, posting course materials, incorporating multimedia, tracking progress, and more with this customizable course management tool. WebTutor Advantage™ saves you time and enhances your students' learning, pairing advanced course management capabilities with text-specific learning tools. On WebCT: 0-495-13061-3; On Blackboard: 0-495-13062-1

Student Resources

THOMSONNOW FOR KAIL/CAVANAUGH'S HUMAN DEVELOPMENT This web-based program, by David Ward of Arkansas Tech University, helps students discover the areas of text where they need to focus their efforts through a series of diagnostic pretests and posttests, personalized study plans with learning modules that parallel the modules in the book, eBook files, and other integrated media elements. ISBN: 0-495-17175-1

STUDY GUIDE Dea K. DeWolff and Terri A. Tarr of Indiana University–Purdue University, Indianapolis, have revised their dynamic *Study Guide* to accompany the Fourth Edition. Organized by main headings and learning objectives that mirror the main text, each chapter in this comprehensive *Study Guide* includes fill-ins for key terms, true/false questions, an explanation of each learning objective, summary paragraphs with fill-ins, and a "Test Yourself" section with multiple-choice and essay questions. ISBN: 0-495-13056-7

ART AND LECTURE OUTLINES By Ed Morris, Owensboro Community College. These printed lecture outlines, along with selected text figures likely to be shown in class, include space for notes. Students will save time and be able to focus more on listening and participating in class. ISBN: 0-495-13064-8

LIFE-SPAN: A MULTIMEDIA INTRODUCTION TO DEVELOPMENT CD-ROM This comprehensive CD-ROM explores the major developmental milestones from conception to death in seven interactive learning modules. Each module features narrated concept overviews with key terms, explanatory art and videos, critical thinking applications, drag-and-drop games for review of key terms and concepts, section quizzes, and a final test. This updated CD-ROM also includes a video selector, multimedia glossary, and links to the Internet for further study. ISBN: 0-495-05882-3

BOOK COMPANION WEBSITE http://psychology.wadsworth.com/kail_cavanaugh4e/ This site includes instructor resources and a variety of chapter-specific study aids, including *Spotlight on Research* critical thinking questions and related websites, and quizzes for students.

CASEBOOK FOR LIFE-SPAN DEVELOPMENT By Barbara M. Newman, University of Rhode Island; Philip R. Newman, University of Rhode Island; Laura Landry-Meyer, Bowling Green State University; and Brenda J. Lohman, Iowa State University. Created to engage and stimulate students, these contemporary case studies illustrate developmental transitions and challenges in every stage of life. Together with thought-provoking questions for analysis, the case studies help readers use multiple perspectives to analyze and interpret life events. ISBN: 0-534-59767-X

CURRENT PERSPECTIVES: READINGS FROM INFOTRAC® COLLEGE EDITION Compiled by Gabriela Martorell (Portland State University), this reader includes articles on the nature/nurture debate as they relate to stages of development. Each article is followed by two or three critical thinking questions appropriate for in-class discussions or homework assignments. ISBN: 0-495-00724-2

INFOTRAC® COLLEGE EDITION WITH INFOMARKS® Four months' access to this online database—featuring full-length articles from thousands of academic journals and periodicals—is available with this text. Your subscription includes access to Info-Marks®—stable URLs that you can link to articles, journals, and searches to save you time when doing research—and to InfoWrite for writing and critical thinking guidelines. Visit www.thomsonedu.com.

WEBTUTOR™ ADVANTAGE ON WEBCT® AND BLACKBOARD® http://webtutor .thomsonlearning.com. For students, *WebTutor* offers real-time access to a full array of study tools, including chapter outlines, summaries, learning objectives, glossary flashcards (with audio), practice quizzes, InfoTrac College Edition exercises, and Web links. *WebTutor Advantage* extends the benefits of *WebTutor* with additional enhancements that increase interactivity and bring topics to life, such as animations and videos. On WebCT: 0-495-13061-3; On Blackboard: 0-495-13062-1.

ACKNOWLEDGMENTS

Textbook authors do not produce books on their own. We owe a debt of thanks to many people who helped take this project from a first draft to a bound book. Thanks to Jim Brace-Thompson, for his enthusiasm, good humor, and sage advice at the beginning of this project; to Michele Sordi for taking the reins and guiding the Fourth Edition; to Kristin Makarewycz, for providing helpful feedback as we revised; and to Mary Noel, for shepherding the book through production.

We would also like to thank the many reviewers who generously gave their time and effort to help us sharpen our thinking about human development and, in so doing, shape the development of this text.

Reviewers

Fourth Edition Reviewers

L. René Bergeron
University of New Hampshire

Janine P. Buckner
Seton Hall University

Charles Timothy Dickel
Creighton University

Douglas Friedrich
University of West Florida

Lana-Lee Hardacre
Conestoga College

Julie A. Haseleu
Kirkwood Community College

Brett Heintz
Delgado Community College

Heather M. Hill
University of Texas, San Antonio

Mary Anne O'Neill
Rollins College Hamilton Holt School

Shana Pack
Western Kentucky University

Ian Payton
Bethune-Cookman College

Third Edition Reviewers

Gary Allen
University of South Carolina

Kenneth E. Bell
University of New Hampshire

Belinda Bevins-Knabe
University of Arkansas at Little Rock

Catherine Deering
Clayton College and State University

Judith Dieterle
Daytona Beach Community College

Sandy Eggers
University of Memphis

William Fabricius
Arizona State University

Douglas Friedrich
University of West Florida

Tresmaine R. Grimes
Iona College

Susan Horton
Mesa Community College

Jenefer Husman
University of Alabama

Erwin J. Janek
Henderson State University

Wayne Joose
Calvin College

Margaret D. Kasimatis
Carroll College

Michelle L. Kelley
Old Dominion University

Kirsten D. Linney
University of Northern Iowa

Blake Te-Neil Lloyd
University of South Carolina

Susan Magun-Jackson
University of Memphis

Marion G. Mason
Bloomsburg University of Pennsylvania

Julie Ann McIntyre
Russell Sage College

Edward J. Morris
Owensboro Community College

Janet D. Murray
University of Central Florida

Ellen E. Pastorino
Valencia Community College

Robert F. Rycek
University of Nebraska at Kearney

Jeff Sandoz
University of Louisiana at Lafayette

Brian Schrader
Emporia State University

Carolyn A. Shantz
Wayne State University

Cynthia K. Shinabarger Reed
Tarrant County College

Tracy L. Spinrad
Arizona State University

Kelli W. Taylor
Virginia Commonwealth University

Lorraine C. Taylor
University of South Carolina

Barbara Turnage
University of Central Florida

Yolanda van Ecke
Mission College

Carol G. Weatherford
Clemson University

Sandy Wurtele
University of Colorado at Colorado Springs

Second Edition Reviewers

Gary L. Allen
University of South Carolina

Ann MB Austin
Utah State University

David Bishop
Luther College

ELIZABETH M. BLUNK
Southwest Texas State University

JOSETTE BONEWITZ
Vincennes University

LANTHAN D. CAMBLIN, JR.
University of Cincinnati

SHELLEY M. DRAZEN
SUNY, Binghampton

KENNETH ELLIOTT
University of Maine, Augusta

NOLEN EMBRY
Lexington Community College

JAMES GARBARINO
Cornell University

CATHERINE HACKETT RENNER
West Chester University

SANDRA HELLYER
*Indiana University-Purdue University
    at Indianapolis*

JOHN KLEIN
Castleton State College

WENDY KLIEWER
Virginia Commonwealth University

NANCY MACDONALD
University of South Carolina, Sumter

LISA McGUIRE
Allegheny College

MARTIN D. MURPHY
University of Akron

JOHN PFISTER
Dartmouth College

BRADFORD PILLOW
Northern Illinois University

GARY POPOLI
Hartford Community College

ROBERT PORESKY
Kansas State University

JOSEPH M. PRICE
San Diego State University

ROSEMARY ROSSER
University of Arizona

TIMOTHY O. SHEARON
Albertson College of Idaho

MARCIA SOMER
*University of Hawaii-Kapiolani
    Community College*

NANCI STEWART WOODS
Austin Peay State University

ANNE WATSON
West Virginia University

FRED A. WILSON
Appalachian State University

KAREN YANOWITZ
Arkansas State University

CHRISTINE ZIEGLER
Kennesaw State University

First Edition Reviewers

POLLY APPLEFIELD
*University of North Carolina
    at Wilmington*

DANIEL R. BELLACK
Trident Technical College

DAVID BISHOP
Luther College

LANTHAN CAMBLIN, JR.
University of Cincinnati

KENNETH ELLIOTT
University of Maine at Augusta

MARTHA ELLIS
Collin County Community College

LINDA FLICKINGER
St. Clair County Community College

STEVE FINKS
University of Tennessee

REBECCA GLOVER
University of North Texas

J. A. GREAVES
Jefferson State Community College

PATRICIA GUTH
Westmoreland County Community College

PHYLLIS HEATH
Central Michigan University

MYRA HEINRICH
Mesa State College

SANDRA HELLYER
*Indiana University-Purdue University
    at Indianapolis*

SHIRLEY-ANNE HENSCH
University of Wisconsin Center

THOMAS HESS
North Carolina State University

KATHLEEN HURLBURT
University of Massachusetts-Lowell

HEIDI INDERBITZEN
University of Nebraska at Lincoln

SANFORD LOPATER
Christopher Newport University

BILL MEREDITH
University of Nebraska at Omaha

MARIBETH PALMER-KING
Broome Community College

HARVE RAWSON
Franklin College

VIRGINIA WYLY
*State University of New York College
    at Buffalo*

About the Authors

ROBERT V. KAIL

ROBERT V. KAIL is Professor of Psychological Sciences at Purdue University. His undergraduate degree is from Ohio Wesleyan University and his Ph.D. is from the University of Michigan. Kail is editor of the *Journal of Experimental Child Psychology* and of *Advances in Child Development and Behavior*. He received the McCandless Young Scientist Award from the American Psychological Association, was named the Distinguished Sesquicentennial Alumnus in Psychology by Ohio Wesleyan University, and is a fellow of the American Psychological Society. Kail has also written *Children and Their Development*. His research focuses on cognitive development during childhood and adolescence. Away from the office, he enjoys photography and working out.

JOHN C. CAVANAUGH

JOHN C. CAVANAUGH is president of the University of West Florida. He received his undergraduate degree from the University of Delaware and his Ph.D. from the University of Notre Dame. Cavanaugh is a fellow of the American Psychological Association, the American Psychological Society, and the Gerontological Society of America, and has served as president of the Adult Development and Aging Division (Division 20) of the APA. Cavanaugh has also written (with Fredda Blanchard-Fields) *Adult Development and Aging*. His research interests in gerontology concern family caregiving as well as the role of beliefs in older adults' cognitive performance. For enjoyment he backpacks, writes poetry, and, while eating chocolate, ponders the relative administrative abilities of James T. Kirk, Jean-Luc Picard, Kathryn Janeway, Benjamin Sisko, and Jonathan Archer.

HUMAN DEVELOPMENT

A Life-Span View

1.1 How to Use This Book
Learning and Study Aids
Terminology
Organization

1.2 Thinking About Development
Recurring Issues in Human
Development
Basic Forces in Human Develop-
ment: The Biopsychosocial
Framework

1.3 Developmental Theories
Psychodynamic Theory
Learning Theory
Cognitive-Developmental Theory
The Ecological and Systems
Approach
Life-Span Perspective, Selec-
tive Optimization With Com-
pensation, and Life Course
Perspective

REAL PEOPLE: APPLYING
HUMAN DEVELOPMENT:
Sarah and Elizabeth Delany

The Big Picture

**1.4 Doing Developmental
Research**
Measurement in Human Devel-
opment Research
General Designs for Research
Designs for Studying
Development

SPOTLIGHT ON RESEARCH:
Stability and Change in Life
Satisfaction

Integrating Findings From Different Studies

Conducting Research Ethically

Communicating Research Results

Applying Research Results:
Social Policy

CURRENT CONTROVERSIES:
Stem Cell Research

Putting It All Together

Summary

Key Terms

Learn More About It

CHAPTER 1

The Study of Human Development

Y ou are about to begin an exciting personal journey. In this course, you will have the opportunity to ask some of life's most basic questions: How did your life begin? How did you go from a single cell, about the size of the period at the end of a sentence in this text, to the fully grown, complex adult person you are today? Will you be the same or different by the time you reach late life? How do you influence other people's lives? How do they influence yours? How do the various roles you have throughout life—child, teenager, partner, spouse, parent, worker, grandparent—shape your development? How do we deal with our own and others' deaths?

These are examples of the questions that create the scientific foundation of **human development,** *the multidisciplinary study of how people change and how they remain the same over time.* Answering them requires us to draw on theories and research in the physical and social sciences, including biology, genetics, chemistry, medicine, psychology, sociology, demography, ethnography, economics, and anthropology. The science of human development reflects the complexity and uniqueness of each person and each person's experiences as well as commonalities and patterns across people. As a science, human development is firmly grounded in theory and research and seeks to understand human behavior.

Before our journey begins, we need to collect some things to make the trip more rewarding. In this chapter, we pick up the necessary road maps that point us in the proper direction: tips on how to use this book, a framework to organize theories and research, common issues and influences on development, and the methods developmentalists use to make discoveries. Pack well, and bon voyage.

1.1

HOW TO USE THIS BOOK

Human Development is written with you, the student, in mind. In the next few pages, we describe several features of the book that will make it easier for you to learn. Please don't skip this material; it will save you time in the long run.

LEARNING AND STUDY AIDS

Each chapter includes several distinctive features to help you learn the material and organize your studying.

■ Each chapter opens with an overview of the main topics and a detailed outline.

■ Each major section within a chapter begins with a set of learning objectives. There is also a brief vignette introducing one of the topics to be covered in that section and providing an example of the developmental issues people face.

■ When key terms are introduced in the text, they appear in **boldfaced italics.** The definition of the key term appears in *italics.* This should make key terms easy to find and learn.

■ Key developmental theories are introduced in Chapter 1 and are referred to throughout the text.

■ Critical thinking questions appear in the margins. These *Think About It* questions are designed to help you make connections across sections within a chapter or across chapters.

■ The end of each section includes a feature called *Test Yourself,* which will help you check your knowledge of major ideas you just read about. The Test Yourself questions serve two purposes. First, they give you a chance to spot-check your understanding of the material. Second, at times the questions will relate the material you have just read to other facts, theories, or the bio-psychosocial framework you read about earlier.

■ Text features that expand or highlight a specific topic are integrated with the rest of the material. This book includes the following three features, each identified by a distinctive icon.

  ■ *Spotlight on Research* elaborates a specific research study discussed in the text and provides more details on the design and methods used.

  ■ *Current Controversies* offers thought-provoking discussions about current issues affecting development.

  ■ *Real People: Applying Human Development* is a case study that illustrates how an issue in human development is manifested in the life of a real person.

■ The end of each chapter includes several special study tools. *Putting It All Together* returns to each vignette to reprise the major topics of the chapter. A *Summary* organized by major section headings provides a review of the key ideas in the chapter. Next is a list of *Key Terms* that appear in the chapter. Drawing the chapter to a close is *Learn More About It,* which contains a list of *Readings* and *Websites* where you can find more information about human development.

We strongly encourage you to take advantage of these learning and study aids as you read the book. We have also left room in the margins for you to make notes to yourself on the material, so you can more easily integrate the text with your class and lecture material.

Your instructor will probably assign about one chapter per week. Don't try to read an entire chapter in one sitting. Instead, on the first day, preview the chapter. Read the introduction and notice how the chapter fits into the entire book; then page through the chapter, reading the learning objectives, vignettes, and major headings. Also read the italicized sentences and the boldfaced terms. Your goal is to get a general overview of the entire chapter—a sense of what it's all about.

Now you're ready to begin reading. Go to the first major section and preview it again, reminding yourself of the topics covered. Then start to read. As you read, think about what you're reading. Every few paragraphs, stop briefly. Try to summarize the main ideas in your own words; ask yourself if the ideas describe your own experience or that of others you know; tell a friend about something interesting in the material.

In other words, read actively—get involved in what you're reading. Don't just stare glassy-eyed at the page!

Continue this pattern—reading, summarizing, thinking—until you finish the section. Then answer the Test Yourself questions to determine how well you've learned what you've read. If you've followed the read-summarize-think cycle as you worked your way through the section, you should be able to answer most of the questions.

The next time you sit down to read (preferably the next day), start by reviewing the second major section. Then complete it with the read-summarize-think cycle. Repeat this procedure for all the major sections.

When you've finished the last major section, wait a day or two and then review each major section. Pay careful attention to the italicized sentences, the boldfaced terms, and the Test Yourself questions. Also, use the study aids at the end of the chapter to help you integrate the ideas in the chapters.

With this approach, it should take several 30- to 45-minute study sessions to complete each chapter. Don't be tempted to rush through an entire chapter in a single session. Research consistently shows that you learn more effectively by having daily (or nearly daily) study sessions devoted to both reviewing familiar material *and* taking on a relatively small amount of new material.

TERMINOLOGY

A few words about terminology before we embark. Certain terms will be used to refer to different periods of the life span. Although you may already be familiar with the terms, we would like to clarify how they will be used in this text. The following terms will refer to a specific range of ages:

Newborn: birth to 1 month

Infant: 1 month to 1 year

Toddler: 1 year to 2 years

Preschooler: 2 years to 6 years

School-age child: 6 years to 12 years

Adolescent: 12 years to 20 years

Young adult: 20 years to 40 years

Middle-age adult: 40 years to 60 years

Young-old adult: 60 years to 80 years

Old-old adult: 80 years and beyond

Sometimes, for the sake of variety, we will use other terms that are less tied to specific ages, such as babies, youngsters, and older adults. However, you will be able to determine the specific ages from the context.

ORGANIZATION

Authors of textbooks on human development always face the problem of deciding how to organize the material into meaningful segments across the life span. This book is organized in four parts: Prenatal Development, Infancy, and Early Childhood; School-Age Children and Adolescents; Young and Middle Adulthood; and Later Adulthood. We believe this organization achieves two major goals. First, it divides the life span in ways that relate to the divisions encountered in everyday life. Second, it enables us to provide a more complete account of adulthood than other books do.

Because some developmental issues pertain only to a specific point in the life span, some chapters are organized around specific ages. Overall, the text begins with conception and proceeds through childhood, adolescence, adulthood, and old age to death. But because some developmental processes unfold over longer periods of time, some of the chapters are organized around specific topics.

Part 1 covers prenatal development, infancy, and early childhood. Here we will see how genetic inheritance operates and how the prenatal environment affects a person's future development. During the first 2 years of life, the rate of change in both motor and perceptual arenas is amazing. How young children acquire language and begin to think about their world is as intriguing as it is rapid. Early childhood also marks the emergence of social relationships, as well as an understanding of gender roles and identity. By the end of this period, a child is reasonably proficient as a thinker, uses language in sophisticated ways, and is ready for the major transition into formal education.

Part 2 covers the years from elementary school through high school. In middle childhood and adolescence, the cognitive skills formed earlier in life evolve to adult-like levels in many areas. Family and peer relationships expand. During adolescence, there is increased attention to work and sexuality emerges. The young person begins to learn how to face difficult issues in life. By the end of this period, a person is on the verge of legal adulthood. The typical individual uses logic and has been introduced to most of the issues that adults face.

Part 3 covers young adulthood and middle age. During this period, most people achieve their most advanced modes of thinking, achieve peak physical performance, form intimate relationships, start families of their own, begin and advance within their occupations, manage to balance many conflicting roles, and begin to confront aging. Over these years, many people go from breaking away from their families to having their children break away from them. Relationships with parents are redefined, and the pressures of being caught between the younger and older generations are felt. By the end of this period, most people have shifted focus from time since birth to time until death.

Part 4 covers the last decades of life. The biological, physical, cognitive, and social changes associated with aging become apparent. Although many changes reflect decline, many other aspects of old age represent positive elements: wisdom, retirement, friendships, and family relationships. We conclude this section, and the text, with a discussion of the end of life. Through our consideration of death, we will gain additional insights into the meaning of life and human development.

We hope the organization and learning features of the text are helpful to you—making it easier for you to learn about human development. After all, this book tells the story of people's lives, and understanding the story is what it's all about.

1.2

THINKING ABOUT DEVELOPMENT

Javier Suarez smiled broadly as he held his newborn grandson for the first time. So many thoughts rushed into his mind—What would Ricardo experience growing up? Would the poor neighborhood they live in prevent him from reaching his potential? Would the family genes for good health be passed on? How would Ricardo's life growing up as a Latino in the United States be different from Javier's own experiences in Mexico?

LIKE MANY GRANDPARENTS, Javier wonders what the future holds for his grandson. The questions he asks are interesting in their own right, but they are important for another reason: They bear on general issues of human development that have intrigued philosophers and scientists for centuries. In the next few pages, we introduce some of these issues, which surface when any aspect of development is being investigated.

RECURRING ISSUES IN HUMAN DEVELOPMENT

Three fundamental issues pervade modern research on human development: nature versus nurture, continuity versus discontinuity, and universal versus context-specific development. These issues cut across virtually all the topics in this book, so let's examine each one.

Nature Versus Nurture

Think for a minute about a particular characteristic that you and several people in your family have, such as intelligence, good looks, or a friendly, outgoing personality.

Why is this trait so prevalent? Is it because you inherited the trait from your parents? Or is it because of where and how you and your parents were brought up? *Answers to these questions illustrate different positions on the **nature-nurture issue,** which involves the degree to which genetic or hereditary influences (nature) and experiential or environmental influences (nurture) determine the kind of person you are.* Scientists once hoped to answer these questions by identifying either heredity or environment as *the* cause of a particular aspect of development. The goal was to be able to say, for example, that intelligence was due to heredity or that personality was due to experience. Today, however, we know that virtually no features of life-span development are due exclusively to either heredity or environment. Instead, development is always shaped by both: Nature and nurture are mutually interactive influences.

For example, in Chapter 2 you will see that some individuals inherit a disease that leads to mental retardation if they eat dairy products. However, if their environment contains no dairy products, they develop normal intelligence. Similarly, in Chapter 10 you will learn that one risk factor for cardiovascular disease is heredity, but that lifestyle factors such as diet and smoking play important roles in determining who has heart attacks.

As these examples illustrate, a major aim of modern developmental science is to understand how heredity and environment jointly determine development. For Javier, it means his grandson's development will surely be shaped both by the genes he inherited and by the experiences he will have.

Hi and Lois

Continuity Versus Discontinuity

Think of some ways in which you remain similar to how you were as a 5-year-old. Maybe you were outgoing and friendly at that age and remain outgoing and friendly today. Examples like these suggest a great deal of continuity in development. Once a person begins down a particular developmental pathway—for example, toward friendliness or intelligence—he or she stays on that path throughout life. According to this view, if Ricardo is a friendly and smart 5-year-old, he should be friendly and smart as a 25- and 75-year-old.

The other view—that development is not always continuous—is illustrated in the Hi and Lois cartoon. Sweet and cooperative Trixie has become assertive and demanding. In this view, people can change from one developmental path to another, perhaps several times in their lives. Consequently, Ricardo might be smart and friendly at age 5, smart but obnoxious at 25, and wise but aloof at 75!

The **continuity-discontinuity issue** *concerns whether a particular developmental phenomenon represents a smooth progression throughout the life span (continuity) or a series of abrupt shifts (discontinuity).* Throughout this book, you will find examples of both continuities and discontinuities. For example, in Chapter 5 you will see evidence of continuity: Infants who have satisfying emotional relationships with their parents typically become children with satisfying peer relationships. But in Chapter 15 you will see an instance of discontinuity: After spending most of adulthood trying to ensure the success of the next generation and to leave a legacy, older adults turn to evaluating their own lives, in search of closure and a sense that what they have done has been worthwhile.

Universal Versus Context-Specific Development

The **universal versus context-specific development issue** *concerns whether there is just one path of development or several.* In some cities in Brazil, 10- to 12-year-olds sell fruit and candy to pedestrians and passengers on buses. Although they have little formal education and often cannot identify the numbers on the money, they handle money proficiently (Saxe, 1988).

Life for Brazilian street vendors contrasts sharply with childhood in the United States, where 10- to 12-year-olds are formally taught at home or school to identify numbers and to perform the kinds of arithmetic needed to handle money. Can one theory explain development in both groups of children? Perhaps. Some theorists argue that despite what look like differences in development, there is really only one fundamental developmental process for everyone. According to this view, differences in development are simply variations on a fundamental developmental process, in much the same way that cars as different as a Chevrolet, a Honda, and a Porsche are all products of fundamentally the same manufacturing process.

The opposing view is that differences among people may not be just variations on a theme. Advocates of this view argue that human development is inextricably intertwined with the context within which it occurs. A person's development is a product of complex interaction with the environment, and that interaction is *not* fundamentally the same in all environments. Each environment has its own set of unique procedures that shape development, just as the "recipes" for cars, milkshakes, and fly swatters have little in common.

Putting all three issues together, and using personality to illustrate, we can ask how heredity and environment interact to influence the development of personality, whether the development of personality is continuous or discontinuous, and whether personality develops in much the same way around the world. To answer these kinds of questions, we need to look at the forces that combine to shape human development.

BASIC FORCES IN HUMAN DEVELOPMENT: THE BIOPSYCHOSOCIAL FRAMEWORK

When trying to explain why people develop as they do, scientists usually consider four interactive forces:

- ■ ***Biological forces*** include all genetic and health-related factors that affect development.
- ■ ***Psychological forces*** include all internal perceptual, cognitive, emotional, and personality factors that affect development.
- ■ ***Sociocultural forces*** include interpersonal, societal, cultural, and ethnic factors that affect development.
- ■ ***Life-cycle forces*** reflect differences in how the same event affects people of different ages.

Mathias Oppersdorff /Photo Researchers, Inc.

Even with little formal education, this Brazilian boy has well-developed mathematical skills, an example of cultural contextual forces on development.

Each person is a product of a unique combination of these forces. No two individuals, even in the same family, experience these forces in the same way; even identical twins eventually have different friendship networks, partners, and occupations.

To see why each of these forces is important, think about whether a mother decides to breast-feed her infant. Her decision will be based on biological variables (e.g., the quality and amount of milk she produces), her attitudes about the virtues of breast-feeding, the influences of other people (e.g., the father), and her cultural traditions about appropriate ways to feed infants. Additionally, her decision will reflect her age and stage of life. Only by focusing on all of these forces can we have a complete view of the mother's decision.

One useful way to organize the biological, psychological, and sociocultural forces on human development is with the **biopsychosocial framework.** As you can see in Figure 1.1, the biopsychosocial framework emphasizes that human development is more than any one of the basic forces considered alone. Rather, each force interacts with the others to make

■ **Figure 1.1**
The biopsychosocial framework shows that human development results from interacting forces.

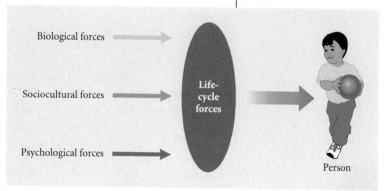

up development. Let's look at the different elements of the biopsychosocial model in more detail.

Biological Forces

Prenatal development, brain maturation, puberty, menopause, facial wrinkling, and change in cardiovascular functioning all illustrate biological forces. Many of these biological forces are determined by our genetic code, which is discussed in Chapters 2, 3, 8, 13, and 14. For example, many children resemble their parents, which shows biological influences on development. But biological forces also include the effects of lifestyle factors, such as diet and exercise; these and other examples are explored in Chapters 2, 8, 9, 13, and 14.

Collectively, biological forces can be viewed as providing the raw material necessary (in the case of genetics) and as setting the boundary conditions (in the case of one's general health) for development.

Biological influences on development help explain why relatives tend to look alike.

Psychological Forces

Psychological forces probably seem familiar because they are the ones used most often to describe the characteristics of a person. For example, think about how you describe yourself when you meet others. Most of us say that we have a nice personality and are intelligent, honest, self-confident, or something along those lines. Concepts like these reflect psychological forces.

In general, psychological forces are all the internal cognitive, emotional, personality, perceptual, and related factors that influence behavior. Psychological forces have received the most attention of the three main developmental forces. Much of what we discuss throughout the text reflects psychological forces. For example, we will see how the development of intelligence enables individuals to experience and think about their world in different ways. We'll also see how the emergence of self-esteem is related to the beliefs people have about their abilities, which in turn influence what they do.

Collectively, psychological factors provide the things we notice most about what makes people the way they are, as well as the interesting variations that make us individuals.

Sociocultural Forces

People develop in the world, not in a vacuum. To understand human development, we need to know how people and their environments interact and relate to each other. In other words, we need to view an individual's development as part of a much larger system, in which no part of the system can act without influencing all other aspects of the system. This larger system includes one's parents, children, and siblings as well as important individuals outside the family, such as friends, teachers, and coworkers. The system also includes institutions that influence development, such as schools, television, and the workplace.

All of these people and institutions fit together to form a person's culture—the knowledge, attitudes, and behavior associated with a group of people. Culture can be linked to a particular country or people (e.g., French culture), to a specific point in time (e.g., popular culture of the 2000s), or to groups of individuals who maintain specific, identifiable cultural traditions (e.g., African Americans). Knowing the culture from which a person comes provides some general information about important influences that may appear throughout the life span.

Understanding the impact of culture is particularly important in the United States, the most diverse country in the world. Hundreds of different languages are spoken, and in many states no racial or ethnic group accounts (or soon will) for more than half the population. The many customs people bring add to a growing richness that offers insights into the broad spectrum of human experience and attest to the diversity of the U.S. population.

Although the U.S. population is changing rapidly, much of the research we describe in this text was conducted on middle-class European Americans. Accordingly, we must be careful *not* to assume that findings from this group necessarily apply to people in other groups. You may feel frustrated at times, wondering whether results obtained with one group apply to other groups as well. Indeed, there is a great need for research on different cultural groups. Perhaps, as a result of taking this course, you will help fill this need by becoming a developmental researcher yourself.

Although many people may describe themselves as Latino, their different countries of origin imply key cultural differences.

Another practical problem that we face is how to describe each group. Terminology changes over time. For example, the terms *colored people, Negroes, Black Americans,* and *African Americans* have all been used to describe Americans of African ancestry. In this book, we use *African American* because it emphasizes the unique cultural heritage of that group of people. Following the same line of reasoning, we use *European American* (instead of *Caucasian* or *White*), *Native American* (instead of *Indian* or *American Indian*), *Asian American,* and *Latino American.*

These labels are not perfect. In some cases, they blur distinctions among ethnic groups. For example, people from both Guatemala and Mexico may be described as Latinos. However, their cultural backgrounds vary on several important dimensions, so we should not view them as being from a homogenous group. Similarly, the term *European American* ignores differences between individuals of northern or southern European ancestry; the term *Asian American* blurs variations among people whose heritage is, for example, Japanese, Chinese, or Korean. Whenever researchers have identified the subgroups in their research sample, we will use the more specific terms in describing results. When we use the more general terms, remember that conclusions may not apply to all subgroups within the more general term.

The Forces Interact

So far, we've described biological, psychological, and sociocultural forces in the biopsychosocial framework as if they were independent. But as we pointed out earlier in introducing the notion of the biopsychosocial framework, each shapes the others.

Consider eating habits. When the authors of this text were growing up, a "red meat and potatoes" diet was common and was thought to be healthy. Subsequently, it became known that high-fat diets may lead to cardiovascular disease and some forms of cancer. Consequently, social pressures began to change what people eat; advertising campaigns were begun; and restaurants began to indicate which menu items were low in fat. Thus, the biological forces of fat in the diet were influenced by the social forces of the times, whether in support of or in opposition to having beef every evening. Finally, as your authors became more educated about diets and their effects on health, the psychological forces of thinking and reasoning also influenced their choice of diets. (We confess, however, that chocolate remains a passion for one of us!) This example illustrates that no aspect of human development can be fully understood by examining only one or two of the forces. All three must be considered in interaction.

To understand the effects of genetic variation, we may need to examine some specific aspect of behavior in a particular social context. To understand the effects of a sociocultural force such as poverty, we may need to look at how poverty affects people's health. In fact, we'll see later in this chapter that integration across the three major forces of the biopsychosocial framework is one criterion by which the adequacy of a developmental theory can be judged. Before we do that, however, we need to consider one more aspect of this framework: The point in life at which a specific combination of biological, psychological, and sociocultural forces operates matters a great deal.

Timing Is Everything: Life-Cycle Forces

Consider the following two situations. Jacqui, a 32-year-old woman, has been happily married for 6 years. She and her husband have a steady income. They decide to start a family, and a month later Jacqui learns she is pregnant. Jenny, a 14-year-old girl, lives in the same neighborhood as Jacqui. She has been sexually active for about 6 months but is not in a stable relationship. After missing her period, Jenny took a pregnancy test and discovered that she is pregnant.

Although both Jacqui and Jenny became pregnant, the outcome of each pregnancy will certainly be affected by factors in each woman's situation such as her age, financial situation, and the extent of her social support systems. The example illustrates life-cycle forces—the same event can have different effects, depending on when it happens in a person's life. In the scenarios with Jacqui and Jenny, the same event—pregnancy—produces happiness and eager anticipation for one woman but anxiety and concern for the other.

The influence of life-cycle forces is depicted in Figure 1.2 as a unified spiral consisting of biological, psychological, and sociocultural forces. The spiral illustrates how a particular issue or event may recur, as indicated by the X's on the spiral, and how a person's accumulated experience, represented by the vertical arrow labeled "development," comes into play. For example, trust is an issue that is addressed throughout life (Erikson, 1982). From its beginnings as an infant's trust in parents, represented by the lowest "X" on the spiral, it develops into progressively more complex forms of trust over the life span for friends and/or lovers, as Jacqui can attest and Jenny will ultimately learn. Each time a person revisits trust issues he or she builds on past experiences in light of intervening development. This accumulated experience means that the person will deal with trust in a new way and that trust is shown in different ways across the life span.

By combining the four developmental forces, we can take a view of human development that encompasses the life span, appreciating the unique aspects of each phase of life. Indeed, the remainder of the book is based on this combination.

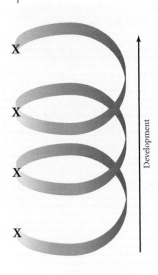

■ Figure 1.2
Life-cycle forces can be depicted as a spiral because similar issues recur at various points throughout life but are dealt with in different ways.

THINK ABOUT IT

Getting a college degree is another event that has different effects based on when it happens in a person's life. Can you think of other events like these?

TEST YOURSELF

1. The nature-nurture issue involves the degree to which _____ and the environment influence human development.

2. Azar remarked that her 14-year-old son is incredibly shy and has been ever since he was a little baby. This illustrates the _____ of development.

3. _____ forces include genetic and health factors.

How does the biopsychosocial framework provide insight into the recurring issues of development (nature-nurture, continuity-discontinuity, universal–context-specific)?

Answers: (1) genetics, (2) continuity, (3) Biological

1.3

DEVELOPMENTAL THEORIES

Marcus has just graduated from high school, first in his class. For his proud mother, Betty, this is a time to reflect on her son's past and ponder his future. Marcus has always been a happy, easy-going child—a joy to rear. And he's constantly been interested in learning. Betty wonders why he is so perpetually good-natured and so curious. If she knew the secret, she laughed, she could write a best-selling book and be a guest on Oprah!

LEARNING OBJECTIVES

How do psychodynamic theories account for development?

What is the focus of learning theories of development?

How do cognitive-developmental theories explain changes in thinking?

What are the main points in the ecological and systems approach?

What are the major tenets of life-span and life course theories?

To answer Betty's questions about her son's growth, developmental researchers would provide a theory of his development. Unfortunately, for many people, the word *theory* means "boring." But that's not true. If you want to understand human development, theories are essential because they provide the "why's" for development. What is a theory? *In human development, a **theory** is an organized set of ideas that is designed to explain development.* For example, suppose friends of yours have a baby who cries often. You could imagine several explanations for her crying. Maybe the baby cries because she's hungry; maybe she cries to get her parents to hold her; maybe she cries because she's simply a cranky, unhappy baby. Each of these explanations is a very simple theory: It tries to explain why the baby cries so much. Of course, actual sophisticated theories in human development are much more complicated, but the purpose is the same—to explain behavior and development.

There are no truly comprehensive theories of human development (Lerner, 2002). Instead, five general perspectives guide modern research on human development. These perspectives are summarized in Table 1.1; in the next few pages, we'll look at each of them.

PSYCHODYNAMIC THEORY

Psychodynamic theories propose that human behavior is largely governed by motives and drives that are internal and often unconscious. These hidden forces influence all aspects of our behavior, thought, and personality, essentially shaping every part of our lives. Psychodynamic theories postulate that development occurs in a sequence of universal stages. This perspective underlies the oldest of the modern theories of human development, tracing its roots to Freud's work in the late 19th and early 20th centuries.

Freud's various theories of development included the idea that personality has several components that emerge over time. It also led to the development of the first comprehensive life-span view, Erik Erikson's psychosocial theory, which remains an important theoretical framework today.

Erikson's Theory

In Freud's view, development is largely complete by adolescence. In contrast, one of Freud's students, Erik Erikson (1902–1994) believed that development continues throughout life. Erikson took the foundation laid by Freud and extended it through adulthood and into late life.

*In his **psychosocial theory,** Erikson proposed that personality development is determined by the interaction of an internal maturational plan and external societal demands.* He proposed that the life cycle is composed of eight stages and that the order of the

Erik Erikson

TABLE 1.1

Theoretical Perspectives on Human Development

Perspective	Examples	Main Idea	Emphases in Biopsychosocial Framework	Positions on Developmental Issues
Psychodynamic	Erikson's psychosocial theory	Personality develops through sequence of stages	Psychological, social, and life-cycle forces crucial; less emphasis on biological	Nature-nurture interaction, discontinuity, universal sequence but individual differences in rate
Learning	Behaviorism (Watson, Skinner)	Environment controls behavior	In all theories, some emphasis on biological and psychological, major focus on social, little recognition of life cycle	In all theories, strongly nurture, continuity, and universal principles of learning
	Social learning theory (Bandura)	People learn through modeling and observing		
Cognitive	Piaget's theory (and extensions) Kohlberg's moral reasoning theory	For Piaget and Kohlberg, thinking develops in a sequence of stages	For Piaget and Kohlberg, main emphasis on biological and social forces, less on psychological, little on life cycle	For Piaget and Kohlberg, strongly nature, discontinuity, and universal sequence of stages
	Information-processing theory	Thought develops by increases in efficiency at handling information	Emphasis on biological and psychological, less on social and life cycle	Nature-nurture interaction, continuity, individual differences in universal structures
	Vygotsky's theory	Development influenced by culture	Emphasis on psychological and social forces	Nature-nurture interaction, continuity, individual differences
Ecological and Systems	Bronfenbrenner's theory	Developing person embedded in a series of interacting systems	Low emphasis on biological, moderate on psychological and life cycle, heavy on social	Nature-nurture interaction, continuity, context-specific
	Competence–environmental press (Lawton and Nahemow)	Adaptation is optimal when ability and demands are in balance	Strong emphasis on biological, psychological, and social, moderate on life cycle	Nature-nurture interaction, continuity, context-specific
Life-Span Perspective/SOC and	Baltes's life-span perspective and selective optimization with compensation (SOC)	Development is multiply determined; optimization of goals	Strong emphasis on the interactions of all four forces; cannot consider any in isolation	Nature-nurture interaction, continuity and discontinuity, context-specific
Life Course Perspective	Life course theory	Life course transitions decreasingly tied to age; increased continuity over time; specific life paths across domains are interdependent	Strong emphasis on psychological, sociocultural, life cycle; less on biological	Nature-nurture interaction, continuity and discontinuity, context-specific

TABLE **1.2**

The Eight Stages of Psychosocial Development in Erikson's Theory

Psychosocial Stage	Age	Challenge
Basic trust vs. mistrust	Birth to 1 year	To develop a sense that the world is safe, a "good place"
Autonomy vs. shame and doubt	1 to 3 years	To realize that one is an independent person who can make decisions
Initiative vs. guilt	3 to 6 years	To develop the ability to try new things and to handle failure
Industry vs. inferiority	6 years to adolescence	To learn basic skills and to work with others
Identity vs. identity confusion	Adolescence	To develop a lasting, integrated sense of self
Intimacy vs. isolation	Young adulthood	To commit to another in a loving relationship
Generativity vs. stagnation	Middle adulthood	To contribute to younger people, through child rearing, child care, or other productive work
Integrity vs. despair	Late life	To view one's life as satisfactory and worth living

stages is biologically fixed. The complete theory included the eight stages shown in Table 1.2. You can see that the name of each stage reflects the challenge people face at a particular age. For example, the challenge for young adults is to become involved in a loving relationship. Challenges are met through a combination of both inner psychological and outer social influences. When challenges are met successfully, people are well prepared to meet the challenge of the next stage.

The sequence of stages in Erikson's theory is based on the **epigenetic principle,** *which means that each psychosocial strength has its own special time of ascendancy or period of particular importance.* The eight stages represent the order of this ascendancy. Because the stages extend across the whole life span, it takes a lifetime to acquire all of the psychosocial strengths. Moreover, Erikson realizes that present and future behavior must have its roots in the past, because later stages are built on the foundation laid in previous ones.

We examine each of Erikson's stages in more detail later in the book. In general, we can view them as a cycle that repeats (Logan, 1986): The first cycle goes from basic trust versus mistrust through identity versus identity confusion; the second cycle goes from intimacy versus isolation through integrity versus despair. In this view, the primary developmental progression is trust, achievement, wholeness. Throughout life, we first establish that we can trust others and ourselves, represented by basic trust versus mistrust in the first cycle. In the second cycle, we search for a person we can trust enough to establish a close relationship, represented by intimacy versus isolation. In achievement, we have a need to create something of our own, seen in the first cycle in the initiative versus guilt and industry versus inferiority stages, and in the second cycle in the generativity versus stagnation stage. Finally, we seek to answer the question of who we are, which in the first cycle is the identity versus identity confusion stage, and in the second cycle the integrity versus despair stage. From Erikson's perspective, we only confront a few issues in life, and we periodically return to them in order to reach higher resolutions of them. This return to certain key issues is a good example of the life-cycle forces we discussed earlier (page 10).

The psychodynamic perspective emphasizes that the trek to adulthood is difficult because the path is strewn with challenges. Outcomes of development reflect the manner and ease with which children surmount life's barriers. When children overcome early obstacles easily, they are better able to handle the later ones. A psychodynamic

THINK ABOUT IT

How do Erikson's eight stages of psychosocial development relate to life experiences you or people you know have had?

theorist would tell Betty that her son's cheerful disposition and his academic record suggest that he has handled life's early obstacles well, which is a good sign for his future development.

LEARNING THEORY

In contrast to psychodynamic theory, learning theory concentrates on how learning influences a person's behavior. This perspective emphasizes the role of experience, examining whether a person's behavior is rewarded or punished. This perspective also emphasizes that people learn from watching others around them. Two influential theories in this perspective are behaviorism and social learning theory.

Behaviorism

© Bettmann /Corbis

B. F. Skinner

At about the same time in the early 20th century that psychodynamic theory was attracting increased attention, John Watson (1878–1958) was among the first psychologists to champion the English philosopher John Locke's view that the infant's mind is a blank slate on which experience writes. Watson argued that learning determines what children will be. He assumed that, with the correct techniques, anything could be learned by almost anyone. In other words, in Watson's view, experience was just about all that mattered in determining the course of development.

Watson did little research to support his claims; B. F. Skinner (1904–1990) filled this gap. *Skinner studied **operant conditioning**, in which the consequences of a behavior determine whether a behavior is repeated in the future.* Skinner showed that two kinds of consequences were especially influential. *A **reinforcement** is a consequence that increases the future likelihood of the behavior that it follows.* Positive reinforcement consists of giving a reward such as chocolate, gold stars, or paychecks to increase the likelihood of a previous behavior. A father who wants to encourage his daughter to help with chores may reinforce her with praise, food treats, or money whenever she cleans her room. Negative reinforcement consists of rewarding people by taking away unpleasant things. The same father could use negative reinforcement by saying that whenever his daughter cleans her room she doesn't have to wash the dishes or fold laundry.

*A **punishment** is a consequence that decreases the future likelihood of the behavior that it follows.* Punishment suppresses a behavior either by adding something aversive or by withholding a pleasant event. Should the daughter fail to clean her room, the father may punish her by nagging (adding something aversive) or by not allowing her to watch television (withholding a pleasant event).

Skinner's research was done primarily with animals, but human development researchers showed that the principles of operant conditioning could be extended readily to people too (Baer & Wolf, 1968). Applied properly, reinforcement and punishment are indeed powerful influences on children, adolescents, and adults.

Social Learning Theory

Researchers discovered that people sometimes learn in ways that are not readily explained by operant conditioning. The most important of these is that people sometimes learn without reinforcement or punishment. *People learn much by simply watching those around them, which is known as **imitation or observational learning**.* Imitation is occurring when one toddler throws a toy after seeing a peer do so or when a school-age child offers to help an older adult carry groceries because she's seen her parents do the same.

Perhaps imitation makes you think of "monkey-see, monkey-do," in which people simply mimic what they see. Early investigators had this view too, but research quickly showed that this was wrong. People do not always imitate what they see around them. People are more likely to imitate if the person they see is popular, smart, or talented. They're also more likely to imitate when the behavior they see is rewarded than when it is punished. Findings like these imply that imitation is more complex than sheer mimicry. People are not mechanically copying what they see and hear; instead, they look to others for information about appropriate behavior. When popular, smart peers are reinforced for behaving in a particular way, it makes sense to imitate them.

Albert Bandura (1918–) based his **social cognitive theory** *on this more complex view of reward, punishment, and imitation.* Bandura's theory is "cognitive" because he believes people actively try to understand what goes on in their world; the theory is "social" because, along with reinforcement and punishment, what other people do is an important source of information about the world.

Bandura also argues that experience gives people a sense of **self-efficacy,** *which refers to people's beliefs about their own abilities and talents.* Self-efficacy beliefs help to determine when people will imitate others. A child who sees herself as athletically untalented, for example, will not try to imitate Shaquille O'Neal dunking a basketball despite the fact that he is obviously talented and popular. Thus, whether people imitate others depends on who the other person is, whether that person's behavior is rewarded, and the person's beliefs about his or her own talents.

Bandura's social cognitive theory is a far cry from Skinner's operant conditioning. The operant conditioned person who responds mechanically to reinforcement and punishment has been replaced by the social cognitive person who actively interprets these and other events. Nevertheless, Skinner, Bandura, and all learning theorists share the view that experience propels people along their developmental journeys. They would tell Betty that she can thank experience for making Marcus both happy and successful academically.

Albert Bandura

COGNITIVE-DEVELOPMENTAL THEORY

Still another way to approach development is to focus on thought processes and the construction of knowledge. In cognitive-developmental theory, the key is how people think and how thinking changes over time. Two distinct approaches have developed.

One approach postulates that thinking develops in a universal sequence of stages; Piaget's theory of cognitive development (and its recent extensions) and Kohlberg's theory of moral reasoning are two examples. The other approach proposes that people process information much like computers, becoming more efficient over much of the life span; information-processing theory is an example of this view.

Piaget's Theory

The cognitive-developmental perspective focuses on how children construct knowledge and how their constructions change over time. Jean Piaget (1896–1980), who was the most influential developmental psychologist of the 20th century, proposed the best known of these theories. Piaget believed children naturally try to make sense of their world. Throughout infancy, childhood, and adolescence, youngsters want to understand the workings of both the physical and the social world. For example, infants want to know about objects: "What happens when I push this toy off the table?" And they want to know about people: "Who is this person who feeds and cares for me?" In their efforts to comprehend their world, Piaget argued that children act like scientists, creating theories about the physical and social worlds. Children try to weave all that they know about objects and people into a complete theory, and these theories are tested daily by experience because their theories lead them to expect certain things to happen. As with real scientific theories, when the predicted events do occur, a child's belief in her theory grows stronger. When the predicted events do not occur, the child must revise her theory.

For example, an infant's theory of objects might include the idea that "Toys pushed off the table fall to the floor." If the infant pushes some other object—a plate or an article of clothing—she will find that it, too, falls to the floor and she can make the theory more general: "Objects pushed off the table fall to the floor." Piaget also believed

	TABLE **1.3**	
	Piaget's Four Stages of Cognitive Development	
Stage	Approximate Age	Characteristics
Sensorimotor	Birth to 2 years	Infant's knowledge of the world is based on senses and motor skills. By the end of the period, uses mental representation.
Preoperational thought	2 to 6 years	Child learns how to use symbols such as words and numbers to represent aspects of the world but relates to the world only through his or her perspective.
Concrete operational thought	7 years to early adolescence	Child understands and applies logical operations to experiences provided they are focused on the here and now.
Formal operational thought	Adolescence and beyond	Adolescent or adult thinks abstractly, deals with hypothetical situations, and speculates about what may be possible.

© Bettmann /Corbis

Jean Piaget

THINK ABOUT IT

Try to use the basic ideas of operant conditioning (page 14) to explain how children create theories of the physical and social world.

children begin to construct knowledge in new ways at a few critical points in development. When this happens, they revise their theories radically. These changes are so fundamental that the revised theory is, in many respects, a brand-new theory. Piaget claimed that these changes occur three times in development: once at about age 2 years, a second time at about age 7, and a third time just before adolescence. These changes mean that children go through four distinct stages in cognitive development. Each stage represents a fundamental change in how children understand and organize their environment, and each stage is characterized by more sophisticated types of reasoning. For example, the sensorimotor stage begins at birth and lasts until about 2 years of age. As the name implies, sensorimotor thinking refers to an infant's constructing knowledge through sensory and motor skills. This stage and the three later stages are shown in Table 1.3.

Piaget's theory has had an enormous influence on how developmentalists and practitioners think about cognitive development. The theory has been applied in many ways—from the creation of discovery learning toys for children to the ways teachers plan lessons.

However, Piaget's theory has also been criticized. Some say that Piaget underestimated the abilities of infants and young children. Also, the universality of his sequence of stages is not entirely supported by evidence from different cultures. More recently, Piaget's theory has been extended to include important cognitive changes in adulthood. We consider these issues in more detail in Chapters 4, 6, and 10.

Kohlberg's Theory

Because Piaget's theory attempts to tie together maturation and experience on one hand and cognitive and social development on the other, it has inspired developmentalists with a wide variety of interests. One of the most influential of these was Lawrence Kohlberg (1927–1987), who built his theory of moral reasoning on the foundation of Piaget's theory of overall cognitive development. As we'll see in detail in Chapter 8, Kohlberg described a sequence of fixed stages that reflect the different ways people think about moral dilemmas. Kohlberg's stages correspond fairly well to Piaget's stages, but they involve levels of thinking beyond Piaget's final stage. In this respect, Kohlberg's theory constitutes an extension of Piaget's work.

Information-Processing Theory

Not all cognitive-developmental theorists view development as a sequence of stages. Information-processing theorists, for example, draw heavily on how computers work to explain thinking and how it develops through childhood and adolescence. *Just as com-*

puters consist of both hardware (disk drives, random-access memory, and central processing unit) and software (the programs we use), ***information-processing theory*** *proposes that human cognition consists of mental hardware and mental software.* Mental hardware refers to cognitive structures, including different memories where information is stored. Mental software includes organized sets of cognitive processes that enable people to complete specific tasks, such as reading a sentence, playing a video game, or hitting a baseball. For example, an information-processing psychologist would say that, for a student to do well on an exam, she must encode the information as she studies, store it in memory, then retrieve the necessary information during the test.

Information-processing theory helps explain how this woman learns, stores, and retrieves information so she can pass this exam.

How do information-processing psychologists explain developmental changes in thinking? To answer this question, think about improvements in personal computers. Today's personal computers can accomplish much more than computers built just a few years ago. Why? Today's computers have better hardware (e.g., more memory and a faster central processing unit) and more sophisticated software that takes advantage of the better hardware. Like modern computers, older children and adolescents have better hardware and better software than younger children, who are more like last year's out-of-date model. For example, older children typically solve math word problems better than younger children because they have greater memory capacity to store the facts in the problem and because their methods for performing arithmetic operations are more efficient.

Some researchers also point to deterioration of the mental hardware, along with declines in the mental software, as explanations of cognitive aging. We will see in Chapter 14, for example, that normal aging brings with it significant changes in people's ability to process information.

Vygotsky's Theory

One of the first theorists to emphasize that children's thinking does not develop in a vacuum, but is influenced by the sociocultural context in which children grow up, was Lev Vygotsky (1896–1934). A Russian psychologist, Vygotsky focused on ways that adults convey to children the beliefs, customs, and skills of their culture. Vygotsky believed that because a fundamental aim of all societies is to enable children to acquire essential cultural values and skills, every aspect of a child's development must be considered against this backdrop. For example, most parents in the United States want their children to work hard in school and be admitted to college, because earning a degree is one of the keys to getting a good job. In the same way, parents in Efe (a developing nation in Africa) want their children to learn to hunt, build houses, and gather food, because these skills are key to survival in their environment. Vygotsky viewed development as an apprenticeship in which children develop when they work with skilled adults, including teachers and parents.

For Piaget, Kohlberg, information-processing theorists, and Vygotsky, children's thinking becomes more sophisticated as they develop. Piaget and Kohlberg explain this change as resulting from the more sophisticated knowledge that children construct from more sophisticated thinking; information-processing psychologists attribute it to more sophisticated mental hardware and mental software. None of these theorists would have much to say to Betty about Marcus's good nature. As to his academic success, Piaget and Kohlberg would explain that all children naturally want to understand their world; Marcus is simply unusually skilled in this regard. An information-processing psychologist would point to superior hardware and superior software as the keys to his academic success. In contrast, Vygotsky would say that Betty communicated key aspects of the culture to Marcus, which influenced both his good nature and his performance in school.

THE ECOLOGICAL AND SYSTEMS APPROACH

Most developmentalists agree that the environment is an important force in many aspects of development. However, only ecological theories have focused on the complexities of environments and their links to development. *In **ecological theory,** which gets its name from the branch of biology dealing with the relation of living things to their environment and to one another, human development is inseparable from the environmental contexts in which a person develops.* The ecological approach is broad; it proposes that all aspects of development are interconnected, much like the threads of a spider's web are intertwined. Interconnectedness means that no aspect of development can be isolated from others and understood independently. An ecological theorist would emphasize that, if we want to understand why adolescents behave as they do, we need to consider the many different systems that influence them, including parents, peers, teachers, television, the neighborhood, and social policy.

We will consider two examples of the ecological and systems approach: Bronfenbrenner's theory and the competence–environmental press framework.

Bronfenbrenner's Theory

The best-known proponent of the ecological approach is Urie Bronfenbrenner (1979, 1989, 1995), who proposes that the developing person is embedded in a series of complex and interactive systems. Bronfenbrenner divides the environment into the four levels shown in Figure 1.3: the microsystem, the mesosystem, the exosystem, and the macrosystem.

*At any point in life, the **microsystem** consists of the people and objects in an individual's immediate environment.* These are the people closest to a child, such as parents or siblings. Some children may have more than one microsystem; for example, a young child might have the microsystems of the family and of the day care setting. As you can imagine, microsystems strongly influence development.

■ **Figure 1.3**
Bronfenbrenner's ecological approach emphasizes the interaction across different systems in which people operate.

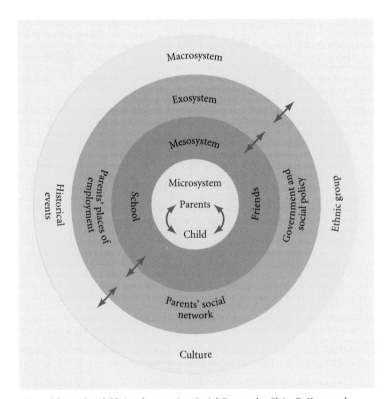

Adapted from *The Child: Development in a Social Context,* by Claire B. Kopp and Joanne B. Krakow, p. 648. Copyright © 1982 Addison-Wesley Publishing Co., Inc. Used with permission.

*Microsystems themselves are connected to create the **mesosystem.*** The mesosystem provides connections across microsystems, because what happens in one microsystem is likely to influence others. Perhaps you've found that if you have a stressful day at work or school you're often grouchy at home. This indicates that your mesosystem is alive and well; your microsystems of home and work are interconnected emotionally for you.

*The **exosystem** refers to social settings that a person may not experience firsthand but that still influence development.* For example, changes in government policy regarding welfare may mean that poor children have less opportunity for enriched preschool experiences. Although the influence of the exosystem is at least secondhand, its effects on human development can be quite strong.

*The broadest environmental context is the **macrosystem,*** *the subcultures and cultures in which the microsystem, mesosystem, and exosystem are embedded.* A mother, her workplace, her child, and the child's school are part of a larger cultural setting, such as Asian Americans living in Southern California or Italian Americans living in large cities on the East Coast. Members of these cultural groups share a common identity, a common heritage, and common values. The macrosystem evolves over time; what is true about a particular culture today may or may not have been true in the past and may or may not be true in the future. Thus, each successive generation may develop in a unique macrosystem.

Competence–Environmental Press Theory

A second, less complex approach that also emphasizes the interaction of individuals with their environment is Lawton and Nahemow's (1973) competence–environmental press theory. As we will see in greater detail in Chapter 15, this theory was originally proposed to account for the ways in which older adults function in their environment. However, it can be used to understand how people of all ages deal with their environments.

Basically, according to the theory, how well people adapt depends on the match between their competence, or abilities, and the environmental press, or the demands put on them by the environment. This notion of "best match" or "best fit" leading to adaptation could be extended across the life span. For example, how well a child's social skills match her peer group's demands could account for whether she will be accepted by the peer group or not. As with Bronfenbrenner's theory, competence–environmental press theory emphasizes that in order to understand people's functioning, it is essential to understand the systems in which they live.

Ecological theorists would agree with learning theorists in telling Betty that the environment has been pivotal in her son's amiable disposition and his academic achievements. However, the ecological theorist would insist that environment means much more than the reinforcements, punishments, and observations that are central to learning theory. The ecological theorist would emphasize the different levels of environmental influence on Marcus. Betty's ability to balance home (microsystem) and work (mesosystem) so skillfully (which meant that she was usually in a good mood herself) contributed positively to Marcus's development as did Betty's membership in a cultural group (exosystem) that emphasized the value of doing well in school.

LIFE-SPAN PERSPECTIVE, SELECTIVE OPTIMIZATION WITH COMPENSATION, AND LIFE COURSE PERSPECTIVE

One criticism of most of the theories of human development we have considered thus far is that they pay little or no specific attention to the adult years of the life span. Historically, adulthood was downplayed due to the belief that it was a time when abilities had reached a plateau (rather than continuing to develop) and that adulthood was followed by inevitable decline in old age. However, the field of adult development and aging has evolved greatly since the late 1940s. As a result, new theoretical perspectives emphasize the importance of viewing human development as a lifelong process. These perspectives view development in terms of where a person has been and where he or she is heading.

Life-Span Perspective and Selective Optimization With Compensation

What would it be like to try to understand your best friend without knowing anything about his or her life? We cannot understand adults' experiences without appreciating their childhood and adolescence. Placing adults' lives in this broader context is what the life-span perspective does.

According to the **life-span perspective,** *human development is multiply determined and cannot be understood within the scope of a single framework.* Matilda Riley, the person most responsible for first developing the life-span perspective, insists that human development must be viewed from the biopsychosocial framework. The basic premises of the life-span perspective, in which aging is viewed in the context of the rest of the life span, are as follows (Riley, 1979):

■ Aging is a lifelong process of growing up and growing old, beginning with conception and ending with death. No single period of a person's life (such as childhood, adolescence, or middle age) can be understood apart from its origins and its consequences. To understand a specific period, we must know what came before and what comes after.

■ How one's life is played out is affected by social, environmental, and historical change. Thus, the experiences of one generation may not be the same as those of another.

■ New patterns of development can cause social change. For example, the realization over the past few decades that severe physical punishment harms psychological development resulted in the passage of laws restricting parents' rights to use this form of punishment. Thus, not only does social change influence people's development, but patterns of development influence society.

The life-span perspective divides human development into two phases: an early phase (childhood and adolescence) and a later phase (young adulthood, middle age, and old age). The early phase is characterized by rapid age-related increases in people's physical size and abilities. These changes also occur in the later phase, but more slowly; people's abilities continue to develop as they adapt to the environment (Baltes, Lindenberger, & Staudinger, 1998; Baltes & Smith, 2003). When development is viewed from a life-span perspective, it is a complex phenomenon that cannot be understood from the vantage point of a single discipline. Understanding how people change requires input from many perspectives.

Paul Baltes and colleagues provide many of the main approaches to human development from a life-span perspective (Baltes, 1987; Baltes et al., 1998; Baltes & Smith, 2003; Baltes, Staudinger, & Lindenberger, 1999). They identify four key features of the life-span perspective:

■ *Multidirectionality:* Development involves both growth and decline; as people grow in one area they may lose in another and at different rates. For example, people's vocabulary ability tends to increase throughout life, but reaction time tends to slow down.

■ *Plasticity:* One's capacity is not predetermined or carved in stone. Many skills can be learned or improved with practice, even in late life. For example, people can learn ways to help themselves remember information, which may help them deal with declines in memory ability with age. There are limits to the degree of potential improvement, though, as described in later chapters.

■ *Historical context:* Each of us develops within a particular set of circumstances determined by the historical time in which we are born and the cul-

Paul Baltes

ture in which we grow up. For example, living in a middle-class suburb in the 1950s was very different from living in a poor Latino neighborhood in Texas in the 1990s.

■ *Multiple causation:* How we develop results from biological, psychological, sociocultural, and life-cycle forces, which we considered earlier in this chapter. For example, two children growing up in the same family will have different experiences if one has a developmental disability and one does not.

Based on these principles, Baltes and colleagues (1998) propose that life-span development consists of the dynamic interplay between growth, maintenance, and loss regulation. Figure 1.4 shows the developmental courses of several hypothetical processes.

Notice that different processes have different developmental trajectories. In their view, four factors are critical to understanding these differences across processes:

■ There is an age-related reduction in the amount and quality of biologically based resources as people grow older.

■ There is an age-related increase in the amount and quality of culture needed to generate continuously higher growth, usually resulting in a net slowing of growth as people mature and grow old.

■ There is an age-related decline in the efficiency with which cultural resources are used.

■ There is a lack of cultural support structures for growing old.

These four factors create the need to shift increasing resources to maintain function and deal with biologically related losses as we grow old, leaving fewer resources to be devoted to continued growth.

Taken together, the principles of the life-span perspective create a way to describe and explain the successful adaptation of people to the changes that occur with aging by proposing an interaction between three processes: selection, compensation, and optimization (Baltes, 1997; B. Baltes & Heydens-Gahir, 2003; M. Baltes & Carstensen, 1999). Selection processes serve to choose goals, life domains, and life tasks; optimization and compensation concern maintaining or enhancing chosen goals. *The basic assumption of the* **selective optimization with compensation (SOC) model** *is that the three processes form a system of behavioral action that generates and regulates development and aging.*

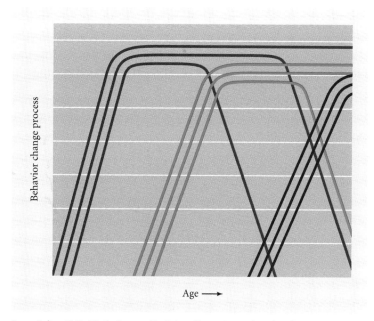

Figure 1.4
In Baltes and colleagues' model, different aspects of development show different courses of development. Note that different behaviors can start at any point in the life span and have different developmental trajectories.

Behavior change process

Age ⟶

From Baltes, P. B., Lindenberger, U., & Staudinger, U. M. (1988). Life-span theory in developmental psychology. In W. Damon (Ed.), *Handbook of child psychology, Vol. 1. Theoretical models of human development* (5th ed.). New York: Wiley, p. 1044.

As people mature and grow old, they select from a range of possibilities or opportunities. This selection occurs for two main reasons. *Elective selection* occurs when one chooses to reduce one's involvement to fewer domains as a result of new demands or tasks, such as when a college student drops out of some organizations due to the amount of work required in the courses she is taking that term. *Loss-based selection* occurs when this reduced involvement happens as a result of anticipated losses in personal or environmental resources, such as when an older person stops going to church because he can no longer drive. In either case, selection can involve the continuation of previous goals on a lesser scale, or the substitution of new goals, and may be proactive or reactive.

Compensation occurs when a person can no longer function well in a particular domain because the necessary behavioral skills have been lost or have fallen below the level necessary for adequate functioning. When a person compensates, she searches for an alternative way to accomplish the goal; for example, if one loses the ability to drive to work due to an injury, one might compensate by taking the bus. Sometimes, compensation requires learning a new skill; for example, an older adult who is experiencing short-term memory problems might compensate by learning to use a PDA device. Thus, compensation differs from selection in that the task or goal is maintained but other means are used to achieve it.

Optimization involves the minimization of losses and the maximization of gains. The main idea is to find the best match possible between one's resources (biological, psychological, and sociocultural) and one's desired goals. Because people cannot achieve optimal outcomes in everything, development becomes a dynamic balancing process between selecting the right goals and compensating when possible to help maximize the odds of achieving them.

One can see the SOC model at work in many situations. For example, aging musicians may reduce the number of pieces they play (selection), rehearse them more often (optimization), and sing them in a lower key (compensation). This way, they can continue playing concerts later in life. Or, a college athlete who excels at ice hockey and baseball may decide to concentrate on hockey (selection), work on training all year (optimization), and develop a wicked wrist shot to make up for a mediocre slap shot (compensation).

The life-span perspective and the SOC model have provided important approaches to the contemporary study of human development. The emphasis on the need for a multidisciplinary approach and recognition of many interactive forces will be developed throughout this text.

Life Course Perspective

If you ask an adult to describe his or her life, what you are likely to hear is a story that includes several key life transitions (e.g., going to school, getting a first job, getting married, having children). Such stories show how people move through their lives and experience unique interactions of the four forces of development.

The **life course perspective** *describes the ways in which various generations experience the biological, psychological, and sociocultural forces of development in their respective historical contexts.* Specifically, it lets researchers examine how historical time affects how people create their lives (Hagestad & Dannefer, 2001; Hareven, 1995, 2002; O'Rand & Campbell, 1999). A key feature of the life course perspective is the dynamic interplay between the individual and society. This interplay creates three major dimensions, all of which involve timing, which underlie the life course perspective:

- The individual timing of life events in relation to external historical events. This dimension addresses the question: How do people time and sequence their lives (e.g., getting a first job) in the context of changing historical conditions (e.g., economic good times or recession)?
- The synchronization of individual transitions with collective familial ones. This dimension addresses the question: How do people balance their own lives (e.g., work obligations) with those of their family (e.g., children's soccer games)?

■ The impact of earlier life events, as shaped by historical events, on subsequent ones. This dimension addresses the question: How does experiencing an event earlier in life (e.g., a male turning 18 years old) at a particular point in history (e.g., when there is a military draft) affect one's subsequent life (e.g., choosing a particular career)?

Research from the life course perspective has clearly shown that major life transitions such as marriage, childbearing, starting and ending a career, and completing one's education occur at many different ages across people and generations. These differences begin appearing after adolescence when people begin to have much more control over the course of their lives. Research has also shown that life transitions are more continuous and multidirectional than previously thought. For example, in traditional models completing an education was relegated to early adulthood; current trends toward lifelong learning make this view obsolete. Finally, research shows that the various domains of people's lives are highly interdependent; for example, the decision to have a child is often made in the context of where one is in one's career and education.

The emphasis in the life course perspective on the interrelations between the individual and society through the emphasis on historical time has made it a dominant view in the social sciences. In particular, it is very useful in helping researchers understand how the various aspects of people's experiences (work, family, education) interact to create unique lives. Sadie and Bessie Delany, discussed in the Real People feature, are good examples of this.

REAL PEOPLE: Applying Human Development

SARAH AND ELIZABETH DELANY

Overall, life-span and life-cycle theories have greatly enhanced the general body of developmental theory by drawing attention to the role of aging in the broader context: "When you get real old, honey," said Elizabeth (Bessie) Delany, "you lay it all on the table."

There's an old saying: "Only little children and old folks tell the truth." With her sister Sarah (Sadie), Bessie lived through and was shaped by some of the most important historical events of the late 19th and 20th centuries. They grew up during a time when segregation was the rule in the South, so they experienced many forms of discrimination, as well as the civil rights and the women's movements. They were born more than a decade before the invention of the airplane, and they lived to see people travel to space and walk on the moon. Each rose to professional prominence, Bessie as the second African American woman to become a licensed dentist in New York and Sadie as the first African American to teach domestic science on the high school level in New York City public schools.

They never married. Bessie died at age 104 in 1995, and Sadie died at age 109 in 1999. Discover for yourself how social and historical events affected their lives by reading their story, listed in the readings at the end of this chapter.

AP /Wide World Photos

Sadie Delany (attending her sister Bessie's funeral) is an example of how historical events can shape a life.

Overall, life-span and life-cycle theories have greatly enhanced the general body of developmental theory by drawing attention to the role of aging in the broader context of human development. These theories have played a major role in conceptualizing adulthood and have greatly influenced the research we consider in Chapters 10 through 15. And life-span and life course perspective theorists would tell Betty that Marcus will continue to develop throughout his adult years, and that this developmental journey will be influenced by biopsychosocial forces, including his own family.

THE BIG PICTURE

Each of the theories provides ways of explaining how the biological, psychological, sociocultural, and life-cycle forces create human development. But because no single theory provides a complete explanation of all aspects of development, we must rely on the biopsychosocial framework to help piece together an account based on many different theories. Throughout the remainder of this text, you will read about many theories that differ in focus and in scope. To help you understand them better, each theory will be introduced in the context of the issues that it addresses.

Because one of the criteria for a theory is that it be testable, developmentalists have adopted certain methods to help accomplish this. The next section provides an overview of the methods by which developmentalists conduct research and test their theories.

TEST YOURSELF

1. _____ organize knowledge in order to provide testable explanations of human behaviors and the ways in which they change over time.

2. The _____ perspective proposes that development is determined by the interaction of an internal maturational plan and external societal demands.

3. According to social cognitive theory, people learn from reinforcements, from punishments, and through _____.

4. Piaget's theory, Kohlberg's theory, and _____ theory are examples of the cognitive-developmental perspective.

5. According to Bronfenbrenner, development occurs in the context of the _____, mesosystem, exosystem, and macrosystem.

6. A belief that human development is characterized by multidirectionality and plasticity is fundamental to the _____ perspective.

How are the psychodynamic perspective and Piaget's theory similar? How are they different?

Answers: (1) Theories, (2) psychosocial, (3) observing others, (4) information-processing, (5) microsystem, (6) life-span

---

1.4

DOING DEVELOPMENTAL RESEARCH

LEARNING OBJECTIVES

How do scientists measure topics of interest in studying human development?

What general research designs are used in human development research? What designs are unique to human development research?

What ethical procedures must researchers follow?

Leah and Joan are both mothers of 10-year-old boys. Their sons have many friends, but the basis for the friendships is not obvious to the mothers. Leah believes "opposites attract"—children form friendships with peers who have complementary interests and abilities. Joan doubts this; her son seems to seek out other boys who are near clones of himself in terms of interests and abilities.

SUPPOSE LEAH AND JOAN KNOW THAT YOU'RE TAKING A COURSE IN HUMAN DEVELOPMENT, so they ask you to settle their argument. Leah believes complementary children are more often friends, whereas Joan believes similar children are more often friends. You know that research could show whose ideas are supported under which circumstances, but how? In fact, human development researchers must make several important decisions as they prepare to study a topic. They need to decide how to measure the topic of interest; they must design their study; they must choose a method for studying development; and they must decide whether their plan respects the rights of the individuals who would participate in the research.

Human development researchers do not always stick to this sequence of steps. For example, often researchers will consider the rights of research participants as they make the other decisions, perhaps rejecting a measurement procedure because it violates the rights of participants. Nevertheless, for simplicity, we will use this sequence as we describe each of the steps in doing developmental research.

MEASUREMENT IN HUMAN DEVELOPMENT RESEARCH

Researchers usually begin by deciding how to measure the topic or behavior of interest. For example, the first step toward answering Leah and Joan's question about friendships would be to decide how to measure friendships.

Human development researchers typically use one of four approaches: observing systematically, using tasks to sample behavior, asking people for self reports, and taking physiological measures.

Systematic Observation

As the name implies, **systematic observation** *involves watching people and carefully recording what they do or say.* Two forms of systematic observation are common. *In* **naturalistic observation,** *people are observed as they behave spontaneously in some real-life situation.* Of course, researchers can't keep track of everything that someone does, so beforehand they must decide what variables to record. For example, researchers studying friendship might decide to observe children at the start of the first year in a middle school (chosen because many children will be making new friends at this time). They could decide to record where children sit in the lunchroom and who talks to whom.

Structured observations *differ from naturalistic observations in that the researcher creates a setting that is particularly likely to elicit the behavior of interest.* Structured observations are particularly useful for studying behaviors that are difficult to observe naturally. Some phenomena occur rarely, such as emergencies. An investigator relying on natural observations to study people's responses to emergencies wouldn't make much progress with naturalistic observation because, by definition, emergencies don't occur at predetermined times and locations. However, using a structured observation, an investigator might stage an emergency—perhaps cooperating with authorities to simulate an accident—to observe other people's responses.

Other behaviors are difficult for researchers to observe because they occur in private settings, not public ones. For example, much interaction between friends takes place at home, where it would be difficult for investigators to observe unobtrusively. However, friends could be asked to come to the researcher's laboratory, which might be furnished to resemble a family room in a typical house. Friends would then be asked to perform some activity typical of friends, such as discussing a problem together or deciding what movie to see. The researchers would then observe their activity from another room, through a one-way mirror, or by videotaping them.

Structured observations are valuable in enabling researchers to observe behavior(s) that would otherwise be difficult to study. However, investigators using this approach must be careful that the settings they create do not disturb the behavior of interest. For example, observing friends as they discuss a problem in a mock family room has many artificial aspects to it: The friends are not in their own homes, they were told in general terms what to do, and they know they're being observed. Any or all of these factors may cause friends to behave differently than they would in the real world. This issue relates to the validity of the research. For example, are observations of friends in a mock family room telling us about friends' interactions as they occur naturally? If they are, then they represent a valid measure of people's behavior. Investigators must take great care to document the validity of their measures.

■ **Figure 1.5**
In this example of sampling behavior with tasks, the child is to select the face that looks happy.

Sampling Behavior With Tasks

When investigators can't observe a behavior directly, another popular alternative is to create tasks that are thought to sample the behavior of interest. One task often used to measure older adults' memory is digit span: Adults listen as a sequence of digits is presented aloud. After the last digit is presented, they try to repeat the digits in order. Another example is shown in Figure 1.5. To study the ability to recognize emotions, the child has been asked to look at the photographs and point to the face that looks happy.

A child's answers on this sort of task are useful in determining his or her ability to recognize emotions. This approach is popular with human development researchers primarily because it is so convenient. The main problem with this approach is validity: Does the task provide a realistic sample of the behavior of interest? For example, asking children to judge emotions from photographs may not be valid because it underestimates what they do in real life. Can you think of reasons this might be the case? We mention several reasons on page 38, just after Test Yourself.

Self Reports

Self reports actually represent a special case of using tasks to measure people's behavior. *Self reports are simply people's answers to questions about the topic of interest.*

When questions are posed in written form, the self report is a questionnaire; when questions are posed orally, the self report is an interview. In either format, questions are created that probe different aspects of the topic of interest. For example, if you believe children are more often friends when they have interests in common, then you might tell your research participants the following:

> Tom and Dave just met each other at school. Tom likes to read, plays the clarinet in the school orchestra, and is not interested in sports; Dave likes to IM his friends, tinker with his car, and is a star on the football team. Do you think Tom and Dave will become friends?

The participants would then decide, perhaps using a rating scale, whether the boys are likely to become friends.

Self reports are useful because they can lead directly to information on the topic of interest. They are also relatively convenient, particularly when they can be administered to groups of participants.

However, self reports are not always valid measures of people's behavior because answers are sometimes inaccurate. Why? When asked about past events, people may not remember them accurately. For example, an older adult asked about adolescent friends may not remember those friendships well. Sometimes people answer incorrectly due to response bias. For many questions, some responses are more socially acceptable than others. People are more likely to select socially acceptable answers than socially unacceptable ones. For example, many people would be reluctant to admit that they have no friends at all. As long as investigators keep these weaknesses in mind, self report is a valuable tool for human development research.

THINK ABOUT IT

If you were studying middle-aged adults caring for their aging parents, what would be the advantages of systematic observation, sampling behavior with tasks, and self reports?

Physiological Measures

A final approach to measurement is less common but can be very powerful—measuring people's physiological responses. Heart rate, for example, often slows down when people are paying close attention to something interesting. Consequently, researchers often measure heart rate to determine a person's degree of attention. As another example, the hormone *cortisol* is often secreted in response to stress. By measuring cortisol levels in people's saliva, scientists can determine when they are experiencing stress.

As both of these examples suggest, physiological measures are usually specialized—they focus on a particular aspect of a person's behavior (attention and stress in the two examples). What's more, they're often used alongside other behaviorally oriented methods. A researcher studying stress might observe several people, looking for overt signs of stress, ask parents/partners/friends to rate the target people's stress, and also measure cortisol in the target people's saliva. If all three measures lead to the same conclusions about stress, then the researcher can be much more confident about those conclusions.

Another important group of physiological measure includes those used to study brain activity. For centuries, philosophers and scientists could only guess about the role of the brain in thinking and feeling. But techniques developed in the past 25 years allow today's scientists to record many facets of brain functioning in real time as people perform specific tasks. Neuroscientists are making great strides in identifying the brain regions associated with reasoning, memory, emotions, and other psychological functions.

The strengths and weaknesses of the four approaches to measurement are summarized in Table 1.4.

Reliability and Validity

After researchers choose a method, they must show that it is both reliable and valid. *The* **reliability** *of a measure is the extent to which it provides a consistent index of a characteristic.* A measure of friendship, for example, is reliable to the extent that it gives a consistent estimate of a person's friendship network each time you administer it. All measures used in human development research must be shown to be reliable, or they cannot be used.

The **validity** *of a measure refers to whether it really measures what researchers think it measures.* For example, a measure of friendship is valid only if it can be shown to actually measure friendship (and not love, for example). Validity is often established by showing that the measure in question is closely related to another measure known to be valid. Because it is possible to have a measure that is reliable but not valid (e.g., a ruler is a reliable measure of length but not a valid measure of friendship), researchers must ensure that their measures are both reliable and valid.

TABLE 1.4

Measuring Behaviors of Interest in Human Development Research

Method	Strength	Weakness
Systematic observation		
Naturalistic observation	Captures people's behavior in its natural setting	Difficult to use with behaviors that are rare or that typically occur in private settings
Structured observation	Can be used to study behaviors that are rare or that typically occur in private settings	May be invalid if structured setting distorts the behavior
Sampling behavior with tasks	Convenient—can be used to study most behaviors	May be invalid if the task does not sample behavior as it occurs naturally
Self reports	Convenient—can be used to study most behaviors	May be invalid because people answer incorrectly (due to either forgetting or response bias)
Physiological measures	Provide a more direct measure of underlying behavior	Highly specific in what they measure, and thus cannot be applied broadly

Throughout this book, you'll see many studies using different methods. In addition, you'll often see that studies of the same topic or behavior use different methods. That is, each of the approaches will be used in different studies. This can be particularly valuable: Because the approaches to measurement have different strengths and weaknesses, finding the same results regardless of the approach leads to particularly strong conclusions.

Representative Sampling

Valid measures also depend on the people who are tested. *Researchers are usually interested in broad groups of people called* **populations.** Examples of populations would be all American 7-year-olds or all African American grandparents. *Virtually all studies include only a* **sample** *of people, which is a subset of the population.* Researchers must take care that their sample really is representative of the population of interest. An unrepresentative sample can lead to invalid research. For example, what would you think of a study of older adults' friendship if you learned that the sample consisted entirely of adults who had no siblings? You would, quite correctly, decide that this sample is not representative of the population of older adults and question whether its results apply to adults with siblings.

As you read on, you'll soon discover that much of the research we describe was conducted with samples of middle-class European American people. Are these samples representative of all people in the United States? Of all people in the world? Sometimes, but not always. Be careful *not* to assume that findings from this group necessarily apply to people in other groups. Additionally, some developmental issues have not been studied in all ethnic and racial groups. For example, the U.S. government does not consistently report its statistics for all ethnic groups.

In an effort to make samples more representative, some federal agencies now require the inclusion of certain groups unless there is a compelling reason not to do so. For example, the National Institutes of Health require the inclusion of ethnic minorities, women, and children in research funded by them. These steps may make it possible to obtain a broader view of developmental processes. Until we have representative samples in all developmental research, we cannot know whether a particular phenomenon applies only to the group studied or to people more generally.

GENERAL DESIGNS FOR RESEARCH

Having selected a way to measure the topic or behavior of interest, researchers next must embed this measure in a research design that yields useful, relevant results. Human development researchers rely on two primary designs in planning their work: correlational and experimental studies.

Correlational Studies

In a **correlational study,** *investigators look at relations between variables as they exist naturally in the world.* In the simplest possible correlational study, a researcher would measure two variables, then see how they are related. Imagine a researcher who wants to test the idea that smarter people have more friends. To test this claim, the researcher would measure two variables for each person in the sample. One would be the number of friends that the person has; the other would be the person's intelligence.

The results of a correlational study are usually measured by calculating a **correlation coefficient,** *abbreviated* r, *which expresses the strength and direction of a relation between two variables.* Correlations can range from -1.0 to 1.0 and reflect three different relations between intelligence and the number of friends:

- When *r* equals 0, two variables are completely unrelated: People's intelligence is unrelated to the number of friends they have.
- When *r* is greater than 0, scores are related positively: People who are smart tend to have more friends than people who are not as smart. That is, *more* intelligence is associated with having *more* friends.

■ When *r* is less than 0, scores are related, but inversely: People who are smart tend to have fewer friends than people who are not as smart. That is, *more* intelligence is associated with having *fewer* friends.

In interpreting a correlation coefficient, you need to consider both the sign *and* the size of the correlation. The sign indicates the *direction* of the relation between variables: a positive sign means that larger values on one variable are associated with larger values on the second variable, whereas a negative sign means that larger values on one variable are associated with smaller values on a second variable.

The *strength* of a relation is measured by how much the correlation differs from 0, either positively or negatively. If the correlation between intelligence and number of friends were .9, the relation between these variables would be very strong: Knowing a person's intelligence, you could accurately predict how many friends the person has. If, instead, the correlation were .3, the link between intelligence and number of friends would be relatively weak: Although more intelligent people would have more friends on the average, there would be many exceptions to this rule. Similarly, a correlation of −.9 would indicate a strong negative relation between intelligence and number of friends, but a correlation of −.3 would indicate a weak negative relation.

A researcher conducting a correlational study can determine whether the variables are related. However, this design doesn't address the question of cause and effect between the variables. For example, suppose a researcher finds that the correlation between intelligence and number of friends is .7. This would mean that people who are smarter have more friends than people who are not as smart. How would you interpret this correlation? Figure 1.6 shows that three interpretations are possible. First, maybe being smart causes people to have more friends. Another interpretation is that having more friends causes people to be smarter. A third interpretation is that neither variable causes the other; instead, intelligence and number of friends are caused by a third variable that was not measured in the study. Perhaps parents who are warm and supportive tend to have children who grow up to both be smarter and have many friends. Any of these interpretations could be true. But they cannot be distinguished in a correlational study. When investigators want to track down causes, they resort to a different design, an experimental study.

■ **Figure 1.6**
There are three basic interpretations of a correlation coefficient because there is no direct way to assess cause and effect.

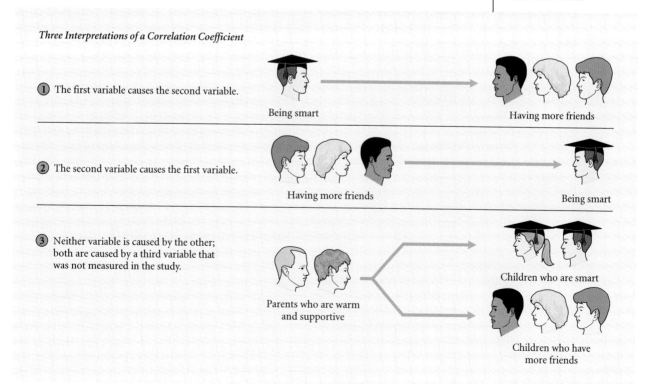

Three Interpretations of a Correlation Coefficient

① The first variable causes the second variable.

Being smart → Having more friends

② The second variable causes the first variable.

Having more friends → Being smart

③ Neither variable is caused by the other; both are caused by a third variable that was not measured in the study.

Parents who are warm and supportive → Children who are smart / Children who have more friends

Experimental Studies

An **experiment** *is a systematic way of manipulating the key factor(s) that the investigator thinks causes a particular behavior. The factor being manipulated is called the **independent variable;** the behavior being observed is called the **dependent variable.*** In human development, an experiment requires that the investigator begin with one or more treatments, circumstances, or events (independent variables) that are thought to affect behavior. People are then assigned randomly to conditions that differ in the treatment they are given; then an appropriate measure (the dependent variable) is taken of all participants to see whether the treatment or treatments had the expected effect. Because each person has an equal chance of being assigned to each treatment condition (the definition of random assignment), the groups should be the same except in the treatment they have received. Any differences between the groups can be attributed to the differential treatment people received in the experiment rather than to other factors.

Suppose, for example, that an investigator believes adolescents can learn more from a short story in a quiet room than in a room in which loud music is playing. Figure 1.7 shows how we might test this hypothesis. Adolescents come to the testing site (perhaps a room in a school) where they read a brief story prepared specially for the study. Based on random assignment, individual adolescents read the story either while the room is quiet or while loud music is played.

The loud music is always the same music, played at the same volume, for all adolescents in the loud-music condition. All the participants read the identical story under circumstances held as constant as possible except for the presence or absence of the music. They all get the same amount of time to read the story and are given the same test afterward. If scores on the test are, on average, better in the quiet condition than in the loud-music condition, the investigator may say with confidence that the music has an unfavorable effect on learning the story. Conclusions about cause and effect are possible in this example because the direct manipulation occurred under controlled conditions.

Human development researchers usually conduct experiments in laboratory-like settings because this allows full control over the variables that may influence the outcome of the research. A shortcoming of laboratory work is that the behavior of interest is not studied in its natural setting. Consequently, there is always the potential problem that the results may be invalid because they are artificial—specific to the laboratory setting and not representative of the behavior in the "real world."

Each research design used by developmentalists has both strengths and weaknesses. There is no one best method. Consequently, no single investigation can definitely settle a question. Researchers rarely rely on one study or even one method to reach conclusions. Instead, they prefer to find converging evidence from as many different kinds of studies as possible.

DESIGNS FOR STUDYING DEVELOPMENT

Sometimes human development research is directed at a single age group, such as the adolescent students in the example on the impact of music on studying. Or we might study retirement planning in 55-year-olds or marital satisfaction in couples married 25 years. In each of these cases, after an investigator has decided how to mea-

■ **Figure 1.7**
Basic outline of an experiment of an experiment that assesses the effects of studying with music.

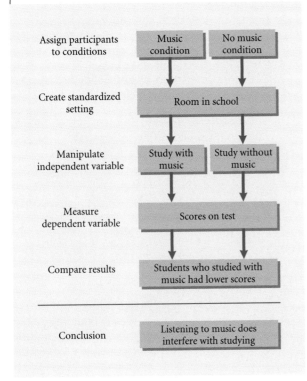

sure the behavior of interest and whether the study will be correlational or experimental, the investigator could skip directly to the last step—determine whether the study is ethical.

However, much research in human development concerns changes that occur as people develop. In these cases, investigators must also choose one of three designs that allow them to examine development: longitudinal, cross-sectional, or sequential designs.

Longitudinal Studies

In a **longitudinal study,** *the same individuals are observed or tested repeatedly at different points in their lives.* As the name implies, the longitudinal approach involves a lengthwise account of development and is the most direct way to watch growth occur.

The longitudinal approach is well suited to studying almost any aspect of the course of development. More important, it is the only way to answer certain questions about the stability or instability of behavior: Will characteristics such as aggression, dependency, or mistrust observed in infancy or early childhood persist into adulthood? How long will the beneficial effects of special academic training in the preschool years last? Will a regular exercise program begun in middle age have benefits in later life? Does people's satisfaction with their lives remain the same or change across adulthood? Such questions can be explored only by testing people at one point in development and then retesting them later in their development. The Spotlight on Research feature focuses on the last question about life satisfaction.

SPOTLIGHT ON RESEARCH

STABILITY AND CHANGE IN LIFE SATISFACTION

Who were the investigators and what was the aim of the study? Frank Fujita and Ed Diener (2005) were interested in learning whether life satisfaction stays the same or changes across adulthood. So they compared measures of life satisfaction to physiological and demographic data over a 17-year period.

How did the investigators measure the topic of interest? Life satisfaction was measured by self ratings to the question "How happy are you at present with your life as a whole?" from 0 (totally unhappy) to 10 (totally happy). Monthly household income was also obtained through self report. Additionally, measures of height, weight, body mass index, systolic and diastolic blood pressure, and personality traits (measured by the NEO personality scale) were obtained.

Who were the participants in the study? The participants were 3,608 Germans (1,709 males and 1,899 females)

who had answered a question about life satisfaction every year from 1984 to 2000 as part of the German Socio-Economic Panel study. The sample is a nationally representative sample of German adults born between 1902 and 1968.

What was the design of the study? The study used a longitudinal design, with assessments conducted annually.

Were there ethical concerns with the study? All of the participants were provided information about the purpose of the study and the tests they would take. Each participant provided informed consent.

What were the results? As you can see in Figure 1.8, there was modest stability in adults' life satisfaction from year to year, but there is an overall decrease as the time between comparison periods increases over the 17 years. Roughly 25% of the sample changed significantly in their life satisfaction ratings over the course of the study. The

stability of life satisfaction was lower than that for personality traits. Stabilities were highest for height, weight, and body mass index.

What did the investigators conclude? Fujita and Diener argue that life satisfaction is somewhat stable, but can vary over time. This is important, particularly for people whose life satisfaction may be low; there is the chance that things could improve.

What converging evidence would strengthen these conclusions? Because the sample only included German adults, it would be necessary to study people from other cultures to find out whether the results generalize cross-culturally.

To enhance your understanding of this research, go to http://psychology .wadsworth.com/kail_cavanaugh4e/ to complete critical thinking questions and explore related websites.

■ **Figure 1.8**
Note that overall life satisfaction showed some decrease over a 17-year period compared to height, weight, body mass index, and personality, but was less stable over time than personality.

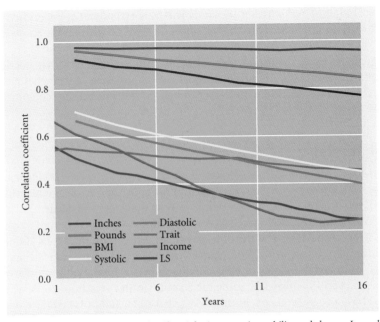

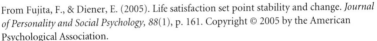

From Fujita, F., & Diener, E. (2005). Life satisfaction set point stability and change. *Journal of Personality and Social Psychology, 88*(1), p. 161. Copyright © 2005 by the American Psychological Association.

The longitudinal approach, however, has disadvantages that frequently offset its strengths. An obvious one is cost: The expense of merely keeping up with a large sample of individuals can be staggering. A related problem is the constancy of the sample over the course of the research. Experience has shown how difficult it is to maintain contact with people over several years (or several decades in some longitudinal studies!) in a highly mobile society. And even among those who do not move away, some lose interest and choose not to continue. These "dropouts" are often significantly different from their more research-minded peers, and this fact may also distort the outcome. For example, a group of older adults may seem to show intellectual stability late in life. What may have happened, however, is that those who found earlier testing most difficult quit the study and thereby raised the group average on the next round.

Even if the sample remains constant, though, the fact that people are given the same test many times may make them "test-wise." Improvement over time may be attributed to development when it actually stems from practice with a particular test. Changing the test from year to year solves the practice problem but raises the question of how to compare responses to different tests. Because of this and other problems with the longitudinal method, human development researchers often use cross-sectional studies instead.

Cross-Sectional Studies

*In a **cross-sectional study,** developmental differences are identified by testing people of different ages in the study.* Development is charted by noting the differences between individuals of different ages at the same point in calendar time. The cross-sectional approach avoids almost all the problems associated with repeated testing; it avoids costly record keeping and sample loss as well. But cross-sectional research has its own weaknesses. Because people are tested at only one point in their development, we learn nothing about the continuity of development. Consequently, we cannot tell whether an aggressive 14-year-old remains aggressive at age 30 because the person would be tested at age 14 or age 30, but not at both ages.

*Cross-sectional studies are also affected by **cohort effects,** meaning that differences between age groups (cohorts) may result as easily from environmental events as from devel-*

opmental processes. In a typical simple cross-sectional study, we compare people from two age groups. If we find differences, we attribute them to the difference in age, but this needn't be the case. Why? The cross-sectional study assumes that when the older people were younger they resembled the people in the younger age group. This isn't always true, and this fact rather than difference in age may be responsible for differences between the groups. An example of a cohort effect might come from a study measuring creativity in young and middle-aged adults. If the young adults were found to be more imaginative than middle-aged adults, should we conclude that imagination declines between these ages? Not necessarily. Perhaps a new curriculum to nourish creativity was introduced after the middle-aged adults completed school. Because the younger adults experienced the curriculum but the middle-aged adults did not, the difference between them is difficult to interpret.

When the two general research designs shown in Table 1.5 are combined with the two designs that are unique to development, four prototypic designs are possible: cross-sectional correlational studies, cross-sectional experimental studies, longitudinal-correlational studies, and longitudinal-experimental studies. You'll read about each of these designs in this book, although the two cross-sectional designs occur more frequently than the two longitudinal designs. Why? For most developmentalists, the ease of conducting cross-sectional studies more than compensates for their limitations.

Sequential Studies

Some researchers who study human development and aging use another, more complex research approach, called a **sequential design,** *which is based on cross-sectional and longitudinal designs.* Basically, a sequential design begins with a simple cross-sectional or longitudinal design. At some regular interval, the researcher then adds additional cross-sectional or longitudinal designs, resulting in a sequence of these designs. For example, suppose a researcher wants to learn whether adults' memory ability changes with age. One way to do this would be to follow several groups of people of different ages over time, creating a sequence of longitudinal studies. The start would be a typical cross-

TABLE 1.5
Designs Used in Human Development Research

Type of Design	Definition	Strengths	Weaknesses
General Designs			
Correlational	Observe variables as they exist in the world and determine their relations.	Behavior is measured as it occurs naturally.	Cannot determine cause and effect.
Experimental	Manipulate independent variable and determine effect on dependent variable.	Control of variables allows conclusions about cause and effect.	Work is often laboratory-based, which can be artificial.
Developmental Designs			
Longitudinal	One group of people is tested repeatedly as they develop.	Only way to chart an individual's development and look at the stability of behavior over time.	Expensive, participants drop out, and repeated testing can distort performance.
Cross-sectional	People of different ages are tested at the same time.	Convenient—solves all problems associated with longitudinal studies.	Cannot study stability of behavior; cohort effects complicate interpretation of differences between groups.
Sequential	Multiple groups of people are tested over time, based on either multiple longitudinal or cross-sectional designs.	Best way to address limitation of single longitudinal and cross-sectional designs.	Very expensive and time consuming; may not completely solve limitations of longitudinal and cross-sectional designs.

sectional study in which 60- and 75-year-olds are tested. Then, every 3 years, the two groups would be retested, creating two separate longitudinal studies.

Although sequential designs are relatively rare because they are so expensive to conduct, they have several advantages. Most important, they help address most of the limitations described earlier concerning single cross-sectional and longitudinal studies. For example, sequential designs help isolate cohort effects, and they help determine whether age-related changes are due to participant dropout or to some other cause. We will encounter examples of sequential designs when we consider some of the large studies examining the normal processes of aging in Chapter 14.

INTEGRATING FINDINGS FROM DIFFERENT STUDIES

Regardless of which research method or design one chooses for a research study, no single study will provide conclusive evidence on a particular topic in human development. Multiple studies on a topic using different methods must be conducted for such evidence to emerge. The advantage of this approach, of course, is that conclusions are most convincing when the results are the same regardless of method.

In reality, though, findings are often inconsistent. Suppose, for example, many researchers find that people often share personal things with friends, some researchers find that people share occasionally with friends, and a few researchers find that people never share with friends. What results should we believe? What should we conclude? ***Meta-analysis** is a tool that allows researchers to synthesize the results of many studies to estimate relations between variables* (Becker, 2003). In conducting a meta-analysis, investigators find all studies published on a topic over a substantial period of time (e.g., 10 to 20 years), then record and analyze the results and important methodological variables.

The usefulness of meta-analysis is illustrated in a study by McClure (2000), who asked whether boys and girls differ in their ability to recognize emotions in facial expressions. She found 60 studies, published between 1931 and 1999, that included nearly 10,000 children and adults. In each study, participants were administered some sort of task, like the one shown in Figure 1.5 in which the aim is to select a face expressing a particular emotion. Analyzing across the results of all 60 studies, McClure found that overall girls recognized emotions in facial expressions more accurately than boys. The gender difference was constant from 4 to 16 years of age and was the same when the faces were shown as photos and as drawings. However, the gender difference was larger when participants judged emotions in children's faces than when they judged emotions in adults' faces.

Thus, meta-analysis is a particularly powerful tool because it allows scientists to determine whether a finding generalizes across many studies that used different methods. In addition, meta-analysis can reveal the impact of those different methods on results.

CONDUCTING RESEARCH ETHICALLY

Choosing a good research design involves more than just selecting a particular method. Researchers must determine whether the methods they plan on using are ethical. That is, when designing a research study, investigators must do so in a way that does not violate the rights of people who participate in the study. To verify that every research project has these protections, investigators must present their proposed studies for formal review by a local panel of experts and community representatives prior to any data collection. Only with the approval of this panel can they begin their study. If the review panel objects to some aspects of the proposed study, the researcher must revise those aspects and present them anew for the panel's approval. Likewise, each time a component of a study is changed, the review panel must be informed and give its approval.

To guide review panels, professional organizations (e.g., the American Psychological Association) and government agencies (e.g., the National Institutes of Health) have codes of conduct that specify the rights of research participants and procedures to protect these participants. The following essential guidelines are included in all of these codes:

- ■ *Minimize risks to research participants.* Use methods that have the least potential for causing harm or stress for research participants. During the research, monitor the procedures to be sure to avoid any unforeseen stress or harm.

- ■ *Describe the research to potential participants so they can determine whether they wish to participate.* Prospective participants must be told the purpose of the project, what they will be asked to do, whether there are any risks or potential harm, any benefits they may receive, that they are free to discontinue participation at any time without penalty, that they are entitled to a complete debriefing at the end of the project, and any other relevant information the review panel deems appropriate. After the study has been explained, participants sign a document that says they understand what they will do in the study. Special caution must be exercised in obtaining consent for the participation of children and adolescents, as well as people who have conditions that affect intellectual functioning (e.g., Alzheimer's disease, severe head injury). In these cases, consent from a parent, legal guardian, or other responsible person, in addition to the agreement of the person him- or herself, is necessary for participation.

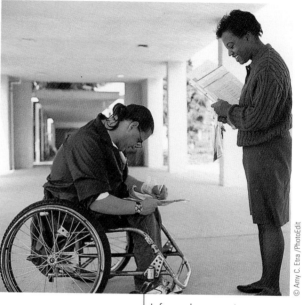

Informed consent is a necessary aspect of any research effort in human development.

- ■ *Avoid deception; if participants must be deceived, provide a thorough explanation of the true nature of the experiment as soon as possible.* Providing complete information about a study in advance sometimes biases or distorts a person's responses. Consequently, investigators may provide participants with partial information about the study or even mislead them about its true purpose. As soon as it is feasible—typically just after the experiment—any false information that was given to research participants must be corrected, and the reasons for the deception must be provided.

- ■ *Results should be anonymous or confidential.* Research results should be anonymous, which means that people's data cannot be linked to their name. When anonymity is not possible, research results should be confidential, which means the identity of participants is known only to the investigator conducting the study.

Conducting research ethically is an obligation of every investigator. If you conduct a project, even in connection with a course, you should submit your procedures for review. If you are a participant in someone else's project, make sure you are given appropriate and complete information, and read it thoroughly.

COMMUNICATING RESEARCH RESULTS

When the study is complete and the data analyzed, researchers will write a report of their work. This report describes, in great detail, what the researchers did and why, their results, and the meaning(s) behind their results. The researchers will submit the report to one of several scientific journals that specialize in human development research. Some of these are *Child Development, Developmental Psychology, Psychology and Aging,* and the *Journals of Gerontology.* If the editor of the journal accepts the report, it will appear in the journal where other human development researchers can learn of the results.

These reports of research are the basis for virtually all the information we present in this book. As you read, you'll see names in parentheses, followed by a date, like this:

(Alexander & Bowen, 2004)

This indicates the person(s) who did the research and the year in which it was published. By looking in the References at the end of the book, which are organized alphabetically by the first author's last name, you can find the title of the article and the journal where it was published.

Maybe all of these different steps in research seem tedious and involved to you. For a human development researcher, however, much of the fun of doing research is planning a study that no one has done before and that will provide useful information to other specialists. This is one of the most creative and challenging parts of human development research.

The Spotlight on Research features that appear in each chapter of this book are designed to convey both the creativity and the challenge of doing human development research. Each feature focuses on a specific study. Some are studies that have just appeared in the journals; others are classics that helped define a new area of investigation or provided definitive results in an existing area. In each of these features, we'll trace the decisions researchers made as they planned their study. We focus on the research question addressed, the design of the study, the measures used, ethical concerns, key findings, and the researchers' conclusions. Some of the studies provide examples of difficult decisions researchers must make in designing good research, as well as constraints on investigators examining development in real-world contexts. By reading these features, you'll see the ingenuity of researchers as they pursue questions of human development. You'll also see that any individual study has limitations; the way around these limits is to have converging evidence from different designs. We can have the most confidence when many studies—each using a unique combination of measurement methods and designs—all point to the same conclusion.

APPLYING RESEARCH RESULTS: SOCIAL POLICY

One question many people have about research is whether any of it really matters. Actually, research on human development has a strong influence on policymakers and politicians. For example, every state in the United States as well as many countries around the world has laws against child abuse and child labor practices. Many countries have laws setting minimum ages for certain activities such as consuming alcohol. Some states in the United States are changing the way older drivers are screened when they renew their driver's licenses.

These and many other examples demonstrate that the research done by developmentalists influences many aspects of daily life that are governed by laws and societal rules. Much of the debate over Social Security and Medicare in the U.S. presidential campaigns of 2000 and 2004, and in President George W. Bush's plans to reform Social Security, hinged on different interpretations of data about older adults.

At several points in the text, we will describe some of the most important connections between human development research and social policy. As you will see, these connections are broad ranging and include areas that you may even take for granted. For example, you may know that lead-based paint cannot be used any more in the United States. You may not know that the ban stemmed from the results of several research studies by developmentalists showing that infants and young children who were exposed to lead-based paint (and who sometimes ate paint chips as they flaked off) suffered brain damage and learning problems. Research on human development not only provides many insights into what makes people tick but can also provide ways to improve the quality of life.

Sometimes, though, the views of scientists, ethicists, public citizens, and government collide in ways that result in significant debate of research. Such is the case with stem cell research, a very controversial topic explored in the Current Controversies feature.

CURRENT CONTROVERSIES

STEM CELL RESEARCH

Imagine you were unable to walk because of a severe spinal cord injury received in an accident. Imagine further that there was a possible cure in the making: getting the damaged nerve cells in your spine to regenerate, thereby enabling you to walk again. Would you support every effort possible to ensure that this research was pursued, especially if you knew that there were positive outcomes in research on other animal species (Nistor et al., 2005)? But what if you also knew that for this research to be applied to humans it would involve using stem cells from human embryos? Would that affect your opinion about the research?

Research on regeneration of nerve cells and for treatment of other diseases, such as Alzheimer's disease, leukemia, and Parkinson's disease, could be revolutionized through the use of stem cells. Researchers such as Dr. Hans Keirstead believe that stem cell research represents the future for medical treatment breakthroughs. *Stem cells are unspecialized human or animal cells that can produce mature specialized body cells and at the same time replicate themselves.* Embryonic stem cells are derived from a blastocyst, which is a very young embryo that contains 200 to 250 cells and is shaped like a hollow sphere (for more information see Chapter 2). The stem cells themselves are the cells in the blastocyst that ultimately would develop into a person or animal. "Adult" stem cells are derived from the umbilical cord and placenta or from blood, bone marrow, skin, and other tissues. Germ line cells, similar to stem cells, come from a fetus that is 5 to 9 weeks old and are derived from tissue that would have developed into the ovaries or testes.

Medical researchers are interested in using stem cells to repair or replace damaged body tissues because stem cells are less likely than other foreign cells to be rejected by the immune system when they are implanted in the body. Embryonic stem cells have the capacity to develop into every type of tissue found in an adult. Stem cells have been used experimentally to form the blood-making cells of the bone marrow and heart, blood vessel, muscle, and insulin-producing tissue. Embryonic germ line cells have been used to help paralyzed mice regain some of the ability to move. Since the 1990s umbilical cord blood stem cells have sometimes been used to treat heart and other defects in children who have rare metabolic diseases and to treat children with certain anemias and leukemias. Stem cells from this blood can migrate to damaged tissues and repair them.

Even though stem cell research may hold much promise, and has already been shown to be effective in treating some conditions, it is extremely controversial. The Bush administration has restricted federally funded research to certain existing colonies of stem cells, pointing out that creating additional such cells involves the destruction of human embryos. But proponents of the research claim that some of the existing colonies may be contaminated. They also argue that early embryos have no feeling or consciousness and that most of them used in research are left over from fertility clinics and are destined to be discarded anyway.

At this point, many states are making their own decisions about whether to support stem cell research. For example, voters in California passed Proposition 71 in 2004, which resulted in $3 billion in state funding for stem cell research and established a 29-member stem cell research review board. The proposition was supported by Republican Governor Arnold Schwarzenegger. One thing is certain, though: The debate on whether to provide public funding (federal or state) for stem cell research will continue for many years to come.

TEST YOURSELF

1. In _____, people are observed as they behave spontaneously in a real-life setting.

2. A _____ is a group of individuals thought to be representative of some larger population of interest.

3. The _____ variable is measured in an experiment to evaluate the impact of the variable that was manipulated.

4. Problems of longitudinal studies include the length of time to complete the work, loss of research participants over time, and _____.

5. Human development researchers must submit their plans for research to a review board that determines whether the research _____.

How could a longitudinal design be used to test Piaget's theory?

Answers: (1) naturalistic observation, (2) sample, (3) dependent, (4) influence of repeated testing on a person's performance, (5) preserves the rights of research participants

Problems With Using Photographs to Measure Understanding of Emotions

On page 26, we invited you to consider why asking children to judge emotions from photos may not be valid. Children's judgments of the emotions depicted in photographs may be less accurate than they would be in real life because (1) in real life, facial features are usually moving—not still as in the photographs—and movement may be one of the clues children naturally use to judge emotions; (2) in real life, facial expressions are often accompanied by sounds, and children use both sight and sound to judge emotions; and (3) in real life, children most often judge facial expressions of people they know (parents, siblings, peers, teachers), and knowing the "usual" appearance of a face may help children judge emotions accurately.

Putting It All Together

The opening section of this chapter introduced you to the major study aids built into this text and the terminology conventions used to communicate developmental research and theory effectively. We met Javier Suarez, whose reflections about his newborn grandson led us to the fundamental issues of nature versus nurture, continuity versus discontinuity, and universal versus context-specific development. This, in turn, prompted discussion of the four basic forces of development: biological, psychological, sociocultural, and life-cycle forces. Marcus and his mother, Betty, led us to several different theories about why people develop the way they do and how these theories connect to the three fundamental issues and the four basic forces of development. And we learned how Leah and Joan could rigorously determine why people form friendships with certain people and not with others.

The topics presented in this chapter form the foundation for all the information in the chapters that follow, so be sure you understand this material very well before you continue reading.

Summary

1.2 Thinking About Development

Recurring Issues in Human Development

■ Three main issues are prominent in the study of human development. The nature-nurture issue involves the degree to which genetics and the environment influence human development. In general, theorists and researchers view nature and nurture as mutually interactive influences; development is always shaped by both. The continuity-discontinuity issue concerns whether the same explanations (continuity) or different explanations (discontinuity) must be used to explain changes in people over time. Continuity approaches emphasize quantitative change; discontinuity approaches emphasize qualitative change. In the issue of universal versus context-specific development, the question is whether development follows the same general path in all people or is fundamentally different, depending on the sociocultural context.

Basic Forces in Human Development: The Biopsychosocial Framework

■ Development is based on the combined impact of four primary forces. Biological forces include all genetic and health-related factors that affect development. Many of these biological forces are determined by our genetic code.

■ Psychological forces include all internal cognitive, emotional, perceptual, and personality factors that influence development. Collectively, psychological forces provide the things we notice most about people.

■ Sociocultural forces include interpersonal, societal, cultural, and ethnic factors that affect development. Culture consists of the knowledge, attitudes, and behavior associated with a group of people. Overall, sociocultural forces provide the context or backdrop for development.

- Life-cycle forces provide a context for understanding how people perceive their current situation and its effects on them.

- The biopsychosocial framework emphasizes that the four forces are mutually interactive; development cannot be understood by examining the forces in isolation. Furthermore, the same event can have different effects, depending on when it happens.

1.3 Developmental Theories

- Developmental theories organize knowledge so as to provide testable explanations of human behaviors and the ways in which they change over time. Current approaches to developmental theory focus on specific aspects of behavior. At present, there is no single unified theory of human development.

Psychodynamic Theory

- Psychodynamic theories propose that behavior is determined by unconscious motives. Erikson proposed a life-span theory of psychosocial development, consisting of eight universal stages, each characterized by a particular struggle.

Learning Theory

- Learning theory focuses on the development of observable behavior. Operant conditioning is based on the notions of reinforcement, punishment, and environmental control of behavior. Social learning theory proposes that people learn by observing others.

Cognitive-Developmental Theory

- Cognitive-developmental theory focuses on thought processes. Piaget proposed a four-stage universal sequence based on the notion that, throughout development, people create their own theories to explain how the world works. Kohlberg expanded on this in the area of moral reasoning. According to information-processing theory, people deal with information like a computer does; development consists of increased efficiency in handling information. Vygotsky emphasized the influence of culture on development.

The Ecological and Systems Approach

- Bronfenbrenner proposed that development occurs in the context of several interconnected systems of increasing complexity. The competence–environmental press theory postulates that there is a "best fit" between a person's abilities and the demands placed on that person by the environment.

Life-Span Perspective, Selective Optimization With Compensation, and Life Course Perspective

- According to the life-span perspective, human development is characterized by multidirectionality, plas-ticity, historical context, and multiple causation. All four developmental forces are key.

- Selective optimization with compensation refers to the developmental trends to focus one's efforts and abilities in successively fewer domains as one ages and to acquire ways to compensate for normative losses.

- The life course perspective refers to understanding human development within the context of the historical time period in which a generation develops, which creates unique sets of experiences.

1.4 Doing Developmental Research

Measurement in Human Development Research

- Research typically begins by determining how to measure the topic of interest. Systematic observation involves recording people's behavior as it takes place, in either a natural environment (naturalistic observation) or a structured setting (structured observation). Researchers sometimes create tasks to obtain samples of behavior. In self reports, people answer questions posed by the experimenter. Physiological measures provide a way to examine body-behavior relationships.

- Researchers must determine that their measures are reliable and valid; they must also obtain a sample representative of some larger population.

General Designs for Research

- In correlational studies, investigators examine relations among variables as they occur naturally. This relation is often measured by a correlation coefficient, r, which can vary from -1 (strong inverse relation) to 0 (no relation) to $+1$ (strong positive relation). Correlational studies cannot determine cause and effect, so researchers do experimental studies in which an independent variable is manipulated and the impact of this manipulation on a dependent variable is recorded. Experimental studies allow conclusions about cause and effect, but the strict control of other variables that is required often makes the situation artificial. The best approach is to use both experimental and correlational studies to provide converging evidence.

Designs for Studying Development

- To study development, some researchers use a longitudinal design in which the same people are observed repeatedly as they grow. This approach provides evidence concerning actual patterns of individual growth but has several shortcomings as well: It is time consuming, some people drop out of the project, and repeated testing can affect performance.

- An alternative, the cross-sectional design, involves testing people of different ages. This design avoids the problems of the longitudinal design but provides no information about individual growth. Also, what appear to be age differences may be cohort effects. Because neither design is problem-free, the best approach is to use both to provide converging evidence.

Integrating Findings From Different Studies

■ Meta-analysis provides a way for researchers to look for trends across multiple studies to estimate the relations among variables.

Conducting Research Ethically

■ Planning research also involves selecting methods that preserve the rights of research participants. Experimenters must minimize the risks to potential research participants, describe the research so that potential participants can decide if they want to participate, avoid deception, and keep results anonymous or confidential.

Communicating Research Results

■ Once research data are collected and analyzed, investigators publish the results in scientific outlets such as journals and books. Such results form the foundation of knowledge about human development.

Applying Research Results: Social Policy

■ Research results are sometimes used to inform and shape public policy. Controversial topics such as stem cell research also form the basis for public policy in terms of what types of research are permitted.

Key Terms

human development (1)

nature-nurture issue (5)

continuity-discontinuity issue (6)

universal versus context-specific development issue (6)

biological forces (7)

psychological forces (7)

sociocultural forces (7)

life-cycle forces (7)

biopsychosocial framework (7)

theory (11)

psychodynamic theories (11)

psychosocial theory (11)

epigenetic principle (13)

operant conditioning (14)

reinforcement (14)

punishment (14)

imitation (observational learning) (14)

social cognitive theory (15)

self-efficacy (15)

information-processing theory (17)

ecological theory (18)

microsystem (18)

mesosystem (19)

exosystem (19)

macrosystem (19)

life-span perspective (20)

selective optimization with compensation (SOC) model (21)

life course perspective (22)

systematic observation (25)

naturalistic observation (25)

structured observations (25)

self reports (26)

reliability (27)

validity (27)

populations (28)

sample (28)

correlational study (28)

correlation coefficient (28)

experiment (30)

independent variable (30)

dependent variable (30)

longitudinal study (31)

cross-sectional study (32)

cohort effects (32)

sequential design (33)

meta-analysis (34)

stem cells (37)

Learn More About It

Readings

BALTES, P. B. (1987). Theoretical propositions of life-span developmental psychology: On the dynamics between growth and decline. *Developmental Psychology, 23,* 611–626. One of the true classics in human development, this is an excellent overview of what it means to take a holistic view of life-span development. Written by one of the leading proponents of this approach, the article is moderately difficult reading.

BALTES, P. B., REESE, H. W., & NESSELROADE, J. R. (1977). *Life-span developmental psychology: Introduction to research methods.* Pacific Grove, CA: Brooks/Cole.

This is one of the classic texts on developmental research methods, and still one of the best. It's very readable and has an easily understood presentation of research designs and methods.

DELANY, S., & DELANY, E. (1993). *Having our say.* New York: Kodansha International. This is the life story of Sadie and Bessie Delany, who are described in the text. Their lives are an excellent example of life course theory. This book was adapted for a popular play.

GARDINER, H. W., MUTTER, J. D., & KOSMITZKI, C. (1998). *Lives across cultures: Cross-cultural human development.* Boston: Allyn & Bacon. A readable introduction to how human development occurs in various world cultures. This book pulls together much of the available research.

LERNER, R. M. (2002). *Concepts and theories of human development* (3rd ed.). Mahwah, NJ: Erlbaum. A good survey of the major theories of human development by a prominent researcher and thinker.

MCLOYD, V. C. (2004). Linking race and ethnicity to culture: Steps along the road from inference to hypothesis testing. *Human Development, 47,* 185–191. A thorough, but high-level discussion of the complexities and dynamics of culture from a theoretical perspective.

Websites

Visit the Human Development companion website for all URLs.

- ■ **The Human Development Book Companion Website**
  See the companion website **http://psychology .wadsworth.com / kail_cavanaugh4e/** for practice quiz questions, Internet links, updates, critical thinking exercises, discussion forums, and more.

- ■ **American Psychological Association**
  The American Psychological Association and the American Psychological Society have numerous sources of information for researchers and consumers on their websites.

- ■ **National Institutes of Health**
  The Office of Human Subjects Research at the National Institutes of Health publishes the Guidelines for the Conduct of Research Involving Human Subjects. These guidelines govern all researchers who use human subjects.

http://www.thomsonedu.com
Go to this site for the link to ThomsonNOW, your one-stop study shop. Take a pre-test for this chapter, and ThomsonNOW will generate a personalized study plan based on your test results. The study plan will identify the topics you need to review and direct you to online resources to help you master those topics. You can then take a post-test to help you determine the concepts you have mastered and what you still need to work on.

PART I

Prenatal Development, Infancy, and Early Childhood

© Lawrence Manning /CORBIS

■ Chapter 2
Biological Foundations
Heredity, Prenatal Development, and Birth

■ Chapter 3
Tools for Exploring the World
Physical Development in Infancy and Early Childhood

■ Chapter 4
The Emergence of Thought and Language
Cognitive Development in Infancy and Early Childhood

■ Chapter 5
Entering the Social World
Socioemotional Development in Infancy and Early Childhood

2.1 In the Beginning: 23 Pairs of Chromosomes
Mechanisms of Heredity
Genetic Disorders
Heredity, Environment, and Development

■ REAL PEOPLE: APPLYING HUMAN DEVELOPMENT: Ben and Matt Pick Their Niches

2.2 From Conception to Birth
Period of the Zygote (Weeks 1–2)

■ CURRENT CONTROVERSIES: Conception in the 21st Century

Period of the Embryo (Weeks 3–8)
Period of the Fetus (Weeks 9–38)

2.3 Influences on Prenatal Development
General Risk Factors
Teratogens: Drugs, Diseases, and Environmental Hazards

■ SPOTLIGHT ON RESEARCH: Impact of Prenatal Exposure to PCBs on Cognitive Functioning

How Teratogens Influence Prenatal Development
Prenatal Diagnosis and Treatment

2.4 Labor and Delivery
Stages of Labor
Approaches to Childbirth
Adjusting to Parenthood
Birth Complications
Infant Mortality

Putting It All Together
Summary
Key Terms
Learn More About It

CHAPTER 2

Biological Foundations

Heredity, Prenatal Development, and Birth

I f you ask parents to name the most memorable experiences of their lives, many immediately mention the events associated with the birth of their children. From the initial exciting news that a woman is pregnant through birth nine months later, the entire experience of pregnancy and birth evokes awe and wonder.

The period before birth is the foundation for all human development and the focus of this chapter. Pregnancy begins when egg and sperm cells unite and exchange hereditary material. In the first section, you'll see how this exchange takes place and, in the process, learn about inherited factors that affect development. The second section of the chapter traces the events that transform sperm and egg into a living, breathing human being. You'll learn about the timetable that governs development before birth and, along the way, get answers to common questions about pregnancy. We talk about some of the problems that can occur during development before birth in the third section of the chapter. The last section focuses on birth and the newborn baby. You'll find out how an expectant mother can prepare for birth and what labor and delivery are like.

2.1

IN THE BEGINNING: 23 PAIRS OF CHROMOSOMES

Leslie and Glenn are excited at the thought of starting their own family. At the same time, they're nervous because Leslie's grandfather had sickle-cell disease and died when he was just 20 years old. Leslie is terrified that her baby may inherit the disease that killed her grandfather. She and Glenn wish that someone could reassure them that their baby will be okay.

LEARNING OBJECTIVES

What are chromosomes and genes? How do they carry hereditary information from one generation to the next?

What are common problems involving chromosomes and what are their consequences?

How is children's heredity influenced by the environment in which they grow up?

How can we reassure Leslie and Glenn? For starters, we need to know more about sickle-cell disease. Red blood cells carry oxygen and carbon dioxide to and from the body. When a person has sickle-cell disease, the red blood cells are long and curved like a sickle. These stiff, misshapen cells cannot pass through small capillaries, so oxygen cannot reach all parts of the body. The trapped sickle cells also block the way of white blood cells that are the body's natural defense against bacteria. As a result, many people with sickle-cell disease—including Leslie's grandfather and many other African Americans, who are more prone to this painful disease than other groups—die from infections before the age of 20.

Sickle-cell disease is inherited and, because Leslie's grandfather had the disorder, it runs in her family. Will Leslie's baby inherit the disease? To answer this question, we need to examine the mechanisms of heredity.

MECHANISMS OF HEREDITY

At conception, egg and sperm unite to create a new organism that incorporates some characteristics of each parent. *Each egg and sperm cell has 23* **chromosomes,** *threadlike structures in the nucleus that contain genetic material.* When a sperm penetrates an egg, their chromosomes combine to produce 23 pairs of chromosomes. *The first 22 pairs of chromosomes are called* **autosomes.** *The 23rd pair determines the sex of the child, so these*

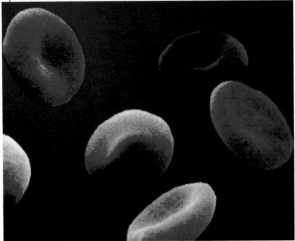

Red blood cells carry oxygen throughout the body.

Kenneth Eward/BioGrafx/Photo Researchers, Inc.

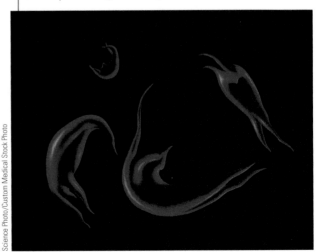

Sickle-shaped blood cells associated with sickle cell disease cannot pass through the body's smallest blood vessels.

Science Photo/Custom Medical Stock Photo

are known as the sex chromosomes. When the 23rd pair consists of an X and a Y chromosome, the result is a boy; two X chromosomes produce a girl.

Each chromosome actually consists of one molecule of deoxyribonucleic acid—DNA for short. To understand the structure of DNA, imagine four different colors of beads placed on two strings. The strings complement each other precisely: Wherever a red bead appears on one string, a blue bead appears on the other; wherever a green bead appears on one string, a yellow one appears on the other. DNA is organized this way, except that the four colors of beads are actually four different chemical compounds—adenine, thymine, guanine, and cytosine. The strings, which are made up of phosphates and sugars, wrap around each other, creating the double helix shown in Figure 2.1.

The order in which the chemical compound "beads" appear is really a code that causes the cell to create specific amino acids, proteins, and enzymes—important biological building blocks. For example, three consecutive thymine "beads" make up the instruction to create the amino acid phenylalanine. *Each group of compounds that provides a specific set of biochemical instructions is a gene.* Thus, genes are the functional units of heredity because they determine production

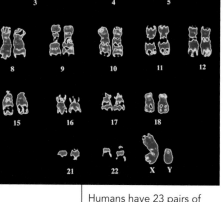

Humans have 23 pairs of chromosomes, 22 pairs of autosomes, and 1 pair of sex chromosomes.

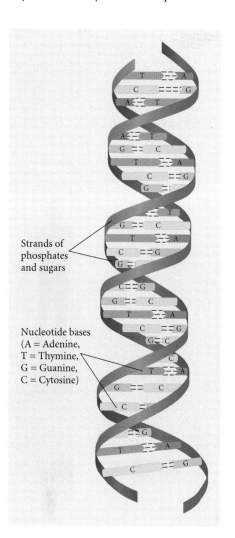

Strands of phosphates and sugars

Nucleotide bases
(A = Adenine,
T = Thymine,
G = Guanine,
C = Cytosine)

■ **Figure 2.1**
DNA is organized in a double helix, with strands of phosphates and sugars linked by nucleotide bases.

of chemical substances that are, ultimately, the basis for all human characteristics and abilities.

Altogether, a person's 46 chromosomes include roughly 30,000 genes. Through biochemical instructions that are coded in DNA, genes regulate the development of all human characteristics and abilities. *The complete set of genes makes up a person's heredity and is known as the person's* **genotype.** *Genetic instructions, in conjunction with environmental influences, produce a* **phenotype,** *an individual's physical, behavioral, and psychological features.*

How do genetic instructions produce the misshapen red blood cells of sickle-cell disease? *Genes come in different forms that are known as* **alleles.** In the case of red blood cells, for example, two alleles can be present on chromosome 11. One allele has instructions for normal red blood cells; another allele has instructions for sickle-shaped red blood cells. *The alleles in the pair of chromosomes are sometimes the same, which is known as being* **homozygous.** *The alleles sometimes differ, which is known as being* **heterozygous.** Leslie's baby would be homozygous if it had two alleles for normal cells *or* two alleles for sickle-shaped cells. The baby would be heterozygous if it had one allele of each type.

How does a genotype produce a phenotype? With sickle-cell disease, for example, how do genotypes lead to specific kinds of blood cells? The answer is simple if a person is homozygous. When both alleles are the same—and therefore have chemical instructions for the same phenotype—that phenotype results. If Leslie's baby had an allele for normal red blood cells on both of its 11th chromosomes, the baby would be almost guaranteed to have normal cells. If, instead, the baby had two alleles for sickle-shaped cells, her baby would almost certainly suffer from the disease.

When a person is heterozygous, the process is more complex. *Often one allele is* **dominant,** *which means that its chemical instructions are followed and those of the other,* **recessive** *allele are ignored.* In sickle-cell disease, the allele for normal cells is dominant, and the allele for sickle-shaped cells is recessive. This is good news for Leslie: As long as either she or Glenn contributes the allele for normal red blood cells, their baby will not develop sickle-cell disease.

Figure 2.2 summarizes what we've learned about sickle-cell disease: *A* denotes the allele for normal blood cells, and *a* denotes the allele for sickle-shaped cells. Depending

■ **Figure 2.2**
In single-gene inheritance, a heterozygous father and a heterozygous mother can have a healthy child, a child with sickle-cell trait, or a child with sickle-cell disease.

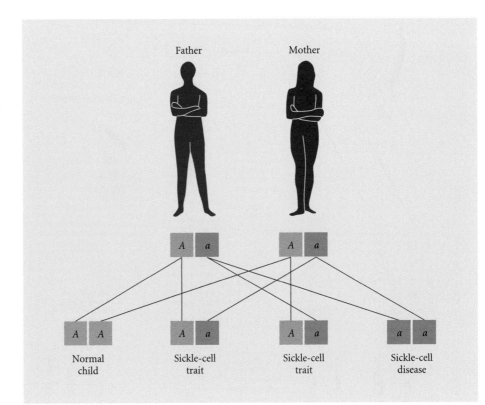

on the alleles in Leslie's egg and in the sperm that fertilizes that egg, three outcomes are possible. Only if the baby inherits two recessive alleles for sickle-shaped cells is it likely to develop sickle-cell disease. But this is unlikely in Glenn's case: He is positive no one in his family has had sickle-cell disease, so he almost certainly has the allele for normal blood cells on both of the chromosomes in his 11th pair.

Even though Glenn's sperm will carry the gene for normal red blood cells, this doesn't guarantee that their baby will be healthy. Why? *Sometimes one allele does not dominate another completely, a situation known as* **incomplete dominance.** In incomplete dominance, the phenotype that results often falls between the phenotype associated with either allele. This is the case for the genes that control red blood cells. *Individuals with one dominant and one recessive allele have* **sickle-cell trait:** *In most situations they have no problems, but when they are seriously short of oxygen, they suffer a temporary, relatively mild form of the disease.* Sickle-cell trait is likely to appear when the person exercises vigorously or is at high altitudes (Sullivan, 1987). Leslie and Glenn's baby would have sickle-cell trait if it inherits a recessive gene from Leslie and a dominant gene from Glenn.

The simple genetic mechanism responsible for sickle-cell disease, involving a single gene pair, with one dominant allele and one recessive allele, is also responsible for numerous other common traits, as shown in Table 2.1. In each of these instances, individuals with the recessive phenotype have two recessive alleles, one from each parent. Individuals with the dominant phenotype have at least one dominant allele.

Most of the traits listed in Table 2.1 are biological and medical phenotypes. These same patterns of inheritance can cause serious disorders, as we'll see in the next section.

GENETIC DISORDERS

Some people are affected by heredity in a special way: They have genetic disorders that disrupt the usual pattern of development. Genetics can derail development in two ways. First, some disorders are inherited. Sickle-cell disease is one example of an inherited dis-

---

TABLE 2.1

Some Common Phenotypes Associated With Single Pairs of Genes

Dominant Phenotype	Recessive Phenotype
Curly hair	Straight hair
Normal hair	Pattern baldness (men)
Dark hair	Blond hair
Thick lips	Thin lips
Cheek dimples	No dimples
Normal hearing	Some types of deafness
Normal vision	Nearsightedness
Farsightedness	Normal vision
Normal color vision	Red-green color blindness
Type A blood	Type O blood
Type B blood	Type O blood
Rh-positive blood	Rh-negative blood

SOURCE: McKusick, 1995

order. Second, sometimes eggs or sperm do not include the usual 23 chromosomes but have more or fewer chromosomes instead. In the next few pages, we'll see how inherited disorders and abnormal numbers of chromosomes can alter a person's development.

Inherited Disorders

You know that sickle-cell disease is a disorder that affects people who inherit two recessive alleles. *Another disorder that involves recessive alleles is **phenylketonuria** (PKU), a disorder in which babies are born lacking an important liver enzyme.* This enzyme converts phenylalanine—a protein found in dairy products, bread, diet soda, and fish—into amino acids that are required for normal body functioning. Without this enzyme, phenylalanine accumulates and produces poisons that harm the nervous system, resulting in mental retardation (Diamond et al., 1997; Mange & Mange, 1990).

Most inherited disorders are like sickle-cell disease and PKU in that they are carried by recessive alleles. Relatively few serious disorders are caused by dominant alleles. Why? If the allele for the disorder is dominant, every person with at least one of these alleles would have the disorder. Individuals affected with these disorders typically do not live long enough to reproduce, so dominant alleles that produce fatal disorders soon vanish from the species. *An exception is **Huntington's disease,** a fatal disease characterized by progressive degeneration of the nervous system.* Huntington's disease is caused by a dominant allele found on chromosome 4. Individuals who inherit this disorder develop normally through childhood, adolescence, and young adulthood. However, during middle age, nerve cells begin to deteriorate, which produces symptoms such as muscle spasms, depression, and significant changes in personality (Shiwach, 1994). By this age, many adults with Huntington's disease have already reproduced, creating children who may well later display the disease themselves.

Abnormal Chromosomes

Sometimes individuals do not receive the normal complement of 46 chromosomes. If they are born with extra, missing, or damaged chromosomes, development is always disturbed. The best example is Down syndrome. People with Down syndrome have almond-shaped eyes and a fold over the eyelid. Their head, neck, and nose are usually smaller than normal. During the first several months of life, development of babies with Down syndrome seems to be normal. Thereafter, their mental and behavioral development begins to lag behind the average child's. For example, a child with Down syndrome might first sit up without help at about 1 year, walk at 2, and talk at 3, reaching each of these developmental milestones months or even years behind children without Down syndrome. By childhood, most aspects of cognitive and social development are seriously retarded. Rearing a child with Down syndrome presents special challenges. During the preschool years, children with Down syndrome need special programs to prepare them for school. Educational achievements of children with Down syndrome are likely to be limited, and their life expectancy ranges from 25 to 60 years (Yang, Rasmussen, & Friedman, 2002). Nevertheless, as you'll see in Chapter 6, many individuals with Down syndrome lead full, satisfying lives.

What causes Down syndrome? Individuals with Down syndrome typically have an extra 21st chromosome that is usually provided by the egg (Antonarakis et al., 1991). Why the mother provides two 21st chromosomes is unknown. However, the odds that a woman will bear a child with Down syndrome increase markedly as she gets older. For a woman in her late 20s, the risk of giving birth to a baby with Down syndrome is about 1 in 1,000; for a woman in her early 40s, the risk is about 1 in 50. Why? A woman's eggs have been in her ovaries since her own prenatal development. Eggs may deteriorate over time as part of aging or because an older woman has a longer history of exposure to hazards in the environment, such as X-rays, that may damage her eggs.

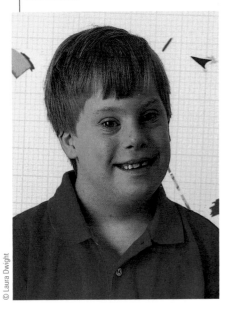

Children with Down syndrome typically have upward slanting eyes with a fold over the eyelid, a flattened facial profile, as well as a smaller than average nose and mouth.

© Laura Dwight

TABLE **2.2**

Common Disorders Associated With the Sex Chromosomes

Disorder	Sex Chromosomes	Frequency	Characteristics
Klinefelter's syndrome	XXY	1 in 500 male births	Tall, small testicles, sterile, below-normal intelligence, passive
XYY complement	XYY	1 in 1,000 male births	Tall, some cases apparently have below-normal intelligence
Turner's syndrome	X	1 in 2,500–5,000 female births	Short, limited development of secondary sex characteristics, problems perceiving spatial relations
XXX syndrome	XXX	1 in 500–1,200 female births	Normal stature but delayed motor and language development

An extra autosome (as in Down syndrome), a missing autosome, or a damaged autosome always has far-reaching consequences for development because the autosomes contain huge amounts of genetic material. In fact, nearly half of all fertilized eggs abort spontaneously within 2 weeks, primarily because of abnormal autosomes. Thus, most eggs that cannot develop normally are removed naturally (Moore & Persaud, 1993).

Abnormal sex chromosomes can also disrupt development. Table 2.2 lists four of the more frequent disorders associated with atypical numbers of X and Y chromosomes. Keep in mind that "frequent" is a relative term; although these disorders are more frequent than PKU or Huntington's disease, most are rare. Notice that there are no disorders consisting solely of Y chromosomes. The presence of an X chromosome appears to be necessary for life.

Fortunately, most of us receive the correct number of chromosomes, and we do not inherit life-threatening illnesses. For most people, heredity reveals its power in creating a unique individual—a person unlike any other.

Now that you understand the basic mechanisms of heredity, we can learn how heredity and environment work together to produce behavioral and psychological development.

HEREDITY, ENVIRONMENT, AND DEVELOPMENT

Many people mistakenly view heredity as a set of phenotypes unfolding automatically from the genotypes that are set at conception. Nothing could be further from the truth. Although genotypes are fixed when the sperm fertilizes the egg, phenotypes are not. Instead, phenotypes depend on both genotypes and the environment in which individuals develop.

To begin our study of heredity and environment, we need to look first at the methods that developmental scientists use.

Behavioral Genetics: Mechanisms and Methods

Behavioral genetics is the branch of genetics that deals with inheritance of behavioral and psychological traits. Behavioral genetics is complex, in part because behavioral and psychological phenotypes are complex. Traits controlled by single genes are usually "either-or" phenotypes. A person either has dimpled cheeks or not; a person either has normal color vision or red-green color blindness; a person's blood either clots normally or it does not. In contrast, most important behavioral and psychological characteristics are *not* "either-or" cases. Instead, an entire range of different outcomes is possible. Take extraversion as an example. Imagine trying to classify 10 people that you know well as

THINK ABOUT IT

Introversion-extraversion is an example of a psychological characteristic that defines a continuum. Think of other psychological characteristics like this, in which outcomes are not "either-or" but represent a range.

either extroverts or introverts. This would be easy for a few extremely outgoing individuals (extroverts) and a few intensely shy persons (introverts). Most are probably neither extroverts nor introverts, but "in between." The result is a distribution of individuals ranging from extreme introversion at one end to extreme extraversion at the other.

Many behavioral and psychological characteristics are distributed in this fashion, including intelligence and many aspects of personality. *When phenotypes reflect the combined activity of many separate genes, the pattern is known as **polygenic inheritance.*** Because so many genes are involved in polygenic inheritance, we usually cannot trace the effects of each gene. But we can use a hypothetical example to show how many genes work together to produce a behavioral phenotype that spans a continuum. Let's suppose that four pairs of genes contribute to extraversion, that the allele for extraversion is dominant, and that the total amount of extraversion is simply the sum of the dominant alleles. If we continue to use uppercase letters to represent dominant alleles and lowercase letters to represent the recessive allele, the four gene pairs would be Aa, Bb, Cc, and Dd.

These four pairs of genes produce 81 different genotypes and 9 distinct phenotypes. For example, a person with the genotype AABBCCDD has 8 alleles for extraversion (the proverbial party animal). A person with the genotype aabbccdd has no alleles for extraversion (the proverbial wallflower). All other genotypes involve some combinations of dominant and recessive alleles, so these are associated with phenotypes representing intermediate levels of extraversion. In fact, Figure 2.3 shows that the most common outcome is for people to inherit exactly 4 dominant and 4 recessive alleles: 19 of the 81 genotypes produce this pattern (e.g., AABBccDd, aaBbcCD). A few extreme cases (very outgoing or very shy), when coupled with many intermediate cases, produce the familiar bell-shaped distribution that characterizes many behavioral and psychological traits.

Remember, this example is completely hypothetical. Extraversion is *not* based on the combined influence of eight pairs of genes. However, the sample shows how several genes working together *could* produce a continuum of phenotypes. Something like our example is probably involved in the inheritance of many human behavioral traits, ex-

■ **Figure 2.3**
Many behavioral phenotypes represent a continuum (with many people falling at the middle of the continuum), an outcome that can be caused by many genes working together.

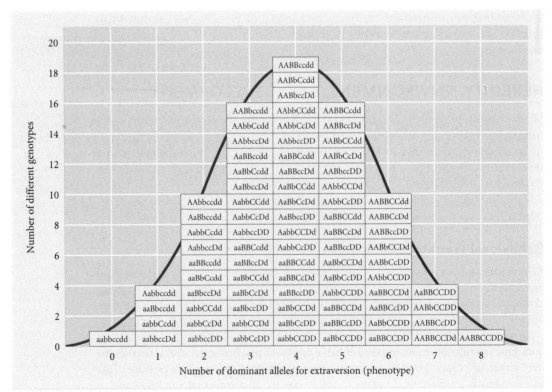

cept that many more pairs of genes are involved. What's more, the environment also influences the phenotype.

If many behavioral phenotypes involve countless genes, how can we hope to unravel the influence of heredity? Twins and adopted children provide some important clues to the role of heredity. In twin studies, researchers compare identical and fraternal twins. *Identical twins are called* **monozygotic twins** *because they come from a single fertilized egg that splits in two.* Because identical twins come from the same fertilized egg, the same genes control their body structure, height, and facial features, which explains why identical twins look alike. *In contrast, fraternal or* **dizygotic twins** *come from two separate eggs fertilized by two separate sperm.* Genetically, fraternal twins are just like any other siblings—on average, about half their genes are the same. In twin studies, scientists compare identical and fraternal twins to measure the influence of heredity. If identical twins are more alike than are fraternal twins, this implicates heredity (Phelps, Davis, & Schartz, 1997).

Identical twins are called monozygotic twins because they came from a single fertilized egg that split in two and, consequently, have identical genes.

A similar logic is used in adoption studies, in which adopted children are compared with their biological parents and their adoptive parents. The idea here is that biological parents provide their child's genes, but adoptive parents provide the child's environment. Consequently, if a behavior has important genetic roots, then adopted children should behave more like their biological parents than like their adoptive parents.

These and other methods are not foolproof. Maybe you thought of a potential flaw in twin studies: Parents and other people may treat monozygotic twins more similarly than they treat dizygotic twins. This would make monozygotic twins more similar than dizygotic twins in their experiences as well as in their genes. Because each method has its unique pitfalls, when different methods converge on the same conclusion about the influence of heredity, we can be confident of that result. Throughout this book, you'll see many instances where twin studies and adoption studies have pointed to genetic influences on human development.

Behavioral geneticists are now moving beyond traditional methods such as twin and adoption studies (Dick & Rose, 2002; Plomin & Crabbe, 2000). Today it is possible to isolate particular segments of DNA in human chromosomes. These segments then serve as markers for identifying specific alleles. The procedure is complicated, but the basic approach often begins by identifying people who differ in the behavioral or psychological trait of interest. For example, researchers might identify children who are outgoing and children who are shy. Or they might identify children who read well and children who read poorly. The children rub the inside of their mouths with a cotton swab, which yields cheek cells that contain DNA. The cells are analyzed in a lab, and the DNA markers for the two groups are compared. If the markers differ consistently, then the alleles near the marker probably contribute to the differences between the groups.

Techniques like these have the potential to identify the many different genes that contribute to complex behavioral and psychological traits. Of course, these new methods have limits. Some require very large samples of people, which can be hard to obtain when studying a rare disorder. Also, some require that an investigator have an idea, before even beginning the study, about which chromosomes to search and where. These can be major hurdles. But, when used with traditional methods of behavioral genetics (e.g., adoption studies), the new methods promise a much greater understanding of how genes influence behavior and development.

Throughout the rest of this book, you'll encounter many instances that show the interactive influences of heredity and environment on human development. In the next few pages, however, we want to mention some general principles of heredity-environment interactions.

Paths From Genes to Behavior

How do genes work together, for example, to make some children brighter than others and some children more outgoing than others? That is, how does the information in strands of DNA influence a child's behavioral and psychological development? The specific paths from genes to behavior are largely uncharted, but in the next few pages we'll discover some of their general properties.

1. *The behavioral consequences of genetic instructions depend on the environment in which those instructions are implemented.* In other words, a genotype can lead to many different phenotypes, depending on the specific environment in which the genotype is expressed (Gottesman & Hanson, 2005). ***Reaction range*** *refers to the fact that the same genotype can produce a range of phenotypes, in reaction to the environment where development takes place.* For example, imagine two children with the same genotype for "average intelligence." The children's phenotypic intelligence would depend on the environments in which they develop. If one child is brought up in an impoverished, unstimulating environment, his or her phenotypic intelligence may be below average. In contrast, if the second child is brought up in an enriched environment filled with stimulation, this child's phenotypic intelligence may be above average. Thus the same genotype for intelligence can lead to a range of phenotypes, depending on the quality of the rearing environment. Of course, what makes a "good" or "rich" environment is not the same for all facets of behavioral or psychological development. Throughout this book, you will see how specific kinds of environments influence very particular aspects of development (Wachs, 1983).

    This principle is responsible for the following warning that you'll find in the fine print on a can of diet soda (and some other food products):

    "Phenylketonurics: contains phenylalanine."

    Why? Children with phenylketonuria (PKU) are missing an enzyme that breaks down phenylalanine. When phenylalanine accumulates, it damages the nervous system and leads to mental retardation. Today, most American hospitals check for PKU at birth—with a blood or urine test. Newborns who have the disease are immediately placed on a diet that limits intake of phenylalanine, and mental retardation is avoided. Thus an individual who has the genotype for PKU but is not exposed to phenylalanine has normal intelligence. PKU illustrates that development depends on heredity and a child's dietary environment.

2. *Heredity and environment interact dynamically throughout development.* A simple-minded view of heredity and environment is that heredity provides the clay of life and experience does the sculpting. In fact, genes and environments constantly influence each other throughout a person's life (Gottesman & Hanson, 2005). This principle actually has two parts. First, genes are expressed—"turned on"—throughout the life span. For example, genes initiate the onset of menstruation in the early teens and the graying of hair in midlife. Second, the environment can trigger genetic expression: A person's experiences can help to determine how and when genes are activated (Gottlieb, 2000). For instance, teenage girls begin to menstruate at a younger age if they've had a stressful childhood. The exact pathway of influence is unknown (though it probably involves the hormones that are triggered by stress and those that initiate ovulation), but this is a clear case in which the environment advances the developmental clock (Ellis, 2004).

    Returning to the analogy of sculpting clay, a more realistic view is that new clay is constantly being added to the sculpture, leading to resculpting, which causes more clay to be added, and the cycle continues. Hereditary clay and environmental sculpting are continuously interweaving and influencing each other.

3. *Genes can influence the kind of environment to which a person is exposed.* In other words, "nature" can help to determine the kind of "nurturing" that a child receives (Scarr, 1992; Scarr & McCartney, 1983). A person's genotype can lead others to respond to the person in a specific way. For example, imagine someone who is bright and outgoing (both due, in part, to his or her genes). As a child, he or she may receive plenty of attention and encouragement from teachers. In contrast, someone who is not as bright and is more withdrawn (again, due in part to heredity) may be easily overlooked by teachers. In addition, as children grow and are more independent, they actively seek environments related to their genetic makeup. Children who are bright (due in part to heredity) may actively seek peers, adults, and activities that strengthen their intellectual development. Similarly, people who are outgoing (due in part to heredity) seek the company of other people, particularly extroverts like themselves. *This process of deliberately seeking environments that fit one's heredity is called* **niche-picking.** Niche-picking is first seen in childhood and becomes more common as children get older and can control their environments. The "Real People" feature shows niche-picking in action.

Children who are outgoing often like to be with other people, and they deliberately seek them out, a phenomenon known as niche-picking.

© Jeff Greenberg/PhotoEdit

REAL PEOPLE: Applying Human Development

BEN AND MATT PICK THEIR NICHES

Ben and Matt Kail were born 25 months apart. Even as a young baby, Ben was always a "people person." He relished contact with other people and preferred play that involved others. From the beginning, Matt was different. He was more withdrawn and was quite happy to play alone. The first separation from parents was harder for Ben than for Matt, because Ben relished parental contact more. When they entered school, Ben enjoyed increasing the scope of his friendships; Matt liked all the different activities that were available and barely noticed the new faces. Though brothers, Ben and Matt are quite dissimilar in terms of their sociability, a characteristic known to have important genetic components (Braungart et al., 1992).

As Ben and Matt have grown up (they're now young adults), they have consistently sought environments that fit their differing needs for social stimulation. Ben was involved in team sports and now enjoys working in the theater. Matt took art and photography classes and now is happy when he's reading, drawing, or working at his computer. Ben and Matt have chosen very different niches, and their choices have been driven in part by the genes that regulate sociability.

4. *Environmental influences typically make children within a family different.* One of the fruits of behavioral genetic research is greater understanding of the manner in which environments influence people. Traditionally, scientists considered some environments beneficial for people and others detrimental. This view has been especially strong in regard to family environments. Some parenting practices are thought to be more effective than others, and parents who use these effective practices are believed to have children who are, on average, better off than children of parents who don't use these practices. This view leads to a simple prediction: Children within a family should be similar because they all receive the same type of effective (or ineffective) parenting. However, dozens of behavioral genetic studies show that, in reality, siblings are not very much alike in their cognitive and social development (Plomin & Spinath, 2004).

Children's experiences within a family typically make them different from one another, not more alike.

Does this mean that family environment is not important? No. *These findings point to the importance of **nonshared environmental influences,** the forces within a family that make children different from one another.* Although the family environment is important, it usually affects each child in a unique way, which makes siblings differ. Each child is likely to have different experiences in daily family life. For example, parents may be more affectionate with one child than another, they may use more physical punishment with one child than another, or they may have higher expectations for school achievement for one child than another. All these contrasting parental influences tend to make siblings different, not alike (Turkheimer & Waldron, 2000). Family environments are important, but, as we describe their influence throughout this book, you should remember that families really create multiple unique environments, one for each person in the family.

Much of what we have said about genes, environment, and development is summarized in Figure 2.4 (Lytton, 2000). Parents are the source of children's genes and, at least for young children, the primary source of children's experiences. Children's genes also influence the experiences they have and the impact of those experiences on them. However, to capture the idea of nonshared environmental influences, we would need a separate diagram for each child, reflecting the fact that parents provide unique genes and a unique family environment for each of their offspring.

Most of this book explains the links between nature, nurture, and development. We can first see the interaction of nature and nurture during prenatal development, which we examine in the next section of this chapter.

■ **Figure 2.4**
Parents influence their children by providing genes and by providing experiences; children's genes and their environments work together to shape development.

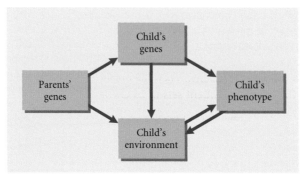

TEST YOURSELF

1. The first 22 pairs of chromosomes are called _____.

2. _____ reflects the combined activity of a number of distinct genes.

3. Individuals with _____ have an extra 21st chromosome, usually inherited from the mother.

4. When a fertilized egg has defective autosomes, the usual result is that _____.

5. Children who inherit PKU can develop normal intelligence if _____.

6. The term _____ refers to the fact that the same genotype can be associated with many different phenotypes.

7. Nonshared environmental influences tend to make siblings _____.

How might niche-picking work in the domain of intelligence?

Answers: (1) autosomes, (2) Polygenic inheritance, (3) Down syndrome, (4) the fertilized egg is aborted spontaneously, (5) they have a special diet that is low in phenylalanine, (6) reaction range, (7) different from each other

2.2

FROM CONCEPTION TO BIRTH

Eun Jung has just learned that she is pregnant with her first child. Like many other parents-to-be, she and her husband, Kinam, are ecstatic. But they also soon realize how little they know about "what happens when" during pregnancy. Eun Jung is eager to visit her obstetrician to learn more about the normal timetable of events during pregnancy.

LEARNING OBJECTIVES

What happens to a fertilized egg in the first two weeks after conception?

When do body structures and internal organs emerge in prenatal development?

When do body systems begin to function well enough to support life?

PRENATAL DEVELOPMENT BEGINS when a sperm successfully fertilizes an egg. *The many changes that transform the fertilized egg into a newborn human are known as* **prenatal development.** Prenatal development takes an average of 38 weeks, which are divided into three periods: the period of the zygote, the period of the embryo, and the period of the fetus.* Each period gets its name from the scientific term used to describe the baby-to-be at that point in prenatal development.

In this section, we'll trace the major developments of each of these periods. As we do, you'll learn the answers to the "what happens when" question that intrigues Eun Jung.

PERIOD OF THE ZYGOTE (WEEKS 1–2)

The teaspoon or so of seminal fluid produced during a fertile male's ejaculation contains from 200 to 500 million sperm. Of the sperm released into the vagina, only a few hundred will actually complete the 6- or 7-inch journey to the Fallopian tubes. Here, an egg arrives monthly, hours after it is released by an ovary. If an egg is present, many sperm will simultaneously begin to burrow their way through the cluster of nurturing cells that surround the egg. When one sperm finally penetrates the cellular wall of the egg, chemical changes occur in the wall immediately, blocking out all other sperm. Then the nuclei of the egg and sperm fuse, and the two independent sets of 23 chromosomes are interchanged. The development of a new human being is under way!

For nearly all of history, sexual intercourse was the only way for egg and sperm to unite and begin the development that results in a human being. This is no longer the only way, as we see in the Current Controversies feature.

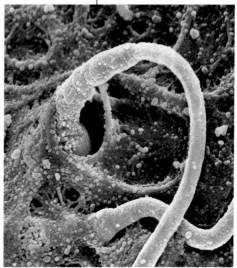

Fertilization begins when sperm cells burrow their way through the outer layers of an egg cell. In this photo the tails of the sperm can be seen clearly, but one sperm has burrowed so deeply that the head is barely visible.

© Lennart Nilsson

CURRENT CONTROVERSIES

CONCEPTION IN THE 21ST CENTURY

More than 25 years ago, Louise Brown captured the world's attention as the first test-tube baby—conceived in a petri dish instead of in her mother's body.

Today, this reproductive technology is no longer experimental; it is used more than 100,000 times annually by American women, producing nearly 50,000 babies

each year (U.S. Department of Health and Human Services, 2004a). Many new techniques are available to couples who cannot conceive a child through sexual

---

*Maybe you've heard that pregnancy lasts 40 weeks and wonder why we say that prenatal development lasts 38 weeks. The reason is that the 40 weeks of pregnancy are measured from the start of a woman's last menstrual period, which typically is about two weeks before conception.

intercourse. *The best known, **in vitro fertilization,** involves mixing sperm and egg together in a petri dish and then placing several fertilized eggs in the mother's uterus, with the hope that they will become implanted in the uterine wall.* Other methods include injecting many sperm directly into the Fallopian tubes or a single sperm directly into an egg.

The sperm and egg usually come from the prospective parents, but sometimes they are provided by donors. Typically, the fertilized eggs are placed in the uterus of the prospective mother, but sometimes they are placed in the uterus of a surrogate mother, who carries the baby to term. This means that a baby could have as many as five "parents": the man and woman who provided the sperm and egg; the surrogate mother who carried the baby; and the mother and father who will rear the baby.

New reproductive techniques offer hope for couples who have long wanted a child, and studies of the first generation of children conceived via these techniques indicates that their social and emotional development is perfectly normal (Golombok, MacCallum, & Goodman, 2001; Golombok et al., 2004). But there are difficulties as well. Only about one third of attempts at in vitro fertiliza-

tion succeed. What's more, when a woman becomes pregnant, she is more likely to have twins or triplets because multiple eggs are transferred to increase the odds that at least one fertilized egg will implant in the mother's uterus. She is also at greater risk for giving birth to a baby with low birth weight or birth defects. Finally, the procedure is expensive—the average cost in the United States of a single cycle of treatment is about $10,000—and typically it is not covered by health insurance (Katz, Nachtigall, & Showstack, 2002).

These problems emphasize that, although technology has increased the alternatives for infertile couples, pregnancy on demand is still in the realm of science fiction. At the same time, the new technologies have led to much controversy because of some complex ethical issues associated with their use. One concerns the prospective parents' right to select particular egg and sperm cells; another involves who should be able to use this technology.

Pick your egg and sperm cells from a catalog? Until recently, prospective parents have known nothing about egg and sperm donors. Today, however, they are sometimes able to select egg and sperm based on physical and psychological

characteristics of the donors, including appearance and race. Some claim that such prospective parents have a right to be fully informed about the person who provides the genetic material for their baby. *Others argue that this amounts to **eugenics,** which is the effort to improve the human species by allowing only certain people to mate and pass along their genes to subsequent generations.*

Available to all? Most couples who use in vitro fertilization are in their 30s and 40s, but a number of older women have begun to use the technology. Many of these women cannot conceive naturally because they have gone through menopause and no longer ovulate. Some argue that it is unfair to a child to have parents who may not live until the child reaches adulthood. Others point out that people are living longer and that middle-aged (or older) adults make better parents. (We discuss this in more depth in Chapter 13.)

What do you think? Should prospective parents be allowed to browse a catalog with photos and biographies of prospective donors? Should new reproductive technologies be available to all, regardless of age?

---

*Whether by artificial means like those we've just described or by natural means, fertilization begins the period of the **zygote,** the technical term for the fertilized egg.* This period ends when the zygote implants itself in the wall of the uterus. During these 2 weeks, the zygote grows rapidly through cell division. Figure 2.5 traces the egg cell from the time it is released from the ovary until the zygote becomes implanted in the wall of the uterus. The zygote travels down the Fallopian tube toward the uterus. Within hours, the zygote divides for the first time, then continues to do so every 12 hours. Occasionally, the zygote separates into two clusters that develop into identical twins. Fraternal twins, which are more common, are created when two eggs are released and each is fertilized by a different sperm cell.

After about 4 days, the zygote includes about 100 cells and resembles a hollow ball. The inner part of the ball is destined to become the baby. The outer layer of cells will form a number of structures that provide a life-support system throughout prenatal development.

By the end of the first week, the zygote reaches the uterus. *The next step is **implantation,** in which the zygote burrows into the uterine wall and establishes connections with a woman's blood vessels.* Implantation takes about a week to complete and triggers hormonal changes that prevent menstruation, letting the woman know that she has conceived.

The implanted zygote is less than a millimeter in diameter, yet its cells have already begun to differentiate. *A small cluster of cells near the center of the zygote, the **germ disc,** will eventually develop into the baby.* The other cells are destined to become structures

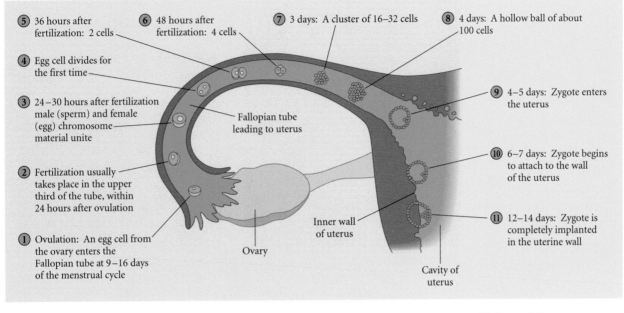

(5) 36 hours after fertilization: 2 cells

(6) 48 hours after fertilization: 4 cells

(7) 3 days: A cluster of 16–32 cells

(8) 4 days: A hollow ball of about 100 cells

(4) Egg cell divides for the first time

(3) 24–30 hours after fertilization male (sperm) and female (egg) chromosome material unite

Fallopian tube leading to uterus

(9) 4–5 days: Zygote enters the uterus

(2) Fertilization usually takes place in the upper third of the tube, within 24 hours after ovulation

(10) 6–7 days: Zygote begins to attach to the wall of the uterus

(1) Ovulation: An egg cell from the ovary enters the Fallopian tube at 9–16 days of the menstrual cycle

Ovary

Inner wall of uterus

Cavity of uterus

(11) 12–14 days: Zygote is completely implanted in the uterine wall

■ **Figure 2.5**
The period of the zygote spans 14 days, beginning with fertilization of the egg in the Fallopian tube and ending with implantation of the fertilized egg in the wall of the uterus.

that support, nourish, and protect the developing organism. *For example, the layer of cells closest to the uterus will become the* **placenta,** *a structure through which nutrients and wastes are exchanged between the mother and the developing organism.*

Implantation and differentiation of cells mark the end of the period of the zygote. Comfortably settled in the shelter of the uterus, the zygote is well prepared for the remaining 36 weeks of the marvelous trek leading up to birth.

PERIOD OF THE EMBRYO (WEEKS 3–8)

Once the zygote is completely embedded in the uterine wall, it is called an **embryo.** This new period typically begins the third week after conception and lasts until the end of the eighth week. During the period of the embryo, body structures and internal organs develop. At the beginning of this period, three layers begin to form in the embryo. *The outer layer or* **ectoderm** *becomes hair, the outer layer of skin, and the nervous system; the middle layer or* **mesoderm** *forms muscles, bones, and the circulatory system; the inner layer or* **endoderm** *forms the digestive system and the lungs.*

One dramatic way to see these changes is to compare a 3-week-old embryo with an 8-week-old embryo. The 3-week-old embryo is about 2 millimeters long. Specialization of cells is under way, but the organism looks more like a salamander than a human being. However, growth and specialization proceed so rapidly that an 8-week-old embryo looks very different: You can see eyes, jaw, arms, and legs. The brain and the nervous system are developing rapidly, and the heart has been beating for nearly a month. Most of the organs found in a mature human are in place, in some form. (The sex organs are a notable exception.) Yet, being only an inch long and weighing a fraction of an ounce, the embryo is much too small for the mother to feel its presence.

The embryo's environment is shown in Figure 2.6. *The embryo rests in a sac called the* **amnion,** *which is filled with* **amniotic fluid** *that cushions the embryo and maintains a constant temperature.* The embryo is linked to the mother via two structures. *The* **umbilical cord** *houses blood vessels that join the embryo to the placenta.* In the placenta, the blood vessels from the umbilical cord run close to the mother's blood vessels, but aren't actu-

© Lennart Nilsson

By the end of the period of the zygote, the fertilized egg has been implanted in the wall of the uterus and has begun to make connections with the mother's blood vessels.

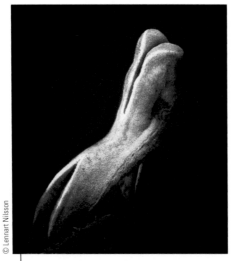

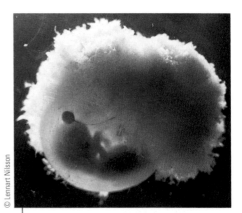

At 3 weeks after conception, the fertilized egg is about 2 millimeters long and resembles a salamander.

At 8 weeks after conception, near the end of the period of the embryo, the fertilized egg is obviously recognizable as a baby-to-be.

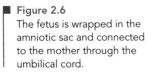

◼ Figure 2.6
The fetus is wrapped in the amniotic sac and connected to the mother through the umbilical cord.

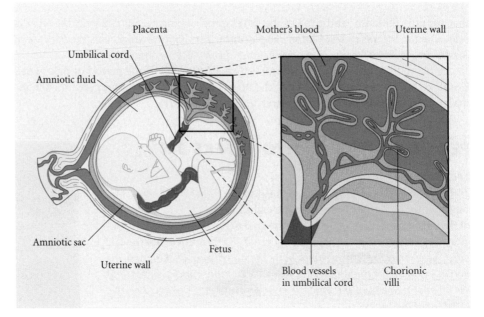

ally connected to them. The close proximity of the blood vessels allows nutrients, oxygen, vitamins, and waste products to be exchanged between mother and embryo.

Growth in the period of the embryo follows two important principles: First, the head develops before the rest of the body. *Such growth from the head to the base of the spine illustrates the* **cephalocaudal principle.** Second, arms and legs develop before hands and feet. *Growth of parts near the center of the body before those that are more distant illustrates the* **proximodistal principle.** Growth after birth also follows these principles.

With body structures and internal organs in place, the embryo has passed another major milestone in prenatal development. What's left is for these structures and organs to begin working properly. This is accomplished in the final period of prenatal development, as we'll see next.

PERIOD OF THE FETUS (WEEKS 9–38)

*The final and longest phase of prenatal development, the **period of the fetus,** begins at the ninth week (when cartilage begins to turn to bone) and ends at birth.* During this period, the baby-to-be becomes much larger and its bodily systems begin to work. The increase in size is remarkable. At the beginning of this period, the fetus weighs less than an ounce. At about 4 months, the fetus weighs roughly 4 to 8 ounces, which is large enough for the mother to feel its movements. In the last 5 months of pregnancy, the fetus will gain an additional 7 or 8 pounds before birth. Figure 2.7, which depicts the fetus at one eighth of its actual size, shows these incredible increases in size.

During the fetal period, the finishing touches are placed on the many systems that are essential to human life, such as respiration, digestion, and vision. Some highlights of this period include the following:

■ In the fifth and sixth months after conception, eyebrows, eyelashes, and scalp hair emerge. *The skin thickens and is covered with a thick greasy substance, **vernix,** which protects the fetus during its long bath in amniotic fluid.*

■ Near the end of the embryonic period, male embryos develop testes and female embryos develop ovaries. In the third month, the testes in a male fetus secrete a hormone that causes a set of cells to become a penis and scrotum; in a female fetus, this hormone is absent, so the same cells become a vagina and labia.

■ At 4 weeks after conception, a flat set of cells curls to form a tube. One end of the tube swells to form the brain; the rest forms the spinal cord. By the start of the fetal period, the brain has distinct structures and has begun to regulate body functions. *During the period of the fetus, all regions of the brain grow, particularly the **cerebral cortex,** the wrinkled surface of the brain that regulates many important human behaviors.*

*With these and other rapid changes, by 22 to 28 weeks most systems function well enough that a fetus born at this time has a chance to survive, which is why this age range is called the **age of viability.*** By this age, the fetus has a distinctly baby-like look, but babies born this early have trouble breathing because their lungs are not yet mature. Also, they cannot regulate their body temperature very well because they lack the insulating

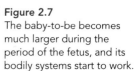

■ **Figure 2.7**
The baby-to-be becomes much larger during the period of the fetus, and its bodily systems start to work.

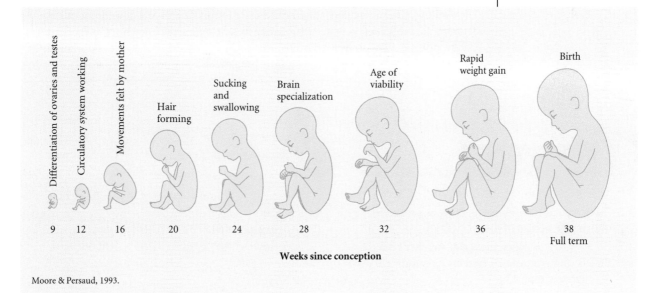

Moore & Persaud, 1993.

From *Before We Are Born,* Fourth Edition, by K. L. Moore and T. V. N. Persaud, p. 130. Copyright © 1993 W. B. Saunders. Reprinted with permission.

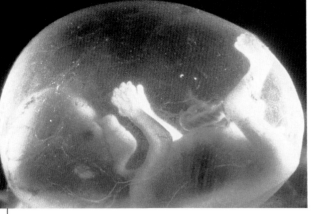

At 22–28 weeks after conception, the fetus has achieved the age of viability, meaning that it has a chance of surviving if born prematurely.

THINK ABOUT IT

Health care professionals often divide pregnancy into three 3-month trimesters. How do these three trimesters correspond to the periods of the zygote, embryo, and fetus?

layer of fat that appears in the eighth month after conception. With modern neonatal intensive care, infants born this early can survive, but they face other challenges, as we'll see later in this chapter.

During the fetal period, the fetus actually starts to behave (Joseph, 2000). The delicate movements that were barely noticeable at 4 months are now obvious. In fact, the fetus is a budding gymnast and kick-boxer rolled into one. It will punch or kick and turn somersaults. When active, the fetus moves about once a minute (DiPietro et al., 2004). These bursts of activity are followed by times when the fetus is still, as regular activity cycles emerge. Although movement is common in a healthy pregnancy, some fetuses are more active than others, and these differences predict infants' behavior: An active fetus is more likely than an inactive fetus to be an unhappy, difficult baby (DiPietro et al., 1996).

Another sign of growing behavioral maturity is that the senses work. There's not much to see in the uterus (imagine being in a cave with a flashlight that has a weak battery), but there are sounds galore. The fetus can hear the mother's heart beating and can hear her food digesting. More important, the fetus can hear her speak and hear others speak to her (Lecanuet, Granier-Deferre, & Busnel, 1995). And there are tastes: As the fetus swallows amniotic fluid, it responds to different flavors in the fluid.

Not only can the fetus detect sounds and flavors, sensory experiences from pregnancy can have lasting effects. In one study (Mennella, Jagnow, & Beauchamp, 2001), women drank carrot juice several days a week during the last month of pregnancy. When their infants were 5 and 6 months old, they preferred cereal with carrot juice. In another study, pregnant women read aloud *The Cat in the Hat* daily for the last several weeks of pregnancy (DeCasper & Spence, 1986). After birth, the newborns were allowed to suck on a special pacifier that controlled a tape recorder. The newborns would suck to hear a tape of their mother reading *The Cat in the Hat* but not to hear her reading other stories. Evidently, newborns recognized the familiar, rhythmic quality of *The Cat in the Hat* from their prenatal story times. The ability of the fetuses in these studies to learn from experience shows that prenatal development leaves babies well prepared for life outside the uterus.

Findings like these tell us that the last few months of prenatal development leave the fetus remarkably well prepared for independent living as a newborn baby. Unfortunately, not all babies arrive well prepared. Sometimes their prenatal development is disrupted. In the next section, we'll see how prenatal development can go awry.

TEST YOURSELF

1. The period of the zygote ends _____.
2. Body structures and internal organs are created during the period of the _____.
3. _____ is called the age of viability because this is when most body systems function well enough to support life.
4. In the last few months of prenatal development, the fetus has regular periods of activity and _____, which are the first signs of fetal behavior.

A friend of yours says, "The environment starts to influence a child's development at birth." Do you agree? Why or why not?

Answers: (1) at 2 weeks after conception (when the zygote is completely implanted in the wall of the uterus), (2) embryo, (3) Between 22 and 28 weeks, (4) the eyes and ears respond to stimulation

2.3

INFLUENCES ON PRENATAL DEVELOPMENT

LEARNING OBJECTIVES

How is prenatal development influenced by a pregnant woman's age, her nutrition, and the stress she experiences while pregnant?

How do diseases, drugs, and environmental hazards sometimes affect prenatal development?

What general principles affect the ways that prenatal development can be harmed?

How can prenatal development be monitored? Can abnormal prenatal development be corrected?

Chloe was 2 months pregnant at her first prenatal checkup. As her appointment drew near, she began a list of questions to ask her obstetrician. "I spend much of my workday at a computer. Is radiation from the monitor harmful to my baby?" "When my husband and I get home from work, we'll have a glass of wine to help unwind from the stress of the day. Is moderate drinking like this okay?" "I'm 38. I know older women give birth to babies with mental retardation more often. Can I know if my baby will be mentally retarded?"

Each of Chloe's questions concerns harm to her baby-to-be. She worries about the safety of her computer monitor, about her nightly glass of wine, and about her age. Chloe's concerns are well founded. Many factors influence the course of prenatal development, and they are the focus of this section. If you're sure you can answer *all* of Chloe's questions, skip this section and go directly to page 74. Otherwise, read on to learn about problems that sometimes arise in pregnancy.

GENERAL RISK FACTORS

As the name implies, general risk factors can have widespread effects on prenatal development. Scientists have identified three general risk factors: nutrition, stress, and a mother's age.

Nutrition

The mother is the developing child's sole source of nutrition, so a balanced diet that includes foods from each of the five major food groups is vital. Most pregnant women need to increase their intake of calories by about 10 to 20% to meet the needs of prenatal development. A woman should expect to gain between 25 and 35 pounds during pregnancy, assuming that her weight was normal before pregnancy. A woman who was underweight before becoming pregnant may gain as much as 40 pounds; a woman who was overweight should gain at least 15 pounds (Institute of Medicine, 1990). Of this gain, about one third reflects the weight of the baby, the placenta, and the fluid in the amniotic sac; another third comes from increases in a woman's fat stores; yet another third comes from the increased volume of blood and increases in the size of the woman's breasts and uterus (Whitney & Hamilton, 1987).

Sheer amount of food is only part of the equation for a healthy pregnancy. *What* a pregnant woman eats is also very important. Proteins, vitamins, and minerals are essential for normal prenatal development. For example, folic acid, one of the B vitamins, is important for the baby's nervous system to develop properly (Shaw et al., 1995). *When mothers do not consume adequate amounts of folic acid, their babies are at risk for **spina bifida,** a disorder in which the embryo's neural tube does not close properly during the first month of pregnancy.* Since the neural tube develops into the brain and spinal cord, when it does not close properly, the result is permanent damage to the spinal cord and the nervous system. Many children with spina bifida need crutches, braces, or wheelchairs.

Other prenatal problems have also been traced to inadequate proteins, vitamins, or minerals, so health care providers typically recommend that pregnant women supplement their diet with additional proteins, vitamins, and minerals.

When a pregnant woman does not provide adequate nourishment, the infant is likely to be born prematurely and to be underweight. Inadequate nourishment during the last few months of pregnancy can particularly affect the nervous system because this is a time of rapid brain growth. Finally, babies who do not receive adequate nourishment are vulnerable to illness (Guttmacher & Kaiser, 1986).

Stress

Does a pregnant woman's mood affect the zygote, embryo, or fetus in her uterus? Is a woman who is happy during pregnancy more likely to give birth to a happy baby? Is a harried office worker more likely to give birth to an irritable baby? *These questions address the impact on prenatal development of chronic* **stress,** *which refers to a person's physical and psychological responses to threatening or challenging situations.* We can answer these questions with some certainty for nonhumans. When pregnant female animals experience constant stress—such as repeated electric shocks or intense overcrowding—their offspring are often smaller than average and prone to other physical and behavioral problems (DiPietro, 2004). In addition, stress seems to cause greater harm when experienced early in pregnancy (Schneider et al., 1999).

Determining the impact of stress on human pregnancy is more difficult because we must rely solely on correlational studies. (It would be unethical to do an experiment that assigned some pregnant women to a condition of extreme stress.) Studies typically show that women who report greater anxiety during pregnancy more often give birth early or have babies who weigh less than average (Copper et al., 1996; Paarlberg et al., 1995). What's more, when women are anxious throughout pregnancy, their children are less able to pay attention as infants and more prone to behavioral problems as preschoolers (Huizink et al., 2002; O'Conner et al., 2002).

Increased stress can harm prenatal development in several ways. First, when a pregnant woman experiences stress, her body secretes hormones that reduce the flow of oxygen to the fetus while increasing its heart rate and activity level (Monk et al., 2000). Second, stress can weaken a pregnant woman's immune system, making her more susceptible to illness (Cohen & Williamson, 1991), which can, in turn, damage fetal development. Third, pregnant women under stress are more likely to smoke or drink alcohol and are less likely to rest, exercise, and eat properly (DiPietro et al., 2004). All these behaviors endanger prenatal development.

We want to emphasize that the results described here apply to women who experience prolonged, extreme stress. Virtually all women sometimes become anxious or upset while pregnant. Occasional, relatively mild anxiety is not thought to have any harmful consequences for prenatal development.

Michael Krasowitz /Getty Images

When pregnant women experience chronic stress, they're more likely to give birth early or have smaller babies, but this may be because women who are stressed are more likely to smoke or drink and less likely to rest, exercise, and eat properly.

Mother's Age

Traditionally, the 20s were thought to be the prime childbearing years. Teenage women as well as women who were 30 or older were considered less fit for the rigors of pregnancy. Is being a 20-something really important for a successful pregnancy? Let's answer this question separately for teenage and older women. Compared to women in their 20s, teenage women are more likely to have problems during pregnancy, labor, and delivery. This is largely because pregnant teenagers are more likely to be economically disadvantaged and to lack good prenatal care, either because they are unaware of the need for it or because they cannot afford it. For example, in one study (Turley, 2003) children of teenage moms were compared with their cousins, whose mothers were the older sisters of the teenage moms but had given birth when they were in their 20s. The two groups of children were very similar in academic skills and behavioral problems, indicating that it's the typical family background of teenage moms that is the obstacle, not their age. Similarly, research done on African American adolescents indicates that when differences in prenatal care are taken into account, teenagers are just as likely as women in their 20s to have problem-free pregnancies and to give birth to healthy babies (Goldenberg & Klerman, 1995).

Nevertheless, even when a teenager receives adequate prenatal care and gives birth to a healthy baby, all is not rosy. Children of teenage mothers generally do less well in school and more often have behavioral problems (Fergusson & Woodward, 2000). The problems of teenage motherhood—incomplete education, poverty, and marital difficulties—affect the child's later development (Moore & Brooks-Gunn, 2002).

Of course, not all teenage mothers and their infants follow this dismal life course. Some teenage mothers finish school, find good jobs, and have happy marriages; their children do well in school, academically and socially. These "success stories" are more likely when teenage moms live with a relative—typically the child's grandmother (Gordon, Chase-Lansdale, & Brooks-Gunn, 2004). However, teenage pregnancies with "happy endings" are definitely the exception; for most teenage mothers and their children, life is a struggle. Educating teenagers about the true consequences of teen pregnancy is crucial.

Are older women better suited for pregnancy? This is an important question because today's American woman is waiting longer than ever to have her first child. Completing an education and beginning a career often delay childbearing. In fact, the birth rate in the early 2000s among 30- to 44-year-olds was nearly double what it was in 1980 (Martin et al., 2002).

Traditionally, older women were thought to have more difficult pregnancies and more complicated labor and deliveries. Today, we know that women in their 20s are twice as fertile as women in their 30s (Dunson et al., 2002). For women 35 years of age and older, the risks of miscarriage and stillbirth increase rapidly. Among 40- to 45-year-olds, for example, nearly half of all pregnancies result in miscarriage (Andersen et al., 2000). What's more, women in their 40s are more liable to give birth to babies with Down syndrome.

In general, then, prenatal development is most likely to proceed normally when women are between 20 and 35 years of age, are healthy and eat right, get good health care, and lead lives that are free of chronic stress. But even in these optimal cases, prenatal development can be disrupted, as we'll see in the next section.

Older women have more difficulty getting pregnant and are more likely to have miscarriages.

TERATOGENS: DRUGS, DISEASES, AND ENVIRONMENTAL HAZARDS

In the late 1950s, many pregnant women in Germany took thalidomide, a drug that helped them sleep. Soon, however, came reports that many of these women were giving birth to babies with deformed arms, legs, hands, or fingers. *Thalidomide is a powerful te-*

TABLE 2.3

Teratogenic Drugs and Their Consequences

Drug	Potential Consequences
Alcohol	Fetal alcohol syndrome, cognitive deficits, heart damage, retarded growth
Aspirin	Deficits in intelligence, attention, and motor skills
Caffeine	Lower birth weight, decreased muscle tone
Cocaine and heroin	Retarded growth, irritability in newborns
Marijuana	Lower birth weight, less motor control
Nicotine	Retarded growth, possible cognitive impairments

ratogen, an agent that causes abnormal prenatal development. Ultimately, more than 7,000 babies worldwide were harmed before thalidomide was withdrawn from the market (Kolberg, 1999).

Prompted by the thalidomide disaster, scientists began to study teratogens extensively. Today, we know a great deal about many teratogens that affect prenatal development. Most teratogens fall into one of three categories: drugs, diseases, or environmental hazards. Let's look at each.

Drugs

Thalidomide illustrates the harm that drugs can cause during prenatal development. Table 2.3 lists several other drugs that are known teratogens. Most of the drugs in the list are substances you may use routinely—alcohol, aspirin, caffeine, nicotine. Nevertheless, when consumed by pregnant women, they do present special dangers (Behnke & Eyler, 1993).

Cigarette smoking is typical of the potential harm from teratogenic drugs (Cornelius et al., 1995; Fried, O'Connell, & Watkinson, 1992). The nicotine in cigarette smoke constricts blood vessels and thus reduces the oxygen and nutrients that can reach the fetus over the placenta. Therefore, pregnant women who smoke are more likely to miscarry (abort the fetus spontaneously) and to bear children who are smaller than average at birth (Cnattingius, 2004; Ernst, Moolchan, & Robinson, 2001). And, as children develop, they are more likely to show signs of impaired attention, language, and cognitive skills, along with behavioral problems (Brennan et al., 2002). Finally, even second-hand smoke harms the fetus: When pregnant women don't smoke but fathers do, babies tend to be smaller at birth (Friedman & Polifka, 1996). The message is clear and simple: Pregnant women shouldn't smoke, and they should avoid others who do.

Alcohol also carries serious risk. *Pregnant women who consume large quantities of alcoholic beverages often give birth to babies with* **fetal alcohol syndrome** *(FAS).* Children with FAS usually grow more slowly than normal and have heart problems and misshapen faces. Youngsters with FAS often have a small head, a thin upper lip, a short nose, and widely spaced eyes. FAS is the leading cause of mental retardation in the United States, and children with FAS have serious attentional, cognitive, and behavioral problems. FAS is most common among pregnant women who are heavy recreational drinkers—that is, women who drink 5 or more ounces of alcohol a few times each week (Jacobson & Jacobson, 2000; Lee, Mattson, & Riley, 2004).

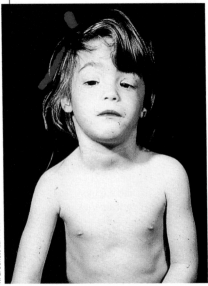

When pregnant women drink large amounts of alcohol, their children often have fetal alcohol syndrome, in which they tend to have a small head and a thin upper lip as well as retarded mental development.

K. L. Jones / LLR Research

Fetal alcohol syndrome is most likely when pregnant women drink three or more ounces of alcohol daily. Does this mean that moderate drinking is safe? No. When women drink moderately throughout pregnancy, their children often have lower scores on tests of attention, memory, and intelligence (Streissguth et al., 1994).

Is there any amount of drinking that's safe during pregnancy? Maybe, but scientists have yet to determine one. This inconclusiveness stems from two factors. First, drinking is often estimated from women's responses to interviews or questionnaires. These replies may be incorrect, leading to inaccurate estimates of the harm associated with drinking. Second, any safe level of consumption is probably not the same for all women. Based on their health and heredity, some women may be able to consume more alcohol safely than others.

These factors make it impossible to offer guaranteed statements about safe levels of alcohol or any of the other drugs listed in Table 2.3. For this reason, the best policy is for women to avoid all drugs throughout pregnancy.

Diseases

Sometimes women become ill while pregnant. Most diseases, such as colds and many strains of the flu, do not affect the fetus. However, several bacterial and viral infections can be quite harmful; five are listed in Table 2.4.

Some diseases pass from the mother through the placenta to attack the embryo or fetus directly. AIDS, cytomegalovirus, rubella, and syphilis are examples of diseases that are transmitted through the placenta. Other diseases attack during birth: The virus is present in the lining of the birth canal and babies are infected as they pass through the canal. AIDS and genital herpes are two such diseases.

The only way to guarantee that these diseases will not harm prenatal development is for a woman to be sure that she does not contract the disease, before or during her pregnancy. Medicines that may help to treat a woman after she has become ill do not prevent the disease from damaging the fetus.

Environmental Hazards

As a by-product of life in an industrialized world, people are often exposed to toxins in food they eat, fluids they drink, and air they breathe. Chemicals associated with industrial waste are the most common form of environmental teratogens. The quantity involved is usually minute; however, as was true for drugs, amounts that go unnoticed in an adult can cause serious damage to the fetus. Several environmental hazards that are known teratogens are listed in Table 2.5.

> **THINK ABOUT IT**
>
> A pregnant woman reluctant to give up her morning cup of coffee and nightly glass of wine says, "I drink so little coffee and wine that it couldn't possibly hurt my baby." What do you think?

TABLE **2.4**

Teratogenic Diseases and Their Consequences

Disease	Potential Consequences
AIDS	Frequent infections, neurological disorders, death
Cytomegalovirus	Deafness, blindness, abnormally small head, mental retardation
Genital herpes	Encephalitis, enlarged spleen, improper blood clotting
Rubella (German measles)	Mental retardation; damage to eyes, ears, and heart
Syphilis	Damage to the central nervous system, teeth, and bones

TABLE 2.5

Environmental Teratogens and Their Consequences

Hazard	Potential Consequences
Lead	Mental retardation
Mercury	Retarded growth, mental retardation, cerebral palsy
PCBs	Impaired memory and verbal skills
X-rays	Retarded growth, leukemia, mental retardation

You'll notice that although X-rays are included in the table, radiation associated with computer monitors or video-display terminals (VDTs) is not. Several major studies have examined the impact of exposure to the electromagnetic fields generated by VDTs. For example, Schnorr and her colleagues (1991) compared the outcomes of pregnancies in telephone operators who worked at VDTs at least 25 hours weekly with operators who never used VDTs. For both groups of women, about 15% of the pregnancies ended in miscarriage. Further, other studies have not found links between exposure to VDTs and birth defects (Parazzini et al., 1993). Evidently, VDTs can be used safely by pregnant women.

In the Spotlight on Research feature, we look at one of these environmental teratogens in detail.

 # SPOTLIGHT ON RESEARCH

IMPACT OF PRENATAL EXPOSURE TO PCBS ON COGNITIVE FUNCTIONING

Who were the investigators, and what was the aim of the study? For many years, polychlorinated biphenyls (PCBs) were used in electrical transformers and paints, but the U.S. government banned them in the 1970s. Like many industrial by-products, they seeped into the waterways, contaminating fish and wildlife. The amount of PCBs in a typical contaminated fish does not affect adults, but Joseph Jacobson and Sandra Jacobson (1996) wanted to determine if this level of exposure was harmful to prenatal development. In particular, they knew from earlier work that substantial prenatal exposure to PCBs affected cognitive skills in infants and preschoolers; they hoped to determine if prenatal exposure similarly affected cognitive skills in school-age children.

How did the investigators measure the topic of interest? Jacobson and Jacobson needed to measure prenatal exposure to PCBs and cognitive skill. To measure prenatal exposure, they measured concentrations of PCBs in (a) blood obtained from the umbilical cord and (b) breast milk of mothers who were breast-feeding. To measure cognitive skill, they used a standardized test of intelligence and a standardized test of reading comprehension.

Who were the children in the study? The sample included 212 children who were born in western Michigan in 1980 and 1981. This region was chosen because, at the time, Lake Michigan contained many contaminated salmon and lake trout.

What was the design of the study? The study was correlational because the investigators were interested in the relation that existed naturally between two variables: exposure to PCBs and cognitive skill. The study was longitudinal because children were tested several times: Their exposure to PCBs was measured immediately after birth, and their cognitive skill was measured at three ages: 7 months, 4 years, and 11 years.

Were there ethical concerns with the study? No. The children had been exposed to PCBs naturally prior to the start of the study. (Obviously, it would not have been ethical for researchers to do an experiment that involved asking pregnant women to eat contaminated fish.) The investigators obtained permission from the parents for the children to participate.

What were the results? PCB exposure affects intelligence and reading comprehension. However, as you can see in Figure 2.8, lower levels of exposure to PCBs apparently had little effect on intelligence and reading comprehension. Only children with high levels of exposure to PCBs were affected.

What did the investigators conclude? Prenatal exposure to PCBs affects children's cognitive skills. Although the children's scores were in the normal range, their reduced cognitive skills may create special hurdles in school.

What converging evidence would strengthen these conclusions? The

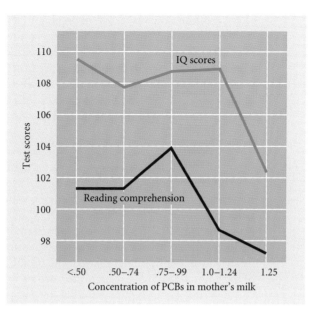

■ **Figure 2.8**
Children with the highest level of exposure to PCBs had the lowest scores on IQ and reading comprehension tests.

results show that PCBs affect children's scores on standardized tests. More convincing would be longitudinal studies showing that children exposed to PCBs were more likely to be diagnosed with a learning disability or language impairment, more likely to repeat a grade, or less likely to graduate from high school.

To enhance your understanding of this research, go to http://psychology .wadsworth.com/kail_cavanaugh4e/ to complete critical thinking questions and explore related websites.

Environmental teratogens are treacherous because people are unaware of their presence in the environment. The women in the Jacobson, Jacobson, and Humphrey (1990) study, for example, did not realize they were eating PCB-laden fish. This invisibility makes it more difficult for a pregnant woman to protect herself from environmental teratogens. The best advice is for a pregnant woman to be particularly careful of the foods she eats and the air she breathes. Be sure that all foods are cleaned thoroughly to rid them of insecticides. Avoid convenience foods, which often contain many chemical additives. Stay away from air that's been contaminated by household products such as cleansers, paint strippers, and fertilizers. Women in jobs such as housecleaning or hairdressing that require contact with potential teratogens should try to switch to less potent chemicals. For example, they should use baking soda instead of more chemically laden cleansers. And they should wear protective gloves, aprons, and masks to reduce their contact with potential teratogens. Finally, because environmental teratogens continue to increase, check with a health care provider to learn whether other materials should be avoided.

HOW TERATOGENS INFLUENCE PRENATAL DEVELOPMENT

By assembling all the evidence on the harm caused by drugs, diseases, and environmental hazards, scientists have identified five important general principles about how teratogens usually work (Hogge, 1990; Jacobson & Jacobson, 2000; Vorhees & Mollnow, 1987).

1. *The impact of a teratogen depends on the genotype of the organism.* A substance may be harmful to one species but not to another. To determine its

safety, thalidomide was tested on pregnant rats and rabbits, and their offspring had normal limbs. Yet, when pregnant women took the same drug in comparable doses, many had children with deformed limbs. Moreover, some women who took thalidomide gave birth to babies with normal limbs whereas others, taking comparable doses of thalidomide at the same time in their pregnancies, gave birth to babies with deformed arms and legs. Apparently, heredity makes some individuals more susceptible than others to a teratogen.

2. *The impact of teratogens changes over the course of prenatal development.* The timing of exposure to a teratogen is very important. Teratogens typically have different effects in the three periods of prenatal development. Figure 2.9 shows how the consequences of teratogens differ for the periods of the zygote, embryo, and fetus. During the period of the zygote, exposure to teratogens usually results in spontaneous abortion of the fertilized egg. During the period of the embryo, exposure to teratogens produces major defects in bodily structure. For example, women who took thalidomide during the period of the embryo had babies with ill-formed or missing limbs. Women who contract rubella during the period of the embryo have babies with heart defects. During the period of the fetus, exposure to teratogens either produces minor defects in bodily structure or causes body systems to function improperly. For example, when women drink large quantities of alcohol during this period, the fetus develops fewer brain cells.

Even within the different periods of prenatal development, developing body parts and systems are more vulnerable at some times than others. The

■ **Figure 2.9**
The consequences of a teratogen depend on the stage of prenatal development.

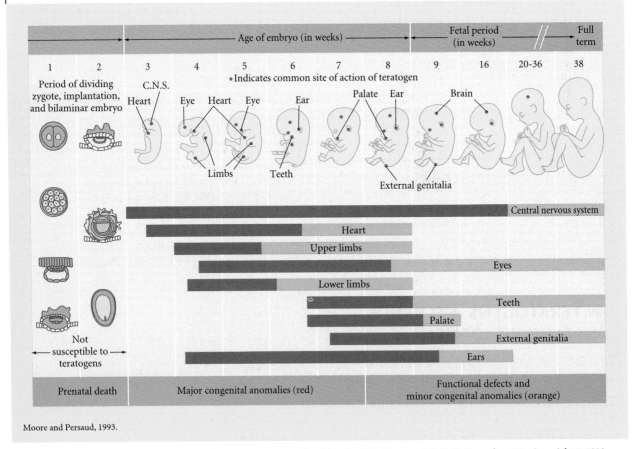

Moore and Persaud, 1993.

From *Before We Are Born,* Fourth Edition, by K. L. Moore and T. V. N. Persaud, p. 130. Copyright © 1993 W. B. Saunders. Reprinted with permission.

red shading in the chart indicates a time of maximum vulnerability; orange shading indicates a time when the developing organism is less vulnerable. The heart, for example, is most sensitive to teratogens during the first half of the embryonic period. Exposure to teratogens before this time rarely produces heart damage; exposure after results in milder damage.

3. *Each teratogen affects a specific aspect (or aspects) of prenatal development.* Said another way, teratogens do not harm all body systems; instead, damage is selective. When women contract rubella, their babies often have problems with their eyes, ears, and heart, but they have normal limbs. When mothers consume PCB-contaminated fish, their babies typically have normal body parts and normal motor skill but below-average verbal and memory skills.

4. *The impact of teratogens depends on the dose.* Just as a single drop of oil won't pollute a lake, small doses of teratogens may not harm the fetus. In research on PCBs, for example, cognitive skills were affected only among children who had the greatest prenatal exposure to these by-products. In general, the greater the exposure, the greater the risk for damage (Adams, 1999). An implication of this principle is that researchers should be able to determine safe levels for a teratogen. In reality, this is very difficult because sensitivity to teratogens is not the same for all people (and it's not practical to establish separate safe amounts for each person). Hence, the safest rule is zero exposure to teratogens.

5. *Damage from teratogens is not always evident at birth but may appear later in life.* In the case of malformed limbs or babies born addicted to cocaine, the effects of a teratogen are obvious immediately. Sometimes, however, the damage from a teratogen becomes evident only as the child develops. For example, when women ate PCB-contaminated fish, their babies were normal at birth. Their below-average cognitive skills were not evident until several months later.

   An even more dramatic example of the delayed impact of a teratogen involves the drug diethylstilbestrol (DES). Between 1947 and 1971, many pregnant women took DES to prevent miscarriages. Their babies were apparently normal at birth. However, as adults, daughters of women who took DES are more likely to have a rare cancer of the vagina and to have difficulties becoming pregnant themselves. Sons of women who took DES may be less fertile and at risk for cancer of the testes (Sharpe & Skakkebaek, 1993). Here is a case in which the impact of the teratogen is not evident until decades after birth.

The Real World of Prenatal Risk

We have discussed risk factors individually, as if each was the only potential threat to prenatal development. In reality, many infants are exposed to multiple general risks and multiple teratogens. Pregnant women who drink alcohol often smoke and drink coffee (Haslam & Lawrence, 2004). Pregnant women who are under stress often drink alcohol (Giberson & Weinberg, 1992). Many of these same women may have poor nutrition. When all of the risks are combined, unfortunately, prenatal development will rarely be optimal (Schneider, Roughton, & Lubach, 1997).

This pattern explains why it's often challenging for human development researchers to determine the harm associated with individual teratogens. Cocaine is a perfect example. You may remember stories in newspapers and magazines about "crack babies" and their developmental problems. In fact, the jury is still out on the issue of cocaine as a teratogen. Some investigators (e.g., Singer et al., 2002) find the harmful effects that made headlines in the 1990s, but others (e.g., Brown et al., 2004; Frank et al., 2001) argue that most of the effects attributed to cocaine actually stem from concurrent smoking and drinking and to the inadequate parenting that these children receive.

From what we've said so far in this section, you may think that the developing child has little chance of escaping harm. But most babies *are* born in good health. Of course, a good policy for pregnant women is to avoid diseases, drugs, and environmental hazards that are known teratogens. This, coupled with thorough prenatal medical care and adequate nutrition, is the best recipe for normal prenatal development.

PRENATAL DIAGNOSIS AND TREATMENT

"I really don't care whether I have a boy or girl, just as long as it's healthy." Legions of parents worldwide have felt this way, but until recently, all they could do was hope for the best. Today, however, advances in technology mean that parents can have a much better idea of whether their baby is developing normally.

Genetic Counseling

Often the first step in deciding whether a couple's baby is likely to be at risk is genetic counseling. A counselor asks about family medical history and constructs a family tree for each parent to assess the odds that their child would inherit a disorder. If the family tree suggests that a parent is likely to be a carrier of the disorder, blood tests can determine the parent's genotype. With this information, a genetic counselor then advises prospective parents about their choices. A couple might simply go ahead and attempt to conceive a child "naturally." Or, they may decide to use sperm or eggs from other people. Yet another choice might be adoption.

Prenatal Diagnosis

After a woman is pregnant, how can we know whether prenatal development is progressing normally? Traditionally, obstetricians tracked the progress of prenatal development by feeling the size and position of the fetus through a woman's abdomen. This technique was not very precise and, of course, couldn't be done at all until the fetus was large enough to feel. Today, however, several new techniques have revolutionized our ability to monitor prenatal growth and development. *A standard part of prenatal care in the United States is* **ultrasound,** *in which sound waves are used to generate a picture of the fetus.* In this procedure, a tool about the size of a hair dryer is rubbed over the woman's abdomen; the image is shown on a nearby computer monitor. The pictures generated are hardly portrait quality; they are grainy, and it takes an expert's eye to distinguish what's what. Nevertheless, parents are often thrilled to see their baby and to watch it move.

Ultrasound typically can be used as early as 4 or 5 weeks after conception; prior to this time the embryo is not large enough to generate an interpretable image. Ultrasound pictures are quite useful for determining the position of the fetus within the uterus and, at 16–20 weeks after conception, its sex. Ultrasound is also helpful in detecting twins or triplets. Finally, ultrasound is used to identify gross physical deformities, such as abnormal growth of the head.

In pregnancies where a genetic disorder is suspected, two other techniques are particularly valuable because they provide a sample of fetal cells that can be analyzed. *In* **amniocentesis** *a needle is inserted through the mother's abdomen to obtain a sample of the amniotic fluid that surrounds the fetus.* As you can see in Figure 2.10, ultrasound is used to guide the needle into the uterus. The fluid contains skin cells that can be grown in a laboratory dish and then analyzed to determine the genotype of the fetus.

A drawback to amniocentesis is that although the amniotic fluid is extracted at about 16 weeks af-

A standard part of prenatal care is ultrasound, in which sound waves are used to generate an image of the fetus that can be used to determine the position of the fetus in the uterus.

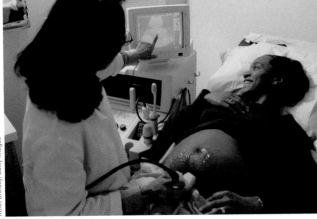

Keith Brofsky/Getty Images

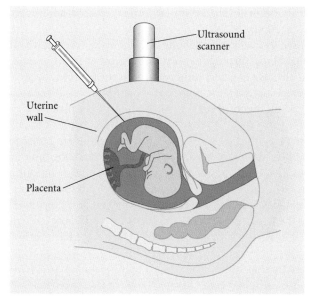

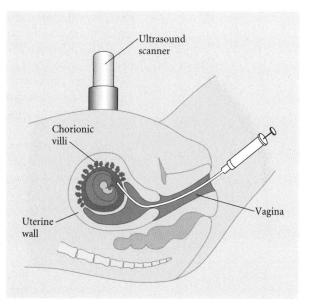

■ **Figure 2.10**
In amniocentesis, a sample of fetal cells is extracted from the fluid in the amniotic sac.

■ **Figure 2.11**
In chorionic villus sampling, fetal cells are extracted from the placenta.

ter conception, another 3 weeks must pass for the individual cells to grow sufficiently to allow testing. *A procedure that can be used much earlier in pregnancy is* **chorionic villus sampling** *in which a sample of tissue is obtained from part of the placenta.* Figure 2.11 shows that a small tube—typically inserted through the vagina and into the uterus but sometimes through the abdomen—is used to collect a small plug of cells from the placenta. This procedure can be used within 8 or 9 weeks after conception, and results are available within 24 hours.

With the samples obtained from either amniocentesis or chorionic villus sampling, roughly 200 different genetic disorders, including Down syndrome, can be detected. These procedures are virtually error-free but at a price: Miscarriages are slightly more likely—1 or 2%—after amniocentesis or chorionic villus sampling (Wilson, 2000). A woman must decide whether the information gained from amniocentesis or chorionic villus sampling justifies the slight risks of a possible miscarriage.

Fetal Medicine

Ultrasound, amniocentesis, and chorionic villus sampling have made it much easier to determine whether prenatal development is progressing normally. But what happens when it is not? Traditionally, a woman's options have been limited: She could continue the pregnancy or end it. Today the list of options is expanding. *A whole new field called* **fetal medicine** *is concerned with treating prenatal problems before birth.* Many tools are now available to solve problems that are detected during pregnancy (Evans, Platt, & De La Cruz, 2001). One approach is to treat disorders medically, by administering drugs or hormones to the fetus. For example, in fetal hypothyroidism, the fetal thyroid gland does not produce enough hormones, leading to retarded physical and mental development. This disorder can be treated by injecting the necessary hormones directly into the amniotic cavity, resulting in normal growth. Another example is congenital adrenal hyperplasia, an inherited disorder in which the fetal adrenal glands produce too much androgen, causing early maturation of boys or masculinization of girls. In this case, treatment consists of injecting hormones into the mother that reduce the amount of androgen secreted by the fetal adrenal glands (Evans et al., 2001).

Another way to correct prenatal problems is fetal surgery. For example, more than 200 cases of spina bifida have been corrected with fetal surgery in the seventh or eighth month of pregnancy. Surgeons cut through the mother's abdominal wall to expose the

THINK ABOUT IT

Imagine that you are 42 years old and pregnant. Would you want to have amniocentesis or chorionic villus sampling to determine the genotype of the fetus? Why or why not?

fetus, then cut through the fetal abdominal wall; the spinal cord is repaired, and the fetus is returned to the uterus (Okie, 2000).

Fetal surgery has also been used to treat a disorder affecting identical twins in which one twin—the "donor"—pumps blood through its own and the other twin's circulatory system. The donor twin usually fails to grow; surgery corrects the problem by sealing off the unnecessary blood vessels between the twins (McCormick, 2000). Fetal surgery holds great promise, but it is still highly experimental and therefore considered as a last resort.

Yet another approach is genetic engineering in which defective genes are replaced by synthetic normal genes. Take PKU as an example. Remember that if a baby inherits the recessive allele for PKU from both parents, toxins that cause mental retardation accumulate. In theory, it should be possible to take a sample of cells from the fetus, remove the recessive genes, and replace them with the dominant genes. These "repaired" cells would then be injected into the fetus, where they would multiply and cause enough enzyme to be produced to break down phenylalanine, thereby avoiding PKU (Verma, 1990).

Translating this idea into practice has been difficult, and there are many problems yet to be solved (Cooke, 2005). Nevertheless, gene therapy has been successful in a few cases. In one, a preschool girl was suffering from a hereditary disease of the immune system that left her unprotected against infection. Doctors took some of the girl's cells and inserted the immune gene into them. The cells were then injected into her bloodstream, where they help ward off infection.

These techniques are highly experimental and failures are common. However, this area of medicine is advancing rapidly, and prenatal treatment should become much more common in the 21st century.

Answers to Chloe's Questions. Now you can return to Chloe's questions in the section-opening vignette (page 63) and answer them for her. If you're not certain, here are the pages in this chapter where the answers appear:

- About her computer monitor—page 68
- About her nightly glass of wine—page 66
- About giving birth to a baby with mental retardation—page 65

TEST YOURSELF

1. General risk factors in pregnancy include a woman's nutrition, _____, and her age.

2. _____ are some of the most dangerous teratogens because a pregnant woman is often unaware of their presence.

3. During the period of the zygote, exposure to a teratogen typically results in _____.

4. Two techniques used to determine whether a fetus has a hereditary disorder are amniocentesis and _____.

Describe how the impact of teratogens on the fetus shows nature and nurture in action during prenatal development.

Answers: (1) prolonged stress, (2) Environmental hazards, (3) spontaneous abortion of the fertilized egg, (4) chorionic villus sampling

2.4

LABOR AND DELIVERY

Marlea is about to begin classes to prepare for her baby's birth. She is relieved that the classes are finally starting because this means the end of pregnancy is in sight. But all the talk she has heard about "breathing exercises" and "coaching" sounds pretty silly to her. Marlea would prefer to get knocked out for the delivery and wake up when everything is over.

LEARNING OBJECTIVES

What are the different phases of labor and delivery?

What are "natural" ways of coping with the pain of childbirth? Is childbirth at home safe?

What are some complications that can occur during birth?

As women like Marlea near the end of pregnancy, they find that sleeping and breathing become more difficult, that they tire more rapidly, that they become constipated, and that their legs and feet swell. Women look forward to birth, both to relieve their discomfort and, of course, to see their baby. In this section, you'll see the different steps involved in birth, review different approaches to childbirth, and look at problems that can arise. Along the way, we'll look at classes like those Marlea will take and the exercises that she'll learn.

STAGES OF LABOR

Labor is an appropriate name for childbirth, which is the most intense, prolonged physical effort that humans experience. Labor is usually divided into the three stages shown in Figure 2.12.

- In stage 1, which may last from 12 to 24 hours for a first birth, the uterus starts to contract. The first contractions are weak and irregular. Gradually, they become stronger and more rhythmic, enlarging the cervix (the opening from the uterus to the vagina) to approximately 10 centimeters.
- In stage 2, the baby passes through the cervix and enters the vagina. The mother helps push the baby along by contracting muscles in her abdomen. *Soon the top of the baby's head appears, an event known as **crowning**.* Within about an hour, the baby is delivered.
- In stage 3, which lasts only minutes, the mother pushes a few more times to expel the placenta (also called, appropriately, the *afterbirth*).

■ **Figure 2.12**
Labor includes three stages, beginning when the uterus contracts and ending when the placenta is expelled.

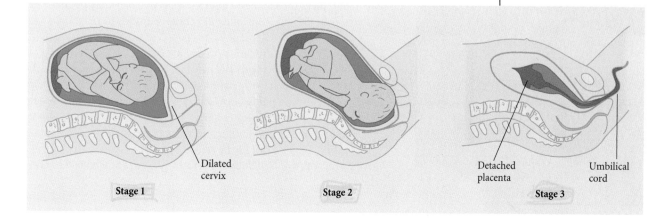

Stage 1 — Dilated cervix

Stage 2

Stage 3 — Detached placenta — Umbilical cord

The times given for each of the stages are only approximations; the actual times vary greatly among women. For most women, labor with their second and subsequent children is much more rapid. Stage 1 may last 4 to 6 hours, and stage 2 may be as brief as 20 minutes.

APPROACHES TO CHILDBIRTH

When your authors were born in the 1950s, women in labor were admitted to a hospital and administered a general anesthetic. Fathers waited anxiously in a nearby room for news of the baby. These were standard hospital procedures in 1950, and virtually all American babies were born this way.

But no longer is this true. In the middle of the 20th century, two European physicians—Grantly Dick-Read (1959) and Ferdinand Lamaze (1958)—criticized the traditional view in which labor and delivery had come to involve elaborate medical procedures that were often unnecessary and that often left women afraid of giving birth. Their fear led them to be tense, thereby increasing the pain they experienced during labor. These physicians argued for a more "natural" or prepared approach to childbirth, viewing labor and delivery as life events to be celebrated, rather than medical procedures to be endured.

Today many varieties of prepared childbirth are available to pregnant women. However, most share some fundamental beliefs. One is that birth is more likely to be problem-free and rewarding when mothers and fathers understand what's happening during pregnancy, labor, and delivery. Consequently, prepared childbirth means going to classes to learn basic facts about pregnancy and childbirth (like the material presented in this chapter).

A second common element is that natural methods of dealing with pain are emphasized over medication. Why? When a woman is anesthetized, with either general anesthesia or regional anesthesia (in which only the lower body is numbed), she can't use her abdominal muscles to help push the baby through the birth canal. Without this pushing, the obstetrician may have to use mechanical devices to pull the baby through the birth canal, which involves some risk to the baby (Johanson et al., 1993). Also, drugs that reduce the pain of childbirth cross the placenta and can affect the baby. Conse-

During childbirth preparation classes, pregnant women learn exercises that help them to relax and reduce the pain associated with childbirth.

© James Marshall / The Image Works

quently, when a woman receives large doses of pain-relieving medication, her baby is often withdrawn or irritable for days or even weeks (Brazelton, Nugent, & Lester, 1987; Ransjoe-Arvidson et al., 2001). These effects are temporary, but they may give the new mother the impression that she has a difficult baby. It is best, therefore, to minimize the use of pain-relieving drugs during birth.

Relaxation is the key to reducing birth pain without drugs. Because pain often feels greater when a person is tense, pregnant women learn to relax during labor, through deep breathing or by visualizing a reassuring, pleasant scene or experience. Whenever they begin to experience pain during labor, they use these methods to relax.

A third common element of prepared childbirth is to involve a supportive "coach." The father-to-be, a relative, or a close friend attends childbirth classes with the mother-to-be. The coach learns the techniques for coping with pain and practices them with the pregnant woman. During labor and delivery, the coach is present to help the woman use the techniques she has learned and to offer support and encouragement. *Sometimes the coach is accompanied by a **doula**, a person familiar with childbirth who is not part of the medical staff but instead provides emotional and physical support throughout labor and delivery.*

Although Marlea, the pregnant woman in the vignette, may have her doubts about these classes, research shows that they *are* useful (Hetherington, 1990). Most mothers who attend childbirth classes use some medication to reduce the pain of labor, but they typically use less than mothers who do not attend childbirth classes. Also, mothers and fathers who attend childbirth classes feel more positively about labor and birth when compared to mothers and fathers who have not attended classes.

Another element of the trend to natural childbirth is the idea that birth need not always take place in a hospital. Virtually all babies in the United States are born in hospitals—only 1% are born at home (Curtain & Park, 1999). However, home birth is a common practice in Europe. In the Netherlands, for example, about one third of all births take place at home (Wiegers, Zee, & Keirse, 1998).

Advocates note that home delivery is less expensive and that most women are more relaxed during labor in their homes. Advocates also point out that many women enjoy the greater control they have over labor and birth in a home delivery. A health care professional is present in the home during labor and delivery. This is sometimes a doctor but is more often a trained nurse-midwife.

For Americans accustomed to hospital delivery, home delivery can seem like a risky proposition. Is home delivery safe? Yes, but with a very important catch. Birth problems are no more common in babies delivered at home than in babies delivered in a hospital, but only when the woman is healthy, her pregnancy has been problem-free, the labor and delivery are expected to be problem-free, and a trained health care professional assists with the delivery (Olsen, 1997). If there is *any* reason to believe that labor and delivery may encounter problems that require medical assistance, labor and delivery should take place in the hospital, not at home.

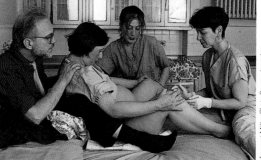

American women who are reluctant to give birth at home can turn to birth centers. These are typically smaller clinics that are independent of a hospital. A woman, her coach, and other family members and friends are assigned a birthing room that is often decorated to look more homelike. A doctor or nurse-midwife assists in labor and delivery, which takes place entirely in the birthing room, where it can be observed by all. Like home deliveries, birthing centers are best for deliveries that should be trouble-free.

In many countries around the world and, to a lesser extent in the United States, a nurse-midwife is present to deliver the baby.

ADJUSTING TO PARENTHOOD

For parents, the time immediately after a trouble-free birth is full of excitement, pride, and joy—the much anticipated baby is finally here! But it is also a time of adjustments for parents. A woman experiences many physical changes after birth. Her breasts begin to produce milk and her uterus gradually becomes smaller, returning to its normal size in 5 or 6 weeks. And levels of female hormones (e.g., estrogen) drop.

Parents must also adjust psychologically. They reorganize old routines, particularly for first-born children, to fit the young baby's sleep-wake cycle. In the process, fathers sometimes feel left out when mothers devote most of their attention to the baby.

Researchers once believed that an important part of parents' adjustment involved forming an emotional bond to the infant. That is, the first few days of life were thought to be a critical period for close physical contact between parents and babies; without such contact, parents and babies would find it difficult to bond emotionally (Klaus & Kennell, 1976). Today, however, we know that such contact in the first few days after birth—although beneficial for babies and pleasurable for babies and parents alike—is not essential for normal development (Eyer, 1992).

Becoming a parent can be a huge adjustment, so it's not surprising that roughly half of all new mothers find that their initial excitement gives way to irritation, resentment, and crying spells. These feelings usually last a week or two and probably reflect both the stress of caring for a new baby and the physiological changes that take place as a woman's body returns to a nonpregnant state (Brockington, 1996).

For 10 to 15% of new mothers, however, irritability continues for months and is often accompanied by feelings of low self-worth, disturbed sleep, poor appetite, and apathy—a condition known as postpartum depression. Postpartum depression does not strike randomly. Biology contributes: Particularly high levels of hormones during the later phases of pregnancy place women at risk for postpartum depression (Harris et al., 1994). Experience also contributes: Women are more likely to experience postpartum depression when they were depressed before pregnancy, are coping with other life stresses (e.g., death of a loved one or moving to a new residence), did not plan to become pregnant, and lack other adults (e.g., the father) to support their adjustment to motherhood (Brockington, 1996; Campbell et al., 1992).

Women who are lethargic and emotionless do not mother warmly and enthusiastically. They don't touch and cuddle their new babies much or talk to them. If the depression lasts only a few weeks, babies are unaffected. However, if postpartum depression lasts for months and months, children of depressed mothers are more likely to become depressed themselves and are also at risk for other behavior problems (e.g., Dawson et al., 2003). For example, in one study (Hay et al., 2003), when mothers had postpartum depression, as 11-year-olds their children were more likely to be involved in aggressive behavior with peers (e.g., bullying them). One explanation of this finding emphasizes the role of early interactions with a mother in helping babies learn to regulate their emotions: When hungry, tired, uncomfortable, or frightened, infants with nondepressed moms soon learn that mom usually responds quickly and makes them feel better; over time, these infants become less upset when hungry or tired because they know that their discomfort will be brief. In contrast, when moms are depressed, they often fail to respond promptly to their infant's needs, causing infants to become frustrated and angry with their lingering discomfort.

Thus, postpartum depression is a serious condition that can harm moms and babies alike; if a mom's depression doesn't lift after a few weeks, she should seek help. Home visits by trained health care professionals can be valuable. During these visits, these visitors show mom better ways to cope with the many changes that accompany her new baby. They also provide emotional support by being a caring, sensitive listener, and, if necessary, they can refer the mother to other needed resources in the community. Finally, one simple way to reduce the risk of postpartum depression is worth mentioning—breast-feeding. Moms who breast-feed are less likely to become depressed, perhaps because breast-feeding releases hormones that act as antidepressants (Gagliardi, 2005).

BIRTH COMPLICATIONS

Women who are healthy when they become pregnant usually have a normal pregnancy, labor, and delivery. When women are not healthy or don't receive adequate prenatal care, problems can surface during labor and delivery. (Of course, even healthy women can have problems, but not as often.) The more common birth complications are listed in Table 2.6.

TABLE 2.6

Common Birth Complications

Complication	Features
Cephalopelvic disproportion	When the infant's head is larger than the pelvis, making it impossible for the baby to pass through the birth canal
Irregular position	In shoulder presentation, the baby is lying crosswise in the uterus and the shoulder appears first; in breech presentation, the buttocks appear first.
Preeclampsia	A pregnant woman has high blood pressure, protein in her urine, and swelling in her extremities (due to fluid retention).
Prolapsed umbilical cord	The umbilical cord precedes the baby through the birth canal and is squeezed shut, cutting off oxygen to the baby.

Some of these complications, such as a prolapsed umbilical cord, are dangerous because they can disrupt the flow of blood through the umbilical cord. *If this flow of blood is disrupted, infants do not receive adequate oxygen, a condition known as* **hypoxia.** Hypoxia sometimes occurs during labor and delivery because the umbilical cord is pinched or squeezed shut, cutting off the flow of blood. Hypoxia is very serious because it can lead to mental retardation or death (Petrie, 1991).

To guard against hypoxia, fetal heart rate is monitored during labor, either by ultrasound or with a tiny electrode that is passed through the vagina and attached to the scalp of the fetus. An abrupt change in heart rate can be a sign that the fetus is not receiving enough oxygen. If the heart rate does change suddenly, a health care professional will try to confirm that the fetus is in distress, perhaps by measuring fetal heart rate with a stethoscope on the mother's abdomen.

When a fetus is in distress or when the fetus is in an irregular position or is too large to pass through the birth canal, a physician may decide to remove it from the mother's uterus surgically (Guillemin, 1993). *In a* **cesarean section** *(or* **C-section***) an incision is made in the abdomen to remove the baby from the uterus.* A C-section is riskier for mothers than a vaginal delivery because of increased bleeding and greater danger of infection. A C-section poses little risk for babies, although they are often briefly depressed from the anesthesia that the mother receives before the operation. And mother-infant interactions are much the same for babies delivered vaginally or by planned or unplanned C-sections (Durik, Hyde, & Clark, 2000).

Birth complications are hazardous not just for a newborn's health—they have long-term effects too. When babies experience many birth complications, they are at risk for becoming aggressive or violent and for developing schizophrenia (e.g., Cannon et al., 2000; Kandel & Mednick, 1991). This is particularly true for newborns with birth complications who later experience family adversity, such as living in poverty (Arseneault et al., 2002). These outcomes underscore the importance of excellent health care through pregnancy and labor and the need for a supportive environment throughout childhood.

Problems also arise when babies are born too early or too small. Normally, a baby spends about 38 weeks developing before being born. *Babies born before the 36th week are called* **preterm** *or* **premature.** In the first year or so, premature infants often lag behind full-term infants in many facets of development. However, by 2 or 3 years of age, such differences have vanished, and most premature infants develop normally (Greenberg & Crnic, 1988).

Prospects are usually not as bright for babies who are "small for date." These infants are most often born to women who smoke or drink alcohol frequently during pregnancy or who do not eat enough nutritious food (Chomitz, Cheung, & Lieberman, 1995). *Newborns who weigh 2,500 grams (5.5 pounds) or less are said to have* **low birth weight;** *newborns weighing less than 1,500 grams (3.3 pounds) are said to have* **very low birth weight;** *and those weighing less than 1,000 grams (2.2 pounds) are said to have* **extremely low birth weight.**

Babies with very or extremely low birth weight do not fare well. Many do not survive; those who live often lag behind in the development of intellectual and motor skills (Sykes et al., 1997; Ventura et al., 1994). The odds are better for newborns who weigh more than 1,500 grams. Most survive. Their prospects are better if they receive appropriate care. Small-for-date babies are typically placed in special, sealed beds where temperature and air quality are regulated carefully. These beds effectively isolate infants, depriving them of environmental stimulation. You might think that stimulation is the last thing that these fragile creatures need, but, in fact, sensory stimulation helps small-for-date babies to develop. Consequently, they often receive auditory stimulation, such as a tape recording of soothing music or their mother's voice, or visual stimulation provided from a mobile placed over the bed. Infants also receive tactile stimulation—they are "massaged" several times daily. These forms of stimulation foster physical and cognitive development in small-for-date babies (Field, Hernandez-Reif, & Freedman, 2004; Teti, 2005).

This special care should continue when infants leave the hospital for home. Consequently, intervention programs for small-for-date babies typically include training

THINK ABOUT IT

A friend of yours has just given birth 6 weeks prematurely. The baby is average size for a baby born prematurely and seems to be faring well, but your friend is concerned nonetheless. What could you say to reassure your friend?

programs designed for parents of infants and young children. In these programs, parents learn how to respond appropriately to their child's behaviors. For example, they are taught the signs that a baby is in distress, overstimulated, or ready to interact. Parents also learn games and activities to use to foster their child's development. In addition, children are enrolled in high-quality child care centers where the curriculum is coordinated with parent training. This sensitive care promotes development in low-birth-weight babies; for example, sometimes they catch up to full-term infants in terms of cognitive development (Hill, Brooks-Gunn, & Waldfogel, 2003).

Long-term positive outcomes for these infants depend critically on providing a supportive and stimulating home environment. Unfortunately, not all at-risk babies have optimal experiences. Many receive inadequate medical care because their families live in poverty. Others experience stress and disorder in their family life. For these low-birth-weight babies, development is usually delayed and sometimes permanently diminished.

The importance of a supportive environment for low-birth-weight babies is underscored by the results of a 30-year longitudinal study by Werner (1989, 1995) covering all children born on the Hawaiian island of Kauai in 1955. When low-birth-weight children grew up in stable homes—defined as the presence of two, mentally healthy parents throughout childhood—they were indistinguishable from children born without birth complications. However, when low-birth-weight children experienced an unstable family environment—defined as experiencing divorce, parental alcoholism, or parental mental illness—they lagged behind their peers in intellectual and social development.

Thus, when biological and sociocultural forces are both harmful—low birth weight *plus* inadequate medical care or family stress—the prognosis for babies is grim. The message to parents of low-birth-weight newborns is clear: Do not despair because excellent caregiving can compensate for all but the most severe birth problems (Werner, 1994; Werner & Smith, 1992).

INFANT MORTALITY

In many respects, medical facilities in the United States are the finest in the world. Nevertheless, American babies don't fare well compared to infants from other countries. **Infant mortality** *is the number of infants out of 1,000 births who die before their first birthday.* In the United States, about 7 babies out of 1,000—slightly less than 1%—live less than a year. This number places the United States near the bottom of the industrialized countries of the world, as you can see in Figure 2.13 (UNICEF, 2004).

Why do so many American babies die? Low birth weight is part of the answer. The United States has more babies with low birth weight than any of the other countries listed in the graph, and we've already seen that low birth weight places an infant at risk. Low birth weight can usually be prevented when a pregnant woman has regular prenatal care, but many pregnant women in the United States receive inadequate or no prenatal care. Virtually all of the countries that rank ahead of the United States provide extensive prenatal care, at little or no cost. In addition, many of these countries provide for paid leaves of absence for pregnant women (Kamerman, 1993).

Prenatal development is the foundation of all development and only with regular prenatal checkups can we know whether this foundation is being laid properly. Pregnant women and the children they carry *need* this care.

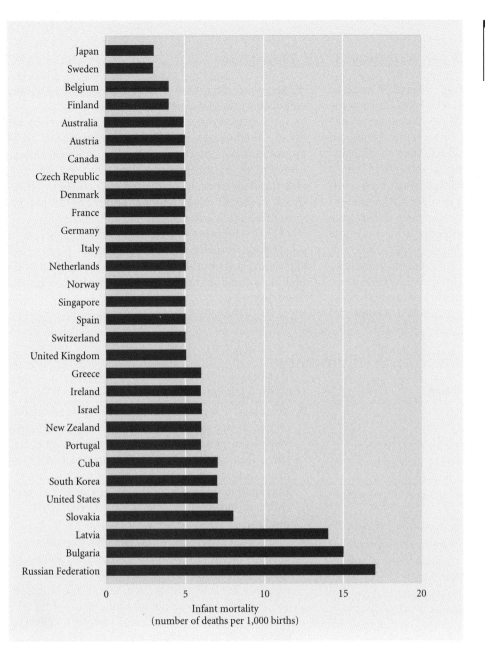

■ **Figure 2.13**
Compared to most developed countries, the United States has a high mortality rate.

Infant mortality
(number of deaths per 1,000 births)

Based on UNICEF, 2003.

TEST YOURSELF

1. In the third stage of labor, the _____ is delivered.

2. Two problems with using anesthesia during labor are that a woman can't use her abdominal muscles to help push the baby down the birth canal and _____.

3. Home delivery is safe when a pregnant woman is healthy, has had a problem-free pregnancy, expects to have a problem-free delivery, and _____.

4. When the supply of oxygen to the fetus is disrupted because the umbilical cord is squeezed shut, _____ results.

Do studies on the long-term effects of prematurity and low birth weight provide evidence for continuity in development or discontinuity? Why?

Answers: (1) placenta, (2) the pain-relieving medication crosses the placenta and affects the baby, (3) when trained health care professionals are present to deliver the baby, (4) hypoxia

Putting It All Together

This chapter began with conception, covered 38 weeks of prenatal development, and ended with birth. You saw the mighty impact of the shuffling of genes that occurs at conception. Sometimes single genes influence development, as in the case of the sickle-cell disease that so frightens Leslie. More often, many genes work together to influence growth, with the outcome depending strongly on the impact of the environment. You learned that structures and processes unfold in a predictable sequence during prenatal development, and this knowledge answered some of Eun Jung's questions about her pregnancy. You also learned how and why prenatal development sometimes goes awry and used this information to address Chloe's concerns about how her health and behavior might affect her baby's development. Finally, you looked at labor and delivery, including some of the advantages of a prepared childbirth such as Marlea plans to have.

This chapter, more than most of the others in this book, has emphasized the biological components of the biopsychosocial framework. Even here, however, biological forces do not operate in isolation but in interaction with the other elements of the framework. Prenatal development reflects biologically programmed events plus environmental influences on the fetus.

The development we have traced in this chapter serves as a prelude to the life span of human development. Each succeeding stage builds on the themes established in the prelude, as we'll see in the next chapter, which is devoted to infancy.

Summary

2.1 In the Beginning: 23 Pairs of Chromosomes

Mechanisms of Heredity

■ At conception, the 23 chromosomes in the sperm merge with the 23 chromosomes in the egg. Each chromosome is one molecule of DNA; a section of DNA that provides specific biochemical instructions is called a gene.

■ All of a person's genes make up a genotype; the phenotype refers to the physical, behavioral, and psychological characteristics that develop when the genotype is exposed to a specific environment.

■ Different forms of the same gene are called alleles. A person who inherits the same allele on a pair of chromosomes is homozygous; in this case, the biochemical instructions on the allele are followed. A person who inherits different alleles is heterozygous; in this case, the instructions of the dominant allele are followed and those of the recessive allele ignored.

Genetic Disorders

■ Most inherited disorders are carried by recessive alleles. Examples include sickle-cell disease and phenylketonuria, in which toxins accumulate and cause mental retardation. Sometimes fertilized eggs do not have 46 chromosomes. Usually they are aborted spontaneously soon after conception. An exception is Down syndrome, in which individuals usually have an extra 21st chromosome. Down syndrome individuals have a distinctive appearance and are mentally retarded. Disorders of the sex chromosomes are more common because these chromosomes contain less genetic material than do autosomes.

Heredity, Environment, and Development

■ Behavioral and psychological phenotypes that reflect an underlying continuum (such as intelligence) often involve polygenic inheritance. In polygenic inheritance, the phenotype reflects the combined activity of many distinct genes. Polygenic inheritance has been examined traditionally by studying twins and adopted children, and more recently, by identifying DNA markers.

■ The impact of heredity on a child's development depends on the environment in which the genetic instructions are carried out, and these heredity-environment interactions occur throughout a child's life. A child's genotype can affect the kinds of experiences the child has; children and adolescents often actively seek environments related to their genetic makeup. Family environments affect siblings differently (nonshared environmental influence); parents provide a unique environment for each child in the family.

2.2 From Conception to Birth

Period of the Zygote (Weeks 1–2)

■ The first period of prenatal development lasts 2 weeks. It begins when the egg is fertilized by the sperm in the Fallopian tube and ends when the fertilized egg has implanted in the wall of the uterus. By the end of this period, cells have begun to differentiate.

Period of the Embryo (Weeks 3–8)

■ The second period of prenatal development begins 2 weeks after conception and ends 8 weeks after. This is a period of rapid growth in which most major body structures are created. Growth in this period is cephalocaudal (the head develops first) and proximodistal (parts near the center of the body develop first).

Period of the Fetus (Weeks 9–38)

■ The third period of prenatal development begins 9 weeks after conception and lasts until birth. The highlights of this period are a remarkable increase in the size of the fetus and changes in body systems that are necessary for life. By 7 months, most body systems function well enough to support life.

2.3 Influences on Prenatal Development

General Risk Factors

■ Parents' age can affect prenatal development. Teenagers often have problem pregnancies, mainly because they rarely receive adequate prenatal care. After age 35, pregnant women are more likely to have a miscarriage or to give birth to a child with mental retardation. Prenatal development can also be harmed if a pregnant mother has inadequate nutrition or experiences considerable stress.

Teratogens: Drugs, Diseases, and Environmental Hazards

■ Teratogens are agents that can cause abnormal prenatal development. Many drugs that adults take are teratogens. For most drugs, scientists have not established amounts that can be consumed safely.

■ Several diseases are teratogens. Only by avoiding these diseases entirely can a pregnant woman escape their harmful consequences.

■ Environmental teratogens are particularly dangerous because a pregnant woman may not know that these substances are present in the environment.

How Teratogens Influence Prenatal Development

■ The impact of teratogens depends on the genotype of the organism, the period of prenatal development when the organism is exposed to the teratogen, and the amount of exposure. Sometimes the impact of a teratogen is not evident until later in life.

Prenatal Diagnosis and Treatment

■ Many techniques are used to track the progress of prenatal development. A common component of prenatal care is ultrasound, which uses sound waves to generate a picture of the fetus. This picture can be used to determine the position of the fetus, its sex, and whether there are gross physical deformities.

■ When genetic disorders are suspected, amniocentesis and chorionic villus sampling are used to determine the genotype of the fetus.

■ Fetal medicine is a new field in which problems of prenatal development are corrected medically, with surgery, or by using genetic engineering.

2.4 Labor and Delivery

Stages of Labor

■ Labor consists of three stages. In stage 1, the muscles of the uterus contract. The contractions, which are weak at first and gradually become stronger, cause the cervix to enlarge. In stage 2, the baby moves through the birth canal. In stage 3, the placenta is delivered.

Approaches to Childbirth

■ Natural or prepared childbirth is based on the assumption that parents should understand what takes place during pregnancy and birth. In natural childbirth, pain-relieving medications are avoided because this medication prevents women from pushing during labor and because it affects the fetus. Instead, women learn to cope with pain through relaxation, imagery, and with the help of a supportive coach.

■ Most American babies are born in hospitals, but many European babies are born at home. Home delivery is safe when the mother is healthy, pregnancy and birth are trouble-free, and a health care professional is present to deliver the baby.

Adjusting to Parenthood

■ Following the birth of a child, a woman's body undergoes several changes: her breasts become filled with milk, her uterus becomes smaller, and hormone levels drop. Both parents also adjust psychologically, and sometimes fathers feel left out. After giving birth, some women experience postpartum depression: they are irritable, have poor appetite and disturbed sleep, and are apathetic.

Birth Complications

■ During labor and delivery, the flow of blood to the fetus can be disrupted because the umbilical cord is squeezed shut. This causes hypoxia, a lack of oxygen to the fetus. Some babies are born prematurely and others are small for date. Premature babies develop more slowly at first but catch up by 2 or 3 years of age. Small-for-date babies often do not fare well, particularly if they weigh less than 1,500 grams at birth and if their environment is stressful.

Infant Mortality

■ Infant mortality is relatively high in the United States, primarily due to low birth weight and inadequate prenatal care.

Key Terms

chromosomes (46)
autosomes (46)
sex chromosomes (47)
deoxyribonucleic acid (DNA) (47)
gene (47)
genotype (48)
phenotype (48)
alleles (48)
homozygous (48)
heterozygous (48)
dominant (48)
recessive (48)
incomplete dominance (49)
sickle-cell trait (49)
phenylketonuria (50)
Huntington's disease (50)
behavioral genetics (51)
polygenic inheritance (52)
monozygotic twins (53)
dizygotic twins (53)
reaction range (54)

niche-picking (55)
nonshared environmental influences (56)
prenatal development (57)
in vitro fertilization (58)
eugenics (58)
zygote (58)
implantation (58)
germ disc (58)
placenta (59)
embryo (59)
ectoderm (59)
mesoderm (59)
endoderm (59)
amnion (59)
amniotic fluid (59)
umbilical cord (59)
cephalocaudal principle (60)
proximodistal principle (60)
period of the fetus (61)
vernix (61)

cerebral cortex (61)
age of viability (61)
spina bifida (63)
stress (64)
teratogen (66)
fetal alcohol syndrome (66)
ultrasound (72)
amniocentesis (72)
chorionic villus sampling (73)
fetal medicine (73)
crowning (75)
doula (76)
hypoxia (79)
cesarean section (C-section) (79)
preterm (premature) (79)
low birth weight (79)
very low birth weight (79)
extremely low birth weight (79)
infant mortality (80)

Learn More About It

Readings

ALFRED, H. (1997). *Pregnancy and birth sourcebook.* Detroit: Omnigraphics. This is a comprehensive but readable reference book that covers all aspects of pregnancy, including genetic counseling, prenatal care, prenatal development, labor and delivery, and common disorders of pregnancy.

DeSALLE, R., & YUDELL, M. (2004). *Welcome to the genome: A user's guide to the genetic past, present, and future.* New York: Wiley. The authors provide an excellent account of the history of genetics research and describe cutting-edge research on the human genome. They also talk about the ethical and social implications of greater understanding of the genome.

NILSSON, L., & HAMBERGER, L. (2003). *A child is born* (4th ed). New York: Delacorte. This book is the source of many of the photos of prenatal development in this chapter. Nilsson developed a variety of techniques to photograph the fetus as it was developing; Hamberger provides an entertaining and informative text to accompany the photos.

PLOMIN, R. (1990). *Nature and nurture.* Pacific Grove, CA: Brooks/Cole. Despite its age, this brief book provides a very readable introduction to modern research on the role of genetics in human behavior, written by one of the leading researchers in the field.

RIDLEY, M. (2000). *Genome: The autobiography of a species in 23 chapters.* New York: HarperCollins. The author describes progress in genetics research by telling fascinating stories about the impact of chromosomes on intelligence, language, cancer, and sex, to name just a few topics.

Websites

Visit the Human Development book companion website for all URLs.

■ **The Human Development Book Companion Website**
See **http://www.psychology.wadsworth.com/kail_cavanaugh4e/** for practice quiz questions, Internet links, updates, critical thinking exercises, discussion forums, and more. Also accessible from the Wadsworth Psychology Study Center (http://psychology.wadsworth.com).

■ **New York Online Access to Health (NOAH)**
NOAH provides a wealth of information about all aspects of pregnancy and prenatal care.

- ■ **Down Syndrome**
  The Down Syndrome website includes information about children who have this genetic disorder.

- ■ **Human Genome Project**
  At the Human Genome Project website, you can see maps of each chromosome showing the location of known genes.

Life-Span CD-ROM

For more information on the concepts covered in this chapter, go to
Module 1: Prenatal Development, Birth, and the Newborn

- • *Prenatal Development*
- • *Birth*

http://www.thomsonedu.com
Go to this site for the link to ThomsonNOW, your one-stop study shop. Take a pre-test for this chapter, and ThomsonNOW will generate a personalized study plan based on your test results. The study plan will identify the topics you need to review and direct you to online resources to help you master those topics. You can then take a post-test to help you determine the concepts you have mastered and what you still need to work on.

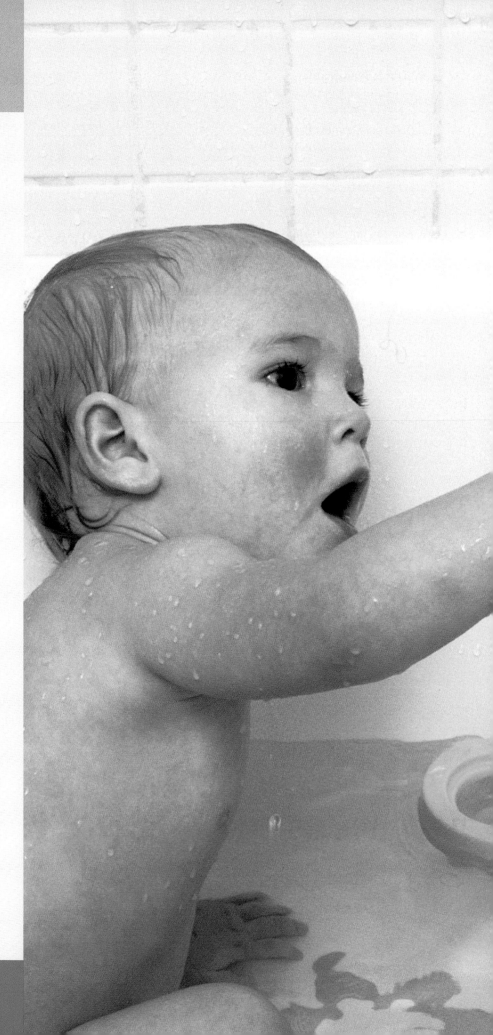

3.1 The Newborn
The Newborn's Reflexes
Assessing the Newborn
The Newborn's States
Temperament

3.2 Physical Development
Growth of the Body
The Emerging Nervous System

3.3 Moving and Grasping—Early Motor Skills
Locomotion
Fine Motor Skills

3.4 Coming to Know the World: Perception
Smell, Taste, and Touch
Hearing
Seeing

SPOTLIGHT ON RESEARCH: How Infants Become Face Experts

Integrating Sensory Information

3.5 Becoming Self-Aware
Origins of Self-Concept
Theory of Mind

REAL PEOPLE: APPLYING HUMAN DEVELOPMENT: "Seeing Is Believing . . ." for 3-Year-Olds

Putting It All Together

Summary

Key Terms

Learn More About It

CHAPTER 3

Tools for Exploring the World

Physical, Perceptual, and Motor Development

Think about what you were like 2 years ago. Whatever you were doing, you probably look, act, think, and feel in much the same way today as you did then. Two years in an adult's life usually doesn't result in profound changes, but 2 years makes a big difference early in life. The changes that occur in the first few years after birth are incredible. In less than 2 years, an infant is transformed from a seemingly helpless newborn into a talking, walking, havoc-wreaking toddler. No changes at any other point in the life span come close to the drama and excitement of these early years.

In this chapter, our tour of these 2 years begins with the newborn, then moves to physical growth—changes in the body and the brain. The third section of the chapter examines motor skills. You'll discover how babies learn to walk and how they learn to use their hands to hold and then manipulate objects. In the fourth section, we'll examine changes in infants' sensory abilities that allow them to comprehend their world.

As children begin to explore their world and learn more about it, they also learn more about themselves. They learn to recognize themselves and begin to understand more about their thoughts and others' thoughts. We'll explore these changes in the last section of the chapter.

3.1

THE NEWBORN

LEARNING OBJECTIVES

How do reflexes help
newborns interact with
the world?

How do we determine
whether a baby is healthy
and adjusting to life outside
the uterus?

What behavioral states are
common among newborns?

What are the different
features of temperament?
Do they change as
children grow?

----

*Lisa and Steve, proud but exhausted parents, are astonished at
how their lives revolve around 10-day-old Dan's eating and sleeping.
Lisa feels as if she is feeding Dan around the clock. When Dan
naps, Lisa thinks of many things she should do, but usually naps
herself because she is so tired. Steve wonders when Dan will start
sleeping through the night, so that he and Lisa can get a good night's
sleep themselves.*

THE NEWBORN BABY THAT THRILLS PARENTS LIKE LISA AND STEVE is actually rather homely. Newborns arrive covered with blood and vernix, a white-colored "wax" that protected the skin during the many months of prenatal development. In addition, the baby's head is temporarily distorted from its journey through the birth canal, and the newborn has a beer belly and is bowlegged.

What can newborns like Dan do? We'll answer that question in this section and, as we do, you'll learn when Lisa and Steve can expect to resume a full night's sleep.

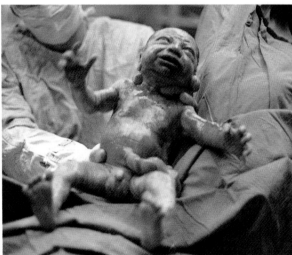

Robert V. Kail

This newborn baby (Ben Kail at 20 seconds old) is covered with vernix, is bowlegged, and his head is distorted from the journey down the birth canal.

THE NEWBORN'S REFLEXES

Most newborns are well prepared to begin interacting with their world. *The newborn is endowed with a rich set of* **reflexes,** *unlearned responses that are triggered by a specific form of stimulation.* Table 3.1 shows the variety of reflexes commonly found in newborn babies.

You can see that some reflexes are designed to pave the way for newborns to get the nutrients that they need to grow: The rooting and sucking reflexes ensure that the newborn is well prepared to begin a new diet of life-sustaining milk. Others seem designed to protect the newborn from danger in the environment. The eye blink and withdrawal reflexes, for example, help newborns avoid unpleasant stimulation.

Still other reflexes serve as the foundation for larger, voluntary patterns of motor activity. For example, the stepping reflex motions look like precursors to walking, so it probably won't surprise you to learn that babies who practice the stepping reflex often learn to walk earlier than those who don't practice this (Zelazo, 1993).

Reflexes are also important because they can be a useful way to determine whether the newborn's nervous system is working properly. For example, infants with damage to the sciatic nerve, which is found in the spinal cord, do not show the withdrawal reflex. Infants who have problems with the lower part of the spine do not show the Babinski reflex. If these or other reflexes are weak or missing altogether, a thorough physical and behavioral assessment is called for. Similarly, many of these reflexes normally vanish during infancy; if they linger, this too indicates the need for a thorough physical examination.

TABLE 3.1

Some Major Reflexes Found in Newborns

Name	Response	Significance
Babinski	A baby's toes fan out when the sole of the foot is stroked from heel to toe.	Perhaps a remnant of evolution
Blink	A baby's eyes close in response to bright light or loud noise.	Protects the eyes
Moro	A baby throws its arms out and then inward (as if embracing) in response to loud noise or when its head falls.	May help a baby cling to its mother
Palmar	A baby grasps an object placed in the palm of its hand.	Precursor to voluntary walking
Rooting	When a baby's cheek is stroked, it turns its head toward the stroking and opens its mouth.	Helps a baby find the nipple
Stepping	A baby who is held upright by an adult and is then moved forward begins to step rhythmically.	Precursor to voluntary walking
Sucking	A baby sucks when an object is placed in its mouth.	Permits feeding
Withdrawal	A baby withdraws its foot when the sole is pricked with a pin.	Protects a baby from unpleasant stimulation

ASSESSING THE NEWBORN

Imagine that a mother has just asked you if her newborn baby is healthy. How would you decide? You would probably check to see whether the baby seems to be breathing and if her heart seems to be beating. In fact, breathing and heartbeat are two vital signs included in the Apgar score, which provides a quick, approximate assessment of the newborn's status, by focusing on the body systems needed to sustain life. The other vital signs are muscle tone, presence of reflexes such as coughing, and skin tone. Each of the five vital signs receives a score of 0, 1, or 2, with 2 being the optimal score. For example, a newborn whose muscles are completely limp receives a 0; a baby who shows strong movements of arms and legs receives a 2. The five scores are added together, with a score of 7 or more indicating a baby who is in good physical condition. A score of 4–6 means that the newborn needs special attention and care. A score of 3 or less signals a life-threatening situation that requires emergency medical care (Apgar, 1953).

Newborns step reflexively when they are held upright and moved forward.

For a comprehensive evaluation of the newborn's well-being, pediatricians and other child-development specialists sometimes administer the Neonatal Behavioral Assessment Scale or NBAS for short (Brazelton & Nugent, 1995). The NBAS is used with newborns to 2-month-olds to provide a detailed portrait of the baby's behavioral repertoire. The scale includes 28 behavioral items along with 18 items that test reflexes. The baby's performance is used to evaluate the functioning of these four systems:

■ Autonomic: the newborn's ability to control body functions such as breathing and temperature regulation
■ Motor: the newborn's ability to control body movements and activity level
■ State: the newborn's ability to maintain a state (e.g., staying alert or staying asleep)
■ Social: the newborn's ability to interact with people

The NBAS is based on the view that newborns are remarkably competent individuals who are well prepared to interact with the environment. Reflecting this view, examiners go to great lengths to bring out a baby's best performance. They do everything possible to make a baby feel comfortable and secure during testing. And if the infant does not at first succeed on an item, the examiner provides some assistance (Alberts, 2005).

The NBAS, along with a thorough physical examination, can determine whether a newborn is functioning normally. Scores from the NBAS can, for example, be used to diagnose disorders of the central nervous system.

THE NEWBORN'S STATES

Newborns spend most of each day alternating among four different states (St. James-Roberts & Plewis, 1996; Wolff, 1987):

- *Alert inactivity*—*The baby is calm with eyes open and attentive; the baby seems to be deliberately inspecting the environment.*
- *Waking activity*—*The baby's eyes are open but they seem unfocused; the arms or legs move in bursts of uncoordinated motion.*
- *Crying*—*The baby cries vigorously, usually accompanied by agitated but uncoordinated motion.*
- *Sleeping*—*The baby alternates from being still and breathing regularly to moving gently and breathing irregularly; eyes are closed throughout.*

Of these states, crying and sleeping have captured the attention of parents and researchers alike.

Crying

Newborns spend 2–3 hours each day crying or on the verge of crying. If you've not spent much time around newborns, you might think that all crying is pretty much alike. In fact, scientists and parents can identify three distinctive types of cries (Snow, 1998). A **basic cry** *starts softly, then gradually becomes more intense and usually occurs when a baby is hungry or tired; a* **mad cry** *is a more intense version of a basic cry; and a* **pain cry** *begins with a sudden, long burst of crying, followed by a long pause, and gasping.* Thus, crying represents the newborn's first venture into interpersonal communication; by crying, babies tell their parents that they are hungry or tired, angry or hurt. By responding to these cries, parents are encouraging their newborn's efforts to communicate.

Parents are naturally concerned when their baby cries, and if they can't quiet a crying baby, their concern mounts and can easily give way to frustration and annoyance. It's no surprise, then, that parents develop little tricks for soothing their babies. Many Western parents lift a baby to the shoulder and walk or gently rock the baby. Sometimes they will also sing lullabies, pat the baby's back, or give the baby a pacifier. Yet another method is to put a newborn into a car seat and go for a drive; this technique was used once, as a last resort, at 2 a.m. with Ben Kail when he was 10 days old. After about the 12th time around the block, he finally stopped crying and fell asleep! Finally, in some countries around the world, wrapping an infant tightly in a blanket, or swaddling, is used to soothe a crying baby (Delaney, 2000). All these techniques work, and they probably calm babies by providing moderate stimulation.

Parents are sometimes reluctant to respond to their crying infant for fear of producing a baby who cries constantly. Yet they hear their baby's cry as a call for help that they shouldn't ignore. What to do?

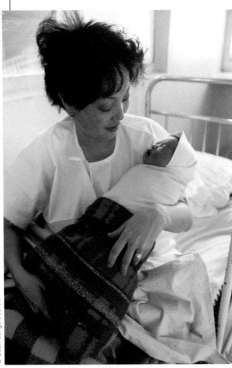

In many countries worldwide, infants are wrapped tightly in blankets as a way to keep them soothed.

© Dean Conger/Corbis

Should parents respond? "Yes, usually" is probably the best answer (Hubbard & van IJzendoorn, 1991). If parents respond *immediately, every time* their infant cries, the result may well be a fussy, whiny baby. Instead, parents need to consider why their infant is crying and the intensity of the crying. When a baby wakes during the night and cries quietly, a parent might wait before responding, giving the baby a chance to calm herself. However, when parents hear a loud noise from an infant's bedroom followed by a mad cry, they should respond immediately. Parents need to remember that crying is actually the newborn's first attempt to communicate with others. They need to decide what the infant is trying to tell them and whether that warrants a quick response or whether they should let the baby soothe herself.

Sleeping

Crying may get parents' attention, but sleep is what newborns do more than anything else. They sleep 16–18 hours daily. The problem for tired parents is that newborns sleep in naps taken round-the-clock. Newborns typically go through a cycle of wakefulness and sleep about every 4 hours. That is, they will be awake for about an hour, sleep for 3 hours, then start the cycle anew. During the hour when newborns are awake, they regularly move between the different waking states several times. Cycles of alert inactivity, waking activity, and crying are common.

As babies grow older, the sleep-wake cycle gradually begins to correspond to the day-night cycle (St. James-Roberts & Plewis, 1996). Most babies begin sleeping through the night by about 3 or 4 months of age, a major milestone for bleary-eyed parents like Lisa and Steve.

*Roughly half of newborns' sleep is **irregular** or **rapid-eye-movement (REM) sleep,** a time when the body is quite active.* During REM sleep, newborns move their arms and legs, they may grimace, and their eyes may dart beneath their eyelids. Brain waves register fast activity, the heart beats more rapidly, and breathing is more rapid. *In **regular** or **nonREM sleep,** breathing, heart rate, and brain activity are steady, and newborns lie quietly without the twitching associated with REM sleep.* REM sleep becomes less frequent as infants grow. By 4 months, only 40% of sleep is REM sleep. By the first birthday, REM sleep will drop to 25%, not far from the adult average of 20% (Halpern, MacLean, & Baumeister, 1995).

The function of REM sleep is still debated. Older children and adults dream during REM sleep, and brain waves during REM sleep resemble those of an alert, awake person. Consequently, many scientists believe that REM sleep provides stimulation for the brain that fosters growth in the nervous system (Halpern et al., 1995; Roffwarg, Muzio, & Dement, 1966).

Mothers (and fathers) of newborns are often tired because their babies take naps 24/7 instead of sleeping through the night.

By the toddler and preschool years, sleep routines are well established. Most 2-year-olds spend about 13 hours sleeping, compared to just under 11 hours for 6-year-olds. At about age 4, most youngsters give up their afternoon nap and sleep longer at nighttime to compensate. This can be a challenging time for parents and caregivers who use naptime as an opportunity to complete some work or to relax.

Following an active day, most preschool children drift off to sleep easily. However, most children will have an occasional night when bedtime is a struggle. Furthermore, for approximately 20 to 30% of preschool children, bedtime struggles occur nightly (Lozoff, Wolf, & Davis, 1985). More often than not, these bedtime problems reflect the absence of a regular bedtime routine that's followed consistently. The key to a pleasant bedtime is to establish a nighttime routine that helps children to "wind down" from busy daytime activities. This routine should start at about the same time every night ("It's time to get ready for bed . . .") and end at about the same time (when the parent leaves the child and the child tries to fall asleep). This nighttime routine may be anywhere from 15 to 45 minutes long, depending on the child. Also, as children get older, parents can expect them to perform more of these tasks independently. A 2-year-old will need help all along the way, but a 5-year-old can do many of these tasks alone. But remember to follow the routine consistently; this way children know that each step is getting them closer to bedtime and falling asleep.

After preschool children are asleep, they will sleep peacefully through most nights. *Many children have* **nightmares,** *vivid, frightening dreams occurring toward morning that usually wake the child.* Occasional nightmares are normal and need nothing more than on-the-spot parental comforting and reassurance. Should nightmares occur repeatedly or trouble the child during waking hours, parents should try to pinpoint the cause of the nightmare and, if need be, seek professional help (Mindell & Cashman, 1995).

Two other sleep disturbances are much rarer than nightmares but are quick to capture a parent's attention. *In* **night terrors,** *children appear to wake in a panicked state and are often breathing rapidly and perspiring heavily.* Nevertheless, children often don't respond to parents (because they are not fully awake), typically go back to sleep quickly, and, unlike nightmares, don't remember the episode the following morning. Night terrors usually occur early in the night and seem to be a by-product of wakening too rapidly from a deep sleep. Although often very frightening to parents, night terrors rarely indicate any underlying problem in children; parents can usually safely ignore the episode (Adair & Bauchner, 1993).

A second sleep disturbance is **sleepwalking,** *in which during deep sleep children get out of bed and walk.* For example, 4-year-old Ricky once sleepwalked into his sister's bedroom, opened the closet door, and squared off as if to pee into the closet. Fortunately, his mom got him directed to the bathroom just in time! The only real danger in sleepwalking is that children can injure themselves. Consequently, parents should wake sleepwalking children and get them back in bed. And, if children sleepwalk regularly, parents should be sure that the child's environment has no special hazards, such as unguarded stairways.

A final disturbance is bedwetting. Most U.S. children are toilet trained as 2- or 3-year-olds. Once trained, they are usually quite successful at staying dry during the day. At nighttime, however, many preschoolers—more boys than girls—wet the bed. For example, about 25% of 4-year-olds wet their bed occasionally (Wille, 1994). Such bedwetting in preschool children is perfectly normal; almost all preschool children grow out of the problem by age 5 or 6. If the problem persists, there are a number of simple, effective methods to help children stay dry at night, such as bedwetting alarms that alert sleeping children when they are starting to urinate and exercises to help children control the sphincter muscles that regulate urination (American Psychiatric Association, 1994; Rappaport, 1993).

Sudden Infant Death Syndrome

For many parents of young babies, however, sleep is a cause of concern. *In* **sudden infant death syndrome (SIDS),** *a healthy baby dies suddenly, for no apparent reason.* Approximately 1–3 of every 1,000 American babies dies from SIDS. Most of them are between 2 and 4 months of age (Wegman, 1994).

Scientists don't know the exact causes of SIDS, but they do know several contributing factors. Babies are more vulnerable to SIDS if they were born prematurely or with low birth weight. They are also more vulnerable if their parents smoke. SIDS is more likely when a baby sleeps on its stomach (face down) than when it sleeps on its back (face up). Finally, SIDS is more likely during winter when babies sometimes become overheated from too many blankets and too heavy sleepwear (Carroll & Loughlin, 1994). Evidently, SIDS infants, many of whom were born prematurely or with low birth weight, are less able to withstand physiological stresses and imbalances that are brought on by cigarette smoke, breathing that is temporarily interrupted, or by overheating (Simpson, 2001).

In 1992, based on mounting evidence that SIDS more often occurred when infants slept on their stomachs, the American Academy of Pediatrics (AAP) began advising parents to put babies to sleep on their backs or sides. In 1994 the AAP joined forces with the U.S. Public Health Service to launch a national program to educate parents about the dangers of SIDS and the importance of putting babies to sleep on their backs. The "Back to Sleep" campaign was widely publicized through brochures, posters like the one shown in Figure 3.1, and videos. Since the "Back to Sleep" campaign began, research shows that far more infants are now sleeping on their backs and that the incidence of SIDS has dropped (NIH, 2000b).

However, it became clear that African American infants were still twice as likely to die from SIDS, apparently because they were much more likely to be placed on their stomachs to sleep. Consequently, in the 21st century the National Institutes of Health has partnered with groups such as the Women in the NAACP and the National Council of 100 Black Women to train thousands of people to convey the "Back to Sleep" message in a culturally appropriate manner to African American communities (NICHD, 2004). The goal is for African American infants to benefit from the life saving benefits of the "Back to Sleep" program. The message for all parents—particularly if their babies were premature or small-for-date—is to keep their babies away from smoke, to put them on their backs to sleep, and don't overdress them or wrap them too tightly in blankets (Willinger, 1995).

TEMPERAMENT

So far, we've talked as if all babies are alike. But, if you've seen a number of babies together, you know this isn't true. Perhaps you've seen some babies who are quiet most of the time alongside others who cried often and impatiently? Maybe you've known infants who responded warmly to strangers next to others who seemed shy? *These characteristics of infants indicate a consistent style or pattern to an infant's behavior and, collectively, they define an infant's* **temperament.**

Alexander Thomas and Stella Chess (Thomas, Chess, & Birch, 1968) pioneered the study of temperament with the New York Longitudinal Study, in which they traced the lives of 141 individuals from infancy through adulthood. Thomas and Chess gathered their initial data by interviewing the babies' parents and asking individuals unfamiliar with the children to observe them at home. Based on these interviews and observations, Thomas and Chess suggested that infants' behavior varied along nine temperamental dimensions. One dimension was activity, which referred to an infant's typical level of motor activity. A second was persistence, which referred to the amount of time an infant devoted to an activity, particularly when obstacles were present.

The New York Longitudinal Study launched research on infant temperament, but today we know that Thomas and Chess overestimated the number of temperamental dimensions. Instead of nine dimensions, scientists now propose two to six dimensions (Rothbart & Bates, 1998). For example, Table 3.2 lists five dimensions of temperament included in most current accounts of temperament (Caspi, 1998).

Some theories have fewer dimensions because they combine dimensions listed in the table. For example, one view is that activity level and positive affect are really a common dimension that refers to a child's enthusiasm for approaching and engaging novel situations. Other theories have more dimensions because dimensions listed in the table are subdivided. An example would be negative affect: Sometimes this is divided into *fearful distress,* a response to a novel social situation or a novel object, and *irritated*

National Institute of Child Health and Development

■ **Figure 3.1**
This poster is one part of an effective campaign to reduce SIDS by encouraging parents to have their babies sleep on their backs.

TABLE 3.2

Five Dimensions of Temperament

Dimension	Description
Activity level	The amount of physical and motor activity in daily situations
Positive affect	The extent to which the child expresses pleasure, enthusiasm, and contentment
Persistence	The amount of time a child devotes to an activity, particularly when obstacles or distractions are present, and the child's ability to resist distraction from competing stimuli
Inhibition	The extent to which a child is shy and withdrawn, particularly in unfamiliar settings
Negative affect	The extent to which a child is irritable, easily distresses, and is prone to anger

distress, a response to frustrating situations (Wachs & Bates, 2001). These fine points of temperament are still being studied.

Some temperamental characteristics are more common in some cultures than in others. Asian babies tend to be less emotional than European American babies. For instance, Asian babies cry less often and less intensely than European American babies (Kagan et al., 1994; Lewis, Ramsay, & Kawakami, 1993).

Hereditary and Environmental Contributions to Temperament

Most theories agree that temperament reflects both heredity and experience. The influence of heredity is shown in twin studies: Identical twins are more alike in most aspects of temperament than fraternal twins. For example, Goldsmith, Buss, and Lemery (1997) found that the correlation for identical twins' activity level was .72 but the correlation for fraternal twins was only .38. In other words, if one identical twin is tem-

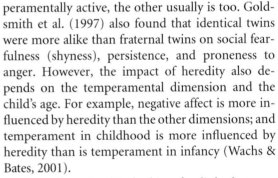

peramentally active, the other usually is too. Goldsmith et al. (1997) also found that identical twins were more alike than fraternal twins on social fearfulness (shyness), persistence, and proneness to anger. However, the impact of heredity also depends on the temperamental dimension and the child's age. For example, negative affect is more influenced by heredity than the other dimensions; and temperament in childhood is more influenced by heredity than is temperament in infancy (Wachs & Bates, 2001).

Recently, scientists looking for links between genes and temperament came up with a surprising finding: Infants and toddlers who are upset by novel stimulation (and who often become shy preschoolers) have narrower faces than youngsters who respond calmly to novel stimulation (Arcus & Kagan, 1995). This observation is provocative because the

Twin studies show the impact of heredity on temperament: If one identical twin is active, the other one usually is.

brain and the facial skeleton originate in the same set of cells in prenatal development. Thus, one fascinating hypothesis is that genes influence levels of hormones that affect both facial growth and temperament.

The environment also contributes to children's temperament. Positive emotionality —youngsters who laugh often, seem to be generally happy, and express pleasure often— seems to reflect environmental influences (Goldsmith et al., 1997). Conversely, infants more often develop intense, difficult temperaments when mothers are abrupt in dealing with them and lack confidence (Belsky, Fish, & Isabella, 1991).

There's no question that heredity and experience cause babies' temperaments to differ, but how stable is temperament? We'll find out in the next section.

Stability of Temperament

Do calm, easygoing babies grow up to be calm, easygoing children, adolescents, and adults? Are difficult, irritable infants destined to grow up to be cranky, whiny children? The first answers to these questions came from the Fels Longitudinal Project, a study of many aspects of physical and psychological development from infancy. Although not a study of temperament per se, Jerome Kagan and his collaborators (Kagan, 1989; Kagan & Moss, 1962) found that fearful preschoolers in the Fels project tended to be inhibited as older children and adolescents.

Spurred by findings like this one, later investigators attempted to learn more about the stability of temperament. Their research shows that temperament is somewhat stable during the infant and toddler years. An active fetus is more likely to be an active infant, and is also more likely to be a difficult, unadaptive infant (DiPietro et al., 1996). Newborns who cry under moderate stress tend, as 5-month-olds, to cry when they are placed in stressful situations (Stifter & Fox, 1990). In addition, inhibited 2-year-olds tend to be shy as 4-year-olds, particularly when their moms are intrusive (e.g., provide help when it's not needed) or frequently make snide remarks about their shyness, such as "Don't be such a baby!" (Rubin, Burgess, & Hastings, 2002).

Children's temperament influences the way that adults treat them: For example, parents engage in more vigorous play when their children are temperamentally active.

Thus, evidence suggests that temperament is at least somewhat stable throughout infancy and the toddler years (Lemery et al., 1999). Of course, the links are not perfect. Sam, an emotional 1-year-old, is more likely to be emotional as a 12-year-old than Dave, an unemotional 1-year-old. However, it's not a "sure thing" that Sam will still be emotional as a 12-year-old. Instead, think of temperament as a predisposition. Some infants are naturally predisposed to be sociable, emotional, or active; others *can* act in these ways too, but only if the behaviors are nurtured by parents and others.

Though temperament is only moderately stable during infancy and toddlerhood, it can still shape development in important ways. For example, an infant's temperament may determine the experiences that parents provide. Parents may read more to quiet babies but play more physical games with their active babies. These different experiences, driven by the infants' temperament, contribute to each infant's development despite the fact that the infants' temperament may change over the years. Thus, although infants have many features in common, temperament characteristics remind us that each baby also seems to have its own unique personality from the very start.

THINK ABOUT IT

How would a learning theorist explain why children have different temperaments?

TEST YOURSELF

1. Some reflexes help infants get necessary nutrients, other reflexes protect infants from danger, and still other reflexes _____.

2. The _____ is based on five vital functions and provides a quick indication of a newborn's physical health.

3. A baby lying calmly with its eyes open and focused is in a state of _____.

4. Newborns spend more time asleep than awake, and about half this time asleep is spent in _____, a time thought to foster growth in the central nervous system.

5. The campaign to reduce SIDS emphasizes that infants should _____.

6. Research on the stability of temperament in infants and young children typically finds that

_____.

Max, a father-to-be, says, "I'm sure I'll worry a lot about our baby, because babies are so helpless; they can't do anything." What might you say to Max to reassure him that, all things considered, newborns are quite talented?

Answers: (1) serve as the basis for later motor behaviors, (2) Apgar score, (3) alert inactivity, (4) REM sleep, (5) sleep on their backs, (6) temperament is moderately stable in these years

PHYSICAL DEVELOPMENT

While crossing the street, 4-year-old Martin was struck by a passing car. He was in a coma for a week but then gradually became more alert. Now he seems to be aware of his surroundings. Needless to say, Martin's mother is grateful that he survived the accident, but she wonders what the future holds for her son.

F OR PARENTS AND CHILDREN ALIKE, physical growth is a topic of great interest and a source of pride. Parents marvel at the speed with which babies add pounds and inches; 2-year-olds proudly proclaim, "I bigger now!" In this section, we examine some of the basic features of physical growth, see how the brain develops, and discover how the accident affected Martin's development.

GROWTH OF THE BODY

Growth is more rapid in infancy than during any other period after birth. Typically, infants double their birth weight by 3 months of age and triple it by their first birthday. This rate of growth is so rapid that if it continued throughout childhood, a typical 10-year-old boy would be nearly as long as an airliner and weigh almost as much (McCall, 1979).

Average heights and weights for young children are represented by the lines marked 50th percentile in Figure 3.2. An average girl weighs about 7 pounds at birth, about 21 pounds at 12 months, and about 26 pounds at 24 months. If perfectly average, she would be 19–20 inches long at birth, grow to 29–30 inches at 12 months, and 34–35 inches at 24 months. Figures for an average boy are similar, but weights are slightly larger at ages 12 and 24 months.

These charts also highlight how much children of the same age vary in weight and height. The lines marked 90th percentile in Figure 3.2 represent heights and weights for children who are larger than 90% of their peers; the lines marked 10th percentile represent heights and weights for children who are smaller than 90% of their peers. Any heights and weights between these lines are considered normal. At age 1, for example, normal weights for boys range from about 19 to 27 pounds. This means that an extremely light but normal boy weighs only two thirds as much as his extremely heavy but normal peer!

The important message here is that average height and normal height are not one and the same. Many children are much taller or shorter than average but are still perfectly normal. This applies to all of the age norms that we mention in this book. Whenever we provide a typical or average age for a developmental milestone, remember that the normal range for passing the milestone is much wider.

Whether an infant is short or tall depends largely on heredity. Both parents contribute to their children's height. In fact, the correlation between the average of the two parents' heights and their child's height at 2 years of age is about .7 (Plomin, 1990). As a general rule, two tall parents will have tall offspring; two short parents will have short offspring; and, one tall parent and one short parent will have offspring of medium height.

So far we have emphasized the quantitative aspects of growth, such as height. This ignores an important fact: Infants are not simply scaled-down versions of adults. Figure 3.3 shows that compared to adolescents and adults, infants and young children look

LEARNING OBJECTIVES

How do height and weight change from birth to 2 years of age?

What nutrients do young children need? How are they best provided?

What are the consequences of malnutrition? How can it be treated?

What are nerve cells, and how are they organized in the brain?

How does the brain develop? When does it begin to function?

THINK ABOUT IT

In Chapter 2 we explained how polygenic inheritance is often involved when phenotypes form a continuum. Height is such a phenotype. Propose a simple polygenic model to explain how height might be inherited.

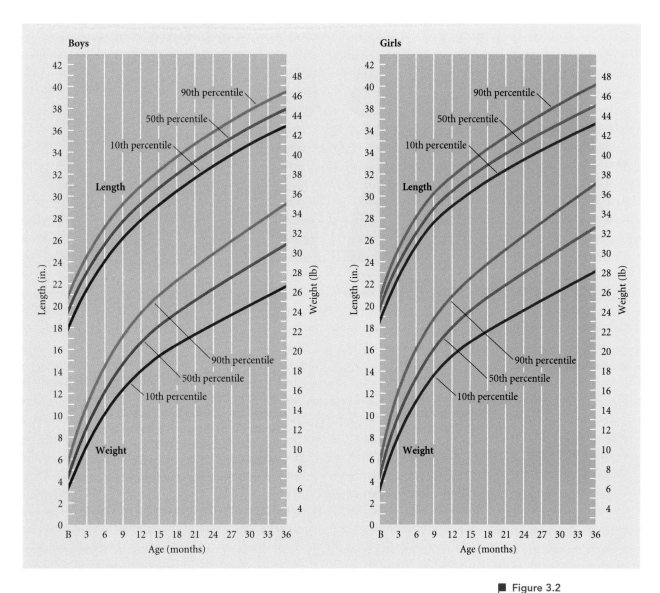

■ **Figure 3.2**
Boys and girls grow taller and heavier from birth to 3 years of age, but the range of normal heights and weights is quite wide.

top-heavy because their heads and trunks are disproportionately large. As growth of the hips, legs, and feet catches up later in childhood, their bodies take on more adult proportions. This pattern of growth, in which the head and trunk develop first, follows the cephalocaudal principle introduced in Chapter 2 (page 60).

Growth of this sort requires energy. Let's see how food and drink provide the fuel to grow.

"You Are What You Eat"—Nutrition and Growth

In a typical 2-month-old, roughly 40% of the body's energy is devoted to growth. Most of the remaining energy is used for basic bodily functions such as digestion and respiration. A much smaller portion is consumed in physical activity.

Because growth requires so much high energy, young babies must consume an enormous number of calories relative to their body weight. A typical, 12-pound 3-month-old, for example, should ingest about 600 calories daily, representing about 50 calories per pound of body weight. An adult, by contrast, needs to consume approximately 15–20 calories per pound, depending on the person's level of activity (National Research Council, 1989).

Breast-feeding is the best way to ensure that babies get the nourishment they need. Human milk contains the proper amounts of carbohydrates, fats, protein, vitamins, and

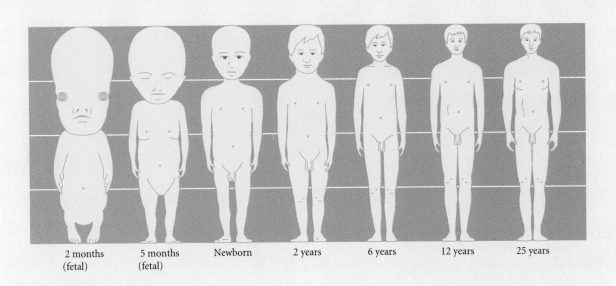

| 2 months (fetal) | 5 months (fetal) | Newborn | 2 years | 6 years | 12 years | 25 years |

Based on Eichorn, 1969.

■ **Figure 3.3**
The head and trunk develop before the hips, legs, and feet, which gives young children a top-heavy appearance.

minerals for babies. Breast-feeding also has several other advantages compared to bottle-feeding (Shelov, 1993; Sullivan & Birch, 1990). First, breast-fed babies are ill less often because breast milk contains the mother's antibodies. Second, breast-fed babies are less prone to diarrhea and constipation. Third, breast-fed babies typically make the transition to solid foods more easily, apparently because they are accustomed to changes in the taste of breast milk that reflect a mother's diet. Fourth, breast milk cannot be contaminated, which is a significant problem in developing countries when formula is used to bottle-feed babies.

Because of these many advantages, the American Academy of Pediatrics recommends that children be breast-fed for the first year, with iron-enriched solid foods introduced gradually. Cereal is a good first semi-solid food, followed by vegetables, fruits, and then meats. A good rule is to introduce only one food at a time. A 7-month-old having cheese for the first time, for instance, should have no other new foods for a few days. In this way, allergies that may develop—skin rash or diarrhea—can be linked to a particular food, making it easier to prevent recurrences.

The many benefits of breast-feeding do not mean that bottle-feeding is harmful. Formula, when prepared in sanitary conditions, provides generally the same nutrients as human milk. But infants are more prone to develop allergies from formula, and formula does not protect infants from disease. However, bottle-feeding has advantages of its own. A mother who cannot readily breast-feed can still enjoy the intimacy of feeding her baby, and other family members can participate in feeding. In fact, long-term longitudinal studies typically find that breast- and bottle-fed babies are similar in physical and psychological development (Fergusson, Horwood, & Shannon, 1987), so women in industrialized countries can choose either method and know that their babies' dietary needs will be met.

In developing nations, bottle-feeding is potentially disastrous. Often the only water available to prepare formula is contaminated; the result is that infants have chronic diarrhea, leading to dehydration and, sometimes, death. Or, in an effort to conserve valuable formula, parents may ignore instructions and use less formula than indicated in making milk; the resulting "weak" milk leads to malnutrition. For these reasons, the World Health Organization strongly advocates breast-feeding as the primary source of nutrition for infants and toddlers in developing nations.

By 2 years, growth slows, so children need less to eat. This is also a time when many children become picky eaters, and toddlers and preschool children may find foods they once ate willingly "yucky." As a toddler, Laura Kail loved green beans. When she reached 2, she decided that green beans were awful and adamantly refused to eat them. Though such finickiness can be annoying, it may actually be adaptive for increasingly independent preschoolers. Because toddlers don't know what is safe to eat and what isn't, eating only familiar foods protects them from potential harm (Birch & Fisher, 1995).

Parents should not be overly concerned about this finicky period. Although some children do eat less than before (in terms of calories per pound), virtually all picky eaters get adequate food for growth. Nevertheless, picky-eating children can make mealtime miserable for all. What's a parent to do? Experts recommend several guidelines for encouraging children to be more open-minded about foods and to deal with them when they aren't (Leach, 1991):

Toddlers and preschool children often become picky eaters. This can be annoying but should not concern parents.

- When possible, allow children to pick among different healthy foods (e.g., milk versus yogurt).
- Allow children to eat foods in any order they want.
- Offer children new foods one at a time and in small amounts; encourage but don't force children to eat new foods.
- Don't force children to "clean their plates."
- Don't spend mealtimes talking about what the child is or is not eating; instead, talk about other topics that interest the child.
- Never use food to reward or punish children.

By following these guidelines, mealtimes can be pleasant and children can receive the nutrition they need to grow.

Malnutrition

An adequate diet is only a dream to many of the world's children. *Worldwide, about 1 in 3 children under age 5 is **malnourished,** as indicated by being small for his or her age* (Grantham-McGregor, Ani, & Fernald, 2001). Many malnourished children live in developing countries, but malnutrition is regrettably common in industrialized countries too. Many American children growing up homeless and in poverty are malnourished. Approximately 20% of U.S. children receive inadequate amounts of iron, and 10% go to bed hungry (Children's Defense Fund, 1996; Pollitt, 1994).

Malnourished children tend to develop less rapidly than their peers. Malnourishment is especially damaging during infancy because growth is ordinarily so rapid during these years. This is well illustrated by a longitudinal study conducted in Barbados in the West Indies (Galler & Ramsey, 1989; Galler, Ramsey, & Forde, 1986). Included were more than 100 children who were severely malnourished as infants, as well as 100 children whose family environments were similar but who had adequate nutrition as infants. The children who experienced malnutrition during infancy were indistinguishable from their peers physically—they were just as tall and weighed just as much. However, children with a history of infant malnutrition had much lower scores on intelligence tests. Also, many of the children who were malnourished during infancy had difficulty maintaining attention in school; they were easily distracted. Many similar studies suggest that malnourished youngsters tire easily, are more wary, and are often inattentive (Lozoff et al., 1998). In addition, malnutrition during rapid periods of growth may cause substantial and potentially irreversible damage to the brain (Morgane et al., 1993).

Malnutrition would seem to have a simple cure—an adequate diet. But the solution is more complex than you might expect. Malnourished children are often listless and

Many children around the world are malnourished.

inactive (Ricciuti, 1993). They are unusually quiet and express little interest in what goes on around them. These behaviors are useful to children whose diet is inadequate because they conserve limited energy. Unfortunately, these behaviors may also deprive youngsters of experiences that would further their development. For example, when children are routinely unresponsive and lethargic, parents often come to believe that their actions have little impact on the children. That is, when children do not respond to parents' efforts to stimulate their development, this discourages parents from providing additional stimulation in the future. Over time, parents tend to provide fewer experiences that foster their children's development. The result is a self-perpetuating cycle in which malnourished children are forsaken by parents who feel as if they can do little to contribute to their children's growth. A biological influence—lethargy stemming from insufficient nourishment—causes a profound change in the experiences—parental teaching—that shape a child's development (Worobey, 2005).

To break the vicious cycle, these children need more than an improved diet. Their parents must be taught how to foster their children's development and must be encouraged to do so. Programs that combine dietary supplements with parent training offer promise in treating malnutrition (Grantham-McGregor et al., 2001). Children in these programs often catch up with their peers in physical and intellectual growth, showing that the best way to reduce the effect of malnutrition on psychological forces is by addressing both biological and sociocultural forces (Super, Herrera, & Mora, 1990).

THE EMERGING NERVOUS SYSTEM

The physical changes we see as infants grow are impressive. Even more awe-inspiring are the changes we cannot see—those involving the brain and the nervous system. An infant's feelings of hunger or pain, its smiles or laughs, and its efforts to sit upright or to hold a rattle all reflect the functioning of the brain and the rest of the emerging nervous system.

How does the brain accomplish these many tasks? To begin to answer this question, we need to look at the organization of the brain. *The basic unit in the brain and the rest of the nervous system is the **neuron,** a cell that specializes in receiving and transmitting information.* Neurons have the basic elements shown in Figure 3.4. *The **cell body,** in the center of the cell, contains the basic biological machinery that keeps the neuron alive. The receiving end of the neuron, the **dendrite,** looks like a tree with its many branches.* This structure allows one neuron to receive input from thousands of other neurons (Morgan & Gibson, 1991). *The tubelike structure that emerges from the other side of the cell body, the **axon,** transmits information to other neurons. At the end of the axon are small knobs called **terminal buttons,** which release chemicals called **neurotransmitters.*** These neurotransmitters are the messengers that carry information to nearby neurons.

Take 50–100 billion neurons like these, and you have the beginnings of a human brain. An adult's brain weighs a little less than 3 pounds and would easily fit into your hands. *The wrinkled surface of the brain is the **cerebral cortex;** made up of 10 billion neurons, the cortex regulates many of the functions that we think of as distinctly human. The cortex consists of left and right halves, called **hemispheres,** linked by a thick bundle of neu-*

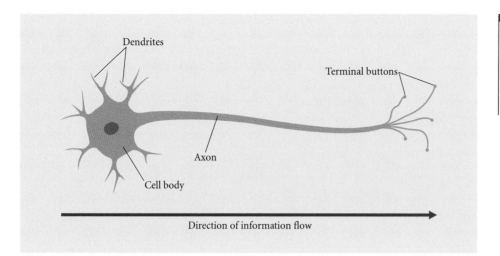

■ **Figure 3.4**
A nerve cell includes dendrites that receive information, a cell body that has life-sustaining machinery, and, for sending information, an axon that ends in terminal buttons.

rons called the **corpus callosum.** The characteristics you value the most—your engaging personality, your "way with words," or your uncanny knack for "reading" others' emotions—are all controlled by specific regions in the cortex. *For example, your personality and your ability to make and carry out plans are largely centered in an area in the front of the cortex called (appropriately enough) the **frontal cortex.*** For most people, the ability to produce and understand language is mainly housed in neurons in the left hemisphere of the cortex. When you recognize that others are happy or sad, neurons in your right hemisphere are usually at work.

Now that we know a bit about the organization of the mature brain, let's look at how the brain grows and begins to function.

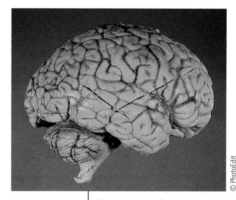

The cortex is the outer, wrinkled surface of the brain.

The Making of the Working Brain

The brain weighs only three-quarters of a pound at birth, which is roughly 25% of the weight of an adult brain. However, you can see from Figure 3.5 that the brain grows rapidly during infancy and the preschool years. At 3 years of age, for example, the brain has achieved 80% of its ultimate weight. Brain weight doesn't tell us much, however, about the fascinating sequence of changes that take place to create a working brain. Instead, we need to move back to prenatal development.

Emerging Brain Structures

The beginnings of the brain can be traced to the period of the zygote. *At roughly 3 weeks after conception, a group of cells form a flat structure known as the **neural plate.*** At 4 weeks, the neural plate folds to form a tube that ultimately becomes the brain and spinal cord. When the ends of the tube fuse shut, neurons are produced in one small region of the neural tube. Production of neurons begins about 10 weeks after conception, and by 28 weeks, the developing brain has virtually all the neurons it will ever have. During these weeks, neurons form at the incredible rate of more than 4,000 per second (Kolb, 1989).

From the neuron-manufacturing site in the neural tube, neurons migrate to their final positions in the brain. The brain is built in stages, beginning with the innermost layers. Neurons in the deepest layer are positioned first, followed by neurons in the second layer, and so on. This layering process continues until all six layers of the mature brain are in place, which occurs about 7 months after conception (Rakic, 1995).

*In the fourth month of prenatal development, axons begin to acquire **myelin**—the fatty wrap that speeds neural transmission.* This process continues through infancy and into childhood and adolescence (Casaer, 1993). Neurons that carry sensory information are

■ Figure 3.5
The brain grows rapidly during infancy and the toddler years, achieving 80% of its adult weight by age 3.

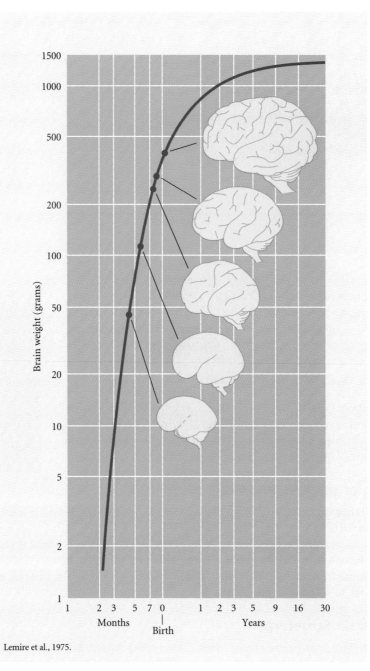

Lemire et al., 1975.

From *Normal and Abnormal Development of the Nervous System,* by R. J. Lemire, J. D. Loesser, R. W. Leech, and E. C. Alvord Jr., p. 236. Copyright © J. B. Lippincott Company. Reprinted with permission.

the first to acquire myelin; neurons in the cortex are among the last. You can see the effect of more myelin in improved coordination and reaction times. The older the infant and, later, the child, the more rapid and coordinated his or her reactions.

In the months after birth, the brain grows rapidly. Axons and dendrites grow longer, and, like a maturing tree, dendrites quickly sprout new limbs. As the number of dendrites increases, so does the number of synapses, reaching a peak at about the first birthday. *Soon after, synapses begin to disappear gradually, a phenomenon known as* **synaptic pruning.** Thus, beginning in infancy and continuing into early adolescence, the brain goes through its own version of "downsizing," weeding out unnecessary connections between neurons. This pruning depends on the activity of the neural circuits—synapses

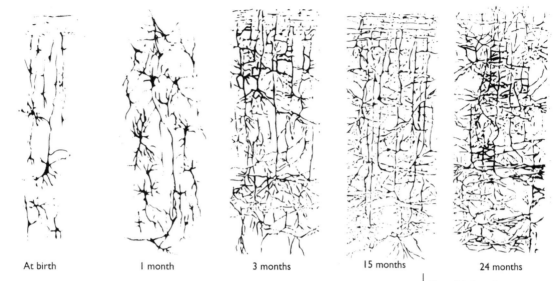

| At birth | 1 month | 3 months | 15 months | 24 months |

From birth to 2 years, neurons grow and create many new synapses with other neurons.

that are active are preserved, but those that aren't are eliminated (Webb, Monk, & Nelson, 2001).

Structure and Function

Since the mature brain is specialized, with different psychological functions localized in particular regions, a natural question for developmental researchers is, "How early in development does brain functioning become localized?" To answer this question, scientists have used many different methods to map functions onto particular brain regions.

- ■ *Studies of children with brain damage:* Children who suffer brain injuries provide valuable insights into brain structure and function. If a region of the brain regulates a particular function (e.g., understanding speech), then damage to that region should impair the function.

- ■ *Studies of electrical activity: Metal electrodes placed on an infant's scalp produce an **electroencephalogram (EEG),** a pattern of brain waves.* If a region of the brain regulates a function, then the region should show distinctive EEG patterns while a child is using that function.

Electrodes placed on an infant's scalp can detect electrical activity that is used to create an electroencephalogram, a pattern of the brain's response to stimulation.

- ■ *Studies using imaging techniques: One method,* **functional magnetic resonance imaging (fMRI),** *uses magnetic fields to track the flow of blood in the brain.* In this method the research participant's brain is literally wrapped in an incredibly powerful magnet that can track blood flow as participants perform different cognitive tasks (Casey et al., 2005).

Alexander Tsiaras/Stock Boston, Inc.

None of these methods is perfect; each has drawbacks. When studying children with brain injuries, for example, multiple areas of the brain may be damaged, making it hard to link impaired functioning to a particular brain region. fMRI is used sparingly because it's very expensive and participants must lie still for several minutes at a time.

Despite these limits, the combined outcome of research using these different approaches indicates that many areas of the cortex begin to function in infancy. Early specialization of the frontal cortex is shown by the finding that damage to this region in infancy results in impaired decision making and abnormal emotional responses (Anderson et al., 2001). Similarly, EEG studies show that a newborn infant's left hemisphere

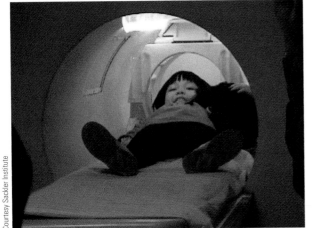

In fMRI, a magnet is used to track the flow of blood to different regions of the brain as children and adults perform cognitive tasks.

> **THINK ABOUT IT**
>
> When you're trying to comprehend a difficult paragraph in a textbook, what part of your brain is probably particularly active?

generates more electrical activity in response to speech than the right hemisphere (Molfese & Burger-Judisch, 1991). Thus, by birth, the cortex of the left hemisphere is already specialized for language processing. Finally, studies of children with prenatal brain damage indicate that by infancy the right hemisphere is specialized for understanding certain kinds of spatial relations (Stiles et al., 2005).

Of course, early specialization does not mean that the brain is functionally mature. Over the remainder of childhood and into adulthood, the brain continues to become more specialized. In Chapter 14, we'll see that some regions of the brain continue to develop into old age, whereas other areas are sometimes destroyed by diseases associated with aging.

Brain Plasticity

Neuroplasticity refers to the extent to which brain organization is flexible. How plastic is the human brain? Answers to this question reflect the familiar views on the nature-nurture issue (Nelson, 1999; Stiles, 2001). Some theorists believe that organization of brain function is predetermined genetically; it's simply in most children's genes that, for example, the left hemisphere will specialize in language processing. In this view, the brain is like a house —a structure that's specialized from the very beginning, with some rooms designed for cooking, others for sleeping, others for bathing. Other theorists believe that few functions are rigidly assigned to specific brain sites at conception. Instead, experience helps determine the functional organization of the brain. In this view, the brain is more like an office building—an all-purpose structure with rooms designed to be used flexibly to meet the different business needs of the companies with offices in the building.

Research designed to test these views shows that the brain has some plasticity. Remember Martin, the preschooler whose brain was damaged when he was hit by a car? His language skills were impaired after the accident. This was not surprising because the left hemisphere of Martin's brain had absorbed most of the force of the accident. But within several months Martin had completely recovered his language skills. Apparently other neurons took over language-related processing from the damaged neurons. This recovery of function is not uncommon—particularly for young children—and shows the brain is plastic. In other words, young children often recover more skills after brain injury than older children and adults, apparently because functions are more easily reassigned in the young brain (Stiles et al., 2005).

However, the brain is not completely plastic—brains have a similar structure and similar mapping of functions on those structures. Visual cortex, for example, is almost always near the back of the brain. Sensory and motor cortex always run across the middle of the brain. But if a neuron's function is not specified at conception, how do different neurons take on different functions and in much the same pattern for most people? Researchers are trying to answer this question, and many details still need to be worked out. The answer probably lies in complex biochemical processes (Barinaga, 1997; Kunzig, 1998). You can get an idea of what's involved by imagining people arriving for a football game at a stadium where there are no reserved seats. As fans enter the stadium, they see others wearing their own school colors and move in that direction. Of course, not everyone does this. Some fans sit with friends from the other team. Some pick seats based on other factors (e.g., to avoid looking into the sun, to be close to the concession stand). In general, though, by game time most fans have taken seats on their respective sides of the field.

In much the same way, as neurons are created and begin migrating through the layers of cortex, cellular biochemistry makes some paths more attractive than others. Yet, just as each fan can potentially sit anywhere because there are no reserved seats, an individual neuron can end up in many different locations because genetic instructions do not assign specific brain regions. Thus, the human brain is plastic—its organization and function can be affected by experience—but its development follows some general biochemical instructions that ensure that most people end up with brains organized along similar lines.

Finally, it's important to emphasize the role of environmental stimulation in normal brain development. To return to the analogy of the brain as a building, the newborn's brain is perhaps best conceived as a partially finished, partially furnished house: A general organization is there, with preliminary neural pathways designed to perform certain functions. The left hemisphere no doubt has some language pathways, and the frontal cortex has some emotion-related pathways. However, completing the typical organization of the mature brain requires input from the environment that stimulates other "general purpose" neurons to specialize. When infants hear speech, these experiences may stimulate other neurons in the brain to specialize in language processing. In this manner, experience is the catalyst that converts the partially furnished, partially finished newborn brain into a mature, specialized brain (Johnson, 2000; Webb et al., 2001).

TEST YOURSELF

1. Compared to older children and adults, an infant's head and trunk are _____.

2. Because of the high demands of growth, infants need _____ calories per pound than adults.

3. The most effective treatment for malnutrition is improved diet and _____.

4. The _____ is the part of the neuron that contains the basic machinery to keep the cell alive.

5. The frontal cortex is the seat of personality and regulates _____.

6. Human speech typically elicits the greatest electrical activity from the _____ of an infant's brain.

7. A good example of brain plasticity is that, although children with brain damage often have impaired cognitive processes, _____.

How does malnutrition illustrate the influence on development of life-cycle forces in the biopsychosocial framework?

Answers: (1) disproportionately large, (2) more, (3) parent training, (4) cell body, (5) goal-directed behavior, (6) left hemisphere, (7) over time, they often regain their earlier skills

---

3.3

MOVING AND GRASPING— EARLY MOTOR SKILLS

LEARNING OBJECTIVES

What are the component skills involved in learning to walk? At what age do infants master them?

How do infants learn to coordinate the use of their hands?

How do maturation and experience influence mastery of motor skills?

Nancy is 14 months old and a world-class crawler. Using hands and knees, she can go just about anywhere she wants to. Nancy does not walk and seems uninterested in learning how. Nancy's dad wonders whether he should be doing something to help Nancy progress beyond crawling. Deep down, he worries that perhaps he was negligent in not providing more exercise for Nancy when she was younger.

Do you remember what it was like to learn to type, to drive a car with a stick shift, to play a musical instrument, or to play a sport? *Each of these activities involves **motor skills**—coordinated movements of the muscles and limbs.* Success demands that each movement be done in a precise way, in exactly the right sequence, and at exactly the right time. For example, in the few seconds that it takes you to type "human development," if you don't move your fingers in exactly the correct sequence to the precise location on the keyboard, you get "jinsj drveo;nrwnt."

These activities are demanding for adults, but think about similar challenges for infants. *Infants must learn to move about in the world, to* **locomote.** At first unable to move independently, infants soon learn to crawl, to stand, and to walk. Once the child can move through the environment upright, the arms and hands are free. To take advantage of this arrangement, the human hand has fully independent fingers (instead of a paw), with the thumb opposing the remaining four fingers. *Infants must learn the* **fine motor skills** *associated with grasping, holding, and manipulating objects.* In the case of feeding, for example, infants progress from being fed by others, to holding a bottle, to feeding themselves with their fingers, to eating with utensils.

Together, locomotion and fine motor skills give children access to an enormous variety of information about shapes, textures, and features in their environment. In this section, we'll see how locomotion and fine motor skills develop and, as we do, we'll see whether Nancy's dad should worry about her lack of interest in walking.

LOCOMOTION

■ **Figure 3.6**
Locomotor skills improve rapidly in the 15 months after birth, and progress can be measured by many developmental milestones.

Advances in posture and locomotion transform the infant in little more than a year. Figure 3.6 shows some of the important milestones in motor development and the age by

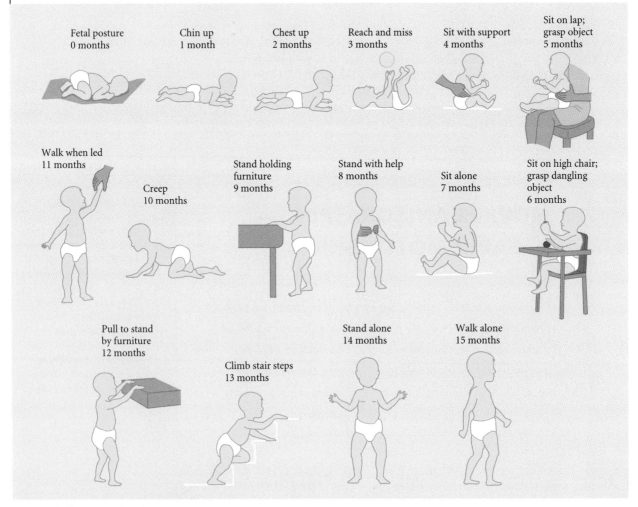

Based on Shirley, 1931, and Bayley, 1969.

which most infants have achieved them. By about 5 months of age, most babies will have rolled from back to front and will be able to sit upright with support. By 7 months, infants can sit alone, and by 10 months, they can creep. A typical 14-month-old is able to stand alone briefly and walk with assistance. *This early, unsteady form of walking is called* **toddling** *(hence the term* **toddler***).* Of course, not all children walk at exactly the same age. Some walk before their first birthday; others, like Nancy, the world-class crawler in the vignette, take their first steps as late as 18 or 19 months of age. By 24 months, most children can climb steps, walk backwards, and kick a ball.

Researchers once thought these developmental milestones reflected maturation (e.g., McGraw, 1935). Walking, for example, emerged naturally when the necessary muscles and neural circuits matured. Today, however, locomotion—and, in fact, all of motor development—is viewed from a new perspective. *According to* **dynamic systems theory,** *motor development involves many distinct skills that are organized and reorganized over time to meet the demands of specific tasks.* For example, walking includes maintaining balance, moving limbs, perceiving the environment, and having a reason to move. Only by understanding each of these skills and how they are combined to allow movement in a specific situation can we understand walking (Thelen & Smith, 1998).

Posture and Balance

The ability to maintain an upright posture is fundamental to walking. But upright posture is virtually impossible for newborns and young infants because of the shape of their body. Cephalocaudal growth means that an infant is top-heavy. Consequently, as soon as a young infant starts to lose her balance, she tumbles over. Only with growth of the legs and muscles can infants maintain an upright posture (Thelen, Ulrich, & Jensen, 1989).

Once infants can stand upright, they must continuously adjust their posture to avoid falling down. By a few months after birth, infants begin to use visual cues and an inner-ear mechanism to adjust their posture. To show the use of visual cues for balance, researchers had babies sit in a room with striped walls that moved. When adults sit in such a room, they perceive themselves as moving (not the walls) and adjust their posture accordingly; so do infants, which shows that they use vision to maintain upright posture (Bertenthal & Clifton, 1998). In addition, when 4-month-olds who are propped in a sitting position lose their balance, they try to keep their head upright. They do this even when blindfolded, which means they are using cues from their inner ear to maintain balance (Woollacott, Shumway-Cook, & Williams, 1989).

Balance is not, however, something that infants master just once. Instead, infants must relearn balancing for sitting, crawling, walking, and other postures. Why? The body rotates around different points in each posture (e.g., the wrists for crawling versus the ankles for walking), and different muscle groups are used to generate compensating motions when infants begin to lose their balance. Consequently, it's hardly surprising that infants who easily maintain their balance while sitting topple over time after time when crawling. Infants must recalibrate the balance system as they take on each new posture, just as basketball players recalibrate their muscle movements when they move from dunking to shooting a three pointer (Adolph, 2000, 2003).

Stepping

Another essential element of walking is moving the legs alternately, repeatedly transferring the weight of the body from one foot to the other. Children don't step spontaneously until approximately 10 months because they must be able to stand to step.

Can younger children step if they are held upright? Thelen and Ulrich (1991) devised a clever procedure to answer this question. Infants were placed on a treadmill and held upright by an adult. When the belt on the treadmill started to move, infants could respond one of several ways. They might simply let both legs be dragged rearward by the belt. Or they might let their legs be dragged briefly, then move them forward together in a hopping motion. Many 6- and 7-month-olds demonstrated the mature pattern of alternating steps on each leg. Even more amazing is that when the treadmill was

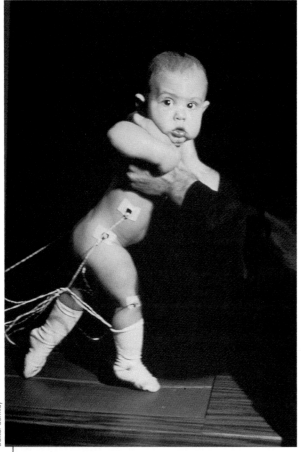

Infants are capable of stepping—moving the legs alternately—long before they can walk alone.

equipped with separate belts for each leg that moved at different speeds, babies adjusted, stepping more rapidly on the faster belt.

Apparently, the alternate stepping motion that is essential for walking is evident long before infants walk alone. Walking unassisted is not possible, though, until other component skills are mastered.

Perceptual Factors

Many infants learn to walk in the relative security of flat, uncluttered floors at home. But they soon discover that the environment offers a variety of surfaces, some more conducive to walking than others. Infants use perceptual information to judge whether a surface is suitable for walking. When placed on a surface that gives way underfoot (e.g., a waterbed), they quickly judge it unsuitable for walking and resort to crawling (Gibson et al., 1987). And, when toddlers encounter a surface that slopes down steeply, few try to walk down, which would result in a fall. Instead, they slide or scoot backwards (Adolph, 1997; Adolph, Eppler, & Gibson, 1993). Results like these show that infants use perceptual cues to decide whether a surface is safe for walking.

Coordinating Skills

Dynamic systems theory emphasizes that learning to walk demands orchestration of many individual skills. Each component skill must first be mastered alone and then integrated with the other skills (Werner, 1948). *That is, mastery of intricate motions requires both* **differentiation**—*mastery of component skills*—*and their* **integration**—*combining them in proper sequence into a coherent, working whole.* In the case of walking, not until 12 to 15 months of age have children mastered the component skills so that they can be coordinated to allow independent, unsupported walking.

Mastering individual skills and coordinating them well does not happen overnight. Instead, they take time and repeated practice. For example, when parents give their infants daily practice in sitting, their infants master sitting at a younger age. However, such practice has no effect on stepping because different muscles and movements are involved (Zelazo et al., 1993). Similarly, when infants practice crawling on their bellies, this helps them crawl on hands and feet because many of the motions are the same (Adolph, Vereijken, & Denny, 1998). But when infants practice crawling on steep slopes, there is no transfer to walking on steep slopes because the motions differ (Adolph, 1997). Thus, experience can improve the rate of motor development, but the improvement is limited to the movements that were trained. In other words, just as daily practice kicking a soccer ball won't improve your golf game, infants who receive much practice in one motor skill usually don't improve in others.

These findings from laboratory research are not the only evidence that practice promotes motor development; cross-cultural research points to the same conclusion. Compared to infants growing up in Europe and North America, many infants from traditional African cultures reach the motor milestones shown in Figure 3.6 at an early age. For example, traditional African infants sit and walk at younger ages. Careful observations of these infants reveal two factors responsible for this early advantage in motor development. First, many common child care practices in traditional African societies have the unanticipated benefit of improving motor skills. For example, infants are commonly carried by their parents "piggyback" style, which helps develop muscles in the infants' trunk and legs. Second, mothers in traditional African cultures believe practice is essential for motor skills to develop normally, and they (or siblings) provide daily training sessions. For example, they may help children learn to sit by having them sit while propped up (Super, 1981). The combined effect of this unintentional and deliberate training is to provide additional opportunities for children to learn the elements of different motor skills. Not surprisingly, African infants with these opportunities learn to sit and walk earlier.

Beyond Walking

If you can recall the feeling of freedom that accompanied your first driver's license, you can imagine how the world expands for infants and toddlers as they learn to move independently. The first tentative steps are soon followed by others that are more skilled. With more experience, infants take longer, straighter steps. And, like adults, they begin to swing their arms, rotating the left arm forward as the right leg moves, then repeating with the right arm and left leg (Ledebt, 2000; Ledebt, van Wieringen, & Savelsbergh, 2004).

Most children learn to run a few months after they walk alone. Most 2-year-olds have a "hurried walk" instead of a true run; they move their legs stiffly (rather than bending them at the knees) and are not "airborne" as is the case when running. By 5 or 6 years, children run easily, quickly changing directions or speed. Hopping also shows young children's growing skill: A typical 2- or 3-year-old will hop a few times on one foot, typically keeping the upper body very stiff; by 5 or 6, children can hop long distances on one foot or alternate hopping first on one foot a few times, then on the other.

With their advanced motor skills, older preschoolers delight in unstructured play. They enjoy swinging, climbing over jungle gyms, and balancing on a beam. Some learn to ride a tricycle or to swim.

FINE MOTOR SKILLS

A major accomplishment of infancy is skilled use of the hands (Bertenthal & Clifton, 1998). Newborns have little apparent control of their hands, but 1-year-olds are extraordinarily talented.

Reaching and Grasping

At about 4 months, infants can successfully reach for objects (Bertenthal & Clifton, 1998). These early reaches often look clumsy and for a good reason. When infants reach, they don't move their arm and hand directly and smoothly to the desired object (as older children and adults do). Instead, the infant's hand moves like a ship under the direction of an unskilled navigator—it moves a short distance, slows, then moves again in a slightly different direction, a process that's repeated until the hand finally contacts the object (McCarty & Ashmead, 1999). As infants grow, their reaches have fewer movements, though they are still not as continuous and smooth as older children's and adults' reaches (Berthier, 1996).

Reaching requires that an infant move the hand to the location of a desired object. Grasping poses a different challenge: Now the infant must coordinate movements of individual fingers to grab an object. Grasping, too, becomes more efficient during infancy. Most 4-month-olds just use their fingers to hold objects, wrapping the object tightly with their fingers alone. Not until 7 or 8 months do most infants use their thumbs to hold

In many African cultures, infants are routinely carried piggyback style, which strengthens the infant's legs, allowing them to walk at a younger age.

> ### THINK ABOUT IT
>
> How does learning to hop on one foot demonstrate differentiation and integration of motor skills?

Locomotor skills develop rapidly in preschool children, making it possible for them to play vigorously.

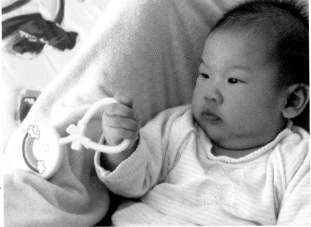

A typical 4-month-old grasps an object with fingers alone.

objects (Siddiqui, 1995). At about this same age, infants begin to position their hands to make it easier to grasp an object. If trying to grasp a long thin rod, for example, infants place their fingers perpendicular to the rod, which is the best position for grasping (Wentworth, Benson, & Haith, 2000). Infants need not see their hand to position it correctly: They position the hand just as accurately in reaching for a lighted object in a darkened room as when reaching in a lighted room (McCarty et al., 2001).

Infants' growing control of each hand is accompanied by greater coordination of the two hands. Although 4-month-olds use both hands, their motions are not coordinated; rather, each hand seems to have a mind of its own. Infants may hold a toy motionless in one hand while shaking a rattle in the other. At roughly 5 to 6 months of age, infants can coordinate the motions of their hands so that each hand performs different actions that serve a common goal. So a child might, for example, hold a toy animal in one hand and pet it with the other (Karniol, 1989). These skills continue to improve after children's first birthday: 1-year-olds reach for most objects with one hand; by 2 years, they reach with one or two hands, as appropriate, depending on the size of the object (van Hof, van der Kamp, & Savelsbergh, 2002).

These gradual changes in fine motor coordination are well illustrated by the ways children feed themselves. Beginning at roughly 6 months of age, many infants experiment with "finger foods" such as sliced bananas and green beans. Infants can easily pick up such foods, but getting them into their mouths is another story. The hand grasping the food may be raised to the cheek, then moved to the edge of the lips, and finally shoved into the mouth. Mission accomplished, but only after many detours along the way! However, infants' eye-hand coordination improves rapidly, and foods varying in size, shape, and texture are soon placed directly in the mouth.

At about the first birthday, many parents allow their children to try eating with a spoon. Youngsters first simply play with the spoon, dipping it in and out of a dish filled with food or sucking on an empty spoon. Soon they learn to fill the spoon with food and place it in their mouth, but the motions are awkward. For example, most 1-year-olds fill a spoon by first placing it directly over a dish. Then, they lower it until the bowl of the spoon is full. In contrast, 2-year-olds typically scoop food from a dish by rotating their wrist, which is the same motion adults use.

As preschoolers, children become much more dextrous, able to make many precise and delicate movements with their hands and fingers. Greater fine motor skill means that preschool children can begin to care for themselves. No longer must they rely primarily on parents to feed and clothe them; instead, they become increasingly skilled at feeding and dressing themselves. A 2- or 3-year-old, for example, can put on some simple clothing and use zippers but not buttons; by 3 or 4 years, children can fasten buttons and take off their clothes when going to the bathroom; most 5-year-olds can dress and undress themselves, except for tying shoes, which children typically master at about age 6.

By age 5, fine motor skills are developed to the point that most youngsters can dress themselves.

Greater fine motor coordination also leads to improvements in preschool children's printing and drawing. Given a crayon or marker, 2-year-olds will scribble, expressing delight in the simple lines that are created just by moving a crayon or marker across paper. By 4 or 5 years of age, children use their drawings to depict recognizable objects.

All of these actions illustrate the principles of differentiation and integration that were introduced in our discussion of locomotion. Complex acts involve many constituent movements.

Each must be performed correctly and in the proper sequence. Development involves first mastering the separate elements and then assembling them into a smoothly functioning whole.

Handedness

Are you right-handed or left-handed? If you're right-handed, you're in the majority. About 90% of the people worldwide prefer to use their right hand, although this figure varies somewhat from place to place, reflecting cultural influences. Most of the remaining 10% are left-handed; a relatively small percentage of people are truly ambidextrous.

When young babies reach for objects, they don't seem to prefer one hand over the other; they use their left and right hands interchangeably. They may shake a rattle with their left hand and, moments later, pick up blocks with their right. In one study, infants and toddlers were videotaped as they played with toys that could be manipulated with two hands, such as a pinwheel (Cornwell, Harris, & Fitzgerald, 1991). The 9-month-olds used their left and right hands equally, but by 13 months, most grasped the toy with their right hand. Then they used their left hand to steady the toy while the right hand manipulated the object.

This early preference for one hand becomes stronger and more consistent during the toddler and preschool years. By age 2 a child's hand preference is clear; most children—about 90%—use their right hand in fine motor skills such as coloring, brushing teeth, or zipping a jacket. At this age, youngsters occasionally use their nonpreferred hand for tasks, but by age 5 children typically use their nonpreferred hand only when the preferred hand is busy doing something else. By the time children are ready to enter kindergarten, handedness is well established and very difficult to reverse (McManus et al., 1988).

What determines whether children become left- or right-handed? Some scientists believe that a gene biases children toward right-handedness (Annett, 2002). Consistent with this idea, identical twins are more likely than fraternal twins to have the same handedness—both are right-handed or both are left-handed (Sicotte, Woods, & Mazziotta, 1999). But experience also contributes to handedness. Modern industrial cultures favor right-handedness. School desks, scissors, and can openers, for example, are designed for right-handed people and can be used by left-handers only with difficulty. In the United States, elementary school teachers used to urge left-handed children to use their right hands. As this practice has diminished in the last 50 years, the percentage of left-handed children has risen steadily (Levy, 1976). Thus, handedness seems to have both hereditary and environmental influences.

TEST YOURSELF

1. According to _____, motor development involves many distinct skills that are organized and reorganized over time, depending on task demands.

2. When 4-month-olds tumble from a sitting position, they usually try to keep their head upright. This happens even when they are blindfolded, which means that the important cues to balance come from _____.

3. Skills important in learning to walk include maintaining upright posture and balance, stepping, and _____.

4. Akira uses both hands simultaneously, but not in a coordinated manner; each hand seems to be "doing its own thing." Akira is probably _____ months old.

5. Before the age of _____, children show no signs of handedness; they use their left and right hands interchangeably.

Describe how the mastery of a fine motor skill such as learning to use a spoon or a crayon illustrates the integration of biological, psychological, and sociocultural forces in the biopsychosocial framework.

Answers: (1) dynamic systems theory, (2) the inner ear, (3) using perceptual information, (4) 4, (5) 1 year

3.4

COMING TO KNOW THE WORLD: PERCEPTION

Darla is mesmerized by her newborn daughter, Olivia. Darla loves holding Olivia, talking to her, and simply watching her. Darla is certain that Olivia is already getting to know her, coming to recognize her face and the sound of her voice. Darla's husband, Steve, thinks she is crazy: "Everyone knows that babies are born blind, and they probably can't hear much either." Darla doubts Steve and wishes someone could tell her the truth about Olivia's vision and hearing.

LEARNING OBJECTIVES

Are infants able to smell, to taste, and to experience pain?

Can infants hear? How do they use sound to locate objects?

How well can infants see? Can they see color and depth?

How do infants coordinate information between different sensory modalities, such as between vision and hearing?

To answer Darla's questions, we need to define what it means for an infant to experience or sense the world. Humans have several kinds of sense organs, each of which is receptive to a different kind of physical energy. For example, the retina at the back of the eye is sensitive to some types of electromagnetic energy, and sight is the result. The eardrum detects changes in air pressure, and hearing is the result. Cells at the top of the nasal passage detect the passage of airborne molecules, and smell is the result. In each case, the sense organ translates the physical stimulus into nerve impulses that are sent to the brain. *The processes by which the brain receives, selects, modifies, and organizes these impulses is known as* **perception.** This is simply the first step in the complex process of accumulating information that eventually results in "knowing."

Darla's questions are really about her newborn daughter's perceptual skills. By the end of this section, you'll be able to answer her questions because we're going to look at how infants use different senses to experience the world. We begin with smell, taste, and touch because they are among the most mature senses at birth.

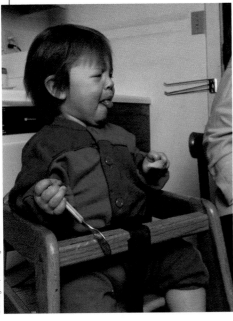

Infants and toddlers do *not* like bitter and sour tastes!

Dion Ogust/The Image Works

SMELL, TASTE, AND TOUCH

Newborns have a keen sense of smell. Infants respond positively to pleasant smells and negatively to unpleasant smells (Mennella & Beauchamp, 1997). They have a relaxed, contented-looking facial expression when they smell honey or chocolate, but frown, grimace, or turn away when they smell rotten eggs or ammonia. Young babies can also recognize familiar odors. Newborns will look in the direction of a pad that is saturated with their own amniotic fluid (Schaal, Marlier, & Soussignan, 1998). They will also turn toward a pad saturated with the odor of their mother's breast or her perfume (Porter & Winburg, 1999).

Newborns also have a highly developed sense of taste. They readily differentiate salty, sour, bitter, and sweet tastes (Rostenstein & Oster, 1997). Most infants seem to have a "sweet tooth." They react to sweet substances by smiling, sucking, and licking their lips (Steiner et al., 2001) but grimace when fed bitter- or sour-tasting substances (Kaijura, Cowart, & Beauchamp, 1992). Infants are also sensitive to changes in the taste of breast milk that reflect a mother's diet. Infants will nurse more after their mother has consumed a sweet-tasting substance such as vanilla (Mennella & Beauchamp, 1996).

Newborns are sensitive to touch. As we saw earlier in this chapter, many areas of the newborn's body respond reflexively when touched. Touching an infant's cheek, mouth, hand, or foot produces reflexive movements, documenting that infants perceive touch.

If babies react to touch, does this mean they experience pain? This is difficult to answer because pain has such a subjective element to it. The same pain-eliciting stimulus that leads some adults to complain of mild discomfort causes others to report that they are in agony. Since infants cannot express their pain to us directly, we must use indirect evidence.

The infant's nervous system definitely is capable of transmitting pain: Receptors for pain in the skin are just as plentiful in infants as they are in adults (Anand & Hickey, 1987). Furthermore, babies' behavior in response to apparent pain-provoking stimuli also suggests that they experience pain (Buchholz et al., 1998). For example, when a baby is receiving an inoculation, she lowers her eyebrows, purses her lips and, of course, opens her mouth to cry. Although we can't hear her, the sound of her cry is probably the unique pattern associated with pain. The pain cry begins suddenly, is high-pitched, and is not easily soothed. The baby is also agitated, moving her hands, arms, and legs (Craig et al., 1993; Goubet, Clifton, & Shah, 2001). All together, these signs strongly suggest that babies experience pain.

Perceptual skills are extraordinarily useful to newborns and young babies. Smell and touch help them recognize their mothers. Smell and taste make it much easier for them to learn to eat. Early development of smell, taste, and touch prepares newborns and young babies to learn about the world.

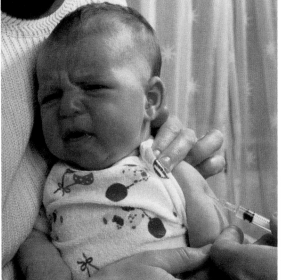

An infant's response to an inoculation—a distinctive facial expression coupled with a distinctive cry—clearly suggests that the baby feels pain.

HEARING

Do you remember, from Chapter 2, the study in which mothers read aloud *The Cat in the Hat* late in pregnancy? This research showed that the fetus can hear at 7 or 8 months after conception. As you would expect from these results, newborns typically respond to sounds in their surroundings. If a parent is quiet but then coughs, an infant may startle, blink his eyes, and move his arms or legs. These responses may seem natural, but they do indeed indicate that infants are sensitive to sound.

Overall, adults can hear better than infants (Aslin, Jusczyk, & Pisoni, 1998). Adults can hear some very quiet sounds that infants can't. More interestingly, infants best hear sounds that have pitches in the range of human speech—neither very high- nor very low-pitched. Infants can differentiate speech sounds, such as vowels from consonant sounds and by 4½ months, they can recognize their own names (Jusczyk, 1995; Mandel, Jusczyk, & Pisoni, 1995).

Infants also can distinguish different musical sounds and can remember lullabies and songs that parents sing to them (Trainor, Wu, & Tsang, 2004). They can distinguish different melodies and prefer melodies that are pleasant sounding over those that are unpleasant sounding or dissonant (Trainor & Heinmiller, 1998). And infants are sensitive to the rhythmic structure of music. After infants have heard a simple sequence of notes, they can tell the difference between a new sequence that fits the original versus one that doesn't (Hannon & Trehub, 2005). This early sensitivity to music is remarkable but perhaps not so surprising when you consider that music is (and has been) central in all cultures.

In addition to carrying a message through words or music, sound can reveal much about its source. When we hear a person speak, the pitch of the speech can be used to judge the age and sex of the speaker; if the speech contains many relatively lower-pitched sounds, then the speaker is probably a man. The loudness of the speech tells us about the speaker's distance; if it can barely be heard, the speaker is far away. Also, differences in the time it takes sound to travel to the left and right ears tell us about the speaker's location; if the sounds arrive at exactly the same time, the speaker must be directly ahead or directly behind us.

Even infants can extract much of this information in sound. Young babies can distinguish sounds of different pitches; 6-month-olds do so nearly as accurately as adults (Spetner & Olsho, 1990). They are also able to differentiate speech sounds, such as different vowel and consonant sounds (a topic we examine in more detail in Chapter 4).

Like adults, infants use sound to locate objects, looking toward the source of sound (Morrongiello, Fenwick, & Chance, 1990). Infants also use sound to decide whether objects are near or far. In one study (Clifton, Perris, & Bullinger, 1991), 7-month-olds were shown a rattle. Next, the experimenters darkened the room and shook the rattle, either 6 inches away from the infant or about 2 feet away. Infants would often reach for the rattle in the dark when it was 6 inches away but not when it was 2 feet away. These 7-month-olds were quite capable of using sound to estimate distance—in this case, distinguishing a toy they could reach from one they could not.

Thus, by the middle of the first year, infants are responding to much of the information that is provided by sound. In Chapter 4, we will reach the same conclusion when we examine the perception of language-related sounds.

SEEING

If you've ever watched infants, you've probably noticed that they spend much of their waking time looking around. Sometimes they seem to be generally scanning their environment, and sometimes they seem to be focusing on nearby objects. What do they see as a result? Perhaps their visual world is a sea of confusing gray blobs. Or maybe they see the world essentially as adults do. Actually, neither of these descriptions is entirely accurate, but the second is closer to the truth.

The various elements of the visual system—the eye, the optic nerve, and the brain—are relatively well developed at birth. Newborns respond to light and can track moving objects with their eyes. How well do infants see? *The clarity of vision, called **visual acuity**, is defined as the smallest pattern that can be distinguished dependably.* You've undoubtedly had your acuity measured, probably by being asked to read rows of progressively smaller letters or numbers from a chart. The same approach is used to assess newborns' acuity, adjusted to compensate for the fact that we can't use words to explain to infants what we'd like them to do. Most infants will look at patterned stimuli instead of plain, patternless stimuli (Snow, 1998). For example, if we were to show the two stimuli in Figure 3.7 to an infant, most babies would look longer at the striped pattern than at the gray pattern. As we make the lines narrower (along with the spaces between them), there comes a point at which the black and white stripes become so fine that they simply blend together and appear gray—just like the other pattern.

To estimate an infant's acuity, we pair the gray square with squares in which the widths of the stripes differ, like the ones in Figure 3.8: When infants look at the two stimuli equally, this indicates that they are no longer able to distinguish the stripes of the

■ **Figure 3.7**
Infants usually like to look at striped patterns over plain ones, a preference that can be used to measure an infant's visual acuity.

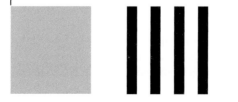

■ **Figure 3.8**
An infant's acuity can be measured by determining the thinnest stripes that the infant prefers to view.

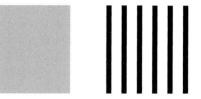

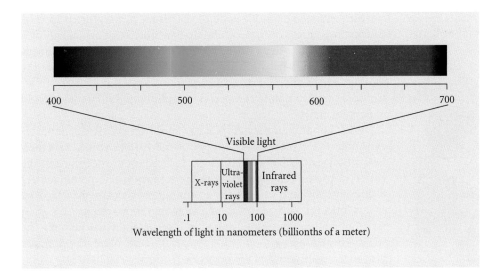

patterned stimulus. By measuring the width of the stripes and their distance from an infant's eye, we can estimate acuity, with detection of thinner stripes indicating better acuity. Measurements of this sort indicate that newborns and 1-month-olds see at 20 feet what normal adults would see at 200–400 feet. By the first birthday, infants' acuity is essentially the same as that of an adult with normal vision (Kellman & Banks, 1998).

Color

Not only do infants begin to see the world with greater acuity during the first year, they also begin to see it in color! How do we perceive color? The wavelength of light is the basis of color perception. In Figure 3.9, light that we see as red has a relatively long wavelength, whereas violet, at the other end of the color spectrum, has a much shorter wavelength. *Concentrated in the back of the eye, along the retina, are specialized neurons called* **cones.** Some cones are particularly sensitive to short-wavelength light (blues and violets). Others are sensitive to medium-wavelength light (greens and yellows); still others are sensitive to long-wavelength light (reds and oranges). These different kinds of cones are linked by complex circuits of neurons, and this circuitry is responsible for our ability to see the world in colors.

These circuits gradually begin to function in the first few months after birth. Newborns and young babies can perceive few colors, but by 3 months the three kinds of cones and their associated circuits are working and infants are able to see the full range of colors (Kellman & Banks, 1998). In fact, by 3 to 4 months, infants' color perception seems similar to that of adults (Adams & Courage, 1995; Franklin, Pilling, & Davies, 2005). In particular, infants, like adults, tend to see categories of color. That is, infants see the spectrum as consisting of broad categories of colors that are separated by narrow regions where color changes rapidly (Dannemiller, 1998).

Depth

People see objects as having three dimensions: height, width, and depth. The retina of the eye is flat, so height and width can be represented directly on its two-dimensional surface. But the third dimension, depth, cannot be represented directly on this flat surface, so how do we perceive depth? We use perceptual processing to *infer* depth.

Depth perception tells us whether objects are near or far, which was the basis for some classic research by Eleanor Gibson and Richard Walk (1960) on the origins of depth perception. *In their work, babies were placed on a glass-covered platform, a device known as the* **visual cliff.** On one side of the platform, a checkerboard pattern appeared directly under the glass; on the other side, the pattern appeared several feet below the glass. The result was that the first side looked shallow but the other looked deep, like a cliff.

Infants avoid the "deep side" of the visual cliff, indicating that they perceive depth.

Mothers stood on each side of the visual cliff and tried to coax their infants across the deep or the shallow side. Most babies willingly crawled to their mothers when they stood on the shallow side. In contrast, almost every baby refused to cross the deep side, even when the mothers called them by name and tried to lure them with an attractive toy. Clearly, infants can perceive depth by the time they are old enough to crawl.

What about younger babies who cannot yet crawl? When babies as young as 1½ months are simply placed on the visual cliff, their hearts beat more slowly when they are placed on the deep side of the cliff. Heart rate often decelerates when people notice something interesting, so this would suggest that 1½-month-olds notice that the deep side is different. At 7 months, infants' heart rate accelerates, a sign of fear. Thus, although young babies can detect a difference between the shallow and the deep sides of the visual cliff, only older, crawling babies are actually afraid of the deep side (Campos et al., 1978).

How do infants infer depth, on the visual cliff or anywhere? They use several kinds of cues. *Among the first are* **kinetic cues**, *in which motion is used to estimate depth.* ***Visual expansion*** *refers to the fact that as an object moves closer, it fills an ever-greater proportion of the retina.* Visual expansion is why we flinch when someone unexpectedly tosses a soda can toward us, and it's what allows a batter to estimate when a baseball will arrive over the plate. *Another cue,* **motion parallax,** *refers to the fact that nearby moving objects move across our visual field faster than those at a distance.* Motion parallax is in action when you look out the side window in a moving car: Trees next to the road move rapidly across the visual field, but mountains in the distance move much more slowly. Babies use these cues in the first weeks after birth; for example, 1-month-olds blink if a moving object looks as if it's going to hit them in the face (Nanez & Yonas, 1994).

Another cue becomes important at about 4 months. ***Retinal disparity*** *is based on the fact that the left and right eyes often see slightly different versions of the same scene.* When objects are distant, the retinal images are nearly identical; when they are nearby, the images differ. Thus, greater disparity in retinal images signifies that an object is close. By 4–6 months of age, infants use retinal disparity as a depth cue, correctly inferring that objects are nearby when disparity is great (Kellman & Banks, 1998; Yonas & Owsley, 1987).

By 7 months, infants use several cues for depth that depend on the arrangement of objects in the environment. *These are sometimes called* **pictorial cues** *because they're the same cues that artists used to convey depth in drawings and paintings.* Here are two examples of pictorial cues that 7-month-olds use to infer depth.

- ■ ***Linear perspective:*** *Parallel lines come together at a single point in the distance.* Thus, we use the space between the lines as a cue to distance and, consequently, decide the train is far away because the parallel tracks grow close together.
- ■ ***Texture gradient:*** *The texture of objects changes from coarse but distinct for nearby objects to finer and less distinct for distant objects.* We judge distinct flowers to be close and blurred ones, distant.

Not only do infants use visual cues to judge depth, they also use sound. Remember that infants correctly judge quieter objects to be more distant than louder objects. Given such an assortment of cues, it is not surprising that infants gauge depth so accurately.

Perceiving Objects

Perceptual processes enable us to interpret patterns of lines, textures, and colors as objects. That is, our perception actually creates an object from sensory stimulation. This is particularly challenging because we often see only parts of objects—nearby objects of-

THINK ABOUT IT

Psychologists often refer to "perceptual-motor skills," which implies that the two are closely related. Based on what you've learned in this chapter, how might motor skills influence perception? How could perception influence motor skills?

© Mark Richards/PhotoEdit

© Charles O'Rear/Corbis

Linear perspective is one cue to depth: We interpret the railroad tracks that are close together as being more distant than the tracks that are far apart.

© Jose Fuste Raga/Corbis

Texture gradient is used to infer depth: We interpret the distinct flowers as being closer than the flowers with the course texture.

ten obscure parts of more distant objects. Nevertheless, we recognize these objects despite this complexity in our visual environment.

Perception of objects is limited in newborns, but develops rapidly in the first few months after birth (Johnson, 2001). By 4 months, infants use a number of cues to determine which elements go together to form objects. One important cue is motion: Elements that move together are usually part of the same object (Kellman & Banks, 1998). For example, at the left of Figure 3.10, a pencil appears to be moving back and forth behind a colored square. If the square were removed, you would be surprised to see a pair of pencil stubs, as shown on the right side of the diagram. The common movement of the pencil's eraser and point leads us to believe that they're part of the same pencil.

Young infants, too, are surprised by demonstrations like this. If they see a display like the moving pencils, they will then look very briefly at a whole pencil, apparently because they expected it. In contrast, if after seeing the moving pencil they're shown the two pencil stubs, they look much longer, as if trying to figure out what happened (Eizenman & Bertenthal, 1998; Johnson & Aslin, 1995). Evidently, even very young babies use common motion to create objects from different parts.

Motion is one clue to object unity, but infants use others too, including color, texture, and aligned edges. As you can see in Figure 3.11,

Many cues tell us that these are two objects, not one unusually shaped object: The two objects differ slightly in color, the glass of juice has a different texture than the orange, and the glass has a well-defined edge.

GoodShoot/SuperStock

When you look at this pattern, what do you see? You probably recognize it as part of a human eyeball, even though all that's physically present in the photo are many different colored dots.

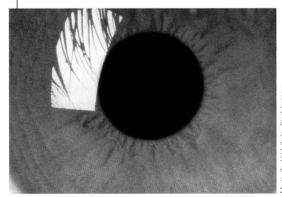

Martin Paul Ltd./Index Stock Imagery

▪ Figure 3.10
After infants have seen the pencil ends moving behind the square, they are surprised to see two pencils when the square is removed; this shows that babies use common motion as a way to determine what makes up an object.

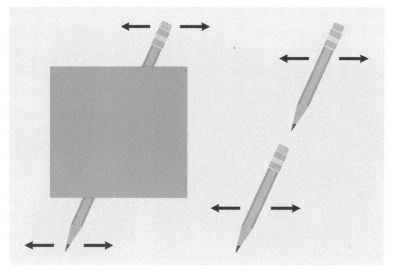

infants more often group features together (i.e., believe they're part of the same object) when they're the same color, have the same texture, and when their edges are aligned (Johnson, 2001).

One object that's particularly important for infants is the human face. Young babies readily look at faces. Typically, 1-month-olds look mostly at the outer edges of a face. In contrast, the pattern of eye fixations in Figure 3.12 shows that 3-month-olds focus almost entirely on the interior of the face, particularly the eyes and lips.

Some theorists argue that babies are innately attracted to stimuli that are facelike. The claim here is that some aspect of the face—perhaps two eyes and a mouth in the correct arrangement—constitutes a distinctive stimulus that is readily recognized, even by newborns. For example, newborns turn their eyes to follow a moving face more than they turn their eyes for nonface stimuli (Mondloch et al., 1999; Morton & Johnson, 1991). This preference for faces over facelike stimuli supports the view that infants are innately attracted to faces. However, preference for tracking a moving face changes abruptly at about 4 weeks of age—infants now track all moving stimuli. One idea is that newborns' face tracking is a reflex, based on primitive circuits in the brain, designed to enhance attention to facelike stimuli. Starting at about 4 weeks, circuits in the brain's cortex begin to control infants' looking at faces and other stimuli (Morton & Johnson, 1991).

Other scientists, however, are skeptical. They believe that general principles of perception explain how infants perceive faces (Turati, 2004). They argue that infants are attracted to faces because faces have stimuli that move (the eyes and mouth) and stimuli with dark and light contrast (the eyes, lips, and teeth). Research by Easterbrooks and her colleagues (1999) supports this view. They found that when face and nonface stimuli are matched for a number of important variables, newborns turn their head and eyes equally for face and nonface stimuli. These results go along with the idea that infants look at faces because of general perceptual principles (for example, babies prefer contrasting stimuli), not because faces are intrinsically attractive to infants. In much the same vein, infants may look at attractive faces simply because those faces contain features that draw attention to any stimulus (not just faces) such as symmetry (Gangestad & Thornhill, 1997).

More research is needed to decide whether face perception follows general perceptual principles or represents a special case. What is clear, though, is that by 3 or 4 months babies have the perceptual skills that enable them to begin to distinguish individual faces (Carey, 1992). And they gradually use more information to recognize faces: 3-month-olds rely mostly on the overall configuration of a face, but 5- and 6-month-olds also rely on more fine-grained spatial relations, such as the distances between the eyes and between the nose and lips (Bhatt et al., 2005). And, as we'll see in the Spotlight on Research feature, by 9 months, these skills have become specific to human faces.

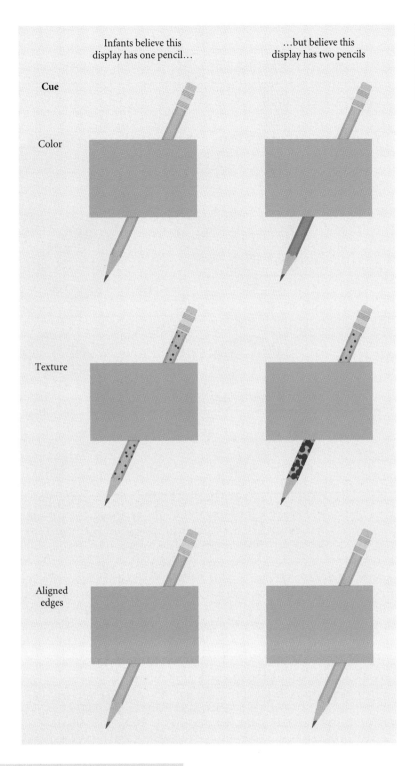

Infants believe this display has one pencil... ...but believe this display has two pencils

Cue

Color

Texture

Aligned edges

Figure 3.11
In addition to common motion, infants use common color, common texture, and aligned edges as clues to object unity.

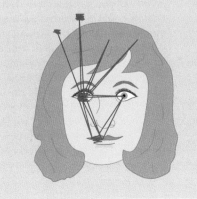

Figure 3.12
When 3-month-olds look at a face, they pay attention to the interior of the face, particularly the eyes and lips.

Adapted from Figure 3.21 on p. 201 from "Pattern Perception in Infancy," Chapter 3, pp. 133–234, by Philip Salapatek. In L. B. Cohen and P. Salapatek (Eds.), *Infant Cognition: From Sensation to Perception.* Copyright © 1975, with permission from Elsevier.

SPOTLIGHT ON RESEARCH

HOW INFANTS BECOME FACE EXPERTS

Who were the investigators, and what was the aim of the study? Over the first year, infants rapidly become more skilled at recognizing human faces, presumably as they are exposed to an ever-larger number of faces and are able to fine-tune their face-recognition processes. If this argument is correct, infants might also *lose* the ability to recognize some facelike stimuli. For example, a monkey's face has many of the same basic features of a human face —eyes, nose, and mouth in the familiar configuration. A young infant's broadly tuned face-recognition processes might work well for monkey faces, but an older infant's more finely tuned processes might not. Testing this hypothesis was the aim of a study by Olivier Pascalis, Michelle de Haan, and Charles A. Nelson (2002).

How did the investigators measure the topic of interest? Pascalis and colleagues wanted to determine whether 6-month-olds, 9-month-olds, and adults could recognize human faces and monkey faces. Consequently, they had infants and adults view a photo of a monkey face or a human face. Then that face was paired with a novel face of the same species. Experimenters recorded participants' looking at the two faces— the expectation was that, if the participants recognized the familiar stimulus, they would look longer at the novel stimulus.

Who were the participants in the study? The study included 30 6-month-olds, 30 9-month-olds, and 11 adults. Half the infants at each age saw human faces; the others saw monkey faces. Adults saw both human and monkey faces.

What was the design of the study? This study was experimental. The independent variables included the type of face (human, monkey) and the familiarity of the face on the test trial (novel, familiar). The dependent variable was the participants' looking at the two faces on the test trials. The study was cross-sectional because it included 6-month-olds, 9-month-olds, and adults, each tested once.

Were there ethical concerns with the study? No. There was no obvious harm

Reprinted with permission from Pascalis et al., *Science* 296: 1321–1323. Copyright 2002, AAAS.

Pascalis and colleagues had participants in their study view one of the human faces or one of the monkey faces. Then that face was shown with the other face of the same type (e.g., both human faces if the participant had seen the human face first). If participants remember the first face, they should look longer at the novel face.

associated with looking at pictures of faces.

What were the results? If participants recognized the familiar face, they should look more at the novel face; if they did not recognize the familiar face, they should look equally at the novel and familiar faces. Figure 3.13 shows the percentage of time that participants looked at the novel face. When human faces were shown, all three age groups looked longer at the novel face (more than 50% preference for the novel face). In contrast, when monkey faces were shown, 6-month-olds looked longer at the novel face, but 9-month-olds and adults looked at novel and familiar faces equally. Remarkably, 6-month-olds showed greater skill than older infants and adults—they were the only group to recognize a monkey face that had been shown before.

What did the investigators conclude? Pascalis and colleagues (2002) con-

cluded that their findings "support the hypothesis that the perceptual window narrows with age and that during the first year of life the face processing system is tuned to a human template" (p. 1322). That is, from experience infants finely tune their face-processing systems to include only human faces.

What converging evidence would strengthen these conclusions? These findings show that 6-month-olds' face-processing systems work equally well on human and monkey faces. The investigators could determine how broadly the system is tuned by studying young infants' recognition of other species that have faces in a humanlike configuration. In addition, it would be beneficial to use brain mapping methods (described on page 103) to determine whether the brain regions associated with face recognition change as face-processing systems become more finely tuned between 6 and 9 months.

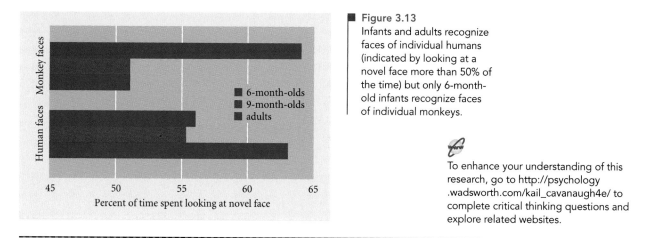

■ **Figure 3.13**
Infants and adults recognize faces of individual humans (indicated by looking at a novel face more than 50% of the time) but only 6-month-old infants recognize faces of individual monkeys.

To enhance your understanding of this research, go to http://psychology .wadsworth.com/kail_cavanaugh4e/ to complete critical thinking questions and explore related websites.

These rapid changes in face-recognition skill are adaptive, for they provide the basis for social relationships that infants form during the rest of the first year, which we'll examine in Chapter 5. And there's a practical benefit as well: If you see a giant ape in New York City and wonder whether it's really King Kong or an imposter, you'll know to ask a 6-month-old.

INTEGRATING SENSORY INFORMATION

So far, we have discussed infants' sensory systems separately. In reality, of course, most infant experiences are better described as "multimedia events." For example, a nursing mother provides visual and taste cues to her baby. A rattle stimulates vision, hearing, and touch. In fact, much stimulation is not specific to one sense but spans multiple senses. Temporal information, such as duration or tempo, can be seen or heard. For example, you can detect the rhythm of a person clapping by seeing the hands meet or by hearing the sound of hands striking. Similarly, the texture of a surface—whether it's rough or smooth—can be detected by sight or by feel.

Infants readily perceive many of these relations. For example, infants can recognize visually an object that they have only touched previously. Similarly, they can detect relations between information presented visually and auditorily. They know, for example, that an object moving into the distance looks smaller and is harder to hear (Bahrick & Lickliter, 2002). And they can link the temporal properties of visual and auditory stimulation, such as duration and rhythm (Lewkowicz, 2000a).

Traditionally, coordinating information from different senses (e.g., vision with hearing, vision with touch) was thought to be a challenging task for infants. *More recently, however, some researchers have argued that the infant's sensory systems are particularly attuned to **intersensory redundancy,** that is, to information that is presented simultaneously to different sensory modes* (Bahrick & Lickliter, 2002). Perception is best when information is presented redundantly to multiple senses. When an infant sees and hears the mother clapping (visual, auditory information), he focuses on the information conveyed to both senses and pays less attention to information that's only available in one sense, such as the color of the mother's nail polish or the sounds of her humming along with the tune. Or the infant can learn that the mom's lips are chapped from seeing the flaking skin and by feeling the roughness as the mother kisses him. According to intersensory redundancy

A mother who breast-feeds provides her baby with a multimedia event: the baby sees, smells, hears, feels, and tastes her!

Getty Images

theory, it's as if infants follow the rule "Any information that's presented in multiple senses must be important, so pay attention to it!"

Integrating information from different senses is yet another variation on the theme that has dominated this module: Infants' sensory and perceptual skills are impressive. Darla's newborn daughter, from the opening vignette, can definitely smell, taste, and feel pain. She can distinguish sounds, and at about 7 months she will use sound to locate objects. Her vision is a little blurry now but will improve rapidly; in a few months, she'll see the full range of colors and perceive depth. In short, Darla's daughter, like most infants, is exceptionally well prepared to begin to make sense out of her environment.

TEST YOURSELF

1. Infants respond negatively to substances that taste sour or _____.

2. Infants respond to _____ with a high-pitched cry that is hard to soothe.

3. If an infant seated in a completely darkened room hears the sound of her favorite rattle nearby, she will reach for it; this demonstrates _____.

4. At age _____, infants' acuity is like that of an adult with normal vision.

5. _____ are specialized neurons in the retina that are sensitive to color.

6. The term _____ refers to the fact that images of an object in the left and right eyes differ for nearby objects.

7. When elements consistently move together, infants decide that they are _____.

8. Infants readily integrate information from different senses, and their sensory systems seem to be particularly attuned to _____.

What features of infants' perceptual skills show the influence of nature? What features show the influence of nurture?

Answers: (1) bitter, (2) pain, (3) the use of sound to judge distances, (4) 1 year, (5) Cones, (6) retinal disparity, (7) part of the same object, (8) information presented redundantly to multiple senses

---

3.5

BECOMING SELF-AWARE

LEARNING OBJECTIVES

When do children begin to realize that they exist?

What are toddlers' and preschoolers' self-concepts like?

When do preschool children begin to acquire a theory of mind?

When Ximena brushes her teeth, she puts her 20-month-old son, Christof, in an infant seat facing the bathroom mirror. She's been doing this for months, and Christof always seems to enjoy looking at the images in the mirror. Lately, he seems to pay special attention to his own reflection. Ximena thinks that sometimes Christof deliberately frowns or laughs just to see what he looks like. Is this possible, Ximena wonders, or is her imagination simply running wild?

AS INFANTS' PHYSICAL, MOTOR, AND PERCEPTUAL SKILLS GROW, they learn more and more about the world around them. As part of this learning, infants and toddlers begin to realize that they exist independently of other people and objects in the environment and that their existence continues over time. In this last section, you'll see how children become self-aware and learn what Christof knows about himself.

ORIGINS OF SELF-CONCEPT

When do children begin to understand that they exist? Measuring the onset of this awareness is not easy. Obviously, we can't simply ask a 3-year-old, "So, tell me, when did you first realize you existed and weren't just part of the furniture?" Investigators need a less direct approach, and a mirror offers one route. Babies sometimes touch the face in the mirror or wave at it, but none of their behaviors indicates that they recognize themselves in the mirror. Instead, babies act as if the face in the mirror is simply a very interesting stimulus.

How would we know that infants recognize themselves in a mirror? One clever approach is to have mothers place a red mark on their infant's nose; they do this surreptitiously, while wiping the baby's face. Then the infant is returned to the mirror. Many 1-year-olds touch the red mark on the mirror, showing that they notice the mark on the face in the mirror. By 15 months, however, an important change occurs: Babies see the red mark in the mirror, then reach up and touch their own noses. By age 2, virtually all children do this (Bullock & Lütkenhaus, 1990; Lewis & Brooks-Gunn, 1979). When these older children notice the red mark in the mirror, they understand that the funny looking nose in the mirror is their own!

We don't need to rely solely on the mirror task to know that self-awareness emerges between 18 and 24 months. During this same period, toddlers look more at photographs of themselves than at photos of other children. They also refer to themselves by name or with a personal pronoun, such as "I" or "me," and sometimes they know their age and their gender. These changes, which often occur together, suggest that self-awareness is well established in most children by age 2 (Lewis & Ramsay, 2004; Pinquart, 2005).

Soon toddlers and young children begin to recognize continuity in the self over time; the "I" in the present is linked to the "I" in the past (Nelson, 2001). Awareness of a self that is extended in time is fostered by conversations with parents about the past and the future. Through such conversations, a 3-year-old celebrating a birthday understands that she's an older version of the same person who had a birthday a year previously.

Children's growing awareness of a self extended in time is also revealed by their understanding of ownership (Fasig, 2000). When a toddler sees his favorite toy and says "mine," this implies awareness of continuity of the self over time: "In the past, I played with that." And when toddlers say "Mine!" they are often not being aggressive or selfish; instead, "mine" is a way of indicating ownership and in the process defining themselves. They are not trying to deny the toy to another but simply saying that playing with this toy is part of who they are (Levine, 1983).

Not until 15 to 18 months of age do babies recognize themselves in the mirror, which is an important step in becoming self-aware.

Once children fully understand that they exist, they begin to wonder who they are. They want to define themselves. Throughout the preschool years, possessions continue to be one of the ways in which children define themselves. Preschoolers are also likely to mention physical characteristics ("I have blue eyes"), their preferences ("I like spaghetti"), and their competencies ("I can count to 50"). What these features have in common is a focus on a child's characteristics that are observable and concrete (Damon & Hart, 1988).

As children enter school, their self-concepts become even more elaborate (Harter, 1994), changes that we'll explore in Chapter 9.

THEORY OF MIND

As youngsters gain more insights into themselves as thinking beings, they begin to realize that people have thoughts, beliefs, and intentions. They also understand that thoughts, beliefs, and intentions often cause people to behave as they do. Amazingly, even infants understand that people's behavior is often intentional—designed to achieve a goal.

Preschool children use their toys to define themselves; saying "Mine" is shorthand for "This is my doll and I like to play with dolls a lot!"

Imagine a father who says, "Where are the crackers?" in front of his 1-year-old daughter, then begins opening kitchen cabinets, moving some objects to look behind them. Finding the box of crackers, he says, "There they are!" An infant who understands intentionality would realize how her father's actions—searching, moving objects—were related to the goal —finding the crackers.

Many clever experiments have revealed that 1-year-olds do indeed have this understanding of intentionality (Sommerville & Woodward, 2005). For example, in one study (Meltzoff, 1995) 18-month-olds watched an experimenter perform an action but fail to achieve an apparent goal. The experimenter might, for example, look as if she wanted to drop a bead necklace in a jar but instead it falls onto the table. Or an experimenter looks as if she wants to use a stick to push a button, but she misses. When 18-month-olds were given the same objects, they typically imitated the experimenter's intended action— placing the necklace in the jar or pushing the button—not what she really did. Infants' interpretations emphasized what the actions were to accomplish, not the actions per se.

From this early understanding of intentionality, young children's naïve psychology expands rapidly. *Between 2 and 5, children develop a* **theory of mind,** *a naïve understanding of the relations between mind and behavior.* One of the leading researchers on theory of mind, Henry Wellman (1993, 2002), believes that children's theory of mind moves through three phases during the preschool years. In the earliest phase, 2-year-olds are aware of desires and often speak of their wants and likes, as in "Lemme see" or "I wanna sit." And they often link their desires to their behavior, such as "I happy there more cookies" (Wellman, 1993). Thus, by age 2 children understand that people have desires and that desires can cause behavior.

By about age 3, children clearly distinguish the mental world from the physical world. For example, if told about a girl who has a cookie and another who is thinking about a cookie, 3-year-olds know that only the first girl can see, touch, and eat her cookie (Harris et al., 1991). And, most 3-year-olds use "mental verbs" like "think," "believe," "remember," and "forget," which suggests that they have a beginning understanding of different mental states (Bartsch & Wellman, 1995). Although 3-year-olds talk about thoughts and beliefs, they nevertheless emphasize desires when trying to explain why people act as they do.

Not until 4 years of age do mental states really take center stage in children's understanding of their and others' actions. That is, by age 4, children understand that behavior is often based on a person's beliefs about events and situations, even when those beliefs are wrong. This developmental transformation is particularly evident when children are tested on false-belief tasks such as the one shown in Figure 3.14. In all false-belief tasks, a situation is set up so that the child being tested has accurate information but someone else does not. For example, in the story in Figure 3.14, the child being tested knows the ball is really in the box, but Sally, the girl in the story, believes that the ball is still in the basket. Remarkably, although 4-year-olds correctly say that Sally will look for the ball in the basket (acting on her false belief), most 3-year-olds claim that she will look for the ball in the box. The 4-year-olds understand that Sally's behavior is based on her beliefs, despite the fact that her beliefs are incorrect (Frye, 1993).

This basic developmental progression is remarkably robust. Wellman, Cross, and Watson (2001) conducted a meta-analysis of approximately 175 studies in which more than 4,000 young children were tested on false-belief tasks. Before 3½ years, children typically make the false-belief error: Attributing their own knowledge of the ball's location to Sally, they say she will search in the correct location. Yet six short months later, children now understand that Sally's false belief will cause her to look for the ball in the box. This rapid developmental transition from incorrect to correct performance is unaffected by many procedural variables (e.g., whether Sally is a doll, a picture, a person in a videotape, or a real person) and is much the same whether the children are from Europe, North America, Africa, or Asia.

■ **Figure 3.14**
Most 3-year-olds say that Sally will look for the ball in the box, showing that they do not understand how people can act on their beliefs (where the ball is) even when those beliefs are wrong.

Thus, this pattern signifies a fundamental change in children's understanding of the centrality of beliefs in a person's thinking about the world. By age 4 children "realize that people not only have thoughts and beliefs, but also that thoughts and beliefs are crucial to explaining why people do things; that is, actors' pursuits of their desires are inevitably shaped by their beliefs about the world" (Bartsch & Wellman, 1995, p. 144).

Preschoolers understand false belief at a younger age if they have older siblings (Ruffman et al., 1998). During play, older brothers and sisters often talk with their younger siblings about internal states—who is happy or sad and why—and these conversations may help youngsters to see the link between beliefs and behavior.

You can see preschool children's growing understanding of false belief in the Real People feature.

THINK ABOUT IT

Suppose you believe that a theory of mind develops faster when preschoolers spend much time with other children. What sort of correlational study would you devise to test this hypothesis? How could you do an experimental study to test the same hypothesis?

REAL PEOPLE: Applying Human Development

"SEEING IS BELIEVING . . ." FOR 3-YEAR-OLDS

Preschoolers gradually recognize that people's behavior is sometimes guided by mistaken beliefs. We once witnessed an episode at a day care center that documented this growing understanding. After lunch, Karen, a 2-year-old, saw ketchup on the floor and squealed, "blood, blood!" Lonna, a 3-year-old, said in a disgusted tone, "It's not blood—it's ketchup." Then, Shenan, a 4-year-old, interjected, "Yeah, but Karen *thought* it was blood." A similar incident took place a few weeks later, on the day after Halloween. This time Lonna put on a monster mask and scared Karen. When Karen began to cry, Lonna said, "Oh stop. It's just a mask." Shenan broke in again, saying, "You know it's just a mask. But she *thinks* it's a monster." In both cases, only Shenan understood that Karen's behavior was based on her beliefs (that the ketchup is blood and that the monster is real), even though her beliefs were false.

Preschool children's growing knowledge of the mind is not an isolated accomplishment. This understanding is simply part of the profound cognitive growth that occurs during the preschool years. We'll examine this cognitive growth next, in Chapter 4.

TEST YOURSELF

1. Apparently children are first self-aware at age 2 because this is when they first recognize themselves in the mirror and in photographs and when they first use _____.

2. During the preschool years, children's self-concepts emphasize _____, physical characteristics, preferences, and competencies.

3. Unlike 4-year-olds, most 3-year-olds don't understand that other people's behavior is sometimes based on _____.

During the preschool years, children acquire a more sophisticated understanding of the mind. Do you think this change occurs in much the same way in all cultures, or does it vary from one culture to another?

Answers: (1) personal pronouns such as "I" and "me," (2) possessions, (3) false beliefs

Putting It All Together

The first years of life are remarkable. We saw that newborn babies are endowed with reflexes that prepare them well for life outside of the uterus and that their behavior is already well organized into a number of distinct states. We learned that physical growth is extraordinarily rapid but can be slowed when children are malnourished. Different regions of the infant's brain are already regulating distinct functions, such as goal-directed behavior. This pattern of specialization helps to explain the impact of Martin's injury on his language skills.

We also looked at improvements in motor skills. Infants gradually become more mobile during the first year.

Most begin to walk soon after their first birthday, reflecting biological maturation and integration of the different component skills involved in walking. Paralleling changes in locomotion are changes in fine motor skills: During the first year, infants become more skilled at grasping and manipulating objects.

We saw that infants are endowed with powerful perceptual skills. Even newborn babies can smell, taste, feel, hear, and see—in some cases with remarkable accuracy. Finally, we discovered that children gradually become self-aware and understand that others think too.

Summary

3.1 The Newborn

The Newborn's Reflexes

■ Babies are born with a number of different reflexes. Some help them adjust to life outside of the uterus, some help protect them from danger, and some serve as the basis for later voluntary motor behavior.

Assessing the Newborn

■ The Apgar scale measures five vital signs to determine a newborn baby's physical well-being. The Neonatal Behavioral Assessment Scale provides a comprehensive evaluation of a baby's behavioral and physical status.

The Newborn's States

■ Newborns spend their day in one of four states: alert inactivity, waking activity, crying, and sleeping. A newborn's crying includes a basic cry, a mad cry, and a pain cry. The best way to calm a crying baby is by putting it on the shoulder and rocking.

■ Newborns spend approximately two thirds of every day asleep and go through a complete sleep-wake cycle once every 4 hours. By 3 or 4 months, babies sleep through the night. Newborns spend about half of their time asleep in REM sleep, an active form of sleep that may stimulate growth in the nervous system. Sleep-related problems include nightmares, night terrors, sleepwalking, and bedwetting.

- Some healthy babies die from sudden infant death syndrome. Factors that contribute to SIDS are prematurity, low birth weight, and smoking. Also, babies are vulnerable to SIDS when they sleep on their stomach and when they are overheated. The goal of the Back to Sleep campaign is to prevent SIDS by encouraging parents to have infants sleep on their backs.

Temperament

- Temperament refers to a consistent style or pattern to an infant's behavior. Modern theories list two to six dimensions of temperament, including, for example, activity level and positive affect. Temperament is influenced by both heredity and environment and is a reasonably stable characteristic of infants and young children.

3.2 Physical Development

Growth of the Body

- Physical growth is particularly rapid during infancy, but babies of the same age differ considerably in their height and weight. Size at maturity is largely determined by heredity.

- Growth follows the cephalocaudal principle, in which the head and trunk develop before the legs. Consequently, infants and young children have disproportionately large heads and trunks.

- Infants must consume a large number of calories, relative to their body weight, primarily because of the energy required for growth. Breast-feeding and bottle-feeding both provide babies with adequate nutrition.

- Malnutrition is a worldwide problem that is particularly harmful during infancy, when growth is so rapid. Treating malnutrition adequately requires improving children's diets and training their parents to provide stimulating environments.

The Emerging Nervous System

- A nerve cell, called a neuron, includes a cell body, a dendrite, and an axon. The mature brain consists of billions of neurons, organized into nearly identical left and right hemispheres connected by the corpus callosum. The cerebral cortex regulates most of the functions we think of as distinctively human. The frontal cortex is associated with personality and goal-directed behavior; the left hemisphere of the cortex with language; and the right hemisphere of the cortex

with nonverbal processes such as perceiving music and regulating emotions.

- The brain specializes early in development; during infancy, the left hemisphere is specialized for language, the right hemisphere is specialized for some forms of spatial processing, and the frontal cortex is specialized for emotionality.

- The brain is moderately plastic. Most brains are organized in much the same way, but following a brain injury, cognitive processes are sometimes transferred to undamaged neurons.

3.3 Moving and Grasping—Early Motor Skills

Locomotion

- Infants acquire a series of locomotor skills during their first year, culminating in walking a few months after the first birthday. Like most motor skills, learning to walk involves differentiation of individual skills, such as maintaining balance and using the legs alternately, and then integrating these skills into a coherent whole.

Fine Motor Skills

- Infants first use only one hand at a time, then both hands independently, then both hands in common actions, and, finally, at about 5 months of age, both hands in different actions with a common purpose.

- Most people are right-handed, a preference that emerges after the first birthday and becomes well established during the preschool years. Handedness is determined by heredity but can also be influenced by cultural values.

3.4 Coming to Know the World: Perception

Smell, Taste, and Touch

- Newborns are able to smell, and some can recognize their mother's odor; they also taste, preferring sweet substances and responding negatively to bitter and sour tastes.

- Infants respond to touch. They probably experience pain because their responses to painful stimuli are similar to those of older children.

Hearing

- Babies can hear. More important, they can distinguish different sounds and use sound to locate objects in space.

Seeing

- A newborn's visual acuity is relatively poor, but 1-year-olds can see as well as an adult with normal vision. Color vision develops as different sets of cones begin to function, a process that seems to be complete by 3 or 4 months of age. Infants perceive depth, based on kinetic cues, retinal disparity, and pictorial cues. They also use motion to recognize objects. Infants are particularly attracted to faces, but whether this reflects special face-processing mechanisms is uncertain.

Integrating Sensory Information

■ Infants coordinate information from different senses. They can recognize, by sight, an object they've felt previously. Infants are often particularly attentive to information presented redundantly to multiple senses.

3.5 Becoming Self-Aware

Origins of Self-Concept

■ Beginning at about 15 months, infants begin to recognize themselves in the mirror, which is one of the first signs of self-recognition. They also begin to prefer to look at pictures of themselves, begin to refer to themselves by name (or use personal pronouns), and sometimes know their age and gender. Evidently, by 2 years of age most children are self-aware.

■ Preschoolers often define themselves in terms of observable characteristics, such as possessions, physical characteristics, preferences, and competencies.

Theory of Mind

■ Theory of mind, which refers to a person's ideas about connections between thoughts, beliefs, intentions, and behavior, develops rapidly during the preschool years. Most 2-year-olds know that people have desires and that desires can cause behavior. By age 3, children distinguish the mental world from the physical world but still emphasize desire in explaining others' actions. By age 4, however, children understand that behavior is based on beliefs about the world, even when those beliefs are wrong.

Key Terms

reflexes (88)
alert inactivity (90)
waking activity (90)
crying (90)
sleeping (90)
basic cry (90)
mad cry (90)
pain cry (90)
irregular or rapid-eye-movement (REM) sleep (91)
regular (nonREM) sleep (91)
nightmares (92)
night terrors (92)
sleepwalking (92)
sudden infant death syndrome (SIDS) (92)
temperament (93)
malnourished (99)
neuron (100)

cell body (100)
dendrite (100)
axon (100)
terminal button (100)
neurotransmitter (100)
cerebral cortex (100)
hemispheres (100)
corpus callosum (101)
frontal cortex (101)
neural plate (101)
myelin (101)
synaptic pruning (102)
electroencephalogram (EEG) (103)
functional magnetic resonance imaging (fMRI) (103)
neuroplasticity (104)
motor skills (105)
locomote (106)
fine motor skills (106)

toddling (107)
toddler (107)
dynamic systems theory (107)
differentiation (108)
integration (108)
perception (112)
visual acuity (114)
cones (115)
visual cliff (115)
kinetic cues (116)
visual expansion (116)
motion parallax (116)
retinal disparity (116)
pictorial cues (116)
linear perspective (116)
texture gradient (116)
intersensory redundancy (121)
theory of mind (124)

Learn More About It

Readings

ACREDOLO, L., & GOODWYN, S. (2000). *Baby minds: Brain-building games your baby will love.* New York: Bantam. The authors, both child psychologists, use modern research on child development as the basis for techniques and activities that foster children's cognitive development.

BRAZELTON, T. B., & GREENSPAN, S. I. (2000). *The irreducible needs of children: What every child must have to grow, learn, and flourish.* Cambridge, MA: Perseus.

The first author is a famous pediatrician and creator of the Neonatal Behavioral Assessment Scale (NBAS); the second author is a well-known child psychiatrist. Together they outline what they see as the basic needs of children, then show how modern society often does not meet these needs.

ELIOT, L. (1999). *What's going on in there? How the brain and mind develop in the first five years of life.* New York: Bantam. The author, a neurobiologist, provides a comprehensive but readable account of the development of the brain and of the senses.

KOPP, C. (2003). *Baby steps: The "whys" of your child's behavior in the first two years* (2nd ed.). New York: Henry Holt. As the title indicates, this book is not only about newborns. However, we recommend the book because the author begins with newborn babies and traces the changes that occur in physical, motor, mental, and socioemotional development.

Websites

Visit the Human Development book companion website for all URLs.

- **The Human Development Book Companion Website**
  See **http://www.psychology.wadsworth.com/kail_cavanaugh4e/** for practice quiz questions, Internet links, updates, critical thinking exercises, discussion forums, and more. Also accessible from the Wadsworth Psychology Study Center (http://psychology.wadsworth.com).

- **Human Development and Family Science Extension, Ohio State University**
  Visit this website for more information about infants and toddlers.

- **Kidshealth**
  This website, maintained by the Nemours Foundation, has information about children's growth and nutrition.

- **Total Baby Care**
  Pampers (the diaper company) maintains this website, which has information about infant and toddler development.

- **Kids Nutrition**
  The Baylor College of Medicine maintains this website with information about children's nutrition.

- **Society for Neuroscience, "Brain Briefings"**
  The society's website has a feature called "brain briefings," which features newsletters summarizing research findings, including topics related to the developing brain.

Life-Span CD-ROM

For more information on the concepts covered in this chapter, go to

Module 1: Prenatal Development, Birth, and the Newborn

- *The Newborn*

Module 2: Infancy and Toddlerhood

- *Physical Growth and Motor Development*

Module 3: Early and Middle Childhood

- *Physical Growth and Motor Development*

http://www.thomsonedu.com
Go to this site for the link to ThomsonNOW, your one-stop study shop. Take a pre-test for this chapter, and ThomsonNOW will generate a personalized study plan based on your test results. The study plan will identify the topics you need to review and direct you to online resources to help you master those topics. You can then take a post-test to help you determine the concepts you have mastered and what you still need to work on.

4.1 The Onset of Thinking: Piaget's Account
Basic Principles of Cognitive Development
Sensorimotor Thinking
Preoperational Thinking

REAL PEOPLE: APPLYING HUMAN DEVELOPMENT: Christine, Egocentrism, and Animism

SPOTLIGHT ON RESEARCH: Finding Toys in a Shrunken Room

Evaluating Piaget's Theory
Extending Piaget's Account: Children's Naive Theories

4.2 Information Processing During Infancy and Early Childhood
General Principles of Information Processing
Attention
Learning
Memory

CURRENT CONTROVERSIES: Preschoolers on the Witness Stand

Learning Number Skills

4.3 Mind and Culture: Vygotsky's Theory
The Zone of Proximal Development
Scaffolding
Private Speech

4.4 Language
The Road to Speech
First Words and Many More
Speaking in Sentences: Grammatical Development
Communicating With Others

Putting It All Together

Summary

Key Terms

Learn More About It

CHAPTER 4

The Emergence of Thought and Language

Cognitive Development in Infancy and Early Childhood

O n the TV show *Family Guy,* Stewie is a 1-year-old who can't stand his mother (Stewie: "Hey, mother, I come bearing a gift. I'll give you a hint. It's in my diaper and it's not a toaster.") and hopes to dominate the world. Much of the humor, of course, turns on the idea that babies are capable of sophisticated thinking—they just can't express it. But what thoughts *do* lurk in the mind of an infant who is not yet speaking? How does cognition develop during infancy and early childhood? What makes these changes possible?

These questions provide the focus of this chapter. We begin with what has long been considered the definitive account of cognitive development, Jean Piaget's theory. In this theory, thinking progresses through four distinct stages between infancy and adulthood.

The next two sections of the chapter concern alternative accounts of cognitive development. One account, the information-processing perspective, traces children's emerging cognitive skills in many specific domains, among them memory skills. The other, Lev Vygotsky's theory, emphasizes the cultural origins of cognitive development and explains why children sometimes talk to themselves as they play or work.

Throughout development, children express their thoughts in oral and written language. In the last section of this chapter, you'll see how children master the sounds, words, and grammar of their native language.

4.1

THE ONSET OF THINKING: PIAGET'S ACCOUNT

Three-year-old Jamila loves talking to her grandmother ("Gram") on the telephone. Sometimes these conversations are not very successful because Gram asks questions and Jamila replies by nodding her head "yes" or "no." Jamila's dad has explained that Gram (and others on the phone) can't see her nodding—that she needs to say "yes" or "no." But Jamila invariably returns to head-nodding. Her dad can't see why such a bright and talkative child doesn't realize that nodding is meaningless over the phone.

LEARNING OBJECTIVES

According to Piaget, how do assimilation, accommodation, and organization provide the foundation for cognitive development throughout the life span?

How do schemes become more advanced as infants progress through the sensorimotor stage?

What are the distinguishing characteristics of thinking during the preoperational stage?

What are some of the shortcomings of Piaget's account of cognitive development?

W HY DOES JAMILA INSIST ON NODDING HER HEAD when she's talking on the phone? This behavior is quite typical according to the famous Swiss psychologist, Jean Piaget (1896–1980). In Piaget's theory, children's thinking progresses through four qualitatively different stages. In this section, we'll begin by describing some of the general features of Piaget's theory, then examine Piaget's account of thinking during infancy and during the preschool years, and, finally, consider some of the strengths and weaknesses of the theory.

BASIC PRINCIPLES OF COGNITIVE DEVELOPMENT

Piaget believed that children are naturally curious. They constantly want to make sense of their experience and, in the process, construct their understanding of the world. For Piaget, children at all ages are like scientists in that they create theories about how the world works. Of course, children's theories are often incomplete. Nevertheless, children's theories are valuable to them because they make the world seem more predictable.

According to Piaget, children understand the world with **schemes,** *psychological structures that organize experience.* Schemes are mental categories of related events, objects, and knowledge. During infancy, most schemes are based on actions. That is, infants group objects based on the actions they can perform on them. For example, infants suck and grasp, and they use these actions to create categories of objects that can be sucked and objects that can be grasped.

Schemes are just as important after infancy, but they are now based primarily on functional or conceptual relationships, not action. For example, preschoolers learn that forks, knives, and spoons form a functional category of "things I use to eat." Or they learn that dogs, cats, and goldfish form a conceptual category of "pets."

Like preschoolers, older children and adolescents have schemes based on functional and conceptual schemes. But they also have schemes that are based on increasingly abstract properties. For example, an adolescent might put fascism, racism, and sexism in a category of "ideologies I despise."

Thus, schemes of related objects, events, and ideas are present throughout development. But as children develop, their rules for creating schemes shift from physical activity to functional, conceptual, and, later, abstract properties of objects, events, and ideas.

Assimilation and Accommodation

Schemes change constantly, adapting to children's experiences. In fact, intellectual adaptation involves two processes working together: assimilation and accommodation. *Assimilation occurs when new experiences are readily incorporated into existing schemes.*

Imagine a baby who has the familiar grasping scheme. She will soon discover that the grasping scheme also works well on blocks, toy cars, and other small objects. Extending the existing grasping scheme to new objects illustrates assimilation. ***Accommodation*** *occurs when schemes are modified based on experience.* Soon the infant learns that some objects can only be lifted with two hands and that some can't be lifted at all. Changing the scheme so that it works for new objects (e.g., using two hands to grasp heavy objects) illustrates accommodation.

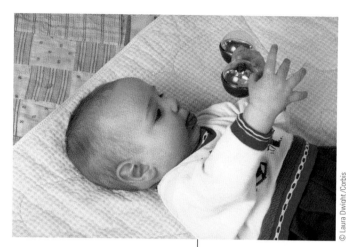

This baby will learn that many objects can be grasped easily with one hand—illustrating assimilation—but will also discover that bigger, heavier objects can be grasped only with two hands—illustrating accommodation.

Assimilation and accommodation are often easier to understand when you remember Piaget's belief that infants, children, and adolescents create theories to try to understand events and objects around them. The infant whose theory is that objects can be lifted with one hand finds that her theory is confirmed when she tries to pick up small objects, but she's in for a surprise when she tries to pick up a heavy book. The unexpected result forces the infant, like a good scientist, to revise her theory to include this new finding.

Equilibration and Stages of Cognitive Development

Assimilation and accommodation are usually in balance, or equilibrium. Children find that many experiences are readily assimilated into their existing schemes but that they sometimes need to accommodate their schemes to adjust to new experiences. This balance between assimilation and accommodation is illustrated by the baby with the theory about lifting objects. Periodically, however, this balance is upset, and a state of disequilibrium results. That is, children discover that their current schemes are not adequate because they are spending much time accommodating and much less time assimilating. *When disequilibrium occurs, children reorganize their schemes to return to a state of equilibrium, a process that Piaget called* ***equilibration.*** To restore the balance, current but now-outmoded ways of thinking are replaced by a qualitatively different, more advanced set of schemes.

One way to understand equilibration is to return to the metaphor of the child as a scientist. As we discussed in Chapter 1, good scientific theories readily explain some phenomena but usually must be revised to explain others. Children's theories allow them to understand many experiences by predicting, for example, what will happen ("It's morning, so it's time for breakfast") or who will do what ("Mom's gone to work, so Dad will take me to school"), but the theories must be modified when predictions go awry ("Dad thinks I'm old enough to walk to school, so he won't take me").

Sometimes scientists find that their theories contain critical flaws that can't be fixed simply by revising; instead, they must create a new theory that draws upon the older theory but is fundamentally different. For example, when the astronomer Copernicus realized that the earth-centered theory of the solar system was fundamentally wrong, his new theory built on the assumption that the sun is the center of the solar system. In much the same way, periodically children reach states in which their current theories seem to be wrong much of the time, so they abandon these theories in favor of more advanced ways of thinking about their physical and social worlds.

According to Piaget, these revolutionary changes in thought occur three times over the life span, at approximately 2, 7, and 11 years of age. This divides cognitive development into the following four stages:

Period of Development	Age Range
Sensorimotor period	Infancy (0–2 years)
Preoperational period	Preschool and early elementary school years (2–7 years)
Concrete operational period	Middle and late elementary school years (7–11 years)
Formal operational period	Adolescence and adulthood (11 years and up)

The ages listed are only approximate. Some youngsters move through the periods more rapidly than others, depending on their ability and their experience. However, the only route to formal operations—the most sophisticated type of thought—is through the first three periods, in sequence. Sensorimotor thinking always gives rise to preoperational thinking; a child cannot "skip" preoperational thinking and move directly from the sensorimotor to the concrete operational period.

In the next few pages of this chapter, we consider Piaget's account of sensorimotor and preoperational thinking, the periods from birth to approximately 7 years of age. In Chapter 6, we will return to Piaget's theory to examine his account of concrete and formal operational thinking in older children and adolescents.

SENSORIMOTOR THINKING

Piaget (1951, 1952, 1954) believed that the first 2 years of life form a distinct phase in human development. *The **sensorimotor period**, from birth to roughly 2 years of age, is the first of Piaget's four periods of cognitive development.* In the 24 months of this stage, infants' thinking progresses remarkably along three important fronts.

Adapting to and Exploring the Environment

Newborns respond reflexively to many stimuli, but between 1 and 4 months reflexes are first modified by experience. An infant may inadvertently touch his lips with his thumb, thereby initiating sucking and the pleasing sensations associated with sucking. Later, the infant tries to re-create these sensations by guiding his thumb to his mouth. Sucking no longer occurs only reflexively when a mother places a nipple at the infant's mouth; instead, the infant has found a way to initiate sucking himself.

At about 8 months, infants reach a watershed: the onset of deliberate, intentional behavior. For the first time, the "means" and "end" of activities are distinct. If, for example, a father places his hand in front of a toy, an infant will move his hand to be able to play with the toy. "The moving the hand" scheme is the means to achieve the goal of "grasping the toy." Using one action as a means to achieve another end is the first indication of purposeful, goal-directed behavior during infancy.

Beginning at about 12 months, infants become active experimenters. An infant may deliberately shake a number of different objects trying to discover which produce sounds and which do not. Or an infant may decide to drop different objects to see what happens. An infant will discover that stuffed animals land quietly, whereas bigger toys often make a more satisfying "clunk" when they hit the ground. These actions represent a significant extension of intentional behavior; now babies repeat actions with different objects solely for the purpose of seeing what will happen.

Understanding Objects

Objects fill the world. Some, including dogs, spiders, and college students, are animate; others, including cheeseburgers, socks, and this textbook, are inanimate. But they all share a fundamental property—they exist independently of our actions and thoughts toward them. Much as we may dislike spiders, they still exist when we close our eyes or wish they would go away. *Piaget's term for this understanding that objects exist independently is **object permanence**.* And Piaget made the astonishing claim that infants lacked this understanding for much of the first year. That is, he proposed that an infant's understanding of objects could be summarized as "out of sight, out of mind." For infants, objects are ephemeral, existing when in sight and no longer existing when out of sight.

Piaget concluded that infants have little understanding of objects. If a tempting object such as an attractive toy is placed in front of a 4- to 8-month-old, the infant will probably reach and grasp the object. If, however, the object is then hidden by a barrier or covered with a cloth, the infant will neither reach nor search. Instead, the infant seems to lose all interest in the object, as if the now hidden object no longer exists. Paraphrasing the familiar phrase, "out of sight, out of existence!"

Beginning at about 8 months, infants search for an object that an experimenter has covered with a cloth. In fact, many 8- to 12-month-olds love to play this game—an adult covers the object and the infant sweeps away the cover, laughing and smiling all the while! But despite this accomplishment, their understanding of object permanence remains incomplete according to Piaget. If 8- to 10-month-olds see an object hidden under one container several times, then see it hidden under a second container, they usually look for the toy under the first container. Piaget claimed that this behavior shows only a fragmentary understanding of objects because infants do not distinguish the object from the actions they use to locate it, such as lifting a particular container.

When interesting toys are covered so that they can't be seen, young babies lose interest, as if "out of sight" means "out of existence."

Piaget argued that not until approximately 18 months do infants have full understanding of object permanence. However, in a few pages, we'll see that infants know more about objects than Piaget claimed.

Using Symbols

By 18 months, most infants have begun to talk and gesture, evidence of the emerging capacity to use symbols. Words and gestures are symbols that stand for something else. When a baby waves, it is just as effective and symbolic as saying "good-bye" to bid farewell. Children also begin to engage in pretend play, another use of symbols. A 20-month-old may move her hand back and forth in front of her mouth, pretending to brush her teeth.

Once infants can use symbols, they can begin to anticipate the consequences of actions mentally instead of having to perform them. Imagine that an infant and parent construct a tower of blocks next to an open door. Leaving the room, a 12- to 18-month-old might close the door, knocking over the tower, because he cannot foresee the outcome of closing the door. But an 18- to 24-month-old can anticipate the consequence of closing the door and move the tower beforehand.

In just 2 years, the infant progresses from reflexive responding to actively exploring the world, understanding objects, and using symbols. These achievements are remarkable and set the stage for preoperational thinking, which we'll examine next.

Toddlers frequently gesture, a sign of their growing competence at using symbols.

PREOPERATIONAL THINKING

Once they have crossed into preoperational thinking, the magical power of symbols is available to young children. Of course, mastering this power is a lifelong process; the preschool child's efforts are tentative and sometimes incorrect (DeLoache, 1995). Piaget identified a number of characteristic shortcomings in preschoolers' fledgling symbolic skills. Let's look at three.

Egocentrism

Preoperational children typically believe that others see the world—both literally and figuratively—exactly as they do. **Egocentrism** *is difficulty in seeing the world from another's outlook.* When youngsters stubbornly cling to their own way, they are not simply being contrary. Preoperational children simply do not comprehend that other people differ in their ideas, convictions, and emotions.

■ **Figure 4.1**
When asked to select the photograph that shows the mountains as the adult sees them, preschool children often select the photograph that shows how the mountain looks to them, demonstrating egocentrism.

One of Piaget's famous experiments, the three-mountains problem, demonstrates preoperational children's egocentrism (Piaget & Inhelder, 1956, chap. 8). Youngsters were seated at a table like the one shown in Figure 4.1. When preoperational children were asked to choose the photograph that corresponded to another person's view of the mountains, they usually picked the photograph that showed their own view of the mountains, not the other person's. Preoperational youngsters evidently suppose that the mountains are seen the same way by all; they presume that theirs is the only view, not one of many conceivable views. According to Piaget, only concrete operational children fully understand that all people do not experience an event in exactly the same way.

Recall that in the vignette, 3-year-old Jamila nods her head during phone conversations with her grandmother. This, too, reflects preoperational egocentrism. Jamila assumes that because she is aware that her head is moving up and down (or side-to-side), her grandmother must be aware of it too. In the Real People feature, we see yet another manifestation of this egocentrism.

 ## REAL PEOPLE: Applying Human Development

CHRISTINE, EGOCENTRISM, AND ANIMISM

Because of their egocentrism, preoperational youngsters often attribute their own thoughts and feelings to others. *They may even credit inanimate objects with life and lifelike properties, a phenomenon known as* **animism** (Piaget, 1929). A 3½-year-old we know, Christine, illustrated this in a conversation we had with her recently on a dreary, rainy day when she was forced to stay indoors.

CHRISTINE: Mr. Sun is very sad today.
US: Why?
CHRISTINE: Because it's cloudy. He can't shine. And he can't see me!
US: That's too bad.
CHRISTINE: Trike [tricycle] is sad too.
US: Why is that?
CHRISTINE: Because I can't ride him. And because he's all alone in the garage, where it's dark.

Caught up in her egocentrism, preoperational Christine believes that objects like the sun and her tricycle think and feel as she does. That is, because she has thoughts and feelings, she believes that other people and inanimate objects have them too.

Centration

A second characteristic of preoperational thinking is that children seem to have the psychological equivalent of tunnel vision: They often concentrate on one aspect of a problem but totally ignore other, equally relevant aspects. *Centration* *is Piaget's term for this narrowly focused thought that characterizes preoperational youngsters.*

Piaget demonstrated centration in his experiments involving conservation. In the conservation experiments, Piaget wanted to determine when children realize that important characteristics of objects (or sets of objects) stay the same despite changes in their physical appearance. Some tasks that Piaget used to study conservation are shown in Figure 4.2. Each begins with identical objects (or sets of objects). Then one of the objects (or sets) is transformed, and children are asked if the objects are the same in terms of some important feature.

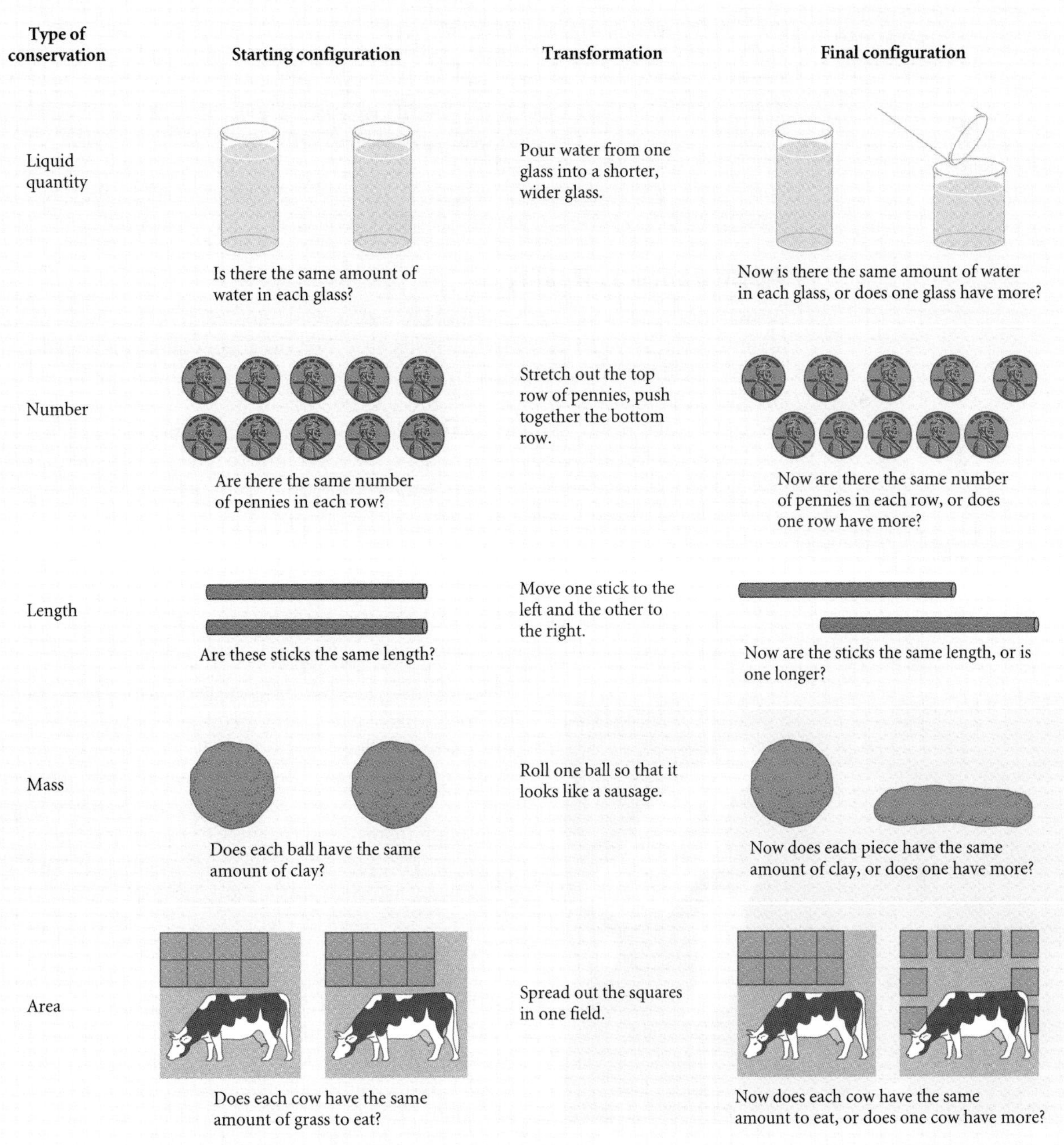

■ **Figure 4.2**
Children in the preoperational stage of development typically have difficulty solving conservation problems, in which important features of an object (or objects) stay the same despite changes in physical appearance.

Type of conservation	Starting configuration	Transformation	Final configuration
Liquid quantity	Is there the same amount of water in each glass?	Pour water from one glass into a shorter, wider glass.	Now is there the same amount of water in each glass, or does one glass have more?
Number	Are there the same number of pennies in each row?	Stretch out the top row of pennies, push together the bottom row.	Now are there the same number of pennies in each row, or does one row have more?
Length	Are these sticks the same length?	Move one stick to the left and the other to the right.	Now are the sticks the same length, or is one longer?
Mass	Does each ball have the same amount of clay?	Roll one ball so that it looks like a sausage.	Now does each piece have the same amount of clay, or does one have more?
Area	Does each cow have the same amount of grass to eat?	Spread out the squares in one field.	Now does each cow have the same amount to eat, or does one cow have more?

In conservation problems, preschool children typically do not believe that the quantity of a liquid remains the same when it is poured into a taller, more slender beaker.

A typical conservation problem involves conservation of liquid quantity. Children are shown identical beakers filled with the same amount of juice. After children agree that the two beakers have the same amount of juice, the juice is poured from one beaker into a taller, thinner beaker. The juice looks different in the tall, thin beaker—it rises higher—but of course the amount is unchanged. Nevertheless, preoperational children claim that the tall, thin beaker has more juice than the original beaker. (And, if the juice is poured into a wider beaker, they believe it has less.)

What is happening here? According to Piaget, preoperational children center on the level of the juice in the beaker. If the juice is higher after it is poured, preoperational children believe that there must be more juice now than before. Because preoperational thinking is centered, these youngsters ignore the fact that the change in the level of the juice is always accompanied by a change in the diameter of the beaker.

In other conservation problems, preoperational children also tend to focus on only one aspect of the problem. In conservation of number, for example, preoperational children concentrate on the fact that, after the transformation, one row of objects is now longer than the other. In conservation of length, preoperational children concentrate on the fact that, after the transformation, the end of one stick is farther to the right than the end of the other. Preoperational children's centered thinking means that they overlook other parts of the problem that would tell them the quantity is unchanged.

Appearance as Reality

A final feature of preoperational thinking is that preschool children believe an object's appearance tells what the object is really like. For instance, many a 3-year-old has watched with quiet fascination as an older brother or sister put on a ghoulish costume only to erupt in frightened tears when their sibling put on scary makeup. The scary made-up face is reality, not just something that looks frightening but really isn't.

Confusion between appearance and reality is not limited to costumes and masks. It is a general characteristic of preoperational thinking. Consider the following cases where appearances and reality conflict:

For young children, appearance is often reality, so they are frightened when familiar people wear scary masks.

- A boy is angry because a friend is being mean but smiles because he's afraid the friend will leave if he reveals his anger.
- A glass of milk looks brown when seen through sunglasses.
- A piece of hard rubber looks like food (e.g., like a piece of pizza).

Older children and adults know that the boy looks happy, the milk looks brown, and the object looks like food but that the boy is really angry, the milk is really white, and the object is really rubber. Preoperational children, however, confuse appearance and reality, thinking the boy is happy, the milk is brown, and the piece of rubber is edible.

Distinguishing appearance and reality is particularly difficult for children in the early years of preoperational thinking. This difficulty is evident in research on children's use of scale models, which are objects that also symbolize some much larger object. A model of a house, for example, can be an interesting object in its own right as well as a representation of an actual house. The ability to use scale models develops early in the preoperational period. If young children watch an adult hide a toy in a full-size room, then try to find the toy in a scale model of the room that contains all the principal features of the full-scale room (e.g., carpet, window, furniture), 3-year-olds find the hidden toy readily but 2½-year-olds do not (DeLoache, 1995).

Why is this task so easy for 3-year-olds and so difficult for 2½-year-olds? Judy DeLoache believes that 2½-year-olds' "attention to a scale model as an interesting and attractive object makes it difficult for them to simultaneously think about its relation to something else" (DeLoache, Miller, & Rosengren, 1997, p. 308). In other words, for young children the appearance of the object is reality and, consequently, they find it hard to think about the model as a symbol of something else (i.e., the full-size room).

If this argument is correct, 2½-year-olds should be more successful using the model if they don't have to think of it as a symbol for the full-size room. DeLoache tested this hypothesis in the study described in the Spotlight on Research feature. (This is one of our favorite studies of all time, for reasons that will soon be obvious.)

SPOTLIGHT ON RESEARCH

FINDING TOYS IN A SHRUNKEN ROOM

Who were the investigators and what was the aim of the study? Judy De-Loache, Kevin Miller, and Karl Rosengren (1997) believed that 2½-year-olds could not find the toy in the model because it was difficult for them to think of the model as an object *and* as a symbol of the full-size room. To test this argument, they created a condition designed to eliminate the need for children to think of the model as an object and as a symbol. Children were told that a machine could shrink the full-size room. In this case, the model is no longer a symbol of the full-size room; it *is* the room, just shrunken. Consequently, DeLoache and her colleagues expected 2½-year-olds to find the hidden toy because they believed the model was the full-size room shrunken to miniature size.

How did the investigators measure the topic of interest? Some children were tested with the usual procedures: hiding the toy in the full-size room and asking children to find it in the scale model. Other children were tested in the new condition designed to help them find the toy. Children were shown an oscilloscope, which was described as a shrinking machine. They saw a toy doll, "Terry the Troll," placed in front of the oscilloscope; then the experimenter and child left the room briefly while a tape-recorder played sounds that were described as sounds "the machine makes when it's shrinking something." When experimenter and child returned, Terry

When children were led to believe that the oscilloscope was a machine that could shrink a room to the size of a scale model, they were able to find a hidden toy; this shows that children have difficulty thinking of scale models as objects and as symbols of something else.

Judy DeLoache

had shrunk from 8 inches to 2 inches. Next, Terry was hidden in the full-size room, the experimenter aimed the "shrinking machine" at the full-size room, then experimenter and child left the room. While the tape recorder played shrinking sounds, research assistants quickly removed everything from the full-size room and substituted the model. Experimenter and child returned, and the child was asked to find Terry. This procedure was repeated, so that

children searched for Terry on four separate trials.

Who were the children in the study? DeLoache and her colleagues tested 32 children whose average age was 2½ years.

What was the design of the study? The study was experimental. The independent variable was the presence or absence of the shrinking machine. The dependent variable was the percentage of trials on which the children found Terry.

Were there ethical concerns with the study? For children tested with the "shrinking machine," the study involved deception. Parents were fully informed about the shrinking machine before they gave consent, and parents were present throughout the experiment. Immediately after the experiment, children were told that the machine could not really shrink objects. They were shown the model, the full-size room, and both small and large versions of Terry. The deception seemed warranted, and no children seemed upset when they were told what really happened.

What were the results? The top part of Figure 4.3 shows the percentage of trials that children found the toy. Children rarely found the toy in the standard condition, but they did frequently in the "shrinking machine" condition. The bottom part of the graph shows the percentage of children who found Terry on at least three of the four trials. No children in the standard condition were

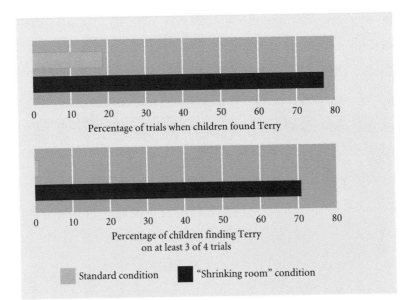

this accurate, but most children in the "shrinking machine" condition were.

What did the investigators conclude? When 2½-year-olds must think of the model as an object *and* as a symbol, they find this very difficult and, consequently, cannot find the hidden toy, even though the model is an exact replica of the full-size room. When children need only think of the model as the original room, but much smaller, they readily find the toy.

What converging evidence would strengthen these conclusions? Because the changes observed by DeLoache and her colleagues appeared across a fairly narrow age range, this would be an ideal opportunity to conduct a microgenetic study: The goal would be to show, for individual children, the age at which they understand the model is a symbol of something else. Additional useful evidence would be to compare the results with other situations in which

an object also serves a symbolic function (e.g., children's understanding that a map is a colorful piece of paper as well as a symbol of a much larger physical space).

To enhance your understanding of this research, go to http://psychology.wadsworth.com/kail_cavanaugh4e/ to complete critical thinking questions and explore related websites.

The appearance of a colorful, interesting object that beckons "come play with me" is reality for 2½-year-olds; they cannot "see through" the model to realize that in this task the model really is a symbol for something else (DeLoache, 2000). Difficulty in distinguishing appearance and reality is a deep-seated characteristic of preoperational thinking (especially in the early years of this stage), as are egocentrism and centration. These defining characteristics of preoperational thought are summarized in Table 4.1.

EVALUATING PIAGET'S THEORY

Because Piaget's theory is so comprehensive, it has stimulated much research. Much of this work supports Piaget's view that children actively try to understand the world around them and organize their knowledge and that cognitive development includes major qualitative changes (Brainerd, 1996; Flavell, 1996).

One important contribution of Piaget's theory is that many teachers and parents have found it a rich source of ideas about ways to foster children's development. In fact, the theory has several straightforward implications for teaching practices that promote cognitive growth:

■ Cognitive growth occurs as children construct their own understanding of the world, so the teacher's role is to create environments where children can

THINK ABOUT IT

Children with low birth weight often have delayed intellectual development. According to Piaget, what form might the delay take?

TABLE 4.1
Characteristics of Preoperational Thinking

Characteristic	Definition	Example
Egocentrism	Child believes that all people see the world as he or she does.	A child gestures during a telephone conversation, not realizing that the listener cannot see the gestures.
Centration	Child focuses on one aspect of a problem or situation but ignores other relevant aspects.	In conservation of liquid quantity, child pays attention to the height of the liquid in the beaker but ignores the diameter of the beaker.
Appearance as reality	Child assumes that an object really is what it appears to be.	Child believes that a person smiling at another person is really happy even though the other person is being mean.

discover for themselves how the world works. A teacher shouldn't simply try to tell children how addition and subtraction are complementary but instead should provide children with materials that allow them to discover the complementarity themselves.

■ Children profit from experience only when they can interpret this experience with their current cognitive structures. It follows, then, that the best teaching experiences are slightly ahead of the children's current level of thinking. As youngsters begin to master basic addition, don't jump right to subtraction but go to slightly more difficult addition problems.

■ Cognitive growth can be particularly rapid when children discover inconsistencies and errors in their own thinking. Teachers should therefore encourage children to look at the consistency of their thinking but then let children take the lead in sorting out the inconsistencies. If a child is making mistakes in borrowing on subtraction problems, a teacher shouldn't correct the error directly but should encourage the child to look at a large number of these errors to discover what he or she is doing wrong.

Despite these important contributions of Piaget's theory, some aspects of his theory have been challenged (Siegler & Alibali, 2005). Let's look at some of the criticisms that have been raised.

Alternative Explanations of Performance

As we have seen, Piaget explained cognitive development by using constructs like accommodation, assimilation, and schemes. However, subsequent researchers have found that children's performance on Piaget's tasks is often better explained by other theoretical constructs. For example, preoperational children's performance on the conservation task appears to reflect, at least in part, their growing sensitivity to the nuances of language, rather than purely their lack of reversibility. The phrasing of the questions concerning the amount of water turns out to be critical (Winer, Craig, & Weinbaum, 1992). Remember that in this procedure, youngsters are twice asked if the amount of water in the two beakers is the same—once before the water is poured and once after. In everyday conversation, a question is usually repeated like this because the answer was wrong the first time. Or it may be repeated because the answer was correct at first but something has changed so that it is now wrong. Both of these rules about questions would lead young children who had answered "yes" to the first question to wonder whether they were wrong and perhaps say "no" the second time. In fact, when the procedure is changed (e.g., by asking the question only once) preschoolers are more likely to answer correctly. Thus, children's performance on conservation problems is based partly on language development, not just the concepts that Piaget included in his theory.

Researchers have also questioned Piaget's studies of infants' understanding of objects (Goubet & Clifton, 1998; Munakata et al., 1997). According to Piaget, one of the milestones of infancy is the understanding that objects exist independently of oneself and one's actions. He claimed that 1- to 4-month-olds—who are in Stage 2 of the sensorimotor period—believe that objects no longer exist when they disappear from view (out of sight, out of mind). As astounding as this may seem, if you take a favorite toy from a 3-month-old and hide it under a cloth directly in front of her, she will not look for it. This is true even though the shape of the toy is clearly visible under the cloth and within reach!

Beginning at about 4 or 5 months, Piaget found that infants will search for objects. Understanding of objects is far from complete, because even older infants are sometimes unable to find hidden objects. If 9-month-olds see an object hidden under one container, then see it hidden under a second container, most of them routinely look for the toy under the first container. Piaget claimed that this showed 9-month-olds' fragmentary understanding of objects. Infants do not distinguish the object per se from the actions they used to locate it, such as lifting a particular container. Not until approximately 18 months of age do infants apparently have full understanding of the permanence of objects.

Investigators have since questioned Piaget's conclusions (Smith et al., 1999). Some fairly minor changes in procedures can affect 8- to 10-month-olds' success on the hidden object task. An infant is more likely to look under the correct container if, for example, the interval between hiding and looking is brief and if the containers are easily distinguished from each other. Therefore, infants who are unsuccessful on this task may be showing poor memory rather than inadequate understanding of the nature of objects (Marcovitch & Zelazo, 1999; Wellman, Cross, & Bartsch, 1986).

In addition, by devising some clever procedures, other investigators have shown that babies understand objects much earlier than Piaget claimed. Renée Baillargeon (1987, 1994), for example, assessed object permanence using the method shown in Figure 4.4. Infants first saw a silver screen that appeared to be rotating back and forth. When they

■ **Figure 4.4**
Infants are surprised to see the silver screen rotate flat, which suggests that they understand the "permanence" of the orange box.

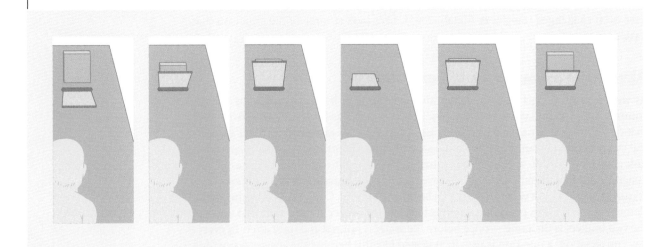

were familiar with this display, one of two new displays was shown. In the *possible event,* a yellow box appeared in a position behind the screen, making it impossible for the screen to rotate as far back as it had previously. Instead, the screen rotated until it made contact with the box, then rotated forward. In the *impossible event,* the yellow box appeared, but the screen continued to rotate as before. The screen rotated back until it was flat, then rotated forward, again revealing the yellow box. The illusion was possible because the box was mounted on a movable platform that allowed it to drop out of the way of the moving screen. However, from the infant's perspective, it appeared as if the box vanished behind the screen, only to reappear.

The disappearance and reappearance of the box violates the idea that objects exist permanently. Consequently, an infant who understands the permanence of objects should find the impossible event a truly novel stimulus and look at it longer than the possible event. Baillargeon found that $4\frac{1}{2}$-month-olds consistently looked longer at the impossible event than the possible event. Infants apparently thought that the impossible event was novel, just as we are surprised when an object vanishes from a magician's scarf.

Evidently, infants have some understanding of the permanence of objects at a much younger age than Piaget's theory would predict. Why the difference? Remember that Piaget usually based his assessments on tasks in which infants had to search for missing objects. Search requires locomotor skills—reaching and grasping, for example—and apparently it is these skills that are limited in younger infants, not their understanding that objects are permanent.

The contrary findings regarding infants' understanding of object permanence and conservation do not mean that Piaget's theory is fundamentally wrong. In some cases, the theory needs to be revised to include important constructs that Piaget overlooked.

Consistency in Performance

In Piaget's view, each stage of intellectual development consists of a unified set of mental structures that pervades children's thinking. For example, preoperational thinking should leave its mark on all of a child's activities. On conservation and three-mountains tasks, a 4-year-old should always respond in a preoperational way: He should claim that the water is not the same after pouring and believe that the other person sees the mountains as he does. In fact, research reveals some consistency in performance on various tasks, but exceptions are common too (Siegler, 1981). A youngster may be advanced on the conservation task, perfectly average on the three-mountains task, and somewhat delayed on other Piagetian tasks. This variability is not readily incorporated into Piaget's view of uniform stages that should leave the same characteristic imprint in all domains.

These criticisms do not mean that Piaget's theory is invalid or should be ignored. As noted earlier, it remains the most complete account of cognitive development. However, in recent years researchers have attempted to round out our understanding of cognitive development, using other theoretical perspectives such as the information-processing approach that is examined later in this chapter.

EXTENDING PIAGET'S ACCOUNT: CHILDREN'S NAIVE THEORIES

Piaget believed that children, like scientists, formulate theories about how the world works. Children's theories are usually called "naive theories" because, unlike real scientific theories, they are not created by specialists and are rarely evaluated by formal experimentation. Naive theories are nevertheless valuable because they allow children (and adults) to understand new experiences and predict future events.

In Piaget's view, children formulate a grand, comprehensive theory that attempts to explain an enormous variety of phenomena, including reasoning about objects, people, and morals, for example, within a common framework. More recent views cling to the idea of children as theorists, but propose that children, like real scientists, develop specialized theories about much narrower areas. *For example, according to the **core knowledge hypothesis,** infants are born with rudimentary knowledge of the world; this knowledge is elaborated based on children's experiences* (Carey & Spelke, 1994). Some of the theories young children first develop concern physics, psychology, and biology. That is, infants and toddlers rapidly develop theories that organize their knowledge about properties of objects, people, and living things (Wellman & Gelman, 1998).

We examined children's developing theory of mind in Chapter 3; in the next few pages, we'll look at children's naive theories of physics and biology.

Naive Physics

As adults, we know much about objects and their properties. For example, we know that, if we place a coffee cup on a table, it will remain there unless moved by another person: It will not move by itself or simply disappear. And we don't release a coffee cup in mid-air because we know that an unsupported object will fall. Child development researchers have long been interested in young children's understanding of objects, in part because Piaget claimed that understanding of objects develops slowly, taking many months to become complete. However, we've already seen that other investigators have shown that babies understand objects much earlier than Piaget claimed (Baillargeon, 1994).

Of course, understanding that objects exist independently is just a start; objects have many other important properties, and infants know many of them. Infants know, for instance, that objects move along connected, continuous paths and that objects cannot move "through" other objects (Hespos & Baillargeon, 2001a; Spelke, 1994). Infants look longer at objects that violate these properties than at objects that are consistent with them. For example, imagine one ball that rolls through a hole in a wall and a second ball that rolls directly through a hole-less wall. By 5 months, infants look much longer at the second ball, apparently because they are surprised when objects move in ways not predicted by their naive theory of physics. By the middle of the first year, babies also understand that one object striking a second object will cause the latter to move (Kotovsky & Baillargeon, 1998; Spelke, 1994).

Later in the first year, if infants are shown the two situations illustrated in Figure 4.5, they will look intently at the object that appears unsupported, apparently because it violates their expectations about what happens to unsupported objects (Baillargeon, 1998). And infants are surprised when a tall object is completely hidden when placed behind a shorter object, apparently because it violates their expectations about concealment (Hespos & Baillargeon, 2001b).

These amazing demonstrations attest to the fact that the infant is indeed an accomplished naive physicist (Baillargeon, 2004). Of course, the infant's theories are far from complete; physical properties can be understood at many different levels (Hood, Carey,

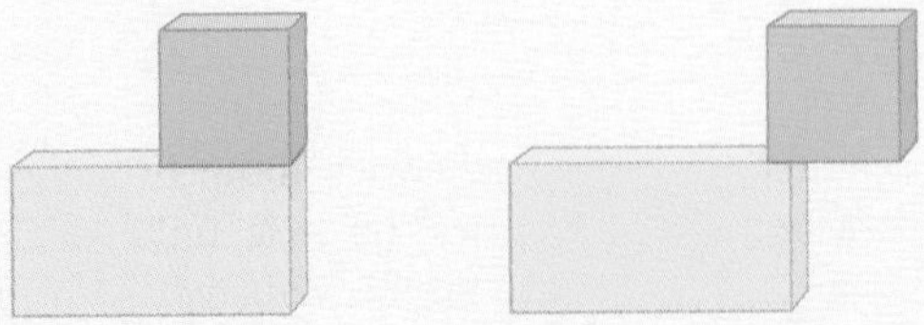

Figure 4.5
Infants are surprised when an unsupported box doesn't fall, which suggests that they have some understanding that objects should be supported.

A realistic configuration in which the small box rests on the larger one

An impossible configuration in which the small box has no apparent means of support

& Prosada, 2000). Using gravity as an example, infants can expect that unsupported objects will fall, elementary-school children know that such objects fall due to gravity, and physics students know that the force of gravity equals the mass of an object times the acceleration caused by gravity. Obviously, infants do not understand objects at the level of physics students. However, the important point is that infants rapidly create a reasonably accurate theory of some basic properties of objects, a theory that helps them to expect that objects such as toys will act in predictable ways.

Naive Biology

Fundamental to adults' naive theories is the distinction between living and nonliving things. Adults know that living things, for example, are made of cells, inherit properties from parents, and move spontaneously. Adults' theories of living things begin in infancy, when youngsters first distinguish animate objects (e.g., people, insects, other animals) from inanimate objects (e.g., rocks, plants, furniture, tools). Motion is critical in early understanding of the difference between animate and inanimate objects: That is, infants and toddlers use motion to identify animate objects, and by 12–15 months they have determined that animate objects are self-propelled, can move in irregular paths, and act to achieve goals (Rakison & Hahn, 2004; Rakison & Poulin-Dubois, 2001).

By the preschool years, children's naive theories of biology have come to include many of the specific properties associated with living things (Wellman & Gelman, 1998). Many 4-year-olds' theories of biology include the following elements:

- *Movement:* Children understand that animals can move themselves but inanimate objects can be moved only by other objects or by people. Shown an animal and a toy hopping across a table in exactly the same manner, preschoolers claim that only the animal can move itself (Gelman & Gottfried, 1996).

- *Growth:* Children understand that, from their first appearance, animals get bigger and physically more complex but that inanimate objects do not change in this way. They believe, for example, that sea otters and termites become larger as time goes by but that teakettles and teddy bears do not (Rosengren et al., 1991).

- *Internal parts:* Children know that the insides of animate objects contain different materials than the insides of inanimate objects. Preschool children judge that blood and bones are more likely to be inside an animate object but that cotton and metal are more likely to be inside an inanimate object (Simons & Keil, 1995).

- *Inheritance:* Children realize that only living things have offspring that resemble their parents. Asked to explain why a dog is pink, preschoolers believe that some biological characteristic of the parents probably made the dog pink; asked to explain why a can is pink, preschoolers rely on mechanical causes (e.g., a worker used a machine), not biological ones (Springer & Keil, 1991; Weissman & Kalish, 1999). And both U.S. and Brazilian children believe that a baby pig that is adopted by a cow will grow up to look like and behave like a pig (Sousa, Altran, & Medin, 2002).

- *Illness:* Preschoolers believe that permanent illnesses such as color blindness or food allergies are more likely to be inherited from parents but that temporary illnesses such as a sore throat or a runny nose are more likely to be transmitted through contact with other people (Raman & Gelman, 2005).

- *Healing:* Children understand that when injured, animate things heal by regrowth whereas inanimate things must be fixed by humans. Preschoolers know that hair will grow back when cut from a child's head but must be repaired by a person when cut from a doll's head (Backscheider, Shatz, & Gelman, 1993).

Where do children get this knowledge of living things? Some of it comes just by watching animals, which children love to do. But mothers also contribute: When reading books about animals to preschoolers, mothers frequently mention the properties that distinguish animals, including self-initiated motion (e.g., "the seal is jumping in the water") and psychological properties (e.g., the bear is really mad!"). Such talk helps to highlight important characteristics of animals for youngsters (Gelman et al., 1998).

Of course, although preschoolers' naive theories of biology are complex, their theories aren't complete. Preschoolers don't know, for instance, that genes are the biological basis for inheritance (Springer & Keil, 1991). And preschoolers' theories include some misconceptions. They believe that body parts have intentions—that the heart "wants" to pump blood and bones "want" to grow (Morris, Taplin, & Gelman, 2000). And, although preschoolers know that plants grow and heal, they nevertheless don't consider plants to be living things. It's not until 7 or 8 years of age that children routinely decide that plants are alive. Preschoolers' reluctance to call plants living things may stem from their belief in goal-directed motion as a key property of living things. This is not easy to see in plants, but when 5-year-olds are told that plants move in goal-directed ways—for example, tree roots turn toward a source of water or a venus flytrap closes its leaves to trap an insect—they decide that plants are alive after all (Opfer & Siegler, 2004).

Despite these limits, children's naive theories of biology, when joined with their naive theory of physics, provide powerful tools for making sense of their world and for understanding new experiences.

TEST YOURSELF

1. The term _____ means modification of schemes based on experience.

2. According to Piaget, _____ are psychological structures that organize experience.

3. Piaget believed that infants' understanding of objects could be summarized as _____.

4. By 18 months, most infants talk and gesture, which shows that they have the capacity _____.

5. Preschoolers are often _____, meaning that they are unable to take another person's viewpoint.

6. Preoperational children sometimes attribute thoughts and feelings to inanimate objects. This is called _____.

7. One criticism of Piaget's theory is that children's performance on tasks like conservation and object performance is _____.

8. Most 4-year-olds know that living things move, _____, have internal parts, resemble their parents, and heal when injured.

What forces in the biopsychosocial framework can you see in an infant's progress through the sensorimotor period?

Answers: (1) accommodation, (2) schemes, (3) "out of sight, out of mind," (4) to use symbols, (5) egocentric, (6) animism, (7) better explained by ideas that are not part of Piaget's theory, (8) grow

4.2

INFORMATION PROCESSING DURING INFANCY AND EARLY CHILDHOOD

A few days ago, 4-year-old Cheryl told her mother a disturbing story. Several months ago, she said, Mr. Johnson, a neighbor and long-time family friend, had taken down her pants and touched her "private parts." Her mother was shocked. She had always believed Mr. Johnson to be an honest, decent man, which made her wonder if Cheryl's imagination had simply run wild. Yet Mr. Johnson had sometimes seemed a bit peculiar, so her daughter's claim did have a ring of truth.

LEARNING OBJECTIVES

What is the basis of the information-processing approach?

How well do young children pay attention?

Do infants and preschool children remember?

What are the shortcomings of preschoolers' eyewitness testimony? What can we do to make it more reliable?

Can infants discriminate different quantities?

How do preschoolers count?

Today, many developmentalists borrow from computer science to formulate their ideas about human thinking and how it develops (Kail & Bisanz, 1992; Plunkett, 1996). As you recall from Chapter 1, this approach is called information processing. In this section, we'll see what information processing has revealed about young children's thinking, and, along the way, see whether we should believe Cheryl.

GENERAL PRINCIPLES OF INFORMATION PROCESSING

In the information-processing view, human thinking is based on both mental hardware and mental software. **Mental hardware** *refers to mental and neural structures that are built in and that allow the mind to operate.* **Mental software** *refers to mental programs that are the basis for performing particular tasks.* According to information-processing psychologists, it is the combination of mental hardware and mental software that allows children to accomplish a specific task. Information-processing psychologists claim that as children develop, their mental software becomes more complex, more powerful, and more efficient.

In the next few pages, we'll look at the development of many important cognitive processes in infants, toddlers, and preschoolers, beginning with attention.

ATTENTION

Linda was only 3 days old and was often startled by the sounds of traffic outside their apartment. Linda's parents worried that she might not get enough sleep. Yet, within a few days, traffic sounds no longer disturbed Linda; she slept blissfully. Why was a noise that had been so troubling no longer a problem? *The key is* **attention,** *a process that determines which sensory information receives additional cognitive processing.*

Linda's response was normal not only for infants but also for children and adolescents. *When presented with a strong or unfamiliar stimulus, an* **orienting response** *usually occurs: A person starts, fixes the eyes on the stimulus, and shows changes in heart rate and brain wave activity.* Collectively, these responses indicate that the infant has noticed the stimulus. Remember, too, that Linda soon ignored the sounds of trucks. After repeated presentations of a stimulus, people recognize it as familiar and the orienting response gradually disappears. **Habituation** *is the diminished response to a stimulus as it becomes more familiar.*

Infants (and older children) pay attention to loud stimuli at first, but then ignore them if they aren't interesting or dangerous.

Paul Chesley/Getty Images

The orienting response and habituation are both useful to infants. On one hand, orienting makes the infant aware of potentially important or dangerous events in the environment. On the other hand, constantly responding to insignificant stimuli is wasteful, so habituation keeps infants from wasting too much energy on biologically nonsignificant events (Rovee-Collier, 1987).

Preschool children gradually learn how to focus their attention, but when compared to older children and adults, they are often not very attentive (Ruff, Capozzoli, & Weissberg, 1998). Preschoolers are easily distracted by extraneous information. However, we can help children to pay attention better. One straightforward approach is to make relevant information stand out. For example, closing a classroom door may not eliminate competing sounds and smells entirely, but it does make them less noticeable. When preschoolers are working at a table or desk, we can remove other objects that are not necessary for the task. Another useful tack, particularly for young children, is to remind them to pay attention to relevant information and ignore the rest.

LEARNING

An infant is always learning. For example, a 5-month-old learns that a new toy makes a noise every time she shakes it. Infants are born with many mechanisms that enable them to learn from experience. This learning can take many forms, including habituation, classical conditioning, operant conditioning, and imitation.

Classical Conditioning

Some of the most famous experiments in psychology were conducted with dogs by the Russian physiologist, Ivan Pavlov. Dogs salivate when fed. Pavlov discovered that if something always happened just before feeding—for example, a bell sounded—dogs would begin to salivate to that event. *In **classical conditioning,** a neutral stimulus elicits a response that was originally produced by another stimulus.* In Pavlov's experiments, the bell was a neutral stimulus that did not naturally cause dogs to salivate. However, by repeatedly pairing the bell with food, the bell began to elicit salivation. Similarly, infants will suck reflexively when sugar water is placed in their mouth with a dropper; if a tone precedes the drops of sugar water, infants will suck when they hear the tone (Lipsitt, 1990).

Classical conditioning is important because it gives infants a sense of order in their environment. That is, through classical conditioning, infants learn that a stimulus is a signal for what will happen next. A youngster may smile when she hears the family dog's collar because she knows the dog is coming to play with her. Or a toddler may smile when he hears water running in the bathroom because he realizes this means it's time for a bath.

Infants and toddlers are definitely capable of classical conditioning when the stimuli are associated with feeding or other pleasant events. It is much more difficult to demonstrate classical conditioning in infants and toddlers when the stimuli are aversive, such as loud noises or shock (Fitzgerald & Brackbill, 1976). Because adults care for and protect very young children, learning about potentially dangerous stimulation is not a common biological problem for infants and toddlers (Rovee-Collier, 1987).

Operant Conditioning

In classical conditioning, infants form expectations about what will happen in their environment. ***Operant conditioning*** *focuses on the relation between the consequences of behavior and the likelihood that the behavior will recur.* When a child's behavior leads to pleasant consequences, the child will probably behave similarly in the future; when the child's behavior leads to unpleasant consequences, the child will probably not repeat the behavior. When a baby smiles, an adult may hug the baby in return; this pleasing consequence makes the baby more likely to smile in the future. When a baby grabs a family heirloom, an adult may become angry and shout at the baby; these unpleasant consequences make the baby less likely to grab the heirloom in the future.

Imitation

Older children, adolescents, and young adults learn much simply by watching others behave. For example, children learn new sports moves by watching pro athletes, they learn how to pursue romantic relationships by watching TV, and they learn how to play new computer games by watching peers. Infants, too, are capable of imitation (Barr & Hayne, 1999). A 10-month-old may imitate an adult waving her finger back-and-forth or imitate another infant who knocks down a tower of blocks.

More startling is the claim that even newborns imitate. Meltzoff and Moore (1989, 1994) found that 2- to 3-week-olds would stick out their tongue or open and close their mouth to match an adult's acts. This work is controversial because other researchers do not consistently obtain these results. In addition, because the newborns' behavior is not novel—newborns are already capable of sticking out their tongues as well as opening and closing their mouths—some researchers do not consider this to be a "true" form of imitation (Anisfeld, 1991, 1996). This work may well represent an early, limited form of imitation; over the course of the first year of life, infants are able to imitate a rapidly expanding range of behaviors.

Children often smile as they hear the family dog coming closer, which is a by-product of classical conditioning.

© Myrleen Ferguson Cate/PhotoEdit

MEMORY

Young babies remember events for days or even weeks at a time. Some of the studies that opened our eyes to the infant's ability to remember used the following method (Rovee-Collier, 1997, 1999). A ribbon from a mobile is attached to a 2- or 3-month-old's leg; within a few minutes, the babies learn to kick to make the mobile move. When Rovee-Collier brought the mobile to the infants' homes several days or a couple of weeks later, babies would still kick to make the mobile move. If Rovee-Collier waited several weeks to return, most babies forgot that kicking moved the mobile. When that happened, Rovee-Collier gave them a reminder—she moved the mobile herself without attaching the ribbon to their foot. Then she would return the next day, hook up the apparatus, and the babies would kick to move the mobile.

Rovee-Collier's experiments show that three important features of memory exist as early as 2 and 3 months of age: (1) an event from the past is remembered, (2) over time, the event can no longer be recalled, and (3) a cue can serve to dredge up a memory that seems to have been forgotten.

From these humble origins, memory improves rapidly in older infants and toddlers. Youngsters can recall more of what they experience and remember it longer (Courage & Howe, 2004; Pelphrey et al., 2004). When youngsters are shown novel actions with toys and later are asked to imitate what they saw, toddlers can remember more than infants and remember the actions for longer periods (Bauer, Burch, & Kleinknecht, 2003). For example, if shown how to make a rattle by first placing a wooden block inside a con-

Newborns imitate an adult's facial expressions.

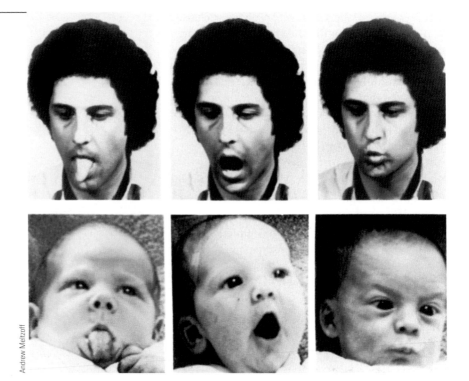

Andrew Meltzoff

Several days after infants have learned that kicking moves a mobile, they will kick when they see the mobile, showing that they remember the connection between kicking and the mobile's movements.

Courtesy of Dr. Carolyn Rovee-Collier

tainer, then putting a lid on the container, toddlers are more likely than infants to remember the necessary sequence of steps.

These improvements in memory can be traced, in part, to growth in the brain regions that support memory (Bauer, 2004). The brain structures primarily responsible for the initial storage of information, including the hippocampus and amygdala, seem to develop very early—by 6 months after birth. The structures responsible for retrieving these stored memories, the frontal cortex, develop much later—into the second year. Development of memory over the first 2 years reflects growth in these two different brain regions.

Autobiographical Memory

A novel feature of memory emerges in the preschool years. ***Autobiographical memory*** *refers to people's memory of the significant events and experiences of their own lives.* You can access your own autobiographical memory by answering these questions:

Who was your teacher in fourth grade?

Where (and with whom!) was your first kiss?

Was your high school graduation indoors or outdoors?

In answering these questions, you searched memory, just as you would search memory to answer questions such as "What is the capital of Ohio?" and "Who invented the sewing machine?" However, answers to questions about Ohio and sewing machines are based on general knowledge that you have not experienced personally; answers to questions about *your* fourth-grade teacher, *your* first kiss, and *your* high school graduation are based on knowledge unique to your own life. Autobiographical memory is important because it helps people construct a personal life history. In addition, autobiographical memory allows people to relate their experiences to others, creating socially shared memories (Conway & Pleydell-Pearce, 2000; Nelson, 1993).

Autobiographical memory originates in the preschool years. According to one influential theory (Nelson & Fivush, 2004), autobiographical memory emerges gradually, as children acquire the component skills. Infants and toddlers have the basic memory skills that enable them to remember past events. Layered on top of these memory skills during the preschool years are language skills and a child's sense of self. Language allows children to become conversational partners. After infants begin to talk, parents often converse with them about past and future events, particularly about personal experiences in the child's past and future. Parents may talk about what the child did today at day care or remind the child about what the child will be doing this weekend. In conversations like these, parents teach their children the important features of events and how events are organized. Children's autobiographical memories are richer when parents talk about past events in detail and encourage their children to participate in these conversations. In contrast, when parents' talk is limited to direct questions that can be answered "yes" or "no," children's autobiographical memories are less extensive.

How does an emergent sense of self contribute to autobiographical memory? One- and 2-year-olds rapidly acquire a sense that they exist independently in space and time. An emerging sense of self thus provides coherence and continuity to children's experience. Children realize that the self who went to the park a few days ago is the same self who is now at a birthday party and is the same self who will read a book with dad before bedtime. The self provides a personal timeline and anchors a child's recall of the past (and anticipation of the future). Thus, a sense of self, language skills that enable children to converse with parents about past and future, and basic memory skills all contribute to the emergence of autobiographical memory in preschool children.

Research on children's autobiographical memory has played a central role in cases of suspected child abuse. When abuse is suspected, the victim is usually the sole witness. To prosecute the alleged abuser, the child's testimony is needed. But can preschoolers accurately recall these events? We'll try to answer this question in the Current Controversies feature.

CURRENT CONTROVERSIES

PRESCHOOLERS ON THE WITNESS STAND

Remember Cheryl, the 4-year-old who claimed that a neighbor had touched her "private parts"? Regrettably, episodes like this one are all too common in America today. When abuse is suspected, the victim is usually the sole eyewitness. Can preschool children like Cheryl provide reliable testimony?

Answering this question is not as easy as it might seem. One obstacle to accurate testimony is that young children are often interviewed repeatedly during legal proceedings, which can cause them to confuse what actually happened with what others suggest may have happened. When the questioner is an adult in a position of authority, children often believe that what is suggested by the adult actually happened (Ceci & Bruck, 1995, 1998; Lampinen & Smith, 1995). They will tell a convincing tale about "what really happened" simply because adults have led them to believe things must have happened that way. Young children's storytelling can be so convincing that even though enforcement officials and child protection workers believe they can

usually tell if children are telling the truth, professionals often cannot distinguish true and false reports (Gordon, Baker-Ward, & Ornstein, 2001). Perhaps you doubt that interviewers routinely ask the leading or suggestive questions that are the seeds of false memories. But analyses of videotapes of actual interviews reveal that trained investigators often ask children leading questions and make suggestive comments (Lamb, Steinberg, & Esplin, 2000).

Adults aren't the only ones who taint children's memories; peers can too! When, for example, some children in a class experience an event (e.g., a class field trip, a special class visitor), they often talk about the event with classmates who weren't there; later,

When questioned by a person in a position of authority, young children often go along with an adult's description of events.

these absent classmates readily describe what happened and often insist they were actually there (Principe & Ceci, 2002).

Preschool children are particularly suggestible. Why? One idea is that preschool children are more suggestible due to limited source-monitoring skills (Poole & Lindsay, 1995). Older children, adolescents, and adults often know the source of information that they remember. For example, a father recalling his daughter's piano recitals will know the source of many of his memories: Some are from personal experience (he attended the recital), some he saw on videotape, and some are based on his daughter's descriptions. Preschool children are not particularly skilled at such source monitoring. When recalling past events, preschoolers are often confused about who did or said what, and when confused in this manner, they frequently assume that they must have experienced something personally. Consequently, when preschool children are asked leading questions (e.g., "When the man touched you, did it hurt?"), this information is also stored in memory, but without the source. Because preschool children are not skilled at monitoring sources, they have trouble distinguishing what they actually experienced from what interviewers imply that they experienced.

Although preschoolers are easily misled, they can provide reliable testimony. Here are guidelines for improving the reliability of child witnesses (Ceci & Bruck, 1995, 1998; Gordon et al., 2001):

- Warn children that interviewers may sometimes try to trick them or suggest things that didn't happen.

- Interviewers' questions should evaluate alternative explanations of what happened and who was involved.
- Children should not be questioned repeatedly on a single issue.

Following these guidelines can foster the conditions under which preschoolers (and older children too) are more likely to provide accurate testimony. More important, with greater understanding of the circumstances that give rise to abuse—a topic of Chapter 7—we should be able to prevent its occurrence altogether.

LEARNING NUMBER SKILLS

Powerful learning and memory skills allow infants and preschoolers to learn much about their worlds. This rapid growth is well illustrated by research on children's understanding of number. Basic number skills originate in infancy, long before babies learn names of numbers. Many babies experience daily variation in quantity. They play with two blocks and see that another baby has three; they watch as a father sorts laundry and finds two black socks but only one blue sock, and they eat one hot dog for lunch while an older brother eats three.

From these experiences, babies apparently come to appreciate that quantity or amount is one of the ways in which objects in the world can differ. That is, research suggests that 5-month-olds can distinguish two objects from three and, less often, three objects from four (Canfield & Smith, 1996; Wynn, 1996). Apparently, infants' perceptual processes enable them to distinguish differences in quantity. That is, just as colors (reds, blues) and shapes (triangles, squares) are basic perceptual properties, small quantities ("twoness" and "threeness") are too.

What's more, young babies can do very simple addition and subtraction. In experiments using the method shown in Figure 4.6, infants view a stage with one mouse. A

■ **Figure 4.6**
Infants are surprised when they see objects added or removed but the original number of objects are still present when the screen is removed; this pattern suggests some basic understanding of addition and subtraction.

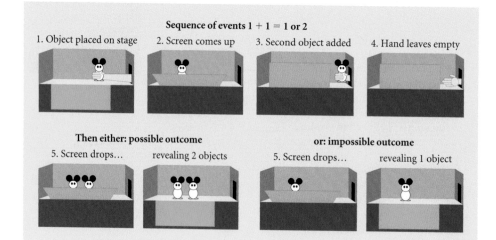

Adapted from Karen Wynn, "Addition and Subtraction by Human Infants," *Nature, 358* (August 27, 1992), 749.

screen hides the mouse, and then a hand appears with a second mouse, which is placed behind the screen. When the screen is removed and reveals one mouse, 5-month-olds look longer than when two mice appear. Apparently, 5-month-olds expect that one mouse plus another mouse should equal two mice, and they look longer when this expectancy is violated (Wynn, 1992). And when the stage first has two mice, one of which is removed, infants are surprised when the screen is removed and two mice are still on the stage. These experiments only work with very small numbers, indicating that the means by which infants add and subtract are very simple and probably unlike the processes that older children use (Mix, Huttenlocher, & Levine, 2002).

Finally, somewhat older infants are aware of "more than" and "less than" relations. *Ordinality refers to the fact that numbers can differ in magnitude; some values are greater than others.* Near the first birthday, infants can identify the larger set. If 10-month-olds watch an adult place two crackers in one container and three crackers in a second container, the infants usually reach for the container with more crackers (Feigenson, Carey, & Hauser, 2002), showing early sensitivity to the ordinal properties of sets.

Learning to Count

By 2 years of age, most youngsters know some number words, and they have begun to count. Usually, their counting is full of mistakes. They might count "1, 2, 6, 7"—skipping 3, 4, and 5. Gelman and Meck (1986) charted preschoolers' understanding of counting. They simply placed several objects in front of a child and asked, "How many?" By analyzing children's answers to many of these questions, Gelman and Meck discovered that by age 3 most children have mastered three basic principles of counting, at least when it comes to counting up to five objects.

■ *One-to-one principle: There must be one and only one number name for each object that is counted.* A child who counts three objects as "1, 2, a" understands this principle because the number of number words matches the number of objects to be counted.

■ *Stable-order principle: Number names must be counted in the same order.* A child who counts in the same sequence—for example, consistently counting four objects as "1, 2, 4, 5"—shows understanding of this principle.

■ *Cardinality principle: The last number name differs from the previous ones in a counting sequence by denoting the number of objects.* Typically, 3-year-olds reveal their understanding of this principle by repeating the last number name, often with emphasis: "1, 2, 4, 8 . . . EIGHT!"

During the preschool years, children master these basic principles and apply them to ever larger sets of objects. By age 5, most youngsters apply these counting principles to as many as nine objects. Of course, children's understanding of these principles does not mean that they always count accurately. To the contrary, children can apply all these principles consistently while counting incorrectly. They must master the conventional sequence of the number names and the counting principles to learn to count accurately.

Learning the number names beyond 9 is easier because the counting words can be generated based on rules for combining decade number names (e.g., 20, 30, 40) with unit names (1, 2, 3, 4). And later, similar rules are used for hundreds, thousands, and so on. By age 4, most youngsters know the numbers to 20, and some can count to 99. Usually, they stop counting at a number ending in 9 (29, 59), apparently because they don't know the next decade name (Siegler & Robinson, 1982).

Learning to count beyond 10 is more complicated in English than in other languages. For example, *eleven* and *twelve* are completely irregular names, following no rules. Also, the remaining "teen" number names differ from the 20s, 30s, and the rest in that the decade number name comes after the unit (thir-*teen,* four-*teen*) rather

Preschool children in Asian countries often learn to count at younger ages than children in North America because in many Asian languages number names correspond directly to the base-ten system.

than before (*twenty*-three, *thirty*-four). Also, some decade names only loosely correspond to the unit names on which they are based: twenty, thirty, and fifty resemble two, three, and five but are not the same.

In contrast, the Chinese, Japanese, and Korean number systems are almost perfectly regular. *Eleven* and *twelve* are expressed as *ten-one* and *ten-two*. There are no special names for the decades: *Two-ten* and *two-ten-one* are names for 20 and 21. These simplified number names help explain why youngsters growing up in Asian countries count more accurately than U.S. preschool children of the same age (Miller et al., 1995). Furthermore, the direct correspondence between the number names and the base-ten system makes it easier for Asian youngsters to learn base-ten concepts (Miura et al., 1988).

Thus far we have not considered the impact of the social context on children's thinking. In the next section, we'll examine a theory developed by Vygotsky, who believed that cognitive development has its roots in social interactions.

TEST YOURSELF

1. One way to improve preschool children's attention is to make irrelevant stimuli _____.

2. Four-month-old Tanya has forgotten that kicking moves a mobile. To remind her of the link between kicking and the mobile's movement, we could _____.

3. Preschoolers' testimony is more likely to be reliable if interviewers test alternative hypotheses and avoid repeated questioning, and if we warn the children that _____.

4. When a child who is counting a set of objects repeats the last number, usually with emphasis, this indicates the child's understanding of the _____ principle of counting.

Think back to the changes in attention and memory that we've described in this section. Were the changes all quantitative in nature, or were some qualitative, like those emphasized by Piaget?

Answers: (1) less noticeable, (2) let her view a moving mobile, (3) interviewers may try to trick them, (4) cardinality

---

LEARNING OBJECTIVES

What is the zone of proximal development? How does it help explain how children accomplish more when they collaborate with others?

What is a particularly effective way of teaching youngsters new tasks?

When and why do children talk to themselves as they solve problems?

MIND AND CULTURE: VYGOTSKY'S THEORY

Victoria, a 4-year-old, enjoys solving jigsaw puzzles, coloring, and building towers with blocks. While busy with these activities, she often talks to herself. For example, once as she was coloring a picture, she said, "Where's the red crayon? Stay inside the lines. Color the blocks blue." These remarks were not directed at anyone else; after all, Victoria was alone. Why did she say these things? What purpose did they serve?

Human development is often referred to as a journey that takes people along many different paths. For Piaget and for information-processing psychologists, children make the journey alone. Other people (and culture in general) certainly influence the direction that children take, but fundamentally the child is a solitary adventurer-explorer, boldly forging ahead. Lev Vygotsky (1896–1934), a Russian psychologist, proposed a very different account: Development is an apprenticeship, in which children advance when they collaborate with others who are more skilled. According to Vygotsky (1934/1986), children rarely make much headway on the developmental path when they walk alone; they progress when they walk hand in hand with an expert partner.

Vygotsky died of tuberculosis at the age of 37, so he never had the opportunity to develop his theory fully. He did not provide a complete theory of cognitive development throughout childhood and adolescence (as Piaget did), nor did he give definitive accounts of cognitive change in specific domains (as information-processing theorists do). However, many of his ideas are influential, largely because they fill in some gaps in the Piagetian and information-processing accounts. In the next few pages, we'll look at three of Vygotsky's most important contributions—the zone of proximal development, scaffolding, and private speech—and discover why Victoria talks to herself.

THE ZONE OF PROXIMAL DEVELOPMENT

Four-year-old Ian and his father often solve puzzles together. Although Ian does most of the work, his father encourages him, sometimes finds a piece that he needs, or shows Ian how to put parts together. When Ian tries to assemble the same puzzles by himself, he can rarely complete them. *The difference between what Ian can do with assistance and what he does alone defines his **zone of proximal development.*** That is, the zone is the area between the level of performance a child can achieve when working independently and a higher level of performance that is possible when working under the guidance or direction of more skilled adults or peers (Wertsch & Tulviste, 1992). For example, elementary-school children are often asked to solve arithmetic story problems. Many youngsters have trouble with these problems, often because they simply don't know where to begin. By structuring the task for them—"first decide what you're supposed to figure out, then decide what information you're told in the problem"—teachers can help children accomplish what they cannot do by themselves. Thus, just as training wheels help children learn to ride a bike by allowing them to concentrate on certain aspects of bicycling, collaborators help children perform more effectively by providing structure, hints, and reminders.

The idea of a zone of proximal development follows naturally from Vygotsky's basic premise: Cognition develops first in a social setting and only gradually comes under the child's independent control. What factors aid this shift? This leads us to the second of Vygotsky's key contributions.

SCAFFOLDING

Have you ever had the good fortune to work with a master teacher, one who seemed to know exactly when to say something to help you over an obstacle but otherwise let you work uninterrupted? *Scaffolding is a style in which teachers gauge the amount of assistance they offer to match the learner's needs.* Early in learning a new task, children know little, so teachers give much direct instruction about

Young children can often accomplish far more with some adult guidance than they can accomplish alone; Vygotsky referred to this difference as the zone of proximal development.

© David Young-Wolff/PhotoEdit

how to do all the different elements of a task. As the children catch on, teachers need to provide much less direct instruction; they are more likely to be giving reminders.

Worldwide, parents attempt to scaffold their children's learning, but not always using the same methods. Rogoff and her colleagues (1993) observed mothers in four countries—Guatemala, India, Turkey, and the United States—as they showed their toddlers how to operate a novel toy. In all cultures, most mothers attempted to scaffold their children's learning, either by dividing a difficult task into easier subtasks or by doing parts of the task themselves, particularly the more complicated parts. However, mothers in different cultures accomplish scaffolding in different ways. Mothers in Turkey and the United States relied primarily on verbal instruction. Mothers in India and Guatemala used verbal instruction, but they also used touches (e.g., nudging a child's elbow) or gaze (e.g., winking or staring) to guide their youngsters. Evidently, parents worldwide try to simplify learning tasks for their children, but they use different methods.

The defining characteristic of scaffolding—giving help but not more than is needed—clearly promotes learning (Plumert & Nichols-Whitehead, 1996). Youngsters do not learn readily when they are constantly told what to do or when they are simply left to struggle through a problem unaided. However, when teachers collaborate with them, allowing children to take on more and more of a task as they master its different elements, they learn more effectively (Murphy & Messer, 2000). Scaffolding is an important technique for transferring skills from others to the child, both in formal settings such as schools and in informal settings such as the home or playground.

PRIVATE SPEECH

Remember Victoria, the 4-year-old in the vignette who talked to herself as she colored? *Her behavior demonstrates **private speech:** comments that are not intended for others but are designed to help children regulate their own behavior* (Vygotsky, 1934/1986). Thus, Victoria's remarks are simply an effort to help herself color the picture.

Vygotsky viewed private speech as an intermediate step toward self-regulation of cognitive skills. At first, children's behavior is regulated by speech from other people that is directed toward them. When youngsters first try to control their own behavior and thoughts, without others present, they instruct themselves by speaking aloud. Private speech seems to be children's way of guiding themselves, of making sure that they do all the required steps in solving a problem. Finally, as children gain ever greater skill, private speech becomes *inner speech,* which was Vygotsky's term for thought (Behrend, Rosengran, & Perlmutter, 1992).

If private speech functions in this way, can you imagine when a child would be most likely to use it? We should see children using private speech more often on difficult tasks than on easy tasks, because children are most likely to need extra guidance on harder tasks. Also, children should be more likely to use private speech after a mistake than after a correct response. These predictions are generally supported by research (Berk, 1992), which suggests the power of language in helping children learn to control their own behavior and thinking.

Thus, Vygotsky's work has characterized cognitive development not as a solitary undertaking but as a collaboration between expert and novice. His work reminds us of the importance of language, which we'll examine in detail in the last section of this chapter.

Young children often regulate their own behavior by talking to themselves, particularly when they perform difficult tasks.

THINK ABOUT IT

Vygotsky emphasized cognitive development as collaboration. How could such collaboration be included in Piaget's theory? In information processing?

© Eric A. Wessman./Stock Boston, Inc.

TEST YOURSELF

1. The _____ is the difference between the level of performance that youngsters can achieve with assistance and the level they can achieve alone.

2. The term _____ refers to a style in which teachers adjust their assistance to match a child's needs.

3. According to Vygotsky, _____ is an intermediate step between speech from others and inner speech.

Compare the role of sociocultural influences in Piaget's theory, the information-processing approach, and Vygotsky's theory.

Answers: (1) zone of proximal development, (2) scaffolding, (3) private speech

---

4.4

LANGUAGE

Nabina is just a few weeks away from her first birthday. For the past month, she has seemed to understand much of her mother's speech. If her mom asks, "Where's Garfield?" (the family cat), Nabina scans the room and points toward Garfield. Yet Nabina's own speech is still gibberish: She "talks" constantly, but her mom can't understand a word of it. If Nabina apparently understands others' speech, why can't she speak herself?

LEARNING OBJECTIVES

When do infants first hear and make speech sounds?

When do children start to talk? Why?

How do youngsters learn the meanings of words?

How do young children progress from two-word speech to more complex sentences?

How well do youngsters communicate?

AN EXTRAORDINARY HUMAN ACHIEVEMENT OCCURS soon after the first birthday: Most children speak their first word, which is followed in the ensuing months by several hundred more. This marks the beginning of a child's ability to communicate orally with others. Through speech, youngsters impart their ideas, beliefs, and feelings to family, friends, and others.

Actually, the first spoken words represent the climax of a year's worth of language growth. To tell the story of language acquisition properly and explain Nabina's seemingly strange behavior, we must begin with the months preceding the first words.

THE ROAD TO SPEECH

When a baby is upset, a concerned mother tries to console it. This familiar situation is rich in language-related information. The infant, not yet able to talk, is conveying its displeasure by one of the few means of communication available to it—crying. The mother, for her part, is using both verbal and nonverbal measures to cheer her baby, to send the message that the world is really not as bad as it may seem now.

The situation also raises two questions about infants as nonspeaking creatures. First, can babies who are unable to speak understand any of the speech that is directed at them? Second, how do infants progress from crying to more effective methods of oral communication, such as speech? Let's start by answering the first question.

A baby's first form of communication—crying—is soon joined by other, language-based ways of communicating.

Perceiving Speech

Even newborn infants hear remarkably well (page 113), but can babies distinguish speech sounds? To answer this question, we first need to know more about the elements of speech. *The basic building blocks of language are* **phonemes,** *which are unique sounds that can be joined to create words.* Phonemes include consonant sounds, such as the sound of *t* in *toe* and *tap,* along with vowel sounds such as the sound of *e* in *get* and *bed.* Infants can distinguish many of these sounds, some of them as early as 1 month after birth (Aslin, Jusczyk, & Pisoni, 1998).

How do we know that infants can distinguish different vowels and consonants? Researchers have devised a number of clever techniques to determine whether babies respond differently to distinct sounds. In one approach, a rubber nipple is connected to a tape recorder so that sucking turns on the tape and sound comes out of a loudspeaker. In just a few minutes, 1-month-olds learn the relation between their sucking and the sound: They suck rapidly to hear a tape that consists of nothing more than the sound of *p* as in *pin, pet,* and *pat* (pronounced "puh").

After a few more minutes, infants seemingly tire of this repetitive sound and suck less often, which represents the habituation phenomenon described on page 147. But, if the tape is changed to a different sound, such as the sound of *b* in *bed, bat,* or *bird* (pronounced "buh"), babies begin sucking rapidly again. Evidently, they recognize that the sound of *b* is different from *p* because they suck more often to hear the new sound (Jusczyk, 1995).

Of course, the language environment for young infants is not solely auditory; much exposure to language comes in face-to-face interaction with adults. These interactions provide many visual cues about sounds, and infants' use of these cues: Shown a video of an adult saying "ba," infants notice when the adult looks to be saying "sha" even though the audio still presents "ba" (Patterson & Werker, 2003).

THE IMPACT OF LANGUAGE EXPOSURE. Not all languages use the same set of phonemes; a distinction that is important in one language may be ignored in another. For example, unlike English, French and Polish differentiate between nasal and non-nasal vowels. To hear the difference, say the word *rod.* Now repeat it, but holding your nose. The subtle difference between the two sounds illustrates a nonnasal vowel (the first version of *rod*) and a nasal one (the second).

Because an infant might be exposed to any of the world's languages, it would be adaptive for young infants to be able to perceive a wide range of phonemes. In fact, research shows that infants can distinguish phonemes that are not used in their native language. For example, Japanese does not distinguish the consonant sound of *r* in *rip* from the sound of *l* in *lip,* and Japanese adults trying to learn English have great difficulty distinguishing these sounds. At about 6 months, infants in both Japanese- and English-speaking environments can distinguish them, but by 11 or 12 months, only infants in English-speaking environments can (Werker & Tees, 1999).

Newborns apparently are biologically capable of hearing the entire range of phonemes in all languages worldwide. But as babies grow and are more exposed to a particular language, they notice only the linguistic distinctions that are meaningful in their own language. Thus, specializing in one language apparently comes at the cost of making it more difficult to hear sounds in other languages (Best, 1995).

IDENTIFYING WORDS. Of course, hearing individual phonemes is only the first step in perceiving speech. One of the biggest challenges for infants is identifying recurring patterns of sounds—words. Imagine, for example, an infant overhearing this conversation between a parent and an older sibling:

SIBLING: Jerry got a new *bike.*
PARENT: Was his old *bike* broken?
SIBLING: No. He'd saved his allowance to buy a new mountain *bike.*

An infant listening to this conversation hears *bike* three times. Can the infant learn from this experience? Yes. When 7- to 8-month-olds hear a word repeatedly in different sentences, they later pay more attention to this word than to words they haven't heard previously. Evidently, 7- and 8-month-olds can listen to sentences and recognize the sound patterns that they hear repeatedly (Houston & Jusczyk, 2003; Saffran, Aslin, & Newport, 1996). And, by 6 months, infants pay more attention to content words (e.g., nouns, verbs) than to function words (e.g., articles, prepositions) and they look at the correct parent when they hear "mommy" or "daddy" (Shi & Werker, 2001; Tincoff & Jusczyk, 1999).

In normal conversation, there are no silent gaps between words, so how do infants pick out words? Stress is one important clue. English contains many one-syllable words that are stressed and many two-syllable words that have a stressed syllable followed by an unstressed syllable (e.g., *dough'-nut, tooth'-paste, bas'-ket*). Infants pay more attention to stressed syllables than unstressed syllables, which is a good strategy for identifying the beginnings of words (Mattys et al., 1999; Thiessen & Saffran, 2003).

Of course, stress is not a foolproof sign. Many two-syllable words have stress on the second syllable (e.g., *gui-tar', sur-prise'*), so infants need other methods to identify words in speech. One method is statistical. Infants notice syllables that go together frequently (Jusczyk, 2002). For example, in a study by Aslin, Saffran, and Newport (1998), 8-month-olds heard the following sounds, which consisted of 4 three-syllable artificial words, said over and over in random order.

<u>*pa bi ku*</u> <u>*go la tu*</u> <u>*da ro pi*</u> <u>*ti bu do*</u> <u>*da ro pi*</u> <u>*go la tu*</u> <u>*pa bi ku*</u> <u>*da ro pi*</u>...

We've underlined the words and inserted gaps between them so you can see them more easily, but in the study there were no breaks at all—just a steady flow of syllables for 3 minutes. Later, infants listened to these words less than to new words that were novel combinations of the same syllables. They had detected *pa bi ku, go la tu, da ro pi,* and *ti bu do* as familiar patterns and listened to them less than to words like *tu da ro,* a new word made up from syllables they'd already heard.

Yet another way that infants identify words is through their emerging knowledge of how sounds are used in their native language. For example, think about these two pairs of sounds: *s* followed by *t* and *s* followed by *d.* Both pairs of sounds are quite common at the end of one word and the beginning of the next: bu*s t*akes, kis*s t*ook; thi*s d*og, pas*s d*irectly. However, *s* and *t* occur frequently within a word (*st*op, li*st*, pe*st*, *st*ink) but *s* and *d* do not. Consequently, when *d* follows an *s,* it probably starts a new word. In fact, 9-month-olds follow rules like this one because when they hear novel words embedded in continuous speech, they're more likely to identify the novel word when the final sound in the preceding word occurs infrequently with the first sound of the novel word (Mattys & Jusczyk, 2001). Thus, infants use many powerful tools to identify words in speech. Of course, they don't yet understand the meanings of these words; they just recognize a word as a distinct configuration of sounds.

Parents (and other adults) often help infants master language sounds by talking in a distinctive style. In **infant-directed speech,** *adults speak slowly and with exaggerated changes in pitch and loudness.* If you listen to a mother talking to her baby, you will notice that she alternates between speaking softly and loudly and between high and low pitches and that her speech seems very expressive emotionally (Trainor, Austin, & Desjardins, 2000). Infant-directed speech is also known as *motherese,* because this form of speaking was first noted in mothers, although it's now known that most caregivers talk this way to infants.

Infant-directed speech may attract infants' attention more than adult-directed speech (Kaplan et al., 1995; Lewkowicz, 2000b) because its slower pace and accentuated changes provide infants with more and more salient language clues. Infant-directed

Andy Cox/Getty Images

When mothers and other adults talk to young children, they often use infant-directed speech, in which they speak slowly and with exaggerated changes in pitch and loudness.

speech includes especially good examples of vowels (Kuhl et al., 1997), which may help infants learn to distinguish these sounds. And when talking to infants, speaking clearly is a good idea. In one study (Liu, Kuhl, & Tsao, 2003), infants who could best distinguish speech sounds had mothers who spoke most clearly.

Infant-directed speech, then, helps infants perceive the sounds that are fundamental to their language. But how do infants accomplish the next step, producing speech? We answer this question next.

Steps to Speech

As any new parent can testify, newborns and young babies make many sounds—they cry, burp, and sneeze. Language-based sounds don't appear immediately. *At two months, infants begin to produce vowel-like sounds, such as "ooooooo" or "ahhhhhh," a phenomenon known as **cooing.*** Sometimes infants become quite excited as they coo, perhaps reflecting the joy of simply playing with sounds.

*After cooing comes **babbling**, speechlike sound that has no meaning.* A typical 6-month-old might say "dah" or "bah," utterances that sound like a single syllable consisting of a consonant and a vowel. Over the next few months, babbling becomes more elaborate as babies apparently experiment with more complex speech sounds. Older infants sometimes repeat a sound, as in "bahbahbah," and begin to combine different sounds, such as "dahmahbah" (Hoff, 2005).

Babbling is not just mindless playing with sounds; it is a precursor to real speech. We know this, in part, from video records of people's mouths while speaking. When adults speak, their mouth is open somewhat wider on the right side than on the left side, reflecting the left hemisphere's control of language and muscle movements on the body's right side (Graves & Landis, 1990). Infants do the same when they babble, but not when making other nonbabbling sounds, which suggests that babbling is fundamentally linguistic (Holowka & Petitto, 2002).

Other evidence for the linguistic nature of babbling comes from studies of developmental change in babbling: At roughly 8 to 11 months, infants' babbling sounds more like real speech because infants stress some syllables and vary the pitch of their speech (Davis et al., 2000). In English declarative sentences, for example, pitch first rises, then falls toward the end of the sentence. In questions, however, the pitch is level, then rises toward the end of the question. Older babies' babbling reflects these patterns: Babies who are brought up by English-speaking parents have both the declarative and question patterns of intonation in their babbling. Babies exposed to a language with different patterns of intonation, such as Japanese or French, reflect their language's intonation in their babbling (Levitt & Utman, 1992).

The appearance of intonation in babbling indicates a strong link between perception and production of speech: Infants' babbling is influenced by the characteristics of the speech that they hear. Beginning in the middle of the first year, infants try to reproduce the sounds of language that others use in trying to communicate with them (or, in the case of deaf infants with deaf parents, the signs that others use). Hearing *dog*, an infant may first say "dod," then "gog" before finally saying "dog" correctly. In the same way that beginning typists gradually link movements of their fingers with particular keys, through babbling infants learn to use their lips, tongue, and teeth to produce specific sounds, gradually making sounds that approximate real words (Poulson et al., 1991). Fortunately, learning to produce language sounds is easier for most babies than the following cartoon suggests!

These developments in production of sound, coupled with the 1-year-old's advanced ability to perceive speech sounds, clearly set the stage for the infant's first true words.

THINK ABOUT IT

Compare and contrast the steps in learning to make speech sounds with Piaget's account of the sensorimotor period.

B.C. © 1993. Reprinted by permission of Johnny Hart and Creators Syndicate, Inc.

FIRST WORDS AND MANY MORE

Remember that Nabina, the 1-year-old in the vignette, looks at the family cat when she hears its name. This phenomenon is common in 10- to 14-month-olds. They appear to understand what others say despite the fact that they have yet to speak. In response to "Where is the book?" children will go find the book. They grasp the question, even though their own speech is limited to advanced babbling (Fenson et al., 1994; Hoff-Ginsberg, 1997). Evidently, children have made the link between speech sounds and particular objects, even though they cannot yet manufacture the sounds themselves. As fluent adult speakers, we forget that speech is a motor skill requiring perfect timing and tremendous coordination.

A few months later, most youngsters utter their first words. Typically, these words have a structure borrowed from their advanced babbling, consisting of a consonant-vowel pair that may be repeated. *Mama* and *dada* are common examples of this type of construction. Other common words in early vocabularies denote animals, food, and toys (Caselli et al., 1995; Nelson, 1973). Also common are words that denote actions (e.g., *go*). By the age of 2, youngsters have a vocabulary of a few hundred words; by 6, a typical child's vocabulary includes more than 10,000 words (Anglin, 1993). However, children differ markedly in the size of their vocabulary (Fenson et al., 1994). At 16 months, vocabularies typically range from as few as 10 words to as many as 150; at 2½ years, from 375 words to 650.

The Grand Insight: Words as Symbols

To make the transition from babbling to real speech, infants need to learn that speech is more than just entertaining sound. They need to know that particular sounds form words that can refer to objects, actions, and properties. Put another way, infants must recognize that words are symbols, entities that stand for other entities.

A vivid account of this insight came from Helen Keller, an American essayist. Born in 1880 and left blind and deaf from an illness during infancy, she had no means to communicate with other people. When Helen was 7 years old, a tutor attempted to teach her words by spelling them in her hands. For Helen, the hurdle was to link the finger spelling with concepts she already knew; in her case, awareness came suddenly (Keller, 1965, p. 21):

> Someone was drawing water and my teacher placed my hand under the spout. As the cool stream gushed over one hand she spelled into the other the word *water*, first slowly, then

Helen Keller became deaf and blind in infancy but learned to speak at 7 years of age.

© Bettmann/Corbis

rapidly. I stood still, my whole attention fixed upon the motions of her fingers. Suddenly I felt a misty consciousness as of something forgotten—a thrill of returning thought; and somehow the mystery of language was revealed to me. I knew then that "w-a-t-e-r" meant the wonderful and cool something that was flowing over my hand. That living word awakened my soul, gave it light, hope, joy, set it free!

When do youngsters who can hear and see have this insight? Piaget believed that it occurs at roughly 18 months of age and that it marks the beginning of transition from the sensorimotor to the preoperational stage. However, a glimmer of understanding of symbols occurs earlier, soon after the first birthday. By this age, children have already formed concepts such as "round, bouncy things" or "furry things that bark," based on their own experiences. With the insight that speech sounds can denote these concepts, infants begin to identify a word that goes with each concept (Reich, 1986).

If this argument is correct, we should find that children use symbols in other areas, not just in language. They do. Gestures are symbols, and infants begin to gesture shortly before their first birthday (Goodwyn & Acredolo, 1993). Young children may smack their lips to indicate hunger or wave "bye-bye" when leaving. In these cases, gestures and words convey a message equally well.

What's more, gesture sometimes paves the way for language. Before knowing an object's name, infants often point to it or pick it up for a listener, as if saying, "I want this!" or "What's this?" In one study, 50% of all objects were first referred to by gesture and, about 3 months later, by word (Iverson & Goldin-Meadow, 2005). After children know that objects have names, a gesture is a convenient substitute for pronouns like "it" or "that" and often causes an adult to say the object's name.

One of the challenges for theories of language learning is to explain how children figure out that the parent's words refer to the object, not to its color or texture and not to her actions.

© Roman Barnes

What's What? Fast Mapping of Words

Once children have the insight that a word can symbolize an object or action, their vocabularies grow slowly at first. A typical 15-month-old, for example, may learn 2 to 3 new words each week. However, at about 18 months, many children experience a naming explosion during which they learn new words—particularly names of objects—much more rapidly than before. Children now learn 10 or more new words each week (Fenson et al., 1994).

This rapid rate of word learning is astonishing when we realize that most words have many plausible but incorrect referents. To illustrate, imagine what's going through the mind of a child when her mother points to a flower and says, "Flower. This is a flower. See the flower." This all seems crystal clear to you and incredibly straightforward. But what might the child learn from this episode? Perhaps the correct referent for "flower." But a youngster could, just as reasonably, conclude that "flower" refers to a petal, to the color of the flower, or to the mother's actions in pointing at the flower.

Surprisingly, though, most youngsters learn the proper meanings of simple words in just a few presentations. *Children's ability to connect new words to referents so rapidly that they cannot be considering all possible meanings for the new word is termed* **fast mapping.** How can young children learn new words so rapidly? Researchers believe that many distinct factors contribute to young children's rapid word learning (Hollich, Hirsh-Pasek, & Golinkoff, 2000).

JOINT ATTENTION. Parents encourage word learning by carefully watching what interests their children. When toddlers touch or look at an object, parents often label it for them. When a youngster points to a banana, a parent may say, "Banana, that's a banana." And parents do their best to simplify the task for children by typically using just one label for an object (Callanan & Sabbagh, 2004).

Of course, to take advantage of this help, infants must be able to tell when parents are labeling instead of just conversing. In fact, when adults label an unfamiliar object, 18- to 20-month-olds assume that the label is the object's name *only* when adults show signs that they are referring to the object. For example, toddlers are more likely to learn the name of an object or action when adults look at the object or action while saying its name than when adults look elsewhere while labeling (Diesendruck et al., 2004; Poulin-Dubois & Forbes, 2002). Thus, beginning in the toddler years, parents and children work together to create conditions that foster word learning: Parents label objects and youngsters rely on adults' behavior to interpret the words they hear.

Although joint attention helps children to learn words, it is not required: Children learn new words that are used in ongoing conversation and when they overhear others use novel words (Akhtar, Jipson, & Callanan, 2001). And when speakers appear unfamiliar with a novel person or object, 4- and 5-year-olds are less likely to learn new words, as if they doubt that speakers know what they're talking about (Birch & Bloom, 2002; Jaswal, 2004).

CONSTRAINTS ON WORD NAMES. Joint attention simplifies word learning for children, but the problem still remains: How does a toddler know that banana refers to the object that she's touching, as opposed to her activity (touching) or to the object's color? Many researchers believe that young children follow several simple rules that limit their conclusions about what labels mean.

A study by Au and Glusman (1990) shows how researchers have identified rules that young children use. Au and Glusman presented preschoolers with a stuffed animal with pink horns that otherwise resembled a monkey and called it a *mido*. *Mido* was then repeated several times, always referring to the monkey-like stuffed animal with pink horns. Later, these youngsters were asked to find a *theri* in a set of stuffed animals that included several *mido*. Never having heard of a *theri*, what did the children do? They never picked a *mido*; instead, they selected other stuffed animals. Knowing that *mido* referred to monkey-like animals with pink horns, evidently they decided that *theri* had to refer to one of the other stuffed animals.

Apparently children were following this simple but effective rule for learning new words:

- If an unfamiliar word is heard in the presence of objects that already have names and objects that don't, the word refers to one of the objects that doesn't have a name.

Researchers have discovered several other simple rules that help children match words with the correct referent (Hoff, 2005; Woodward & Markman, 1998):

- A name refers to a whole object, not its parts or its relation to other objects, and refers not just to this particular object but to all objects of the same type. For example, when a grandparent points to a stuffed animal on a shelf and says "dinosaur," children conclude that *dinosaur* refers to the entire dinosaur, not just its ears or nose, not to the fact that the dinosaur is on a shelf, and not to this specific dinosaur but to all dinosaurlike objects.
- If an object already has a name and another name is presented, the new name denotes a subcategory of the original name. If the child who knows the meaning of *dinosaur* sees a brother point to another dinosaur and hears the brother say "T-rex," the child will conclude that *T-rex* is a special type of dinosaur.
- Given many similar category members, a word applied consistently to only one of them is a proper noun. If a child who knows *dinosaur* sees that one of a group of dinosaurs is always called "Dino," the child will conclude that *Dino* is the name of that dinosaur.

Rules like these make it possible for children like Nabina, the child in the vignette, to learn words rapidly because they reduce the number of possible referents. The child being shown a flower follows these rules to decide that *flower* refers to the entire object, not its parts or the action of pointing to it.

SENTENCE CUES. Children hear many unfamiliar words embedded in sentences containing words they already know. The other words and the overall sentence structure can be helpful clues to a word's meaning.

For example, when a parent describes an event using familiar words but an unfamiliar verb, children often infer that the verb refers to the action performed by the subject of the sentence (Fisher, 1996; Woodward & Markman, 1998). When youngsters hear, "The man is juggling," they will infer that *juggling* refers to the man's actions with the bowling pins, because they already know *man* and because *-ing* refers to ongoing actions.

As another example of how sentence context aids word learning, look at the blocks in Figure 4.7 and point to the "boz block." You probably pointed to the middle block. Why? In English, adjectives usually precede the nouns they modify, so you inferred that *boz* is an adjective describing *block*. Since *the* before *boz* implies that only one block is *boz,* you picked the middle one, having decided that *boz* means "winged." Toddlers, too, use sentence cues like these to judge word meanings. Hearing "This is a Zav," 2-year-olds will interpret *zav* as a category name, but hearing "This is Zav" (without the *a*), they interpret *zav* as a proper name (Hall, Lee, & Belanger, 2001).

COGNITIVE FACTORS. The naming explosion coincides with a time of rapid cognitive growth, and children's increased cognitive skill helps them to learn new words. As children's thinking becomes more sophisticated and, in particular, as they start to have goals and intentions, language becomes a means to express those goals and to achieve them. Thus, intention provides children with an important motive to learn language—to help achieve their goals (Bloom & Tinker, 2001).

In addition, young children's improving attentional and perceptual skills also promote word learning. Smith (2000), for example, argues that shape plays a central role in learning words. Infants and young children spontaneously pay attention to an object's shape, and they use this bias to learn new words. In Smith's theory, children first associate names with a single object: "ball" is associated with a specific tennis ball, and "cup" is associated with a favorite sippy cup. As children encounter new balls and new cups, however, they hear the same words applied to similarly shaped objects and reach the conclusion that balls are round and cups are cylinders with handles. With further experience, children derive an even more general rule: Objects that have the same shape have the same name. From this, children realize that paying attention to shape is an easy way to learn names. Consistent with this theory, the shape bias and the naming explosion typically occur at about the same time (Gershkoff-Stowe & Smith, 2004).

NAMING ERRORS. Of course, these rules for learning new words are not perfect; initial mappings of words onto meanings are often only partially correct (Hoff & Naigles, 2002). *A common mistake is* **underextension,** *defining a word too narrowly.* Using *car* to refer only to the family car and *ball* to a favorite toy ball are examples of underextension. *Between 1 and 3 years, children sometimes make the opposite error,* **overextension,** *defining a word too broadly.* Children may use *car* to also refer to buses and trucks or use *doggie* to refer to all four-legged animals.

The overextension error occurs more frequently when children are producing words than when they are comprehending words. Two-year-old Jason may say "doggie"

■ **Figure 4.7**
"The boz block" probably refers to the middle block because "the" implies that only one block is "boz" and the middle block is the only one with wings.

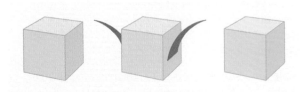

to refer to a goat but nevertheless correctly point to a picture of a goat when asked. Because overextension is more common in word production, it may actually reflect another fast-mapping rule that children follow: "If you can't remember the name for an object, say the name of a related object" (Naigles & Gelman, 1995). Both underextension and overextension disappear gradually as youngsters refine meanings for words as they have more exposure to language.

Individual Differences in Word Learning

The naming explosion typically occurs at about 18 months, but like many developmental milestones, the timing of this event varies widely for individual children. Some youngsters have a naming explosion as early as 14 months, but for others it may be as late as 22 months (Goldfield & Reznick, 1990). Another way to make this point is to look at variation in the size of children's vocabulary at a specific age. At 18 months, for example, an average child's vocabulary would have about 75 words, but a child in the 90th percentile would know nearly 250 words, and a child in the 10th percentile fewer than 25 words (Fenson et al., 1994).

The range in vocabulary size for normal 18-month-olds is huge—from 25 to 250 words! What can account for this difference? Heredity contributes: Twin studies find that vocabulary size is more similar in identical twins than in fraternal twins (Dionne et al., 2003). But the difference is fairly small, indicating a relatively minor role for genetics.

More important are two other factors. *One is **phonological memory,** the ability to remember speech sounds briefly.* This is often measured by saying a nonsense word to children—"ballop" or "glistering"—and asking them to repeat it immediately. Children's skill in recalling such words is strongly related to the size of their vocabulary (Gathercole et al., 1992). Children who have difficulty remembering speech sounds accurately find word learning particularly challenging, which is not surprising because word learning involves associating meaning with an unfamiliar sequence of speech sounds.

However, the single most important factor in growth of vocabulary is the child's language environment. Children have larger vocabularies when they are exposed to much high-quality language. The more words that children hear, the better. Specifically, children learn more words when their parents' speech is rich in different words and is grammatically sophisticated (Hoff, 2003; Hoff & Naigles, 2002) and when parents respond promptly and appropriately to their children's talk (Tamis-Lemonda & Bornstein, 2002).

BILINGUALISM. Millions of American children grow up in bilingual households; these youngsters usually speak English and another language. When 1- and 2-year-olds learn two languages simultaneously, they often progress somewhat slowly at first because they mix words from the two languages. By age 3 or 4, however, children separate the languages; and by the time they begin elementary school, they are proficient in both languages (Baker, 1993; Lanza, 1992). When each language is considered separately, bilingual children often have somewhat smaller vocabularies than monolingual children (Umbel et al., 1992). However, because bilingual youngsters often know words in one language but not the other, their total vocabulary (i.e., words known in both languages plus words known in either language but not both) is greater than that of monolingual children. What's more, bilingual children also better understand that words are simply arbitrary symbols. Bilingual youngsters, for instance, are more likely than monolingual children to understand that, as long as all English speakers agreed, *dog* could refer to cats and *cat* could refer to dogs (Bialystok, 1988; Campbell & Sais, 1995).

WORD LEARNING STYLES. As youngsters expand their vocabulary, they often adopt a distinctive style of learning language (Bates, Bretherton, & Snyder, 1988; Nelson, 1973). *Some children have a **referential style;** their vocabularies mainly consist of words that name objects, persons, or actions.* For example, Rachel, a referential child, had 41 name words in her 50-word vocabulary but only 2 words for social interaction or questions.

THINK ABOUT IT

Gavin and Mitch are both 16-month-olds. Gavin's vocabulary includes about 14 words, but Mitch's has about 150 words, more than 10 times as many as Gavin. What factors contribute to this difference?

Other children have an **expressive style;** *their vocabularies include some names but also many social phrases that are used like a single word, such as "go away," "what'd you want?" and "I want it."* Elizabeth, an expressive child, had a more balanced vocabulary, with 14 words for social interactions and questions and 24 name words.

Referential and expressive styles represent end points on a continuum; most children are somewhere in between. For children with referential emphasis, language is primarily an intellectual tool—a means of learning and talking about objects (Masur, 1995). In contrast, for children with expressive emphasis, language is more of a social tool—a way of enhancing interactions with others. Of course, both of these functions—intellectual and social—are important functions of language, which explains why most children blend the referential and expressive styles of learning language.

Encouraging Language Growth

How can parents and other adults help children learn words? For children to expand their vocabularies, they need to hear others speak. Not surprisingly, then, children learn words more rapidly if their parents speak to them frequently (Huttenlocher et al., 1991; Roberts, Burchinal, & Durham, 1999). Of course, sheer quantity of parental speech is not all that matters. Parents can foster word learning by naming objects that are the focus of a child's attention (Dunham, Dunham, & Curwin, 1993). Parents can name different products on store shelves as they point to them. During a walk, parents can label the objects—birds, plants, vehicles—that the child sees.

Parents can also help children learn words by reading books with them. Reading together is fun for parents and children alike and provides opportunities for children to learn new words. However, the way that parents read makes a difference. When parents carefully describe pictures as they read, preschoolers' vocabularies increase (Reese & Cox, 1999). Asking children questions during reading also helps (Sénéchal, Thomas, & Monker, 1995). When an adult reads a sentence (e.g., Arthur is angling), then asks a question (e.g., What is Arthur doing?), a child must match the new word (*angling*) with the pictured activity (*fishing*) and say the word aloud. When parents read without questioning, children can ignore words they don't understand. Questioning forces children to identify meanings of new words and practice saying them.

Watching television can help word learning under some circumstances. For example, preschool children who frequently view *Sesame Street* often have larger vocabularies by the time they enter kindergarten than do preschoolers who watch *Sesame Street*

Children can learn words from TV programs that actively engage them in language-related activities such as naming, singing, or counting.

less often (Rice et al., 1990). Other kinds of television programs—notably cartoons—do not have this positive influence.

What accounts for the difference? The key to success is encouraging children to become actively involved in language-related activities. Video segments that encourage youngsters to name objects, to sing, and to count help children increase their vocabulary. Apparently, the fundamental principle is much the same for television and for parents: Children expand their vocabularies when they have experiences that engage and challenge their emerging language talents.

SPEAKING IN SENTENCES: GRAMMATICAL DEVELOPMENT

Within months after children say their first words, they begin to form simple two-word sentences. Such sentences are based on "formulas" that children figure out from their own experiences (Braine, 1976; Radford, 1995). Armed with a few formulas, children can express an enormous variety of ideas:

Formula	Example
actor + action	Mommy sleep, Timmy run
action + object	Gimme cookie, throw ball
possessor + possession	Kimmy pail, Maya shovel

Each child develops a unique repertoire of formulas, reflecting his or her own experiences. However, the formulas listed here are commonly used by many children growing up in different countries around the world.

From Two Words to Complex Sentences

Children rapidly move beyond two-word sentences, first doing so by linking two-word statements together: "Rachel kick" and "Kick ball" become "Rachel kick ball." Even longer sentences soon follow; sentences with 10 or more words are common in 3-year-olds' speech. For example, at 1½ years, Laura Kail would say, "Gimme juice" or "Bye-bye Ben." As a 2½-year-old, she had progressed to "When I finish my ice cream, I'll take a shower, okay?" and "Don't turn the light out—I can't see better!"

Children's two- and three-word sentences often fall short of adults' standards of grammar. Youngsters will say, "He eating" rather than "He is eating," or "two cat" rather than "two cats." *This sort of speech is called* **telegraphic** *because, like telegrams of days gone by, children's speech includes only words directly relevant to meaning, and nothing more.* Before cell phones and e-mail, people sent urgent messages by telegraph, and the cost was based on the number of words. Consequently, telegrams were brief and to the point, containing only the important nouns, verbs, adjectives, and adverbs, much like children's two-word speech. *The missing elements,* **grammatical morphemes,** *are words or endings of words (such as -ing, -ed, or -s) that make a sentence grammatical.* During the preschool years, children gradually acquire the grammatical morphemes, first mastering those that express simple relations like *-ing*, which is used to denote that the action expressed by the verb is ongoing. More complex forms, such as appropriate use of the various forms of the verb *to be*, are mastered later (Peters, 1995).

Children's use of grammatical morphemes is based on their growing knowledge of grammatical rules, not simply memory for individual words. This was first demonstrated in a landmark study by Berko (1958), in which preschoolers were shown pictures of nonsense objects like the one in Figure 4.8. The experimenter labeled it, saying, "This is a wug." Then youngsters were shown pictures of two of the objects, and the ex-

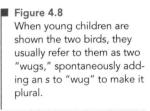
■ Figure 4.8
When young children are shown the two birds, they usually refer to them as two "wugs," spontaneously adding an s to "wug" to make it plural.

This is a wug.

Now there is another one.
There are two of them.
There are two _____.

From Berko, 1958.

perimenter said, "These are two." Most children spontaneously said, "wugs." Because both the singular and plural forms of this word were novel for these youngsters, they could have generated the correct plural form only by applying the familiar rule of adding -s.

Children growing up in homes where English is spoken face the problem that their native tongue is highly irregular, with many exceptions to the rules. *Sometimes children apply rules to words that are exceptions to the rule, errors called* **overregularizations.** With plurals, for example, youngsters may incorrectly add an -s instead of using an irregular plural—two "mans" instead of two "men." With the past tense, children may add -ed instead of using an irregular past tense: "I goed home" instead of "I went home" (Marcus et al., 1992; Mervis & Johnson, 1991).

These examples give some insight into the complexities of mastering the grammatical rules of one's language. Not only must children learn an extensive set of specific rules, but they must also absorb, on a case-by-case basis, all of the exceptions. Despite the enormity of this task, most children have mastered the basics of their native tongue by the time they enter school. How do they do it? Biological, psychological, and sociocultural forces all contribute.

How Do Children Acquire Grammar?

Most youngsters can neither read nor do arithmetic when they enter school, but virtually all have mastered the fundamentals of grammar of their native tongue. How do they do it? Theorists have proposed several different answers to this question.

THE BEHAVIORIST ANSWER. If you were asked to explain how children master grammar, you might propose that children learn to speak grammatically by imitating the grammatical forms they hear. In fact, B. F. Skinner (1957) and other learning theorists once claimed that all aspects of language—sounds, words, grammar, and communication—are learned through imitation and reinforcement (Whitehurst & Vasta, 1975).

Critics were quick to point to some flaws in this theory. One problem is that children produce many sentences they've never even heard. In fact, most of children's sentences are novel, which is difficult to explain in terms of simple imitation of adults' speech. For example, when young children create questions by inserting a *wh* word at the beginning of a sentence ("What she doing?"), who are they imitating? Also troublesome is that, even when children imitate adult sentences, they do not imitate adult grammar. In simply trying to repeat "I am drawing a picture," young children will say "I draw picture." Finally, linguists (Chomsky, 1957, 1995) argued that grammatical rules are far too complex for toddlers and preschoolers to infer them solely on the basis of speech that they hear.

THE LINGUISTIC ANSWER. Many scientists believe that children are born with mechanisms that simplify the task of learning grammar (Slobin, 1985). According to this view, children are born with neural circuits in the brain that allow them to infer the grammar of the language that they hear. That is, grammar itself is not built into the child's nervous system, but processes that guide the learning of grammar are. Many findings indirectly support this view:

1. If children are born with a "grammar-learning processor," specific regions of the brain should be involved in learning grammar. As we discussed on page 104, the left hemisphere of the brain plays a critical role in understanding language.

2. If learning grammar depends on specialized neural mechanisms that are unique to humans, then efforts to teach grammar to nonhumans should fail. This prediction has been tested by trying to teach grammar to chimpanzees, the species closest to humans on the evolutionary ladder. The result: Chimps master a handful of grammatical rules governing two-word speech, but only

with massive effort that is completely unlike the preschool child's learning of grammar (Savage-Rumbaugh et al., 1993; Seyfarth & Cheney, 1996).

3. The period from birth to about 12 years is a critical period for acquiring language generally and mastering grammar particularly. If children do not acquire language in this period, they never truly master language later (Newport, 1991; Rymer, 1993).

Although these findings are consistent with the idea that children have innate grammar-learning mechanisms, they do not prove the existence of such mechanisms. Consequently, scientists have continued to look for other explanations.

THE COGNITIVE ANSWER. Some theorists (Braine, 1992) believe that children learn grammar through powerful cognitive skills that help them rapidly detect regularities in their environment, including patterns in the speech they hear. According to this approach, it's as if children establish a huge Excel spread sheet that has the speech they've heard in one column and the context in which they heard it in a second column; periodically infants scan the columns looking for recurring patterns (Maratsos, 1998). For example, children might be confused the first time they hear -s added to the end of a familiar noun. However, as the database expands to include many instances of familiar nouns with an added -s, children discover that -s is always added to a noun when there are multiple instances of the object. Thus, they create the rule: noun + -s = plural. With this view, children learn language by searching for regularities across many examples that are stored in memory, not through an inborn grammar-learning device.

THE SOCIAL-INTERACTION ANSWER. This approach is eclectic, drawing on each of the views we've considered. From the behaviorist approach, it takes an emphasis on the environment; from the linguistic approach, that language learning is distinct; and, from the cognitive view, that children have powerful cognitive skills they can use to master language. The unique contribution of this perspective is emphasizing that much language learning takes place in the context of interactions between children and adults, with both parties eager for better communication (Bloom & Tinker, 2001). Children have an ever-expanding repertoire of ideas and intentions that they wish to convey to others, and caring adults want to understand their children, so both parties work to improve language skills as a means toward better communication. Thus, improved communication provides an incentive for children to master language and for adults to help them.

None of these accounts provides a comprehensive account of how grammar is mastered. But many scientists believe the final explanation will include contributions from the linguistic, cognitive, and social-interaction accounts. That is, children's learning of grammar will be explained in terms of some mechanisms specific to learning grammar, children actively seeking to identify regularities in their environment, and linguistically rich interactions between children and adults (MacWhinney, 1998).

COMMUNICATING WITH OTHERS

Imagining two preschoolers arguing is an excellent way to learn what is needed for effective communication. Both youngsters probably try to speak at the same time; their remarks may be rambling or incoherent; and they neglect to listen to each other altogether. These actions reveal three key elements in effective oral communication with others (Grice, 1975):

- People should take turns, alternating as speaker and listener.
- When speaking, remarks should be clear to the listener, from his or her own perspective.
- When listening, pay attention and let the speaker know if his or her remarks don't make sense.

Arguments can often be traced to people's failure to follow fundamental conversational rules, including (1) take turns, (2) speak clearly, and (3) listen carefully.

Complete mastery of these elements is a lifelong pursuit. After all, even adults often miscommunicate with one another, violating each of these prescriptions in the process. However, youngsters grasp many of the basics of communication early in life.

Taking Turns

Many parents begin to encourage turn-taking long before infants have said their first words (Field & Widmayer, 1982):

PARENT: Can you see the bird?
INFANT: (cooing) ooooh.
PARENT: It *is* a pretty bird.
INFANT: ooooh.
PARENT: You're right, it's a cardinal.

Soon after 1-year-olds begin to speak, parents encourage their youngsters to participate in conversational turn-taking. To help their children along, parents often carry both sides of the conversation to show how the roles of speaker and listener are alternated (Hoff, 2005):

PARENT: (initiating conversation) What's Kendra eating?
PARENT: (illustrating reply for child) She's eating a cookie.

Help of this sort is needed less often by age 2, when spontaneous turn-taking is common in conversations between youngsters and adults (Barton & Tomasello, 1991). By

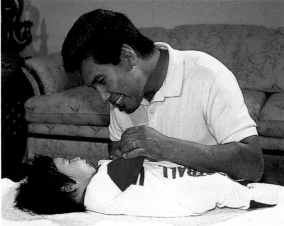

In early parent-child "conversations," parents usually carry both sides of the conversation, alternating as speaker and listener.

3 years of age, children have progressed to the point that if a listener fails to reply promptly, the child will often repeat his or her remarks to elicit a response and keep the conversation moving (Garvey & Berninger, 1981).

Speaking Effectively

When do children first try to initiate communications with others? In fact, what appear to be the first deliberate attempts to communicate typically emerge at 10 months (Bates et al., 1979; Golinkoff, 1993). Infants at this age may touch or point to an object while simultaneously looking at another person. They continue this behavior until the person acknowledges them. It's as if the child is saying, "This is a neat toy! I want you to see it too."

Beginning at 10 months, an infant may point, touch, or make noises to get an adult to do something. An infant in a playpen who wants a toy that is out of reach may make noises while pointing to the toy. The noises capture an adult's attention, and the pointing indicates what the baby wants (Blake, O'Rourke, & Borzellino, 1994). The communication may be a bit primitive by adult standards, but it works for babies!

After the first birthday, children begin to use speech to communicate and often initiate conversations with adults (Bloom et al., 1996). Toddlers' first conversations are about themselves, but their conversational scope expands rapidly to include objects in the environment (e.g., toys, food). Later, conversations begin to include more abstract notions, such as hypothetical objects and past or future events (Foster, 1986).

Of course, young children are not always skilled conversational partners. At times their communications are confusing, leaving a listener to wonder, "What was that all about?" Every message—whether an informal conversation or a formal lecture—

should have a clear meaning. But saying something clearly is often difficult because clarity can only be judged by considering the listener's age, experience, and knowledge of the topic, along with the context of the conversation. For example, think about the simple request, "Please hand me the Phillips screwdriver." This message may be clear to older listeners who are familiar with variants of screwdrivers, but it is vague to younger listeners, to whom all screwdrivers come from the same mold. Of course, if the toolbox is filled with Phillips screwdrivers of assorted sizes, the message is ambiguous even to a knowledgeable listener.

Consistently constructing clear messages is a fine art, which we would hardly expect young children to have mastered. By the preschool years, however, youngsters have made their initial attempts to calibrate messages, adjusting them to match the listener and the context. For example, preschool children give more elaborate messages to listeners who lack access to critical information than to listeners who have this information (Nadig & Sedivy, 2002; O'Neill, 1996). For example, a child describing where to find a toy will give more detailed directions to a listener whose eyes were covered when the toy was hidden. And, if listeners appear to misunderstand, 2- and 3-year-olds will clarify their messages (Shwe & Markman, 1997). These findings show that preschoolers are already sensitive to the importance of the listener's skill and understanding in formulating a clear message.

Listening Well

Sometimes messages are vague or confusing; in such situations, a listener needs to ask the speaker to clarify the message. Preschoolers do not always realize when a message is ambiguous. Told to find "the red toy," they may promptly select the red ball from a pile that includes a red toy car, a red block, and a red toy hammer. Instead of asking the speaker to refer to a specific red toy, preschool listeners often assume they know which toy the speaker had in mind (Beal & Belgrad, 1990). During the elementary-school years, youngsters gradually master the many elements involved in determining whether another person's message is consistent and clear (Ackerman, 1993).

Improvement in communication skill is yet another astonishing accomplishment in language during the first 5 years of life; changes are summarized in Table 4.2. By the time children are ready to enter kindergarten, they use language with remarkable proficiency and are able to communicate with growing skill.

THINK ABOUT IT

Compare Piaget's theory, Vygotsky's theory, and the information-processing approach in their emphasis on the role of language in cognitive development.

TABLE **4.2**

Major Milestones of Language Development

Age	Milestones
Birth to 1 year	Babies hear phonemes; they begin to coo and then babble.
About the 1st birthday	Babies begin to talk and to gesture, showing they have begun to use symbols.
1–2 years	Vocabulary expands rapidly (due to fast mapping); reflective and expressive language learning styles appear; two-word sentences emerge in telegraphic speech; and turn-taking is evident in communication.
3–5 years	Vocabulary continues to expand; grammatical morphemes are added; and children begin to adjust speech to listener but, as listeners, often ignore problems in messages they receive.

TEST YOURSELF

1. _____ are fundamental sounds used to create words.

2. Infants' mastery of language sounds may be fostered by _____, in which adults speak slowly and exaggerate changes in pitch and loudness.

3. Older infants' babbling often includes _____, a pattern of rising and falling pitch that distinguishes statements from questions.

4. Youngsters with a(n) _____ style have early vocabularies dominated by words that are names, and use language primarily as an intellectual tool.

5. In _____, a young child's meaning of a word is broader than an adult's meaning.

6. Noam Chomsky, a noted linguist, emphasized the role of _____ in children's acquisition of grammar.

7. When talking to listeners who lack critical information, preschoolers _____.

According to Piaget's theory, preschoolers are egocentric. How should this egocentrism influence their ability to communicate? Are the findings we have described on children's communication skills consistent with Piaget's view?

Answers: (1) Phonemes, (2) infant-directed speech, (3) intonation, (4) referential, (5) overextension, (6) biological mechanisms, (7) provide more elaborate messages.

Putting It All Together

The preschool years mark the transition from an infant who routinely depends on others to an independent 5-year-old ready to begin the long process of schooling. Piaget explained this transition in terms of a progression through qualitatively different stages. The first 2 years form the sensorimotor period, which has as its climax the ability to use symbols. The years 2–7 form the preoperational period, when children begin to explore the power of symbolic thought. Their thinking has limits, however, including the egocentrism that explains Jamila's head-nodding during phone conversations.

We also looked at the information-processing approach, in which cognitive development is described in terms of both general and task-specific processes. We saw that the basic skills of attention and memory improve considerably during the preschool years. However, there are imperfections in children's memory, so preschoolers like Cheryl (the child involved in an alleged case of abuse) do not always provide reliable testimony.

Next, we examined Vygotsky's view of cognitive development—that is, an apprenticeship in which children progress when collaborating with others who are more knowledgeable than they. We learned that children like Victoria talk to themselves during a transition period in which the control of cognitive processes is transferred from others to self.

In the last section, we saw that infants and preschoolers master the sounds, meanings, and grammar of their native language early in life. For example, infants like Nabina often understand words long before they have spoken. However, effective use of language to communicate is much slower to develop, continuing throughout the life span.

As a result of this growing intellectual and linguistic power, children are able to have more elaborate interactions and relationships with others, as we'll see in Chapter 5.

Summary

4.1 The Onset of Thinking: Piaget's Account

Basic Principles of Cognitive Development

■ In Piaget's view, children construct their own understanding of the world by creating schemes, categories of related events, objects, and knowledge. Infants' schemes are based on actions, but older children's and adolescents' schemes are based on functional, conceptual, and abstract properties.

■ Schemes change constantly. In assimilation, experiences are readily incorporated into existing schemes. In accommodation, experiences cause schemes to be modified.

■ When accommodation becomes much more common than assimilation, this is a sign that children's schemes are inadequate, so children reorganize them. This reorganization produces four different phases of mental development from infancy through adulthood.

Sensorimotor Thinking

■ The first 2 years of life constitute Piaget's sensorimotor period. Over these 2 years, infants begin to adapt to and explore their environment, understand objects, and learn to use symbols.

Preoperational Thinking

■ From 2 to 7 years of age, children are in Piaget's preoperational period. Although now capable of using symbols, their thinking is limited by egocentrism, the inability to see the world from another's point of view. Preoperational children are also centered in their thinking and sometimes confuse appearance with reality.

Evaluating Piaget's Theory

■ One important contribution of Piaget's theory is the view that children actively try to understand their world. Another contribution is specifying conditions that foster cognitive development. However, the theory has been criticized because children's performance on tasks is sometimes better explained by ideas that are not part of his theory. Another shortcoming is that children's performance from one task to the next is not as consistent as the theory predicts it to be.

Extending Piaget's Account: Children's Naive Theories

■ In contrast to Piaget's idea that children create a comprehensive theory that integrates all their knowledge, the modern view is that children are specialists, generating naive theories in particular domains, including physics and biology. Infants understand many properties of objects; they know how objects move, what happens when objects collide, and that objects fall when not supported.

■ Infants understand the difference between animate and inanimate objects. As preschoolers, children know that, unlike inanimate objects, animate objects move themselves, grow, have distinct internal parts, resemble their parents, and repair through healing.

4.2 Information Processing During Infancy and Early Childhood

General Principles of Information Processing

■ According to the information-processing view, cognitive development involves changes in mental hardware and in mental software.

Attention

■ Infant use habituation to filter unimportant stimuli. Compared to older children, preschoolers are less able to pay attention to task-relevant information. Their attention can be improved by making irrelevant stimuli less noticeable.

Learning

■ Infants are capable of many forms of learning, including classical conditioning, operant conditioning, and imitation.

Memory

■ Infants can remember and can be reminded of events they seem to have forgotten. Preschool children can remember events they experienced more than 1 year previously. Autobiographical memory emerges in the preschool years, reflecting children's growing language skills and their sense of self.

■ Preschoolers sometimes testify in cases of child abuse. When they are questioned repeatedly, preschoolers often have difficulty distinguishing what they experienced from what others may suggest they have experienced. Inaccuracies of this sort can be minimized by following certain guidelines when interviewing children, such as warning them that interviewers may try to trick them.

Learning Number Skills

■ Infants are able to distinguish small quantities, such as "twoness" from "threeness." By 3 years of age, children can count small sets of objects and in so doing adhere to the one-to-one, stable-order, and cardinality principles.

■ Learning to count to larger numbers involves learning rules about unit and decade names. This learning is more difficult for English-speaking children compared to children from Asian countries because names for numbers are irregular in English.

4.3 Mind and Culture: Vygotsky's Theory

The Zone of Proximal Development

■ Vygotsky believed that cognition develops first in a social setting and only gradually comes under the child's independent control. The difference between what children can do with assistance and what they can do alone constitutes the zone of proximal development.

Scaffolding

■ Control of cognitive skills is most readily transferred to the child through scaffolding, a teaching style in which teachers let children take on more and more of a task as they master its different components. Scaffolding is common worldwide, but the specific techniques for scaffolding children's learning vary from one cultural setting to the next.

Private Speech

■ Children often talk to themselves, particularly when the task is difficult or after they have made a mistake. Such private speech is one way that children regulate their behavior, and it represents an intermediate step in the transfer of control of thinking from others to the self.

4.4 Language

The Road to Speech

■ Phonemes are the basic units of sound from which words are constructed. Infants can hear phonemes soon after birth. They can even hear phonemes that are not used in their native language, but this ability diminishes after the first birthday.

■ Infant-directed speech is adults' speech to infants that is slower and has greater variation in pitch and loudness. Infants prefer infant-directed speech, perhaps because it gives them additional language clues.

■ Newborns' communication is limited to crying, but at about 3 months of age, babies coo. Babbling soon follows, consisting of a single syllable; over several months, infants' babbling comes to include longer syllables and intonation.

First Words and Many More

■ After a brief period in which children appear to understand others' speech but do not speak themselves, most infants begin to speak around the first birthday. The first use of words is triggered by the realization that words are symbols. Soon after, the child's vocabulary expands rapidly.

■ Most children learn the meanings of words much too rapidly for them to consider all plausible meanings systematically. Instead, children use certain rules to determine the probable meanings of new words. The rules do not always yield the correct meaning. An underextension is a child's meaning that is narrower than an adult's meaning; an overextension is a child's meaning that is broader.

■ Individual children differ in vocabulary size, differences attributable to phonological memory and the quality of the child's language environment. Bilingual children learn language readily and better understand the arbitrary nature of words. Some youngsters use a referential word-learning style that emphasizes words as names and that views language as an intellectual tool. Other children use an expressive style that emphasizes phrases and views language as a social tool.

■ Children's vocabulary is stimulated by experience. Both parents and television can foster the growth of vocabulary. The key ingredient is to actively involve children in language-related activities.

Speaking in Sentences: Grammatical Development

■ Soon after children begin to speak, they create two-word sentences that are derived from their own experiences. Moving from two-word to more complex sentences involves adding grammatical morphemes. Children first master grammatical morphemes that express simple relations, then those that denote complex relations. Mastery of grammatical morphemes involves learning rules as well as exceptions to the rules.

■ Behaviorists proposed that children acquire grammar through imitation, but that explanation is incorrect. Today's explanations come from three perspectives: the linguistic emphasizes inborn mechanisms that allow children to infer the grammatical rules of their native language, the cognitive perspective emphasizes cognitive processes that allow children to find recurring patterns in the speech they hear, and the social-interaction perspective emphasizes social interactions with adults in which both parties want improved communication.

Communicating With Others

■ Parents encourage turn-taking even before infants begin to talk and, later, demonstrate both the speaker and listener roles for their children. By 3 years of age, children spontaneously take turns and prompt one another to take their turn.

■ Preschool children adjust their speech in a rudimentary fashion to fit the listener's needs. However, preschoolers are unlikely to identify ambiguities in another's speech; instead, they are likely to assume they knew what the speaker meant.

Key Terms

scheme (132)

assimilation (132)

accommodation (133)

equilibration (133)

sensorimotor period (134)

object permanence (134)

egocentrism (135)

animism (136)

centration (137)

core knowledge hypothesis (144)

mental hardware (147)

mental software (147)

attention (147)

orienting response (147)

habituation (147)

classical conditioning (148)

operant conditioning (148)

autobiographical memory (150)

ordinality (153)

one-to-one principle (153)

stable-order principle (153)

cardinality principle (153)

zone of proximal development (155)

scaffolding (155)

private speech (156)

phonemes (158)

infant-directed speech (159)

cooing (160)

babbling (160)

fast mapping (162)

underextension (164)

overextension (164)

phonological memory (165)

referential style (165)

expressive style (166)

telegraphic speech (167)

grammatical morpheme (167)

overregularization (168)

Learn More About It

Readings

FLAVELL, J. H., MILLER, P. H., & MILLER, S. A. (2001). *Cognitive development* (4th ed.). Englewood Cliffs, NJ: Prentice-Hall. This book, written by a trio of leading researchers, describes cognitive development during infancy and the preschool years. Piaget's and Vygotsky's theories are presented, as is the information-processing perspective. This is probably the best general-purpose reference book on cognitive development for undergraduates.

GOLINKOFF, R. M., & HIRSH-PASEK, K. (1999). *How babies talk: The magic and mystery of language in the first three years of life.* New York: Dutton/Penguin. This engaging book, written by two specialists in child language, shows how children master language in the first 3 years of life. It is filled with many entertaining examples of children's talk.

KAIL, R. (1990). *The development of memory in children* (3rd ed.). New York: Freeman. This book describes memory in infants and toddlers, as well as in older children and adolescents. Much research is discussed, but in a straightforward, easy-to-read style.

POOLE, D. A., & LAMB, M. E. (2003). *Investigative interviews of children: A guide for helping professionals.* Washington, DC: American Psychological Association. Written by leading experts on the proper use of children as witnesses, the authors describe how best to ensure that interviews with child witnesses are conducted sensitively and professionally.

SIEGLER, R. S., & ALIBALI, M. W. (2005). *Children's thinking* (4th ed.). Upper Saddle River, NJ: Prentice-Hall. The authors are leading proponents of the information-processing approach to cognitive development, and this book reflects that orientation. They discuss Piaget's theory and language, but the best coverage is given to information-processing topics such as memory, problem solving, and academic skills.

Websites

Visit the Human Development book companion website for all URLs.

■ **The Human Development Book Companion Website**
See **http://www.psychology.wadsworth.com/kail _cavanaugh4e/** for practice quiz questions, Internet links, updates, critical thinking exercises, discussion forums, and more. Also accessible from the Wadsworth Psychology Study Center (http://psychology .wadsworth.com).

■ **The Jean Piaget Society**
This website includes biographical information about Piaget, suggested readings on Piaget's life and theory, and articles about cognitive development.

■ **The American Speech-Language-Hearing Association**
At this website you will find information about communication and communication disorders.

■ **The American Sign Language Browser**
The browser has a dictionary that shows the signs for many words and also has links to sites where you can learn more about American Sign Language.

Life-Span CD-ROM

For more information on the concepts covered in this chapter, go to
Module 2: Infancy and Toddlerhood

- *Cognitive Development*
- *Language Development*

Module 3: Early and Middle Childhood

- *Cognitive Development*
- *Language Development*

http://www.thomsonedu.com
Go to this site for the link to ThomsonNOW, your one-stop study shop. Take a pre-test for this chapter, and ThomsonNOW will generate a personalized study plan based on your test results. The study plan will identify the topics you need to review and direct you to online resources to help you master those topics. You can then take a post-test to help you determine the concepts you have mastered and what you still need to work on.

5.1 Beginnings: Trust and Attachment
Erikson's Stages of Early Psychosocial Development
The Growth of Attachment
What Determines Quality of Attachment?
Attachment, Work, and Alternative Caregiving
REAL PEOPLE: APPLYING HUMAN DEVELOPMENT: Lois, Bill, and Sarah

5.2 Emerging Emotions
Experiencing and Expressing Emotions
Recognizing and Using Others' Emotions
Regulating Emotions

5.3 Interacting With Others
The Joys of Play
Learning to Cooperate
Helping Others
SPOTLIGHT ON RESEARCH: Are Empathic Children More Likely to Help?

5.4 Gender Roles and Gender Identity
Images of Men and Women: Facts and Fantasy
Gender Typing
Biological Influences
Evolving Gender Roles

Putting It All Together

Summary

Key Terms

Learn More About It

CHAPTER 5

Entering the Social World

Socioemotional Development in Infancy and Early Childhood

Will Rogers, a famous American humorist in the 1920s and 1930s, once claimed, "I never met a man I didn't like." It certainly is true that humans enjoy one another's company. Social relationships of all sorts—friends, lovers, spouses, parents and children, coworkers, and team-mates—make our lives both interesting and satisfying.

In this chapter, we trace the origins of these social relationships. We begin with the first social relationship—between an infant and a parent. You will also see how this relationship is affected by the separation that comes when parents work full-time. Interactions with parents and others are often full of emotions—happiness, satisfaction, anger, and guilt, to name just a few. In the second section, you'll see how children express different emotions and how they recognize others' emotions.

In the third section, you'll learn how children's social horizons ex-pand beyond parents to include peers. Then you'll discover some of the factors that determine whether children cooperate and whether they help others in distress.

As children's interactions with others become more wide-ranging, they begin to learn about the social roles they are expected to play. Among the first social roles children learn are those associated with gender—how society expects boys and girls to behave. We'll explore children's awareness of gender roles in the last section of the chapter.

5.1

BEGINNINGS: TRUST AND ATTACHMENT

Kendra's son Roosevelt is a happy, affectionate 18-month-old. Kendra so loves spending time with him that she is avoiding an important decision. She wants to return to her job as a loan officer at the local bank. Kendra knows a woman in the neighborhood who has cared for some of her friends' children, and they all think she is a fantastic baby-sitter. But Kendra still has a nagging feeling that going back to work isn't a "motherly" thing to do —that being away during the day may hamper Roosevelt's development.

THE SOCIOEMOTIONAL RELATIONSHIP THAT DEVELOPS between an infant and a parent (usually, but not necessarily, the mother) is special. This is a baby's first relationship, and scientists and parents believe it should be satisfying and trouble free to set the stage for later relationships. In this section, we'll look at the steps involved in creating the baby's first emotional relationship. Along the way, you'll see how this relationship is affected by the separation that sometimes comes when a parent like Kendra works full-time.

ERIKSON'S STAGES OF EARLY PSYCHOSOCIAL DEVELOPMENT

Some of our keenest insights into the nature of psychosocial development come from a theory proposed by Erik Erikson (1982). We first encountered Erikson's theory in Chapter 1; recall that he describes development as a series of eight stages, each with a unique crisis for psychosocial growth. When a crisis is resolved successfully, an area of psychosocial strength is established. When the crisis is not resolved, that aspect of psychosocial development is stunted, which may limit the individual's ability to resolve future crises.

In Erikson's theory, infancy and the preschool years are represented by three stages, shown in Table 5.1. Let's take a closer look at each stage.

Basic Trust Versus Mistrust

Erikson argues that a sense of trust in oneself and others is the foundation of human development. Newborns leave the warmth and security of the uterus for an unfamiliar world. If parents respond to their infant's needs consistently, the infant comes to trust and feel secure in the world. Of course, the world is not always pleasant and can some-

TABLE 5.1

Erikson's First Three Stages

Age	Crisis	Strength
Infancy	Basic trust vs. mistrust	Hope
1–3 years	Autonomy vs. shame and doubt	Will
3–5 years	Initiative vs. guilt	Purpose

times be dangerous. Parents may not always reach a falling baby in time, or they may accidentally feed an infant food that is too hot. Erikson sees value in these experiences, because infants learn mistrust. *With a proper balance of trust and mistrust, infants can acquire **hope,** which is an openness to new experience tempered by wariness that discomfort or danger may arise.*

Autonomy Versus Shame and Doubt

Between 1 and 3 years of age, children gradually come to understand that they can control their own actions. With this understanding, children strive for autonomy, for independence from others. However, autonomy is counteracted by doubt that the child can handle demanding situations and by shame that may result from failure. *A blend of autonomy, shame, and doubt gives rise to **will,** the knowledge that, within limits, youngsters can act on their world intentionally.*

Initiative Versus Guilt

Most parents have their 3- and 4-year-olds take some responsibility for themselves (by dressing themselves, for example). Youngsters also begin to identify with adults and their parents; they begin to understand the opportunities that are available in their culture. Play begins to have purpose as children explore adult roles, such as mother, father, teacher, athlete, or writer. Youngsters start to explore the environment on their own, ask innumerable questions about the world, and imagine possibilities for themselves.

This initiative is moderated by guilt as children realize that their initiative may place them in conflict with others; they cannot pursue their ambitions with abandon. ***Purpose** is achieved with a balance between individual initiative and a willingness to cooperate with others.*

One of the strengths of Erikson's theory is its ability to tie together important psychosocial developments across the entire life span. We will return to the remaining stages in later chapters. For now, let's concentrate on the first of Erikson's crises—the establishment of trust in the world—and look at the formation of bonds between infants and parents.

THE GROWTH OF ATTACHMENT

In explaining the essential ingredients of these early social relationships, most modern accounts take an evolutionary perspective. *According to **evolutionary psychology,** many human behaviors represent successful adaptation to the environment.* That is, over human history, some behaviors have made it more likely that people will reproduce and pass on their genes to following generations. For example, we take it for granted that most people enjoy being with other people. But evolutionary psychologists argue that our "social nature" is a product of evolution: For early humans, being in a group offered protection from predators and made it easier to locate food. Thus, early humans who were social were more likely than their asocial peers to live long enough to reproduce, passing on their social orientation to their offspring (Gaulin & McBurney, 2001). Over many, many generations, "being social" had such a survival advantage that nearly all people are socially oriented (though in varying amounts, as we know from research on temperament discussed in Chapter 3).

Applied to child development, evolutionary psychology highlights the adaptive value of children's behavior at different points in development (Bjorklund & Pellegrini, 2000). For example, think about the time and energy parents invest in child rearing. Without such effort, infants and young children would die before they were sexually mature, which means that a parent's genes could not be passed along to grandchildren (Geary, 2002). Here, too, parenting just seems "natural" but really represents an adaptation to the problem of guaranteeing that one's helpless offspring can survive until they're sexually mature.

Evolutionary psychology emphasizes the adaptive value of parents nurturing their offspring.

THINK ABOUT IT

Based on Piaget's description of infancy (pages 134–135), what cognitive skills might be important prerequisites for the formation of an attachment relationship?

When infants have an attachment relationship with the mother, they use her as a secure base from which to explore the environment.

Steps Toward Attachment

An evolutionary perspective of early human relationships comes from John Bowlby (1969, 1991). According to Bowlby, *children who form an **attachment** to an adult—that is, an enduring socioemotional relationship —are more likely to survive.* This person is usually the mother but need not be; the key is a strong emotional relationship with a responsive, caring person. Attachments can form with fathers, grandparents, or someone else. Bowlby described four phases in the growth of attachment:

- *Preattachment* (birth to 6–8 weeks). Evolution has endowed infants with many behaviors that elicit caregiving from an adult. When babies cry, smile, or gaze intently at a parent's face, the parent usually smiles back or holds the baby. The infant's behaviors and the responses they evoke in adults create an interactive system that is the first step in the formation of attachment relationships.

- *Attachment in the making* (6–8 weeks to 6–8 months). During these months, babies begin to behave differently in the presence of familiar caregivers and unfamiliar adults. Babies now smile and laugh more often with the primary caregiver. And when babies are upset, they're more easily consoled by the primary caregiver. Babies are gradually identifying the primary caregiver as the person they can depend on when they're anxious or distressed.

- *True attachment* (6–8 months to 18 months). By approximately 7 or 8 months, most infants have singled out the attachment figure— usually the mother—as a special individual. The attachment figure is now the infant's stable socioemotional base. For example, a 7-month-old will explore a novel environment but periodically look toward his mother, as if seeking reassurance that all is well. The behavior suggests that the infant trusts his mother and indicates that the attachment relationship has been established. In addition, this behavior reflects important cognitive growth: It means that the infant has a mental representation of the mother, an understanding that she will be there to meet the infant's needs (Lewis et al., 1997).

- *Reciprocal relationships* (18 months on). Infants' growing cognitive and language skills and their accumulated experience with their primary caregivers make infants better able to act as true partners in the attachment relationship. They often take the initiative in interactions and negotiate with parents ("Please read me another story!"). They begin to understand parents' feelings and goals and sometimes use this knowledge to guide their own behavior (e.g., social referencing, described on pages 190– 191). In addition, they cope with separation more effectively because they can anticipate that parents will return.

Father-Infant Relationships

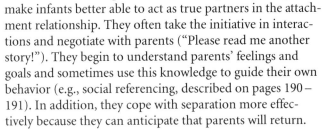

Attachment typically first develops between infants and their mothers because mothers are usually the primary caregivers of American infants. Babies soon become attached to fathers too, despite some consistent differences in the ways American mothers and fathers interact with infants. In a typical two-parent family, fathers spend far less time than mothers with infants and are far less likely than mothers to be responsible for child care tasks. For example, in a nationally representative sample of mothers and fathers of infants and toddlers, fathers spent an average of 32 minutes each day in caregiving tasks (e.g., feeding, bathing) compared to 70 minutes for mothers (Yeung et al., 2001). Over the past 40 years, child care has shifted some from being "women's work" to being a responsibility that can be shared equally by mothers and fathers. But women are still far more likely to be involved in direct care of infants and toddlers, despite no evidence that they provide better care than fathers do (Parke, 2002).

Another difference between mothers and fathers is *how* they interact with young children. Fathers typically spend much more time playing with their babies than taking care of them. And even their style of play differs. Physical play is the norm for fathers, whereas mothers spend more time reading and talking to babies, showing them toys, and playing games like patty-cake (Parke, 2002). Given the opportunity to play with mothers or fathers, infants more often choose their fathers. However, when infants are distressed, mothers are preferred (Field, 1990). Thus, although most infants become attached to both parents, mothers and fathers typically have distinctive roles in their children's early social development.

Forms of Attachment

Thanks to biology, virtually all infants behave in ways that elicit caregiving from adults, and because of this behavior attachment almost always develops between infant and caregiver by 8 or 9 months of age. However, attachment can take different forms, and environmental factors help determine the quality of attachment between infants and caregivers. Mary Ainsworth (1978, 1993) pioneered the study of attachment relationships using a procedure that has come to be known as the Strange Situation. You can see in Table 5.2 that the Strange Situation involves a series of episodes, each about 3 minutes long. The mother and infant enter an unfamiliar room filled with interesting toys. The mother leaves briefly, then mother and baby are reunited. Meanwhile, the experimenter observes the baby, recording its response to both separation and reunion.

Based on how the infant reacts to separation from, and reunion with, the mother, Ainsworth and other researchers have discovered four primary types of attachment relationships (Ainsworth, 1993; Main & Cassidy, 1988). One is a secure attachment and three are different types of insecure attachment (avoidant, resistant, disorganized):

■ ***Secure attachment:*** *The baby may or may not cry when the mother leaves, but when she returns, the baby wants to be with her, and if the baby is crying, it stops.* Babies in this group seem to be saying, "I missed you terribly, I'm delighted to see you, but now that all is well, I'll get back to what I was doing." Approximately 60–65% of American babies have secure attachment relationships.

Fathers and mothers differ in how they play with children. Fathers are much more likely to engage in vigorous physical play.

© Dorothy Littell Greco/The Image Works

TABLE 5.2

Sequence of Events in the Strange Situation

1. An observer shows the experimental room to the mother and infant, then leaves the room.

2. The infant is allowed to explore the playroom for 3 minutes; the mother watches but does not participate.

3. A stranger enters the room and remains silent for 1 minute, then talks to the baby for a minute, then approaches the baby. The mother leaves unobtrusively.

4. The stranger does not play with the baby but attempts to comfort it if necessary.

5. After 3 minutes, the mother returns, greets, and consoles the baby.

6. When the baby has returned to play, the mother leaves again, this time saying "bye-bye" as she leaves.

7. The stranger attempts to calm and play with the baby.

8. After 3 minutes, the mother returns, and the stranger leaves.

■ **Avoidant attachment:** *The baby is not upset when the mother leaves and, when she returns, may ignore her by looking or turning away.* Infants with an avoidant attachment look as if they're saying, "You left me *again.* I always have to take care of myself!" About 20% of American infants have avoidant attachment relationships, which is one of the three forms of insecure attachment.

■ **Resistant attachment:** *The baby is upset when the mother leaves and remains upset or even angry when she returns, and is difficult to console.* These babies seem to be telling the mother, "Why do you do this? I need you desperately and yet you just leave me without warning. I get so angry when you're like this." About 10–15% of American babies have this resistant attachment relationship, which is another form of insecure attachment.

■ **Disorganized (disoriented) attachment:** *The baby seems confused when the mother leaves and when she returns, as if not really understanding what's happening.* The baby often behaves in contradictory ways, such as nearing the mother when she returns but not looking at her, as if wondering, "What's happening? I want you to be here, but you left and now you're back. I don't get what's going on!" About 5–10% of American babies have this disorganized attachment relationship, the last of the three kinds of insecure attachment.

When infants who have a resistant attachment relationship are reunited with the mother, they're typically tearful, angry, and difficult to console.

More than 30 years later, the Strange Situation remains an important tool for studying attachment. But some scientists have criticized its emphasis on separation and reunion as the primary means for assessing quality of attachment; they suggest that what is considered an appropriate response to separation may not be the same in all cultures (Rothbaum et al., 2000). Consequently, investigators now use other methods to complement the Strange Situation. One of them, the Attachment Q-Set, can be used with young children as well as infants and toddlers. In this method, trained observers watch mothers and children interact at home; then the observer rates the interaction on many attachment-related behaviors (e.g., "Child greets mother with a big smile when she enters the room"). The ratings are totaled to provide a measure of the security of the child's attachment. Scores obtained with the Q-Set converge with assessments derived from the Strange Situation (van IJzendoorn et al., 2004).

Whether measured with the Strange Situation or the Attachment Q-Set, the quality of attachment during infancy predicts parent-child relations during childhood, adolescence, and young adulthood. Infants with secure attachment relationships tend to report, as adolescents and young adults, that they depend on their parents for care and support. In contrast, infants with insecure attachment relationships often report, as adolescents and young adults, being angry with their parents or deny being close to them. However, consistency is far from perfect. Stressful life events—death of a parent, divorce, life-threatening illness, poverty—help to determine stability and change in attachment. Stressful life events are associated with insecure attachments during adolescence and young adulthood. Consequently, when infants with insecure attachments experience stressful life events, their attachment tends to remain insecure; when infants with secure attachment experience these same events, their attachment often becomes insecure, perhaps because stress makes parents less available and less responsive to their children (Hamilton, 2000; Waters et al., 2000).

Consequences of Attachment

Erikson and other theorists (e.g., Waters & Cummings, 2000) believe that infant-parent attachment, the first social relationship, lays the foundation for all of the infant's later social relationships. In this view, infants who experience the trust and compassion of a secure attachment should develop into preschool children who interact confidently and successfully with their peers. In contrast, infants who do not experience a successful, satisfying first relationship should be more prone to problems in their social interactions as preschoolers.

Many findings are consistent with these predictions. For example, children with secure attachment relationships have higher-quality friendships and fewer conflicts in their friendships than children with insecure attachment relationships (Lieberman, Doyle, & Markiewicz, 1999.) And school-age children are less likely to have behavior problems if they have secure attachment relationships and more likely to have behavior problems if they have insecure attachment relationships (Carlson, 1998; Moss et al., 1998).

However, the most compelling evidence comes from a meta-analysis of 63 studies that had examined possible links between parent-child attachment and children's peer relations (Schneider, Atkinson, & Tardif, 2001). As predicted, children with secure attachments tended to have better relations with their peers and, in particular, had higher-quality friendships. Although some theorists (Thompson, 1998) have argued that an insecure attachment is particularly detrimental to peer relations in children who are exposed to other risk factors (e.g., those with a history of maltreatment or whose parents have a psychiatric disorder), the positive relation between attachment and peer relations was evident in children from high- and low-risk groups.

The conclusion seems inescapable: Secure attachment serves as the prototype for later successful social interactions. That is, a secure attachment evidently promotes trust and confidence in other humans, which leads to more skilled social interactions later in childhood (Thompson, 1998).

Of course, attachment is only the first of many steps along the long road of social development. Infants with insecure attachments are not forever damned, but this initial misstep *can* interfere with their social development. Consequently, we need to look at the conditions that determine the quality of attachment.

WHAT DETERMINES QUALITY OF ATTACHMENT?

Because secure attachment is so important to a child's later development, researchers have tried to identify the factors involved. Undoubtedly the most important is the interaction between parents and their babies (De Wolff & van IJzendoorn, 1997). A secure attachment is most likely when parents respond to infants predictably and appropriately. For example, when the mother promptly responds to her baby's crying and reassures the baby, the mother's behavior evidently conveys that social interactions are predictable and satisfying. This behavior seems to instill in infants the trust and confidence that are the hallmarks of secure attachment.

Why does predictable and responsive parenting promote secure attachment relationships? To answer this question, think about your own friendships and romantic relationships. These relationships are usually most satisfying when we believe we can trust the other people and depend on them in times of need. The same formula seems to hold for infants. *Infants develop an* **internal working model,** *a set of expectations about parents' availability and responsiveness, generally and in times of stress.* When parents are dependable and caring, babies come to trust them, knowing they can be relied on for comfort. That is, babies develop an internal working model in which they believe their parents are concerned about their needs and will try to meet them (Huth-Bocks et al., 2004; Thompson, 2000).

Many research findings attest to the importance of a caregiver's sensitivity for developing secure attachment:

- In a longitudinal study, infants were more likely to have a secure attachment relationship at 12 months when their parents were sensitive and responded quickly and appropriately to their infant at 3 months (Cox et al., 1992).

Perhaps the most important ingredient in fostering a secure attachment relationship is responding predictably and appropriately to the infant's needs.

© David Young-Wolff /PhotoEdit

■ In a study conducted in Israel, infants were less likely to develop secure attachment when they slept in dormitories with other children under 12, where they received inconsistent (if any) attention when they became upset overnight (Sagi et al., 1994).

■ In a study conducted in the Netherlands, infants were more likely to form a secure attachment when their mother had 3 months of training that emphasized monitoring an infant's signals and responding appropriately and promptly (van den Boom, 1994, 1995).

Thus, secure attachment is most likely when parents are sensitive and responsive. Of course, not all caregivers react to babies in a reliable and reassuring manner. Some respond intermittently or only after the infant has cried long and hard. And when these caregivers finally respond, they are sometimes annoyed by the infant's demands and may misinterpret the infant's intent. Over time, these babies tend to see social relationships as inconsistent and often frustrating, conditions that do little to foster trust and confidence.

Another factor contributing to the quality of attachment is temperament. Babies with difficult temperaments are somewhat less likely to form secure attachment relationships (Goldsmith & Harman, 1994; Seifer et al., 1996). That is, babies who fuss often and are difficult to console are more prone to insecure attachment. This may be particularly likely when a difficult, emotional infant has a mother whose personality is rigid and traditional than when the mother is accepting and flexible (Mangelsdorf et al., 1990). Rigid mothers do not adjust well to the often erratic demands of their difficult babies; instead, they want the baby to adjust to them. This means that rigid mothers less often provide the responsive, sensitive care that leads to secure attachment.

Fortunately, even brief training for mothers of newborns can help them respond to their babies more effectively (Bakermans-Kranenburg, Van IJzendoorn, & Juffer, 2003). Mothers can be taught how to interact more sensitively, affectionately, and responsively, paving the way for secure attachment and the lifelong benefits associated with a positive internal working model of interpersonal relationships.

The formation of attachment illustrates well the combined influence of the different components of the biopsychosocial framework. Many infant behaviors that elicit caregiving in adults—smiling and crying, for example—are biological in origin. When the caregiver is responsive to the infant (a sociocultural force), a secure attachment forms in which the infant trusts caregivers and knows that they can be relied on in stressful situations (a psychological force).

ATTACHMENT, WORK, AND ALTERNATIVE CAREGIVING

Since the 1970s, more women in the workforce and more single-parent households have made child care a fact of life for many American families. Today approximately 6 million infants and toddlers are cared for by someone other than their mother. About one third of America's infants and preschoolers are cared for in their home, typically by the father or a grandparent. Another third receive care in the provider's home. The provider is often but not always a relative. Finally, another third attend day care or nursery school programs. The patterns are very similar for European American, African American, and Latino American youngsters (Singer et al., 1998; U.S. Census Bureau, 1995).

Parents and policymakers alike have been concerned about the impact of such care on children generally and, specifically, its impact on attachment. Is there, for example, a maximum amount of time per week that infants should spend in care outside the home? Is there a minimum age below which infants should not be placed in care outside the home? To answer these questions, a comprehensive longitudinal study of early child care was initiated by the National Institute of

Roughly one third of American infants and preschoolers attend day care or nursery school programs.

© Ellen Senisi / The Image Works

Child Health and Human Development (NICHD), which was created in 1962 to study children's physical, emotional, and cognitive development. Planning for the early child care study began in 1989, and by 1991 the study was under way. Researchers recruited 1,364 mothers and their newborns from 12 U.S. cities. Both mothers and children have been tested repeatedly (and the testing continues because the study is ongoing).

From the outset, one of the concerns was the impact of early child care on mother-infant attachment. In fact, the results so far show no overall effects of child care experience on mother-infant attachment, for either 15- or 36-month-olds (NICHD Early Child Care Research Network, 1997, 2001). In other words, a secure mother-infant attachment was just as likely regardless of the quality of child care, the amount of time the child spent in care, the age when the child began care, how frequently the parents changed child care arrangements, or the type of child care (e.g., a child care center or in the home with a nonrelative).

However, when the effects of child care were considered along with characteristics of the mothers, an important pattern was detected: At 15 and 36 months, insecure attachments were more common when less sensitive mothering was combined with low-quality or large amounts of child care (NICHD Early Child Care Research Network, 1997, 2001). As the investigators put it, "poor quality, unstable, or more than minimal amounts of child care apparently added to the risks already inherent in poor mothering, so that the combined effects were worse than those of low maternal sensitivity and responsiveness alone" (1997, p. 877). These conclusions are particularly convincing because the same pattern of results was found in Israel in a large-scale study of child care and attachment that was modeled after the NICHD early child care study (Sagi et al., 2002).

These results provide clear guidelines for parents like Kendra, the mother in the vignette. They can enroll their infants and toddlers in high-quality day care programs with no fear of harmful consequences. When children are enrolled in high-quality day care, other factors (e.g., the type of child care or the amount of time the child spends in child care) typically do not affect the mother-child attachment relationship.

The results of the early child care study are reassuring for parents, who often have misgivings about their infants and toddlers spending so much time in the care of others. Nevertheless, they raise another, equally important question: What are the features of high-quality child care? That is, what should parents look for when trying to find care for their children? In general, high-quality child care has the following features (Burchinal et al., 2000; Lamb, 1999; Rosenthal & Vandell, 1996):

- A low ratio of children to caregivers
- Well-trained, experienced staff
- Low staff turnover
- Ample opportunities for educational and social stimulation
- Effective communication between parents and day care workers concerning the general aims and routine functioning of the program

Collectively, these variables do *not* guarantee that a child will receive high-quality care. Sensitive, responsive caregiving—the same behavior that promotes secure attachment relationships—is the real key to high-quality child care. Centers that have well-trained, experienced staff caring for a relatively small number of children are more likely to provide good care, but the only way to know the quality of care with certainty is to see for yourself (Lamb, 1999).

Fortunately, employers have begun to realize that convenient, high-quality child care makes for a better employee. In Flint, Michigan, for example, child care was part of the contract negotiated between the United Auto Workers and General Motors. Many cities have

THINK ABOUT IT

Imagine that your best friend is the mother of a 3-month-old. Your friend is about to return to her job as a social worker, but she's afraid she'll harm her baby by going back to work. What could you say to reassure her?

Responding to the needs of working families, many employers now provide child care on site.

© Boulton-Wilson /Jeroboam

modified their zoning codes so that new shopping complexes and office buildings include child care facilities. Businesses are realizing that the availability of excellent child care helps attract and retain a skilled labor force.

With effort, organization, and help from the community and business, full-time employment and high-quality caregiving *can* be compatible. We will return to this issue in Chapter 12, from the perspective of the parents. For now, the Real People feature provides one example of a father who stays home to care for his daughter while her mother works full-time.

REAL PEOPLE: Applying Human Development

LOIS, BILL, AND SARAH

Lois, 46, and Bill, 61, had been married nearly 4 years when Lois gave birth to Sarah. Lois, a kindergarten teacher, returned to work full-time 4 months after Sarah was born. Bill, who had been half-heartedly pursuing a Ph.D. in education, became a full-time househusband. Bill does the cooking and takes care of Sarah during the day. Lois comes home from school at noon so that the family can eat lunch together, and she is home from work by 4 in the afternoon. Once a week, Bill takes Sarah to a parent-infant play program. The other parents, all mothers in their 20s or 30s, first assumed that Bill was Sarah's grandfather and had trouble relating to him as an older father. Soon, however, he was an accepted member of the group. On weekends, Lois's and Bill's grown children from previous marriages often visit and enjoy caring for and playing with Sarah. By all accounts, Sarah looks to be a healthy, happy, outgoing 9-month-old. Is this arrangement nontraditional? Clearly. Is it effective for Sarah, Lois, and Bill? Definitely. Sarah receives the nurturing care she needs, Lois goes to work assured that Sarah is in Bill's knowing and caring hands, and Bill relishes being the primary caregiver.

TEST YOURSELF

1. _____ proposed that maturational and social factors come together to pose eight unique challenges for psychosocial growth during the life span.

2. Infants must balance trust and mistrust to achieve _____, an openness to new experience that is coupled with awareness of possible danger.

3. By approximately _____ months of age, most infants have identified a special individual—usually but not always the mother—as the attachment figure.

4. Joan, a 12-month-old, was separated from her mother for about 15 minutes. When they were reunited, Joan would not let her mother pick her up. When her mother approached, Joan would look the other way or toddle to another part of the room. This behavior suggests that Joan has a(n) _____ attachment relationship.

5. The single most important factor in fostering a secure attachment relationship is _____.

6. Tim and Douglas, both 3-year-olds, rarely argue; when they disagree, one goes along with the other's ideas. The odds are good that both boys have _____ attachment relationships with their parents.

7. An insecure attachment relationship is likely when an infant receives poor-quality child care and _____.

Most research on attachment has relied on Ainsworth's Strange Situation. What are some of the assets of this method? What are some potential problems?

Answers: (1) Erik Erikson, (2) hope, (3) 6 or 7, (4) avoidant insecure, (5) responding consistently and appropriately, (6) secure, (7) insensitive, unresponsive mothering

5.2

EMERGING EMOTIONS

Nicole is ecstatic that she is finally going to see her 7-month-old nephew, Claude. She rushes into the house, and seeing Claude playing on the floor with blocks, sweeps him up in a big hug. After a brief, puzzled look, Claude bursts into angry tears and begins thrashing his arms and legs, as if saying to Nicole, "Who are you? What do you want? Put me down! Now!" Nicole quickly hands Claude to his mother, who is surprised by her baby's outburst and even more surprised that he continues to sob while she rocks him.

LEARNING OBJECTIVES

At what ages do children begin to express basic emotions?

———

What are complex emotions, and when do they develop?

———

When do children begin to understand other people's emotions? How do they use this information to guide their own behavior?

THIS VIGNETTE ILLUSTRATES THREE COMMON EMOTIONS. Nicole's initial joy, Claude's anger, and his mother's surprise are familiar to all of us. In this section, we look at when children first express emotions, how children come to understand emotions in others, and, finally, how children regulate their emotions. As we do, we'll learn why Claude reacted to Nicole as he did and how Nicole could have prevented Claude's outburst.

EXPERIENCING AND EXPRESSING EMOTIONS

The three emotions from the vignette—joy, anger, and fear—are considered "basic emotions," as are interest, disgust, distress, sadness, and surprise (Dragh-Lorenz, Reddy, & Costall, 2001). **Basic emotions** *are experienced by people worldwide, and each consists of three elements: a subjective feeling, a physiological change, and an overt behavior* (Izard, 1991). For example, suppose you wake to the sound of a thunderstorm and then discover your roommate has left for class with your umbrella. Subjectively, you might feel ready to explode with anger; physiologically, your heart would beat faster; and behaviorally, you would probably be scowling.

Measuring Emotions

How can we determine when infants first experience basic emotions? Overt behaviors such as facial expression provide important clues. Infants' facial expressions are revealing, but do these distinctive facial expressions mean the infants are actually experiencing these emotions? Not necessarily. Facial expressions are only one component of emotion—the behavioral manifestation. Emotion also involves physiological responses and subjective feelings. Of course, infants can't express their feelings to us verbally, so we don't know much about their subjective experiences. But at least some of the physiological responses that accompany facial expressions are the same in infants and adults.

Facial expressions often reveal an infant's emotions.

For example, when infants and adults smile—which suggests they're happy—the left frontal cortex of the brain tends to have more electrical activity than the right frontal cortex (Fox, 1991).

Research has revealed several other reasons to believe that facial expressions are an accurate barometer of an infant's emotional state:

■ Infants (and adults) worldwide express basic emotions in much the same way (Izard, 1991). For example, eyes open wide, eyebrows raised, and mouth relaxed but slightly open are universal signs of fear. The universality of emotional expression suggests that humans are biologically programmed to express basic emotions in a specific way.

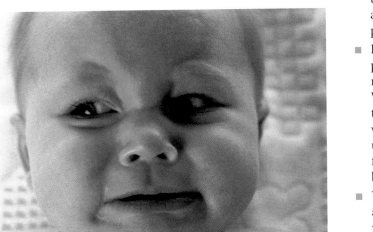

The universal signs of fear: eyes wide open, eyebrows raised, and mouth relaxed but open slightly.

■ By 5 to 6 months, infants' facial expressions change predictably and meaningfully in response to events. When a happy mother greets her baby, the baby usually smiles in return; when a tired, distracted mother picks up her baby roughly, the baby usually frowns at her (Izard et al., 1995; Weinberg & Tronick, 1994).

■ When adults are really happy or amused, they smile differently than when they smile to greet an acquaintance or to hide hurt feelings. In "joyful" smiles, the muscles around the eyes contract, which lifts the cheeks.

Similarly, infants smile at both moms and other interesting objects, but they are more likely to raise their cheeks during smiling when looking at mom (Messinger, 2002). The close parallel between the details of infants' and adults' smiles suggests that smiling has the same meaning, emotionally, for infants and adults.

Collectively, these findings make it reasonable to assume that facial expressions reflect an infant's underlying emotional state.

Development of Basic Emotions

Using facial expressions and other overt behaviors, scientists have traced the growth of basic emotions in infants. According to one influential theory (Lewis, 2000), newborns experience only two general emotions: pleasure and distress. Rapidly, though, more discrete emotions emerge, and by 8 or 9 months of age, infants are thought to experience all basic emotions. For example, joy emerges at about 2 or 3 months. *At this age **social smiles** first appear; infants smile when they see another human face.* Sometimes social smiling is accompanied by cooing, the early form of vocalization described in Chapter 4 (Sroufe & Waters, 1976). Smiling and cooing seem to be the infant's way of expressing pleasure at seeing another person. Sadness is also observed at about this age: Infants look sad, for example, when their mothers stop playing with them (Lewis, 2000).

Anger typically emerges between 4 and 6 months. Infants will become angry, for example, if a favorite food or toy is taken away (Sternberg & Campos, 1990). Reflecting their growing understanding of goal-directed behavior (see page 134), infants also become angry when their attempts to achieve a goal are frustrated. For example, if a parent restrains an infant trying to pick up a toy, the guaranteed result is a very angry baby.

Like anger, fear emerges later in the first year. *At about 6 months, infants become wary in the presence of an unfamiliar adult, a reaction known as **stranger wariness.*** When a stranger approaches, a 6-month-old typically looks away and begins to fuss (Mangelsdorf, Shapiro, & Marzolf, 1995). If a grandmother picks up her grandchild without giving the infant a chance to warm up to her, the outcome is as predictable as it was with

THINK ABOUT IT

How might an infant's ability to express emotions relate to the formation of attachment? To the temperamental characteristics described on pages 93–95?

Claude, the baby boy in the vignette who was frightened by his aunt: He cries, looks frightened, and reaches with arms outstretched in the direction of someone familiar.

How wary an infant feels around strangers depends on a number of factors (Thompson & Limber, 1991). First, infants tend to be less fearful of strangers when the environment is familiar and more fearful when it is not. Many parents know this firsthand from traveling with their infants: Enter a friend's house for the first time and the baby clings tightly to its mother. Second, the amount of anxiety depends on the stranger's behavior. Instead of rushing to greet or pick up the baby, as Nicole did in the vignette, a stranger should talk with other adults and, in a while, perhaps offer the baby a toy (Mangelsdorf, 1992). Handled this way, many infants will soon be curious about the stranger instead of afraid.

Wariness of strangers is adaptive because it emerges at the same time that children begin to master creeping and crawling (described on pages 106–109). Like Curious George, the monkey in a famous series of children's books, babies are inquisitive and want to use their new locomotor skills to explore their world. Being wary of strangers provides a natural restraint against the tendency to wander away from familiar caregivers. However, as youngsters learn to interpret facial expressions and recognize when a person is friendly, their wariness of strangers declines.

Young babies are often wary of strangers; consequently, they're unhappy when strangers hold them without giving them a chance to "warm up."

Emergence of Complex Emotions

In addition to basic emotions such as joy and anger, people feel complex emotions such as pride, guilt, and embarrassment. Most scientists (e.g., Lewis, 2000) believe that complex emotions don't surface until 18 to 24 months of age because they depend on the child having some understanding of the self, which typically occurs between 15 and 18 months. Children feel guilty or embarrassed, for example, when they've done something they know they shouldn't have done (Kochanska et al., 2002). For example, a child who breaks a toy is thinking, "You told me to be careful. But I wasn't!" Similarly, children feel pride when they accomplish a challenging task for the first time. Thus, children's growing understanding of themselves enables them to experience complex emotions like pride and guilt (Lewis, 2000).

THINK ABOUT IT

Explain how the different forces in the biopsychosocial framework contribute to the development of basic and complex emotions.

Later Developments

As children grow, they continue to experience basic and complex emotions, but different situations or events elicit these emotions. In the case of complex emotions, cognitive growth means that elementary-school children experience shame and guilt in situations they would not have when they were younger (Reimer, 1996). For example, unlike preschool children, many school-age children would be ashamed if they neglected to defend a classmate who had been wrongly accused of a theft.

Fear is another emotion that can be elicited in different ways, depending on a child's age. Many preschool children are afraid of the dark and of imaginary creatures. These fears typically diminish during the elementary-school years as children grow cognitively and better understand the difference between appearance and reality. Replacing these fears are concerns about school, health, and personal harm (Silverman, La Greca, & Wasserstein, 1995). Such worries are common and not cause for concern in most children. In some youngsters, however, they become so extreme they overwhelm the child (Chorpita & Barlow, 1998). For example, a 7-year-old's worries about school would not be unusual unless her concern grew to the point that she refused to go to school.

Cultural Differences in Emotional Expression

Children worldwide express many of the same basic and complex emotions. However, cultures differ in the extent to which emotional expression is encouraged (Hess & Kirouac, 2000). In many Asian countries, for example, outward displays of emotion are discouraged in favor of emotional restraint. Consistent with these differences, in one study (Camras et al., 1998), European American 11-month-olds cried and smiled

American children are often quite proud of personal achievement, but Asian children would be embarrassed by such a public display of individual accomplishments.

more often than Chinese 11-month-olds. In another study (Zahn-Waxler et al., 1996), U.S. preschoolers were more likely than Japanese preschoolers to express anger in interpersonal conflicts.

And cultures differ in the events that trigger emotions, particularly complex emotions. Situations that evoke pride in one culture may evoke embarrassment or shame in another. For example, American elementary-school children often show pride at personal achievement, such as getting the highest grade on a test or coming in first place in a county fair. In contrast, Asian elementary-school children are embarrassed by a public display of individual achievement but show great pride when their entire class is honored for an achievement (Stevenson & Stigler, 1992).

Expression of anger also varies around the world. For example, think about the following two events: (a) a friend grabs and eats a piece of candy just as you were about to eat it yourself, and (b) you fall down while running and your friend laughs at you. Most American children respond to these and similar events with anger. In contrast, children growing up in east Asian countries that practice Buddhism (e.g., Mongolia, Thailand, Nepal) rarely respond with anger because this goes against the Buddhist tenet to extend loving kindness to all people, even those whose actions hurt others (Cole, Bruschi, & Tamang, 2002).

Thus, culture can influence when and how much children express emotion. Of course, expressing emotion is only part of the developmental story. Children must also learn to recognize others' emotions, which is our next topic.

RECOGNIZING AND USING OTHERS' EMOTIONS

Imagine you are broke (only temporarily, of course) and plan to borrow $20 from your roommate when she returns from class. Shortly, she storms into your apartment, slams the door, and throws her backpack on the floor. Immediately, you change your plans, realizing that now is hardly a good time to ask for a loan. This example reminds us that we often need to recognize others' emotions and sometimes change our behavior as a consequence.

When can infants first identify emotions in others? Perhaps as early as 4 months and definitely by 6 months infants begin to distinguish facial expressions associated with different emotions. They can, for example, distinguish a happy, smiling face from a sad, frowning face (Bornstein & Arterberry, 2003; Montague & Walker-Andrews, 2001). Of course, infants might be able to distinguish an angry face from a happy one but not know the emotional significance of the two faces. How can we tell whether infants understand the emotions expressed in a face? The best evidence is that infants often match their own emotions to other people's emotions. When happy mothers smile and talk in a pleasant voice, infants express happiness themselves. If mothers are angry or sad, infants become distressed too (Haviland & Lelwica, 1987; Montague & Walker-Andrews, 2001).

Also like adults, infants use others' emotions to direct their behavior. *Infants in an unfamiliar or ambiguous environment often look at their mother or father, as if searching for cues to help them interpret the situation, a phenomenon known as* **social referencing.** If a parent looks afraid when shown a novel object, 12-month-olds are less likely to play with the toy than if a parent looks happy (Repacholi, 1998). Furthermore, an infant can use parents' facial expressions or their vocal expressions alone to decide whether they want to explore an unfamiliar object (Mumme, Fernald, & Herrera, 1996). And infants' use of parents' cues is precise (see Figure 5.1). If two unfamiliar toys are shown to a parent, who expresses disgust at one toy but not the other, 12-month-olds will avoid the toy that elicited the disgust but not the other toy (Moses et al., 2001). And by 14 months,

■ Figure 5.1
When parents seem frightened by an unfamiliar object, babies are also wary or even afraid of it too.

infants remember this information: They avoid a toy that elicited disgust an hour earlier (Hertenstein & Campos, 2004). Thus, social referencing shows that infants are remarkably skilled in using their parents' emotions to help them direct their own behavior.

As children's cognitive skills continue to grow in childhood, they become more adept at identifying others' emotions and more adept at modifying their behavior accordingly (Boone & Cunningham, 1998; Dunn, Brown, & Maguire, 1995). Children learn that sometimes they should conceal their emotions (Jones, Abbey, & Cumberland, 1998). And, they begin to understand why people feel as they do and how emotions can influence a person's behavior. Preschool children, for example, understand that an angry child is more likely than a happy child to hurt someone (Russell & Paris, 1994).

What experiences contribute to children's understanding of emotions? Parents and children frequently talk about past emotions and why people felt as they did; this is particularly true for negative emotions such as fear and anger (Lagattuta & Wellman, 2002). Not surprisingly, children learn about emotions when parents talk about feelings, explaining how they differ and the situations that elicit them (Brown & Dunn, 1996; Cervantes & Callanan, 1998). Also, a positive, rewarding relationship with parents and siblings is related to children's understanding of emotions (Brown & Dunn, 1996; Thompson, Laible, & Ontai, 2003). The nature of this connection is still a mystery. One possibility is that within positive parent-child and sibling relationships, people express a fuller range of emotions (and do so more often) and are more willing to talk about why they feel as they do, providing children with more opportunities to learn about emotions.

REGULATING EMOTIONS

Think back to a time when you were *really* angry at a good friend. Did you shout at the friend? Did you try to discuss matters calmly? Or did you simply ignore the situation altogether? Shouting is a direct expression of anger, but calm conversation and overlooking a situation are purposeful attempts to regulate emotion. People often regulate emotions; for example, we routinely try to suppress fear (because we know there's no real need to be afraid of the dark), anger (because we don't want to let a friend know just how upset we are), and joy (because we don't want to seem like we're gloating over our good fortune).

Child development researchers have studied two aspects of emotion regulation: its origins and its links to social competence. Emotion regulation clearly begins in infancy. By 4 to 6 months, infants use simple strategies to regulate their emotions (Buss & Goldsmith, 1998; Rothbart & Rueda, 2005). When something frightens or confuses an infant —for example, a stranger or a mother who suddenly stops responding—he or she often looks away (just as older children and even adults often turn away or close their eyes to block out disturbing stimuli). Frightened infants also move closer to a parent, another effective way of helping to control their fear (Parritz, 1996). By 24 months, a distressed toddler's face typically expresses sadness instead of fear or anger; apparently by this age toddlers have learned that a sad facial expression is the best way to get a mother's attention and support (Buss & Kiel, 2004).

Older children and adolescents encounter a wider range of emotional situations, so it's fortunate they develop a number of related new ways to regulate emotion (Eisenberg & Morris, 2002):

- Children begin to regulate their own emotions and rely less on others to do this for them. A fearful child no longer runs to a parent but instead devises her own methods for dealing with fear (e.g., "I know the thunderstorm won't last long, and I'm safe inside the house").
- Children more often rely on mental strategies to regulate emotions. For example, a child might reduce his disappointment at not receiving a much-expected gift by telling himself that he didn't really want the gift in the first place.
- Children more accurately match the strategies for regulating emotion with the particular setting. For example, when faced with emotional situations that are unavoidable (e.g., a child must go to the dentist to have a cavity filled), children adjust to the situation (e.g., thinking of the positive consequences of treating the tooth) instead of trying to avoid it.

Collectively, these age-related trends give children tools for regulating emotions.

Unfortunately, not all children regulate their emotions well, and those who don't tend to have problems interacting with peers and have adjustment problems (Eisenberg & Morris, 2002; Eisenberg et al., 2005). When children can't control their anger, worry, or sadness, they often have difficulty resolving the conflicts that inevitably surface in peer relationships (Fabes et al., 1999). For example, when children are faced with a dispute over who gets to play with a toy, their unregulated anger interferes with finding a mutually satisfying solution. Thus, ineffective regulation of emotions leads to more frequent conflicts with peers, and, consequently, less satisfying peer relationships and less adaptive adjustment to school (Eisenberg et al., 2001; Olson et al., 2005).

 **TEST YOURSELF**

1. Basic emotions include a subjective feeling, a physiological change, and _____.
2. The first detectable form of fear is _____, which emerges at about 6 months.
3. Wariness of strangers is adaptive because it emerges at about the same time that _____.
4. Complex emotions, such as guilt and shame, emerge later than basic emotions because _____.
5. In social referencing, infants use a parent's facial expression _____.

6. Infants often control fear by looking away from a frightening event or by _____.

Most theories of cognitive development, such as Piaget's and the information-processing approach, don't explicitly consider emotion. How might emotions affect thinking? How could these theories include emotions?

Answers: (1) an overt behavior, (2) wariness of strangers, (3) infants master creeping and crawling, (4) complex emotions require more advanced cognitive skills, (5) to direct their own behavior (e.g., deciding if an unfamiliar situation is safe or frightening), (6) moving closer to a parent

5.3

INTERACTING WITH OTHERS

Six-year-old Juan got his finger trapped in the VCR when he tried to remove a tape. While he cried and cried, his 3-year-old brother, Antonio, and his 2-year-old sister, Carla, watched but did not help. Later, when their mother had soothed Juan and concluded that his finger was not injured, she worried about her younger children's reactions. In the face of their brother's obvious distress, why did Antonio and Carla do nothing?

LEARNING OBJECTIVES

When do youngsters first begin to play with each other? How does play change during infancy and the preschool years?

——————

What determines whether preschool children cooperate with one another?

——————

What determines whether children help one another? What experiences make children more inclined to help?

Infants' initial interactions are with parents, but soon they begin to interact with other people, notably their peers. In this section, we'll trace the development of these interactions and learn why children like Antonio and Carla don't always help others.

THE JOYS OF PLAY

If you watch two 5-month-olds together, hoping to see some social interaction, you'll be disappointed. The infants will look at each other, but you won't observe anything that qualifies as an interaction. However, at about 6 months, the first signs of peer interactions appear: Now an infant may point to or smile at another infant (Hartup, 1983).

*Soon after the first birthday, children begin **parallel play**, in which each youngster plays alone but maintains a keen interest in what another is doing.* Two toddlers may each have his or her own toys, but each will watch the other's play too. Exchanges between youngsters also become more common. When one toddler talks or smiles, the other usually responds (Howes, Unger, & Seidner, 1990).

Beginning at roughly 15 to 18 months, toddlers no longer simply watch one another at play. *Instead, they engage in similar activities and talk or smile at one another, illustrating **simple social play.*** Play has now become truly interactive. For example, youngsters now offer toys to one another (Howes & Matheson, 1992).

*Toward the second birthday, **cooperative play** is observed: Now a distinct theme organizes children's play, and they take on special roles based on the theme.* They may play "hide-and-seek" and alternate the roles of hider

In parallel play, children play independently but actively watch what other children are doing.

Cooperative play, which involves well-defined roles (e.g., a hider and a seeker), is first observed at about 2 years of age.

Make-believe—a favorite of preschoolers everywhere—fosters their cognitive development.

and finder, or they may have a tea party and take turns being the host and the guest (Parten, 1932).

The nature of young children's play changes dramatically in a few years (Howes & Matheson, 1992). In a typical day care center, 1- and 2-year-olds spend most of their time in parallel play; other forms of play are relatively rare. In contrast, among 3- and 4-year-olds, parallel play is much less common, and cooperative play is the norm.

Make-Believe

During the preschool years, cooperative play often takes the form of make-believe. Preschoolers have telephone conversations with imaginary partners or pretend to drink imaginary juice. In the early phases of make-believe, children rely on realistic props to support their play. While pretending to drink, younger preschoolers use a real cup; while pretending to drive a car, they use a toy steering wheel. In the later phases of make-believe, children no longer need realistic props; instead, they can imagine that a block is the cup or that a paper plate is the steering wheel. Of course, this gradual movement toward more abstract make-believe is possible because of cognitive growth that occurs during the preschool years (Harris & Kavanaugh, 1993).

As you might suspect, make-believe reflects the values important in a child's culture. This influence is apparent in the results of research by Farver and Shin (1997), who studied European American and Korean American preschoolers. The Korean American children came from families who had recently immigrated to the United States and who still stressed the importance of traditional Korean values such as emphasis on the family and favoring harmony over conflict. The two groups of children differed in the themes common during make-believe. Adventure and fantasy were common themes for European American youngsters, but family roles and everyday activities were common for the Korean American youngsters. In addition, the groups differed in their style of play during make-believe. European American children were more assertive in their make-believe and more likely to disagree with their play partner's ideas about pretending ("*I* want to be the king; *you* be the mom!"). In contrast, Korean American children were more polite and more likely to strive for harmony in their play ("Could I *please* be king?"). Thus, cultural values influence both the form and the content of make-believe.

Make-believe play is not only entertaining for children, it seems to promote children's cognitive development (Berk, 1994). Children who spend much time in make-believe play tend to be more advanced in their language, memory, and reasoning. They also tend to be more sophisticated in their understanding of other people's thoughts, beliefs, and feelings (Howe, Petrakos, & Rinaldi, 1998; Youngblade & Dunn, 1995).

Another benefit of make-believe is that it allows children to explore topics that frighten them. Children who are afraid of the dark may reassure a doll who is also afraid of the dark. By explaining to the doll why she need not be afraid, children come to understand and regulate their own fear of darkness. Or children may pretend that a doll has misbehaved and must be punished, which allows them to experience the parent's anger and the doll's guilt. With make-believe, children explore other emotions as well, including joy and affection (Gottman, 1986).

For many preschool children, make-believe play involves imaginary companions. These children can easily describe their imaginary playmates, mentioning their sex and age as well as the color of their hair and eyes. Imaginary companions were once thought to be fairly rare and a sign of possible developmental problems. But more recent research shows that many children report imaginary companions (Taylor et al., 2004). What's more, the presence of an imaginary companion is actually associated with many *positive* social characteristics: Preschoolers with imaginary companions tend to be more

THINK ABOUT IT

How might Jean Piaget have explained the emergence of make-believe during the preschool years? How would Erik Erikson explain it?

sociable and have more real friends than preschoolers without imaginary companions. Furthermore, vivid fantasy play with imaginary companions does *not* mean that the distinction between fantasy and reality is blurred: Children with imaginary companions can distinguish fantasy from reality just as readily as youngsters who do not have imaginary companions (Taylor, Cartwright, & Carlson, 1993).

Solitary Play

At times throughout the preschool years, many children prefer to play alone. Should parents be worried? Usually, no. Solitary play comes in many forms and most are normal—even healthy. Spending playtime alone coloring, solving puzzles, or assembling Legos® is not a sign of maladjustment. Many youngsters enjoy solitary activities and, at other times, choose very social play.

However, some forms of solitary play *are* signs that children are uneasy interacting with others (Coplan et al., 2004; Harrist et al., 1997). One type of unhealthy solitary play is wandering aimlessly. Sometimes children go from one preschool activity center to the next, as if trying to decide what to do. But really they just keep wandering, never settling into play with others or constructive solitary play. Another unhealthy type of solitary play is hovering: A child stands nearby peers who are playing, watching them play but not participating. Over time, these behaviors do not bode well for youngsters, so it's best for these youngsters to see a professional who can help them overcome their reticence in social situations (Gazelle & Ladd, 2003).

Gender Differences in Play

Between 2 and 3 years of age, most youngsters begin to prefer playing with peers of their own sex (Martin & Fabes, 2001). This preference increases during childhood, reaching a peak in preadolescence (McHale et al., 2004). This tendency for boys to play with boys and girls with girls has several distinctive features (Maccoby, 1998):

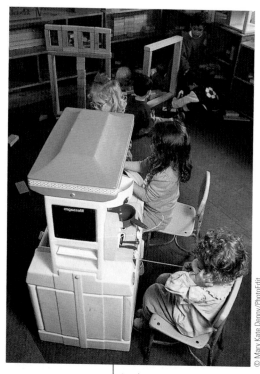

At about 2 or 3 years of age, boys and girls start to prefer playing with members of their own sex.

- In some cultures, adults select playmates for children. However, in cultures where children choose playmates, boys select boys as playmates and girls select girls.

- Children spontaneously select same-sex playmates. Adult pressure ("James, why don't you play with John, not Amy,") is not necessary.

- Children resist parents' efforts to get them to play with members of the opposite sex. Girls are often unhappy when parents encourage them to play with boys, and boys are unhappy when parents urge them to play with girls.

- Children's reluctance to play with members of the opposite sex is not restricted to gender-typed games, such as playing house or playing with cars. Boys and girls prefer same-sex playmates even in gender-neutral activities such as playing tag or doing puzzles.

Why do boys and girls seem so attracted to same-sex play partners? Eleanor Maccoby (1990, 1998) believes that two factors are critical. First, boys specifically prefer rough-and-tumble play and generally are more competitive and dominating in their interactions. Girls' play is not as rough and is less competitive, so Maccoby argues that boys' style of play may be aversive to girls.

Second, when girls and boys play together, girls do not readily influence boys. *Girls' interactions with one another are typically* **enabling**—*their actions and remarks tend to support others and sustain the interaction. In contrast, boy's interactions are often* **constricting**—*one partner tries to emerge as the victor by threatening or contradicting the* *other, by exaggerating, and so on.* When these styles are brought together, girls find their enabling style is ineffective with boys. The same subtle overtures that work with other girls have no impact on boys. Boys ignore girls' polite suggestions about what to do and ignore girls' efforts to resolve conflicts with discussion (Leman, Ahmed, & Ozarow, 2005).

Some theorists believe that these contrasting styles may have an evolutionary basis (Geary et al., 2003). Boys' concerns about dominating others may stem from a concern with establishing one's rank among a group of males because those males at the upper ranks have better access to mates and better access to resources needed for offspring. Girls' concerns about affiliation may be a by-product of the fact that women traditionally left their own communities (and relatives) to live in a husband's community. Having no relatives nearby enhanced the value of a close friend, which placed a premium on the affiliative behaviors that lead to and maintain friendships.

Whatever the exact cause, the preference to play with same-sex peers that emerges in the preschool years is a constant throughout the life span (Moller, Hymel, & Rubin, 1992). As we will see in Chapters 7, 10, and 11, time spent at leisure (and later, at work) is commonly segregated by sex during adolescence and adulthood.

Parental Influence

Parents get involved in their preschool children's play in several ways (Isley et al., 1999). Sometimes they take the role of playmate (and many parents deserve an Oscar for their performances). They use the opportunity to scaffold their children's play, often raising it to more sophisticated levels (Tamis-LeMonda & Bornstein, 1996). For example, if a toddler is stacking toy plates, a parent might help the child stack the plates (play at the same level) or might pretend to wash each plate (play at a more advanced level). When parents demonstrate more advanced forms of play, their children often play at the more advanced levels later (Bornstein et al., 1996).

Another parental role during preschoolers' play is mediator (Colwell et al., 2002). Preschoolers often disagree, argue, and sometimes fight. Children play more cooperatively and longer when parents are present to help iron out conflicts (Mize, Pettit, & Brown, 1995). When young children can't agree on what to play, a parent can negotiate a mutually acceptable activity. When both youngsters want to play with the same toy, a parent can arrange for them to share. Here, too, parents scaffold their preschoolers' play, smoothing the interaction by providing some of the social skills preschoolers lack.

Yet another parental role is coach. Preschool children often encounter social problems that, although minor from an adult's perspective, seem overwhelming to the child. For example, a child might be coloring when another child approaches and demands the crayon the child is using. Parents can help their preschoolers understand and handle such problems. When parents coach—and their advice is constructive—their children tend to be skilled socially and less aggressive (Mize & Pettit, 1997).

Parents also influence the success of their children's peer interactions in a much less direct manner. Children's relationships with peers are most successful when, as infants, they had a secure attachment relationship with their mother (Ladd & LeSieur, 1995; Lieberman et al., 1999).

Why does quality of attachment predict the success of children's peer relationships? One view is that a child's relationship with his or her parents is the internal working model for all future social relationships. When the parent-child relationship is of high quality and emotionally satisfying, children are encouraged to form relationships with other people. Another possibility is that a secure attachment relationship with the mother makes an infant feel more confident about exploring the environment, which,

Parents influence their children's play in many ways, perhaps none more important than mediating disputes that always arise when preschoolers play.

in turn, provides more opportunities to interact with peers. These two views are not mutually exclusive; both may contribute to the relative ease with which securely attached children interact with their peers (Hartup, 1992).

Learning to Cooperate

Play is built on the implicit and sometimes explicit agreement that all players will adhere to certain rules for the common benefit. Hide-and-seek, for example, is no fun when one child only wants to hide and refuses to take a turn as the seeker. Of course, although cooperation may be the ideal, children do not always play together well: Conflicts and arguments are common.

What are some factors that determine whether children cooperate? Age is one. Older children are less egocentric, and knowing that others view things differently helps reduce conflicts. Also, preschoolers' growing communicative and social skills make it easier for them to cooperate (Lourenco, 1993).

Cooperation is also influenced by other factors. Children are more likely to cooperate if they see peers who are cooperative and can observe, firsthand, that cooperation works. Children who observe successful cooperation more often cooperate when given the opportunity (Liebert, Sprafkin, & Poulos, 1975).

Children's eagerness to cooperate is strongly influenced by the response to their cooperative overtures (Brady, Newcomb, & Hartup, 1983). When children try to cooperate but their peers do not go along, the incentive to cooperate vanishes rapidly; instead, youngsters look after their own interests. In contrast, when one child's cooperative gesture leads to another youngster's cooperative response, children see for themselves the beauty of working together and cooperation flourishes.

Piecing these findings together, we see why longlasting cooperation is so fragile. Cooperation works only when all participants agree to cooperate; a few people—or perhaps even just one person—who fail to go along can undermine all the benefits of cooperation. Young children in particular need to be directed by their parents into practical cooperative relationships so that they can directly experience the benefits associated with greater cooperation (Parke & Bahvnagri, 1989).

Cooperation often begets more cooperation.

Some cultures go to greater lengths than others to encourage cooperation. In the United States, the rights of the individual are emphasized, and self-reliance is encouraged. Other cultures, such as China, place a premium on what is good for all; people are seen as being strongly interdependent. Reflecting these cultural differences, Chinese children tend to be substantially more cooperative than North American children (Domino, 1992). For example, in one study (Orlick, Zhou, & Partington, 1990) investigators recorded the frequency of cooperation among kindergartners in Beijing, China, and in Ottawa, Canada. In the Canadian kindergartens, 22% of the interactions were cooperative, which meant that children supported or helped a peer. In the Chinese kindergartens, 85% of the interactions were cooperative. These findings reveal that young children *can* be cooperative if they view such behavior as mutually beneficial and if their culture expects them to cooperate.

HELPING OTHERS

Prosocial behavior is any behavior that benefits another person. Cooperation—that is, working together toward a common goal—is one form of prosocial behavior. Of course, cooperation often "works" because individuals gain more than they would by not cooperating. *In contrast, **altruism** is behavior that is driven by feelings of responsibility toward other people, such as helping and sharing, in which individuals do not benefit directly from their actions.* If two youngsters pool their funds to buy a candy bar to share, this is

By 18 months of age, toddlers try to comfort others who are hurt or upset.

When children can empathize with others who are sad or upset, they're more likely to offer to help.

cooperative behavior. If one youngster gives half of her lunch to a peer who forgot his own, this is altruism.

Many scientists believe that humans are biologically predisposed to be helpful, to share, to cooperate, and to be concerned for others (Hoffman, 2000; Wilson, 1975). Why has prosocial behavior evolved over time? The best explanation has nothing to do with lofty moral principles; it's much more pragmatic: People who frequently help others are more likely to receive help themselves, which increases the odds that they'll pass along their genes to future generations. In fact, basic acts of altruism can be seen by 18 months of age. When toddlers see other people who are obviously hurt or upset, they will appear concerned, try to comfort the person who is in pain (by hugging or patting), and try to determine why the person is upset (Zahn-Waxler et al., 1992). Apparently, at this early age, they recognize some of the qualities of states of distress. During the toddler and preschool years, children gradually begin to understand others' needs and learn appropriate altruistic responses (van der Mark, van IJzendoorn, & Bakermans-Kranenburg, 2002). When 3-year-old Alexis sees that her infant brother is crying because he's dropped his favorite bear, she retrieves it for him; when 4-year-old Darren sees his mom crying while watching a TV show, he may turn off the TV. These early attempts at altruistic behavior are limited because young children's knowledge of what they can do to help is modest. As youngsters acquire more strategies to help others, their preferred strategies become more adultlike (Eisenberg, Fabes, & Spinrad, 2006).

Let's look at some specific skills that set the stage for altruistic behaviors.

Skills Underlying Altruistic Behavior

Remember from Chapter 4 that preschool children are often egocentric, so they may not see the need for altruistic behavior. For example, young children might not share candy with a younger sibling because they cannot imagine how unhappy the sibling is without the candy. In contrast, school-age children, who can more easily take another person's perspective, would perceive the unhappiness and would be more inclined to share. In fact, research consistently indicates that altruistic behavior is related to perspective-taking skill. Youngsters who understand others' thoughts and feelings share better with others and help them more often (Strayer & Roberts, 2004).

Related to perspective-taking is **empathy,** *which is the actual experiencing of another's feelings.* Children who deeply feel another individual's fear, disappointment, sorrow, or loneliness are more inclined to help that person than children who do not feel those emotions (Eisenberg et al., 2006). In other words, youngsters who are obviously distressed by what they are seeing are most likely to help if they can. The Spotlight on Research feature describes a study that investigated this link between empathy and prosocial behavior.

SPOTLIGHT ON RESEARCH

ARE EMPATHIC CHILDREN MORE LIKELY TO HELP?

What was the aim of the study, and who were the investigators? A common idea in many theories of helping is that children (and adults) who "feel" another person's discomfort or distress should be more likely to help that person. That is, children and adults who are more empathic are thought to be more likely to help. Paul Miller and his colleagues, Nancy Eisenberg, Richard Fabes, and

Rita Shell (1996), tested this claim by measuring children's emotional responding and their tendency to help.

How did the investigators measure the topic of interest? Miller and his colleagues prepared brief films in which children appeared to hurt themselves when they fell. After watching the films, the children in the study were asked how they felt. Children responded by

pointing to a happy, sad, sorry, or neutral face. Next, they were asked if they felt a little bit this way, kind of, or very much this way. Next, children were told that the child in the film was in the hospital and that the experimenter wanted to send that child some crayons. However, the crayons were loose in a large box and needed to be put into smaller boxes before they could be sent to the hospitalized child. The children were shown some toys and told that they could help sort the crayons or they could play with the toys. Thus, the measures were the type and intensity of the child's emotional response to the films and the number of crayons that they sorted.

Who were the children in the study? The researchers tested 74 5- and 6-year-old boys and girls.

What was the design of the study? This study was correlational because the investigators looked at the relations that existed naturally between helping (as measured by the number of crayons sorted) and the emotions that children experienced while watching the film. The study included only 5- and 6-year-olds, so it was neither longitudinal nor cross-sectional.

Were there ethical concerns with the study? No. The emotional episodes depicted in the films were fairly mild and similar to what children might experience in their own lives.

What were the results? Figure 5.2 shows the correlations between children's emotions and their helping. Helping was greatest when children said they were sad after watching the film and least when they said they were happy after the film. Neutral or sorry emotional responses were unrelated to helping.

What did the investigators conclude? As predicted, children who are saddened by another person's discomfort are most likely to help that person. Chil-

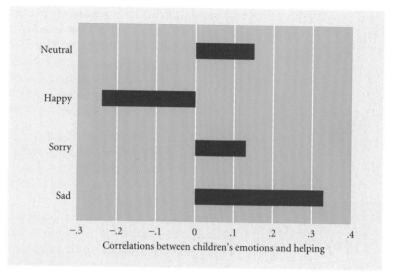

■ **Figure 5.2**
When children respond empathically to another person's misfortune (they're sorry or sad after they watch a movie in which a child is hurt), they're more likely to help others.

dren who are happy (perhaps because they think it is funny to see others make mistakes, such as falling down) are unlikely to help.

What converging evidence would strengthen these conclusions? One interesting extension of this study would be to obtain different kinds of measures of helping and emotional responding. For example, parents might be asked to report on their children's emotional responding and teachers could rate their students' willingness to help. Doing this

research as part of a cross-sectional study would also be useful in determining whether the relation between helping and emotional responding changes as children grow.

To enhance your understanding of this research, go to http://psychology.wadsworth.com/kail_cavanaugh4e/ to complete critical thinking questions and explore related websites.

Of course, responding empathically does not guarantee that children will act altruistically. Some caring children who would like to help others may not be able to do so. An older brother might want to share candy with a younger sibling but will not because a parent forbids it. Sometimes children may not help because they lack the time or believe that others will help. It is necessary to consider the context in which behavior occurs, as this helps determine whether a child will act altruistically. A number of contextual features are known to influence children's altruism.

■ *Feelings of responsibility.* Children act altruistically when they feel responsible for the person in need. Children may help siblings and friends, for example, more often than strangers simply because they feel a direct responsibility for people they know well (Costin & Jones, 1992).

■ *Feelings of competence.* Children act altruistically when they feel they have the skills to help the person in need. Suppose, for example, that a preschooler is growing more and more upset because she can't figure out how to work a computer game; a peer who knows little about computer games is not likely to come to the young girl's aid because the peer doesn't know what to do to help. If the peer tries to help, he or she could end up looking foolish (Peterson, 1983).

■ *Mood.* Children act altruistically when they are happy or feeling successful but not when they are sad or feeling as if they have failed. A preschool child who has just spent an exciting morning as the "leader" in nursery school is more inclined to share treats with siblings than is a preschooler who was punished by the teacher (Eisenberg, 2000).

■ *Costs of altruism.* Children act altruistically when such actions entail few or modest sacrifices. A preschool child who was given a snack that she doesn't particularly like is more inclined to share it with others than one who was given her very favorite food (Eisenberg & Shell, 1986).

So when are children most likely to help? They help when they feel responsible for the person in need, have the needed skills, are happy, and believe they will give up little by helping. When are children least likely to help? They are less likely to help when they feel neither responsible nor capable of helping, are in a bad mood, and believe that helping will entail a large personal sacrifice.

With these guidelines in mind, can you explain why Antonio and Carla, the children in the opening vignette, watched idly as their older brother cried? The last two factors—mood and costs—are not likely to be involved. However, the first two factors may explain the failure of Antonio and Carla to help their older brother. Our explanation appears on page 201, just before Test Yourself.

So far, we've seen that altruistic behavior is determined by children's skills (such as perspective-taking) and by characteristics of situations (such as whether children feel competent to help in a particular situation). Whether children are altruistic is also determined by socialization, the topic of the next section.

Socialization of Altruism

Dr. Martin Luther King Jr. said that his pursuit of civil rights for African Americans was particularly influenced by three people: Henry David Thoreau (a 19th-century American philosopher), Mohandas Gandhi (the leader of the Indian movement for independence from England), and his father, Dr. Martin Luther King Sr. As is true of many humanitarians, Dr. King's prosocial behavior started in childhood, at home. But how do parents foster altruism in their children? Several factors contribute:

■ *Modeling.* When children see adults helping and caring for others, they often imitate such prosocial behavior (Eisenberg et al., 2006). Of course, parents are the models to whom children are most continuously exposed, so they exert a powerful influence. Parents who report frequent feelings of warmth and concern for others tend to have children who experience stronger feelings of empathy. When a mother is helpful and responsive, her children often imitate her by being cooperative, helpful, sharing, and less critical of others. In a particularly powerful demonstration of the impact of parental modeling, people who had risked their lives during World War II to protect Jews from the Nazis often reported their parents' emphasis on caring for all people (Oliner & Oliner, 1988).

■ *Disciplinary practices.* Children behave prosocially more often when their parents are warm and supportive, set guidelines, and provide feedback; in contrast, prosocial behavior is less common when parenting is harsh, threatening, and includes frequent physical punishment (Asbury et al., 2003; Eisenberg & Fabes, 1998). Particularly important is parents' use of reasoning as a disciplinary tactic, with the goal of helping children see how their actions affect others. For example, after 4-year-old Annie grabbed some crayons from a playmate, her father told Annie, "You shouldn't just grab things away from people. It makes them angry and unhappy. Ask first, and if they say 'no,' then you mustn't take them."

■ *Opportunities to behave prosocially.* You need to practice to improve motor skills and the same is true of prosocial behaviors—children and adolescents are more likely to act prosocially when they're routinely given the opportunity to help and cooperate with others. At home, children can help with

THINK ABOUT IT

Suppose some kindergarten children want to raise money for a gift for one of their classmates who is ill. Based on the information presented here, what advice can you give the children as they plan their fund-raising?

household tasks, such as cleaning and setting the table. Adolescents can be encouraged to participate in community service, such as working at a food bank or tutoring younger children. Experiences like these help sensitize children and adolescents to the needs of others and allow them to enjoy the satisfaction of helping (Grusec, Goodnow, & Cohen, 1996; McLellan & Youniss, 2003).

Thus, parents can foster altruism in their youngsters by behaving altruistically themselves, using reasoning to discipline their children, and encouraging their children to help at home and elsewhere. Also, contextual factors play a role, and altruism requires perspective-taking and empathy. Combining these ingredients, we can give a general account of children's altruistic behavior. As children get older, their perspective-taking and empathic skills develop, which enables them to see and feel another's needs. Nonetheless, children are never invariably altruistic (or, fortunately, invariably nonaltruistic) because particular contexts affect altruistic behavior too.

Postscript: Why Didn't Antonio and Carla Help?

Here are our explanations. First, neither Antonio nor Carla may have felt sufficiently responsible to help, because (a) with two children who could help, each child's feeling of individual responsibility is reduced, and (b) younger children are less likely to feel responsible for an older sibling. Second, it's our guess that neither child has had many opportunities to use the VCR. In fact, it's likely that they both have been strongly discouraged from venturing near it. Consequently, they don't feel very competent to help because neither knows how it works or what they should do to help Juan remove his finger.

> **THINK ABOUT IT**
>
> Paula worries that her son Elliot is too selfish and wishes that he were more caring and compassionate. As a parent, what could Paula do to encourage Elliot to be more concerned about others' welfare?

TEST YOURSELF

1. Toddlers who are 12–15 months old often engage in _____ play, in which they play separately but look at one another and sometimes communicate verbally.

2. One of the advantages of _____ play is that children can explore topics that frighten them.

3. When girls interact, conflicts are typically resolved through _____; boys more often resort to intimidation.

4. Compared to young children in North America, youngsters in China are _____ cooperative.

5. _____ is the ability to understand and feel another person's emotions.

6. Contextual influences on prosocial behavior include feelings of responsibility, feelings of competence, _____, and the costs associated with behaving prosocially.

7. Parents can foster altruism in their youngsters by behaving altruistically themselves, using reasoning to discipline their children, and _____.

How might children's temperament, which we discussed in Chapter 2, influence the development of their play with peers?

Answers: (1) parallel, (2) make-believe, (3) discussion and compromise, (4) more, (5) Empathy, (6) mood, (7) providing children with opportunities to practice being altruistic

5.4

GENDER ROLES AND GENDER IDENTITY

Meda and Frank are in their early 50s. Though not married, they have lived together since the early 1970s, when both were active in protests against the war in Vietnam. Their daughter Hope is now 6 years old. True to their countercultural roots, both Meda and Frank want their daughter to pick activities, friends, and, ultimately, a career based on her interests and abilities, not on her gender. Both are now astonished that Hope seems to be totally indistinguishable from other 6-year-olds reared by parents with conventional outlooks. Hope's close friends are all girls, and they often play "house" or play with dolls. What seems to be going wrong with Meda and Frank's plans for a "gender-neutral" girl?

FAMILY AND WELL-WISHERS ARE ALWAYS EAGER to know the sex of a newborn. Why are people so interested in a baby's sex? The answer is that being a "boy" or "girl" is not simply a biological distinction. Instead, these terms are associated with distinct social roles. *Like a role in a play, a* **social role** *is a set of cultural guidelines as to how a person should behave, particularly with other people.* The roles associated with gender are among the first that children learn, starting in infancy. Youngsters rapidly learn about the behaviors that are assigned to males and females in their culture. At the same time, they begin to identify with one of these groups. As they do, they take on an identity as a boy or a girl.

In this section, you'll learn about the "female role" and the "male role" in North America today, and you'll also discover why Meda and Frank are having so much trouble rearing a gender-neutral girl.

IMAGES OF MEN AND WOMEN: FACTS AND FANTASY

All cultures have **gender stereotypes**—*beliefs and images about males and females that may or may not be true.* For example, many men and women believe that males are rational, active, independent, competitive, and aggressive. At the same time, many men and women claim that females are emotional, passive, dependent, sensitive, and gentle (Best, 2001; Lueptow, Garovich-Szabo, & Lueptow, 2001; Lutz & Ruble, 1995).

Based on gender stereotypes, we expect males and females to act and feel in particular ways, and we respond to their behavior differently, depending on their gender (Smith & Mackie, 2000). For example, if you saw a toddler playing with a doll, you would probably assume that she is a girl, based on her taste in toys. What's more, your assumption would lead you to believe (a) that she plays more quietly and (b) that she is more readily frightened than a boy would be (Stern & Karraker, 1989). Once we assume the child is a girl, our gender stereotypes lead to a whole host of inferences about behavior and personality.

Learning Gender Stereotypes

Children don't live in a gender-neutral world for long. Although 12-month-old boys and girls look equally at gender-stereotyped toys, 18-month-olds do not: Girls look longer at pictures of dolls than pictures of trucks, but boys

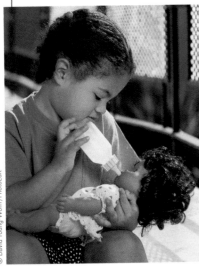

If you assume the child is a girl, this leads to a host of other inferences about her personality and behavior.

look longer at pictures of trucks (Serbin et al., 2001). By 4 years of age, children's knowledge of gender-stereotyped activities is extensive: They believe girls play hopscotch but boys play football; girls help bake cookies but boys take out the trash; and women feed babies but men chop wood (Gelman, Taylor, & Nguyen, 2004). And they've begun to learn about behaviors and traits that are stereotypically masculine or feminine. Preschoolers believe boys are more often aggressive physically but girls tend to be aggressive verbally (Giles & Heyman, 2005).

By the time children are ready to enter elementary school, they are well on their way to learning gender stereotypes. For example, 5-year-olds believe boys are strong and dominant and girls are emotional and gentle (Best et al., 1977; Etaugh & Liss, 1992).

Beyond the preschool years, children learn more about stereotypes, but they also have greater flexibility when it comes to gender stereotypes (Serbin, Powlishta, & Gulko, 1993). They understand that it is often acceptable for children to deviate from gender stereotypes—a girl can be ambitious and a boy can be gentle (Levy, Taylor, & Gelman, 1995). And they learn that traits and occupations associated with males such as lawyers and engineers have higher social status than those associated with females such as social workers and flight attendants (Liben, Bigler, & Krogh, 2001).

Gender-Related Differences

So far we've only considered people's *beliefs* about differences between males and females, and many of them are false. Research reveals that males and females often *do not* differ in the ways specified by cultural stereotypes. What are the bona fide differences between males and females? Of course, in addition to the obvious anatomical differences, males are typically larger and stronger than females throughout most of the life span. Beginning in infancy, boys are more active than girls (Eaton & Enns, 1986). In contrast, girls have a lower mortality rate and are less susceptible to stress and disease (Zaslow & Hayes, 1986).

When it comes to social roles, activities for males tend to be more strenuous, involve more cooperation with others, and often require travel. Activities for females are usually less demanding physically, more solitary, and take place closer to home. This division of roles is much the same worldwide (Whiting & Edwards, 1988).

The extent of gender differences in the intellectual and psychosocial arenas remains uncertain. Research suggests differences between males and females in several areas:

- *Verbal ability.* During the toddler years, girls have larger vocabularies than boys (Leaper & Smith, 2004). During elementary school and high school, girls read, write, and spell better than boys, and more boys have reading and other language-related problems such as stuttering (Halpern, 2004; Wicks-Nelson & Israel, 2006).

- *Mathematics.* Males tend to get higher grades on math achievement tests, but girls often get better grades in math courses (Beller & Gafni, 1996; Halpern, 2004).

- *Spatial ability.* On problems like those in Figure 5.3, which measure the ability to manipulate visual information mentally, you must decide which figures are rotated variants of the standard shown at the left. Males typically respond more rapidly and accurately than females (Govier & Salisbury, 2000; Voyer, Voyer, & Bryden, 1995).

- *Social influence.* Girls are more likely than boys to comply with the directions of adults (Maccoby & Jacklin, 1974). Girls and women are also more readily influenced by others in a variety of situations, particularly when they are under group pressure (Becker, 1986; Eagly, Karau, & Makhijani, 1995). However, these gender differences may stem from the fact that females value group harmony more than males do and thus seem to give in to others (Miller, Danaher, & Forbes, 1986; Strough & Berg, 2000). For instance, at a meeting to plan a school function, girls are just as likely as boys to recognize the flaws in a bad idea, but girls are more willing to go along simply because they don't want the group to start arguing.

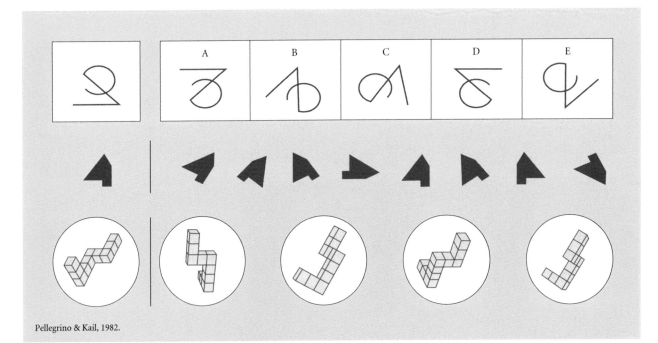

Pellegrino & Kail, 1982.

Figure 5.3
On spatial ability tasks, which involve visualizing information in different orientations, males tend to respond more rapidly and more accurately than females.

From "Process Analysis of Spatial Aptitude," by J. W. Pellegrino and R. V. Kail. In R. J. Sternberg (Ed.), *Advances in the Psychology of Human Intelligence, Vol. 1*, p. 316. Copyright © 1982 Lawrence Erlbaum Associates, Inc. Reprinted with permission.

- *Aggression.* In virtually all cultures that have been studied, males are more physically aggressive, particularly when aggression is not provoked by others (Martin & Ross, 2005). This difference begins as early as the preschool years and remains throughout the life span (Sanson et al., 1993). *In contrast, girls are more likely to resort to* **relational aggression** *in which they try to hurt others by damaging their relationships with peers.* They may call children names, make fun of them, spread rumors about them, or pointedly ignore them (Crick & Grotpeter, 1995).

- *Emotional sensitivity.* Girls are better able to express their emotions and interpret others' emotions (Hall & Halberstadt, 1981; Weinberg et al., 1999). For example, throughout infancy and childhood, girls identify facial expressions (e.g., a happy face versus a sad face) more accurately than boys do (McClure, 2000).

In most other intellectual and social domains, boys and girls are similar. When thinking about areas in which sex differences have been found, keep in mind that gender differences often depend on a person's experiences (Casey, 1996; Serbin et al., 1993). Also, gender differences may fluctuate over time, reflecting historical change in the contexts of childhood for boys and girls. Finally, each result just described refers to a difference in the *average* performance of boys and girls. These differences tend to be small, which means that they do not apply to all boys and girls. Many girls have greater spatial ability than many boys; many boys are more susceptible to social influence than are some girls.

GENDER TYPING

Folklore holds that parents and other adults—teachers and television characters, for example—directly shape children's behavior toward the roles associated with their sex. Boys are rewarded for boyish behavior and punished for girlish behavior. The folklore even has a theoretical basis. According to social cognitive theorists Albert Bandura

(1977, 1986; Bandura & Bussey, 2004) and Walter Mischel (1970), children learn gender roles in much the same way they learn other social behaviors—by watching the world around them and learning the outcomes of different actions. Parents and others thus shape appropriate gender roles in children, and children learn what their culture considers appropriate behavior for males and females by simply watching how adults and peers act.

How well does research support social learning theory? The best answer to this question comes from an extensive meta-analysis of 172 studies involving 27,836 children (Lytton & Romney, 1991) that found that parents often treat sons and daughters similarly: Parents interact equally with sons and daughters, are equally warm to both, and encourage both sons and daughters to achieve and be independent. However, in behavior related to gender roles, parents respond differently to sons and daughters (Lytton & Romney, 1991). Activities such as playing with dolls, dressing up, or helping an adult are encouraged more often in daughters than in sons; rough-and-tumble play and playing with blocks are encouraged more in sons than in daughters. And parents tolerate mild aggression more in sons than in daughters (Martin & Ross, 2005).

Fathers are more likely than mothers to treat sons and daughters differently. More than mothers, fathers often encourage gender-related play. Fathers punish their sons more, but they accept dependence in their daughters (Snow, Jacklin, & Maccoby, 1983). A father, for example, may urge his frightened young son to jump off the diving board ("Be a man!") but not insist that his daughter do so ("That's okay, honey"). Apparently mothers are more likely to respond based on their knowledge of the needs of individual children, but fathers respond based on gender stereotypes. A mother responds to her son knowing that he's smart but unsure of himself; a father may respond based on what he thinks boys generally should be like.

Of course, adults differ in their views on the relative rights and roles of males and females. Some have very traditional views, believing, for example, that men should be hired preferentially for some jobs and that it's more important for sons than daughters to attend college; others have more gender-neutral views, believing, for example, that women should have the same business and professional opportunities as men and that daughters should have the same educational opportunities as sons. It would be surprising if parents did not convey these attitudes to their children, and indeed they do. A meta-analysis of 48 studies including more than 10,000 pairs of parents and children showed that children's gender-related interests, attitudes, and self-concepts are more traditional when their parents have traditional views and more gender-neutral when their parents have nontraditional views (Tenenbaum & Leaper, 2002).

Peers are also influential. Preschoolers are critical of peers who engage in cross-gender play (Langlois & Downs, 1980). This is particularly true of boys who like feminine toys or who play at feminine activities. A boy who plays with dolls and a girl who plays with trucks will both be ignored, teased, or ridiculed by their peers, but the boy will be treated more harshly than the girl (Levy et al., 1995). Once children learn rules about gender-typical play, they often harshly punish peers who violate those rules.

Peers influence gender roles in another way too. We've seen that by 2 and 3 years of age, children most often play with same-sex peers (Martin & Fabes, 2001). This early segregation of playmates based on a child's sex play means that boys learn primarily from boys and girls from girls. This helps solidify a youngster's emerging sense of membership in a particular gender group and sharpens the contrast between their own gender and the other gender.

Thus, through encouraging words, critical looks, and other forms of praise and punishment, other people influence boys and girls to behave differently (Jacobs & Eccles,

Fathers are more likely than mothers to encourage their children's gender-related play.

Preschoolers discourage peers from cross-gender play.

1992). However, children learn more than simply the specific behaviors associated with their gender. *A child gradually begins to identify with one group and to develop a* **gender identity**—*a sense of the self as a male or a female.*

Gender Identity

If you were to listen to a typical conversation between two preschoolers, you might hear something like this:

MARIA: When I grow up, I'm going to be a singer.
JUANITA: When I grow up, I'm going to be a papa.
MARIA: No, you can't be a papa—you'll be a mama.
JUANITA: No, I wanna be a papa.
MARIA: You can't be a papa. Only boys can be papas, and you're a girl!

Obviously, Maria's understanding of gender is more developed than Juanita's. How can we explain these differences? According to Lawrence Kohlberg (1966; Kohlberg & Ullian, 1974), children gradually develop a basic understanding that they are of either the female or the male sex. Gender then serves to organize many perceptions, attitudes, values, and behaviors. Full understanding of gender is said to develop gradually in three steps:

■ *Gender labeling: By age 2 or 3, children understand that they are either boys or girls, and label themselves accordingly.*

■ *Gender stability: During the preschool years, children begin to understand that gender is stable: Boys become men and girls become women.* However, children in this stage believe that a girl who wears her hair like a boy will become a boy and a boy who plays with dolls will become a girl (Fagot, 1985).

■ *Gender constancy: Between 4 and 7 years, most children understand that maleness and femaleness do not change over situations or according to personal wishes.* They understand that a child's sex is unaffected by the clothing a child wears or the toys a child likes. Juanita and Maria both know that they're girls, but Maria has developed a greater sense of gender stability and gender constancy.

Kohlberg's theory specifies *when* children begin learning about gender-appropriate behavior and activities (once they understand gender constancy) but not *how* such learning takes place. A theory proposed by Carol Martin (Martin & Ruble, 2004; Martin et al., 1999) addresses how children learn about gender (see Figure 5.4). *In* **gender-schema theory,** *children first decide if an object, activity, or behavior is associated with females or males, then use this information to decide whether they should learn more about the object, activity, or behavior.* That is, once children know their gender, they pay attention primarily to experiences and events that are gender appropriate (Martin & Halverson, 1987). According to gender-schema theory, a preschool boy watching a group of girls playing in sand will decide that playing in sand is for girls and that, because he is a boy, playing in sand is not for him. Seeing a group of older boys playing football, he will decide that football is for boys, and because he is a boy, football is acceptable and he should learn more about it.

According to gender-schema theory, after children understand gender, it's as if they see the world through special glasses that allow only gender-typical activities to be in focus (Liben & Bigler, 2002). This pattern was evident in a study by Martin and Little (1990), who measured preschool children's understanding of gender and their knowledge of gender-stereotyped activities (for example, that girls play with dolls and that boys play with airplanes). The youngest children in their study—3½-year-olds—did

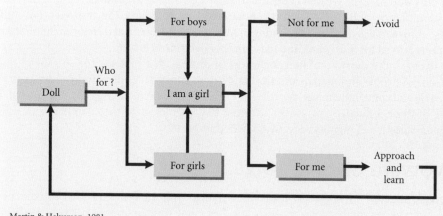

Martin & Halverson, 1981.

■ **Figure 5.4**
According to gender-schema theory, children decide if an object, activity, or behavior is for females or males, then learn more about objects, activities, or behaviors that are appropriate for their own sex.

From "A Schematic Processing Model of Sex Typing and Stereotyping in Children," by C. L. Martin and D. F. Halverson, 1981, *Child Development, 52,* p. 1121. Copyright © 1981 Society for Research on Child Development, Inc. Reprinted with permission.

not understand gender constancy and knew little of gender-stereotyped activities. But by 4½ years of age, many children understood gender constancy and knew gender-typical and gender-atypical activities.

After children understand gender, their tastes in TV programs begin to shift along gender-specific lines (Luecke-Aleksa et al., 1995). In addition, they begin to use gender labels to evaluate toys and activities. Shown an unfamiliar toy and told that children of a specific sex *really* like this toy, children like the toy much more if others of their sex do too (Martin, Eisenbud, & Rose, 1995). As Martin and Ruble (2004) put it, "Children are gender detectives who search for cues about gender—who should or should not engage in a particular activity, who can play with whom, and why girls and boys are different" (p. 67).

This selective viewing of the world explains a great deal about children's learning of gender roles, but one final important element needs to be considered: biology.

BIOLOGICAL INFLUENCES

Most child-development researchers agree that biology contributes to gender roles and gender identity. Evolutionary developmental psychology, for example, reminds us that men and women performed vastly different roles for much of human history: Women were more invested in child rearing, and men were more invested in providing important resources (e.g., food, protection) for their offspring (Geary, 2002). In adapting to these roles, different traits and behaviors evolved for men and women. For example, men became more aggressive because that was adaptive in helping them ward off predators.

Another way to consider biological influences on gender is in terms of the impact of hormones on gender-stereotyped play. *Some fascinating insights come from studies of children with* **congenital adrenal hyperplasia (CAH),** *a genetic disorder in which, beginning in prenatal development, the adrenal glands secrete large amounts of androgen.* The extra androgen doesn't affect a baby boy's physical development; but in baby girls it can enlarge the clitoris so that it resembles a penis. Girls affected by CAH have surgery during infancy to correct their physical appearance, and they receive hormone therapy to correct the imbalance of androgen. Nevertheless, during childhood and adolescence, girls with CAH prefer masculine activities (such as playing with cars instead of dolls) and male playmates to a much greater extent than girls not exposed to these amounts of androgen (Berenbaum & Snyder, 1995; Collaer & Hines, 1995). These effects are largest for girls who have the greatest exposure to androgen during prenatal development (Berenbaum, Duck, & Bryk, 2000; Servin et al., 2003). Apparently, the androgen not only masculinizes the genitals in baby girls but also affects the prenatal development of brain regions critical for masculine and feminine gender-role behavior.

Perhaps the most accurate conclusion to draw is that biology, the socializing influence of people and media, and the child's own efforts to understand gender-typical behavior all contribute to gender roles and differences. Recognizing the interactive nature of these influences on gender learning also enables us to better understand how gender roles are changing today, which we consider next.

EVOLVING GENDER ROLES

Gender roles are not etched in stone; they change with the times. In the United States the range of acceptable roles for girls and boys and women and men has never been greater than today. For example, some fathers stay home to be primary caregivers for children, and some mothers work full-time as sole support for the family. What is the impact of these changes on gender roles? Some insights come from the results of the Family Lifestyles Project (Weisner & Wilson-Mitchell, 1990). This research has examined families in which the adults were members of the counterculture of the 1960s and 1970s. Some of the families are deeply committed to living their own lives and to rearing their children without traditional gender stereotypes. In these families, men and women share the household, financial, and child care tasks.

The results of this project show that parents like Meda and Frank, from the opening vignette, can influence some aspects of gender stereotyping more readily than others. On the one hand, children in these families tend to have same-sex friends and to like sex-typed activities: The boys enjoy physical play, and the girls enjoy drawing and reading. On the other hand, the children have few stereotypes concerning occupations: They agree that girls can be president of the United States and drive trucks and that boys can be nurses and secretaries. They also have fewer sex-typed attitudes about the use of objects. They claim that boys and girls are equally likely to use an iron, a shovel, a hammer and nails, and a needle and thread.

Despite the wide range of roles acceptable today for men and women, boys and girls still tend to have same-sex friends and to enjoy many sex-typed activities.

Apparently, some features of gender roles and identities are more readily influenced by experience than others. This is as it should be. For most of our history as a species, Homo sapiens have existed in small groups of families, hunting animals and gathering vegetation. Women have given birth to the children and cared for them. Over the course of human history, it has been adaptive for women to be caring and nurturing because this increases the odds of a secure attachment and, ultimately, the survival of the infant. Men's responsibilities have included protecting the family unit from predators and hunting with other males, roles for which physical strength and aggressiveness are crucial.

Circumstances of life at the start of the 21st century are, of course, substantially different. Men can rear children, and women can generate income to purchase food for the family. The range of acceptable roles for girls and boys and women and men has never been wider. At the same time, the cultural changes of the past few decades cannot erase hundreds of thousands of years of evolutionary history (Kenrick, 1987). Consequently, we should not be surprised to find that boys and girls often differ in their styles of play, that girls tend to be more supportive of one another in their interactions, and that boys are usually more aggressive.

TEST YOURSELF

1. _____ are beliefs and images about males and females that may or may not be true.

2. Research on intellectual functioning and social behavior has revealed sex differences in verbal ability, mathematics, _____, social influence, and aggression.

3. _____ may be particularly influential in teaching gender roles, because they more often treat sons and daughters differently.

4. According to Kohlberg's theory, understanding of gender includes gender labeling, gender stability, and _____.

5. Children studied in the Family Lifestyles Project, whose parents were members of the counterculture of the 1960s and 1970s, had traditional gender-related views toward friends and _____.

How do the different forces in the biopsychosocial framework contribute to the development of gender roles?

Answers: (1) Gender stereotypes, (2) spatial ability, (3) Fathers, (4) gender constancy, (5) preferred activities

Putting It All Together

Though the cartoon is funny, you probably wouldn't care to consider living alone because interactions with other people are so important throughout life. Having completed this chapter, you now know that these interactions start early in life. In the first part of this chapter, we saw that responsive caregiving often leads to the formation of a secure attachment between infant and parent. When infants who have had secure attachments grow up, they tend to interact more successfully with other people. Infants who spend much time in early alternative child care also form secure attachments unless the child care is of low quality and the mother is unresponsive. Children like Roosevelt, Kendra's 18-month-old, are not harmed by time spent in early alternative child care as long as the care is of high quality and mothers remain responsive and sensitive.

We showed that infants like Claude can express basic emotions such as happiness and anger. By age 2, children experience complex emotions such as guilt. Babies use others' emotions to guide their behavior, and this skill improves as children grow cognitively.

We traced how children's social relations expand from parents to peers. Even babies play with others, and play rapidly becomes more complex over the preschool years. Toddlers also show concern for others. However, as children grow older, whether they actually help others depends on perspective-taking and empathic skills, the context in which help is required, and styles of parental discipline. For example, in the vignette, Antonio and Carla did not help their older brother because they did not feel great responsibility to help and because they did not feel capable of helping.

As children's social horizons continue to expand, they soon learn that they are expected to play certain roles in society based on their gender. By the end of the preschool years, most children know that gender is fixed, and they begin to use this knowledge to select activities and objects that are appropriate for them. These choices are influenced by parents' values and expectations, but some aspects of gender roles are easier to change than others. For example, Meda and Frank, the parents in the vignette, will probably find it easier to modify their daughter's career goals than to modify her style of play.

Of course, despite the rapid and sometimes dramatic change we've witnessed in this chapter, social and interpersonal development is far from complete by the end of the preschool years. Much additional change takes place in school-age children and adolescents, as we'll see in Chapter 7.

THE FAR SIDE® BY GARY LARSON

**Hot off the press, the very first edition of
the *Desert Island Times* caused the
newspaper to quickly fold.**

Summary

5.1 Beginnings: Trust and Attachment

Erikson's Stages of Early Psychosocial Development

■ In Erikson's theory of psychosocial development, individuals face certain psychosocial crises at different phases in development. The crisis of infancy is to establish a balance between trust and mistrust of the world, producing hope; between 1 and 3 years of age, youngsters must blend autonomy and shame to produce will; and between 3 and 5 years of age, initiative and guilt must be balanced to achieve purpose.

The Growth of Attachment

■ Attachment is an enduring socioemotional relationship between infant and parent. For both adults and infants, many of the behaviors that contribute to the formation of attachment are biologically programmed. Bowlby's theory of attachment is rooted in evolutionary psychology and describes four stages

in the development of attachment: preattachment, attachment in the making, true attachment, and reciprocal relationships.

■ Research with the Strange Situation, in which infant and mother are separated briefly, reveals four primary forms of attachment. Most common is a secure attachment, in which infants have complete trust in the mother. Less common are three types of attachment relationships in which this trust is lacking. In avoidant relationships, infants deal with the lack of trust by ignoring the mother; in resistant relationships, infants often seem angry with her; in disorganized relationships, infants do not appear to understand the mother's absence.

■ Children who have had secure attachment relationships during infancy often interact with their peers more readily and more skillfully. Secure attachment is most likely to occur when mothers respond sensitively and consistently to their infants' needs.

What Determines Quality of Attachment?

▪ Responsive caregiving results in infants developing an internal working model that parents will try to meet their needs. Secure attachment can be harder to achieve when infants are temperamentally difficult.

Attachment, Work, and Alternative Caregiving

▪ Many U.S. children are cared for at home by a father or other relative, in a day care provider's home, or in a day care center. Infants and young children are not harmed by such care as long as the care is of high quality and parents remain responsive to their children.

5.2 Emerging Emotions

Experiencing and Expressing Emotions

▪ Basic emotions, which include joy, anger, and fear, emerge in the first year. Fear first appears in infancy as stranger wariness. Complex emotions have an evaluative component and include guilt, embarrassment, and pride. They appear between 18 and 24 months and require more sophisticated cognitive skills than the basic emotions of happiness and fear. Cultures differ in the rules for expressing emotions and the situations that elicit particular emotions.

Recognizing and Using Others' Emotions

▪ By 6 months, infants have begun to recognize the emotions associated with different facial expressions. They use this information to help them evaluate unfamiliar situations. Beyond infancy, children learn more about the causes of different emotions.

Regulating Emotions

▪ Infants use simple strategies to regulate emotions such as fear. As children grow, they become better skilled at regulating their emotions. Children who do not regulate emotions well tend to have problems interacting with others.

5.3 Interacting With Others

The Joys of Play

▪ Even infants notice and respond to one another, but the first real interactions, at about 12 to 15 months, take the form of parallel play, in which toddlers play alone while watching each other. A few months later, simple social play emerges, in which toddlers engage in similar activities and interact with one another. At about 2 years of age, cooperative play organized around a theme becomes common. Make-believe play is also common; in addition to being fun, it allows children to examine frightening topics. Most forms of solitary play are harmless.

Learning to Cooperate

▪ Cooperation becomes more common as children get older. Children cooperate more readily if they are shown that cooperation is effective and if peers respond to their cooperation with further cooperation. Cooperation is also influenced by societal values; it is more common in cultures that prize cooperation more highly than competition.

Helping Others

▪ Prosocial behaviors, such as helping or sharing, are more common in children who understand (perspective-taking) and experience (empathy) another's feelings.

▪ Prosocial behavior is more likely when children feel responsible for the person in distress. Also, children help more often when they believe they have the skills needed, when they are feeling happy or successful, and when they perceive that the costs of helping are small.

▪ Parents can foster altruism in their youngsters by behaving altruistically themselves, using reasoning to discipline their children, and encouraging their children to help at home and elsewhere.

5.4 Gender Roles and Gender Identity

Images of Men and Women: Facts and Fantasy

▪ Gender stereotypes are beliefs about males and females that are often used to make inferences about a person, simply based on his or her gender; by 4 years of age, children know these stereotypes well.

▪ Studies of gender differences reveal that girls have greater verbal skill and get better grades in math courses but that boys have greater spatial skill and get higher scores on math achievement tests. Girls are better able to interpret emotions and are more prone to social influence, but boys are more aggressive. These differences vary based on a number of factors, including the historical period.

Gender Typing

▪ Parents treat sons and daughters similarly, except in sex-typed activities. Fathers may be particularly important in sex typing because they are more likely to treat sons and daughters differently.

▪ In Kohlberg's theory, children gradually learn that gender is stable over time and cannot be changed according to personal wishes. After children understand gender stability, they begin to learn gender-typical behavior. According to gender-schema theory, children learn about gender by paying attention to behaviors of members of their own sex and ignoring behaviors of members of the other sex.

Biological Influences

■ Evolutionary developmental psychology reminds us that different roles for males and females caused different traits and behaviors to evolve for men and women. The idea that biology influences some aspects of gender roles is also supported by research on females exposed to male hormones during prenatal development.

Evolving Gender Roles

■ Gender roles are changing. However, studies of nontraditional families indicate that some components of gender stereotypes are more readily changed than others.

Key Terms

hope (179)
will (179)
purpose (179)
evolutionary psychology (179)
attachment (180)
secure attachment (181)
avoidant attachment (182)
resistant attachment (182)
disorganized (disoriented) attachment (182)
internal working model (183)

basic emotions (187)
social smiles (188)
stranger wariness (188)
social referencing (190)
parallel play (193)
simple social play (193)
cooperative play (193)
enabling actions (195)
constricting actions (195)
prosocial behavior (197)
altruism (197)

empathy (198)
social role (202)
gender stereotypes (202)
relational aggression (204)
gender identity (206)
gender labeling (206)
gender stability (206)
gender constancy (206)
gender-schema theory (206)
congenital adrenal hyperplasia (CAH) (207)

Learn More About It

Readings

BRAZELTON, T. B., & SPARROW, J. D. (2002). *Touchpoints 3 to 6: Your child's emotional and behavioral development.* Boulder, CO: Perseus. This book, written by a well-known pediatrician and his colleague, focuses on four prototypic children to illustrate the developmental milestones and common problems encountered during the preschool years.

ERIKSON, E. H. (1982). *The life cycle completed: A review.* New York: Norton. Erikson summarizes his theory.

RIDLEY, M. (2003). *The red queen: Sex and the evolution of human nature.* New York: Harper Perennial. The author, a well-known science writer, examines how the biological imperative to reproduce has influenced human behavior and contributed to differences between males and females.

SAARNI, C. (1999). *The development of emotional competence.* New York: Guilford. A leading investigator of emotional development focuses on the growth of eight key emotional skills in children. The author discusses the effects of day care on children, reviews the research, describes the elements of high-quality care, and explains how to obtain such care. Written in a straightforward style.

Websites

Visit the Human Development book companion website for all URLs.

■ **The Human Development Book Companion Website**
See **http://www.psychology.wadsworth.com/kail_cavanaugh4e/** for practice quiz questions, Internet links, updates, critical thinking exercises, discussion forums, and more. Also accessible from the Wadsworth Psychology Study Center (http://psychology.wadsworth.com).

■ **State University of New York at Stony Brook**
The site provides information about attachment theory and describes observational methods used to assess quality of attachment.

■ **American Psychological Association**
This site includes information about why children care for others and gives tips for parents who want to encourage their children to be more altruistic.

■ **American Academy of Family Physicians**
This site provides guidelines for selecting a good day care facility.

Life-Span CD-ROM

For more information on the concepts covered in this chapter, go to

Module 2: Infancy and Toddlerhood

- *Emotional and Social Development*

Module 3: Early and Middle Childhood

- *Emotional and Social Development*

http://www.thomsonedu.com
Go to this site for the link to ThomsonNOW, your one-stop study shop. Take a pre-test for this chapter, and ThomsonNOW will generate a personalized study plan based on your test results. The study plan will identify the topics you need to review and direct you to online resources to help you master those topics. You can then take a post-test to help you determine the concepts you have mastered and what you still need to work on.

Exploring Infancy and Early Childhood

T he first 5 years of life are profoundly influential for all children. The events of these early years initiate and direct a lifelong developmental journey.

Infant Development

Infants' brains grow rapidly and the neurons become more efficient.

Physical

Newborns are born with a set of reflexes that enable them to get nutrients for growth (e.g,. rooting and sucking reflexes), protect them from dangers (e.g., eye blink and withdrawal reflexes), and are the foundation of larger patterns of motor activity (e.g., stepping reflex).

Infants typically double their birth weight by 3 months, and triple it by 1 year.

Learning to walk requires integrating many motor skills and perceptual cues; most children walk unassisted by 15 months of age.

Infants' hand control increases rapidly in the first year; handedness is established by age 2.

Infants begin to recognize themselves in the mirror by about 15 months of age. Self-awareness is established by age 2.

Infant Development of the Five Senses	
Smell	Recognize familiar odors
Taste	Differentiate sweet, salty, sour, bitter
Touch	Sensitive to touch; likely feel pain
Hearing	Hear pitches in the range of human speech
Sight	Prefer patterned to plain stimuli

Socioemotional

Bowlby argued that children who form an attachment to an adult are more likely to survive, and infant behaviors (e.g., crying, clinging, sucking, and smiling) are likely to elicit caregiving.

By about 6 to 7 months of age, most infants designate their first attachment figure (usually their mother); attachments to others soon follow.

Basic emotions (e.g., joy, anger, fear) emerge in the first year of life. Complex emotions (e.g., guilt, embarrassment, pride) emerge between 18 and 24 months.

Parallel play begins at about 12 to 15 months of age, followed by simple social play. By age 2, cooperative play emerges.

Cognitive

Infants mentally group objects (called *schemes)* based on the actions they can perform on them. Schemes change constantly as a result of an infant's new experiences.

At about 18 months of age, infants fully understand object permanence.

Infants prefer infant-directed speech, which is slower and has greater variation in pitch and volume.

Many infants begin to talk at about 1 year, although they appear to understand others' speech before they speak themselves. Soon after learning to talk, children begin to speak in two-word sentences, called *telegraphic speech.*

Types of Attachment	
Secure	Infants have complete trust in mother
Disorganized	Infants don't understand mother's absence
Avoidant	Infants ignore mother
Resistant	Infants seem angry with mother

Development in Early Childhood

Physical

Children grow steadily taller and heavier during the preschool years, but their bodies are top heavy because growth of the head and trunk outpaces growth of the legs.

During these years, nerve cells continue to acquire myelin, a natural insulator that allows them to transmit information more rapidly. At the same time, synapses that are unused are gradually eliminated.

Preschoolers' brains are very flexible (called *brain plasticity*) and can sometimes completely recover from injuries as healthy neurons take over from damaged neurons.

Fine motor control becomes more developed, and preschoolers can dress and feed themselves fairly efficiently.

Nicola Sutton / Life File /Getty Images

Photolink/Getty Images

Preschoolers gradually learn to focus their attention but are easily distracted.

© Tom Prettyman /PhotoEdit

Cognitive

Preschoolers mentally group objects (schemes) based on functional or conceptual relationships. Schemes change based on new experiences.

Vygotsky proposed that children learn best when they collaborate with others who are more skilled. Vygotsky's ideas include the *zone of proximal development, scaffolding,* and *private speech.*

Preschool children can remember events they experienced more than 1 year previously, although they are impressionable to what others suggest they may have experienced.

Preschoolers adjust their speech to fit the listener's needs. By age 3, sentences of 10 or more words are common.

Piaget's Four Stages of Thinking	
0-2 years	Sensorimotor thinking
2-7 years	Preoperational thinking
7-11 years	Concrete operations
11 years up	Formal operations

Socioemotional

Erikson's theory proposes three stages for infancy through the preschool years, in which the child must resolve crises for psychosocial growth: *trust vs. mistrust* (0-1 year), *autonomy vs. shame and doubt* (1-3 years), and *initiative vs. guilt* (3-5 years).

Prosocial behavior (e.g. helping, sharing) is more likely when children are empathetic, feel responsible for the person in distress, feel they have the necessary skills, feel happy, and perceive that the costs of helping are small.

Children gradually learn that gender is stable over time and cannot be changed. Children begin to learn gender-typical behavior by observing members of their own sex.

As children grow, they become better skilled at cooperation and at regulating their emotions; those who don't tend to have problems interacting with others.

David Buffinton /Getty Images

PART II

School-Age Children and Adolescents

■ CHAPTER 6
Off to School
*Cognitive and Physical
Development in Middle Childhood*

■ CHAPTER 7
**Expanding Social
Horizons**
*Socioemotional Development
in Middle Childhood*

■ CHAPTER 8
Rites of Passage
*Physical and Cognitive
Development in Adolescence*

■ CHAPTER 9
**Moving Into the Adult
Social World**
*Socioemotional Development
in Adolescence*

Getty Images

6.1 Cognitive Development
More Sophisticated Thinking: Piaget's Version

■ REAL PEOPLE: APPLYING HUMAN DEVELOPMENT: Combinatorial Reasoning Goes to the Races

Information-Processing Strategies for Learning and Remembering

6.2 Aptitudes for School
Theories of Intelligence
Binet and the Development of Intelligence Testing
Do Tests Work?
Hereditary and Environmental Factors
The Impact of Ethnicity and Socioeconomic Status

6.3 Special Children, Special Needs
Gifted and Creative Children
Children With Mental Retardation
Children With Learning Disabilities

■ SPOTLIGHT ON RESEARCH: Improving Reading Skill in Children With Reading Disability

Attention-Deficit Hyperactivity Disorder

6.4 Academic Skills
Reading
Writing
Math Skills

■ REAL PEOPLE: APPLYING HUMAN DEVELOPMENT: Shin-ying Loves School

Effective Schools, Effective Teachers

■ CURRENT CONTROVERSIES: Computers in the Classroom

6.5 Physical Development
Growth
Development of Motor Skills
Physical Fitness
Participating in Sports

Putting It All Together
Summary
Key Terms
Learn More About It

CHAPTER 6

Off to School

Cognitive and Physical Development in Middle Childhood

Every fall, American 5- and 6-year-olds trot off to kindergarten, starting an educational journey that lasts 13 or more years. As the journey begins, many children can read only a few words and know little math; by the end, most can read complete books and many have learned algebra and geometry. This mastery of complex academic skills is possible because of profound changes in children's thinking, changes described in the first section of this chapter.

For most American schoolchildren, intelligence and aptitude tests are a common part of their educational travels. In the second section of this chapter, you'll see what tests measure and why some children get lower scores on tests. In the third section, you'll discover how tests are often used to identify schoolchildren with atypical or special needs.

Next we look at the way that students learn to read, write, and do math. In this section, you'll discover some of the educational practices that seem to foster students' learning.

Finally, children's growing cognitive skills, when coupled with improved motor coordination, enable them to participate in sports. In the last section, we'll look at such participation and the physical changes that make it possible.

6.1

COGNITIVE DEVELOPMENT

Adrian, a sixth grader who is starting middle school, just took his first social studies test—and failed. He is shocked because he'd always gotten A's and B's in elementary school. Adrian realizes that glancing through the textbook chapter once before a test is probably not going to work in middle school, but he's not sure what else he should be doing.

YOU'RE ABOUT ONE THIRD OF THE WAY THROUGH THE BOOK and deserve a break. Try this joke:

> Mr. Jones went into a restaurant and ordered a whole pizza for dinner. When the waiter asked if he wanted it cut into six or eight pieces, Mr. Jones said: "Oh, you'd better make it six! I could never eat eight!" (McGhee, 1976, p. 422)

Okay, this is not such a great joke (to put it mildly). However, many 6- to 8-year-olds think it's hilarious. To understand why children find this joke so funny and to learn more about the skills that will save Adrian's social studies grade, we need to learn more about cognitive development. Let's start with Piaget's theory, then look at information-processing accounts.

MORE SOPHISTICATED THINKING: PIAGET'S VERSION

You probably remember Jean Piaget, from Chapters 1 and 4. Piaget believed that thought develops in a sequence of stages. The first two stages, sensorimotor and preoperational thinking, characterize infancy and the preschool years. In the next few pages, we describe the remaining two stages, the concrete-operational and formal-operational stages, which apply to school-age children and adolescents.

The Concrete-Operational Period

Let's start by reviewing three important limits of preoperational thinking described in Chapter 4:

- Preschoolers are egocentric, believing that others see the world as they do.
- Preschoolers sometimes confuse appearances with reality.
- Preschoolers are unable to reverse their thinking.

None of these limits applies to children in the concrete-operational stage, which extends from approximately 7 to 11 years. Egocentrism wanes gradually. Why? As youngsters have more experiences with friends and siblings who assert their own perspectives on the world, children realize that theirs is not the only view (LeMare & Rubin, 1987). The understanding that events can be interpreted in different ways leads to the realization that appearances can be deceiving. *Also, thought can be reversed, because school-age children have acquired* **mental operations,** *which are actions that can be performed on objects or ideas and that consistently yield a result.* Recall from Chapter 4 that on the conservation task, concrete-operational children realize that the amount of liquid is the same after it has been poured into a different beaker, pointing out that the pouring can always be reversed.

Now you can understand why 7-year-olds laugh at the joke about cutting a pizza into six pieces instead of eight. Think of a joke as a puzzle in which the aim is to determine why a particular remark is funny or incongruous. Generally, people like jokes that are

---

LEARNING OBJECTIVES

What are the distinguishing characteristics of thought during Piaget's concrete-operational and formal-operational stages?

What are some of the limitations of Piaget's account of thinking during the formal-operational stage?

How do children use strategies to improve learning and remembering?

What is the role of monitoring in successful learning and remembering?

neither too simple nor too complex to figure out. Jokes are best when understanding the punch line involves an intermediate level of difficulty (Brodzinsky & Rightmyer, 1980). For children just entering the concrete-operational stage, knowing that the amount of pizza is the same whether it is cut into six or eight pieces taps their newly acquired understanding of conservation, so they laugh (McGhee, 1976).

In discussing the concrete-operational period, we have emphasized how acquiring mental operations is advantageous to children. At the same time, as the name implies, concrete-operational thinking is limited to the tangible and real, to the here and now. The concrete-operational youngster takes "an earthbound, concrete, practical-minded sort of problem-solving approach" (Flavell, 1985, p. 98). Thinking abstractly and hypothetically is beyond the ability of concrete-operational children; these skills are acquired in the formal-operational period, as you'll see in the next section.

THINK ABOUT IT

Piaget, Freud, and Erikson each propose unique stages for ages 7 to 11 years. How similar are the stages they propose? How do they differ?

The Formal-Operational Period

With the onset of the formal-operational period, which extends from roughly age 11 into adulthood, children and adolescents expand beyond thinking about only the concrete and the real. Instead, they apply psychological operations to abstract entities too; they are able to think hypothetically and reason abstractly (Bond, 1995).

To illustrate these differences, let's look at problem solving, where formal-operational adolescents often take a very different approach from concrete-operational children. In one of Piaget's experiments (Inhelder & Piaget, 1958), children and adolescents were presented with several flasks, each containing what appeared to be the same clear liquid. They were told that one combination of the clear liquids would produce a blue liquid; they were asked to determine the necessary combination. A typical concrete-operational youngster plunges right in, mixing liquids from different flasks in a haphazard way. In contrast, formal-operational adolescents understand that setting up the problem in abstract terms is the key. The problem is not really about pouring liquids but about combining different elements until all possible combinations have been tested. So a teenager might mix liquid from the first flask with liquids from each of the other flasks. If none of those combinations produces a blue liquid, the teenager would conclude that the liquid in the first flask is not an essential part of the mixture. The next step would be to mix the liquid in the second flask with each of the remaining liquids. A formal-operational thinker would continue in this manner until he or she finds the critical pair that produces the blue liquid. For adolescents, the problem is not one of concrete acts of pouring and mixing. Instead, they understand that it involves identifying possible combinations and then evaluating each one. This sort of adolescent combinatorial reasoning is illustrated in the Real People feature.

Concrete-operational thinkers often solve problems haphazardly, but formal-operational thinkers more often set up problems in abstract terms.

REAL PEOPLE: Applying Human Development

COMBINATORIAL REASONING GOES TO THE RACES

As a 15-year-old, Robert Kail delivered the *Indianapolis Star.* In the spring of 1965, the newspaper announced a contest for all newspaper carriers. The task was to list the most words that could be created from the letters contained in the words "SAFE RACE." Whoever listed the most words would win two tickets to the Indianapolis 500 auto race.

Kail realized that this was a problem in combinatorial reasoning. All he needed to do was create all possible combinations of letters, then look them up. Following this procedure, he had to win (or, at worst, tie). So he created exhaustive lists of possible words, beginning with each of the letters individually, then all possible combinations of two letters, and working his way up to all possible combinations of all eight letters (e.g., SCAREEFA, SCAREEAF). This was monotonous enough, but no more so than the next step: looking up all those possible words in a dictionary. (Remember, this was in the days before computerized spell-checkers.) Weeks later, he had generated a list of 126 words. As predicted, a few months later, he learned that he had won the contest. Combinatorial reasoning has its payoffs!

---

*Adolescents' more sophisticated thinking is also shown in their ability to make appropriate conclusions from facts, which is known as **deductive reasoning.*** Suppose we tell a person the following statement:

> If you hit a glass with a hammer, the glass will break.

If you then tell the person, "You hit the glass with a hammer" he or she would conclude, of course, that "The glass will break,"—a conclusion that formal-operational adolescents do reach.

Concrete-operational youngsters sometimes reach this conclusion too—but based on their experience, not because the conclusion is logically necessary. To see the difference, imagine that the statement now is:

> If you hit a glass with a feather, the glass will break.

Told "You hit the glass with a feather," the conclusion "the glass will break" follows just as logically as it did in the first example. In this instance, however, the conclusion is contrary to fact—it goes against what experience tells us is really true. Concrete-operational 10-year-olds resist reaching conclusions that are contrary to known facts, whereas formal-operational 15-year-olds reach them much of the time (Markovits & Vachon, 1989). Formal-operational teenagers understand that these problems are about abstractions that need not correspond to real-world relations. In contrast, concrete-operational youngsters reach conclusions based on their knowledge of the world.

Comments on Piaget's View

As mentioned in Chapter 4, although Piaget provides our single most comprehensive theory of cognitive development, his account of mental development during the early years has some shortcomings. The same is true of his description of formal-operational thinking (Siegler & Alibali, 2005). Let's look at two questionable aspects.

1. *Formal-operational thinking as a capability.* Simply because adolescents have attained the formal-operational stage does not mean that they always reason at this level. Adolescents (and adults) often fail to reason logically, even when they are capable of doing so and when it would be beneficial to them (Klaczynski, 2004). Adolescents typically show more sophisticated reasoning when the problems are relevant to them personally (e.g., if they concern driving a car) than when they are presented in an abstract form using symbols (Ward & Overton, 1990). And, as you'll see in Chapter 8, adolescents' thinking is sometimes egocentric and irrational. Consequently, Piaget's account of formal operations is really a description of how adolescents *can* think, not how they always or even usually *do* think.

2. *Formal operations as an end point.* Cognitive development is complete by age 12 or 13 in Piaget's theory. After adolescents have attained the formal-operational level, their thinking is said to remain the same qualitatively. Of course, people continue to acquire more knowledge and skills, but the fundamental processes of thinking do not change, according to Piaget. Many theorists have criticized this aspect of the theory and have proposed further developmental changes in thinking during late adolescence and adulthood (Moshman, 1998), which we'll discuss in Chapter 9.

Because of these limits to Piaget's theory, we need to look at other approaches to complete our account of mental development during childhood and adolescence. In the next few pages, we'll focus on the information-processing approach we examined in Chapter 4.

INFORMATION-PROCESSING STRATEGIES FOR LEARNING AND REMEMBERING

Once one of us had just written four pages for this book that would have made John Grisham green with envy, when the unthinkable happened: A power failure knocked out the computer, and all those wonderful words were lost. If only the text had been saved to the hard drive . . . but it hadn't.

This tale of woe sets the stage for a main issue of the information-processing approach. As you'll remember from Chapter 4, information-processing psychologists believe that cognitive development proceeds by increases in the efficiency with which children process information.

One of the key issues in this approach is the means by which children store information in permanent memory and retrieve it when needed later. *According to information-processing psychologists, most human thought takes place in* **working memory,** *where a relatively small number of thoughts and ideas can be stored briefly*. As you read these sentences, for example, the information is stored in working memory. However, as you read additional sentences, they displace the contents of sentences you read earlier. *For you to learn this information, it must be transferred to* **long-term memory,** *a permanent storehouse of knowledge that has unlimited capacity*. If information you read is not transferred to long-term memory, it is lost, just as our words vanished from the computer's memory when the power failed.

High school and college students often use efficient strategies, such as highlighting, to help them remember information.

Memory Strategies

How do you try to learn the information in this or your other textbooks? If you're like many college students, you will probably use some combination of highlighting key sentences, outlining chapters, taking notes, writing summaries, and testing yourself. These are all effective learning strategies that make it easier for you to store text information in long-term memory.

Children begin to use simple strategies fairly early. For example, 7- or 8-year-olds use rehearsal, a strategy of repetitively naming information that is to be remembered. As children get older, they learn other memory strategies. *One is* **organization**—*structuring information to be remembered so that related information is placed together*. For example, a sixth grader trying to remember major battles of the American Civil War could organize them geographically (e.g., Shiloh and Fort Donelson in Tennessee, Antietam and Monocacy in Maryland) or chronologically (e.g., Fort Sumter and First Manassas in 1861, Gettysburg and Vicksburg in 1863).

Another strategy is **elaboration**—*embellishing information to be remembered to make it more memorable*. To see elaboration in action, imagine a child who can never remember if the second syllable of *rehearsal* is spelled *her* (as it sounds) or *hear*. The child could remember the correct spelling by reminding herself that *rehearsal* is like *re-hear-ing*. Thus, thinking about the derivation of *rehearsal* makes it easier to remember how to spell it. Finally, as children grow, they're also more likely to use external aids to memory: They are more likely to make notes and to write down information on calendars so they won't forget future events (Eskritt & Lee, 2002).

One efficient memory strategy is to use external devices, like a calendar, to help remember future events.

Metacognition

Just as there's not much value to a filled toolbox if you don't know how to use the tools, memory strategies aren't much good unless children know when to use them. For example, rehearsal is a great strategy for remembering phone numbers but lousy for remembering amendments to the U.S. Constitution or the plot of *Hamlet.* During the elementary-school years and adolescence, children gradually learn to identify different kinds of memory problems and the memory strategies most appropriate to each. For example, when reading a textbook or watching a television newscast, outlining or writing a summary are good strategies because they identify the main points and organize them. Children gradually become more skilled at selecting appropriate strategies, but even high school students do not always use effective learning strategies when they should (Kuhn, 2000; Pierce & Lange, 2000).

After children choose a memory strategy, they need to monitor its effectiveness. That is, they need to decide if the strategy is working. If it's not, they need to begin anew, reanalyzing the memory task to select a better approach. If the strategy is working, they should determine the portion of the material they have not yet mastered and concentrate their efforts there. Monitoring improves gradually with age. For example, elementary-school children can accurately identify which material they have not yet learned, but they do not consistently focus their study efforts on this material (Kail, 1990).

*Diagnosing memory problems accurately and monitoring the effectiveness of memory strategies are two important elements of **metamemory**, which refers to a child's intuitive understanding of memory.* That is, as children develop, they learn more about how memory operates and devise naive theories of memory that represent an extension of the theory of mind described on pages 123–126. For example, children learn that memory is fallible (i.e., they sometimes forget!) and that some types of memory tasks are easier than others (e.g., remembering the main idea of the Gettysburg address is simpler than remembering it word-for-word). This growing knowledge of memory helps children to use memory strategies more effectively, just as an experienced carpenter's accumulated knowledge of wood tells her when to use nails, screws, or glue to join two boards.

Of course, children's growing understanding of memory is paralleled by their increased understanding of all cognitive processes. *Such knowledge and awareness of cognitive processes is called **metacognitive knowledge.*** Metacognitive knowledge grows rapidly during the elementary-school years: Children come to know much about perception, attention, intentions, knowledge, and thinking (Flavell, 1999, 2000). For example, school-age children know that sometimes they deliberately direct their attention—as in searching for a parent's face in a crowd—but that sometimes events capture attention—as with an unexpected clap of thunder (Parault & Schwanenflugel, 2000).

One of the most important features of children's metacognitive knowledge is their understanding of the connections among goals, strategies, monitoring, and outcomes, shown in Figure 6.1. Children come to realize that on a broad spectrum of tasks—ranging from learning words in a spelling list to learning to spike a volleyball to learning to get along with an overly talkative classmate seated nearby—they need to regulate their learning by understanding the goal and selecting a means to achieve that goal. Then they determine whether the chosen method is working. *Effective **cognitive self-regulation**— that is, skill at identifying goals, selecting effective strategies, and monitoring accurately —is a characteristic of successful students* (McCormick & Pressley, 1997; Zimmerman, 2001). A student may decide that writing each spelling word twice before the test is a good way to get all the words right. When the student gets only 70% correct on the first

THINK ABOUT IT

Which elements of the biopsychosocial framework are emphasized in the information-processing approach to cognitive development?

test, he switches to a new strategy (e.g., writing each word four times, plus writing its definition), showing the adaptive nature of cognitive processes in self-regulated learners.

Perhaps this has a familiar ring to it. It should, for the diagram simply summarizes an important set of study skills. Analyzing, strategizing, and monitoring are key elements of productive studying. The study goals change when you move from this book to your math text to a novel that you are reading for English, but the basic sequence still holds. Studying should always begin with a clear understanding of what goal you are trying to achieve because this sets the stage for all the events that follow. Too often we see students like Adrian—the student in the vignette—who just read text material, without any clear idea of what they should be getting out of it. Instead, students should be active readers (Adams, Treiman, & Pressley, 1998). Always study with a plan. Start by skimming the text to become familiar with the material. Before you read more carefully, try to anticipate some of the topics that the author will cover

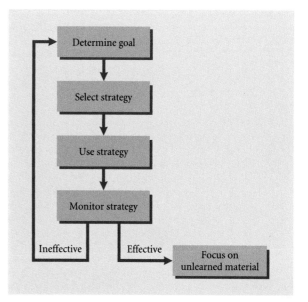

in detail. When you reach natural breaks in the material, try to summarize what you've read and think of questions that a teacher might ask about the material. Finally, when you don't understand something in the text, stop and determine the source of your confusion. Perhaps you don't know a word's meaning. Maybe you skipped or misunderstood an earlier section of the material. By reading actively, using strategies like these, you'll be much more likely to understand and remember what you've read (Adams et al., 1998; Brown et al., 1996).

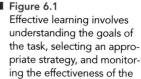

Figure 6.1
Effective learning involves understanding the goals of the task, selecting an appropriate strategy, and monitoring the effectiveness of the chosen strategy.

 **TEST YOURSELF**

1. During Piaget's _____ stage, children are first able to represent objects mentally in different ways and to perform mental operations.

2. Hypothetical and deductive reasoning are characteristic of children in Piaget's _____ stage.

3. Piaget's account of formal operations has been criticized because adolescents' reasoning is often less sophisticated than the theory predicts and because _____.

4. Children and adolescents often select a memory strategy after they have _____.

5. The term _____ refers to periodic evaluation of a strategy to determine whether it is working.

Formal-operational adolescents are able to reason abstractly. How might this ability help them use the study skills shown in Figure 6.1 more effectively?

Answers: (1) concrete-operational, (2) formal-operational, (3) the formal-operational stage is portrayed as the final stage of intellectual development, (4) determined the goal of the memory task, (5) monitoring

6.2

APTITUDES FOR SCHOOL

Max is 12 years old and is moderately mentally retarded. That is, he performs most tasks at the level of a nonretarded 5- or 6-year-old. For example, he can't do many of Piaget's conservation tasks, and he reads very slowly and with much effort. Nevertheless, if Max hears a song on the radio, he can immediately sit down at the piano and play the melody flawlessly, despite having had no musical training. Everyone who sees Max do this is astonished. How can a person who is otherwise so limited intellectually perform such an amazing feat?

LEARNING OBJECTIVES

Why were intelligence tests first developed? What are their features?

How well do intelligence tests work?

What is the nature of intelligence?

How and why do test scores vary for different racial and ethnic groups?

How do heredity and environment influence intelligence?

Before you read further, how would you define intelligence? If you're typical of most Americans, your definition probably includes the ability to reason logically, connect ideas, and solve real problems. You might mention verbal ability, meaning the ability to speak clearly and articulately. You might also mention social competence, referring, for example, to an interest in the world at large and an ability to admit when you make a mistake (Sternberg & Kaufman, 1998).

As you'll see in this section, many of these ideas about intelligence are included in psychological theories of intelligence. We'll begin by considering the theories of intelligence, where we'll get some insights into Max's uncanny musical skill. Next, you'll see how intelligence tests were devised initially to assess individual differences in intellectual ability. Then we'll look at a simple question: "How well do modern tests work?" Finally, we'll examine how race, ethnicity, social class, gender, environment, and heredity influence intelligence.

THEORIES OF INTELLIGENCE

Psychometricians are psychologists who specialize in measuring psychological characteristics such as intelligence and personality. When psychometricians want to research a particular question, they usually begin by administering a large number of tests to many individuals. Then they look for patterns in performance across the different tests. The basic logic underlying this technique is similar to the logic a jungle hunter uses to decide whether some dark blobs in a river are three separate rotting logs or a single alligator (Cattell, 1965). If the blobs move together, the hunter decides they are part of the same structure, an alligator. If they do not move together, they are three different structures, three logs. Similarly, if changes in performance on one test are accompanied by changes in performance on a second test—that is, they move together—one could assume that the tests are measuring the same attribute or factor.

Suppose, for example, that you believe there is such a thing as general intelligence. That is, you believe that some people are smart regardless of the situation, task, or problem, whereas others are not so smart. According to this view, children's performance should be very consistent across tasks. Smart children should always receive high scores, and the less smart youngsters should always get lower scores. As early as 1904, Charles Spearman reported findings supporting the idea that a general factor for intelligence, or *g,* is responsible for performance on all mental tests.

Other researchers, however, have found that intelligence consists of distinct abilities. For example, Thurstone and Thurstone (1941) analyzed performance on a wide range of tasks and identified seven distinct patterns, each reflecting a unique ability: percep-

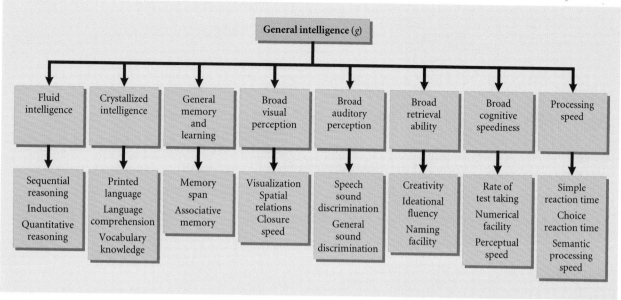

From Carroll, 1993.

■ Figure 6.2
Hierarchical theories of intelligence have different levels that range from general intelligence (g) to very specific skills.

tual speed, word comprehension, word fluency, space, number, memory, and induction. Thurstone and Thurstone also acknowledged a general factor that operated in all tasks, but they emphasized that the specific factors were more useful in assessing and understanding intellectual ability.

The Hierarchical View of Intelligence

These conflicting findings have led many psychometric theorists to propose hierarchical theories of intelligence that include both general and specific components. John Carroll (1993), for example, proposed the hierarchical theory with three levels shown in Figure 6.2. At the top of the hierarchy is *g*, general intelligence. In the level underneath *g* are eight broad categories of intellectual skill, ranging from fluid intelligence to processing speed. Each of the abilities in the second level is further divided into the skills listed in the third and most specific level. Crystallized intelligence, for example, includes understanding printed language, comprehending language, and knowing vocabulary.

Carroll's hierarchical theory is, in essence, a compromise between the two views of intelligence—general versus distinct abilities. But some critics find it unsatisfactory because it ignores the research and theory on cognitive development. They believe we need to look beyond the psychometric approach to understand intelligence. In the remainder of this section, then, we'll look at two newer theories that have gained a following.

Gardner's Theory of Multiple Intelligences

Only recently have developmental psychologists viewed intelligence from the perspective of Piaget's theory and information-processing psychology. These new theories present a much broader theory of intelligence and how it develops. Among the most ambitious is Howard Gardner's (1983, 1999, 2002) theory of multiple intelligences. Rather than using test scores as the basis for his theory, Gardner draws on research in child development, studies of brain-damaged persons, and studies of exceptionally talented people. Using these criteria, Gardner identified seven distinct intelligences when he first proposed the theory in 1983. In subsequent work, Gardner (1999, 2002) has identified two additional intelligences; the complete list is shown in Table 6.1.

The first three intelligences in this list—linguistic intelligence, logical-mathematical intelligence, and spatial intelligence—are included in psychometric theories of intelligence. The last six intelligences are not: Musical, bodily-kinesthetic, interpersonal, intrapersonal, naturalistic, and existential intelligences are unique to Gardner's theory.

TABLE 6.1

Nine Intelligences in Gardner's Theory of Multiple Intelligences

Type of Intelligence	Definition
Linguistic	Knowing the meanings of words, having the ability to use words to understand new ideas, and using language to convey ideas to others
Logical-mathematical	Understanding relations that exist among objects, actions, and ideas, as well as the logical or mathematical operations that can be performed on them
Spatial	Perceiving objects accurately and imagining in the "mind's eye" the appearance of an object before and after it has been transformed
Musical	Comprehending and producing sounds varying in pitch, rhythm, and emotional tone
Bodily-kinesthetic	Using one's body in highly differentiated ways, as dancers, craftspeople, and athletes do
Interpersonal	Identifying different feelings, moods, motivations, and intentions in others
Intrapersonal	Understanding one's emotions and knowing one's strengths and weaknesses
Naturalistic	Recognizing and distinguishing among members of a group (species) and describing relations between such groups
Existential	Considering "ultimate" issues, such as the purpose of life and the nature of death

SOURCE: Gardner, 1983, 1999, & 2002

Savants are individuals with mental retardation who nevertheless are exceptionally talented in one domain, such as music.

Paul Merideth

According to Gardner, Yo-Yo Ma's wizardry on the cello, the Williams sisters' remarkable shots on the tennis court, and Oprah Winfrey's grace and charm in dealing with people are all features of intelligence that are totally ignored in traditional theories.

How did Gardner arrive at these nine distinct intelligences? First, each has a unique developmental history. Linguistic intelligence, for example, develops much earlier than the others. Second, each intelligence is regulated by distinct regions of the brain, as shown in studies of brain-damaged persons. Spatial intelligence, for example, is regulated by particular regions in the right hemisphere of the brain. Third, each has special cases of talented individuals. *Musical intelligence is often shown by savants, individuals with mental retardation who are extremely talented in one domain* (Miller, 1999). Max, the 12-year-old in the opening vignette, is a savant whose special talent is music. Max can play a tune correctly after a single hearing and without ever having had formal musical training (Shuter-Dyson, 1982).

Prompted by Gardner's theory, researchers have begun to look at other nontraditional aspects of intelligence. *Probably the best known is **emotional intelligence**, which is the ability to use one's own and others' emotions effectively for solving problems and living happily.* Emotional intelligence made headlines in 1995 due to a best-selling book, *Emotional Intelligence,* in which Daniel Goleman (1995) argued that "emotions [are] at the center of aptitudes for living" (p. xiii). In fact, research shows that emotional intelligence has a number of different components, including perceiving emotions accurately (in others and in oneself) and regulating one's emotions. People who are emotionally intelligent tend to have high scores on traditional IQ tests, have higher self-esteem, and are more sociable (Mayer, Caruso, & Salovey, 1999; Mayer, Salovey, & Caruso, 2000).

The theory of multiple intelligences has important implications for education. Gardner (1993, 1995) believes schools should foster all intelligences, not just the traditional linguistic and logical-mathematical intelligences. Teachers should capitalize on the strongest intelligences of individual children. Some students may best understand unfamiliar cultures, for example, by studying their dance; other students may best understand these cultures by studying their music.

These guidelines do not mean that teachers should gear instruction solely to a child's strongest intelligence, pigeon-holing youngsters as "numerical learners" or "spatial learners." Instead, whether the topic is the signing of the Declaration of Independence or Shakespeare's *Hamlet,* instruction should try to engage as many different intelligences as possible (Gardner, 1999, 2002). The typical result is a much richer understanding of the topic by all students.

Some American schools have enthusiastically embraced Gardner's ideas (Gardner, 1993). Are these schools better? Educators in schools using the theory think so; they claim that their students have higher test scores and better discipline and that their parents are more involved (Project Zero, 1999). Although these findings are encouraging, they need to be supported by research that evaluates children's learning and achievement, not educators' opinions. In the mean time, there is no doubt that Gardner's work has helped liberate researchers from narrow psychometric-based views of intelligence. A comparably broad but different view of intelligence comes from another new theory that we'll look at in the next section.

Sternberg's Theory of Successful Intelligence

Robert Sternberg has studied intelligence for more than 30 years. He began by asking how adults solve problems on intelligence tests. Over the years, this work led to a comprehensive theory of intelligence, one in which intelligence is defined as using one's abilities skillfully to achieve one's personal goals (Sternberg, 1999). Goals can be short-term, such as getting an A on a test, making a snack in the microwave, or winning the 100-meter hurdles, or longer term, such as having a successful career and a happy family life. Achieving these goals by using one's skills defines successful intelligence.

In achieving personal goals, people use three different kinds of abilities. ***Analytic ability*** *involves analyzing problems and generating different solutions.* Suppose a 12-year-old wants to download songs to her MP3 player, but something isn't working. Analytic intelligence is shown in considering different causes of the problem—maybe the MP3 player is broken or maybe the software to download songs wasn't installed correctly. Analytic intelligence also involves thinking of different solutions: She could surf the Internet for clues about what's wrong or ask a sibling for help.

Creative ability *involves dealing adaptively with novel situations and problems.* Returning to our 12-year-old, suppose that she discovers her MP3 player is broken just as she's ready to leave on a day-long car trip. Lacking the time (and money) to buy a new player, creative intelligence is shown in dealing successfully with a novel goal: finding something enjoyable to do to pass the time on a long drive.

Finally, ***practical ability*** *involves knowing what solution or plan will actually work.* Problems can be solved in different ways in principle, but in reality only one solution may be practical. Our 12-year-old may realize that the only way to figure out why her MP3 player isn't working is to surf the net: She doesn't want to ask for help because her parents wouldn't approve of many of the songs, and she doesn't want a sibling to know that she's downloading them anyway.

Like Gardner, Sternberg (1999) argues that instruction is most effective when it is geared to a child's strength. A child with strong analytic ability, for example, may find algebra simpler when the course emphasizes analyses and evaluation; a child with strong practical ability may be at his best when the material is organized around practical applications. Thus, the theory of successful intelligence shows how instruction can be matched to students' strongest abilities, enhancing students' prospects for mastering the material (Grigorenko, Jarvin, & Sternberg, 2002).

For street vendors in Brazil, successful intelligence involves sophisticated arithmetic operations for buying products, making change, and keeping track of sales.

Stock Boston, Inc.

Sternberg emphasizes that successful intelligence is revealed in people's pursuit of goals. Of course, these goals vary from one person to the next and, just as important, often vary even more in different cultural or ethnic groups. That is, intelligence is always partly defined by the demands of an environment or cultural context. What is intelligent for children growing up in cities in North America may not be intelligent for children growing up in the Sahara desert, the Australian outback, or on a remote island in the Pacific Ocean. For example, in Brazil, many elementary-school-age boys sell candy and fruit to bus passengers and pedestrians. These children often cannot identify the numbers on paper money, yet they know how to purchase their goods from wholesale stores, make change for customers, and keep track of their sales (Saxe, 1988b).

If the Brazilian vendors were given the tests that measure intelligence in American students, they would fare poorly. Does this mean they are less intelligent than American children? Of course not. The skills important to American conceptions of intelligence and that are assessed on our intelligence tests are less valued in these other cultures and so are not cultivated in the young. Each culture defines what it means to be intelligent, and the specialized computing skills of vendors are just as intelligent in their cultural settings as verbal skills are in American culture (Sternberg & Kaufman, 1998).

As with Gardner's theory, researchers are still evaluating Sternberg's theory and still debating the question of what intelligence is. However it is defined, the fact is that individuals differ substantially in intellectual ability, and numerous tests have been devised to measure these differences. We'll examine the construction, properties, and limitations of these tests in the next section.

BINET AND THE DEVELOPMENT OF INTELLIGENCE TESTING

American schools faced a crisis at the beginning of the 20th century. Between 1890 and 1915, school enrollment nearly doubled nationally because of an influx of immigrants and because reforms restricted child labor and emphasized education (Chapman, 1988). With the increased enrollment, teachers were confronted by ever-greater numbers of students who did not learn as readily as the "select few" students who had populated their classes previously. How to deal with "feebleminded" children was one of the pressing issues of the day for U.S. educators.

These problems were not unique to the United States. In 1904 the Minister of Public Instruction in France asked two noted psychologists of the day, Alfred Binet and Theophile Simon, to formulate a way to recognize children who would be unable to learn in school without special instruction. Binet and Simon's approach was to select simple tasks that French children of different ages ought to be able to do, such as naming colors, counting backward, and remembering numbers in order. Based on preliminary testing, Binet and Simon identified problems that normal 3-year-olds could solve, that normal 4-year-olds could solve, and so on. *Children's mental age, or MA, referred to the difficulty of the problems they could solve correctly.* A child who solved problems that the average 7-year-old could solve would have an MA of 7.

Binet and Simon used mental age to distinguish "bright" from "dull" children. A bright child would have the MA of an older child—for example, a 6-year-old with an MA of 9. A dull child would have the MA of a younger child—for example, a 6-year-old with an MA of 4. Binet and Simon confirmed that bright children identified using their test did better in school than dull children. Voilà—the first objective measure of intelligence!

THINK ABOUT IT

If Jean Piaget were to create an intelligence test, how would it differ from the type of test Binet created?

The Stanford-Binet

Lewis Terman, of Stanford University, revised Binet and Simon's test substantially and published a version known as the Stanford-Binet in 1916. *Terman described performance* *as an **intelligence quotient,** or **IQ,** which was simply the ratio of mental age to chronological age, multiplied by 100:*

IQ = MA/CA × 100

At any age, children who are perfectly average have an IQ of 100, because their mental age equals their chronological age. Furthermore, roughly two thirds of children taking a test will have IQ scores between 85 and 115. The IQ score can also be used to compare intelligence in children of different ages. A 4-year-old girl with an MA of 5 has an IQ of 125 (5/4 × 100), just like that of an 8-year-old boy with an MA of 10 (10/8 × 100).

IQ scores are no longer computed in this manner. Instead, children's IQ scores are determined by comparing their test performance to that of others their age. When children perform at the average for their age, their IQ is 100. Children who perform above the average have IQs greater than 100; children who perform below the average have IQs less than 100. Nevertheless, the concept of IQ as the ratio of MA to CA helped to popularize the Stanford-Binet test.

By the 1920s the Stanford-Binet had been joined by many other intelligence tests. Educators greeted these new devices enthusiastically because they seemed to offer an efficient and objective way to assess a student's chances of succeeding in school (Chapman, 1988). Today, more than 80 years later, the Stanford-Binet remains a popular test; the latest version was revised in 2003. Like the earlier versions, the modern Stanford-Binet consists of various cognitive and motor tasks, ranging from the extremely easy to the extremely difficult. The Stanford-Binet, the Wechsler Intelligence Scale for Children-III (WISC-III), and the Kaufman Assessment Battery for Children (K-ABC) are the primary individualized tests of intelligence in use today.

DO TESTS WORK?

To answer this question, two separate issues are important: reliability and validity. First, we need to know whether a test is reliable, which means that it yields scores that are consistent. Reliability is often measured by administering similar forms of a test on two occasions. On a reliable test, a person will have similar scores on both occasions. In fact, modern intelligence tests are quite reliable. If a child takes an intelligence test and then retakes it days or a few weeks later, the two scores are usually quite similar (Wechsler, 1991).

What do these scores *mean*? Are they really measuring intelligence? These questions raise the issue of validity, which refers to the extent to which a test really measures what it claims to measure. Validity is usually assessed by determining the relation between test scores and other, independent measures of the construct that the test is thought to measure. For example, to measure the validity of a test of extraversion, we would first have children take the test. Then we would observe these same youngsters in some social setting, such as during a school recess, and record who is outgoing and who is shy. The test would be valid if scores correlated highly with our independent observations of extraverted behavior.

How can this approach be extended to intelligence tests? Ideally, we would administer the intelligence tests and then correlate the scores with other, independent estimates of intelligence. Therein lies the problem. There are no other independent ways to estimate intelligence; the only way to measure intelligence is with tests. Consequently, many follow Binet's lead and obtain measures of performance in school, such as grades or teachers' ratings of their students. The correlations between these measures and scores on intelligence tests typically fall somewhere between .4 and .6 (Neisser et al., 1996). For example, the correlation between scores on the WISC-III and grade-point average is .47 (Wechsler, 1991). That is, children with high scores on the WISC-III tend to get better grades. However, the correlation is far from perfect, which means that some youngsters with high test scores do not excel in school, whereas others with low scores get good grades. In general, however, tests do a reasonable job of predicting school success.

Not only are intelligence tests reasonable predictors of performance in school, they also predict performance in the workplace, particularly for more complex jobs (Gottfredson, 1997; Schmidt & Hunter, 1998). Workers with higher IQ scores tend to be more successful in their on-the-job training and, following training, more successful in their actual work performance. If, for example, two teenagers have summer jobs running tests in a biology lab, the one with the higher IQ score will probably learn the procedures more rapidly and, once learned, conduct them more accurately.

Increasing Validity With Dynamic Testing

Traditional tests of intelligence such as the Stanford-Binet and the WISC-III measure knowledge and skills that a child has accumulated up to the time of testing. These tests do *not* directly measure a child's potential for future learning; instead, the usual assumption is that children who have learned more in the past will probably learn more in the future. Critics argue that tests would be more valid if they directly assessed a child's potential for future learning.

Dynamic testing measures a child's learning potential by having the child learn something new in the presence of the examiner and with the examiner's help. Thus, dynamic testing is interactive and measures new achievement rather than past achievement. It is based on Vygotsky's ideas of the zone of proximal development and scaffolding (pages 155–156). Learning potential can be estimated by the amount of material the child learns during interaction with the examiner and from the amount of help the child needs to learn the new material (Grigorenko & Sternberg, 1998; Sternberg & Grigorenko, 2002).

To understand the difference between traditional, static methods of intelligence testing and new, dynamic approaches, imagine a group of children attending a week-long soccer camp. On the first day, all children are tested on a range of soccer skills and receive a score that indicates their overall level of soccer skill. If this score were shown to predict later success in soccer, such as number of goals scored in a season, this would be a valid static measure of soccer skill. To make this a dynamic measure of soccer skill, children would spend all week at camp being instructed in new skills. At the end of the week, the test of soccer skills would be administered again. The amount of the child's improvement over the week would measure learning potential, with greater improvement indicating greater learning potential.

Dynamic testing is a recent innovation and is still being evaluated. Preliminary research does indicate, however, that static and dynamic testing both provide useful and independent information. If the aim is to predict future levels of a child's skill, it is valuable to know a child's current level of skill (static testing) as well as the child's potential to acquire greater skill (dynamic testing). By combining both forms of testing, we achieve a more comprehensive view of a child's talents than by relying on either method alone (Day et al., 1997).

HEREDITARY AND ENVIRONMENTAL FACTORS

Joanna, a 7-year-old girl, was administered the WISC-III and obtained a score of 112. Ted, a 7-year-old boy, took the same test and received a score of 92. What accounts for the 20-point difference in these youngsters' scores? Heredity and experience both matter.

Some of the evidence for hereditary factors is shown in Figure 6.3. If genes influence intelligence, then siblings' test scores should become more alike as siblings become more similar genetically (Plomin & Petrill, 1997). In other words, because identical twins are identical genetically, they should have virtually identical test scores, which would be a correlation of 1. Fraternal twins have about 50% of their genes in common, just like other siblings of the same biological parents. Consequently, their test scores should be (a) less similar than scores for identical twins, (b) similar to other siblings who have the same biological parents, and (c) more similar than the scores of children and their adopted siblings. You can see in Figure 6.3 that each of these predictions is supported.

Heredity also influences patterns of developmental change in IQ scores (Wilson, 1983). Patterns of developmental change in IQ are more alike for identical twins than

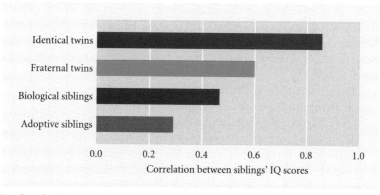

Based on the data in Bouchard and McGue, 1981.

■ **Figure 6.3**
Siblings' IQ scores become more similar as the siblings become more similar genetically, which is evidence for a hereditary basis for intelligence.

for fraternal twins. If one identical twin gets higher IQ scores with age, the other twin almost certainly will too. In contrast, if one fraternal twin gets higher scores with age, the other twin may not necessarily show the same pattern. Thus, identical twins are not only more alike in overall IQ but in developmental change in IQ as well.

Studies of adopted children suggest that the impact of heredity increases during childhood and adolescence: If heredity helps determine IQ, then children's IQs should be more like their biological parents' IQs than their adoptive parents' IQs. In fact, these correlations were computed in the Colorado Adoption Project (Plomin et al., 1997), which included adopted children as well as their biological and adoptive parents. Biological parents' IQ was measured before the child was born; adoptive parents' IQ was measured before the child's first birthday; children's IQs were tested repeatedly in childhood and adolescence. The results, shown in Figure 6.4, are clear. At every age, the correlation between children's IQ and their biological parents' IQ (shown by the blue line) is greater than the correlation between children's IQ and their adoptive parents' IQ (shown by the red line). In fact, children's IQ scores are essentially unrelated to their adoptive parents' IQs.

Notice, too, that the relation between children's IQs and their biological parents' IQ actually gets *stronger* as children get older. In other words, as adopted children get older, their test scores increasingly resemble their biological parents' scores. These results are evidence for the greater impact of heredity on IQ as a child grows.

Do these results mean that heredity is the sole determiner of intelligence? No. Three areas of research show the importance of environment on intelligence: characteristics of the home environment, changes in IQ scores, and intervention programs. Let's start with research on the characteristics of families and homes. If intelligence were solely due

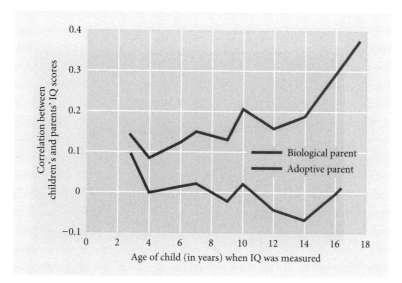

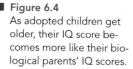

■ **Figure 6.4**
As adopted children get older, their IQ score becomes more like their biological parents' IQ scores.

to heredity, environment should have little or no impact on children's intelligence. But we know that many characteristics of parents' behavior and home environments are related to children's intelligence. For example, children with high test scores tend to come from homes that are well organized and have plenty of appropriate play materials (Bradley et al., 1989).

The impact of the environment on intelligence is also implicated by research on historical change in IQ scores. During most of the 20th century, IQ test scores rose dramatically (Flynn, 1998; Sundet, Barlaug, & Torjussen, 2004). For example, scores on the WISC increased by nearly 10 points over a 25-year-period (Flynn, 1999). Heredity cannot account for such a rapid increase over a few decades (a mere fraction of a second in genetic time). Consequently, the rise must reflect the impact of some aspect of the environment. The change might reflect smaller, better-educated families with more leisure time (Daley et al., 2003; Dickens & Flynn, 2001). Or it might be due to movies, television, and more recently, the computer and Internet, providing children with an incredible wealth of virtual experience (Greenfield, 1998). Although the exact cause remains a mystery, the increase per se shows the impact of changing environmental conditions on intelligence.

The importance of a stimulating environment for intelligence is also demonstrated by intervention programs that prepare economically disadvantaged children for school. When children grow up in never-ending poverty, the cycle is predictable and tragic: Youngsters have few of the intellectual skills to succeed in school, so they fail; lacking an education, they find minimal jobs (if they can work at all), guaranteeing that their children, too, are destined to grow up in poverty.

Since Project Head Start began in 1965, massive educational intervention has been an important tool in the effort to break this repeated cycle of poverty. Head Start and other intervention programs teach preschool youngsters basic school readiness skills and social skills and offer guidance to parents (Campbell et al., 2001; Ramey & Ramey, 1990). When children participate in these enrichment programs, their test scores go up and school achievement improves, particularly when intervention programs are extended beyond preschool into the elementary-school years (Reynolds & Temple, 1998).

One of the success stories is the Carolina Abecedarian Project designed by Frances Campbell and Craig Ramey (1994; Campbell et al., 2001; Ramey & Campbell, 1991). This project included 111 children; most were born to African American mothers who had less than a high school education, an average IQ score of 85, and typically no income. About half the children were assigned to a control group in which they received no special attention. The others attended a special day care facility daily from 4 months until 5 years. The curriculum emphasized mental, linguistic, and social development for infants, and prereading skills for preschoolers.

Every few years, the children were assessed on a battery of tests. The results for IQ scores are shown in Figure 6.5. You can see that during the period of the intervention

■ **Figure 6.5**
Intervention that focuses on children's linguistic, cognitive, and reading skills can have a long-term effect on children.

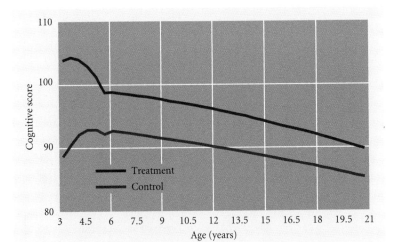

(i.e., the preschool years), the groups differ substantially: Youngsters in the treatment group have above average IQ scores, but those in the control group have below average scores. For the remaining 15 years, scores for both groups decline slowly, but the children who participated in the special preschool programs always have higher scores, even as young adults. Intervention had a similar benefit on students' reading and math achievement.

Thus, intervention works. An improvement of 7 to 10 points may not strike you as very much, but it is a substantial improvement from a practical standpoint. Of course, massive intervention over many years is expensive. But so are the economic consequences of poverty, unemployment, and their by-products. Programs like the Abecedarian Project show that the repetitive cycle of school failure and education can be broken. And, in the process, they show that intelligence is fostered by a stimulating and responsive environment.

THE IMPACT OF ETHNICITY AND SOCIOECONOMIC STATUS

On many intelligence tests, ethnic groups differ in their average scores: Asian Americans tend to have the highest scores, followed by European Americans, Latino Americans, and African Americans (Loehlin, 2000). To a certain extent, these differences in test scores reflect group differences in socioeconomic status. Children from economically advantaged homes tend to have higher test scores than children from economically disadvantaged homes, and European American and Asian American families are more likely to be economically advantaged whereas Latino American and African American families are more likely to be economically disadvantaged. Nevertheless, when children from comparable socioeconomic status are compared, group differences in IQ test scores are reduced but not eliminated (Brooks-Gunn, Klebanov, & Duncan, 1996). Let's look at four explanations for this difference.

A Role for Genetics?

On pages 232–233, you learned that heredity helps determine a child's intelligence: Smart parents tend to beget smart children. Does this also mean that group differences in IQ scores reflect genetic differences between groups? No. Most researchers agree that there is no evidence that some ethnic groups have more "smart genes" than others. Instead, they believe that the environment is largely responsible for these differences (Bronfenbrenner & Morris, 1998; Neisser et al., 1996).

A popular analogy (Lewontin, 1976) demonstrates the thinking here. Imagine two kinds of corn: Each kind produces both short and tall plants, and height is known to be due to heredity. If one kind of corn grows in a good soil—plenty of water and nutrients—the mature plants will reach their genetically determined heights: some short, some tall. If the other kind of corn grows in poor soil, few of the plants will reach their full height, and overall the plants of this kind will be much shorter. Thus, even though height is quite heritable for each type of corn, the difference in height between the two groups is due solely to the quality of the environment.

The same conclusion applies to ethnic groups. Differences within ethnic groups are partly due to heredity, but differences between groups apparently reflect environmental influences. Three potential influences have been studied, and we'll look at these next.

Experience With Test Contents

Some critics contend that differences in test scores reflect bias in the tests themselves. They argue that test items reflect the cultural heritage of the test creators, most of whom are economically advantaged European Americans, and so tests are biased against economically disadvantaged children from other groups. They point to test items like this one:

A conductor is to an orchestra as a teacher is to what?
book   school   class   eraser

■ **Figure 6.6**
Culture-fair intelligence tests
are designed to minimize
the impact of experiences
that are unique to some cultures or to some children
within a culture.

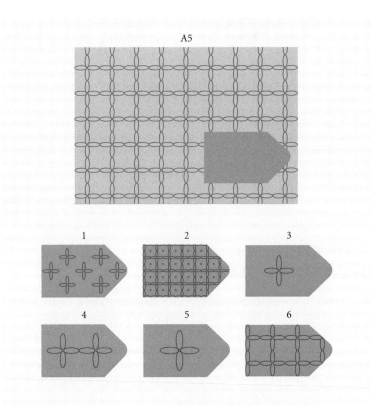

Figure 6.6
Culture-fair intelligence tests are designed to minimize the impact of experiences that are unique to some cultures or to some children within a culture.

Children whose background includes exposure to orchestras are more likely to answer this question correctly than children who lack this exposure.

The problem of bias has led to the development of **culture-fair intelligence tests,** *which include test items based on experiences common to many cultures.* An example is Raven's Progressive Matrices, which consists solely of items like the one shown in Figure 6.6. Examinees are asked to select the piece that would complete the design correctly (6, in this case). Although items like this are thought to reduce the impact of specific experience on test performance, ethnic group differences remain on so-called culture-fair intelligence tests (Anastasi, 1988; Herrnstein & Murray, 1994). Apparently, familiarity with test-related items per se is not the key factor responsible for group differences.

Test-Taking Skills

The impact of experience and cultural values can extend beyond particular items to a child's familiarity with the entire testing situation. Tests underestimate a child's intelligence if, for example, the child's culture encourages children to solve problems in collaboration with others and discourages them from excelling as individuals. Moreover, because they are wary of questions posed by unfamiliar adults, many economically disadvantaged children often answer test questions by saying, "I don't know." Obviously, this strategy guarantees an artificially low test score. When these children are given extra time to feel at ease with the examiner, they respond less often with "I don't know," and their test scores improve considerably (Zigler & Finn-Stevenson, 1992).

Stereotype Threat

When people know that they belong to a group that is said to lack skill in a domain, this makes them anxious when performing in that domain for fear of confirming the stereotype, and they often do poorly as a result. *This self-fulfilling prophecy, in which knowledge of stereotypes leads to anxiety and reduced performance consistent with the original stereotype, is called* **stereotype threat.** Applied to intelligence, the argument is that African

American children experience stereotype threat when they take intelligence tests, and this contributes to their lower scores (Steele, 1997; Steele & Aronson, 1995). For example, imagine two 10-year-olds taking an intelligence test for admission to a special program for gifted children. The European American child worries that if he fails the test he won't be admitted to the program. The African American child has the same fears but also worries that if he does poorly it will confirm the stereotype that African American children don't get good scores on IQ tests (Suzuki & Aronson, 2005).

Interpreting Test Scores

If all tests reflect cultural influences, at least to some degree, how should we interpret test scores? Remember that tests assess successful adaptation to a particular cultural context. Most intelligence tests predict success in a school environment, which usually espouses middle-class values. Regardless of ethnic group—African American, Hispanic American, or European American—a child with a high test score has the intellectual skills needed for academic work based on middle-class values. A child with a low test score apparently lacks those skills. Does a low score mean that a child is destined to fail in school? No. It simply means that, based on the child's current skills, he or she is unlikely to do well. We know from the Abecedarian Project that improving children's skills improves their school performance.

By focusing on groups of people, it's easy to overlook the fact that individuals within these groups differ in intelligence. The average difference in IQ scores between various ethnic groups is relatively small compared to the entire range of scores for these groups. You can easily find youngsters with high IQ scores from all ethnic groups, just as you can find youngsters with low IQ scores from all groups. And, in the next section, we'll look at children at the extremes of ability.

TEST YOURSELF

1. If some children consistently have high scores on different intelligence tests while other children consistently have lower scores on the same tests, this would support the view that intelligence _____.

2. According to _____ theories, intelligence includes both general intelligence and more specific abilities, such as verbal and spatial skill.

3. Gardner's theory of multiple intelligences includes linguistic, logical-mathematical, and spatial intelligences, which are included in psychometric theories, as well as musical, _____, interpersonal, and intrapersonal intelligences, which are ignored in psychometric theories.

4. Based on Gardner's view of intelligence, teachers should _____.

5. According to Sternberg, successful intelligence depends on _____, creative, and practical abilities.

6. Modern intelligence tests are typically validated by _____.

7. As adopted children get older, their IQ scores increasingly resemble the IQ scores of their _____ parents.

8. Evidence for the impact of environment on children's intelligence comes from studies of children's homes, from historical change in IQ scores, and from _____.

9. The problem of cultural bias on intelligence tests led to the development of _____.

Compare and contrast the major perspectives on intelligence in terms of the extent to which they make connections between different aspects of development. That is, to what extent does each perspective emphasize cognitive processes versus integrating physical, cognitive, social, and emotional development?

Answers: (1) consists of a general factor, (2) hierarchical , (3) bodily-kinesthetic, (4) teach in a manner that engages as many different intelligences as possible, (5) analytic, (6) showing that test scores correlate with school grades, (7) biological, (8) intervention studies, (9) culture-fair intelligence tests

6.3

LEARNING OBJECTIVES

What are the characteristics of gifted and creative children?

What are the different forms of mental retardation?

What is learning disability?

What are the distinguishing features of hyperactivity?

SPECIAL CHILDREN, SPECIAL NEEDS

Sanjit, a second grader, has taken two separate intelligence tests, and both times he had above-average scores. His parents took him to an ophthalmologist, who determined that his vision is 20-30 — nothing wrong with his eyes. Nevertheless, Sanjit absolutely cannot read. Letters and words are as mysterious to him as Metallica's music would be to Mozart. What is wrong?

THROUGHOUT HISTORY, societies have recognized children with unusual abilities and talents. Today, we know much about the extremes of human skill. Let's begin with a glimpse at gifted and creative children.

GIFTED AND CREATIVE CHILDREN

Traditionally, giftedness was defined by scores on intelligence tests: a score of 130 or greater was the criterion for being gifted. Today, however, definitions of giftedness are broader and include exceptional talent in an assortment of areas, such as art, music, creative writing, and dance (Robinson & Clinkenbeard, 1998; Winner, 2000).

Exceptional talent—whether defined solely by IQ scores or more broadly—seems to have several prerequisites (Feldman & Goldsmith, 1991; Rathunde & Csikszentmihalyi, 1993):

- The child's love for the subject and overwhelming desire to master it
- Instruction, beginning at an early age, with inspiring and talented teachers
- Support and help from parents, who are committed to promoting their child's talent

The message here is that exceptional talent must be nurtured. Without encouragement and support from stimulating and challenging mentors, a youngster's talents will wither, not flourish. Talented children need a curriculum that is challenging and complex; they need teachers who know how to foster talent; and they need like-minded peers who stimulate their interests (Feldhusen, 1996).

What of the stereotype that gifted children are emotionally troubled and unable to get along with their peers? Research discredits the stereotype of gifted people as distressed and socially inept. Actually, gifted youngsters tend to be more mature than their peers and to have fewer emotional problems (Luthar, Zigler, & Goldstein, 1992).

Creativity

Mozart and Salieri were rival composers in Europe during the 18th century. Both were talented, ambitious musicians. Yet more than 200 years later, Mozart's work is revered but Salieri's is all but forgotten. Why? Then and now, Mozart's work was recognized as creative, but Salieri's was not. What is creativity, and how does it differ from intelligence? *Intelligence is often associated with __convergent thinking__, which means using the information provided to determine a standard, correct answer. In contrast, creativity is often linked to __divergent thinking__, in which the aim is not a single correct answer (often there isn't one) but instead to think in novel and unusual directions* (Callahan, 2000).

Divergent thinking is often measured by asking children to produce a large number of ideas in response to some specific stimulus (Kogan, 1983). Children might be asked to name different uses for a common object, such as a coat hanger. Or they might be shown a page filled with circles and be asked to draw as many different pictures as they can, as shown in Figure 6.7. Both the number of responses and their originality are used to measure creativity.

Creativity, like giftedness, must be cultivated. Youngsters are more likely to be creative when their home and school environments value nonconformity and encourage children to be curious. When schools, for example, emphasize mastery of factual material and discourage self-expression and exploration, creativity usually suffers (Thomas & Berk, 1981). In contrast, creativity can be enhanced by experiences that stimulate children to be flexible in their thinking and to explore alternatives (Starko, 1988).

Gifted and creative children represent one extreme of human ability. Who are at the other extreme? Youngsters with mental retardation, the topic of the next section.

CHILDREN WITH MENTAL RETARDATION

"Little David" was the oldest of four children. He learned to sit days before his first birthday, he began to walk at 2, and said his first words as a 3-year-old. At 5 years of age, David's development was far behind that of his age-mates. A century ago, David would have been called "feebleminded" or "mentally defective." In fact, David has Down syndrome, which we first described in Chapter 2 (see page 50). David had an extra 21st chromosome; as a consequence of this extra gene, David experienced retarded mental development.

Mental retardation refers to substantially below-average intelligence and problems adapting to an environment that emerge before the age of 18. Below-average intelligence is defined as a score of 70 or less on an intelligence test such as the Stanford-Binet. Adaptive behavior is usually evaluated from interviews with a parent or other caregiver and refers to those daily living skills needed to live, work, and play in the community, such as caring for oneself and social skills. Only individuals who are under 18 and have problems in these areas *and* IQ scores of 70 or less are considered mentally retarded (Detterman, Gabriel, & Ruthsatz, 2000).

Types of Mental Retardation

Your image of a child with mental retardation may be someone with Down syndrome, but in reality, individuals with mental retardation are just as varied as are people without retardation. How should we describe this variety? One approach is to distinguish the causes of mental retardation (Baumeister & Baumeister, 1995). *Some cases of mental retardation—no more than 25%—can be traced to a specific biological or physical problem and are known as organic mental retardation.* Down syndrome is the most common organic form of mental retardation. Other forms of organic mental retardation can be linked to prenatal exposure to teratogens (described in Chapter 2). Other types of mental retardation apparently do not involve biological damage. *Familial mental retardation simply represents the lower end of the normal distribution of intelligence.*

Varieties of mental retardation are also distinguished based on the person's level of functioning. The American Association on Mental Retardation identifies four levels of retardation. The levels, along with the range of IQ scores associated with each level, are shown in Figure 6.8. Also shown are the three levels of retardation typically used by educators in the United States (Cipani, 1991). The more extreme forms of mental retardation—for example, profound, severe, and moderate in the AAMR system—are usually organic in origin; the less extreme forms are usually familial.

■ **Figure 6.7**
One way to measure creativity is to determine how many original responses children can make to a specific stimulus.

> **THINK ABOUT IT**
>
> How might our definitions of giftedness and mental retardation differ if they were based on Gardner's theory of multiple intelligences?

Individuals with mild mental retardation can work productively.

Becky Huffman/Resources and Residential Alternatives, Inc.

■ **Figure 6.8**
IQ scores are used to distinguish different varieties of mental retardation.

AAMR	Profound	Severe	Moderate		Mild
IQ level	10 20 30		40 50		60 70
Educators	Custodial		Trainable	Educable	

The most severe forms of mental retardation are, fortunately, relatively uncommon. Profound, severe, and moderate retardation together make up only 10% of all cases. Individuals with profound and severe retardation usually have so few skills that they must be supervised constantly. Consequently, they usually live in institutions where they can sometimes be taught self-help skills such as dressing, feeding, and toileting (Reid, Wilson, & Faw, 1991).

Persons with moderate retardation may develop the intellectual skills of a nonretarded 7- or 8-year-old. With this level of functioning, they sometimes find employment working on simple tasks under close supervision. They do not live independently but receive care from relatives or in institutions (Editorial Board, 1996).

The remaining 90% of individuals with mental retardation are classified as mildly or educably mentally retarded. These individuals go to school and can master many academic skills, but at an older age than a nonretarded child. Individuals with mild mental retardation can lead independent lives, and many mildly retarded people have jobs. Some marry. Comprehensive training programs that focus on vocational and social skills help individuals with mild mental retardation be productive citizens and satisfied human beings (Baumeister & Baumeister, 1995).

From these descriptions, it's clear that "mental retardation" is a catch-all term. Some individuals with mental retardation have substantial disability, but others have a much smaller disability. What they have in common, though, is that with support from family, health care professionals, and the community, many individuals with mental retardation can become contributing members of society.

Mental retardation represents one end of the intelligence spectrum; gifted children's precocity represents the other. Falling between these two extremes are other special children: those who have learning disability.

CHILDREN WITH LEARNING DISABILITIES

For some children with normal intelligence, learning is a struggle. *These youngsters suffer from **learning disability**, a term that refers to a child who (a) has difficulty mastering one or more academic subjects, (b) has normal intelligence, and (c) is not suffering from other conditions that could explain poor performance, such as sensory impairment or inadequate instruction* (Lyon, 1996).

In the United States, about 5% of school-age children are classified as learning disabled, which translates into nearly 3 million affected youngsters (Torgesen, 2004). The number of distinct disabilities and the degree of overlap among them is still hotly contested. However, one common classification scheme distinguishes disability in language (including listening, speaking, and writing), in reading, and in arithmetic (Dockrell & McShane, 1993).

The variety of learning disabilities complicates the task for teachers and researchers because it suggests that each type

Children with reading disability often have trouble associating sounds with letters.

of learning disability may have its own cause and treatment (Lyon, 1996). Reading is the most common area of learning disability, and many children with reading disability have problems in phonological awareness, which refers to understanding and using the sounds in written and oral language. For a reading-disabled child like Sanjit (in the vignette), all vowels sound alike. Thus *pin* sounds like *pen*, which sounds like *pan*. These youngsters benefit from explicit, extensive instruction on the connections between letters and their sounds (Lyon, 1996). The Spotlight on Research feature looks at one such successful training program.

SPOTLIGHT ON RESEARCH

IMPROVING READING SKILL IN CHILDREN WITH READING DISABILITY

Who were the investigators, and what was the aim of the study? Most reading experts agree that, compared to children who read normally, children with reading disability have problems translating print into sound. Experts also agree that the aim of treatment should be to improve such translation skills. Where experts disagree is in the best way to achieve this aim. Some emphasize exercises in which children manipulate sounds and letters in syllables (e.g., "Which one is 'ook'?" "Which is 'koo'?"). Other experts emphasize articulatory awareness in which children learn the positions of their mouth and tongue as they make different vowel and consonant sounds. Barbara Wise, Jerry Ring, and Richard Olson (1999) wanted to compare the effects of these two approaches in improving reading in children with reading disability.

How did the investigators measure the topic of interest? Children in the study were assigned to one of four conditions. Some were in a control group that received no special treatment. Others were in a sound manipulation condition, an articulatory awareness condition, or a condition that included both sound manipulation and articulatory awareness. The training included exercises like those that we just mentioned and lasted six months. All children were tested on a large battery of reading-related tests before and after training. For simplicity, we'll focus on just one outcome measure: children's ability to read individual words accurately.

Who were the children in the study? Wise and her colleagues tested 122 children with reading disability from grades 2 to 5. About one fourth of the chil-

dren were assigned to each of the four conditions.

What was the design of the study? The study was experimental. The independent variable was the condition to which the child was assigned; the dependent variable was the number of words that children read accurately. The study was also longitudinal: Students were tested in October and again in May of the same school year.

Were there ethical concerns with the study? No. Parental permission was obtained for all children who participated. You may question the ethics of denying treatment to one fourth of the children (those in the control group). However, all these children were promised treatment in the following school year, and this was deemed an acceptable risk by the review panel at the University of Colorado, where the study was conducted.

What were the results? As we mentioned, the children were administered a large battery of tasks. On some of the tasks, the training groups differed.

For example, children who had sound manipulation training were more accurate on phoneme deletion tasks (e.g., "Say 'pran' without the 'r'."). But the most important result is shown in Figure 6.9: In actual reading, the various training methods were equally effective. That is, in terms of the increase in reading skill from before training to after training, all three groups improved 12 to 15% compared to 4% for the control group.

What did the investigators conclude? Children with reading disability must learn about language sounds, but apparently there is no single best method. Consequently, teachers can be successful with either method and can alter their approach based on their own background and their students' strengths.

What converging evidence would strengthen these conclusions? Two types of findings would complement the results of this study. First, it would be useful to include a group of children who read normally as another way to

■ **Figure 6.9**
Children's reading scores increased when they had training identifying sounds or practiced actually making different vowel and consonant sounds.

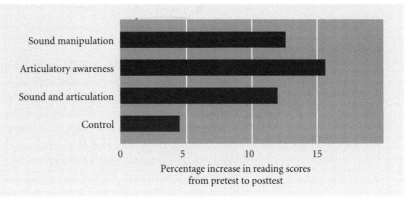

Percentage increase in reading scores
from pretest to posttest

assess the effectiveness of training (i.e., after training, are children with reading disability reading normally?). Second, it would be important to test these children in subsequent years to determine

whether the training has long-lasting benefits.

⌇

To enhance your understanding of this research, go to http://psychology

.wadsworth.com/kail_cavanaugh4e/ to complete critical thinking questions and explore related websites.

The findings in the Spotlight on Research feature are good news for children with learning disabilities, such as reading disability. The key to helping these children is to move beyond the generic label learning disability to pinpoint specific cognitive and academic deficits that hamper an individual child's performance in school (e.g., for children with reading disability, processing language sounds). Then instruction can be specifically tailored to improve the child's skills (Moats & Lyon, 1993).

This is much easier said than done because diagnosing learning disabilities remains so difficult. Some children have both reading and language disabilities; others have reading and arithmetic disabilities; still others have learning disability and another problem, attention-deficit hyperactivity disorder, which we discuss next.

ATTENTION-DEFICIT HYPERACTIVITY DISORDER

Let's begin with a case study of Stuart, an 8-year-old:

> [His] mother reported that Stuart was overly active as an infant and toddler. His teachers found him difficult to control once he started school. He is described as extremely impulsive and distractible, moving tirelessly from one activity to the next. . . . His teacher reports that he is immature and restless, responds best in a structured, one-on-one situation, but is considered the class pest because he is continually annoying the other children and is disobedient. (Rapaport & Ismond, 1990, p. 120)

For many years, children like Stuart, who were restless and impulsive, were said to have "hyperactive child syndrome" (Barkley, 1996). In the 1960s and 1970s, researchers realized that these children often also had difficulty paying attention. By the 1980s, the disorder had been renamed, attention-deficit hyperactivity disorder (ADHD).

Roughly 3 to 5% of all school-age children are diagnosed with ADHD (Rapport, 1995); boys outnumber girls by a 3:1 ratio (Wicks-Nelson & Israel, 2006). Three symptoms are at the heart of ADHD (Rapport, 1995):

- *Overactivity.* Children with ADHD are unusually energetic, fidgety, and unable to keep still, especially in situations where they need to limit their activity, such as school classrooms.

- *Inattention.* Youngsters with ADHD do not pay attention in class and seem unable to concentrate on schoolwork; instead, they skip from one task to another.

- *Impulsivity.* Children with ADHD often act before thinking; they may run into a street before looking for traffic or interrupt others who are already speaking.

Not all children with ADHD show all these symptoms to the same degree. Some may be primarily hyperactive and impulsive. Others may be primarily inattentive and show fewer signs of hyperactivity and impulsivity; their disorder is often described simply as attention-deficit disorder (Barkley, 1990). Children with ADHD often have problems with conduct and academic performance. Like Stuart, many hyperactive children are aggressive and therefore are not liked by their peers (Barkley, 1990; McGee, Williams, & Feehan, 1992). Although youngsters with ADHD usually have normal intelligence, their scores on reading, spelling, and arithmetic achievement tests are often below average (Pennington, Groisser, & Welsh, 1993).

Many myths surround ADHD. Some concern causes. At one time or another, TV, food allergies, sugar, and poor home life have all been proposed as causes of ADHD, but research does not consistently support any of these (e.g., Wolraich et al., 1994). Instead, heredity is an important factor. Twin studies show that identical twins are often both diagnosed with ADHD, but this is uncommon for fraternal twins (Pennington, Willcutt, & Rhee, 2005). Similarly, adoption studies show that children are more prone to ADHD when a biological parent has been diagnosed with ADHD than when an adoptive parent has (Sherman, Iacono, & McGue, 1997). In addition, prenatal exposure to alcohol and other drugs can place children at risk for ADHD (Milberger et al., 1997).

Another myth is that most children "grow out of" ADHD in adolescence or young adulthood. More than half of the children diagnosed with ADHD will have problems related to overactivity, inattention, and impulsivity in adolescence and adulthood. Few of these young adults complete college, and some will have work- and family-related problems (Fischer et al., 1993; Rapport, 1995). One final myth is that many healthy children are wrongly diagnosed with ADHD. The number of children diagnosed with ADHD has increased substantially over the past 10 to 15 years, but not because children are being routinely misdiagnosed; the increased numbers reflect growing awareness of ADHD and more frequent diagnoses of ADHD in girls and adolescents (Goldman et al., 1998).

Because ADHD affects academic and social success throughout childhood and adolescence, researchers have worked hard to find effective treatments. By the mid 1980s, it was clear that ADHD could be treated. For example, children with ADHD often respond well to stimulant drugs such as Ritalin. It may seem odd that stimulants are given to children who are already overactive, but these drugs stimulate the parts of the brain that normally inhibit hyperactive and impulsive behavior. Thus, stimulants actually have a calming influence for many youngsters with ADHD, allowing them to focus their attention (Aman, Roberts, & Pennington, 1998).

Drug therapy was not the only approach: Psychosocial treatments also worked and were designed to improve children's cognitive and social skills and often included home-based intervention and intensive summer programs (Richters et al., 1995). For example, children can be taught to remind themselves to read instructions before starting assignments. And they can be reinforced by others for inhibiting impulsive and hyperactive behavior (Barkley, 1994).

These treatments were well known by the late 1980s, yet many researchers were troubled by large gaps in our understanding. One gap concerned the long-term success of treatment. Most studies had measured the impact of weeks or months of treatment; virtually nothing was known about the effectiveness of treatment over longer periods. Another gap concerned the most effective combination of treatments, and whether this was the same for all children. That is, is medication plus psychosocial treatment best for all children and for all facets of children's development (i.e., academic and social)?

Prompted by these concerns, in the early 1990s the National Institute of Mental Health initiated the Multimodal Treatment Study of Children with ADHD—the MTA for short (Richters et al., 1995). The MTA involves 18 scientists who are experts on ADHD and nearly 600 elementary-school children with ADHD. The children were assigned to different treatment modes, and the impact of treatment is measured in several different domains of children's development.

The MTA is ongoing, but initial results show that medical treatment alone is the best way to treat hyperactivity per se. However, for a variety of other measures, including academic and social skills as well as parent-child relations, medication plus psychosocial treatment is slightly more effective than drug therapy alone. The MTA also makes it clear that medication treatment is effective only when dosage is monitored carefully, with regular follow-up visits to a health care professional, and there is regular communication with schools regarding children's functioning (Jensen et al., 2001).

Thus, effective treatment of ADHD addresses the biological, psychological, and sociocultural contributions to the disorder. Such comprehensive treatment enables children with ADHD to become more attentive and to improve their schoolwork (Carlson et al., 1992).

TEST YOURSELF

1. A problem with defining giftedness solely in terms of IQ scores is that _____.

2. Creativity is associated with _____ thinking, in which the goal is to think in novel and unusual directions.

3. Cases of _____ mental retardation can be linked to specific biological or physical problems.

4. Individuals with _____ mental retardation often go to school, have jobs, and marry.

5. The most common form of learning disability is _____.

6. Key symptoms of attention-deficit hyperactivity disorder are overactivity, _____, and impulsivity.

7. The results of the MTA show that the best way to treat the full spectrum of symptoms of ADHD is through stimulant drugs combined with _____.

How might Jean Piaget have explained differences in intellectual functioning between children with mental retardation and children without mental retardation? How might an information-processing psychologist explain these differences?

Answers: (1) it excludes talents in areas such as art, music, and dance, (2) divergent, (3) organic, (4) mild or educable, (5) reading disability, (6) inattentiveness, (7) psychosocial treatment that improves children's cognitive and social skills

---

6.4

ACADEMIC SKILLS

Angelique is a fifth grader who absolutely loves to read. As a preschooler, Angelique's parents read Dr. Seuss stories to her, and now she has progressed to the point where she can read (and understand!) 400-page novels intended for teens. Her parents marvel at this accomplishment and wish they better understood the skills that were involved so they could help Angelique's younger brother learn to read as well as his sister does.

LEARNING OBJECTIVES

What are the components of skilled reading?

As children develop, how does their writing improve?

When do children understand and use quantitative skills?

What are the hallmarks of effective schools and effective teachers?

READING IS INDEED A COMPLEX TASK and learning to read well is a wonderful accomplishment. Much the same can be said for writing and arithmetic. We'll examine each of these academic skills in this section. As we do, you'll learn about the skills that underlie Angelique's mastery of reading. We'll end the section by looking at characteristics that make some schools and some teachers better than others.

READING

Try reading the following sentence:

Sumisu-san wa nawa o naifu de kirimashita.

You probably didn't make much headway, did you? (Unless you know Japanese.) Now try this one:

Snore secretary green plastic sleep trucks.

These are English words, and you probably read them quite easily, but did you get anything more out of this sentence than the one in Japanese?

These examples show two important processes involved in skilled reading. ***Word recognition*** *is the process of identifying a unique pattern of letters.* Unless you know Japanese, your word recognition was not successful in the first sentence. You did not know that *nawa* means *rope* or that *kirimashita* is the past tense of the English verb *cut.* Furthermore, because you could not recognize individual words, you had no idea of the meaning of the sentence. ***Comprehension*** *is the process of extracting meaning from a sequence of words.* In the second sentence, your word recognition was perfect, but comprehension was still impossible because the words were presented in a random sequence. These examples remind us just how difficult learning to read can be.

In the next few pages, we'll look at some of the skills children must acquire if they are to learn to read and to read well. We'll start with prereading skills, then move to word recognition and comprehension.

Foundations of Reading Skill

English words are made up of individual letters, so children need to know their letters before they can learn to read. Consequently, it's not surprising that knowledge of letter names is consistently one of the best predictors of success in learning to read: That is, youngsters who know most of their letters learn to read more easily than their peers who don't know their letters (Treiman & Kessler, 2003).

A second essential skill is sensitivity to language sounds. The ability to hear the distinctive sounds of letters is a skill known as ***phonological awareness.*** One way to measure phonological awareness is to present several words—*fun, pin, bun, gun*—then ask the child to pick the word that didn't rhyme with the others. Another way is to ask children to say the first, last, or middle sound of a word: "What's the first sound in *cat?*" These measures have been used in dozens of studies, and the outcome is always the same: Phonological awareness is strongly related to success in learning to read (Muter et al., 2004). That is, children who can readily distinguish language sounds learn to read more readily than children who do not.

As children get older, phonological skill continues to be an excellent predictor of reading ability (Wagner et al., 1999). Furthermore, phonological skills are not only important in learning to read in alphabet-based languages such as English; they are also important for children learning to read in non–alphabet-based languages such as Chinese (McBride-Chang & Kail, 2002).

If phonological skills are so essential, how can we help children master them? Reading to children is one approach that's fun for children and parents alike. When parents read stories, their children learn many language-related skills that prepare them for reading (Sénéchal & LeFevre, 2002).

Recognizing Words

The first step in actual reading is identifying individual words. One way to do this is to say the sounds associated with each letter, and then blend the sounds to produce a recognizable word. Such "sounding out" is a common technique among beginning readers. Older children sometimes sound out words, but only when they are unfamiliar, which points to another common way of recognizing words (Coltheart et al., 1993). Words are recognized through direct retrieval from long-term memory: As the individual letters in a word are identified, long-term memory is searched to see if there is a matching sequence of letters. Knowing that the letters are, in sequence, *c-a-t,* long-term memory is searched for a match, and the child recognizes the word as *cat* (Rayner et al., 2001).

So far, word recognition may seem like a one-way street where readers first recognize letters and then recognize words. In reality, readers constantly use context to help them recognize letters and words. For example, readers typically recognize *t* faster in *cast* than in *asct.* That is, readers recognize letters faster when they appear in words than in nonwords. How do the nearby letters in *cast* help readers to recognize the *t*? As children recognize the first letters in the word as *c, a,* and *s,* the possibilities for the last letter become more limited. Because English only includes four 4-letter words that start with *cas* (well, five if you include *Cass*), the last letter can only be *e, h, k,* or *t.* In contrast, there are no four-letter words (in English) that begin with *acs,* so all 26 letters must be checked, which takes more time than just checking four letters. In this way, a reader's knowledge of words simplifies the task of recognizing letters, which in turn makes it easier to recognize words (Seidenberg & McClelland, 1989).

Readers also use the sentence context to speed word recognition. Read these two sentences:

> The last word in this sentence is cat.
> The little girl's pet dog chased the cat.

Most readers recognize cat more rapidly in the second sentence because the first seven words put severe limits on the last word: It must be something "chaseable," and because the "chaser" is a *dog, cat* is a very likely candidate. In contrast, the first seven words in the first sentence put no limits on the last word; virtually any word could end the sentence. Beginning and skilled readers both use sentence context like this to help them recognize words (Archer & Bryant, 2001; Kim & Goetz, 1994).

As you can imagine, most beginning readers rely more heavily on "sounding out" because they know fewer words. As they gain more reading experience, they are more likely to be able to retrieve a word directly from long-term memory. You might be tempted to summarize this as, "Beginning readers sound out and more advanced readers retrieve directly." Don't! From their very first efforts to read, most children use direct retrieval for a few words. From that point on, the general strategy is to try retrieval first and, if that fails, children sound out the word or ask a more skilled reader for help (Booth, Perfetti, & MacWhinney, 1999; Siegler, 1986). For example, shown a sentence like this:

> Mark saw the fat cat run.

a beginning reader might say, "Mark s-s-s. . . ah-h. . . wuh . . . saw the fat cat er-r-r. . . uh-h-h . . n-n-n . . . run." Familiar words like *Mark, the, fat,* and *cat* are retrieved rapidly, but the unfamiliar ones are slowly sounded out. With more experience, fewer words are sounded out and more are retrieved (Siegler, 1986). That is, by sounding out novel words, children store information about words in long-term memory that can be used for direct retrieval (Cunningham et al., 2002; Share, 1999). Of course, all readers sometimes fall back on sounding out when they confront unfamiliar words. Try reading this sentence:

> The rock star rode to the concert in a palanquin.

You may well need to do some sounding out, then consult a dictionary (or look for the answer prior to Test Yourself) for the correct meaning.

Beginning readers usually rely heavily on "sounding out" a word.

Comprehension

Once individual words are recognized, reading begins to have a lot in common with understanding speech. That is, the means by which people understand a sequence of words is much the same whether the source of words is printed text or speech or, for that matter, Braille or sign language (Crowder & Wagner, 1992). *In all of these cases, children derive meaning by combining words to form* **propositions** *or ideas and then combining propositions.* For example, as you read this sentence:

> The tall boy rode his bike.

you spontaneously derive a number of propositions, including "There is a boy," "The boy is tall," and "The boy was riding." If this sentence were part of a larger body of text, you would derive propositions for each sentence, then link the propositions together to derive meaning for the passage as a whole (Perfetti & Curtis, 1986).

As children gain more reading experience, they better comprehend what they read. Several factors contribute to this improved comprehension (Siegler & Alibali, 2005):

- *Working memory capacity increases.* Older and better readers can store more of a sentence in memory as they try to identify the propositions it contains (De Beni & Palladino, 2000; Nation et al., 1999). This extra capacity is handy when readers move from sentences like "Kevin hit the ball" to "In the bottom of the ninth, with the bases loaded and the Cardinals down 7–4, Kevin put a line drive into the left-field bleachers, his fourth home run of the Series."

- *Children acquire more general knowledge of their physical, social, and psychological worlds.* This allows them to understand more of what they read (Ferreol-Barbey, Piolat, & Roussey, 2000; Graesser, Singer, & Trabasso, 1994): For example, even if a 6-year-old could recognize all of the words in the longer sentence about Kevin's home run, the child would not fully comprehend the meaning of the passage because he or she lacks the necessary knowledge of baseball.

- *With experience, children use more appropriate reading strategies.* The goal of reading and the nature of the text dictate how you read. When reading a novel, for example, do you often skip sentences (or perhaps paragraphs or entire pages) to get to "the good parts"? This approach makes sense for pleasure reading but not for reading textbooks or recipes or how-to manuals. Reading a textbook requires attention to both the overall organization and the relation of details to that organization. Older, more experienced readers are better able to select a reading strategy that suits the material being read (Brown et al., 1996; Cain, 1999).

- *With experience, children better monitor their comprehension.* When readers don't grasp the meaning of a passage because it is difficult or confusing, they read it again (Baker, 1994). Try this sentence (adapted from Carpenter & Daneman, 1981): "The Midwest State Fishing Contest would draw fishermen from all around the region, including some of the best bass guitarists in Michigan." When you first encountered "bass guitarists" you probably interpreted "bass" as a fish. This didn't make much sense, so you reread the phrase to determine that "bass" refers to a type of guitar. Older readers are better able to realize that their understanding is not complete and take corrective action.

Thus, several factors contribute to improved comprehension as children get older. And greater comprehension, along with improved word recognition skills, explains why children like Angelique are able to read ever-more complex texts as they grow.

WRITING

Though few of us end up being a Maya Angelou, a Sandra Cisneros, or a John Grisham, most adults do write, both at home and at work. The basics of good writing are remarkably straightforward (Williams, 1997), but writing skill develops very gradually during childhood, adolescence, and young adulthood. Research indicates that a number of factors contribute to improved writing as children develop (Adams et al., 1998; Siegler & Alibali, 2005).

Knowledge About Topics

Writing is about telling "something" to others. With age, children have more to tell as they gain more knowledge about the world and incorporate this knowledge into their writing (Benton et al., 1995). For example, asked to write about a mayoral election, 8-year-olds are apt to describe it as much like a popularity contest; 12-year-olds more

THINK ABOUT IT

Reading and speaking are both important elements of literacy. How is learning to read like learning to speak? How do they differ?

often describe it in terms of political issues that are both subtle and complex. Of course, students are sometimes asked to write about topics quite unfamiliar to them. In this case, older children's and adolescents' writing is usually better because they are more adept at finding useful reference material and incorporating it into their writing.

Organizing Writing

One difficult aspect of writing is organization, arranging all the necessary information in a manner that readers find clear and interesting. In fact, children and young adolescents organize their writing differently than do older adolescents and adults (Bereiter & Scardamalia, 1987). *Young writers often use a* **knowledge-telling strategy,** *writing down information on the topic as they retrieve it from memory.* For example, asked to write about the day's events at school, a second grader wrote:

> It is a rainy day. We hope the sun will shine. We got new spelling books. We had our pictures taken. We sang Happy Birthday to Barbara. (Waters, 1980, p. 155)

The story has no obvious structure. The first two sentences are about the weather, but the last three deal with completely independent topics. Apparently, the writer simply described each event as it came to mind.

Toward the end of the elementary-school years, children begin to use a **knowledge-transforming strategy,** *deciding what information to include and how best to organize it for the point they wish to convey to their reader.* This approach involves considering the purpose of writing (e.g., to inform, to persuade, to entertain) and the information needed to achieve this purpose. It also involves considering the needs, interests, and knowledge of the anticipated audience.

Asked to describe the day's events, older children's writing can take many forms, depending on the purpose and audience. An essay written to entertain peers about humorous events at school would differ from one written to convince parents about problems in schoolwork. And both of these essays would differ from one written to inform an exchange student about a typical day in a U.S. middle school. In other words, although children's knowledge-telling strategy gets words on paper, the more mature knowledge-transforming strategy produces a more cohesive text for the reader.

The Mechanical Requirements of Writing

Compared to speaking, writing is more difficult because we need to worry about spelling, punctuation, and actually forming the letters. These many mechanical aspects of writing can be a burden for all writers, but particularly for young writers. For example, when youngsters are absorbed by the task of printing letters correctly, the quality of their writing usually suffers (Graham, Harris, & Fink, 2000; Jones & Christensen, 1999). As children master printed and cursive letters, they can pay more attention to other aspects of writing. Similarly, correct spelling and good sentence structure are particularly hard for younger writers; as they learn to spell and to generate clear sentences, they write more easily and more effectively (Graham et al., 1997; McCutchen et al., 1994).

Writing can be particularly hard for young children who are still learning how to print or write cursive letters.

© Joel Gordon

Skill in Revising

Few authors get it down right the first time. Instead, they revise and revise, then revise some more. In the words of one expert, "Experienced writers get something down on paper as fast as they can, just so they can revise it into something clearer" (Williams, 1997, p. 11). Unfortunately, young writers often don't revise at all—the first draft is usually the final draft. To make matters worse, when young writers revise, the changes do not necessarily improve their writing (Fitzgerald, 1987). Effective revising requires being able to detect problems and to know how to correct them (Baker & Brown, 1984; Beal, 1996). As children develop, they're better able to find problems and to know how to correct them, particularly when the topic is familiar to them (Chanquoy, 2001; McCutchen, Francis, & Kerr, 1997).

Considering all the factors involved, it's quite clear why good writing is so long in developing. Many different skills are involved, and each is complicated in its own right. Mastering them collectively is a huge challenge, one that spans all of childhood, adolescence, and adulthood. Much the same could be said for mastering quantitative skills, as we'll see in the next section.

MATH SKILLS

In Chapter 4 we saw that preschoolers understand many of the principles underlying counting, even if they sometimes stumble over the mechanics of counting. By kindergarten, children have mastered counting, and they use this skill as the starting point for learning to add. For instance, suppose you ask a kindergartner to solve the following problem: "John had four oranges. Then Mary gave him two more oranges. How many oranges does John have now?" Many 6-year-old children solve the problem by counting. They first count out four fingers on one hand, then count out two more on the other. Finally, they count all six fingers on both hands. To subtract, they do the same procedure in reverse (Siegler & Jenkins, 1989; Siegler & Shrager, 1984).

Youngsters soon abandon this approach for a slightly more efficient method. Instead of counting the fingers on the first hand, they simultaneously extend the number of fingers on the first hand corresponding to the larger of the two numbers to be added. Next, they count out the smaller number, with fingers on the second hand. Finally, they count all of the fingers to determine the sum (Groen & Resnick, 1977).

After children begin to receive formal arithmetic instruction in first grade, addition problems are less often solved by counting aloud or by counting fingers. Instead, children add and subtract by counting mentally. That is, children act as if they are counting silently, beginning with the larger number, and adding on. By age 8 or 9, children have learned the addition tables so well that sums of the single-digit integers (from 0 to 9) are facts that are simply retrieved from memory (Ashcraft, 1982).

These counting strategies do not occur in a rigid developmental sequence. Individual children use many or all of these strategies, depending upon the problem. Children usually begin by trying to retrieve an answer from memory. If they are not reasonably confident that the retrieved answer is correct, they resort to counting aloud or on fingers (Siegler, 1988). Retrieval is most likely for problems with small numbers (e.g., 1 + 2, 2 + 4) because these problems are presented frequently in textbooks and by teachers. Consequently, the sum is highly associated with the problem, which makes the child confident that the retrieved answer is correct. In contrast, problems with larger addends, such as 9 + 8, are presented less often. The result is a weaker link between the addends and the sum and, consequently, a greater chance that children will need to determine an answer by counting.

Of course, arithmetic skills continue to improve as children move through elementary school. They become more proficient in addition and subtraction, learn multiplication and division, and move on to the more sophisticated mathematical concepts involved in algebra, geometry, trigonometry, and calculus.

Young children often solve addition problems by counting, either on their fingers or in their head.

THINK ABOUT IT

What information-processing skills may contribute to growth in children's arithmetic skills?

Comparing U.S. Students With Students in Other Countries

When compared to students worldwide in terms of math skills, American eighth-grade students don't fare well. For example, Figure 6.10 shows the results of a major inter-

■ **Figure 6.10**
Compared to eighth-grade students in other developed countries, U.S. students often fare relatively poorly on tests of math skills.

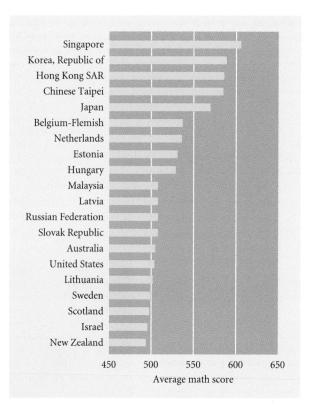

From International Association for the Evaluation of Educational Achievement (IEA), *Trends in International Mathematics and Science Study* (TIMSS), 2003, p. 5.

national comparison involving students in 20 countries (Gonzalez et al., 2004). Students in the United States have substantially lower scores than students in the leading nations. Phrased another way, the very best U.S. students only perform at the level of average students in Asian countries like Singapore and Korea. Furthermore, the cultural differences in math achievement hold for both math operations and math problem solving (Stevenson & Lee, 1990).

Why do American students rate so poorly? The Real People feature has some answers.

REAL PEOPLE: Applying Human Development

SHIN-YING LOVES SCHOOL

Shin-ying is an 11-year-old attending school in Taipei, the largest city in Taiwan. Like most fifth graders, Shin-ying is in school from 8 a.m. until 4 p.m. daily. Most evenings, she spends 2 to 3 hours doing homework. This academic routine is grueling by U.S. standards, where fifth graders typically spend 6 to 7 hours in school each day and less than an hour doing homework. We asked Shin-ying what she thought of school and schoolwork. Her answers surprised us.

US: Why do you go to school?
SHIN-YING: I like what we study.
US: Any other reasons?
SHIN-YING: The things that I learn in school are useful.
US: What about homework? Why do you do it?
SHIN-YING: My teacher and my parents think it's important. And I like doing it.
US: Do you think you would do nearly as well in school if you didn't work so hard?

SHIN-YING: Oh no. The best students are always the ones who work the hardest.

Schoolwork is the focal point of Shin-ying's life. Although many American schoolchildren are unhappy when schoolwork intrudes on time for play and television, Shin-ying is enthusiastic about school and school-related activities.

Shin-ying is not unusual among Asian elementary-school students. Many of her comments are typical of students from a comprehensive comparison of students in Japan, Taiwan, and the United States (Stevenson & Lee, 1990):

- *Time in school and how it is used.* By fifth grade, students in Japan and Taiwan spend 50% more time than American students in school, and more of this time is devoted to academic activities than in the United States.

- *Time spent on homework and attitudes toward it.* Students in Taiwan and Japan spend more time on homework and value homework more than American students.

- *Parents' attitudes.* American parents are more often satisfied with their children's performance in school; in contrast, Japanese and Taiwanese parents set much higher standards for their children.

- *Parents' beliefs about effort and ability.* Japanese and Taiwanese parents believe more strongly than American parents that effort, not native ability, is the key factor in school success.

Thus, students in Japan and Taiwan excel because they spend more time both in and out of school on academic tasks. What's more, their parents (and teachers) set loftier scholastic goals and believe that students can attain these goals with hard work. Japanese classrooms even post a motto describing ideal students: *gambaru kodomo*—they who strive the hardest.

Parents underscore the importance of schoolwork in many ways to their children. For example, even though homes and apartments in Japan and China are very small by U.S. standards, Asian youngsters typically have a desk in a quiet area where they can study undisturbed (Stevenson & Lee, 1990). For Japanese and Taiwanese teachers and parents, academic excellence is paramount, and it shows in their children's success.

What can Americans learn from Japanese and Taiwanese educational systems? From their experiences with Asian students, teachers, and schools, Stevenson and Stigler (1992) suggest several ways U.S. schools could be improved:

- Give teachers more free time to prepare lessons and correct students' work.

- Improve teachers' training by allowing them to work closely with older, more experienced teachers.

- Organize instruction around sound principles of learning such as providing multiple examples of concepts and giving students adequate opportunities to practice newly acquired skills.

Schoolchildren in Asian countries often have a quiet place at home where they can study.

Audrey Gottlieb

■ Set higher standards for children, who need to spend more time and effort in school-related activities to achieve those standards.

Changing teaching practices and attitudes toward achievement would begin to reduce the gap between American students and students in other industrialized countries, particularly Asian countries. Ignoring the problem will mean an increasingly undereducated workforce and citizenry in a more complex world—an alarming prospect for the 21st century.

EFFECTIVE SCHOOLS, EFFECTIVE TEACHERS

Because education is run locally in the United States, American education is a smorgasbord. Schools differ on many dimensions, including their emphasis on academic goals and the involvement of parents. Teachers, too, differ in many ways, such as how they run their classrooms and how they teach. These and other variables do affect student achievement, as you'll see in the next few pages. Let's begin with school-based influences.

School-Based Influences on Student Achievement

Roosevelt High School, in the center of Detroit, has an enrollment of 3,500 students in grades 9–12. Opened in 1936, the building shows its age. The rooms are drafty, the desks are decorated with generations of graffiti, and new technology means an overhead projector. Nevertheless, attendance at Roosevelt is good. Most students graduate, and many continue their education at community colleges and state universities. Southport High School, in Newark, has about the same enrollment as Roosevelt High, and the building is about the same age. Yet truancy is commonplace at Southport, where fewer than half the students graduate and almost none go to college.

Although these schools are hypothetical, they accurately depict a common outcome in the United States. Some schools are much more successful than others, whether success is defined in terms of the percentage of students who are literate, graduate, or go to college. Why? Researchers (Good & Brophy, 1994; Stevenson & Stigler, 1992; Walberg, 1995) have identified a number of characteristics of schools where students typically succeed rather than fail:

In successful schools, parents are involved, often as tutors.

■ *Staff and students alike understand that academic excellence is the primary goal of the school and of every student in the school.* The school day emphasizes instruction (not simply filling time from 8:30 to 3:30 with nonacademic activities), and students are recognized publicly for their academic accomplishments.

■ *The school climate is safe and nurturant.* Students know that they can devote their energy to learning (instead of worrying about being harmed in school) and that the staff truly cares that they succeed.

■ *Parents are involved.* In some cases, this may be through formal arrangements, such as parent-teacher organizations. Or it may be informal. Parents may spend some time each week in school grading papers or tutoring a child. Such involvement signals both teachers and students that parents are committed to students' success.

■ *Progress of students, teachers, and programs is monitored.* The only way to know whether schools are succeeding is by measuring performance. Students, teachers, and programs need to be evaluated regularly, using objective measures that reflect academic goals.

In schools where these guidelines are followed regularly, students usually succeed. In schools where the guidelines are ignored, students more often fail.

© Mary Kate Denny/PhotoEdit

Some educators argue that schools should take greater advantage of technology—primarily computers—to improve instruction. Opponents believe that computers remove the all-important human factor from learning. The Current Controversies feature examines this issue.

CURRENT CONTROVERSIES

Know

COMPUTERS IN THE CLASSROOM

New technologies—whether TV, videotape, or pocket calculator—soon find their way into the classroom. Personal computers are no exception; virtually all U.S. public schools now use personal computers to aid instruction. A primary function of computers in the schools is as a tutor (Lepper & Gurtner, 1989). Children use computers to learn reading, spelling, arithmetic, science, and social studies. Computers allow instruction to be individualized and interactive. Students proceed at their own pace, receiving feedback and help when necessary.

Computers are also valuable as a medium for experiential learning (Lepper & Gurtner, 1989). Simulation programs allow students to explore the world in ways that would be impossible or dangerous otherwise. Students can change the law of gravity or see what happens to a city when no taxes are imposed.

Finally, the computer is a multipurpose tool that can help students achieve traditional academic goals (Steelman, 1994). A graphics program enables artistically untalented students to produce beautiful illustrations. A word-processing program relieves much of the drudgery associated with revising, thereby encouraging better writing.

Not all parents and teachers are enthusiastic about computers in classrooms. Some critics fear that computers eliminate an important human element in learning. To some, "a classroom in which children spend the day plugged into their own individual desktop computers seems a chilling spectacle" (Lepper & Gurtner, 1989, p. 172). Many worry that computers isolate students from each other and from the teacher and make learning a solitary activity. In reality, students interact with each other more when computers are introduced into the classroom, not less (Pozzi, Healy, & Hoyles, 1993). Students often cluster around one student as he or she works, and they often consult the class "expert" on a particular program. Teachers, freed from many of the drill-type tasks that occupied the school day, can turn their attention to other aspects of instruction.

Although some critics worry that computers will isolate students from one another, the more typical result is that students work together.

© David M. Grossman

Of course, on a daily basis, individual teachers have the most potential for impact. Let's see how teachers can influence their students' achievement.

Teacher-Based Influences on Student Achievement

Take a moment to recall your teachers in elementary school, middle school, and high school. You probably remember some fondly because they were enthusiastic and innovative, and they made learning fun. You may remember others with bitterness. They seemed to have lost their love of teaching and children, making class a living hell. Your experiences tell you that some teachers are better than others, but what is it that makes an effective teacher? Personality and enthusiasm are *not* the key elements. Although you may enjoy warm and eager teachers, research (Good & Brophy, 1994; Stevenson & Stigler, 1992; Walberg, 1995) has revealed that several other factors are critical when it comes to students' achievement. Students tend to learn the most when teachers do the following:

- *Manage the classroom effectively so they can devote most of their time to instruction.* When teachers spend a lot of time disciplining students, or when students do not move smoothly from one class activity to the next, instructional time is wasted, and students are apt to learn less.

- *Believe they are responsible for their students' learning and that their students will learn when taught well.* When students don't understand a new topic, these teachers may repeat the original instruction (in case the student missed something) or create new instructions (in case the student heard everything but just didn't "get it"). These teachers keep plugging away because they feel at fault if students don't learn.

- *Emphasize mastery of topics.* Teachers should introduce a topic, then give students many opportunities to understand, practice, and apply the topic. Just as you'd find it hard to go directly from driver's ed to driving a race car, students more often achieve when they grasp a new topic thoroughly, then gradually move on to other, more advanced topics.

- *Teach actively.* Teachers don't just talk or give students an endless stream of worksheets. Instead, they demonstrate topics concretely or have hands-on demonstrations for students. They also have students participate in class activities, and they encourage students to interact, generating ideas and solving problems together.

- *Pay careful attention to pacing.* Teachers present material slowly enough so that students can understand a new concept, but not so slowly that students get bored.

- *Value tutoring.* Teachers work with students individually or in small groups so they can gear their instruction to each student's level and check each student's understanding. They also encourage peer tutoring, in which more capable students tutor less capable students. Children who are tutored by peers *do* learn, and so do the tutors, evidently because teaching helps tutors to organize their knowledge.

- *Teach children techniques for monitoring and managing their own learning.* Students are more likely to achieve when they are taught how to recognize the aims of school tasks and know effective strategies for achieving those aims (like those described on pages 223–225).

When teachers rely on most of these guidelines for effective teaching most of the time, their students generally learn the material and enjoy doing so. When teachers rely on few of them, their students often fail, or, at the very least, find learning difficult and school tedious (Good & Brophy, 1994; Stevenson & Stigler, 1992; Walberg, 1995).

Definition for page 246: A palanquin is a covered couch resting on two horizontal poles that are carried by four people, one at each end of the poles.

Peer tutoring can be very effective; both tutor and tutee usually learn.

© David M. Grossman

THINK ABOUT IT

Would some of these ways to promote students' learning be more appropriate for students in Piaget's concrete-operational stage? Would some be better for students in the formal-operational stage?

TEST YOURSELF

1. Important prereading skills include knowing letters and _____.

2. Beginning readers typically recognize words by sounding them out; with greater experience, readers are more likely able to _____.

3. Older and more experienced readers understand more of what they read because the capacity of working memory increases, they have more general knowledge of the world, _____, and they are more likely to use appropriate reading strategies.

4. Children typically use a _____ to organize their writing.

5. Children revise best when revising other children's writing and when _____.

6. The simplest way of solving addition problems is to _____; the most advanced way is to retrieve sums from long-term memory.

7. Compared to students in U.S. elementary schools, students in Japan and Taiwan spend more time in school, and a greater proportion of that time is _____.

8. In schools where students usually succeed, academic excellence is a priority, the school is safe and nurturant, progress of students and teachers is monitored, and _____.

9. Effective teachers manage classrooms well, believe they are responsible for their students' learning, _____, teach actively, pay attention to pacing, value tutoring, and show children how to monitor their own learning.

Imagine two children just entering first grade. One has mastered prereading skills, can sound out many words, and recognizes a rapidly growing set of words. The second child knows most of the letters of the alphabet but knows only a handful of letter-sound correspondences. How are these differences in reading skills likely to lead to different experiences in first grade?

Answers: (1) sounds associated with each letter, (2) retrieve words from long-term memory, (3) they monitor their comprehension more effectively, (4) knowledge-telling strategy, (5) the topic is familiar to them, (6) count on one's fingers, (7) devoted to academic activities, (8) parents are involved, (9) emphasize mastery of topics

---

6.5

PHYSICAL DEVELOPMENT

LEARNING OBJECTIVES

How much do school-age children grow?

How do motor skills improve during the elementary school years?

Are American children physically fit?

What are the consequences of participating in sports?

Miguel and Dan are 9-year-olds playing organized baseball for the first time. Miguel's coach is always upbeat. He constantly emphasizes the positive. When they lost a game 12 to 2, the coach complimented all the players on their play in the field and at bat. In contrast, Dan's coach was livid when the team lost, and he was very critical of three players who made errors that contributed to the loss. Miguel thinks that baseball is great, but Dan can hardly wait for the season to be over.

DURING THE ELEMENTARY-SCHOOL YEARS, children steadily grow, and their motor skills continue to improve. We'll trace these changes in the first two parts of this section. Then we'll see whether U.S. children are physically fit. We'll end the section by examining children's participation in sports and see how coaches like those in the vignette influence children in organized sports.

■ **Figure 6.11**
Height and weight increase steadily during the elementary-school years.

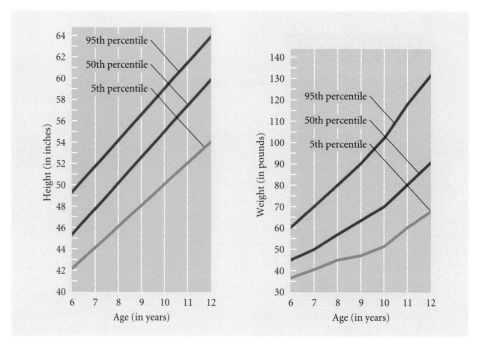

GROWTH

Physical growth during the elementary-school years continues at the steady pace established during the preschool years. From Figure 6.11 you can see that a typical 6-year-old weighs about 45 pounds and is 45 inches tall but grows to about 90 pounds and 60 inches by age 12. In other words, most children gain about 8 pounds and 2 to 3 inches per year. Many parents notice that their elementary-school children outgrow shoes and pants more rapidly than they outgrow sweaters, shirts, or jackets; this is because most of the increase in height comes from the legs, not the trunk.

Boys and girls are about the same size for most of these years (which is why they are combined in the figure), but girls are much more likely than boys to enter puberty toward the end of the elementary-school years. Once girls enter puberty, they grow rapidly and become much bigger than the boys their age. (We have more to say about this in Chapter 8.) Thus, at ages 11 and 12, the average girl is about a half-inch taller than the average boy.

As was true in infancy and early childhood, individuals of the same age often differ markedly in their height and weight. Ethnic differences are also evident in children's growth. In these years, African American children tend to be taller than European American children, who are taller than Asian American children (Webber et al., 1995).

To support this growth and to provide energy for their busy lives, school-age children need to eat more. Although preschool children need only consume about 1,500 to 1,700 calories per day, the average 7- to 10-year-old needs about 2,400 calories each day. Of course, the exact figure depends on the child's age and size and can range anywhere from roughly 1,700 to 3,300 calories daily.

As was true for preschool children, elementary-school children need a well-balanced diet. They should eat regularly from each of the major food groups: grains, vegetables, fruits, milk, meat and beans. Too often children consume calories from sweets that are "empty"—they have very little nutritional value.

During the elementary- and middle-school years, some children are typically much taller than average, and others are much shorter than average.

Anne Ackermann /Getty Images

It's also important that school-age children eat breakfast. At this age, many children skip breakfast, often because they're too rushed in the morning. In fact, breakfast should provide about one fourth of a child's daily calories. When children don't eat breakfast, they often have difficulty paying attention or remembering in school (Pollitt, 1995). Consequently, parents should organize their mornings so that their children have enough time for breakfast.

DEVELOPMENT OF MOTOR SKILLS

Elementary-school children's greater size and strength contributes to improved motor skills. During these years, children steadily run faster and jump farther. For example, Figure 6.12 shows how far a typical boy and girl can throw a ball and how far they can jump (in the standing long jump). By the time children are 11 years old, they can throw a ball three times farther than they could at age 6, and they can jump nearly twice as far.

Fine motor skills also improve as children move through the elementary-school years. Children's greater dexterity is evident in a host of activities ranging from typing, writing, and drawing to working on puzzles, playing the piano, and building model cars. Children gain much greater control over their fingers and hands, making them much more nimble. This greater fine-motor coordination is obvious in children's handwriting.

Children do better in school when they've had breakfast.

Gender Differences in Motor Skills

In both gross and fine motor skills, there are gender differences in performance levels. Girls tend to excel in fine motor skills; their handwriting tends to be better than that of boys, for example. Girls also excel on gross motor skills that require flexibility and balance, such as tumbling. On gross motor skills that emphasize strength, boys usually have the advantage. Figure 6.12 shows that boys throw and jump farther than girls.

■ **Figure 6.12**
Between 6 and 11 years, children's motor skills improve considerably.

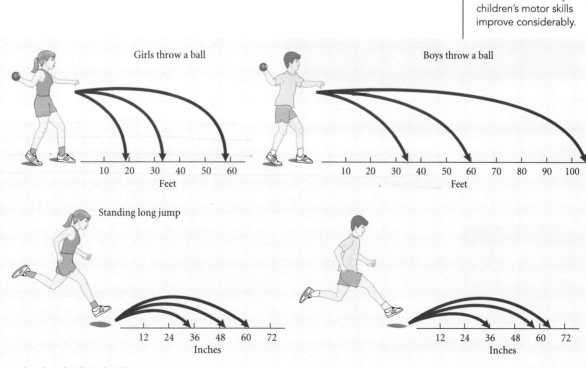

■ Age 6 ■ Age 8 ■ Age 11

Some of the gender differences in gross motor skills that require strength reflect the fact that as children approach and enter puberty, girls' bodies have proportionately more fat and less muscle than boys' bodies. This difference explains why, for example, boys can hang from a bar using their arms and hands much longer than girls can. However, for other gross motor skills, such as running, throwing, and catching, body composition is much less important (Smoll & Schutz, 1990). In these cases, children's experience is crucial. During recess, elementary-school girls are more often found on a swing set, jumping rope, or perhaps talking quietly in a group; in contrast, boys are playing football or shooting baskets. Many girls and their parents believe that sports and physical fitness are less valuable for girls than boys. Consequently, girls spend less time in these sports and fitness-related activities than boys, depriving them of opportunities to practice, which is essential for developing motor skills (Fredricks & Eccles, 2005).

PHYSICAL FITNESS

Being active physically has many benefits for children: it helps to promote growth of muscles and bone, promotes cardiovascular health (National High Blood Pressure Education Program Working Group, 1996), and can help to establish a lifelong pattern of exercise. During the elementary-school years, most U.S. school-age children meet the current guidelines of being physically active at least 60 minutes daily (President's Council on Physical Fitness and Sports, 2004). For example, in one study in which children wore devices similar to pedometers, children in grades 1–3 spent 3 hours daily in moderate-to-vigorous physical activity, and children in grades 4–6 spent 2 hours daily (Trost et al., 2002). Thus, the average school-age child in the United States is physically fit.

© Cindy Charles/PhotoEdit

Participating in sports can enhance children's physical, motor, cognitive, and social development.

THINK ABOUT IT

What skills of concrete-operational thinking make it possible for children to participate in organized sports?

PARTICIPATING IN SPORTS

Children's greater motor skill means they are able to participate in many team sports, including baseball, softball, basketball, and soccer. Obviously, when children play sports, they get exercise and improve their motor skills. But there are other hidden benefits as well. Sports can provide children with a chance to learn important social skills, such as how to work effectively as part of a group, often in complementary roles. And playing sports allows children to use their emerging cognitive skills as they devise new playing strategies or modify the rules of a game.

In days gone by, children gathered together informally—at a playground, a vacant lot, or someone's backyard—to play these sports. However, when today's children participate, the setting is often an official league, organized and run by adults. This turns out to be a mixed blessing. Adults' involvement in children's sports has several advantages: Children learn how to improve their skills and get knowledgeable feedback, and they can enjoy spending time with a positive role model. But there are disadvantages as well. Adults sometimes overemphasize competition instead of skill development, they can be so controlling that children have little opportunity to learn leadership skills, and they may so emphasize drills, strategy, and performance that the activity becomes more like "work" rather than "play."

When adult coaches like the one in the opening vignette encourage their players and emphasize skill development, children usually enjoy playing, often improve their skills, and increase their self-esteem (Smith & Smoll, 1997; Smoll et al., 1993). In contrast, when coaches emphasize winning over skill development and criticize or punish players for bad plays, children lose interest and stop playing (Bailey & Rasmussen, 1996; Smith & Smoll, 1996).

Many youth sports organizations provide guidelines for players, coaches, and parents, so that children will enjoy participating. For example, the American Youth Soccer Organization has a code for coaches that includes the following principles:

- Coach positively: Praise children, don't criticize them.
- Be sure that children have fun!
- Have realistic expectations for children and use these to form reasonable demands.
- Develop children's respect for their opponents, opposing coaches, referees, and the game itself.
- Be a good role model for children.

When adult coaches emphasize winning or frequently criticize players, children lose interest and quit.

© David Young-Wolff/PhotoEdit

When coaches (and parents) follow these guidelines, it's a good bet that their players will have fun and continue to play the sport. And everyone involved needs to remember that this is the whole point: Children (and adults) play games for recreation, to have fun!

TEST YOURSELF

1. Boys and girls grow at about the same rate during elementary-school years, but at the end of this period, girls _____.
2. When children skip breakfast, _____.
3. Boys typically have the advantage on gross motor skills that emphasize strength, but girls tend to have the advantage on _____.
4. Having parents as coaches has many drawbacks, including that they sometimes overemphasize competition, _____, and emphasis drills, strategy, and performance so much that it turns "play" into "work."

How does participation in sports illustrate connections between physical, motor, and cognitive development?

Answers: (1) are more likely to enter puberty and grow rapidly, (2) they often have difficulty paying attention and remembering in school, (3) fine motor skills that emphasize dexterity, (4) are so controlling that children do not have the opportunity to experience leadership

Putting It All Together

We began the chapter by examining children's cognitive development. At about the same time that children begin school, they enter Piaget's period of concrete operations. As they grow, their thinking moves beyond the concrete to the abstract. Like Adrian, they gradually pick up the study strategies that are essential for school achievement.

Next, we traced the origins of intelligence testing and examined how tests are used today. Test scores predict school achievement because they tap the knowledge and skills that are prerequisites for school success. Low test scores, like the one reported for Charlene, indicate that the student probably lacks the skills needed for school success.

We also examined the spectrum of special children, ranging from children who are gifted to those with mental retardation and those with learning disabilities and ADHD. We saw that each group has a distinct profile of cognitive skills.

Then we looked at some of the reasons children's academic skills improve during childhood and adolescence.

We saw that improvements in reading, writing, and arithmetic often can be traced to changes in basic cognitive processes. Angelique's skilled reading comprehension, for example, reflects changes in working memory and comprehension monitoring. In addition, research points to several school- and teacher-related factors that enhance students' achievement.

Finally, we traced children's physical development and motor development during the school-age years. These changes allow children to participate in organized sports, which can be very beneficial when children are fortunate to have coaches like Miguel's who are encouraging and emphasize improving skills rather than winning.

Summary

6.1 Cognitive Development

More Sophisticated Thinking: Piaget's Version

- In progressing to Piaget's stage of concrete operations, children become less egocentric, rarely confuse appearances with reality, and are able to reverse their thinking. They now solve perspective-taking, conservation, and class-inclusion problems correctly. Thinking at this stage is limited to the concrete and the real.

- With the onset of formal-operational thinking, adolescents can think hypothetically and reason abstractly. In deductive reasoning, they understand that conclusions are based on logic, not on experience.

- Critics of Piaget's account of formal-operational thinking point to two shortcomings. First, in everyday thinking, adolescents' reasoning is often less sophisticated than would be expected of formal-operational thinkers. Second, Piaget assumed that after the formal-operational stage is reached, thinking never again changes qualitatively.

Information-Processing Strategies for Learning and Remembering

- Rehearsal and other memory strategies are used to transfer information from working memory, a temporary store of information, to long-term memory, a permanent store of knowledge. Children begin to rehearse at about age 7 or 8 and take up other strategies as they get older.

- Effective use of strategies for learning and remembering begins with an analysis of the goals of any learning task. It also includes monitoring one's performance to determine whether the strategy is working. Collectively, these processes make up an important group of study skills.

6.2 Aptitudes for School

Theories of Intelligence

- Psychometric approaches to intelligence include theories that describe intelligence as a general factor as well as theories that include specific factors. Hierarchical theories include both general intelligence

and various specific skills, such as verbal and spatial ability.

- Gardner's theory of multiple intelligences proposes seven distinct intelligences. Three are found in psychometric theories (linguistic, logical-mathematical, and spatial intelligence), but six are new (musical, bodily-kinesthetic, interpersonal, intrapersonal, naturalistic, and existential intelligence). Gardner's theory has stimulated research on nontraditional forms of intelligence, such as social-cognitive flexibility. The theory also has implications for education, suggesting, for example, that schools should adjust teaching to each child's unique intellectual strengths.

- According to Robert Sternberg, intelligence is defined as using abilities to achieve short- and long-term goals and depends on three abilities: analytic ability to analyze a problem and generate a solution, creative ability to deal adaptively with novel situations, and practical ability to know what solutions will work.

Binet and the Development of Intelligence Testing

- Binet created the first intelligence test in order to identify students who would have difficulty in school. Using this work, Terman created the Stanford-Binet in 1916; it remains an important intelligence test. The Stanford-Binet introduced the concept of the intelligence quotient (IQ): $MA/CA \times 100$.

Do Tests Work?

- Intelligence tests are reasonably valid measures of achievement in school. They also predict people's performance in the workplace. Dynamic tests are designed to improve validity by measuring children's potential for future learning.

Hereditary and Environmental Factors

- Evidence for the impact of heredity on IQ comes from the findings that (a) siblings' IQ scores become more alike as siblings become more similar genetically, and (b) adopted children's IQ scores are more like their biological parents' test scores than their adoptive parents' scores. Evidence for the impact of the environment comes from the finding that children who live in responsive, well-organized home environments tend to have higher IQ scores, as do children who participate in intervention programs.

The Impact of Ethnicity and Socioeconomic Status

■ The average IQ score for African Americans is lower than the average score for European Americans, a difference attributed to the fact that more African American children live in poverty and that the test assesses knowledge based on middle-class experiences. IQ scores remain valid predictors of school success because middle-class experience is often a prerequisite for school success.

6.3 Special Children, Special Needs

Gifted and Creative Children

■ Traditionally, gifted children have been those with high scores on IQ tests. Modern definitions of giftedness have been broadened to include exceptional talent in, for example, the arts. However defined, giftedness must be nurtured by parents and teachers alike. Contrary to folklore, gifted children are socially mature and emotionally stable.

■ Creativity is associated with divergent thinking, in which the aim is to think in novel and unusual directions. Tests of divergent thinking can predict which children are most likely to be creative. Creativity can be fostered by experiences that encourage children to think flexibly and to explore alternatives.

Children With Mental Retardation

■ Individuals with mental retardation have IQ scores of 70 or lower and deficits in adaptive behavior. Organic mental retardation, which is severe but relatively infrequent, can be linked to specific biological or physical causes; familial mental retardation, which is less severe but more common, reflects the lower end of the normal distribution of intelligence. Most retarded persons are classified as mildly or educably retarded; they attend school, work, and have families.

Children With Learning Disabilities

■ Children with learning disabilities have normal intelligence but have difficulty mastering specific academic subjects. The most common is reading disability, which often can be traced to inadequate understanding and use of language sounds.

Attention-Deficit Hyperactivity Disorder

■ Children with ADHD are distinguished by being over-active, inattentive, and impulsive. They often have conduct problems and do poorly in school. ADHD is due to heredity and ineffective parenting brought on by children's impulsive behavior. Children with ADHD are often administered stimulants, which

calm them. They can also be taught more effective ways of regulating their behavior and attention.

6.4 Academic Skills

Reading

■ Reading includes a number of component skills. Pre-reading skills include knowing letters and the sounds associated with them. Word recognition is the process of identifying a word. Beginning readers more often accomplish this by sounding out words; advanced readers more often retrieve a word from long-term memory. Comprehension, the act of extracting meaning from text, improves with age due to several factors: working memory capacity increases, readers gain more world knowledge, and readers are better able to monitor what they read and to match their reading strategies to the goals of the reading task.

Writing

■ As children develop, their writing improves, reflecting several factors: They know more about the world, so they have more to say; they use more effective ways of organizing their writing; they master the mechanics of writing (e.g., handwriting, spelling); and they become more skilled at revising their writing.

Math Skills

■ Children first add and subtract by counting, but soon they use more effective strategies such as retrieving addition facts directly from memory. In mathematics, U.S. students lag behind students in most other industrialized countries, chiefly because of cultural differences in time spent on schoolwork and homework and in parents' attitudes toward school, effort, and ability.

Effective Schools, Effective Teachers

■ Schools influence students' achievement in many ways. Students are most likely to achieve when their school emphasizes academic excellence, has a safe and nurturing environment, monitors pupils' and teachers' progress, and encourages parents to be involved.

■ Students achieve at higher levels when their teachers manage classrooms effectively, take responsibility for their students' learning, teach mastery of material, pace material well, value tutoring, and show children how to monitor their own learning.

6.5 Physical Development

Growth

■ Elementary-school children grow at a steady pace, more so in their legs than in the trunk. Boys and girls tend to be about the same size for much of these years, but there are large individual differences and ethnic differences.

■ School-age children need approximately 2,400 calories daily, preferably drawn from each of the basic food groups. Children need to eat breakfast. This meal should provide approximately one fourth of their calories; without breakfast, children often have trouble concentrating in school.

Development of Motor Skills

■ Fine and gross motor skills improve substantially over the elementary-school years, reflecting children's greater size and strength. Girls tend to excel in fine motor skills that emphasize dexterity as well as gross motor skills that require flexibility and balance; boys tend to excel in gross motor skills that emphasize strength. Although some of these differences reflect differences in body makeup, they also reflect differing cultural expectations regarding motor skills for boys and girls.

Physical Fitness

■ Most American schoolchildren meet today's standards for being physically fit.

Participating in Sports

■ Many school-age children participate in team sports. Adult coaches can help children to improve their skills, but they sometimes overemphasize competition, are so controlling that children have little opportunity to experience leadership, and overemphasize drills, strategy, and performance, which turns "play" into "work."

Key Terms

mental operations (220)	emotional intelligence (228)	mental retardation (239)
deductive reasoning (222)	analytic ability (229)	organic mental retardation (239)
working memory (223)	creative ability (229)	familial mental retardation (239)
long-term memory (223)	practical ability (229)	learning disability (240)
organization (223)	mental age (MA) (230)	word recognition (245)
elaboration (223)	intelligence quotient (IQ) (231)	comprehension (245)
metamemory (224)	dynamic testing (232)	phonological awareness (245)
metacognitive knowledge (224)	culture-fair intelligence tests (236)	propositions (246)
cognitive self-regulation (224)	stereotype threat (236)	knowledge-telling strategy (248)
psychometricians (226)	convergent thinking (238)	knowledge-transforming strategy (248)
savants (228)	divergent thinking (238)	

Learn More About It

Readings

BARKLEY, R. A. (2000). *Taking charge of ADHD: The complete, authoritative guide for parents* (revised edition). New York: Guilford. Written by one of the leading experts on ADHD, this book clearly describes what research has revealed about the nature of ADHD. The book also provides a wealth of practical information for parents and teachers on many topics, such as the effects of medications and how to improve children's performance in the classroom.

FISKE, E. B. (1992). *Smart schools, smart kids.* New York: Touchstone. The author examines some exceptional U.S. schools to discover the key ingredients of a successful school.

FLAVELL, J. H., MILLER, P. H., & MILLER, S. A. (2003). *Cognitive development* (4th ed.). Englewood Cliffs, NJ: Prentice-Hall. We recommended this book in Chapter 4 as a good source of information about cognitive development in young children, but it also covers the development of thinking in school-age children and adolescents.

GARDNER, H. (2000). *Intelligence reframed: Multiple intelligences for the 21st century.* New York: Basic Books. The author explains his theory of intelligence and describes how the theory has been used in some schools to boost students' achievement.

McBRIDE-CHANG, C. (2004). *Children's literacy development.* London: Arnold. The author, an expert on reading, examines the different skills children master in order to read, write, and spell well.

Websites

Visit the Human Development book companion website for all URLs.

■ **Human Development Book Companion Website**
See **http://www.psychology.wadsworth.com/kail_cavanaugh4e/** for practice quiz questions, Internet links, updates, critical thinking exercises, discussion forums, and more. Also accessible from the Wadsworth Psychology Study Center (http://psychology.wadsworth.com).

■ **Twenty-First Century Teachers**
A nationwide volunteer initiative to encourage teachers to use technology in their teaching, this site includes information on the use of computers and other technology in schools.

■ *Skeptic* **Magazine**
This site includes an interview with Robert Sternberg in which Sternberg talks about his triarchic theory, the influence of heredity and environment on intelligence, and Gardner's model of multiple intelligences.

■ **Howard Gardner**
For more information about Howard Gardner's theory of multiple intelligences and its application in teaching, visit this website.

■ **National Association for Gifted Children**
This site contains information for parents of gifted children and has links to related sites.

Life-Span CD-ROM

For more information on the concepts covered in this chapter, go to
Module 3: Early and Middle Childhood

• *Cognitive Development*

http://www.thomsonedu.com
Go to this site for the link to ThomsonNOW, your one-stop study shop. Take a pre-test for this chapter, and ThomsonNOW will generate a personalized study plan based on your test results. The study plan will identify the topics you need to review and direct you to online resources to help you master those topics. You can then take a post-test to help you determine the concepts you have mastered and what you still need to work on.

7.1 Family Relationships
The Family as a System
Dimensions and Styles of
    Parenting
Siblings
Divorce and Remarriage
Parent-Child Relationships Gone
    Awry: Child Abuse

7.2 Peers
Friendships
■ SPOTLIGHT ON RESEARCH:
   Influences of Best Friends
     on Sexual Activity
Groups
Popularity and Rejection
Aggressive Children and Their
    Victims

**7.3 Television: Boob Tube or
Window on the World?**
Influence on Attitudes and Social
    Behavior
Influences on Cognition
Criticisms of TV

7.4 Understanding Others
Describing Others
■ REAL PEOPLE: APPLYING
   HUMAN DEVELOPMENT:
   Tell Me About a Girl That You
     Like a Lot
Understanding What Others
    Think
Prejudice

Putting It All Together
Summary
Key Terms
Learn More About It

CHAPTER 7

Expanding Social Horizons

Socioemotional Development in Middle Childhood

Although you've never had a course called "Culture 101," your knowledge of your culture is deep. Like all human beings, you have been learning, since birth, to live in your culture. *Teaching children the values, roles, and behaviors of their culture—**socialization**—is a major goal of all peoples.* In most cultures, the task of socialization falls initially to parents. In the first section of this chapter, we see how parents set and try to enforce standards of behavior for their children.

Soon other powerful forces contribute to socialization. In the second section, you'll discover how peers become influential, through both individual friendships and social groups. Next, you'll learn how the media—particularly television—contribute to socialization as well.

As children become socialized, they begin to understand more about other people. We'll examine this growing understanding in the last section of the chapter.

7.1

FANILY RELATIONSHIPS

LEARNING OBJECTIVES

What are the primary dimensions of parenting? How do they affect children's development?

What determines how siblings get along? How do first-born, later-born, and only children differ?

How do divorce and remarriage affect children?

What factors contribute to child abuse?

Tanya and Sheila, both sixth-graders, wanted to go to a Kelly Clarkson concert with two boys from their school. When Tanya asked if she could go, her mom said, "No way!" Tanya replied defiantly, "Why not?" Her mother blew up: "Because I say so. That's why. Stop bugging me." Sheila wasn't allowed to go either. When she asked why, her mom said, "I just think that you're still too young to be dating. I don't mind your going to the concert. If you want to go just with Tanya, that would be fine. What do you think of that?"

THE VIGNETTE ILLUSTRATES WHAT WE ALL KNOW WELL from personal experience— parents go about child rearing in many different ways. We'll study these different approaches in this chapter and learn how Tanya and Sheila are likely to be affected by their mothers' styles of parenting. But first we'll start by considering parents as key components of a broader family system.

THE FAMILY AS A SYSTEM

Families are rare in the animal kingdom. Only human beings and a handful of other species form family-like units. Why? Compared to the young in other species, children develop slowly. And because children are immature—unable to care for themselves —for many years, the family structure evolved as a way to protect and nurture young children during their development (Bjorklund, Yunger, & Pellegrini, 2002). Of course, modern families serve many other functions as well—they're economic units, and they provide emotional support—but child rearing remains the most salient and probably the most important family function.

As we think about how families function, it's tempting to believe that parents' actions are all that really matter. That is, through their behavior, parents directly and indirectly determine their children's development. This view of parents as "all powerful" was part of early psychological theories (e.g., Watson, 1925) and is held even today by some first-time parents. But most theorists now view families from a contextual perspective (described in Chapter 1). That is, families form a system of interacting elements —parents and children influence one another (Bronfenbrenner & Morris, 2006; Cox & Paley, 2003), and families are part of a much larger system that includes extended family, friends, and teachers as well as institutions that influence development (e.g., schools).

In the systems view, parents still influence their children, both directly—for example, by encouraging them to study hard—and indirectly—for example, by being generous and kind to others. However, the influence is no longer exclusively from parents to children but is mutual: Children influence their parents too. By their behaviors, attitudes, and interests, children affect how their parents behave toward them. When children resist discipline, for example, parents may become less willing to reason and more inclined to use force (Ritchie, 1999).

Even more subtle influences become apparent when families are viewed as systems of interacting elements. For example, fathers' behaviors can affect mother-child relationships—a demanding husband may leave his wife with little time, energy, or interest in helping her daughter with her homework. Or, when siblings argue constantly, parents may become preoccupied with avoiding problems rather than encouraging their children's development.

These many examples show that narrowly focusing on parents' impact on children misses the complexities of family life. But there is even more to the systems view. The family itself is embedded in other social systems, such as neighborhoods and religious institutions (Parke & Buriel, 1998). These other institutions can affect family dynamics. Sometimes they simplify child rearing, as when neighbors are trusted friends and can help care for each others' children. Sometimes, however, they complicate child rearing. Grandparents who live nearby and visit constantly can create friction within the family. At times, the impact of the larger systems is indirect, as when work schedules cause a parent to be away from home or when schools must eliminate programs that benefit children.

Figure 7.1 summarizes the numerous interactive influences that exist in a systems view of families. In the remainder of this section, we'll describe parents' influences on children and then how children affect their parents' behavior.

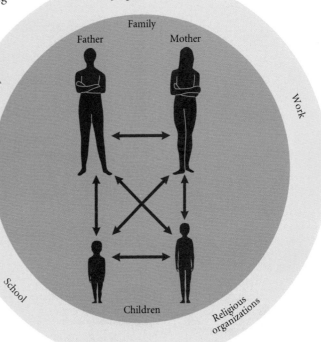

DIMENSIONS AND STYLES OF PARENTING

Parenting can be described in terms of general dimensions that are like personality traits in that they represent stable aspects of parental behavior—aspects that hold across different situations (Holden & Miller, 1999). When parenting is viewed in this way, two general dimensions of parental behavior emerge. One is the degree of warmth and responsiveness that parents show their children. At one end of the spectrum are parents who are openly warm and affectionate with their children. They are involved with them, respond to their emotional needs, and spend considerable time with them. At the other end of the spectrum are parents who are relatively uninvolved with their children and sometimes even hostile toward them. These parents often seem more focused on their own needs and interests than on those of their children. Warm parents enjoy hearing their children describe the day's activities; uninvolved or hostile parents aren't interested, considering it a waste of their time. Warm parents see when their children are upset and try to comfort them; uninvolved or hostile parents pay little attention to their children's emotional states and invest little effort in comforting them when they're upset. As you might expect, children benefit from warm and responsive parenting (Pettit, Bates, & Dodge, 1997; Zhou et al., 2002).

A second general dimension of parental behavior involves control. Some parents are dictatorial: They try to regulate every facet of their children's lives, like a puppeteer controlling a marionette. At the other extreme are parents who exert little or no control over their children: These children do whatever they want without asking parents first or worrying about their parents' response. What's best for children is an intermediate amount of control, when parents set reasonable standards for their children's behavior, expect their children to meet them, and monitor their children's behavior (i.e., they also usually know where their children are, what they're doing, and with whom). When parents have reasonable expectations for their children and keep tabs on their activities —for example, a mother knows that her 12-year-old is staying after school for choir practice, then going to the library—their children tend to be better adjusted (Kilgore, Snyder, & Lentz, 2000).

■ Figure 7.1
In a systems view of families, parents and children influence each other; this interacting family unit is also influenced by other forces outside of the family.

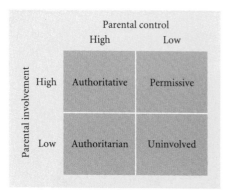

Figure 7.2

Combining the two dimensions of parental behavior (warmth and control) creates four prototypic styles of parenting.

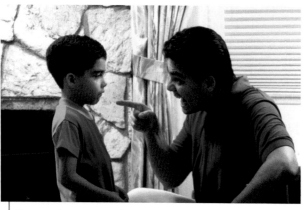

Parents who use an authoritarian style are controlling but not very warm; they expect children to obey them without question.

Parenting Styles

Combining the dimensions of warmth and control produces four prototypic styles of parenting, as shown in Figure 7.2 (Baumrind, 1975, 1991).

■ ***Authoritarian parenting*** *combines high control with little warmth.* These parents lay down the rules and expect them to be followed without discussion. Hard work, respect, and obedience are what authoritarian parents wish to cultivate in their children. There is little give-and-take between parent and child because authoritarian parents do not consider children's needs or wishes. This style is illustrated by Tanya's mother in the opening vignette. She feels no obligation whatsoever to explain her decision.

■ ***Authoritative parenting*** *combines a fair degree of parental control with being warm and responsive to children.* Authoritative parents explain rules and encourage discussion. This style is exemplified by Sheila's mother in the opening vignette. She explained why she did not want the girls going to the concert with the boys and encouraged her daughter to discuss the issue with her.

■ ***Permissive parenting*** *offers warmth and caring but little parental control.* These parents generally accept their children's behavior and punish them infrequently. An indulgent-permissive parent would readily agree to Tanya's or Sheila's request to go to the concert, simply because it is something the child wants to do.

■ ***Uninvolved parenting*** *provides neither warmth nor control.* Indifferent-uninvolved parents provide for their children's basic physical and emotional needs but little else. They try to minimize the amount of time spent with their children and avoid becoming emotionally involved with them. If Tanya or Sheila had parents with this style, she might have simply gone to the concert without asking, knowing that her parents wouldn't care and would rather not be bothered.

Research consistently shows the authoritative parenting is best for most children most of the time. Children with authoritative parents tend to have higher grades and are responsible, self-reliant, and friendly (Amato & Fowler, 2002; Aunola, Stattin, & Nurmi, 2000). In contrast, children with authoritarian parents are often unhappy, have low self-esteem, and frequently are overly aggressive (e.g., Silk et al., 2003). Finally, children with permissive parents are often impulsive and have little self-control, whereas children with uninvolved parents often do poorly in school and are aggressive (Aunola et al., 2000; Barber & Olsen, 1997). Thus, children typically thrive on a parental style that combines control, warmth, and affection.

VARIATIONS ASSOCIATED WITH CULTURE AND SOCIOECONOMIC STATUS. The general aim of child rearing—helping children become contributing members of their culture—is much the same worldwide (Whiting & Child, 1953), and warmth and control are universal aspects of parents' behavior. But views about the "proper" amount of warmth and the "proper" amount of control vary with particular cultures. European Americans want their children to be happy and self-reliant individuals, and they believe these goals are best achieved when parents are warm and exert moderate control (Goodnow, 1992). In many Asian and Latin American countries, however, individualism is less important than cooperation and collaboration (Okagaki & Sternberg, 1993). In China, for example, Confucian principles dictate that parents are always right and that emotional restraint is the key to family harmony (Chao, 2001). In fact, consistent with their cultural values, mothers and fathers in China are more likely to emphasize parental control and less likely to express affection than are mothers and fathers in the United States (Lin & Fu, 1990). Thus, cultural values help specify appropriate ways for parents to interact with their offspring.

Not only do parental styles vary across cultures, they vary within cultures, depending on parents' socioeconomic status. Within the United States, parents with lower socioeconomic status tend to be more controlling and more punitive—characteristics associated with the authoritarian parenting style—than are parents with higher socioeconomic status (Hoff-Ginsberg & Tardif, 1995). This difference may reflect educational differences that help to define socioeconomic status. Parents with higher socioeconomic status are, by definition, more educated and, consequently often see development as a more complex process that requires the more nuanced and child-friendly approach that marks authoritative parenting (Skinner, 1985). And parents who are relatively uneducated often find themselves employed in positions where they're used to taking orders from others; when they're at home, these parents reverse roles and order their children around (Greenberger, O'Neil, & Nagel, 1994).

Another contributing factor derives from another variable that defines socioeconomic status—income. Due to their limited financial resources, parents with lower socioeconomic status often lead more stressful lives (e.g., they wonder whether they'll have enough money at the end of the month for groceries) and are far more likely to live in neighborhoods where violence, drugs, and crime are commonplace. Thus, parents with lower socioeconomic status may be too stressed to invest the energy needed for authoritative parenting, and the authoritarian approach—with its emphasis on the child's immediate compliance—may actually protect children growing up in dangerous neighborhoods (Parke & Buriel, 1998).

As important as these different dimensions and styles are for understanding parenting, there is more to effective child rearing, as we'll see in the next section.

Parental Behavior

Dimensions and styles are general characterizations of how parents typically behave. If, for example, we describe a parent as warm or controlling, you immediately have a sense of that parent's usual style in dealing with his or her children. Nevertheless, the price for such a broad description is that it tells us little about how parents behave in specific situations and how these parental behaviors influence children's development. Put another way, what specific behaviors can parents use to influence their children? Researchers who study parents name three: direct instruction, modeling, and feedback.

DIRECT INSTRUCTION. Parents often tell their children what to do. But simply playing the role of drill sergeant and ordering children around—"Clean your room!" "Turn off the TV!"—is not very effective. *A better approach is **direct instruction**, which involves telling a child what to do, when, and why.* Instead of just shouting, "Share your candy with your brother!" a parent should explain when and why it's important to share with a sibling.

In addition, just as coaches help athletes master sports skills, parents can help their youngsters master social and emotional skills. Parents can explain links between emotions and behavior—"Catlin is sad because you broke her crayon" (Gottman, Katz, & Hooven, 1996). They can also teach children how to deal with difficult social situations —"When you ask Lindsey if she can sleep over, do it privately so you won't hurt Kaycee's or Hannah's feelings" (Mize & Pettit, 1997). In general, children who get this sort of parental "coaching" tend to be more socially skilled and, not surprisingly, get along better with their peers.

Direct instruction and coaching are particularly powerful when paired with modeling. Urging children to act in a particular way, such as sharing with others, is more compelling when children also see others sharing. In the next section, we'll see how children learn by observing others.

MODELING. Children learn a great deal from parents simply by watching them. The parents' modeling and the youngsters' observational learning leads to imitation, so chil-

When children see older siblings punished, younger children also get the message and are less likely to behave in ways that lead to punishment.

dren's behavior resembles the behavior they observe. *Observational learning can also produce* **counterimitation,** *learning what should not be done.* If an older sibling kicks a friend and parents punish the older sibling, the younger child may learn not to kick others.

Sometimes observational learning leads to **disinhibition,** *an increase in all behaviors like those observed.* Children who watch their parents shouting angrily, for example, are more likely to yell at or push a younger sibling. In other words, observation can lead to a general increase in aggression, or put still another way, aggressive responses become disinhibited. *The opposite effect, in which an entire class of behaviors is made less likely, is known as* **inhibition.** When a child sees parents punish a sibling, the child is less likely to behave in the ways that led to the sibling being punished. Inhibition is similar to counterimitation in some ways but is a much broader concept that affects a whole range of behaviors rather than a specific act.

So far, we've seen that parents influence their children's development by direct instruction and by acting as models that children can observe. In the next section, we'll see how parents use feedback to affect children's behavior.

FEEDBACK. By giving feedback to their children, parents indicate whether a behavior is appropriate and should continue or is inappropriate and should stop. Feedback comes in two general forms. **Reinforcement** *is any action that increases the likelihood of the response that it follows.* Parents may use praise to reinforce a child's studying or give a reward for completing household chores. **Punishment** *is any action that discourages the recurrence of the response that it follows.* Parents may forbid children to watch television when they get poor grades in school or make children go to bed early for neglecting household chores.

Of course, parents have been rewarding and punishing their children for centuries, so what do psychologists know that parents don't know already? In fact, researchers have made some surprising discoveries concerning the nature of reward and punishment. *Parents often unwittingly reinforce the very behaviors they want to discourage, a situation called the* **negative reinforcement trap** (Patterson, 1980). The negative reinforcement trap occurs in three steps, most often between a mother and her son. In the first step, the mother tells her son to do something he doesn't want to do. She might tell him to clean up his room, to come inside while he's outdoors playing with friends, or to study instead of watching television. In the next step, the son responds with some behavior that most parents find intolerable: He argues, complains, or whines—not just briefly, but for an extended period of time. In the last step, the mother gives in—saying that the son needn't do as she told him initially—simply to get the son to stop the behavior that is so intolerable.

The feedback to the son is that arguing (or complaining or whining) works; the mother rewards that behavior by withdrawing the request that the son did not like. That is, although we usually think a behavior is strengthened when it is followed by the presentation of something that is valued, behavior is also strengthened when it is followed by removing something that is disliked.

As for punishment, research (Parke, 1977) shows that punishment works best when

- administered directly after the undesired behavior occurs, not hours later.
- an undesired behavior *always* leads to punishment, not usually or occasionally.

- accompanied by an explanation of why the child was punished and how punishment can be avoided in the future.
- the child has a warm, affectionate relationship with the person administering the punishment.

At the same time, research reveals some serious drawbacks to punishment. One is that punishment is primarily suppressive: Punished responses are stopped, but only temporarily if children do not learn new behaviors to replace those that were punished. For example, denying TV to brothers who are fighting stops the undesirable behavior, but fighting is likely to recur unless the boys learn new ways of solving their disputes.

A second drawback is that punishment can have undesirable side effects. Children become upset when they are being punished, which makes it unlikely that they will understand the feedback punishment is meant to convey. A child denied TV for misbehaving may become angry over the punishment itself and ignore why he's being punished. Furthermore, when children are punished physically, they often imitate this behavior with peers and younger siblings (Whitehurst & Vasta, 1977). Children who are spanked often use aggression to resolve their disputes with others.

An effective form of punishment is time-out, in which children sit alone briefly.

One method combines the best features of punishment while avoiding its shortcomings. *In **time-out,** a child who misbehaves must briefly sit alone in a quiet, unstimulating location.* Some parents have children sit alone in a bathroom; others have children sit in a corner of a room. Time-out is punishing because it interrupts the child's ongoing activity and isolates the child from other family members, toys, books, and, generally, all forms of rewarding stimulation.

The period is sufficiently brief—usually just a few minutes—for a parent to use the method consistently. During time-out, both parent and child typically calm down. Then, when time-out is over, a parent can talk with the child and explain why the punished behavior is objectionable and what the child should do instead. "Reasoning" like this—even with preschool children—is effective because it emphasizes why a parent punished initially and how punishment can be avoided in the future.

Thus, parents can influence children by direct instruction, by modeling behavior that they value and not modeling what they don't want their children to learn, by giving feedback, and through the parenting styles that we examined in the beginning of this section. In the next section, we'll explore less direct ways that parents influence their children's development.

Influences of the Marital System

When Derek returned from 7-Eleven with a six-pack of beer and chips instead of diapers and baby food, Anita exploded in anger. "How could you! I used the last diaper an hour ago!" Huddled in the corner of the kitchen, their son Randy watched yet another episode in the daily soap opera that featured Derek and Anita.

Although Derek and Anita aren't arguing about Randy—in fact, they're so wrapped up in their conflict that they forget he's in the room—it's hard to conceive that a child would emerge unscathed from such constant parental conflict. And research indeed shows that chronic parental conflict is harmful for children. Parental conflict affects children's development through three distinct mechanisms. First, seeing parents fight jeopardizes a child's feeling that the family is stable and secure, making a child feel anxious, frightened, and sad (Davies, Cummings, & Winter, in press). Second, chronic conflict between parents often spills over into the parent-child relationship. A wife who finds herself frequently arguing with and confronting her husband may adopt a similar ineffective style in interacting with her children (Cox, Paley, & Harter, 2001). Third, when parents invest time and energy fighting with each other, they're often too tired or too preoccupied to invest themselves in high-quality parenting (Katz & Woodin, 2002).

Of course, all long-term relationships experience conflict at some point. Does this mean that all children bear at least some scars? Not necessarily. Many parents resolve conflicts in a manner that's constructive instead of destructive. To see this, suppose one parent believes their child should attend a summer camp but the other parent believes it's too expensive and not worth it because the child attended the previous summer. Instead of shouting and name-calling (e.g., "You're always such a cheapskate!"), some parents seek mutually acceptable solutions: The child could attend the camp if she earns money to cover part of the cost, or the child could attend a different, less expensive camp. When disagreements are routinely resolved in this way, children actually respond positively to conflict, apparently because it shows that their family is cohesive and able to withstand life's problems (Goeke-Moray et al., 2003).

The extent and resolution of conflict is an obvious way in which the parental system affects children, but it's not the only way. Many mothers and fathers form an effective parental team, working together in a coordinated and complementary fashion toward goals that they share for their child's development. For example, parents may agree that their daughter is smart and athletically skilled and that she should excel in both domains. Consequently, they're quite happy to help her achieve these goals. One parent gives her basketball tips and the other edits her writing.

But not all parents work well together. Sometimes they don't agree on goals: One parent values sports over schoolwork and the other reverses these priorities. Sometimes parents actively compete for their child's attention: One parent may want to take the child shopping but the other wants to take her to a ball game. Finally, parents sometimes act as gatekeepers, limiting one another's participation in parenting. A mother may feel that infant care is solely her turf and not allow the father to participate. Or the father may claim all school-related tasks and discourage the mother from getting involved.

Just as a doubles tennis team won't win many matches if each player ignores the other, parenting is far less effective when each parent tries to "go it alone" instead of working together to achieve shared goals using methods that they both accept. When parents don't work together, when they compete, or when they limit each other's access to their children, problems can result: for example, children can become withdrawn (McHale et al., 2002). Thus, in understanding the impact parents have on children's development, we need to consider the nature of the marital relationship as well as parenting styles and specific parenting behaviors (e.g., parents' use of feedback).

In the next few pages, we'll switch perspectives and see how children affect parenting behavior.

Children's Contributions: Reciprocal Influence

At the beginning of this chapter, we emphasized that the family is a dynamic, interactive system with parents and children influencing each other. In fact, children begin at birth to influence the way their parents treat them. Let's look at two characteristics of children that influence how parents treat them.

■ *Age.* Parenting changes as children grow. The same parenting that is marvelously effective with infants and toddlers is inappropriate for adolescents. These age-related changes in parenting are evident in the two basic dimensions of parental behavior—warmth and control. Warmth is beneficial throughout development—toddlers and teens alike enjoy knowing that others care about them. But the manifestation of parental affection changes, becoming more reserved as children develop. The enthusiastic hugging and kissing that delights toddlers embarrasses adolescents. Parental control also changes as children develop (Maccoby, 1984; Vazsonyi, Hibbert, & Snider, 2003). As children develop cognitively and are better able to make their own decisions, parents gradually relinquish control and expect children to be responsible for themselves. For instance, parents of elementary-school children often keep track of their children's progress on school assignments, but parents of adolescents don't, expecting their children to do this themselves.

■ *Temperament and behavior.* A child's temperament can have a powerful effect on parental behavior (Brody & Ge, 2001). To illustrate the reciprocal influence of parents and children, imagine two children with different temperaments as they respond to a parent's authoritative style. The first child has an "easy" temperament and readily complies with parental requests and responds well to family discussions about parental expectations. These parent-child relations are a textbook example of successful authoritative parenting. But suppose the second child has a "difficult temperament" and complies reluctantly and sometimes not at all. Over time, the parent becomes more controlling and less affectionate. The child in turn complies even less in the future, leading the parent to adopt an authoritarian parenting style (Bates et al., 1998).

When children respond defiantly to discipline, parents often resort to harsher discipline in the future.

As this example illustrates, parenting behaviors and styles often evolve as a consequence of the child's behavior. With a moderately active young child who is eager to please adults, a parent may discover that a modest amount of control is adequate. But for a very active child who is not as eager to please, a parent may need to be more controlling and directive (Brody & Ge, 2001; Hastings & Rubin, 1999). Influence is reciprocal: Children's behavior helps determine how parents treat them, and the resulting parental behavior influences children's behavior, which in turn causes parents to again change their behavior (Stoolmiller, 2001).

As time goes by, these reciprocal influences lead many families to adopt routine ways of interacting with each other. Some families end up functioning smoothly: Parents and children cooperate, anticipate each other's needs, and are generally happy. Unfortunately, other families end up troubled: Disagreements are common, parents spend much time trying unsuccessfully to control their defiant children, and everyone is often angry and upset (Belsky, Woodworth, & Crnic, 1996; Kochanska, 1997).

Over the long term, such troubled families do not fare well, so it's important that these negative reciprocal influences be nipped in the bud (Carrere & Gottman, 1999; Christensen & Heavey, 1999). When parents recognize the problem early on, they can modify their own behavior. For example, they can try to be less controlling, which sometimes causes children to be less defiant. We are *not* suggesting that parents allow children to do as they please. Instead, parents should decide aspects of children's lives where they need less control and relinquish it.

Parents should also discuss expectations for appropriate behavior with their preschoolers (e.g., about the need to share toys or snacks with playmates). Such discussions may seem odd for children so young, but, phrased properly, these conversations can help parents and children to better understand one another. And, just as important, they help to establish a style for dealing with family issues that will serve everyone well as the children grow.

Of course, many parents find it hard to view family functioning objectively because they are, after all, an integral part of that family. And parents often lack the expertise needed to change their children's behavior. In these circumstances, a family therapist can provide invaluable assistance, identifying the obstacles to successful family functioning and suggesting ways to eliminate them.

A reciprocal parent-child relationship is central to human development, but other relationships within the family are also influential. For many children, relationships with siblings are very important, as we'll see in the next few pages.

SIBLINGS

For most of a year, all first-born children are only children. Some children remain "onlies" forever, but most get brothers and sisters. Some first-borns are joined by many siblings in rapid succession; others are simply joined by a single brother or sister. As the family acquires these new members, parent-child relationships become more complex. Parents can no longer focus on a single child but must adjust to the needs of multiple children. Just as important, siblings influence each other's development.

From the very beginning, sibling relationships are complicated. On the one hand, most expectant parents are excited by the prospect of another child, and their enthusiasm is contagious: Their children, too, eagerly await the arrival of the newest family member. On the other hand, the birth of a sibling is often distressing for older children, who may become withdrawn or return to more childish behavior because of the changes that occur in their lives, particularly the need to share parental attention and affection (Gottlieb & Mendelson, 1990). However, distress can be avoided if parents remain responsive to their older children's needs (Howe & Ross, 1990). In fact, one of the benefits of a sibling's birth is that fathers become more involved with their older children as mothers must devote more time to a newborn (Stewart et al., 1987).

Many older siblings enjoy helping their parents take care of newborns. Older children play with the baby, console it, feed it, or change its diapers. In middle-class Western families, such caregiving often occurs in the context of play, with parents nearby. But in some cultures children—particularly girls—play an important role in providing care for their younger siblings (Zukow-Goldring, 2002). As the infant grows, interactions between siblings become more frequent and more complicated. For example, toddlers tend to talk more to parents than to older siblings. But by the time the younger sibling is 4 years old, the situation is reversed: Now young siblings talk more to older siblings than to their mother (Brown & Dunn, 1992). Older siblings become a source of care and comfort for younger siblings when they are distressed or upset (Garner, Jones, & Palmer, 1994). And older siblings serve as teachers for their younger siblings, teaching them to play games or how to cook simple foods (Maynard, 2002). Finally, when older children do well in school and are popular with peers, younger siblings often follow suit (Brody et al., 2003).

As time goes by, some siblings grow close, becoming best friends in ways that nonsiblings can never be. Other siblings constantly argue, compete, and, overall simply do not get along with each other. The basic pattern of sibling interaction seems to be established early in development and remains fairly stable. Dunn, Slomkowski, and Beardsall (1994), for example, interviewed mothers twice about their children's interaction, first when the children were 3- and 5-year-olds and again 7 years later, when the children were 10- and 12-year-olds. Dunn and her colleagues found that siblings who got along as preschoolers often continued to get along as young adolescents, whereas siblings who quarreled as preschoolers often quarreled as young adolescents.

Why are some sibling relationships so filled with love and respect, whereas others are dominated by jealousy and resentment? Put more simply, what factors contribute to the quality of sibling relationships? Biological, psychological, and sociocultural forces all help determine how well siblings get along. Among the biological forces are the child's sex and temperament. Sibling relations are more likely to be warm and harmo-

In many cultures, older siblings regularly provide care for younger siblings.

Terri Wright

nious between siblings of the same sex than between siblings of the opposite sex (Dunn & Kendrick, 1981) and when neither sibling is temperamentally emotional (Brody, Stoneman, & McCoy, 1994). Age is also important: Sibling relationships generally improve as the younger child approaches adolescence because siblings begin to perceive one another as equals (Buhrmester & Furman, 1990).

Parents contribute to the quality of sibling relationships, both directly and indirectly (Brody, 1998). The direct influence stems from parents' treatment. Siblings more often get along when they believe that parents have no "favorites" but treat all siblings fairly (Kowal & Kramer, 1997). When parents lavishly praise one child's accomplishments while ignoring another's, children notice the difference, and their sibling relationship suffers (Updegraff et al., 2005).

This doesn't mean that parents must treat all their children the same. Children understand that parents should treat their kids differently—based on their age or personal needs. Only when differential treatment is not justified do sibling relationships deteriorate (Kowal & Kramer, 1997). In fact, during adolescence, siblings get along better when each has a unique, well-defined relationship with parents (Feinberg et al., 2003).

The indirect influence of parents on sibling relationships stems from the quality of the parents' relationship with each other: A warm, harmonious relationship between parents fosters positive sibling relationships; conflict between parents is associated with conflict between siblings (Erel, Margolin, & John, 1998; Volling & Belsky, 1992). When parents don't get along, they no longer treat their children the same, leading to conflict among siblings (Brody et al., 1994).

A biopsychosocial perspective on sibling relationships makes it clear that, in their pursuit of family harmony (what many parents call "peace and quiet"), parents can influence some of the factors affecting sibling relationships but not others. Parents *can* help reduce friction between siblings by being equally affectionate, responsive, and caring to all of their children, and by caring for one another. At the same time, parents (and prospective parents!) must realize that some dissension is natural in families, especially those with young boys and girls. Children's different interests lead to conflicts that youngsters cannot resolve because their social skills are limited.

Adopted Children

The U.S. government doesn't keep official statistics on the number of adopted children, but the best estimate is that 2 to 4% of U.S. children are adopted. The majority of adoptive parents are middle-class, European Americans, and until the 1960s so were adopted children. However, improved birth control and legalized abortion meant that few European American infants were relinquished for adoption. Consequently, parents began to adopt children from other races and from other countries. Also, adoption of children with special needs, such as those with chronic medical problems or exposure to maltreatment, became more common (Brodzinsky & Pinderhughes, 2002; Gunnar, Bruce, & Grotevant, 2000).

With these increases in adoptions, the myth of the "adopted child syndrome" blossomed. According to this myth, adopted children are more prone to behavioral problems, substance use, and criminal activity (Finley, 1999). Is there any truth to the myth? In fact, when compared to children living with biological parents, adopted children are quite similar in terms of temperament, mother-infant attachment, and cognitive development (Brodzinsky & Pinderhughes, 2002). Adopted children *are* more prone to problems adjusting to school and to conduct disorders, such as being overly aggressive (Miller et al., 2000). To a certain extent, this finding reflects the fact that adoptive parents are more likely to seek help for their adoptive children because they are more affluent and can afford it. Also, the extent of these problems hinges on the age when the

> **THINK ABOUT IT**
>
> Calvin, age 8, and his younger sister, Hope, argue over just about everything and constantly compete for their parents' attention. Teenage sisters Hillary and Elizabeth love doing everything together and enjoy sharing clothes and secrets about their teen romances. Why might Calvin and Hope get along so poorly but Elizabeth and Hillary get along so well?

Beginning in the 1960s, many European American parents adopted children from other racial and ethnic groups.

© Paul Conklin / PhotoEdit

child was adopted and the quality of care prior to adoption (Brodzinsky & Pinder-hughes, 2002; Gunnar et al., 2000). Problems are much more common when children are adopted at an older age (and thus probably separated from an attachment figure) and when their care before adoption was poor (e.g., they were institutionalized or lived in a series of foster homes).

Perhaps the best way to summarize this research is that adoption per se is not a fundamental developmental challenge for most children. But quality of life before adoption certainly places some adopted children at risk. And it's important to remember that most adopted children fare quite well.

Impact of Birth Order

First-born children are often "guinea pigs" for most parents, who have lots of enthusiasm but little practical experience rearing children. Parents typically have high expectations for their first-borns (Furman, 1995). They are both more affectionate and more punitive toward them. As more children arrive, most parents become more adept at their roles, having learned "the tricks of the trade" from earlier children. With later-born children, parents have more realistic expectations and are more relaxed in their discipline (Baskett, 1985).

The different approaches that parents use with their first- and later-born children help explain differences that are commonly observed between these children. First-born children generally have higher scores on intelligence tests and are more likely to go to college. They are also more willing to conform to parents' and adults' requests. In contrast, perhaps because later-born children are less concerned about pleasing parents and adults, they are more popular with their peers and more innovative (Herrera et al., 2003; Sulloway, 1995).

What about only children? According to conventional wisdom, parents dote on onlies, who therefore become selfish and egotistical. Is the folklore correct? In a comprehensive analysis of more than 100 studies, only children were not worse off than other children on any measure. In fact, only children were found to succeed more in school and to have higher levels of intelligence, leadership, autonomy, and maturity (Falbo & Polit, 1986).

This general pattern is not limited to only children in North America. In China, only children are common because of governmental efforts to limit population growth. Comparisons between only children and children with siblings often find no differences; when differences are found, the advantage usually goes to the only child (Jiao, Ji, & Jing, 1996; Yang et al., 1995). Thus, contrary to the popular stereotype, only children are not "spoiled brats" (nor, in China, are they "little emperors" who boss around parents, peers, and teachers). Instead, only children are, for the most part, much like children who grow up with siblings.

Contrary to the folklore, only children are often more mature and are smarter.

Whether U.S. children grow up with siblings or as onlies, they are more likely than children in other countries to have their family relationships disrupted by divorce. What is the impact of divorce on children and adolescents?

DIVORCE AND REMARRIAGE

In the 1990s, nearly half of all North American children experienced their parents' divorce (Amato, 2001). According to all theories of child development, divorce is distressing for children because it involves conflict between parents and, usually, separation from one of them. (Of course, divorce is also distressing to parents, as we describe in Chapter 11.) Do the disruptions, conflict, and stress associated with divorce affect children? Of course they do. Having answered this easy question, however, many more difficult questions remain: Are all aspects of children's lives affected equally by divorce? How does divorce influence development? Why is divorce more stressful for some children than for others?

What Aspects of Children's Lives Are Affected by Divorce?

By 2000, nearly 200 studies on divorce had been conducted, involving tens of thousands of preschool- through college-age children. Amato (2001; Amato & Keith, 1991) conducted comprehensive meta-analyses of this research. The outcome? In school achievement, conduct, adjustment, self-concept, and parent-child relations, children whose parents had divorced fared poorly compared to children from intact families. However, the effects of divorce dropped from the 1970s to the 1980s, perhaps because as divorce became more frequent in the 1980s it became more familiar and less frightening. The effects of divorce increased again in the 1990s, perhaps reflecting a widening gap in income between single- and two-parent families (Amato, 2001).

When children of divorced parents become adults, the effects of divorce persist. As adults, children of divorce are more likely to experience conflict in their own marriages, to have negative attitudes toward marriage, and to become divorced themselves. Also, they report less satisfaction with life and are more likely to become depressed (Hetherington & Kelly, 2002; Segrin, Taylor, & Altman, 2005). These findings don't mean that children of divorce are destined to have unhappy, conflict-ridden marriages that inevitably lead to divorce, but children of divorce are at greater risk for such an outcome.

The first year following a divorce is often rocky for parents and children alike. But beginning in the second year, most children begin to adjust to their new circumstances (Hetherington & Kelly, 2002). Children adjust to divorce more readily if their divorced parents cooperate with each other, especially on disciplinary matters (Buchanan & Heiges, 2001). *In **joint custody,** both parents retain legal custody of the children.* Children benefit from joint custody if their parents get along (Bauserman, 2002).

Of course, many parents do not get along after a divorce, which eliminates joint custody as an option. Traditionally, mothers have been awarded custody; but in recent years growing numbers of fathers have been given custody, especially of sons. This practice coincides with findings that children often adjust better when they live with same-sex parents: Boys often fare better with fathers and girls fare better with mothers (McLanahan, 1999). One reason boys are often better off with their fathers is that boys are likely to become involved in negative reinforcement traps (described on page 270) with their mothers. Another explanation is that both boys and girls may forge stronger emotional relationships with same-sex parents than with opposite-sex parents (Zimiles & Lee, 1991).

How Does Divorce Influence Development?

Divorce usually results in several changes to family life that affect children (Amato & Keith, 1991). First, the absence of one parent means that children lose a role model, a source of parental help and emotional support, and a supervisor. For instance, a single parent may have to choose between helping one child complete an important paper or watching another child perform in a school play. She can't do both, and one child will miss out.

Second, single-parent families experience economic hardship, which creates stress and often means that activities once taken for granted are no longer affordable (Goodman, Emery, & Haugaard, 1998). A family may no longer be able to pay for books for pleasure reading, music lessons, or other activities that promote child development. Moreover, when a single parent worries about having enough money for food and rent, she has less energy and effort to devote to parenting.

Third, conflict between parents is extremely distressing to children and adolescents (Leon, 2003), particularly for children who are emotionally insecure (Davies & Cummings, 1998). In fact, many of the problems ascribed to divorce are really caused by marital conflict occurring before the divorce (Erel & Burman, 1995; Shaw, Winslow, & Flanagan, 1999). Children whose parents are married but fight constantly often show many of the same effects associated with divorce (Katz & Woodin, 2002).

WHICH CHILDREN ARE MOST AFFECTED BY DIVORCE? Why are some children more affected by divorce than others? Amato and Keith's (1991) analysis, for example, showed that although the overall impact of divorce is the same for boys and girls, divorce is more harmful when it occurs during childhood and adolescence than during the preschool or college years. Also, children who are temperamentally more emotional tend to be more affected by divorce (Lengua et al., 1999).

Some children suffer more from divorce because of their tendency to interpret events negatively. Suppose, for example, that a father forgets to take a child on a promised outing. One child might believe that an emergency prevented the father from taking the child. A second child might believe that the father hadn't really wanted to spend time with the child in the first place and will never make similar plans again. Children like the second child—who tend to interpret life events negatively—are more likely to have behavioral problems following divorce (Mazur et al., 1999).

Finally, when children actively cope with problems brought on by divorce—either by trying to solve them or by trying to make them feel less threatening—they gain confidence in their ability to control future events in their lives. This confidence acts as a buffer against anxiety or depression, which can be triggered when children feel that problems brought on by divorce are insurmountable (Sandler et al., 2000).

Just as children can reduce the harm of divorce by being active problem solvers, parents can reduce divorce-related stress and help children adjust to their new life circumstances. Parents should explain together to children why they are divorcing and what their children can expect to happen to them. They should reassure children that they will always love them and always be their parents; parents must back up these words with actions by remaining involved in their children's lives despite the increased difficulty of doing so. Finally, parents must expect that their children will sometimes be angry or sad about the divorce, and they should encourage children to discuss these feelings with them.

To help children deal with divorce, parents should *not* compete with each other for their children's love and attention; children adjust to divorce best when they maintain good relationships with both parents. Parents should neither take out their anger with each other on their children nor criticize their ex-spouse in front of the children. Finally, parents should not ask children to mediate disputes; parents should work out problems without putting the children in the middle.

Following all these rules all the time is not easy. After all, divorce is stressful and painful for adults too. But parents owe it to their children to try to follow most of these rules most of the time to minimize the disruptive effects of divorce on their children's development.

Following divorce, most men and women remarry, creating a blended family.

© David Young-Wolff/PhotoEdit

Blended Families

Following divorce, most children live in a single-parent household for about 5 years. However, more than two thirds of men and women eventually remarry (Glick, 1989; Glick & Lin, 1986). *The resulting unit, consisting of a biological parent, stepparent, and children, is known as a **blended family.*** (Other terms for this family configuration are "remarried family" and "reconstituted family.")

Because mothers are more often granted custody of children, the most common form of blended family is a mother, her children, and a stepfather. Most stepfathers do not participate actively in child rearing; they often seem reluctant to become involved (Clarke-Stewart & Bretano, 2005). Nevertheless, boys typically benefit from the presence of a stepfather, particularly when he is warm and involved. Preadolescent girls, however, do not adjust readily to their mother's remarriage, apparently because it disrupts the intimate relationship they have established with her (Bray, 1999; Visher, Visher, & Pasley, 2003).

These adjustments are more difficult when mothers of adolescents remarry. Adolescents do not adapt to the new family circumstances as easily as children do; they're more likely to challenge a stepfather's authority. And adjustment is more difficult when a stepfather brings his own biological children. In such families, parents sometimes favor their biological children over their stepchildren—they're more involved with and warmer toward their biological children. Such preferential treatment almost always leads to conflict and unhappiness (Dunn & Davies, 2001; Hetherington, Bridges, & Insabella, 1998). And when the mother and stepfather argue, children usually side with their biological parents (Dunn, O'Connor, & Cheng, 2005).

The best strategy for stepfathers is to be interested in their new stepchildren but avoid encroaching on established relationships. Newly remarried mothers must be careful that their enthusiasm for their new spouse does not come at the expense of time and affection for their children. And both parents and children need to have realistic expectations. The blended family can be successful, but it takes effort because of the complicated relationships, conflicting loyalties, and jealousies that usually exist (Anderson et al., 1999; White & Gilbreth, 2001).

Much less is known about blended families consisting of a father, his children, and a stepmother, though several factors make a father's remarriage difficult for his children. First, fathers are often awarded custody when judges believe that children are unruly and will profit from a father's "firm hand." Consequently, many children living with their fathers do not adjust well to many of life's challenges, which certainly includes a father's remarriage. Second, fathers are sometimes granted custody because they have a particularly close relationship with their children, especially their sons. When this is the case, children sometimes fear that their father's remarriage will disturb their relationship (Buchanan, Maccoby, & Dornbusch, 1996). Finally, noncustodial mothers are more likely than noncustodial fathers to maintain close and frequent contact with their children (Maccoby et al., 1993). The constant presence of the noncustodial mother may interfere with a stepmother's efforts to establish close relationships with her stepchildren, particularly with her stepdaughters.

Over time, children adjust to the blended family. If the marriage is happy, most children profit from the presence of two caring adults. Unfortunately, second marriages are slightly more likely than first marriages to end in divorce, so many children relive the trauma. As you can imagine, another divorce—and possibly another remarriage—severely disrupts children's development, accentuating the problems that followed the initial divorce (Dunn, 2002).

Regrettably, divorce is not the only way that parents can disturb their children's development. As you'll see in the next few pages, some parents harm their children more directly, by abusing them.

PARENT-CHILD RELATIONSHIPS GONE AWRY: CHILD ABUSE

The first time that 7-year-old Max came to school with bruises on his face, he explained to his teacher that he had fallen down the basement steps. When Max had similar bruises a few weeks later, his teacher spoke with the school principal, who contacted local authorities. It turned out that Max's mother thrashed him with a paddle for even minor misconduct; for serious transgressions, she beat Max and made him sleep alone in a dark, unheated basement.

Unfortunately, cases like Max's occur far too often. Maltreatment comes in many forms (Cicchetti & Toth, 2006):

- *Physical abuse,* involving assault that leads to injuries including cuts, welts, bruises, and broken bones
- *Sexual abuse,* involving fondling, intercourse, or other sexual behaviors
- *Psychological abuse,* involving ridicule, rejection, or humiliation
- *Neglect,* in which children do not receive adequate food, clothing, or medical care

The frequency of child maltreatment is difficult to estimate because so many cases go unreported. According to the U.S. Department of Health and Human Services (2005), approximately 1 million children annually suffer maltreatment or neglect. About 60% are neglected, about 20% are abused physically, about 10% are abused sexually, and 10% are maltreated psychologically.

Who Are the Abusing Parents?

Parents who abuse their children were once thought to be severely disturbed or deranged. Today, we know that the vast majority of abusing parents cannot be distinguished from other parents in terms of standard psychiatric criteria (Wolfe, 1985). In fact, modern explanations of child abuse no longer look to a single or even a small number of causes. Instead, a host of factors combine to place some children at risk for abuse and to protect others; the number and combination of factors determine whether the child is a likely target for abuse (Cicchetti & Toth, 2006). Let's look at three of the most important factors: those associated with the cultural context, those associated with parents, and those associated with children themselves.

The most general category of contributing factors are those dealing with cultural values and the social conditions in which parents rear their children. Many countries in Europe and Asia have strong cultural prohibitions against physical punishment. It simply isn't done and would be viewed in much the same way we would view an American parent who punished by not feeding the child for a few days. In Sweden, for example, spanking is against the law, and children can report their parents to the police. But spanking is common in the United States. Countries that do not condone physical punishment tend to have lower rates of child maltreatment than the United States (U.S. Department of State, 2002).

What social conditions seem to foster maltreatment? Poverty is one. Maltreatment is more common among children living in poverty, in part because lack of money increases the stress of daily life (Coulton et al., 1995). When parents are worrying about whether they can buy groceries or pay rent, they are more likely to punish their children physically instead of making the extra effort to reason with them.

Social isolation is a second force. Abuse is more likely when families are socially isolated from other relatives or neighbors. When a family lives in relative isolation, it deprives children of adults who could protect them and deprives parents of social support that would help them better deal with life's stresses (Coulton, Korbin, & Su, 1999).

Cultural factors clearly contribute to child abuse, but they are only part of the puzzle. Although maltreatment *is* more common among families living in poverty, it does not occur in a majority of these families, and it does occur in middle- and upper-

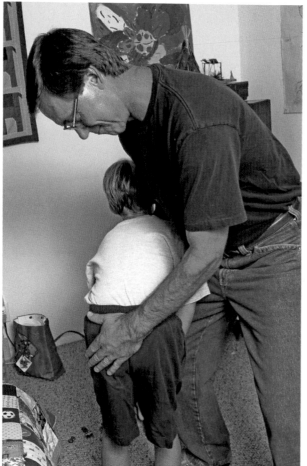

Child abuse is more common in societies that condone physical punishment.

© Cindy Charles/PhotoEdit

class families too. Consequently, we need to look for additional factors to explain why abuse occurs in some families but not in others.

Child development researchers have identified several important factors (Azar, 2002; Bugental & Happaney, 2004). First, parents who maltreat their children often were maltreated themselves, which may lead them to believe that abuse is simply a normal part of childhood. This does not mean that abused children inevitably become abusing parents—only about one third do. But a history of child abuse clearly places adults at risk for mistreating their own children (Cicchetti & Toth, 2006; Serbin & Karp, 2003). Second, parents who mistreat their children often use ineffective parenting techniques (e.g., inconsistent discipline), have such unrealistic expectations that their children can never meet them, and often believe that they are powerless to control their children. For example, when abusive parents do not get along with their children, they often chalk this up to factors out of their control, such as children having a difficult temperament or being tired that day; they're less likely to think that their own behavior contributed to unpleasant interactions. Third, in families where abuse occurs, the couple's interactions are often unpredictable, unsupportive, and unsatisfying for both husbands and wives. In other words, mistreatment of children is simply one symptom of family dysfunction. This marital discord makes life more stressful and more difficult for parents to invest effort in child rearing.

To place the last few pieces in the puzzle, we must look at the abused children themselves. Our earlier discussion of the reciprocal influence between parents and children should remind you that children may inadvertently, through their behavior, contribute to their own abuse. In fact, infants and preschoolers are more often abused than older children, probably because they are less able to regulate aversive behaviors that may elicit abuse (Sidebotham et al., 2003). You've probably heard stories about a parent who shakes a baby to death because the baby wouldn't stop crying. Because younger children are more likely to cry or whine excessively—behaviors that irritate all parents sooner or later—they are more likely to be the targets of abuse.

For much the same reason, children who are frequently ill are more often abused. When children are sick, they're more likely to cry and whine, annoying parents. Also, when children are sick, they need medical care (which means additional expense) and can't go to school (which often means that working parents must arrange alternative child care). Because sick children increase the level of stress in a family, they can inadvertently become the targets of abuse. By behaving immaturely or being ill, children unintentionally place themselves at risk for maltreatment (Rogosch et al., 1995).

Stepchildren form another group at risk for abuse (Daly & Wilson, 1996). Just as Cinderella's stepmother doted on her biological children but abused Cinderella, so stepchildren are more prone to abuse and neglect than biological children. Adults are less invested emotionally in their stepchildren, and this lack of emotional investment leaves stepchildren more vulnerable.

Thus, cultural, parental, and child factors all contribute to child maltreatment. Any single factor will usually not result in abuse. For instance, a sick infant who cries constantly would not be maltreated in countries where physical punishment is not tolerated. Maltreatment becomes a possibility only when cultures condone physical punishment, parents lack effective skills for dealing with children, and a child's behavior is frequently aversive.

Effects of Abuse on Children

You probably aren't surprised to learn that the prognosis for youngsters like Max is not very good. Some, of course, suffer permanent physical damage. Even when there is no lasting physical damage, the children's social and emotional development is often disrupted. They tend to have poor relationships with peers, often because they are too aggressive (Bolger & Patterson, 2001; Cicchetti & Toth, 2006). Their cognitive development and academic performance are also disturbed. Abused youngsters tend to get lower grades in school, score lower on standardized achievement tests, and be retained in a grade rather than promoted. Also, school-related behavior problems, such as being disruptive in class, are common, in part because maltreated children don't regulate their emotions well (Maughan & Cicchetti, 2002; Shonk & Cicchetti, 2001).

Adults who were abused as children often experience emotional problems such as depression or anxiety, are more prone to think about or attempt suicide, and are more likely to abuse spouses and their own children (Malinosky-Rummell & Hansen, 1993). In short, when children are maltreated, virtually all aspects of their development are affected, and these effects do not vanish with time.

Some children are less affected by maltreatment than others. For example, in one study of children who had been abused sexually (Lynsky & Fergusson, 1997), approximately 75% of these children as adults had psychiatric disorders or adjustment difficulties, such as depression, anxiety, and substance abuse. However, 25% reported no problems of this sort. Why did these individuals escape the harm that was typical for sexual abuse? Two factors contributed: One was the adolescent peer group, and the other was the relationship with the father. Specifically, sexually abused children were more likely to avoid long-term difficulties when (a) as adolescents they avoided delinquent or substance-abusing peers, and (b) their father was supportive, caring, and nurturant. Thus, the type of peers and the type of father-child relationship can help to mitigate the long-term consequences of childhood sexual abuse.

Preventing Abuse and Maltreatment

The complexity of child abuse dashes any hopes for a simple solution. Because maltreatment is more apt to occur when several contributing factors are present, eradicating child maltreatment requires many different approaches.

American attitudes toward "acceptable" levels of punishment and poverty would have to change. American children will be abused as long as physical punishment is considered acceptable and effective and as long as poverty-stricken families live in chronic stress from simply trying to provide food and shelter. Parents also need counseling and training in parenting skills. Abuse will continue as long as parents remain ignorant of effective methods of parenting and discipline.

It would be naive to expect all of these changes to occur overnight. However, by focusing on some of the more manageable factors, the risk of maltreatment can be reduced. Social supports help. When parents know they can turn to other helpful adults for advice and reassurance, they better manage the stresses of child rearing that might otherwise lead to abuse. And families can be taught more effective ways of coping with situations that might otherwise trigger abuse (Wicks-Nelson & Israel, 2006). Through role-playing sessions, parents can learn the benefits of authoritative parenting and effective ways of using feedback and modeling to regulate children's behavior.

Providing social supports and teaching effective parenting are typically done when maltreatment and abuse have already occurred. Of course, preventing maltreatment in the first place is more desirable and more cost-effective. For prevention, one useful tool is familiar—early childhood intervention programs. That is, maltreatment and abuse can be cut in half when families participate for 2 or more years in intervention programs that include preschool education along with family support activities aimed at encouraging parents to become more involved in their children's education (Reynolds & Robertson, 2003). When parents participate in these programs, they become more committed to their children's education. This leads their children to be more successful in school, reducing a source of stress and enhancing parents' confidence in their child-rearing skills, reducing the risks of maltreatment in the process.

Finally, we need to remember that most parents who have mistreated their children need our help. Although we must not tolerate child maltreatment, most of these parents and children are attached to each other; maltreatment is a consequence of ignorance and burden, not malice.

TEST YOURSELF

1. According to the systems approach, the family consists of interacting elements that influence each other, and the family itself is _____.

2. A(n) _____ parental style combines high control with low involvement.

3. Most children seem to benefit when parents rely on a(n) _____ style.

4. Parental behaviors that influence children include direct instruction, modeling (learning through observation), and _____.

5. Some parents do not make a good team: they don't work together, they compete with each other for their children's attention, and _____.

6. With later-born children, parents often have more realistic expectations and are _____.

7. Among the effects of divorce on children are inadequate supervision of children, conflict between parents, and _____.

8. When mothers remarry, daughters do not adjust as readily as sons because _____.

9. Children are more likely to be abused when they are younger and when they are _____.

How can child abuse be explained in terms of the biological, psychological, and sociocultural forces in the biopsychosocial framework?

Answers: (1) embedded in other social systems, such as neighborhoods, (2) authoritarian, (3) authoritative, (4) feedback (reward and punishment), (5) they limit each other's access to the child, (6) more relaxed in their discipline, (7) economic hardship, (8) the remarriage disrupts an intimate mother–daughter relationship, (9) often ill

---

7.2

PEERS

- -

Only 36 hours had passed since the campers arrived at Crab Orchard Summer Camp. Nevertheless, groups had already formed spontaneously based on the campers' main interests: arts and crafts, hiking, and swimming. Within each group, leaders and followers had already emerged. This happens every year, but the staff is always astonished at how quickly a "social network" emerges at camp.

LEARNING OBJECTIVES

What are the benefits of friendship?

What are the important features of groups of children and adolescents? How do these groups influence individuals?

Why are some children more popular than others? What are the causes and consequences of being rejected?

Why are some children so aggressive? Why are others frequent targets of aggression?

THE GROUPS THAT FORM AT SUMMER CAMPS—as well as in schools and neighborhoods—represent one of the more complex forms of peer relationships: Many children are involved, and there are multiple relationships. We'll examine these kinds of interactions later in this section. Let's start by looking at a simpler social relationship, friendship.

FRIENDSHIPS

Over time children develop special relationships with certain peers. *Friendship is a voluntary relationship between two people involving mutual liking.* By age 4 or 5, most children claim to have a "best friend." If you ask them how they can tell a child is their best friend, their response will probably resemble 5-year-old Katelyn's:

INTERVIEWER: Why is Heidi your best friend?
KATELYN: Because she plays with me. And she's nice to me.
INTERVIEWER: Are there any other reasons?
KATELYN: Yeah, Heidi lets me play with her dolls.

Thus, the key elements of friendship for younger children are that children like each other and enjoy playing together.

As children develop, their friendships become more complex. For older elementary-school children (ages 8 to 11), mutual liking and shared activities are joined by features that are more psychological in nature—trust and assistance. At this age, children expect that they can depend on their friends—their friends will be nice to them, will keep their promises, and won't say mean things about them to others. And they expect friends to step forward in times of need: A friend should willingly help with homework or willingly share a snack.

Adolescence adds another layer of complexity to friendships. Mutual liking, common interests, and trust remain. In fact, trust becomes even more important in adolescent friendships. New to adolescence is intimacy—friends now confide in one another, sharing personal thoughts and feelings. Teenagers will reveal their excitement over a new romance or disappointment at not being cast in a school musical. Intimacy is more common in friendships among girls, who are more likely than boys to have one exclusive "best friend" (Markovits, Benenson, & Dolenszky, 2001). Because intimacy is at the core of their friendships, girls are also more likely to be concerned about the faithfulness of their friends and worry about being rejected (Benenson & Christakos, 2003).

The emergence of intimacy in adolescent friendships means that friends also come to be seen as sources of social and emotional support. Elementary-school children generally rely on close family members—parents, siblings, and grandparents—as primary sources of support when they need help or are bothered by something. But adolescents turn to close friends instead. Because adolescent friends share intimate thoughts and feelings, they can provide support during emotional or stressful periods (Levitt, Guacci-Franco, & Levitt, 1993).

Hand in hand with the emphasis on intimacy is loyalty. Having confided in friends, adolescents expect friends to stick with them through good and bad times. If a friend is disloyal, adolescents are afraid that they may be humiliated because their intimate thoughts and feelings will become known to a much broader circle of people (Berndt & Perry, 1990).

Who Are Friends?

Most friends are alike in age, gender, and race (Hamm, 2000). Because friends are supposed to treat each other as equals, friendships are rare between an older, more experienced child and a younger, less experienced child. Because children typically play with same-sex peers, boys and girls rarely become friends.

Friendships are more common between children from the same race or ethnic group than between children from different groups, reflecting racial segregation in American society. Friendships among children of different groups are more common in schools where classes are smaller (Hallinan & Teixeira, 1987) and when a child's school and neighborhood are ethnically diverse (Quillian & Campbell, 2003).

Friends tend to be alike in age, race, and sex.

© David Young-Wolff/PhotoEdit

Children and adolescents are also drawn together because they have similar attitudes toward school, recreation, and the future (Newcomb & Bagwell, 1995). Tom, who enjoys school, likes to read, and plans to go to Harvard, will probably not befriend Barry, who thinks that school is stupid, listens to his MP3 player constantly, and plans to quit high school to become a rock star (Haselager et al., 1998). As time passes, friends become more similar in their attitudes and values (Berndt & Murphy, 2002). Nevertheless, friends are not photocopies of each other; friends are less similar, for example, than spouses or fraternal twins (Rushton & Bons, 2005).

Although children's friendships are overwhelmingly with members of their own sex, a few children have friendships with opposite-sex children. Who are these children, and why do they have opposite-sex friendships? Boys and girls are equally likely to have opposite-sex friendships. The important factor in understanding these children is whether they have same- *and* opposite-sex friends or *only* opposite-sex friends. Children with same- and opposite-sex friendships tend to be very well adjusted, whereas children with only opposite-sex friendships tend to be unpopular, less competent academically and socially, and have lower self-esteem. Apparently, children with both same- and opposite-sex friends are so socially skilled and popular that both boys and girls are eager to be their friends. In contrast, children with only opposite-sex friendships are socially unskilled, unpopular youngsters who are rejected by their same-sex peers and form friendships with opposite-sex children as a last resort (Kovacs, Parker, & Hoffman, 1996).

Quality and Consequences of Friendships

If you think back to your childhood friendships, you probably remember some that were long-lasting and satisfying as well as others that rapidly wore thin and soon dissolved. What accounts for these differences in the quality and longevity of friendships? Sometimes friendships are brief because children lack the skills to sustain them (Jiao, 1999; Parker & Seal, 1996). As friends they can't keep secrets, or they're too bossy. Sometimes friendships end because, when conflicts arise, children are more concerned about their own interests and are unwilling to compromise or negotiate (Fonzi et al., 1997; Rose & Asher, 1999). And, sometimes friendships end when children discover that their needs and interests aren't as similar as they thought initially (Gavin & Furman, 1996).

When youth have good friends, they're better able to cope with life's stresses.

Considering that friendships disintegrate for many reasons, you're probably reminded that truly good friends are to be treasured. In fact, researchers consistently find that children benefit from having good friends (Berndt & Murphy, 2002). Compared to children who lack friends, children with good friends have higher self-esteem, are less likely to be lonely and depressed, and more often act prosocially—sharing and cooperating with others (Hartup & Stevens, 1999; Ladd, 1998). Children with good friends cope better with life stresses, such as the transition from elementary school to middle school or junior high (Berndt & Keefe, 1995), and they're less likely to be victimized by peers (Hodges et al., 1999). The benefits of friendship are also long-lasting: Children who have friends have greater self-worth as young adults (Bagwell, Newcomb, & Bukowski, 1998).

We need to recognize, however, that not all friendships are beneficial for children and adolescents (Bagwell, 2004). For example, when aggressive children are friends, they become more antisocial as time goes by (Dishion, Poulin, & Burraston, 2001). Similarly, when teens engage in risky behavior (e.g., they drink, smoke, or have sex), they often encourage each other's risky behavior (Curran, Stice, & Chassin, 1997). The Spotlight on Research feature describes a study that shows this impact of friends.

© Image Source/Alamy

SPOTLIGHT ON RESEARCH

INFLUENCE OF BEST FRIENDS ON SEXUAL ACTIVITY

Who were the investigators, and what was the aim of the study? James Jaccard, Hart Blanton, and Tonya Dodge (2005) set out to determine whether close friends influence adolescents' sexual behavior. That is, they wanted to know whether adolescents were more likely to be sexually active when their closest same-sex friend was sexually active.

How did the investigators measure the topic of interest? Jaccard and his colleagues used data from the Add Health database, which includes information obtained from more than 20,000 U.S. adolescents in grades 7 through 12 who completed questionnaires and were interviewed on a wide range of topics concerning adolescent health and development. Jaccard and colleagues focused on two variables: Best friends were determined by asking adolescents to name five same-sex friends and then indicate the time spent with each in the past week. Sexual activity was determined by asking teens whether they had ever had sexual intercourse, and, if so, how recently.

Who were the children in the study? The investigators focused on a subsample of nearly 1,700 adolescents —837 boys, 851 girls—who were interviewed twice and who were not married.

What was the design of the study? This study was correlational because Jaccard and colleagues were interested in the relation that existed naturally between two variables: whether an adolescent was sexually active and whether an adolescent's best friend was sexually active. The study was longitudinal because adolescents were interviewed twice, approximately a year apart.

Were there ethical concerns with the study? You bet. This is one of the few human development studies that's been debated on the floor of the U.S. Congress! The initial version of the project, proposed in the late 1980s, was motivated by the growing AIDS epidemic and focused solely on adolescent sexual risk-taking. After the National Institutes of Health (NIH) decided to fund the project, many conservative groups protested, arguing that the project actually endorsed the adolescent sexual behaviors that it was designed to study. The NIH withdrew the funds, but a compromise was reached in 1993: Congress passed legislation calling for a much broader longitudinal study, one that would examine adolescent health and well-being, the factors that jeopardize adolescent health, and behaviors that promote health. The result was the National Longitudinal Study of Adolescent Health, or Add Health for short.

Parents and adolescents both gave consent to participate. In addition, the Add Health project has gone to great lengths to ensure that no individual's name can be linked to his or her responses to any question. For example, for questions on sensitive topics, adolescents listened to questions played on a tape recorder, and the answers were entered directly into a laptop computer.

What were the results? When adolescents were interviewed the first time, the correlation between an adolescent being sexually active and an adolescent's best friend being sexually active was .34 for boys and .40 for girls. This shows a tendency for best friends to be alike in their sexual experience. But are adolescents more likely to be sexually active when their best friends are? The investigators answered this question by examining adolescents' sexual activity over the year. They found that when best friends were sexually active over the year, 56% of adolescents were sexu-

ally active during the same period; in contrast, when best friends were sexually inactive, only 24% of adolescents were sexually active. Thus, over time, adolescents were more likely to be sexually active when their best friend was too. This was true for adolescents who were sexually active at the initial interview as well as for those who had been inactive sexually.

What did the investigators conclude? Adolescent friendships are based on similarity and, once formed, like-minded friends can encourage and support each other's behavior. In this case, they can support each other's sexual activity or inactivity. However, friendships are not all-powerful in this regard. When adolescents' best friends were sexually active over the year, 56% of the adolescents followed their friends in becoming sexually active, but 44% did not. As Jaccard et al. put it, "adolescent peer and social networks exert considerable impact on a wide range of behaviors, such as musical interests, clothing preference, and extracurricular activities. . . . [However,] peer influence is just one of a number of factors that contribute to adolescent risk behavior" (p. 144).

What converging evidence would strengthen these conclusions? One useful step would be to continue the longitudinal study to examine the influence of friends over a longer term. Another important addition would be to examine the impact of an extended peer network, not simply an adolescent's best friend.

To enhance your understanding of this research, go to http://psychology .wadsworth.com/kail_cavanaugh4e/ to complete critical thinking questions and explore related websites.

Thus, friends are one important way in which peers influence children's development. Peers also influence development through groups, the topic of the next section.

GROUPS

At the summer camp in the vignette, new campers form groups based on common interests. Groups are just as prevalent in American schools. "Jocks," "preps," "burnouts," "druggies," "nerds," and "brains"—you may remember these or similar terms referring to groups of older children and adolescents. During late childhood and early adolescence, the peer group becomes the focal point of social relationships for youth (Rubin, Bukowski, & Parker, 1998). *The starting point is often a* **clique**—*a small group of children or adolescents who are friends and tend to be similar in age, sex, race, and attitudes.* Members of a clique spend time together and often dress, talk, and act alike. *Several cliques that have similar values and attitudes sometimes become part of a larger group called a* **crowd,** *known by a label such as "jocks" or "nerds."*

Some crowds have more status than others. For example, students in many junior and senior high schools say that the "jocks" are the most prestigious crowd, whereas the "burnouts" are among the least prestigious. Self-esteem in older children and adolescents often reflects the status of their crowd. During the school years, young people from high-status crowds tend to have greater self-esteem than those from low-status crowds (Brown & Lohr, 1987).

Why do some students become nerds but others join the burnouts? Parenting style is part of the answer. A study by Brown and his colleagues (1993) examined the impact of three parental practices on students' membership in particular crowds. The investigators measured the extent to which parents emphasized academic achievement, monitored their children's out-of-school activities, and involved their children in joint decision making. When parents emphasized achievement, their children were more likely to be in the popular, jock, and normal crowds and less likely to be in the druggie crowd. When parents monitored their children's out-of-school behavior, their children were more likely to be in the brain crowd and less likely to be in the druggie crowd. Finally, when parents included their children in joint decision making, their children were more likely to be in the brain and normal crowds and less likely to be in the druggie crowd. These relations were true for African American, Asian American, European American, and Hispanic American children and their parents.

What seems to happen is that when parents use the practices associated with authoritative parenting—control coupled with warmth—their children become involved with crowds that endorse adult standards of behavior (e.g., normals, jocks, brains). However, when parents' style is uninvolved or indulgent, their children are less likely to identify with adult standards of behavior. In fact, they become involved with crowds like druggies, who disavow these standards.

Group Structure

Groups—be they in school, at a summer camp as in the vignette, or elsewhere—typically have a well-defined structure. *Often groups have a* **dominance hierarchy,** *headed by a leader to whom all other members of the group defer.* Other members know their position in the hierarchy. They yield to members who are above them in the hierarchy and assert themselves over members who are below them. A dominance hierarchy is useful in reducing conflict within groups because every member knows his or her place.

What determines where members stand in the hierarchy? In children, especially boys, physical power is often the basis for the dominance hierarchy. The leader is usually the member who is the most intimidating physically (Hawley, 1999). Among girls and older boys, hierarchies are often based on individual traits that relate to the group's main function. At Crab Orchard Summer Camp, for example, the leaders are most often the children with the greatest camping experience. Among Girl Scouts, girls chosen to be patrol leaders tend to be bright and goal-oriented and to have new ideas (Edwards, 1994). These characteristics are appropriate, because the primary function of patrols is to help plan activities for an entire troop of Girl Scouts. Thus, this type of group structure is effective; the people with the most useful skills have the greatest influence (Rubin et al., 1998).

Group leaders tend to be those who have skills valuable to the group: Girl Scout patrol leaders, for example, tend to be goal-oriented and have good ideas.

© Mary Kate Denny/PhotoEdit

THINK ABOUT IT

Chapter 5 described important differences in the ways that boys and girls interact with same-sex peers. How might these differences help explain why boys' and girls' dominance hierarchies differ?

Peer Pressure

Groups establish norms—standards of behavior that apply to all group members—and may pressure members to conform to these norms. Such "peer pressure" is often characterized as an irresistible, harmful force. The stereotype is that teenagers exert enormous pressure on each other to behave antisocially. In reality, peer pressure is neither all-powerful nor always evil. For example, most junior and senior high students *resist* peer pressure to behave in ways that are clearly antisocial, such as stealing (Brown, Lohr, & McClenahan, 1986). Peer pressure can be positive too, urging peers to participate in school activities, such as trying out for a play or working on the yearbook, or becoming involved in community-action projects, such as Habitat for Humanity. Peer pressure is most powerful when the standards for appropriate behavior are not clear-cut. Tastes in music and clothing, for example, are completely subjective; consequently, youth conform to peer group guidelines.

Similarly, standards concerning smoking, drinking, and using drugs are often fuzzy. Drinking is a good case in point. Parents and groups like SADD (Students Against Driving Drunk) may discourage teens from drinking, yet American culture is filled with youthful models who drink, seem to enjoy it, and suffer no apparent ill effects. To the contrary, they seem to enjoy life even more. With such contradictory messages, it is not surprising that youth look to their peers for answers (Urberg, Değirmencioğlu, & Pilgrim, 1997). Consequently, some youth *will* drink (or smoke, use drugs, have sex) to conform to *their* group's norms; others will abstain, again, reflecting their group's norms.

Even when standards are fuzzy, not all teenagers are equally susceptible to peer influence (Vitaro et al., 1997). Adolescents are less likely to be influenced by peer pressure when their parents use an authoritative style and more likely to be influenced when their parents are not authoritative (Mounts & Steinberg, 1995).

POPULARITY AND REJECTION

Eileen is, without question, the most popular child in her fourth-grade class. Most of the other youngsters like to play with her and want to sit near her at lunch or on the school bus. Whenever the class must vote to pick a child for something special—to be class representative to the student council, to recite the class poem on Martin Luther King Day, or to lead the classroom to the lunchroom—Eileen invariably wins.

Peer pressure is greatest in areas where standards are fuzzy, such as style of clothing.

© Spencer Grant/PhotoEdit

Jay is not as fortunate as Eileen. In fact, he is the least popular child in the class. His presence is obviously unwanted in any situation. When he sits down at the lunch table, other kids move away. When he tries to join a game of four-square, the others quit. Students in the class detest Jay as much as they like Eileen.

Popular and rejected children like Eileen and Jay are common. In fact, studies of popularity (Hymel et al., 2004) reveal that most children in elementary-school classrooms can be placed, fairly consistently, in one of these five categories:

- *Popular children* are liked by many classmates.
- *Rejected children* are disliked by many classmates.
- *Controversial children* are both liked and disliked by classmates.
- *Average children* are liked and disliked by some classmates, but without the intensity found for popular, rejected, or controversial children.
- *Neglected children* are ignored by classmates.

Of these categories, we know most about popular and rejected children. Each of these categories actually includes two subtypes. Most popular children are skilled academically and socially. They are good students who are usually friendly, cooperative, and helpful. They are more skillful at communicating and better at integrating themselves into an ongoing conversation or play session—they "fit in" instead of "barging in" (Rubin, Bukowski, & Parker, 2006). A smaller group of popular children includes physically aggressive boys who pick fights with peers and relationally aggressive girls who, like the "Plastics" in the film *Mean Girls,* thrive on manipulating social relationships. Although these youth are not particularly friendly, their antisocial behavior nevertheless apparently has a certain appeal to peers (Cillesen & Rose, 2005; Rose, Swenson, & Waller, 2004).

Being well liked seems straightforward: Be pleasant and friendly, not obnoxious. Share, cooperate, and help instead of being disruptive. These results don't apply just to American children; they hold for children in many areas of the world, including Canada, Europe, Israel, and China. Sometimes, however, popular children have other characteristics unique to their cultural setting. In Israel, for example, popular children are more likely to be assertive and direct than in other countries (Krispin, Sternberg, & Lamb, 1992). In China, popular children are more likely to be shy than in other countries (Chen, Rubin, & Li, 1995). Evidently, good social skills are at the core of popularity in most countries, but other features are important, reflecting culturally specific values.

> **THINK ABOUT IT**
>
> Effective parents and popular children have many characteristics in common. What are they?

As for rejected children, many are overly aggressive, hyperactive, socially unskilled, and unable to regulate their emotions. These children are usually much more hostile than popular-aggressive children and seem to be aggressive for the sheer fun of it—which peers dislike—instead of using aggression as a means toward other ends—which peers may not actually like but grudgingly respect (Prinstein & Cillessen, 2003). Other rejected children are shy, withdrawn, timid, and, not surprisingly, lonely (Asher & Paquette, 2003; Hart et al., 2000).

Causes and Consequences of Rejection

No one enjoys being rejected. For children, repeated peer rejection in childhood can have serious long-term consequences less often seen in other groups, including dropping out of school, committing juvenile offenses, and suffering from psychopathology (Bagwell et al., 1998; Rubin et al., 1998).

Peer rejection can be traced, at least in part, to the influences of parents (Ladd, 1998). As expected from Bandura's social cognitive theory, children see how their parents respond in different social situations and often imitate these responses later. Parents who are friendly and cooperative with others demonstrate effective social skills for their youngsters. Parents who are belligerent and combative demonstrate tactics that are much less effective. In particular, when parents typically respond to interpersonal conflict with intimidation or aggression, their children may imitate them, hampering

Some rejected children learn ineffective social skills by watching parents who use intimidation or conflict in their own relationship.

the development of their social skills and making them less popular in the long run (Keane, Brown, & Crenshaw, 1990).

Parents also contribute to their children's social skills and popularity through their disciplinary practices. Inconsistent discipline—punishing a child for misbehaving one day and ignoring the same behavior the next—is associated with antisocial, aggressive behavior, paving the way for rejection. Consistent punishment that does not rely on power assertion but is tied to parental love and affection is more likely to promote social skills and, in the process, popularity (Dekovic & Janssens, 1992; Rubin, Stewart, & Chen, 1995).

Thus, the origins of rejection are clear: Socially awkward, aggressive children are often rejected because they rely on an aggressive interpersonal style, which can be traced to parenting. The implication is that by teaching youngsters (and their parents) more effective ways of interacting with others, we can make rejection less likely. With improved social skills, rejected children would not need to resort to antisocial behaviors that peers deplore. Training of this sort *does* work. Rejected children can learn skills that lead to peer acceptance and thereby avoid the long-term harm associated with being rejected (La-Greca, 1993; Mize & Ladd, 1990).

AGGRESSIVE CHILDREN AND THEIR VICTIMS

By the time toddlers are old enough to play with one another, they show aggression. For example, 1- and 2-year-olds sometimes use physical aggression to resolve their conflicts (Coie & Dodge, 1998). *In **instrumental aggression**, a child uses aggression to achieve an explicit goal.* By the start of the elementary-school years, another form of aggression emerges (Coie et al., 1991). ***Hostile aggression** is unprovoked and seems to have as its sole goal to intimidate, harass, or humiliate another child.* Hostile aggression is illustrated by a child who spontaneously says, "You're stupid!" and then kicks the child. A third form of aggression is relational aggression, in which children try to hurt others by undermining their social relationships (see Chapter 5). Examples would include telling friends to avoid a particular classmate or spreading malicious gossip (Crick et al., 2004).

Children's tendencies to behave aggressively are stable over time, particularly among those children who are highly aggressive at a young age. For example, in one study among 7-year-old boys who were highly aggressive, more than half had committed serious acts of delinquency (e.g., stealing a car, attacking others) by age 17 (Raine et al., 2005). Similarly, in another study 6-year-old girls who were disobedient or bullied classmates were, as teenagers, 4 or 5 times more likely to be chronically aggressive, destroy property, and lie or steal (Coté et al., 2001). And violent behavior in adulthood is not the only long-term outcome of childhood aggression; poor adjustment to high school (e.g., dropping out, failing a grade) and unemployment are others (Ladd, 2003). Clearly, aggression is not simply a case of playful pushing and shoving that children always outgrow. To the contrary, a small minority of children who are highly aggressive develop into young adults who create havoc in society.

Most schoolchildren are the targets of an occasional aggressive act—a shove or kick to gain a desired toy, or a stinging insult by someone trying to save face. However, a small percentage of children are chronic targets of bullying. In both Europe and the United States, about 10% of elementary-school children and adolescents are chronic victims of aggression (Kochenderfer & Ladd, 1996; Olweus, 1994). Victimization can occur through physical aggression (e.g., a child who is beat up daily on the playground) and through relational aggression (e.g., a child who is constantly the subject of rumors spread by their classmates (Crick, Casas, & Nelson, 2002).

As you can imagine, being tormented daily by their peers is hard on children. When children are chronic victims of aggression, they're often lonely, anxious, and depressed; they dislike school and have low self-esteem (Graham & Juvonen, 1998; Ladd & Ladd, 1998). Although most children are happier when no longer victimized, the harmful effects linger for some children: They are still lonely and sad despite not having been victims for 1 or 2 years (Kochenderfer-Ladd & Wardrop, 2001).

Why do some children suffer the sad fate of being victims? Some victims are actually aggressive themselves (Olweus, 1978; Schwartz et al., 1997). These youngsters often overreact, are restless, and are easily irritated. Their aggressive peers soon learn that these children are easily baited. A group of children will, for example, insult or ridicule them, knowing that they will probably start a fight even though they are outnumbered. Other victims tend to be withdrawn and submissive. They are unwilling or unable to defend themselves from their peers' aggression, and so they are usually referred to as passive victims (Ladd & Ladd, 1998; Olweus, 1978). When attacked, they show obvious signs of distress and usually give in to their attackers, thereby rewarding the aggressive behavior. Thus, both aggressive and withdrawn-submissive children end up as victims; and this pattern holds for children in China as well as for children in North America (Schwartz, Chang, & Farver, 2001).

Children are likely to become chronic victims of aggression if they refuse to defend themselves.

Victimized children can be taught ways of dealing with aggression; they can be encouraged to not respond in kind when insulted and to not show fear when threatened. In addition, increasing self-esteem can help. When attacked, children with low self-esteem may think, "I'm a loser and have to put up with this because I have no choice." Increasing children's self-esteem makes them less tolerant of personal attacks (Egan & Perry, 1998). Finally, one of the easiest ways to help victims is to foster their friendships with peers. When children have friends, they're not as likely to be victimized (Bollmer et al., 2005).

TEST YOURSELF

1. Friends are usually similar in age, sex, race, and _____.

2. Children with friends have higher self-esteem, are less likely to be lonely, and _____ than children without friends.

3. As a group forms, a _____ typically emerges, with the leader at the top.

4. Peer pressure is most powerful when _____.

5. Popular children often share, cooperate, and are _____.

6. Rejected youngsters are more likely to drop out of school, to commit juvenile offenses, and _____.

7. Some children who are chronic victims of aggression overreact and are easily irritated; other chronic victims are _____.

How could developmental change in the nature of friendship be explain in terms of Piaget's stages of intellectual development, discussed in Chapters 4 and 6?

Answers: (1) interests, (2) more often act prosocially (sharing and cooperating), (3) dominance hierarchy, (4) standards for appropriate behavior are vague, (5) socially skilled, (6) to suffer from psychopathology, (7) unwilling or unable to defend themselves

7.3

TELEVISION: BOOB TUBE OR WINDOW ON THE WORLD?

Every day, 7-year-old Roberto follows the same routine when he gets home from school: He watches one action-adventure cartoon after another until it's time for dinner. Roberto's mother is disturbed by her son's constant TV viewing, particularly because of the amount of violence in the shows he likes. Her husband tells her to stop worrying: "Let him watch what he wants to. It won't hurt him and, besides, it keeps him out of your hair."

THE CARTOON EXAGGERATES TV'S IMPACT ON NORTH AMERICAN CHILDREN, but only somewhat. After all, think about how much time you spent in front of a TV while you were growing up. If you were a typical U.S. child and adolescent, you spent much more time watching TV than you did interacting with your parents or in school. The numbers tell an incredible story. School-age children spend 20 to 25 hours each week watching TV (Roberts, Foehr, & Rideout, 2005). Extrapolated through adolescence, the typical U.S. high school graduate has watched 20,000 hours of TV—the equivalent of 2 full years of watching TV 24 hours daily! No wonder social scientists and laypeople alike have come to see TV as an important contributor to the socialization of North American children.

Of course, not all children watch the same amount of TV. For most youngsters, however, viewing time increases gradually during the preschool and elementary school years, reaching a peak at about 11 or 12 years of age. Boys watch more TV than girls. Also, children with lower IQs watch more than those with higher IQs; children from lower-income families watch more TV than children from higher-income families (Huston & Wright, 1998).

It is hard to imagine that such massive viewing of TV would have no effect on children's behavior. After all, 30-second TV ads are designed to influence children's preferences in toys, cereals, and hamburgers, so the programs themselves ought to have even more impact.

INFLUENCE ON ATTITUDES AND SOCIAL BEHAVIOR

Ever since television became a common fixture in American homes in the 1950s, citizens have been concerned about violence on TV. For good reason: children's cartoons typically have one violent act every 3 minutes. (The term *violence* here refers to use of physical force against another person.) The average North American youngster will see several thousand murders on TV before reaching adolescence (Waters, 1993).

What is the impact of this steady diet of televised mayhem and violence? According to Bandura's (1986) social cognitive theory, which we first described in Chapter 1, children learn by observing others; they watch others and often imitate what they see. Applied to TV, this theory predicts more aggressive behavior from children who watch violent TV. And, in fact, research results consistently find that frequent exposure to TV violence causes children to be more aggressive (Huston & Wright, 1998).

"MRS. HORTON, COULD YOU STOP BY SCHOOL TODAY?"

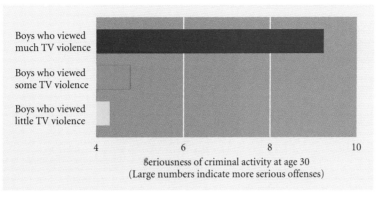

■ **Figure 7.3**
Boys who viewed much TV violence were much more likely to have committed serious crimes as adults.

Based on data in Huesmann and Miller, 1994.

One of the most compelling studies examined the impact of children's TV viewing at age 8 on criminal activity at age 30 (Huesmann & Miller, 1994). Figure 7.3 shows quite clearly that 8-year-olds exposed to large doses of TV violence had the most extensive criminal records as 30-year-olds. The link was found for both males and females, although females' level of criminal activity was much lower overall.

More recent studies (e.g., Johnson et al., 2002) confirm the long-term impact of TV on aggression and violence, particularly for boys, even when confounding variables such as parents' education and family income are controlled. What's more, playing violent video games seems to lead to violence in much the same way that watching violent TV does (Anderson & Bushman, 2001). Children and adolescents who play violent video games frequently tend to be more aggressive and less altruistic.

Thus, children like Roberto, who are frequent viewers of TV violence, learn to resort to aggression in their interactions with others. For some, their aggression eventually puts them behind bars. Of course, violence is only one part of what children see on TV. Let's examine other ways in which TV is an important influence on children as they develop.

Stereotypes

TV is said to provide a "window on the world." Unfortunately, the view on prime time TV is distorted, particularly when it comes to minorities, women, and the elderly. For example, when women are shown on TV, they are often passive and emotional. Most are not employed; those who have jobs are often in stereotypical female careers such as teachers or secretaries (Huston & Wright, 1998). And the impact of the stereotyped presentation of males and females is clear: children who watch TV frequently end up with more stereotyped views of males and females. For example, in a classic study, Kimball (1986) examined sex-role stereotypes in a small Canadian town that was located in a valley and could not receive TV programs. Two years after a transmitter was installed nearby in 1974, views of personality traits, behaviors, occupations, and peer relations were again measured in the town's children. Figure 7.4 shows that boys' and girls' views on these issues became more stereotyped after TV was introduced. For example, after the introduction of TV, girls had more stereotyped views of peer relations. They believed that boasting and swearing were

Cartoons frequently depict violent acts; children who watch many cartoons are more likely to behave aggressively.

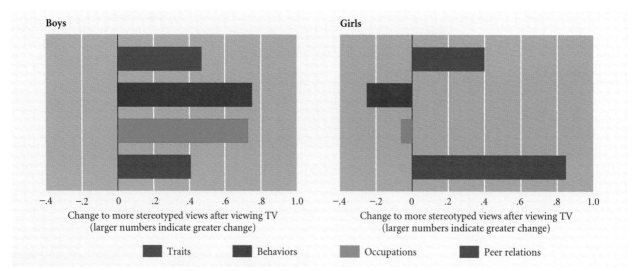

Boys

Girls

Change to more stereotyped views after viewing TV
(larger numbers indicate greater change)

Change to more stereotyped views after viewing TV
(larger numbers indicate greater change)

■ Traits ■ Behaviors ■ Occupations ■ Peer relations

Based on data in Kimball, 1986.

■ **Figure 7.4**
In the Kimball study, after children began watching TV, boys had more stereotyped views of traits, behaviors, occupations, and peer relations; girls had more stereotyped views of traits and peer relations.

TV commercials are effective; children often urge parents to buy products they've seen on TV.

characteristic of boys but that sharing and helping were characteristic of girls. The boys in the town acquired more stereotyped views of occupations, believing that girls could be teachers and cooks, whereas boys could be physicians and judges.

Findings like these indicate that TV viewing causes children to adopt many of the stereotypes that dominate television programming (Signorielli & Lears, 1992). For many children and adolescents, TV's slanted depiction of the world *becomes* reality.

Consumer Behavior

Sugary cereals, hamburgers and french fries, snack foods, expensive toys—these products are the focus of a phenomenal amount of TV advertising directed toward children. A typical youngster may see more than 100 commercials a day (Linn, 2004). As early as 3 years of age, children distinguish commercials from programs. However, preschool children often believe that commercials are simply a different form of entertainment—one designed to inform viewers. Not until 8 or 9 years of age do most children understand the persuasive intent of commercials; a few years later, children realize that commercials are not always truthful (Linn, 2005). They understand that a toy rocket will not really fly or that a doll will not really talk, contrary to how they're shown in commercials.

Commercials are effective sales tools with children. Children grow to like many of the products advertised on TV. They may urge parents to buy products they have seen on television. This selling power of TV commercials has long concerned advocates for children, because so many ads focus on children's foods that have little nutritional value and that are associated with problems such as obesity and tooth decay. The U.S. government once regulated the amount and type of advertising on children's TV programs (Huston, Watkins, & Kunkel, 1989), but today the responsibility falls largely to parents. Here are some ways for parents to regulate their children's TV viewing:

■ Children need absolute rules concerning the amount of TV and the types of programs they can watch. These rules must be enforced consistently!

■ Children shouldn't fall into the trap of "I'm bored, so I'll watch TV." Children should be encouraged to know what they want to watch *before* they turn on the TV set.

- Adults should watch TV with children and discuss the programs. Parents can, for example, express their disapproval of a character's use of aggression and suggest other means of resolving conflicts. Parents can also point to the stereotypes that are depicted. The aim is for children to learn that TV's account of the world is often inaccurate and to encourage children to watch TV critically.

- Parents need to be good TV viewers themselves. The first two tips listed here apply to viewers of all ages. When a child is present, parents shouldn't watch violent programs or others that are inappropriate for the young. And parents should watch TV deliberately and selectively, not mindlessly flip between channels.

Prosocial Behavior

TV is clearly a potent influence on children's aggression and on the stereotypes they form. Can this power be put to more prosocial goals? Can TV viewing help children learn to be more generous, to be more cooperative, and to have greater self-control? Yes: youngsters who watch TV shows that emphasize prosocial behavior, such as *Mister Rogers' Neighborhood,* are more likely to behave prosocially (Calvert & Kotler, 2003; Huston & Wright, 1998; Sanders, Montgomery, & Brechman-Toussaint, 2000). Nevertheless, two important factors restrict the actual prosocial impact of TV viewing. First, prosocial behaviors are portrayed on TV programs far less frequently than aggressive behaviors; opportunities to learn prosocial behaviors from television are limited. Second, in the real world of TV watching, the relatively small number of prosocial programs must compete with other kinds of television programs, as well as other activities, for children's time. Children simply may not watch the few prosocial programs that are televised. Clearly, we are far from harnessing the power of television for prosocial uses.

INFLUENCES ON COGNITION

You undoubtedly know Big Bird, Kermit the Frog, Cookie Monster, Oscar the Grouch, and their friends, for they are the cast of *Sesame Street,* one of the longest-running shows in TV history. First appearing in 1969, *Sesame Street* has helped educate generations of preschoolers. Produced by Children's Television Workshop, the goal of *Sesame Street* was to use the power of video and animation to foster skills like recognizing letters and numbers, counting, and vocabulary in preschool children. Evaluations conducted in the early years of *Sesame Street* showed that the program achieved its goals—preschoolers who watched *Sesame Street* regularly were more proficient at the targeted academic skills than were children who watched less often. And frequent viewers adjusted to school more readily, according to teachers' ratings (Bogatz & Ball, 1972).

Today, mothers and fathers who watched *Sesame Street* as preschoolers are watching with their own youngsters. Remarkably, the time preschool children spend watching *Sesame Street* predicts their grades in high school and the amount of time they spend reading as adolescents (Anderson et al., 2001).

Building on the success of *Sesame Street,* Children's Television Workshop developed a number of other successful programs. *Electric Company* was designed to teach reading skills, *3-2-1 Contact* has a science and technology focus, and *Square One TV* aims at mathematics (Fisch & McCann, 1993). More recent programs have included *Reading Rainbow, Ghostwriter, Where in the World Is Carmen Sandiego?* and *Bill Nye Science Guy.* Although these programs are no longer in production (except for *Sesame Street*), they are still shown on cable networks and demonstrate that children can learn academic skills and useful social skills from TV. Thus, TV can be beneficial if parents monitor their youngsters' viewing and if they insist that the television industry improves the quality and variety of programs available for children and adolescents.

CRITICISMS OF TV

Television has its critics. Although they concede that some TV programs help children learn, they also argue that the medium itself—independent of the content of programs—has several harmful effects on viewers, particularly children (Huston & Wright, 1998). One common criticism is that because TV programs consist of many brief segments presented in rapid succession, children who watch a lot of TV develop short attention spans and have difficulty concentrating in school. Another concern heard frequently is that because TV provides ready-made, simple-to-interpret images, children who watch a lot of TV become passive, lazy thinkers and become less creative.

In fact, as stated, neither of these criticisms is consistently supported by research (Huston & Wright, 1998). The first criticism—TV watching reduces attention—is the easiest to dismiss. Research repeatedly shows that increased TV viewing does not lead to reduced attention, greater impulsivity, reduced task persistence, or increased activity levels. The contents of TV programs can influence these dimensions of children's behavior—children who watch impulsive models behave more impulsively themselves—but TV per se does not harm children's ability to pay attention.

As for the criticism that TV viewing fosters lazy thinking and stifles creativity, the evidence is mixed. Many studies find no link between amount of TV viewing and creativity (e.g., Anderson et al., 2001). Some find a negative relation in which, as children watch more TV, they tend to get lower scores on tests of creativity (Valkenburg & van der Voort, 1994, 1995). Child development researchers don't know why the negative effects aren't found more consistently, although one idea is that the effects depend on what programs children watch, not simply the amount of TV watched.

In general, then, although the content of TV programs can clearly influence children (positively or negatively, depending on what children watch), there is no strong evidence that TV watching per se has harmful effects on children.

TEST YOURSELF

1. When children watch a lot of TV violence, they often become _____.

2. Preschool children believe that commercials _____.

3. Youngsters who watch *Sesame Street* frequently improve their academic skills, and, according to their teachers, _____.

4. Contrary to popular criticisms, frequent TV viewing is not consistently related to reduced attention or to a lack of _____.

Use the difference between divergent and convergent thinking, explained in Chapter 6, to describe the impact of TV viewing on children.

Answers: (1) more aggressive, (2) represent a different, informative type of program but do not understand the intent to persuade, (3) adjust to school more readily, (4) creativity

---

7.4

UNDERSTANDING OTHERS

LEARNING OBJECTIVES

As children develop, how do they describe others differently?

How does understanding of others' thinking change as children develop?

When do children develop prejudice toward others?

When 12-year-old Ian agreed to baby-sit his 5-year-old brother, Kyle, their mother reminded Ian to keep Kyle out of the basement because Kyle's birthday presents were there, unwrapped. But as soon as their mother left, Kyle wanted to go to the basement to ride his tricycle. When Ian told him no, Kyle burst into angry tears and shouted, "I'm gonna tell Mom that you were mean to me!" Ian wished he could explain to Kyle,

but he knew that would just cause more trouble!

A s children spend more time with other people (either directly or vicariously, through television), they begin to understand other people better. In this vignette, for example, Ian realizes why Kyle is angry, and he knows that if he gives in to Kyle now, his mother will be angry when she returns. Children's growing understanding of others is the focus of this section. We begin by looking at how children describe others, then examine their understanding of how others think. Finally, we'll also see how children's recognition of different social groups can lead to prejudices.

DESCRIBING OTHERS

As children develop, more sophisticated cognitive processes cause self-descriptions to become richer, more abstract, and more psychological. These same changes occur in children's descriptions of others. Children begin by describing other people in terms of concrete features, such as behavior, and progress to describing them in terms of abstract traits (Barenboim, 1981; Livesley & Bromley, 1973). The Real People feature shows this progression in one child.

 # REAL PEOPLE: Applying Human Development

TELL ME ABOUT A GIRL THAT YOU LIKE A LOT

Every few years, Tamsen was asked to describe a girl that she liked a lot. Each time, she described a different girl. More important, the contents of her descriptions changed, focusing less on behavior and emphasizing psychological properties. Let's start with the description she gave as a 7-year-old:

> Vanessa is short. She has black hair and brown eyes. She uses a wheelchair because she can't walk. She's in my class. She has dolls just like mine. She likes to sing and read.

Tamsen's description of Vanessa is probably not too different from the way she would have described herself: The emphasis is on concrete characteristics, such as Vanessa's appearance, posses-sions, and preferences. Contrast this with the following description, which Tamsen gave as a 10-year-old:

> Kate lives in my apartment. She is a very good reader and is also good at math and science. She's nice to everyone in our class. And she's very funny. Sometimes her jokes make me laugh so-o-o hard! She takes piano lessons and likes to play soccer.

Tamsen's account still includes concrete features, such as where Kate lives and what she likes to do. However, psycho-logical traits are also evident: Tamsen describes Kate as nice and funny. By age 10, children move beyond the purely concrete and observable in describing others. During adolescence, descrip-tions become even more complex, as you can see in the following, from Tamsen as a 16-year-old:

> Jeannie is very understanding. Whenever anyone at school is upset, she's there to give a helping hand. Yet, in private, Jeannie can be so sarcastic. She can say some really nasty things about people. But I know she'd never say that stuff if she thought people would hear it because she wouldn't want to hurt their feelings.

This description is more abstract: Tamsen now focuses on psychological traits like understanding and concern for others' feelings. It's also more integrated: Tamsen tries to explain how Jeannie can be both understanding and sarcastic.

Each of Tamsen's three descriptions is very typical. As a 7-year-old, she emphasized concrete characteristics; as a 10-year-old, she began to include psychological traits; and as a 16-year-old, she tried to integrate traits to form a cohesive account.

The progression in how children perceive others was illustrated vividly in a classic study by Livesley and Bromley (1973). They interviewed 320 students, 7 to 15 years old, who attended school in Merseyside, England (near Liverpool, home of the Beatles). All participants were asked to describe eight people they knew: two boys, two girls, two men, and two women. The examiner told the participants, "I want you to describe what

■ **Figure 7.5**
In describing other people, personality becomes more important with development, and general information, appearance, and possessions become less important.

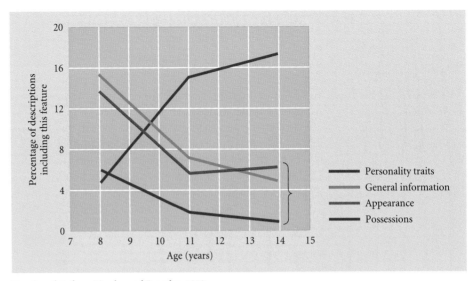

Based on data from Livesley and Bromley, 1973.

sort of person they are. I want you to tell me what you think about them and what they are like" (p. 97).

The participants at different ages typically produced descriptions much like Tamsen's at different ages. Livesley and Bromley then categorized the contents of the descriptions. Some of their results appear in Figure 7.5. Descriptions referring to appearances or possessions become less common as children grow older, as do descriptions giving general information, such as the person's age, gender, religion, or school. In contrast, descriptions of personality traits (e.g., "friendly" or "conceited") increase between 8 and 14 years of age. Thus, children's descriptions of others begin with the concrete and later become more conceptual.

By the time they enter school, children use the information in their descriptions to predict others' future behavior (Heyman & Gelman, 1999; Yuill & Pearson, 1998). To illustrate, suppose kindergarten children are told that Alissa did something nice (e.g., helped another child finish a difficult puzzle) but that Celeste did something mean (e.g., scribbled in another child's favorite book). Kindergarten children will judge that, in the future, Alissa is more likely than Celeste to help a child who is hurt, to give money to a needy child, and to hope that an elaborate art project turns out well for the child who created it. Thus, descriptions of others are useful, even for young children, because they allow children to predict how others will behave in the future.

UNDERSTANDING WHAT OTHERS THINK

One trademark of the preschooler's thinking is difficulty in seeing the world from another's view. Piaget's term for this is *egocentrism,* and it is a defining characteristic of his preoperational stage of development. As children move beyond the preschool years, though, they realize that others see the world differently, both literally and figuratively. For example, in the vignette, Ian knows why his little brother Kyle is angry: Kyle thinks that Ian is being bossy and mean. Ian understands that Kyle doesn't know there is a good reason why he can't go to the basement.

Sophisticated understanding of how others think is achieved gradually throughout childhood and adolescence. According to a theory proposed by Robert Selman (1980, 1981), understanding other people begins with the egocentric thinking characteristic of preoperational children—they think others think as they do. As children develop, they become able to take the perspective of other people. In Selman's theory, this perspective-taking skill progresses through five different stages, which are shown in Table 7.1.

TABLE 7.1

Selman's Stages of Perspective-Taking

Stage	Approximate Ages	Description
Undifferentiated	3–6 years	Children know that self and others can have different thoughts and feelings but often confuse the two.
Social-informational	4–9 years	Children know that perspectives differ because people have access to different information.
Self-reflective	7–12 years	Children can step into another's shoes and view themselves as others do. They know that others can do the same.
Third-person	10–15 years	Children can step outside of the immediate situation to see how they and another person are viewed by a third person.
Societal	14 years to adult	Adolescents realize that a third person's perspective is influenced by broader personal, social, and cultural contexts.

To see children's understanding at each of these stages, let's look at one of the stories that Selman (1980) used.

> Holly is an 8-year-old girl who likes to climb trees. She is the best tree climber in the neighborhood. One day while climbing down from a tall tree she falls off the bottom branch but does not hurt herself. Her father sees her fall. He is upset and asks her to promise not to climb trees anymore. Holly promises.
>
> Later that day, Holly and her friends meet Sean. Sean's kitten is caught up in a tree and cannot get down. Something has to be done right away or the kitten may fall. Holly is the only one who climbs well enough to reach the kitten and get it down, but she remembers her promise to her father. (Selman & Byrne, 1974, p. 805)

This dilemma is typical in that it includes several people who don't share the same knowledge about the events taking place. After hearing the story, children and adolescents were asked questions to investigate their ability to take on each character's view and predict what would happen to Holly.

The first stage is called undifferentiated, because children in this stage get confused about "who thinks what." A child in this stage might reply, "Holly's father will be happy because he likes kittens." This answer confuses Holly's feelings with her father's and ignores Holly's promise. Children in the social-informational stage might say, "If Holly's father knew why she climbed the tree, he probably wouldn't be angry." This answer indicates that the child understands that the father's response depends on whether or not he knows the reason for Holly's behavior.

In the self-reflective stage, a child might say, "Holly's father would understand that she thought saving the kitten's life was really important, so he wouldn't be mad. He'd probably be proud." This comment shows Holly's father stepping into Holly's shoes, the defining characteristic of the self-reflective stage.

At the next level, the third-person stage, a child might respond, "Holly remembers the promise, but she doesn't think her father will be angry when she explains that she wouldn't have climbed the tree except to save the kitten's life. Her father might wish that Holly had asked an adult for help, but he'd also understand why it was important to Holly to save the kitten." This child simultaneously considers both Holly's and her father's perspectives on the dilemma. That is, in answering, the child has stepped outside the immediate situation to take the perspective of a neutral third party who can look at both Holly's and her father's views.

At the most advanced level, the societal stage, an adolescent might reply, "Holly and her father both know that she almost always obeys him. So, they'd both know that if she disobeyed him to climb the tree, there would have to be an awfully good reason. So, they'd talk about it." This child's answer, like the previous one, considers Holly's and her

THINK ABOUT IT

How do Selman's stages of perspective-taking correspond to Piaget's and Erikson's stages?

father's perspectives simultaneously. The difference is that this comment puts the issue in the broader context of the history of their father-daughter relationship.

As predicted by Selman's theory, research shows that as children develop their reasoning moves through each stage, in sequence. In addition, regardless of age, children at more advanced cognitive levels tend to be at more advanced stages in perspective-taking (Gurucharri & Selman, 1982; Krebs & Gillmore, 1982).

Other support for Selman's theory comes from studies of the connections between perspective-taking and social behavior. Children who can anticipate what others are thinking should get along better with their peers, and research indicates that they do. For example, children with good perspective-taking skills are typically well liked by their peers (LeMare & Rubin, 1987). Of course, mere understanding does not guarantee good social behavior; sometimes children who understand what another child is thinking take advantage of that child. But, in general, greater understanding of others seems to promote positive interactions with others.

Socially skilled youth understand what others are thinking; in this case, they invite the girl on the sideline to join them.

PREJUDICE

As children learn more about others, they discover that people belong to different social groups, based on variables such as gender, ethnicity, and social class. By the preschool years, most children can distinguish males from females and can identify people from different ethnic groups (Aboud, 1993). *Once children learn their membership in a specific group, they typically show* **prejudice,** *a negative view of others based on their membership in a specific group.* Actually, in young children prejudice is not so much a negative view of others as it is an enhanced view of one's own group. That is, preschool and kindergarten children attribute to their own group many positive traits such as being friendly and smart and few negative traits such as being mean (Bigler, Jones, & Lobliner, 1997; Black-Gutman & Hickson, 1996).

Negative views of other groups form more slowly. In young children, negative views typically don't involve overt hostility; it's simply that other groups "come up short" when compared to one's own group (Aboud, 2003). However, when children believe that children from other groups dislike them or think they're better, children's views of other groups become more negative (Nesdale et al., 2005).

As children move into the elementary-school years, prejudice usually declines somewhat (Powlishta et al., 1994). Cognitive development explains the decline. Preschool and kindergarten children usually view people in social groups as much more homogeneous than they really are. People from other groups are seen as all alike and, typically, not as good as people from the child's own group. As children grow, they begin to understand that people in social groups are heterogeneous—they know that individual European Americans, girls, and obese children, for example, are not all alike. And they have learned that people from different groups may be more alike than people from the same group. Gary, an African American whose passion is computers, finds that he enjoys being with Vic, an Italian American who shares his love of computers, but not Curtis, another African American whose passion is music. As children realize that social groups consist of all kinds of different people, prejudice lessens.

At the same time, children's knowledge of racial stereotypes and prejudices increases steadily. In one study relatively few 7-year-olds were aware of broadly held racial stereotypes, but most 10- and 11-year-olds were (McKown & Weinstein, 2003). What's more, children from groups that are often victims of discrimination (e.g., Latino, African American) were aware of racial stereotypes at a younger age than children from other groups.

As children learn more about stereotypes, they also learn norms that discourage openly favoring their own group over others. For example, Rutland and colleagues (2005) videotaped some children and adolescents as they completed questionnaires dealing with racial attitudes and told the participants that adults might watch the videotapes later; other children and adolescents were not videotaped and were led to believe that their responses were completely anonymous. When children and adolescents believed that their response might be made public, they were less enthusiastic about their own group and less negative about other groups.

During early adolescence, prejudice often increases again. This resurgence apparently reflects two different processes (Black-Gutman & Hickson, 1996; Teichman, 2001). One is experiential: Exposed to prejudices of those around them, children and adolescents internalize some of these views. A second process concerns adolescents' identity. In their search for identity (see pages 340–343), adolescents' preference for their own group often intensifies. Thus, greater prejudice in older children and adolescents reflects both a more positive view of their own group and a more negative view of other groups. Bob, a 14-year-old European American growing up in Arizona, becomes more prejudiced because he views his own European American heritage more positively and acquires prejudicial attitudes toward Native Americans from his parents and peers.

Identifying *how* children form actual prejudices is challenging because ethical concerns limit us to correlational studies. (Obviously, we could not do an experiment in which some children are deliberately exposed to biased information about actual groups of children.) Consequently, to study the processes underlying prejudice, researchers sometimes conduct experiments in which children are temporarily assigned to different groups.

To illustrate this approach, many researchers believe that social status contributes to prejudice: Children are more likely to develop strong preferences for their group when it has high status. In experimentation designed to test this prediction (Bigler, Brown, & Markell, 2001; Brown & Bigler, 2002), children attending a summer school program were assigned to wear either a blue or yellow T-shirt. To increase the status of children wearing yellow shirts, children were told that in the previous summer, students wearing yellow shirts were smarter, better leaders, and better athletes. Throughout the 4-week program, teachers mentioned T-shirt color frequently (e.g., had children sit with others wearing the same color of shirt), but did *not* favor one group over the other. Nevertheless, at the end of the program, children wearing yellow shirts viewed themselves much more positively than they viewed children wearing blue shirts; in contrast, children wearing blue shirts (low status) had no biases. Thus, high status breeds a preference for one's own group (Nesdale & Flesser, 2001).

What can parents, teachers, and other adults do to rid children of prejudice? One way is to encourage friendly and constructive contacts between children from different groups. However, contact alone usually accomplishes little. Intergroup contact reduces prejudice only when the participating groups of children are equal in status, when the contact between groups involves pursuing common goals (not competing), and when parents and teachers support the goal of reducing prejudice (Killen & McGlothlin, 2005). To illustrate, adults might have children from different groups work together toward common goals. In school, this might be a class project. In sports, it might be mastering a new skill. By working together, Gary starts to realize that Vic acts, thinks, and feels as he does simply because he's Vic, not because he's an Italian American.

Another useful approach is to ask children to play different roles (Davidson & Davidson, 1994). They can be asked to imagine that, because of their race, ethnic background, or gender, they have been insulted verbally or not allowed to participate in special activities. A child might be asked to imagine that she can't go to a private swimming club because she's African American or that she

One effective way to reduce prejudice is for children from different races to work together toward a common goal, such as completing a class project.

© Bob Daemmrich/Stock Boston, Inc.

wasn't invited to a party because she's Hispanic American. Afterward, children reflect on how they felt when prejudice and discrimination was directed at them. And they're asked to think about what would be fair—What should be done in situations like these?

From experiences like these, children and adolescents discover for themselves that a person's membership in a social group tells us very little about that person. They learn, instead, that all children are different, each a unique mix of experiences, skills, and values.

TEST YOURSELF

1. When adolescents describe others, they usually _____.

2. In the most advanced stage of Selman's theory, adolescents _____.

3. Prejudice declines some as children get older because _____.

How might an information-processing theorist describe the stages of Selman's perspective-taking theory?

Answers: (1) try to provide a cohesive, integrated account, (2) provide a third person's perspective on situations and recognize the influence of context on this perspective, (3) with cognitive development, children realize that social groups are heterogeneous

Putting It All Together

In this chapter we've examined some of the many forces that contribute to socialization. Parents, peers, and TV emerged as mighty shapers of children's development. We learned that parental style influences both cognitive and social development. Children reared by parents with the authoritarian style favored by Tanya's mother often have low self-esteem and low social skill; children reared by parents with the authoritative style used by Sheila's mother tend to be self-reliant and friendly and to do well in school. We saw that groups like those at Crab Orchard Summer Camp are an important element of social life among older children and adolescents and that their impact is greatest when behavioral standards are not clear. We saw that TV's influence is tremendous. It can cause children like Roberto to rely on aggression to resolve in-terpersonal conflict, and it can give them a stereotyped view of the world. Finally, we learned that children's descriptions and understanding of others become more complex with age, so that young adolescents like Ian are often fully aware of what others are thinking. And, we saw that prejudice declines with age, especially when children interact with peers from other groups.

Thus, parents, siblings, peers, and television define much of the sociocultural context of development for American children, and their impact is considerable. Through the combined power of parents, siblings, peers, and television, children acquire the beliefs and behaviors of their culture. Full, adult membership in their culture is not far away. Only adolescence remains, and that topic will be examined in Chapter 8.

Summary

7.1 Family Relationships

The Family as a System

■ According to the systems approach, the family consists of interacting elements; that is, parents and children influence each other. The family itself is influenced by other social systems, such as neighborhoods and religious organizations.

Dimensions and Styles of Parenting

■ One key factor in parent-child relationships is the degree of warmth that parents express: Children clearly benefit from warm, caring parents. A second factor is control, which is complicated because neither too much nor too little control is desirable. Effective parental control involves setting appropriate standards, enforcing them, and trying to anticipate conflicts.

■ Taking into account both warmth and control, four prototypic parental styles emerge: Authoritarian parents are controlling but uninvolved; authoritative parents are fairly controlling but are also responsive to their children; permissive parents are loving but exert little control; and uninvolved parents are neither warm nor controlling. Authoritative parenting seems best for children in terms of both cognitive and social development, but there are important exceptions associated with culture and socioeconomic status.

■ Parents influence development by direct instruction and coaching. In addition, parents serve as models for their children, who sometimes imitate parents' behavior directly; sometimes children behave in ways that are similar to what they have seen (disinhibition), and sometimes in ways that are the opposite of what they've seen (counterimitation).

■ Parents also use feedback to influence children's behavior. Sometimes parents fall into the negative reinforcement trap, inadvertently reinforcing behaviors that they want to discourage.

■ Punishment is effective when it is prompt, consistent, accompanied by an explanation, and delivered by a person with whom the child has a warm relationship. Punishment has limited value because it suppresses behaviors but does not eliminate them, and it often has side effects. Time-out is one useful form of punishment.

■ Chronic conflict is harmful to children, but children can actually benefit when their parents solve problems constructively. Parenting is a team sport, but not all parents play well together because they may disagree in child-rearing goals or parenting methods.

■ Parenting is influenced by characteristics of children themselves. A child's age and temperament will influence how a parent tries to exert control over the child.

Siblings

■ The birth of a sibling can be stressful for children, particularly when they are still young and when parents ignore their needs. Siblings get along better when they are of the same sex, believe that parents treat them similarly, enter adolescence, and have parents who get along well.

■ As adoption became more common in the United States, a myth grew that adopted children are more prone to problems. Research shows that adopted children are similar to children living with biological parents in many respects, but they are more prone to some problems, such as adjusting to school and conduct disorders. However, these results depend strongly on the child's age when adopted and the quality of care prior to adoption, which suggests that adoption per se is not a problem for children's development.

■ Parents have higher expectations for first-born children, which explains why such children are more intelligent and more likely to go to college. Later-born children are more popular and more innovative. Contradicting the folklore, only children are almost never worse off than children with siblings. In some respects (such as intelligence, achievement, and autonomy), they are often better off.

Divorce and Remarriage

■ Divorce can harm children in a number of areas, ranging from school achievement to adjustment. The impact of divorce stems from less supervision of children following divorce, economic hardship, and conflict between parents. Children often benefit when parents have joint custody following divorce, or when they live with the same-sex parent.

■ When a mother remarries, daughters sometimes have difficulty adjusting because the new stepfather encroaches on an intimate mother-daughter relationship. A father's remarriage can cause problems because children fear that the stepmother will disturb intimate father-child relationships and because of tension between the stepmother and the noncustodial mother.

Parent-Child Relationships Gone Awry: Child Abuse

■ Cultural factors contributing to child abuse include a culture's views on violence, poverty, and social isolation. Parents who abuse their children were often neglected or abused themselves and tend to be unhappy, socially unskilled individuals. Younger or unhealthy children are more likely to be targets of abuse. Children who are abused often lag behind in cognitive and social development.

7.2 Peers

Friendships

■ Friendships among preschoolers are based on common interests and getting along well. As children grow, loyalty, trust, and intimacy become more important features in their friendships. Friends are usually similar in age, sex, race, and attitudes. Children with friends are more skilled socially and better adjusted.

Groups

■ Older children and adolescents often form cliques—small groups of like-minded individuals—that become part of a crowd. Some crowds have higher status than others, and members of higher-status crowds often have higher self-esteem than members of lower-status crowds.

- Common to most groups is a dominance hierarchy, a well-defined structure with a leader at the top. Physical power often determines the dominance hierarchy, particularly among boys. However, with older children and adolescents, dominance hierarchies are more often based on skills that are important to the group.

- Peer pressure is neither totally powerful nor totally evil. In fact, groups influence individuals primarily in areas where standards of behavior are unclear, such as tastes in music or clothing, or concerning drinking, drug use, and sex.

Popularity and Rejection

- Most popular children are socially skilled. They often share, cooperate, and help others. A far smaller number of popular children use aggression to achieve their social goals.

- Some children are rejected by their peers because they are too aggressive. Others are rejected for being too timid or withdrawn. Repeated peer rejection often leads to school failure and behavioral problems.

Aggressive Children and Their Victims

- Many highly aggressive children end up being violent and poorly adjusted as adults. Children who are chronic victims of aggression either overreact or refuse to defend themselves.

7.3 Television: Boob Tube or Window on the World?

Influence on Attitudes and Social Behavior

- Children's social behaviors and attitudes are influenced by what they see on TV. Youngsters who frequently watch televised violence become more aggressive, whereas those who watch prosocial TV become more socially skilled. Children who watch TV frequently may adopt TV's distorted view of women, minorities, and older people.

Influences on Cognition

- TV programs designed to foster children's cognitive skills, such as *Sesame Street,* are effective. Children frequently improve their academic skills and often adjust more readily to school.

Criticisms of TV

- Many popular criticisms of TV as a medium are not consistently supported by research. TV watching per se does not shorten children's attention span and does not consistently lead to reduced creativity.

7.4 Understanding Others

Describing Others

- Children's descriptions of others change in much the same way that children's descriptions of themselves change. During the early elementary-school years, descriptions emphasize concrete characteristics. In the late elementary-school years, they emphasize personality traits. In adolescence, they emphasize providing an integrated picture of others.

Understanding What Others Think

- According to Selman's theory, children's understanding of how others think progresses through five stages. In the first, the undifferentiated stage, children often confuse their own and another's view. In the last, the societal stage, adolescents can take a third person's perspective and know that this perspective is influenced by context.

Prejudice

- Prejudice emerges in the preschool years, soon after children recognize different social groups. Prejudice declines during childhood, as children's cognitive growth helps them understand that social groups are heterogeneous, not homogeneous. However, older children and adolescents still show prejudice, which is best reduced by additional exposure to individuals from other social groups.

Key Terms

socialization (265)
authoritarian parenting (268)
authoritative parenting (268)
permissive parenting (268)
uninvolved parenting (268)
direct instruction (269)
counterimitation (270)
disinhibition (270)
inhibition (270)

reinforcement (270)
punishment (270)
negative reinforcement trap (270)
time-out (271)
joint custody (277)
blended family (278)
friendship (283)
clique (287)
crowd (287)

dominance hierarchy (287)
popular children (289)
rejected children (289)
controversial children (289)
average children (289)
neglected children (289)
instrumental aggression (290)
hostile aggression (290)
prejudice (300)

Learn More About It

Readings

CANTOR, J. (1998). *Mommy, I'm scared: How TV and movies frighten children and what we can do to protect them.* New York: Harvest Books. The author shows some of the consequences of violent programs and movies on children, gives some age-related guidelines for what kind of material is likely to scare children, and describes ways to comfort frightened children. An excellent resource for parents.

DUNN, J. (2004). *Children's friendships: The beginnings of intimacy.* Malden, MA: Blackwell. A leading expert provides a straightforward and entertaining account of children's friendships; she includes practical guidelines for parents who want to help when children have problems with friendships.

GARDERE, J. (2002). *Smart parenting for African Americans: Helping your kids thrive in a difficult world.* New York: Dafina. The author, a clinical psychologist, is a familiar face on TV talk shows and, in fact, this book was featured on *Oprah.* He uses his clinical experience to provide solutions to many problems that parents face. Although written with African Americans in mind, this book is interesting and provocative reading for all parents and prospective parents.

HETHERINGTON, E. M., & KELLY, J. (2003). *For better or worse: Divorce reconsidered.* New York: W. W. Norton. The authors, the world's foremost authority on divorce and a professional writer, trace the findings from a 30-year study to explain how divorce affects families. They also provide many practical suggestions for dealing with problems associated with divorce.

Websites

Visit the Human Development book companion website for all URLs.

- **The Human Development Book Companion Website**
  See **http://www.psychology.wadsworth.com/kail _cavanaugh4e/** for practice quiz questions, Internet links, updates, critical thinking exercises, discussion forums, and more. Also accessible from the Wadsworth Psychology Study Center (http://psychology .wadsworth.com).

- **Today's Parent**
  This site offers tips on how to deal with the different problems—large and small—that come up in rearing children.

- **MedlinePlus**
  Maintained by the National Library of Medicine and the National Institutes of Health, you can find a variety of information about child abuse at this site.

- **The National Youth Violence Prevention Resource Center**
  Sponsored by the Centers for Disease Control and Prevention, this site includes useful information about aggressive behavior and violence in youth.

- **National Coalition Building Institute**
  This site describes methods to eliminate prejudice and discrimination.

Life-Span CD-ROM

For more information on the concepts covered in this chapter, go to

Module 3: Early and Middle Childhood
- *Emotional and Social Development*

Module 4: Adolescence
- *Emotional and Social Development*

Thomson NOW!

http://www.thomsonedu.com
Go to this site for the link to ThomsonNOW, your one-stop study shop. Take a pre-test for this chapter, and ThomsonNOW will generate a personalized study plan based on your test results. The study plan will identify the topics you need to review and direct you to online resources to help you master those topics. You can then take a post-test to help you determine the concepts you have mastered and what you still need to work on.

8.1 Pubertal Changes
Signs of Physical Maturation
Mechanisms of Maturation
Psychological Impact of Puberty

8.2 Health
Nutrition
Physical Fitness
Threats to Adolescent Well-Being

8.3 Information Processing During Adolescence
How Does Information Processing Improve in Adolescence?
Limits on Information Processing
SPOTLIGHT ON RESEARCH: Beliefs Can Interfere With Effective Reasoning

8.4 Reasoning About Moral Issues
Kohlberg's Theory
REAL PEOPLE: APPLYING HUMAN DEVELOPMENT: Schindler's List
Cultural Differences in Moral Reasoning
Beyond Kohlberg's Theory
Promoting Moral Reasoning

Putting It All Together

Summary

Key Terms

Learn More About It

CHAPTER 8

Rites of Passage

Physical and Cognitive Development in Adolescence

At age 12, Michelle Kwan finished 6th in the U.S. national figure skating championships; at age 15, she won her first world title; and at age 17, she earned a silver medal in the 1998 Olympics in Nagano, Japan. Michelle's steady march to the top of her sport over her adolescent years is a remarkable feat. Yet, in a less dramatic and less public way, these years are times of profound changes for *all* adolescents. In this chapter, we'll examine the physical and cognitive developments in adolescence. We'll begin by describing the important features of physical growth in the teenage years. Then we'll consider some of the necessary ingredients for healthy growth in adolescence. Next, we'll examine the nature of information processing during adolescence. Finally, we'll end the chapter by examining how adolescents reason about moral issues.

8.1

PUBERTAL CHANGES

----

*Pete just celebrated his 15th birthday, but as far as he is concerned,
there is no reason to celebrate. Although most of his friends have grown
about 6 inches in the past year or so, have a much larger penis and larger
testicles, and mounds of pubic hair, Pete looks just as he did when he was
10 years old. He is embarrassed by his appearance, particularly in the
locker room, where he looks like a little boy among men.
"Won't I ever change?" he wonders.*

LEARNING OBJECTIVES

What physical changes
occur in adolescence that
mark the transition to a
mature young adult?

What factors cause the
physical changes associated
with puberty?

How do physical changes
affect adolescents' psychological development?

THE APPEARANCE OF BODY HAIR, the emergence of breasts, and the enlargement of
the penis and testicles are all signs that the child is gone and the adolescent has arrived. Many adolescents take great satisfaction in these signs of maturity. Others, like
Pete, worry through their teenage years as they wait for the physical signs of adolescence.

In this section, we'll begin by describing the normal pattern of physical changes that
take place in adolescence and look at the mechanisms responsible for them. Then we'll
discover the impact of these physical changes on adolescents' psychological functioning.
As we do, we'll learn about the possible effects of Pete's maturing later than his peers.

SIGNS OF PHYSICAL MATURATION

*Puberty denotes two general types of physical changes that mark the transition from child-
hood to young adulthood.* The first are bodily changes, including a dramatic increase in
height and weight, as well as changes in the body's fat and muscle content. The second
concern sexual maturation, including change in the reproductive organs and the appearance of secondary sexual characteristics, such as facial and body hair and the growth
of the breasts.

Physical Growth

When it comes to physical growth, the elementary-school years represent the calm before the adolescent storm. As Figure 8.1 shows, in an average year, a typical 6- to 10-

∎ **Figure 8.1**
Children grow steadily taller
and heavier until puberty,
when they experience a
rapid increase known as the
adolescent growth spurt.

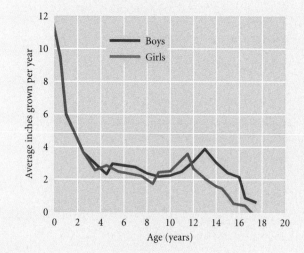

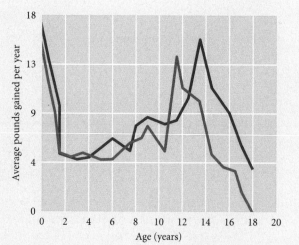

During the growth spurt, girls are often much taller than boys of the same age.

year-old girl or boy gains about 5 to 7 pounds and grows 2 to 3 inches. In contrast, during the peak of the adolescent growth spurt, a girl may gain as much as 20 pounds in a year and a boy 25 pounds (Tanner, 1970).

Figure 8.1 also shows that girls typically begin their growth spurt about 2 years before boys do. That is, girls typically start the growth spurt at about age 11, reach their peak rate of growth at about 12, and achieve their mature stature at about 15. In contrast, boys start the growth spurt at age 13, hit peak growth at 14, and reach mature stature at 17. This 2-year difference in the growth spurt can lead to awkward social interactions between 11- and 12-year-old boys and girls because the girls are often taller and look much more mature than the boys.

Body parts don't all mature at the same rate. Instead, the head, hands, and feet usually begin to grow first, followed by growth in the arms and legs. The trunk and shoulders are the last to grow (Tanner, 1990). The result of these differing growth rates is that an adolescent's body sometimes seems to be out of proportion—teens have a head and hands that are too big for the rest of their body. Fortunately, these imbalances don't last long as the later developing parts catch up.

During the growth spurt, bones become longer (which, of course, is why adolescents grow taller) and denser. Bone growth is accompanied by several other changes that differ for boys and girls. Muscle fibers become thicker and denser during adolescence, producing substantial increases in strength. However, muscle growth is much more pronounced in boys than in girls (Smoll & Schutz, 1990). Body fat also increases during adolescence, but much more rapidly in girls than in boys. Finally, heart and lung capacity increases more in adolescent boys than in adolescent girls. Together, these changes help to explain why the typical adolescent boy is stronger, quicker, and has greater endurance than the typical adolescent girl.

Sexual Maturation

Not only do adolescents become taller and heavier, they also become mature sexually. *Sexual maturation includes change in **primary sex characteristics,** which refer to organs that are directly involved in reproduction.* These include the ovaries, uterus, and vagina in girls and the scrotum, testes, and penis in boys. *Sexual maturation also includes changes in **secondary sex characteristics,** which are physical signs of maturity not directly linked to the reproductive organs.* These include the growth of breasts and the widening of the pelvis in girls, the appearance of facial hair and the broadening of shoulders in boys, and the appearance of body hair and changes in voice and skin in both boys and girls.

Changes in primary and secondary sexual characteristics occur in a predictable sequence for boys and for girls. Figure 8.2 shows these changes and the ages when they

THINK ABOUT IT

Compare and contrast the events of puberty for boys and girls.

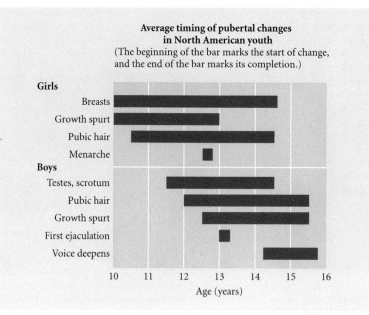

From Malina & Buchard, 1991.

typically occur for boys and girls. For girls, puberty begins with growth of the breasts and the growth spurt, followed by the appearance of pubic hair. **Menarche,** *the onset of menstruation, typically occurs at about age 13.* Early menstrual cycles are usually irregular and without ovulation.

For boys, puberty usually commences with the growth of the testes and scrotum, followed by the appearance of pubic hair, the start of the growth spurt, and growth of the penis. *At about age 13, most boys reach* **spermarche,** *the first spontaneous ejaculation of sperm-laden fluid.* Initial ejaculations often contain relatively few sperm; only months or sometimes years later are there sufficient sperm to fertilize an egg (Chilman, 1983).

MECHANISMS OF MATURATION

What causes the many physical changes that occur during puberty? The pituitary gland is the key player: It helps to regulate physical development by releasing growth hormone. In addition, the pituitary regulates pubertal changes by signaling other glands to secrete hormones. During the early elementary-school years—long before there are any outward signs of puberty—the pituitary signals the adrenal glands to release androgens, initiating the biochemical changes that will produce body hair. A few years later, in girls the pituitary signals the ovaries to release estrogen, which causes the breasts to enlarge, the female genitals to mature, and fat to accumulate. In boys the pituitary signals the testes to release the androgen hormone testosterone, which causes the male genitals to mature and muscle mass to increase.

Although estrogen is often described as a "female hormone" and androgen as a "male hormone," estrogen and androgen are present in both boys and girls. As we've seen, in girls the adrenal glands secrete androgens. The amount is very small compared to that secreted by boys' testes but is enough to influence the emergence of body hair. In boys, the testes secrete very small amounts of estrogen, which explains why some boys' breasts enlarge, temporarily, early in adolescence.

The timing of pubertal events is regulated, in part, by genetics. This is shown by the closer synchrony of pubertal events in identical twins than in fraternal twins: If one identical twin has body hair, the odds are that the other twin will too (Mustanski et al., 2004). Genetic influence is also shown by the fact that a mother's age at menarche is related to her daughter's age at menarche (Weichold & Silbereisen, 2005). However, these genetic forces are strongly influenced by the environment, particularly an adolescent's nutrition and health. In general, puberty occurs earlier in adolescents who are well nourished and healthy than in adolescents who are not. For example, puberty occurs earlier in girls who are heavier and taller but later in girls who are afflicted with chronic illnesses or who receive inadequate nutrition (St. George, Williams, & Silva, 1994).

Two other findings underscore the importance of nutrition and health in the onset of puberty. Cross-cultural comparisons reveal that menarche occurs earlier in areas of the world where nutrition and health care are adequate. For example, menarche occurs an average of 2 to 3 years earlier in Western European and North American countries than in African countries. And, within regions, socioeconomic status matters: Girls from affluent homes are more likely to receive adequate nutrition and health care and, consequently, reach menarche earlier (Steinberg, 1999).

Historical data point to the same conclusion concerning the importance of nutrition and health care. In many industrialized countries around the world, the average age of menarche has declined steadily over the past 150 years. For example, in Europe the average age of menarche was 17 in 1840, compared to about 13 today. This drop reflects improvements in nutrition and better health care over this period. In these countries, age of menarche is no longer dropping, which suggests that with adequate nutrition the genetic lower limit for menarche is, on average, about 13 years.

What may surprise you is that the social environment also influences the onset of puberty, at least for girls. Menarche occurs at younger ages in girls who experience chronic stress or who are depressed (Belsky, Steinberg, & Draper, 1991; Moffit et al., 1992). For example, Ellis and Garber (2000) found that girls entered puberty at a younger age when their mothers' romantic relationships were stressful. Other research shows that girls begin puberty at a younger age when their father is no longer living at home (Hoier, 2003).

The exact nature of these links is not known, but many explanations focus on the circumstances that would trigger the release of hormones that regulate menarches. One proposal is that when young girls experience chronic socioemotional stress—their family life is harsh and they lack warm, supportive parents—the hormones elicited by this stress may help to activate the hormones that trigger menarche. This mechanism would even have an evolutionary advantage: If events of a girl's life suggest that her future reproductive success is uncertain—as indicated by chronic socioemotional stress—then it may be adaptive to reproduce as soon as possible instead of waiting until later when she would be more mature and better able to care for her offspring. That is, the evolutionary gamble in this case might favor "lower quality" offspring early over "higher quality" offspring later (Ellis, 2004).

One variant of this theory is paternal investment theory (Ellis & Garber, 2000; Ellis et al., 2003), which emphasizes the role of fathers in determining the timing of puberty. In this theory, when girls' childhood experiences indicate that fathers are invested in child rearing, this may delay the timing of maturation. But when those experiences indicate that fathers are uninvolved, this may trigger early maturation. Delaying puberty is adaptive when high-quality fathers are plentiful, because it allows the girl to mature herself; but accelerating puberty is adaptive when high-quality fathers are rare, because it allows a girl to be mature sexually should a high-quality father become available and because it means that her mother is likely to be young enough to help with child care. In fact, girls who have infrequent or negative interactions with their fathers enter puberty earlier than girls who have frequent or positive interactions with their fathers; infrequent or negative experiences would indicate that the environment has few high-quality fathers (Ellis et al., 1999).

These and other explanations are being actively studied today. Scientists already agree, however, that the onset of menarche is not solely under genetic and biological control—social and emotional factors also contribute.

PSYCHOLOGICAL IMPACT OF PUBERTY

Of course, teenagers are well aware of the changes taking places in their bodies. Not surprisingly, some of these changes affect adolescents' psychological development.

Body Image

Compared to children and adults, adolescents are much more concerned about their overall appearance. Many teenagers look in the mirror regularly, checking for signs of additional physical change. Generally, girls worry more than boys about appearance and are more likely to be dissatisfied with their appearance (Vander Wal & Thelen, 2000).

Young adolescents are often quite concerned about their appearance.

Girls are particularly likely to be unhappy with their appearance when appearance is a frequent topic of conversation with friends, leading girls to spend more time comparing their own appearance with that of their peers. Peers have relatively little influence on boys' satisfaction with their appearance; instead, boys are unhappy with their appearance when they expect to have an idealized strong, muscular body but don't (Carlson Jones, 2004).

Response to Menarche and Spermarche

Carrie was horror writer Stephen King's first novel (and later a movie starring Sissy Spacek); it opens with a riveting scene in which the title character has her first menstrual period in the shower at school and, not knowing what is happening, fears that she will bleed to death. Fortunately, most adolescent girls today know about menstruation beforehand—usually from discussions with their mothers. Being prepared, their responses are usually fairly mild. Most girls are moderately pleased at this new sign of maturity but moderately irritated by the inconvenience and messiness of menstruation (Brooks-Gunn & Ruble, 1982). Girls usually tell their moms about menarche right away, and after two or three menstrual periods, they tell their friends too (Brooks-Gunn & Ruble, 1982).

Menarche is usually a private occasion for adolescents living in industrialized countries, but it is often celebrated in traditional cultures. For example, the Western Apache, who live in the southwest portion of the United States, traditionally have a spectacular ceremony to celebrate a girl's menarche (Basso, 1970). After a girl's first period, a group of older adults decide when the ceremony will be held and select a sponsor—a woman of good character and wealth (she helps to pay for the ceremony) who is unrelated to the initiate. On the day before the ceremony, the sponsor serves a large feast for the girl and her family; at the end of the ceremony, the family reciprocates, symbolizing that the sponsor is now a member of their family.

The ceremony itself begins at sunrise and lasts a few hours. The ceremony includes eight distinct phases in which the initiate, dressed in ceremonial attire, dances or chants, sometimes accompanied by her sponsor or a medicine man. The intent of these actions is to transform the girl into "Changing Woman," a heroic figure in Apache myth. With this transformation comes longevity and perpetual strength. The ceremony is a signal to all in the community that the initiate is now an adult, and it tells the initiate herself that her community now has adultlike expectations for her.

In contrast to menarche, much less is known about boys' reactions to spermarche. Most boys know about spontaneous ejaculations beforehand, and they get their information by reading, not by asking parents (Gaddis & Brooks-Gunn, 1985). When boys are prepared for spermarche, they feel more positively about it. Nevertheless, boys rarely tell parents or friends about this new development (Stein & Reiser, 1994).

Moodiness

Adolescents are often thought to be extraordinarily moody, moving from joy to sadness to irritation to anger over the course of a morning or afternoon. And the source of teenage moodiness is often presumed to be the influx of hormones associated with puberty —"hormones running wild." In fact, evidence indicates that adolescents are moodier than children or adults, but not primarily due to hormones (Steinberg, 1999). Scientists

THINK ABOUT IT

The Apache have an elaborate celebration for menarche. Can you think of other similar ceremonies—perhaps not as elaborate—that take place to celebrate other milestones of adolescent development?

The Apache celebrate menarche with a special ceremony in which a girl is said to become a legendary hero.

Because children enter puberty at different ages, early-maturing teens tower over their later-maturing agemates.

often find that rapid increases in hormone levels are associated with greater irritability and greater impulsivity, but the correlations tend to be small and are found primarily in early adolescence (Buchanan, Eccles, & Becker, 1992).

If hormones are not responsible, what causes teenage moodiness? Some insights come from an elaborate study in which teenagers carried electronic pagers for a week (Csikszentmihalyi & Larson, 1984). When paged by researchers, the adolescents briefly described what they were doing and how they felt. The record of a typical adolescent is shown in Figure 8.3. His mood shifts frequently from positive to negative, sometimes several times in a single day. For this boy, like most of the adolescents in the study, mood shifts were associated with changes in activities and social settings. Teens are more likely to report being in a good mood when with friends or when recreating; they tend to report being in a bad mood when in adult-regulated settings such as school classrooms or at a part-time job. Because adolescents often change activities and social settings many times in a single day, they appear to be moodier than adults.

Rate of Maturation

Although puberty begins at age 10 in the average girl and age 12 in the average boy, for many children puberty begins months or even years before or after these norms. An early-maturing boy might begin puberty at age 11, whereas a late-maturing boy might start at 15 or 16. An early-maturing girl might start puberty at age 9, a late-maturing girl at 14 or 15.

Maturing early or late has psychological consequences that differ for boys and girls. Several longitudinal studies show that early maturation can be harmful for girls. Girls who mature early often lack self-confidence, are less popular, are more likely to be depressed and have behavior problems, and are more likely to smoke and drink (Dick

The Week of Gregory Stone

Mood (raw score)

		Negative				Positive			
		−24	−16	−8	0	8	16	24	What he was doing and thinking about

Monday	12:45 P.M.	Walking down the hall at school with a friend
	2:52	Walking to work with a girl
	6:40	On a dinner break at work, heading for Arby's; "I'm hungry."
	8:30	At work, rearranging women's personal products; "I was hoping I wouldn't get beeped right now."
	10:25	Lying in bed, daydreaming about the Prom; listening to music
Tuesday	8:44 A.M.	In English Lit, discussing Lord Tennyson's "Memoriam," thinking about "the Creeds in the poem"
	11:00	In Chemistry, watching movie; complaining to teacher that the sound is too loud; "This movie is terrible."
	12:35 P.M.	Outside at school; "Rapping to a friend"
	2:05	In Sociology, listening to teacher talk about "living together"
	5:15	At work, cleaning shelves; just dropped wristwatch
	7:05	Getting off work; rushing to catch the el train; "I want to get home and eat."
Wednesday	7:30 A.M.	In kitchen, pulling toast from the toaster, talking to sister
	10:30	In Chemistry, taking notes on the reactions of hydrogen and oxygen
	12:15 P.M.	"Rapping to friends" on the school mall; admiring graffiti
	1:30	In Typing class, typing a letter; being bored
	3:00	Walking to work alone; staring at a squirrel
	4:25	At work; pricing and stocking Q-tips
	6:00	At work, making room for new products; listening to the radio
	8:55	Doing homework in room; listening to new wave music
Thursday	8:50 A.M.	In English Lit, studying the poem "Prospice"
	12:30 P.M.	In the cafeteria with friends; looking at girls with blond hair
	2:10	In Sociology, daydreaming and wondering "Should I call my girlfriend tonight?"
	6:00	Eating dinner and talking with brother; watching TV
	7:05	In night school English class. "Pondering if I would like to be an author of children's books"
	10:00	Talking to brother in bedroom; listening to stereo
Friday	9:05 A.M.	Walking to Gym class; "Will this be another Drugland weekend?"
	11:30	In Chemistry; "Spacing off"
	12:15 P.M.	At home, watching "Bozo's Circus," heating a sandwich for lunch
	1:20	In Sociology, handing in a test
	3:15	Taking out the garbage at work; "Checking out a girl"
	4:55	At work, bringing stock out from the back room
	6:45	Mopping the bathroom at work; thinking about "a lecture on the E.R.A. I attended a few weeks ago"
	8:15	At girlfriend's, watching a game of backgammon; drinking beer
	10:20	At girlfriend's taking a hit off a joint; talking and reminiscing: "We're wasted."
Sunday	1:20 P.M.	Starting on a bike ride; talking with a girl
	6:15	At home, watching a "60 Minutes" presentation on Arthur Ashe; "I never knew he was black."
	8:30	In bedroom, resting and listening to music; "Should I call my girlfriend?"
Monday	7:20 A.M.	Talking to mother in kitchen; "Should I eat pizza with my mother tonight?"
	10:30	In Chemistry; daydreaming about the girl and the bike ride

From Csikszentmihalyi & Larson, 1984.

■ **Figure 8.3**
For most adolescents, mood shifts many times daily (from positive to negative and back), reflecting the many different activities and settings (some positive, some negative) that adolescents experience daily.

et al., 2000; Ge, Conger, & Elder, 2001; Stice, Presnell, & Bearman, 2001). Early maturation may hamper girls' development by leading them to associate with older adolescents who apparently encourage them to engage in age-inappropriate activities, such as drinking, smoking, and sex, for which they are ill prepared. And early maturation can have life-changing effects on early-maturing girls who are pressured into sex and become mothers while still teenagers (Weichold & Silbereisen, 2005). The good news here is that the harmful effects of early maturation can be offset by other factors: When early-maturing girls have warm, supportive parents, for example, they are less likely to suffer the consequences of early maturation (Ge et al., 2002).

The findings for boys are much more confusing. Some early studies suggested that early maturation benefits boys. For example, in an extensive longitudinal study of adolescents growing up in Milwaukee during the 1970s (Simmons & Blyth, 1987), the early-maturing boys dated more often and had more positive feelings about their physical development and their athletic abilities. But other studies have supported the "off-time hypothesis" for boys. In this view, being early or late is stressful for boys, who strongly prefer to be "on time" in their physical development. Yet another view is that puberty per se is stressful for boys, but the timing is not (Ge et al., 2003).

Scientists cannot yet explain this bewildering pattern of results, but it's clear that the transition to puberty seems to have few long-lasting effects for boys. In contrast to what happens with girls, by young adulthood, the effects associated with puberty and its timing vanish. When Pete, the late-maturing boy in the vignette, finally matures, others will treat him like an adult, and the few extra years of being treated like a child will not be harmful (Weichold & Silbereisen, 2005).

TEST YOURSELF

1. Puberty refers to changes in height and weight, to changes in the body's fat and muscle contents, and to _____.

2. Girls tend to have their growth spurts about _____ earlier than boys.

3. During adolescent physical growth, boys have greater muscle growth than girls, acquire less _____, and have greater increases in heart and lung capacity.

4. Primary sex characteristics are organs directly related to reproduction, whereas secondary sex characteristics are _____.

5. During puberty, the ovaries secrete estrogen, which causes the breasts to enlarge, the genitals to mature, and _____.

6. We know that nutrition and health determine the timing of puberty because puberty is earlier in girls who are taller and heavier, in regions of the world where nutrition and health care are adequate, and _____.

7. Adolescents are moodier than children and adults primarily because _____.

8. Early maturation tends to be harmful to girls because _____.

At first blush, the onset of puberty would seem to be due entirely to biology. In fact, the child's environment influences the onset of puberty. Summarize the ways in which biology and experience interact to trigger the onset of puberty.

Answers: (1) sexual maturation, (2) 2 years, (3) fat, (4) physical signs of maturity that are not linked directly to reproductive organs, such as the appearance of body hair, (5) fat to accumulate, (6) today, compared to earlier in history, (7) they change activities and social settings frequently, and their moods track these changes, (8) it leads them to associate with older adolescents and, consequently, they may become involved in activities for which they are ill prepared, such as drinking and sex.

8.2

HEALTH

Dana had just started the seventh grade and was overjoyed that he could try out for the middle school football team. He'd always excelled in sports and was usually the star when he played football on the playground or in gym class. But this was Dana's first opportunity to play on an actual team—with a real helmet, jersey, pads, and everything—and he was jazzed! Dana's dad played football in high school and thought Dana could benefit from the experience. His mom wasn't so sure—

LEARNING OBJECTIVES

What are the elements of a healthy diet for adolescents? Why do some adolescents suffer from eating disorders?

Do adolescents get enough exercise? What are the pros and cons of participating in sports in high school?

What are common obstacles to healthy growth in adolescence?

she was afraid that he'd be hurt and have to deal with the injury
for the rest of his life.

ADOLESCENCE IS A TIME OF TRANSITION when it comes to health. On the one hand, teens are much less affected by the minor illnesses that would have kept them at home, in bed, as children. On the other hand, teens are at much greater risk for harm because of their own unhealthy and risky behaviors. In this section, we'll look at some of the factors essential to adolescent health and see whether Dana's mother should be worried about sports-related injuries. We'll start with nutrition.

NUTRITION

The physical growth associated with puberty means that the body has special nutritional needs. A typical teenage girl should consume about 2,200 calories per day; a typical boy should consume about 2,700 calories. (The exact levels depend on a number of factors, including body composition, growth rate, and activity level.) Teenagers also need calcium for bone growth and iron to make extra hemoglobin, the matter in red blood cells that carries oxygen. Boys need additional hemoglobin because of their increased muscle mass; girls need hemoglobin to replace that lost during menstruation.

Unfortunately, although many U.S. teenagers consume enough calories each day, too much of their intake consists of fast food rather than well-balanced meals. The result of too many meals of burgers, french fries, and a shake is that teens may get inadequate iron or calcium and far too much sodium and fat. With inadequate iron, teens are often listless and moody; with inadequate calcium, bones may not develop fully, placing the person at risk later in life for osteoporosis.

Many American teenagers eat far too many fast food meals, which are notoriously high in calories.

Obesity

In part because of a diet high in fast foods, many American children and adolescents are overweight. *The technical definition for overweight is based on the **body mass index** (BMI), which is an adjusted ratio of weight to height.* Children and adolescents who are in the upper 5% (very heavy for their height) are defined as being overweight. Using these standards, in 2001 the U.S. Surgeon General announced that childhood obesity had reached epidemic proportions. In the past 25 to 30 years, the number of overweight children has doubled, and the number of overweight adolescents has tripled. Today roughly one child or adolescent out of seven is overweight (U.S. Department of Health and Human Services, 2001).

Overweight youngsters are often unpopular and have low self-esteem (Braet, Mervielde, & Vandereycken, 1997). What's more, they are at risk for many medical problems throughout life, including high blood pressure and diabetes, because the vast majority of overweight children and adolescents become overweight adults (Serdula et al., 1993).

Heredity plays an important role in juvenile obesity. In adoption studies, children's and adolescents' weight is related to the weight of their biological parents, not to the weight of their adoptive parents (Stunkard et al., 1986). Genes may influence obesity by influencing a person's activity level. In other words, being genetically more prone to inactivity makes it more difficult to burn off calories and easier to gain weight. *Heredity may also help set the **basal metabolic rate,** the speed at which the body consumes calories.*

Children and adolescents with a slower basal metabolic rate burn off calories less rapidly, making it easier for them to gain weight (Epstein & Cluss, 1986).

One's environment is also influential. Television advertising, for example, encourages youth to eat tasty but fattening foods. Parents play a role too. They may inadvertently encourage obesity by emphasizing external eating signals rather than internal. Thus, obese children and adolescents may overeat because they rely on external cues and disregard internal cues to stop (Birch, 1991).

Obese youth *can* lose weight. The most effective programs have several features in common (Epstein et al., 1995; Foreyt & Goodrick, 1995; Israel et al., 1994):

- The focus of the program is to change obese children's eating habits, encourage them to become more active, and discourage sedentary behavior.

- As part of the treatment, children learn to monitor their eating, exercise, and sedentary behavior. Goals are established in each area, and rewards are earned when the goals are met.

- Parents are trained to help children set realistic goals and to use behavioral principles to help children meet these goals. Parents also monitor their own lifestyles to be sure they aren't accidentally fostering their child's obesity.

Childhood obesity has reached epidemic proportions in the United States.

When programs incorporate these features, obese children do lose weight. However, even after losing weight, many of these children remain overweight. Consequently, it is best to avoid overweight and obesity in the first place; the *Surgeon General's Call for Action* emphasizes the role of increased physical activity and good eating habits in warding off overweight and obesity (U.S. Department of Health and Human Services, 2001).

Fast food is not the only risky diet common among adolescents. Many teenage girls worry about their weight and are attracted to the "lose 10 pounds in 2 weeks!" diets advertised on TV and in teen magazines. Many of these diets are flatly unhealthy—they deprive youth of the many substances necessary for growth. Similarly, for philosophical or health reasons, many adolescents decide to eliminate meat from their diets. Vegetarian diets can be healthy for teens, but only when adolescents do more than eliminate meat. That is, vegetarians need to adjust the rest of their diet to assure that they have adequate sources of protein, calcium, and iron.

Yet another food-related problem common in adolescence are two similar eating disorders, anorexia and bulimia.

Anorexia and Bulimia

Just days after turning 18, Mary-Kate Olsen, a TV and movie star and successful businesswoman, entered a rehabilitation clinic. She was rail thin and was being treated for an eating disorder. ***Anorexia nervosa*** *is a disorder marked by a persistent refusal to eat and an irrational fear of being overweight.* Individuals with anorexia nervosa have a grossly distorted image of their own body and claim to be overweight despite being painfully thin (Wilson, Heffernan, & Black, 1996). Anorexia is a very serious disorder, often leading to heart damage. Without treatment, as many as 15% of adolescents with anorexia die (Wang & Brownell, 2005).

A related eating disorder is bulimia nervosa. *Individuals with* **bulimia nervosa** *alternate between binge eating periods, when they eat uncontrollably, and purging through self-induced vomiting or with laxatives.* The frequency of binge eating varies remarkably among people with bulimia nervosa, from a few times a week to more than 30 times a week. What's common to all is the feeling that they cannot stop eating (Mizes, Scott, & Tonya, 1995).

© David Young-Wolff/PhotoEdit

Adolescent girls with anorexia nervosa believe that they are overweight and refuse to eat.

THINK ABOUT IT

Describe how obesity, anorexia, and bulimia represent the different forces in the biopsychosocial network.

Anorexia and bulimia are alike in many respects. Both disorders primarily affect females and emerge in adolescence (Wang & Brownell, 2005), and many of the same factors put teenage girls at risk for both eating disorders. Corinna Jacobi and her colleagues (2004) conducted a meta-analysis of more than 300 longitudinal and cross-sectional studies of individuals with eating disorders. They concluded that heredity puts some girls at risk and that psychosocial factors amplify that risk:

■ During childhood, a history of eating problems, such as being a picky eater or being diagnosed with pica, which refers to eating nonfood objects such as chalk, paper, or dirt

■ During adolescence, negative self-esteem, a mood or anxiety disorder and, most strongly of all, being overly concerned about one's body and weight and having a history of dieting

The meta-analysis also identified some risk factors that are unique to anorexia and bulimia. For example, overprotective parenting is associated with anorexia but not bulimia. In contrast, obesity in childhood is associated with bulimia but not anorexia.

Although eating disorders are far more common in girls, boys make up about 10% of diagnosed cases of eating disorders. Because boys with eating disorders are far less common, researchers have conducted much less research. However, some of the known risk factors are childhood obesity, low self-esteem, pressure from parents and peers to lose weight, and participating in sports that emphasize being lean (Ricciardelli & McCabe, 2004).

Fortunately, there are programs that can help protect teens from eating disorders (Stice & Shaw, 2004). The most effective programs are designed for at-risk youth: for example, for those who already say they are unhappy with their body. The best programs are interactive, enabling youth to become involved and to learn new skills, such as ways to resist social pressure to be thin. And they work to change critical attitudes (such as ideals regarding thinness) and critical behaviors (such as dieting and overeating). At-risk adolescents who participate in these programs are helped; they are more satisfied with their appearance and less likely to diet or overeat. And for those teens affected by eating disorders, treatment is available: Like prevention programs, treatment typically focuses on modifying key attitudes and behaviors (Puhl & Brownell, 2005).

PHYSICAL FITNESS

Being physically active promotes mental and physical health, both during adolescence and throughout adulthood. Individuals who regularly engage in physical activity reduce their risk for obesity, cancer, heart disease, diabetes, and psychological disorders, including depression and anxiety. "Regular activity" typically means exercising for 30 minutes, at least three times a week, at a pace that keeps an adolescent's heart rate at about 140 beats per minute (President's Council on Physical Fitness and Sports, 2004). Running, vigorous walking, swimming, aerobic dancing, biking, and cross-country skiing are all examples of activities that can provide this level of intensity.

Unfortunately, all the evidence indicates that most adolescents rarely get enough exercise. For example, in one study the researchers (Kann et al., 1995) asked high school students whether they had exercised at least three times for 20 minutes during the past week at a level that made them sweat and breathe hard. In 9th grade, about 75% of boys

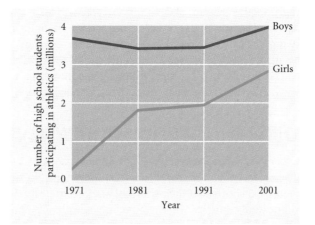

and 65% of girls said they had; by 12th grade, these figures had dropped to 65% for boys and 40% for girls. Part of the problem here is that, for many high school students, physical education classes provide the only regular opportunity for exercise, yet a minority of high school students are enrolled in physical education and most who are enrolled do not attend daily.

Many teenagers get exercise by participating in organized sports. Today, approximately 3.9 million boys and 2.8 million girls participate in sports. Although about 1.1 million more boys than girls participate, Figure 8.4 shows that the difference is smaller than it once was. In 1971, about 3.7 million boys participated, compared to only about 300,000 girls. However, in 1972 the U.S. government required that schools receiving public funds provide equal educational and athletic opportunities for boys and girls. Since that time, girls' participation in sports has grown steadily (National Federation of State High School Associations, 2004).

The most popular sport for boys is football; more than a million boys play high school football. The next most popular sports are basketball, track and field, and baseball. For girls, the most popular sport is basketball; approximately half a million girls play high school basketball. The next most popular sports are track and field, volleyball, and fast-pitch softball (National Federation of State High School Associations, 2004).

Participating in sports has many benefits for youth. In addition to improved physical fitness, sports can enhance participants' self-esteem and can help them to learn initiative (Larson, 2000; Whitehead & Corbin, 1997). Athletes also learn about teamwork and competitiveness. At the same time, there are some potential costs. About 15% of high school athletes will be injured and require some medical treatment. Boys are most likely to be injured while playing football or wrestling; girls are injured while participating in cross-country or soccer (Rice, 1993). Fortunately, most of these injuries are not serious ones but are more likely to involve bruises or strained muscles (Nelson, 1996). Dana's mom can rest easy; the odds are that he won't be injured, and if he is, it won't be serious.

A more serious problem is the use of illegal drugs to improve performance (American Academy of Pediatrics, 1997). Some athletes use anabolic steroids, drugs that are chemically similar to the male hormone testosterone, to increase muscle size and strength and to promote more rapid recovery from injury. Approximately 5 to 10% of high school boys and 1 to 2½% of high school girls report having used anabolic steroids. This is disturbing because steroid use can damage the liver,

THINK ABOUT IT

Many teenagers do not eat well-balanced meals, and many do not get enough exercise. What would you do to improve teenagers' dietary and exercise habits?

Nearly half a million U.S. girls play high school basketball.

reproductive system, skeleton, and cardiovascular system (increasing blood pressure and cholesterol levels); in addition, use of anabolic steroids is associated with mood swings, aggression, and depression. Parents, coaches, and health professionals need to be sure that high school athletes are aware of the dangers of steroids and should encourage youth to meet their athletic goals through alternative methods that do not involve drug use (American Academy of Pediatrics, 1997).

THREATS TO ADOLESCENT WELL-BEING

Every year, approximately 1 U.S. adolescent out of 1,000 dies. Relatively few die from disease; instead, they are killed in accidents, typically involving automobiles or firearms. Figure 8.5 shows that the pattern of adolescent death depends, to a very large extent, on gender and ethnicity. Among boys, most deaths are due to accidents involving motor vehicles or firearms. For European American, Latino American, and Asian American boys, motor vehicles are more deadly than guns, but the reverse is true for African American boys. Among girls, most deaths are due to natural causes or accidents involving motor vehicles. For European American girls, motor vehicle accidents account for nearly half of all deaths; for African American girls, natural causes account for nearly half of all deaths; and for Latina American and Asian American girls, natural causes and motor vehicles account for about the same number of deaths and together account for about two thirds of all deaths (Federal Interagency Forum on Child and Family Statistics, 2005).

Sadly, many of these deaths are completely preventable. Deaths in automobile accidents are often linked to driving too fast, drinking alcohol, and not wearing seatbelts (U.S. Department of Health and Human Services, 1997). And deaths due to guns are often linked to "all-too-easy" access to firearms in the home (Rivara & Grossman, 1996).

Adolescent deaths from accidents can be explained, in part, because adolescents take risks that adults often find unacceptable (Nell, 2002). Teens take unnecessary risks

Figure 8.5
Adolescent boys are much more likely than adolescent girls to die from accidents or use of firearms, and this is particularly true for African American and Latino American teenage boys.

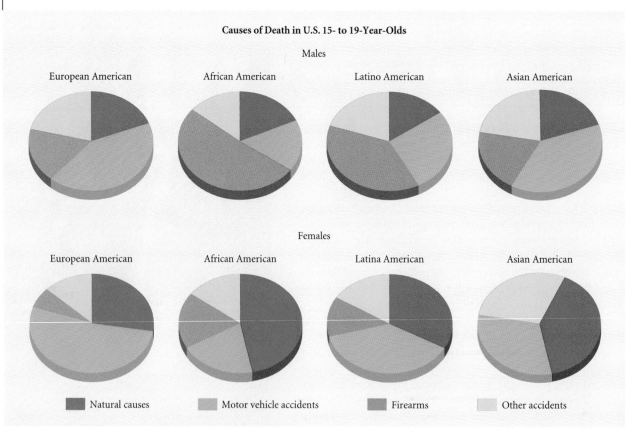

From Federal Interagency Forum on Child and Family Statistics, 2005.

while riding skateboards, scooters, or bicycles. They drive cars recklessly, engage in unprotected sex, and sometimes use illegal and dangerous drugs (we'll discuss this more in Chapter 9). Although it is tempting to call such behavior "stupid" or "irrational," research suggests that adolescents and adults often make decisions in a similar manner, even though the outcome of that decision-making process sometimes differs for adolescents and adults (Fischoff & Quadrel, 1995). Specifically, adolescents and adults typically follow this process:

■ Determine the alternative courses of action available

■ Determine the consequences of each action

■ Determine the desirability and likelihood of these consequences

Then they integrate this information to make a decision.

To see this decision making in action, consider a teen deciding whether to drive home from a party with friends who have been drinking alcohol. She decides that she has two alternatives: (1) try to find a ride with people who haven't been drinking but that she doesn't know well, or (2) ask her parents to come get her. Her analysis might run something like this:

> If I go home with my friends, I won't upset them (+) but I might be in an accident (−). If I go home with other people, I'll definitely make my friends mad (−) but will probably make it home safely (+). If I call my parents, I'll definitely upset my friends (−), probably annoy other people at the party (−), but I'll get home safely (+).

This basic analysis is sound and not much different from what an adult might do. The difference comes in the adolescent's weighting of the desirability of different consequences. Adolescents are likely to place greater emphasis on the social consequences of their decisions, such as upsetting their friends, and less emphasis on the health consequences, such as getting home safely (Steinberg, 1999). And, as we saw in Chapter 7, they're particularly likely to consider these social consequences when the standards for appropriate behavior are not clear, which is often the case when it comes to drinking or having sex.

© Dennis MacDonald/PhotoEdit

Adolescents are far more accident prone than children or adults, in part because they're particularly concerned about the social consequences of their behavior and less concerned about the risks.

TEST YOURSELF

1. An adolescent's diet should contain adequate calories, _____, and iron.

2. A vegetarian diet can be healthy for teens, but only when adolescents _____.

3. Individuals with _____ alternate between binge eating and purging.

4. During adolescence, the most important risk factors for anorexia and bulimia are _____.

5. Regular physical activity helps to promote _____ and physical health.

6. Girls' participation in sports has grown steadily since 1972 when _____.

7. Some teenage athletes use anabolic steroids to increase muscular strength and to _____.

8. More teenage girls die from _____ than any other single cause.

9. Because they place greater emphasis on the _____ consequences of their actions, adolescents make what adults think are risky decisions.

How does adolescent risk taking illustrate the idea that individuals help to shape their own development?

Answers: (1) calcium, (2) adjust the rest of their diet so they consume adequate protein, calcium, and iron, (3) bulimia nervosa, (4) being overly concerned about one's body and a history of dieting, (5) mental health, (6) the U.S. government required that schools receiving public funds provide equal athletic opportunities for boys and girls, (7) promote more rapid recovery from an injury, (8) automobile accidents, (9) social

INFORMATION PROCESSING DURING ADOLESCENCE

Calvin, a 14-year-old boy, was an enigma to his mother, Crystal. On one hand, Calvin's growing reasoning skills impressed and sometimes even surprised her. He not only readily grasped technical discussions of her medical work, but he was becoming adept at finding loopholes in her explanations of why he wasn't allowed to do some things with his friends. On the other hand, sometimes Calvin was a real teenage "space cadet." Simple problem solving stumped him, or he made silly mistakes and got the wrong answer. Calvin didn't correspond to Crystal's image of the formal-operational thinker that she remembered from her college child development class.

According to information-processing theories, many important cognitive processes reach mature levels of functioning during adolescence. We'll look at some of these processes in the first part of this section. Of course, that doesn't mean that adolescents' thinking is always flawless; it's not, and in this section we'll see why adolescents like Crystal's son don't always think in the sophisticated manner predicted by theories of cognitive development.

HOW DOES INFORMATION PROCESSING IMPROVE IN ADOLESCENCE?

For information-processing theorists, adolescence does not represent a distinct, qualitatively different stage of cognitive development. Instead, adolescence is considered to be a transitional period between the rapidly changing cognitive processes of childhood and the mature cognitive processes of young adulthood. Cognitive changes do take place in adolescence, but they are small compared to those seen in childhood. Adolescence is a time when cognitive processes are "tweaked" to adult levels.

These changes take place in several different areas of information processing.

Working Memory and Processing Speed

Working memory is the site of ongoing cognitive processing, and processing speed is the speed with which individuals complete basic cognitive processes. Both achieve adultlike levels during adolescence. Adolescents' working memory has about the same capacity as adults' working memory, which means teenagers are better able to store information needed for ongoing cognitive processes. In addition, Figure 8.6 illustrates changes in processing speed, exemplified in this case by performance on a simple response-time task in which individuals press a button as rapidly as possible in response to a visual stimulus. Simple response time declines steadily during childhood—from about one third of a second at age 8 to one quarter of a second at age 12—but changes little thereafter. This pattern of change is not specific to simple response time but is, instead, found for a wide range of cognitive tasks: Adolescents generally process information just about as quickly as young adults (Kail, 2004). Change in working memory and processing speed means that, compared to children, adolescents process information very efficiently.

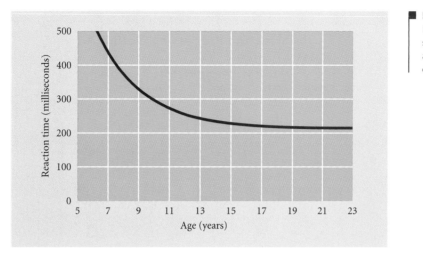

■ Figure 8.6
Response time declines
steadily during childhood
and reaches adultlike values
during middle adolescence.

Content Knowledge

As children move into adolescence, they acquire adult-like levels of knowledge and understanding in many domains. Children, for example, may enjoy baseball or computers, but as adolescents they acquire true expertise. For example, many parents turn to their teens for help learning how to navigate the Internet. This increased knowledge is useful for its own sake, but it also has the indirect effect of enabling adolescents to learn, understand, and remember more of new experiences (Schneider & Bjorklund, 1998; Schneider & Pressley, 1997). Imagine two middle school students—one a baseball expert, the other not—watching a baseball game. Compared to the novice, the adolescent expert would understand many of the nuances of the game and, later, remember many more features of the game.

Adolescents often have adultlike skills in some domains, such as using computers, which allows them to teach adults.

Strategies and Metacognitive Skill

Adolescents become much better skilled at identifying strategies appropriate for a specific task, then monitoring the chosen strategy to verify that it is working (Schneider

Many adolescents use a variety of study skills, such as highlighting important information and outlining a text, to help them prepare for tests.

TABLE **8.1**	
Information Processing During Adolescence	
Feature	State in Adolescence
Working memory and processing speed	Adolescents have adultlike working memory capacity and processing speed, enabling them to process information efficiently.
Content knowledge	Adolescents' greater knowledge of the world facilitates understanding and memory of new experiences.
Strategies and metacognition	Adolescents are better able to identify task-appropriate strategies and to monitor the effectiveness of those strategies.

THINK ABOUT IT

Students typically are introduced to the study of complex topics such as philosophy and experimental science during adolescence. Explain how their maturing cognitive skills contribute to the study of these and other subject areas.

& Pressley, 1997). For example, adolescents are more likely to outline and highlight information in a text. They are more likely to make lists of material they don't know well and should study more. And they more often embed these activities in a master study plan (e.g., a list of assignments, quizzes, and tests for a 2-week period). All these activities help adolescents learn more effectively and remember more accurately (Schneider & Pressley, 1997; Thomas et al., 1993).

These changing features of information processing are summarized in Table 8.1. Change in each of these elements of information processing occurs gradually. When combined, they contribute to the steady progress to mature thinking that is the destination of adolescent cognitive development.

LIMITS ON INFORMATION PROCESSING

Adolescents' improved information processing affords them much greater cognitive power. Of course, adolescents may not always use their skills effectively. Sometimes they resort to simpler, less mature ways of thinking because such thinking takes less effort—it's easier. And, as we'll see in the Spotlight on Research feature, sometimes adolescents' beliefs interfere with effective thinking.

SPOTLIGHT ON RESEARCH

BELIEFS CAN INTERFERE WITH EFFECTIVE REASONING

Who were the investigators, and what was the aim of the study? People's beliefs sometimes interfere with their ability to think clearly. When evidence is inconsistent with their beliefs, people may dismiss the evidence as being irrelevant or try to reinterpret the evidence to make it consistent with their beliefs. Paul Klaczynski and Gayathri Narasimham (1998) wanted to determine whether children and adolescents would show such biases in their scientific reasoning.

How did the investigators measure the topic of interest? The experiment was conducted in two sessions. In one session, participants completed a num-

ber of questionnaires, including one in which they indicated their religious preference. In a second session, participants read brief descriptions of hypothetical research studies that involved members of different religious groups. The studies were tailored so that each participant read about some studies that presented results depicting the participant's religion positively, some that presented results depicting the participant's religion negatively, and some that did not involve the participant's own religion. For example, if the participant was Lutheran, one study might conclude that Lutherans make better parents (favorable out-

come), a second might conclude that Lutherans are less creative than Catholics (unfavorable outcome), and a third might conclude that Baptists handle stress more effectively than Mormons (neutral outcome). After reading about each hypothetical study, participants rated how well the study was conducted on a 9-point scale ranging from 1, extremely poorly conducted, to 9, extremely well conducted. (In fact, each hypothetical study had a serious flaw, so there was reason to be critical of the results.)

Who were the children in the study? Klaczynski and Narasimham tested 41 10-year-olds, 42 13-year-olds, and

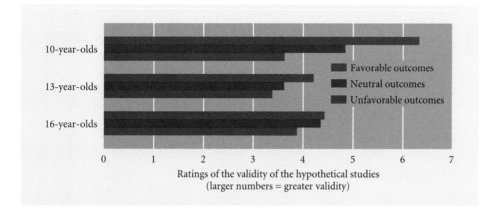

■ Figure 8.7
Children and adolescents often are biased in their reasoning. They believe that research with findings consistent with their own values is more valid than research with findings that are inconsistent with their own values.

41 16-year-olds. The sample included approximately the same number of boys and girls at each age.

What was the design of the study? This study was experimental because Klaczynski and Narasimham included two independent variables: the age of the participant and the nature of the outcome in the results of the hypothetical study (favorable, unfavorable, neutral). The dependent variable was the participant's rating of the validity of the results (i.e., how well the study had been conducted). The study was cross-sectional because 10-, 13-, and 16-year-olds were all tested at approximately the same time.

Were there ethical concerns with the study? No. As soon as the participants had completed the second session, they were told that the studies they had read were completely hypothetical.

What were the results? The results are illustrated in Figure 8.7 and show the average ratings for the three types of studies separately for the three age groups. The same pattern is evident at each age. Relative to studies that had neutral outcomes, children and adolescents believed that studies with favorable outcomes were conducted better and that studies with unfavorable out-

comes were conducted worse. In other words, participants were quick to find flaws in studies when the results were inconsistent with their beliefs but overlooked similar flaws when the results were consistent with their beliefs. This pattern is particularly strong for the 10-year-olds, but it was also found for the 13- and 16-year-olds.

What did the investigators conclude? Klaczynski and Narasimham believe that adolescents use their scientific reasoning skills selectively, raising their standards to dismiss findings that threaten their beliefs and lowering them to admit findings compatible with their beliefs. Such biased reasoning can be traced to two factors. One concerns self-esteem: When outcomes favor groups to which a person belongs, self-esteem is enhanced; consequently, people overlook flaws in studies that produce results favorable to their groups. That is, children and adolescents may have ignored flaws in studies that were critical about their own religious group because accepting the evidence would have reduced their own self-esteem. A second factor concerns people's naive theories of the world (like those described in Chapter 4). Such theories are often created over long periods of time, and individuals

come to believe them to be self-evident and true. Consequently, a person's naive theories are protected by adjusting standards depending on the fit of the results with the person's theory. That is, children and adolescents may have ignored flaws in studies that were critical about their own religious group because accepting the flaws would force them to revise a well-developed and well-believed naive theory about their religious group.

What converging evidence would strengthen these conclusions? An obvious way to bolster these results would be to show that they are not specific to religious beliefs but, instead, extend to other types of beliefs. For example, they might study political beliefs (although this would be difficult with the younger participants in the study). The prediction is that adolescents who, for example, identified themselves with the Democratic Party would be less likely to detect flaws in studies that portrayed Democrats positively.

To enhance your understanding of this research, go to http://psychology.wadsworth.com/kail_cavanaugh4e/ to complete critical thinking questions and explore related websites.

The Spotlight on Research feature tells us that Crystal, the mother in the opening vignette, should not be so perplexed by her son's seemingly erratic thinking: Adolescents (and adults, for that matter) do not always use the most powerful levels of thinking that they possess. The information-processing account of intellectual functioning in adolescence is really a description of how children and adolescents *can* think, not how they always or even usually think.

TEST YOURSELF

1. According to information-processing theorists, adolescence is a time of important changes in working memory, processing speed, _____, strategies, and metacognition.

2. Information-processing theorists view adolescence as a time of _____.

3. When evidence is inconsistent with their beliefs, adolescents often _____.

The information-processing account of cognitive change in adolescence emphasizes working memory, knowledge, and strategies. How might each of these factors be influenced by nature? By nurture?

Answers: (1) content knowledge, (2) gradual cognitive change, (3) ignore or dismiss the evidence

---

LEARNING OBJECTIVES

How do adolescents reason about moral issues?

Is moral reasoning similar in all cultures?

How do concern for justice and caring for other people contribute to moral reasoning?

What factors help promote more sophisticated reasoning about moral issues?

8.4

REASONING ABOUT MORAL ISSUES

Howard, the least popular boy in the entire eighth grade, had been wrongly accused of stealing a sixth grader's CD player. Min-shen, another eighth grader, knew that Howard was innocent but said nothing to the school principal for fear of what his friends would say about siding with Howard. A few days later, when Min-shen's father heard about the incident, he was upset that his son apparently had so little "moral fiber." Why hadn't Min-shen acted in the face of an injustice?

ONE DAY THE LOCAL PAPER HAD TWO ARTICLES about youth from the area. One article was about a 15-year-old girl who was badly burned while saving her younger brothers from a fire in their apartment. Her mother said she wasn't surprised by her daughter's actions because she had always been an extraordinarily caring person. The other article was about two 17-year-old boys who had beaten an elderly man to death. They had only planned to steal his wallet, but when he insulted them and tried to punch them, they became enraged.

Reading articles like these, you can't help but question why some teenagers (and adults, as well) act in ways that earn our deepest respect and admiration, whereas others earn our utter contempt as well as our pity. And, at a more mundane level, we wonder why Min-shen didn't tell the truth about the stolen CD player to the principal. In this section, we'll start our exploration of moral reasoning with an influential theory proposed by Lawrence Kohlberg.

KOHLBERG'S THEORY

Some of the world's great novels are based on moral dilemmas. Victor Hugo's *Les Misérables,* for example, begins with the protagonist, Jean Valjean, stealing a loaf of bread to feed his sister's starving child. You could probably think of many reasons Valjean should have stolen the bread as well as arguments why he shouldn't have stolen the bread. Lawrence Kohlberg created stories like this one in which decisions were difficult because every alternative involved some undesirable consequences. In fact, there is no "correct" answer—that's why the stories are referred to as moral "dilemmas." Kohlberg was primarily interested in the reasoning used to justify a decision—Why should Jean Valjean steal the bread? Why should he not steal the bread?—not the decision itself.

Kohlberg's (1969) best known moral dilemma is this story about Heinz, whose wife is dying:

> In Europe, a woman was near death from cancer. One drug might save her, a form of radium that a druggist in the same town had recently discovered. The druggist was charging $2,000, ten times what the drug cost him to make. The sick woman's husband, Heinz, went to everyone he knew to borrow the money, but he could only get together about half of what it cost. He told the druggist that his wife was dying and asked him to sell it cheaper or let him pay later. But the druggist said, "No." The husband got desperate and broke into the man's store to steal the drug for his wife. (p. 379)

Thus, Heinz and Jean Valjean both face moral dilemmas in which the various alternative courses of action have desirable and undesirable features.

Kohlberg analyzed children's, adolescents', and adults' responses to a large number of dilemmas and identified three levels of moral reasoning, each divided into 2 stages. Across the six stages, the basis for moral reasoning shifts. In the earliest stages, moral reasoning is based on external forces, such as the promise of reward or the threat of punishment. At the most advanced levels, moral reasoning is based on a personal, internal moral code and is unaffected by others' views or society's expectations. Let's take a closer look.

Kohlberg identified three levels of moral reasoning: preconventional, conventional, and postconventional. Each level is further subdivided into two substages. *At the **preconventional level,** moral reasoning is based on external forces.* For most children, many adolescents, and some adults, moral reasoning is controlled almost exclusively by rewards and punishments. *Individuals in Stage 1 moral reasoning assume an **obedience orientation,** which means believing that authority figures know what is right and wrong.* Consequently, Stage 1 individuals do what authorities say is right to avoid being punished. At this stage, one might argue that Heinz shouldn't steal the drug because an authority figure (e.g., parent or police officer) said he shouldn't do it. Alternatively, one might argue that he should steal the drug because he would get into trouble if he let his wife die.

*In Stage 2 of the preconventional level, people adopt an **instrumental orientation,** in which they look out for their own needs.* Stage 2 individuals are nice to others because they expect the favor to be returned in the future. Someone at this stage could justify stealing the drug because Heinz's wife might do something nice for Heinz in return. Or, they might argue that Heinz shouldn't steal the drug because it will create more problems for him if his wife remains bedridden and he is burdened with caring for her.

*At the **conventional level,** adolescents and adults look to society's norms for moral guidance.* In other words, people's moral reasoning is largely determined by others' expectations of them. *In Stage 3, adolescents' and adults' moral reasoning is based on **interpersonal norms.*** The aim is to win the approval of other people by behaving as "good boys" and "good girls" would. Stage 3 individuals might argue that Heinz shouldn't steal the drug because he must keep his reputation as an honest man, or that no one would think negatively of him for trying to save his wife's life.

*Stage 4 of the conventional level focuses on **social system morality.*** Here, adolescents and adults believe that social roles, expectations, and laws exist to maintain order within society and to promote the good of all people. Stage 4 individuals might reason that Heinz shouldn't steal the drug, even though his wife might die, because it is illegal and no one is above the law. Alternatively, they might claim that he should steal it to live up to his marriage vow of protecting his wife, even though he will face negative consequences for his theft.

*At the **postconventional level,** moral reasoning is based on a personal moral code.* The emphasis is no longer on external forces like punishment, reward, or social roles. *In Stage 5, people base their moral reasoning on a **social contract.*** Adults agree that members of social groups adhere to a social contract because a common set of expectations and laws benefits all group members. However, if these expectations and laws no longer promote the welfare of individuals, they become invalid. Consequently, Stage 5 individuals might reason that Heinz should steal the drug because social rules about property rights no longer benefit individuals' welfare. (Indeed, the Declaration of Independence, written by Thomas Jefferson in 1776, made a similar argument about the laws of England.) They could alternatively argue that he shouldn't steal it because it would create social anarchy.

Finally, in Stage 6 of the postconventional level, **universal ethical principles** *dominate moral reasoning.* Abstract principles such as justice, compassion, and equality form the basis of a personal code that may sometimes conflict with society's expectations and laws. Stage 6 individuals might argue that Heinz should steal the drug because saving a life takes precedence over everything, including the law. Or they might claim that Heinz's wife has a right to die and that he should not force his views on her by stealing and administering the drug.

Putting the stages together, the entire sequence of moral development looks like this:

Preconventional Level: Punishment and Reward

Stage 1: Obedience to authority

Stage 2: Nice behavior in exchange for future favors

Conventional Level: Social Norms

Stage 3: Live up to others' expectations

Stage 4: Follow rules to maintain social order

Postconventional Level: Moral Codes

Stage 5: Adhere to a social contract when it is valid

Stage 6: Personal moral system based on abstract principles

The developmental sequence described by Kohlberg usually takes many years to unfold. But on occasion, we may see the process occur much more dramatically, such as when individuals undergo a major transformation in their moral motivation. One noteworthy example of such a transformation was depicted in Steven Spielberg's Oscar-winning movie *Schindler's List,* as described in the Real People feature.

REAL PEOPLE: Applying Human Development

SCHINDLER'S LIST

The outbreak of war typically provides numerous opportunities for shrewd businesspeople to profit from the increased demand for manufactured goods. The outbreak of World War II in Europe in 1939 was no exception. Oskar Schindler was one such entrepreneur who made a great deal of money working for the Germans after they conquered Poland. His flamboyant demeanor brought him to the attention of the local German commanders, for whom Schindler did favors. Motivated at first strictly by the potential for personal profit, he opened a factory in which he employed Jews as slave labor, with few, if any, qualms.

Schindler's company was quite successful. But as the war continued, official German policy toward Jews changed to one of extermination. Jewish citizens in Poland and other countries were rounded up and shipped to concentration camps or summarily executed. Schindler was deeply disturbed by this, and his attitudes began to change. His employees suggested that he give the Germans a list of workers essential to the factory's continued operation. The list provided protection because the plant's products were used in the war effort. This, of course, also kept the profits rolling in. But Schindler's motivation gradually underwent a profound transformation as well. No longer driven by profit, he went to great lengths to preserve life, at no small danger to himself. He created cover stories to support his claims that certain employees were essential, and he went to Auschwitz to

During World War II, Oskar Schindler saved the lives of many Jews by adding their names to lists of employees who were essential for his factory's operation.

AP Photo/Peter Hillebrecht

rescue employees who were sent there by mistake.

Oskar Schindler's list saved many lives. Profits were made (and helped provide the perfect cover), but he employed Jews in his factory primarily to save them from the gas chamber. Schindler may have begun the war at Kohlberg's preconventional level—where he was motivated solely by personal profit—but he ultimately moved to the postconventional level—where he was motivated by the higher principle of saving lives. And it is at the postconventional level that heroes are made.

Support for Kohlberg's Theory

Kohlberg proposed that his stages form an invariant sequence. That is, individuals move through the six stages in the order listed and only in that order. If his stage theory is right, then level of moral reasoning should be strongly associated with age and level of cognitive development: Older and more advanced thinkers should, on average, be more advanced in their moral development, and indeed, they usually are (Stewart & Pascual-Leone, 1992).

For example, Figure 8.8 shows developmental change in the percentage of individuals who reason at Kohlberg's different stages. Stages 1 and 2 are common among children and young adolescents but not older adolescents and adults. Stages 3 and 4 are common among older adolescents and adults. The figure also shows that most individuals do not progress to the final stages. Most adults' moral reasoning is at Stages 3 and 4.

Support for Kohlberg's invariant sequence of stages also comes from longitudinal studies measuring individuals' level of reasoning over several years. Individuals do progress through each stage in sequence, and virtually no individuals skip any stages (Colby et al., 1983). Longitudinal studies also show that, over time, individuals become more advanced in their level of moral reasoning or remain at the same level. They do not regress to a lower level (Walker & Taylor, 1991).

Additional support for Kohlberg's theory comes from research on the link between moral reasoning and moral behavior. In general, level of moral reasoning should be linked to moral behavior. Remember that less advanced moral reasoning reflects the influence of external forces such as rewards and social norms, whereas more advanced reasoning is based on a personal moral code. Therefore, individuals at the preconventional and conventional levels would act morally when external forces demand, but otherwise they may not. In contrast, individuals at the postconventional level, where reasoning is based on personal principles, should be compelled to moral action even when external forces may not favor it.

> **THINK ABOUT IT**
>
> How might cognitive-developmental level and stage of moral reasoning be raised?

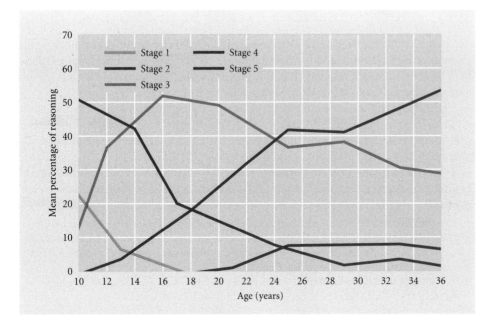

■ **Figure 8.8**
During adolescence and young adulthood, reasoning at Kohlberg's Stage 4 becomes more common, but reasoning at Stages 1 and 2 becomes less common.

Let's return to the example in the vignette. Suppose you know that one of the least popular students has been wrongly accused of stealing a CD player; you know that some friends in your group are actually responsible. What would you do? Speaking out on behalf of the unpopular student is unlikely to lead to a reward. Furthermore, there are strong social norms against "squealing" on friends. So if you are in the preconventional or conventional level of moral reasoning, like Min-shen, the boy in the vignette, you would probably let the unpopular student be punished unfairly. But if you are at the postconventional level and see the situation in terms of principles of justice and fairness, you would be more likely to identify the real perpetrators, despite the price to be paid in rejection by the group.

Many researchers report findings that support the hypothesized link between moral reasoning and moral action. In one study (Gibbs et al., 1986), high school teachers were asked to judge whether their students would defend their principles in difficult situations, or if they would act morally only when it was fashionable or handy. High school students who were judged by their teachers to have greater moral courage tended to be more advanced in Kohlberg's stages than students who were judged less courageous. That is, students who protest social conditions tend to have higher moral reasoning scores. The converse is also true: Delinquent adolescents, whose actions are more likely to be morally offensive, tend to have lower moral reasoning scores than nondelinquent adolescents (Chandler & Moran, 1990). That is, delinquent adolescents are more likely to emphasize punishment and reward in their moral reasoning, not social norms and personal moral codes.

On another point of Kohlberg's theory, support is mixed. Kohlberg claimed that his sequence of stages is universal: All people in all cultures progress through the six-stage sequence. Some research shows that children and adolescents in cultures worldwide reason about moral dilemmas at Stage 2 or 3, just like North American children and adolescents. But as we'll see in the next section, beyond the earliest stages, moral reasoning in other cultures is often not described well by Kohlberg's theory (Turiel & Neff, 2000).

Teenagers who engage in moral behavior, such as participating in protest marches, often reason at high levels in Kohlberg's theory.

THINK ABOUT IT

Research shows that people sometimes do not reason at the most advanced levels of which they are capable; instead, they revert to simpler, less mature levels. Might this happen in the realm of moral reasoning too? What factors might make it more likely for a person's moral reasoning to revert to a less sophisticated level?

CULTURAL DIFFERENCES IN MORAL REASONING

Many critics note that Kohlberg's emphasis on individual rights and justice reflects traditional American culture and Judeo-Christian theology. Not all cultures and religions share this emphasis; consequently, moral reasoning might be based on different values in other cultures (Carlo et al., 1996; Keller et al., 1998).

The Hindu religion, for example, emphasizes duty and responsibility to others, not individual rights and justice (Simpson, 1974). Accordingly, children and adults reared with traditional Hindu beliefs might emphasize caring for others in their moral reasoning more than individuals brought up in the Judeo-Christian tradition.

Miller and Bersoff (1992) tested the hypothesis that cultural differences affect moral reasoning by constructing dilemmas with both justice- and care-based solutions. For example:

> Ben planned to travel to San Francisco in order to attend the wedding of his best friend. He needed to catch the very next train if he was to be on time for the ceremony, as he had to deliver the wedding rings. However, Ben's wallet was stolen in the train station. He lost all of his money as well as his ticket to San Francisco.
>
> Ben approached several officials as well as passengers . . . and asked them to loan him money to buy a new ticket. But, because he was a stranger, no one was willing to lend him the money he needed.

While Ben . . . was trying to decide what to do next, a well-dressed man sitting next to him walked away. . . . Ben noticed that the man had left his coat unattended. Sticking out of the man's coat pocket was a train ticket to San Francisco. . . . He also saw that the man had more than enough money in his coat pocket to buy another train ticket. (p. 545)

One solution emphasized individual rights and justice:

Ben should not take the ticket from the man's coat pocket even though it means not getting to San Francisco in time to deliver the wedding rings to his best friend. (p. 545)

The other solution placed a priority on caring for others:

Ben should go to San Francisco to deliver the wedding rings to his best friend even if it means taking the train ticket from the other man's coat pocket. (p. 545)

When children and adults living in the United States responded to dilemmas like this one about Ben, a slight majority selected the justice-based alternative. In contrast, when Hindu children and adults living in India responded to the same dilemmas, the overwhelming majority selected the care-based alternative.

Clearly, moral reasoning reflects the culture in which a person is reared. Consistent with Kohlberg's theory, judgments by American children and adults reflect their culture's emphasis on individual rights and justice. But judgments by Indian children and adults reflect their culture's emphasis on caring for other people. The bases of moral reasoning are not universal as Kohlberg claimed; instead, they reflect cultural values.

In their thinking about moral dilemmas, Hindu children and adults living in India often emphasize responsibility for others.

BEYOND KOHLBERG'S THEORY

Kohlberg's theory obviously is not the final word on moral development. Much about his theory seems valid, but some research findings indicate that Kohlberg's theory applies primarily to cultures with Western philosophical and religious traditions. In the next few pages, we describe some work that helps to complete our picture of moral reasoning.

Gilligan's Ethic of Caring

Researcher Carol Gilligan (1982; Gilligan & Attanucci, 1988) questions how applicable Kohlberg's theory is even within the Western tradition. Gilligan argues that Kohlberg's emphasis on justice applies more to men than to women, whose reasoning about moral issues is often rooted in concern for others. Gilligan (1982) writes, "The moral imperative that emerges repeatedly in interviews with women is an injunction to care, a responsibility to discern and alleviate the real and recognizable trouble of this world" (p. 100).

Gilligan proposed a developmental progression in which individuals gain greater understanding of caring and responsibility. In the first stage, children are preoccupied with their own needs. In the second stage, people care for others, particularly those who are less able to care for themselves, such as infants and the aged. The third stage unites caring for others and for oneself by emphasizing caring in all human relationships and by denouncing exploitation and violence between people. For example, consider why a teen might be helping at a homeless shelter. She does so not because she believes the homeless are needy but because she believes, first, that all humans should care for each other, and, second, that many people are in the shelter because they've been exploited.

Like Kohlberg, Gilligan also believes that moral reasoning becomes qualitatively more sophisticated as individuals develop, progressing through a number of distinct stages. However, Gilligan emphasizes care (helping people in need) instead of justice (treating people fairly).

What does research tell us about the importance of justice and care in moral reasoning? Do females and males differ in the bases of their moral reasoning? The best answer to these questions comes from a comprehensive meta-analysis conducted by Jaffee

According to Gilligan, moral reasoning is driven by the need to care for others.

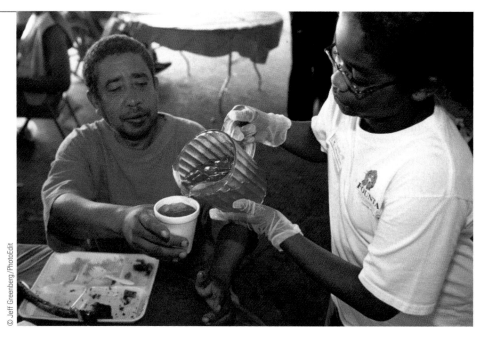

© Jeff Greenberg/PhotoEdit

and Hyde (2000) that included 113 studies with more than 12,000 participants. Overall, boys and men tended to get slightly higher scores on problems that emphasized justice, whereas girls and women tended to get slightly higher scores on problems that emphasized caring. But the differences are small and do not indicate that moral reasoning is predominated by a concern with care for females and a concern with justice for males. Instead, girls and boys as well as men and women reason about moral issues similarly; both often think about moral issues in terms of care and interpersonal relationships (Turiel, 2006).

Eisenberg's Levels of Prosocial Reasoning

Nancy Eisenberg (1982; Eisenberg et al., 1995) argues that Kohlberg's theory is flawed because the dilemmas are unrealistic. They involve breaking a law or disobeying a person in authority. In real life, says Eisenberg, most children's moral dilemmas involve choosing between self-interest and helping others. For example, in one of Eisenberg's moral dilemmas, a child walking to a party comes upon a child injured from a fall. The first child must decide whether to continue to the party or help the second child and miss the party.

Like Kohlberg, Eisenberg focuses on how children explain their choices. *Most preschool and many elementary-school children have a* **hedonistic orientation:** *They pursue their own pleasure.* These children do not help the injured child because they would miss the party. Or they might help because they expect that the injured child would return the favor in the future. In either case, self-interest is the basis of their decision.

Some preschool and many elementary-school children have a **needs-oriented orientation:** *They are concerned about others' needs and want to help.* Children at this stage have learned a simple rule, to help others. They often explain their desire to help as a straightforward "He needs my help." Their desire to help is not based on imagining how the injured child feels or on a personal moral code.

Many elementary-school children and adolescents have a stereotyped, **approval-focused orientation:** *They behave as they think society expects "good people" to behave.* Children and adolescents with this orientation believe that their helpful behavior will cause others to like them more.

Finally, some children and many adolescents develop an **empathic orientation:** *They consider the injured child's perspective and how their own actions will make them feel.* An adolescent with this orientation might say, "He'd be in pain, so I'd feel bad if I didn't help."

The same kinds of evidence that support Kohlberg's theory support Eisenberg's. For example, longitudinal studies indicate that children in many countries move through Eisenberg's different orientations in sequence (Eisenberg, 1986; Eisenberg et al., 1995). Moreover, children who reason at more advanced levels are more likely to actually help others than children who reason at less advanced levels (Miller et al., 1996).

Eisenberg's theory is like Kohlberg's in emphasizing that moral development involves a developmental shift away from self-centered thinking to social norms and moral principles. Her theory is like Gilligan's in emphasizing that caring for others is an important element in everyday moral reasoning.

PROMOTING MORAL REASONING

Whether it is based on justice or care, most cultures and most parents want to encourage adolescents to think carefully about moral issues. What can be done to help adolescents develop more mature forms of moral reasoning? Sometimes simply being exposed to more advanced moral reasoning is sufficient to promote developmental change (Walker, 1980). Adolescents may notice, for example, that older friends do not wait to be rewarded to help others. Or a teenager may notice that respected peers take courageous positions regardless of the social consequences. Such experiences apparently cause adolescents to reevaluate their reasoning on moral issues and propel them toward more sophisticated thinking.

Adolescents often do good deeds because they believe this will make others think better of them.

When adolescents discuss moral issues together, the thinking of those at lower stages in Kohlberg's theory is often influenced by those whose thinking is at the higher stages; that is, individuals who reason at the lower levels typically move their thinking to a more sophisticated stage.

Kohlberg himself wasn't content to simply chart how moral reasoning changed with age. He also wanted to devise ways to foster sophisticated moral reasoning. Kohlberg discovered that discussion can be particularly effective in revealing shortcomings in moral reasoning. When people reason about moral issues with others whose reasoning is at a higher level, the usual result is that individuals reasoning at lower levels improve (Berkowitz & Gibbs, 1985). This is particularly true when the conversational partner with the more sophisticated reasoning makes an effort to understand the other's view by requesting clarification or paraphrasing what the other child is saying (Walker, Hennig, & Krettenauer, 2000). Imagine, for example, two 13-year-olds discussing the Heinz dilemma. Suppose one takes the position that Heinz should not steal the drug because he might get caught—reasoning at the preconventional level. The other argues that Heinz should steal the drug because a husband should do anything to save his wife's life—reasoning at the conventional level. During conversations of this sort, individuals at the preconventional level usually adopt the logic of the children arguing at the higher conventional level.

To foster discussion and expose students to more advanced moral thinking, Kohlberg and his colleagues set up "Just Communities," special groups of students and teachers within public high schools (Higgins, 1991; Power, Higgins, & Kohlberg, 1989). Teachers and students met weekly to plan school activities and discuss school policies. Decisions were reached democratically, with teachers and students alike each

having one vote. However, during discussions, teachers acted as facilitators, encouraging students to consider the moral consequences of different courses of action. Students who participated in Just Communities tended to be more advanced in their moral thinking (Higgins, 1991; Power et al., 1989).

Research findings such as these send an important message to parents: Discussion is probably the best way for parents to help their children think about moral issues in more mature terms (Walker & Taylor, 1991). Research consistently shows that mature moral reasoning comes about when adolescents are free to express their opinions on moral issues to their parents, who are, in turn, expressing their own opinions and, consequently, exposing their adolescent children to more mature moral reasoning (Hoffman, 1988, 1994).

TEST YOURSELF

1. Kohlberg's theory includes the preconventional, conventional, and _____ levels.

2. For children and adolescents in the preconventional level, moral reasoning is strongly influenced by _____.

3. Supporting Kohlberg's theory are findings that level of moral reasoning is associated with age, that people progress through the stages in the predicted sequence, and that _____.

4. Gilligan's view of morality emphasizes _____ instead of justice.

5. When boys' and girls' moral reasoning is compared, the typical result is that _____.

6. Eisenberg's theory of prosocial reasoning is like Kohlberg's theory in claiming that moral reasoning

involves a shift away from self-centered thinking; her theory is like Gilligan's in _____.

7. In Just Communities, teachers encourage students to _____.

8. If parents wish to foster their children's moral development, they should _____ with them.

How similar is Piaget's stage of formal operational thought to Kohlberg's stage of conventional moral reasoning?

Answers: (1) postconventional, (2) reward or punishment, (3) more advanced moral reasoning is associated with moral action, (4) caring for others, (5) they do not differ, (6) its emphasis on caring for others as an important feature in moral reasoning, (7) consider the moral consequences of their decisions, (8) discuss moral issues

Putting It All Together

Teenagers are "nearly" adults, and throughout this chapter we've seen many of the factors that contribute to this remarkable push toward maturity. We began with the physical changes associated with puberty. These outward signs of looming adulthood come early in adolescence for some, but for others, like Pete, they come much later. Next we looked at adolescent health, where we learned of the importance of adequate nutrition and exercise but discovered that many teenagers receive inadequate nutrition and do not exercise regularly. We discovered that for adolescents like Dana who participate in sports, dangerous injuries are uncommon.

From health we moved to information processing, which improves gradually during the teenage years be-

cause of increased working memory and processing speed, greater content knowledge, and more efficient strategies. Adolescents like Crystal's son Calvin do not always think as effectively as they could, sometimes because their beliefs interfere with effective cognition.

We ended the chapter by examining moral reasoning. As children and adolescents develop, their moral reasoning is more likely to be guided by moral principles than by rewards and punishments, but adolescents' moral thinking is based on their desire to win others' approval, which explains why Min-shen did not tell the school principal who really stole the CD player.

Summary

8.1 Pubertal Changes

Signs of Physical Maturation

■ Puberty includes bodily changes in height and weight as well as sexual maturation. Girls typically begin the growth spurt earlier than boys, who acquire more muscle, less fat, and greater heart and lung capacity. Sexual maturation, which includes primary and secondary sex characteristics, occurs in predictable sequences for boys and girls.

Mechanisms of Maturation

■ Pubertal changes take place when the pituitary gland signals the adrenal gland, ovaries, and testes to secrete hormones that initiate physical changes. The timing of puberty is influenced strongly by health and nutrition. In addition, the timing of puberty is influenced by the social environment, coming earlier when girls experience family conflict or depression.

Psychological Impact of Puberty

■ Pubertal changes affect adolescents' psychological functioning. Teens, particularly girls, become concerned about their appearance. When forewarned, adolescents respond positively to menarche and spermarche. Adolescents are moodier than children or adults primarily because their moods shift in response to frequent changes in activities and social setting. Early maturation tends to be harmful to girls.

8.2 Health

Nutrition

■ For proper growth, teenagers need to consume adequate calories, calcium, and iron. Unfortunately, many teenagers do not eat properly and do not receive adequate nutrition.

■ Anorexia and bulimia are eating disorders that typically affect adolescent girls. They are characterized by an irrational fear of being overweight. Several factors contribute to these disorders, including heredity, a childhood history of eating problems, and, during adolescence, negative self-esteem and a preoccupation with one's body and weight. Treatment and prevention programs emphasize changing adolescents' views toward thinness and their eating-related behaviors.

Physical Fitness

■ Individuals who work out at least three times weekly often have improved physical and mental health. Unfortunately, many high school students do not get enough exercise.

■ Millions of American boys and girls participate in sports. Football and basketball are the most popular sports for boys and girls, respectively. The benefits of participating in sports include improved physical fitness, enhanced self-esteem, and understanding about teamwork. The potential costs include injury and abuse of performance-enhancing drugs.

Threats to Adolescent Well-Being

■ Accidents involving automobiles or firearms are the most common cause of death in American teenagers. Many of these deaths could be prevented if, for example, adolescents did not drive recklessly (e.g., too fast and without wearing seatbelts). Adolescents and adults often make decisions similarly, considering the alternatives available, the consequences of each alternative, and the desirability and likelihood of these consequences. The outcomes of decision making sometimes differ because adolescents are more likely to emphasize the social consequences of actions.

8.3 Information Processing During Adolescence

How Does Information Processing Improve in Adolescence?

■ According to information-processing theorists, adolescence is a time of gradual cognitive change. Working memory and processing speed achieve adultlike levels; content knowledge increases, to expertlike levels in some domains; and strategies and metacognitive skills become much more sophisticated.

Limits on Information Processing

■ Adolescents do not always think as effectively as they can. Sometimes they resort to simpler, less mature levels of thinking, and sometimes their beliefs blind them to more sophisticated forms of thought.

8.4 Reasoning About Moral Issues

Kohlberg's Theory

■ Kohlberg proposed that moral reasoning includes preconventional, conventional, and postconventional levels. Moral reasoning is first based on rewards and punishments and, much later, on personal moral codes. As predicted by Kohlberg's theory, people progress though the stages in sequence and do not regress, and morally advanced reasoning is associated with more frequent moral behavior. However, few people attain the most advanced levels, and cultures differ in the bases of moral reasoning.

Cultural Differences in Moral Reasoning

■ Not all cultures emphasize justice in moral reasoning. The Hindu religion emphasizes duty and responsibility to others and, consistent with these beliefs, Hindu children and Indians emphasize caring for other people in their moral reasoning.

Beyond Kohlberg's Theory

■ Gilligan proposed that females' moral reasoning is based on caring and responsibility for others, not justice. Research does not support consistent sex differences in moral reasoning but has found that males and females both consider caring as well as justice in their moral judgments, depending on the situation. According to Eisenberg, reasoning about prosocial

dilemmas shifts gradually from a self-interested, hedonistic orientation to concern for others based on empathy.

Promoting Moral Reasoning

■ Many factors can promote more sophisticated moral reasoning, including (a) noticing that one's current thinking is inadequate (is contradictory or does not lead to clear actions), (b) observing others reasoning at more advanced levels, and (c) discussing moral issues with peers, teachers, and parents.

Key Terms

puberty (308)

primary sex characteristics (309)

secondary sex characteristics (309)

menarche (310)

spermarche (311)

body mass index (316)

basal metabolic rate (316)

anorexia nervosa (317)

bulimia nervosa (317)

preconventional level (327)

obedience orientation (327)

instrumental orientation (327)

conventional level (327)

interpersonal norms (327)

social system morality (327)

postconventional level (327)

social contract (327)

universal ethical principles (328)

hedonistic orientation (332)

needs-oriented orientation (332)

approval-focused orientation (332)

empathic orientation (332)

Learn More About It

Readings

ARNOLD, C. (2004). *Running on empty: A diary of anorexia and recovery.* Livonia, MI: First Page. This autobiography traces the author's 15-year struggle with anorexia.

COLBY, A., & DAMON, W. (1992). *Some who do care: Contemporary lives of moral commitment.* Glencoe, IL: Free Press. The authors, developmental psychologists interested in moral development, use biographies of humanitarians to identify the forces that make some people commit their lives to helping others.

COOPER, K. (1999). *Fit kids.* Nashville, TN: Broadman & Holman. The originator of the concept of aerobic fitness describes a program of diet and exercise developed just for children and adolescents.

ROZAKIS, L., & CAIN, D. (2002). *Super study skills.* New York: Scholastic Reference. This book provides a wide range of excellent tips on effective ways to read and study as well as how to prepare for and take tests.

SLAP, G. A., & JABLOW, M. M. (1994). *Teenage health care.* New York: Pocket Books. The authors provide excellent general information about puberty, exercise, and nutrition but also discuss a variety of specific topics including headaches, cancer, drug abuse, and mental health.

Websites

Visit the Human Development book companion website for all URLs.

■ **The Human Development Book Companion Website**
See **http://www.psychology.wadsworth.com/kail_cavanaugh4e/** for practice quiz questions, Internet links, updates, critical thinking exercises, discussion forums, and more. Also accessible from the Wadsworth Psychology Study Center (http://psychology.wadsworth.com).

■ **Anorexia Nervosa and Relating Eating Disorders, Inc.**
This website describes different eating disorders, their causes, and treatments.

■ **United States Holocaust Memorial Museum**
This site has an online exhibit describing individuals like Oskar Schindler who, during World War II, risked imprisonment and death to save Jews in German-occupied Europe.

■ **President's Council on Physical Fitness and Sports**
Go to this website for statistics on levels of adolescent fitness and ways to encourage adolescents to stay active and fit.

Life-Span CD-ROM

For more information on the concepts covered in this chapter, go to
Module 4: Adolescence

- *Physical Development*
- *Cognitive Development*
- *Emotional and Social Development*

http://www.thomsonedu.com
Go to this site for the link to ThomsonNOW, your one-stop study shop. Take a pre-test for this chapter, and ThomsonNOW will generate a personalized study plan based on your test results. The study plan will identify the topics you need to review and direct you to online resources to help you master those topics. You can then take a post-test to help you determine the concepts you have mastered and what you still need to work on.

9.1 Identity and Self-Esteem
The Search for Identity
Ethnic Identity
Self-Esteem in Adolescence
The Myth of Storm and Stress

9.2 Romantic Relationships and Sexuality
Romantic Relationships
Sexual Behavior
Sexual Orientation
Sexual Coercion

■ SPOTLIGHT ON RESEARCH:
Why Are Some Boys More Likely
to Perpetrate Dating Violence?

9.3 The World of Work
Career Development

■ REAL PEOPLE: APPLYING
HUMAN DEVELOPMENT:
"The Life of Lynne," a Drama
in Three Acts

Part-Time Employment

9.4 The Dark Side
Drug Use
Depression
Delinquency

■ CURRENT CONTROVERSIES:
When Juveniles Commit Serious
Crimes, Should They Be Tried
as Adults?

Putting It All Together
Summary
Key Terms
Learn More About It

CHAPTER 9

Moving into the Adult Social World

Socioemotional Development in Adolescence

You probably have vivid memories of your teenage years. Remember the exhilarating moments—high school graduation, your first paycheck from a part-time job, and your first feelings of love and sexuality? There were, of course, also painful times—your first day on the job when you couldn't do anything right, not knowing what to say on a date with a person you desperately wanted to impress, and countless arguments with your parents. Feelings of pride and accomplishment accompanied by feelings of embarrassment and bewilderment are common to individuals who are on the threshold of adulthood.

Adolescence represents the transition from childhood to adulthood and is a time when individuals grapple with their identity; many have their first experiences with love and sex, and some enter the world of work. In the first three sections of this chapter, we investigate these challenging developmental issues. Then we look at the special obstacles adolescents sometimes encounter that make adolescence difficult to handle.

9.1

IDENTITY AND SELF-ESTEEM

Dea was born in Seoul of Korean parents but was adopted by a Dutch couple in Michigan when she was 3 months old. Growing up, she considered herself a red-blooded American. In college, however, Dea realized that others saw her as an Asian American, an identity about which she had never given much thought. She began to wonder, "Who am I really? American? Dutch American? Asian American?"

LIKE DEA, DO YOU SOMETIMES WONDER WHO YOU ARE? Self-concept refers to the attitudes, behaviors, and values that make a person unique. In adolescence, self-concept takes on special significance as individuals struggle to achieve an identity that will allow them to participate in the adult world. Through self-reflection, youth search for an identity to integrate the many different and sometimes conflicting elements of the self. In this section we'll learn more about the adolescent search for an identity. Along the way, we'll learn more about Dea's struggle to learn who she is.

THE SEARCH FOR IDENTITY

Erik Erikson's (1968) account of identity formation has been particularly influential in our understanding of adolescence. Erikson argued that adolescents face a crisis between identity and role confusion. This crisis involves balancing the desire to try out many possible selves and the need to select a single self. Adolescents who achieve a sense of identity are well prepared to face the next developmental challenge—establishing intimate, sharing relationships with others. However, Erikson believed that teenagers who are confused about their identity can never experience identity in any human relationship. Instead, throughout their lives they remain isolated and respond to others stereotypically.

How do adolescents achieve an identity? They use the hypothetical reasoning skills of the formal-operational stage to experiment with different selves to learn more about possible identities (Nurmi, Poole, & Kalakoski, 1996). Adolescents' advanced cognitive skills enable them to imagine themselves in different roles.

Much of the testing and experimentation is career oriented. Some adolescents may envision themselves as rock stars; others may imagine being professional athletes, Peace Corps workers, or best-selling novelists. Other testing is romantically oriented. Teens may fall in love and imagine living with the loved one. Still other exploration involves religious and political beliefs (King, Elder, & Whitbeck, 1997; Yates & Youniss, 1996). Teens give different identities a trial run just as you might test-drive different cars before selecting one. By fantasizing about their future, adolescents begin to discover who they will be.

As adolescents strive to achieve an identity, they often progress through different phases or statuses as shown in Table 9.1 (Marcia, 1980, 1991). Unlike Piaget's stages, these four phases do not necessarily occur in sequence. Most young adolescents are in a state of diffusion or foreclosure.

The common element in these phases is that teens are not exploring alternative identities. They are avoiding the crisis altogether or have resolved it by taking on an identity suggested by parents or other adults. However, as individuals move into young adulthood, they have more opportunity to explore alternative identities. Diffusion and

As part of their search for an identity, adolescents often try on different roles, trying to imagine what life might be like as, for example, a rock star.

© Lawrence Manning/Corbis

✱ Kroco

TABLE 9.1

Marcia's Four Identity Statuses

Status	Definition	Example
Diffusion	The individual is overwhelmed by the task of achieving an identity and does little to accomplish the task.	Larry hates the idea of deciding what to do with his future, so he spends most of his free time playing video games.
Foreclosure	The individual has a status determined by adults rather than from personal exploration.	For as long as she can remember, Sakura's parents have told her that she should be an attorney and join the family law firm. She plans to study prelaw in college, though she's never given the matter much thought.
Moratorium	The individual is examining different alternatives but has yet to find one that's satisfactory.	Brad enjoys almost all of his high school classes. Some days he thinks it would be fun to be chemist, some days he wants to be a novelist, and some days he'd like to be an elementary-school teacher. He thinks it's a little weird to change his mind so often, but he also enjoys thinking about different jobs.
Achievement	The individual has explored alternatives and has deliberately chosen a specific identity.	Throughout middle school, Efrat wanted to play in the WNBA. During 9th and 10th grades, she thought it would be cool to be a physician. In 11th grade, she took a computing course and everything finally "clicked"—she'd found her niche. She knew that she wanted to study computer science in college.

foreclosure become less common in young adults, and as Figure 9.1 shows, achievement and moratorium become more common (Kroger, 2005).

Typically, young people do not reach the achievement status for all aspects of identity at the same time (Dellas & Jernigan, 1990; Kroger & Green, 1996). Some adolescents may reach the achievement status for occupations before achieving it for religion and politics. Others reach the achievement status for religion before other domains. Evidently, few youth achieve a sense of identity all at once; instead, the crisis of identity is first resolved in some areas and then in others.

■ **Figure 9.1**

Most 15-year-olds are still searching for an identity (diffusion state), but many 21-year-olds have achieved an identity.

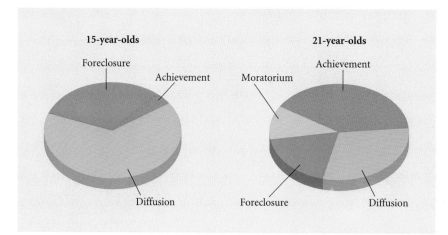

When the achievement status is attained, the period of active experimentation ends, and individuals have a well-defined sense of self. However, during adulthood, an individual's identity is sometimes reworked in response to new life challenges and circumstances. Consequently, individuals may return to the moratorium status for a period of time, only to reemerge with a changed identity. In fact, adults may go through these changes several times, creating "MAMA" cycles in which they alternate between the *m*oratorium and *a*chievement statuses as they explore new alternatives in response to personal and family crises (Marcia, 1991). For example, a man who has placed career above all else but finds himself unemployed may reorganize his life around family and become the primary caregiver of his children.

During the search for identity, adolescents reveal a number of characteristic ways of thinking. They are often very self-oriented. *The self-absorption that marks the teenage search for identity is referred to as* **adolescent egocentrism** (Elkind, 1978). Unlike preschoolers, adolescents know that others have different perspectives on the world. Adolescents are simply *much* more interested in their own feelings and experiences than in anyone else's experiences. In addition, as they search for an identity, many adolescents wrongly believe that they are the focus of others' thinking. A teen who spills food on herself may imagine that all her friends are thinking only about the stain on her blouse and how sloppy she is. *Many adolescents feel that they are, in effect, actors whose performance is watched constantly by their peers, a phenomenon known as the* **imaginary audience.**

Although an identity is first formed in adolescence, it may evolve as adults respond to life events; a man may abandon a career-related identity in favor of one centered on being a primary caregiver.

Adolescent self-absorption is also demonstrated by the **personal fable,** *teenagers' tendency to believe that their experiences and feelings are unique, that no one has ever felt or thought as they do.* Whether it is the excitement of first love, the despair of a broken relationship, or the confusion of planning for the future, adolescents often believe they are the first to experience these feelings and that no one else could possibly understand the power of their emotions (Elkind & Bowen, 1979). *Adolescents' belief in their uniqueness also contributes to an* **illusion of invulnerability**—*the belief that misfortune only happens to others.* They think they can have sex without becoming pregnant, and they can drive recklessly without being in an auto accident. These characteristics of adolescents' thinking are summarized in Table 9.2.

As adolescents make progress toward achieving an identity, adolescent egocentrism, imaginary audiences, personal fables, and the illusion of invulnerability become less common. What circumstances help adolescents achieve identity? Parents are influential (Marcia, 1980). When parents encourage discussion and recognize children's auton-

TABLE 9.2

Characteristics of Adolescents' Thinking

Feature	Definition	Example
Adolescent egocentrism	Adolescents are overly concerned with their own thoughts and feelings.	When Levi's grandmother died unexpectedly, Levi was preoccupied with how the funeral would affect his weekend plans and ignored how upset his mother was by her own mother's death.
Imaginary audience	Adolescents believe that others are watching them constantly.	Tom had to ride his bike to football practice because his dad wouldn't let him have the car; he was sure that all his car-driving friends would see and make fun of him.
Personal fable	Adolescents believe that their experiences and feelings are unique.	When Rosa's boyfriend decided to date another girl, Rosa cried and cried. She couldn't believe how sad she was, and she was sure her mom had never felt this way.
Illusion of invulnerability	Adolescents think that misfortune only happens to others.	Kumares and his girlfriend had been having sex for about 6 months. Although she thought it would be a good idea to use birth control, he thought it was unnecessary: There was no way his girlfriend would get pregnant.

omy, their children are more likely to reach the achievement status. Apparently these youth feel encouraged to undertake the personal experimentation that leads to identity. In contrast, when parents set rules with little justification and enforce them without explanation, children are more likely to remain in the foreclosure status. These teens are discouraged from experimenting personally; instead, their parents simply tell them what identity to adopt. Overall, adolescents are most likely to establish a well-defined identity in a family atmosphere where parents encourage children to explore alternatives on their own but do not pressure or provide explicit direction (Harter, 1990, 1999).

Sean Murphy/Getty Images

Adolescents often believe that others are constantly watching them, a phenomenon known as imaginary audience; consequently, they're often upset or embarrassed when they make obvious mistakes or blunders, such as spilling food or drink.

ETHNIC IDENTITY

Roughly one third of the adolescents and young adults living in the United States are members of ethnic minority groups, including African Americans, Asian Americans, Latino Americans, and Native Americans. *These individuals typically develop an* **ethnic identity:** *They feel a part of their ethnic group and learn the special customs and traditions of their group's culture and heritage* (Phinney, 2005).

Achieving an ethnic identity seems to occur in three phases. Initially, adolescents have not examined their ethnic roots. A teenage African American girl in this phase remarked, "Why do I need to learn about who was the first Black woman to do this or that? I'm just not too interested" (Phinney, 1989, p. 44). For this girl, ethnic identity is not yet an important personal issue.

In the second phase, adolescents begin to explore the personal impact of their ethnic heritage. The curiosity and questioning that is characteristic of this stage is captured in the comments of a teenage Mexican American girl who said, "I want to know what we do and how our culture is different from others. Going to festivals and cultural events helps me to learn more about my own culture and about myself" (Phinney, 1989, p. 44). Part of this phase involves learning cultural traditions; for example, many adolescents learn to prepare ethnic food.

In the third phase, individuals achieve a distinct ethnic self-concept. One Asian American adolescent explained his ethnic identification like this: "I have been born Fil-

THINK ABOUT IT

Although Piaget's theory of cognitive development was not concerned with identity formation, how might his theory explain why identity is a central issue in adolescence?

Part of the search for an ethnic identity involves learning cultural traditions, such as learning how to prepare foods associated with one's ethnic group.

ipino and am born to be Filipino. . . . I'm here in America, and people of many different cultures are here, too. So I don't consider myself only Filipino, but also American" (Phinney, 1989, p. 44).

To see if you understand the differences between these stages of ethnic identity, reread the vignette on page 340 about Dea, the Dutch-Asian-American college student. Then decide which stage applies to her. The answer appears on page 347, just before Test Yourself.

Older adolescents are more likely than younger ones to have achieved an ethnic identity because they are more likely to have had opportunities to explore their cultural heritage (Phinney & Chavira, 1992). Also, as is the case with overall identity, adolescents are most likely to achieve an ethnic self-concept when their parents encourage them to explore alternatives instead of pressuring them to adopt a particular ethnic identity (Rosenthal & Feldman, 1992).

Ethnic identity poses a special challenge for immigrant adolescents. Unlike native-born ethnic children, who have exposure to mainstream and ethnic culture from a young age, from the time immigrant adolescents enter a new country, they face the task of negotiating a culture largely unfamiliar to them. And many immigrant adolescents have already established a strong identity with their native land. Consequently, it's not surprising that immigrant adolescents do not immediately identify with their new culture. For example, in one study (Berman & Trickett, 2001), Jewish adolescents who had fled the former Soviet Union report that, although they acted like most American teenagers (e.g., they ate American food, spent time with native-born American teens), they still "felt Russian" despite having lived in the United States for nearly 10 years.

Do adolescents benefit from a strong ethnic identity? Yes. Adolescents who have achieved an ethnic identity tend to have higher self-esteem and find their interactions with family and friends more satisfying (Roberts et al., 1999). In addition, many investigators have found that adolescents with a strong ethnic identity do better in school than adolescents whose ethnic identities are weaker. For example, Chavous and colleagues (2003) found that African American adolescents were most likely to stay in high school and go on to college when they had a strong African American identity coupled with awareness of racism in American society.

Some individuals achieve a well-defined ethnic self-concept and, at the same time, identify strongly with the mainstream culture. In the United States, for example, many Chinese Americans embrace both Chinese and American culture; in England many Indians identify with both Indian and British cultures. In contrast, for other individuals, the cost of strong ethnic identification is a weakened tie to mainstream culture. For example, some researchers report that strong identification with American culture is associated with a weaker ethnic self-concept for Latino Americans (Phinney, 1990).

We shouldn't be too surprised that identifying with mainstream culture weakens ethnic identity in some groups but not others. Racial and ethnic groups living in the United States are diverse. African American, Asian American, Latino American, and Native American cultures and heritages differ, and so we should expect that the nature and consequences of a strong ethnic self-concept will differ across these and other ethnic groups (Phinney, 2005).

Even within any particular group, the nature and consequences of ethnic identity may change over successive generations (Cuellar et al., 1997). As successive generations become more acculturated to mainstream culture, they may identify less strongly with ethnic culture. Thus parents may maintain strong feelings of ethnic identity that their children don't share (Phinney, Ong, & Madden, 2000).

Finally, let's think about adolescents for whom an ethnic identity is a particular challenge—those whose parents come from different racial or ethnic groups. As recently as 1970, only 1% of U.S. children were multiracial; now 5% are (National Center for Health Statistics, 1999). When children have one European American parent and the

THINK ABOUT IT

What factors in the biopsychosocial framework are shown by adolescents who develop an ethnic identity?

other is African American, Asian American, or Latino, children tend to adopt the ethnic minority identity. A child with an Asian mother and a European American father will probably consider herself Asian (Herman, 2004).

SELF-ESTEEM IN ADOLESCENCE

Self-esteem is normally very high in preschool children but declines gradually during the early elementary-school years as children compare themselves to others. By the later elementary-school years, self-esteem has usually stabilized—it neither increases nor decreases in these years (Harter, Whitesell, & Kowalski, 1992). Evidently, children learn their place in the "pecking order" of different domains and adjust their self-esteem accordingly. However, self-esteem sometimes drops when children move from elementary school to middle school or junior high (Twenge & Campbell, 2001). Apparently, when students from different elementary schools enter the same middle school or junior high, they know where they stand compared to their old elementary-school classmates but not compared to students from other elementary schools. Thus peer comparisons begin anew, and self-esteem often suffers temporarily. As a new school becomes familiar and students gradually adjust to the new pecking order, self-esteem again increases.

These changes in overall level of self-esteem are accompanied by another important change: Self-esteem becomes more differentiated as children enter adolescence (Boivin, Vitaro, & Gagnon, 1992). Youth are able to evaluate themselves in more domains as they develop, and their evaluations in each domain are increasingly independent. That is, children's ratings of self-esteem are often consistent across different dimensions of self-esteem, but adolescents' ratings more often vary from one domain to another. For example, a 9-year-old may have high self-esteem in the academic, social, and physical domains, but a 15-year-old might have high self-esteem in the academic domain, moderate self-esteem in the social domain, and low self-esteem in the physical domain.

As children progress through elementary school and enter junior high or middle school, their academic self-concepts become particularly well defined (Byrne & Gavin, 1996; Marsh & Yeung, 1997). As students accumulate successes and failures in school, they form beliefs about their ability in different content areas (e.g., English, math, science), and these beliefs contribute to their overall academic self-concept. A teen who believes she is skilled at English and math but not so skilled in science will probably have a positive academic self-concept overall. But a teen who believes he is untalented in most academic areas will have a negative academic self-concept.

During adolescence, the social component of self-esteem becomes particularly well differentiated. Adolescents distinguish self-worth in many different social relationships. A teenager may, for example, feel very positive about her relationships with her parents but believe that she's a loser in romantic relationships. Another teen may feel loved and valued by his parents but believe the coworkers at his part-time job can't stand him (Harter, Waters, & Whitesell, 1998).

Thus between the late preschool years and adolescence, self-esteem becomes more complex as older children and adolescents identify distinct domains of self-worth. This growing complexity is not surprising—it reflects the older child's and adolescent's greater cognitive skill and the more extensive social world of older children and adolescents.

Influences on Adolescents' Self-Esteem

What factors contribute to adolescents' self-esteem? Research indicates two important sources. One is based on children's actual competence in domains that are important to them: Children's self-worth is greater when they are skilled in areas that matter to them. Think about two students who are struggling in math. This performance will probably create feelings of low self-worth in a student who believes that she's really smart and expect to get straight A's. But the same performance wouldn't phase a student who couldn't care less about math because her life revolves around boys and hanging out at the mall.

Phrased more positively, for children to feel good about themselves overall, they don't need to be superstars in everything. Doing well in something that matters to them —getting good grades, being popular, excelling in athletics—is enough for children and adolescents to have positive feelings of self-worth (Harter, 2005).

Children's and adolescents' self-worth is also affected by how others view them, particularly other people who are important to them. Parents matter, of course, even to adolescents. Children are more likely to view themselves positively when their parents are affectionate toward them and involved with them (Lord, Eccles, & McCarthy, 1994). Around the world, children have higher self-esteem when families live in harmony and parents nurture their children (Scott, Scott, & McCabe, 1991). A father who routinely hugs his daughter and gladly takes her to piano lessons is saying to her, "You are important to me." When children hear this regularly from parents, they evidently internalize the message and come to see themselves positively.

Parents' discipline also is related to self-esteem. Children with high self-esteem generally have parents who aren't afraid to set rules but are also willing to discuss rules and discipline with their children (Coopersmith, 1967). Parents who fail to set rules are, in effect, telling their children that they don't care—they don't value them enough to go to the trouble of creating rules and enforcing them. In much the same way, parents who refuse to discuss discipline with their children are saying, "Your opinions don't matter to me." Not surprisingly, when children internalize these messages, the result is lower overall self-worth.

Peers' views are important too. Children's and particularly adolescents' self-worth is greater when they believe that their peers think highly of them (Harter, 2005). Maddy's self-worth increases, for example, when she hears that Pedro, Matt, and Michael think she's the hottest girl in the eighth grade.

Thus children's and adolescents' self-worth depends on their being competent at something they value and in being valued by people who are important to them. By encouraging children to find their special talents and by being genuinely interested in their progress, parents and teachers can enhance the self-esteem of all students.

THE MYTH OF STORM AND STRESS

Parent-child relations change during adolescence. As teens become more independent, their relationships with their parents become more egalitarian. Parents must adjust to their children's growing sense of autonomy by treating them more like equals (Laursen & Collins, 1994). This growing independence means that teens spend less time with their parents, are less affectionate toward them, and argue more often with them about matters of style, taste, and freedom. In addition, teenagers are more likely to enjoy spending some time alone (Larson, 1997; Wolfson & Carskadon, 1998).

According to American novelists and filmmakers, adolescence is often a time of storm and stress—a period in which parent-child relationships deteriorate in the face of a combative, argumentative youth. Although this view may make for best-selling novels and hit movies, in reality the rebellious teen is largely a myth. Think about these conclusions derived from research findings (Steinberg, 1990):

- Most adolescents admire and love their parents.
- Most adolescents rely upon their parents for advice.
- Most adolescents embrace many of their parents' values.
- Most adolescents feel loved by their parents.

Not exactly the image of the rebel, is it?

Cross-cultural research provides further evidence that adolescence is not necessarily a time of turmoil and conflict. Offer and his colleagues (1988) interviewed adolescents from 10 countries: the United States, Australia, Germany, Italy, Israel, Hungary, Turkey, Japan, Taiwan, and Bangladesh. These investigators found most adolescents moving confidently and happily toward adulthood. As Figure 9.2 shows, most adolescents around the world reported that they were usually happy, and few avoided their homes.

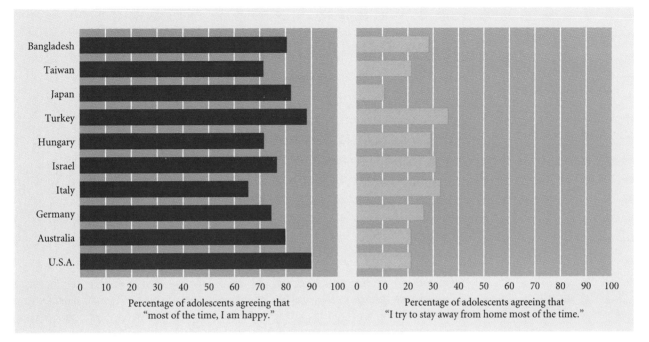

| Percentage of adolescents agreeing that "most of the time, I am happy." | Percentage of adolescents agreeing that "I try to stay away from home most of the time." |

■ **Figure 9.2**
Although the myth is that adolescence is inherently a period of storm and stress, in reality most adolescents worldwide claim to be happy and do not avoid their homes.

Adolescence is definitely an interesting and challenging time for youth and their parents as both parties deal with challenges brought on by an evolving parent-child relationship in which the "child" is nearly a fully independent young adult (Steinberg, 1990). However, it is not inherently tempestuous as the myth of "storm and stress" would lead us to believe.

RESPONSE TO QUESTION ON PAGE 344 ABOUT DEA'S ETHNIC IDENTITY. Dea, the Dutch Asian American college student, doesn't know how to integrate the Korean heritage of her biological parents with the Dutch American culture in which she was reared. This would put her in the second phase of acquiring an ethnic identity. On the one hand, she is examining her ethnic roots, which means she's progressed beyond the initial stages. On the other hand, she has not yet integrated her Asian and European roots and so has not reached the third and final phase.

TEST YOURSELF

1. According to Erikson, adolescents face a crisis between identity and _____ .

2. The _____ status would describe an adolescent who has attained an identity based almost entirely on her parents' advice and urging.

3. A person who has simply put off searching for an identity because it seems too confusing and too overwhelming is in the _____ status.

4. _____ refers to the fact that adolescents sometimes believe that their lives are a performance, with their peers watching them constantly.

5. Adolescents are most likely to achieve an identity when parents encourage them _____.

6. In the second phase of achieving an ethnic identity, adolescents _____.

7. When individuals have a strong ethnic identity, their identification with mainstream culture

_____.

8. Self-esteem often drops when students enter middle school or junior high school because young adolescents _____.

Your local newspaper has just printed a feature describing all the "storm and stress" that typifies adolescence. Write a letter to the editor in which you set the record straight.

Answers: (1) role confusion, (2) foreclosure, (3) diffusion, (4) imaginary audience, (5) to explore alternative identities but do not pressure them or provide direction, (6) start to explore the personal impact of their ethnic roots, (7) is sometimes strong and sometimes weak, depending on specific circumstances, (8) no longer know where they stand among their peers, so they must establish a new "pecking order."

9.2

ROMANTIC RELATIONSHIPS AND SEXUALITY

For 6 months, 15-year-old Gretchen has been dating Jeff, a 17-year-old. She thinks she is truly in love for the first time, and she often imagines being married to Jeff. They have had sex a few times, each time without contraception. It sometimes crosses Gretchen's mind that if she gets pregnant she could move into her own apartment and begin a family.

THE FIRES OF ROMANTIC RELATIONSHIPS have long warmed the hearts of American adolescents. Often, as with Jeff and Gretchen, romance leads to sex. In this section, we'll explore adolescent dating and sexual behavior. As we do, you'll better understand Gretchen's reasons for having unprotected sex with Jeff.

ROMANTIC RELATIONSHIPS

The social landscape adds a distinctive landmark in adolescence—romantic relationships. These are uncommon during elementary school, but in one study of U.S. children and adolescents, about 50% of 15-year-olds and 70% of 18-year-olds had had a romantic relationship within the past 1½ years. Most 18-year-olds had been involved in a romance lasting nearly a year (Carver, Joyner, & Udry, 2003).

Not only do romantic relationships become more common as children develop, their function changes: For younger adolescents, romantic relationships offer companionship like that provided by a best friend and an outlet for sexual exploration. For older adolescents, trust and support become important features of romantic relationships (Shulman & Kipnis, 2001).

As you might suspect, cultural factors strongly influence dating patterns. For example, European American parents tend to encourage independence in their teenagers more than traditional Latino American and Asian American parents, who emphasize family ties and loyalty to parents. Dating is a sign of independence and usually results in less time spent with family, which explains why Latino American and Asian American adolescents often begin to date at an older age and date less frequently (Xiaohe & Whyte, 1990).

It's tempting to dismiss teen romances as nothing more than "puppy love," but they are often developmentally significant. On the one hand, adolescents involved in a romantic relationship are often more self-confident (Harter, 2006). On the other hand, they report more emotional upheaval and conflict (Joyner & Udry, 2000). In addition, early dating with many different partners is associated with a host of problems in adolescence (e.g., drug use, lower grades) and is associated with less satisfying romantic relationships in adulthood (Collins, 2003; Zimmer-Gembeck, Siebenbruner, & Collins, 2001).

SEXUAL BEHAVIOR

We've already seen that sexual exploration is an important feature of romantic relationships for younger adolescents. In fact, by the end of high school, roughly two thirds of American adolescents will have had intercourse at least once (U.S. Department of Health and Human Services, 2004b). But there are gender, regional, and ethnic differences in the prevalence of adolescent sexual activity. About 25% more boys have had sex than girls. African American adolescents begin sexual activity at a younger age than other groups, and teenagers living in rural areas and inner cities are more likely to be sexually active than teens living in the suburbs (Steinberg, 1999). Most teenagers have had intercourse with only one partner.

Why are some adolescents sexually active? Parents are influential: Adolescents are less likely to have sex when they feel close to their parents, when parents monitor their teenagers' activities, and when parents' values discourage sex (Miller, Benson, & Galbraith, 2001). Peers matter too. Adolescents are more likely to have sex when their peers approve and when they believe their peers are also having sex (Brown & Theobald, 1999).

Although a majority of boys and girls have sex at some point during adolescence, sexual activity has very different meanings for boys and girls (Brooks-Gunn & Paikoff, 1993). Girls tend to describe their first sexual partner as "someone they love," but boys describe their first partner as a "casual date." Girls report stronger feelings of love for their first sexual partner than for a later partner, but boys don't. Girls have mixed feelings after their first sexual experience—fear and guilt mixed with happiness and excitement—whereas boys' feelings are more uniformly positive. Finally, when describing their sexual experiences to peers, girls' peers typically express some disapproval, but boys' peers typically do not. In short, for boys sexual behavior is viewed as recreational and self-oriented; for girls sexual behavior is viewed as romantic and is interpreted through their capacity to form intimate interpersonal relationships (Steinberg, 1999).

Sexually Transmitted Diseases

Adolescent sexual activity is cause for concern because a number of diseases are transmitted from one person to another through sexual intercourse. Table 9.3 lists several of the most common types of sexually transmitted diseases (STDs). Some STDs, such as chlamydia and syphilis, are caused by bacteria; others, such as herpes and hepatitis B, are caused by a virus.

You can see from the table that several STDs can have serious complications if left untreated. Most are cured readily with antibiotics. In contrast, the prognosis is bleak for individuals who contract the human immunodeficiency virus (HIV), which typically leads to acquired immunodeficiency syndrome (AIDS). In persons with AIDS, the immune system is no longer able to protect the body from infections, and they often die from one of these infections.

Adolescents and young adults—those age 24 and younger—account for roughly 15% of all AIDS cases in the United States (Centers for Disease Control and Prevention, 2004b). Most of these people contracted the disease during adolescence. Many factors make adolescents especially susceptible to AIDS. Teenagers and young adults are more likely than older adults to engage in unprotected sex and to use intravenous drugs—common pathways for the transmission of AIDS.

Teenage Pregnancy and Contraception

Adolescents' sexual behavior is a cause for concern because approximately 1 in 11 American adolescent girls becomes pregnant; about half of them give birth. The result is that nearly a half million babies are born to American teenagers annually. African American, Native American, and Latino American adolescents are the most likely to become teenage moms; Asian American adolescents are the least likely (Martin et al., 2005).

Teenage mothers and their children usually face bleak futures. If this is the case, why do so many teens become pregnant? The answer is simple: Only about half of teenagers use contraception when they first have intercourse; and about 10% of teens who are sexually active do not use contraception. Those who do often use ineffective methods, such as withdrawal, or practice contraception inconsistently (Besharov & Gardiner, 1997; Kirby, 2001).

> **THINK ABOUT IT**
>
> According to the "storm and stress" view of adolescence, sexual behavior would be one way for adolescents to rebel against their parents. Does research on adolescent sexuality support this prediction?

TABLE 9.3

Features of Sexually Transmitted Diseases (STDs)

Disease	Frequency	Symptoms	Complications
Caused by bacteria			
Chlamydia	2.8 million Americans annually	75% of women and 50% of men have no symptoms; sometimes abnormal discharge of pus from the vagina or penis, or pain while urinating	Infections of the cervix and Fallopian tubes that can lead to infertility; rare in men
Gonorrhea	About 750,000 Americans annually	Often no symptoms at all; pus discharged from the penis or vagina, pain associated with urination; for women, pain during intercourse; for men, swollen testicles	Pelvic inflammatory disease, a serious infection of the female reproductive tract that can lead to infertility; in men, epididymitis, an infection of the testicles that can lead to infertility
Syphilis	About 30,000 annually	A sore, called a chancre, at the site of the infection, usually the penis, vulva, or vagina	Left untreated, can damage internal organs such as the brain, nerves, eyes, heart, bones, and joints
Caused by virus			
Genital herpes	At least 45 million Americans 12 and older (roughly one out of 5 adolescents and adults)	Itching, burning, or pain in the genital or anal area; sores on the mouth, penis, or vagina	Recurrent sores; pregnant women can pass the virus to the fetus, which can be fatal
Genital human papilloma virus (HPV)	20 million Americans	Usually no symptoms; sometimes genital warts or discharge from the penis or vagina	Usually goes away; in rare cases leads to cervical cancer
Hepatitis B	About 75,000 Americans annually	Jaundice, fatigue, loss of appetite, abdominal pain	Death from chronic liver disease
HIV	About 40,000 Americans diagnosed annually	Initially a flu-like illness; later, enlarged lymph nodes, lack of energy, weight loss, frequent fevers	Loss of immune cells (AIDS), cancer, death

SOURCE: Centers for Disease Control and Prevention (2005).

45 million have disease [handwritten annotation]

Why do some adolescents not use contraceptives consistently? Several factors contribute (Adler, 1994; Gordon, 1996):

- *Ignorance:* Many adolescents are seriously misinformed about the facts of conception. For example, many do not know when conception is most likely to occur during the menstrual cycle.
- *Illusion of invulnerability:* Too many adolescents deny reality. They believe they are invincible—"It couldn't happen to me"—only others become pregnant.
- *Lack of motivation:* For some adolescent girls, becoming pregnant is appealing. Like Gretchen in the vignette, they think having a child is a way to break away from parents, gain status as an independent-living adult, and have "someone to love them."
- *Lack of access:* Some teenagers do not know where to obtain contraceptives, and others are embarrassed to buy them. Still others don't know how to use contraceptives.

What's the best way to reduce adolescent sexual behavior and teen pregnancy? Programs that focus primarily on abstinence receive lots of headlines, but they are not consistently effective; some versions may work, but many do not (Kirby, 2002). In contrast, comprehensive sex education programs *are* effective (Kirby, 2001). These programs teach the biological aspects of sex and emphasize responsible sexual behavior or abstaining from premarital sex altogether. They also include discussions of the pressures to become involved sexually and ways to respond to this pressure. A key element is that in role-playing sessions students practice strategies for refusing to have sex. Youth who participate in programs like these are less likely to have intercourse; when they do have intercourse, they are more likely to use contraceptives (Kirby, 2001).

SEXUAL ORIENTATION

For most adolescents, dating and romance involve members of the opposite sex. However, in early and mid-adolescence, roughly 15% of teens experience a period of sexual questioning during which they sometimes report emotional and sexual attractions to members of their own sex (Carver, Egan, & Perry, 2004). For most adolescents, these experiences are simply a part of the larger process of role experimentation common to adolescence. However, about 5% of teenage boys and girls identify their sexual orientation as gay or lesbian (Rotherman-Borus & Langabeer, 2001). This identification usually occurs in mid-adolescence, but not until young adulthood do most gay individuals express their sexual orientation publicly (D'Augelli, 1996).

Why do gay adolescents wait so long—3 to 5 years on average—before declaring their sexual orientation? Many believe, correctly, that their peers are not likely to support them (Newman & Muzzonigro, 1993). For example, in one national survey, only 40% of 15- to 19-year-old boys agreed that they could befriend a gay person (Marsiglio, 1993). Adolescents who said that they could not befriend a gay peer were most often younger, identified themselves as religious fundamentalists, and had parents who were less educated.

The roots of sexual orientation are poorly understood. Scientists have, however, discredited several theories of sexual orientation. Research (Golombok & Tasker, 1996; Patterson, 1992) shows that each of the following statements is *false:*

About 5% of adolescents find themselves attracted to members of their own sex, and about 5% identify themselves as gay or lesbian.

- Sons become gay when raised by a domineering mother and a weak father.
- Girls become lesbians when their father is their primary role model.
- Children raised by gay or lesbian parents usually adopt their parents' sexual orientation.
- Gay and lesbian adults were, as children, seduced by an older person of their sex.

If all these statements are false, what determines a person's sexual orientation? The exact factors probably differ from one person to the next, but many scientists today believe that biology plays an important role (Lalumière, Blanchard, & Zucker, 2000). Some evidence suggests that heredity and hormones influence sexual orientation (Bailey, Dunne, & Martin, 2000). Another idea is based on the finding that men are more often gay when they have older brothers, and this effect gets stronger with each additional older brother; the explanation for this effect is that a pregnant woman's immune system responds to some biochemical feature of a male fetus. The response is weak at first but increases with each successive male, ultimately affecting brain development in later-born sons (Bogaert, 2003).

Yet another intriguing idea—one that applies to males and females—is that genes and hormones don't produce sexual orientation per se but lead to temperaments that affect children's preferences for same- and opposite-sex activities (Bem, 1996). Children who do not enjoy gender-typical activities come to see themselves as different and thus ultimately acquire a different gender identity.

Though the origins of sexual orientation may not be obvious, it is clear that gay and lesbian individuals face many special challenges. Their family and peer relationships may be disrupted. They are often attacked, both verbally and physically. Given these problems, it's not surprising that gay and lesbian youth often experience mental health problems such as anxiety and depression (D'Augelli, 2002).

In recent years, social changes have helped gay and lesbian youth respond more effectively to these unique challenges. The "official" stigma associated with being gay or lesbian was removed in 1973 when the American Psychological Association and the American Psychiatric Association declared that homosexuality was not a psychological disorder. Other helpful changes include more (and more visible) gay role models (e.g., popular TV programs such as *Queer Eye for the Straight Guy*) and numerous centers in cities for gay and lesbian youth. These resources are making it easier for gay and lesbian youth to understand their sexual orientation and to cope with the many other demands of adolescence.

SEXUAL COERCION

Cindy reported that her date "lifted up my skirt and took off my panties when I was drunk. Then he laid down on top of me and went to work." *Like Cindy, many adolescent and young women are forced to have sexual intercourse by males they know, a situation known as* **date rape** *or* **acquaintance rape** (Ogletree, 1993). Firm numbers are hard to come by because many cases of rape go unreported. However, in the United States it is estimated that about 10% of high school girls and 20 to 25% of college-age women have been victims of rape or attempted rape (National Center for Injury Prevention and Control, 2005). In addition, many females experience dating violence, in which they're kicked, pushed, choked, or beaten up.

A number of circumstances place an adolescent girl or young woman at risk. One of the most important is drug and alcohol use: Heavy drinking usually impairs a female's ability to send a clear message regarding her intentions and makes males less able and less inclined to interpret such messages (Champion et al., 2004). Females are more at risk when they adhere to more traditional gender stereotypes, apparently because their view of the female gender role includes being relatively submissive to a male's desires (Foshee et al., 2004).

What factors make teenage boys likely to commit acts of violence? One contributing factor is a boy's home life: Boys are more at risk when they were abused as children or witnessed domestic violence, apparently because this leads them to believe that violence is a normal part of romantic relationships (National Center for Injury Prevention and Control, 2005).

In the Spotlight on Research feature, you'll learn about some other factors that make boys more likely to be violent while dating.

SPOTLIGHT ON RESEARCH

WHY ARE SOME BOYS MORE LIKELY TO PERPETRATE DATING VIOLENCE?

Who were the investigators, and what was the aim of the study? Is any teenage boy likely to perpetrate violence while dating? Or are there factors that make some boys a greater risk when it comes to dating violence? If so, what are those factors? Vangie Foshee and her colleagues (2001) designed a study to answer these questions.

How did the investigators measure the topic of interest? The investigators measured dating violence by asking teenage boys whether they

had ever committed any of a list of 18 violent acts while on a date. The list included hitting, choking, slapping, and kicking a partner, as well as whether they had forced a partner to have sex. In addition, several other questionnaires were created that measured factors that might make a boy more at risk for perpetrating dating violence. Some of these factors included peers, other problem behaviors (e.g., drinking), and personal competencies (e.g., self-esteem, communication skills).

Who were the children in the study? The study included 576 boys in eighth and ninth grades who reported that they had begun dating. About 75% of the sample was European American. (The study also included girls, but for simplicity, we're going to concentrate on the results for boys.)

What was the design of the study? This study was correlational because Foshee and her colleagues were interested in the relations that existed naturally between boys' perpetration of violence and other variables that might be related to perpetration of violence. The study was longitudinal because adolescents were tested first in eighth or ninth grade and a second time, about 18 months later. Again, for simplicity, we're going to describe only the results from the first testing.

Were there ethical concerns with the study? Yes. Obviously, violence is a sensitive topic, and the investigators were careful to be sure that they obtained consent from parents and adolescents and that the adolescents' responses were confidential.

What were the results? Most boys said that they had never perpetrated dating violence. However, 10% said that they had used one of the milder forms (e.g., slapped, pushed), and 4% said that they had used one of the more severe forms (e.g., choked, burned, assaulted with a gun or knife). Personal competence was not related to dating violence, but two factors

were linked. One was alcohol use: Boys were 1.31 times more likely to perpetrate violence if they reported frequent use of alcohol. The second was having a friend who had perpetrated dating violence: Boys were 3.57 times more likely to perpetrate violence if they had a friend who had perpetrated violence.

What did the investigators conclude? Some boys definitely represent a greater risk for dating violence. Boys are more likely to perpetrate violence when they drink, which parallels the finding that girls are more likely to be victims when they drink. Drinking and dating are clearly a bad, bad mix. Second, boys more often perpetrate violence when they believe that their friends are doing the same. As we saw in Chapter 7, friends can be powerful forces, for good or for bad.

What converging evidence would strengthen these conclusions? The main limitation of the study concerns the source of the data—questionnaires

completed by the boys themselves. The results hinge on the assumption that adolescent boys' reports are accurate, and there's good reason to doubt the accuracy of these reports. To take an obvious choice, some boys may be reluctant to admit that they've been violent on a date. These findings would be more compelling if there was converging information from another source about frequency of violence during dating. For example, boys and girls who are actively dating could each complete questionnaires, and researchers could compare the boy's responses to questions about perpetration of violence with the girl's responses to questions about being a victim.

To enhance your understanding of this research, go to http://psychology .wadsworth.com/kail_cavanaugh4e/ to complete critical thinking questions and explore related websites.

According to the Foshee et al. (2001) study, the level of dating violence is surprisingly high in boys who have just begun to date. At the start of high school, about one boy in seven admits to having perpetrated violence, which underscores the importance of effective prevention programs. One effective program for reducing sexual violence is "Safe Dates" (Foshee & Langwick, 2004). Targeted for middle and high school students, the program features a brief play, nine hour-long interactive sessions devoted to topics such as overcoming gender stereotypes and how to prevent sexual assault, and a poster contest. Teens who participate in Safe Date are less likely to be victims of sexual violence and are less likely to perpetrate it (Foshee et al., 2004).

Most colleges and universities offer workshops on date rape. These workshops often emphasize the importance of communication. The ad shown in Figure 9.3 is part of one approach to encourage males and females to communicate about sex. Here are some guidelines that are often presented at such workshops; you may find them useful (Allgeier & Allgeier, 2000):

1. Know your own sexual policies. Decide when sexual intimacy is acceptable for *you*.

2. Communicate these policies openly and clearly.

3. Avoid being alone with a person until you have communicated these policies and believe that you can trust the person.

4. Avoid using alcohol or other drugs when you are with a person with whom you do not wish to become sexually intimate.

5. If someone tries to force you to have sex, make your objections known: Talk first, but struggle and scream if necessary.

■ **Figure 9.3**
Posters like this one are designed to reduce dating violence by encouraging men to listen to and respect a woman's intentions.

If you don't take no for an answer, these could be your new roommates.

If she says, "No, stop!" and you don't listen, you're committing rape. A felony. And you could go to jail. Where it may take you a while to get used to the guys in your new dorm.

Against her will is against the law.

This tagline is used with permission from Pi Kappa Phi.

©1992 Rape Treatment Center, Santa Monica Hospital.

© Rape Treatment Center, Santa Monica Hospital

TEST YOURSELF

1. For younger adolescents, romantic relationships offer companionship and _____.

2. Boys more often view sexual behavior as _____, but girls view sex as romantic.

3. When parents approve of sex, their adolescent children are _____.

4. Adolescents and young adults are at particular risk for contracting AIDS because they _____ and use intravenous drugs.

5. Adolescents often fail to use contraception due to ignorance, the illusion of invulnerability, and _____.

6. Not until _____ do most gay and lesbian individuals express their sexual orientation publicly.

7. _____ apparently plays a key role in determining sexual orientation.

8. A girl is more likely to be a victim of sexual violence if she has been drinking and if she _____.

Some sexually active teenagers do not use contraceptives. How do the reasons for this failure show connections between cognitive, social, and emotional development?

Answers: (1) an outlet for sexual exploration, (2) recreational, (3) more likely to be active sexually, (4) engage in unprotected sex, (5) lack of access to contraceptives, (6) young adulthood, (7) Biology, (8) holds traditional views of gender roles

---

9.3

THE WORLD OF WORK

LEARNING OBJECTIVES

How do adolescents select an occupation?

What is the impact of part-time employment on adolescents?

When 15-year-old Aaron announced that he wanted an after-school job at the local supermarket, his mother was delighted, believing that he would learn much from the experience. Five months later, she has her doubts. Aaron has lost interest in school, and they argue constantly about how he spends his money.

"WHAT DO YOU WANT TO BE WHEN YOU GROW UP?" Children are often asked this question in fun. Beginning in adolescence, however, it takes on special significance because work is such an important element of the adult life that is looming on the horizon. A job—be it as a bricklayer, reporter, or child care worker—helps define who we are. In this section, we'll see how adolescents begin to think about possible occupations. We'll also look at adolescents' first exposure to the world of work, which usually comes about with part-time jobs after school or on weekends. As we do, we'll see if Aaron's changed behavior is typical of teens who work part time.

CAREER DEVELOPMENT

Faced with the challenge of selecting a career, many adolescents may be attracted by the approach taken by the teenage boy in the cartoon. Choosing a career is difficult, in part because it involves determining the kinds of jobs that will be available in the future. Predicting the future is risky, but the U.S. Bureau of Labor Statistics projects that by the year 2012, nearly 80% of all jobs will be in service industries, such as education, health care, and banking. About 15% of jobs will be associated with the production of goods. In the future, there will be fewer jobs in agriculture, forestry, and manufacturing (Berman, 2004).

"Your son has made a career choice, Mildred.
He's going to win the lottery and travel a lot."

Knowing the types of jobs that experts predict will be plentiful, how do adolescents begin the long process of selecting an occupation that will bring fame and fortune? Theories of vocational choice describe this process. According to a theory proposed by Donald Super (1976, 1980), identity is a primary force in an adolescent's choice of a career. *At about age 13 or 14, adolescents use their emerging identity as a source of ideas about careers, a process called* **crystallization**. Teenagers use their ideas about their own talents and interests to limit potential career prospects. A teenager who is extroverted and sociable may decide that working with people would be the career for him. Another who excels in math and science may decide she'd like to teach math. Decisions are provisional, and adolescents experiment with hypothetical careers, trying to envision what each might be like.

At about age 18, adolescents extend the activities associated with crystallization and enter a new phase. *During* **specification,** *individuals further limit their career possibilities by learning more about specific lines of work and starting to obtain the training required for a specific job.* The extroverted teenager who wants to work with people may decide that a career in sales would be a good match for his abilities and interests. The teen who likes math may have learned more about careers and decided she'd like to be an accountant. Some teens may begin an apprenticeship as a way to learn a trade.

In the specification stage of career development, adolescents try to learn more about different careers, sometimes by serving an apprenticeship.

The end of the teenage years or the early 20s marks the beginning of the third phase. *During* **implementation,** *individuals enter the workforce and learn firsthand about jobs.* This is a time of learning about responsibility and productivity, of learning to get along with coworkers, and of altering one's lifestyle to accommodate work. This period is often unstable; individuals may change jobs frequently as they adjust to the reality of life in the workplace.

In the Real People feature, you can see these three phases in one young woman's career development.

REAL PEOPLE: Applying Human Development

"THE LIFE OF LYNNE," A DRAMA IN THREE ACTS

Act 1: Crystallization. Throughout high school, Lynne was active in a number of organizations. She enjoyed being busy and liked the constant contact with people. Lynne was often nominated for office, and more often than not, she asked to be treasurer. Not that she was greedy or had her hand in the till; she simply found it satisfying to keep the financial records in order. By the end of her junior year, Lynne decided that she wanted to study business in college, a decision that fit with her good grades in English and math.

Act 2: Specification. Lynne was accepted into the business school of a large state university. She decided that accounting fit her skills and temperament, so this became her major. During the summers, she worked as a cashier at Target. This helped to pay for college and gave her experience in the world of retail sales.

Act 3: Implementation. A few months after graduation, Lynne was offered a junior accounting position with Wal-Mart. Her job required that she work Tuesday through Friday, auditing Wal-Mart stores

in several nearby cities. Lynne liked the pay, the company car, the pay, the feeling of independence, and the pay. However, having to hit the road every morning by 7:30 a.m. was a jolt to someone used to rising casually at 10 a.m. Also, Lynne often found it awkward to deal with store managers, many of whom were twice her age and very intimidating. She was coming to the conclusion that there was much more to a successful career as an accountant than simply having the numbers add up correctly.

"The Life of Lynne" illustrates the progressive refinement that takes place in a person's career development. An initial interest in math and finance led to a degree in business, which led to a job as an accountant. However, one other aspect of Lynne's life sheds more light on Super's theory. After 18 months on the job, Lynne's accounting group was merged with another; this would have required Lynne to move to another state, so she quit. After 6 months looking for another accounting job, Lynne gave up and began to study to become a real estate agent. The moral? Economic conditions and opportunities also shape career development. Changing times can force individuals to take new, often unexpected career paths.

Personality-Type Theory

Super's (1976, 1980) work helps to explain how self-concept and career aspirations develop hand in hand, but it does not explain why particular individuals are attracted to one line of work rather than another. Explaining the match between people and occupations has been the aim of a theory devised by John Holland (1985, 1987, 1996). *According to Holland's* **personality-type theory,** *people find work fulfilling when the important features of a job or profession fit the worker's personality.* Holland identified six prototypic personalities that are relevant to the world of work. Each one is best suited to a specific set of occupations, as indicated in the right-hand column of Table 9.4. Remember, these are merely prototypes. Most people do not match any one personality type exactly. Instead, their work-related personalities are a blend of the six.

This model is useful in describing the career preferences of African, Asian, European, Native, and Latino American adolescents; it is also useful for both males and females (Day, Rounds, & Swaney, 1998). When people have jobs that match their personality type, in the short run they are more productive employees, and in the long run they

TABLE 9.4

Personality Types in Holland's Theory

Personality Type	Description	Careers
Realistic	Individuals enjoy physical labor and working with their hands, and they like to solve concrete problems.	mechanic, truck driver, construction worker
Investigative	Individuals are task-oriented and enjoy thinking about abstract relations.	scientist, technical writer
Social	Individuals are skilled verbally and interpersonally, and they enjoy solving problems using these skills.	teacher, counselor, social worker
Conventional	Individuals have verbal and quantitative skills that they like to apply to structured, well-defined tasks assigned to them by others.	bank teller, payroll clerk, traffic manager
Enterprising	Individuals enjoy using their verbal skills in positions of power, status, and leadership.	business executive, television producer, real estate agent
Artistic	Individuals enjoy expressing themselves through unstructured tasks.	poet, musician, actor

have more stable career paths (Holland, 1996). For example, an enterprising youth is likely to be successful in business because he will enjoy positions of power in which he can use his verbal skills.

Of course, there's more to job satisfaction than the match between a personality type and important features of a job. In fact, the correlation between the degree of match and job satisfaction is relatively small—only about .2 (Arnold, 2004). What this tells us is that even when people are well matched to a job, some will find the work more satisfying than others because of a host of factors, including pay, stress in the workplace, and the frequency of conflicts between work and family obligations (Hammer et al., 2005). Nevertheless, the person-job match is a good place to start thinking about a vocation.

Combining Holland's work-related personality types with Super's theory of career development gives us a very comprehensive picture of vocational growth. On the one hand, Super's theory explains the developmental progression by which individuals translate general interests into a specific career; on the other hand, Holland's theory explains what makes a good match between specific interests and specific careers.

Of course, trying to match interests to occupations can be difficult. Fortunately, several tests can be used to describe a person's work-related personality and the jobs for which he or she is best suited. In the Strong Interest Inventory (SII), for example, people express their liking of different occupations, school subjects, activities, and types of people (e.g., the elderly, people who live dangerously). These answers are compared to the responses obtained from a representative sample of individuals from different occupations.

If you are still undecided about a career, we encourage you to visit your college's counseling center and arrange to take a test like the SII. The results will help you to focus on careers that would match your interests and help you to choose a college major that would lead to those careers.

Even if you are fairly certain of your vocational plans, you might take one of these tests anyway. As we saw with Lynne, career development does not end with the first job.

© Michael Newman/PhotoEdit

According to Holland's personality-type theory, people are satisfied with a job when it matches their personality; for example, adolescents with an enterprising personality type enjoy working in business because this allows them to use verbal skills in positions of leadership.

THINK ABOUT IT

How do the different personality types in Holland's theory relate to the different types of intelligence proposed by Howard Gardner, described in Chapter 6?

People continuously refine their career aspirations over the life span, and these test results might be useful later in your life.

Many American adolescents hold part-time jobs; these can be beneficial but not when adolescents work more than 20 hours weekly.

PART-TIME EMPLOYMENT

Today, about 25% of high school freshmen have a part-time job, and about 75% of high school seniors do (Bureau of Labor Statistics, 2005). About two thirds of these youth work in retail, and half of those working in retail are employed in the food and beverage industry (U.S. Department of Labor, 2000).

Part-time work is a new aspect of adolescence. In the 1970s, only 25% of high school students worked part time compared to 75% in the 1980s and 1990s. This development is unique to the United States. In other industrialized countries in Western Europe and Asia, high school students who also hold part-time jobs are a clear minority. But compared to high school students in these countries, U.S. students have a shorter school day and much less homework, which means they have time to work (Reubens, Harrison, & Kupp, 1981).

Most adults praise teens for working, believing that early exposure to the workplace teaches adolescents self-discipline, self-confidence, and important job skills (Snedeker, 1982). For most adolescents, however, the reality is very different. Part-time work can actually be harmful, for several reasons:

1. *School performance suffers.* When students work more than approximately 15 hours per week, they devote less time to homework and are more apt to cut classes. Not surprisingly, their grades are lower than those of their peers who work less or not at all (Steinberg, Fegley, & Dornbusch, 1993). Why should 15 hours of work be so detrimental to school performance? A 15-hour work schedule usually means four 3-hour shifts after school and another 3-hour shift on the weekend. This would seem to leave ample opportunity to study, but only if students use their time effectively. In fact, many high school students apparently do not have the foresight and discipline necessary to consistently meet the combined demands of work and school. Many teens have great difficulty balancing work, study, and sleep.

When adolescents work long hours in a part-time job, they often have trouble juggling the demands of work, school, and sleep!

2. *Mental health and behavioral problems.* Adolescents who work long hours—more than 15 or 20 hours a week—are more likely to experience anxiety and depression, and their self-esteem often suffers. Many adolescents find themselves in jobs that are repetitive and boring but stressful, and such conditions undermine self-esteem and breed anxiety.

Extensive part-time work frequently leads to substance abuse, including cigarettes, alcohol, marijuana, and cocaine (Mortimer et al., 1996; Valois et al., 1999). Extensive work is also associated with more frequent problem behavior, including violence toward others, trouble with police, and arguments with parents (Staff & Uggen, 2003).

Why employment is associated with all of these problems is not clear. Perhaps employed adolescents turn to drugs to help them cope with the anxiety and depression brought on by work. Arguments with parents may become more common because anxious, depressed adolescents are more prone to argue or because wage-earning adolescents may believe that their freedom should match their income. Whatever the exact mechanism, extensive part-time work is clearly detrimental to the mental health of most adolescents.

3. *Misleading affluence.* Adults sometimes argue that work is good for teenagers because it teaches them "the value of a dollar." Here, too, reality is at odds with the adage. The typical teenage pattern is to "earn and spend." Working adolescents spend most of their earnings on themselves—to buy clothing, snack food, or cosmetics, and to pay for entertainment. Few working teens set aside much of their income for future goals, such as a college education, or use it to contribute to their family's expenses (Shanahan et al., 1996b). Because parents customarily pay for many of the essential expenses associated with truly independent living—rent, utilities, and groceries, for example—working adolescents often have a vastly higher percentage of their income available for discretionary spending than do working adults. Thus, for many teens the part-time work experience provides unrealistic expectations about how income can be allocated (Bachman, 1983).

The message that emerges repeatedly from research on part-time employment is hardly encouraging. Like Aaron, the teenage boy in the vignette, adolescents who work long hours at part-time jobs do not benefit from the experience. To the contrary, they do worse in school, are more likely to have behavioral problems, and learn how to spend money rather than how to manage it. These effects are similar for adolescents from different ethnic groups (Steinberg & Dornbusch, 1991) and are comparable for boys and girls (Bachman & Schulenberg, 1993). Ironically, though, there is a long-term benefit: Young adults who had a stressful part-time job as an adolescent are better able to cope with stressful adult jobs (Mortimer & Staff, 2004). They're apparently better prepared to cope with the corresponding stresses of full-time employment.

Does this mean that teenagers who are still in school should never work part time? Not necessarily. Part-time employment can be a good experience, depending on the circumstances. One key is the number of hours of work. Although the exact number of hours varies, of course, from one student to the next, most students could easily work 5 hours weekly without harm, and many could work 10 hours weekly. Another key is the type of job. When adolescents have jobs that allow them to use their skills (e.g., bookkeeping, computing, or typing) and acquire new ones, self-esteem is enhanced, and they learn from their work experience (Mortimer, Hartley, & Staff, 2002). Yet another factor is how teens spend their earnings. When they save their money or use it to pay for clothes and school expenses, their parent-child relationships often improve (Shanahan et al., 1996a).

By these criteria, who is likely to show the harmful effects of part-time work? A teen who spends 30 hours a week bagging groceries and spends most of it on CDs or videos. And who is likely to benefit from part-time work? A teen who likes to tinker with cars and spends Saturdays working in a repair shop and who sets aside some of his earnings for college.

Finally, summer jobs typically do not involve conflict between work and school. Consequently, many of the harmful effects associated with part-time employment during the school year do not hold for summer employment. In fact, such employment sometimes enhances adolescents' self-esteem, especially when they save part of their income for future plans (Marsh, 1991).

THINK ABOUT IT

Think back to your own high school years and those of your friends. Can you think of students (including yourself!) who showed harmful effects from part-time work? Can you think of people who benefited from part-time work?

TEST YOURSELF

1. During the _____ phase of vocational choice, adolescents learn more about specific lines of work and begin training.

2. Individuals with a(n) _____ personality type are best suited for a career as a teacher or counselor.

3. Adolescents who work extensively at part-time jobs during the school year often get lower grades, have behavior problems, and _____.

4. Part-time employment during the school year can be beneficial if adolescents limit the number of hours they work and _____.

Based on the description of Lynne's career, how would you describe continuity of vocational development during adolescence and young adulthood?

Answers: (1) specification, (2) social, (3) experience misleading affluence, (4) hold jobs that allow them to use and develop skills

---

9.4

THE DARK SIDE

Rod was an excellent student and a starter on his high school basketball team. He was looking forward to going to the senior prom with Peggy, his long-time girlfriend, and then going to the state college with her in the fall. Then, without a hint that anything was wrong in their relationship, Peggy dropped Rod and moved in with the drummer of a local rock band. Rod was stunned and miserable. Without Peggy, life meant so little. Basketball and college seemed pointless. Some days Rod wondered if he should just kill himself to make the pain go away.

LEARNING OBJECTIVES

Why do teenagers drink?

What leads some adolescents to become depressed? How can depression be treated?

What are the causes of juvenile delinquency?

SOME YOUNG PEOPLE DO NOT ADAPT WELL to the new demands and responsibilities of adolescence and respond in ways that are unhealthy. In this last section of Chapter 9, we look at three problems, often interrelated, that create the "three D's" of adolescent development: drugs, depression, and delinquency. As we look at these problems, you'll understand why Rod feels so miserable without Peggy.

DRUG USE

Throughout history, people have used substances that alter their behavior, thoughts, or emotions. Today, drugs used commonly in the United States include alcohol, tobacco, marijuana, hallucinogens (like LSD), heroin, cocaine, barbiturates, and amphetamines. Figure 9.4 provides a picture of the use of these drugs by U.S. adolescents (Johnston et al., 2004). In fact, most adolescents avoid drugs, with one glaring exception—alcohol. A majority of high school seniors have drunk alcohol within the past month (Johnston et al., 2004).

Teenage Drinking

For many teens, drinking alcohol is simply part of the experimentation that is one of the defining characteristics of adolescence. Of course, many adolescents never drink, and

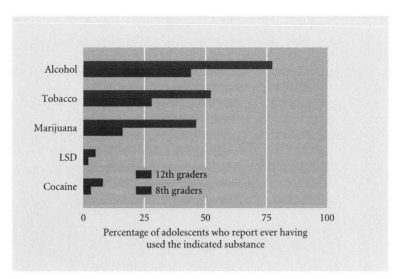

■ Figure 9.4
Alcohol and tobacco are the substances used most frequently by adolescents.

others experiment briefly with drinking, then decide it is not for them. But the majority of American teenagers drink, some heavily.

What determines whether an adolescent joins the majority who drink? At least three factors are important:

■ *Parents.* Teens are more likely to drink (a) when drinking is an important part of parents' social lives—for example, stopping at a bar after work, and (b) when parents are relatively uninvolved in their teenager's life or set arbitrary or unreasonable standards for their teens (Reesman & Hogan, 2005).

■ *Peers.* Many adolescents drink because their peers do so and exert pressure on them to join the group (Simons-Morton et al., 2001).

■ *Stress.* Like adults, many adolescents drink to cope with stress. Teens who report frequent life stresses—problems with parents, with interpersonal relationships, or at school—are more likely to drink and to drink more often (Chassin et al., 2003).

Adolescents often drink because peers encourage them to.

Because teenage drinking has so many causes, no single approach is likely to eliminate alcohol abuse. Adolescents who drink to reduce their tension can profit from therapy designed to teach them more effective means of coping with stress. School-based programs that are interactive—featuring student-led discussion—can be effective in teaching the facts about drinking and strategies for resisting peer pressure to drink (Fitzgerald, 2005). Stopping teens from drinking before it becomes habitual is essential because adolescents who drink are at risk for becoming alcohol-dependent as adults (Bonomo et al., 2004).

Teenage Smoking

Many youth experiment with cigarette smoking at some point in their teenage years. For much of the 1980s, about 15% of 8th graders and 30% of 12th graders said that they had smoked a cigarette within the past 30 days. You can see in Figure 9.5 that those numbers increased steadily in the early 1990s, then return to earlier levels by the turn of the century (Johnson et al., 2004). Compared to the rest of the world, American teenagers are about average. However, in some countries (e.g., Chile, the Russian Federation) more than a third of 13- to 15-year-olds smoke regularly (Global Youth Tobacco Survey Collaborative Group, 2002).

American teenagers typically begin to smoke sometime between sixth and ninth grade. As was true for teenage drinking, parents and peers are influential in determining whether youth smoke. When parents smoke, their teenage children are more likely to smoke too. But the parent-child relationship also contributes: Teens are less likely to smoke when they experience the supportive parenting associated with authoritative parenting (Gallagher, Bruzzese, & McCann-Doyle, 2005). Like parents, peer influences can be direct and indirect. Teenagers more often smoke when their friends do (Kobus, 2003). However, a more subtle influence of peers on teen smoking comes from informal school norms. When most students in a school think it's okay to smoke—even though many of them do not themselves smoke—teens are more likely to start smoking (Kumar et al., 2002).

The dangers of cigarette smoking for adults are well known. Many teenagers (particularly those who smoke) are convinced that cigarette smoking is harmless for healthy adolescents, but they're absolutely wrong. Smoking can interfere with the growth of the lungs, and when teens smoke, they more often have a variety of health problems such as respiratory illnesses. What's more, smoking is often the fateful first step on the path to abuse of more powerful substances, including alcohol, marijuana, and cocaine (Chen et al., 2002).

Faced with these many harmful consequences of teenage smoking, health care professionals and human development researchers have worked hard to create effective programs to discourage adolescents from smoking. In fact, just as comprehensive school-based programs can reduce teenage sex, such programs are effective in reducing teenage smoking (U.S. Department of Health and Human Services, 2000). These programs typically include many common features:

■ Schools have no-smoking policies for all students, staff, and school visitors.

■ The program provides information about short- and long-term health and social consequences of smoking and provides students with effective ways to respond to peer pressure to smoke.

■ The program goes beyond the school to involve parents and communities.

■ **Figure 9.5**
Teenage smoking hit a peak in the mid 1990s and has dropped since then.

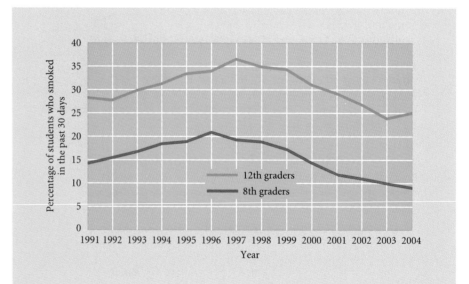

These programs can reduce teenage smoking by more than one third, but they have been implemented in only a handful of schools. By encouraging more schools to provide comprehensive anti-smoking programs, we could vastly reduce the number of teens who start to smoke (Gallagher et al., 2005).

DEPRESSION

Sometime in your life you have probably had the blues—days when you had little energy or enthusiasm for activities that you usually enjoy. You wanted to be alone, and you may have doubted your abilities. These feelings are perfectly normal, can usually be explained as reactions to specific events, and vanish in a matter of hours or days. For example, after an exciting vacation with family and friends, you may be depressed at the thought of returning to school to start new and difficult courses. Yet your mood improves as you renew friendships and become involved in activities on campus.

Now imagine experiencing these same symptoms continuously for weeks or months. Also suppose that you lost your appetite, slept poorly, and were unable to concentrate. *Pervasive feelings of sadness, irritability, and low self-esteem characterize an individual with **depression**.* In early to mid-adolescence, fewer than 5% of adolescents are depressed; by late adolescence, depression is much more common, with nearly 25% of adolescent girls and 10% of adolescent boys experiencing depression (Wicks-Nelson & Israel, 2006).

Research reveals that unhappiness, anger, and irritation often dominate the lives of depressed adolescents. They believe that family members, friends, and classmates are not friendly to them (Cole & Jordan, 1995). Depressed adolescents wish to be left alone much more often than do nondepressed adolescents (Larson et al., 1990). Rather than being satisfying and rewarding, life is empty and joyless for depressed adolescents.

Depression often begins with a situation in which an adolescent feels helpless to control the outcome. Think back to Rod, the adolescent in the vignette at the beginning of this section. His girlfriend had been the center of his life. When she left him unexpectedly, he felt helpless to control his own destiny. Similarly, an athlete may play poorly in the championship game because of illness, or a high school senior may get a lower score on the SAT exam due to a family crisis the night before taking the test. In each case, the adolescent could do nothing to avoid an undesirable result. Most teens recognize that such feelings of helplessness are specific to the particular situation. *In **learned helplessness**, however, adolescents and adults generalize these feelings of helplessness and believe that they are always at the mercy of external events, with no ability to control their own destinies.* Such feelings of learned helplessness often give rise to depression (Peterson, Maier, & Seligman, 1993).

Experiences like these do not lead all adolescents to become depressed. Some adolescents seem more vulnerable to depression than others, which has led scientists to look for biological factors. Studies of twins and adopted children indicate that heredity definitely plays a part in depression. The exact biochemical mechanism seems to involve neurotransmitters (Wicks-Nelson & Israel, 2006). *Some depressed adolescents have reduced levels of **norepinephrine** and **serotonin**, neurotransmitters that help regulate brain centers that allow people to experience pleasure.* Some adolescents may feel depressed because lower levels of neurotransmitters make it difficult for them to experience happiness, joy, and other pleasurable emotions (Peterson, 1996).

THINK ABOUT IT

How does depression illustrate the interaction of biological, psychological, and sociocultural forces on development?

Treating Depression

It is essential to treat depression; otherwise, depressed adolescents are prone to more serious problems. Two general approaches are commonly used in treating depression (Wicks-Nelson & Israel, 2006). One is to administer antidepressant drugs designed to correct the imbalance in neurotransmitters. The well-known drug Prozac, for example, is designed to reduce depression by increasing levels of serotonin (Peterson, 1996). The

Adolescents sometimes become depressed when they feel as if they've lost control of their lives.

© Peter Byron/PhotoEdit

other approach is psychotherapy. Many different forms are available (Lewinsohn & Gotlib, 1995; Sacco & Beck, 1995), but the most effective are based on a cognitive-behavioral perspective that focuses on social skills. The goals are to improve depressed adolescents' social skills, so that they can have rewarding social interactions, and to restructure their interpretation of events, so that they can recognize situations where they can exert control over their lives (Hollon, Thase, & Markowitz, 2002).

Preventing Teen Suicides

Suicide is the third most frequent cause of death (after accidents and homicide) among U.S. adolescents. Roughly 10 adolescents in 100 report having attempted suicide at least once, but only 1 in 10,000 actually commits suicide. Suicide is rare before 15 years of age, and it is uncommon in girls throughout adolescence. Suicide is far more frequent in older adolescent boys, but the rates differ across ethnic groups. As you can see in Figure 9.6, Native American teenage boys have the highest suicide rate by far; Asian Americans and African Americans have the lowest rates (Anderson & Smith, 2005).

Depression is one frequent precursor of suicide; substance abuse is another (Rich, Sherman, & Fowler, 1990; Summerville, Kaslow, & Doepke, 1996). Few suicides are truly spontaneous; in most cases there are warning signals (Atwater, 1992). Here are some common signs:

- Threats of suicide
- Preoccupation with death
- Change in eating or sleeping habits
- Loss of interest in activities that were once important
- Marked changes in personality
- Persistent feelings of gloom and helplessness
- Giving away valued possessions

If someone you know shows these signs, *don't ignore them,* hoping that they aren't for real. Instead, ask the person if he or she is planning on hurting him- or herself. Be calm and supportive and, if the person appears to have made preparations to commit suicide,

Figure 9.6
Suicide is far more common among Native Americans than any other group.

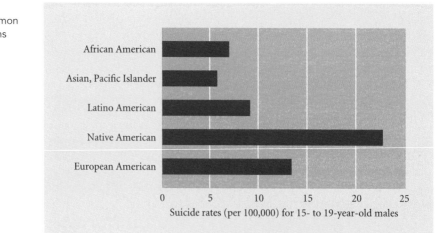

Suicide rates (per 100,000) for 15- to 19-year-old males

don't leave him or her alone. Stay with the person until other friends or relatives can come. More important, *insist* that the adolescent seek professional help. Therapy is essential to treat the feelings of depression and hopelessness that give rise to thoughts of suicide (Capuzzi & Gross, 2004).

DELINQUENCY

Skipping school. Shoplifting. Selling cocaine. Murder. *When adolescents commit acts like these, which are illegal as well as destructive toward themselves or others, this represents **juvenile delinquency.*** Because delinquency applies to such a broad range of activities, it is useful to identify different forms of delinquent behavior. ***Status offenses*** *are acts that are not crimes if committed by an adult, such as truancy, sexual promiscuity, and running away from home.* (An adult is someone older than 16, 17, 18, or 19, depending on the state.) ***Index offenses*** *are acts such as robbery, rape, and arson, which are crimes regardless of the age of the perpetrator.*

Adolescents are responsible for many of the index offenses committed in the United States. For example, adolescents represent about 15% of all arrests for violent crimes (Children's Defense Fund, 2001), and ethnic minority youth are more likely to be arrested for violent crimes (Foster, 2005).

Causes of Delinquency

Why is delinquent behavior so common among adolescents? It's important to distinguish two kinds of delinquent behavior (Moffitt, 1993; Moffitt et al., 2002). The most common form is relatively mild: ***Adolescent-limited antisocial behavior*** *refers to youth who engage in relatively minor criminal acts yet aren't consistently antisocial.* These youth may become involved in petty crimes, such as shoplifting or using drugs, but may be careful to follow all school rules. And, as the name implies, their antisocial behavior is short-lived, usually vanishing in late adolescence or early adulthood.

A second form of delinquent behavior is far more serious and, fortunately, much less common. ***Life-course persistent antisocial behavior*** *refers to antisocial behavior that emerges at an early age and continues throughout life.* These individuals may start with hitting at 3 years of age, then progress to shoplifting at age 12, and then to car theft at age 16. Perhaps only 5% of youth fit this pattern of antisocial behavior, but they account for most adolescent criminal activity. Researchers have identified several forces that contribute to this type of antisocial and delinquent behavior (Vitulano, 2005).

1. *Biological contributions. Born to be Bad* is the title of at least two movies, two CDs (one by George Thorogood and one by Joan Jett), and three books. Implicit in this popular title is the idea that from birth some individuals follow a developmental track that leads to destructive, violent, or criminal behavior. In other words, the claim is that biology pushes people to be aggressive long before experience can affect development.

    Is there any truth to this idea? In fact, biology and heredity do contribute to aggressive and violent behavior, but not in the manner suggested by "born to be bad." Twin studies make it clear that heredity contributes: Identical twins are usually more alike in their levels of physical aggression than fraternal twins (Dionne et al., 2003). But these studies do not tell us that antisocial behavior per se is inherited; instead, they indicate that some children inherit factors that place them at risk for aggressive or violent behavior. Temperament seems to be one such factor: Youngsters who are temperamentally difficult, overly emotional or inattentive, are, for example, more likely to be aggressive (Campbell, 2000; Olson et al., 2000). And levels of hormones contribute: Boys with higher levels of the hormone testosterone are often more irritable and have greater body mass (Olweus et al., 1988; Tremblay et al., 1998).

Neither difficult temperament nor higher levels of testosterone cause a child to be antisocial, but they do make aggressive behavior more likely. For instance, children who are emotional and easily irritated may be disliked by their peers and frequently in conflict with them, opening the door for aggressive responses. Biological factors place children and adolescents at risk for antisocial behavior, but to understand which children actually become aggressive, we need to look elsewhere.

2. *Cognitive processes.* The perceptual and cognitive skills described in Chapters 6 and 8 also play a role in antisocial behavior. Adolescent boys often respond aggressively because they are not skilled at interpreting other people's intentions. Without a clear interpretation in mind, they respond aggressively by default. That is, aggressive boys far too often think, "I don't know what you're up to, and when in doubt, attack" (Crick & Dodge, 1994; Dodge & Rabiner, 2004). Antisocial adolescents are often inclined to act impulsively, and they often are unable or unwilling to postpone pleasure (Patterson, 1995). Seeing a fancy new CD player or a car, delinquent youth are tempted to steal it, simply so that they can have it *right now.* When others inadvertently get in their way, delinquent adolescents often respond without regard to the nature of the other person's acts or intentions.

3. *Family processes.* Delinquent behavior is often related to inadequate parental supervision. Adolescents who are unsupervised—either because their parents are not around or because their parents aren't keeping track of their activities—are much more likely to become involved in delinquent acts (Pettit et al., 2001). Parents may also contribute to delinquent behavior if their marital relationship is marked by constant conflict. When parents constantly argue and fight, their children are much more likely to be antisocial (Ingoldsby et al., 1999). Of course, children have ringside seats for many of these confrontations, and thus they can see firsthand how parents use verbal and physical aggression against each other. And, sadly, children come to believe that these patterns of interacting represent "natural" ways of solving problems (Graham-Bermann & Brescoll, 2000).

4. *Poverty.* Aggressive and antisocial behavior is more common among children living in poverty than among children who are economically advantaged (Keiley et al., 2000). Some of the impact of poverty can be explained by factors that we've already considered. For example, living in poverty is extremely stressful for parents and often leads to the very parental behaviors that promote aggression—harsh discipline and lax monitoring (Tolan, Gorman-Smith, & Henry, 2003). But other links from poverty to violent behavior are new. For example, violent crime is far more common in poverty-stricken neighborhoods. Older children and adolescents exposed to such violence are, as they get older, more likely to be aggressive and violent themselves (Binghenheimer, Brennan, & Earls, 2005).

Treatment and Prevention

Given the wide-ranging causes of delinquency, it would be naive to expect a single or simple cure. Instead, delinquency must be attacked along several fronts simultaneously:

- Delinquent adolescents can be taught more effective social skills and better methods of self-control.
- Parents of delinquent youth can be taught the importance of supervising and monitoring their children's behavior and the necessity for consistent discipline.
- Families of delinquents can learn to function more effectively as a unit, with special emphasis on better means of resolving conflict.

THINK ABOUT IT

A letter to the editor of your local paper claims that "juvenile delinquents should be thrown in jail because they're born as 'bad apples' and will always be that way." Write a reply that states the facts correctly.

- Schools can develop programs that motivate delinquent youth to become invested in their school performance.
- Communities can improve economic conditions in neighborhoods where delinquency reigns.

Programs that include many of these strategies have met with success; adolescents who participate are less likely to be arrested again. The programs thereby address a major problem affecting not only adolescent development but all of North American society (Wicks-Nelson & Israel, 2006).

One effective method for preventing violent behavior and delinquency, developed by John Reid at the Oregon Social Learning Center, is called Linking the Interests of Families and Teachers (LIFT). The aim of the LIFT program is to nip aggressive behavior in the bud during the elementary-school years. LIFT includes a 10-week intervention that attacks aggressive behavior on many fronts. Parents receive training on discipline, resolving disputes with their children, and monitoring their children's schoolwork. Children receive training designed to improve their social skills, with a particular emphasis on effective problem solving and nonaggressive play. At school, teachers are taught effective ways of dealing with off-task and disruptive behavior, and playground and cafeteria monitors are trained to reward children for positive social interactions and to prevent children from bullying peers. Finally, each classroom has a dedicated phone line with an answering machine so that teachers can record daily homework assignments and parents can leave messages for teachers.

In the short run, LIFT is effective in reducing aggression at school (particularly among those children who were most aggressive initially) and in improving children's behavior in the classroom (Eddy et al., 2003; Stoolmiller, Eddy, & Reid, 2000). In addition, family interactions were smoother, with fewer disputes over discipline. Three years later, children who had participated in LIFT remained better behaved in the classroom and were less likely to begin drinking alcohol. Obviously, the ultimate proof of LIFT's success will be the demonstration that, as adolescents and young adults, LIFT participants are less likely to be involved in criminal activity. In the interim, the evidence clearly indicates that fewer youngsters are taking the first steps down the path to criminal activity. LIFT serves as a wonderful example of a model program that draws upon child-development research to create an effective approach to solving a pressing social problem.

In the Current Controversies feature, we describe a very different approach to dealing with adolescent crime.

CURRENT CONTROVERSIES

WHEN JUVENILES COMMIT SERIOUS CRIMES, SHOULD THEY BE TRIED AS ADULTS?

Traditionally, when adolescents under 18 commit crimes, the case is handled in the juvenile justice system. Although procedures vary from state to state, most adolescents who are arrested do not go to court; instead, law enforcement and legal authorities have considerable discretionary power. They may, for example, release arrested adolescents into the custody of their parents. However, when adolescents commit serious or violent crimes, there will be a hearing with a judge. This hearing is closed to the press and public; no jury is involved. Instead, the judge receives reports from police, probation officers, school officials, medical authorities, and other interested parties. Adolescents judged guilty can be placed on probation at home, in foster care outside the home, or in a facility for youth offenders.

Because juveniles are committing more serious crimes, many law enforcement and legal authorities believe that juveniles should be tried as adults. Advocates of this position argue for lowering the minimum age for mandatory transfer of a case to adult courts, increasing the range of offenses that must be tried in adult court, and giving prosecutors more authority to file cases with juveniles in adult criminal court. Critics argue that treating juvenile offenders as adults ignores the fact that juveniles are less able than adults to understand the nature and consequences of committing a crime. Also, they argue, punishments appropriate for adults are inappropriate for juveniles (Steinberg et al., 2003).

What do you think? Should we lower the age at which juveniles are tried as adults? Based on the theories of development we have discussed, what guidelines would you propose in deciding when a juvenile should be tried as an adult?

TEST YOURSELF

1. The main factors that determine whether teenagers drink include parents, peers, and _____.

2. Peers influence teenage smoking indirectly by _____.

3. Depression has been linked to situations in which teenagers feel helpless and to _____.

4. Treatments for depression include drugs that correct imbalances in neurotransmitters and therapy that emphasizes _____.

5. Acts like truancy and running away from home, which are not crimes when committed by adults, are known as _____.

6. The factors that contribute to juvenile delinquency include biology, cognitive processes, _____, and poverty.

Describe potential biological and environmental contributions to delinquency.

Answers: (1) stress, (2) establishing an informal school norm in which smoking is approved, (3) an imbalance in neurotransmitters, (4) the development of social skills, (5) status offenses, (6) family processes

Putting It All Together

In the voyage from the land of childhood to the land of adulthood, the choppy waters of adolescence must be navigated. Most teens complete the journey successfully, becoming adults who will someday watch their own children make the same trip. As one writer noted:

> It is easy to forget that a personality unfurling itself can be glorious as well as inconvenient. No doubt Jesus was considered a pain by his elders, as was Gandhi. The young need to check out their wingspreads, and adults need to be adult enough to withstand the onslaught . . . and challenge to every sensible norm. (Pacy, 1993, p. 35)

The spreading of wings that characterizes adolescence is evident in all its splendor and aggravation in this chapter.

We began by looking at the struggle to achieve an identity. Adolescents and young adults often experiment with different roles in their efforts to realize an identity. When parents support this experimentation, the search for identity is more likely to succeed. For example, Dea came to realize that she is uniquely blessed with roots in three different cultures; she loves elements of each, and she is forging a novel Dutch-Asian-American identity.

Our next stop was romance and sex. Interest in sex mounts in the teenage years, and many adolescents become sexually active. Like Gretchen, many teenagers have unprotected sex, which can lead to pregnancy and sexually transmitted diseases.

From romance and sex we moved to the world of work. We saw that selecting a career involves matching interests and aptitudes with specific occupations, then determining the skills and education needed for the chosen line of work. Aaron's experiences in part-time work are typical. Adolescents rarely balance school and heavy part-time work effectively.

We ended the chapter by looking at the dark side of adolescence. Some young people do not handle adolescent difficulties well, leading to use of illegal drugs, depression (like Rod, the basketball player in the throes of first love), and delinquency.

Summary

9.1 Identity and Self-Esteem

The Search for Identity

■ The task for adolescents is to find an identity. This search typically involves four statuses. Diffusion and foreclosure are more common in early adolescence; moratorium and achievement are more common in late adolescence and young adulthood. As they seek identity, adolescents often believe that others are always watching them and that no one else has felt as they do.

■ Adolescents are more likely to achieve an identity when parents encourage discussion and recognize their autonomy; they are least likely to achieve an identity when parents set rules and enforce them without explanation.

Ethnic Identity

■ Adolescents from ethnic groups often progress through three phases in acquiring an ethnic identity: initial disinterest, exploration, and identity achievement. Achieving an ethnic identity usually results in higher self-esteem but is not consistently related to the strength of one's identification with mainstream culture.

Self-Esteem in Adolescence

■ Social comparisons begin anew when children move from elementary school to middle or junior high school, and, consequently, self-esteem usually declines somewhat during this transition. However, self-esteem begins to rise in middle and late adolescence as teenagers see themselves acquiring more adult skills and responsibilities. Self-esteem is linked to adolescents' actual competence in domains that matter to them and to how parents and peers view them.

The Myth of Storm and Stress

■ The parent-child relationship becomes more egalitarian during the adolescent years, reflecting adolescents' growing independence. Contrary to myth, adolescence is not usually a period of storm and stress. Most adolescents love their parents, feel loved by them, rely on them for advice, and adopt their values.

9.2 Romantic Relationships and Sexuality

Romantic Relationships

■ Romantic relationships emerge in mid-adolescence. For younger adolescents, dating is for both companionship and sexual exploration; for older adolescents, it is a source of trust and support.

Sexual Behavior

■ By the end of adolescence, most American boys and girls have had sexual intercourse, which boys view as recreational but girls see as romantic. Adolescents are more likely to be sexually active if they believe that their parents and peers approve of sex. Sexually transmitted diseases and pregnancy are two common consequences of adolescent sexual behavior because sexually active adolescents use contraceptives infrequently.

Sexual Orientation

■ A small percentage of adolescents are attracted to members of their own sex. Sexual orientation probably has its roots in biology. Gay and lesbian youth face many special challenges and consequently often suffer from mental health problems.

Sexual Coercion

■ Adolescent and young adult females are sometimes forced into sex against their will. Girls are more likely to be victims of sexual violence when they've been drinking and when they hold traditional views of gender. Boys are more likely to perpetrate violence when they've experienced violence at home, when they drink, and when their friends perpetrate sexual violence. Date-rape workshops strive to improve communication between males and females.

9.3 The World of Work

Career Development

■ In his theory of vocational choice, Super proposes three phases of vocational development during adolescence and young adulthood: crystallization, in which basic interests are identified; specification, in which jobs associated with interests are identified; and implementation, which marks entry into the workforce.

■ Holland proposes six different work-related personalities: realistic, investigative, social, conventional, enterprising, and artistic. Each is uniquely suited to certain jobs. People are happier when their personality fits their job and less happy when it does not.

Part-Time Employment

■ Most adolescents in the United States have part-time jobs. Adolescents who are employed more than 15 hours per week during the school year typically do poorly in school, often have lowered self-esteem and increased anxiety, and have problems interacting with others. Employed adolescents save relatively little of their income. Instead, they spend it on clothing, food, and their entertainment, which can give misleading expectations about how to allocate income.

■ Part-time employment can be beneficial if adolescents work relatively few hours, if the work allows them to use existing skills or acquire new ones, and if teens save some of their earnings. Summer employment, which does not conflict with the demands of school, can also be beneficial.

9.4 The Dark Side

Drug Use

■ Today many adolescents drink alcohol regularly. The primary factors that influence whether adolescents drink are encouragements from others (parents and peers) and stress. Similarly, teenage smoking is influenced by parents and peers.

Depression

■ Depressed adolescents have little enthusiasm for life, believe that others are unfriendly, and wish to be left alone. Depression can be triggered by an event that deprives them of rewarding experiences, by an event in which they feel unable to control their own destiny, or by an imbalance in neurotransmitters. Treating depression relies on medications that correct the levels of neurotransmitters and on therapy designed to improve social skills and restructure adolescents' interpretation of life events.

Delinquency

■ Many young people engage in antisocial behavior briefly during adolescence. In contrast, the small percentage of adolescents who engage in life-course persistent antisocial behavior are involved in one fourth to half of the serious crimes committed in the United States. Life-course persistent antisocial behavior has been linked to biology, cognitive processes, family processes, and poverty. Efforts to reduce adolescent criminal activity must address all of these variables.

Key Terms

adolescent egocentrism (342)
imaginary audience (342)
personal fable (342)
illusion of invulnerability (342)
ethnic identity (343)
date (acquaintance) rape (352)
crystallization (355)

specification (355)
implementation (356)
personality-type theory (356)
depression (363)
learned helplessness (363)
norepinephrine (363)
serotonin (363)

juvenile delinquency (365)
status offense (365)
index offense (365)
adolescent-limited antisocial behavior (365)
life-course persistent antisocial behavior (365)

Learn More About It

Readings

GALLO, D. R. (Ed.) (1997). *No easy answers: Short stories about teenagers making tough choices.* New York: Basic Books. This readable collection of short stories shows youth dealing with common problems of adolescence, including peer pressure, substance abuse, and teen pregnancy.

KROGER, J. (2005). *Identity in adolescence: The balance between self and other* (3rd ed.). New York: Routledge. The author discusses the adolescent search for identity from many perspectives, including that of Erik Erikson.

STEINBERG, L. D., & LEVINE, A. (1997). *You and your adolescent.* New York: Harper Perennial. This outstanding book has a number of useful guidelines to help parents recognize when their teenager has a problem that may require professional help.

WALSH, D., & BENNETT, N. (2004). *Why do they act that way? A survival guide to the adolescent brain for you and your teen.* New York: Free Press. The authors explore many of the problems that adolescents confront—sex, drugs, and inability to get along with parents. Case studies show how parents can help teenagers through these years.

Websites

Visit the Human Development book companion website for all URLs.

■ **The Human Development Book Companion Website**
See **http://www.psychology.wadsworth.com/kail_cavanaugh4e/** for practice quiz questions, Internet links, updates, critical thinking exercises, discussion forums, and more. Also accessible from the Wadsworth Psychology Study Center (http://psychology.wadsworth.com).

■ **Centers for Disease Control and Prevention**
This organization devotes a portion of its website to STDs, including how they are harmful, how they can be prevented, and how they can be treated.

■ **National Institutes of Health**
This website includes information on the symptoms, causes, and treatment of depression in adolescents.

■ **Oregon Social Learning Center**
This site has a wealth of information on the factors that contribute to violent and aggressive behaviors, as well as ways to discourage such behaviors.

Life-Span CD-ROM

For more information on the concepts covered in this chapter, go to
Module 4: Adolescence

• *Emotional and Social Development*

http://www.thomsonedu.com
Go to this site for the link to ThomsonNOW, your one-stop study shop. Take a pre-test for this chapter, and ThomsonNOW will generate a personalized study plan based on your test results. The study plan will identify the topics you need to review and direct you to online resources to help you master those topics. You can then take a post-test to help you determine the concepts you have mastered and what you still need to work on.

Exploring Middle Childhood and Adolescence

C hildhood and adolescence are times of remarkable change: At the beginning of childhood, children are still dependent on parents, rarely venture far from home, and their futures are uncertain; by the end of adolescence, they are largely independent, often travel widely, and have goals for their adult years.

Development in Middle Childhood

Physical

School-aged children grow at a steady pace; most increases in height come from the legs, not the trunk.

Motor skills continue to improve as strength and dexterity increase. Boys tend to excel on motor skills requiring strength; girls excel in fine motor skills and those requiring flexibility and balance.

School-aged children need at least 60 minutes of physical activity per day. Most U.S. elementary school children are physically fit.

Participation in sports improves motor skills and helps children learn social skills and use emerging cognitive skills.

Cognitive

From about ages 7 to 11, children are in Piaget's *concrete operational stage,* in which they become less egocentric, realize that appearances can be deceiving, and acquire mental operations.

At about age 11, school-aged children begin *formal-operational thinking,* in which they can think hypothetically, reason abstractly, and use deductive reasoning.

Children begin to use memory strategies at about 7 to 8 years of age and learn to self-monitor the effectiveness of their memory strategies.

Major theories of intelligence include Carroll's hierarchical view, Gardner's theory of multiple intelligences, and Sternberg's triarchic theory.

The Stanford-Binet intelligence test introduced the concept of IQ, which predicts school achievement. Ethnic groups differ in their average scores, in part due to social class differences.

Children with learning disabilities have normal intelligence but struggle to master specific academic subjects.

U.S. students typically fall behind academically compared to many other industrialized countries, particularly those in Asia.

Although giftedness used to be defined by IQ, today giftedness is more broadly defined to include exceptional talent in specific areas.

Socioemotional

In the systems view, parents and children influence each other: parents by instruction and behavior modeling; children by age and temperament. The family is influenced by other social systems (e.g., school, work, religious organizations, the neighborhood, and extended family).

Two key factors in parent-child relationships are parental warmth and control.

Types of Parenting Styles	
Authoritarian	High control; little warmth
Authoritative	Medium control; lots of warmth
Indulgent-permissive	Little control; lots of warmth
Indifferent-uninvolved	Little control; little warmth

Punishment is most effective when it is immediate, consistent, explained, and administered by a caring parent.

School-aged friendships are based on loyalty, trust, and intimacy. Friends are usually similar in age, race, and attitudes. Older children and adolescents often form *cliques.*

Highly aggressive children can end up being violent and poorly adjusted as adults. Chronically bullied children either overreact or don't defend themselves.

Development in Adolescence

Physical

Puberty includes physical growth and sexual maturation. Girls typically begin puberty 2 years ahead of boys, at about age 10.

The timing of puberty is strongly influenced by genetics, health, nutrition, and (for girls) social environment. Early maturation tends to be harmful for girls but beneficial to boys.

Adolescents are very concerned with appearance. Many American teens are

overweight, which increases the likelihood of being unpopular and having low self-esteem and future medical problems.

Due to cultural norms idealizing thinness, some teens (90% females, 10% males) develop eating disorders. Individuals with anorexia refuse to eat and irrationally fear becoming overweight; those with bulimia alternate between binge eating and purging.

Many high school students do not get enough exercise. Participation in sports improves physical fitness, self-esteem, and teaches initiative and teamwork.

Socioemotional

Adolescents seek to find an identity by experimenting with different roles, and they are more likely to achieve a well-defined sense of self when parents encourage discussion and autonomy.

Teens who achieve an ethnic identity tend to have higher self-esteem and do better in school.

Self-esteem often drops when children begin middle school or junior high.

Self-esteem is linked to adolescents' actual competence in

domains they value and how their parents and peers view them.

As teens become more independent, parents treat them more like equals. Most adolescents love and feel loved by their parents, seek their advice, and embrace their values.

Romantic relationships emerge in mid-adolescence. By the end of high school, about two-thirds of U.S. teens have had intercourse. Because many teens do not use contraceptives, STDs and pregnancy are two common consequences of adolescent sexual behavior.

Many adolescents drink alcohol regularly. Parents, peers, and stress influence whether adolescents drink and smoke.

By late adolescence, 25% of adolescent girls and 10% of adolescent boys are depressed. Medication and improving social skills can help.

Many youth briefly engage in minor criminal acts, but only about 5% engage in *life-course persistent antisocial behavior.* Several factors contribute to antisocial behavior: biology, cognitive processes, family dynamics, and poverty.

Cognitive

Cognitive changes in adolescence are not as rapid as in childhood. Adolescents' cognitive processes are like adults' in terms of

working memory, processing speed, content knowledge, and ability to identify task-appropriate strategies.

Although capable of adultlike cognition, teens may revert to simpler thinking. Their beliefs can blind them to more sophisticated thought processes.

Theories of What Drives Moral Reasoning	
Kohlberg	Moral reasoning is rooted in justice. One progresses sequentially through *preconventional, conventional,* and *postconventional* levels.
Gilligan	Moral reasoning is rooted in caring.
Eisenberg	Children's moral dilemmas involve choosing between self-interest and helping others.

Most high school students hold part-time jobs. Working more than 15 hours per week can be detrimental.

Young and Middle Adulthood

■ **Chapter 10**
Becoming an Adult
Physical, Cognitive, and Personality Development

■ **Chapter 11**
Being With Others
Forming Relationships in Young and Middle Adulthood

■ **Chapter 12**
Work and Leisure
Occupational and Lifestyle Issues in Young and Middle Adulthood

■ **Chapter 13**
Making It in Midlife
The Unique Challenges of Middle Adulthood

10.1 **When Does Adulthood Begin?**
Role Transitions Marking Adulthood
Going to College
Psychological Views
So When Do People Become Adults?

REAL PEOPLE: APPLYING HUMAN DEVELOPMENT: Britney Spears's Transition to Adulthood

10.2 **Physical Development and Health**
Growth, Strength, and Physical Functioning
Health Status
Lifestyle Factors

CURRENT CONTROVERSIES: Binge Drinking on College Campuses

Social, Gender, and Ethnic Issues in Health

10.3 **Cognitive Development**
How Should We View Intelligence in Adults?
What Happens to Intelligence in Adulthood?

SPOTLIGHT ON RESEARCH: The Seattle Longitudinal Study

Going Beyond Formal Operations: Thinking in Adulthood
The Role of Stereotypes in Thinking

10.4 **Who Do You Want to Be? Personality in Young Adulthood**
Creating Scenarios and Life Stories
Possible Selves
Personal Control Beliefs

Putting It All Together

Summary

Key Terms

Learn More About It

Becoming an Adult

*Physical, Cognitive,
and Personality Development*

There comes a time in life when we turn away from childhood and aspire to being adults. In some societies, the transition to adulthood is abrupt and dramatic, marked by clear rites of passage. In Western society, it is fuzzier; the only apparent marker may be a birthday ritual. We may even ask "real" adults what it's like to be one. Adulthood is marked in numerous ways, some of which we explore in the first section.

Without question, young adulthood is the peak of physical processes and health. It is also a time when people who acquired unhealthy habits earlier in life may decide to adopt a healthier lifestyle. Young adulthood also marks the peak of some cognitive abilities, and the continued development of others.

On a more personal level, young adulthood is a time when we make plans and dream of what lies ahead. It is a time when we think about what life as an adult will be like. But above all, young adulthood is a time when we lay the foundation for the developmental changes we will experience during the rest of our lives. For these reasons, young adulthood is a very important time in our lives. We will consider these issues as we examine young adulthood in this chapter.

10.1

WHEN DOES ADULTHOOD BEGIN?

Marcus woke up with the worst headache he ever remembered having. "If this is adulthood, they can keep it," he muttered to himself. Like many young adults in the United States, Marcus spent his 21st birthday celebrating at a nightclub. But the phone call from his mother that woke him in the first place reminds him that he isn't an adult in every way; she called to see if he needs money.

IMAGINE THAT YOU ARE MARCUS. Think for a minute about the first time you felt like an adult. When was it? What was the context? Who were you with? How did you feel?

Now think about yourself between the ages of 18 and 22. Is this the period when you completed the transition to adulthood? Why or why not?

Even though becoming an adult is one of our most important life transitions, it is difficult to pin down exactly when it occurs in Western societies. Birthday celebrations marking the achievement of a certain age, such as 21, are helpful but do not signal a clean break with youth and full acceptance as an adult. Certainly Marcus may feel like an adult because he can purchase alcohol legally, but he may not feel that way in other respects, such as supporting himself financially.

In this section, we examine some of the ways societies mark the transition to adulthood, and we'll see that the criteria vary widely from culture to culture.

ROLE TRANSITIONS MARKING ADULTHOOD

One cool spring evening, a group of former high school classmates got together to catch up on what had been going on in their lives. The conversation eventually turned to the topic of growing up and becoming adults, as each of them would be turning 21 in the

Milestone birthdays such as turning 21 are often marked with celebrations.

Image 100/Alamy

next few months. Joyce looked older than her 20 years. Her 5-year-old son was playing quietly on the floor. Next to Joyce sat Sheree, an art major. She wore the latest style clothes, purchased at the store where she works part-time. The third young woman, Marcia, looked a bit tired from her long day as an intern at Accenture, a global technology consulting services and outsourcing company; she's also an MBA student at the local university. Joyce spoke first. "I had Jimmy when I was 15. I thought it would make me grown up and give me someone who would love me. But it gave me grown-up bills and no job. I still can't afford my own place, so I live with my mom." Sheree declared, "It's like, sure, I'm an adult. I can do whatever I want, whenever I want. It's like, I don't have to answer to anybody, okay?" Marcia had a different view: "As for me, I don't think I'll *really* be an adult until I complete my education, can support myself, and get married." Are these young people adults? Yes and no. As we will see, it depends on how you define adulthood.

Role Transitions in Western Cultures

The most widely used criteria for deciding whether a person has reached adulthood are **role transitions,** *which involve assuming new responsibilities and duties.* Certain role transitions have long been recognized in Western society as key markers for attaining adulthood: completing education, beginning full-time employment, establishing an independent household, getting married, and becoming a parent (Hogan & Astone, 1986).

The age at which people tend to experience marker events varies over time. Such changes are examples of cohort effects, described in Chapter 1. For example, in the United States the average age for completing all of one's formal schooling rose steadily during the 20th century as the proportion of people going to college increased from roughly 10% in the early part of the century to more than 50% today. In contrast, the average age of first marriage and parenthood dropped steadily from 1900 to around 1960, before rising sharply from 1960 to the late 1980s, when the rate of increase slowed down (U.S. Census Bureau, 2005a).

Beyond these marker events, Western society has very few formal rituals that clearly mark the transition to adulthood (Ivory, 2004). As a result, college students may create their own rituals of initiation, such as outdoor challenges or drinking alcohol (a topic we explore later in this chapter). Such complexities make it difficult to use any one event as the transition for becoming an adult. Although the trend is that living independently from one's parents, financial independence, and romantic involvement are associated with increased assumption of adult roles, individual patterns are extremely diverse. Like the three women we encountered earlier, people experience some marker events but not others, further complicating the issue. Such is not the case in all cultures, however.

Cross-Cultural Evidence of Role Transitions

Non-Western cultures tend to be clearer about when a person becomes an adult and put greater emphasis on specific practices that mark the transition (Nelson, Badger, & Wu, 2004). In these cultures, marriage is the most important determinant of adult status (Schlegel & Barry, 1991).

Many non-Western cultures also have a well-defined set of requirements that boys must meet to become men (Gilmore, 1990). These requirements typically focus on three key features: being able to provide, protect, and impregnate. In contrast, most cultures rely on menarche as the primary, and usually the only, marker of adulthood for girls (Gilmore, 1990).

Rituals marking initiation into adulthood, often among the most important ones in a culture, are termed **rites of passage.** Rites of passage may involve highly elaborate steps that take days or weeks, or they may be compressed into a few minutes. Initiates are usually dressed in apparel re-

This couple from India reflects that the passage to adulthood for many occurs with marriage.

served for the ritual to denote their special position. Traces of these rites remain in Western culture; consider, for example, the ritual attire for graduations or weddings. Tribal rituals marking the transition to adulthood tend to be public and may involve pain or mutilation. Because rites change little over the years, they provide continuity throughout the life span (Keith, 1990); older adults lead young people through the same rites they themselves experienced years earlier. Western counterparts are much less formalized and are diffuse; indeed, you may be hard pressed to think of any. A father buying his son his first razor or a mother helping her daughter with her first menstrual period may be as close as we get in the larger society. Certain ethnic groups maintain more formal rites, such as bar and bat mitzvahs. Through rites of passage, cultures the world over maintain contact and social continuity across the generations.

GOING TO COLLEGE

One of the most common markers of adulthood in the United States is completing one's education. For 65% of high school graduates, this means going to college (Smith, 2001), which has been known for many years to serve as a catalyst for intellectual and personal growth (Kitchener & King, 1989; Perry, 1970). We examine some of these cognitive changes later in this chapter.

We commonly think of people between the ages of 18 and 25 as college students. However, the face of college campuses is changing rapidly, as you can probably tell by looking around your own. Although students who attend full-time tend to be the traditional age (under 25), as you can see in Figure 10.1, a relatively large number of undergraduates are older, with most of them being part-time. *Colleges usually refer to students over age 25 as **returning adult students,** which implies that these individuals have already reached adulthood.*

Overall, returning adult students tend to be problem solvers, self-directed, and pragmatic, and they have relevant life experiences they can integrate with their course work (Harringer, 1994). Returning adult students often have to balance employment and families along with their college courses, resulting in additional stress; however, support from family and the positive effects of continuing one's education act as stress reducers (Kirby et al., 2004).

Americans with disabilities are experiencing the going-to-college-as-passage-into-adulthood in greater numbers since the Americans with Disabilities Act (ADA) became

■ **Figure 10.1**
Undergraduate enrollment is changing at college campuses, with many undergraduates being older and attending only part-time.

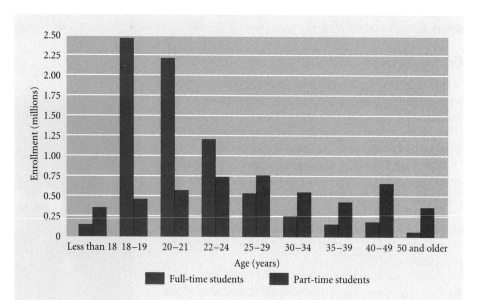

From U.S. Department of Education, National Center for Education Statistics. Integrated Postsecondary Education Data System, fall enrollment survey, fall 2002. Prepared by the Center for Policy Analysis, American Council on Education.

law in 1990. This act recognizes the rights of people with disabilities, and an increasing number of college students have identified themselves as having disabilities. The ADA prohibits discrimination on the basis of disability in employment, state and local government, public accommodations, commercial facilities, transportation, and telecommunications, and it also applies to the United States Congress (U.S. Department of Justice, 2001). To be protected by the ADA, a person must have a disability or have a relationship or association with someone with a disability. This means that a person must have a physical or mental impairment that substantially limits one or more major life activities, have a history or record of this impairment, be perceived by others as having this impairment, or be related to someone who meets one of the other criteria. The ADA does not provide a list of the impairments that are covered, leaving the courts to make this determination.

Returning adult students are typically more motivated and focused on their studies.

The most visible signs that the ADA has had an effect on society are the structural changes to buildings, such as entrance ramps. Such changes have had profound effects on the lives of people with disabilities by providing them with a way to use these facilities. Many other changes due to the ADA are less visible, but equally important, such as requiring all websites to be accessible to people with disabilities. Several are the result of legal complaints filed in court.

These court cases have proven very important for many people, including college students. Jackie Okin, an aspiring college student in 1994 who has cerebral palsy, discovered that the Scholastic Aptitude Test (SAT) was offered on several dates for students without disabilities but only once for students who needed accommodation. She felt that this was unfair and filed a complaint under the ADA. The U.S. Justice Department ruled that Jackie was right. She took the exam and went on to graduate from Tufts University in 1999 and the American University Law School. Students who have a disability simply need to contact the campus office on disabilities to receive accommodations, such as longer time to complete examinations or assistance obtaining course material in alternative formats.

THINK ABOUT IT

Why do Western cultures lack clear-cut transitions to adulthood?

Professional golfer Casey Martin won a lawsuit under the ADA that allowed him to use a cart during tournaments.

Another case that created a national debate beginning in 1998 involved Casey Martin, a professional golfer who played on the same college team as Tiger Woods. As a child, Casey was diagnosed with Klippel-Trenaunay-Webber syndrome in his right leg, an incurable disease that restricts blood flow and causes great pain. Casey filed suit under the ADA against the PGA Tour to be allowed to use a golf cart, which he was allowed to use in college. His court battles were all successful; in 2001 the U.S. Supreme Court ruled that he must be allowed to use a cart during tournaments.

In sum, the ADA has fundamentally changed the way people with disabilities participate in society. Physical, social, and psychological barriers that once prevented such participation are coming down. There is still much to do, but substantial progress is being made.

PSYCHOLOGICAL VIEWS

From a psychological perspective, becoming an adult means interacting with the world in a fundamentally different way. Cognitively, young adults think in different ways than adolescents (King & Kitchener, 2004). Behaviorally, a major difference between adolescence and adulthood is the significant drop in the frequency of reckless behavior such as driving at high speed, having sex without contraception, or committing antisocial acts like vandalism (Arnett & Taber, 1994). From this perspective, young adults maintain a higher degree of self-control and compliance with social conventions (Hart, 1992).

On the psychosocial front, young adulthood marks the transition from concern with identity (see Section 10.4) to concern with autonomy and intimacy, which we explore here and in Chapter 11 (Erikson, 1982). Becoming independent from one's parents entails being able to fend for oneself, but it does not imply a complete severing of the relationship. On the contrary, adult children usually establish a rewarding relationship with their parents, as we will see in Chapter 13.

Establishing Intimacy

According to Erikson, the major task for young adults is dealing with the psychosocial conflict of **intimacy versus isolation.** This is the sixth step in Erikson's theory of psychosocial development, the basic tenets of which are summarized in Chapter 1. Once a person's identity had been established, Erikson (1982) believed he or she was ready to create a shared identity with another, the key ingredient for intimacy. Without a clear sense of identity, Erikson argued, young adults would be afraid of committing to a long-term relationship or might become overly dependent on the partner for his or her identity.

Some studies support this view. For example, Montgomery (2005) found that a stronger sense of identity was related to higher levels of intimacy in young adults. However, some research shows different results. For example, Berliner (2000) also found that identity formation correlated with intimacy in adults aged 35 to 45. But this relationship held even for those people who demonstrated diffusion, the lowest level of identity formation, which Erikson argued should not be the case. Consequently, the extent to which successful resolution of identity is necessary for the successful development of intimacy is still unresolved.

Another key question is whether the relation between identity and intimacy holds equally for men and women. The results of this research are also equivocal. Apparently, most men and career-oriented women resolve identity issues before intimacy issues (Dyk & Adams, 1990; Patterson, Sochting, & Marcia, 1992). These individuals complete their education and make initial career choices before becoming involved in a committed relationship.

But some women resolve intimacy issues before identity issues by marrying and rearing children, and only after their children have grown and moved away do they deal with the question of their own identity. Still other women deal with both identity and intimacy issues simultaneously—for example, by entering into relationships that allow them to develop identities based on caring for others (Dyk & Adams, 1990).

Thus, this part of Erikson's theory is most applicable in the cases of men and career-oriented women. But many women confront and resolve the issues of identity and intimacy in young adulthood in reverse order or even simultaneously.

SO WHEN DO PEOPLE BECOME ADULTS?

Increasingly, researchers and writers are arguing that the years between 18 and 25 may reflect a distinct life stage. Apter (2001) coined the term "thresholders" to describe the fact that these young adults are no longer adolescents but are not yet full-fledged adults either. Economic and social realities now mean that more than 50% of college students expect to live with their parents again for some period of time after graduation (Smith, 2001). Robbins and Wilner (2001), who are both in their 20s and authors of a popular book about being 20-something, write that life in one's 20s is far from easy as individuals struggle to find their way.

The perspectives considered in this section do not provide any definitive answers to the question of when people become adults. All we can say is that the transition depends on culture and a number of psychological factors. In cultures without clearly defined rites of passage, defining oneself as an adult rests on one's perception of whether personally relevant key criteria have been met. In U.S. society, this can be very complicated, for example, when success comes at a young age. Is Britney Spears, discussed in the Real People feature, an adult?

REAL PEOPLE: Applying Human Development

BRITNEY SPEARS'S TRANSITION TO ADULTHOOD

Britney Spears is a huge international star and one of the most successful young recording artists of today. Only 17 when her debut album was released, she worked hard to maintain her image as a wholesome teen. However, the sales from the album quickly made her a multimillionaire and a worldwide celebrity. Clearly, she had achieved financial independence.

By 2002 Britney had three extremely successful albums, numerous lucrative contracts including a major product endorsement for Pepsi, and many awards. Her heavily publicized relationships indicated that she was beginning to deal with Erikson's stage of intimacy versus isolation. During this period, a key issue was a need to change her image from teen idol to adult female pop star.

One way Britney tried to emphasize the change was through her dress, which became more revealing. One of her now famous routines during this period had her take off a more modest costume to reveal a more risqué one. Addition-

AP/Wide World Photos

AP/Wide World Photos

Britney Spears's transition from teen pop star to married mother represents the achievement of adulthood in the public eye.

ally, her two marriages, first to Jason Allen Alexander for 2 days in 2004 and second to Kevin Federline, and her subsequent pregnancy may be indica-

tors of her transition from adolescent pop star to adult woman.

What do you think?

TEST YOURSELF

1. The most widely used criteria for deciding whether a person has reached adulthood are _____.

2. Rituals marking initiation into adulthood are called _____.

3. Students over 25 are referred to as _____.

4. Behaviorally, a major difference between adolescence and adulthood is a significant drop in the frequency of _____.

5. Research indicates that Erikson's idea of resolving identity followed by intimacy best describes men and _____.

Why are formal rites of passage important? What has Western society lost by eliminating them? What have we gained?

Answers: (1) role transitions, (2) rites of passage, (3) returning adult students, (4) reckless behavior, (5) career-oriented women

10.2

PHYSICAL DEVELOPMENT AND HEALTH

Juan is a 25-year-old who started smoking cigarettes in high school to be popular. Juan wants to quit, but he knows it will be difficult. He has also heard that it doesn't really matter if he quits or not because his health will never recover. Juan wonders whether it is worthwhile to try.

JUAN IS AT THE PEAK OF HIS PHYSICAL FUNCTIONING. Most young adults are in the best physical shape of their lives. Indeed, the early 20s are the best years for strenuous work, trouble-free reproduction, and peak athletic performance. These achievements reflect a physical system at its peak. But people's physical functioning is affected by several health-related behaviors, including smoking.

GROWTH, STRENGTH, AND PHYSICAL FUNCTIONING

Professional basketball player Cheryl Ford is an example of being at one's physical peak during one's 20s.

© Rebecca Cook / Reuters /Corbis

As a young adult, you're as tall as you will ever be (Whitbourne, 1999). Height remains stable through middle adulthood, declining somewhat in old age (as described in Chapter 14). Although men have more muscle mass and tend to be stronger than women, physical strength in both sexes peaks during the late 20s and early 30s, declining slowly throughout the rest of life (Whitbourne, 1996). Coordination and dexterity peak around the same time (Whitbourne, 1996). Because of these trends, few professional athletes remain at the top of their sport in their mid-30s. Indeed, individuals such as Jerry Rice, a wide receiver in the NFL into his early 40s, and Nolan Ryan, who pitched for the Texas Rangers until his mid-40s, are famous partly because they are exceptions. Most sports stars are in their 20s.

Sensory acuity is also at its peak in the early 20s (Fozard & Gordon-Salant, 2001). Visual acuity remains high until middle age, when people tend to become farsighted and require glasses for reading. Hearing begins to decline somewhat by the late 20s, especially for high-pitched tones. By old age, this hearing loss may affect one's ability to understand speech. People's ability to smell, taste, feel pain and changes in temperature, and maintain balance remain largely unchanged until late life.

HEALTH STATUS

How is your overall health? If you are a young adult, chances are better than 90% that you will say that your health is as good as or better than it was in childhood (National Center for Health Statistics, 2004a). Relatively speaking, young adults get many fewer colds and respiratory infections than they did when they were children. Indeed, only about 1% of young adults are limited in their ability to function because of a health-related condition.

Because of the overall healthy status of American young adults, death from disease, especially during the early 20s, is relatively rare (National Center for Health Statistics, 2004a).

For example, the death rate due to cancer for people aged 15 to 24 is less than 5 people per 100,000 population, compared with about 123 per 100,000 for people aged 45 to 54, and more than 1,700 per 100,000 for people over age 85. So what are the leading causes of death among young adults in the United States? Between the ages of 25 and 44, accidents are the leading cause, followed by cancer, cardiovascular disease, suicide, and homicide.

There are important gender and ethnic differences in these statistics. Young adult men aged 25 to 34 are nearly 2.5 times as likely to die as women of the same age; men are most likely to die in auto accidents and women from cancer. African American and Latino young adult males are roughly 2 to 2.5 times as likely to die as their European American male counterparts, but Asian and Pacific Islander young adult males are likely to die at only half the rate of their European American male counterparts (National Center for Health Statistics, 2004a).

LIFESTYLE FACTORS

If you are trying to maintain good health, you should *not* smoke. Lifestyle factors such as smoking, drinking alcohol, and eating poorly negatively affect health. We return to this theme in Chapter 13 when we examine additional aspects of health promotion, especially concerning cardiovascular disease and exercise.

Smoking

Smoking is the single biggest contributor to health problems, a fact known for decades. In the United States alone, roughly 440,000 people die each year, and medical treatment of smoking-related ailments costs more than $100 billion annually (National Cancer Institute, 2005).

Smoking is the worst life-style choice one can make from a health perspective.

The risks of smoking are many. The American Cancer Society estimates that more than half of all cancers (including cancer of the lung, larynx, mouth, esophagus, bladder, kidney, pancreas, and cervix) are related to smoking. Emphysema, a disease that destroys the air sacs in the lungs, is primarily caused by smoking, and the carbon monoxide and nicotine inhaled in cigarette smoke foster the development of cardiovascular disease (Centers for Disease Control and Prevention, 2001). As noted in Chapter 2, nicotine in cigarettes is a potent teratogen; smoking during pregnancy can cause stillbirth, low birth weight, or perinatal death. And smoking during one's lifetime has a small, but measurable negative impact on cognitive functioning in later life (Whalley et al., 2005).

Nonsmokers who breathe secondhand smoke are also at considerably higher risk for smoking-related diseases; each year 3,000 adult nonsmokers die from lung cancer, and 35,000 to 40,000 adult nonsmokers die from cardiovascular disease. Hundreds of thousands of children suffer from lung problems annually in the United States due to environmental smoke (American Cancer Society, 2005b). For these reasons, many states and communities have passed stricter legislation banning smoking in public buildings, and smoking is banned entirely on airline flights within the United States and on many international flights. Still, secondhand smoke remains a major problem; two thirds of the respondents to one survey indicated that they had been exposed to secondhand smoke in the past week (Landreck, Wallace, & Neuberger, 2000).

Juan, the young man in the vignette, is typical of people who want to stop smoking. Most people who try to stop smoking begin the process in young adulthood. Although some smokers who want to quit find formal programs helpful, more than 90% of those who stop do so on their own. But as Juan suspects, quitting is not easy; 70 to 80% of those who try to quit relapse at least once (Cohen et al., 1989). For most people, success is attained only after a long period of stopping and relapsing.

Regardless of how it happens, quitting smoking has enormous health benefits (American Cancer Society, 2005a). For example, women who have stopped smoking significantly reduce their chances of dying prematurely (Surgeon General, 2001). Women who have quit for 3 years have a risk of heart attack equivalent to women who have never smoked (Rosenberg, Palmer, & Shapiro, 1990). The risk of cardiovascular disease returns to normal after a period of roughly 15 years (American Cancer Society, 2005a). Even people who do not quit until late life (even after age 70) show marked improvements in health (LaCroix et al., 1991). In sum, the evidence is clear: If you don't smoke, don't start. If you do, you're never too old to stop. Check out the American Cancer Society's website (www.cancer.org) for key information about how to quit and a quiz about which way of quitting will work best for you.

Drinking Alcohol

If you are between the ages of 25 and 44, chances are you drink occasionally; about 63% of the people in the United States currently drink alcohol regularly (National Center for Health Statistics, 2004a). Total consumption of alcohol in industrialized countries has declined for the past few decades (Hanson, 2005), partly in response to tougher laws regarding underage drinking and drinking and driving.

For the majority of people, drinking alcohol poses no serious health problems as long as they do not drink and drive. In fact, numerous studies show that for people who

© John Feingersh /Corbis

Moderate consumption of alcohol can have health benefits, but drinking heavily has serious negative consequences.

drink no more than two glasses of wine per day, alcohol consumption may be beneficial. For example, light drinkers (one glass of beer or wine per day) have a lower risk of stroke than either abstainers or heavy drinkers, even after controlling for hypertension, smoking, and medication (Ebersole, Hess, & Luggen, 2004).

*One type of drinking that is particularly troublesome among young adults, especially college students, is **binge drinking,** defined for men as consuming five or more drinks in a row and for women as consuming four or more drinks in a row within the past 2 weeks.* Binge drinking has been identified as a major national health problem (Gomez, 2000; Schoenborn & Adams, 2001; Wechsler et al., 1994) and is the focus of several efforts to reduce the number of college students who binge. These efforts include establishing low tolerance levels for the antisocial behaviors associated with binge drinking, working with fraternities and sororities, changing the expectations of incoming freshmen, and increasing the number of nonalcoholic activities available to students (Bishop, 2000). As discussed in the Current Controversies feature, these efforts come at a time when national attention is directed at the problem.

CURRENT CONTROVERSIES

BINGE DRINKING ON COLLEGE CAMPUSES

A widely held notion about college life is that it is a time when young adults "cut loose" and enjoy all available social activities. For many students, this involves drinking alcohol. Indeed, to many students, college parties and drinking alcohol are virtually synonymous.

Unfortunately, drinking among college students often goes beyond moderate intake. Binge drinking is on the upswing in U.S. colleges. In two repre-

sentative national surveys of more than 17,500 undergraduate students (in 1993) and 14,000 undergraduates (in 1999), 44% of the students reported that they were binge drinkers (Wechsler et al., 1994, 2002).

Although students between the ages of 17 and 23 are more likely than older students to binge drink, there is no relation between year in school and binge drinking rates. Which students are most

likely to binge drink? Research shows that binge drinking students are more likely to have observed family members binge drinking at home, meaning that they have been socialized into this drinking pattern (Gomez, 2000). They are also more likely to be members of fraternities and sororities (Gomez, 2000); intention to affiliate with a Greek organization also predicts binge drinking for men but not for women (Read et al., 2002). Other predictors include race, class, use of other drugs in the past 30 days, positive alcohol expectancies, perception of minimal risk, perception that friends do not disapprove of binge drinking, and perception of high normative drinking (Strano, Cuomo, & Venable, 2004). Being male, European American, a freshman, having a fraternity membership, perceiving that friends do not disapprove, and using other drugs distinguished high-frequency from low-frequency binge drinkers. Men are sometimes shown to binge drink more than women, such as in Sardinia (DiGrande et al., 2000), but in other studies, such as one in Britain, women sometimes have higher rates (Pickard et al., 2000; Reifman & Watson, 2004).

Research indicates that students binge drink for several reasons, including insecure attachment to parents and impaired ability to express emotion (Camlibel, 2000) and stressful life events during late adolescence (Aseltine & Gore, 2000). Incoming students who believe drinking is part of the social experience of college are more likely to be binge drinkers; males are particularly likely to show this pattern (Read et al., 2002).

Binge drinking is extremely dangerous. But coma and death are only two of its numerous ill effects. As you can see in Figure 10.2, the rate of drinking-related problems, including missing class and engaging in unwanted sexual behavior, is much higher in binge drinkers, especially those who binge three or more times within a 2-week period ("frequent binge drinkers"). These problems have important long-lasting consequences, from poorer grades and unplanned pregnancies to contracting sexually transmitted diseases.

Equally important, but often overlooked, are secondhand drinking effects, those negative drinking-related consequences experienced by others. For example, a nondrinker may be insulted, assaulted, or have to care for an ill binge drinker, which may in turn have important academic consequences for these students. These negative social outcomes need to be viewed as part of the overall problem posed by binge drinking (Vicary & Karshin, 2002).

Many colleges and universities are developing programs to respond to this growing problem. Because students who participate in extracurricular activities, work at part-time jobs, or study more than 4 hours a day are less likely to binge drink (Wechsler et al., 1995), programs to get students involved in such activities may have some success. Other programs focus on education, working with fraternities and sororities, and offering social activities without alcohol (Bishop, 2000). Because binge drinking college students are more likely to have been binge drinkers in high school, strategies that focus on younger students are also important. Taken together, the key elements in reducing binge drinking appear to be student participation and involvement in designing the program, campuswide informational and educational processes, and changes in the campus culture that involve tougher regulations (Ziemelis, Bucknam, & Elfessi, 2002).

The key is changing the culture that is strongly supportive of binge drinking to one in which binge drinking is something popular people do not do. Focusing on the negative behavioral outcomes may be a key to program success (Alexander & Bowen, 2004). What appears not to work are efforts to limit access to alcohol (Wechsler et al., 2004). Whether programs now in place actually lower the rate of binge drinking remains to be seen. However, one thing is certain—binge drinking must be dealt with. But it will not be easy. Wechsler and colleagues (2002) note that the national rates of binge drinking showed little overall change between 1994 and 2001, remaining around 41%. Examined more closely, rates had increased for women who attend all-women's colleges. Despite educational and disciplinary efforts, the number of frequent binge drinkers has actually increased. Clearly, changing the culture for young adult college students is extremely difficult.

■ **Figure 10.2**
Troublesome behaviors increase with binge drinking. Note that all binge drinkers report more problems than non–binge drinkers.

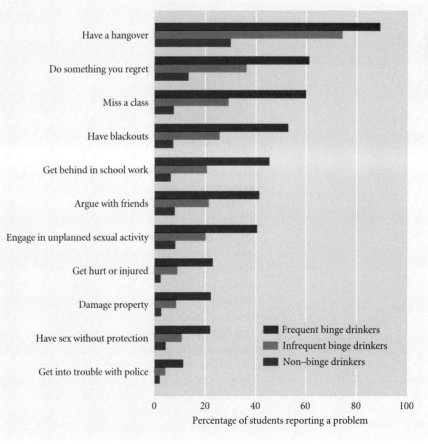

THINK ABOUT IT

What would be some specific strategies to reduce binge drinking on your campus?

Nearly 14 million people in the United States—1 in every 13 adults—abuse alcohol or are alcoholic. However, more men than women are alcohol dependent or experience alcohol-related problems. In addition, rates of alcohol problems are highest among young adults ages 18 to 29 and lowest among adults 65 years and older (National Institute on Alcohol Abuse and Alcoholism [NIAAA], 1998). The risk of alcoholism is increased in children of alcoholics, especially when they engage in binge drinking as adolescents and young adults (Chassin, Pitts, & Prost, 2002).

Alcoholism is viewed by most experts as a form of **addiction,** *which means that alcoholics demonstrate physical dependence on alcohol and experience withdrawal symptoms when they do not drink.* Dependence occurs when a drug, such as alcohol, becomes so incorporated into the functioning of the body's cells that the drug becomes necessary for normal functioning (Mayo Clinic, 2005a). Alcohol addiction occurs over time as drinking alcohol alters the balance of some chemicals in the brain, causing a strong desire for more alcohol. These chemicals include gamma-aminobutyric acid (GABA), which inhibits impulsiveness; glutamate, which excites the nervous system; norepinephrine, which is released in response to stress; and dopamine, serotonin, and opioid peptides, which are responsible for pleasurable feelings. Excessive, long-term drinking can deplete or increase the levels of some of these chemicals, causing the body to crave alcohol to restore good feelings or to avoid negative feelings. Additionally, other factors come into play, including genetics; high stress, anxiety, or emotional pain; close friends or partners who drink excessively; and sociocultural factors that glorify alcohol.

Most people seeking treatment are young adults (NIAAA, 1998). The most widely known treatment option is Alcoholics Anonymous, founded in Akron, Ohio, in 1935 by two recovering alcoholics. Other treatment approaches include inpatient and outpatient programs at treatment centers, behavior modification, cognitive behavioral therapy, aversion therapy, motivational enhancement therapy, and acupuncture (Mayo Clinic, 2005a). Typically, the goal of these programs is abstinence. Unfortunately, we know very little about the long-term success of the various programs.

Nutrition

How many times did your parents tell you to eat your vegetables? Or perhaps they said, "You are what you eat." Most people have disagreements with parents about food while growing up, but as adults they later realize that those lima beans and other despised foods really are healthful.

Experts agree that nutrition directly affects one's mental, emotional, and physical functioning (Mayo Clinic, 2005b). For example, diet has been linked to cancer, cardiovascular disease, diabetes, anemia, and digestive disorders. Nutritional requirements and eating habits change across the life span. *This change is due mainly to differences in* **metabolism,** *or how much energy the body needs.* Body metabolism and the digestive process slow down with age (Rowe & Kahn, 1998).

Every 5 years the U.S. Department of Agriculture publishes dietary guidelines based on current research. In its *Dietary Guidelines for Americans 2005* (U.S. Department of Agriculture, 2005a), the USDA recommends that we eat a variety of nutrient-dense foods and beverages across the basic food groups. Most important, we should choose foods that limit the intake of saturated and *trans* fats, cholesterol, added sugars, salt, and alcohol. The USDA has roughly equivalent nutritional guidelines for younger, middle-aged, and older adults, with a few modifications; for example, they recommend that women of childbearing age consume more iron-rich foods, that adults over 50 consume vitamin B_{12} in its crystalline form, and that older adults with dark skin or who do not get enough sunlight consume more vitamin D. Because of slowing metabolic rates with age, older adults need fewer calories than younger adults, who in turn need more carbohydrates. Older adults are also at higher risk for dehydration, so they should drink more water. Older adults also need more protein.

Did you ever worry as you were eating a triple-dip cone of premium ice cream that you really should be eating fat-free frozen yogurt instead? If so, you are among the people who have taken to heart (literally) the link between diet and cardiovascular disease. The

American Heart Association (2005b) makes it clear that foods high in saturated fat (such as our beloved ice cream) should be replaced with foods low in fat (such as fat-free frozen yogurt). (The American Heart Association provides a website at www.deliciousdecisions.org with recipes and alternatives for a heart-healthy diet.)

The main goal of these recommendations is to lower your level of cholesterol because high cholesterol is one risk factor for cardiovascular disease. There is an important difference between two different types of cholesterol, which are defined by their effect on blood flow. Lipoproteins are fatty chemicals attached to proteins carried in the blood. *Low-density lipoproteins (LDLs) cause fatty deposits to accumulate in arteries, impeding blood flow, whereas* **high-density lipoproteins (HDLs)** *help keep arteries clear and break down LDLs.* It is not so much the overall cholesterol number but the ratio of LDLs to HDLs that matters most in cholesterol screening. High levels of LDLs are a risk factor in cardiovascular disease, and high levels of HDLs are considered a protective factor. Reducing LDL levels is effective in diminishing the risk of cardiovascular disease in adults of all ages; in healthy adults a high level of LDL (over 160 mg/dL) indicates a higher risk for cardiovascular disease (American Heart Association, 2005a). In contrast, higher levels of HDL are good (in healthy adults, levels above 40 mg/dL). LDL levels can be lowered and HDL levels can be raised through various interventions such as exercise and a high-fiber diet. Weight control is also an important component.

Eating a heart-healthy diet is an important part of preventing cardiovascular disease.

Numerous medications exist for treating cholesterol problems. The most popular of these drugs are from a family of medications called *statins* (e.g., Lipitor, Crestor). These medications lower LDL and moderately increase HDL. Because of potential side effects on liver functioning, patients taking cholesterol-lowering medications should be monitored on a regular basis.

Obesity is a growing health problem related to diet. One good way to assess your own status is to compute your body mass index. *Body mass index (BMI) is a ratio of body weight and height and is related to total body fat.* You can compute BMI as follows:

$$BMI = w/h^2$$

Where: w = weight in kilograms (or weight in pounds divided by 2.2), h = height in meters (or inches divided by 39.37). The National Institutes of Health and the American Heart Foundation define healthy weight as having a BMI less than 25. However, this calculation may overestimate body fat in very muscular people and underestimate body fat in those who appear of normal weight but have little muscle mass.

BMI is related to the risk of serious medical conditions and mortality: the higher one's BMI, the higher one's risk (Centers for Disease Control and Prevention, 2004a). Figure 10.3 shows the increased risk for several diseases and mortality associated with increased BMI. Based on these estimates, you may want to lower your BMI if it's above 25. But be careful—lowering your BMI too much may not be healthy either. Very low BMIs may indicate malnutrition, which is also related to increased mortality.

SOCIAL, GENDER, AND ETHNIC ISSUES IN HEALTH

We have indicated that although most young adults are very healthy there are important individual differences. Let's see what they are.

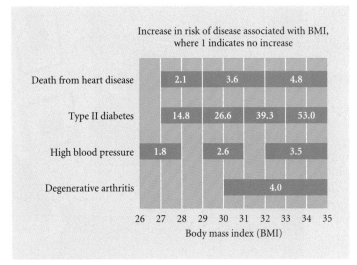

Increase in risk of disease associated with BMI, where 1 indicates no increase

Death from heart disease	2.1	3.6	4.8
Type II diabetes	14.8	26.6	39.3	53.0
High blood pressure	1.8	2.6	3.5
Degenerative arthritis		4.0	

Body mass index (BMI)

From National Institutes of Health, 1999.

■ **Figure 10.3**
Your body mass index (BMI) is related to health and mortality. The higher one's BMI, the higher the risk of disease.

Social Factors

The two most important social influences on health are socioeconomic status and education. In the United States, income level is a major determinant of how healthy a person is likely to be, mainly because income is linked to having access to adequate health care. Regardless of ethnic group, people who live in poverty are more likely to be in poor health than people who do not.

Related to income is education. College graduates are less likely to develop chronic diseases such as hypertension and cardiovascular disease than people who do not go to college. In fact, people who have less education are not only more likely to contract a chronic disease, they are more likely to die from it. In one of the largest studies examining this issue ever conducted, results show that in a representative sample of 5,652 working adults between the ages of 18 and 64, educational level was associated with good health even when the effects of age, gender, ethnicity, and smoking were accounted for (Pincus, Callahan, & Burkhauser, 1987).

Does education *cause* good health? Not exactly. Higher educational level is associated with higher income, as well as more awareness of dietary and lifestyle influences on health. Thus, more highly educated people are in a better position to afford health care and to know about the kinds of foods and lifestyle that affect health.

Gender

Are men or women healthier? This question is difficult to answer, primarily because women were not routinely included in many major studies of health until the 1990s (Kolata, 1990). For example, most of the longitudinal data about risk factors for cardiovascular disease comes from studies of men. We do know that women live longer than men, for reasons discussed in Chapter 14. Women also use health services more often because they tend to pay more attention to changes in their bodies (Ebersole et al., 2004).

Ethnic Group Differences

In the United States, the poorest health conditions exist in inner-city neighborhoods. For example, African American men in large urban areas have a lower life expectancy than men in some developing countries (U.S. Census Bureau, 2005b). Many inner-city residents rely on overcrowded clinics. Why is this the case?

The main reasons are poverty and racism. As noted earlier, poverty is associated with inadequate health care and higher mortality throughout life in many countries (McLaughlin, Stokes, & Nonoyama, 2001; Underlid, 2005). Even when poor minorities have access to health care, they are less likely than European Americans to receive treatment for chronic disease (National Center for Health Statistics, 2004a).

But there is another factor: stress related to racism. Unlike men in most developing countries, African American men are the targets of racism. Research demonstrates that people who suppress their anger are at increased risk of hypertension (al'Absi, Bongard, & Lovallo, 2000), although this relationship is moderated by age, with older African American adults having the highest blood pressures (Peters, 2004). People who are subjected to racism may not feel they can show their anger and therefore keep it bottled up.

To the extent that other ethnic groups suffer from poverty and cannot obtain adequate health care, they also have poorer health. Thus, until poverty and access to health care and racism are addressed, inner-city minority groups will be at a serious disadvantage in terms of health.

Many inner-city residents must rely on overcrowded clinics for their primary health care.

© Tom Carter/PhotoEdit

TEST YOURSELF

1. In young adulthood, most people reach their maximum _____.

2. Sensory acuity peaks during the _____.

3. During the early 20s, death from disease is _____.

4. Young adult _____ are the most likely to die.

5. _____ is the biggest contributor to health problems.

6. Alcoholism is viewed by most experts as a form of _____.

7. The two most important social influences on health are education and _____.

8. In the United States, the poorest health conditions exist for African Americans living in _____.

How could you design a health care system that provides strong incentives for healthy lifestyles during young adulthood?

Answers: (1) height, (2) 20s, (3) rare, (4) men, (5) Smoking, (6) addiction, (7) socioeconomic status, (8) inner-city neighborhoods

10.3

COGNITIVE DEVELOPMENT

Susan, a 33-year-old woman recently laid off from her job as a secretary, slides into her seat on her first day of college classes. She is clearly nervous. "I'm worried that I won't be able to compete with these younger students, that I may not be smart enough," she sighs. "Guess we'll find out soon enough, though, huh?"

LEARNING OBJECTIVES

What is intelligence in adulthood?
_____

What types of abilities have been identified? How do they change?
_____

What is postformal thought? How does it differ from formal operations?
_____

How do stereotypes influence thinking?

MANY RETURNING ADULT STUDENTS LIKE SUSAN worry that they may not be "smart enough" to keep up with 18- or 19-year-olds. Are these fears realistic? In this section, we examine the evidence concerning intellectual performance in adulthood.

We will see how the answer to this question depends on the types of intellectual skills being used.

HOW SHOULD WE VIEW INTELLIGENCE IN ADULTS?

We interrupt this section for a brief exercise. Take a sheet of paper and write down all the abilities that you think reflect intelligence in adults. When you have finished, read further to see how your perceptions match research results.

It's a safe bet that you listed more than one ability as reflecting adults' intelligence. You are not alone. *Most theories of intelligence are **multidimensional**—that is, they identify several types of intellectual abilities.* As discussed in Chapter 6, there is disagreement about the number and types of abilities, but virtually everyone agrees that no single generic type of intelligence is responsible for all the different kinds of mental activities we perform.

Sternberg (1985, 2003) emphasized multidimensionality in his theory of successful intelligence (discussed in Chapter 6). Based on the life-span perspective (described in Chapter 1), Baltes and colleagues (Baltes, 1997; Baltes et al., 1998, 1999; Schaie, 1995) introduced three other concepts as vital to intellectual development in adults: multidirectionality, interindividual variability, and plasticity. Let's look at each of these concepts in turn.

*Over time, the various abilities underlying adults' intelligence show **multidirectionality:** Some aspects of intelligence improve and other aspects decline during adulthood. Closely related to this is **interindividual variability:** These patterns of change also vary from one person to another.* In the next two sections, we will see evidence for both multidirectionality and interindividual variability when we examine developmental trends for specific sets of intellectual abilities. *Finally, people's abilities reflect **plasticity:** They are not fixed but can be modified under the right conditions at just about any point in adulthood.* Because most research on plasticity has focused on older adults, we return to this topic in Chapter 14.

Baltes and colleagues emphasize that intelligence has many components and these components show varying development in different abilities and different people. Let's turn our attention to the evidence that supports this theoretical view.

WHAT HAPPENS TO INTELLIGENCE IN ADULTHOOD?

Given that intelligence in adults is a complex, multifaceted construct, how might we study adult intelligence? Two common ways involve formal testing and assessing practical problem-solving skills. Formal testing typically assesses primary or secondary abilities and involves tests from which we can compute overall IQ scores like those discussed in Chapter 6. Tests involving practical problems assess people's ability to use intelligence in everyday situations. So what happens in each type of ability?

Primary Abilities

From our previous discussion, we know that intelligence consists of many different skills and abilities. *Since the 1930s, researchers have agreed that intellectual abilities can be studied as groups of related skills (such as memory or spatial ability) organized into hypothetical constructs called **primary mental abilities.*** Roughly 25 primary mental abilities have been identified (Horn, 1982). Because it is difficult to study all of the primary mental abilities, researchers have focused on five representative ones:

- *Number:* the basic skills underlying our mathematical reasoning
- *Word fluency:* how easily we produce verbal descriptions of things
- *Verbal meaning:* our vocabulary ability
- *Inductive reasoning:* our ability to extrapolate from particular facts to general concepts

Testing sessions such as the one shown here are used to assess intellectual functioning.

© Frank Siteman/PhotoEdit

■ *Spatial orientation:* our ability to reason in the three-dimensional world in which we live

Do these primary abilities show change in adulthood? One answer is examined in the Spotlight on Research feature.

SPOTLIGHT ON RESEARCH

THE SEATTLE LONGITUDINAL STUDY

Who was the investigator and what was the aim of the study? In the 1950s, little information was available concerning longitudinal changes in adults' intellectual abilities. What little there was showed a developmental pattern quite different from the picture of across-the-board decline obtained in cross-sectional studies. To provide a more thorough picture of intellectual change, K. Warner Schaie began the Seattle Longitudinal Study in 1956.

How did the investigator measure the topic of interest? Schaie used standardized tests of primary mental abilities to assess a wide range of abilities such as logical reasoning and spatial ability.

Who were the participants in the study? Over the course of the study, more than 5,000 individuals were tested at seven testing cycles (1956, 1963, 1970, 1977, 1984, 1991, and 1998). The participants were representative of the upper 75% of the socioeconomic spectrum and were recruited through a very large health maintenance organization in Seattle. Extensions of the study include longitudinal data on second-generation family members and on the grandchildren of some of the original participants.

What was the design of the study? To provide a thorough view of intellectual change over time, Schaie invented a new type of research design—the sequential design (see Chapter 1). Participants were tested every 7 years. Like most longitudinal studies, Schaie's sequential study encountered selectivity effects—that is, people who return over the years for retesting tend to do better initially than those who fail to return (in other words, those who don't perform well initially tend to drop out of the study). However, an advantage of Schaie's sequential design is that by bringing in new groups of participants, he was able to estimate the importance

of selection effects, a major improvement over previous research.

Were there ethical concerns with the study? The most serious issue in any study in which participants are followed over time is confidentiality. Because people's names must be retained for future contact, the researchers were very careful about keeping personal information secure.

What were the results? Among the many important findings from the study are differential changes in abilities over time and cohort effects. As you can see in Figure 10.4, scores on tests of primary mental abilities improve gradually until the late 30s or early 40s. Small declines begin in the 50s, increase as people age

into their 60s, and become increasingly large in the 70s (Schaie, 1994).

Cohort differences were also found. Figure 10.5 shows that on some skills, such as inductive reasoning ability, but not others, more recently born younger and middle-aged cohorts performed better than cohorts born earlier. An example of the latter is that older cohorts outperformed younger ones on number skills (Schaie, 1994). These cohort effects probably reflect differences in educational experiences; younger groups' education emphasized figuring things out on one's own, whereas older groups' education emphasized rote learning. Additionally, older groups did not have calculators or computers, so

■ **Figure 10.4**
Longitudinal changes in intellectual abilities follow similar patterns for all abilities.

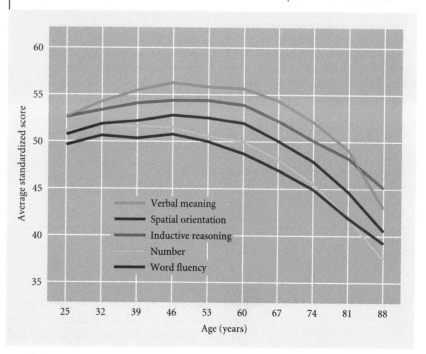

From "The Course of Adult Intellectual Development" by K. W. Schaie, 1994, *American Psychologist, 49,* 304–313. Copyright © 1994 by the American Psychological Association. Reprinted with permission of the author.

■ **Figure 10.5**
Intellectual abilities differ across cohorts.

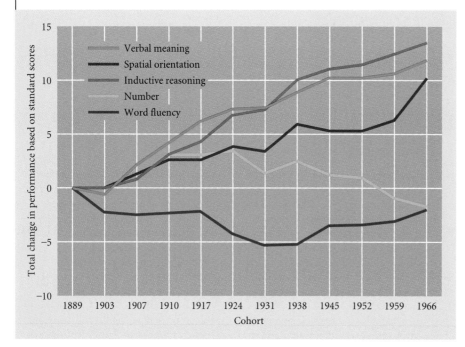

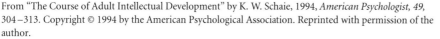

From "The Course of Adult Intellectual Development" by K. W. Schaie, 1994, *American Psychologist, 49,* 304–313. Copyright © 1994 by the American Psychological Association. Reprinted with permission of the author.

- Having a flexible personality style in middle age
- Being married to a person with high cognitive status
- Being satisfied with one's life achievements in middle age

What did the investigator conclude? Three points are clear. First, intellectual development during adulthood is marked by a gradual leveling off of gains, followed by a period of relative stability, and then a time of gradual decline in most abilities. Second, these trends vary from one cohort to another. Third, individual patterns of change vary considerably from person to person.

Overall, Schaie's findings indicate that intellectual development in adulthood is influenced by a wide variety of health, environmental, personality, and relationship factors. By attending to these influences throughout adulthood, we can at least stack the deck in favor of maintaining good intellectual functioning in late life.

What converging evidence would strengthen these conclusions? Although Schaie's study is one of the most comprehensive ever conducted, it is limited. Studying people who live in different locations around the world would provide evidence as to whether the results are limited geographically. Additional cross-cultural evidence comparing people with different economic backgrounds and differing access to health care would also provide insight into the effects of these variables on intellectual development.

To enhance your understanding of this research, go to http://psychology .wadsworth.com/kail_cavanaugh4e/ to complete critical thinking questions and explore related websites.

they had to do mathematical problems by hand.

Schaie uncovered many individual differences as well; some people showed developmental patterns closely approximating the overall trends, but others showed unusual patterns. For example, some individuals showed steady declines in most abilities beginning in their 40s and 50s, others showed declines in some abilities but not others, but some people showed little change in most abilities over a 14-year period. Such individual variation in developmental patterns means that average trends, like those depicted in the figures, must be interpreted cautiously; they reflect group averages and do not represent the patterns shown by each person in the group.

Another key finding is that how intellectual abilities are organized in people does not change over time (Schaie et al., 1998). This finding is important because it means that the tests, which presuppose a particular organizational structure of intellectual abilities, can be used across different ages. Additionally, Schaie (1994) identified several variables that appear to reduce the risk of cognitive decline in old age:

- Absence of cardiovascular and other chronic diseases
- Living in favorable environmental conditions (such as good housing)
- Remaining cognitively active through reading and lifelong learning

Secondary Mental Abilities

Rather than focusing separately on specific primary abilities, some researchers argue that it makes more sense to study a half dozen or so broader skills, termed **secondary mental abilities,** *that subsume and organize the primary abilities.* Figure 10.6 shows how performance data, primary mental abilities, and secondary mental abilities relate to each other. Notice that as you move up to secondary mental abilities you are moving away from the data. Two secondary mental abilities have received a great deal of attention in adult developmental research: fluid intelligence and crystallized intelligence (Horn, 1982).

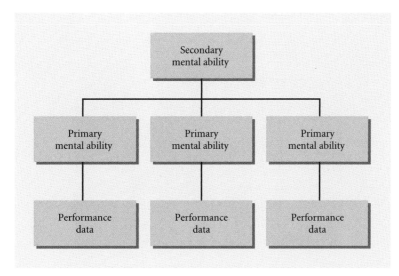

Fluid intelligence consists of the abilities that make you a flexible and adaptive thinker, that allow you to make inferences, and that enable you to understand the relations among concepts. It includes the abilities you need to understand and respond to any situation, but especially new ones: inductive reasoning, integration, abstract thinking, and the like (Horn, 1982). An example of a question that taps fluid abilities is the following: What letter comes next in the series *d f i m r x e?** Other typical ways of testing fluid intelligence include mazes, puzzles, and relations among shapes. Most of the time, these tests are timed, and higher scores are associated with faster solutions.

Crystallized intelligence is the knowledge you have acquired through life experience and education in a particular culture. Crystallized intelligence includes your breadth of knowledge, comprehension of communication, judgment, and sophistication with information (Horn, 1982). Your ability to remember historical facts, definitions of words, knowledge of literature, and sports trivia information are some examples. Many popular television game shows (such as *Who Wants to Be a Millionaire?, Jeopardy,* and *Wheel of Fortune*) are based on contestants' accumulated crystallized intelligence.

Even though crystallized intelligence involves cultural knowledge, it is based partly on the quality of a person's underlying fluid intelligence (Horn, 1982; Horn & Hofer, 1992). For example, the breadth of your vocabulary depends to some extent on how quickly you are able to make connections between new words you read and information already known, which is a component of fluid intelligence.

Developmentally, fluid and crystallized intelligence follow two very different paths, as you can see in Figure 10.7. Notice that fluid intelligence declines throughout adulthood, whereas crystallized intelligence improves. Although we do not yet fully understand why fluid intelligence declines, it may be related to underlying changes in the brain from the accumulated effects of disease, injury, and aging or from lack of practice (Horn & Hofer, 1992). In contrast, the increase in crystallized intelligence (at least until late life) indicates that people continue adding knowledge every day.

What do these different developmental trends imply? First, they indicate that although learning continues through adulthood, it becomes more difficult the older one gets. Consider what happens when Michael, age 17, and Marge, age 50, learn a second language. Although Marge's verbal skills in her native language (a component of crystallized intelligence) are probably better than Michael's, his probable superiority in the fluid abilities necessary to learn another language will usually make it easier for him to do so.

Second, these developmental trends point out once again that intellectual development varies a great deal from one set of skills to another. Beyond the differences in

---

*The next letter is *m*. The rule is to increase the difference between adjacent letters in the series by one each time *and* use a continuous circle of the alphabet for counting. Thus, *f* is two letters from *d, i* is three letters from *f,* and *e* is seven letters from *x*.

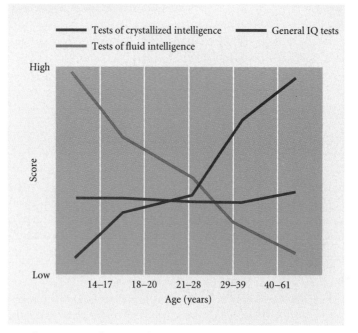

From "Organization of Data on Life-Span Development of Human Abilities" by J. L. Horn. In L. R. Goulet and P. B. Baltes (Eds.), *Life-Span Developmental Psychology: Research and Theory*, p. 463. Copyright © 1970 Academic Press.

overall trends, differences in individuals' fluid and crystallized intelligence also vary. Whereas individual differences in fluid intelligence remain relatively uniform over time, individual differences in crystallized intelligence increase with age, largely because maintaining crystallized intelligence depends on being in situations that require its use (Horn, 1982; Horn & Hofer, 1992). For example, few adults get much practice in solving complex letter series tasks like the one on page 395. But because people can improve their vocabulary skills by reading, and because people differ considerably in how much they read, differences are likely to emerge. In short, crystallized intelligence provides a rich knowledge base to draw on when material is somewhat familiar, whereas fluid intelligence provides the power to deal with learning in novel situations.

GOING BEYOND FORMAL OPERATIONS: THINKING IN ADULTHOOD

Suppose you are faced with the following dilemma. You are a member of your institution's student judicial board and are currently hearing a case involving plagiarism. The student handbook indicates that plagiarism is a serious offense that results in expulsion. The student accused of plagiarizing a paper admits copying but says that she has never been told that she needed to use a formal citation and quotation marks. Do you vote to expel the student?

When this and similar problems are presented to adolescents and adults, interesting differences emerge. Adolescents tend to point out that the student handbook is clear, the student ignored it, and conclude that the student should be expelled. Adolescents thus tend to approach the problem in formal-operational terms, as discussed in Chapter 6. They reason deductively from the information given to come to a single solution grounded in their own experience. Formal-operational thinkers are certain that such solutions are right because they are based on their own experience and are logically driven.

But many adults are reluctant to draw any conclusions based on the limited information in the problem, especially when the problem can be interpreted in different ways (Sinnott, 1998). They point out that there is much about the student we don't know:

Has she ever been taught the proper procedure for using sources? Was the faculty member clear about what plagiarism is? From this perspective, the problem is much more ambiguous. Adults may eventually decide that the student is (or is not) expelled, but they do so only after considering aspects of the situation that go well beyond the information given in the problem. Such thinking shows a recognition that other people's experiences may be quite different from one's own.

Clearly, the thought process these adults use is different from formal operations (King & Kitchener, 2004). Unlike formal-operational thinking, this approach involves considering situational constraints and circumstances, realizing that reality sometimes constrains solutions, and knowing that feelings matter.

Perry (1970) first uncovered adults' different thinking and traced its development. He found that 18-year-old first-year students tend to rely heavily on the expertise of authority figures (for example, experts, professors, police, parents) to determine which ways of thinking are right and which are wrong. For these students, thinking is tightly tied to logic, as Piaget had argued, and the only legitimate answers are ones that are logically derived.

Perceptions change over the next few years. Students go through a phase in which they are much less sure of which answers are right—or whether there are any right answers at all. However, by the time they are ready to graduate, students are fairly adept at examining different sides of an issue and have developed commitments to particular viewpoints. They recognize that they are the source of their own authority, that they must take a position on an issue, and that other people may hold different positions from theirs but be equally committed. During the college years, then, individuals become able to understand many perspectives on an issue, choose one, and still acknowledge the right of others to hold differing views. Perry concluded that this kind of thinking is very different from formal operations and represents another level of cognitive development.

Based on several additional longitudinal studies and numerous cross-sectional investigations, researchers have concluded that this type of thinking represents a qualitative change beyond formal operations (King & Kitchener, 1994, 2004; Kitchener & King, 1989; Kramer et al., 1991; Sinnott, 1998). *Postformal thought is characterized by a recognition that truth (the correct answer) may vary from situation to situation, that solutions must be realistic to be reasonable, that ambiguity and contradiction are the rule rather than the exception, and that emotion and subjective factors usually play a role in thinking.* In general, the research evidence indicates that postformal thinking has its origins in young adulthood (King & Kitchener, 2004; Sinnott, 1998).

Several research-based descriptions of the development of thinking in adulthood have been offered. *One of the best is the description of the development of **reflective judgment**, a way in which adults reason through dilemmas involving current affairs, religion, science, personal relationships, and the like.* Based on decades of longitudinal and cross-sectional research, Kitchener and King (1989; King & Kitchener, 1994, 2004) refined descriptions and identified a systematic progression of reflective judgment in young adulthood, which is described in Table 10.1.

The first three stages in the model represent prereflective thought. People in these stages typically do not acknowledge and may not even perceive that knowledge is uncertain. Consequently, they do not understand that some problems exist for which there is not a clearly and absolutely correct answer. For example, Martina's pressuring of her instructor for the "right" theory to explain human development reflects this stage. She is also likely to hold firm positions on controversial issues, but she does so without acknowledging other people's ability to reach a different, but nevertheless equally logical, position.

About halfway through the developmental progression, Martina thinks very differently. In Stages 4 and 5, she is likely to say that nothing can be known for certain and to change her conclusions based on the situation and the evidence. At this point, she argues that knowledge is quite subjective. She is also less persuasive with her positions on controversial issues: "Each person is entitled to his or her own view; I cannot force my opinions on anyone else." Kitchener and King refer to thinking in these stages as quasi-reflective thinking.

TABLE 10.1

Description of the Stages of Reflective Judgment

Stage 1

View of knowledge: Knowledge is assumed to exist absolutely and concretely. It can be obtained with absolute certainty through direct observation.

Concept of justification: Beliefs need no justification because there is assumed to be an absolute correspondence between what is believed and what is true. There are no alternatives.

Stage 2

View of knowledge: Knowledge is absolutely certain, or certain but not immediately available. Knowledge can be obtained via direct observation or via authorities.

Concept of justification: Beliefs are justified via authority, such as a teacher or parent, or are unexamined and unjustified. Most issues are assumed to have a right answer, so there is little or no conflict in making decisions about disputed issues.

Stage 3

View of knowledge: Knowledge is assumed to be absolutely certain or temporarily uncertain. In areas of temporary uncertainty, we can know only via intuition and bias until absolute knowledge is obtained.

Concept of justification: In areas in which answers exist, beliefs are justified via authorities. In areas in which answers do not exist, because there is no rational way to justify beliefs, they are justified arationally or intuitively.

Stage 4

View of knowledge: Knowledge is uncertain and idiosyncratic because situational variables (for example, incorrect reporting of data, data lost over time) dictate that we cannot know with certainty. Therefore, we can only know our own beliefs about the world.

Concept of justification: Beliefs often are justified by reference to evidence but still are based on idiosyncratic reasons, such as choosing evidence that fits an established belief.

Stage 5

View of knowledge: Knowledge is contextual and subjective. Because what is known is known via perceptual filters, we cannot know directly. We may know only interpretations of the material world.

Concept of justification: Beliefs are justified within a particular context via the rules of inquiry for that context. Justifications are assumed to be context specific or are balanced against each other, delaying conclusions.

Stage 6

View of knowledge: Knowledge is personally constructed via evaluations of evidence, opinions of others, and so forth across contexts. Thus we may know our own and other's personal constructions of issues.

Concept of justification: Beliefs are justified by comparing evidence and opinion on different sides of an issue or across contexts and by constructing solutions that are evaluated by personal criteria, such as one's personal values or the pragmatic need for action.

Stage 7

View of knowledge: Knowledge is constructed via the process of reasonable inquiry into generalizable conjectures about the material world or solutions for the problem at hand, such as what is most probable based on the current evidence or how far it is along the continuum of how things seem to be.

Concept of justification: Beliefs are justified probabilistically via evidence and argument or as the most complete or compelling understanding of an issue.

SOURCE: Adapted from King, P. M., & Kitchener, K. S. (1994). *Developing reflective judgment: Understanding and promoting intellectual growth and critical thinking in adolescents and adults.* Copyright © 1994. This material is used by permission of John Wiley & Sons, Inc.

As Martina continues her development into Stages 6 and 7, she begins to show true reflective judgment, understanding that people construct knowledge using evidence and argument after very careful analysis of the problem or situation. She once again holds very firm convictions, but she reaches them only after careful consideration of several points of view. Martina also realizes that she has to continually reevaluate her beliefs in view of new evidence.

How does a person like Martina move from prereflective judgment to reflective judgment? Is the progression a gradual one or one involving qualitative shifts? Kitchener and Fischer (1990) argue that the progression involves both, depending on which aspect of development one emphasizes. Their view is based on the distinction between optimal level and skill acquisition aspects of development. *The **optimal level of development** is the highest level of information-processing capacity that a person is capable of doing.* The optimal level increases with age and is marked by abrupt changes ("growth spurts") followed by periods of stability. Each spurt represents the emergence of a new developmental level (stage) of thinking; the period of stability reflects the time needed to become proficient at using the newly acquired skills. ***Skill acquisition** is the gradual, somewhat haphazard process by which people learn new abilities.* People progress through many small steps in acquiring skills before they are ready for the next growth spurt.

One's optimal level indicates the highest stage a person has achieved in cognitive development but probably does not indicate the level he or she will use most of the time (King & Kitchener, 1994, 2004). Why is this the case? Mostly it is because the environment does not provide the supports necessary for high-level performance, especially for issues concerning knowledge. For example, exams in most courses require you to have one and only one correct response, despite the fact that there may be multiple correct answers to the problem. However, if pushed and if given the necessary supports, people demonstrate a level of thinking and performance far higher than they typically show on a daily basis. This discrepancy may explain why fewer people are found at each more complex level of thinking who consistently use it.

The reflective judgment model is not the only way to describe the development of thinking in adulthood. Other researchers describe similar trends. For example, Kramer (1989; Kramer et al., 1991) reported a developmental process involving three stages: absolutist, relativistic, and dialectical. Absolutist thinking involves firmly believing that there is only one correct solution to a problem and that personal experience is the basis for all truth. People aged 18 to 22 tend to think this way. Relativistic thinking involves realizing that there are many sides to an issue and that correct actions or solutions depend on circumstances. Adults in their late 20s through early middle age use this style most. One potential danger with relativistic thinking is that it can lead to a cynical approach to life: "I'll do my thing and you do yours." Because relativistic thinkers tend to reason things out on a case-by-case basis, they are unlikely to be committed to any one position for long. The final stage, dialectical thinking, solves this problem. Dialectical thinkers see the merits in different viewpoints but are able to synthesize them into a workable solution to which they are strongly committed (Kramer & Kahlbaugh, 1994; Sinnott, 1994a, 1994c, 1998).

Although the various approaches to postformal thinking differ in some details, they all agree that some, but not all, adults progress from believing in one and only one right way of thinking and acting to accepting the fact that there are multiple solutions, each potentially equally acceptable (or equally flawed). This progression is important; it allows for the integration of emotion with thought in dealing with practical, everyday problems, as we will see next.

> **THINK ABOUT IT**
>
> Why are formal operations inadequate for integrating emotion and thought?

Integrating Emotion and Logic in Life Problems

One theme in descriptions of postformal thinking is the movement from thinking "I'm right because I've experienced it" to thinking "I'm not so sure who's right because your experience is different from mine." Problem situations that had seemed pretty straightforward now appear much more complicated; the "right thing to do" is much tougher to figure out.

Differences in thinking styles have major implications for dealing with life problems. For example, couples who are able to understand and synthesize each other's point of view are much more likely to resolve conflicts; couples not able to do so are more likely to feel resentful, drift apart, or even break up (Kramer, 1989; Kramer et al., 1991).

In addition to an increasing understanding that there is more than one "right" answer, Labouvie-Vief (1997, 2005; Zhang & Labouvie-Vief, 2004; Labouvie-Vief & Diehl, 2000) argues that adult thinking is characterized by the integration of emotion with logic. Beginning in young adulthood and continuing through middle age, people gradually shift from an orientation emphasizing conformity and context-free principles to one emphasizing change and context-dependent principles.

As they age, adults tend to make decisions and analyze problems not so much on logical grounds but rather on pragmatic and emotional grounds. Rules and norms are not viewed as absolute but as relative. Mature thinkers realize that thinking is an inherently social enterprise that demands making compromises with other people and tolerating contradiction and ambiguity. Such shifts mean that one's sense of self also undergoes a fundamental change (Labouvie-Vief, 2005; Magai, 2001).

A good example of this developmental shift would be the differences between the way late adolescents and young adults view an emotionally charged issue such as cheating on one's partner compared to the views of middle-aged adults. The younger people may view such behavior as completely inexcusable with the inescapable outcome being the end of the relationship. Middle-aged adults may take contextual factors into consideration and consider everyone's feelings. Researchers might argue that this is because the topic is too emotionally charged for adolescents to deal with intellectually, whereas adults are better able to incorporate emotion into their thinking. But is this interpretation reasonable?

It appears to be. In a now classic study, high school students, college students, and middle-aged adults were given three dilemmas to resolve (Blanchard-Fields, 1986). One dilemma had low emotional involvement, involving conflicting accounts of a war between two fictitious countries, North and South Livia, written by a partisan from each country. The other two dilemmas had high emotional involvement. In one, parents and their adolescent son disagreed about going to visit the grandparents (the son did not want to go). In the other, a man and a woman had to resolve an unintentional pregnancy (the man was anti-abortion, the woman was pro-choice).

The results are shown in Figure 10.8. You should note two important findings. First, there were clear developmental trends in reasoning level, with the middle-aged adults best able to integrate emotion into thinking. Second, the high school and college students were equivalent on the fictitious war dilemma, but the young adult students more readily integrated emotion and thought on the visit and pregnancy dilemmas. These results support the kinds of developmental shifts suggested by Labouvie-Vief. To continue the earlier example, dealing with a cheating partner may require the integration of thought and emotion, which is done better by middle-aged adults.

The mounting evidence of continued cognitive development in adulthood paints a more positive view of adulthood than that of Piaget, who focused only on logical thinking. The integration of emotion with logic that happens in adulthood provides the basis for decision making in the very personal and sometimes difficult arenas of love and work, which we examine in detail in Chapters 11 and 12, respectively. In the present context, it sets the stage for envisioning one's future life, a topic we take up later in this chapter.

THE ROLE OF STEREOTYPES IN THINKING

Thus far we have concentrated on the developmental course of thinking in adulthood. One powerful influence on the use of these intellectual powers is revealed in how social knowledge structures and social beliefs guide behavior. What are social knowledge structures and social beliefs? They are defined in terms of how we represent and interpret the behavior of others in a social situation (Fiske, 1993). They come in many different forms. For example,

◼ **Figure 10.8**
Developmental differences in reasoning level can be seen across these three story types. Middle-aged adults tend to use higher levels of thinking than adolescents or younger adults.

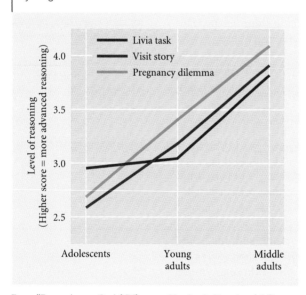

From "Reasoning on Social Dilemmas Varying in Emotional Saliency: An Adult Developmental Study," by F. Blanchard-Fields, 1986, *Psychology and Aging, 1,* 325–333. Copyright © 1986 by the American Psychological Association. Reprinted with permission of the author.

© Michael Newman/PhotoEdit

Digital Vision/Getty Images

Write down all of the things that come to mind when you look at the people in these photographs. Did you use rather general descriptions about them that reflect stereotypes?

we have scripted knowledge structures regarding everyday activities such as what people should do when they go to the doctor's office or a restaurant. We also have stereotypes of groups of people and how we feel they will act in certain situations. Finally, we have been socialized to adhere to and believe in social rules, or how to behave in specific social situations such as how a husband should act toward his wife.

One important type of social knowledge structure is stereotypes. *Stereotypes are a special type of social knowledge structure or social belief that represent organized prior knowledge about a group of people that affects how we interpret new information.* In other words, stereotypes are used to help us process information when we are engaged in social interactions (Cuddy & Fiske, 2002). We use our stereotypes to size up people when we first meet them. They help us understand why people behave the way they do and guide us in our behavior toward other people. Stereotypes are not inherently negative in their effect, but too many times they are applied in ways that underestimate the potential of the person we are observing.

Social psychologists suggest that stereotypes are automatically activated because they become overlearned and thus spontaneously activated when you encounter a member or members of a stereotyped group, such as older adults or African Americans (Devine, 1989; Greenwald, McGhee, & Schwartz, 1998). *The activation of strong stereotypes is not only automatic but also nonconscious, making it more likely that they will influence your behavior without you being aware of it, an effect called* **implicit stereotyping.** The effects of such implicit stereotyping are illustrated in a clever study conducted by Bargh and colleagues (1996). They demonstrated that if you subliminally (out of conscious awareness) prime young people with the image of an older adult, the young people's behavior is influenced in an age-related manner. In this case, the implicitly primed young adults walked down the hall more slowly after the experiment than young adults who were not primed with the older adult image. This is a powerful demonstration of how our unconscious stereotypes of aging can guide our behavior.

Measuring implicit aging stereotyping is a challenge because by definition it is inaccessible. However, recent research using a clever technique called the Age Attitude IAT (Implicit Attitudes Test; Hummert et al., 2002) has overcome this challenge. In this test individuals categorize photographs of faces by indicating as fast as they can whether the photo is a young or older person. They are asked to press a button with their right hand to indicate young and with their left hand to indicate old. Then they categorize other photographs as pleasant or unpleasant with the right hand indicating pleasant and the left hand indicating unpleasant. Next is the two-part test of implicit aging stereotypes. Part one consists of a combination of the young-old and pleasant-unpleasant categorization task using the same hands as indicated previously. In this test the right hand is associated with both young and pleasant whereas the left hand is associated with both old and unpleasant. The second part reverses the hands for young-old. Now, the right hand is associated with old and the left hand is associated with young. The right hand is still associated with pleasant and the left hand with unpleasant. The logic is this: if you have a negative stereotype regarding aging, you will be much slower in your response during the second test. In other words, it becomes difficult to use your right hand to indicate old because it is also associated with pleasant. This difficulty slows your response down.

Using this methodology, Hummert and colleagues (2002) found that people of all ages were faster to respond to young-pleasant and old-unpleasant trials than to old-pleasant and young-unpleasant trials. Furthermore, all individuals had implicit age attitudes that strongly favored the young over the old. If you would like to experiment with this test, the Internet home page for all the different variations of the Implicit Attitudes Test is at https://implicit.harvard.edu/implicit/demo/measureyourattitudes .html. These experiments and others (Levy, 2003) demonstrate that activation of our negative stereotypes about aging affects our behavior without us being aware of it.

Implicit stereotyping is illustrated in many different domains of our behavior toward others as well. Steele and colleagues (Spencer, Steele, & Quinn, 1999; Steele, 1997; Steele & Aronson, 1995) conducted a number of studies suggesting that stigmatized groups such as African Americans and women are vulnerable to stereotype threat. **Stereotype threat** *is an evoked fear of being judged in accordance with a negative stereotype about a group to which you belong.* For example, if you are African American, you may be vulnerable to cues in your environment that activate stereotype threat about academic ability. In turn, you may perform more poorly on a task associated with that stereotype regardless of high competence in academic settings.

In a seminal study, African Americans at Stanford University were divided into two groups. Both groups scored very high on their SAT verbal scores. However, one group was told that they were going to take a test that was highly diagnostic of their verbal ability. The other group did not receive this highly evaluative instruction. When scores were compared on verbal tests for both groups, despite the fact that all participants were highly verbal, the group that received the diagnostic instructions performed more poorly. Caucasians in the diagnostic evaluation did not differ from Caucasians in the nondiagnostic group. However, they outperformed African Americans in the diagnostic condition. Importantly, there were no differences between African Americans and Caucasians in the nondiagnostic group. Why? Steele argues that the performance of African Americans in the diagnostic condition suffered because they felt threatened by the negative stereotype that African Americans perform poorly on academic ability tests. This same type of effect was found when women were told that a test evaluated their mathematical competence. In this case, women are the stigmatized group because of negative stereotypes suggesting that women are less capable at math than men.

Implicit Social Beliefs

Stereotypes are only one of many types of belief systems that differ in content across age groups and also influence behavior. There are three important considerations in understanding age differences in social belief systems (Blanchard-Fields & Hertzog, 2000).

First, we must examine the specific content of social beliefs (i.e., the particular beliefs and knowledge people have about rules, norms, and patterns of social behavior). Second, we must consider the strength of these beliefs to know under what conditions they may influence behavior. Third, we need to know the likelihood that these beliefs will be activated automatically when they are violated or questioned. If these three aspects of the belief system are understood, it is possible to explain when and why age differences occur in social judgments. In other words, middle-aged and older adults may hold different beliefs than other age groups (e.g., different rules for appropriate social behavior during dating). Furthermore, how strongly people hold these beliefs may vary as a function of how particular generations were socialized. For example, although many adults of all ages may believe couples should not live together before marriage, older generations may be more adamant and rigid about this belief.

A good portion of the research literature focuses on age differences in the content of attitudes, beliefs, and values. However, evidence of age differences in the content of social beliefs does not completely account for age differences in how and when such beliefs are activated and how they influence behavior.

Social cognition researchers argue that individual differences in the strength of social representations of rules, beliefs, and attitudes are linked to specific situations (Mischel & Shoda, 1995). Such representations can be both cognitive (how we conceptualize the situation) and emotional (how we react to the situation). When one encounters a specific situation, the person's belief system triggers an emotional reaction and related goals tied to the content of that situation. This in turn drives social judgments. Consider the belief that couples should not live together before marriage. If you were socialized from childhood to believe in this rule, you would evaluate anyone violating the rule negatively. For example, suppose you were told about a man named Allen who put pressure on Joan to live with him before they were married, and they subsequently broke up. You may have a negative emotional response and blame Allen for the breakup of the relationship because he was lobbying for cohabitation.

A study exploring social beliefs found age differences in the types of social rules and evaluations evoked in different types of situations (Blanchard-Fields, 1996, 1999). For example, when subjects considered a husband who chooses to work long hours instead of spending more time with his wife and children, the social evaluation "marriage is more important than a career" tended to increase in importance with age. As can be seen in Figure 10.9, this was particularly evident from age 24 to age 65. The figure also shows that the social rule "the marriage was already in trouble" was also produced and has an inverted *U*-shaped relationship. In other words, adults around age 35 to 55 years produced this social evaluation the most.

These findings may relate to how the oldest generation was socialized with respect to the social rules of marriage. Your grandparents' generation probably was socialized very differently from your generation in terms of appropriate behavior by husbands and wives. Thus, these findings may reflect cohort differences. Alternatively, viewing marriage as more important than one's career may relate to the particular life stage and life circumstances different age groups confront. During mid-career and mid–childrearing stages, making a living and proving oneself in a career may take precedence. In contrast, during the retirement and empty nest phase, the importance of a marital relationship may reemerge. On the other hand, the middle-aged group may not have relied on social rules to guide their thinking about the problem situation and focused more on the marital conflict itself. This could possibly reflect the 1960s focus on communicating

■ **Figure 10.9**
There are age differences in social rules and relationships evoked in different situations. Note the increase in belief that marriage is more important than achieving in one's career as one gets older, and that older and younger couples may have different explanations than middle-aged adults of why marriages fail.

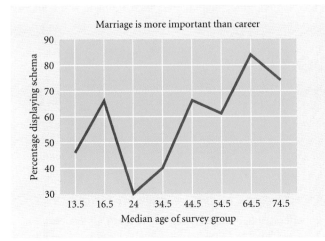

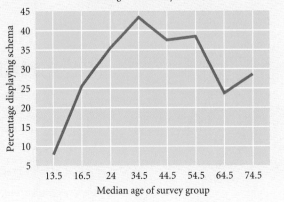

feelings. These are only a few examples of sociocultural experiential factors that may influence different social beliefs.

For a situation involving a young couple who eloped despite the objections of their parents, the social rules "parents should have talked to, not provoked, the young couple" and "they were too young" also showed an inverted *U*-shaped relationship with age. In other words, middle-aged people endorsed these rules, whereas younger and older people did not. On the other hand, the social rule "you can't stop true love" showed a *U*-shaped relationship with age. In other words, younger and older age groups endorsed this rule, whereas people in middle adulthood did not. It may be that in middle adulthood, between ages 30 and 45, people are not focusing on issues of true love. This makes sense because they are in the stage of life where the pragmatics of building a career are important. They also emphasized the pragmatics of age (e.g., being too young) as an important factor in marriage decisions.

One possible explanation for these findings is that cohort effects or generational differences (as we discussed in Chapter 1) influenced whether strong family social rules would be activated. For example, older women adopted the social rule "marriage is more important than career" much more than men of their same generation and more than women and men of younger generations. The fact that older women endorsed this social rule more strongly than the other age groups is a good example of how emotionally laden values are evoked in these situations.

TEST YOURSELF

1. Most modern theories of intelligence are _____ because they identify many domains of intellectual abilities.

2. Number, verbal fluency, and spatial orientation are some of the _____ mental abilities.

3. _____ reflects knowledge that you have acquired through life experience and education in a particular culture.

4. Kitchener and King describe a kind of postformal thinking called _____.

5. _____ are a special type of social knowledge structure or social belief that represent organized prior knowledge about a group of people that affects how we interpret new information.

Many young adult college students seemingly get more confused about what they want to major in and less certain about what they know as they progress through college. From a cognitive-developmental approach, why does this happen?

Answers: (1) multidimensional, (2) primary, (3) Crystallized intelligence, (4) reflective judgment, (5) Stereotypes

---

10.4

LEARNING OBJECTIVES

What is the life-span construct? How do adults create scenarios and life stories?

What are possible selves? Do they show differences during adulthood?

What are personal control beliefs?

WHO DO YOU WANT TO BE? PERSONALITY IN YOUNG ADULTHOOD

Felicia is a 19-year-old sophomore at a community college. She expects her study of early childhood education to be difficult but rewarding. She figures that along the way she will meet a great guy, whom she will marry soon after graduation. They will have two children before she turns 30. Felicia sees herself getting a good job teaching preschool children and some day

owning her own day care center.

IN CHAPTER 9, we saw how children and adolescents deal with the question "What do you want to be when you grow up?" As a young adult, Felicia has arrived at the "grown up" part and is experimenting with some idealistic answers to the question. Are Felicia's answers typical of most young adults?

In this section, we examine how the search for identity in adolescence meets the cognitive, social, and personal reality of adulthood. In particular, we will see how people create life scenarios and life stories, possible selves, self-concept, and personal control beliefs. Let's begin by considering how Felicia and the rest of us construct images of our adult lives.

CREATING SCENARIOS AND LIFE STORIES

Figuring out what (and who) you want to be as an adult takes lots of thought, hard work, and time. *Based on personal experience and input from other people, young adults create a* **life-span construct** *that represents a unified sense of the past, present, and future.* Several factors influence the development of a life-span construct; identity, values, and society are only a few. Together they not only shape the creation of the life-span construct, they influence the way it is played out and whether it remains stable (Fraley & Roberts, 2005). The life-span construct represents a link between Erikson's notion of identity, which is a major focus during adolescence, and our adult view of ourselves.

The first way the life-span construct is manifested is through the **scenario,** *which consists of expectations about the future.* The scenario takes aspects of a person's identity that are particularly important now and projects them into a plan for the future. For example, you may find yourself thinking about the day you will graduate and be able to apply all of the knowledge and skills you have learned. In short, a scenario is a game plan for how your life will play out in the future.

Felicia, the sophomore human development student, has a fairly typical scenario. She plans on completing a degree in early childhood education, marrying after graduation, and having two children by age 30. *Tagging future events with a particular time or age by which they are to be completed creates a* **social clock.** This personal timetable gives people a way to track progress through adulthood. They use biological markers of time (such as menopause), social aspects of time (such as getting married), and historical time (such as the turn of the century) (Hagestad & Neugarten, 1985).

Felicia will use her scenario to evaluate her progress toward her personal goals. With each new event, she will check where she is against where her scenario says she should be. If she is ahead of her plan, she may be proud of having made it. If she is lagging behind, she may chastise herself for being slow. But if she criticizes herself too much, she may change her scenario altogether. For example, if she does not go to college, she may decide to change her career goals entirely: Instead of owning her own day care center, she may aim to be a manager in a department store.

McAdams's Life-Story Model

McAdams (1994, 1999, 2001b; Bauer & McAdams, 2004; Bauer, McAdams, & Sakaeda, 2005) argues that a person's sense of identity cannot be understood using the language of dispositional traits or personal concerns. It is not just a collection of traits, nor is it a collection of plans, strategies, or goals. Instead, it is based on a story of how the person came into being, where the person has been, where he or she is going, and who he or she will become. *One's* **life story** *is a personal narrative that organizes past events into a coherent sequence.* Our life story becomes our autobiography as we move through adulthood.

McAdams argues that people create a life story that is an internalized narrative with a beginning, a middle, and an anticipated ending. The life story is created and revised throughout adulthood as people change and the changing environment places different demands on them.

McAdams and colleagues' research indicates that people in Western society begin forming their life story in late adolescence and early adulthood, but it has its roots in the development of one's earliest attachments in infancy. As in Erikson's theory, adolescence marks the full initiation into forming an identity, and thus, a coherent life story begins. In early adulthood it is continued and refined, and from midlife and beyond it is refashioned in the wake of major and minor life changes. Generativity marks the attempt to create an appealing story "ending" that will generate new beginnings for future generations (we discuss this in detail in Chapter 13).

Paramount to these life stories is the changing personal identity reflected in the emotions conveyed in the story (from tragedy to optimism or through comic and romantic descriptions). In addition, motivations change and are reflected in the person repeatedly trying to attain his or her goals over time. The two most common goal themes are agency (reflecting power, achievement, and autonomy) and communion (reflecting love, intimacy, and belongingness). Finally, stories indicate one's beliefs and values, or the ideology, a person uses to set the context for his or her actions.

Every life story contains episodes that provide insight into perceived change and continuity in life. People prove to themselves and others that they have either changed or remained the same by pointing to specific events that support the appropriate claim. The main characters in people's lives represent idealizations of the self, such as "the dutiful mother" or "the reliable worker." Integrating these various aspects of the self is a major challenge of midlife and later adulthood. Finally, all life stories need an ending through which the self is able to leave a legacy that creates new beginnings. Life stories in middle-aged and older adults have a clear quality of "giving birth to" a new generation, a notion essentially identical to generativity.

One of the more popular methods for examining the development of life stories is through autobiographical memory (Bluck, 2003; Bluck & Habermas, 2000; Thorne, 2000). When people tell their life story to others it is a joint product of the speaker and the audience (Pasupathi, 2001; Pasupathi & Carstensen, 2003). Pasupathi finds that the responses of the audience affect how the teller remembers his or her experiences. For example, if the listener finds that particular experience interesting, it's likely to be retold again; if the listener doesn't provide positive feedback, it's less likely. This is a good example of conversational remembering much like collaborative cognition discussed in Chapter 9.

Overall, McAdams (1994, 1999, 2001b; Bauer & McAdams, 2004; Bauer, McAdams, & Sakaeda, 2005) believes that the model for change in identity over time is a process of fashioning and refashioning one's life story. This process appears to be strongly influenced by culture. At times, the reformulation may be at a conscious level, such as when people make explicit decisions about changing careers. At other times, the revision process is unconscious and implicit, growing out of everyday activities. The goal is to create a life story that is coherent, credible, open to new possibilities, richly differentiated, reconciling of opposite aspects of oneself, and integrated within one's sociocultural context.

POSSIBLE SELVES

Another important aspect of self-concept and creating a scenario about ourselves is the ability to project ourselves into the future and to speculate about what we might be like (Markus & Nurius, 1986). How do we do this? *Projecting ourselves into the future involves creating* **possible selves** *that represent what we could become, what we would like to become, and what we are afraid of becoming.* What we could or would like to become often reflects personal goals; we may see ourselves as leaders, as rich and famous, or as in shape. What we are afraid of becoming may show up in our fear of being undervalued, or overweight, or lonely. Our possible selves are very powerful motivators; indeed, much of our behavior can be viewed as efforts to approach or avoid these various possible selves and to protect the current view of self (Markus & Nurius, 1986).

The topic of possible selves offers a way to understand how both stability and change operate in adults' personality. On one hand, possible selves tend to remain stable for at least some period of time and are measurable with psychometrically sound scales (Hooker, 1999, 2002). On the other hand, possible selves may change in response to efforts at personal growth (Frazier et al., 2000, 2002), which would be expected from ego development theory. In particular, possible selves facilitate adaptation to new roles across the life span. For example, a full-time mother who pictures herself as an executive once her child goes to school may begin to take evening courses to acquire new skills. Thus, possible selves offer a way to bridge the experience of the current self and our imagined future self.

Researchers have begun studying age differences in the construction of possible selves (Frazier et al., 2000, 2002; Hooker, 1999; Morfei et al., 2001). In a set of similar studies conducted by Cross and Markus (1991) and Hooker and colleagues (Frazier et al., 2000, 2002; Hooker, 1999; Hooker et al., 1996; Morfei et al., 2001), people across the adult life span were asked to describe their hoped-for and feared possible selves. Responses are grouped into categories (such as family, personal, material, relationships, occupation).

Several interesting age differences emerged. In terms of hoped-for selves, young adults listed as most important family concerns, for instance, marrying the right person (Cross & Markus, 1991), whereas Hooker and colleagues (1996) found getting started in an occupation was also important in this age group. In contrast, middle adults listed family concerns last; their main issues concerned personal things, such as being a more loving and caring person (Cross & Markus, 1991). By ages 40 to 59, Cross and Markus found that family issues again became most common, such as being a parent who can "let go" of his or her children. Hooker and Kaus (1994) also found that reaching and maintaining satisfactory performance in one's occupational career and accepting and adjusting to the physiological changes of middle age were important to this age group.

As shown in Figure 10.10, health becomes an increasingly important factor in defining the self as people grow older. Both sets of studies found that for the two younger groups, being overweight and, for women, becoming wrinkled and unattractive when

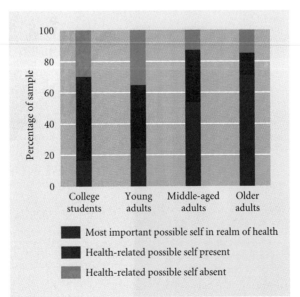

■ **Figure 10.10**
Health plays an increasingly important role in defining the self as people age.

Reprinted from Hooker, K. (1999). Possible Selves in Adulthood: Incorporating Teleonomic Relevance Into Studies of the Self. In T. M. Hess & F. Blanchard-Fields (eds.), *Social Cognition and Aging,* p. 107, with permission from Elsevier.

old were commonly mentioned as feared-for selves. For the middle-aged and older adult groups, fear of having Alzheimer's disease or being unable to care for oneself were frequent responses.

For adults over 60, researchers find that personal issues are most prominent, for example, being able to be active and healthy for another decade at least (Cross & Markus, 1991; Smith & Freund, 2002). Similarly, Hooker and colleagues (Frazier et al., 2000, 2002; Morfei et al., 2001) found that continuity in possible selves was much more prevalent than change in later life especially in independence, physical, and lifestyle areas. However, they also found that change did occur in older age. The greatest amount of change occurred in the health domain: Health became the most important domain for hoped-for and feared-for selves. The health domain is the most sensitive and central to the self in the context of aging (Frazier et al., 2000).

Overall, adolescents and young adults are far more likely to have multiple possible selves and to believe more strongly that they can actually become the hoped-for self and successfully avoid the feared self. By old age, though, both the number of possible selves and the strength of belief have decreased. Older adults are more likely to believe that neither the hoped-for nor the feared self is under their personal control. These findings may reflect differences with age in personal motivation, beliefs in personal control, and the need to explore new options.

Other researchers have examined possible selves in a different way by asking adults to describe their present, past, future, and ideal self (Keyes & Ryff, 1999; Ryff, 1991). Instead of examining categories of possible selves, this approach focuses on people's perceptions of change over time. The data indicate that young and middle-aged adults see themselves as improving with age and expecting to continue getting better in the future. In contrast, older adults see themselves as having remained stable over time, but they foresee decline in their future. These findings may indicate that the older group has internalized negative stereotypes about aging, especially in view of the fact that they tend to be healthy and well educated.

AP/Wide World Photos

PERSONAL CONTROL BELIEFS

As you were reading about adults creating scenarios, life stories, and possible selves (and perhaps reflecting on your own), you may have thought about the degree to which you feel that you are in control of your life. Such beliefs are becoming an important element of theories about how adults create their lives (Antonucci, 2001). **Personal control beliefs** *reflect the degree to which you believe your performance in a situation depends on something you do.* For example, suppose you don't get a job you think you should have gotten. Was it your fault? Or was it because the company was too shortsighted to recognize your true talent? Which option you select provides insight into a general tendency. Do you generally believe that outcomes depend on the things you do? Or are they due to factors outside of yourself, such as luck or the power of others?

A high sense of personal control implies a belief that performance is up to you, whereas a low sense of personal control implies that your performance is under the influence of forces other than your own. Personal control has become an extremely important idea in a wide variety of settings because of the way it guides behavior (Brandstädter, 1999; Soederberg Miller & Lachman, 1999). Successful leaders such as President George W. Bush need to exude a high sense of personal control to demonstrate that they are in charge.

THINK ABOUT IT

How might the development of possible selves be related to cognitive development?

President George W. Bush shows a high level of personal control in his job.

Personal control is a very important concept that can be applied broadly to several domains including social networks and health (Antonucci, 2001). For example, personal control beliefs are not only important in personality development but also (as we will see in Chapter 14) in memory performance in late life. Research indicates that people experience four types of personal control (Tiffany & Tiffany, 1996): control from within oneself, control over oneself, control over the environment, and control from the environment.

Despite its importance, we do not have a clear picture of the developmental course of personal control beliefs. Evidence from both cross-sectional studies and longitudinal studies (Lang & Heckhausen, 2001) is contradictory. Some data indicate that younger adults are less likely to hold internal control beliefs (i.e., believe they are in control of outcomes) than are older adults. Other research finds the opposite.

The contradiction may derive from the complex nature of personal control beliefs (Lachman, 1985). These beliefs vary depending on which domain, such as intelligence or health, is being assessed. Indeed, other research shows that perceived control over one's development declines with age, whereas perceived control over marital happiness increases (Brandtstädter, 1989). Additionally, younger adults are more satisfied when attributing success in attaining a goal to their own efforts, whereas older adults are more satisfied when they attribute such success to their ability (Lang & Heckhausen, 2001). Clearly, people of all ages and cultures try to influence their environment irrespective of whether they believe they will be successful.

Schulz and Heckhausen (1999) pulled together the various perspectives on control beliefs and proposed a life-span model to describe this striving that distinguishes between primary and secondary control. *Primary control* is behavior aimed at affecting the individual's external world; working a second job to increase one's earnings is an example. One's ability to influence the environment is heavily influenced by biological factors (e.g., stamina to work two jobs), so it changes over time, from very low influence during early childhood to high influence during middle age, to very low again in very late life. *Secondary control* is behavior or cognition aimed at affecting the individual's internal world; believing that one is capable of success even when faced with challenges is an example.

The developmental patterns of both are shown in Figure 10.11. The figure also shows that people of all ages strive to control their environment, but how they do this changes over time. Note that for the first half of life, primary and secondary control operate in parallel. During midlife, primary control begins to decline but secondary control does not. Thus, the desire for control does not change; whether we can actually affect our environment or whether we need to think about things differently is what differs with age.

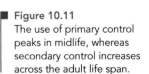

Figure 10.11
The use of primary control peaks in midlife, whereas secondary control increases across the adult life span.

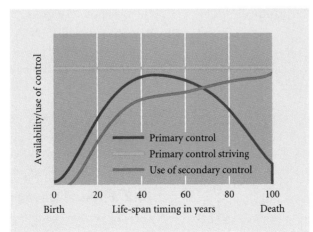

Adapted from R. Schulz and J. Heckhausen (1996). A Lifespan Model of Successful Aging, *American Psychologist, 51,* 702–714. Copyright © 1996 by the American Psychological Association. Adapted with permission.

TEST YOURSELF

1. A _____ is a unified sense of a person's past, present, and future.

2. A personal narrative that organizes past events into a coherent sequence is a _____.

3. Representations of what we could become, what we would like to be, and what we are afraid of becoming are our _____.

4. _____ reflect the degree to which a person's performance in a situation is believed to be under his or her control.

How might people's scenarios, life stories, and other aspects of personality vary as a function of cognitive-developmental level and self-definition as an adult?

Answers: (1) life-span construct, (2) life story, (3) possible selves, (4) Personal control beliefs

---

Putting It All Together

In this chapter, we have seen how people make the transition from adolescence to adulthood. For many people, like Marcus, the transition is fuzzy, having more to do with arbitrary legal issues than anything else. In some cultures, though, there are clear, formalized rites of passage that make it much easier to pinpoint the beginning of adulthood. Young adults are fine physical specimens, reaching their peak in most areas of functioning. It is a time when people like Juan think about abandoning unhealthy habits acquired earlier in life in favor of healthier lifestyles. People like Susan decide to return to college to further their education. Indeed, young adulthood is a time when intellectual growth continues in some areas but decline begins in others. Young adults also tend to dream about their future like Felicia does, mapping out their lives in detail.

All in all, young adulthood is an exciting time of life. In many respects, life will never be this good, at least physically, ever again. New avenues are opened, and adult responsibilities are undertaken. The most important of these responsibilities are the topics for the next two chapters: love and work.

Summary

10.1 When Does Adulthood Begin?

Role Transitions Marking Adulthood

■ The most widely used criteria for deciding whether a person has reached adulthood are role transitions, which involve assuming new responsibilities and duties.

■ Some societies use rituals, called rites of passage, to mark this transition clearly. However, such rituals are largely absent in Western culture.

Going to College

■ Over half of all college students are over age 25. These students tend to be more motivated and have many other positive characteristics.

■ College serves as a catalyst for cognitive development.

Psychological Views

■ Adolescents and adults differ in their abilities to acquire knowledge and to apply knowledge and skills.

■ A second major difference is a drop in the rate of participation in reckless behavior.

So When Do People Become Adults?

■ In cultures without clearly defined rites of passage, people become adults when they fully feel like adults.

10.2 Physical Development and Health

Growth, Strength, and Physical Functioning

■ Young adulthood is the time when certain physical abilities peak: strength, muscle development, coordination, dexterity, and sensory acuity. Most of these abilities begin to decline in middle age.

Health Status

■ Young adults are also at the peak of health. Death from disease is relatively rare, especially during the 20s. Accidents are the leading cause of death. However, homicide and violence are major factors in some groups. Poor ethnic minorities have less access to good health care, and poverty is also a major barrier to good health.

Lifestyle Factors

■ Smoking is the single biggest contributor to health problems. One is never too old to quit smoking.

■ Smoking is related to half of all cancers and is a primary cause of respiratory and cardiovascular disease. Although it is difficult, quitting smoking has many health benefits.

■ For most people, drinking alcohol poses few health risks. Several treatment approaches are available for alcoholics.

■ Nutritional needs change somewhat during adulthood, mostly due to changes in metabolism. Some nutrient needs, such as carbohydrates, change. The ratio of LDLs to HDLs in serum cholesterol, which can be controlled through diet or medication in most people, is an important risk factor in cardiovascular disease.

Social, Gender, and Ethnic Issues in Health

■ The two most important social factors in health are socioeconomic status and education. The poorest health conditions exist for African Americans living in poor, inner-city neighborhoods. Other ethnic groups who have limited access to health care also suffer.

■ Whether women or men are healthier is difficult to answer because women have been excluded from much health research.

■ Higher education is associated with better health due to better access to health care and more knowledge about proper diet and lifestyle.

10.3 Cognitive Development

How Should We View Intelligence in Adults?

■ Most modern theories of intelligence are multidimensional. For instance, Baltes's research shows that development varies among individuals and across different categories of abilities.

What Happens to Intelligence in Adulthood?

■ Intellectual abilities can be studied as groups of related skills called primary mental abilities. These abilities develop differently and change in succeeding cohorts. More recent cohorts perform better on some skills, such as inductive reasoning, but older cohorts perform better on number skills.

■ Fluid intelligence consists of abilities that make people flexible and adaptive thinkers. Fluid abilities generally decline during adulthood.

■ Crystallized intelligence reflects knowledge that people acquire through life experience and education in a particular culture. Crystallized abilities improve until late life.

Going Beyond Formal Operations: Thinking in Adulthood

■ Postformal thought is characterized by a recognition that truth may vary from one situation to another, that solutions must be realistic, that ambiguity and contradiction are the rule, and that emotion and subjectivity play a role in thinking. One example of postformal thought is reflective judgment.

The Role of Stereotypes in Thinking

■ Stereotypes are a special type of social knowledge structure or social belief that represent organized prior knowledge about a group of people that affects how we interpret new information. Activating stereotypes can have a powerful effect on cognitive processing.

10.4 Who Do You Want to Be? Personality in Young Adulthood

Creating Scenarios and Life Stories

■ Young adults create a life-span construct that represents a unified sense of the past, present, and future. This is manifested in two ways: through a scenario that maps the future based on a social clock, and in the life story, which creates an autobiography.

Possible Selves

■ People create possible selves by projecting themselves into the future and thinking about what they would like to become, what they could become, and what they are afraid of becoming.

■ Age differences in these projections depend on the dimension examined. In hoped-for selves, 18- to 24-year-olds and 40- to 59-year-olds report family issues as most important, whereas 25- to 39-year-olds and older adults consider personal issues to be most important. However, all groups include physical aspects as part of their most feared selves.

Personal Control Beliefs

■ Personal control is an important concept with broad applicability. However, the developmental trends are complex because personal control beliefs vary considerably from one domain to another.

Key Terms

role transitions (379)

rites of passage (379)

returning adult students (380)

intimacy versus isolation (382)

binge drinking (386)

addiction (388)

metabolism (388)

low-density lipoproteins (LDLs) (389)

high-density lipoproteins (HDLs) (389)

body mass index (BMI) (389)

multidimensional (392)

multidirectionality (392)

interindividual variability (392)

plasticity (392)

primary mental abilities (392)

secondary mental abilities (394)

fluid intelligence (395)

crystallized intelligence (395)

postformal thought (397)

reflective judgment (397)

optimal level of development (399)

skill acquisition (399)

stereotypes (401)

implicit stereotyping (401)

stereotype threat (402)

life-span construct (405)

scenario (405)

social clock (405)

life story (405)

possible selves (406)

personal control beliefs (408)

Learn More About It

Readings

DAVEY, J. D., & DAVEY, L. D. (2001). *The conscience of the campus: Case studies in moral reasoning among today's college students.* Westport, CT: Praeger. Discusses how college students deal with contemporary moral issues such as race, poverty, sex, educational funding, and constitutional rights.

ROBBINS, A., & WILNER, A. (2001). *Quarterlife crisis: The unique challenges of life in your twenties.* New York: Putnam. An intriguing book written by two people in their 20s.

SCHAIE, K. W. (1996). *Intellectual development in adulthood: The Seattle longitudinal study.* New York: Cambridge University Press. This is an excellent summary of the history and findings of the most extensive study of intellectual development across adulthood.

SINNOTT, J. D. (1998). *The development of logic in adulthood: Postformal thought and its applications.* New York: Plenum. This book provides both a history of research on postformal thinking and Sinnott's own ideas.

Websites

Visit the Human Development book companion website for all URLs.

■ **The Human Development Book Companion Website**
See the companion website **http://psychology .wadsworth.com/kail_cavanaugh4e/** for practice quiz questions, Internet links, updates, critical thinking exercises, discussion forums, and more.

■ **Centers for Disease Control and Prevention**
The CDC provides a well-organized collection of resources about tobacco. Included in the site are resources for people who want to quit smoking.

■ **National Institute on Alcohol Abuse and Alcoholism**
The NIAAA provides a wide variety of information for consumers and researchers. The list of frequently asked questions on the home page is especially helpful.

■ **American Heart Association**
The American Heart Association provides a wealth of information about cardiovascular disease and diet, including a wide assortment of recipes for heart-healthy eating.

■ **Institute on Race, Health Care, and the Law**
The Institute on Race, Health Care, and the Law is dedicated to improving the health status of all ethnic minorities in the United States by providing information to legislators, health and human rights activists, lawyers, health care professionals, and consumers.

Life-Span CD

For more information about the concepts covered in this chapter, go to
Module 5: Early and Middle Adulthood

- *Physical Development*
- *Cognitive Development*

http://www.thomsonedu.com
Go to this site for the link to ThomsonNOW, your one-stop study shop. Take a pre-test for this chapter, and ThomsonNOW will generate a personalized study plan based on your test results. The study plan will identify the topics you need to review and direct you to online resources to help you master those topics. You can then take a post-test to help you determine the concepts you have mastered and what you still need to work on.

11.1 Relationships
Friendships
Love Relationships

■ SPOTLIGHT ON RESEARCH:
Patterns and Universals
of Romantic Attachment
Around the World

The Dark Side of Relationships:
Violence

11.2 Lifestyles
Singlehood
Cohabitation
Gay and Lesbian Couples

■ REAL PEOPLE: APPLYING
HUMAN DEVELOPMENT:
Maggie O'Carroll's Story

Marriage

11.3 The Family Life Cycle
Deciding Whether to Have
Children
The Parental Role

11.4 Divorce and Remarriage
Divorce

■ CURRENT CONTROVERSIES:
"Covenant Marriage," A Way
to Keep Couples Together?

Remarriage

Putting It All Together

Summary

Key Terms

Learn More About It

CHAPTER 11

Being with Others

Forming Relationships in Young and Middle Adulthood

I magine yourself years from now. Your children are grown and have children and grandchildren of their own. In honor of your 80th birthday, they have all come together, along with your friends, to celebrate. Their present to you is an assemblage of hundreds of photographs and dozens of home videos. As you look at them, you realize how lucky you've been to have so many wonderful people in your life. Your relationships have made your adult life fun and worthwhile. As you watch the videos and look at the pictures, you wonder what it must be like to go through life totally alone. You think of all the wonderful experiences you would have missed in early and middle adulthood—never knowing what friendship is all about, never being in love, never dreaming about children and becoming a parent.

That is what we'll explore in this chapter—the ways in which we share our lives with others. First, we consider what makes good friendships and love relationships. Because these relationships form the basis of our lifestyle, we examine these next. In the third section, we consider what it is like to be a parent. Finally, we see what happens when marriages end. Throughout this chapter, the emphasis is on aspects of relationships that nearly everyone experiences during young adulthood and middle age. In Chapter 12, we examine aspects of relationships specific to middle-aged adults; in Chapter 14, we do the same for relationships in later life.

RELATIONSHIPS

Jamal and Deb, both 25, have been madly in love since they met at a party about a month ago. They spend as much time together as possible and pledge that they will stay together forever. Deb finds herself daydreaming about Jamal at work and can't wait to go over to his apartment. She wants to move in, but her coworkers tell her to slow down.

LEARNING OBJECTIVES

What types of friendships do adults have? How do adult friendships develop?

What is love? How does it begin? How does it develop through adulthood?

What is the nature of violence in some relationships?

You know what Jamal and Deb are going through. Each of us wants to be wanted by someone else. What would your life be like if you had no one to share it with? There would be no one to go shopping or hang out with, no one to talk to on the phone, no one to cuddle close to while watching the sunset at a mountain lake. Although there are times when being alone is desirable, for the most part we are social creatures. We need people. Without friends and lovers, life would be pretty lonely.

In the next sections, we explore both life-enhancing and life-diminishing relationships. We consider friendships, what happens when love enters the picture, and how people find mates. Unfortunately, some relationships turn violent; we'll also examine the factors underlying aggressive behaviors between partners.

FRIENDSHIPS

What is an adult friend? Someone who is there when you need to share? Someone not afraid to tell you the truth? Someone to have fun with? Friends, of course, are all of these and more.

Friends are very different from family and represent a point of contrast (de Vries, 1996). Friendships are predominantly based on feelings and are grounded in reciprocity and choice. Friendships are different from love relationships in that they are less emotionally intense and involve less sexual energy or contact (Rose & Zand, 2000). Having good friendships helps boost self-esteem (Bagwell et al., 2005). They also help us become socialized into new roles throughout adulthood.

Friendship in Adulthood

From a developmental perspective, adult friendships can be viewed as having identifiable stages (Levinger, 1980, 1983): Acquaintanceship, Buildup, Continuation, Deterioration, and Ending. This ABCDE model describes not only the stages of friendships but also the processes by which they change. For example, whether a friendship will develop from Acquaintanceship to Buildup depends on where the individuals fall on several dimensions, such as the basis of the attraction, what each person knows about the other, how good the communication is between the partners, the perceived importance of the friendship, and so on. Although many friendships reach the Deterioration stage, whether a friendship ultimately ends depends importantly on the availability of alternative relationships. If new potential friends appear, old friendships may end; if not, they may continue even though they may no longer be considered important by either person.

People tend to have more friends and acquaintances during young adulthood than at any subsequent period (Sherman, de Vries, & Lansford, 2000). Friendships are important throughout adulthood, in part because a person's life satisfaction is strongly related to the quantity and quality of contacts with friends. College students who have strong friendship networks adjust better to stressful life events (Brissette, Scheier, & Carver, 2002) and have better self-esteem (Bagwell et al., 2005). The importance of maintaining contacts with friends cuts across ethnic lines as well. Additionally, people who have friendships that cross ethnic groups have more positive attitudes toward people with different backgrounds (Aberson, Shoemaker, & Tomolillo, 2004). Thus, regardless of one's background, friendships play a major role in determining how much we enjoy life.

Researchers have uncovered three broad themes that underlie adult friendships (de Vries, 1996):

- The most frequently mentioned dimension represents the *affective* or emotional basis of friendship. This dimension refers to self-disclosure and expressions of intimacy, appreciation, affection, and support, all of which are based on trust, loyalty, and commitment.

- A second theme reflects the *shared or communal* nature of friendship, in which friends participate in or support activities of mutual interest.

- The third dimension represents *sociability and compatibility;* our friends keep us entertained and are sources of amusement, fun, and recreation.

If these women decide to form a friendship, they will move through several stages.

These three dimensions are found in friendships among adults of all ages (de Vries, 1996). They characterize both traditional (e.g., face-to-face) and new forms (e.g., online) of friendships (Ridings & Gefen, 2004).

In the case of online friendships, trust develops on the basis of four sources: (1) reputation, whether grounded in a pseudonym or offline identity; (2) performance, due to the scope for enhanced performance in online communication; (3) pre-commitment, through self-disclosure, which in turn encourages a "leap of faith" and reciprocal self-disclosure; and (4) situational factors, especially the premium placed on intimacy and the relationship in contemporary societies (Henderson & Gilding, 2004). Online environments are more conducive to people who are lonely, providing an opportunity to meet others in an initially more anonymous interaction in which social interaction and intimacy levels can be carefully controlled (Morahan-Martin & Schumacher, 2003). This relative anonymity provides a supportive context for the subsequent development of friendships online.

One special type of friendship exists with one's siblings. Although little research has focused on the development and maintenance of sibling friendships across adulthood, we know that the importance of these relationships varies with age. As you can see in Figure 11.1, women place more importance on sibling ties across adulthood than do men; however, for both the strength of these ties is greatest in adolescence and late life (Schmeeckle, Giarusso, & Wang, 1998). We will consider sibling relationships in more detail in Chapter 15.

■ **Figure 11.1**
The importance men and women place on sibling relationships varies across adulthood, being weakest for both during middle age.

Gender Differences in Friendships

Men's and women's friendships tend to differ in adulthood, reflecting continuity in the learned behaviors from childhood (Fehr, 1996; Sherman et al., 2000). Women tend to base their friendships on more intimate and emotional sharing and use friendship as a means to confide in others. For women, getting together with friends often takes the form of getting together to discuss personal matters. Confiding in others is a basis of women's friendships. In contrast, men tend to base friendships on shared activities or interests. They are more likely to go bowling or fishing or to talk sports

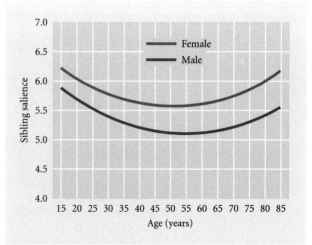

From Schmeeckle, M., Giarusso, R., and Wang, O. (1998, November). When being a brother or sister is important to one's identity: Life stage and gender differences. Paper presented at the annual meeting of the Gerontological Society, Philadelphia.

with their friends. For men, confiding in others is inconsistent with the need to compete; this may be one reason men are reluctant to do so (Cutrona, 1996). Rather, competition often is a part of men's friendships, as evidenced in basketball games with friends. However, the competition usually is set up so that the social interaction is the most important element, not who wins or loses (Rawlins, 1992). Men's friendships usually are less intimate than women's, no matter how one defines intimacy (Fehr, 1996).

Women tend to have more close relationships than do men. Although you may think this puts women at an advantage, research shows that this is not always the case. Sometimes friends can get on people's nerves or make high demands. When these things happen, women tend to be less happy even when they have lots of friends (Antonucci, Akiyama, & Lansford, 1998).

Why are women's friendships typically more intimate than men's? Compared to men, women have much more experience with such intimate sharing from early childhood, and they are more comfortable with vulnerability. Social pressure on men to be brave and strong may actually inhibit their ability to form close friendships (Rawlins, 1992).

LOVE RELATIONSHIPS

Love is one of those things everybody feels but nobody can define completely. (Test yourself: Can you explain fully what you mean when you look at someone special and say, "I love you"?) One way researchers have tried to understand love is to think about what components are essential. In an interesting series of studies, Sternberg (1986) found that love has three basic components: (1) *passion,* an intense physiological desire for someone; (2) *intimacy,* the feeling that one can share all one's thoughts and actions with another; and (3) *commitment,* the willingness to stay with a person through good and bad times. Ideally, a true love relationship has all three components. As we will see next, the balance among these components often shifts as time passes.

Love Through Adulthood

The different combinations of love can be used to understand how relationships develop (Sternberg, 1986). Early in any relationship, passion is usually high, but intimacy and commitment tend to be low. This is infatuation: an intense, physically based relationship in which the two people have a high risk of misunderstanding and jealousy.

But infatuation is short-lived. Whereas even the smallest touch is enough to drive each partner into wild, lustful ecstasy in the beginning, with time it takes more and more effort to get the same level of feeling. As passion fades, either a relationship acquires emotional intimacy or it is likely to end. Trust, honesty, openness, and acceptance must be a part of any strong relationship; when they are present, romantic love develops.

Given more time, people who work at their relationship may become committed to each other. They spend much of their time together, make decisions together, care for each other, share possessions, and develop ways to settle conflicts. Couples usually show outward signs of commitment, such as wearing a lover's ring, having children together, or simply sharing the mundane details of daily life, from making toast at breakfast to before-bed rituals.

Lemieux and Hale (2002) demonstrated that these developmental trends hold in romantically involved couples between 17 and 75 years of age. As the length of the relationship increases, intimacy and passion decrease, but commitment increases.

Falling in Love

Everybody wants to be loved by somebody, but actually having it happen is fraught with difficulties. In his book *The Prophet,* Kahlil Gibran points out that love is two-sided: Just as it can give you great ecstasy, so can it cause you great pain. Yet most of us are willing to take the risk.

As you may have experienced, taking the risk is fun (at times) and difficult (at other times). Making a connection can be ritualized, as when people use pickup lines in a bar, or it can happen almost by accident, as when two people literally run into each other in a crowded corridor. The question that confronts us is "How do people fall in love?" Do birds of a feather flock together? Or do opposites attract?

*The best explanation of the process is the theory of **assortative mating**, which states that people find partners based on their similarity to each other.* Assortative mating occurs along many dimensions, including religious beliefs, physical traits, age, socioeconomic status, intelligence, and political ideology, among others (Sher, 1996). Such nonrandom mating occurs most often in Western societies, which allow people to have more control over their own dating and pairing behaviors. Common activities are one basis for identifying potential mates. But does where people meet influence the likelihood that they will "click" on particular dimensions and will form a couple?

Kalmijn and Flap (2001) found that it did. Using data from more than 1,500 couples, they found that meeting at school promoted most forms of homogamy, or the degree to which people are similar. Meeting through other methods (being from the same neighborhood or through family networks) did not promote most forms of homogamy other than religious. Not surprisingly, the pool of available people to meet is strongly shaped by the opportunities available, which in turn constrain the type of people one is likely to meet.

Once people have met someone compatible, what happens next? Some researchers believe that couples progress in stages. According to Murstein's (1987) classic theory, people apply three filters, representing discrete stages, when they meet someone:

THE FAR SIDE® BY GARY LARSON

"Say, honey ... didn't I meet you last night at the feeding frenzy?"

Stimulus: Do the person's physical appearance, social class, and manners match your own?

Values: Do the person's values regarding sex, religion, politics, and so on match your own?

Role: Do the person's ideas about the relationship, communication style, gender roles, and so on match your own?

If the answer to all three filters is "yes," then you are likely to form a couple.

An important aspect in understanding how adults form couples relates to the attachments they made to adults in infancy and childhood as described in Chapter 5 (Hazan & Shaver, 1987). Researchers have shown that each of us tends to re-create in our partnership relationships the kind of attachments we had as children to key adults (e.g., Hazan & Shaver, 1987; Kobak, 1994; Main, 1996). For example, Hazan and Shaver (1987, 1990) found that adults who get close to people fairly easily (*secure style*) had the strongest relationships as children; those who are lonely had trouble forming close relationships (*avoidant style*) as children. Similarity in attachment styles is an important element for assortative mating (Collins & Read, 1990). Persons with a secure style tend to have high levels of flexibility in their descriptions of the ideal image of the spouse (Tolmacz, Goldzweig, & Guttman, 2004).

It also turns out that whether a couple find each other physically attractive is more important in love relationships than most people realize. Certainly, physical attractiveness acts as an initial filter, as described earlier. However, a study of nearly 2,000 Span-

THINK ABOUT IT

What are the effects of increasing interactions among cultures on mate selection?

Physical attraction is a very important aspect in forming a love relationship.

ish respondents showed that physical attractiveness was important in sporadic relationships, but it also influences the way in which people fall in love and is linked to feelings and thoughts associated with love (intimacy, passion, commitment) and to satisfaction with the relationship (Sangrador & Yela, 2000).

How do these couple-forming behaviors compare cross-culturally? A few studies have examined the factors that attract people to each other in different cultures. In one now-classic study, Buss and a large team of researchers (1990) identified the effects of culture and gender on heterosexual mate preferences in 37 cultures worldwide. Men and women in each culture displayed unique orderings of their preferences concerning the ideal characteristics of a mate. When all of the orderings and preferences were compared, two main dimensions emerged.

In the first main dimension, the characteristics of a desirable mate changed because of cultural values—that is, whether the respondents' country has more traditional values or Western-industrial values. In traditional cultures, men place a high value on a woman's chastity, desire for home and children, and being a good cook and housekeeper; women place a high value on a man's ambition and industry, being a good financial prospect, and holding favorable social status. China, India, Iran, and Nigeria represent the traditional end of this dimension. In contrast, people in Western-industrial cultures value these qualities to a much lesser extent. The Netherlands, Great Britain, Finland, and Sweden represent this end of the dimension.

The second main dimension reflects the relative importance of education, intelligence, and social refinement, as opposed to a pleasing disposition, in choosing a mate. People in Spain, Colombia, and Greece, for example, highly value education, intelligence, and social refinement; in contrast, people in Indonesia place a greater emphasis on having a pleasing disposition. Note that this dimension emphasizes the same traits for both men and women.

Chastity proved to be the characteristic showing the most variability across cultures, being highly desired in some cultures but mattering little in others. Interestingly, in their respective search for mates, men around the world value physical attractiveness in women, whereas women around the world look for men capable of being good providers. But men and women around the world agree that love and mutual attraction are most important, and nearly all cultures rate dependability, emotional stability, kindness, and understanding as important factors. Attraction, it seems, has some characteristics that transcend culture.

Overall, Buss and his colleagues concluded that mate selection is a complex process no matter where you live. However, each culture has a describable set of high-priority traits that men and women look for in the perfect mate. The study also shows that socialization within a culture plays a key role in being attractive to the opposite sex; characteristics that are highly desirable in one culture may not be so desirable in another.

In the Spotlight on Research feature, Schmitt and his team of colleagues (2004) had 17,804 participants from 62 cultural regions complete the Relationship Questionnaire (RQ), a self-report measure of adult romantic attachment. They showed that secure romantic attachment was the norm in nearly 80% of cultures and that preoccupied romantic attachment was particularly common in East Asian cultures. In general, what these large multicultural studies show is that there are global patterns in mate selection and romantic relationships. The romantic attachment profiles of individual nations were correlated with sociocultural indicators in ways that supported evolutionary theories of romantic attachment and basic human mating strategies.

SPOTLIGHT ON RESEARCH

PATTERNS AND UNIVERSALS OF ROMANTIC ATTACHMENT AROUND THE WORLD

Who were the investigators and what was the aim of the study? One's attachment style may have a major influence on how one forms romantic relationships. In order to test this hypothesis, David Schmitt assembled a large international team of researchers.

How did the investigators measure the topic of interest? Great care was taken to ensure equivalent translation of the survey across the 62 cultural regions included. The survey was a two-dimension four-category measure of adult romantic attachment (the Relationship Questionnaire) that measured secure romantic attachment (high scores indicate positive models of self and others), dismissing romantic attachment (high scores indicate a positive model of self and a negative model of others), preoccupied romantic attachment (high scores indicate a negative model of self and a positive model of others), and fearful romantic attachment (high scores indicate negative models of self and others). An overall score of model of self is computed by adding together the secure and dismissing scores and subtracting the combination of preoccupied and fearful scores. The overall model of others score is computed by adding together the secure and preoccupied scores and subtracting the combination of dismissing and fearful scores.

Additionally, there were measures of self-esteem, personality traits, and sociocultural correlates of romantic attachment (e.g., fertility rate, national profiles of individualism versus collectivism).

Who were the participants in the study? A total of 17,804 people (7,432 men and 10,372 women) from 62 cultural regions around the world took part in the study. Such large and diverse samples are unusual in developmental research.

What was the design of the study? Data for this cross-sectional, nonexperimental study were gathered by research

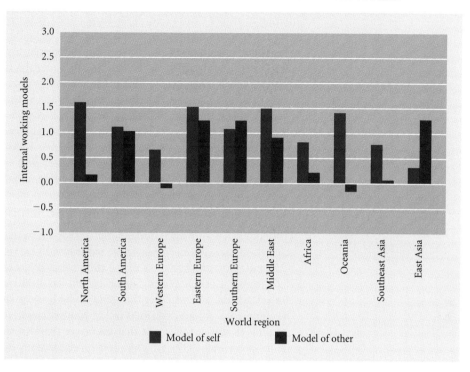

Figure 11.2
In this model of self and other levels across 10 world regions, note that only in East Asian cultures was model of other scores significantly higher than model of self scores.

teams in each country. The principal researchers asked the research collaborators to administer a nine-page survey to the participants that took 20 minutes to complete.

Were there ethical concerns with the study? Because the study involved volunteers, there were no ethical concerns. However, ensuring that all participants' rights were protected was a challenge because of the number of countries and cultures involved.

What were the results? The researchers first demonstrated that the model of self and others measures were valid across cultural regions, which provided general support for the independence of measures (i.e., they measure different things). Specific analyses showed that 79% of the cultural groups studied demonstrated secure romantic attachments, but that East Asian cultures tended to be high on preoccupied romantic attachment. These patterns are shown in Figure 11.2. Note that all the cultural regions except East Asia showed the pattern of model of self scores higher than model of others scores.

What have the investigators concluded? Overall, Schmitt and colleagues concluded that although the same attachment pattern holds across most cultures, no one pattern holds across all of them. East Asian cultures in particular tend to fit a pattern in which people report that others do not get as emotionally close as the respondent would like, and that respondents find it difficult to trust others or to depend on them.

What converging evidence would strengthen these conclusions? Although this is one of the best designed among large cross-cultural studies, several additional lines of evidence would help bolster the conclusions. Most important, representative samples from the countries under study would provide more accurate insights into people's romantic attachment patterns.

To enhance your understanding of this research, go to http://psychology.wadsworth.com/kail_cavanaugh4e/ to complete critical thinking questions and explore related websites.

The power of culture in shaping mate selection choices must not be underestimated. For example, despite decades of sociopolitical change in China (the socialist transformation in the 1950s, the Cultural Revolution in the 1960s, and the economic reforms in the 1990s), research indicates that the same status hierarchy norms govern assortative mating in urban China (Xu, Ji, & Tung, 2000). Clearly, cultural norms are sometimes very resistant to change. Arranged marriages are a major way some cultures ensure an appropriate match on key dimensions. For example, loyalty of the individual to the family is a very important value in India; consequently, many marriages are carefully arranged to avoid selecting inappropriate mates. Data show that this approach appears to work; among urban professionals polled in one study, 81% said their marriages had been arranged, and 94% of them rated their marriage as "very successful" (Lakshmanan, 1997). Similarly, Islamic societies use matchmaking as a way to preserve family consistency and continuity, and to ensure that couples follow the prohibition on premarital relationships between men and women (Adler, 2001). Matchmaking in these societies occurs through both family connections and personal advertisements in newspapers.

Developmental Forces and Relationships

From our discussion and your experience, you know that finding a relationship is a complicated matter. Many things must work just right: timing, meeting the right person, luck, and effort are but a few of the things that shape the course of a relationship. As is clear from the ABCDE and Sternberg models, adult relationships are complex. Who chooses whom, and whether the feelings will be mutual, results from the interaction of developmental forces described in the biopsychosocial model presented in Chapter 1.

Biologically, it turns out that there are two distinct stages, attraction and attachment (Liebowitz, 1983), which reflect fundamentally different neurochemical processes (Fisher, 1994). *Attraction* is associated with neurochemicals related to the amphetamines, which account for the exhilaration of falling in love. *Attachment,* which some people might call long-term commitment and tranquility, is reflected neurochemically in substances related to morphine, a powerful narcotic. People with a predilection to fall in love also tend to show left hemisphere chemical dominance and several changes in neurochemical processing (Kurup & Kurup, 2003). (Love really does do a number on your brain!)

Psychologically, as we saw in Chapter 9, an important developmental issue is intimacy; according to Erikson, mature relationships are impossible without it. Additionally, the kinds of relationships you saw and experienced as a child (and whether they involved violence) affect how you define and act in relationships you develop as an adult. Sociocultural forces shape the characteristics you find desirable in a mate and determine whether you are likely to encounter resistance from your family when you have made your choice. Life-cycle forces matter too; different aspects of love are more or less important, depending on your stage in life.

In short, to understand adult relationships, we must take the forces of the biopsychosocial model into account. Relying too heavily on one or two of the forces provides an incomplete description of why people are successful (or not) in finding a partner or a friend. Unfortunately, the developmental forces do not only influence good relationships. As we will see next, sometimes relationships turn violent.

THE DARK SIDE OF RELATIONSHIPS: VIOLENCE

Up to this point, we have been considering relationships that are healthy and positive. Sadly, this is not always the case. *Sometimes relationships become violent; one person becomes aggressive toward the partner, creating an **abusive relationship**.* Such relationships have received increasing attention since the early 1980s, when the U.S. criminal justice system ruled that, under some circumstances, abusive relationships can be used as an explanation for one's behavior (Walker, 1984). *For example, **battered woman syndrome** occurs when a woman believes that she cannot leave the abusive situation and may even go so far as to kill her abuser.*

From "Through a Psychological Lens: Personality Traits, Personality Disorders, and Levels of Violence" by K. D. O'Leary. In R. J. Gelles and R. D. Loeske (Eds.), *Current Controversies on Family Violence*, pp. 7–30. Copyright © 1993 by Sage Publications, Inc. Reprinted by permission of Sage Publications, Inc.

What kind of aggressive behaviors occur in abusive relationships? What causes such abuse? Researchers are beginning to find answers to these and related questions. Based on considerable research on abusive partners, O'Leary (1993) argues that there is a continuum of aggressive behaviors toward a spouse, which progresses as follows: verbally aggressive behaviors, physically aggressive behaviors, severe physically aggressive behaviors, and murder of the partner. The causes of the abuse also vary with the type of abusive behavior being expressed. O'Leary's continuum is shown in Figure 11.3.

Two points about the continuum should be noted. First, there may be fundamental differences in the types of aggression independent of level of severity. Lower levels of physically aggressive behavior, such as pushing or slapping, are common; 25 to 40% of men and women who are in committed relationships display such behaviors on occasion (Riggs & O'Leary, 1992). In contrast, some men are extremely abusive from the outset of the relationship; they are thought to comprise the subset of batterers who seriously physically injure their partners and exert coercive control over their lives (Stark, 1992).

The second interesting point, depicted in the figure, is that the suspected underlying causes of aggressive behaviors differ as the type of aggressive behaviors change (O'Leary, 1993). Although anger and hostility in the perpetrator are associated with various forms of physical abuse, the exact nature of this relationship remains elusive (Norlander & Eckhardt, 2005).

The Feminist Majority Foundation (2005) reports other key findings. Roughly 40 to 50% of women who experience physical abuse are injured during an attack. Women who are separated or divorced from their partners are most vulnerable to physical abuse. Latina women are least likely to be physically abused in all age groups.

As can be seen in the figure, the number of suspected causes of aggressive behavior increases as the level of aggression increases. Thus, the causes of aggressive behavior become more complex as the level of aggression worsens. Such differences in cause imply that the approaches to treating abusers should vary with the nature of the aggressive behavior (O'Leary, 1993). Situational factors that contribute to all levels of aggression are alcoholism, job stressors, and unemployment; the presence of these factors increases the likelihood that violence will occur in the relationship (O'Leary, 1993).

Johnson (1995, 2001; Johnson & Ferraro, 2000) goes even further in making a very important distinction in the types of violence that occur in relationships, distinguishing between common couple violence and patriarchal terrorism. ***Common couple violence*** *refers to violence that occurs occasionally and that can be instigated by either partner.* ***Patriarchal terrorism*** *(or intimate terrorism) refers to women who are victims of systematic violence from men.* Data supporting this distinction clearly show that women are not as violent as men in relationships (e.g., Johnson, 2001) and that this distinction holds well across various types of offenders (Graham-Kevan & Archer, 2003). Additional research has uncovered different patterns within common couple violence that range from aggressive to abusive (Olson, 2000).

Gender differences in some of the underlying causes of aggressive behavior in relationships have been reported (O'Leary, 1993). Most important, the triad of need to control, misuse of power, and jealousy is a more pertinent cause for men than for women. For example, men are more likely than women to act aggressively because they want to make sure their partner knows "who the boss is" and who makes the rules.

Culture is also an important contextual factor. For example, cultures that emphasize honor and portray females as passive, nurturing supporters of men's activities and that emphasize loyalty and sacrifice for the family may contribute to tolerating abuse. Vandello (2000) reported two studies of Latino Americans, southern Anglo Americans, and northern Anglo Americans that examined these ideas. Latino Americans and southern Anglo Americans placed more value on honor. These groups rated a woman in an abusive relationship more positively if she stayed with the man, and communicated less disapproval of a woman who they witnessed being shoved and restrained if she portrayed herself as contrite and self-blaming than did northern Anglo Americans, who rated the woman more positively if she left the man.

Chinese Americans are more likely to define domestic violence in terms of physical and sexual aggression, and not include psychological forms of abuse (Yick, 2000). And South Asian immigrants to the United States report the use of social isolation (e.g., not being able to interact with family, friends, or coworkers) as a very painful form of abuse that is often tied to being financially dependent on the husband and traditional cultural gender roles (M. Abraham, 2000).

Shelters like this one provide protection for women who are victims of abuse.

AP/Wide World Photos

Additionally, international data indicate that rates of abuse are higher in cultures that emphasize female purity, male status, and family honor. For example, a common cause of women's murders in Arab countries is brothers or other male relatives killing the victim because the woman violated the family's honor (Kulwicki, 2002). Intimate partner violence is prevalent in China (43% lifetime risk in one study), with strong associations with male patriarchal values and conflict resolutions (Xu et al., 2005).

Many college students report experiencing abuse in a dating relationship; one study found 7% reported physical abuse and 36% reported emotional abuse from their partner (Knox, Custis, & Zusman, 2000). Being female, being involved in a love relationship, living together, being 20 years of age or older, having been physically abused by one's partner, and having abused a partner increased the chances of experiencing emotional abuse. Although overall national rates of sexual assault have been declining since the early 1990s, acquaintance rape or date rape is experienced by roughly 1 in 4 college women (Rape, Abuse, and Incest National Network, 2005).

Alarmed at the seriousness of abuse, many communities have established shelters for battered women and their children and programs that treat abusive men. However, the legal system in many localities is still not set up to deal with domestic violence; women in some locations cannot sue their husbands for assault, and restraining orders all too often offer little real protection from additional violence. Much remains to be done to protect women and their children from the fear and the reality of continued abuse.

TEST YOURSELF

1. Friendships based on intimacy and emotional sharing are more characteristic of _____.

2. Competition is a major part of most friendships among _____.

3. Love relationships in which intimacy and passion are present but commitment is not are termed _____.

4. Chastity is an important quality that men look for in a potential female mate in _____ cultures.

5. Aggressive behavior that is based on abuse of power, jealousy, or the need to control is more likely to be displayed by _____.

Why is intimacy (discussed in Chapter 9) a necessary prerequisite for adult relationships, according to Erikson? What aspects of relationships discussed here support (and refute) this view?

Answers: (1) women, (2) men, (3) romantic love, (4) traditional, (5) men

11.2

LIFESTYLES

Kevin and Beth are on cloud nine. They got married one month ago and have recently returned from their honeymoon. Everyone who sees them can tell that they love each other a lot. They are highly compatible and have much in common, sharing most of their leisure activities. Kevin and Beth wonder what lies ahead in their marriage.

LEARNING OBJECTIVES

Why do some people decide not to marry, and what are these people like?

What are the characteristics of cohabiting people?

What are gay and lesbian relationships like?

What is marriage like through the course of adulthood?

Dᴇᴠᴇʟᴏᴘɪɴɢ ʀᴇʟᴀᴛɪᴏɴsʜɪᴘs is only part of the picture in understanding how adults live their lives with other people. Putting relationships like Kevin and Beth's in context is important for us to understand how relationships come into existence and how they change over time. In the following sections, we explore relationship lifestyles: singlehood, cohabitation, gay and lesbian couples, and marriage.

SINGLEHOOD

When Susan graduated from college with a degree in accounting, she took a job at a consulting firm. For the first several years in her job, she spent more time traveling than she did at home. During this time, she had a series of love relationships, but none resulted in commitment even though she had marriage as a goal. By the time she was in her mid-30s, Susan had decided that she no longer wanted to get married. "I'm now a partner in my firm, I enjoy traveling, and I'm pretty flexible in terms of moving if something better comes along," she stated to her friend Michele. "But I do miss being with someone to share my day or to just hang around with."

During early adulthood, most men and women are single, like Susan, defined as not living with an intimate partner. Estimates are that approximately 80% of men and 70% of women between ages 20 and 24 are unmarried, with increasing numbers deciding to stay that way (U.S. Census Bureau, 2005b).

Susan's experience is common among women who ultimately decide not to marry (Dalton, 1992). Many women and men focus on establishing their careers rather than marriage or relationships. Others report that they simply did not meet "the right person" or prefer singlehood (Lamanna & Riedmann, 2003). However, the pressure to marry is especially strong for women; frequent questions such as "Any good prospects yet?" may leave women feeling conspicuous or left out as many of their friends marry. Research indicates that single women have unresolved or unrecognized ambivalences about being single (Lewis & Moon, 1997). Such feelings result from being aware of the advantages and disadvantages of being single and ambivalence about the reasons they are single.

Men tend to remain single longer in young adulthood because they tend to marry at a later age than women (U.S. Census Bureau, 2005b). Fewer men than women remain unmarried throughout adulthood, largely because men find partners more easily as they select from a larger age range of unmarried women. Because men also tend to "marry down" in social status, women with higher levels of education are overrepresented among unmarried adults compared with men with similar levels of education.

Ethnic differences in singlehood reflect both differences in age at marriage and social factors. For example, nearly twice as many African Americans are single during young adulthood as European Americans, and more are choosing to stay that way (U.S. Census Bureau, 2005b). Major reasons for this trend are the shortage of marriageable African American men, poor economic opportunities, and lower life expectancy (Benokraitis, 2005). Singlehood is also increasing among Latinos, in part because the average age of Latinos in the United States is lower than other ethnic groups, and in part due to poor economic opportunities for many Latinos (Lamanna & Riedmann, 2003). However, Latino men expect to marry (even if they do not) because it indicates achievement.

An important distinction is between adults who are temporarily single (i.e., those who are single only until they find a suitable marriage partner) and those who choose to remain single. Results from an in-depth interview study with never-married women in their 30s revealed three distinct groups: some suffer with acute distress about being single and long to be married with children; others describe experiencing the emotional continuum of desiring to be married and desiring to remain single; and others say that they are quite happy with a healthy self-image and high quality of life (Cole, 2000). For most singles, the decision to never marry is a gradual one. This transition is represented by a change in self-attributed status that occurs over time and is associated with a cultural timetable for marriage. It marks the experience of "becoming single" that occurs when an individual identifies more with singlehood than with marriage (Davies, 2003). Still, a key question is what marks the decision to remain single? For some, it is reaching a milestone birthday (e.g., 30) and still being single, although the particular age that

Young adult African Americans are more likely to remain single than are European Americans.

reflects this varies a great deal (Davies, 2000). For many middle-aged single women, purchasing a house marks the decision:

> I always thought you got married, you bought a house. Well, I bought a house and I'm not married. . . . I've laid down roots. . . . You're sort of saying, "Okay, this is it." And it makes you feel more settled. (Davies, 2000, p. 12)

For most, though, the transition to permanent singlehood is a gradual one they drift into by circumstance rather than a lifestyle they choose, such as having to care for parents or other family members instead of attending to personal goals related to marriage, family, education, or career (Connidis, 2001).

In general, singles recognize the pluses and minuses in their lifestyles. They enjoy the freedom and flexibility but also feel loneliness, dissatisfaction with dating, limited social life in a couple-oriented society, and less sense of security (Chasteen, 1994). Gender differences are evident between single men and women. Single men have higher mortality rates and higher incidence of alcoholism, suicide, and mental health problems (Whitbourne, 1996). However, single women experience more problems overall than single men (Lamanna & Riedmann, 2003). Because they tend to live alone, single women are more likely than their married counterparts to be mugged, raped, or burglarized, and to encounter problems when traveling. Single women are also more likely to be asked to perform extra functions at work because they are perceived as having no other duties to perform. Despite the challenges, though, most singles who choose to stay that way are content with their lives.

COHABITATION

Being unmarried does not necessarily mean living alone. *People in committed, intimate, sexual relationships may decide that living together, or **cohabitation**, provides a way to share daily life.* Cohabitation is becoming an increasingly popular lifestyle choice in the United States as well as in Canada, Europe, Australia, and elsewhere. As you can see in Figure 11.4, cohabitation in the United States has increased 10-fold over the past three decades from 523,000 in 1970 to 5.5 million in 2000, the most recent year extensive data were collected (U.S. Census Bureau, 2003). The age of people who cohabit has also changed. In 1970, the majority of cohabiting couples were adults over age 45; by 2000,

THINK ABOUT IT

Why might there be large differences in cohabitation rates among countries?

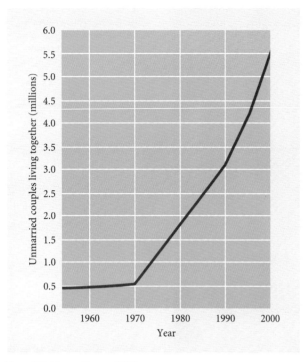

■ **Figure 11.4**
There has been a rapid growth in cohabitation in the United States since 1970.

the majority were adults between 25 and 44. This age change is related to a combination of increasing age of first marriage and the increased divorce rate since 1970.

Couples cohabit for three main reasons (Benokraitis, 2005). Some couples engage in *part-time or limited cohabitation,* which is usually based on convenience, sharing expenses, and sexual accessibility. There is typically no long-term commitment, and marriage is not usually a goal. Research shows that for most American young adult couples, cohabitation is a step toward marriage (King & Scott, 2005). In this *premarital cohabitation,* the couple is actually engaging in a trial marriage. If marriage does not follow, the couple usually separates. Both part-time and premarital cohabitation are the most popular forms among young adults. Finally, some couples use cohabitation as a *substitute marriage,* which is a long-term commitment between two people without a legal marriage. Research indicates that this form is especially popular with older couples who may lose financial benefits (e.g., survivor's benefits from deceased spouses) if they remarry (King & Scott, 2005).

The picture is quite different in most European, South American, and Caribbean countries where cohabitation is a common alternative to marriage for young adults. For example, cohabitation is extremely common in the Netherlands, Norway, and Sweden, where this lifestyle is part of the culture; 99% of married couples in Sweden lived together before they married and nearly one in four couples are not legally married. Couples living together there are just as devoted to each other as are married couples, and they believe that such relationships are grounded in love and commitment to each other (Kaslow, Hansson, & Lundblad, 1994). Decisions to marry in these countries are typically made to legalize the relationship after children are born, in contrast to Americans, who marry to confirm their love and commitment to each other.

Cohabitation rates are lower in Africa and Asia. For example, in China, cohabitation is largely limited to rural villages where couples below the legal age for marriage live together (Neft & Levine, 1997).

Interestingly, having cohabited does not seem to make American or Canadian marriages any better; in fact, it may do more harm than good, resulting in marriages that are less happy and with a higher risk of divorce (Hall & Zhao, 1995). Other research indicates that transitioning to marriage from cohabitation does not lessen depression, and concern about getting approval from friends increases distress for cohabitors who marry (Marcussen, 2001). Why is this the case? Part of the answer may be that cohabiting couples tend to be less conventional, less religious, and come from lower socioeconomic backgrounds, which may put them at higher risk for divorce (DeMaris & Rao, 1992). Part of the reason may also be that marrying after already having lived with someone represents much less of a change in the relationship than when a couple marries who have not been cohabiting; such couples lack the newly wedded bliss seen in couples who have not cohabited (Thomson & Colella, 1992).

Data indicate that the negative relation between cohabiting and marital stability may be weakening somewhat (McRae, 1997). Why would this be the case? Much of the previous data comes from a time when cohabitation was viewed as unconventional. As cohabitation becomes more common, and perhaps the majority pattern, this negative link is likely to grow progressively weaker (McRae, 1997). For example, more recent longitudinal studies find few differences in couples' behavior after living together for many years regardless of whether they married without cohabiting, cohabited then married, or simply cohabited (Stafford, Kline, & Rankin, 2004). Additionally, many countries are now extending the same rights and benefits to cohabiting couples as they do to married couples. For instance, Argentina provides pension rights to cohabiting partners, Canada extends insurance benefits, and Australia has laws governing the disposition of property when cohabiting couples sever their relationship (Neft & Levine, 1997).

GAY AND LESBIAN COUPLES

Less is known about the developmental course of gay and lesbian relationships than heterosexual relationships, largely because they were almost never the focus of research. To date, gay and lesbian relationships have been studied most often in comparison to married heterosexual couples. What is it like to be in a gay or lesbian relationship? One woman shares her experience in the Real People feature.

REAL PEOPLE: Applying Human Development

MAGGIE O'CARROLL'S STORY

I am a 35-year-old woman who believes that each person is here with a purpose to fulfill in his or her lifetime. "Add your light to the sum of light" are words I live by in my teaching career, my personal life with friends and family, and living in general. I do not believe that our creator makes mistakes, although at times I am very discouraged by the level of hatred that is evident in the world against many groups, but against homosexuals in particular.

For me, being a lesbian is the most natural state of being. I do not think of it as a mishap of genetics, a result of an unhappy or traumatic childhood, or an unnatural tendency. From the time I was a child I had a definite and strong sense of my sexual identity. However, I am aware of the homophobia that is present at all levels of my own life and in the community. That is where my sense of self and living in the world collide.

Society does not value diversity. We, as a people, do not look to people who are different and acknowledge the strength it takes to live in this society. Being gay in a homophobic, heterosexist society is a burden that manifests itself in many forms, such as through alcohol and drug abuse rates that are much higher than in the heterosexual community. The lack of acknowledgment of gay people's partners by family members, coworkers, and society at large is a stamp of nonexistence and invisibility. How can we build a life with a partner and then not share that person with society?

I consider myself a fortunate gay person in that I have a supportive family. Of the five children in my family, two of us are gay. My parents are supportive and love our partners. My siblings vary in their attitudes. One sister invited me and my partner to her wedding. Nine years

later, my other sister refused to do that. Her discomfort over my sexual orientation meant that I spent a special event without my partner at my side. However, my straight brother was allowed to bring a date. It was very hurtful and hard to forgive.

In the larger community, I have been surprised by the blatant hatred I have experienced. I have demeaning comments aimed at me. The home I live in has been defaced with obscenities. But on a more positive note, I have never been more strongly certain of who I am. I am indebted to those who have supported me over the years with love and enlightenment, knowing that who I am is not a mistake. As I age, it becomes clearer to me that I am meant to share the message that our differences are to be appreciated and respected.

Like heterosexuals, gay and lesbian couples must deal with issues related to effective communication, power, and household responsibilities. For the most part, the relationships of gay and lesbian couples show similar stressors to those of heterosexual couples: conflicts tend to be about finances, lack of equality in the relationship, possessiveness, personal flaws, dissatisfaction over the sexual relationship, and physical absence due to work or education commitments (Kurdek, 1995a, 1995b). However, heterosexual couples are more likely to argue over personal values, social and political issues, and relationships with in-laws, whereas gay and lesbian couples reported more distrust, especially regarding former lovers (Kurdek, 1995a, 1995b). Most gay and lesbian couples are in dual-worker relationships, much like the majority of married couples. Thus, they are likely to share household chores. In general, though, the same factors predict long-term success of couples regardless of sexual orientation (Mackey, Diemer, & O'Brien, 2004).

Gay and lesbian couples experience stresses in relationships similar to those of heterosexual couples.

Gender differences are more important than differences in sexual orientation (Huston & Schwartz, 1995). Gay men, like heterosexual men, tend to separate love and sex and have more short-term relationships (Missildine et al., 2005); both lesbian and heterosexual women are more likely to connect sex and emotional intimacy in fewer, longer lasting relationships. Men in any type of relationship tend to want more power if they earn more money. Women in any type of relationship are likely to be more egalitarian and to view money as a way to maintain independence from one's partner.

Gay and lesbian couples often report less support from family members than do either married or cohabiting couples (Benokraitis, 2005). The more that one's family holds traditional ethnic or religious values, the less likely it is that the family will provide support. At a societal level, the lack of legal recognition for gay and lesbian relationships in the United States also means that certain rights and privileges are not granted. For example, it is difficult for gay and lesbian partners to inherit property from their partners in the absence of a will, and sometimes they are denied visitation rights when their partner is hospitalized. Although the legal status of gay and lesbian couples is changing in some countries (most notably in Scandinavia), few countries provide them with the same legal rights as married couples.

MARRIAGE

Most adults want their love relationships to result in marriage. However, U.S. residents are in less of a hurry to achieve this goal; the median age at first marriage for adults in the United States has been rising for several decades. As you can see in Figure 11.5, between 1970 and 2000, the median age for first marriage rose nearly 4 years for both men and women, from roughly 23 to 27 for men, and from roughly 21 to 25 for women (U.S. Census Bureau, 2005b). This trend is not bad; women under age 20 at the time they are first married are three times more likely to end up divorced than women who first marry in their 20s, and six times more likely to end up divorced than first-time wives in their 30s (U.S. Census Bureau, 2005b). Let's explore age and other factors that keep marriages going strong over time.

■ **Figure 11.5**
Median age at first marriage in the United States has increased more for women than men since 1970.

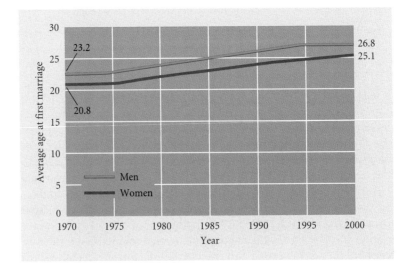

TABLE 11.1

Beliefs About Marriage

1. A husband's marital satisfaction is usually lower if his wife is employed full time than if she is a full-time homemaker.	True	False
2. Marriages that last many years almost always have a higher level of satisfaction than marriages that last only a few years.	True	False
3. In most marriages, having a child improves marital satisfaction for both spouses.	True	False
4. The best single predictor of marital satisfaction is the quality of the couple's sex life.	True	False
5. Overall, married women are physically healthier than married men.	True	False
6. African American women are happier in marriage than African American men.	True	False
7. Marital satisfaction for a wife is usually lower if she is employed full time than if she is a full-time homemaker.	True	False
8. "If my spouse loves me, he/she should instinctively know what I want and need to make me happy."	True	False
9. In a marriage in which the wife is employed full time, the husband usually shares equally in the housekeeping tasks.	True	False
10. "No matter how I behave, my spouse should love me because he/she is my spouse."	True	False
11. European American husbands spend more time on household work than do Latino husbands.	True	False
12. Husbands usually make more lifestyle adjustments in marriage than do wives.	True	False
13. "I can change my spouse by pointing out his/her inadequacies and bad habits."	True	False
14. The more a spouse discloses positive and negative information to his/her partner, the greater the marital satisfaction of both partners.	True	False
15. For most couples, maintaining romantic love is the key to marital happiness over the life span.	True	False

All of the items are false. The more "True" responses you gave, the greater your belief in stereotypes about marriage.

SOURCE: From Benokraitis, 1999, p. 235.

What Factors Help Marriages Succeed?

Why do some marriages succeed? Answer the questions in Table 11.1 and you may get some good ideas. Take time to think about your responses and why you answered the way you did. Your responses are the result of many factors, including the socialization you had about marriage. As we explore the research data about marital satisfaction, think about these and other widely held beliefs about marriage.

Although marriages, like other relationships, differ from one another, some important predictors of future success can be identified. One key factor in enduring marriages is the relative maturity of the two partners at the time they are married. In general, the younger the partners are, the lower the odds that the marriage will last, especially when the people are in their teens or early 20s (U.S. Bureau of the Census, 2005b). In part, the age issue relates to Erikson's (1982) belief that intimacy cannot be achieved until after one's identity is established (see Chapter 10). Other reasons that determine whether marriages last include low financial security and pregnancy at the time of the marriage.

A second important predictor of successful marriage is **homogamy,** *or similarity of values and interests.* As we saw in relation to choosing a mate, the extent that the partners share similar values, goals, attitudes, socioeconomic status, and ethnic background increases the likelihood that their relationship will succeed.

A third factor in predicting marital success is a feeling that the relationship is equal. *According to **exchange theory,** marriage is based on each partner contributing something to the relationship that the other would be hard-pressed to provide.* Satisfying and happy marriages result when both partners perceive that there is a fair exchange, or equity, in all the dimensions of the relationship. Problems achieving such equity can arise because of the competing demands of work and family, an issue we take up again in Chapter 12.

At their wedding, couples tend to be very happy and in love.

Do Married Couples Stay Happy?

Few sights are happier than a couple on their wedding day. Newlyweds like Kevin and Beth, in the vignette, are at the peak of marital bliss. The beliefs people bring into a marriage (which you identified in Table 11.1 in the quiz you took) influence how satisfied they will be as the marriage develops. As you might suspect, a couple's feelings change over time. Like any relationship, marriage has its peaks and valleys.

Much research has been conducted on marital satisfaction across adulthood. Research shows that for most couples overall marital satisfaction is highest at the beginning of the marriage, falls until the children begin leaving home, and rises again in later life (see Figure 11.6; Miller, Hemesath, & Nelson, 1997). However, for some couples, satisfaction never rebounds and remains low; in essence, they have become emotionally divorced.

Overall, marital satisfaction ebbs and flows over time. The pattern of a particular marriage over the years is determined by the nature of the dependence of each spouse on the other. When dependence is mutual and about equal, the marriage is strong and close. When the dependence of one partner is much higher than that of the other, however, the marriage is likely to be characterized by stress and conflict. Changes in individual lives over adulthood shift the balance of dependence from one partner to the other; for example, one partner may go back to school, become ill, or lose status. Learning how to deal with these changes is the secret to long and happy marriages.

■ **Figure 11.6**
Marital satisfaction is highest early on and in later life, dropping off during the child-rearing years.

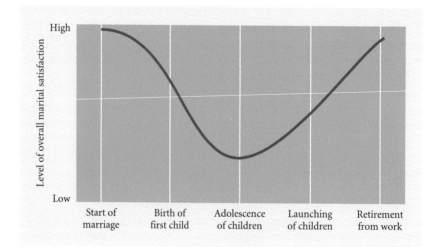

The fact that marital satisfaction has a general downward trend but varies widely across couples led Karney and Bradbury (1995) to propose a vulnerability–stress–adaptation model of marriage. This model sees marital quality as a dynamic process resulting from the couple's ability to handle stressful events in the context of their particular vulnerabilities and resources. For example, as a couple's ability to adapt to stressful situations gets better over time, the quality of the marriage probably will improve.

The Early Years

Marriages are most intense in their early days. When husbands and wives share many activities and are open to new experiences together, bliss results (Olson & McCubbin, 1983). When there is marital conflict, the intensity of the early phase may create considerable unhappiness (Faulkner, Davey, & Davey, 2005).

Early in a marriage, the couple must learn to adjust to the different perceptions and expectations each person has for the other. Many wives tend to be more concerned than their husbands with keeping close ties with their friends. Women are also more likely to identify problems in the marriage and want to talk about them (Peplau & Gordon, 1985). The couple must also learn to handle confrontation. Indeed, learning effective strategies for resolving conflict is an essential component of a strong marriage, as these strategies provide ways for couples to discuss their problems maturely.

Early in a marriage, couples tend to have global adoration for their spouse regarding the spouse's qualities (Neff & Karney, 2005). For wives, but not for husbands, more accurate specific perceptions of what their spouses are really like were associated with their supportive behaviors, feelings of control in the marriage, and whether or not the marriage ended in divorce. Thus, love grounded in specific accuracy of one's perceptions of one's spouse's qualities appears to be stronger than love that is "blind" to one's spouse's true qualities.

Less-educated couples experience greater dissatisfaction with their marriages, as do couples who do not pool their financial resources (Kurdek, 1991a). This occurs because less-educated couples face many additional stressors (e.g., higher rates of unemployment, lower financial security), and the failure to pool resources may reflect a lack of trust in the partner.

As couples settle into a routine, marital satisfaction tends to decline (Lamanna & Riedmann, 2003). Research shows that the primary reason for this drop for most couples is the birth of children (Carstensen et al., 1996). Indeed, for most couples having children means strong pressures to engage in traditional gender-role behaviors for mothers and fathers (Carstensen et al., 1996). Parenthood also means having substantially less time to devote to the marriage. Taking care of children is hard work, requiring energy that used to be spent on keeping the marriage alive and well (Acock & Demo, 1994; Noller & Fitzpatrick, 1993). Most couples are ecstatic over having their first child, a tangible product of their love for each other. But soon the reality of child care sets in, with 2:00 A.M. feedings, diaper changing, and the like, not to mention the long-term financial obligations that will continue at least until the child becomes an adult. Both African American and European American couples report an increase in conflict after the birth of their first child (Crohan, 1996).

However, using the birth of a child as the explanation of the drop in marital satisfaction is much too simplistic (Clements & Markman, 1996). In fact, child-free couples also experience a decline in marital satisfaction. It appears that a decline in overall marital satisfaction over time is a common developmental phenomenon, even for couples who choose to remain childless (Clements & Markman, 1996). Additionally, couples without children due to infertility face the stress associated with the inability to have children, which lowers their marital satisfaction (Matthews & Matthews, 1986). Longitudinal research indicates that disillusionment, as demonstrated by a decline in feeling in love, in demonstrations of affection, and in the feeling that one's spouse is responsive, as well as an increase in feelings of ambivalence, is a key predictor of marital dissatisfaction (Huston et al., 2001).

THINK ABOUT IT

What types of interventions would help keep married couples happier?

Marriage at Midlife

For most couples marital satisfaction improves after the children leave, a state called the *empty nest,* which we examine in more detail in Chapter 12. The departure of children usually gives middle-aged couples a chance to relax and spend more time with each other (Rosenberg, 1993).

For some middle-aged couples, however, marital satisfaction continues to be low. They may have grown apart but continue to live together, a situation sometimes referred to as *married singles* (Lamanna & Riedmann, 2003). In essence, they have become emotionally divorced and live more as housemates than as a married couple; for these couples, spending more time together is not a welcome change. Research shows that marital dissatisfaction in midlife is a process that develops over a long period of time and is not spontaneous (Rokach, Cohen, & Dreman, 2004).

Older Couples

As we will discuss in more detail in Chapter 14, marital satisfaction is fairly high in older couples (Miller et al., 1997). However, satisfaction in long-term marriages—that is, marriages of 40 years or more—is a complex issue. In general, however, marital satisfaction among older couples increases shortly after retirement but then decreases with health problems and advancing age (Miller et al., 1997). The level of satisfaction in these marriages appears to be unrelated to the amount of past or present sexual interest or sexual activity, but it is positively related to the degree of social engagement such as interaction with friends (Bennett, 2005). In keeping with the married-singles concept, many older couples have simply developed detached, contented styles (Connidis, 2001; Lamanna & Riedmann, 2003).

Keeping Marriages Happy

Although no two marriages are exactly the same, couples must be flexible and adaptable. Couples who have been happily married for many years show an ability to roll with the punches and to adapt to changing circumstances in the relationship. For example, a serious problem of one spouse may not be detrimental to the relationship and may even make the bond stronger. Likewise, couples' expectations about marriage change over time, gradually becoming more congruent (Weishaus & Field, 1988). In contrast, the physical illness of one spouse almost invariably affects marital quality negatively, even after other factors such as work stress, education, and income are considered (Wickrama et al., 1997).

How well couples communicate their thoughts, actions, and feelings to each other largely determines the level of conflict couples experience, and, by extension, how happy they are likely to be over the long term (Notarius, 1996). And increasing demands from work and family put enormous pressures on a marriage (Rogers & Amato, 1997). It appears that key factors underlying marital satisfaction do not differ between European American and African American couples (Hairston, 2001). It takes a great deal of love, humor, and perseverance to stay happily married a long time. But it *can* be done, providing couples work at these seven key things (Donatelle & Davis, 1997; Enright, Gassin, & Wu, 1992; Knapp & Taylor, 1994):

- Make time for your relationship.
- Express your love to your spouse.
- Be there in times of need.
- Communicate constructively and positively about problems in the relationship.
- Be interested in your spouse's life.
- Confide in your spouse.
- Forgive minor offenses, and try to understand major ones.

TEST YOURSELF

1. A difficulty for many single people is that other people may expect them to _____.
2. Young adults view cohabitation as a _____ marriage.
3. Gay and lesbian relationships are similar to _____.
4. According to _____, marriage is based on each partner contributing something to the rela-

   tionship that the other would be hard-pressed to provide.
5. For most couples, marital satisfaction _____ after the birth of the first child.

What sociocultural forces affect decisions to marry rather than to cohabit indefinitely?

Answers: (1) marry, (2) step toward, (3) marriages, (4) exchange theory, (5) decreases

---

11.3

THE FAMILY LIFE CYCLE

Bob, 32, and Denise, 33, just had their first child, Matthew, after several years of trying. They've heard that having children in their 30s can have advantages, but Bob and Denise wonder whether people are just saying that to be nice to them. They are also concerned about the financial obligations they are likely to face.

LEARNING OBJECTIVES

Why do people have children?

What is it like to be a parent? What differences are there in different types of parenting?

"WHEN ARE YOU GOING TO START A FAMILY?" is a question young couples like Bob and Denise are asked frequently. Most couples want children because they believe they will bring great joy, which they often do. But once the child is born, adults may feel inadequate because children don't come with instructions. Young adults may be surprised when the reality of being totally responsible for another person hits them. Experienced middle-aged parents often smile knowingly to themselves.

Frightening as it might be, the birth of a child transforms a couple (or a single parent) into a family. *The most common form of family in Western societies is the **nuclear family,** consisting only of parent(s) and child(ren). The most common family form around the world is the **extended family,** in which grandparents and other relatives live with parents and children.* Because we have discussed families from the child's perspective in earlier chapters, here we focus on families from the parents' point of view.

DECIDING WHETHER TO HAVE CHILDREN

One of the biggest decisions couples have to make is whether to have children. This decision is more complicated than most people think. A couple must weigh the many benefits of child rearing, such as personal satisfaction, fulfilling personal needs, continuing the family line, and companionship, with the many drawbacks, including expense and lifestyle changes. What influences the decision process? Psychological and marital factors are always important, and career and lifestyle factors matter when the prospective mother works outside the home (Benokraitis, 2005). As you can see in Figure 11.7, these four factors are interconnected.

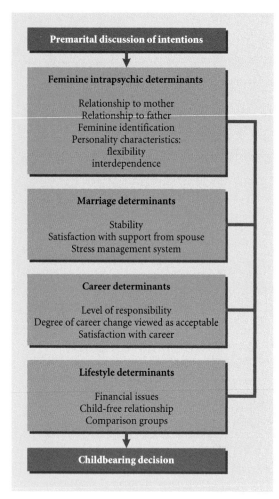

Premarital discussion of intentions

Feminine intrapsychic determinants

Relationship to mother
Relationship to father
Feminine identification
Personality characteristics:
flexibility
interdependence

Marriage determinants

Stability
Satisfaction with support from spouse
Stress management system

Career determinants

Level of responsibility
Degree of career change viewed as acceptable
Satisfaction with career

Lifestyle determinants

Financial issues
Child-free relationship
Comparison groups

Childbearing decision

From *Career, Women, and Childbearing: A Psychological Analysis of the Decision Process,* by D. Wilk. Copyright © 1986 Van Nostrand Reinhold. Reprinted with permission.

■ **Figure 11.7**
Many factors are considered in the decision to have children.

Whether the pregnancy is planned or not (and over half of all pregnancies in the United States are unplanned), a couple's first pregnancy is a milestone event with both benefits and costs (Benokraitis, 2005). Having a child raises many important matters for consideration, such as relationships with one's own parents, marital stability, career satisfaction, and financial issues. Parents largely agree that children add affection, improve family ties, and give parents a feeling of immortality and a sense of accomplishment. Most parents willingly sacrifice a great deal for their children and hope that they grow up to be happy and successful.

Nevertheless, finances are of great concern to most couples because children are expensive. How expensive? According to the U.S. Department of Agriculture (2005b), a family who had a child in 2004 would spend the following estimated amounts by the time the child turned 18: in the lowest income bracket, $177,000; in the middle income bracket, $242,000, and in the highest income bracket $353,000 for food, shelter, and other necessities. College expenses would be an additional expense. No wonder couples are concerned.

For many reasons, such as personal choice, financial instability, and infertility, an increasing number of couples are child-free. In some respects, these couples have several advantages over those who choose to have children (Benokraitis, 2005): higher marital satisfaction, more freedom, and higher standards of living. But the larger society does not tend to view being child-free as something positive when being child-free is by choice and not due to infertility (Lampman & Dowling-Guyer, 1995). Couples who are child-free by choice face social criticism as being self-indulgent and less loving by the larger child-oriented society (Arenofsky, 1993), and they may run the risk of feeling more lonely in old age (Connidis, 2001).

THE PARENTAL ROLE

Today, couples have fewer children and have their first child later than in the past. Indeed, until 1993, couples in which mothers were over 30 when they had their first child were increasing. The slight decline since then is due mainly to smaller numbers of women of childbearing age in cohorts following the baby boomers. Delaying the birth of one's first child has important benefits from both the mother's and the father's perspectives.

Older mothers, like Denise in the vignette, are more at ease being parents, spend more time with their babies, and are more affectionate and sensitive to them (Ragozin et al., 1982). The age of the father also makes a difference in how fathers interact with their children. Remember Bob, the 32-year-old first-time father in the vignette? Compared to men who become fathers in their 20s, men like Bob who become fathers in their 30s are generally more invested in their paternal role and spend up to three times as much time caring for their preschool children as younger fathers do (Cooney et al., 1993). However, men who become fathers in their 30s are also more likely to feel ambivalent and resentful about time lost to their careers (Cooney et al., 1993).

Parenting skills do not come naturally; they must be acquired. Having a child changes all aspects of couples' lives. As we have seen, children place a great deal of stress on a relationship. Both motherhood and fatherhood require major commitment and cooperation. Parenting is full of rewards, but it also takes a great deal of work. Caring for young children is demanding. It may create disagreements over division of labor, especially if both parents are employed outside the home (see Chapters 4 and 11). Even when mothers are employed outside the home (and more than 70% of women with children under age 18 are), they still perform most of the child-rearing tasks. Pleck (1997) estimated that men only spend 44% as much time raising their children as women do.

In general, parents manage to deal with the many challenges of child rearing reasonably well. They learn how to compromise when necessary, and when to apply firm but fair discipline. Given the choice, most parents do not regret their decision to have children.

Having a child later in adulthood has many benefits.

Ethnic Diversity and Parenting

Ethnic background matters in terms of family structure and the parent-child relationship. African American husbands are more likely than their European American counterparts to help with household chores, and they help more with child care (Penha-Lopes, 1995). But African American wives still do more of the traditional household chores such as cooking and cleaning. In low-income families, African American parents often buffer their children from involvement with drugs and other problems (Brooks-Gunn, Klebanov, & Duncan, 1996; Jarrett, 1995). Overall, most African American parents provide a cohesive, loving environment that promotes strong religious beliefs, pride in cultural heritage, self-respect, and cooperation with the family (Brissett-Chapman & Issacs-Shockley, 1997).

A strong sense of tribalism is a major factor in Native American families. This helps promote strong ties to parents, siblings, and grandparents (Garrod & Larimore, 1997). Native American children are viewed as very important family members, and tribal members spend great amounts of time passing cultural values to them, such as cooperation, sharing, personal integrity, generosity, harmony with nature, and spirituality, values very different from European American ones that emphasize competitiveness and individuality (Stauss, 1995). Many Native American parents worry that their children will lose their values if they are overexposed to European American values, such as during college.

Latino families are less likely than either European American or Asian American families to be two-parent families, largely due to higher rates of cohabitation, cultural values, and out-of-wedlock births (del Pinal & Singer, 1997). Two key values among Latino families are familism and the extended family. *Familism refers to the idea that the well-being of the family takes precedence over the concerns of individual family members.* This value is a defining characteristic of Latino families (Benokraitis, 2005). The extended family is also very strong among Latino families, which serves as the venue for a wide range of exchanges of goods and services, such as child care and financial support.

Family ties among Native Americans tend to be very strong.

Many sociopolitical factors influence Asian American families. Like Latinos, Asian Americans value familism and place an even higher value on extended family. Other key values include obtaining good grades in school, maintaining discipline, being concerned about what others think, and conformity. Children are encouraged to mature at an early age, and sibling rivalry and aggressive behavior are not tolerated (Lamanna & Riedmann, 2003). Men have higher status in most Asian American families (Yu, 1995). Among recent immigrants, though, women are expanding their role by working outside the home.

Raising biracial children presents challenges not experienced by parents of same-race children. For ex-

ample, parents of biracial children face prejudice toward themselves and their children by members of both races (Chan & Smith, 1995). These parents also worry that their children may be rejected by members of both racial communities.

As is clear, ethnic groups vary a great deal in how they approach the issue of parenting and what values are most important. Considered together, there is no one parenting standard that applies equally to all groups.

Single Parents

The number of single parents, most of whom are women, is increasing rapidly. Roughly 70% of births to African American mothers, 40% of births to Latina mothers, and 20% of births to European American mothers are to unmarried women (U.S. Census Bureau, 2005b). Among the causes are high divorce rates, the decision to keep children born out of wedlock, different fertility rates across ethnic groups, and the desire of many single adults to have or adopt children. Being a single parent raises important questions. Ethnic group differences are due in part to different rates at which women marry to legitimate a pregnancy (African American women do this the least) and higher rates of cohabitation among some groups (e.g., Latinos; Raley, 1999).

Two main questions arise concerning single parents: How are children affected when only one adult is responsible for child care? and How do single parents meet their own needs for emotional support and intimacy?

Many divorced single parents report complex feelings such as frustration, failure, guilt, and a need to be overindulgent (Lamanna & Riedmann, 2003). Loneliness can be especially difficult to deal with (Anderson et al., 2004). Feelings of guilt may lead to attempts to make up for the child's lack of a father or mother. Some single parents make the mistake of trying to be peers to their children, using inconsistent discipline, or, if they are the noncustodial parent, of spoiling their children with lots of monetary or material goods.

Single parents, regardless of gender, face considerable obstacles. Financially, they are usually much less well-off than their married counterparts. Integrating the roles of work and parenthood are difficult enough for two people; for the single parent, the hardships are compounded. Financially, single mothers are hardest hit.

One particular concern for many divorced single parents is dating. Several common questions asked by single parents involve dating: "How do I become available again?" "How will my children react?" "How do I cope with my own sexual needs?" Research indicates that repartnering happens fairly quickly (Anderson et al., 2004), with half having had some dating experience even prior to the divorce filing. At one-year post filing, typically parents have dated two new partners. Among recent filers, younger parents, those with greater time since separation, and those in households containing other (nonromantic) adults are significantly more likely to have dated. There are typically no differences in dating by ethnic group, but African American parents report significantly longer times since separation.

Alternative Forms of Parenting

Not all parents raise their own biological children. In fact, roughly one third of North American couples become stepparents or foster or adoptive parents some time during their lives.

To be sure, the parenting issues we have discussed thus far are just as important in these situations as when people raise their own biological children. In general, there are few differences among parents who have their own biological children or who become parents in some other way (Ceballo et al., 2004). However, some special problems arise as well.

A big issue for foster parents, adoptive parents, and stepparents is how strongly the child will bond with them. Although infants less than 1 year old will probably bond well, children who are old enough to have formed attachments with their biological parents may have competing loyalties. For example, some stepchildren remain strongly attached to the noncustodial parent and actively resist attempts to integrate them into the new family ("My real mother wouldn't make me do that"), or they may exhibit behavioral problems. Children in blended families also tend not to have as good mental health as children in non-divorced families (Cherlin & Furstenberg, 1994). Stepparents must often deal with continued visitation by the noncustodial parent, which may exacerbate any difficulties. These problems are a major reason second marriages are at high risk for dissolution, as discussed earlier in this chapter.

Still, many stepparents and stepchildren ultimately develop good relationships with each other. Stepparents must be sensitive to the relationship between the step-child and his or her biological, noncustodial parent. Allowing stepchildren to develop the relationship with the stepparent at their own pace also helps. What style of stepparenting ultimately develops is influenced by the expectations of the stepparent, stepchild, spouse, and nonresidential parent (Erera-Weatherley, 1996).

Becoming a stepparent is a very common occurrence in the United States as single parents remarry.

Adoptive parents also contend with attachment to birth parents, but in different ways. Even if they don't remember them, adopted children may wish to locate and meet their birth parents. Wanting to know one's origins is understandable, but such searches can strain the relationships between these children and their adoptive parents, who may interpret these actions as a form of rejection (Rosenberg, 1992).

Foster parents tend to have the most tenuous relationship with their children because the bond can be broken for any of a number of reasons having nothing to do with the quality of the care being provided. For example, a court may award custody back to the birth parents, or another couple may legally adopt the child. Dealing with attachment is difficult; foster parents want to provide secure homes, but they may not have the children long enough to establish continuity. Furthermore, because many children in foster care have been unable to form attachments at all, they

Adopting a child can be a very rewarding experience.

are less likely to form ones that will inevitably be broken. Thus, foster parents must be willing to tolerate considerable ambiguity in the relationship and have few expectations about the future.

Finally, many gay men and lesbian women also want to be parents. Some have biological children themselves, whereas others choose adoption or foster parenting. Although gay men and lesbian women make good parents, they often experience resistance to having children. Actually, research indicates that children reared by gay or lesbian parents do not experience any more problems than children reared by heterosexual parents and are as psychologically healthy as children of heterosexual parents (Lambert, 2005). Substantial evidence exists that children raised by gay or lesbian parents do not develop sexual identity or any other problems any more than children raised by heterosexual parents (Flaks et al., 1995; Patterson, 1992). For example, research evidence indicates that roughly 90% of sons (aged 17 or older) of gay fathers are heterosexual (Bailey et al., 1995).

Additional evidence shows that children raised by gay men may even have some advantages over children raised by heterosexual men. Gay men are often especially concerned about being good and nurturing fathers, and they try hard to raise their children with nonsexist, egalitarian attitudes (Flaks et al., 1995). Children of lesbian couples and heterosexual couples are equally adjusted behaviorally, show equivalent cognitive development, and have similar behaviors in school. Indeed, one study found that the only difference between such couples was that lesbian couples exhibit more awareness of parenting skills than do heterosexual couples (Flaks et al., 1995).

These data will not make the controversy go away as much of it is based on long-held beliefs and prejudices. Admittedly, the data comparing children raised by different types of parents are inadequate; for example, there is very little information about children raised by lesbian women. Only when societal attitudes toward gay men and lesbians become more accepting will there be greater acceptance of their right to be parents like anyone else.

TEST YOURSELF

1. The series of relatively predictable changes that families experience is called _____.
2. Major influences on the decision to have children are marital factors, career factors, lifestyle factors, and _____.
3. A new father who is invested in his parental role, but who may also feel ambivalent about time lost to his career, is probably over age _____.
4. A major issue for foster parents, adoptive parents, and stepparents is _____.

What difference do you think it would make to view children as a financial asset (i.e., a source of income) as opposed to a financial burden (i.e., mainly an expense)? Which of these do you think characterizes most Western societies? Can you think of an example of the other type?

Answers: (1) the family life cycle, (2) psychological factors, (3) 30, (4) how strongly the child will bond with them

11.4

DIVORCE AND REMARRIAGE

LEARNING OBJECTIVES

Who gets divorced? How does divorce affect parental relationships with children?

What are remarriages like? How are they similar to and different from first marriages?

Frank and Marilyn, both in their late 40s, thought their marriage would last forever. They weren't so lucky; they just got divorced. Although two of their children are married, their youngest daughter is still in college. The financial pressures Marilyn feels now that she's on her own are beginning to take their toll. She wonders whether her financial situation is similar to that of other recently divorced women.

D ESPITE WHAT FRANK AND MARILYN PLEDGED on their wedding day, their marriage did not last until death parted them; they dissolved their marriage through divorce. But even though divorce is stressful and difficult, thousands of people each year also choose to try again. Most enter their second (or third or fourth) marriage with renewed expectations of success. Are these new dreams realistic? As we'll see, it depends on many things; among the most important is whether children are involved.

DIVORCE

Most couples enter marriage with the idea that their relationship will be permanent. Unfortunately, fewer and fewer couples experience this permanence. Rather than growing together, couples grow apart.

Who Gets Divorced and Why?

Divorce in the United States is common and the divorce rate is substantially higher than it is in many other countries around the world; as you can see in Figure 11.8, couples have roughly a 50–50 chance of remaining married for life (U.S. Census Bureau, 2005b). In contrast, the divorce rates in Canada, Austria, France, and Germany are substantially lower (United Nations, 2002). However, divorce rates in nearly every developed country have increased significantly over the past several decades (United Nations, 2002).

One factor consistently related to divorce rates in the United States is ethnicity. African Americans are more likely than European Americans to divorce or separate (U.S. Census Bureau, 2005b). Ethnically mixed marriages are at greater risk of divorce than ethnically homogenous ones (Jones, 1996).

Men and women tend to agree on the reasons for divorce (Amato & Previti, 2003). Infidelity is the most commonly reported cause, followed by incompatibility, drinking or drug use, and growing apart. People's specific reasons for divorcing vary with gender, social class, and life course variables. Former husbands and wives are more likely to blame their ex-spouses than themselves for the problems that led to the divorce. Former husbands and wives claim, however, that women are more likely to have initiated the divorce.

Why people divorce has been the focus of much research. Much of the attention has been on the notion that how couples handle conflict is the key to success or failure. Although conflict management is important, it has become clear that there is more to it than that (Fincham, 2003).

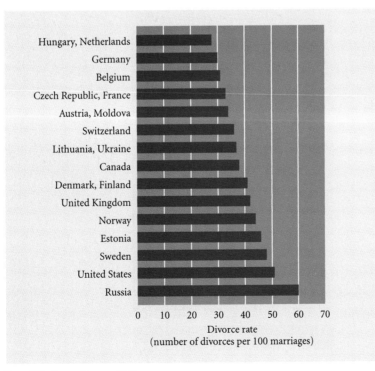

Figure 11.8
The United States has one of the highest divorce rates in the world.

From U.S. Census Bureau, 2001.

Gottman and Levenson (2000) developed two models that predict divorce early (within the first 7 years of marriage) and later (when the first child reaches age 14) with 93% accuracy over the 14-year period of their study. Negative emotions displayed during conflict between the couple predict early divorce, but not later divorce. In general, this reflects a pattern of wife-demand-husband-withdraw (Christensen, 1990) in which, during conflict, the wife places a demand on her husband, who then withdraws either emotionally or physically. In contrast, the lack of positive emotions in a discussion of events-of-the-day and during conflict predict later divorce, but not early divorce. An example would be a wife talking excitedly about a project she had just been given at work and her husband showing disinterest. Such "unrequited" interest and excitement in discussions likely carries over to the rest of the relationship.

Gottman's research is important because it clearly shows that how couples show emotion is critical to marital success. Couples who divorce earlier typically do so because of high levels of negative feelings such as contempt, criticism, defensiveness, and stonewalling experienced as a result of intense marital conflict. But for many couples, such intense conflict is generally absent. Although this makes it easier to stay in a marriage longer, the absence of positive emotions eventually takes its toll and results in later divorce. For a marriage to last, people need to be told that they are loved and that what they do and feel really matters to their partner.

Why people divorce is certainly complex. As shown in Figure 11.9, macro-level social issues, demographic variables, and interpersonal problems all factor into the deci-

Figure 11.9
Many factors on different levels enter into the decision to divorce.

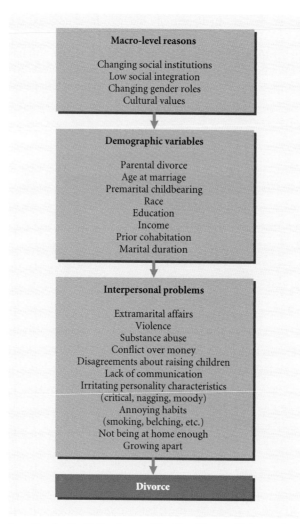

From Benokraitis, N. *Marriages and Families: Changes, Choices, and Constraints*, 4/e, © 2002, p. 401. Reprinted with permission of Pearson Education, Inc., Upper Saddle River, New Jersey.

sion to divorce (Lamanna & Riedmann, 2003). The high divorce rate in the United States and the reasons typically cited for getting divorced have sparked a controversial approach to keeping couples together. As described in the Current Controversies feature, *covenant marriage,* which makes divorce much harder to obtain, is an option being tried in some states. Other proposals, such as the Healthy Marriage Initiative supported by the Heritage Foundation, raise similar issues. Will they work? Read the feature and draw your own conclusion.

CURRENT CONTROVERSIES

"COVENANT MARRIAGE," A WAY TO KEEP COUPLES TOGETHER?

The divorce rate in the United States, one of the highest in the world, has become a national concern. As our society strives to make marriage more successful, numerous approaches, such as mandatory premarital counseling, cooling-off periods, and the abolition of no-fault divorce, are being tried, with varying degrees of success.

In 1997 Louisiana adopted a different and controversial approach. When couples get married, they choose between a "no-fault marriage" and a "covenant marriage." Under a no-fault marriage, a couple may divorce after 6 months of separation without proof of adultery, abuse, neglect, or other basis. Under a covenant marriage, couples seeking divorce must undergo separation for 2 years or verify that one spouse is an adulterer, abuser, deserter, or felon. Couples opting for covenant marriage must also undergo mandatory premari-

tal counseling. Couples already married may recast their vows and their marriage under terms of the covenant. Other states, such as Arizona and Arkansas, have adopted similar measures.

Proponents of covenant marriage point out that about 20% of couples who participate in premarital counseling decide not to marry their partners (Etzioni, 1997). Making divorce harder to obtain addresses lawmakers' concerns that divorce laws are too lenient. It is hoped that the provisions of covenant marriage will get couples to think more seriously about marriage and to make a deeper commitment to each other. Organizations such as the Covenant Marriage Movement (www.covenantmarriage.com) have initiated national meetings of dozens of other organizations to develop a comprehensive approach. Covenant marriage is especially popular among people who are religiously active and

hold conservative gender-role ideologies (Hawkins et al., 2002).

Opponents of covenant marriage argue that the option may force couples to stay together when it is in their and their children's best interest to end the marriage. Bad marriages are not supportive environments for children. Opponents also point out that covenant marriage is a backward step that reintroduces the idea that divorce has to be someone's fault. These opponents also question whether couples really have a choice; that is, peer pressure may force them into covenant marriage.

Will covenant marriage reduce divorce rates? It's too early to tell. Making sure couples who want to marry fully appreciate the emotional and financial realities is good. Whether making divorce more difficult to obtain is equally good for couples and children remains to be seen.

Effects of Divorce on the Couple

Although the changes in attitudes toward divorce have eased the social trauma associated with it, divorce still takes a high toll on the psyche of the couple. Both partners in a failed marriage feel deeply disappointed, misunderstood, and rejected (Brodie, 1999). Unlike the situation when one's spouse dies, divorce often means that the person's ex-spouse is present to provide a reminder of the failure. As a result, divorced people are typically unhappy in general, at least for a while. Indeed, divorced people of all ages are less likely than married, never-married, and widowed people to say that they are "very happy" with their lives (Kurdek, 1991b; Lee, Seccombe, & Shehan, 1991). The effects of a divorce can even be traced to generations not yet born due to long-term negative consequences on education and parent-child relations in future generations (Amato & Cheadle, 2005).

Divorced people sometimes find the transition very difficult; researchers refer to these problems as "divorce hangover" (Walther, 1991). Divorce hangover reflects divorced partners' inability to let go, develop new friendships, or reorient themselves as single parents. Indeed, ex-spouses who are preoccupied with thoughts of their former partner, and who have high feelings of hostility toward him or her, have significantly poorer emotional well-being than ex-spouses who are not preoccupied or who have

THINK ABOUT IT

Given the serious impact of divorce, what changes in mate selection might lower the divorce rate?

feelings of friendship toward the former partner (Masheter, 1997). Forgiving the ex-spouse is also important for eventual adjustment postdivorce (Rye et al., 2004). Both low preoccupation and forgiveness may be indicators that ex-spouses are able to move on with their lives.

Gender differences are also found. Men report being shocked by the breakup, especially if the wife filed for divorce (Arendell, 1995). Men are more likely to be blamed for the problems that led to the divorce, to accept the blame, to move out, and to thereby find their social life disrupted. Women are affected differently (Ross, 1995). For example, divorced mothers have fewer prospects for potential remarriage, and they find it more difficult to establish new friendship networks if they have custody of the children (Albeck & Kaydar, 2002). Women are at a serious financial disadvantage, largely because they usually have custody of the children, are typically paid less than men, and are likely to have inadequate child support from their ex-husbands (Gallagher, 1996; Kurz, 1995). Marilyn, the recently divorced middle-aged woman we met in the vignette, probably has a difficult road ahead as she tries to meet her own expenses as well as help pay her daughter's college tuition.

Divorce in middle age or late life has some special characteristics. If women initiate the divorce, they report self-focused growth and optimism; if they did not initiate the divorce, they tend to ruminate and feel vulnerable (Sakraida, 2005). However, in both cases they report changes in their social networks. Middle-aged and elderly women are at a significant disadvantage for remarriage—an especially traumatic situation for women who obtained much of their identity from their roles as wife and mother. Support groups help people adjust; for men this works best in large groups and for women it works best when the group provides emotional support (Oygard & Hardeng, 2001).

We must not overlook the financial problems faced by middle-aged divorced women (Gallagher, 1996; Kurz, 1995). These problems are especially keen for the middle-aged divorcee who may have spent years as a homemaker and has few marketable job skills. For her, divorce presents an especially difficult financial hardship, which is intensified if she has children in college and the father provides little support (Lamanna & Riedmann, 2003).

Relationships With Young Children

The difficulty in adjusting to divorce often depends on whether young children are involved. Deciding who will have custody of the children often triggers the problems. Roughly 90% of all divorces are not contested and are settled out of court. In these cases, more than 70% of the time the mother receives custody, and the father becomes an occasional parent (Lamanna & Riedmann, 2003). However, when men sue over custody, they win either sole or joint custody up to 70% of the time (Benokraitis, 2005). Women may be forced to agree to lower alimony or child support payments in exchange for custody. Consequently, men are sometimes encouraged to wage an all-out battle for custody, even when they do not want it, simply to gain bargaining power over their financial obligations (Winner, 1996).

Most divorced mothers of young children end up being the primary custodial parent. For many of them, the price they pay for custody is very high; at the same time as their parental responsibilities are increasing, their financial resources are decreasing significantly (Gallagher, 1996; Kurz, 1995). Child care is expensive, and most divorced fathers contribute less than before the separation. Furthermore, in the United States many child support payments are not made; to address this problem, most states have passed laws to enforce child support payments (Gallagher, 1996).

Divorced fathers pay a psychological price. Although many would like to remain active in their children's lives, few actually do. One reason is that children's needs change; anticipating these changes requires frequent contact, which is hard for many men. Additionally, even when child support payments are made, noncustodial fathers find it difficult to develop good relationships with their children, often because their ex-wives express their anger by limiting contact with the children. Child support laws in some states also may limit fathers' contact with their children (Wadlington, 2005). The fact that

Most custodial parents following a divorce are women.

about one fourth of divorced couples end up as bitter enemies only makes matters worse for all concerned (Ahrons & Wallisch, 1986). The unfortunate result is that many divorced fathers become peripheral in their children's lives, often through no fault of their own (Seltzer, 1991).

One hopeful direction that addresses the usually difficult custody situations following divorce is the Collaborative Divorce Project (Pruett, Insabella, & Gustafson, 2005). The Collaborative Divorce Project is an intervention designed to assist the parents of children 6 years old or younger as they begin the separation/divorce process. In addition to positive evaluations from both parents, intervention families benefited through lower conflict, greater father involvement, and better outcomes for children than the control group. Attorneys and court records indicate that intervention families were more cooperative and were less likely to need custody evaluations and other costly services. The Collaborative Divorce Project is evidence that programs can be designed and implemented that benefit all members of the family.

Relationships With Adult Children

We saw in Chapter 5 that young children can be seriously affected by their parents' divorce. But what happens when the parents of adult children divorce? Are adult children affected too? It certainly looks that way. Young adults whose parents divorce experience a great deal of emotional vulnerability and stress (Cooney & Uhlenberg, 1990). One young man put it this way:

> . . . the difficult thing was that it was a time where, you know [you're] making the transition from high school to college . . . your high school friends are dispersed . . . they're all over the place. . . . It's normally a very difficult transition [college], new atmosphere, new work load, meeting new people. You've got to start deciding what you want to do, you've got to sort of start getting more independent, and so forth. And then, at the same time you find out about a divorce. You know, it's just that much more adjustment you have to make. (Cooney et al., 1986)

The effects of experiencing a divorce of one's parents while growing up can be quite long-lasting. Wallerstein and Lewis (2004) report the findings from a 25-year follow-up study of individuals whose parents divorced when they were between 3 and 18 years old. Results show an unexpected gulf between growing up in intact versus divorced families, and the difficulties children of divorce encounter in achieving love, sexual intimacy, and commitment to marriage and parenthood. Clearly, experiencing divorce alters lives.

REMARRIAGE

The trauma of divorce does not deter people from beginning new relationships, which often lead to another marriage. Typically, men and women wait about 4 years before they remarry (De Witt, 1994), with men being quicker to repartner (Wu & Schimmele, 2005). However, remarriage rates vary somewhat across ethnic groups. African Americans remarry a bit more slowly than European Americans, and Hispanics remarry more slowly than either of these other two groups (Ganong & Coleman, 1994). European Americans are more likely to remarry than any other ethnic group, with African Americans being the least likely. African Americans are also more likely to separate without divorcing (Ganong & Coleman, 1994).

Although remarriage is common, adjusting to it can be difficult.

Research indicates that there are few differences between first marriages and remarriages (Coleman & Ganong, 1990). Except for African Americans, second marriages have about a 25% higher risk of dissolution than first marriages, and the divorce rate for remarriages involving stepchildren is about three times higher than the rate for first marriages (Lamanna & Riedmann, 2003; U.S. Census Bureau, 2005b).

Although women are more likely to initiate a divorce, they are less likely to remarry (Buckle, Gallup, & Rodd, 1996) unless they are poor (Schmiege, Richards, & Zvonkovic, 2001). However, women in general tend to benefit more from remarriage than do men, particularly if they have children (Ozawa & Yoon, 2002). Divorced men without children tend to marry women who have never been married; divorced men with children tend to marry divorced women (Buckle et al., 1996). Results from a Canadian study indicate that men with higher educational attainment are more likely to remarry than their female counterparts (Wu, 1994). This appears to be because women with higher educational and socioeconomic status have less to gain from remarriage because they are economically independent. They also have a smaller pool of potential partners as they are less likely than men to marry someone from a lower socioeconomic or educational status.

Adapting to new relationships in remarriage is stressful. For example, partners may have unresolved issues from the previous marriage that may interfere with satisfaction with the new marriage (Faber, 2004).

TEST YOURSELF

1. Following divorce, most women suffer disproportionately in the _____ domain compared to most men.

2. On average, within 2 years after a divorce, _____ fathers remain central in their children's lives.

3. Even many years later, divorced _____ may not experience positive relationships with their adult children.

4. For African American couples, divorce rates for remarried couples are _____ than for first marriages.

Despite greatly increased divorce rates over the past few decades, the rate of marriage has not changed very much. Why do you think this is?

Answers: (1) financial, (2) few, (3) fathers, (4) lower

Putting It All Together

In this chapter, we have seen how people find and develop adult relationships. We considered the important role that friendships play in adulthood. Some relationships, like Jamal and Deb's, turn into love. Although the romantic love they feel won't last forever, their love may evolve so that the relationship can last. Although young love like Jamal and Deb's gets played out the world over, what people look for in a partner varies in different cultures. Turning a love relationship into newly wedded bliss, as Kevin and Beth did, is very common; it's still true that the vast majority of people get married at some point in their lives. If Kevin and Beth have children, their newfound happiness is likely to fade a bit, but as long as they maintain their commitment to each other, their marriage will probably last. Frank and Marilyn's divorce has had fairly typical results: Marilyn is having trouble making financial ends meet. Because Bob and Denise were in their 30s when their first child was born, they will likely be better suited and better prepared for parenthood than many younger parents.

Throughout the chapter, we saw that human relationships are complex. Although there are similarities around the world in how people find partners, culture plays a large part in helping people find the person who will say, "I am for you." Maintaining a strong relationship takes a great deal of work, and many pressures can divert partners' attention from each other.

Summary

11.1 Relationships

Friendships

■ People tend to have more friendships during young adulthood than during any other period. Friendships are especially important for maintaining life satisfaction throughout adulthood.

■ Men tend to have fewer close friendships and to base them on shared activities, such as sports. Women tend to have more close friendships, and to base them on intimate and emotional sharing. Gender differences in same-gender friendship patterns may explain the difficulties men and women have in forming cross-gender friendships.

Love Relationships

■ Passion, intimacy, and commitment are the key components of love.

■ Although styles of love change with age, the priorities within relationships do not. Men tend to be more romantic earlier in relationships than women, who tend to be cautious pragmatists. As the length of the relationship increases, intimacy and passion decrease, but commitment increases.

■ Selecting a mate works best when there are shared values, goals, and interests. There are cross-cultural differences with regard to the specific aspects of these that are considered most important.

The Dark Side of Relationships: Violence

■ Levels of aggressive behavior range from verbal aggression, to physical aggression, to murdering one's partner. The causes of aggressive behaviors become more complex as the level of aggression increases. People remain in abusive relationships for many reasons, including low self-esteem and the belief that they cannot leave.

11.2 Lifestyles

Singlehood

■ Most adults decide by age 30 whether they plan on getting married. Never-married adults often develop a strong network of close friends. Dealing with other people's expectations that they should marry is often difficult for single people.

Cohabitation

■ Young adults usually cohabit as a step toward marriage, and adults of all ages may also cohabit for financial reasons. Cohabitation is only rarely seen as an alternative to marriage. Overall, more similarities than differences exist between cohabiting and married couples.

Gay and Lesbian Couples

■ Gay and lesbian relationships are similar to marriages in terms of relationship issues. Lesbian couples tend to be more egalitarian and are more likely to remain together than gay couples. Frequency of sexual expression differs in gay, lesbian, and heterosexual couples.

Marriage

■ The most important factors in creating stable marriages are creating a stable sense of identity as a foundation for intimacy, similarity of values and interests, effective communication, and the contribution of unique skills by each partner.

■ For couples with children, marital satisfaction tends to decline until the children leave home, although individual differences are apparent, especially in long-term marriages. Most long-term marriages are happy.

11.3 The Family Life Cycle

■ Although the nuclear family is the most common form of family in Western societies, the most common form around the world is the extended family. Families experience a series of relatively predictable changes called the *family life cycle.* This cycle provides a framework for understanding the changes families go through as children mature.

Deciding Whether to Have Children

■ Although having children is stressful and very expensive, most people do it anyway. However, the number of child-free couples is increasing.

The Parental Role

■ The timing of parenthood is important in how involved parents are in their families as opposed to their careers.

■ Single parents are faced with many problems, especially if they are women and are divorced. The main problem is significantly reduced financial resources.

■ A major issue for adoptive parents, foster parents, and stepparents is how strongly the child will bond with them. Each of these relationships has some special characteristics.

■ Gay and lesbian parents also face numerous obstacles, but they usually prove to be good parents.

11.4 Divorce and Remarriage

Divorce

■ Currently, odds are about 50–50 that a new marriage will end in divorce. Conflict styles can predict who divorces. Recovery from divorce is different for men and women. Men tend to have a tougher time in the short run, but women clearly have a harder time in the long run, often for financial reasons.

■ Difficulties between divorced partners usually involve visitation and child support. Disruptions also occur in divorced parents' relationships with their children, whether the children are young or are adults themselves.

Remarriage

■ Most divorced couples remarry. Second marriages are especially vulnerable to stress if spouses must adjust to having stepchildren. Remarriage in middle age and beyond tends to be happy.

Key Terms

assortative mating (419)

abusive relationship (422)

battered woman syndrome (422)

common couple violence (424)

patriarchal terrorism (424)

cohabitation (427)

homogamy (431)

exchange theory (432)

nuclear family (435)

extended family (435)

familism (437)

Learn More About It

Readings

BENGTSON, V. L., ACOCK, A. C., ALLEN, K. R., DILWORTH-ANDERSON, P., & KLEIN, D. M. (2004). *Sourcebook of family theory and research.* Thousand Oaks, CA: Sage. This superb resource book covers all major theories and methods used in family and relationship research.

COONTZ, S. (2005). *Marriage, a history: From obedience to intimacy, or how love conquered marriage.* New York: Viking Adult. An excellent overview of the history of traditional marriage, which turns out not to be so traditional.

PRATHER, H., & PRATHER, G. (1990). *Notes to each other.* New York: Bantam. This collection of reflections on making relationships work, staying happy, and parenting makes easy reading.

STAPLES, R. (Ed.). (1999). *The Black family: Essays and studies* (6th ed.). Belmont, CA: Wadsworth. This book covers many issues in African American families and relationships.

TANNEN, D. (2001). *I only say this because I love you: How the way we talk can make or break family relationships throughout our lives.* New York: Random House. This highly readable and intriguing book discusses the different communication styles people use.

Websites

Visit the Human Development book companion website for all URLs.

- ■ **The Human Development Book Companion Website**

  See the companion website **http://psychology .wadsworth.com / kail_cavanaugh4e/** for practice quiz questions, Internet links, updates, critical thinking exercises, discussion forums, and more.

- ■ **National Council on Family Relations**

  Research findings and professional materials about all aspects of families can be obtained through the National Council on Family Relations.

- ■ **Family Violence Prevention Fund**

  The Family Violence Prevention Fund is a national nonprofit organization that focuses on domestic violence education, prevention, and public policy reform.

- ■ **American Bar Association Section on Family Law**

  The American Bar Association Section on Family Law provides analyses of all aspects of the law pertaining to families.

Life-Span CD-ROM

For more information about the concepts covered in this chapter, go to

Module 5: Early and Middle Adulthood

- • *Emotional and Social Development*

http://www.thomsonedu.com

Go to this site for the link to ThomsonNOW, your one-stop study shop. Take a pre-test for this chapter, and ThomsonNOW will generate a personalized study plan based on your test results. The study plan will identify the topics you need to review and direct you to online resources to help you master those topics. You can then take a post-test to help you determine the concepts you have mastered and what you still need to work on.

12.1 Occupational Selection and Development
The Meaning of Work
Holland's Theory of Occupational Choice Revisited
Occupational Development
Job Satisfaction

■ SPOTLIGHT ON RESEARCH: The Connection Between Job Satisfaction and Employee Turnover

12.2 Gender, Ethnicity, and Discrimination Issues
Gender Differences in Occupational Selection
Women and Occupational Development
Ethnicity and Occupational Development
Bias and Discrimination

■ CURRENT CONTROVERSIES: Is It Sexual Harassment?

12.3 Occupational Transitions
■ REAL PEOPLE: APPLYING HUMAN DEVELOPMENT: Changing Occupations to Find Satisfying Work
Retraining Workers
Occupational Insecurity
Coping With Unemployment

12.4 Work and Family
The Dependent Care Dilemma
Juggling Multiple Roles

12.5 Time to Relax: Leisure Activities
Types of Leisure Activities
Developmental Changes in Leisure
Consequences of Leisure Activities

Putting It All Together
Summary
Key Terms
Learn More About It

CHAPTER 12

Work and Leisure

Occupational and Lifestyle Issues in Young and Middle Adulthood

W ork—it seems as though that's all we do sometimes. From the small chores children do to putting in 12-hour days at the office, we are taught that working is a natural part of life. For some, work *is* life. In this chapter, we explore the world of work first by considering how people choose occupations and develop in them. After that, we examine how women and minorities contend with barriers to their occupational selection and development. Dealing with occupational transitions is considered in the third section. How to balance work and family obligations is a difficult issue for many people; this is discussed in the fourth section. Finally, we will see how people spend their time away from work in leisure activities.

As in Chapter 11, our focus in this chapter is on issues faced by both young and middle-aged adults. No longer is it the case that only young adults have to deal with occupational selection issues. It is increasingly common for middle-aged people to have to confront the issues of occupational selection all over again, as their industry changes or their company downsizes. Similarly, the other topics we consider apply to both younger and middle-aged adults.

Getty Images

12.1

OCCUPATIONAL SELECTION AND DEVELOPMENT

Monique, a 28-year-old senior communications major, wonders about careers. Should she enter the broadcast field as a behind-the-scenes producer, or would she be better suited as a public relations spokesperson? She thinks that her outgoing personality is a factor she should consider.

LEARNING OBJECTIVES

How do people view work? How do occupational priorities vary with age?

How do people choose their occupations?

What factors influence occupational development?

What is the relationship between job satisfaction and age?

CHOOSING ONE'S WORK IS SERIOUS BUSINESS. Like Monique, we try to select a field in which we are trained, and that is also appealing. Work colors much of what we do in life. You may be taking this course as part of your preparation for work. People make friends at work and arrange personal activities around work schedules. Parents often choose child care centers on the basis of their proximity to their place of employment.

In this section, we explore what work means to adults. We also revisit issues pertaining to occupational selection, first introduced in Chapter 8, and examine occupational development. Finally, we will see how satisfaction with one's job changes during adulthood.

THE MEANING OF WORK

Did you ever stop to think about why we fight the commuting crowds to get to work? Studs Terkel, author of the fascinating book *Working* (1974), writes that work is "a search for daily meaning as well as daily bread, for recognition as well as cash, for astonishment rather than torpor; in short, for a sort of life rather than a Monday through Friday sort of dying" (p. xiii). Kahlil Gibran (1923), in his mystical book *The Prophet,* put it this way: "Work is love made visible."

For some of us, work is a source of prestige, social recognition, and a sense of worth. For others, the excitement, creativity, and the opportunity to give something of themselves make work meaningful. But for most, the main purpose of work is to earn a living. This is not to imply, of course, that money is the only reward in a job; friendships, the chance to exercise power, and feeling useful are also important. The meaning most of us derive from working includes both the money that can be exchanged for life's necessities (and maybe a few luxuries too) and the possibility of personal growth.

Hassling with commuting makes us think about why we work.

The kind of occupation appears to have no effect on people's need to derive meaning from work. Even when their occupation consists of highly repetitive work (Isaksen, 2000) or is in a declining industry experiencing a high number of layoffs (Dorton, 2001), people find great personal meaning in what they do. The specific meanings people get from their work vary with the type of occupation and are influenced by socialization (Chetro-Szivos, 2001).

What meanings do people derive from their work? Lips-Wiersma (2003) sought answers to this question by interviewing people in depth about the meanings they derive from work and whether and how these meanings determine work behavior. Despite wide diversity of backgrounds in the participants in her study, Lips-Wiersma found four common meanings: developing self, union with others, expressing self, and serving others. To the extent that these meanings can all be achieved, people experience the workplace as a place of personal fulfillment. These meanings also provide a framework for understanding occupational transitions as ways people may use to find opportunities for better balance among the four main meanings.

Given the various meanings people derive from work, occupation is clearly a key element of a person's sense of identity and self-efficacy (Lang & Lee, 2005). This can be readily observed when adults introduce themselves socially. When asked to tell something about themselves, you've probably noticed that people usually provide information about what they do for a living. Occupation affects your life in a host of ways, often influencing where you live, what friends you make, and even what clothes you wear. In short, the impact of work cuts across all aspects of life. Work, then, is a major social role and influence on adult life. Occupation is an important anchor that complements the other major role of adulthood—love relationships.

As we will see, occupation is part of human development. Young children, in their pretend play, are in the midst of the social preparation for work. Adults are always asking them, "What do you want to be when you grow up?" School curricula, especially in high school and college, are geared toward preparing people for particular occupations. Young adult college students as well as older returning students have formulated perspectives on the meanings they believe they will get from work. Hance (2000) organized these beliefs into three main categories: working to achieve social influence; working to achieve personal fulfillment; and working due to economic reality. These categories reflect fairly well the actual meanings working adults report.

Because work plays such a key role in providing meaning for people, an important question is how people select an occupation. Let's turn our attention to one of the theories explaining how and why people choose the occupations they do.

HOLLAND'S THEORY OF OCCUPATIONAL CHOICE REVISITED

In Chapter 8, we saw that early decisions about what people want to do in the world of work are related to their personalities. Holland's (1997) theory makes explicit an intuitively appealing idea: that people choose occupations to optimize the fit between their individual traits (such as personality, intelligence, skills, and abilities) and their occupational interests. Recall from Table 9.4 (page 357) that Holland categorizes occupations in two ways: by the interpersonal settings in which people must function and by their associated lifestyles. From this perspective, he identifies six personality types that combine these factors: investigative, social, realistic, artistic, conventional, and enterprising.

How does Holland's theory help us understand the continued development of occupational interests in adulthood? Monique's situation helps illustrate this point. Monique, the college senior in the vignette, found a good match between her outgoing nature and her major, communications. Indeed, most college students, regardless of age, tend to like courses and majors best when they provide a good fit with their personalities. Thus, the early occupational choices in adolescence continue to be modified and fine-tuned in adulthood.

Although the relations between personality and occupational choice are important, we must also recognize the limits of the theory as it relates to adults' occupational choices. If we consider the gender and ethnic/racial distributions of Holland's personality types, adult men and women are represented differently, but there are minimal differences across ethnic/racial groups (Fouad & Mohler, 2004). Regardless of age, women are more likely than men to have the social, artistic, and conventional personality types.

THINK ABOUT IT

How does one's level of cognitive development relate to one's choice of occupation?

In part, gender differences reflect different experiences in growing up (e.g., hearing that girls grow up to be nurses whereas boys grow up to be firefighters), differences in personality (e.g., gender-role identity), and differences in socialization (e.g., women being expected to be more outgoing and people-oriented than men). However, if we look within a specific occupational type, women and men are very similar to each other and closely correspond to the interests Holland describes (Betz, Harmon, & Borgen, 1996).

One important limitation in Holland's theory is that it ignores the context in which occupational decisions are made. For example, he overlooks the fact that many people have little choice in the kind of job they can get because of external factors such as family, financial pressures, or ethnicity. Holland takes a static view of both personality and occupations, but it must be recognized that what occupation we choose is not dictated solely by what we are like. Equally important is the dynamic interplay between us and the sociocultural context we find ourselves in—just as one would suspect, given the biopsychosocial model presented in Chapter 1. Occupational selection is a complex developmental process involving interactions among personal, ethnic, gender, and economic factors.

OCCUPATIONAL DEVELOPMENT

For most of us, getting a job is not enough; we would also like to move up the ladder. Promotion is a measure of how well one is doing in one's career. How quickly occupational advancement occurs (or does not) may lead to such labels as "fast-tracker" or "dead-ender." Bill Clinton, inaugurated as the president of the United States at age 46, is an example of a fast-tracker. People who want to advance learn quickly how long to stay at one level and how to seize opportunities as they occur, while others experience the frustration of remaining in the same job, with no chance for promotion.

How a person advances in a career seems to depend on professional socialization, which is the socialization that occurs when people learn the unwritten rules of an organization. These rules include several factors other than those that are important in choosing an occupation; among them are expectations, support from coworkers, priorities, and job satisfaction. Before we consider these aspects, let's look at a general scheme of occupational development.

Super's Theory

Over four decades, Super (1957, 1980) developed a theory of occupational development based on self-concept, first introduced in Chapter 9. He proposed a progression through five distinct stages during adulthood, resulting from changes in individuals' self-concept and adaptation to an occupational role: implementation, establishment, maintenance, deceleration, and retirement (see Figure 12.1). *People are located along a continuum of vocational maturity through their working years; the more congruent their occupational behaviors are with what is expected of them at different ages, the more vocationally mature they are.* The initial two phases of Super's theory, crystallization and specification, occur primarily during adolescence, and the first adulthood phase has its origins then as well. Each of the stages in adulthood has distinctive characteristics:

AP/Wide World Photos

As the second youngest person ever elected president of the United States at age 46, Bill Clinton is a fast-tracker.

- The *implementation* stage begins in late adolescence or the early 20s, when people take a series of temporary jobs to learn firsthand about work roles and to try out some possible career choices. Summer internships that many students use to gain experience are one example.

Implementation ➡ Establishment ➡ Maintenance ➡ Deceleration ➡ Retirement

■ **Figure 12.1**
Super's theory describes the development of occupations.

- The *establishment* stage begins with selecting a specific occupation during young adulthood. It continues as the person advances up the career ladder in the same occupation. Taking a position in a law firm and working one's way up to partner or beginning as a sales clerk in a store in a mall and moving up to store manager are two examples.

- The *maintenance* stage is a transition phase during middle age as workers begin to reduce the amount of time they spend fulfilling work roles. Some middle-aged adults increase the time they spend volunteering as coaches for children's sports teams or for their church; other middle-aged adults spend more time with their families.

- The *deceleration* stage begins as workers begin planning in earnest for their upcoming retirement and separating themselves from their work. Sitting down with a financial planner to review one's retirement savings and starting a hobby that one plans to do after retirement are examples.

- The *retirement* stage begins when people stop working full-time. Ideally, people are then able to implement the plans they made in the previous stage.

In Super's framework, people's occupations evolve in response to changes in their self-concept (Salomone, 1996). So, for example, a high-level executive could decide to take a lower ranking position if her sense of self changed from a high need to be in charge to one with a lower need. Consequently, this is a developmental process that reflects and explains important life changes. This developmental process complements Holland's ideas. Investigative and enterprising types are likely to come from more affluent families, in which the parents tend not to be in investigative or enterprising occupations. Interestingly, initial occupational goals are not as important for social types as for the other two types; social types appeared to be more flexible in eventual occupational choice.

A shortcoming of Super's theory is that the progression assumes that once people choose an occupation, they stay in it for the rest of their working lives. Although this may have been true for many employees in the past, it is not the case for most North American workers today (Cascio, 1995). The downsizing of public and private organizations since the late 1980s has all but eliminated the notion of lifetime job security with a particular employer. It remains to be seen whether new developmental stages will be found to underlie the new occupational reality.

Nevertheless, a longitudinal study of 7,649 individuals born in the United Kingdom showed that occupational aspirations at age 16 predicted actual occupational attainments in science, health professions, or engineering at age 33 (Schoon, 2001). Adult occupational attainment was also related to belief in one's own ability, mathematical test performance, several personality characteristics, sociocultural background, and gender. These results point to the importance of viewing occupational development as a true developmental process, as Super claimed, as well as the importance of personal characteristics, as Holland claimed.

THINK ABOUT IT

What biological, psychological, sociocultural, and life-cycle forces influence the progression of one's career?

Occupational Expectations

As we saw in Chapter 9, individuals form opinions about what work in a particular occupation will be like based on what they learn in school and from their parents, peers, other adults, and the media. People have expectations regarding what they want to become and when they hope to get there. Levinson and his colleagues (1978) built these expectations into their theory of adult male development, which was later extended to women (Levinson & Levinson, 1996). Based on findings from the original longitudinal study begun in the 1940s on men attending an elite private college, Levinson and his colleagues (1978) found considerable similarity among the participants in terms of major life tasks during adulthood. *Forming a **dream**, with one's career playing a prominent role, is one of the young adult's chief tasks.*

Throughout adulthood, people continue to refine and update their occupational expectations. This usually involves trying to achieve the dream, monitoring progress toward it, and changing or even abandoning it as necessary. For some, modifying the dream comes as a result of realizing that interests have changed or that the dream was not a good fit. In other cases, failure leads to changing the dream—for example, dropping a business major because one is failing economics courses. Other causes are age, racial, or sexual discrimination; lack of opportunity; obsolescence of skills; and changing interests. In some cases, one's initial occupational choice may simply have been unrealistic. Some goal modification is essential from time to time, but it usually surprises us to realize that we could have been wrong about what seemed to be a logical choice in the past. As Marie, a 38-year-old advertising manager, put it, "I really thought I wanted to be a pilot; the travel sounded really interesting. But it just wasn't what I expected."

Research supports these personal experiences. Rindfuss, Cooksey, and Sutterlin (1999) examined the stability of occupational expectations during the first 7 years after high school and their correspondence with occupations held at age 30. They found much instability in occupational expectations during the late teens and early 20s. Even when occupational expectations are measured as late as age 25, fewer than half of the men and women studied actually achieved the level of job they expected. When they do not achieve their expectations, work roles at age 30 differed by gender. Men tend to move into higher managerial occupations, whereas women tend to move down or leave the labor force.

Mar Romanelli /Getty Images

Reality shock typically hits younger workers soon after they begin an occupation.

Perhaps the rudest jolt for most of us first comes during the transition from school to the real world (Rindfuss et al., 1999). Reality shock sets in, and things never seem to happen the way we expect. Reality shock befalls everyone, from the young worker to the accountant who learns that the financial forecast that took days to prepare may simply end up in a file cabinet (or, worse yet, in the wastebasket). The visionary aspects of the dream may not disappear altogether, but a good dose of reality goes a long way toward bringing a person down to earth. Such feedback plays an increasingly important role in a person's occupational development and self-concept. For example, the woman who thought that she would receive the same rewards as her male counterparts for comparable work is likely to become increasingly angry and disillusioned when her successes result in smaller raises and fewer promotions.

The Role of Mentors

Imagine how hard it would be to figure out everything you needed to know in a new job with no support from the people around you. Entering an occupation involves more than the relatively short formal training a person receives. Indeed, much of the most critical information is not taught in training seminars. Instead, most people are shown the ropes by coworkers. In many cases, an older, more experienced person makes a specific effort to do this, taking on the role of a *mentor*. Although mentors (or "coaches") by no means provide the only source of guidance in the workplace, they have been studied fairly closely.

A mentor is part teacher, part sponsor, part model, and part counselor (Heimann & Pittenger, 1996). The mentor helps a young worker avoid trouble ("Be careful what you say around Harry"). He or she also provides invaluable information about the unwritten rules that govern day-to-day activities in the workplace (not working too fast on the assembly line, wearing the right clothes, and so on), with mentors being sensitive to the employment situation (such as guarding against playing favorites if the mentee is a direct report, a union environment, or cross-gender mentor/mentee) (Smith, Howard, & Harrington, 2005). As part of the relationship, a mentor makes sure that his or her protégé is noticed and receives credit for good work from supervisors. Thus, occupational success often depends on the quality of the mentor-protégé relationship and the protégé's perceptions of its importance (Eddleston, Baldridge, & Veiga, 2004).

Kram (1985) theorized that the mentor relationship develops through four phases: initiation (mentors and protégés begin the relationship), cultivation (mentors work with protégés), separation (protégés and mentors spend less time together), and redefinition (the mentor-protégé relationship either ends or is transformed into a different type of relationship). Research supports this developmental process, as well as the benefits of having a mentor (Chao, 1997). Clearly, protégés get tangible benefits from having a mentor.

What do mentors get from the relationship? In Chapter 1, we saw that the ideas in Erikson's theory (1982) included important aspects of adulthood related to work. Helping a younger employee learn the job is one way to fulfill aspects of Erikson's phase of generativity. As we will see in more detail in Chapter 13, generativity reflects middle-aged adults' need to ensure the continuity of society through activities such as socialization or having children. In work settings, generativity is most often expressed through mentoring. In particular, the mentor ensures that there is some continuity in the corporation or profession by passing on the knowledge and experience he or she has gained over the years. Additionally, leaders may need to serve as mentors to activate transformational leadership (leadership that changes the direction of an organization) and promote positive work attitudes and career expectations of followers, enabling the mentor to rise to a higher level in his or her own career (Scandura & Williams, 2004).

Some researchers suggest that women have a greater need for mentors than men (Blake-Beard, 2001). For example, Blake-Beard points out that although women have achieved virtual parity with men in entering most organizations, within 5 to 6 years their careers begin to lag behind those of their male counterparts. When paired with mentors, women have higher expectations about career advancement opportunities (Baugh, Lankau, & Scandura, 1996). Female lawyers with mentors earn more, are promoted more often, are treated more fairly, and are integrated better in the firm than women without mentors (Wallace, 2001). However, women seem to have a more difficult time finding adequate mentors; some evidence suggests that only one third of professional women find mentors as young adults (Kittrell, 1998). One reason is that there are few female role models who could serve a mentoring function, especially in upper-level management. Although female lawyer protégés with male mentors may earn more than those with female mentors, those mentored by women report more career satisfaction, more intent to continue practicing law, more achievement of professional expectations, and less work-family conflict (Wallace, 2001).

Women employees typically prefer and may achieve more from a female mentor.

Despite the evidence that having a mentor can have many positive effects on one's occupational development, there is an important caveat. Having a poor mentor is worse than having no mentor at all (Ragins, Cotton, & Miller, 2000). A mentoring program is only as good as the mentor. Consequently, prospective protégés must choose a mentor carefully, and mentorship programs need to select motivated and skilled individuals who are provided with extensive training.

JOB SATISFACTION

What does it mean to be satisfied with one's job or occupation? In a general sense, **job satisfaction** *is the positive feeling that results from an appraisal of one's work.* Job satisfaction tends to increase gradually with age (Sterns & Gray, 1999). Why is this the case? There are several reasons.

First, self-selection factors suggest that people who truly like their jobs tend to stay in them, whereas people who do not tend to leave (Hom & Kinicki, 2001). This connection is explored in more detail in the Spotlight on Research feature. To the extent that this is the case, age differences in job satisfaction may simply reflect the fact that with sufficient time, many people eventually find a job with which they are reasonably happy.

SPOTLIGHT ON RESEARCH

THE CONNECTION BETWEEN JOB SATISFACTION AND EMPLOYEE TURNOVER

Who were the investigators and what was the aim of the study? Hom and Kinicki (2001) tested a model of how employee dissatisfaction results in the decision to leave one's job. Researchers since the 1970s have been studying the various steps between people's attitudes toward their jobs and their ultimate decision to quit. Despite decades of work, the causal mechanisms underlying the dissatisfaction-quit process have yet to be specified clearly. Hom and Kinicki wanted to learn whether avoiding certain jobs (such as avoiding jobs that require supervising others or relocation), interrole conflict, and employment conditions also affect people's decisions to quit.

How did the investigators measure the topic of interest? The researchers used a set of questions for most of the

variables of interest. In addition, they used the following scales. Satisfaction with work hours, team, and duties was measured with 5-point scales. Interrole conflict reported the extent to which jobs interfered with community and personal activities and was measured on a 4-point scale. Participants rated the extent to which job seeking would produce stress, alternative jobs, personal costs, impact on personal and work time, and job interference on 5-point scales. Respondents also indicated how often during the last 3 months they had used methods to prepare or to look for jobs on a 4-point scale.

Who were the participants in the study? Hom and Kinicki used data from a national survey of 438 managers, salespersons, and auto mechanics conducted in the spring of 1997. The aver-

age age of the sample was 31.4 years, 62% were married, and 91% were European Americans.

What was the design of the study? The study used a cross-sectional design for the administration of the survey.

Were there ethical concerns with the study? Because the study involved voluntary completion of a survey, there were no ethical concerns.

What were the results? Hom and Kinicki's findings supported a complex model that provides an explanatory framework for why people leave their jobs (see Figure 12.2). Several aspects of the model are important. First, conflict between work and other aspects of a person's life (interrole conflict) affect job satisfaction and thoughts about leaving the job (withdrawal cognitions). These, in turn, affect whether the person thinks

■ **Figure 12.2**
Whether someone actually leaves a job (turnover) is directly influenced by thoughts about withdrawing from one's company (withdrawal cognitions) and by comparing alternative jobs (compared alternatives), which in turn are influenced by several other variables.

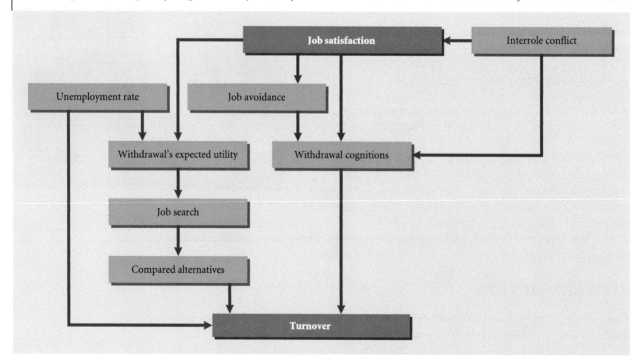

things might be better elsewhere (withdrawal's expected utility), which in turn affects whether the person actually begins a job search. Actually resigning (turnover) results from a combination of thinking about leaving, finding a better alternative (compared alternatives), and the actual unemployment rate.

What have the investigators concluded? The most important finding from the study is the importance of interrole conflict between work and other aspects of a person's life. Prior to this

study, few researchers included this concept in studies of employee turnover. The importance of interrole conflict means that employers need to pay more attention to the balance people need between their work roles and their other roles.

What converging evidence would strengthen these conclusions? Hom and Kinicki's study examined only a few job types. It will be important to test their model with other occupational classifications. Also, it will be important to

study a more diverse group of employees. The present study had overrepresentation by European Americans compared with the actual labor force in the United States.

To enhance your understanding of this research, go to http://psychology .wadsworth.com/kail_cavanaugh4e/ to complete critical thinking questions and explore related websites.

Second, the relationship between worker age and job satisfaction is complex. Satisfaction does not increase in all areas and job types with age. Middle-aged workers are more satisfied with the intrinsic personal aspects of their jobs, such as perceived control and self-efficacy, than they are with the extrinsic aspects, such as pay (Glickman, 2001; Mirabella, 2001). White-collar professionals show an increase in job satisfaction, whereas those in blue-collar positions do not (Sterns, Marsh, & McDaniel, 1994).

Third, increases in job satisfaction may not result from age alone but rather from the degree to which there is a good fit between the worker and the job (Holland, 1997). Middle-aged workers have had more time to find a job that they like or may have resigned themselves to the fact that things are unlikely to improve, resulting in a better congruence between worker desires and job attributes (Glickman, 2001). Middle-aged workers also may have revised their expectations over the years to better reflect the actual state of affairs.

Fourth, as workers get older, they make work less of a focus in their lives, partly because they have achieved occupational success. Consequently, it takes less to keep them satisfied.

Fifth, the type of job and the degree of family responsibilities at different career stages may influence the relationship between age and job satisfaction (Engle et al., 1994). This suggests that the accumulation of experience, changing context, and the stage of one's career development may contribute to the increase in job satisfaction.

Finally, job satisfaction may be cyclical. That is, it may show periodic fluctuations that are not related to age per se but rather to changes people intentionally make in their occupations (Shirom & Mazeh, 1988). The idea is that job satisfaction increases over time because people change jobs or responsibilities on a regular basis, thereby keeping their occupation interesting and challenging.

Alienation and Burnout

No job is perfect; there is always something about it that is not as good as it could be. Perhaps the hours are not optimal, the pay is lower than one would like, or the boss does not have a pleasant personality. For most workers, such negatives are merely annoyances. But for others, extremely stressful situations on the job may result in deeply rooted unhappiness with work: alienation and burnout.

When workers feel that what they are doing is meaningless and that their efforts are devalued, or when they do not see the connection between what they do and the final product, a sense of **alienation** *is likely to result.* Studs Terkel's (1974) classic study in which he interviewed several alienated workers found that all of them expressed the feeling that they were nameless, faceless cogs in a large machine. He reported that employees are most likely to feel alienated when they perform routine, repetitive actions such as those on an assembly line, jobs that are most likely to be replaced by technology. But other workers can become alienated too. Given the large number of companies that have downsized

Air traffic controllers experience high levels of stress in their jobs.

hundreds of thousands of workers over the past few decades, white-collar managers and executives do not have the same level of job security that they once had.

What makes employees become alienated? R. Abraham (2000) found that the personality trait of cynicism was the strongest predictor of organizational cynicism and alienation, which resulted in job dissatisfaction. How can employers avoid alienating workers and improve organizational commitment? Research indicates that trust is key (Chen, Aryee, & Lee, 2005). It is also helpful to involve employees in the decision-making process, create flexible work schedules, and institute employee development and enhancement programs. Indeed, many organizations have instituted new practices such as total quality management and related programs partly as a way to address worker alienation. These approaches make a concerted effort to get employees involved in the operation and administration of their plant or office. Contributing positively to the work environment reduces alienation and improves employee commitment and satisfaction (Freund, 2005).

Sometimes the pace and pressure of the occupation becomes more than a person can bear, resulting in **burnout,** *a depletion of a person's energy and motivation, the loss of occupational idealism, and the feeling that one is being exploited.* Burnout is a state of physical, emotional, and mental exhaustion as a result of job stress (Malach-Pines, 2005). Burnout is most common among people in the helping professions, such as teaching, social work, health care (Bozikas et al., 2000), and occupational therapy (Bird, 2001), and for those in the military (Harrington et al., 2001). For example, nurses have high

High-stress jobs such as intensive care nursing often result in burnout.

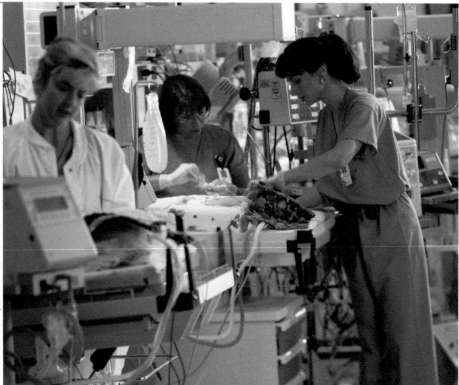

levels of burnout from stress, and as a result are more likely to verbally abuse other nurses (Rowe & Sherlock, 2005). People in these professions must constantly deal with other people's complex problems, usually under difficult time constraints. Dealing with these pressures every day, along with bureaucratic paperwork, may become too much for the worker to bear. Ideals are abandoned, frustration builds, and disillusionment and exhaustion set in. In short, the worker is burned out. And burnout can negatively affect the people who are supposed to receive services from the burned-out employee (Rowe & Sherlock, 2005).

The best defenses against burnout appear to be practicing stress-reduction techniques, lowering people's expectations of themselves, cognitive restructuring of the work situation, and finding alternative ways to enhance personal growth and identity (van Dierendonck, Garssen, & Visser, 2005). No one in the helping professions can resolve all problems perfectly; lowering expectations of what can be realistically accomplished will help workers deal with real-world constraints. Similarly, improving communication among different sections of organizations, to keep workers informed of the outcome of their efforts, gives them a sense that what they do matters in the long run.

In short, making workers feel that they are important to the organization by involving them in decisions, keeping expectations realistic, ensuring good communication, and promoting teamwork helps employees avoid alienation and burnout. As organizations adopt different management styles, perhaps these goals can be achieved.

TEST YOURSELF

1. Compared with workers a few decades ago, workers today are more concerned with individual freedom, personal growth, and _____.

2. Holland's theory deals with the relationship between occupation and _____.

3. Super believes that through their working years, people are located along a continuum of _____.

4. The role of a mentor is part teacher, part sponsor, part model, and part _____.

5. Recent research has shown that job satisfaction does not increase consistently as a person ages; rather, satisfaction may be _____.

6. Two negative aspects of job satisfaction are alienation and _____.

What is the relation between Holland's theory, occupational development, and job satisfaction? Would these relations be different in the case of a person with a good match between personality and occupation rather than a poor match?

Answers: (1) cooperation, (2) personality, (3) vocational maturity, (4) counselor, (5) cyclical, (6) burnout

12.2

GENDER, ETHNICITY, AND DISCRIMINATION ISSUES

Janice, a 35-year-old African American manager at a business consulting firm, is concerned because her career is not progressing as rapidly as she had hoped. Janice works hard and has received excellent performance ratings every year. But she has noticed that there are very few women in upper management positions in her company. Janice wonders whether she will ever be promoted.

LEARNING OBJECTIVES

How do women's and men's occupational expectations differ? How are people viewed when they enter occupations that are not traditional for their gender?

What factors are related to women's occupational development?

What factors affect ethnic minority workers' occupational experiences and occupational development?

What types of bias and discrimination hinder the occupational development of women and ethnic minority workers?

Occupational choice and development are not equally available to all, as Janice is experiencing. Gender, ethnicity, and age may create barriers to achieving one's occupational goals. Although in similar occupations, men and women may come from different backgrounds and may have received somewhat different socialization as children and adolescents, which made it easier or harder for them to set their sights on a career. Bias and discrimination also create barriers to occupational success. In this section, we'll get a better appreciation of the personal and structural barriers that exist for many people.

GENDER DIFFERENCES IN OCCUPATIONAL SELECTION

Traditionally, men have been groomed from childhood for future employment. Boys learn at an early age that men are known by the work they do, and they are strongly encouraged to think about what occupation they would like to have. Occupational achievement is stressed as a core element of masculinity. Important social skills are taught through team games, in which they learn how to play by the rules, to accept setbacks without taking defeat personally, to follow the guidance of a leader, and to move up the leadership hierarchy by demonstrating qualities that are valued by others.

People in similar occupations come from many backgrounds, which affects their experiences.

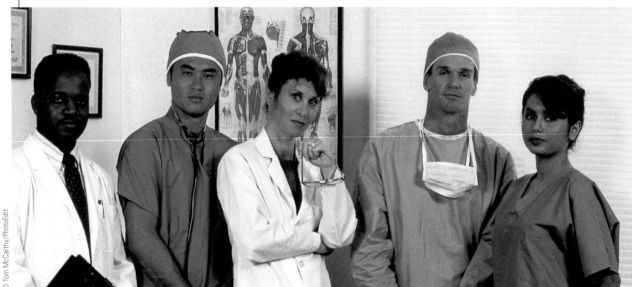

© Tom McCarthy/PhotoEdit

Traditionally, women have not been trained in this manner. The skills that they have learned have been quite different: how to be accommodating, deferential, quiet, and supportive (Shainess, 1984). However, an increasing emphasis has been placed on the importance of providing girls with the necessary skills for occupations outside the home. The growth of women's athletic programs is giving more women the opportunity to learn key skills as well.

Women represent roughly 46% of the total workforce in the United States (U.S. Department of Labor, 2005d). However, major structural barriers to women's occupational selection remain (Maume, 2004; Probert, 2005). Let's take a look at the situation in both traditional and nontraditional occupations.

Traditional and Nontraditional Occupations

In the past, women employed outside the home tended to enter traditional, female-dominated occupations such as secretarial, teaching, and social work jobs. This was due mainly to their socialization into these occupational tracks. However, as more women enter the workforce and as new opportunities are opened for women, a growing number work in occupations that have been traditionally male-dominated, such as construction and engineering. The U.S. Department of Labor (2005c) categorizes women's nontraditional occupations as those in which women comprise 25% or less of the total number of people employed.

Why some women end up in nontraditional occupations appears to be related to personal feelings and experiences as well as to expectations about the occupation and self-efficacy (Aguayo, 2005). Despite the efforts to counteract gender stereotyping of occupations, women who choose nontraditional occupations and are successful tend to be viewed negatively, being described as cold and as having very negative interpersonal characteristics (e.g., in one study, they were described as bitter, quarrelsome, selfish, deceitful, and devious) as compared with similarly successful male managers (Heilman et al., 2004).

In a cross-cultural research study conducted in India, both women and men gave higher "respectability" ratings to males than to females in the same occupation (Kanekar, Kolsawalla, & Nazareth, 1989). People even make inferences about working conditions based on their perception of an occupation as traditionally masculine or feminine. Scozzaro and Subich (1990) report that occupations such as secretarial jobs are perceived as offering nice working conditions, whereas male-dominated occupations are perceived as offering good pay and promotion potential. Worst of all, people are less likely to perceive incidents of sexual coercion as harassing when a woman is in a nontraditional occupation (Burgess & Borgida, 1997).

Taken together, these studies show that we still have a long way to go before people can choose any occupation they want without having to contend with gender-related stereotypes. Although differences in opportunities for women in traditional and nontraditional occupations are narrowing, key differences remain.

WOMEN AND OCCUPATIONAL DEVELOPMENT

If you were to guess what a young woman who has just graduated from college will be doing occupationally 10 years from now, what would you say? Would you guess that she will be strongly committed to her occupation? Will she have abandoned it for other things?

Occupational development for women has undergone major changes over the past several decades. The characteristics and aspirations of women who entered the workforce in the 1950s and those from Generation X (born between 1965 and 1982) are significantly different (Piscione, 2004). For example, women in the 1950s had far fewer occupational choices than their younger counterparts. Table 12.1 presents some quick comparisons.

These differences play out in women's occupational development. In the 21st century, women are starting small businesses at a faster rate than men and are finding that

> **THINK ABOUT IT**
>
> What changes in children's school and other socialization experiences will enable girls to acquire different occupational skills?

TABLE 12.1

Fast Facts About Women in the United States, 1950 Versus 2002

	1950	2002
Population		
Women (in millions)	76,004	143,491
Percent of U.S. population	51%	51%
Percent high school graduates (of total population, age 25 and over)	21	84
Percent college graduates (of total population, age 25 and over)		
1 to 3 years	4	26
4 years or more	3	25
Percent married (of total population)	66	51
Percent working (of total population, age 14 and older)	28.6	60

Women who graduate from college now have more opportunities in the workplace than their grandmothers did.

a home-based business can solve many of the challenges they face in balancing employment and a home life. For those seeking work outside the home, Gen-X women are negotiating beyond the first offer of a job, salary, and benefits package, and are making deals with prospective employers on the work environment best for their career interests and the needs of their family. In this scenario, the employer wins as well; getting a happy employee can provide an employer with cost-savings, increased retention, reduced absenteeism, and greater productivity. These beneficial opportunities for working women include flexible work options, increased personal and vacation time, child care assistance, and benefits that fit individual needs.

Still, some women who work in traditional work environments cite challenges that include pressure to work longer hours, increased commute time, rising child care costs, and limited health care options. The working women in Piscione's (2004) study also report increased financial and emotional stress during their children's summer breaks, or during the after-school hours when their children are home alone. Equally difficult to contend with is the perception in some workplaces of a working mother not being a team player or not being able to do the "tough" work because she may be pulled away by child care needs during a critical time of a project.

Unsupportive or insensitive work environments, organizational politics, and the lack of occupational development opportunities are most important for women working full-time (Silverstein, 2001). In particular, female professionals leave their jobs for two sets of reasons. First, although female professionals need to work interdependently with others to grow professionally, develop personally, and achieve satisfaction in their work, the corporations in which they work are felt to hold contrary values. Corporations more highly value masculine values of working, rewarding individuality, self-sufficiency, and individual contributions, and emphasize tangible outputs, competitiveness, and rationality rather than valuing relationships, interdependence, and collaboration that women seek. Second, women feel disconnected from the workplace. They feel disconnected from their colleagues, clients, and coworkers, derive less meaning from work, and feel alienated from themselves. By mid-career, they conclude that to achieve satisfaction, growth, and development at work, and to be rewarded for the relational skills they considered essential for success, they need to leave corporate life. Clearly, women are focusing on issues that create barriers to their occupational development and personal satisfaction and are looking for ways around these barriers.

Such barriers are a major reason women's workforce participation is discontinuous. Because they cannot find affordable and dependable child care, or freely choose to take on this responsibility, many women stay home while their children are young. Discontinuous participation makes it difficult to maintain an upward trajectory in one's career through promotion, and in terms of maintaining skills. Some women make this choice willingly; however, many find themselves forced into it.

ETHNICITY AND OCCUPATIONAL DEVELOPMENT

What factors are related to occupational selection and development for people from ethnic minorities? Unfortunately, not much research has been conducted from a developmental perspective. Rather, most researchers have focused on the limited opportunities ethnic minorities have and the structural barriers, such as discrimination, that they face. Most of the developmental research to date focuses on occupational selection issues and variables that foster occupational development. Three topics have received the most focus: nontraditional occupations, vocational identity, and issues pertaining to occupational aspirations.

African American women and European American women do not differ in terms of plans to enter nontraditional occupations (Murrell, Frieze, & Frost, 1991). However, African American women who choose nontraditional occupations tend to plan for more formal education than necessary to achieve their goal. This may actually make them overqualified for the jobs they get; for example, a woman with a college degree may be working in a job that does not require that level of education.

Vocational identity is the degree to which one views one's occupation as a key element of identity. Research shows that vocational identity varies with both ethnicity and gender. Compared to European American women and Latino American men, African American and European American men have higher vocational identity when they graduate from college (Steward & Krieshok, 1991). Lower vocational identity means that people define themselves primarily in terms of aspects of their lives other than work.

A person's occupational aspiration is the kind of occupation he or she would like to have. In contrast, occupational expectation is the occupation the person believes he or she will actually get. Latino Americans differ from European Americans in several ways with regard to these variables. They have high occupational aspirations but low expectations, and they differ in their educational attainment as a function of national origin, generational status, and social class (Arbona, 1990).

However, Latino Americans are similar to European Americans in occupational development and work values. In the area of leadership aspiration, or the degree to which one aspires to a leadership position in one's company, African American workers have significantly lower leadership aspirations than European American workers (Clarke-Anderson, 2005).

Research on occupational development of ethnic minority workers is clear on one point: Whether an organization is responsive to the needs of ethnic minorities makes a big difference for employees. Both European American and ethnic minority managers who perceive their organizations as responsive and positive for ethnic minority employees are more satisfied with and committed to the organization (Burke, 1991a, 1991b). But much still remains to be accomplished. African American managers report less choice of jobs, less acceptance, more career dissatisfaction, lower performance evaluations and promotability ratings, and more rapid attainment of plateaus in their careers than European American managers (Greenhaus, Parasuraman, & Wormley, 1990). Over 60% of African American protégés have European American mentors, which is problematic because same-ethnicity mentors provide more psychosocial support than

Daniel Bosler/Getty Images

Whether her company is responsive to the needs of minority employees affects this woman's satisfaction with her employer.

cross-ethnicity mentors (Thomas, 1990). Nevertheless, having any good mentor is more beneficial than having none (Bridges, 1996).

BIAS AND DISCRIMINATION

Since the 1960s, organizations in the United States have been sensitized to the issues of bias and discrimination in the workplace. Hiring, promotion, and termination procedures have come under close scrutiny in numerous court cases, resulting in judicial rulings governing these processes.

Gender Bias and the Glass Ceiling

Even though the majority of women work outside the home, women in high-status jobs are unusual (Mitchell, 2000); only about 5% of senior managers (vice president or above) in Fortune 1500 companies are women. Not until 1981 was a woman, Sandra Day O'Connor, appointed to the U.S. Supreme Court; it took another 12 years before a second woman, Ruth Bader Ginsburg, was appointed. As Janice noticed in the vignette, few women serve in the highest ranks of major corporations, and women are substantially outnumbered at the senior faculty level of most universities and colleges.

Why are there so few women? *The most important reason is **gender discrimination,** denying a job to someone solely on the basis of whether the person is a man or a woman.* Lovoy (2001) points out that gender discrimination is pervasive in the workplace. Despite some progress over the past two decades, sex discrimination is still common: Women are being kept out of high-status jobs by the men at the top (Barnes, 2005; Reid, Miller, & Kerr, 2004).

*Women themselves refer to a **glass ceiling,** the level to which they may rise in a company but beyond which they may not go.* The glass ceiling is a major barrier for women

Associate Justice Sandra Day O'Connor was the first woman on the U.S. Supreme Court. She retired in 2005.

Associate Justice Ruth Bader Ginsburg was the second woman on the U.S. Supreme Court, appointed 12 years after Associate Justice O'Connor.

AP/Wide World Photos

AP/Wide World Photos

(Maume, 2004), and the greatest barrier facing them is at the boundary between lower-tier and upper-tier job grades. Women like Janice tend to move to the top of the lower tier and remain there, whereas men are more readily promoted to the upper tier, even when other factors, such as personal attributes and qualifications and job performance, are controlled (Lovoy, 2001).

Clear evidence of the glass ceiling has been found in private corporations (Lyness & Thompson, 1997), government agencies (Reid et al., 2004), and nonprofit organizations (Shaiko, 1996). The glass ceiling has also been used to account for why African Americans do not advance as much in their careers as European American men (Johnson, 2000; Phelps & Constantine, 2001). It also provides a framework for understanding limitations to women's careers in many countries around the world (Mugadza, 2005; Zafarullah, 2000).

What can be done to begin eliminating the glass ceiling? Mitchell (2000) suggests that companies must begin to value the competencies women develop, such as being more democratic and interpersonally oriented than men, and to assist men in feeling more comfortable with their female colleagues. Mentoring is also an important aspect. Lovoy (2001) adds that companies must be more proactive in promoting diversity, provide better and more detailed feedback about performance and where employees stand regarding promotion, and establish ombuds offices (offices in companies that provide a safe place for employees to complain about working conditions or their supervisor and have protection) that help women deal with difficulties on the job.

In addition to discrimination in hiring and promotion, women are also subject to pay discrimination. According to the U.S. Department of Labor (2004), in many occupations men are paid substantially more than women in the same positions; indeed, on average, women are paid less than 80% of what men are paid on an annual basis. As you can see in Figure 12.3, the wage gap has been narrowing slowly since the late 1970s.

Several solutions to this problem have been promoted. *One of these is* **comparable worth**: *equalizing pay across occupations that are determined to be equivalent in importance but differ in the gender distribution of the people doing the jobs.* Determining which male-dominated occupations should be considered equivalent to which female-dominated occupations for pay purposes can be difficult and controversial. One way to do this is with gender-neutral job evaluations, which examine all positions within an organization to establish fair-pay policies (Castro, 1997).

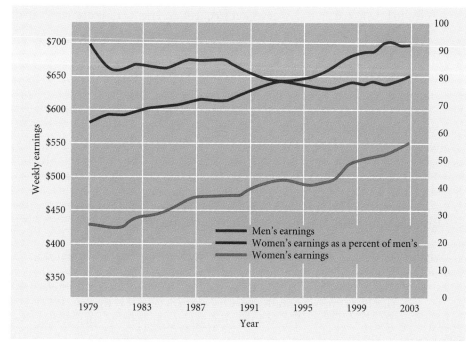

■ **Figure 12.3**
The gap between men's and women's average weekly wages has been closing slowly since the 1970s.

U.S. Department of Labor (2004).

Sexual Harassment

Suppose you have been working very hard on a paper for a course and think you've done a good job. When indeed you receive an "A" for the paper, you are elated. When you discuss your paper (and your excitement) with your instructor, you receive a big hug. How do you feel? What if this situation involved a project at work and the hug came from your boss? Your coworker? What if it were a kiss on your lips instead of a hug?

Whether such behavior is acceptable has become a major topic of debate in the United States over the past few decades. Although sexual harassment of women has been documented for centuries, only more recently has it received much attention from researchers (Sbraga & O'Donohue, 2000). Interest among U.S. researchers increased dramatically after the 1991 Senate hearings involving Supreme Court nominee Clarence Thomas and Anita Hill, who accused him of sexual harassment, the scandals involving military personnel, and charges against President Bill Clinton. By no means is sexual harassment a U.S.-only phenomenon; sad to say, it occurs around the world (Luo, 1996).

Research on sexual harassment focuses on situations in which there is a power differential between two people, most often involving men with more power over women (Berdahl, Magley, & Waldo, 1996). Such situations exist in the workplace and in academic settings (Zappert, 1996). However, peer-to-peer harassment also occurs, such as among classmates in academic settings (Ivy & Hamlet, 1996).

How many people have been sexually harassed? Evidence suggests that about 58% of women report they have experienced potentially harassing behaviors, which typically involve behaviors such as comments, jokes, brushes of hands on shoulders, and so on (Ilies et al., 2003). Reliable statistics on more serious forms of harassment, such as touching and sexual activity, are more difficult to obtain, in part due to the unwillingness of many victims to report harassment and to differences in reporting procedures. Even given these difficulties, evidence from meta-analytic research indicates that at least 28% of women report having been sexually harassed in the workplace (Ilies et al., 2003). Victims are most often single or divorced women under age 35 (Tang & McCollum, 1996).

What effects does being sexually harassed have? Research evidence shows clear, negative job-related, psychological, and physical health outcomes (Lim & Cortina, 2005). Establishing the degree of problems is difficult, though, because many women try to minimize or hide their reactions or feelings (Tang & McCollum, 1996). It is becoming evident, however, that one does not have to experience the worst kinds of sexual harassment to be affected. Even low-level but frequent experience of sexual harassment can have significant negative consequences for women (Schneider, Swan, & Fitzgerald, 1997).

Cultural differences in labeling behaviors as sexually harassing are also important. For example, one study found that U.S. women judged specific interactions as more harassing than U.S. men, but women and men from Australia, Brazil, and Germany did not differ in their judgments (Pryor et al., 1997). Unfortunately, little research has been done to identify what aspects of organizations foster harassment or to determine the impact of educational programs aimed at addressing the problem.

In 1998, the U.S. Supreme Court (*Oncale v. Sundowner Offshore Services*) ruled that sexual harassment is not limited to female victims, but that the relevant laws also protect men. This case is also important for establishing that same-sex harassment is barred by the same laws that ban heterosexual harassment (Knapp & Kustis, 2000). Thus, the standard by which sexual harassment is judged could now be said to be a "reasonable person" standard.

What can be done to provide people with safe work and learning environments, free from sexual harassment? Training in gender awareness is a common approach that often works (Tang & McCollum, 1996). Clearly differentiating between workplace romance and sexual harassment is another essential element (Pierce & Aguinis, 1997). The Current Controversies feature discusses the complexities involved in solving the problem. Take a minute to read it, and ask yourself what you would do.

THINK ABOUT IT

What are the key biological, psychological, sociocultural, and life-cycle factors that should inform training programs concerning sexual harassment?

CURRENT CONTROVERSIES

IS IT SEXUAL HARASSMENT?

What would have to be going on for you to label a behavior sexual harassment? Defining sexual harassment turns out to be much more difficult than many people think. Sure, the most egregious forms (such as requiring a woman to have sex in exchange for a promotion or a grade) are easy. Where it gets more difficult are in the "gray areas" such as brief touches and comments.

Sbraga and O'Donohue (2000) reviewed 30 years of writing in psychology and law concerning the definition of sexual harassment. They point out that definitions disagree on whether a power differential must be present for behaviors to be called sexual harassment, whether a specific location must be identified, whether the behavior must be perceived as harassment by the victim, whether men can be the objects of harassment, whether sexist behavior is included under the guise of sexual harassment, and whether the behaviors are considered to be harassment apart from any negative consequences they create. Lim and Cortina (2005) point out that sexual harassment often occurs in the context of general incivility in workplace settings. Based on considerable research, Fitzgerald and colleagues (1997) proposed three major categories of sexual harassment:

- *Sexual coercion:* an attempt to force sexual compliance in exchange for workplace (or educational) benefits or threats of punishment. It is the least frequently reported type.
- *Unwanted sexual attention:* sexual conduct in the workplace or school that can be either verbal or nonverbal and that is unwanted by the victim and creates an intimidating, hostile, or offensive environment. Common examples include repeated requests

for a date and risqué comments about clothing.
- *Gender harassment:* sexist remarks or behavior based on stereotypes of the sexes, including making sexist jokes, displaying nude photographs, and making comments about another's body. This is the most common form, with up to 70% of women reporting experiencing gender harassment (Sbraga & O'Donohue, 2000).

In general, women are more likely to view such behaviors as offensive than are men (Rotundo, Nguyen, & Sackett, 2001). Specifically, women perceive a broader range of social-sexual behavior as harassing. *Because of this gender gap in perceptions, a federal court, in the case of* Ellison v. Brady, *instituted the "reasonable woman" standard as the appropriate legal criterion for determining whether sexual harassment has occurred.* If a reasonable woman would view a behavior as offensive, the court held, then it is offensive even if the man

did not consider it to be so. Even this standard, though, is more likely to be understood by women than by men (Wiener et al., 1997).

When specific behaviors are examined, touching the cheek of a person of the opposite sex sends particularly strong relational and emotional messages (e.g., flirtation and attraction) and is rated as the most inappropriate and sexually harassing of types of touch (Lee & Guerrero, 2001). Putting one's arm around another's waist is also seen as highly inappropriate and harassing. Shaking hands is viewed as the least offensive form of touch.

Most companies now have training programs to try to eliminate sexual harassment. If designed well, they can be effective in reducing the number of complaints (Sbraga & O'Donohue, 2000). However, it is unlikely that sexual harassment will disappear in the near future. Only through considerable socialization and education can we hope to eliminate it eventually.

Is the situation depicted here an example of sexual harassment?

© Gabe Palmer/Corbis

Age Discrimination

Another structural barrier to occupational development is **age discrimination,** which involves denying a job or promotion to someone solely on the basis of age. The U.S. Age Discrimination in Employment Act of 1986 protects workers over age 40. Similar laws are required in the United Kingdom by December 2006 (Duncan & Loretto, 2004). These laws stipulate that people must be hired based on their ability, not their age. Under this law, employers are banned from refusing to hire and from discharging workers solely on

Employers cannot make a decision not to hire this woman solely on the basis of her age.

the basis of age. Additionally, employers cannot segregate or classify workers or otherwise denote their status on the basis of age.

Employment prospects for middle-aged people around the world are lower than for their younger counterparts. For example, age discrimination toward those over age 45 is common in Germany (Frerichs & Naegele, 1997), Britain (Ginn & Arber, 1996), and Hong Kong (Chiu et al., 2001) resulting in longer periods of unemployment, early retirement, or negative attitudes. Such practices may save companies money in the short run, but the loss of expertise and knowledge comes at a high price. Indeed, global corporations are beginning to realize that retraining and integrating middle-aged workers is a better strategy (Frerichs & Naegele, 1997).

Age discrimination may occur in several ways but is not typically demonstrated by professional human resources staff (Kager, 2000). Age discrimination usually happens prior to or after interaction with human resources staff by other employees making the hiring decisions. For example, employers can make certain types of physical or mental performance a job requirement and argue that older workers cannot meet the standard prior to an interview. Or they can attempt to get rid of older workers by using retirement incentives. Supervisors' stereotyped beliefs sometimes factor in performance evaluations for raises or promotions or in decisions about which employees are eligible for additional training (Chiu et al., 2001).

TEST YOURSELF

1. Women who choose nontraditional occupations are viewed _____ by their peers.

2. Among the reasons women in well-paid occupations leave, _____ are most important for part-time workers.

3. Ethnic minority workers are more satisfied with and committed to organizations that are responsive and provide _____.

4. Three barriers to women's occupational development are sex discrimination, the glass ceiling, and _____.

What steps need to be taken to eliminate gender, ethnic, and age bias in the workplace?

Answers: (1) negatively, (2) family obligations, (3) positive work environments, (4) pay discrimination

---

LEARNING OBJECTIVES

Why do people change occupations?

Is worrying about potential job loss a major source of stress?

How does the timing of job loss affect the amount of stress experienced?

12.3

OCCUPATIONAL TRANSITIONS

Fred has 32 years of service for an automobile manufacturer. Over the years, more and more assembly-line jobs have been eliminated due to robots and other technology and the export of manufacturing jobs to other countries. Although Fred has been assured by his boss that his job is safe, he isn't so sure. He worries that he could be laid off at any time.

IN THE PAST, people like Fred commonly chose an occupation during young adulthood and stayed in it throughout their working years. Today, however, not many people take a job with the expectation that it will last a lifetime. Corporations have restructured globally so often that employees now assume occupational changes are part of the career process. Such corporate actions mean that people's conceptions of work and career are in flux, and that losing one's job does not necessarily have only negative meaning (Haworth & Lewis, 2005). The case of Kevin, told in the Real People feature, exemplifies many of these aspects of occupational change.

REAL PEOPLE: Applying Human Development

CHANGING OCCUPATIONS TO FIND SATISFYING WORK

From the time he was in college, Kevin knew he wanted to be an accountant. His only question was whether it would be in a large public accounting firm or in a private corporation. After much consideration (and several job offers), he chose to work for a major global corporation. Kevin rose through the ranks, and all seemed well. He eventually was in charge of the Far East division of the international tax unit, which allowed him to travel to fun and exotic places.

However, Kevin's company, like many others, went through several rounds of downsizing. Although his job was extremely secure, Kevin saw his staff reduced considerably. These cuts led to many long hours and much more job stress. So, after 17 years with the company, Kevin decided that even though the pay was good, the hours and the stress were not worth it. He left, and began working for a start-up biotechnology firm. At first, conditions were much better. But soon the long hours and stress started in again. This time, he quit with no new job. He needed time to think and re-set his priorities.

After much careful thought, he decided that what he really wanted was to work in a nonprofit organization. Eventually, he ended up with a large foundation that funds minority businesses and other community-based companies. He worked for this non-profit for several years, eventually rising to the position of Chief Operating Officer. But when his wife decided that she wanted to return to the workforce and retrain as a high school science and math teacher, Kevin decided to change occupations again and stay at home with their two sons. Now Kevin does financial and accounting consulting from home, and his choice is working well.

The changes for Kevin have been very successful. Although he makes much less money than he did in the private sector and less than as a COO, he is much happier and less stressed. And for him, this is worth it all.

Several factors have been identified as important in determining who will remain in an occupation and who will change. Some factors—such as whether the person likes the occupation—lead to self-initiated occupation changes like Kevin experienced. For example, people who really like their occupation may seek additional training or accept overtime assignments in hopes of acquiring new skills that will enable them to get better jobs. Others will use the training to become more marketable. However, other factors, such as obsolete skills and economic trends, cause forced occupational changes. For example, continued improvement of robots has caused some auto industry workers to lose their jobs; corporations send jobs overseas to increase profits; and economic recessions usually result in large-scale layoffs. But even forced occupational changes can have benefits. As we saw in Chapter 10, for instance, many adults go to college. Some are taking advantage of educational benefits offered as part of a severance package. Others are pursuing educational opportunities to obtain new skills; still others are looking to advance in their careers.

In this section, we explore the positive and negative aspects of occupational transitions. First we examine the retraining of midcareer and older workers. The increased use of technology, corporate downsizing, and an aging workforce has focused attention on the need to keep older workers' skills current. Later, we will examine occupational insecurity and the effects of job loss.

Seminars such as this are taken by thousands of workers around the world each year as part of worker training and retraining programs.

RETRAINING WORKERS

When you are hired into a specific job, you are selected because your employer believes you offer the best fit between the abilities you already have and those needed to perform the job. As most people can attest, though, the skills needed to perform a job usually change over time. Such changes may be due to the introduction of new technology, additional responsibilities, or promotion.

Unless a person's skills are kept up to date, the outcome is likely to be either job loss or career plateauing (Froman, 1994). *Career plateauing occurs when there is a lack of promotional opportunity in the organization or when a person decides not to seek advancement.* Research in Canada (Lemire, Saba, & Gagnon, 1999) and in Asia (Lee, 2003) shows that feeling that one's career has plateaued results in less organizational commitment, lower job satisfaction, and a greater tendency to leave.

In cases of job loss or career plateauing, retraining may be an appropriate response. Large numbers of employees globally participate each year in programs and courses offered by their employer or by a college or university aimed at improving existing or adding new job skills. For midcareer employees, retraining might focus on how to advance in one's occupation or how to find new career opportunities—for example, through résumé preparation and career counseling. Because of the aging workforce, retraining programs have been developed that focus specifically on them (Armstrong-Stassen & Templer, 2005). Additional research indicates that companies can take several specific steps to address the problems associated with career plateauing (Lemire et al., 1999; Rotondo & Perrewe, 2000). For example, positive activities such as expanding job assignments, mentoring, clearly defined career paths, and new projects or teams result in more positive attitudes and higher perceived performance among career-plateaued employees.

Many corporations, as well as community and technical colleges, offer retraining programs in a variety of fields. Organizations that promote employee development typically promote in-house courses to improve employee skills. Or they may offer tuition reimbursement programs for individuals who successfully complete courses at colleges or universities.

The retraining of midcareer and older workers highlights the need for lifelong learning (Armstrong-Stassen & Templer, 2005; Sinnott, 1994a). If corporations are to meet the challenges of a global economy, it is imperative that they include retraining in their employee development programs. Such programs will help improve people's chances of advancement in their chosen occupations, and they will also assist people in making successful transitions from one occupation to another.

OCCUPATIONAL INSECURITY

Changing economic conditions in the United States over the past few decades (such as the move toward a global economy), as well as changing demographics, have forced many people out of their jobs. Heavy manufacturing and support businesses (such as the steel, oil, and automotive industries) and farming were the hardest hit during the 1970s and 1980s. But no one is immune. Indeed, the corporate takeover frenzy of the 1980s and the recessions of the early 1990s and early 2000s put many middle- and upper-level corporate executives out of work in all kinds of businesses worldwide.

As a result of these trends, many people feel insecure about their jobs. Like Fred, the autoworker in the vignette, many worried workers have numerous years of dedicated service to a corporation. Unfortunately, people who worry about their jobs tend to have poorer physical and psychological well-being (McKee-Ryan et al., 2005). For example, anxiety about one's job may result in negative attitudes about one's employer or even work in general, which in turn may result in diminished desire to be successful. Whether there is any actual basis for people's feelings of job insecurity may not matter; sometimes what people think is true about their work situation is more important than what is actually the case. Just the possibility of losing one's job can negatively affect physical and psychological health.

So how does the possibility of losing one's job affect employees? Mantler and colleagues (2005) examined coping strategies for comparable samples of laid-off and employed high-technology workers. They found that although unemployed participants reported higher levels of stress compared with employed participants, employment uncertainty mediated the association between employment status and perceived stress. That is, people who believe that their job is in jeopardy and that they might lose it, even if that is untrue, show levels of stress similar to unemployed participants. This was due to differences in coping strategies. There are several different ways in which people deal with stress. Two of the more common ways are emotion-focused coping and problem-focused coping. Some people focus on how the stressful situation makes them feel, so focus their coping on making themselves feel better about it. Others focus on the problem itself, and do something to solve it. People who used emotional avoidance as a strategy reported higher levels of stress, particularly under low uncertainty conditions. So even people whose jobs aren't really in jeopardy can report high levels of stress if they tend to use emotion-focused coping strategies.

> **THINK ABOUT IT**
>
> How do recent changes in job security affect the occupational socialization that children and adolescents receive?

COPING WITH UNEMPLOYMENT

What does it feel like to lose one's job after many years of dedicated service? One man put it this way.

> After becoming used to living like a human being, then losing your job, working six days a week just to make the house payment for two years before selling it at a loss, then losing your wife because of all the hardships that were not your fault, then looking endlessly for a decent job only to find jobs for [minimum wage so that I] can't afford an apartment or any place to live so having to live out of a van for the past two-and-one-half years, *how should one feel?* Please, I'm a hard worker and did a good job. I always go to work—check my record! I want to be normal again, like a real human being with a house instead of a van. (Leana & Feldman, 1992, p. 51)

Being unemployed is very stressful.

As this man states so poignantly, losing one's job can have enormous personal impact (Creede, Bloxsome, & Johnston, 2001; Ebberwein, 2001; McKee-Ryan et al., 2005; Waters & Moore, 2001). Since 2000, unemployment in the United States has ranged from a low of 4% in 2000 to a high of 6% in 2003. Unemployed people commonly experience a wide variety of effects (Viinamaki, Koskela, & Niskanen, 1996). Most important, losing one's job has a negative effect on the individual's well-being (McKee-Ryan et al., 2005).

In a comprehensive meta-analysis of the research on the effects of unemployment, McKee-Ryan and colleagues (2005) found several specific results from losing one's job. Unemployed workers had significantly lower mental health, life satisfaction, marital or family satisfaction, and subjective physical health (how they perceive their health to be) than their employed counterparts. With reemployment, these negative effects disappear. Figure 12.4 shows that physical and psychological health following job displacement is influenced by several factors (McKee-Ryan et al., 2005).

The effects of job loss vary with age and gender. In the United States, middle-aged men are more vulnerable to negative effects than older or younger men, largely because they have greater financial responsibilities than the other two groups, but women report a sharper decline in health (Kulik, 2001a). Research in Spain indicates that gender differences are complexly related to family responsibilities and social class (Artazcoz et al., 2004). Specifically, to the extent that work is viewed as your expected contribution to the family, then losing one's job has a more substantial negative effect. Because this tends to be more the case for men than for women, it helps explain the gender differences.

Life-cycle factors are also important in understanding the reaction to job loss. Leana and Feldman (1992) write that workers in their 50s who lose their jobs are not always highly distressed. Some may have been planning to retire in the near future, others may

■ **Figure 12.4**
Psychological and physical well-being after losing one's job is affected by many variables.

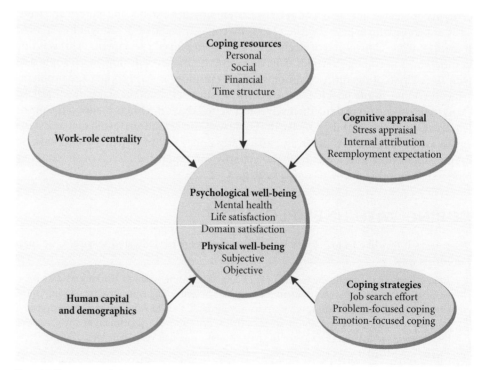

From McKee-Ryan et al. (2005), p. 56.

be hired back as consultants, and still others see it as an opportunity to try something new. If they want to become re-employed, middle-aged people spend more hours per week searching for jobs than do younger adults (Kulik, 2001a).

Because unemployment rates for many ethnic minority groups are substantially higher than for European Americans (U.S. Department of Labor, 2005a), the effects of unemployment are experienced by a greater proportion of people in these groups. As far as is known, however, the nature of the distress resulting from job loss is the same regardless of ethnicity. Compared to European Americans, however, it usually takes minority workers longer to find another job.

Research also offers some advice for adults who are trying to manage occupational transitions (Ebberwein, 2001):

- Approach job loss with a healthy sense of urgency.
- Consider your next career move and what you must do to achieve it, even if there are no prospects for it in sight.
- Admit and react to change as soon as you realize it is there.
- Be cautious of stop-gap employment.
- Identify a realistic goal, and list the steps you must take to achieve it.

These steps may not guarantee that you will find a new job quickly, but they will help create a better sense that you are in control.

THINK ABOUT IT

What are some of the broader effects of unemployment on an individual's personal and family life?

TEST YOURSELF

1. One response to the pressures of a global economy and an aging workforce is to provide _____.

2. Two factors that could cause involuntary occupational change are economic trends and _____.

3. Fear of job loss is often a more important determinant of stress than _____.

4. The age group that is most at risk for negative effects of job loss is _____.

It is likely that the trend toward multiple careers will continue and become the norm. What implications will this have for theories of career development in the future?

Answers: (1) worker retraining, (2) obsolete skills, (3) actual likelihood of job loss, (4) middle-aged adults

---

12.4

WORK AND FAMILY

LEARNING OBJECTIVES

What are the issues faced by employed people who care for dependents?

How do partners view the division of household chores? What is work-family conflict? How does it affect couples' lives?

Jennifer, a 38-year-old sales clerk at a department store, feels that her husband, Bill, doesn't do his share of the housework or child care. Bill says that real men don't do housework, and that he's really tired when he comes home from work. Jennifer thinks that this isn't fair, especially because she works as many hours as her husband.

ONE OF THE MOST DIFFICULT CHALLENGES facing adults like Jennifer is trying to balance the demands of occupation with the demands of family. Over the past few decades, the rapid increase in the number of families in which both parents are employed has fundamentally changed how we view the relationship between work and family. This

Balancing work and family obligations is especially difficult for women.

can even mean taking a young child to work as a way to deal with the pushes and pulls of being an employed parent. In roughly two thirds of two-parent households today, both adults work outside the home (U.S. Department of Labor, 2005a). The main reason? Families need the dual income to pay the bills and maintain a moderate standard of living.

As we will see, dual-earner couples with children experience both benefits and costs from this arrangement. The stresses of living in this arrangement are substantial—and gender differences are clear, especially in the division of household chores.

THE DEPENDENT CARE DILEMMA

Many employed adults must also provide care for dependent children or parents. As we will see, the issues they face are complex.

Employed Caregivers Revisited

Many mothers have no option but to return to work after the birth of a child. In fact, more than half of married mothers and nearly half of unmarried mothers with children under the age of 1 year work for pay (U.S. Department of Labor, 2005b).

Some women, though, grapple with the decision of whether they want to return to work. Surveys of mothers with preschool children reveal that the motivation for returning to work tends to be related to financial need and how attached mothers are to their work. For example, in one survey of Australian mothers, those with high work attachment were more likely to cite intrinsic personal achievement reasons for returning. Those with low work attachment cited pressing financial needs. Those with moderate work attachment were divided between intrinsic and financial reasons (Cotton, Anthill, & Cunningham, 1989). Those who can afford to give up careers and stay home also must deal with changes in identity (Milford, 1997).

Giving up a career means that those aspects of one's identity that came from work must be redefined to come from being a stay-at-home mother. Mothers also worry about conflicts between work and family roles. For some women, returning to work part-time may offer a compromise. Although switching from full-time to part-time work may seem appealing, what matters more is whether mothers are working hours that are close to what they consider ideal and accommodating to their family's needs (Kim, 2000). Perceptions of ideal working hours differ as a function of gender and life-cycle stage regarding children, as shown in Figure 12.5.

An increasing and often overlooked group of employed caregivers are those caring for a parent or partner. Of women in this situation, 60% work at least 35 hours per week (Jenkins, 1997). Because most of these women are middle aged, we will consider their situation in more detail in Chapter 13.

Whether assistance is needed for one's children or parent, key factors in selecting an appropriate care site are quality of care, price, and hours of availability (Helpguide.org, 2005; Mitchell & Messner, 2003–2004). Depending on one's economic situation, it may not be possible to find affordable and quality care that is available when needed. In such cases, there may be no option but to drop out of the workforce or enlist the help of friends and family.

Dependent Care and Effects on Workers

Workers who care for dependents face tough choices. Especially when both partners are employed, dependent care is the central organizing aspect of the couples' lives (Hertz, 1997).

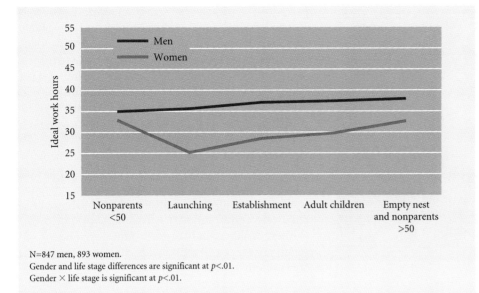

N=847 men, 893 women.
Gender and life stage differences are significant at *p*<.01.
Gender × life stage is significant at *p*<.01.

From P. Moen, *The Cornell Couples and Careers Study,* 1999.

Figure 12.5
The ideal number of hours that men want to work stays about the same regardless of whether they have children; women's ideal number of hours depends on whether they have children and how old they are.

Being responsible for dependent care has significant negative effects, especially for women. For example, when they are responsible for caring for an older parent, women report missing more meetings and being absent from work more often (Gignac, Kelloway, & Gottlieb, 1996). Such women also report higher levels of stress (Jenkins, 1997). Likewise, parents often exhibit poor quality of life and report higher stress and trouble coping with it (Galinsky, Bond, & Friedman, 1996).

How can these negative effects be lessened? When women's partners provide good support and women have average or high control over their jobs, employed mothers are significantly less distressed than employed nonmothers (Roxburgh, 1997) or mothers without support (Rwampororo, 2001). When support and job control are lacking, though, employed mothers are significantly more distressed than employed nonmothers. Clearly, having partner support and being in a job that allows one to have control over such things as one's schedule are key. What employers provide is also important, as we see next.

Dependent Care and Employer Responses

Employed parents with small children are confronted with the difficult act of leaving their children in the care of others. In response to pressure from parents, most developed countries (but not the United States) provide government-supported child care centers for employees as one way to help ease this burden. Does providing a center make a difference in terms of an employee's feelings about work, absenteeism, and productivity?

The answer is that there is no simple answer. Just making a child care center available to employees does not necessarily reduce parents' work-family conflict or their absenteeism, particularly among younger employees (Connelly, Degraff, & Willis, 2004). A "family-friendly" company must also pay attention to the attitudes of their employees and make sure that the company provides broad-based support (Allen, 2001; Grandey, 2001). The keys are how supervisors act and the number and type of benefits the company provides. When the organization adopts a justice approach, in which supervisors are sympathetic and supportive regarding family issues and child care, and provides benefits that employees consider important, employees report less work-family conflict, have lower absenteeism, and report higher job satisfaction.

Research on specific working conditions and benefits that help caregivers perform optimally on the job points to several consistent conclusions. To the extent that employers provide better job security, autonomy, lower productivity demands, supervisor support, and flexible schedules, caregivers fare better (Aryee & Luk, 1996). Job appli-

THINK ABOUT IT

How do the effects of dependent care on mothers relate to the debate of whether children should be placed in day care?

Employers who provide day care centers on-site have more satisfied employees.

cants tend to perceive an organization more positively if it provides flexible work schedules and dependent care and nonwork life assistance (Casper, 2000).

It will be interesting to watch how these issues, especially flexible schedules, play out in the United States where such practices are not yet very common. The passage of the Family and Medical Leave Act in 1993 gave people the right to take unpaid time off to care for their dependents with the right to return to their jobs. Experience from other countries indicates that parental leave affects each parent differently. For example, a large-scale study in Sweden showed that fathers who take parental leave are more likely to continue their involvement in child care and to reduce their work involvement. Regardless of fathers' participation, however, mothers still retain primary responsibility for child care and receive fewer rewards in the labor market.

JUGGLING MULTIPLE ROLES

When both members of a heterosexual couple with dependents are employed, who cleans the house, cooks the meals, and takes care of the children when they are ill? This question gets to the heart of the core dilemma of modern, dual-earner couples: How are household chores divided? How are work and family role conflicts handled?

Dividing Household Chores

Despite much media attention and claims of increased sharing in the duties, women still perform the lion's share of housework, regardless of employment status. As shown in Figure 12.6, working mothers spend up to 50% more hours per week than men in family work, and women bear the greatest responsibility for household and child care tasks (Moen, 1999). This unequal division of labor causes the most arguments and the most unhappiness for dual-earner couples. This is the case with Jennifer and Bill, the couple in the vignette; Jennifer does most of the housework.

A great deal of evidence indicates that since the 1970s women have reduced the amount of time they spend on housework, especially when they are employed, and that men have increased the amount of time they spend on such tasks (Saginak & Saginak, 2005). The increased participation of men in these tasks is not all that it seems, however.

■ **Figure 12.6**
Women spend much more time on household chores than men, even after the children have left (empty nest).

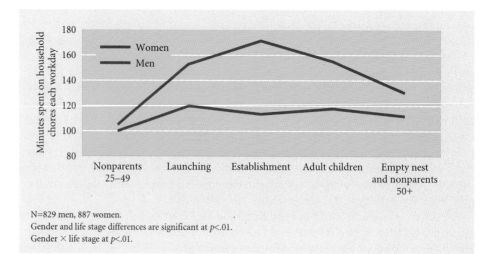

N=829 men, 887 women.
Gender and life stage differences are significant at $p<.01$.
Gender × life stage at $p<.01$.

From P. Moen, *The Cornell Couples and Careers Study,* 1999.

Most of the increase is on weekends, with specific tasks that they agree to perform, and it is largely unrelated to women's employment status. In short, the increase in men's participation has not done much to lower women's burdens around the house.

Men and women view the division of labor in very different terms. Men are often most satisfied with an equitable division of labor based on the number of hours spent, especially if the amount of time needed to perform household tasks is relatively small. Women are often most satisfied when men are willing to perform women's traditional chores (Saginak & Saginak, 2005). When ethnic minorities are studied, much the same is true concerning satisfaction. For example, in African American dual-earner couples, women were twice as likely as men to feel overburdened with housework and to be dissatisfied with their family life (Broman, 1988).

Despite some gains, women still end up doing most of the household tasks, especially those involving child care.

© Left Lane Productions /Corbis

Ethnic differences in the division of household labor are also apparent. In a study of European American, African American, and Latino American men, several interesting patterns emerged (Shelton & John, 1993). African American and Latino American men tend to spend more time doing household tasks than do European American men. In the case of African American men, this finding supports the view that such households are more egalitarian than European American households. Moreover, the increased participation of African American men was primarily true of employed (as opposed to unemployed) men. There was greater participation in traditionally female tasks, such as washing dishes and cooking. Similarly, Latino American men also tended to participate more in these tasks. Overall, European American men spent the least time helping with traditionally female tasks. Clearly, the degree to which men and women divide household tasks varies not only with gender but with ethnicity as well.

International data comparing the United States, Sweden, and The Netherlands indicates that even women who are employed outside the home do much more of the household chores than men in all three countries (Gjerdingen et al., 2000). Not surprisingly, such heavy workloads contribute to poorer health, lower marital satisfaction, and less career advancement. Findings from research in Israel show differences in the amount of gender inequality when women are employed part-time versus full-time; inequality in the division of household chores is greater when women are employed part-time (Stier & Lewin-Epstein, 2000).

In sum, the available evidence from heterosexual couples indicates that women still perform more household tasks than men but that the difference varies with ethnic groups. The discrepancy is greatest when the male endorses traditional masculine gender roles and is less when the male endorses more feminine or androgynous gender roles (Saginak & Saginak, 2005).

Work-Family Conflict

When people have both occupations and children, they must figure out how to balance the demands of each. Parents agonize over how to be at their daughter's ball game at the same time they have to be at an important business meeting. *These competing demands cause **work-family conflict**, which is the feeling of being pulled in multiple directions by incompatible demands from one's job and one's family.*

Dual-earner couples must find a balance between their occupational and family roles. With nearly two thirds of married couples with children comprising dual-earner households (U.S. Department of Labor, 2005a), how to divide the household chores and how to care for the children have become increasingly important.

Many people believe that work and family roles influence each other in such families: When things go badly at work, family suffers, and when there are troubles at home, work suffers. However, this appears not to be the case all the time (Aryee & Luk, 1996).

Whether work influences family or vice versa is a complex function of support resources, type of job, and a host of other factors (Saginak & Saginak, 2005). One key but often overlooked factor is whether the work schedules of both partners mesh (Jacobs & Gerson, 2001).

Of course, it is important that the partners negotiate agreeable arrangements of household and child care tasks, but (as noted earlier) truly equitable divisions of labor are clearly the exception. Most U.S. households with heterosexual dual-worker couples still operate under a gender-segregated system: There are traditional chores for men and women. All of these tasks are important and must be performed to keep homes safe, clean, and sanitary. These tasks also take time. The important point for women is not how much time is spent in performing household chores, but which tasks are performed. What bothers wives the most is not that their husbands are lazy but that they will not perform some "women's work." Men may mow the lawn, wash the car, and even cook, but they rarely vacuum, scrub the toilet, or change the baby's diaper.

The division of labor apparently occurs the way it does because that's how people saw their parents do it, and that's what they are comfortable with. John Cavanaugh had an interesting experience in this regard. While doing some volunteer maintenance work at a battered women's shelter in Appalachia, he had to use the vacuum cleaner. He soon became aware that several women were following him around, pointing at him and talking excitedly. A little later, he asked why they did that. He was told that it was the first time in these adult women's lives that they had ever seen a man use a vacuum cleaner.

So how and when will things change? An important step would be to talk about these issues with your partner. Keep communication lines open all the time, and let your partner know if something is bothering you. Teaching your children that men and women are equally responsible for household chores will also help end the problem. Only by creating true gender equality, without differentiating among household tasks, will the unfair division of labor be ended.

Research provides some evidence of how to deal with work-family conflict successfully. Women in one study were clear in their commitment to their careers, marriage, and children, and they successfully combined them without high levels of distress (Guelzow, Bird, & Koball, 1991). How did they do it? Contrary to popular belief, the age of the children was not a factor in stress level. However, the *number* of children was important, as stress increases greatly with each additional child, irrespective of their ages. Guilt was also not an issue for these women. In the same study, men reported sharing more of the child care tasks as a way of dealing with multiple role pressures. Additionally, stress is lower for men who have a flexible work schedule that allows them to care for sick children and other family matters. Together, these findings are encouraging; they indicate that more heterosexual dual-earner couples are learning how to balance work and family.

This study also indicates the importance of taking a life-stage approach (see Chapter 1) to work-family conflict (Blanchard-Fields, Baldi, & Constantin, 2004). For example, several studies find that the highest conflict between the competing demands of work and family occurs during the peak parenting years when there are at least two preschool children in the home. Interrole conflict diminishes in later life stages, especially when the quality of the marriage is high. Overall, it is important to note that perception of the quality of one's roles (as a spouse or parent) is a key indicator of whether one will experience work-family stress (Reid & Hardy, 1999).

Dual-earner couples often have difficulty finding time for each other, especially if both work long hours. The amount of time together is not necessarily the most important issue; as long as the time is spent in shared activities such as eating, playing, and conversing, couples tend to be happy (Jacobs & Gerson, 2001). Especially when both partners are employed, getting all of the schedules to work together smoothly can be a major challenge. Unfortunately, many couples find themselves in the same position as Hi and Lois; by the time they have an opportunity to be alone together, they are too tired to make the most of it.

Cross-cultural data show that burnout from work and parenting is more likely to affect women. A study of dual-earner married couples in Singapore showed that wives are more likely to suffer from burnout than husbands; wives' burnout resulted from

THINK ABOUT IT

How does the issue of dependent care relate to the level of work-family stress felt by women?

both work and nonwork stress, whereas husbands' burnout resulted only from work stress (Aryee, 1993). Japanese career women's job satisfaction declines and turnover becomes more likely to the extent they have high work-family conflict (Honda-Howard & Homma, 2001). Research comparing sources of work-family conflict in the United States and China reveals that work demand does not differ, indicating that work pressure is a significant source of work-family conflict in both countries (Yang et al., 2000).

So exactly what effects do family matters have on work performance and vice versa? Evidence suggests that our work-family conflict is a major source of stress in couples' lives. In general, women feel the work-to-family spillover to a greater extent than men, but both men and women feel the pressure (Saginak & Saginak, 2005).

 **TEST YOURSELF**

1. Parents report lower work-family conflict and have lower absenteeism when supervisors are sympathetic and supportive regarding _____.
2. Men are satisfied with an equitable division of labor based on _____, whereas women are satisfied _____.

What should organizations do to help ease work-family conflict?

Answers: (1) family issues and child care, (2) the number of hours spent; when men perform traditionally female chores

12.5

TIME TO RELAX: LEISURE ACTIVITIES

Claude is a 55-year-old electrician who has enjoyed outdoor activities his whole life. From the time he was a boy, he has fished and water-skied in the calm inlets of coastal Florida. Although he doesn't compete in slalom races any more, Claude still skis regularly, and he participates in fishing competitions every chance he gets.

LEARNING OBJECTIVES

What activities are leisure activities? How do people choose among them?

What changes in leisure activities occur with age?

What do people derive from leisure activities?

Aᴅᴜʟᴛꜱ ᴅᴏ ɴᴏᴛ ᴡᴏʀᴋ ᴇᴠᴇʀʏ ᴡᴀᴋɪɴɢ ᴍᴏᴍᴇɴᴛ of their lives. As each of us knows, we need to relax sometimes and engage in leisure activities. Intuitively, leisure consists of activities not associated with work. *Leisure is discretionary activity that includes simple relaxation, activities for enjoyment, and creative pursuits.* However, men and women differ in their views of leisure, as do people in different ethnic groups (Henderson, 1990). For example, one study of African American women revealed that they view leisure as both freedom from the constraint of needing to work and as a form of self-expression (Allen & Chin-Sang, 1990).

TYPES OF LEISURE ACTIVITIES

Leisure can include virtually any activity. To organize the options, researchers have classified leisure activities into four categories: cultural—such as attending sporting events, concerts, church services, and meetings; physical—such as basketball, hiking, aerobics, and gardening; social—such as visiting friends and going to parties; and solitary—including reading, listening to music, and watching television (Glamser & Hayslip, 1985). Leisure activities can also be considered in terms of the degree of cognitive, emotional, or physical involvement; backpacker, for example, would have high activity in all three areas.

Adults engage in many different types of leisure activities, including backpacking.

An alternative approach to classifying leisure activities involves the classic distinction between preoccupations and interests (Rapoport & Rapoport, 1975). Preoccupations are much like daydreaming. Sometimes, preoccupations become more focused and are converted to interests. Interests are ideas and feelings about things one would like to do, is curious about, or is attracted to. Jogging, surfing the Web, fishing, and painting are some examples of interests.

Rapoport and Rapoport's distinction draws attention to a key truth about leisure: Any specific activity has different meaning and value, depending on the individual involved. For example, cooking a gourmet meal is an interest, or a leisure activity, for many people. For professional chefs, however, it is work and thus is not leisure at all.

Given the wide range of options, how do people pick their leisure activities? Apparently, each of us has a leisure repertoire, a personal library of intrinsically motivated activities that we do regularly (Mobily, Lemke, & Gisin, 1991). The activities in our repertoire are determined by two things: perceived competence (how good we think we are at the activity compared to other people our age) and psychological comfort (how well we meet our personal goals for performance). Other factors are important as well: income, interest, health, abilities, transportation, education, and social characteristics. For example, some leisure activities, such as downhill skiing, are relatively expensive and require transportation and reasonably good health and physical coordination for maximum enjoyment. In contrast, reading requires minimal finances (if one uses a public library) and is far less physically demanding. Women in all ethnic groups tend to participate less in leisure activities that involve physical activity (Eyler et al., 2002).

The use of computer technology in leisure activities has increased dramatically (Bryce, 2001). Most usage involves either electronic mail or the World Wide Web for such activities as keeping in touch with family and friends, pursuing hobbies, and lifelong learning. Computer gaming on the Web has also increased among adult players.

DEVELOPMENTAL CHANGES IN LEISURE

Cross-sectional studies report age differences in leisure activities. Young adults participate in a greater range of activities than middle-aged adults. Furthermore, young adults tend to prefer intense leisure activities, such as scuba diving and hang gliding. In contrast, middle-aged adults focus more on home- and family-oriented activities. In later middle age, they spend less of their leisure time in strenuous physical activities and more in sedentary activities such as reading and watching television. People of all ages report feelings of freedom during leisure activities (Larson, Gillman, & Richards, 1997).

Longitudinal studies of changes in individuals' leisure activities over time show considerable stability over reasonably long periods (Cutler & Hendricks, 1990). Claude, the 55-year-old in the vignette who likes to fish and ski, is a good example of this overall trend. As Claude demonstrates, frequent participation in particular leisure activities during childhood tends to continue into adulthood. Similar findings hold for the pre- and postretirement years. Apparently, one's preferences for certain types of leisure activities are established early in life; they tend to change over the life span primarily in terms of how physically intense they are.

CONSEQUENCES OF LEISURE ACTIVITIES

What do people gain from participating in leisure activities? Researchers have long known that involvement in leisure activities is related to well-being (Warr, Butcher, & Robertson, 2004). Research shows that participating in leisure activities helps promote better mental health in women (Ponde & Santana, 2000) and buffers the effects of stress and negative life events.

Studies show that leisure activities provide an excellent forum for the interaction of biological, psychological, and sociocultural forces (Kleiber, Hutchinson, & Williams, 2002). Leisure activities are a good way to deal with stress, which as we have seen has significant biological effects. This is especially true for unforeseen negative events (Janoff-Bulman & Berger, 2000). Psychologically, leisure activities have been well documented as one of the primary coping mechanisms people use (Iwasaki & Mannell, 2000; Kleiber et al., 2002). How people cope using leisure varies across cultures depending on the various types of leisure activities that are permissible and available. Likewise, leisure activities vary across social class; basketball is one activity that cuts across class because it is inexpensive, whereas downhill skiing is more associated with people who can afford to get to ski resorts and pay the fees.

Participating in leisure activities improves one's well-being.

How do leisure activities provide protection against stress? Kleiber and colleagues (2002) offer four ways that leisure activities serve as a buffer against negative life events:

- Leisure activities distract us from negative life events.
- Leisure activities generate optimism about the future because they are pleasant.
- Leisure activities connect us to our personal past by allowing us to participate in the same activities over much of our lives.
- Leisure activities can be used as vehicles for personal transformation.

Whether the negative life events we experience are personal, such as the loss of a loved one, or societal, such as a terrorist attack, leisure activities are a common and effective way to deal with them. They truly represent the confluence of biopsychosocial forces and are effective at any point in the life cycle.

Participating with others in leisure activities may also strengthen feelings of attachment to one's partner, friends, and family (Carnelley & Ruscher, 2000). Adults use leisure as a way to explore interpersonal relationships or to seek social approval. In fact, some research suggests that marital satisfaction is helped more when couples spend some leisure time with others than if they spend it just as a couple (Shebilske, 2000).

But what if leisure activities are pursued very seriously? In some cases, people create leisure-family conflict by engaging in leisure activities to extremes (Goff, Fick, & Opplinger, 1997). Only when there is support from others for such extreme involvement are problems avoided (Goff et al., 1997). As in most things, moderation in leisure activities is probably best.

You have probably heard the saying that "no vacation goes unpunished." It appears to be true. Workers report that the high postvacation workloads eliminate most of the positive effects of a vacation (Strauss-Blasche, Ekmekcioglu, & Marktl, 2002). Restful vacations do not prevent declines in mood or in sleep due to one's postvacation workload.

One often overlooked outcome of leisure activity is social acceptance. For persons with disabilities, this is a particularly important consideration (Devine & Lashua, 2002). There is a positive connection between frequency of leisure activities and social acceptance, friendship development, and acceptance of differences. These findings highlight the importance of designing inclusive leisure activity programs.

THINK ABOUT IT

What can employers do to address the postvacation workload problem?

TEST YOURSELF

1. Preoccupations are conscious mental absorptions, whereas interests are _____.
2. Compared to younger adults, middle-aged and older adults prefer leisure activities that are more family- and home-centered and _____.
3. Being involved in leisure activities is related to _____.

How are choices of leisure activities related to physical, cognitive, and social development?

Answers: (1) focused preoccupations, (2) less physically intense, (3) well-being

Putting It All Together

Sigmund Freud once said that the two most important aspects of adulthood are love and work. In this chapter, we have seen how pervasive work is in our lives, and how it is affected by many things. The occupation Monique ultimately chooses is partly influenced by talents or skills she may have inherited from her parents, the kind of environment in which she grew up, and the match between her personality style and her occupational skills.

We saw that occupational development is not an inevitable outcome of hard work. Unfortunately, the world of work also reflects the biases, prejudices, and discrimination people face in the world at large. Janice found that being a woman and a member of an ethnic minority may make it difficult to achieve the levels of advancement in her career that she truly deserves. Work spills over into

our personal lives too. Fred and others like him worry about job security, and this sometimes affects home life. Although retraining may be an option, it may not alleviate all the concerns. Dual-earner couples are forced to think about how to divide household tasks in order to maintain balance. Jennifer and her husband are struggling with this issue; too often, women perform most of the chores at home.

But a life that is all work and no play is dull. Just as children need a certain amount of play for their development, adults like Claude find playful outlets through leisure activities. Such activities may be as quiet as reading a book or as daring as skydiving, but being able to do something besides work gives these activities value.

Summary

12.1 Occupational Selection and Development

The Meaning of Work

■ Although most people work for money, other reasons are highly variable. Occupational priorities have changed over time; younger workers' expectations from their occupations are now lower, and their emphasis on personal growth potential is higher.

Holland's Theory of Occupational Choice Revisited

■ Holland's theory is based on the idea that people choose occupations to optimize the fit between their individual traits and their occupational interests. Six personality types, representing different combinations of these, have been identified. Support for these types has been found in several studies.

Occupational Development

■ Super's developmental view of occupations is based on self-concept and adaptation to an occupational role. Super describes five stages in adulthood: implementation, establishment, maintenance, deceleration, and retirement.

■ Reality shock is the realization that one's expectations about an occupation are different from the reality one experiences. Reality shock is common among young workers.

■ A mentor is a coworker who teaches a new employee the unwritten rules and fosters occupational development. Mentor-protégé relationships develop over time, through stages, like other relationships.

Job Satisfaction

■ Older workers report higher job satisfaction than younger workers, but this may be partly due to self-selection; unhappy workers may quit. Other reasons include intrinsic satisfaction, good fit, lower importance of work, finding nonwork diversions, and life-cycle factors.

■ Alienation and burnout are important considerations in understanding job satisfaction. Both involve significant stress for workers.

12.2 Gender, Ethnicity, and Discrimination Issues

Gender Differences in Occupational Selection

■ Boys and girls are socialized differently for work, and their occupational choices are affected as a result. Women choose nontraditional occupations for many reasons, including expectations and personal feelings. Women in such occupations are still viewed more negatively than men in the same occupations.

Women and Occupational Development

■ Women leave well-paid occupations for many reasons, including family obligations and workplace environment. Women who continue to work full-time have adequate child care and look for ways to further their occupational development.

Ethnicity and Occupational Development

■ Vocational identity and vocational goals vary in different ethnic groups. Whether an organization is sensitive to ethnicity issues is a strong predictor of satisfaction among ethnic minority employees.

Bias and Discrimination

■ Sex discrimination remains the chief barrier to women's occupational development. In many cases, this operates as a glass ceiling. Pay inequity is also a problem; women are often paid less than what men in similar jobs earn.

■ Sexual harassment is a problem in the workplace. Current criteria for judging harassment are based on the "reasonable woman" standard. Denying employment to anyone over 40 because of age is age discrimination.

12.3 Occupational Transitions

Retraining Workers

■ To adapt to the effects of a global economy and an aging workforce, many corporations are providing retraining opportunities for workers. Retraining is especially important in cases of outdated skills and career plateauing.

Occupational Insecurity

■ Important reasons people change occupations include personality, obsolescence, and economic trends. Occupational insecurity is a growing problem. Fear that one may lose one's job is a better predictor of anxiety than the actual likelihood of job loss.

Coping With Unemployment

■ Job loss is a traumatic event that can affect every aspect of a person's life. Degree of financial distress and the extent of attachment to the job are the best predictors of distress.

12.4 Work and Family

The Dependent Care Dilemma

■ Whether a woman returns to work after having a child depends largely on how attached she is to her work. Simply providing child care on-site does not always result in higher job satisfaction. The more important factor is the degree to which supervisors are sympathetic.

Juggling Multiple Roles

■ Although women have reduced the amount of time they spend on household tasks over the past two decades, they still do most of the work. European American men are less likely than either African American or Latino American men to help with traditionally female household tasks.

■ Flexible work schedules and number of children are important factors in role conflict. Recent evidence shows that work stress has a much bigger impact on family life than family stress has on work performance. Some women pay a high personal price for having careers.

12.5 Time to Relax: Leisure Activities

Types of Leisure Activities

■ Preoccupations can become more focused as interests, which can lead to the selection of particular leisure activities. People develop a repertoire of preferred leisure activities.

Developmental Changes in Leisure

■ As people grow older, they tend to engage in leisure activities that are less strenuous and more family-oriented. Leisure preferences in adulthood reflect those earlier in life.

Consequences of Leisure Activities

■ Leisure activities enhance well-being and can benefit all aspects of people's lives.

Key Terms

vocational maturity (454)

dream (456)

job satisfaction (457)

alienation (459)

burnout (460)

gender discrimination (466)

glass ceiling (466)

comparable worth (467)

"reasonable woman" standard (469)

age discrimination (469)

career plateauing (472)

work-family conflict (479)

leisure (482)

Learn More About It

Readings

BOLLES, R. N., & BOLLES, M. E. (2004). *The 2005 what color is your parachute: A practical manual for job-hunters and career changers.* Berkeley, CA: Ten Speed Press. This popular reference is a valuable resource for people in search of careers. It is regularly updated.

BOLTON, M. K. (2000). *The third shift: Managing hard choices in our careers, homes, and lives as women.* San Francisco: Jossey-Bass. Discusses the decisions that factor into women's decisions to have careers and families based on a longitudinal study.

PALKOVITZ, R. J. (2002). *Involved fathering and men's adult development: Provisional balances.* Mahwah, NJ: Erlbaum. A book grounded in research but which offers practical advice to families.

SBRAGA, T. P., & O'DONOHOE, W. (2000). Sexual harassment. *Annual Review of Sex Research, 11,* 258–285. A superb review of the history of sexual harassment writings in the psychology and legal literatures.

Websites

Visit the Human Development book companion website for all URLs.

■ **The Human Development Book Companion Website**
See the companion website **http://psychology.wadsworth.com/kail_cavanaugh4e/** for practice quiz questions, Internet links, updates, critical thinking exercises, discussion forums, and more.

■ **Monster.com**
Monster.com provides a broad range of services for people looking for a job and employers looking for potential employees. They also provide help with creating a résumé, salary data, and information about companies.

■ **U.S. Department of Labor**
The U.S. Department of Labor provides many reports on various aspects of workforce participation, employment, and demographics. The Women's Bureau is especially good for statistics on women's employment status.

■ **U.S. Equal Employment Opportunity Commission**
The EEOC provides an extensive website covering all aspects of discrimination in the workplace as well as information about sexual harassment and other related topics. You can find out how to file a claim and information important to employers.

Life-Span CD-ROM

For more information about the concepts covered in this chapter, go to

Module 5: Early and Middle Adulthood

- *Emotional and Social Development*

Module 6: Late Adulthood

- *Emotional and Social Development*

http://www.thomsonedu.com

Go to this site for the link to ThomsonNOW, your one-stop study shop. Take a pre-test for this chapter, and ThomsonNOW will generate a personalized study plan based on your test results. The study plan will identify the topics you need to review and direct you to online resources to help you master those topics. You can then take a post-test to help you determine the concepts you have mastered and what you still need to work on.

13.1 Physical Changes and Health
Changes in Appearance
Changes in Bones and Joints
Reproductive Changes
■ CURRENT CONTROVERSIES: Hormone Replacement Therapy
Stress and Health
Exercise

13.2 Cognitive Development
Practical Intelligence
Becoming an Expert
Lifelong Learning

13.3 Personality
Stability Is the Rule: The Five-Factor Model
■ SPOTLIGHT ON RESEARCH: Is Personality in Young and Middle Adulthood Set in Plaster?
Change Is the Rule: Changing Priorities in Midlife

13.4 Family Dynamics and Middle Age
Letting Go: Middle-Aged Adults and Their Children
Giving Back: Middle-Aged Adults and Their Aging Parents
■ REAL PEOPLE: APPLYING HUMAN DEVELOPMENT: Taking Care of Mom
Grandparenthood

Putting It All Together
Summary
Key Terms
Learn More About It

CHAPTER 13

Making It In Midlife

The Unique Challenges of Middle Adulthood

There's an old saying that life begins at 40. That's good news for middle-aged adults. As we will see, they face many stressful events, but they also leave many of the pressures of young adulthood behind. In many respects, middle age is the prime of life: People's health is generally good, and their earnings are at their peak.

Of course, during middle age people typically get wrinkles, gray hair, and a bulging waistline. But middle-aged adults also achieve new heights in cognitive development, reevaluate their personal goals and change their behavior if they choose, develop adult relationships with their children, and ease into grandparenthood. Along the way, they must deal with stress, changes in the way they learn, and the challenges of helping their aging parents.

Some of these issues are based more on stereotypes than on hard evidence. Which is which? You will know by the end of the chapter.

13.1

PHYSICAL CHANGES AND HEALTH

By all accounts, Dean is extremely successful. Among other things, he became the head of a moderate-sized manufacturing firm by the time he was 43. Dean has always considered himself to be a rising young star in the company. Then one day he found more than the usual number of hairs in his brush. "Oh no!" he exclaimed. "I can't be going bald! What will people think?" What does Dean think about these changes?

LEARNING OBJECTIVES

How does appearance change in middle age?

───────

What reproductive changes occur in men and women in middle age?

───────

What is stress? How does it affect physical and psychological health?

───────

What benefits are there to exercise?

THE REALITY OF MIDDLE AGE generally strikes early one morning in the bathroom mirror. Standing there, staring through half-awake eyes, you see *it*. One solitary gray hair, or one tiny wrinkle at the corner of your eye, or, like Dean, some excess hairs falling out, and you worry that your youth is gone, your life is over, and you will soon be acting the way your parents did when they totally embarrassed you in your younger days. Middle-aged people become concerned that they are over the hill, sometimes going to great lengths to prove that they are still vibrant.

Crossing the boundary to middle age in the United States is typically associated with turning 40 (or the big four-oh, as many people term it). This event is frequently marked with a special party, and the party often has an "over the hill" motif. Such events are society's attempt at creating a rite of passage between youth and maturity.

As people move into middle age, they begin experiencing some of the physical changes associated with aging. In this section, we focus on the ones most obvious in middle-aged adults: appearance, reproductive capacity, and stress and coping. In Chap-

Turning age 40 is usually marked as the beginning of middle age.

© Steve Chenn /Corbis

ter 14, we will consider changes that may begin in middle age but are usually not apparent until later in life, such as slower reaction time and sensory changes. A critical factor in setting the stage for healthy aging is living a healthy lifestyle in young adulthood and middle age. Eating a healthy diet and exercising regularly across adulthood can help reduce the chances of chronic disease later in life (Leventhal et al., 2002).

CHANGES IN APPEARANCE

On that fateful day when the hard truth stares at you in the bathroom mirror, it probably doesn't matter to you that getting wrinkles and gray hair is universal and inevitable. Wrinkles are caused by changes in the structure of the skin and its connective and supporting tissues, as well as the cumulative effects of damage from exposure to sunlight and smoking cigarettes (Aldwin & Gilmer, 2004). It may not make you feel better to know that gray hair is perfectly natural and caused by a normal cessation of pigment production in hair follicles. Male pattern baldness, a genetic trait in which hair is lost progressively beginning with the top of the head, often begins to appear in middle age. No, the scientific evidence that these changes occur to many people isn't what matters most. What matters is that these changes are affecting *you*.

Finding the first wrinkle is often a traumatic experience.

To make matters worse, you may have also noticed that your clothes aren't fitting properly, even though you watch what you eat. You remember a time not very long ago when you could eat whatever you wanted; now it seems that as soon as you look at food you put on weight. Your perceptions are correct; most people gain weight between their early 30s and mid-50s, producing the infamous "middle-aged bulge" as metabolism slows down (Aldwin & Gilmer, 2004).

People's reactions to these changes in appearance vary. Dean wonders how people will react to him now that he's balding. Some people rush out to purchase hair coloring and wrinkle cream. Others just take it as another stage in life. You've probably experienced several different reactions yourself. There is a wide range of individual differences, especially those between men and women and across cultures.

CHANGES IN BONES AND JOINTS

Another physical change is loss of bone mass, a potentially serious problem. Bone mass peaks in one's 20s, and then declines with age (National Institute of Arthritis, Musculoskeletal and Skin Diseases, 2005). Loss of bone mass makes bones weaker and more brittle, thereby making them easier to break. Because there is less bone mass, bones also

■ **Figure 13.1**
Bone mass loss through
osteoporosis.

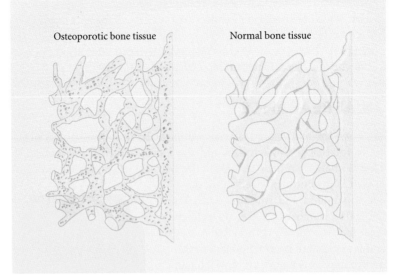

Osteoporotic bone tissue   Normal bone tissue

■ **Figure 13.2**
Notice how osteoporosis
eventually causes a person
to stoop and to lose height
due to compression of the
vertebrae.

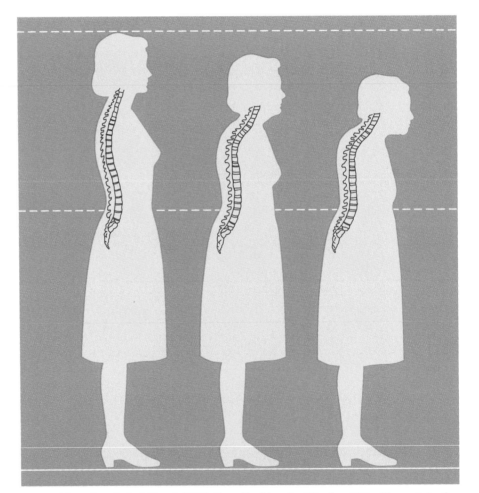

Reprinted from Ebersole, P., & Hess, P. (1998). *Toward healthy aging* (5th ed., p. 395), with permission from
Elsevier Science.

take longer to heal in middle-aged and older adults. *If the loss of bone mass is severe, the
disease* **osteoporosis** *results; bones become porous like honeycombs and extremely easy to
break* (see Figure 13.1). In severe cases, osteoporosis can cause spinal vertebrae to col-
lapse, causing the person to stoop and to become shorter as shown in Figure 13.2 (National Institutes of Health, 2000a). Osteoporosis is the leading cause of broken bones

in older women (Ebersole, Hess, & Luggen, 2004). Although the severe effects of osteoporosis typically are not observed until later life, this disease can occur in people in their 50s.

Osteoporosis is more common in women than men, largely because women have less bone mass in general, because some girls and women do not consume enough calcium to build strong bones from childhood to young adulthood, and because the decrease in estrogen following menopause greatly accelerates bone loss (National Institutes of Health, 2000a). According to a national study of 48,000 postmenopausal women in the United States, 65% of Asian American, 59% of Native American, 56% of Latina, 51% of European American, and 38% of African American women had low bone mass. Additional evidence from bone scans suggests that at least 65% of all women over age 60 and almost all women over age 90 are affected; in all, more than 20 million women in the United States have osteoporosis, with millions more at risk.

Osteoporosis is caused in part by low bone mass at skeletal maturity, deficiencies of calcium and vitamin D, estrogen depletion, and lack of weight-bearing exercise. Other risk factors include smoking, high-protein diets, and excessive alcohol, caffeine, and sodium intake. Women who are being treated for asthma, cancer, rheumatoid arthritis, thyroid problems, and epilepsy are also at increased risk because the medications used can lead to loss of bone mass.

The relationship between dietary calcium intake and osteoporosis is controversial (Aldwin & Gilmer, 2004). There is some evidence that calcium supplements after menopause may slow the rate of bone loss and delay the onset of osteoporosis, but benefits appear to be greater when the supplements are provided before menopause (National Institutes of Health, 2000a). The reasons estrogen depletion affects bone loss are not fully understood, mainly because the effects must be indirect because there are no estrogen receptors in bone tissue. Although estrogen replacement therapy may slow bone loss, this approach must be used cautiously because of potential side effects. (We explore hormone replacement therapy in detail later in the Current Controversies feature when we consider reproductive changes in women.) Additionally, estrogen therapy must be continued indefinitely because bone loss speeds up as soon as the therapy is stopped.

Data showing that vitamin D metabolism plays a causative role in osteoporosis are clear; however, whether supplementary dietary vitamin D retards bone loss is less certain. Some research shows that vitamin D administered after menopause slows bone loss, whereas other research does not (National Institutes of Health, 2000a). To reduce the risk of osteoporosis, the National Institutes of Health recommends dietary, drug, and activity approaches to prevent osteoporosis. People should eat foods high in calcium (such as milk and broccoli), reduce alcohol intake, and take calcium supplements if necessary. Recommended calcium intake for men and women of various ages are shown in Figure 13.3. Some evidence also supports the view that oral ingestion of mag-

Recommended Calcium Intakes	
Children and young adults	**Amount (mg/day)**
1–10 years	800 to 1,200
11–24 years	1,200 to 1,500
Adult women	
Pregnant and lactating	1,200 to 1,500
25–49 years (premenopausal)	1,000
50–64 years (postmenopausal) taking estrogen	1,000
50–64 years (postmenopausal) not on estrogen	1,500
65+ years	1,500
Adult Men	
25–64 years	1,000
65+ years	1,500

■ **Figure 13.3**
Recommended dietary calcium intake.

National Institutes of Health Consensus Panel, Optimal Calcium Intake, 1994.

nesium, zinc, vitamin K, and special forms of fluoride may be effective. Estrogen replacement is clearly effective in preventing women's bone loss after menopause but is controversial due to potential side effects (as discussed later). There is also some evidence that regular exercise is beneficial, but results vary depending on the type and intensity of the regimen. The best results come from a regular regimen of moderate aerobic exercise.

You may have heard some of the claims about using human growth hormone to treat various problems related to changes in the muscles and bones. Some researchers have found positive effects of human growth hormone in studies of normal aging (Welle et al., 1996). But most studies have failed to support the advertised benefits (Taaffe et al., 1996) and some have found harmful side effects such as increased risk of breast cancer (Dorgan et al., 1997).

Many middle-aged adults complain of aching joints. They have good reason. Beginning in the 20s, the protective cartilage in joints shows signs of deterioration, such as thinning and becoming cracked and frayed. *Over time the bones underneath the cartilage become damaged, which can result in* **osteoarthritis,** *a disease marked by gradual onset and progression of pain and disability, with minor signs of inflammation.* The disease usually becomes noticeable in late middle age or early old age, and it is especially common in people whose joints are subjected to routine overuse and abuse, such as athletes and manual laborers (National Institute of Arthritis, Musculoskeletal and Skin Diseases, 2002). Thus, osteoarthritis is a wear-and-tear disease. Pain typically is worse when the joint is used, but skin redness, heat, and swelling are minimal or absent. Osteoarthritis usually affects the hands, spine, hips, and knees, sparing the wrists, elbows, shoulders, and ankles. Effective management approaches consist mainly of certain steroids and anti-inflammatory drugs, rest and nonstressful exercises that focus on range of motion, diet, and a variety of homeopathic remedies.

A second and more common form of arthritis is **rheumatoid arthritis,** *a more destructive disease of the joints that also develops slowly and typically affects different joints and causes different types of pain than osteoarthritis.* Most often, a pattern of morning stiffness and aching develops in the fingers, wrists, and ankles on both sides of the body. Joints appear swollen. The typical therapy for rheumatoid arthritis consists of aspirin or other nonsteroidal anti-inflammatory drugs. Newer chemical therapies (such as methotrexate) and experimental drugs (such as cyclosporine) are showing promising results. Rest and passive range-of-motion exercises are also helpful. Contrary to popular belief, rheumatoid arthritis is not contagious, hereditary, or self-induced by any known diet, habit, job, or exposure. Interestingly, the symptoms often come and go in repeating patterns (National Institute of Arthritis, Musculoskeletal and Skin Diseases, 2004).

REPRODUCTIVE CHANGES

Besides changes in the way we look, middle age brings transitions in our reproductive systems. These changes differ dramatically for women and men. Even in the context of these changes, though, middle-aged adults continue to have active sex lives. In fact, 73% of men and 69% of women between the ages of 40 and 49, and 67% of men and 48% of women between 50 and 59, have sex at least several times a month (Michael et al., 1994). The declines in frequency of sexual activity with age reflect complex biopsychosocial factors, including physiological changes, the stresses of everyday life, and negative social stereotypes about sex and growing older (Michael et al., 1994).

The Climacteric and Menopause

As women enter midlife, they experience a major biological process, called the **climacteric,** *during which they pass from their reproductive to nonreproductive years.* **Menopause** *is the point at which menstruation stops.* Men do not endure such sweeping biological changes but experience several gradual changes. These changes have important psychological implications because midlife is thought by many to be a key time for redefining ourselves.

The major reproductive change in women during adulthood is the loss of the ability to bear children. This change begins in the 40s as menstrual cycles become irregular, and by age 50 to 55 it is usually complete (Avis, 1999). This time of transition is called *perimenopause,* and how long it lasts varies considerably (Mayo Clinic, 2004). The gradual loss and eventual end of monthly periods is accompanied by decreases in estrogen and progesterone levels, changes in the reproductive organs, and changes in sexual functioning (Aldwin & Gilmer, 2004).

A variety of physical and psychological symptoms may accompany perimenopause and menopause due to decreases in hormonal levels (Avis, 1999): hot flashes, night sweats, headaches, mood changes, difficulty concentrating, vaginal dryness, and a variety of aches and pains. Negative effects on sexuality, such as low libido, are common (Myskow, 2002). Although many women report no symptoms at all, most women experience at least some, but there are large ethnic and cultural group differences in how they are expressed (Banger, 2003). For example, studies of European American women reveal a decrease in reported physical symptoms after climacteric. In contrast, African American women reported more physical symptoms after climacteric than before. Although these differences could be a function of the different age groups included in the various studies, they also draw attention to the need to study the experiences of women from different ethnic and racial backgrounds (Jackson, Taylor, & Pyngolil, 1991).

Cultural differences are exemplified in Lock's (1991) classic study of Japanese women. Fewer than 13% of Japanese women whose menstrual periods were becoming irregular reported having hot flashes during the previous 2 weeks, compared with nearly half of Western women. In fact, fewer than 20% of Japanese women in the study had ever had a hot flash, compared with nearly 65% of Western women. However, Japanese women reported more headaches, shoulder stiffness, ringing in the ears, and dizziness than Western women. Why? The answer seems to be the power of sociocultural forces. In Japan, the government considers "menopausal syndrome" to be a modern affliction of women with too much time on their hands. With this official attitude, it is hard to know whether Japanese women actually experience menopause differently or may simply be reluctant to describe their true experience.

Similar findings were reported by Fu, Anderson, and Courtney (2003), who compared Taiwanese and Australian women. Significant differences were found in their attitudes toward menopause, menopausal symptoms, and physical vitality. These results clearly indicate that sociocultural factors are critical in understanding women's experience during menopause.

Women's genital organs undergo progressive change after menopause (Aldwin & Gilmer, 2004). The vaginal walls shrink and become thinner, the size of the vagina decreases, vaginal lubrication is reduced and delayed, and some shrinkage of the external genitalia occurs. These changes have important effects on sexual activity, such as an increased possibility of painful intercourse and a longer time and more stimulation needed to reach orgasm. Failure to achieve orgasm is more common than in a woman's younger years. However, maintaining an active sex life throughout adulthood lowers the degree to which problems are encountered.

Despite the physical changes, there is no physiological reason most women cannot continue sexual activity and enjoy it well into old age. Whether this happens depends more on the availability of a suitable partner than on a woman's desire for sexual relations. This is especially true for older women. The AARP *Modern Maturity* sexuality study (AARP, 1999) found that older married women were far more likely to have an active sex life than unmarried women. The primary reason for the decline in women's sexual activity with age is the lack of a willing or appropriate partner, not a lack of physical ability or desire (AARP, 1999).

Reproductive technology such as fertility drugs and in vitro fertilization (see Chapter 2) has made it possible for postmenopausal women to have children. Indeed, in 1997 Rosanna Dalla Corta, a 63-year-old woman from Viterbo, Italy, gave birth to a baby conceived through in vitro fertilization. Scientists have thus fundamentally changed the rules of reproduction. Even though a woman has gone through the climacteric, she can

THINK ABOUT IT

Why does sexual desire remain largely unchanged despite the biological changes that are occurring?

Rosanna Dalla Corta from Viterbo, Italy, gave birth to a baby at age 63.

still have children. Technology can make her pregnant, if she so chooses and if she has access to the proper medical centers.

What does this do to our understanding of human reproduction? It changes the whole notion of menopause representing an absolute end to childbearing. Some of the women who have given birth after menopause have done so because their daughters were unable to have children; they consider this act another way to show their parental love. Others view it as a way to equalize reproductive potential in middle age between men and women, as men remain fertile throughout adulthood.

Clearly, these are complicated issues that currently affect a very small number of women. But as reproductive technology continues to advance faster than our ability to think through the issues, we will be confronted with increasingly complex ethical questions (Lindlaw, 1997). Should children be born to older parents? Might not there be some advantage, considering the life experience such parents would have, compared to young parents? Are such births merely selfish acts? Are they a viable alternative way for younger adults to have a family? What dangers are there to older pregnant women? How do you feel about it?

Treating Symptoms of Menopause

The decline in estrogen that women experience after menopause is related to increased risk of osteoporosis, cardiovascular disease, stress urinary incontinence (involuntary loss of urine during physical stress, such as exercising, sneezing, or laughing), weight gain, and memory loss (Mayo Clinic, 2003b). In the case of cardiovascular disease, before they turn 50, women have three times less risk of heart attacks than men. Ten years after menopause, when women are about 60, their risk equals that of men.

*Due to these increased risks, and the estrogen-related symptoms women experience, many physicians and researchers advocate the use of **hormone replacement therapy (HRT),** in which women take low doses of estrogen, which is often combined with progestin (synthetic form of progesterone).* HRT is controversial and has been the focus of many research studies (National Heart, Lung, and Blood Institute, 2003). There appear to be both benefits and risks with HRT.

One way to address the symptoms associated with the climacteric is hormone replacement therapy. Although there is evidence that estrogen and progesterone influence the brain mechanisms that underlie learning and memory, the value of hormone replacement therapy as a treatment or deterrent for cognitive impairment remains largely unknown (Dohanich, 2003). For these reasons, as discussed in the Current Controversies feature, probably no other area of medical research has resulted in more contradictory data about the potentially serious side effects (or lack thereof) than has work on hormone replacement therapy.

CURRENT CONTROVERSIES

HORMONE REPLACEMENT THERAPY

For many years, women have had the choice of taking medications to replace the female hormones that are not produced naturally by the body after menopause. Hormone replacement therapy (HRT) may involve taking estrogen alone, or in combination with progesterone (or progestin in its synthetic form). For

many years, it was thought that HRT was beneficial for most women, and results from several studies were positive. However, in 2002 and 2003 results from the Women's Health Initiative research indicated that for some types of HRT there were several potentially very serious side effects.

The Women's Health Initiative (WHI), begun in the United States in 1991, was a very large study (National Heart, Lung, and Blood Institute, 2003). The postmenopausal hormone therapy clinical trial had two parts. The first involved 16,608 postmenopausal women with a uterus who took either estrogen plus progestin therapy or a placebo. The second involved 10,739 women who had a hysterectomy and were taking estrogen alone or a placebo. The estrogen plus progestin trial used 0.625 milligram of estrogens taken daily plus 2.5 milligrams of medroxyprogesterone acetate taken daily (Prempro). This combination was chosen because it is the mostly commonly prescribed form of the combined hormone therapy in the United States, and, in several observational studies, it had appeared to benefit women's health. The women in the WHI estrogen plus progestin study were aged 50 to 79 when they enrolled in the study between 1993 and 1998. The health of study participants was carefully monitored by an independent panel called the Data and Safety Monitoring Board (DSMB). The study was stopped in July 2002 because investigators discovered a significant increased risk for breast cancer and that overall the risks outnumbered the benefits. However, in addition to the increased risk of breast cancer, heart attack, stroke, and blood clots, HRT resulted in fewer hip fractures and colorectal cancer. The risk factors for these diseases can be summarized as follows (National Heart, Lung, and Blood Institute, 2003):

- **Breast cancer.** The increased risk of breast cancer appeared after 4 years of hormone use. After 5.2 years, estrogen plus progestin resulted in a 26% increase in the risk of breast cancer.

Women who had used estrogen plus progestin before entering the study were more likely to develop breast cancer than others, indicating that the therapy may have a cumulative effect.

- **Heart attack.** The risk for heart attack began to increase in the first year of estrogen plus progestin use and became more pronounced in the second year. After 5.2 years, there were 29% more heart attacks in the estrogen plus progestin group than in the placebo group. Unlike earlier research, which involved women with heart disease, the increased risk from estrogen plus progestin did not go back down again.
- **Stroke.** For the first time, estrogen plus progestin was shown to cause more strokes in healthy women. By the end of the study, the estrogen plus progestin group had 41% more strokes than the placebo group.
- **Blood clots.** The risk of total blood clots was greatest during the first 2 years of hormone use—four times higher than that of placebo users. By the end of the study, it had decreased to two times greater.
- **Fractures.** Estrogen plus progestin reduced hip fractures by 34%. This is the first solid evidence from a clinical trial that hormone therapy, in helping to prevent bone loss and osteoporosis, protects women against fractures.
- **Colorectal cancer.** The therapy also lowered the risk of colorectal cancer by 37%. This reduction appeared after 3 years of hormone use and became

more significant thereafter. However, the number of cases of colorectal cancer was relatively small, and more research is needed to confirm the finding.

A newer approach involves a class of compounds called *selective estrogen receptor modulators (SERMs)*, which can be considered "designer estrogens" (Avis, 1999). SERMs have the protective properties of estrogen on bone tissue and the cardiovascular system but seem to block some estrogen effects on breast and uterine tissue. In essence, they have the advantages of traditional HRT with apparently none of the negative side effects. Two SERMs that are being intensively studied are tamoxifen, the first SERM approved for clinical use, and raloxifene. Although both show promise, the potential of increased uterine cancer in the case of tamoxifen and increased hot flashes in the case of raloxifene indicate that neither is perfect (Modelska et al., 2004; National Cancer Institute, 2002).

In sum, women have difficult choices to make when deciding whether to use HRT to combat certain symptoms related to menopause and to protect themselves against other diseases. To date, research evidence about the long-term risks of HRT is clear in the case of the most common estrogen-progesterone combination. The best course of action is to consult closely with one's physician to weigh the benefits and risks.

Alternative approaches to addressing both estrogen-related and somatic symptoms are gaining in popularity (National Heart, Lung, and Blood Institute, 2003). Herbal remedies, especially those rich in phytoestrogens (such as soybeans, chickpeas, and other legumes), used effectively in Asian cultures may be one reason Asian American women report the fewest symptoms (DeAngelis, 1997). The use of a nonpetroleum-based lubricating jelly (such as K-Y Jelly) usually solves the problem of vaginal dryness, which often makes intercourse painful.

Reproductive Changes in Men

Unlike women, men do not have a physiological (and cultural) event to mark reproductive changes although there is a gradual decline in testosterone levels (Seidman, 2003). Men do not experience a complete loss of the ability to father children, but men do experience a normative decline in the quantity of sperm (Lewis, 1995). Sperm production declines by approximately 30% between ages 25 and 60 (Whitbourne, 1996). However, even at age 80 a man is still half as fertile as he was at age 25 and is quite capable of fathering a child.

With increasing age the prostate gland enlarges, becomes stiffer, and may obstruct the urinary tract. Prostate cancer becomes a real threat during middle age; annual screenings are extremely important for men over age 50 (American Cancer Society, 2005d).

The majority of men show a gradual reduction in testosterone levels after the mid-20s (Whitbourne, 1996). However, some men who experience an abnormally rapid decline in testosterone production during their late 60s report symptoms similar to those experienced by some menopausal women, such as hot flashes, chills, rapid heart rate, and nervousness (Ebersole et al., 2004).

Men experience some physiological changes in sexual performance. By old age, men report less perceived demand to ejaculate, a need for longer time and more stimulation to achieve erection and orgasm, and a much longer resolution phase during which erection is impossible (Saxon & Etten, 1994). Older men also report more frequent failures to achieve orgasm and loss of erection during intercourse (AARP, 1999). However, the advent of the drug Viagra, which helps men achieve and maintain an erection, has provided an easy-to-use medical treatment for erectile dysfunction.

As with women, as long as men enjoy sex and have a willing partner, sexual activity is a lifelong option. As for women, the most important ingredient of sexual intimacy for men is a strong relationship with a partner (AARP, 1999). That is a significant reason frequency of intercourse drops by two and three times per month in men over age 50 and 60, respectively (Araujo, Mohr, & McKinlay, 2004).

STRESS AND HEALTH

There's no doubt about it—life is full of stress. Think for a moment about all the things that bother you, such as exams, jobs, relationships, and finances. For most people, this list lengthens quickly. But, you may wonder, isn't this true for people of all ages? Is stress more important in middle age?

Although stress affects people of all ages, it is during middle age that the effects of both short- and long-term stress become most apparent. In part, this is because it takes time for stress disorders to manifest themselves, and in part it is due to the gradual loss of physical capacity, as the normal changes accompanying aging begin to take their toll. As we will see, psychological factors play a major role as well.

Work-related stress is a major problem around the world and can have serious negative effects on physical and psychological health.

© Esbin Anderson / The Image Works

You may think that stress affects health mainly in people who hold certain types of jobs, such as air traffic controllers and high-level business executives. In fact, business executives actually have *fewer* stress-related health problems than waitresses, construction workers, secretaries, laboratory technicians, machine operators, farmworkers, and painters. Why? Even though business executives are often under great stress and tend to be isolated and lonely (Cooper & Quick, 2003), they have better outlets for their stress, such as the ability to delegate problems, and they are in control. What do all of these truly high-stress jobs have in common? These workers have little direct control over their jobs.

Although we understand some important workplace factors related to stress, our knowledge is largely based on research examining middle-aged men. Unfortunately, the relation of stress to age, gender, and ethnic status remains to be researched. Women tend to rate their stressful experiences as more negative and uncontrollable than do men, and report stress most often in family and health areas compared to men's reports of financial and work-related stressors (Matud, 2004). Middle-aged people report the highest levels of stress, whereas people over age 65 report the lowest. Why? As we will see in the next section, part of the reason may be due to the number of pressures middle-aged people feel: Children may be in college, the job has high demands, the mortgage payment and other bills always need paying, the marriage needs some attention, the in-laws would like to visit, and on it goes.

What Is Stress?

Think about the last time you felt stressed. What was it about the situation that made you feel stressed? How did you feel? *The answers to questions like these provide a way to understand the dominant framework used to study stress, the **stress and coping paradigm.***

Figure 13.4
The physical markers of stress are the result of complex and dynamic psychological processes.

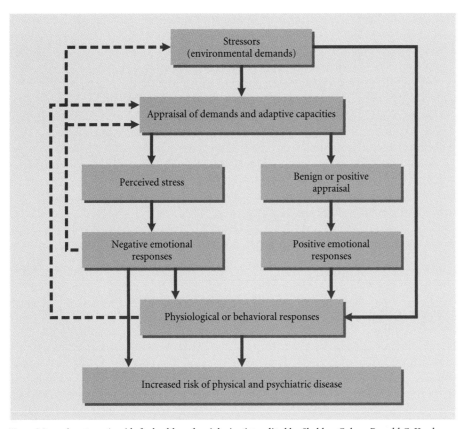

From *Measuring stress: A guide for health and social scientists,* edited by Sheldon Cohen, Ronald C. Kessler, and Lynn Underwood Gordon, copyright © 1995 by Oxford University Press, Inc. Used by permission of Oxford University Press, Inc.

Because the stress and coping paradigm emphasizes the transactions between a person and the environment, it fits well with the biopsychosocial framework. An example of a transactional model of stress is shown in Figure 13.4.

Physiologically, stress refers to a number of specific changes in the body, including increased heart rate, sweaty palms, and hormone secretion (McEwen, 1998). In the short run, stress can be beneficial and may even allow you to perform at your peak. In the long run, though, a high physical toll and even death may result (McEwen, 1998).

Whether you report feeling stressed depends on how you interpret a situation or event (Lazarus & Folkman, 1984). What the situation or event is, or what you do to deal with it, does not matter. *Stress results when you **appraise** a situation or event as taxing or exceeding your personal, social, or other resources and endangering your well-being. It is the day-to-day **hassles,** or the things that upset and annoy us, that prove to be particularly stressful.*

Interestingly, culture plays an important role in how people perceive stress (Laungani, 2001). These differences are grounded in the values people hold. For example, what constitutes stressors varies a great deal between Eastern societies such as India and Western societies such as England. Indians tend to believe that much of life is determined, whereas the British tend to emphasize personal choice and free will. Consequently, frustrations that Britons may feel when free will is thwarted may not be perceived as stressful by Indians. These differences point out the importance of understanding a culture when studying a concept such as stress.

***Coping** is any attempt to deal with stress.* People cope in several different ways (Kinney et al., 2003). Sometimes people cope by trying to solve the problem at hand; for example, you may cope with a messy roommate by moving out. At other times, people focus on how they feel about the situation and deal with things on an emotional level; feeling sad after breaking up with your partner would be one way of coping with the stress of being alone. Sometimes people cope by simply redefining the event as not stressful—saying that it was no big deal that you failed to get the job you wanted would be an example of this approach. Still others focus on religious or spiritual approaches, perhaps asking God for help.

People appraise different types of situations or events as stressful at different times during adulthood. For example, the pressures from work and raising a family are typically greater for younger and middle-aged adults than for older adults. However, stressors due to chronic disease are often more important to older adults than to their younger counterparts. Similarly, the same kind of event may be appraised differently at different ages. For example, uncertainty about one's job security may be less stressful in young adulthood, when one might get another job more easily, than in middle age, when alternative job prospects might diminish. From a biopsychosocial perspective, such life-cycle factors must be taken into account when considering what kinds of stress adults of different ages are experiencing.

THINK ABOUT IT

How might life experience and cognitive developmental level influence the appraisal of and coping with stress?

How Are Stress and Coping Related to Physical Health?

A great deal of research has been conducted over the years examining links between stress and physical health. Being under chronic stress suppresses the immune system, resulting in increased susceptibility to viral infections, increases risk of atherosclerosis (buildup of plaque along the walls of arteries so that the arteries become stiffer and restrict blood flow) and hypertension (high blood pressure), and impaired memory and cognition (Davis, McKay, & Eshelman, 2000). However, these effects depend on the kind of event (Kemeny, 2003). Experiencing negative events results in lower immune function. Likewise, experiencing positive events seems to improve immune functioning.

Many specific diseases and conditions are caused or exacerbated by stress (WebMD, 2004). Stress serves as a major trigger for angina (pain caused by interrupted flood flow to the heart), causes arrhythmias (irregular pulse), causes blood to become stickier (making it more likely to cause a clot in an artery), raises cholesterol, reduces estrogen in women, increases production of certain proteins that damage cells, causes sudden increases in blood pressure, increases the risk of irritable bowel syndrome, causes weight fluctuations, is associated with the development of insulin resistance (a primary factor in diabetes), causes tension headaches, causes sexual dysfunction and fertility, and results in poorer memory and cognitive performance. Clearly, chronic stress is harmful to one's health!

Surprisingly, little research has been conducted testing whether successful coping strategies reverse these health effects of stress. At best, we can only surmise that if stress causes these health problems, effective coping strategies may prevent them.

How Are Stress and Coping Related to Behavior and Psychological Health?

Probably the most well-known connection between stress and behavior involves the link with cardiovascular disease. Due mostly to the pioneering work of Friedman and Rosenman (1974), we know that two behavior patterns differ dramatically in terms of risk of cardiovascular disease. *People who demonstrate a **Type A behavior pattern** tend to be intensely competitive, angry, hostile, restless, aggressive, and impatient. In contrast, people who show a **Type B behavior pattern** tend to be just the opposite.* Type A individuals are at least twice as likely as Type B people to develop cardiovascular disease, even when other risk factors such as smoking and hypertension are taken into account. In fact, Type A behavior is a more important predictor of cardiovascular disease than body weight, alcohol intake, or activity level (Zmuda et al., 1997).

How do these behavior types relate to *recovery* from a heart attack? Although it is relatively rare, Type B people sometimes do have heart attacks. Who recovers better, Type A people or Type B people?

The answer may surprise you. In a classic study, Ragland and Brand (1988) conducted a 22-year longitudinal follow-up of the original Friedman and Rosenman study and discovered that Type A people recover from a heart attack better than Type B people. Why? Some of the characteristics of being Type A may help motivate people to stick to diet and exercise regimens after heart attacks and to have a more positive attitude toward recovery (Ivancevich & Matteson, 1988). Indeed, although the anger and hostility components of Type A behavior increase the risk for cardiovascular disease, the other components appear to aid the recovery process (Ivancevich & Matteson, 1988). In contrast, the laid-back approach to life of Type B people may actually work against them during recovery.

Although experiencing stress is not directly related to psychopathology, it is associated with other psychological processes. For example, chronic stress related to financial pressures and fear of crime promotes social isolation and distrust of others in some adults (Krause, 1991). Thus, although stress does not directly cause psychopathology, it does influence how people behave. For example, the stress many people experienced after the terrorist attacks of September 11, 2001, resulted in higher levels of anxiety experienced through nightmares, flashbacks, insomnia, traumatic grief, emotional numbing, and avoidance (LeDoux & Gorman, 2001).

Data examining ethnic group differences highlight the importance of self-esteem. For example, a national study of Latina American professionals showed that higher self-esteem predicted lower levels of stress, marital stress, family-cultural conflict, and occupational-economic stress (Arellano, 2001). Additionally, results indicated that emotion-focused coping (focusing on controlling emotional reactions to a problem) reflects Western concepts of coping; other traditional approaches to coping do not capture the dynamic process of coping that these women showed. That is, Latinas use more complex and not-so-neatly categorized coping styles that don't fit traditional labels. Mexican immigrant farmworkers who reported high levels of stress due to cultural pressures also reported lower levels of self-esteem and higher levels of symptoms of depression (Hovey & Magana, 2000). Cross-cultural research in Hong Kong indicates that with increased age the effects of stress on one's well-being are reduced (Siu et al., 2001). This could be a result of people learning how to cope better as they gain experience in dealing with stress.

Another way to lessen the effects of stress is to disclose and discuss one's health problems. For example, women who disclose the fact that they have breast cancer, which is a source of considerable stress in their lives, had more optimism and lower reported levels of stress than women who did not disclose their disease (Henderson et al., 2002). How people disclose such information matters. Pennebaker and Graybeal (2001) showed that particular patterns of word use can be analyzed by a computer to predict health and personality style. Such analyses may prove useful to physicians and clinicians in providing guidance to individuals who need help in discussing stressful situations.

On a larger scale, the Health and Safety Commission in the United Kingdom developed an extensive program to lower work-related stress (Cousins et al., 2004; Mackay et al., 2004). The Management Standards that were developed address six key areas that each has a goal and specific behaviors that organizations must address: demands, control, support, relationships, role, and organizational change. Whether this nationwide effort will actually reduce work-related stress in the United Kingdom remains to be seen, but the effort alone is quite significant.

EXERCISE

Ever since the time of Hippocrates, physicians and researchers have known that exercise significantly slows the aging process. Indeed, evidence suggests that a program of regular exercise, in conjunction with the healthy lifestyles discussed in Chapter 10, can slow the physiological aging process (Aldwin & Gilmer, 2004). Being sedentary is hazardous to your health.

*Adults benefit from **aerobic exercise,** which places moderate stress on the heart by maintaining a pulse rate between 60 and 90% of the person's maximum heart rate.* You can calculate your maximum heart rate by subtracting your age from 220. Thus, if you are 40 years old, your target range would be 108–162 beats per minute. The minimum time necessary for aerobic exercise to be of benefit depends on its intensity; at low heart rates, sessions may need to last an hour, whereas at high heart rates, 15 minutes may suf-

Engaging in an aerobic exercise program throughout middle age is a great way to stay fit and stay healthy.

Ryan McVay/Getty Images

fice. Examples of aerobic exercise include jogging, step aerobics, swimming, and cross-country skiing.

What happens when a person exercises aerobically (besides becoming tired and sweaty)? Physiologically, adults of all ages show improved cardiovascular functioning and maximum oxygen consumption; lower blood pressure; and better strength, endurance, flexibility, and coordination (Mayo Clinic, 2003a). Psychologically, people who exercise aerobically report lower levels of stress, better moods, and better cognitive functioning (Mayo Clinic, 2003a).

The best way to gain the benefits of aerobic exercise is to maintain physical fitness through the life span, beginning at least in middle age. The Mayo Clinic's Fitness and Sports Medicine Center provides an excellent place to start. In planning an exercise program, three points should be remembered. First, check with a physician before beginning an aerobic exercise program. Second, bear in mind that moderation is important. A study of nearly 17,000 middle-aged and older men found that those who exercised moderately (walked 9 miles per week or cycled for 6–8 hours per week) had a 21 to 50% lower risk of dying than men who did not exercise, whereas men who exercised strenuously (walked 20 miles per week or cycled more than 15 hours per week) had a significantly higher risk of dying than men who exercised moderately. Third, the reasons people exercise change during adulthood. Younger adults tend to exercise to improve their physical appearance, whereas middle-aged and older adults are more concerned with physical and psychological health (Trujillo, Walsh, & Brougham, 1991).

TEST YOURSELF

1. Severe bone loss may result in the disease _____.

2. The cessation of menstruation is termed _____.

3. Reduction of fertility in men usually occurs _____.

4. The stress and _____ paradigm defines stress on the basis of the person's appraisal of a situation as taxing his or her well-being.

5. Research indicates that Type _____ individuals have a better chance of recovering from a heart attack than Type _____ individuals.

The media are full of advertisements for anti-aging creams, diets, and exercise plans. Based on what you have read in this section, how would you evaluate these ads?

Answers: (1) osteoporosis, (2) menopause, (3) gradually, (4) coping, (5) A, B

13.2

COGNITIVE DEVELOPMENT

Kesha, a 54-year-old social worker, is widely regarded as the resident expert when it comes to working the system of human services. Her coworkers look up to her for her ability to get several agencies to cooperate, which they do not do normally, and to keep clients coming in for routine matters and follow-up visits. Kesha claims there is nothing magical about it— it's just her experience that makes the difference.

LEARNING OBJECTIVES

How does practical intelligence develop in adulthood? What are the developmental trends of exercised and unexercised abilities?

How does a person become an expert?

What is meant by lifelong learning? What differences are there between adults and young people in how they learn?

COMPARED TO THE RAPID COGNITIVE GROWTH OF CHILDHOOD, or the controversies about postformal cognition in young adulthood, cognitive development in middle age is relatively quiet. For the most part, the trends in intellectual development discussed in Chapter 10 are continued and solidified. The hallmark of cognitive development in middle age involves developing higher levels of expertise like Kesha shows and flexibility in solving practical problems, such as dealing with complex forms like the tax form in Figure 13.5. We will also see how important it is to continue learning throughout adulthood.

PRACTICAL INTELLIGENCE

Take a moment to think about the following problems (Denney, 1989, 1990; Denney, Pearce, & Palmer, 1982):

- A middle-aged woman is frying chicken in her home when, all of a sudden, a grease fire breaks out on top of the stove. Flames begin to shoot up. What should she do?
- A man finds that the heater in his apartment is not working. He asks his landlord to send someone out to fix it, and the landlord agrees. But after a week of cold weather and several calls to the landlord, the heater is still not fixed. What should the man do?

These practical problems are different from the examples of measures of fluid and crystallized intelligence in Chapter 10. These problems are more realistic; they reflect real-world situations that people routinely face. One criticism of traditional measures of intelligence is that they do not assess the kinds of skills adults actually use in everyday life (Diehl et al., 2005). Most people spend more time at tasks such as managing their personal finances, dealing with uncooperative people, and juggling busy schedules than they do solving esoteric mazes.

The shortcomings of traditional approaches to testing adults' intelligence led to different ways of viewing intelligence that differentiates academic (or traditional) intelligence from other skills (Diehl et al., 2005; Sternberg & Grigorenko, 2000). *The broad range of skills related to how individuals shape, select, or adapt to their physical and social environments is termed* **practical intelligence.** The examples at the beginning of this section illustrate how practical intelligence is measured. Such real-life problems differ in three main ways from traditional tests (Diehl et al., 2005): People are more motivated to solve them; personal experience is more relevant; and they have more than one correct answer. Research evidence supports the view that practical intelligence is distinct from general cognitive ability (Taub et al., 2001).

Figure 13.5
The tax returns that people complete are an example of everyday problem-solving tasks.

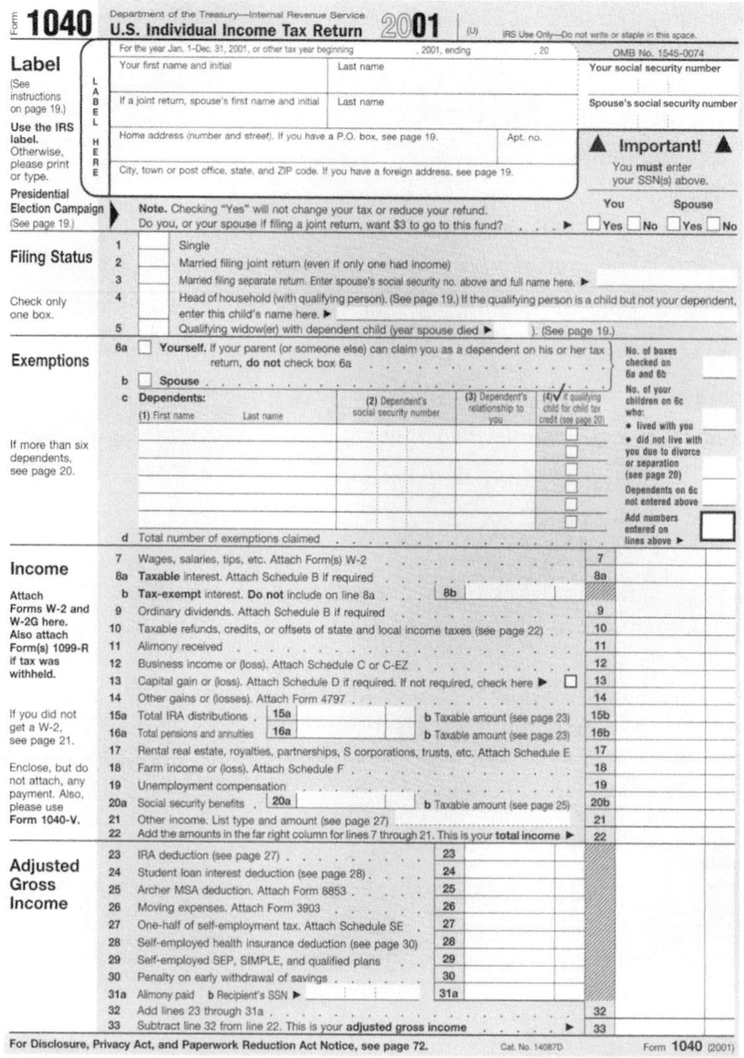

Form **1040** Department of the Treasury—Internal Revenue Service
U.S. Individual Income Tax Return 2001 (U) IRS Use Only—Do not write or staple in this space.

Label (See instructions on page 19.) **Use the IRS label.** Otherwise, please print or type.
LABEL HERE
For the year Jan. 1–Dec. 31, 2001, or other tax year beginning , 2001, ending , 20 | OMB No. 1545-0074
Your first name and initial | Last name | **Your social security number**
If a joint return, spouse's first name and initial | Last name | **Spouse's social security number**
Home address (number and street). If you have a P.O. box, see page 19. | Apt. no.
City, town or post office, state, and ZIP code. If you have a foreign address, see page 19.
▲ **Important!** ▲ You **must** enter your SSN(s) above.

Presidential Election Campaign (See page 19.)
Note. Checking "Yes" will not change your tax or reduce your refund.
Do you, or your spouse if filing a joint return, want $3 to go to this fund? ▶ You ☐Yes ☐No Spouse ☐Yes ☐No

Filing Status
Check only one box.
1 ☐ Single
2 ☐ Married filing joint return (even if only one had income)
3 ☐ Married filing separate return. Enter spouse's social security no. above and full name here. ▶
4 ☐ Head of household (with qualifying person). (See page 19.) If the qualifying person is a child but not your dependent, enter this child's name here. ▶
5 ☐ Qualifying widow(er) with dependent child (year spouse died ▶). (See page 19.)

Exemptions
6a ☐ **Yourself.** If your parent (or someone else) can claim you as a dependent on his or her tax return, **do not** check box 6a
b ☐ **Spouse**
c **Dependents:** (1) First name Last name | (2) Dependent's social security number | (3) Dependent's relationship to you | (4) ✓ if qualifying child for child tax credit (see page 20)
If more than six dependents, see page 20.
d Total number of exemptions claimed
No. of boxes checked on 6a and 6b
No. of your children on 6c who: • lived with you • did not live with you due to divorce or separation (see page 20)
Dependents on 6c not entered above
Add numbers entered on lines above ▶

Income
Attach Forms W-2 and W-2G here. Also attach Form(s) 1099-R if tax was withheld.
If you did not get a W-2, see page 21.
Enclose, but do not attach, any payment. Also, please use Form 1040-V.
7 Wages, salaries, tips, etc. Attach Form(s) W-2 — 7
8a **Taxable** interest. Attach Schedule B if required — 8a
b **Tax-exempt** interest. **Do not** include on line 8a — 8b
9 Ordinary dividends. Attach Schedule B if required — 9
10 Taxable refunds, credits, or offsets of state and local income taxes (see page 22) — 10
11 Alimony received — 11
12 Business income or (loss). Attach Schedule C or C-EZ — 12
13 Capital gain or (loss). Attach Schedule D if required. If not required, check here ▶ ☐ — 13
14 Other gains or (losses). Attach Form 4797 — 14
15a Total IRA distributions 15a — b Taxable amount (see page 23) — 15b
16a Total pensions and annuities 16a — b Taxable amount (see page 23) — 16b
17 Rental real estate, royalties, partnerships, S corporations, trusts, etc. Attach Schedule E — 17
18 Farm income or (loss). Attach Schedule F — 18
19 Unemployment compensation — 19
20a Social security benefits 20a — b Taxable amount (see page 25) — 20b
21 Other income. List type and amount (see page 27) — 21
22 Add the amounts in the far right column for lines 7 through 21. This is your **total income** ▶ — 22

Adjusted Gross Income
23 IRA deduction (see page 27) — 23
24 Student loan interest deduction (see page 28) — 24
25 Archer MSA deduction. Attach Form 8853 — 25
26 Moving expenses. Attach Form 3903 — 26
27 One-half of self-employment tax. Attach Schedule SE — 27
28 Self-employed health insurance deduction (see page 30) — 28
29 Self-employed SEP, SIMPLE, and qualified plans — 29
30 Penalty on early withdrawal of savings — 30
31a Alimony paid b Recipient's SSN ▶ — 31a
32 Add lines 23 through 31a — 32
33 Subtract line 32 from line 22. This is your **adjusted gross income** ▶ — 33

For Disclosure, Privacy Act, and Paperwork Reduction Act Notice, see page 72. Cat. No. 14087D Form **1040** (2001)

Denney's Theory

Denney (1982) postulated that performance on tests of practical intelligence depends on two different components, whose developmental trends are shown in Figure 13.6. *The bottom line represents* ***unexercised ability,*** *the level of performance a person exhibits without practice or training.* Unexercised abilities are those that are not used very often, are not well developed, or are called upon to handle new situations. For example, when you are presented with a problem you have never seen before, the cognitive skills you bring to bear are your unexercised abilities. Unexercised abilities reflect the lower limit to your ability to perform cognitive problems. Notice that performance on traditional laboratory tasks, such as those included in many intelligence tests, closely approximates unexercised ability.

The top line represents ***optimally exercised ability,*** *the level of performance a normal, healthy adult demonstrates under the best conditions of training or practice.* Optimally exercised abilities are those you use the most, or ones you have practiced the most. Problems that tap these abilities are typically performed accurately and more quickly than those that test unexercised abilities, as you can see by comparing the top and bottom lines in Figure 13.6. Optimally exercised abilities, then, reflect areas in which you have greater expertise.

Whether a specific ability is unexercised or optimally exercised varies from individual to individual; for example, one person may have little training in computer programming, whereas the leader of a programming team at Microsoft would be highly

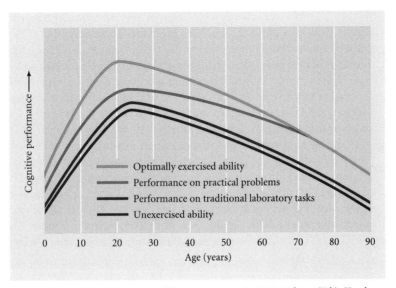

■ **Figure 13.6**
The developmental patterns
of exercised and unexercised
ability: Notice that performance on practical problems
is better than performance
on laboratory problems
across the life span.

From "Aging and Cognitive Changes," by N. W. Denney. In B. B. Wolman (Ed.), *Handbook of Developmental Psychology,* p. 821. Copyright © 1982. Reprinted by permission of Prentice-Hall, Inc. Upper Saddle River, NJ.

skilled. Thus, how an ability is classified depends on the person's experience and expertise; it is not a property of the skill in question. This is an important distinction, as it means that interventions such as additional practice or education could shape the developmental trajectory of a particular ability.

The developmental course of unexercised and optimally exercised abilities is the same: They increase until young adulthood, plateau through middle age, and decline thereafter. As shown in Figure 13.6, the difference between performance on practical problems and optimally exercised ability is hypothesized to close rapidly during middle age. But do the data support Denney's speculations?

When people's answers to practical problems are evaluated in terms of how likely their answers are to be effective, practical intelligence does not appear to decline appreciably until late life (Heidrich & Denney, 1994). Diehl (1998; Diehl et al., 2005) and Allaire and Marsiske (1999) showed that practical intelligence is related to psychometric intelligence; to the extent that everyday problems reflect well-structured challenges in daily life, how well people deal with them is related to traditional psychometric abilities.

Applications of Practical Intelligence

Practical intelligence and postformal thinking across adulthood have been linked (Blanchard-Fields, Janke, & Camp, 1995). Specifically, the extent to which a practical problem evokes an emotional reaction, in conjunction with experience and one's preferred mode of thinking, determines whether one will use a cognitive analysis (thinking one's way through the problem), a problem-focused action (tackling the problem head-on by doing something about it), passive-dependent behavior (withdrawing from the situation), or avoidant thinking and denial (rationalizing to reframe, or redefine, the problem to minimize the seriousness of it). Adults tend to blend emotion with cognition in their approach to practical problems, whereas adolescents tend not to because they get hung up in the logic. For late middle-aged adults, highly emotional problems are associated most with passive-dependent and avoidant-denial approaches. Interestingly, though, problems that deal more with instrumental issues (issues related to daily living such as grocery shopping, getting place to place, etc.) and home management (issues related to living in one's household) are dealt with differently (Blanchard-Fields, Chen, & Norris, 1997). Middle-aged adults use problem-focused strategies more frequently in dealing with instrumental problems than do adolescents or young adults. Clearly, we cannot characterize problem solving in middle age in any one way.

THINK ABOUT IT

How are cognitive analysis, problem-focused action, passive-dependent behavior, and avoidant thinking and denial related to coping with stress?

Other research has shown connections between practical intelligence and Russians' ability to deal with rapid change (Grigorenko & Sternberg, 2001), Yup'ik community members' (in Alaska) competence in life tasks (Grigorenko et al., 2004), and leaders' ability to convince people that their vision is where people need to go (Sternberg, 2002). People higher in practical intelligence are able to deal with a more rapid pace of change (the Russian example), come up with new and more effective ways of solving daily life problems (the Alaskan example), and persuade people to change the way they do things (the leadership example). Practical intelligence has also emerged as an important approach in assessing adults' competence in performing everyday tasks. The Revised Observed Tasks of Daily Living (OTDL) test assesses food preparation, medication intake, and telephone use, three key skills necessary for independent living (Diehl et al., 2005). The Revised OTDL is a useful tool in determining whether adults are capable of living on their own. We will learn more about this issue in Chapter 15 when we consider the topic of frail older adults. Finally, one study comparing European American, African American, and Caribbean American adults showed no differences in practical intelligence (Castro, 2000).

Mechanics and Pragmatics of Intelligence

When we combine the research on practical intelligence with the research on the components or mechanics of intelligence discussed in Chapter 10, we have a more complete description of cognition in adulthood. The two-component model of life-span intelligence (Baltes et al., 1998, 1999) is grounded in the dynamic interplay among the biopsychosocial forces (see Chapter 1). However, as Baltes points out, these forces differentially influence the mechanics and pragmatics of intelligence. Whereas the mechanics of intelligence (those aspects of intelligence discussed as fluid intelligence in Chapter 10) is more directly an expression of the neurophysiological architecture of the mind, the pragmatics of intelligence (those aspects of intelligence discussed as crystallized intelligence in Chapter 10) is associated more with the bodies of knowledge that are available from and mediated through one's culture (Baltes et al., 1998).

This is illustrated in the left portion of Figure 13.7. The mechanics of intelligence in later life is more associated with the fundamental organization of the central nervous system (i.e., biological forces). Thus, it is more closely linked with a gradual loss of brain efficiency with age (Horn & Hofer, 1992).

On the other hand, the pragmatics of intelligence is more closely associated with psychological and sociocultural forces. At the psychological level, knowledge structures change as a function of the accumulated acquisition of knowledge over time. For ex-

■ **Figure 13.7**
The pragmatics of intelligence remain optimal across adulthood whereas the mechanics of fluid intelligence declines.

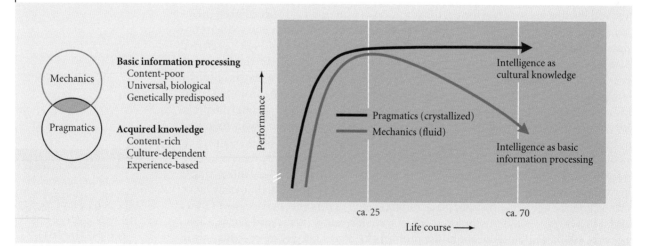

From Baltes, P. B., Staudinger, U. M., and Lindenberger, U. (1999). Lifespan psychology: Theory and application to intellectual functioning. With permission from the *Annual Review of Psychology,* volume 50, 471–507. © 1999 by Annual Reviews, www.AnnualReviews.org.

ample, the more you learn about the American Revolution, the more differentiated your knowledge system becomes, going perhaps from knowing just that the Americans declared their independence from Great Britain and won the war, to a much more elaborated knowledge about how the Americans nearly lost the war and that many people sided with the British. At the sociocultural level, knowledge structures are also influenced by how we are socialized given the particular historical period in which we are raised. For example, people who grew up in the Cold War era were taught and learned that the people in the former Soviet Union were our enemies; those who grew up after the breakup of the former Soviet Union learned that the Russians could be our allies. Such differences reflect the sociocultural and historical contexts of particular points in time. Overall, these knowledge structures influence the way we implement our professional skills, solve everyday problems, and conduct the business of life (Baltes et al., 1998).

Finally, as the right portion of Figure 13.7 suggests, different weightings of the forces of intelligence lead to specific predictions about the developmental pathway they take across the adult life span. Given that biological and genetic forces govern the mechanics more, there is a downward trajectory with age. However, given that the pragmatics of intelligence is governed more by environmental and cultural factors, there is an upward trajectory that is maintained across the adult life span.

BECOMING AN EXPERT

One day John Cavanaugh was driving along when his car suddenly began coughing and sputtering. As deftly as possible, he pulled over to the side of the road, turned off the engine, opened the hood, and proceeded to look inside. It was hopeless; to him, it looked like a jumble of unknown parts. After the car was towed to a garage, a middle-aged mechanic set about fixing it. Within a few minutes, the car was running like new. How?

We saw in Chapter 10 that aspects of intelligence grounded in experience (crystallized intelligence) tend to improve throughout most of adulthood. Some developmentalists have gone so far as to claim that each of us becomes an expert at something that is important to us, such as our work, interpersonal relationships, cooking, sports, or auto repair (Dixon, Kramer, & Baltes, 1985). In this sense, an expert (like the mechanic or Kesha, the social worker in the vignette) is someone who is much better at a task than people who have not put much effort into it (such as John Cavanaugh, in terms of auto repair). We tend to become selective experts in some areas, while remaining rank amateurs or novices at others.

What makes experts better than novices? Most important, experts have built up a wealth of knowledge about alternative ways of solving problems or making decisions. These enable them to bypass steps needed by novices (Ericsson & Smith, 1991). Experts don't always follow the rules as novices do; they are more flexible, creative, and curious; and they have superior strategies for accomplishing a task (Charness & Bosman, 1990). Even though experts may be slower in terms of raw speed because they spend more time planning, their ability to skip steps puts them at a decided advantage. In a way, this represents "the triumph of knowledge over reasoning" (Charness & Bosman, 1990).

Research evidence indicates that expert performance tends to peak in middle age and drops off slightly after that (Masunaga & Horn, 2001). However, the declines in expert performance are not nearly as great as they are for the abilities of information processing, memory, and fluid intelligence that underlie expertise, and expertise may sometimes compensate for declines in underlying cognitive abilities (Masunaga & Horn, 2001; Taylor et al., 2005). Thus, it appears that knowledge based on experience is an important component of expertise.

But why are expertise and information processing, memory, and fluid intelligence not strongly related? After all, we saw in Chapter 10 that the latter abilities underlie good cognitive performance. Rybash, Hoyer, and Roodin (1986) proposed a process called *encapsulation* as the answer. *Their notion is that the **processes of thinking** (information processing, memory, fluid intelligence) become connected or **encapsulated** to the **products***

THINK ABOUT IT

Can expertise be taught? Why or why not?

of thinking (expertise). This process of encapsulation allows expertise to compensate for declines in underlying abilities, perhaps by making thinking more efficient (Hoyer & Rybash, 1994).

Let's consider how encapsulation might work with auto mechanics. As a rule, people who become auto mechanics are taught to think as if they were playing a game of Twenty Questions, in which the optimal strategy is to ask a question such that the answer eliminates half of the remaining possibilities. In the beginning, the mechanic learns the thinking strategy and the content knowledge about automobiles separately. But as the person's experience with repairing automobiles increases, the thinking strategy and content knowledge merge; instead of having to go through a Twenty Questions approach, the expert mechanic just "knows" how to proceed. This cognitive-developmental pattern in adults is very different from the one that occurs in children (Hoyer & Rybash, 1994). In the adult's case, development is directed toward mastery and adaptive competency in specific domains, whereas during childhood it is more uniform across content domains.

One of the outcomes of encapsulation appears to be a decrease in the ability to explain how one arrives at a particular answer (Hoyer & Rybash, 1994). It appears that the increased efficiency that comes through merging the process with the product of thinking comes at the cost of being able to explain to others what one is doing. This could be why some instructors have a difficult time explaining the various steps involved in solving a problem to novice students, but an easier time explaining it to graduate students who have more background and experience. Because these instructors may skip steps, it's harder for those with less elaborated knowledge to fill in the missing steps.

We will return to the topic of expertise in Chapter 14 when we discuss wisdom, which some believe to be the outcome of becoming an expert in living.

LIFELONG LEARNING

Many people work in occupations in which information and technology change rapidly. To keep up with these changes, many organizations and professions now emphasize the importance of learning how to learn, rather than learning specific content that may become outdated in a couple of years. For most people, a college education will probably not be the last educational experience they have in their careers. Workers in many professions, such as medicine, nursing, social work, psychology, auto mechanics, and teaching, are now required to obtain continuing education credits to stay current in their fields. Online learning has made lifelong learning more accessible to professionals and interested adults alike (Fretz, 2001; Ranwez, Leidig, & Crampes, 2000), but open access to computers for these programs needs to be in supportive, quiet environments (Eaton & Salari, 2005).

College campuses are an obvious site for lifelong learning; you probably have seen returning adult students on your campus. Lifelong learning takes place in settings other than college campuses too. Many organizations offer workshops for their employees on a wide range of topics, from specific job-related tasks to leisure-time activities. Additionally, many channels on cable television offer primarily educational programming, and online courses, computer networks, and bulletin boards are available for educational exchanges. Only a few generations ago, a high school education was the ticket to a lifetime of secure employment. Today, lifelong learning is rapidly becoming the norm.

Lifelong learning is gaining acceptance as the best way to approach the need for continuing education and for retraining displaced workers. But should lifelong learning be approached as merely an extension of earlier educational experiences? Knowles, Swanson, and Holton (2005) argue that teaching aimed at children and youth differs from teaching aimed at adults. Adult learners differ from their younger counterparts in several ways:

- ◼ Adults have a higher need to know why they should learn something before undertaking it.
- ◼ Adults enter a learning situation with more and different experience on which to build.

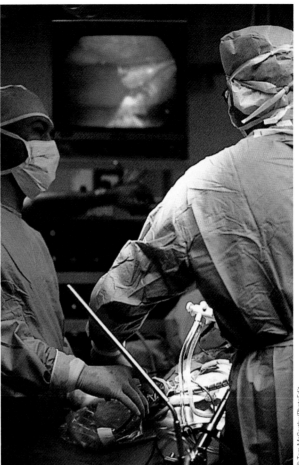

Workers in many professional fields need to engage in lifelong learning to keep up with the latest developments in their fields.

- Adults are most willing to learn those things they believe are necessary to deal with real-world problems rather than abstract, hypothetical situations.

- Most adults are more motivated to learn by internal factors (such as self-esteem or personal satisfaction) than by external factors (such as a job promotion or pay raise).

Lifelong learning is becoming increasingly important, but educators need to keep in mind that learning styles change as people age.

TEST YOURSELF

1. The skills and knowledge necessary for people to function in everyday life make up _____.

2. The difference between performance on practical problems and optimally exercised ability is hypothesized to _____ during middle age.

3. Even though they may be slower in terms of raw speed, experts are at a distinct advantage over novices because they _____.

4. The way in which the process of thinking becomes connected to the products of thinking is termed _____.

5. Due to rapidly changing technology and information, many educators now support the concept of

_____.

Based on the cognitive-developmental changes described in this section, what types of jobs would be done best by middle-aged adults?

Answers: (1) practical intelligence, (2) narrow, (3) can skip steps, (4) encapsulation, (5) lifelong learning

13.3

PERSONALITY

Jim showed all the signs. He divorced his wife of nearly 20 years to enter into a relationship with a woman 15 years younger, sold his ordinary-looking midsize sedan and bought a red sports car, and began working out regularly at the health club after years of being a couch potato. Jim claims he hasn't felt this good in years; he is happy to be making this change in middle age. All of Jim's friends agree: This is a clear case of midlife crisis. Or is it?

LEARNING OBJECTIVES

What is the five-factor model? What evidence is there for stability in personality traits?

What changes occur in people's priorities and personal concerns? How does a person achieve generativity? How is midlife best described?

THE TOPIC OF PERSONALITY DEVELOPMENT in middle age immerses us in one of the hottest debates in theory and research in adult development and aging. Take Jim's case. *Many people believe strongly that middle age brings with it a normative crisis called the **midlife crisis**.* There would appear to be lots of evidence to support this view based on case studies like Jim's. But is everything as it seems? We'll find out in this section.

Unlike most of the other topics we have covered in this chapter, research on personality in middle-aged adults is grounded in several competing theories, one being the psychoanalytic approach we encountered in Chapter 1. Another difference is that much of the research we will consider is longitudinal research, also discussed in Chapter 1.

First, we examine the evidence that personality traits remain fairly stable in adulthood. This position makes the claim that what you are like in young adulthood predicts pretty well what you will be like for the rest of your life. Second, we consider the evidence that people's priorities and personal concerns change throughout adulthood, requiring adults to reassess themselves from time to time. This alternative position claims that change is the rule during adulthood.

At no other point in the life span is the debate about stability versus change as heated as it is concerning personality in middle age. In this section, we consider the evidence for both positions.

STABILITY IS THE RULE: THE FIVE-FACTOR MODEL

One of the most important advances in research on adult development and aging in the past few decades has been the emergence of a personality theory aimed specifically at describing adults. Due mostly to the efforts of Paul Costa Jr. and Robert McCrae (1997; McCrae, 2002), we are able to describe adults' personality traits using five dimensions: neuroticism, extraversion, openness to experience, agreeableness, and conscientiousness. These dimensions are strongly grounded in cross-sectional, longitudinal, and sequential research. First, though, let's take a closer look at each dimension.

- *People who are high on the **neuroticism** dimension tend to be anxious, hostile, self-conscious, depressed, impulsive, and vulnerable.* They may show violent or negative emotions that interfere with their ability to get along with others or to handle problems in everyday life. People who are low on this dimension tend to be calm, even-tempered, self-content, comfortable, unemotional, and hardy.

- *Individuals who are high on the **extraversion** dimension thrive on social interaction, like to talk, take charge easily, readily express their opinions and feelings, like to keep busy, have boundless energy, and prefer stimulating and challenging environments.* Such people tend to enjoy people-oriented jobs, such as social work and sales, and they often have humanitarian goals. People who are low tend to be reserved, quiet, passive, serious, and emotionally unreactive.

- *Being high on the **openness to experience** dimension tends to mean a vivid imagination and dream life, appreciation of art, and a strong desire to try anything once.* These individuals tend to be naturally curious about things and to make decisions based on situational factors rather than absolute rules. People who are readily open to new experiences place a relatively low emphasis on personal economic gain. They tend to choose jobs such as the ministry or counseling, which offer diversity of experience rather than high pay. People who are low on this dimension tend to be down-to-earth, uncreative, conventional, uncurious, and conservative.

- *Scoring high on the **agreeableness** dimension is associated with being accepting, willing to work with others, and caring.* Interestingly, people who score low on this dimension (i.e., demonstrate high levels of *antagonism*) show many of the characteristics of the Type A behavior pattern discussed earlier in this chapter. They tend to be ruthless, suspicious, stingy, antagonistic, critical, and irritable.

- *People who show high levels of **conscientiousness** tend to be hard working, ambitious, energetic, scrupulous, and persevering.* Such people have a strong desire to make something of themselves. People at the opposite end of this scale tend to be negligent, lazy, disorganized, late, aimless, and nonpersistent.

What's the Evidence for Trait Stability?

Costa and McCrae have investigated whether the traits that make up their model remain stable across adulthood (e.g., Costa & McCrae, 1988, 1997; McCrae & Costa, 1994). In fact, they suggest that personality traits stop changing by age 30 and appear to be "set in plaster" (McCrae & Costa, 1994, p. 21). The data from the Costa, McCrae, and colleagues' studies came from the Baltimore Longitudinal Study of Aging for the 114 men who took the Guilford-Zimmerman Temperament Survey (GZTS) on three occasions, with each of the two follow-up testings about 6 years apart. What Costa and colleagues found was surprising. Even over a 12-year period, the 10 traits measured by the GZTS remained highly stable; the correlations ranged from .68 to .85. In much of personality research we might expect to find this degree of stability over a week or two, but to see it over 12 years is noteworthy.

We would normally be skeptical of such consistency over a long period. But similar findings were obtained in other studies. In a longitudinal study of 60-, 80-, and 100-year-old men and women, Martin, Long, and Poon (2003) found that there were no significant changes across age groups in overall personality patterns. However, some interesting changes did occur in the very old. There was an increase in suspiciousness and sensitivity. This could be explained by increased wariness of victimization in older adulthood. Stability was also observed in past longitudinal data conducted over an 8-year span by Siegler, George, and Okun (1979) at Duke University, a 30-year span by Leon, Gillum, Gillum, and Gouze (1979) in Minnesota, and in other longitudinal studies (Schaie & Willis, 1995; Schmitz-Scherzer & Thomae, 1983). Even more amazing was the finding that personality ratings by spouses of each other showed no systematic changes over a 6-year period (Costa & McCrae, 1988). Thus, it appears that individuals change very little in self-reported personality traits over periods of up to 30 years and over the age range of 20 to 90.

This is a truly exciting and important conclusion. Clearly, lots of things change in people's lives over 30 years. They marry, divorce, have children, change jobs, face stressful situations, move, and maybe even retire. Social networks and friendships come and go. Society changes, and economic ups and downs have important effects. Personal changes in appearance and health occur. People read volumes, see dozens of movies, and watch thousands of hours of television. But their underlying personality dispositions hardly change at all. Or do they?

Despite the impressive collection of research findings for personality stability using the five-factor model, there is growing evidence for personality change. First, there are data indicating that certain personality traits (self-confidence, cognitive commitment,

THINK ABOUT IT

Does evidence of stability in traits support the idea that some aspects of personality are genetic? Why or why not?

outgoingness, and dependability) show some change over a 30- to 40-year period (Jones & Meredith, 1996). Second, there are a growing number of studies suggesting that neuroticism may increase and extraversion may decrease as we grow older (Maiden et al., 2003; Small et al., 2003). Third, Srivastava, John, Gosling, and Potter (2003) conducted a large Internet study of more than 130,000 people ranging in age from 21 to 60 examining the Big Five traits. This study, described in detail in the Spotlight on Research feature, is a testament to how changes in our technology allow more in depth analyses of larger samples of individuals. They found that none of the Big Five personality traits remained stable after age 30.

SPOTLIGHT ON RESEARCH

IS PERSONALITY IN YOUNG AND MIDDLE ADULTHOOD SET IN PLASTER?

Who were the investigators and what was the aim of the study? Srivastava and colleagues (2003) wanted to test the notion that the Big Five personality traits are "set in plaster" in adulthood against the contextualist view that they should change over time.

How did the investigators measure the topic of interest? All participants completed the Big Five Inventory that was available through the study websites.

Who were the participants in the study? Srivastava and colleagues had 132,515 people aged 21 to 60 (54% female; 86% European descended) complete a Big Five personality measure on the Internet. This is one of the largest samples ever collected. Participants were all residents of either the United States (90.8%) or Canada (9.2%).

What was the design of the study? The study used a cross-sectional design. To attract a broad and diverse sample, they used two types of web pages. One was a guide called "all about you," which informed individuals that they would take a test on what psychologists considered to be the fundamental dimensions of personality. The second was a "Find your *Star Wars* Twin," which included feedback about the characters from *Star Wars* with whom the participant was most similar based on the Big Five personality test.

Were there ethical concerns with the study? Because the study used volunteers who completed surveys containing no questions about sensitive topics, there were no ethical concerns.

What were the results? The developmental patterns for each of the Big Five dimensions are shown in Figure 13.8. They found that none of the Big Five personality traits remained completely stable after age 30. For example, conscientiousness showed the most differences across early adulthood, a time when adults are advancing in the workforce and forming intimate relationships. Agreeableness increased most during the 30s. Neuroticism differed considerably for women, whereas men showed little change but increased variability (that is, although results for the overall group stayed the same, some men increased and some decreased). Despite differences in respondents across the two Web sites (more women responded to the "all about you" site and more men responded to the "*Star Wars*" site, the developmental patterns were the same.

What did the investigators conclude? Overall, Srivastava and colleagues concluded that the plaster notion for the Big Five was wrong. They found much evidence that personality traits differed across adulthood, and they argue that this is the result of traits and environments interacting.

What converging evidence would strengthen their conclusions? The findings would be strengthened by longitudinal data that would actually track the possibility of personality change over time.

To enhance your understanding of this research, go to http://psychology .wadsworth.com/kail_cavanaugh4e/ to complete critical thinking questions and explore related websites.

Although the five-factor model enjoys great popularity and appears to have much supporting evidence, it is not perfect. Even acknowledging the problems, though, evidence for some stability in personality traits across adulthood is a very important finding. What a person chooses to do with these traits and how their interaction with the environment shapes how they are displayed may not be as consistent.

CHANGE IS THE RULE: CHANGING PRIORITIES IN MIDLIFE

Joyce, a 52-year-old preschool teacher, thought carefully about what she thinks is important in life. "I definitely feel differently about what I want to accomplish. When I was younger, I wanted to advance and be a great teacher. Now, although I still want to be

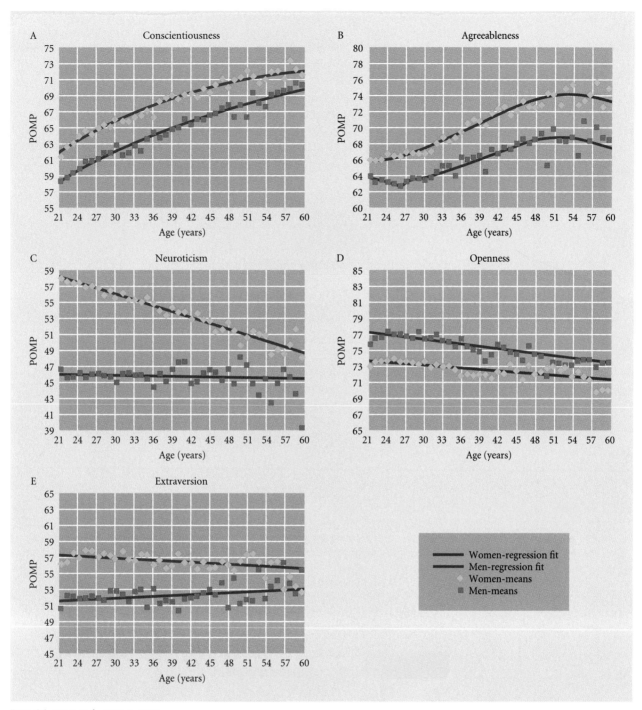

From Srivastava et al., 2005, p. 1047.

■ **Figure 13.8**
Age differences in Big Five personality traits across young adulthood and middle age.

good, I'm more concerned with providing help to the new teachers around here. I've got lots of on-the-job experience that I can pass along."

Joyce is not alone. Despite the evidence that personality traits remain stable during adulthood, many middle-aged people report that their personal priorities change during middle age. In general, they report that they are increasingly concerned with helping younger people achieve rather than with getting ahead themselves. *In his psychosocial theory, Erikson argued that this shift in priorities reflects* **generativity,** *or being productive by helping others in order to ensure the continuation of society by guiding the next generation.*

Achieving generativity can be very enriching. It is grounded in the successful resolution of the previous six phases of Erikson's theory (see Chapter 1). There are many avenues for generativity, such as parenting (Pratt et al., 2001), mentoring (Lucas, 2000; see Chapter 12), volunteering, foster grandparent programs, and many other activities. Sources of generativity do not vary across ethnic groups (Ellen, 2000), but there is some evidence that African Americans express more generative concern than do European Americans (Hart et al., 2001).

Some adults do not achieve generativity. Instead, they become bored, self-indulgent, and unable to contribute to the continuation of society. *Erikson referred to this state as* **stagnation,** *in which people are unable to deal with the needs of their children or to provide mentoring to younger adults.*

What Are Generative People Like?

To describe generativity so that we can recognize it in someone, several researchers have constructed various descriptions of it (Washko, 2001). One of the best is McAdams's model (McAdams, 2001a; McAdams, Hart, & Maruna, 1998), shown in Figure 13.9. This multidimensional model shows how generativity results from the complex interconnections among societal and inner forces, which create a concern for the next generation and a belief in the goodness of the human enterprise, leading to generative commitment, which produces generative actions. A person derives personal meaning from being generative by constructing a life story, or narration, which helps create the person's identity (see Chapter 10).

The components of McAdams's model relate differently to personality traits. For example, generative *concern* relates to life satisfaction and overall happiness, whereas generative *action* does not (de St. Aubin & McAdams, 1995). New grandparents may derive much satisfaction from their grandchildren and are greatly concerned with their well-being, but they have little desire to engage in the daily hassles of caring for them on a regular basis. Women who exhibit high generativity tend to have prosocial personality traits, are personally invested in being a parent, express generative attitudes at work, and exhibit caring behaviors toward others outside their immediate families (Peterson & Klohnen, 1995), as well as show high well-being in their role as a spouse (MacDermid, De Haan, & Heilbrun, 1996). These results have led to the creation of positive and negative generativity indices that reliably identify differences between generative and nongenerative individuals (Himsel et al., 1997).

The growing evidence on generativity indicates that the personal concerns and priorities of middle-aged adults are different from those of younger adults. But is this

■ **Figure 13.9**
McAdams's model of generativity. Note that how one shows generativity (action) is influenced by several factors.

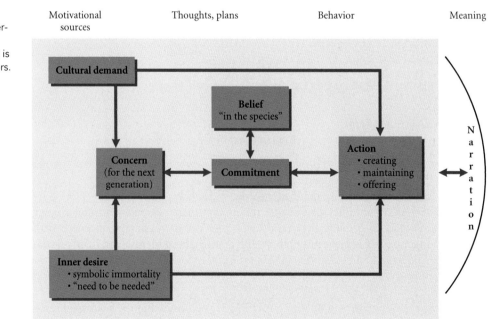

view supported in other aspects of personality? Let's consider gender-role identity as an example.

Does Gender-Role Identity Converge?

People's beliefs about the appropriate characteristics for men and women reflect shared cultural beliefs and stereotypes of "masculinity" and "femininity" (Best & Williams, 1993; Huyck, 1999; Sinnott & Shifren, 2001). Across a wide age range in U.S. society, women are traditionally described as weaker with lower self-esteem, less active, more concerned with affiliation, and more nurturing and deferential. Men are regarded as stronger, more active, and higher in autonomy, risk-taking, achievement, and aggression (Huyck, 1999; Robinson, Johnson, & Benton, 2002). Collectively, such descriptions help form one's gender-role identity.

In addition, some gender stereotypes are sensitive to age (Gutmann, 1994). Old men are seen as less stereotypically masculine or warriorlike and more as powerful elderly men striving for peace. Old women are noted for their greater assertiveness and control; stereotypes include matriarchs overseeing extended families or dangerous witches who use power malevolently. Some cultures view older adults as genderless, having lost the need for differentiated gender-role identity after they concluded their child-rearing duties (Gailey, 1987).

Beginning with Jung (1933), several researchers and theorists argue for a "crossover effect" of gender identity during middle age. As we noted earlier, Jung proposed that in adolescence women initially suppress their masculine aspects and men initially suppress their feminine aspects. Each discovers these suppressed aspects and develops them in midlife, with the goal of achieving a balance between one's masculine and feminine characteristics. For example, during midlife women may place increased emphasis on achievement and accomplishment, and men may place more emphasis on familial and nurturant concerns (Parker & Aldwin, 1997).

Overall, the data on actual changes in people's gender-role identity are mixed. Some studies find a tendency for middle-aged and older adults to endorse similar self-descriptions concerning gender-role identity (Gutmann, 1994). Other studies show decreasing endorsement of traditional feminine traits in both men and women but stable endorsements of masculine traits (Parker & Aldwin, 1997). Collectively, the data indicate that men and women are most different in their gender-role identities in late adolescence and young adulthood but become increasingly similar in midlife and old age (Huyck, 1999).

Longitudinal data on individual development are largely lacking. What evidence is available suggests that a majority (54%) of people remain in the same gender-role category over a 10-year period (Hyde, Krajnik, & Skuldt-Niederberger, 1991). However, this still means that a substantial number of people demonstrate change. As Hyde and coworkers (1991) note, however, we currently have no way of predicting who will change and who will not.

Increasing similarity in self-descriptions does not guarantee increased similarity in the way men and women behave. Thus, the change may be happening more internally than behaviorally (Parker & Aldwin, 1997). Moreover, much of the change may be due to the failing health of elderly men. Because older wives tend to be healthier than their husbands, the balance of power may shift out of necessity to wives, and men may be forced to accept a more dependent role.

Does gender-role identity converge with increasing age? It is still debatable. The lack of consistent behavioral evidence and the statistically small differences in some of the self-assessment data lead some researchers to argue that no changes in personality occur (for example, McCrae & Costa, 1994). In contrast, others see the convergence in self-assessments as evidence that older men and women transcend stereotypes to become essentially gender free (Sinnott & Shifren, 2001). Still others view any change in self-assessment, no matter how small, as at least personally relevant (Gutmann, 1987).

It will be interesting to see whether the trend toward similarity continues over the next few generations. Changes in how younger men and women view themselves as a result of women's new roles in society may shift the trend downward in age or may make it disappear altogether.

Life Transition Theories and the Midlife Crisis

We have seen that theorists such as Erikson believe that adults face several important challenges and that by struggling with these issues people develop new aspects of themselves. Erikson's notion that people experience fundamental changes in their priorities and personal concerns was grounded in the possibility that middle adulthood includes other important changes. Indeed, Carl Jung, one of the founders of psychoanalytic theory, believed that adults may experience a midlife crisis. This belief led to the development of several theories postulating that adulthood consists of alternating periods of stability and transition that people experience in a fixed sequence.

Levinson and colleagues (1978; Levinson & Levinson, 1996), Gould (1978), and Vaillant (1977) developed life transition theories based on longitudinal studies of fairly exclusive and nonrepresentative groups of adults (in some cases only men) over several decades. Data were gathered mainly through interviews and personal reflections of the participants. These approaches led to a popularization of "midlife crisis" so that most people thought that people like Jim, the recently divorced guy with the red sports car in the vignette, were typical. Indeed, few people in the United States would have difficulty providing an example, as most people believe that a midlife crisis is inevitable. In part, this belief is fostered by descriptions of personality development in adulthood that have appeared in the popular press. Surveys of Americans indicate that most people believe they have or will have a midlife crisis (Wethington, 2000).

Despite the popularity of these theories, some of which were turned into best-selling books, the evidence for universal age-related stages is based on far fewer and much more selective samples than are the data from the personality trait research or research on generativity. For several decades the bulk of the research evidence fails to support the idea that most adults experience difficulty at the level of a crisis in midlife. Research involving women and men, using a variety of methods such as interviews and personality tests, shows that unexpected events (such as divorce or job transfers) are much more likely to create stress than are normative midlife events (such as menopause or becoming a grandparent). In fact, it may be the case that those who do experience a crisis are those who are suffering from general problems of psychopathology (Labouvie-Vief & Diehl, 1999). Reanalysis and extension of Costa and McCrae's data, specifically looking for evidence of a midlife crisis, revealed only a handful of men who fit the classic profile, and even then the crisis came anywhere between the ages of 30 and 60 (Rosenberg, Rosenberg, & Farrell, 1999). There may be universal stresses during midlife, but there is no set way of dealing with them (Rosenberg et al., 1999).

Is there a midlife crisis? The evidence indicates that for most people, midlife is no more or no less traumatic than any other period. Even investigators who believed strongly in the existence of a midlife crisis when they began their research admitted that they could find no support for it despite extensive testing and interviewing (Rosenberg et al., 1999). Thus, Jim's behavior may have an explanation, but it's not because he's going through a universal midlife crisis.

Despite the lack of evidence for a universal midlife crisis, as we saw in our consideration of generativity, there is substantial evidence that people do experience some sort of fundamental change in themselves at some point during adulthood. Thus, it may well be that most adults pass through transitions at some point; when those transitions will occur, though, is largely unpredictable. Perhaps it is better to view midlife as a time that presents unique challenges and issues that must be negotiated (Bumpass & Aquilino, 1995).

If midlife is not characterized by a crisis, but does present unique challenges and issues, how do people negotiate it successfully? *The secret seems to be **ego resilience,** a powerful personality resource that enables people to handle midlife changes.* Longitudinal data from two samples indicate that people who enter middle age with high ego resilience are more likely to experience it as an opportunity for change and growth, whereas people with low ego resilience are more likely to experience it as a time of stagnation or decline (Klohnen, Vandewater, & Young, 1996). Individual differences in the timing of such experiences and how people deal with midlife are very large, which probably accounts for the failure to find a universal midlife crisis (Klohnen et al., 1996). Ego resilience may also be the resource that could account for the two outcomes (generativity and stagnation) of Erikson's view of midlife.

In sum, perhaps the best way to view the life transitions associated with middle age is through the words of a 52-year-old woman (Klohnen et al., 1996):

> Middle age. . . . The time when you realize you've moved to the caretaker, senior responsibility role. . . . A time of discomfort because you watch the generation before you, whom you have loved and respected and counted on for emotional back-up, for advice . . . become more dependent on you and then die. Your children grow up, move out, try their wings . . . ; indeed, they attempt to teach you the "truths" they've discovered about life. . . . It's time to make some new choices—groups, friends, activities need not be so child related anymore.

TEST YOURSELF

1. The dimensions in the five-factor theory of personality include anxiety, hostility, _____ and impulsiveness.

2. According to Erikson, an increasing concern with helping younger people achieve is termed _____.

3. According to McAdams, the meaning one derives from being generative happens through the process of _____.

4. Statistical evidence indicates that gender-role identity _____ in middle age.

5. Research indicates that _____ is a key personality factor in predicting who will negotiate midlife successfully.

How can you reconcile the data from trait research, which indicates little change, with the data from other research, which shows substantial change in personality in adulthood?

Answers: (1) neuroticism, (2) generativity, (3) narration, (4) converges, (5) ego resilience

---

13.4

FAMILY DYNAMICS AND MIDDLE AGE

Esther is facing a major milestone: Her youngest child, Megan, is about to head off to college. But instead of feeling depressed, as she thought she would, Esther feels almost elated at the prospect. She and Bill are finally free of the day-to-day parenting duties of the past 30 years. Esther is looking forward to getting to know her husband again. She wonders whether there is something wrong with her for being excited that her daughter is moving away.

LEARNING OBJECTIVES

How does the relationship between middle-aged parents and their young adult children change?

How do middle-aged adults deal with their aging parents?

What styles of grandparenthood do middle-aged adults experience? How do grandchildren and grandparents interact?

PEOPLE LIKE ESTHER CONNECT GENERATIONS. Family ties across the generations provide the context for socialization and for continuity in the family's identity. At the center agewise are members of the middle-aged generation, like Esther, who serve as the links between their aging parents and their own maturing children (Hareven & Adams, 1996). *Middle-aged mothers (more than fathers) tend to take on this role of* **kinkeeper,** *the*

Intergenerational ties in a family help to keep them together and to ensure the transmission of key values.

© Tim Pannell /Corbis

person who gathers family members together for celebrations and keeps them in touch with each other.

Think about the major issues confronting a typical middle-aged couple: maintaining a good marriage, parenting responsibilities, children who are becoming adults themselves, job pressures, and concern about aging parents, just to name a few. Middle-aged adults truly have quite a lot to deal with every day in balancing their responsibilities to their children and their aging parents (Riley & Bowen, 2005). *Indeed, middle-aged adults are sometimes referred to as the **sandwich generation;** they are caught between the competing demands of two generations (their parents and their children).* Being in the sandwich generation means different things for women and men. When middle-aged women assess how well they are dealing with the midlife transition, their most pressing issues relate more to their adolescent children than to their aging parents; for middle-aged men, it is the other way around (Riley & Bowen, 2005).

In this section, we first examine the dynamics of middle-aged parents and their maturing children and discover whether Esther's feelings are typical. Next, we consider the issues facing middle-aged adults and their aging parents. Later, we consider what happens when people become grandparents.

LETTING GO: MIDDLE-AGED ADULTS AND THEIR CHILDREN

Being a parent has a rather strange side when you think about it. After creating children out of love, parents spend considerable time, effort, and money preparing them to become independent and leave. For most parents, the leaving (and sometimes returning) occurs during midlife.

Becoming Friends and the Empty Nest

Some time during middle age, most parents experience two positive developments with regard to their children. Suddenly their children see them in a new light, and the children leave home.

After the strain of raising adolescents, parents generally appreciate the transformation that occurs when their children head into young adulthood. In general, parent-child relationships improve when children become young adults (Troll & Fingerman, 1996). The difference can be dramatic, as in the case of Deb, a middle-aged mother. "When Sacha was 15, she acted as if I was the dumbest person on the planet. But now that she's 21, she acts as if I got smart all of a sudden. I like being around her. She's a great kid, and we're really becoming friends."

A key factor in making this transition as smoothly as possible is the extent to which parents foster and approve of their children's attempts at being independent. Most parents are like Esther, the mother in the vignette, and manage the transition to an empty nest successfully (Lewis & Lin, 1996). That's not to say that parents are heartless. When children leave home, emotional bonds are disrupted. Parents feel the change, although differently; women who define themselves more in their role as a mother tend to report more distress and negative mood (Hobdy, 2000). But only about 25% of mothers and fathers report being very sad and unhappy when the last child leaves home (Lewis & Lin, 1996).

When children become adults, their relationships with their parents turn more into friendship.

Still, parents provide considerable financial help (such as paying college tuition) when possible. Most help in other ways, ranging from the mundane (such as making the washer and dryer available to their college-age children) to the extraordinary (providing the down payment for their child's house). Adult children and their parents generally believe that they have strong, positive relationships and that they can count on each other for help when necessary (Connidis, 2001).

When Children Come Back

Parents' satisfaction with the empty nest is sometimes short-lived. Roughly half of young adults in the United States return to their parents' home at least once after moving out (Osgood et al., 2005). Interestingly, this living arrangement is more common if the parents are in good health and the parents continue to do most of the housework (Ward, Logan, & Spitze, 1992).

Why do children move back? Several demographic and psychological factors influence the decision. Men are more likely to move back than women, as are children who had low college GPAs, low sense of autonomy, and an expectation that their parents would provide a large portion of their income following graduation (Osgood et al., 2005; Steen & Peterson, 2000). Adult children whose parents were verbally or physically abusive are unlikely to move back, as are those who are married.

Adult children sometimes move back with their parents for economic and social reasons.

Caring for one's aging parent can bring both stresses and rewards.

GIVING BACK: MIDDLE-AGED ADULTS AND THEIR AGING PARENTS

No matter how old you may be, being someone's child is a role that people still play well into adulthood and, sometimes, into their 60s and 70s. How do middle-aged adults relate to their parents? What happens when their parents become frail? How do middle-aged adults deal with the need to care for their parents?

Caring for Aging Parents

Most middle-aged adults have parents who are in reasonably good health. For a growing number of people, however, being a middle-aged child of aging parents involves providing some level of care. The job of caring for older parents usually falls to a daughter or a daughter-in-law (Stephens & Franks, 1999). Even after ruling out all other demographic characteristics of adult child caregivers and their care recipients, daughters are more than three times as likely to provide care as sons (Stephens et al., 2001). This gender difference is also found in other cultures. For example, in Japan, even though the oldest son is responsible for parental care, it is his wife who actually does the day-to-day caregiving (Morioka, 1998).

In some situations, older parents must move in with one of their children. Such moves usually occur after decades of both generations living independently. This history of independent living sets the stage for adjustment difficulties following the move; both lifestyles must be accommodated. Most of the time, adult children provide care for their mothers, who may in turn have provided care for their husbands before they died. (Spousal caregiving is discussed in Chapter 14.) In other situations, adult daughters must try to manage care from a distance. As we will see later, irrespective of the location of care, women are under considerable stress from the pressures of caregiving.

As described in the Real People feature, caring for one's parent presents a dilemma, especially for women (Baek, 2005; Stephens et al., 2001). *Most adult children feel a sense of responsibility, termed* **filial obligation,** *to care for their parent if necessary.* For example, adult child caregivers sometimes express the feeling that they "owe it to Mom or Dad" to care for them; after all, their parent provided for them for many years, and now the shoe is on the other foot (Myers & Cavanaugh, 1995). Adult children often provide care when needed to their parents in all Western and non-Western cultures studied (Hareven & Adams, 1996). Viewed from a global perspective, all but a small percentage of care to older adults is provided by adult children and other family members (Hareven & Adams, 1996; Pavalko & Artis, 1997).

REAL PEOPLE: Applying Human Development

TAKING CARE OF MOM

Everything seemed to be going well for Joan. Her career was really taking off, her youngest daughter had just entered high school, and her marriage to Bill was better than ever. So when her phone rang one June afternoon, she was really taken by surprise.

The voice on the other end was matter-of-fact. Joan's mother had had a major stroke and would need someone to care for her. Because her mother did not have sufficient medical and long-term care insurance to afford a nursing home, Joan made the only decision she could—her mom would move in with her, Bill, and Kelly. Joan firmly believed

that because her mom had provided for her, Joan owed it to her mom to do the same now that she was in need.

What Joan didn't count on was that taking care of her mom was both the most difficult thing she ever did, as well as one of the most rewarding. Joan quickly realized that the days of her being able to do the lengthy business trips and seminars were over, as was her quick rise up the company leadership ladder. Other employees were now the ones who brought back the great new ideas and could respond to out-of-town crises quickly. Hard as it was, Joan knew that her career trajectory had taken a

different turn. And she and Bill had more disagreements than she could ever remember, usually about the lessening amount of time they had to spend with each other. Kelly's demands to be taken here and there also added to Joan's stress.

But Joan and her mom were able to develop the kind of relationship that they could not have otherwise and to talk about issues that they had long suppressed. Although caring for a physically disabled mother was extremely taxing, Joan and her mother's ability to connect on a different level made all the difference.

Research indicates that middle-aged adults and other relatives provide 72% of all care to frail older adults and expend a great deal of energy, time, and money helping their older parents (National Academy on an Aging Society, 2000). Caring for an older parent is not easy. It usually doesn't happen by choice; each party would just as soon live apart. The potential for conflict over daily routines and lifestyles is high. Indeed, one major source of conflict between middle-aged daughters and their older mothers is differences in perceived need for care, with middle-aged daughters believing that their mothers needed care more than the mothers believed they did (Fingerman, 1996).

Caregiving Stress

Caregiving is also a major source of stress. Adult children and other family caregivers are especially vulnerable to stress from two main sources (Pearlin et al., 1990):

- Adult children may have trouble coping with declines in their parents' functioning, especially those involving cognitive abilities and problematic behavior, and with the work overload, burnout, and loss of the previous relationship with a parent.

- When the caregiving situation is perceived as confining, or seriously infringes on the adult child's other responsibilities (spouse, parent, employee, etc.), the situation is likely to be perceived negatively, which may lead to family or job conflicts, economic problems, loss of self-identity, and decreased competence.

Caring for a parent entails psychological costs. Even the most devoted adult child caregiver feels depressed, resentful, angry, and guilty at times (Cavanaugh, 1999; Stephens et al., 2001). Many middle-aged caregivers are pressed financially, as they may still be paying child care or college tuition expenses and trying to save adequately for their own retirement. Financial pressures are especially serious for those caring for parents with chronic conditions, such as Alzheimer's disease, that require services that are not covered by medical insurance. In some cases, adult children may even need to quit their jobs to provide care if adequate alternatives, such as adult day care, are unavailable or unaffordable.

The stresses of caring for one's parent are especially difficult for women. In terms of its timing in the life course, caring for a parent is typically something that coincides with women's peak employment years of 35–64. Longitudinal research clearly shows that employment status has no effect on women's decisions to become caregivers (many have little choice), but that becoming a caregiver makes it likely that women will reduce employment hours or stop working (Pavalko & Artis, 1997). When you consider that most women caring for parents are also mothers, wives, and employees, it should come as no surprise that stress from these other roles exacerbates the effects of stress due to caregiving (Baek, 2005; Stephens & Townsend, 1997; Stephens et al., 2001).

What aspects of women's roles reduce the stress of caregiving? Having a secure attachment style to one's parent appears to buffer some aspects of stress (Crispi, Schiaffino, & Berman, 1997). Additionally, the rewards one gains as an employee, but not those from being a wife or mother, also seem to buffer the experience of caregiving stress (Stephens & Townsend, 1997).

Ethnic differences in adult children's experiences of caregiving stress are becoming better documented. Compared to European Americans, Latino American family members are likely to be caring for people who are at higher risk of chronic disease and are more disabled (Aranda & Knight, 1997). Latino American and African American caregivers, compared to European Americans, are more likely to be an adult child, friend, or other relative; report lower levels of caregiver stress, burden, and depression; believe more strongly in filial obligation; and are more likely to use prayer, faith, or religion as a coping strategy (Connell & Gibson, 1997). Such differences show that the relation between caregiving and stress is mediated by beliefs in family cohesiveness versus individual independence, as well as one's socialization. And caregivers also report experiencing rewards (Stephens & Franks, 1999).

From the parent's perspective, things aren't always rosy either. Independence and autonomy are important traditional values in some ethnic groups, and their loss is not taken lightly. Older adults in these groups are more likely to express the desire to pay a professional for assistance rather than ask a family member for help; they may find it demeaning to live with their children (Hamon & Blieszner, 1990). Most move in only as a last resort. As many as two thirds of older adults who receive help with daily activities feel negatively about the help they receive (Newsom, 1999).

Determining whether older parents are satisfied with the help their children provide is a complex issue (Newsom, 1999). Based on a critical review of the research, Newsom (1999) proposes a model of how certain aspects of care can produce negative perceptions of care directly or by affecting the interactions between caregiver and care recipient (see Figure 13.10). The important thing to conclude from the model is that even under the best circumstances there is no guarantee that the help adult children provide their parents will be well received. Misunderstandings can occur, and the frustration caregivers feel can be translated directly into negative interactions.

In sum, taking care of one's aging parents is a difficult task. Despite the numerous challenges and risks of negative psychological and financial outcomes, many caregivers nevertheless experience positive outcomes.

THINK ABOUT IT

Why does parental caregiving fall mainly to women?

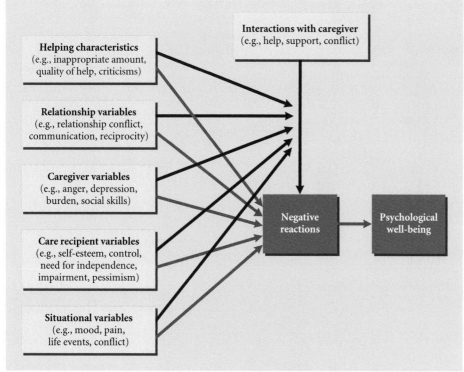

From Newson, J. T. (1999). Another side to caregiving: Negative reactions to being helped. *Current Directions in Psychological Science, 8,* 185. Reprinted by permission of Blackwell Scientific Publications, Ltd.

■ **Figure 13.10**
Whether a care recipient perceives care to be good depends on interactions with the caregiver and whether those interactions are perceived negatively.

GRANDPARENTHOOD

Becoming a grandparent takes some help. Being a parent yourself, of course, is a prerequisite. But it is your children's decisions and actions that determine whether you will experience the transition to grandparenthood, making this role different from most others we experience throughout life. Most people become grandparents in their 40s and 50s, though some are older or perhaps as young as their late 20s or early 30s. In most cases, grandparents are quite likely to still be employed and to have living parents themselves. Thus, although being a grandparent may be an exciting time, it is often only one part of their busy lives.

How Do Grandparents Interact With Grandchildren?

Keisha, an 8-year-old girl, smiled brightly when asked to describe her grandparents. "Nana Mary gives me chocolate ice cream, and that's my favorite! Poppy Bill sometimes takes care of me when Momma and Daddy go out, and plays ball with me." Kyle, a 14-year-old, had a different view. "My grandparents generally tell me stories of what life was like back when they were young."

As Keisha's and Kyle's experiences show, grandparents have many different ways of interacting with their grandchildren. Categorizing these styles has been attempted over the years (e.g., Neugarten & Weinstein, 1964), but none has been overly successful because grandparents use different styles with different grandchildren and styles change as grandparents and grandchildren age (Stephens & Clark, 1996).

Many of the functions grandparents serve can be understood as reflecting different levels of the social and personal dimensions (Cherlin & Furstenberg, 1986). The social dimension includes societal needs and expectations of what grandparents are to do, such as passing on family history to grandchildren. The personal dimension includes the personal satisfaction and individual needs that are fulfilled by being a grand-

Grandparents typically enjoy spending time with their grandchildren, who also like the contact.

parent. Many grandparents pass on skills, as well as religious, social, and vocational values (social dimension) through storytelling and advice, and they may feel great pride and satisfaction (personal dimension) from working with grandchildren on joint projects.

Grandchildren give grandparents a great deal in return. For example, grandchildren keep grandparents in touch with youth and the latest trends. Sharing the excitement of surfing the Web in school may be one way in which grandchildren keep grandparents on the technological forefront.

Being a Grandparent Is Meaningful

Does being a grandparent matter to people? You bet it does, at least to the vast majority of grandparents. Kivnick (1982, 1985) identified five dimensions of meaning that grandparents often assign to their roles, though these may not be independent (Hayslip, Henderson, & Shore, 2003). *For some, grandparenting is the most important thing in their lives, termed **centrality**. For others, meaning comes from being seen as wise (**valued elder**), from spoiling grandchildren (**indulgence**), from recalling the relationship they had with their own grandparents (**reinvolvement with personal past**), or from taking pride in the fact that they will be followed by not one but two generations (**immortality through clan**).*

Most grandparents derive several different meanings, regardless of the style of their relationship with the grandchildren (Alley, 2004). Similar findings are reported when overall satisfaction with being a grandparent is examined; no matter what their style is, grandparents find their role meaningful (Hayslip et al., 2003).

Grandchildren also highly value their relationships with grandparents, even when they are young adults (Alley, 2004). Grandparents are valued as role models, and for their personalities, the activities they share, and the attention they show to grandchildren. Grandchildren also note that when their grandparents are frail, helping their grandparents is a way for them to act on their altruistic beliefs (Kennedy, 1991).

Ethnic Differences

How grandparents and grandchildren interact varies in different ethnic groups. For example, African American grandmothers under age 40 report feeling pressured to provide care for grandchildren they were not eager to have; in contrast, those over age 60 tend to feel that they are fulfilling an important role (Kivett, 1991). African American grandparents tend to be more involved in teaching their grandchildren and more willing to take a grandparent education course than are European American grandparents (Watson & Koblinsky, 1997). African American grandfathers tend to perceive grandparenthood as a central role to a greater degree than European American grandfathers (Kivett, 1991). And Latino American grandparents are more likely to participate in child rearing due to a cultural core value of family (Burnette, 1999).

Grandparenting style also varies with ethnicity, which may sometimes create tension within families. Kornhaber (1985) relates the case of an 18-month-old girl who had one pair of Latino grandparents and one pair of Nordic grandparents. Her Latino grandparents tickled her, frolicked with her, and doted over her. Her Nordic grandparents loved her just as much but tended to just let her be. Her Latina mother thought that the Nordic grandparents were "cold and hard," and her Nordic father accused the Latino grandparents of "driving him crazy" with their displays of affection. The child, though, was flexible enough to adapt to both styles.

THINK ABOUT IT

How is being a grandparent related to generativity?

Native American grandparents appear to have some interactive styles different from those of other groups (Weibel-Orlando, 1990). ***Fictive grandparenting*** *is a style that allows adults to fill in for missing or deceased biological grandparents, functionally creating the role of surrogate grandparent.* These adults provide a connection to the older generation that otherwise would be absent for these children. *In the* **cultural conservator** *style, grandparents request that their grandchildren be allowed to live with them to ensure that the grandchildren learn the native ways.* These grandparents provide grandchildren with a way to connect with their cultural heritage. In general, Native American grandmothers take a more active role in these styles than do grandfathers.

How grandparents and grandchildren interact varies across ethnic groups.

When Grandparents Care for Grandchildren

Grandparenthood today is tougher than it used to be.
Families are more mobile, which means that grandparents are more often separated from their grandchildren by geographical distance. Grandparents are more likely to have independent lives apart from their children and grandchildren. What being a grandparent entails in the 21st century is more ambiguous than it once was (Fuller-Thompson, Hayslip, & Patrick, 2005).

Perhaps the biggest change for grandparents is the increasing number who serve as custodial parents for their grandchildren (Waldrop & Weber, 2001). Estimates are that more than 800,000 U.S. households include a grandparent raising a grandchild under age 18 when neither of the child's parents is present (U.S. Census Bureau, 2005b). These situations result most often when parents are addicted, incarcerated, or unable to raise their children for some other reason (Cox, 2000; Hayslip & Goldberg-Glen, 2000), or because of discipline or behavior problems exhibited by the grandchild (Giarusso et al., 2000). Lack of legal recognition due to the grandparents' lack of legal guardianship also poses problems and challenges, for example, in dealing with schools and obtaining records. Clearly, public policy changes are needed to address these issues (Smith et al., 2000).

Raising grandchildren is not easy. Financial stress, cramped living space, and social isolation are only some of the issues facing custodial grandmothers (Bullock, 2004). Rates of problem behavior, hyperactivity, and learning problems in the grandchildren are high and negatively affect the grandparent-grandchild relationship (Hayslip et al., 1998). The grandchildren's routines, activities, and school-related issues also cause stress (Musil & Standing, 2005). All of these stresses are also reported cross-culturally; for example, full-time custodial grandmothers in Kenya reported higher levels of stress than part-time caregivers (Oburu & Palmérus, 2005).

Even custodial grandparents raising grandchildren without these problems report more stress and role disruption than noncustodial grandparents (Emick & Hayslip, 1999). And custodial grandmothers who are employed report that they arrive late, miss work, must leave work suddenly, or leave early to tend to the grandchild's needs (Pruchno, 1999). But most custodial grandparents consider their situation better for their grandchild than any other alternative and report surprisingly few negative effects on their marriages.

TEST YOURSELF

1. The term _____ refers to middle-aged adults who have both living parents and children of their own.

2. The people who gather the family together for celebrations and keep family members in touch are called _____.

3. Most caregiving for aging parents is provided by _____.

4. The sense of personal responsibility to care for one's parents is called _____.

5. The meaning of _____ grandparenthood refers to the desire to be an esteemed and wise resource to grandchildren.

6. _____ grandparents have a style called cultural conservator.

If you were to create a guide to families for middle-aged adults, what would your most important pieces of advice be? Why did you select these?

Answers: (1) sandwich generation, (2) kinkeepers, (3) daughters and daughters-in-law, (4) filial obligation, (5) valued elder, (6) Native American

Putting It All Together

Is it any wonder why middle age gets bad press? There's a lot to face: signs of biological aging, children leaving, cognitive abilities changing, and parents dying. But middle age also has much going for it from many people's perspective: generally good relationships with children, grandparenthood, and accumulated experience. We saw how middle age is partly a continuation of previous developmental trends (e.g., in aspects of cognitive development and personality) and partly a time of new challenges (such as getting used to physical changes and dealing with different generations in the family).

We learned that Dean, the man who reacted negatively to losing his hair, is pretty typical of many middle-aged people confronting the first signs of aging. Kesha's expertise in social work is also typical of middle-aged adults, many of whom become experts in one area or another. We saw that Jim's behavior is not a reflection of a universal midlife crisis. Esther's joy and relief when her youngest daughter moved out is the reaction of most middle-aged parents who acquire an empty nest (at least until their adult children decide to move back).

Judging from the information in this chapter and in Chapters 10 and 11, middle age has many positive aspects —relatively good health, the best financial security most people ever have, stable relationships with partners, good relations with children, expertise in some area, and the prospect of rewarding relationships with grandchildren. It has its challenges too. Getting used to physical aging can be hard, as is caring for an aging parent. But for many people, on balance these are the best years of their lives.

Summary

13.1 Physical Changes and Health

Changes in Appearance

■ Some of the signs of aging appearing in middle age include wrinkles, gray hair, and weight gain.

Changes in Bones and Joints

■ An important change, especially in women, is loss of bone mass, which in severe form may result in the disease osteoporosis.

■ Osteoarthritis generally becomes noticeable in late middle or early old age. Rheumatoid arthritis is a more common form affecting fingers, wrists, and ankles.

Reproductive Changes

■ The climacteric (loss of the ability to bear children by natural means) and menopause (cessation of menstruation) occur in the 40s and 50s and constitute a major change in reproductive ability in women.

■ Most women do not have severe physical symptoms associated with the hormonal changes. Hormone replacement therapy is a controversial approach to treatment of menopausal symptoms.

- Reproductive changes in men are much less dramatic; even older men are usually still fertile. Physical changes do affect sexual response.

Stress and Health

- In the stress and coping paradigm, stress results from a person's appraisal of an event as taxing his or her resources. Daily hassles are viewed as the primary source of stress.

- The types of situations people appraise as stressful change through adulthood. Family and career issues are more important for young and middle-aged adults; health issues are more important for older adults.

- Type A behavior pattern is characterized by intense competitiveness, anger, hostility, restlessness, aggression, and impatience. It is linked with a person's first heart attack and with cardiovascular disease. Type B behavior pattern is the opposite of Type A; it is associated with lower risk of first heart attack, but the prognosis after an attack is poorer. Following an initial heart attack, Type A behavior pattern individuals have a higher recovery rate.

- Although stress is unrelated to serious psychopathology, it is related to social isolation and distrust.

Exercise

- Aerobic exercise has numerous benefits, especially to cardiovascular health and fitness. The best results are obtained through a moderate exercise program maintained throughout adulthood.

13.2 Cognitive Development

Practical Intelligence

- Research on practical intelligence reveals differences between optimally exercised ability and unexercised ability. This gap closes during middle adulthood. Practical intelligence appears not to decline appreciably until late life.

Becoming an Expert

- People tend to become experts in some areas and not in others. Experts tend to think in more flexible ways than novices and are able to skip steps in solving problems. Expert performance tends to peak in middle age.

Lifelong Learning

- Adults learn differently than children and youth. Older students need practical connections and a rationale for learning and are more motivated by internal factors.

13.3 Personality

Stability Is the Rule: The Five-Factor Model

- The five-factor model postulates five dimensions of personality: neuroticism, extraversion, openness to experience, agreeableness, and conscientiousness. Several longitudinal studies indicate that personality traits show long-term stability, but increasing evidence shows that traits change across adulthood.

Change Is the Rule: Changing Priorities at Midlife

- Erikson believed that middle-aged adults become more concerned with doing for others and passing social values and skills to the next generation—a set of behaviors and beliefs he labeled *generativity*. Those who do not achieve generativity are thought to experience stagnation.

- For the most part, there is little support for theories based on the premise that all adults go through predictable life stages at specific points in time. Individuals may face similar stresses, but transitions may occur at any time in adulthood. Research indicates that not everyone experiences a crisis at midlife.

- There is some evidence that gender-role identity converges in middle age to the extent that men and women are more likely to endorse similar self-descriptions. However, these similar descriptions do not necessarily translate into similar behavior.

13.4 Family Dynamics and Middle Age

- Middle-aged mothers tend to adopt the role of kin-keepers to keep family traditions alive and as a way to link generations.

- Middle age is sometimes referred to as the sandwich generation.

Letting Go: Middle-Aged Adults and Their Children

- Parent-child relations improve dramatically when children emerge from adolescence. Most parents look forward to having an empty nest. Difficulties emerge to the extent that raising children has been a primary source of personal identity for parents. However, once children have left home, parents still provide considerable support.

- Children move back home primarily for financial or child-rearing reasons. Neither parents nor children generally choose this arrangement.

Giving Back: Middle-Aged Adults and Their Aging Parents

- Middle-aged children contact their parents fairly frequently and use the visits to strengthen the relationship.

- Caring for aging parents usually falls to a daughter or daughter-in-law. Caregiving creates a stressful situation due to conflicting feelings and roles. The potential for conflict is high, as is financial pressure.

■ Caregiving stress is usually greater in women, who must deal with multiple roles. Older parents are often dissatisfied with the situation as well.

Grandparenthood

■ Becoming a grandparent means assuming new roles. Styles of interaction vary across grandchildren and with the age of the grandchild. Also relevant are the social and personal dimensions of grandparenting.

■ Grandparents derive several different types of meaning regardless of style: centrality, valued elder, indulgence, reinvolvement with personal past, and immortality through clan. Most children and young adults report positive relationships with grandparents, and young adults feel a responsibility to care for them if necessary.

■ Ethnic differences are found in the extent to which grandparents take an active role in their grandchildren's lives.

■ In an increasingly mobile society, grandparents are more frequently assuming a distant relationship with their grandchildren. An increasing number of grandparents serve as the custodial parent. These arrangements are typically stressful.

Key Terms

osteoporosis (492)

osteoarthritis (494)

rheumatoid arthritis (494)

climacteric (494)

menopause (494)

hormone replacement therapy (HRT) (496)

stress and coping paradigm (498)

appraise (499)

hassles (499)

coping (499)

Type A behavior pattern (500)

Type B behavior pattern (500)

aerobic exercise (501)

practical intelligence (503)

unexercised ability (504)

optimally exercised ability (504)

processes of thinking (507)

encapsulated (507)

products of thinking (508)

midlife crisis (510)

neuroticism (510)

extraversion (510)

openness to experience (511)

agreeableness (511)

conscientiousness (511)

generativity (513)

stagnation (514)

ego resilience (516)

kinkeeper (517)

sandwich generation (518)

filial obligation (520)

centrality (524)

valued elder (524)

indulgence (524)

reinvolvement with personal past (524)

immortality through clan (524)

fictive grandparenting (525)

cultural conservator (525)

Learn More About It

Readings

ARP, D. H., ARP, C. S., STANLEY, S. M., MARKMAN, H. J., & BLUMBERG, S. L. (2000). *Fighting for your empty nest marriage: Reinventing your relationship when the kids leave home.* San Francisco: Jossey-Bass. A research-based guide for married couples to help them get through a difficult period for most marriages.

ESTES, C. P. (1992). *Women who run with the wolves.* New York: Ballantine Books. In this now-classic book, femininity is discussed from a Jungian point of view, as revealed through story and myth.

MCADAMS, D. P., & DE ST. AUBIN, E. (Eds.). (1998). *Generativity and adult development: How and why do we care for the next generation.* Washington, DC: American Psychological Association. Excellent collection of articles about generativity and how people put Erikson's concept into practice.

TAN, A. (1989). *The joy luck club.* New York: Putnam. This novel explores the bond among four Chinese American women and their adult daughters.

WESTHEIMER, R., & KAPLAN, S. (2000). *Grandparenthood.* New York: Routledge. Provides a research-based but practical overview of the major issues in grandparenthood.

ZAL, H. M. (2001). *The sandwich generation: Caught between growing children and aging parents.* New York: Perseus Publishing. A research and theory-based book with good information about caring for parents and the stresses related to being a middle-aged adult child.

Websites

Visit the Human Development book companion website for all URLs.

- **The Human Development Book Companion Website**

  See the companion website **http://psychology .wadsworth.com /kail_cavanaugh4e/** for practice quiz questions, Internet links, updates, critical thinking exercises, discussion forums, and more.

- **Mayo Clinic and WebMD**

  The Mayo Clinic and WebMD provide excellent general sites for information on health. These sites are also worthwhile for general medical information on most specific conditions, such as menopause, and treatments. The Mayo Clinic site includes a Fitness and Sports Medicine Center.

- **The Family Caregiver Alliance**

  The Family Caregiver Alliance National Center on Caregiving provides a wealth of information about medical, policy, and resource issues concerning caregiving. It is aimed at people caring for adults with Alzheimer's disease, stroke, brain injury, and related brain disorders.

- **Helpguide.org**

  Helpguide.org's section on grandparenting is a good source of information about grandparenting resources and a variety of topics about grandparent-grandchild relations.

Life-Span CD-ROM

For more information about the concepts covered in this chapter, go to

Module 5: Early and Middle Adulthood

- *Physical Development*
- *Cognitive Development*
- *Emotional and Social Development*

http://www.thomsonedu.com

Go to this site for the link to ThomsonNOW, your one-stop study shop. Take a pre-test for this chapter, and ThomsonNOW will generate a personalized study plan based on your test results. The study plan will identify the topics you need to review and direct you to online resources to help you master those topics. You can then take a post-test to help you determine the concepts you have mastered and what you still need to work on.

Exploring Young and Middle Adulthood

Young adulthood lays the foundation for development changes people experience throughout their adult lives. In many respects, middle adulthood is the prime of life.

Development in Young Adulthood

Physical

Young adults are at the peak of their physical functioning for strength, muscle development, coordination, dexterity, and sensory acuity. Most of these abilities begin declining in middle age.

Overall health is at its peak, and death from disease is relatively rare. Accidents are the leading cause of death among adults ages 25-44.

Lifestyle factors that negatively affect health include smoking, alcohol abuse, and poor nutrition.

Socioeconomic status and level of education can affect an individual's health.

A healthy lifestyle in young adulthood reduces the chances of chronic disease later in life.

Digital Vision/Getty Images

Socioemotional

According to Erikson, the major task for young adults is dealing with the psychosocial conflict of *intimacy versus isolation*. A key component of intimacy is a clear sense of identity.

Young adults have more friendships than other age groups, and women have more close friends than men. Men base friendships on shared interests while women base friendships on emotional sharing.

Digital Vision/Getty Images

Sternberg's Three Key Components of Love	
Passion	Intense physiological desire for someone
Intimacy	Sharing one's thoughts and actions with someone
Commitment	Staying with someone through good and bad times

Gay, lesbian, and heterosexual relationships all have similar issues. Lesbian couples tend to be more egalitarian.

Marital satisfaction declines over time, for couples both with children and without.

The number of U.S. single parents is increasing. Financially, single mothers are the hardest hit.

Digital Vision./Getty Images

Cognitive

Most modern theories of intelligence recognize that there is no single type of intelligence. Some aspects of intelligence improve and some decline during adulthood.

Primary mental abilities are intellectual abilities that can be studied as groups of related skills (e.g., memory). These skills improve until the early 40s, then begin to decline in the 50s.

Fluid intelligence consists of abilities related to flexible and adaptive thinking. These skills tend to decline during adulthood.

Ryan McVay/Getty Images

Cystallized intelligence reflects knowledge acquired through life experience and education in a particular culture. These skills improve during adulthood until late life.

In the early 20s, individuals become capable of *postformal thought*, progressing from believing that there is only one right way of thinking and acting to accepting the fact that there are multiple approaches.

Mate selection and marriage are most successful when there are shared values, goals, and interests.

Development in Middle Adulthood

Physical

Wrinkles, gray hair, and weight gain appear in middle age. Bone density declines with age, especially in women; severe bone loss may result in osteoporosis. Arthritis often begins in late middle age: *Rheumatoid arthritis* is more common, but people whose joints are subject to overuse, such as athletes and manual laborers, are more prone to *osteoarthritis*.

Most middle-aged adults continue to have active sex lives.

Menopause occurs in women in the 40s or early 50s, and physical changes may affect sexual response. Hormone replacement therapy (HRT) is a controversial treatment for menopausal symptoms.

Although sperm production declines with age, men are still able to father a child in middle age or older. Prostate cancer becomes more likely in middle age.

Regular aerobic exercise slows physiological aging, reduces psychological stress, and improves cardiovascular health and overall fitness.

Middle-aged people report the highest levels of stress. Stress results when a situation is perceived as taxing a person's resources; daily hassles are viewed as the primary source of stress.

© Corbis

Socioemotional

As the length of time a couple has been together increases, commitment also increases while passion and intimacy decrease.

Stockbyte/Getty Images

Marital satisfaction ebbs and flows over time, but often improves after children leave home. Being flexible and adaptable leads to happier marriages.

There is some evidence that gender roles converge starting in middle age, with men and women showing increasing similiarity in self-descriptions.

Adults with high ego resilience are more likely to see middle age as an opportunity for change and growth, whereas adults with low ego resilience see it as a time of stagnation or decline.

Middle-aged mothers tend to adopt the role of kin keepers to maintain family traditions and link generations.

Occupational Choice and Development Theories	
Holland's personality-type theory	People choose occupations that optimize the fit between their individual traits and their occupational interests.
Super's developmental view	People adapt to an occupational role, in which there are five stages: implementation, establishment, maintenance, deceleration, and retirement.

Cognitive

Practical intelligence is maintained in middle age, and does not significantly decline until late life.

Adam Crowley/Getty Images

People become experts in select areas, and expertise usually peaks in middle adulthood. Experts are more flexible thinkers than novices and can skip steps in solving problems.

Middle-aged adults need practical connections and a rationale for learning and are more motivated by internal factors.

Erikson believes middle-aged adults become more concerned with helping younger people achieve than getting ahead themselves—a shift in priorities he labeled *generativity*.

Jack Hollingsworth/Getty Images

Occupation is a key part of a person's identity. Although most people work to earn a living, a key by-product is the possibility of personal growth.

Middle-aged adults have frequent contact with their parents. Most adult children feel responsible for their aging parents, and caring for them can cause stress, conflict, and financial pressure.

Jim Cummins/Getty Images

Late Adulthood

■ Chapter 14
**The Personal Context
of Later Life**
*Physical, Cognitive, and Mental
Health Issues*

■ Chapter 15
**Social Aspects
of Later Life**
*Psychosocial, Retirement,
Relationship, and Societal Issues*

■ Chapter 16
The Final Passage
Dying and Bereavement

Getty Images

14.1 What Are Older Adults Like?
The Demographics of Aging
Longevity
The Third-Fourth Age Distinction
So How Long Will You Live?

14.2 Physical Changes and Health
Biological Theories of Aging
Physiological Changes
Health Issues

14.3 Cognitive Processes
Information Processing
■ CURRENT CONTROVERSIES: Information Processing in Everyday Life: Older Drivers
Memory
Creativity and Wisdom

14.4 Mental Health and Intervention
Depression
Anxiety Disorders
Dementia: Alzheimer's Disease
■ REAL PEOPLE: APPLYING HUMAN DEVELOPMENT: What's the Matter With Mary?
■ SPOTLIGHT ON RESEARCH: Training Persons With Dementia to Be Group Activity Leaders

Putting It All Together
Summary
Key Terms
Learn More About It

The Personal Context of Later Life

Physical, Cognitive, and Mental Health Issues

S TOP! Before you read this chapter, do the following exercise. Take out a piece of paper and write down all the adjectives you can think of that describe aging and older adults, as well as all of the "facts" about aging that you know.

Now that you have your list, look it over carefully. Are most of your descriptors positive or negative? Do you have lots of "facts" written down, or just a few? Most people's lists contain at least some words and phrases that reflect images of older adults as portrayed by the media. Many of the media's images are stereotypes of aging that are only loosely based on reality. For example, people over age 60 are almost never pictured in ads for perfume, but they are shown in ads for wrinkle removers.

In this chapter, our journey through old age begins. Our emphasis in this chapter is on physical and cognitive changes. To begin, we consider the key physical changes and health issues confronting older adults. Changes in cognitive abilities, as well as interventions to help remediate the changes, are discussed next. Finally, some well-known mental health issues are considered, including depression, anxiety disorders, and Alzheimer's disease.

14.1

WHAT ARE OLDER ADULTS LIKE?

Sarah is an 87-year-old African American woman who comes from a family of long-lived individuals. She has never been to a physician in her entire life, and she has never really been seriously ill. Sarah figures it's just as well that she has never needed a physician, because for most of her life she had no health insurance. Because she feels healthy and has more living that she wants to do, Sarah believes that she'll live for several more years.

WHAT IS IT LIKE TO BE OLD? Do you want your own late life to be described by the words and phrases you wrote at the beginning of the chapter? Do you look forward to becoming old, or are you afraid of what may lie ahead?

Most of us probably want to be like Sarah and enjoy a long healthy life. Growing old is not something we think about very much until we have to. Most of us experience the coming of old age the way Jim does in the *Far Side* cartoon. It's as if we go to bed one night middle-aged and wake up the next day feeling old. But we can take comfort in knowing that when that day comes, we will have plenty of company.

THE DEMOGRAPHICS OF AGING

Did you ever stop to think about how many older adults you see in your daily life? Did you ever wonder whether your great-grandparents had the same experience? There have never been as many older adults alive as there are now. The proportion of older adults in the population of industrialized countries has increased tremendously in this century, due mainly to better health care and to lowering women's mortality rate during childbirth.

People who study population trends, called **demographers,** *use a graphic technique called a* **population pyramid** *to illustrate these changes.* Figure 14.1 shows population pyramids for both developed and developing countries. Let's consider developed countries first (they're designated by the darker color in the figure). Notice the shape of the population pyramid in 1950, shown in the top panel of the figure. In the middle of the 20th century, there were fewer people over age 60 than there were people under age 60, so the figure tapers toward the top. Compare that to projections for 2030 (when the last of the baby boomers have reached age 65)—a dramatic change will occur in that the number of people over 65 will equal or outnumber those in other age groups.

These changes also occur in developing countries, shown in the lighter color. Notice that the figures for both 1950 and 1990 look like pyramids because there are substantially fewer older adults than younger people. But by 2030 the number of older adults in developing countries will also have increased dramatically, changing the shape of the figure.

THE FAR SIDE® By GARY LARSON

You never see it coming.

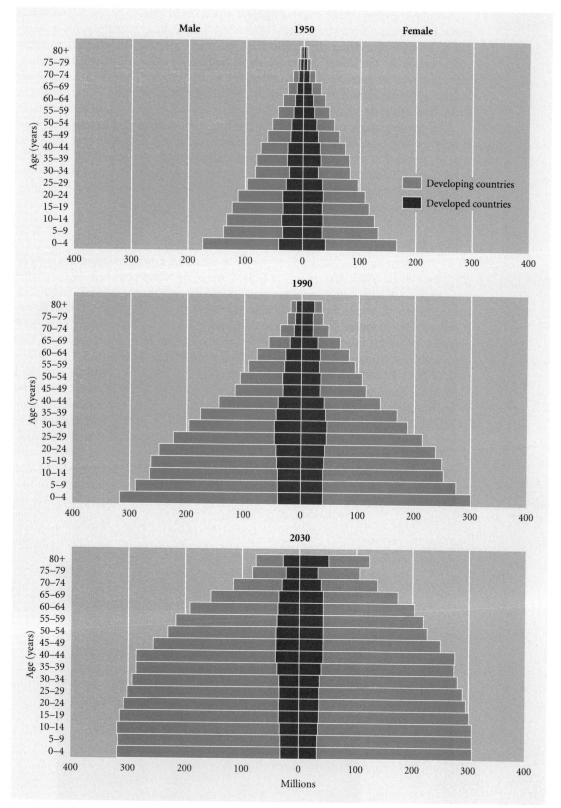

Male   **1950**   Female

☐ Developing countries
■ Developed countries

1990

2030

Millions

From United Nations, 1999, and U.S. Census Bureau, 2000.

■ **Figure 14.1**

Note the changing shapes of the distributions in terms of the proportion of the population that is young versus old over time and as a function of whether countries are considered developed or developing.

THINK ABOUT IT

How will the demographic changes in the first 30 years of the 21st century affect the need for retraining workers?

The rapid increase in the number of older adults (individuals over age 60) will bring profound changes to everyone's lives. In the first half of the 21st century, older adults will be a major marketing target, and they will wield considerable political and economic power. In the United States the sheer number of older adults will place enormous pressure on pension systems (especially Social Security), health care (especially Medicare, Medicaid, and long-term care), and other human services. The costs will be borne by a relatively small number of taxpaying workers in the cohorts behind them.

The growing strain on social service systems will be intensified because the most rapidly growing segment of the U.S. population is the group of people over age 85. In fact, the number of such people will increase 400% between 1995 and 2050 (U.S. Census Bureau, 2005b). As we will see in this chapter and in Chapter 15, individuals over age 85 generally need more assistance with daily living than do people under 85, placing increasing strain on the health care system.

The Diversity of Older Adults

Older adults are no more alike than people at other ages. Older women outnumber older men in all ethnic groups in the United States, for reasons we will explore later. The number of older adults among ethnic minority groups is increasing faster than among European Americans. For example, the number of Native American elderly has increased 65% in recent decades; Asian and Pacific Islander elderly have quadrupled; older adults are the fastest-growing segment of the African American population; and the number of Hispanic American elderly is also increasing rapidly (U.S. Census Bureau, 2005b). Projections for the future diversity of the U.S. population are shown in Figure 14.2. You should note the very large increases in the number of Asian, Native, and Hispanic American older adults relative to European and African American older adults.

Older adults in the future will be better educated too. At present only about half of the people over age 65 have a high school diploma, and 10% have 4 or more years of college. By 2030 it is estimated that 85% will have a high school diploma and 75% will have a college degree (U.S. Census Bureau, 2005b). These dramatic changes will be due mainly to better educational opportunities for more students and greater need for formal schooling (especially college) to find a good job. Also, better-educated people tend

Figure 14.2
Projected changes in the U.S. minority population of older adults. Note that the number of older Latinos will increase the fastest.

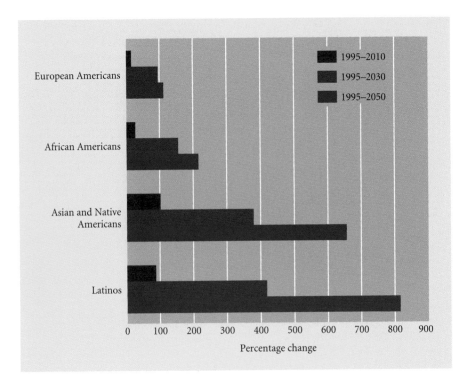

to live longer, mostly because they have higher incomes, which give them better access to good health care and a chance to follow healthier lifestyles.

Internationally, the number of older adults is also growing rapidly, especially among developing countries. To a large extent, these rapid increases are due to improved health care in developing countries. Such increases will literally change the face of the population as more people live to old age.

Economically powerful countries around the world such as Japan are trying to cope with increased numbers of older adults that strain the country's resources. Indeed, the rate of growth of older adults in Japan is the highest in the industrialized world; due to a declining birth rate, by 2025 there will be twice as many adults over age 65 as there will be children (Ministry of Internal Affairs and Communication, 2005). The economic impact will include much higher pension costs and very substantial increases in health care costs, which will have to be borne by far fewer workers (WuDunn, 1997).

Japan and the United States are not alone in facing increased numbers of older adults. As you can see in Figure 14.3, many countries will have substantially more older adults in the population over the next few decades. All of them will need to deal with increased needs for services to older adults and, in some cases, competing demands with children and younger and middle-aged adults for limited resources.

Even though the financial implications of an aging population are predictable, the United States has done surprisingly little to prepare. For example, little research has been done on the characteristics of older workers (even though mandatory retirement has been virtually eliminated for several years), on differences between the young-old (ages 65–80) and the old-old (over age 80), or on specific health care needs of older adults with regard to chronic illness despite a call for such work in 1993 (American Psychological Society, 1993). As of 2005, the U.S. Congress had yet to adopt long-term plans for funding Social Security and Medicare, even though the first baby boomers will turn 60 in 2006. Recommendations made to President Bush in December 2001 by a special commission he established, and his own discussions of them in 2005, reiterated the need to address the problems posed by the coming wave of retirees. These issues will need to be addressed in the very near future so that appropriate policies can be implemented.

LONGEVITY

The number of years a person can expect to live, termed **longevity,** *is jointly determined by genetic and environmental factors.* Researchers distinguish between three types of longevity: average life expectancy, useful life expectancy, and maximum life expectancy.

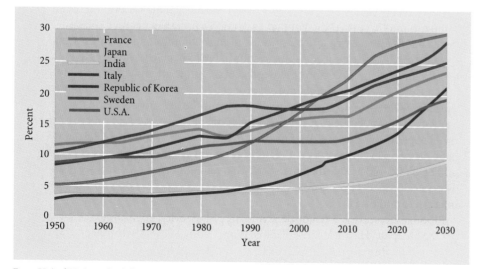

■ **Figure 14.3**
The proportion of older adults (aged 65 years and over) is increasing in many countries and will continue to do so in the coming decades.

From United Nations, Statistics Bureau, MPHPT, Ministry of Health, Labour and Welfare.

■ **Figure 14.4**
Average life expectancy for all people in the United States increased steadily during the 20th century, but women still outlive men by about 6 years.

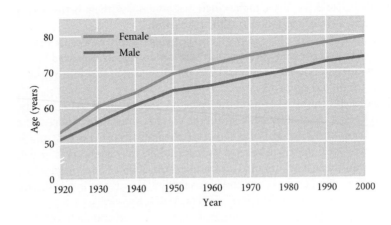

From National Center for Health Statistics, 2001.

Average life expectancy (or median life expectancy) is the age at which half of the people born in a particular year will have died. As you can see in Figure 14.4, average life expectancy for people in the United States increased steadily during the 20th century. This increase was due mainly to significant declines in infant mortality and in the number of women dying during childbirth, the elimination of major diseases such as smallpox and polio, and improvements in medical technology that prolong the lives of people with chronic disease.

Useful life expectancy is the number of years that a person is free from debilitating chronic disease and impairment. Ideally, useful life expectancy exactly matches the actual length of a person's life. However, medical technology sometimes enables people to live for years even though they may be unable to perform routine daily tasks. Accordingly, people are placing greater emphasis on useful life expectancy rather than just the sheer number of years they may live in making medical treatment decisions.

Maximum life expectancy is the oldest age to which any person lives. Currently, scientists estimate that the maximum limit for humans is around 120 years, mostly because the heart and other key organ systems are limited in how long they can last without replacement (Hayflick, 1998).

Genetic and Environmental Factors in Longevity

We have known for a long time that a good way to increase one's chances of a long life is to come from a family with a history of long-lived individuals (Hayflick, 1998). Researchers have suspected that this is due in large part to genetic factors. One exciting line of contemporary research, the Human Genome Project, has mapped the basic human genetic code. This research and its spinoffs in microbiology and behavior genetics and aging have produced some astounding results in terms of genetic linkages to both physical health and disease (Johnson & Krueger, 2005). Some attempts are even being made to treat genetic diseases by implanting "corrected" genes in people in the hopes that the good genes will reproduce and eventually wipe out the defective genes.

Payoffs from such research are already helping us understand how increasing numbers of people are living to 100 or older. For example, Perls and Terry (2003) showed that genetic factors play a major role in determining how well centenarians cope with disease. The oldest-old are hardy because they have a high threshold for disease and show slower rates of disease progression than their peers, who develop chronic diseases at younger ages and die earlier.

Although heredity is a major determinant of longevity, environmental factors also affect the life span (Hayflick, 1998; Perls & Terry, 2003). Some environmental factors are more obvious; diseases, toxins, lifestyle, and social class are among the most important. Diseases, such as cardiovascular disease and Alzheimer's disease, and lifestyle issues, such as smoking and exercise, receive a great deal of attention from researchers.

Environmental toxins, encountered mainly as air and water pollution, are a continuing problem. For example, toxins in fish, bacteria and cancer-causing chemicals in drinking water, and airborne pollutants are major agents in shortening longevity.

The impact of social class on longevity results from the reduced access to goods and services, especially medical care, that characterizes most ethnic minority groups, the poor, and many older adults (National Center for Health Statistics, 2004a). Most of these people have little or no health insurance, and many cannot afford the cost of a more healthful lifestyle. For example, lead poisoning from old water pipes, air pollution, and poor drinking water are serious problems in large urban areas, but many people simply cannot afford to move.

How environmental factors influence average life expectancy changes over time. For example, acquired immunodeficiency syndrome (AIDS) became a factor in longevity during the 1980s and continues to kill millions of people around the world. In contrast, the life expectancy impact of cardiovascular diseases is lessening somewhat as the rates of those diseases decline.

The sad part about most environmental factors is that people are responsible for them. Denying adequate health care to everyone, continuing to pollute our environment, and failing to address the underlying causes of poverty have undeniable consequences: They needlessly shorten lives and dramatically increase the cost of health care.

Ethnic and Gender Differences in Longevity

Ethnic differences in average life expectancy are complex (Go et al., 1995). For example, African Americans' average life expectancy at birth is roughly 6 years lower for men and 5 years lower for women than that of European Americans. By age 65, though, the average life expectancy for African Americans is only about 2 years less for both men and women than it is for European Americans, and by age 85 African Americans tend to live longer (National Center for Health Statistics, 2004b). Perhaps because they do not typically have access to the same quality of care that European Americans usually do, and are at greater risk for disease and accidents, African Americans who survive to age 85 tend to be healthier than their European American counterparts. Like Sarah, the 87-year-old woman in the vignette, they may well have needed little medical care throughout their lives. The complexity of ethnic group differences is evident in the fact that Hispanic Americans' average life expectancy exceeds European Americans' at all ages, despite access problems to health care for many (National Center for Health Statistics, 2004b).

A visit to a senior center or to a nursing home can easily lead to the question "Where are all the very old men?" Women's average longevity is about 7 years more than men's at birth, narrowing to roughly 1 year by age 85 (National Center for Health Statistics, 2004b). These differences are fairly typical of most industrialized countries but not of developing countries. Indeed, the female advantage in average longevity in the United States became apparent only in the early 20th century (Hayflick, 1996). Why? Until then, so many women died in childbirth that their average longevity as a group was reduced to that of men. Death in childbirth still partially explains the lack of a female advantage in developing countries today; however, part of the difference in some countries also results from infanticide of baby girls. Socioeconomic factors such as access to health care, work and educational opportunities, and athletics also help account for the emergence of the female advantage in industrialized countries (Hayflick, 1998).

Many ideas have been offered to explain the significant advantage women have over men in average longevity in industrialized countries (Hayflick, 1996). Overall, men's rates of dying from the top 15 causes of death are significantly higher than women's at nearly every age, and men are also more susceptible to infectious diseases. These differences have led some to speculate that perhaps there is no fundamental biological difference in longevity but rather a much greater susceptibility in men of contracting certain fatal diseases (Hayflick, 1996).

Other researchers disagree; they argue that there are potential biological explanations. These include the fact that women have two X chromosomes, compared with one

THINK ABOUT IT

How do ethnic and gender differences in life expectancy relate to biological, psychological, sociocultural, and life cycle factors?

in men; men have a higher metabolic rate; women have a higher brain-to-body weight ratio; and women have lower testosterone levels. However, none of these explanations has sufficient scientific support to explain why most women in industrialized countries can expect, on average, to outlive most men (Hayflick, 1996).

Despite their longer average longevity, women do not have all the advantages. Interestingly, older men who survive beyond age 90 are the hardiest segment of their birth cohort in terms of performance on cognitive tests (Perls & Terry, 2003). Between ages 65 and 89, women score higher on cognitive tests; beyond age 90, men do much better.

International Differences in Longevity

Countries around the world differ dramatically in how long their populations live on average. As you can see in Figure 14.5, the current range extends from 38 years in Sierra Leone in Africa to 80 years in Japan. Such a wide divergence in life expectancy reflects

■ **Figure 14.5**
International data on average life expectancy at birth. Note the differences between developed and developing countries.

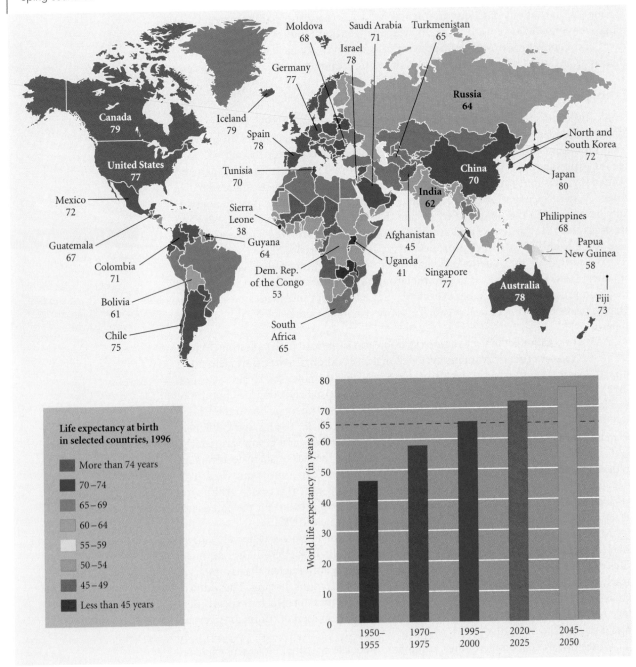

From U.N. Population Division Database, 1996 Revision.

vast discrepancies in genetic, sociocultural and economic conditions, health care, disease, and the like across industrialized and developing nations.

THE THIRD-FOURTH AGE DISTINCTION

The second half of the 20th century was exciting for gerontology. The development of the science of the study of older adults led to cultural, medical, and economic advances for older adults (e.g., longer average longevity, increased quality of life) that in turn resulted in fundamental, positive changes in how older people are viewed in society. Gerontologists and policymakers became optimistic that old age was a time of potential growth rather than of decline. This combination of factors is termed the Third Age (Baltes & Smith, 2003). As we will see in this chapter and in Chapter 15, much research has documented that the young-old (ages 60–80) do indeed have much to look forward to.

However, recent research shows conclusively that the oldest-old (over age 80) typically have a much different experience, which is referred to as the Fourth Age (Baltes & Smith, 2003). The oldest-old are at the limits of their functional capacity, and few interventions have been successful to date. We will see that the rates of diseases such as cancer and dementia increase dramatically in the oldest-old and that other aspects of psychological functioning (e.g., memory) also undergo significant and fairly rapid decline.

Baltes and Smith (2003) view the differences between the Third Age and the Fourth Age as important for research and social policy. They characterize the Third Age as the "good news" about aging, and the Fourth Age as the "bad news":

The "Good News": The Third Age (Young-Old)

- Increased life expectancy, with more older people living longer and aging successfully
- Substantial potential for physical and mental fitness, with improvement in each generation
- Evidence of cognitive and emotional reserves in the aging mind
- High levels of emotional and personal well-being
- Effective strategies to master the gains and losses of later life

The "Bad News": The Fourth Age (Oldest-Old)

- Sizeable losses in cognitive potential and ability to learn
- Increases in the negative effects of chronic stress
- High prevalence of dementia (50% in people over age 90), frailty, and multiple chronic conditions
- Problems with quality of life and dying with dignity

As you proceed through this and the next chapter, keep the distinction between the Third and the Fourth Ages in mind. Note the different developmental patterns shown by the young-old and oldest-old. In Chapter 15, we will consider some of the social policy implications of this distinction.

SO HOW LONG WILL YOU LIVE?

By now you realize that longevity is a complex interaction among genetic and environmental factors. Which specific diseases tend to run in your family, where you live, your lifestyle and health habits, among many other things, influence how long you might expect to live. To get a good idea of how your unique combination of factors might play out for you, visit the website http://www.agingresearch.org/calculator/. There you will find the *Living to 100 Life Expectancy Calculator*. Take a few minutes to answer the questions there, and see for yourself how long you might expect to live, recognizing of course that no predictive test is completely accurate.

TEST YOURSELF

1. The fastest growing segment of the population in the United States is people over age

   _____.

2. The age at which half of the people born in a particular year have died is called _____.

3. The Fourth Age refers to the _____ -old.

Think back to the lifestyle influences on health discussed in Chapter 12. If most people actually followed very healthy lifestyles, what do you think would happen to average life expectancy?

Answers: (1) 85, (2) average life expectancy (3) oldest

14.2

PHYSICAL CHANGES AND HEALTH

LEARNING OBJECTIVES

What are the major biological theories of aging?

What physiological changes normally occur in later life?

What are the principal health issues for older adults?

Frank is an 80-year-old man who has been physically active his whole life. He still enjoys sailing, long-distance biking, and cross-country skiing. Although he considers himself to be in excellent shape, he has noticed that his endurance has decreased, and his hearing isn't quite as sharp as it used to be. Frank wonders: Can he do something to stop these declines, or are they an inevitable part of growing older?

IF YOUR FAMILY HAS KEPT PHOTOGRAPH ALBUMS over many years, you are able to see how your grandparents or great-grandparents changed over the years. Some of the more visible differences are changes in the color and amount of hair and the addition of wrinkles, but many other physical changes are harder to see. In this section, we consider some of these, as well as a few things that adults can do to improve their health. As noted in Chapter 12, many aging changes begin during middle age but typically do not affect people in their daily lives until later in life, as Frank is discovering. But first, we will ask a basic question: Why do people grow old in the first place?

BIOLOGICAL THEORIES OF AGING

Why does everyone who lives long enough grow old and eventually die? To date, there is no one definitive answer, but several complementary biological and other theories, taken together, provide some insights (Timiras, 2002).

There are four major groups of biological theories of aging. *Wear-and-tear theory suggests that the body, much like any machine, gradually deteriorates and finally wears out.* This theory explains some diseases, such as osteoarthritis, rather well. Years of use of the joints causes the protective cartilage lining to deteriorate, resulting in pain and stiffness. However, wear-and-tear theory does not explain most other aspects of aging very well, such as brain diseases like Alzheimer's and Parkinson's disease (Hayflick, 1998).

Cellular theories explain aging by focusing on processes that occur within individual cells, which may lead to the buildup of harmful substances or the deterioration of cells over a lifetime. A second family of ideas points to causes of aging at the cellular level. One notion focuses on the number of times cells can divide, which presumably places limits on the life span of a complex organism. Cells grown in laboratory culture dishes undergo only a fixed number of divisions before dying, with the number of possible divisions dropping depending on the age of the donor organism; this phenomenon is called the Hayflick limit, after its discoverer, Leonard Hayflick (Hayflick, 1996). For example, cells from human fetal tissue are capable of 40 to 60 divisions; cells from a human adult are capable of only about 20. What causes cells to limit their number of divisions? *Evidence suggests that the tips of the chromosomes, called **telomeres,** play a major role* (Timiras, 2002). An enzyme called *telomerase* is needed in DNA replication to fully replicate the telomeres. But telomerase normally is not present in cells, so with each replication the telomeres become shorter. Eventually, the chromosomes become unstable and cannot replicate because the telomeres become too short with age (Lung et al., 2005). Some researchers believe that cancer cells proliferate so quickly in some cases because they can activate telomerase, meaning that the cancer cells may become functionally immortal and take over the organ system (Mera, 1998).

Other cellular theories stress the destructive effects that certain substances have on cellular functioning. *For example, some theorists believe that **free radicals**—chemicals produced randomly during normal cell metabolism, which bond easily to other substances inside cells—cause cellular damage that impairs functioning.* Aging is caused by the cumulative effects of free radicals over the life span. Free radicals may play a role in some diseases, such as atherosclerosis and cancer. The formation of free radicals can be prevented by substances called antioxidants. Although there is growing evidence that taking antioxidants, such as vitamins A, C, and E, postpones the appearance of some age-related diseases, there is little evidence that taking antioxidants or other "anti-aging medicine" increases average longevity (Olshansky, Hayflick, & Perls, 2004a, 2004b).

*Another cellular theory focuses on **cross-linking,** in which some proteins interact randomly with certain body tissues, such as muscles and arteries.* The result of cross-linking is that normal, elastic tissue becomes stiffer, so that muscles and arteries are less flexible over time. The results in some cases can be serious; for example, stiffening in the heart muscle forces the heart to work harder, which may increase the risk of heart attacks. Although we know that these substances accumulate, there is little evidence that cross-linking causes all aspects of aging (Timiras, 2002).

***Metabolic theories** focus on aspects of the body's metabolism to explain why people age.* Two important processes in this approach are caloric intake and stress. There is some evidence that people who limit the number of calories they eat in an otherwise well-balanced diet can expect longer life expectancy and lower rates of disease. For example, Okinawans, who eat only 60% of the normal Japanese diet, have 40 times as many centenarians per capita, and their incidence of cardiovascular disease, diabetes, and cancer is half that of the rest of Japan (Monczunski, 1991). It remains to be seen whether the type of diet (e.g., low-fat) or the number of calories per se is the secret. Another variant of metabolic theory suggests that the hormonal regulatory system's ability to adapt to stress declines with age (Finch & Seeman, 1999). Much research shows that younger adults can tolerate higher levels of physical stress than can older adults (Whitbourne, 1999). It is possible that death occurs because the body can no longer adapt to stress (Hayflick, 1998).

*Finally, **programmed cell death theories** suggest that aging is genetically programmed.* This possibility seems more likely as the explosion of knowledge about human genetics continues to unlock the secrets of our genetic code. Even when cell death appears random, researchers now believe that such losses may be part of a master genetic program (Perls & Terry, 2003; Timiras, 2002). Programmed cell death appears to be a function of physiological processes, the innate ability of cells to self-destruct, and the ability of dying cells to trigger key processes in other cells. At present, we do not know how this self-destruct program is activated, nor do we understand how it works. However, understanding programmed cell death may be the key to understanding how genes and physiological processes interact with psychological and sociocultural forces to produce aging (Perls & Terry, 2003).

It is possible that the other explanations we have considered in this section and the changes we examine throughout this text are the result of a genetic program. For example, there is evidence that osteoarthritis (Charles, 1998), changes in brain cells (Mar-

THINK ABOUT IT

What would be the psychological and sociocultural effects of discovering a single, comprehensive biological theory of aging?

tin, 1998), Alzheimer's disease (Woodruff-Pak & Papka, 1999), certain types of memory (Johansson et al., 1999), and personality (Bouchard, 1997) have key genetic underpinnings. As genetics research continues, it is likely that we will have some exciting answers to the question "Why do we age?"

PHYSIOLOGICAL CHANGES

Growing older brings with it several inevitable physiological changes. Like Frank, whom we met in the vignette, older adults find that their endurance has declined, relative to what it was 20 or 30 years earlier, and that their hearing has declined. In this section, we consider some of the most important physiological changes that occur in neurons, the cardiovascular and respiratory systems, the motor system, and the sensory systems. We also consider general health issues such as sleep, nutrition, and cancer. Throughout this discussion, you should keep in mind that although the changes we will consider happen to everyone, the rate and the amount of change varies a great deal among people.

Changes in the Neurons

The most important normative changes with age involve structural changes in the neurons, the basic cells in the brain, and in communication among neurons (Whitbourne, 1996). Recall the basic structures of the neuron we encountered in Chapter 3 (pages 100 – 101), shown again here in Figure 14.6. Two structures in neurons are most important in understanding aging: the dendrites, which pick up information from other neurons, and the axon, which transmits information inside a neuron from the dendrites to the terminal branches. Each of the changes we consider impairs the neurons' ability to transmit information, which ultimately affects how well the person functions (Vinters, 2001). Three structural changes are most important in normal aging: neurofibrillary tangles, dendritic changes, and neuritic plaques.

*For reasons that are not understood, fibers that compose the axon sometimes become twisted together to form spiral-shaped masses called **neurofibrillary tangles.*** These tangles interfere with the neuron's ability to transmit information down the axon. Some degree of tangling occurs normally with age, but large numbers of neurofibrillary tangles are associated with Alzheimer's disease (Vinters, 2001).

Changes in the dendrites are more complicated. Some dendrites shrivel up and die, making it more difficult for neurons to communicate with each other (Vinters, 2001). However, some dendrites continue to grow (Curcio, Buell, & Coleman, 1982). This may help explain why older adults continue to improve in some areas, as we will discover later in this chapter. Why some dendrites degenerate and others do not is poorly understood; it may reflect the existence of two different families of neurons.

■ **Figure 14.6**
Basic structure of the neuron.

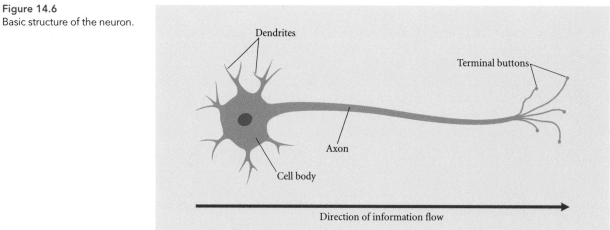

Damaged and dying neurons sometimes collect around a core of protein and produce **neuritic plaques.** It is likely that plaques interfere with normal functioning of healthy neurons. Although large numbers of plaques are associated with dementia (e.g., Alzheimer's disease), researchers have not established an "allowable number" of plaques that indicate a healthy aging brain (Vinters, 2001).

Because neurons do not physically touch each other, they must communicate via chemicals called **neurotransmitters.** With age, the levels of these neurotransmitters decline (Whitbourne, 1999). These declines are believed to be responsible for numerous age-related behavioral changes, including those in memory and sleep, and perhaps in afflictions such as Parkinson's disease.

These changes in neurons are a normal part of aging. However, when these changes occur at a much greater rate, they cause considerable problems and are associated with Alzheimer's or related diseases, conditions we discuss in more detail on pages 567–572. This point is important, as it means that serious behavioral changes such as very severe memory impairment are not a result of normative changes in the brain; rather, they are indicators of disease.

We are learning a great deal about the relations between changes in the brain and changes in behavior through technological advances in noninvasive imaging and in assessing psychological functioning (Dougherty, Rauch, & Rosenbaum, 2004). On the brain imaging front, two types of techniques are used:

- *Structural imaging* provides highly detailed images of anatomical features in the brain. The most commonly used are X-rays, computerized tomography (CT scans), and magnetic resonance imaging (MRI).
- *Functional imaging* provides an indication of brain activity but not high anatomical detail. The most commonly used are single photon emission computerized tomography (SPECT), positron emission tomography (PET), and functional magnetic resonance imaging (fMRI).

These noninvasive imaging techniques coupled with sensitive tests of cognitive processing have shown quite convincingly that age-related changes in the brain are, at least in part, responsible for the age-related declines in cognition we will consider later (Albert & Killiany, 2001). Why these declines occur has yet to be discovered, although fMRI, the newest technique, offers considerable promise in helping researchers unlock this mystery.

Cardiovascular and Respiratory Systems

The incidence of cardiovascular diseases such as heart attack, irregular heartbeat, stroke, and hypertension increases dramatically with age (National Center for Health Statistics, 2004a). However, the overall death rates from these diseases have been declining over recent decades, mainly because fewer adults smoke cigarettes and many people have reduced the amount of fat in their diets. However, the death rate for some ethnic groups, such as African Americans, remains much higher because of poorer preventive health care and less healthy lifestyles due to lack of financial resources (National Center for Health Statistics, 2004b).

Normative changes in the cardiovascular system that contribute to disease begin by young adulthood. Fat deposits are found in and around the heart and in the arteries (Whitbourne, 1999). Eventually, the amount of blood that the heart can pump per minute will decline roughly 30%, on average by the late 70s to 80s. The amount of muscle tissue in the heart also declines due to its replacement by connective tissue. There is also a general stiffening of the arteries due to calcification. These changes appear irrespective of lifestyle, but they occur more slowly in people who exercise, eat low-fat diets, and manage to lower stress effectively (see Chapter 12). In persons who do not have hypertension, blood pressure changes little over adulthood (Pearson et al., 1997).

As people grow older, their chances of having a stroke increase. **Strokes, or cerebral** **vascular accidents,** *are caused by interruptions in the blood flow in the brain due to a* *blockage or to a* **hemorrhage** *in a cerebral artery.* Blockages of arteries may be caused by clots or by deposits of fatty substances due to the disease atherosclerosis. Hemorrhages are caused by ruptures of the artery. *Older adults often experience* **transient ischemic attacks (TIAs),** *which involve an interruption in blood flow to the brain, and are often early warning signs of stroke.* A single, large cerebral vascular accident may produce serious cognitive impairment, such as the loss of the ability to speak, or physical problems, such as the inability to move an arm. The nature and severity of the impairment in functioning a person experiences are usually determined by which specific area of the brain is affected. Recovery from a single stroke depends on many factors, including the extent and type of the loss, the ability of other areas in the brain to assume the functions that were lost, and personal motivation.

Numerous small cerebral vascular accidents can result in a disease termed **vascular dementia.** Unlike Alzheimer's disease, another form of dementia discussed later in this chapter, vascular dementia can have a sudden onset and may or may not progress gradually. Typical symptoms include hypertension, specific and extensive alterations on an MRI, and differential impairment on neuropsychological tests (a pattern of scores showing some functions intact and others significantly below average) that assess the ability to establish or maintain a mental set (that is, the ability to keep focused on a particular task or situation) and visual imagery, with relatively higher scores on tests of delayed recognition memory (Cosentino et al., 2004). Individuals' specific symptom patterns may vary a great deal, depending on which specific areas of the brain are damaged. In some cases, vascular dementia has a much faster course than Alzheimer's disease, resulting in death an average of 2 to 3 years after onset; in others, the disease may progress much more slowly with idiosyncratic symptom patterns.

Single cerebral vascular accidents and vascular dementia are diagnosed similarly. Evidence of damage may be obtained from diagnostic structural imaging (e.g., CT or MRI scan), which provides pictures like the one shown in Figure 14.7, which is then

■ **Figure 14.7**
Example of an MRI image of the brain. The different colors represent different levels of brain activity.

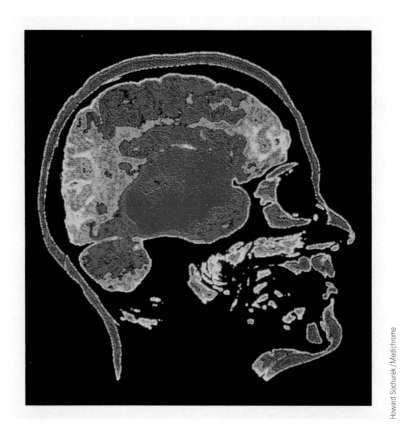

Howard Sochurek/Medichrome

confirmed by neuropsychological tests. Known risk factors for both conditions include hypertension and a family history of the disorders.

The maximum amount of air in one breath drops 40% from age 25 to age 85, due mostly to stiffening of the rib cage and air passages with age, and destruction of the air sacs in the lungs from pollution and smoking (Whitbourne, 1999). This decline is the main cause of shortness of breath after physical exertion in later life. Because of the cumulative effects of breathing polluted air over a lifetime, it is hard to say how much of these changes is strictly age-related. *The most common form of incapacitating respiratory disease among older adults is* **chronic obstructive pulmonary disease (COPD).** COPD can be an extremely debilitating condition, resulting in depression, anxiety, and the need to be continually connected to oxygen (Parmet, Lynm, & Glass, 2003). Emphysema is the most common form of COPD; although most cases of emphysema are due to smoking, some forms are genetic. Asthma is another common type of COPD.

Parkinson's Disease

Parkinson's disease is known primarily for its characteristic motor symptoms: very slow walking, difficulty getting into and out of chairs, and a slow hand tremor. These problems are caused by a deterioration of neurons in the midbrain that produce the neurotransmitter dopamine. Pope John Paul II, who died in 2005, suffered from Parkinson's disease. Former boxing champion Muhammad Ali, former Attorney General Janet Reno, and actor Michael J. Fox are some of the more famous individuals who have Parkinson's disease.

Actor Michael J. Fox is only one of millions of people who have Parkinson's disease.

Symptoms are treated effectively with several medications (Parkinson's Disease Foundation, 2005); the most popular are levodopa, which raises the functional level of dopamine in the brain; Sinemet (a combination of levodopa and carbidopa), which gets more levodopa to the brain; and Stalevo (a combination of Sinemet and entacapone), which extends the effective dosage time of Sinemet. Recent research indicates that a device called a *neurostimulator,* which acts like a brain pacemaker by regulating brain activity when implanted deep inside the brain, may prove effective in eliminating the tremors and shaking when medications fail (National Institute of Neurological Disorders and Stroke, 2005). For reasons we do not yet understand, roughly 30 to 50% of the time Parkinson's disease also involves severe cognitive impairment and eventually dementia (Schapira & Olanow, 2004).

Sensory Changes

Two major kinds of age-related structural changes occur in the eye. One is a decrease in the amount of light that passes through the eye, resulting in the need for more light to do tasks such as reading. As you might suspect, this change is one reason older adults do not see as well in the dark, which may account in part for their reluctance to go places at night. One possible logical response to the need for more light would be to increase illumination levels in general. However, this solution does not work in all situations because we also become increasingly sensitive to glare (Whitbourne, 1999). Additionally, our ability to adjust to changes in illumination, called adaptation, declines. Going from outside into a darkened movie theater involves dark adaptation; going back outside involves light adaptation. Research indicates that the time it takes for both types of adaptation increases with age (Fozard & Gordon-Salant, 2001). These changes are especially important for older drivers, who have more difficulty seeing after being confronted with the headlights of an oncoming car.

The other key structural changes involve the lens. As we grow older, the lens becomes more yellow, causing poorer color discrimination in the green–blue–violet end of the spectrum, and the ability of the lens to adjust and focus declines as the muscles around it stiffen (Fozard & Gordon-Salant, 2001). *This is what causes **presbyopia,** difficulty in seeing close objects clearly, necessitating either longer arms or corrective lenses.* To complicate matters further, the time our eyes need to change focus from near to far (or vice versa) increases (Fozard & Gordon-Salant, 2001). This also poses a major problem in driving. Because drivers are constantly changing their focus from the instrument panel to other autos and signs on the highway, older drivers may miss important information because of their slower refocusing time.

Besides these normative structural changes, some people experience diseases caused by abnormal structural changes. First, opaque spots called cataracts may develop on the lens, which limits the amount of light transmitted. Cataracts often are treated by surgical removal and use of corrective lenses. Second, the fluid in the eye may not drain properly, causing very high pressure; this condition, called glaucoma, can cause internal damage and loss of vision. Glaucoma is a fairly common disease in middle and late adulthood and is usually treated with eye drops.

The second major family of changes in vision result from changes in the retina. The retina lines approximately two thirds of the interior of the eye. The specialized receptor cells in vision, the rods and the cones, are contained in the retina. They are most densely packed toward the rear and especially at the focal point of vision, a region called the macula. At the center of the macula is the fovea, where incoming light is focused for maximum acuity, as when one is reading. With increasing age the probability of degeneration of the macula increases (Fozard & Gordon-Salant, 2001). Macular degeneration involves the progressive and irreversible destruction of receptors from any of a number of causes. This disease results in the loss of the ability to see details; for example, reading is extremely difficult, and television often is reduced to a blur. Roughly 1 in 5 people over age 75, especially smokers and European American women, have macular degeneration, making it the leading cause of functional blindness in older adults.

A second age-related retinal disease is a by-product of diabetes. Diabetes is accompanied by accelerated aging of the arteries, with blindness being one of the more serious side effects. Diabetic retinopathy, as this condition is called, can involve fluid retention in the macula, detachment of the retina, hemorrhage, and aneurysms (Fozard & Gordon-Salant, 2001). Because it takes many years to develop, diabetic retinopathy is more common among people who developed diabetes early in life.

The combined effects of the structural changes in the eye create two other types of changes. First, the ability to see detail and to discriminate different visual patterns, called acuity, declines steadily between ages 20 and 60, with a more rapid decline thereafter. Loss of acuity is especially noticeable at low light levels (Fozard & Gordon-Salant, 2001).

The age-related changes in vision we have considered can significantly affect people's ability to function in their environment. Similarly, age-related changes in hearing can also have this effect and interfere with people's ability to communicate with others. Experiencing hearing loss is one of the well-known normative changes with age (Whitbourne, 1999). A visit to any housing complex for older adults will easily verify this point; you will quickly notice that television sets and radios are turned up fairly loud in most of the apartments. Yet you don't have to be old to experience significant hearing problems. When it became difficult to hear what was being said to him, President Bill Clinton obtained two hearing aids. He was 51 years old at the time, and he attributed his hearing loss to too many high school bands and rock concerts when he was young. His situation is far from unique. Loud noise is the enemy of hearing at any age. You probably have seen people who work in noisy environments wearing protective gear on their ears so that they are not exposed to loud noise over extended periods of time.

But you can do serious damage to your hearing with short exposure too; in 1984, San Francisco punk rock bassist Kathy Peck was performing with her all-female punk band "The Contractions" at the Oakland Coliseum and played so loud that she had ringing in her ears for 3 days and suffered permanent hearing loss. As a result, she founded Hearing Education and Awareness for Rockers (HEAR; http://www.hearnet.com) shortly thereafter to educate musicians about the need to protect their ears (Noonan, 2005). You don't need to be at a concert to damage your hearing either. Using headphones, especially at high volume, can cause the same serious damage and should be avoided. It is especially easy to cause hearing loss with headphones if you wear them while exercising; the increased blood flow to the ear during exercise makes hearing receptors more vulnerable to damage.

The cumulative effects of noise and normative age-related changes create the most common age-related hearing problem: reduced sensitivity to high-pitched tones, called **presbycusis,** *which occurs earlier and more severely than the loss of sensitivity to low-pitched tones.* Research indicates that by the late 70s roughly half of older adults have presbycusis. Men typically have greater loss than women, but this may be because of differential exposure to noisy environments. Hearing loss usually is gradual at first but accelerates during the 40s, a pattern seen clearly in Figure 14.8.

Presbycusis results from four types of changes in the inner ear (Fozard & Gordon-Salant, 2001): sensory, consisting of atrophy and degeneration of receptor cells; neural, consisting of a loss of neurons in the auditory pathway in the brain; metabolic, consisting of a diminished supply of nutrients to the cells in the receptor area; and mechanical, consisting of atrophy and stiffening of the vibrating structures in the receptor area. Knowing the cause of a person's presbycusis is important because the different causes have different implications for other aspects of hearing. Sensory presbycusis has little effect on other hearing abilities. Neural presbycusis seriously affects the ability to understand speech. Metabolic presbycusis produces severe loss of sensitivity to all pitches. Finally, mechanical presbycusis also produces loss across all pitches, but the loss is greatest for high pitches.

Exercising while wearing headphones and listening to music can seriously damage hearing.

© Ken Weingart /Corbis

Because hearing plays a major role in social communication, its progressive loss could have an equally important effect on social adjustment. Loss of hearing in later life can cause numerous adverse emotional reactions, such as loss of independence, social isolation, irritation, paranoia, and depression. Much research indicates hearing loss per se does not cause social maladjustment or emotional disturbance. However, friends and relatives of an older person with hearing loss often attribute emotional changes to hearing loss, which strains the quality of interpersonal relationships (Whitbourne, 1996). Such problems often start, actually, with family and friends becoming impatient at having to repeat everything to the person with hearing loss. Thus, hearing loss may not directly affect older adults' self-concept or emotions, but it may negatively affect how they feel about interpersonal communication. By understanding hearing-loss problems and ways to overcome them, those without hearing loss can play a large part in minimizing the effects of hearing loss on the older people in their lives.

Fortunately, many people with hearing loss can be helped through two types of amplification systems and cochlear implants. Analog hearing aids are the most common and least expensive, but they provide the lowest quality sound. Digital hearing aids include microchips that can be programmed for different hearing situations. Cochlear implants do not amplify sound; rather, a microphone transmits sound to a receiver, which stimulates auditory nerve fibers directly. Although technology continues to improve, none of these devices can duplicate our original equipment, so be kind to your ears.

■ **Figure 14.8**
Hearing loss occurs in all adults but is greatest for high-pitched tones and greater for men than for women.

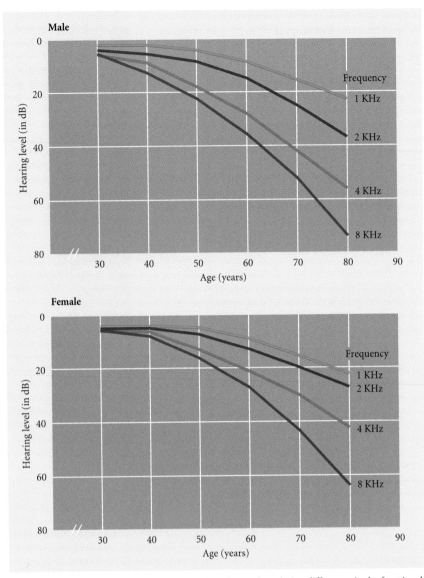

From Ordy, J. M., Brizzee, K. R., Beavers, T., and Medart, P. (1979). Age differences in the functional and structural organization of the auditory system in man. In J. M. Ordy and K. R. Brizzee (Eds.), *Sensory systems and communication in the elderly.* Reprinted by permission of Lippincott, Williams and Wilkins.

The sense of taste remains largely intact in older adults, as do touch, temperature, and pain sensitivity (Whitbourne, 1999). However, substantial age declines in smell occur after age 70 in many people (Ashendorf et al., 2005), and large declines are characteristic of Alzheimer's disease (Suzuki et al., 2004). These changes can be dangerous; for example, very old adults often have difficulty detecting the substance added to natural gas to make leaks noticeable, which can prove fatal.

Changes in balance make older people increasingly likely to fall. Indeed, the fear of falling and getting injured is a real concern for many older adults and can affect their willingness to engage in certain types of activities (Li et al., 2005).

The sensory changes people experience have important implications for their everyday lives (Whitbourne, 1996). Some, such as difficulty reading things close up, are minor annoyances that are easily corrected (by wearing reading glasses). Others are more serious and less easily addressed. For example, the ability to drive a car is affected by changes in vision and in hearing.

Because sensory changes may also lead to accidents around the home, it is important to design a safer environment that takes these changes into account. Many accidents can be prevented by maintaining health through prevention and conditioning. But making some relatively simple environmental changes also helps. For example, falls are the most common cause of accidental serious injury and death among older adults. Here are some steps that can help reduce the potential for falls:

- Illuminate stairways and provide light switches at both the top and the bottom of the stairs.
- Avoid high-gloss floor finishes due to glare and their tendency to be slippery when wet.
- Provide nightlights or bedside remote-control light switches.
- Be sure that both sides of stairways have sturdy handrails.
- Tack down carpeting on stairs or use nonskid treads.
- Remove throw or area rugs that tend to slide on the floor.
- Arrange furniture and other objects so that they are not obstacles.
- Use grab bars on bathroom walls and nonskid mats or strips in bathtubs.
- Keep outdoor steps and walkways in good repair.

> **THINK ABOUT IT**
>
> How might fear of falling and osteoporosis (See Chapter 13, page 492) be linked?

HEALTH ISSUES

In Chapter 13, we examined how lifestyle factors can lower the risk of many chronic diseases. The importance of health promotion does not diminish with increasing age. As we will see, lifestyle factors influence sleep, nutrition, and cancer. In addition, whether an older adult is an immigrant can, at least in the United States, make a significant difference in health status.

Sleep

Older adults have more trouble sleeping than do younger adults, which is probably related to a decreased "ability" to sleep (Ancoli-Israel & Alessi, 2005). Compared to younger adults, older adults report that it takes roughly twice as long to fall asleep, that they get less sleep on an average night, and that they feel more negative effects following a night with little sleep. Some of these problems are due to mental health problems such as depression, physical diseases such as heart disease, arthritis, diabetes, lung diseases, stroke and osteoporosis, and other conditions such as obesity (Foley et al., 2004). *Sleep problems can disrupt a person's* **circadian rhythm,** *or sleep-wake cycle.* Circadian rhythm disruptions can cause problems with attention and memory. Research shows that interventions, such as properly timed exposure to bright light, are effective in correcting circadian rhythm sleep disorders (Terman, 1994).

Nutrition

Most older adults do not need any vitamin or mineral supplements as long as they are eating a well-balanced diet (Ahluwalia, 2004). Even though body metabolism declines with age, older adults need to consume the same amounts of proteins and carbohydrates as young adults because of changes in how readily the body extracts the nutrients from these substances. Because they are typically in poor health, residents of nursing homes (Wallace & Schwartz, 1994) and frail older adults (Keller, 2004) are prone to weight loss and may have various nutritional deficiencies, such as vitamin B_{12} and folic acid, unless closely monitored.

Cancer

One of the most important health promotion steps people can take is cancer screening. In many cases, screening procedures involve little more than tests performed in a physician's office (e.g., screening for colon cancer), at home (e.g., breast self-exams), blood tests (e.g., screening for prostate cancer), or X-rays (e.g., mammograms).

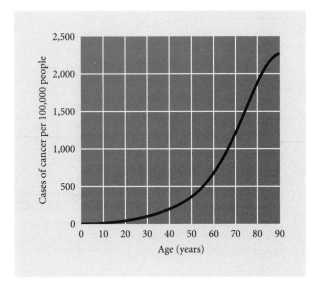

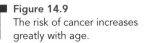

■ **Figure 14.9**
The risk of cancer increases greatly with age.

Why is cancer screening so important? As you can see in Figure 14.9, the risk of getting cancer increases markedly with age (American Cancer Society, 2005d). Why this happens is not fully understood. Unhealthy lifestyles (smoking and poor diet), genetics, and exposure to cancer-causing chemicals certainly are important, but they do not fully explain the age-related increase in risk (American Cancer Society, 2005d). Early detection of cancer even in older adults is essential to maximize the odds of surviving, and survival rates for most cancers are improving (American Cancer Society, 2005d). As our knowledge of the genetic underpinnings of some forms of cancer continues to increase, early detection and lifestyle changes will be increasingly important.

Immigrant Status

Whether an older adult was born in the United States or emigrated from another country affects health. At a basic level, immigrants may have difficulty communicating problems with family members or professionals because they may not be fluent in English (Usita & Blieszner, 2002). Similarly, language and cultural differences need to be considered in performing examinations with immigrants; cultures vary on how comfortable people are allowing strangers (i.e., physicians) to examine them (Bylsma, Ostendorf, & Hofer, 2002), and cultural differences can result in mislabeling or misdiagnosing problems (McConatha, Stoller, & Oboudiat, 2001).

Research comparing the health status of immigrants and U.S.-born older adults shows that even when socioeconomic status is controlled, immigrants show poorer health than U.S.-born people with the same ethnic background (e.g., Angel, Buckley, & Sakamoto, 2001; Berdes & Zych, 2000). Higher rates of depression are reported among older immigrant Mexican Americans who are the least acculturated, which may indicate that language and other barriers affect not only physical health but mental health as well (Gonzalez, Haan, & Hinton, 2001).

TEST YOURSELF

1. The biological theory of aging that includes the factors of free radicals and cross-linking is _____.
2. Damaged and dying neurons that collect around a core of protein produce _____.
3. The risk of getting cancer _____ markedly with age.

In this section we have concentrated on the biological forces in development. Think about the other forces (psychological, social, and life cycle), and list some reasons scientists have yet to propose a purely biological theory that accounts for all aspects of aging.

Answers: (1) cellular theory, (2) neuritic plaques, (3) increases

14.3

COGNITIVE PROCESSES

Rocio is a 75-year-old widow who feels that she does not remember recent events, such as whether she took her medicine, as well as she used to, but she has no trouble remembering things that happened in her 20s. Rocio wonders if this is normal, or whether she should be worried.

LEARNING OBJECTIVES

What changes occur in attention and reaction time as people age? How do these changes relate to everyday life?

What changes occur in memory with age? What can be done to remediate these changes?

What is wisdom, and how is it related to age?

Rocio, LIKE MANY OLDER PEOPLE, takes medications for arthritis, allergies, and high blood pressure. However, each drug has its own pattern; some are taken only with meals, others are taken every 8 hours, and still others are taken twice daily. Keeping these regimens straight is important to avoid potentially dangerous interactions and side effects, and older people face the problem of remembering to take each medication at the proper time.

Such situations place a heavy demand on cognitive resources such as attention and memory. In this section, we examine age-related changes in these and other cognitive processes, including reaction time, intelligence, and wisdom.

INFORMATION PROCESSING

In Chapter 1 we saw that one theoretical framework for studying cognition is information-processing theory. This framework provides a way to identify and study the basic mechanisms by which people take in, store, and remember information. We have already seen in Chapters 4 and 6 that information-processing theory has guided much research on cognition in childhood and adolescence. This approach has also been important to investigators examining age-related differences in basic processes such as attention and reaction time (Stine-Morrow & Soederberg Miller, 1999).

Attention

Researchers view attention as having three major components: selection, vigilance, and control (Parasuraman, 1998). Taken together, these components comprise the processes that enable people to perform a variety of functions.

We are constantly bombarded with stimulation to all of our senses, which we must somehow sort out. For example, when we are talking with someone at a party, we have to focus on what that person is saying and filter out all other noise. *Selective attention involves the selection of relevant information and inhibition of irrelevant information.* Older adults tend to perform poorer than younger adults on most selective attention tasks (McDowd & Shaw, 2000). However, age differences are minimized when the task involves simple searches for target information or when people are given sufficient practice.

Vigilance, also called sustained attention, involves the maintenance of attention over time. Listening for one's name to be called at a take-out restaurant, watching for the traffic light to change, and monitoring a screen connected to security cameras are all examples of vigilance tasks. Whether vigilance ability declines with age is uncertain (Rogers & Fisk, 2001). To the extent that memory demands are minimized, practice on the task is provided, and visual impairments are corrected, age differences are minimized.

*People's abilities to focus, switch, and divide attention are referred to as **attentional control.*** Results concerning age differences in attentional control are mixed (Rogers & Fisk, 2001). If older adults are told where to focus their attention, if a cue is provided to help them shift attention or if the task is simple, then they perform about as well as younger adults. But if the rate at which attention must be shifted is fast or if the task is complex, older adults do less well.

In sum, whether there is an age-related difference in attention depends on many factors, such as task complexity, visual ability, and other cognitive factors. It also turns out that aerobic exercise can improve performance on attention tasks (Kramer et al., 2001). It is clear that there is no simple description of developmental changes in attentional abilities (Rogers & Fisk, 2001).

Psychomotor Speed

You are driving home from a friend's house when all of a sudden a car pulls out of a driveway right into your path. You must hit the brakes as fast as possible, or you will have an accident. How quickly can you move your foot from the accelerator to the brake?

*This real-life situation is an example of **psychomotor speed,** the speed with which a person can make a specific response.* Psychomotor speed (also called reaction time) is one of the most studied phenomena of aging, and hundreds of studies all point to the same conclusion: People slow down as they get older. In fact, the slowing-with-age finding is so well documented that many researchers accept it as the only universal behavioral change in aging yet discovered (Salthouse, 2000). As the cartoon shows, even Garfield feels the effects. Data suggest, however, that the rate at which cognitive processes slow down from young adulthood to late life varies a great deal depending on the task (Madden, 2001; Stine-Morrow & Soederberg Miller, 1999).

The most important reason reaction times slow down is that older adults take longer to decide that they need to respond, especially when the situation involves ambiguous information (Salthouse, 2000). Even when the information presented indicates that a response will definitely be needed, there is an orderly slowing of responding with age. As the uncertainty of whether a response is needed increases, older adults get differentially slower; the difference between them and middle-aged adults increases as the uncertainty level increases.

Although response slowing is inevitable, the amount of the decline can be reduced if older adults are allowed to practice making quick responses or if they are experienced in the task. In a classic study, Salthouse (1984) showed that although older secretaries' reaction times (measured by how fast they could tap their finger) were slower than those of younger secretaries, their computed typing speed was no slower than that of their younger counterparts. Why? Typing speed is calculated on the basis of words typed corrected for errors; because older typists are more accurate, their final speeds were just as good as those of younger secretaries, whose work tended to include more errors. Also, older secretaries are better at anticipating what letters come next (Kail & Salthouse, 1994).

Because psychomotor slowing is a universal phenomenon, many researchers have argued that it may explain a great deal of the age differences in cognition (e.g., Salthouse, 2000). Indeed, psychomotor slowing is a very good predictor of cognitive performance, but there's a catch. The prediction is best when the task requires little effort (Park et al., 1996). When the task requires more effort and is more difficult, then working memory (which we consider later) is a better predictor of performance (Park et al., 1996). Also, older adults who are physically fit do not show as much slowing (Bunce, 2001).

> **THINK ABOUT IT**
>
> What are some of the practical consequences of psychomotor slowing?

Psychomotor slowing with age has also sparked considerable controversy concerning whether older adults should be allowed to drive. As discussed in the Current Controversies feature, knowledge about sensory and cognitive changes has resulted in research on this issue and the development of screening tests.

CURRENT CONTROVERSIES

INFORMATION PROCESSING IN EVERYDAY LIFE: OLDER DRIVERS

On July 16, 2003, an 86-year-old driver killed 10 persons when he lost control of his car while driving through a farmers market in Santa Monica, California. He reportedly confused his brake and gas pedals as he tried to stop (Bowles, 2003). Although only one tragic incident, it represents a growing and controversial issue: Should older adults be allowed to continue driving?

Especially in societies that promote individual independence and that also do not provide extensive public transportation systems, driving a car becomes a basic necessity in order to accomplish many daily tasks, such as purchasing food. However, as we have seen, age-related changes in vision, hearing, attention, and reaction time affect people's competence as drivers. Moreover, the number of older adults is rapidly increasing.

As you can see in Figure 14.10, statistics compiled by the National Highway Traffic Safety Administration (2003) show that the fatality rate for older drivers is higher than that for any age group except 16- to 20-year-olds; it has also increased since 1980, whereas it has dropped for other age groups. Data suggest that this is due to older drivers' age-related decline in key sensory, attentional, and psychomotor abilities (Campagne, Pebayle, & Muzet, 2004; Merat, Anttila, & Luoma, 2005; Satariano et al., 2004).

Experts agree that decisions about whether "at-risk" drivers should be allowed to continue driving must be based on performance measures rather than age or medical diagnosis alone. Since the mid-1980s, researchers have been working to develop these diagnostic measures.

Karlene Ball and her colleagues developed the *Useful Field of View* (UFOV) measure, an area from which one can extract visual information in a single glance without turning one's head or moving one's eyes (Ball & Owsley, 1993), which can easily be assessed via a personal desktop computer (Edwards et al., 2005). The size of the UFOV is important; it may mean the difference between "seeing" a car running a stop sign or a child running out between two parked cars and "not seeing" such information. Clearly, "seeing" and "not seeing" may mean the difference between having an accident and avoiding one (Ball et al., 1993). The UFOV test simulates driving in that it demands quick processing of information, simultaneous monitoring of central and peripheral stimuli, and the extraction of relevant target stimuli from irrelevant background information while performing a task. Importantly, driving performance improves after training in how to expand one's UFOV; for example, people reduce the number of dangerous maneuvers made while driving (Ball, 1997).

Other researchers have focused on alternative diagnostic methods. For example, Freund and colleagues (2005) showed that a new method of scoring the Clock Drawing Test (in which people reproduce various configurations of clock faces from memory) was a highly reliable predictor of how well older adults preformed on a driving simulator. McKenna and colleagues (2004) reported that a neuropsychological test battery was 85% accurate in predicting which of the over-70-year-old participants would fail an on-road driving test.

In the United States research on older drivers has changed the way some states provide license renewals, although states still vary considerably in their procedures. Most states only require older drivers to take a vision test, whereas some states, such as Illinois, also require road tests for drivers over age 75.

To assist states in adopting more uniform standards, the American Automobile Association (2005) created the *AAA Roadwise Review: A Tool to Help Seniors Drive Safely Longer*. The *Roadwise Review* is a screening tool developed by AAA and transportation safety

■ **Figure 14.10**

Motor vehicle traffic fatalities by age group show that drivers 70 years of age and older are at high risk for traffic accidents.

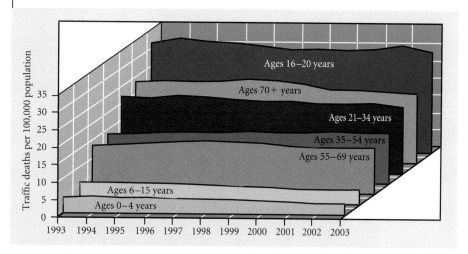

From National Highway Transportation Safety Administration, 2003. Available at http://www-nrd.nhtsa.dot .gov/pdf/nrd-30/NCSA/TSF2003/809766.pdf

researchers and validated in research. Designed to be administered at home, the *Roadwise Review* assesses eight key functional areas: leg strength and general mobility, head and neck flexibility, high-contrast visual acuity, low visual acuity, working memory, visualization of missing information, visual search, and visual information processing speed. Drivers with a significant loss in the functional capabilities tested by *Roadwise Review* are 2 to 5 times more likely to cause a motor vehicle crash than drivers without losses in these key safe driving abilities (American Automobile Association, 2005). You can find out more about *Roadwise Review* at the website http://www.aaa.com.

Should there be mandatory testing of older drivers? The data clearly indicate that the answer should be "yes." What form this testing will take, however, will spark increasing debate over the next few decades.

Working Memory

One evening while you are watching television, you suddenly remember that your lover's birthday is a week from tomorrow. You decide that a nice romantic dinner would be just the thing, so you open the phone book, look up the number for a special restaurant, go over to the phone, and make the call. Remembering the number long enough to dial it successfully requires good working memory. *Working memory involves the processes and structures involved in holding information in mind and simultaneously using it to solve a problem, make a decision, perform some function, or learn new information.*

Working memory is an umbrella term for many similar short-term holding and computational processes relating to a wide range of cognitive skills and knowledge domains (Zacks, Hasher, & Li, 2000). Working memory has a relatively small capacity. Because working memory deals with information that is being used right at the moment, it acts as a kind of mental scratchpad or blackboard. Unless we take some action to keep the information active (perhaps by rehearsal), or pass it along to long-term storage, the page we are using will get filled up quickly; to handle more information, some of the old information must be discarded.

Working memory generally declines with age (Zacks et al., 2000), and several researchers use it to explain age-related differences in cognitive performance on tasks that are difficult and demand considerable effort and resources (Park et al., 1996). Taken together, working memory and psychomotor speed provide a powerful set of explanatory constructs in predicting cognitive performance (Salthouse, 2000).

MEMORY

"Memory is power" (Johnson-Laird, 1988, p. 41). Indeed it is, when you think of the importance of remembering tasks, faces, lists, instructions, and our personal past and identity. Perhaps that is why people put such a premium on maintaining a good memory in old age; like Dagwood in the cartoon, many older adults use it to judge whether their mind is intact. Poor memory is often viewed as an inevitable part of aging. Many people like Rocio, the woman in the vignette, believe that forgetting a loaf of bread at the store when one is 25 is not a big deal, but forgetting it when one is 65 is cause for alarm—a sign of Alzheimer's disease or some other malady. In this section, we sort out the myth and the reality of memory changes with age.

What Changes?

The study of memory aging generally focuses on two types of memory: **explicit memory,** *the deliberate and conscious remembering of information that is learned and remembered at a specific time, and* **implicit memory,** *the unconscious remembering of information learned at some earlier time. Explicit memory is further divided into* **episodic memory,** *the general class of memory having to do with the conscious recollection of information from a specific time or event, and* **semantic memory,** *the general class of memory concerning the remembering of meanings of words or concepts not tied to a specific time or event.*

The results from hundreds of studies point to several conclusions (Bäckman, Small, & Wahlin, 2001). Older adults tend to perform worse than younger adults on tests of episodic memory recall in that they omit more information, include more intrusions, and repeat more previously recalled items. These age differences are large; for example, more than 80% of a sample of adults in their 20s will do better than adults in their 70s (Verhaeghen & Salthouse, 1997). These differences are not reliably lowered by providing slower presentation or by giving cues or reminders during recall. On recognition tests, age differences are smaller but are not eliminated (Zacks et al., 2000). Older adults also tend to be less efficient at spontaneously using memory strategies to help themselves remember (Hertzog & Dunlosky, 2004).

In contrast, age differences on semantic memory tasks are typically absent (Bäckman et al., 2001). However, one area in which older adults have difficulty is in word-finding, such as coming up with the right word based on a definition and having more tip-of-the-tongue experiences. Similarly, age differences are typically absent on tests of implicit memory (Fleischman & Gabrieli, 1998).

A final area of memory research concerns autobiographical memory, memory for events that occur during one's life. An interesting phenomenon arises when the distribution of highly memorable autobiographical events across the life span is examined. As you can see in Figure 14.11, for both younger and older adults vivid memories experienced between ages 10 and 30 are reported more often than those occurring after age 30 (Fitzgerald, 1999). This same pattern holds when people are asked to name Academy Award winners, news stories, and teams that played in the World Series (Rubin, Rahal, & Poon, 1998). It is possible that this earlier period of life has greater importance in defining oneself and thus helps people organize their memories (Fitzgerald, 1999).

In sum, contrary to social stereotypes of a broad-based decline in memory ability with age, research shows that the facts are more complex. Whether memory declines with age depends on the type of memory. But social stereotypes are powerful, as we will see next.

The Impact of Beliefs About Memory Aging

Regardless of the results from research, there is widespread belief that memory inevitably declines. This is significant because research shows that what adults believe about their memory ability is related to how well they perform (Cavanaugh, 1996). This relation is seen in how much effort people exert trying to remember, how well people predict they will perform, and what strategies people use. For example, people who believe that their memory is good work harder at remembering than people who believe their memory is poor. Moreover, these beliefs are also related to the assumptions people

■ **Figure 14.11**
Both younger and older adults remember more life events from their teens and 20s than from any other period of life.

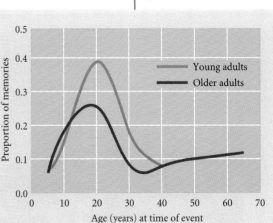

Reprinted from Fitzgerald, J. (1999). Autobiographical memory and social cognition. In T. M. Hess & F. Blanchard-Fields (Eds.), *Social cognition and aging* (p. 161) with permission from Elsevier.

make about the degree to which memory (or other cognitive abilities) is "supposed" to change (Cavanaugh, Feldman, & Hertzog, 1998). For example, if you think that memory is supposed to get much worse as you get older, then your estimate of how much your memory has declined will be much greater than an estimate by someone who thinks memory should decline only a little with age.

Overall, research on memory beliefs shows that although some changes in memory are normal, people can essentially convince themselves that these changes are much worse and more pervasive than they really are (Cavanaugh et al., 1998). It may even be the case that altering your central beliefs about memory aging may help you develop compensatory strategies that lower the magnitude of these changes, or at least help compensate for them (Cavanaugh, 2000).

Still, one's beliefs about memory are influenced by changes in basic information processing, such as working memory (Hertzog & Dunlosky, 2004; Hertzog & Hultsch, 2000). Although beliefs are important, they must also be realistic about normative change.

When Is Memory Change Abnormal?

The older man in the *For Better or For Worse* cartoon voices a concern that many older adults have: that their forgetfulness is indicative of something much worse. Because people are concerned that memory failures may reflect disease, identifying true cases of memory-impairing disease is extremely important. Differentiating normal and abnormal memory changes is usually accomplished through a wide array of tests that are grounded in the various developmental patterns discussed earlier. Such testing focuses on measuring performance and identifying declines in aspects of memory that typically do not change, such as tertiary memory (which is essentially long-term memory) (Edelstein & Kalish, 1999).

Even if a decline is identified in an aspect of memory that is cause for concern, it does not automatically follow that there is a serious problem. A first step is to find out whether the memory problem is interfering with everyday functioning. When the memory problem does interfere with functioning, such as not remembering how to get home or your spouse's name, it is appropriate to suspect a serious, abnormal underlying reason.

Once a serious problem is suspected, the next step is to obtain a thorough examination (Edelstein & Kalish, 1999). This should include a complete physical and neurological examination and a complete battery of neuropsychological tests. These may help identify the nature and extent of the underlying problem and provide information about what steps, if any, can be taken to alleviate the difficulties.

The most important point to keep in mind is that there is no magic number of times that a person must forget something before it becomes a matter for concern. Indeed, many memory-impairing diseases progress slowly, and poor memory performance may only be noticed gradually over an extended period of time. The best course is to have

the person examined; only with complete and thorough testing can these concerns be checked appropriately.

Remediating Memory Problems

Remember Rocio, the person in the vignette who had to remember when to take several different medications? In the face of normal age-related declines, how can her problem be solved?

Support programs can be designed for people to help them remember. Sometimes, people like Rocio who are experiencing normal age-related memory changes need extra help because of the high memory demands they face. At other times, people need help because the memory changes they are experiencing are greater than normal.

Camp and colleagues (1993; Camp, 2001) developed the E-I-E-I-O framework to handle both situations. The E-I-E-I-O framework combines two types of memory: explicit and implicit. The framework also includes two types of memory aids. *External aids are memory aids that rely on environmental resources, such as notebooks or calendars. Internal aids are memory aids that rely on mental processes, such as imagery.* The aha experience that comes with suddenly remembering something (as in, "Oh, I remember!") is the O that follows these E's and I's. As you can see in Figure 14.12, the E-I-E-I-O framework allows different types of memory to be combined with different types of memory aids to provide a broad range of intervention options to help people remember.

You are probably most familiar with the explicit-external and explicit-internal types of memory aids. Explicit-internal aids such as rehearsal help people remember phone numbers. Explicit-external aids are used when information needs to be better organized and remembered, such as taking notes during a visit to the physician (McGuire & Codding, 1998). Implicit-internal aids represent nearly effortless learning, such as the association between the color of the particular wing of the apartment building one lives in and the fact that one's residence is there. Implicit-external aids such as icons representing time of day and the number of pills to take help older adults remember their medication (Morrow et al., 1998).

In general, explicit-external interventions are the most frequently used to remediate the kinds of memory problems older adults face, probably because they are easy to use and widely available (Camp, 2001). For example, virtually everyone owns an address book—whether an electronic one or a physical book—and small notepads are sold in hundreds of stores. Explicit-external interventions have other important applications too. The medication problem is best solved with an explicit-external intervention: a pillbox that is divided into compartments corresponding to days of the week and different times of the day. Research shows that this type of pillbox is the easiest to load and results in the fewest errors (Park, Morrell, & Shifren, 1999). Memory interventions like this can help older adults maintain their independence. Nursing homes also use explicit-external interventions, such as bulletin boards with the date and weather conditions or activities charts, to help residents keep in touch with current events.

The E-I-E-I-O framework can be used to design remediation strategies for any kind of memory problem, including those due to disease or abnormal patterns of aging. Later, we will see how the E-I-E-I-O framework provides insight into how people with Alzheimer's disease can be helped to improve their memory. In the meantime, see how many different categories of memory interventions you can discover.

CREATIVITY AND WISDOM

Two aspects of cognition that have been examined for age-related differences are creativity and wisdom. Each has been the focus of stereotypes: creativity is

> **THINK ABOUT IT**
>
> How might people's beliefs about memory be important elements of memory training programs?

■ **Figure 14.12**
The E-I-E-I-O model of memory helps categorize different types of memory aids.

Type of memory	Type of memory aid	
	External	**Internal**
Explicit	Appointment book	Mental imagery
	Grocery list	Rote rehearsal
Implicit	Color-coded maps	Spaced retrieval
	Sandpaper letters	Conditioning

Posting a calendar with activities in a nursing home is one external device to help residents remember the events for a specific day.

assumed to be a function of young people, whereas wisdom is assumed to be the province of older adults. Let's see whether these views are accurate.

Creativity

What makes a person creative? Is it exceptional productivity? Duke Ellington wrote numerous musical pieces, Diego Rivera painted hundreds of pictures, and Thomas Edison had 1,093 patents (still the record for one person). But Gregor Mendel had only seven scientific papers, yet he endures as a major figure in the history of genetics. Lao Tzu is remembered mostly for the enduring *Tao Te Ching.* Does creativity mean having a career marked by precocity and longevity? Wolfgang Goethe wrote poetry as a teenager, a best-selling novel in his 20s, popular plays in his 30s and 40s, Part I of *Faust* at 59, and Part II at 83. But others are "early bloomers" and decline thereafter, whereas still others are relatively unproductive early and are "late bloomers."

Researchers define creativity in adults as the ability to produce work that is novel, high in demand, and task appropriate (Sternberg & Lubart, 2001). Creative output, in terms of the number of creative ideas a person has or the major contributions a person makes, varies across the adult life span and across disciplines (Simonton, 1997; Sternberg & Lubart, 2001). When considered as a function of age, the overall number of creative ideas a person has tends to increase through one's 20s, plateaus in one's 30s, and declines thereafter, as shown in Figure 14.13. However, the decline does *not* mean that people stop being creative at all; rather, it means that creative people keep producing creative ideas, but fewer of them than they did when they were younger (Dixon & Hultsch, 1999). When translated into a mathematical equation, Figure 14.13 can be used to predict the creative output of a specific individual (e.g., Duke Ellington) or a group of similar people (e.g., jazz composers). In both cases, the figure accurately describes the level of creative output. Thus, creative output peaks in early to middle adulthood and declines thereafter.

What does the trend look like if one compares different disciplines, such as mathematics, biology, and earth science? One way to examine this is to compare three points in a career: the age at the time of the first major contribution, the most important contribution, and the last important contribution (Simonton, 1997). As you can see in Figure 14.14, the overall trend in several scientific disciplines is the same as in Figure 14.13, with a rise, a peak, and a decline with increasing age. The average age at which the people

■ **Figure 14.13**
On average, adults are most creatively productive in their 40s.

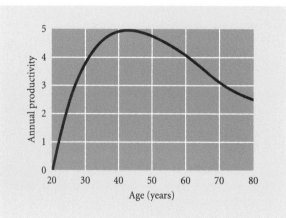

studied died is shown by small crosses. Notice that the specific ages for the three contributions depend on the discipline. For example, mathematics has the youngest age of first major contribution, and earth sciences tends to have the oldest age at last important contribution.

Taken together, Simonton's (1997) analysis provides the most powerful model available to explain individual differences in creative output across adulthood. The trend is clear: Across a variety of disciplines, creative output tends to peak during late young adulthood to early middle age and decline thereafter. This pattern may help explain why senior researchers include many younger scholars in their work. The senior scholar can provide the overall context, while the younger researchers may provide a continuous flow of innovative ideas (Dixon & Hultsch, 1999).

Wisdom

For thousands of years, cultures around the world have greatly admired people who were wise. Tales of wise people, usually older adults, have been passed down from generation to generation to teach lessons about important matters of life and love (Chinen, 1989). What is it about these truths that makes someone who knows them wise?

From a psychological perspective, wisdom has been viewed from three main aspects (Sternberg & Lubart, 2001): the orchestration of mind and virtue, involving the ability to solve difficult real-world problems; postformal thinking (see Chapter 10, page 397); and action-oriented knowledge acquired without direct help from others that allows people to achieve goals they value. A growing body of research has been examining these aspects.

Based on years of research using in-depth think-aloud interviews with young, middle-aged, and older adults about normal and unusual problems that people face, Baltes and Staudinger (1993, 2000) describe four characteristics of wisdom:

- ■ Wisdom deals with important or difficult matters of life and the human condition.
- ■ Wisdom is truly "superior" knowledge, judgment, and advice.
- ■ Wisdom is knowledge with extraordinary scope, depth, and balance, applicable to specific situations.
- ■ Wisdom, when used, is well intended and combines mind and virtue (character).

The researchers used this framework to discover that people who are wise are experts in the basic issues in life (Baltes & Staudinger, 2000). Wise people know a great deal about how to conduct life, how to interpret life events, and what life means.

Research studies indicate that contrary to what many people expect, there is no association between age and wisdom (Baltes & Staudinger, 2000; De Andrade, 2000; Hartman, 2001). As is depicted in Baltes and Staudinger's (2000) model, whether a person is wise depends on whether he or she has extensive life experience with the type of problem given and has the requisite cognitive abilities and personality (see Figure 14.15).

So what specific factors help one become wise? Baltes (1993) identified three factors: (a) *general personal conditions,* such as mental ability; (b) *specific expertise conditions,* such as mentoring or practice; and (c) *facilitative life contexts,* such as education or leadership experience. Other researchers point to additional criteria. For example, Kramer (1990) argues that the *integration of affect and cognition* that occurs during adulthood results in the ability to act wisely. Personal growth during adulthood, reflecting Erikson's concepts of generativity and integrity, helps foster the process as well. All of these fac-

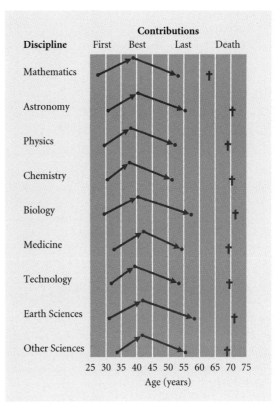

■ **Figure 14.14**
The age at which individuals make their best contribution varies by field, but in no case does it occur in late life.

■ **Figure 14.15**
Although wisdom is influenced by many factors, contrary to what most people think, age is not one of them.

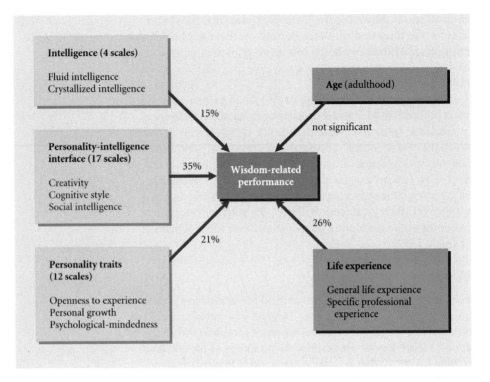

tors take time. Thus, although growing old is no guarantee of wisdom, it does provide the time that, if used well, creates a supportive context for it.

TEST YOURSELF

1. As long as the competing tasks in a test of divided attention are easy, older adults perform _____ younger adults.

2. Compared to age differences in free recall performance, age differences in recognition memory performance are _____.

3. Three factors that help a person become wise are general personal conditions, special expertise conditions, and _____.

How would the view that wisdom involves life experience fit into the discussion of expertise in Chapter 13?

Answers: (1) as well as, (2) smaller, (3) facilitative life contexts

14.4

MENTAL HEALTH AND INTERVENTION

LEARNING OBJECTIVES

How does depression in older adults differ from depression in younger adults? How is it diagnosed and treated?

How are anxiety disorders treated in older adults?

What is Alzheimer's disease? How is it diagnosed and managed? What causes it?

Mary lived by herself for 30 years after her husband died. For all but the last 5 years or so, she managed very well. Little by little, family members and friends began noticing that Mary wasn't behaving quite right. For example, her memory slipped, she sounded confused sometimes, and her moods changed without warning. Her appearance deteriorated. Some of her friends attribute these changes to the fact that Mary is in her 80s. But others wonder whether this is something more than normal aging.

S UPPOSE MARY IS A RELATIVE OF YOURS. How would you deal with the situation? How would you decide whether her behavior is normal? What would you do to try to improve Mary's life? We'll look in on Mary again in the Real People feature later in the chapter.

Every day families turn to mental health professionals for help in dealing with psychological problems their aging relatives are having. Unfortunately, myths interfere with appropriate mental health diagnoses and interventions for older adults. For example, many people mistakenly believe that nearly all older adults are either depressed, demented, or both. When they observe older adults behaving in these ways, they take no action because they believe that nothing can be done.

In this section, we will see that such beliefs are wrong. Only a minority of older adults have mental health problems, and most such problems respond to therapy. Sometimes these problems manifest themselves differently in younger and older adults, so we need to know what to look for. Accurate diagnosis is essential. Let's examine some of the most commonly occurring and widely known disorders: depression, anxiety disorders, and Alzheimer's disease.

DEPRESSION

Most people feel down or sad from time to time, perhaps in reaction to a problem at work or in one's relationships. But does this mean that most people are depressed? How is depression diagnosed? Are there age differences in the symptoms examined in diagnosis? How is depression treated?

First of all, let's dispense with a myth. Contrary to the popular belief that most older adults are depressed, the rate of severe depression *declines* from young adulthood to old age (Gatz, 2000; Qualls, 1999), a fact that also holds cross-culturally (Chou & Chi, 2005). Rates for depression tend to be higher in Latino older adults than for European American and African American older adults (Gonzalez et al., 2001). For those people who do experience depression, let's examine its diagnosis and treatment.

How Is Depression Diagnosed in Older Adults?

Depression in later life is usually diagnosed on the basis of two clusters of symptoms that must be present for at least 2 weeks: feelings and physical changes. *As with younger people, the most prominent symptom of depression in older adults is feeling sad or down, termed dysphoria.* But whereas younger people are likely to label these feelings directly as "feeling depressed," older adults may refer to them as "feeling helpless," or in terms of physical health such as "feeling tired" (Wolfe, Morrow, & Fredrickson, 1996). Older adults are also more likely than younger people to appear apathetic and expressionless, to confine themselves to bed, to neglect themselves, and to make derogatory statements about themselves.

The second cluster of symptoms includes physical changes such as loss of appetite, insomnia, and trouble breathing (Whitbourne, 2000). In young people, these symptoms usually indicate an underlying psychological problem, but in older adults they may simply reflect normal, age-related changes. Thus, older adults' physical symptoms of depression must be evaluated very carefully (Qualls, 1999).

An important step in diagnosis is ruling out other possible causes of the symptoms. For example, other physical health problems, neurological disorders, medication side effects, metabolic conditions, and substance abuse can all cause behaviors that resemble depression (Qualls, 1999). For many minorities, immigration status and degree of acculturation and assimilation are key factors to consider (Black, Markides, & Miller, 1998). An impor-

Although rates of serious depression decline with age, it remains a significant problem for many older adults.

© Eastcott / The Image Works

tant criterion to be established is that the symptoms interfere with daily life; clinical depression involves significant impairment of daily living (Edelstein & Kalish, 1999; Qualls, 1999).

What Causes Depression?

There are two main schools of thought about the causes of depression. One focuses on biological and physiological processes, particularly on imbalances in specific neurotransmitters (see Chapter 9, pages 363–364). Because most neurotransmitter levels decline with age, some researchers believe that depression in later life is likely to be a biochemical problem (Whitbourne, 2000). The general view that depression has a biochemical basis underlies current approaches to drug therapies, discussed a bit later.

The second view focuses on psychosocial factors, such as loss and internal belief systems. Although several types of loss have been associated with depression, including loss of a spouse, a job, or good health, it is how a person interprets a loss, rather than the event itself, that causes depression (Gaylord & Zung, 1987). *In this approach, **internal belief systems,** or what one tells oneself about why certain things are happening, are emphasized as the cause of depression.* For example, experiencing an unpredictable and uncontrollable event such as the death of a spouse may cause depression because you believe the event happened to you because you are a bad person (Beck, 1967). People who are depressed tend to believe that they are personally responsible for all the bad things that happen to them, that things are unlikely to get better, and that their whole life is a shambles.

Gatz (2000) takes a comprehensive view that depression depends on the balance between biological dispositions, stress, and protective factors. Developmentally, biological factors become more important with age, whereas stress factors diminish. Better protective factors, such as coping skills, with age may help explain why the rate of depression decreases across the adult life span.

How Is Depression Treated in Older Adults?

Regardless of how severe depression is, people benefit from treatment, often through a combination of medication and psychotherapy (Qualls, 1999; Wolfe et al., 1996). Medications work by altering the balance of specific neurotransmitters in the brain. *For very severe cases of depression, medications such as **heterocyclic antidepressants (HCAs), monoamine oxidase (MAO) inhibitors,** or **selective serotonin reuptake inhibitors (SSRIs)** can be administered.* Although they are widely prescribed, HCAs cannot be used if the person is also taking medications to control hypertension or has certain metabolic conditions. MAO inhibitors cause very dangerous and potentially fatal interactions with foods containing tyramine or dopamine, such as cheddar cheese, wine, and chicken liver. Consequently, MAO inhibitors are usually used only as a last resort. Selective serotonin reuptake inhibitors (SSRIs) gained wide popularity beginning in the late 1980s because they have the lowest overall side effects of any antidepressant. SSRIs work by boosting the level of serotonin, which is a neurotransmitter involved in regulating moods. One of the SSRIs, Prozac, has been the subject of controversy, as it has been linked in a small number of cases with the serious side effect of high levels of agitation. Other SSRIs, such as Zoloft and Serzone, appear to have fewer adverse reactions.

Psychotherapy is a popular approach to treating depression, based on the idea that focusing on the psychological aspects of depression is helpful. Two forms of psychotherapy have been shown to be effective with older adults. *The basic idea in **behavior therapy** is that depressed people experience too few rewards or reinforcements from their environment.* Thus, the goal of behavior therapy is to increase the good things that happen and minimize the negative things (Lewinsohn, 1975). Often, this is accomplished by having people increase their activities; simply by doing more, the likelihood that something nice will happen is increased. In addition, behavior therapy seeks to get people to reduce the negative things that happen by learning how to avoid them. The net increase in positive events and net decrease in negative events comes about through practice and homework assignments during the course of therapy, such as going out more or joining a club to meet new people.

A second effective approach is **cognitive therapy,** which is based on the idea that maladaptive beliefs or cognitions about oneself are responsible for depression. From this perspective, a depressed person views him- or herself as unworthy and inadequate, the world as insensitive and ungratifying, and the future as bleak and unpromising (Beck et al., 1979). In a cognitive therapy session, a person is taught how to recognize these thoughts and to reevaluate the self, the world, and the future more realistically, resulting in a change in the underlying beliefs.

The most important fact to keep in mind about depression is that it *is* treatable. Thus, if an older person behaves in ways that indicate depression, it is a good idea to have him or her examined by a mental health professional. Even if it turns out not to be depression, another underlying and possibly treatable condition may be uncovered.

ANXIETY DISORDERS

Imagine you are about to give a speech to an audience of several hundred people. During the last few minutes before you begin, you start to feel nervous, your heart begins to pound, your mouth gets very dry, and your palms get sweaty. These feelings, common even to veteran speakers, are similar to those experienced more frequently by people with anxiety disorders.

Anxiety disorders include problems such as feelings of severe anxiety for no apparent reason, phobias with regard to specific things or places, and obsessive-compulsive disorders, in which thoughts or actions are repeatedly performed (Beck & Averill, 2004; Mohlman et al., 2004). Although anxiety disorders occur in adults of all ages, they are particularly common in older adults due to loss of health, relocation stress, isolation, fear of losing independence, and many other reasons. Anxiety disorders are diagnosed in as many as 10% of older women and 5% of older men (Cohen, 1990). The reasons for this gender difference are unknown.

Anxiety disorders can be treated with medication and psychotherapy (Beck & Averill, 2004). The most commonly used medications are benzodiazepine (e.g., Valium and Librium), SSRIs (Paxil, among others), buspirone, and beta-blockers. Though moderately effective, these drugs must be monitored very carefully in older adults because the amount needed to treat the disorder is very low and the potential for side effects is great. For older adults, the clear treatment of choice is psychotherapy, especially relaxation therapy (Beck & Averill, 2004). Relaxation therapy is highly effective, is easily learned, and presents a technique that is useful in many situations (e.g., falling asleep at night).

To this point, we have focused on psychopathologies that can be treated effectively. In the next section, we consider Alzheimer's disease, which at present cannot be treated effectively over the long run, progressively worsening until the person dies.

DEMENTIA: ALZHEIMER'S DISEASE

Arguably the most serious condition associated with aging is **dementia,** a family of diseases involving serious impairment of behavioral and cognitive functioning. Of these disorders, Alzheimer's disease is the most common. The personal side of Alzheimer's disease is explored in the Real People feature, which builds on the scenario at the beginning of this section.

REAL PEOPLE: Applying Human Development

WHAT'S THE MATTER WITH MARY?

Mary lived by herself for 30 years after her husband died. For all but the last 5 years or so, she managed very well. Little by little, though, family members and friends began noticing that Mary wasn't behaving quite right. For example, her memory had slipped badly, she sounded confused sometimes, and her moods changed without warning. Her appearance deteriorated. Some of her friends attributed these changes to the fact that Mary was in her 80s.

However, when Mary started forgetting where she lived, her family and friends knew that something serious was wrong. Her family ultimately realized that Mary could no longer care for herself and moved her to an assisted living facility. Mary's memory continued to decline; she started forgetting the names of her children and grandchildren. When she started to wander at night, Mary was transferred to a nursing home. Her physical abilities declined further, and she lost the ability to feed herself. Toward the end of her life, Mary could not eat solid food and had to be force-fed. Mary died from Alzheimer's disease after 15 years of slow decline.

Alzheimer's disease causes people to change from thinking, communicative human beings to confused, bedridden victims unable to recognize their family members and close friends. As a result, the *fear* of Alzheimer's disease among healthy older adults is a significant problem beyond the actual disease (Youngjohn & Crook, 1996).

Millions of people are afflicted with Alzheimer's disease, including such notable individuals as former U.S. President Ronald Reagan, who died from it in 2004; the disease cuts across ethnic, racial, and socioeconomic groups. The incidence of Alzheimer's disease increases with age, rising from extremely low rates in the 50s to roughly 25% of the people aged 85 and older (Gatz & Smyer, 2001). Women tend to have a higher risk (Henderson, 1997). As the number of older adults increases rapidly over the next several decades, the number of cases is expected to rise substantially.

Alzheimer's disease involves memory loss to the degree that may include forgetting the names of family members.

What Are the Symptoms of Alzheimer's Disease?

*The key symptoms of **Alzheimer's disease** are gradual declines in memory, learning, attention, and judgment; confusion as to time and place; difficulties in communicating and finding the right words; decline in personal hygiene and self-care skills; inappropriate social behavior; and changes in personality.* These classic symptoms may be vague and only occur occasionally in the beginning, but as the disease progresses, they become much more pronounced and are exhibited much more regularly (Golby et al., 2005). Wandering away from home and not being able to remember how to return increases. Delusions, hallucinations, and other related behaviors develop and get worse over time (Piccininni et al., 2005). Spouses become strangers. Patients may not even recognize themselves in a mirror; they wonder who is looking back at them. *In its advanced stages, Alzheimer's disease often causes **incontinence** (the loss of bladder or bowel control) and total loss of mobility.* Victims eventually become completely dependent on others for care. At this point many caregivers seek facilities such as adult day care centers and other sources of help, such as family and friends, in order to provide a safe environment for the Alzheimer's patient while the primary caregiver is at work or needs to do basic errands.

The rate of deterioration in Alzheimer's disease varies widely from one patient to another, although progression usually is faster when onset occurs earlier in adulthood (Wilson et al., 2000). Thus, it is difficult to generalize about the level of a person's im-

© Alan Oddie/PhotoEdit

THINK ABOUT IT

How do the memory problems in Alzheimer's disease differ from those in normal aging?

pairment based solely on how long ago the diagnosis was made. Likewise, it is very difficult to predict how long a specific patient will survive, which only adds to the stress experienced by the caregiver (Cavanaugh & Nocera, 1994).

How Is Alzheimer's Disease Diagnosed?

Given that the behavioral symptoms of Alzheimer's disease eventually become quite obvious, one would assume that diagnosis would be straightforward. Quite the contrary. In fact, absolute certainty that a person has Alzheimer's disease cannot even be achieved while the individual is still alive. Definitive diagnosis must be based on an autopsy of the brain after death because the defining criteria for diagnosing Alzheimer's disease involve documenting large numbers of structural changes in neurons that can only be observed under a microscope after brain tissue has been removed and specially prepared (Ebersole et al., 2004).

Of course, one is still left with the issue of figuring out whether a person probably has Alzheimer's disease while he or she is still alive. Although not definitive, the number and severity of behavioral changes lead clinicians to make fairly accurate diagnoses of *probable* Alzheimer's disease (Golby et al., 2005; Piccininni et al., 2005). But accuracy depends on a broad-based and thorough series of medical and psychological tests, including complete blood tests, metabolic and neurological tests, and neuropsychological tests (Forbes, 2005). A great deal of diagnostic work goes into ruling out virtually all other possible causes of the observed symptoms. This effort is essential. Because Alzheimer's disease is an incurable and fatal disease, every treatable cause of the symptoms must be explored first. In essence, Alzheimer's disease is diagnosed by excluding all other possible explanations. A model plan for making sure the diagnosis is correct is shown in Figure 14.16.

In an attempt to be as thorough as possible, clinicians usually interview family members about their perceptions of the observed behavioral symptoms. Most clinicians view this information as essential to understanding the history of the difficulties the person is experiencing. However, research indicates that spouses are often inaccurate in their assessments of the level of their partner's impairment (McGuire & Cavanaugh, 1992). In part, this inaccuracy is due to lack of knowledge about the disease. Also, spouses wish to portray themselves as in control, either by denying that the symptoms are in fact severe or by exaggerating the severity in order to give the appearance that they are coping well in a very difficult situation. Some spouses describe their partner's symptoms accurately, but family reports should not be the only source of information about the person's ability to function.

A great deal of attention has been given to the development of more definitive tests for Alzheimer's disease while the person is still alive. *Much of this work has focused on **amyloid,** a protein that is produced in abnormally high levels in Alzheimer's patients, perhaps causing the neurofibrillary tangles and neuritic plaques described earlier.* Research is progressing toward developing a way to measure amyloid concentrations in cerebrospinal fluid and blood. Additional work focuses on testing for the presence or absence of specific genes, a topic to which we now turn.

What Causes Alzheimer's Disease?

We do not know for sure what causes Alzheimer's disease (Qualls, 1999; Whitbourne, 2000). Over the years, several hypotheses have been offered, such as aluminum deposits in the brain and a slow-acting virus, but none have explained more than a few cases.

Currently, most research is concentrating on identifying genetic links (Gatz & Smyer, 2001; Schmitt & Estus, 2004). The evidence is growing that at least some forms of Alzheimer's disease are inherited, based on studies of family trees, relatives, and identical twins. Indeed, several sites on various chromosomes have been tentatively identified as being involved in the transmission of Alzheimer's disease, including chromosomes 12, 14, 19, and 21. The most promising work has noted links between the genetic markers and the production of amyloid protein, the major component of neuritic

■ **Figure 14.16**
Diagnosing Alzheimer's disease requires a thorough process of ruling out other possibilities.

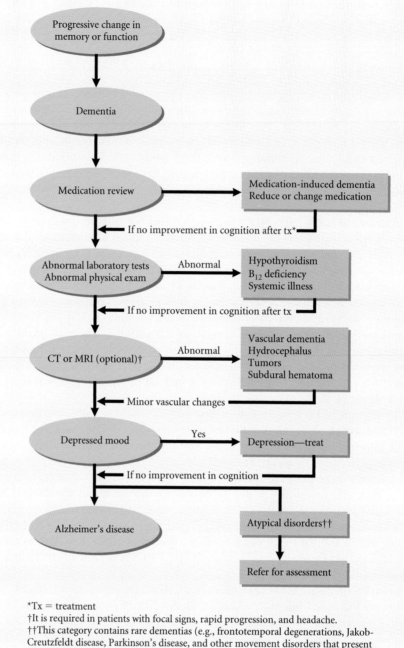

*Tx = treatment
†It is required in patients with focal signs, rapid progression, and headache.
††This category contains rare dementias (e.g., frontotemporal degenerations, Jakob-Creutzfeldt disease, Parkinson's disease, and other movement disorders that present with dementias) that should be considered when unusual clinical features are present or a rapidly progressive course is noted.

From Alzheimer's Association online document. Developed and endorsed by the TriAD Advisory Board. Copyright 1996 Pfizer Inc. and Esai Inc. with special thanks to J. L. Cummings. Algorithm reprinted from TriAD, *Three for the Management of Alzheimer's Disease,* with permission.

plaques (Schmitt & Estus, 2004). Much of this research focuses on apolipoprotein E4 (apo E4), associated with chromosome 19, which may play a central role in creating neuritic plaques. Interestingly, another version, apo E2, seems to have the reverse effect: It decreases the risk of Alzheimer's disease (Gatz et al., 1997). Researchers are also looking for relationships between apolipoprotein E and cognitive functioning (Riley et al., 2000). And researchers have established a link between the cystatin C gene (CST3) and late-onset Alzheimer's disease (Finckh et al., 2000).

Researchers can already identify genetic markers responsible for certain forms of early-onset Alzheimer's disease, and they have developed a test to see whether people have the inheritance pattern (Steinbart et al., 2001). Although research shows no sig-

THE PERSONAL CONTEXT OF LATER LIFE ■ 571

nificant negative consequences to people when they know that they have the marker for Alzheimer's disease (Marteau et al., 2005), difficult choices may remain. For example, individuals who know they have the genes responsible for the disease may be faced with difficult decisions about having children and how to live out their lives. Genetic counseling programs, which currently focus mostly on diseases of childhood, would need to be expanded to help individuals face decisions about diseases occurring later in life.

What Can Be Done for Victims of Alzheimer's Disease?

Even though Alzheimer's disease is incurable, much can be done to alleviate its symptoms. Most of the research has been focused on drugs aimed at improving cognitive functioning. Despite much research with numerous types of drugs, and evidence that some medications ease or slow the progress of symptoms, none currently available permanently reverses the memory symptoms (Voisin et al., 2005). Of these, a group of medications that inhibit acetylcholinesterase has produced the most promising results, even in the later stages of the disease (Voisin et al., 2005).

Other researchers have emphasized the importance of other criteria for therapeutic success besides cognitive function, such as functional abilities, behavior, quality of life, resource utilization, and caregiver burden (Winblad et al., 2001). Medications such as *thioridazine* and *haloperidol* are used to treat severe psychotic symptoms. Antidepressants are effective in alleviating the depression that often accompanies Alzheimer's disease. All of these medications must be used carefully, as older adults have a high risk of side effects such as severe motor impairment and increased cognitive impairment (Brioni & Decker, 1997).

Numerous effective behavioral and educational interventions have also been developed. *One behavioral intervention, based on the E-I-E-I-O approach to memory intervention discussed earlier in this chapter, involves using the implicit-internal memory intervention called **spaced retrieval**.* Adapted by Camp and colleagues (Camp, 2001; Camp & McKitrick, 1991), spaced retrieval involves teaching persons with Alzheimer's disease to remember new information by gradually increasing the time between retrieval attempts. This easy, almost magical technique has been used to teach names of staff members and other information; it holds considerable potential for broad application.

In designing interventions for persons with Alzheimer's disease, the guiding principle should be optimizing the person's functioning. Regardless of the level of impairment, attempts should be made to help the person cope as well as possible with the symptoms. The key is helping all persons maintain their dignity as human beings. This can be achieved in some very creative ways, such as adapting the principles of Montessori methods of education to bring older adults with Alzheimer's disease together with preschool children so that they can perform tasks together (Camp et al., 1997). One example of this approach is discussed in the Spotlight on Research feature.

SPOTLIGHT ON RESEARCH

TRAINING PERSONS WITH DEMENTIA TO BE GROUP ACTIVITY LEADERS

Who were the investigators, and what was the aim of the study? Dementia is marked by progressive and severe cognitive decline. But despite these losses, can people with dementia be trained to be group leaders? Most people might think the answer is "no," but Cameron Camp and Michael Skrajner (2005) decided to find out by using a training technique based on the Montessori method.

How did the investigators measure the topic of interest? The Montessori method is based on self-paced learning and developmentally appropriate activities. As Camp and Skrajner point out, many techniques used in rehabilitation (e.g., task breakdown, guided repetition, moving from simple to complex and concrete to abstract) and in intervention programs with people who have dementia (e.g., use of external cues and implicit memory) are consistent with the Montessori method.

For this study, a program was developed to train group leaders for Memory Bingo (see Camp, 1999a and 1999b, for details about this game). Group leaders had to learn which cards to pick for the game, where the answers were located on the card, where to "discard" the used (but not the winning) cards, and where to put the winning cards. Success in the program was measured by research staff raters, who made ratings of the type and quality of engagement in the task shown by the group leader.

Who were the participants in the study? Camp and Skrajner tested four people who had been diagnosed as probably having dementia who were also residents of a special care unit of a nursing home.

What was the design of the study? The study used a longitudinal design so that Camp and Skrajner could track participants' performance over several weeks.

Were there ethical concerns with the study? Having persons with dementia as research participants raises important issues with informed consent. Because of their serious cognitive impairments, these individuals may not fully understand the procedures. Thus, family members such as a spouse or adult child caregiver are also asked to give informed consent. Additionally, researchers must pay careful attention to participants' emotions; if participants become agitated or frustrated, the training or testing session must be stopped. Camp and Skrajner took all these precautions.

What were the results? Results showed that at least partial adherence to the established game protocols was achieved at a very high rate. Indeed, staff assistance was not required at all for most of the game sessions for any leader. All of the leaders said that they enjoyed their role, and one recruited another resident to become a leader in the next phase of the project.

What did the investigators conclude? It appears that persons with dementia can be taught to be group activity leaders through a procedure based on the Montessori method. This is important as it provides a way for such individuals to become more engaged in an activity and to be more productive.

Although more work is needed to continue refining the technique, applications of the Montessori method offer a promising intervention approach for people with cognitive impairments.

What converging evidence would strengthen these conclusions? Camp and Skrajner studied only four residents; more evidence that the approach works with different types of people would bolster their conclusions. Although the Montessori method is effective for training persons with dementia, the approach has not yet been demonstrated to be effective with all other diseases that cause serious memory loss.

To enhance your understanding of this research, go to http://psychology.wadsworth.com/kail_cavanaugh4e/ to complete critical thinking questions and explore related websites.

One of the best ways to find out about the latest medical and behavioral research, as well as about the educational and support programs available in your area, is to contact your local chapter of the Alzheimer's Association (visit the Human Development book companion website for contact information). The chapter in your area will be happy to supply a range of educational material and information about local programs.

TEST YOURSELF

1. Compared to younger adults, older adults are less likely to label their feelings of sadness as _____.

2. A form of psychotherapy that focuses on people's beliefs about the self, the world, and the future is called _____.

3. Relaxation techniques are an effective therapy for _____.

4. The only way to definitively diagnose Alzheimer's disease is through a _____.

5. Twisted fibers called _____ occur in the axon of neurons in persons with Alzheimer's disease.

After reading about the symptoms of Alzheimer's disease, what do you think would be the most stressful aspects of caring for a parent who has the disease? (You may want to refer to the section on caring for aging parents in Chapter 13.)

Answers: (1) depression, (2) cognitive therapy, (3) anxiety disorders, (4) brain autopsy, (5) neurofibrillary tangles

Putting It All Together

Someone once observed that, all things considered, growing old is much better than the alternative. Based on what we have seen concerning the personal contexts of aging, it is indeed much better in many respects (though not totally rosy, to be sure) than what our cultural conditioning expects it to be. We began by wondering why people like Sarah live a long time and others do not, and we learned that many factors influence longevity. We saw how genetic and environmental factors interact (the biopsychosocial model strikes again!). We encountered Frank, the active 80-year-old, who exemplifies how maintaining fitness throughout life has an important influence on health in the later years. We also discovered how physical changes that began in midlife continue to affect functioning as a person keeps growing older.

Rocio experiences the kinds of changes in recent memory ability common in older adults. Some older people gain wisdom through their experience in living. Thus, cognitive changes in later life are not all a matter of decline. Finally, we saw that psychopathologies can exact a terrible toll among older adults; they must be properly diagnosed in order to separate treatable from untreatable conditions. People with Alzheimer's disease, like Mary, must be examined carefully to identify the most likely cause of the problems.

Many of the stereotypes society holds about older adults are simply untrue. For one thing, only a minority of people over age 65 ever get Alzheimer's disease, whereas the clear majority continue to demonstrate improvement in some cognitive functions such as wisdom. Old age does not imply the across-the-board decline that is often portrayed. Indeed, some segments of society are beginning to understand the beauty and importance of older adults.

Our initial foray into later life reveals the complexity of older adults. Just as it is impossible to characterize all children, adolescents, or young adults as being alike, older adults are also a very diverse group of people. This diversity will continue to be in evidence in the next chapter.

Summary

14.1 What Are Older Adults Like?

The Demographics of Aging

■ The number of older adults is growing rapidly, especially the number of people over age 85. In the future, older adults will be more ethnically diverse and better educated than they are now.

Longevity

■ Average life expectancy has increased dramatically in this century, due mainly to improvements in health care. Useful life expectancy refers to the number of years that a person is free from debilitating disease. Maximum life expectancy is the longest time any human can live.

■ Genetic factors that can influence longevity include familial longevity and a family history of certain diseases. Environmental factors include acquired diseases, toxins, pollutants, and lifestyle.

■ Due to technological advances, there is controversy regarding the quantity of life as against the quality. Women have a longer average life expectancy at birth than men. Ethnic group differences are complex; depending on how old people are, the patterns of differences change.

The Third-Fourth Age Distinction

■ The Third Age refers to changes in research that led to cultural, medical, and economic advances for older adults (e.g., longer average longevity, increased quality of life). In contrast, the Fourth Age reflects the fact that the oldest-old are at the limits of their functional capacity, the rates of diseases such as cancer and dementia increase dramatically, and other aspects of psychological functioning (e.g., memory) also undergo significant and fairly rapid decline.

14.2 Physical Changes and Health

Biological Theories of Aging

■ There are four main biological theories of aging. Wear-and-tear theory postulates that aging is caused by body systems simply wearing out. Cellular theories focus on reactions within cells, involving telomeres, free radicals, and cross-linking. Metabolic theories focus on changes in cell metabolism. Programmed cell death theories propose that aging is genetically programmed. No single theory is sufficient to explain aging.

Physiological Changes

■ Three important structural changes in the neurons are neurofibrillary tangles, dendritic changes, and neuritic plaques. These have important consequences for functioning because they reduce the effectiveness with which neurons transmit information.

■ The risk of cardiovascular disease increases with age. Normal changes in the cardiovascular system include buildup of fat deposits in the heart and arteries, a decrease in the amount of blood the heart can pump, a decline in heart muscle tissue, and stiffening of the arteries. Most of these changes are affected by lifestyle. Stroke and vascular dementia cause significant cognitive impairment, depending on the location of the brain damage.

■ Strictly age-related changes in the respiratory system are hard to identify due to the lifetime effects of pollution. However, older adults suffer shortness of breath, and the risk of chronic obstructive pulmonary disorder increases.

■ Parkinson's disease is caused by insufficient levels of dopamine, and it can be effectively managed with levodopa. In a minority of cases, dementia develops.

■ Age-related declines in vision and hearing are well documented. The main changes in vision concern the structure of the eye and the retina. Changes in hearing mainly involve presbycusis. However, similar changes in taste, smell, touch, pain, and temperature are not as clear.

Health Issues

■ Older adults have more sleep disturbances than younger adults. Nutritionally, most older adults do not need vitamin or mineral supplements. Cancer risk increases sharply with age. Being an immigrant is related to having poorer health status due to communication problems and barriers to care.

14.3 Cognitive Processes

Information Processing

- Older adults are much slower than younger adults at visual search unless there is an advance signal.

- Age differences in attention tasks are complex and depend on the level of difficulty: On easy tasks, there are few differences, but on more difficult tasks, younger adults do better.

- Older adults' psychomotor speed is slower than younger adults'. However, the amount of slowing is lessened if older adults have practice or expertise in the task.

- Sensory and information-processing changes create problems for older drivers. Working memory is another powerful explanatory concept for changes in information processing with age.

Memory

- Older adults typically do worse on tests of episodic recall; age differences are less on recognition tasks. Semantic memory is largely unaffected by aging, as is implicit memory. People tend to remember best those events that occurred to them between ages 10 and 30.

- What people believe to be true about their memory is related to their performance. Beliefs about whether cognitive abilities are supposed to change may be most important.

- Differentiating memory changes associated with aging from memory changes due to disease should be accomplished through comprehensive evaluations.

- Memory training can be achieved in many ways. A useful framework is to combine explicit-implicit memory distinctions with external-internal types of memory aids.

Creativity and Wisdom

- Research indicates that creative output peaks in late young adulthood or early middle age and declines

thereafter, but that the point of peak activity varies across disciplines and occupations.

- Wisdom has more to do with being an expert in living than with age per se. Three factors that help people become wise are general personal conditions, specific expertise conditions, and facilitative life contexts.

14.4 Mental Health and Intervention

Depression

- The key symptom of depression is persistent sadness. Other psychological and physical symptoms also occur, but the importance of these depends on the age of the person reporting them.

- Major causes of depression include imbalances in neurotransmitters and psychosocial forces such as loss and internal belief systems.

- Depression can be treated with medications, such as heterocyclic antidepressants, MAO inhibitors, and selective serotonin reuptake inhibitors, and through psychotherapy, such as behavioral or cognitive therapy.

Anxiety Disorders

- A variety of anxiety disorders afflict many older adults. All of them can be effectively treated with either medications or psychotherapy.

Dementia: Alzheimer's Disease

- Dementia is a family of diseases that cause severe cognitive impairment. Alzheimer's disease is the most common form of irreversible dementia.

- Symptoms of Alzheimer's disease include memory impairment, personality changes, and behavioral changes. These symptoms usually worsen gradually, with rates varying considerably among individuals.

- Definitive diagnosis of Alzheimer's disease can only be made following a brain autopsy. Diagnosis of probable Alzheimer's disease in a living person involves a thorough process through which other potential causes are eliminated.

- Most researchers are focusing on a probable genetic cause of Alzheimer's disease.

- Although Alzheimer's disease is incurable, various therapeutic interventions can improve the quality of the patient's life.

Key Terms

demographers (536)

population pyramid (536)

longevity (539)

average life expectancy (540)

useful life expectancy (540)

maximum life expectancy (540)

wear-and-tear theory (544)

cellular theories (544)

telomeres (545)

free radicals (545)

cross-linking (545)

metabolic theories (545)

programmed cell death theories (545)

neurofibrillary tangles (546)

neuritic plaques (547)

neurotransmitters (547)

strokes (547)

cerebral vascular accidents (547)

hemorrhage (548)

transient ischemic attacks (TIAs) (548)

vascular dementia (548)

chronic obstructive pulmonary
 disease (COPD) (549)
Parkinson's disease (549)
presbyopia (550)
presbycusis (551)
circadian rhythm (553)
selective attention (555)
vigilance (555)
attentional control (555)
psychomotor speed (556)
working memory (558)

explicit memory (558)
implicit memory (558)
episodic memory (558)
semantic memory (558)
external aids (561)
internal aids (561)
dysphoria (565)
internal belief systems (566)
heterocyclic antidepressants
 (HCAs) (566)
monoamine oxidase (MAO)

inhibitors (566)
selective serotonin reuptake
 inhibitors (SSRIs) (566)
behavior therapy (566)
cognitive therapy (567)
anxiety disorders (567)
dementia (567)
Alzheimer's disease (568)
incontinence (568)
amyloid (569)
spaced retrieval (571)

Learn More About It

Readings

ALBOM, M. (1997). *Tuesdays with Morrie.* New York: Doubleday. The true story of a journalist who reconnected with his former teacher who passed on wisdom.

BEERS, M. H., & JONES, T. V. (2004). *The Merck manual of health and aging.* Rahway, NJ: Merck. Everything you want to know about health and aging in a user-friendly volume.

KOTRE, J. (1996). *White gloves: How we create ourselves through memory.* New York: Norton. This is the autobiographical story of a man who explores the meaning of memory after he finds his grandfather's white gloves. Interesting weaving of basic research on memory with everyday experience.

MARTZ, S. H. (Ed.). (1987). *When I am an old woman, I shall wear purple.* (1992) *If I had my life to live over, I would pick more daisies.* Watsonville, CA: Papier-Mache Press. Both of these books are anthologies of poems and short stories about the personal meanings of aging to women.

WHITBOURNE, S. K. (2000). *Psychopathology in later adulthood.* New York: Wiley. A good and very readable overview of the many types of psychopathology experienced by older adults.

Websites

Visit the Human Development book companion website for all URLs.

■ **The Human Development Book Companion Website**

 See the companion website **http://psychology.wadsworth.com/kail_cavanaugh4e/** for practice quiz questions, Internet links, updates, critical thinking exercises, discussion forums, and more.

■ **Division 20, Adult Development and Aging (American Psychological Association)**

 One of the very best sites for starting a search about any aspect of aging is kept by the Adult Development and Aging Division (Division 20) of the American Psychological Association.

■ **Administration on Aging**

 The Administration on Aging keeps a variety of information about older adults. In addition, several reports are available on such things as demographic projections and health.

■ **National Institute on Aging**

 The National Institute on Aging leads the U.S. government's research effort on aging. NIA's website provides access to numerous databases and reports on research related to most aspects of aging.

■ **Alzheimer's Association**

 The Alzheimer's Association maintains an excellent database on the latest research advances about the causes and treatment of Alzheimer's disease as well as the best information for caregivers.

Life-Span CD-ROM

For more information about the concepts covered in this chapter, go to
Module 6: Late Adulthood
 • *Physical Development*
 • *Cognitive Development*
Module 7: Death, Dying, and Bereavement
 • *Theories of Aging*
 • *Stages of Dying*
 • *Bereavement*

http://www.thomsonedu.com
Go to this site for the link to ThomsonNOW, your one-stop study shop. Take a pre-test for this chapter, and ThomsonNOW will generate a personalized study plan based on your test results. The study plan will identify the topics you need to review and direct you to online resources to help you master those topics. You can then take a post-test to help you determine the concepts you have mastered and what you still need to work on.

15.1 Theories of Psychosocial Aging
Continuity Theory
Competence and Environmental Press

■ REAL PEOPLE: APPLYING HUMAN DEVELOPMENT: Still Flying at 91

15.2 Personality, Social Cognition, and Spirituality
Integrity Versus Despair
Well-Being and Social Cognition

■ SPOTLIGHT ON RESEARCH: Understanding the Influences on Subjective Well-Being

Religiosity and Spiritual Support

15.3 I Used to Work at . . . : Living in Retirement
What Does Being Retired Mean?
Why Do People Retire?
Adjustment to Retirement
Keeping Busy in Retirement

15.4 Friends and Family in Late Life
Friends and Siblings
Marriage and Gay and Lesbian Partnerships
Caring for a Partner
Widowhood
Great-Grandparenthood

15.5 Social Issues and Aging
Frail Older Adults
Living in Nursing Homes
Elder Abuse and Neglect
Politics, Social Security, and Medicare

■ CURRENT CONTROVERSIES: Saving Social Security

Putting It All Together
Summary
Key Terms
Learn More About It

CHAPTER 15

Social Aspects of Later Life

Psychosocial, Retirement, Relationship, and Societal Issues

What's it really like to be an older adult? As we saw in Chapter 14, aging brings with it both physical limits (such as declines in vision and hearing) and psychological gains (such as increased expertise). Old age also brings social challenges. Older adults are sometimes stereotyped as marginal and powerless in society, much like children. Psychosocial issues confront older adults as well. How do people think about their lives and bring meaning and closure to them as they approach death? What constitutes well-being for older people? How do they use their time once they are no longer working full time? Do they like being retired? What roles do relationships with friends and family play in their lives? How do older people cope if their partner is ill and requires care? What if their partner should die? Where do older people live who need assistance?

These are a few of the issues we will examine in this chapter. As in Chapter 14, our main focus will be on the majority of older adults who are healthy and live in the community. The distinction made in Chapter 1 between young-old (60- to 80-year-olds) and old-old (80-year-olds and up) adults is important. We know the most about young-old people, even though the old-old reflect the majority of frail elderly and those who live in nursing homes.

Just as at other times in life, getting along in the environment is a complicated issue. We begin by considering a few ideas about how to optimize our fit with the environment. Next, we examine how we bring the story of our lives to a culmination. After that, we consider how interpersonal relationships and retirement provide contexts for life satisfaction. We conclude with an examination of the social contexts of aging.

15.1

THEORIES OF PSYCHOSOCIAL AGING

Since Sandy retired from her job as secretary at the local African Methodist Episcopal Church, she has hardly slowed down. She sings in the gospel choir, is involved in the Black Women's Community Action Committee, and volunteers one day per week at a local Head Start school. Sandy's friends say that she has to stay involved, as that's the only way she's ever known. They claim that you'd never know Sandy is 71 years old.

Understanding how people grow old is not as simple as asking someone how old he or she is, as Sandy shows. As we saw in Chapter 14, aging is an individual process involving many variations in physical changes, cognitive functioning, and mental health. As Dennis the Menace notes, older adults are often marginalized in society. Psychosocial approaches to aging recognize these issues.

Sandy's life reflects several key points. Her level of activity has remained constant across her adult life. This consistency fits well in continuity theory, the first framework considered in this section. Her ability to maintain this level of commitment indicates that the match between her abilities and her environment is just about right, as discussed in competence–environmental press theory a bit later in this section.

CONTINUITY THEORY

People tend to keep doing whatever works for them (Atchley, 1989). *According to **continuity theory**, people tend to cope with daily life in later adulthood by applying familiar strategies based on past experience to maintain and preserve both internal and external structures.* By building on and linking to one's past life, change becomes part of continuity. Thus Sandy's new activities represent both change (because they are new) and continuity (because she has always been engaged in her community). In this sense, continuity represents an evolution, not a complete break with the past (Atchley, 1989).

The degree of continuity in life falls into one of three general categories: too little, too much, and optimal (Atchley, 1989). Too little continuity results in feeling that life is too unpredictable. Too much continuity can create utter boredom or a rut of predictability; there is simply not enough change to make life interesting. Optimal continuity provides just enough change to be challenging and provide interest, but not so much as to overly tax one's resources.

Continuity can be either internal or external (Atchley, 1989). Internal continuity refers to a remembered inner past, such as temperament, experiences, emotions, and skills; in brief, it is one's personal identity. Internal continuity enables you to see that how you are now is connected with your past, even if your current behavior looks different. Internal continuity provides feelings of competence, mastery, ego integrity (discussed later in the chapter), and self-esteem. External continuity concerns remembered physical and social environments, role relationships, and activi-

"WE HAVE A LOT IN COMMON, DON'T WE? I'M TOO YOUNG TO DO MOST EVERYTHING AND YOU'RE TOO OLD TO DO MOST EVERYTHING."

ties. A person feels external continuity from being in familiar environments or with familiar people. For example, continuity theory provides a framework for understanding how friendships in late life provide a way for older adults to maintain connections with people, sometimes over many years (Finchum & Weber, 2000). Similarly, phasing from full-time employment to retirement offers some people (e.g., university faculty) a way to maintain connections with their professional lives and facilitate the adjustment to retirement (Kim & Feldman, 2000). And some people continue a relationship with deceased loved ones (Filanosky, 2004).

Maintaining both internal and external continuity is very important for adaptation in later life (Atchley, 1989). For example, internal discontinuity, if severe enough, can seriously affect mental health. Indeed, one of the most pernicious aspects of Alzheimer's disease is that it destroys internal continuity as it strips away one's identity. Similarly, external discontinuity can have serious consequences for adaptation. For example, if your physical environment becomes much more difficult to negotiate, the resulting problems can eat away at your identity as well.

Clearly, monitoring whether a person is maintaining internal and external continuity matters. Exactly how changes in either affect adaptation is the focus of the competence–environmental press framework, to which we now turn.

THINK ABOUT IT

How do the five-factor theory of personality and the life story approach to personality fit with continuity theory?

COMPETENCE AND ENVIRONMENTAL PRESS

Understanding psychosocial aging requires attention to individuals' needs rather than treating all older adults alike. One way of doing this is to focus on the relation between the person and the environment (Wahl, 2001). As discussed in Chapter 1 (page 19), the competence–environmental press approach is a good example of a theory that incorporates elements of the biopsychosocial model into the person-environment relation (Lawton & Nahemow, 1973; Nahemow, 2000; Wahl, 2001).

Competence is defined as the upper limit of a person's ability to function in five domains: physical health, sensory-perceptual skills, motor skills, cognitive skills, and ego strength. We discussed most of these domains in Chapter 14; ego strength, which is related to Erikson's concept of integrity, is discussed later in this chapter. These domains are viewed as underlying all other abilities and reflect the biological and psychological forces. ***Environmental press** refers to the physical, interpersonal, or social demands that environments put on people.* Physical demands might include having to walk up three flights of stairs to your apartment. Interpersonal demands include having to adjust your behavior patterns to different types of people. Social demands include dealing with laws or customs that place certain expectations on people. These aspects of the theory reflect biological, psychological, and social forces. Both competence and environmental press change as people move through the life span; what you are capable of doing as a 5-year-old differs from what you are capable of doing as a 25-, 45-, 65-, or 85-year-old. Similarly, the demands put on you by the environment change as you age. Thus, the competence–environmental press framework reflects life-cycle factors as well.

The competence and environmental press model, depicted in Figure 15.1, shows how the two are related. Low to high competence is represented on the vertical axis, and weak to strong environmental press is represented on the horizontal axis. Points in the figure represent various combinations of the two. Most important, the shaded areas show that adaptive behavior and positive affect can result from many different combinations of competence and environmental press levels. *Adaptation level is the area where press level is average for a particular level of competence; this is where behavior and affect are normal. Slight increases in press tend to improve performance; this area on the figure is labeled the **zone of maximum performance potential**. Slight decreases in press create the **zone of maximum comfort**, in which people are able to live happily without worrying about environmental demands.* Combinations of competence and environmental press that fall within either of these two zones result in adaptive behavior and positive affect, which translate into a high quality of life.

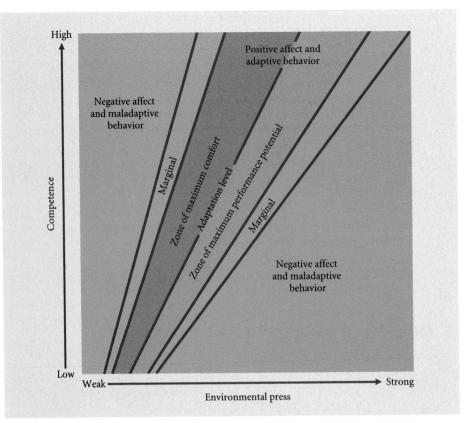

From "Ecology of the Aging Process," by M. P. Lawton and L. Nahemow. In C. Eisdorfer and M. P. Lawton (Eds.), *The Psychology of Adult Development and Aging*, pp. 619–674. Copyright © 1973 American Psychological Association. Reprinted with permission of the authors.

As one moves away from these areas, behavior becomes increasingly maladaptive and affect becomes negative. Notice that these outcomes, too, can result from several different combinations, and for different reasons. For example, too many environmental demands on a person with low competence and too few demands on a person with high competence both result in maladaptive behaviors and negative affect.

What does this mean with regard to late life? Is aging merely an equation relating certain variables? The important thing to realize about the competence–environmental press model is that each person has the potential of being happily adapted to some living situations, but not to all. Whether people are functioning well depends on whether what they are able to do fits what the environment forces them to do. When their abilities match the demands, people adapt; when there is a mismatch, they don't. In this view, aging is more than an equation, as the best fit must be determined on an individual basis.

How do people deal with changes in their particular combinations of environmental press (such as adjusting to a new living situation) and competence (perhaps due to illness)? People respond in two basic ways (Lawton, 1989; Nahemow, 2000). *When people choose new behaviors to meet new desires or needs, they exhibit **proactivity** and exert control over their lives. In contrast, when people allow the situation to dictate the options they have, they demonstrate **docility** and have little control.* Lawton (1989) argues that proactivity is more likely to occur in people with relatively high competence, and docility in people with relatively low competence.

The model has considerable research support. For example, the model accounts for why people choose the activities they do (Lawton, 1982), move to particular kinds of housing (Lawton, 1982), and need to exert some degree of control over their lives (Langer & Rodin, 1976). It helps us understand how well people adapt to various care situations, such as adult day care (Moore, 2005). In short, there is considerable merit

to the view that aging is a complex interaction between a person's competence level and environmental press, mediated by choice. This model can be applied in many different settings.

Understanding how people age usually entails taking a broader perspective than just one theory. The Real People feature about Edna Lockwood, a 91-year-old pilot, shows that both continuity theory and competence–environmental press theory are important.

THINK ABOUT IT

How does the competence–environmental press approach help explain which coping strategies might work best in a particular situation?

REAL PEOPLE: Applying Human Development

STILL FLYING AT 91

Edna Lockwood remembers how badly she longed to fly. At the time, she was a farmer's wife in her mid-30s with five children at home in Goshen, Indiana. Her husband arranged for the flight, and when the pilot let her take the controls briefly, she was hooked. Edna and her husband both became certified pilots—in 1947. At age 91, Edna still loves to fly. In her current plane, a 1976 Piper Warrior, she continues to log about 100 hours per year, mostly flying her friends to her favorite restaurants for lunch. Edna has seen many changes in flying airplanes,

from the days when pilots had to fly using only landmarks on the ground to the current use of global positioning satellite (GPS) data. "I love to fly, just get out [of] the house and fly," she says.

Edna is not the only older adult who loves to fly. In fact, 95-year-old John Miller of Poughkeepsie, New York, formed the United Flying Octogenarians for pilots over age 80. Not surprisingly, Edna is a member.

Edna's long record as a pilot demonstrates her need for internal and external continuity, as well as good competence

in response to environmental demands. She has managed to keep her flying skills sharp (internal continuity and competence) in response to rigorous demands required to keep her pilot's license (environmental press). And she uses her flying to add excitement to her friends' lives and keep the ties strong (external continuity). Edna is a great role model for remaining active in late life. And if you're in northern Indiana, you just might be able to get a ride.

TEST YOURSELF

1. A central premise of _____ theory is that people make adaptive choices to maintain and preserve existing internal and external structures.

2. A person's ability to function in several key domains is termed _____, whereas demands put on a person from external sources are termed _____.

How does continuity theory incorporate aspects of the biopsychosocial model?

Answers: (1) continuity, (2) competence, environmental press

15.2

PERSONALITY, SOCIAL COGNITION, AND SPIRITUALITY

Olive is a spry 88-year-old who spends more time thinking and reflecting about her past than she used to. She also tends to be much less critical now of decisions made years ago than she was at the time. Olive remembers her visions of the woman she wanted to become and concludes that she's come

LEARNING OBJECTIVES

What is integrity in late life? How do people achieve it?

How is well-being defined in adulthood? How do people view themselves differently as they age?

What role does religion play in late life?

pretty close. Olive wonders if this process of reflection is something that most older adults go through.

Tнink for a minute about the older adults you know well. Perhaps they are your grandparents, coworkers, or neighborhood acquaintances. What are they really like? How do they see themselves today? How do they visualize their lives a few years from now? How do they see themselves in the past?

These questions have intrigued authors for many years. In the late 19th century, William James (1890), one of the early pioneers in psychology, wrote that a person's personality traits are set by young adulthood. Some researchers agree; as we saw in Chapter 13, some aspects of personality remain relatively stable throughout adulthood. But people also change in important ways, as Carl Jung (1960/1933) argued, by integrating opposite tendencies, such as masculine and feminine traits. As we have seen, Erik Erikson (1982) was convinced that personality development takes a lifetime, unfolding over a series of stages.

In this section, we explore how people like Olive assemble the final pieces in the personality puzzle and see how important aspects of personality continue to evolve in later life. We begin with the issue of integrity, the process by which people try to make sense of their lives. Next, we see how well-being is achieved and how personal aspirations play themselves out. Finally, we examine how religiosity is an important aspect of many older adults' lives.

INTEGRITY VERSUS DESPAIR

As people enter late life, they begin the struggle of **integrity versus despair,** *which involves the process by which people try to make sense of their lives.* According to Erikson (1982), this struggle comes about as older adults like Olive try to understand their lives in terms of the future of their family and community. Thoughts of a person's own death are balanced by the realization that they will live on through children, grandchildren, great-grandchildren, and the community as a whole. This realization produces what Erikson calls a "life-affirming involvement" in the present.

The struggle of integrity versus despair requires people to engage in a **life review,** *the process by which people reflect on the events and experiences they have had over their lifetimes.* To achieve integrity, a person must come to terms with the choices and events that have made his or her life unique. There must also be an acceptance of the fact that one's life is drawing to a close. Looking back on one's life may resolve some of the second-guessing of decisions that may have occurred earlier in adulthood (Erikson, Erikson, & Kivnick, 1986). People who were unsure whether they made the right choices concerning their children, for example, now feel satisfied that things eventually worked out well. In contrast, others feel bitter about their choices, blame themselves or others for their misfortunes, see their lives as meaningless, and greatly fear death. These people end up in despair rather than integrity.

Research shows a connection between engaging in a life review and achieving integrity. In one study, life review activities done in a group improved the quality of life of older adults, an effect that lasts at least 3 months following the sessions (Hanaoka & Okamura, 2004). A study in Australia showed a connection between "accepting the past" and symptoms of depression (Rylands & Rickwood, 2001). Older women who accepted the past were less likely to show symptoms of depression than older women who did not.

Who reaches integrity? Erikson (1982) emphasizes that there is no one path. They come from many backgrounds and cultures. Such people have made many different choices and follow many different lifestyles; everyone has this opportunity. Those who reach integrity become self-affirming and self-accepting; they judge their lives to have been worthwhile and good. They are glad to have lived the lives they did.

WELL-BEING AND SOCIAL COGNITION

What do you think about your life? Are you reasonably content, or do you think you could be doing better? Answers to these questions provide insight into your subjective well-being. *Subjective well-being is a positive evaluation of one's life that is associated with positive feelings.* In life-span developmental psychology, subjective well-being is usually assessed with measures of life satisfaction, happiness, and self-esteem (Pinquart & Sörensen, 2001).

Whether older adults have high subjective well-being depends on several factors, but hardiness, chronic illness, marital status, social network, and stress are especially important (Krause, 2001; Marshall, 2001; Martin, Grünendahl, & Martin, 2001; Pinquart & Sörensen, 2001; Reinhoudt, 2005). The role of these factors is explored in more detail in the Spotlight on Research feature. Although gender differences are found that increase with age, these are most likely due to the fact that older women are particularly disadvantaged compared with older men with regard to chronic illness, everyday competence, socioeconomic status, and widowhood (Pinquart & Sörensen, 2001). Such gender differences are also smaller in more recent cohorts, indicating that societal changes have influenced how people feel about themselves.

 SPOTLIGHT ON RESEARCH

UNDERSTANDING THE INFLUENCES ON SUBJECTIVE WELL-BEING

Who were the investigators and what was the aim of the study? Research on subjective well-being has suggested that having a good social support system of friends can help improve well-being even when one experiences stress. Martin and colleagues (2001) decided to test this idea by examining the role of social support and stress as influences on people's subjective well-being. Because of conflicting data on the independent roles of social support and stress on well-being, it was unclear what would happen when both of these factors were examined simultaneously.

How did the investigators measure the topic of interest? The main data collection tool was an extensive semistructured interview used in previous longitudinal studies of aging. The interview was conducted and scored by five different interviewers who were highly trained. In the social support section of the interview, participants were asked to rate several components about each of eight social roles: partnership, parent, grandparent, child, relative, friend, acquaintance, and neighbor. The stress section asked about subjectively experienced level of stress in three domains: health, finances, and housing conditions. Subjective well-being was assessed with the revised and standardized Philadelphia Geriatric Center Morale Scale,

which has three parts: agitation, attitude toward one's own aging, and lonely dissatisfaction.

Who were the participants in the study? The data analyses were based on a random, representative sample of 938 middle-aged and older German-speaking residents of German nationality in Germany.

What was the design of the study? The data analyses conducted here were based on a cross-sectional design. However, the overall study from which these analyses come is a longitudinal study.

Were there ethical concerns with the study? No, because the researchers obtained permission from the participants.

What were the results? The researchers compared four models for each of the two age groups (middle-aged and older adults). Figure 15.2 and Figure 15.3 show the best models for each age group. As you can see, in both models social resources has a direct negative effect on stress, stress has a direct negative effect on well-being, and social resources has a direct positive effect on well-being. Social resources does not mediate the effects of stress because stress has no direct effect on social resources, meaning that social resources does not directly counteract the effects of stress on well-being. However, stress does mediate the effects of social re-

sources on well-being because the nature of the relationship between social resources and well-being depends on the level of stress. Finally, there was no age difference in the models; the same basic model works for middle-aged and older adults.

What did the investigators conclude? The results raise three important points about the role of social resources for well-being. First, there are no age differences in perceived quality of social resources or in satisfaction with social activities. However, significant age differences in stress were found; older adults reported higher stress regarding health and lower stress regarding finances and housing conditions. Second, both social resources and stress affect well-being, with stress having a strong negative relation to both. Third, the lack of age differences in the final models indicates stability from middle age to old age in the relations among social resources, stress, and well-being.

What converging evidence would strengthen these conclusions? Because these analyses were conducted on cross-sectional data, they would be strengthened by longitudinal data. The investigators are gathering these data and will be able to reexamine the findings in the future. In addition, because the study was conducted only in Germany,

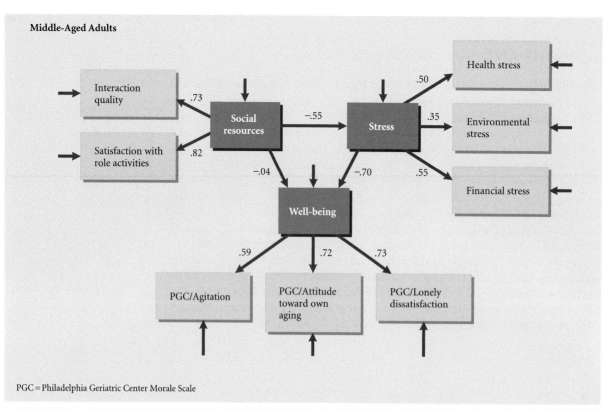

Middle-Aged Adults

PGC = Philadelphia Geriatric Center Morale Scale

Figure 15.2
In middle age, having good social resources, such as a good friendship network, does not buffer the effects of stress on well-being. The numbers on the arrows connecting two of the measures in the figure above indicate the direction and strength of the influence of one variable on another, with absolute values ranging from 0.0 (no influence) to 1.0 (perfect influence).

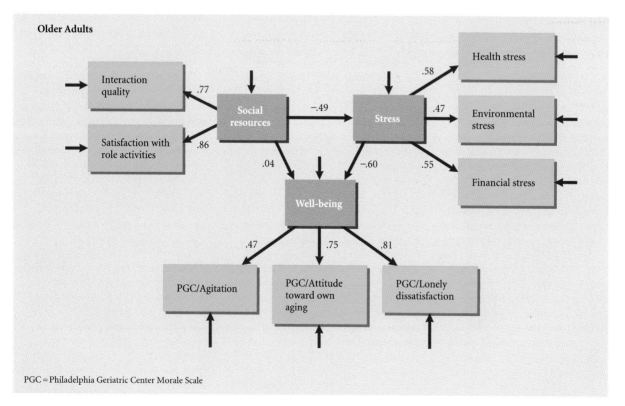

Older Adults

PGC = Philadelphia Geriatric Center Morale Scale

Figure 15.3
For older adults, having good social resources, such as a good friendship network, does not buffer the effects of stress on well-being. The numbers on the arrows connecting two of the measures in the figure above indicate the direction and strength of the influence of one variable on another, with absolute values ranging from 0.0 (no influence) to 1.0 (perfect influence).

samples from other countries would be necessary in order to generalize the findings to other groups.

To enhance your understanding of this research, go to http://psychology

.wadsworth.com/kail_cavanaugh4e/ to complete critical thinking questions and explore related websites.

How people experience their lives also reflects the ways in which they analyze the cause of events in terms of who or what is in control in a specific situation, a concept discussed earlier in Chapter 10 (pages 408–410). Recall that personal control is the degree to which we believe that our performance in a situation depends on something that we personally do.

Brandstädter and Greve (1994) propose that control beliefs in later life involve three interdependent processes. First, people engage in activities that prevent or alleviate losses in domains that are important for self-esteem and identity. Second, people readjust their goals as a way to lessen negative self-evaluations in key domains. Third, people guard against the effects of self-discrepant evidence through denial or by looking for another explanation. This approach, though, has been criticized on the grounds that the losses people experience may not actually threaten the self, and that changes in goals could simply represent normative developmental processes (Carstensen & Freund, 1994).

These interdependent processes mean that the development of personal control into late life is complex, largely because it varies across domains. For example, Soederberg Miller and Lachman (1999) and West and Yassuda (2004) found lower levels of personal control with increasing age in cognitive domains, whereas Brandstädter (1999) found increased personal control with age in the perceived marital support domain. Chipperfield, Campbell, and Perry (2004) found evidence for both increases and decreases in personal control in the health domain. The shape of the developmental function in personal control also varies across domains, as shown in Figure 15.4 (Grob, Little, & Wanner, 1999). As you can see, Grob and colleagues found an increase in perceived control for social (harmony within a close relationship) and personal (personal appearance) domains up to early middle age followed by a general decline. In contrast, perceived control over societal issues (such as pollution) was low across adulthood, with a slow, steady decline.

Why are there different trajectories depending on domain? It may be that people view control differently. For example, Brandstädter (1999) proposes that personal control involves the preservation of a positive view of the self. Similarly, Heckhausen and Schulz (1999) view personal control as a motivational system that regulates behavior over the life span. These views agree that personal control has two parts: *assimilative activities,* or *primary control* (bringing the environment into line with one's desires and goals), and *accommodative activities,* or *secondary control* (bringing oneself into line with the environment). Both views have important implications for aging. Assimilative activities (primary control) increase during childhood as we develop our sense of independence and then plateau across adulthood. However, accommodative activities (secondary control) increase with age across adulthood as we deal with limits imposed on us as our functional competence declines.

Whether this explanation holds across cultures remains to be seen. As Gould (1999) points out, cultures that do not emphasize individualism, such as collectivist soci-

■ **Figure 15.4**
Perceptions of control in the social and personal domains show a very different developmental pattern than perceived control in the societal domain.

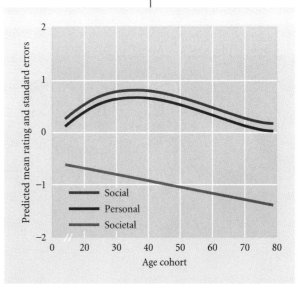

From Grob, A., Little, T. D., & Wanner, B. (1999). Control judgements across the lifespan. *International Journal of Behavioral Decisions, 23,* 844.

eties in Asia, may always place more emphasis on accommodative activities. Clearly, the development of personal control is complex and depends on one's cultural experiences in different domains.

What is clear is that the developmental trajectory matters. An additional aspect of the Chipperfield and colleagues' (2004) study is that whether personal control in matters regarding health increases or decreases affects health outcomes. Older adults whose feelings of control decline also experience declines in physical health. The opposite is true for those whose feelings of control increase. Given that this involves quality of life (if not life itself), personal control beliefs must become a more prominent focus of research.

RELIGIOSITY AND SPIRITUAL SUPPORT

When faced with the daily problems of living, what do most older adults do to help themselves cope? According to research, older adults use their religious faith and spirituality more than anything else, including family or friends (Koenig, 1999; Krause, 2001; McFadden, 1996). Some older adults, more so among African Americans, show a strong attachment to God (Cicirelli, 2004) that they believe helps them deal with the challenges of life.

Evidence shows that older adults who are more involved with and committed to their faith have better physical and mental health than older adults who are not religious (Blazer, 2000; Krause, 2001). Spirituality also helps improve psychological well-being, particularly among frail older adults (Kirby, Coleman, & Daley, 2004; Reinhoudt, 2005). Upchurch and Mueller (2005) found that older African Americans were more likely to be able to perform key activities of daily living if they had higher levels of spirituality.

When asked to describe ways of dealing with problems in life that affect mental health, many people list coping strategies associated with spirituality (Blazer, 2000; Gatz & Smyer, 2001). Of these, the most frequently used were placing trust in God, praying, and getting strength and help from God. These strategies can also be used to augment other ways of coping. Caregivers for people with Alzheimer's disease also report using religion and spiritual practices as primary coping mechanisms (Kinney et al., 2003; Stuckey, 2001).

Researchers are increasingly focusing on **spiritual support,** *which includes seeking pastoral care, participation in organized and nonorganized religious activities, and expressing faith in a God who cares for people as a key factor in understanding how older adults cope.* McFadden (1996) points out that even when under high levels of stress, people who rely on spiritual support report better personal well-being. Krause (1995) reports that feelings of self-worth are lowest in older adults who have very little religious commitment, a finding supported by cross-cultural research with Muslims, Hindus, and Sikhs (Mehta, 1997). However, Pargament (1997) also notes the importance of individual differences in the effectiveness of spiritual support, because some people are helped more than others, some problems are more amenable to religious coping, and certain types of religious coping may be more effective than others.

When people rely on spirituality to cope, how do they do it? Krause and colleagues (2000) asked older adults what they meant when they said that they were "turning it all over to God" and "letting God have it." The older adults in this study reported that turning problems over to God really was a three-step process: (a) differentiating between things that can and cannot be changed; (b) focusing one's own efforts on the parts of the problem that

These Buddhist monks' spirituality can serve as an important coping strategy.

© David Austen/Stock Boston, Inc.

can be changed; and (c) emotionally disconnecting from those aspects of the problem that cannot be changed by focusing on the belief that God will provide the best outcome possible for those. These findings show that reliance on spiritual beliefs acts to help people focus their attention on parts of the problem that may be under their control.

Reliance on religion in times of stress appears to be especially important for many African Americans, who as a group are intensely involved in religious activities (Levin, Taylor, & Chatters, 1994). African Americans tend to identify with their race and religion much more strongly than do European Americans, and they are more committed to their religion (Fife, 2005). Churches offer considerable social support for the African American community, as well as serving an important function for the advocacy of social justice (Roberts, 1980). For example, the civil rights movement in the 1950s and 1960s was led by Dr. Martin Luther King Jr., a Baptist minister, and contemporary congregations often champion equal rights. The role of the church in the majority of African Americans' lives is central; indeed, one of the key predictors of life satisfaction among African Americans is regular church attendance and commitment to their religion (Fife, 2005).

Within the African American community, religion is especially important to many women. The greater importance of the church in the lives of these older African American women is supported by results from four national surveys of African American adults (Levin et al., 1994). The women participants reported that they are more active in church groups and attend services more frequently than African American men or either European American men or women. However, the gender differences diminish in African American people over age 70; among the participants, religion becomes equally important for older African American men. Religion and spiritual support also serve as more important resources for many African American caregivers than for European American caregivers (Picot et al., 1997). In addition, spirituality influences many African American women's daily lives in some less obvious ways (Banks-Wallace & Parks, 2004). For example, many women came to the conclusion that domestic violence was not part of God's plan for their lives. Overall, spiritually based intervention strategies may provide a rich foundation for health promotion programs targeting African American women.

Many older persons of Mexican heritage adopt a different approach. Research indicates that they use *la fé de la gente* ("the faith of the people") as a coping strategy (Villa & Jaime, 1993). The notion of *fé* incorporates varying degrees of faith, spirituality, hope, cultural values, and beliefs. *Fé* does not necessarily imply that people identify with a specific religious community. Rather, they identify with a cultural value or ideology. Spiritual healers play an important part in Mexican culture as well and share many common aspects with cultures such as the !Kung of South Africa and Native American tribes in North America (Finkler, 2004).

Among many Native Americans, the spiritual elders are the wisdom-keepers, the repositories of the sacred ways and philosophies that extend indefinitely back in time (Wall & Arden, 1990). The wisdom-keepers also share dreams and visions, perform healing ceremonies, and may make apocalyptic prophecies. The place of the wisdom-keepers in the tribe is much more central than that of religious leaders in Western society.

Service providers would be well advised to keep in mind the self-reported importance of religion in the lives of many older adults when designing interventions to help them adapt to life stressors. For example, older adults may be more willing to talk with their minister or rabbi about a personal problem than they would be to talk with a psychotherapist. However, when working with people of Mexican heritage, for example, providers should realize that a major source of distress for this group is lack of familial interaction and support. Overall, many churches offer a wide range of programs to assist poor or homebound older adults in the community. Such programs may be more palatable to the people served than programs based in social service agencies. To be successful, service providers should try to view life as their clients see it.

THINK ABOUT IT

What psychological and sociocultural factors make religion and spiritual support important for minority groups?

TEST YOURSELF

1. The Eriksonian struggle that older adults face is termed _____.

2. Personal control has been described as having two components, assimilative activities and _____.

3. The most commonly reported method for coping with life stress among older adults is _____.

Based on research on personal control discussed in this section, what do you think would be good areas to target for interventions designed to improve older adults' well-being?

Answers: (1) integrity versus despair, (2) accommodative activities, (3) religion or spiritual support

---

15.3

I USED TO WORK AT . . . : LIVING IN RETIREMENT

LEARNING OBJECTIVES

What does being retired mean?

Why do people retire?

How satisfied are retired people?

How do retirees keep busy?

Marcus is a 77-year-old retired construction worker who labored hard all of his life. He managed to save a little money, but he and his wife live primarily off of his monthly Social Security checks. Though not rich, they have enough to pay the bills. Marcus is largely happy with retirement, and he stays in touch with his friends. He thinks maybe he's a little strange, though—he has heard that retirees are supposed to be isolated and lonely.

Some retired couples travel to places they have always wanted to visit.

© Bill Bachmann / Photo Network / PictureQuest

YOU PROBABLY TAKE IT FOR GRANTED that some day, after working for many productive years, you will retire. But did you know that until 1934, when a railroad union sponsored a bill promoting mandatory retirement, and 1935, when Social Security was inaugurated, retirement was not even considered a possibility by most Americans like Marcus (Sterns & Gray, 1999)? Only since World War II has there been a substantial number of retired people in the United States (Elder & Pavalko, 1993). Today, the number is increasing rapidly, and the notion that people work a specified time and then retire is built into our most fundamental expectations about work. As we noted in Chapter 12, an increasing number of middle-aged workers either retire prior to age 65 or are planning for retirement.

As more people retire and take advantage of longer lives, a significant social challenge is created (Tsao, 2004). Finding meaningful roles for millions of healthy older adults will raise important questions about stereotypes of older adults, the nature of the workplace, and older adults' desire to contribute to society.

In this section, we explore what retirement is like for older adults. We consider people like Marcus as we examine how retirement is defined, why people retire, how people adjust to being retired, and how retirement affects interpersonal relationships.

WHAT DOES BEING RETIRED MEAN?

It turns out that retirement is more difficult to define than just guessing from someone's age (Henretta, 1997, 2001). One way is to equate retirement with complete withdrawal from the workforce. But this definition is inadequate; many retired people continue to work part time (Mutchler et al., 1997). Another possibility would be to define retirement as a self-described state. However, this definition also lacks universality; one study found that some African Americans define themselves with labels other than "retired" in order to qualify for certain social service programs (Gibson, 1991).

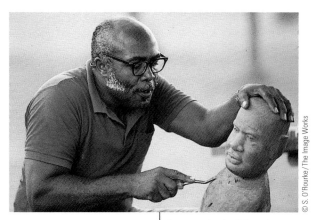

Some retired adults take up hobbies to develop their creative side.

Part of the reason it is difficult to define retirement precisely is that the decision to retire involves the loss of occupational identity (see Chapter 12). What people do for a living is a major part of their identity; we introduce ourselves as postal workers, teachers, builders, or nurses as a way to tell people something about ourselves. Not doing those jobs any more means that we either put that aspect of our lives in the past tense—"I used to work as a manager at the Hilton"—or say nothing at all. Loss of this aspect of ourselves can be difficult to face, so some look for a label other than "retired" to describe themselves.

A useful way to view retirement is as another one of many transitions people experience in life (Schlossberg, 2004). This view makes retirement a complex process by which people withdraw from full-time participation in an occupation (Henretta, 2001; Mutchler et al., 1997; Sterns & Gray, 1999). This withdrawal process can be described as either "crisp" (making a clean break from employment by stopping work entirely) or "blurred" (repeatedly leaving and returning to work, with some unemployment periods) (Mutchler et al., 1997). Bob is a good example of a "<u>crisp</u>" retirement. He retired from TWA at age 65; now in his late 80s, he has done nothing work-related in the interim.

Whereas many people think of retirement as a crisp transition, the evidence shows that less than half of older men who retire fit this pattern (Mutchler et al., 1997). Most men adopt a more gradual or "<u>blurred</u>" process involving part-time work in an effort to maintain economic status. Jack is one of these men. When he retired from DuPont

Some retired adults do volunteer work as a way to stay active.

at age 62, he and a friend began a small consulting company. For about 5 years, Jack worked when he wanted, gradually cutting back over time.

The lack of crisp retirement creates another complicating factor—the idea of a "normal" retirement age such as age 65 may no longer be appropriate because few jobs still have mandatory retirement at age 65 (Sargeant, 2004). Indeed, in the absence of a mandatory retirement age, the concept of "early" retirement has no meaning. Instead, the notion of a typical retirement age changes to a range of ages and one's acceptance of transition, further blurring the meaning of retirement (Schlossberg, 2004). *To reflect these changes, researchers describe a transition phase from career job, the career one has throughout most of adulthood, to* **bridge job,** *the job one holds between one's exit from the career job and final retirement.* Considerable research indicates that an increasing number of workers hold bridge jobs for 10 or fewer years (Quinn, 1999). For some workers, bridge jobs are a continuation of a work history characterized by short-term employment. For others, they reflect a desire to continue working even if it is not financially necessary. In this latter case, generativity may also be a factor in deciding to bridge from full-time employment to retirement (Dendinger, Adams, & Jacobson, 2005). Bridge jobs have been shown to be strongly related to both retirement satisfaction and overall life satisfaction (Kim & Feldman, 2000).

The complexity of the retirement process must be acknowledged in order to understand what retirement means to people in different ethnic groups. For example, whereas middle-class European Americans often use a criterion of full-time employment to define themselves as retired or not, Mexican Americans use any of several different criteria, depending on how the question is asked (Zsembik & Singer, 1990). For example, Mexican Americans are most likely to claim that they are retired when asked directly ("Are you retired?") than when asked indirectly ("What are you doing these days?"). It may be that people want to appear active, so they choose some other descriptor. In contrast, European Americans are just as likely to call themselves retired no matter how they are asked.

WHY DO PEOPLE RETIRE?

Provided that they have good health, more workers retire by choice than for any other reason (Dendinger et al., 2005). Individuals usually retire when they feel financially secure, considering projected income from Social Security, pensions, and personal savings. Of course, some people are forced to retire because they lose their jobs. As corporations downsize in economic downturns or after corporate mergers, some older workers are offered buyout packages involving supplemental payments if they retire. Others are permanently furloughed, laid off, or dismissed.

The decision to retire is complex and is influenced by one's occupational history and goal expectations (Brougham & Walsh, 2005). Whether people perceive that they will achieve their personal goals through work or retirement influences the decision to retire and the connection with health and disability. Health problems that cause functional impairment, such as serious cardiovascular disease or cancer, are the main reason European Americans, African Americans, and Hispanic Americans retire early (Stanford et al., 1991). People in physically demanding jobs also tend to retire earlier (Ucello, 1998). Feeling that retirement is a choice rather than a requirement is associated with an earlier planned retirement age and a better adjustment to retirement (Sterns & Gray, 1999).

Gender Differences

Most of what we know about retirement decisions is based on research on men (Sterns & Gray, 1999). However, women may enter the workforce later, have more discontinuous work histories, spend less time in the workforce, and their financial resources may differ from men's, which may affect women's decisions to retire (Calasanti, 1996;

> **THINK ABOUT IT**
>
> In the absence of mandatory retirement, what does the term "early retirement" really mean?

Sterns & Gray, 1999). Women also tend to spend less time in planning their retirement (Jacobs-Lawson, Hershey, & Neukam, 2004).

Research indicates that men's and women's decisions to retire may be based on different factors. Talaga and Beehr (1995) found that women whose husbands were in poor health or who had more dependents were more likely to retire; the opposite was true for men. However, there were some similarities; having a retired spouse increased the likelihood that spouses would also retire. These factors aside, in general partners have little influence on each other's decision to retire (van Solinge & Henkens, 2005). As more women remain in the workforce for much of their adult lives, focused research will be necessary to understand the extent to which gender differences matter in the decision to retire. At this point, it appears that the male model of retirement is insufficient to account for women's experiences (Sterns & Gray, 1999).

Ethnic Differences

Very little research has been conducted on retirement decisions as a function of ethnicity. A few investigators have examined the characteristics of retired African Americans (e.g., Gibson, 1986, 1987; Jackson & Gibson, 1985). These studies show that African Americans tend to label themselves as retired or not based on subjective disability (the belief that one is disabled whether this is a fact or not), work history, and source of income rather than simply on whether they are currently employed. An important finding is that gender differences appear to be absent among African Americans; men and women base their self-labels on the same variables. Thus, findings based on European American samples must not be generalized to African Americans, and separate theoretical models for African Americans may be needed (Gibson, 1987). The same may be true for other ethnic groups as well.

Older African Americans may not use the same definitions of retirement as other ethnic groups.

ADJUSTMENT TO RETIREMENT

Researchers agree on one point: Retirement is an important life transition. New patterns of involvement must be developed in the context of changing roles and lifestyles, and retirement is no exception (Schlossberg, 2004). Because retirement is now viewed as a process, the "typical" age of retirement has lost its meaning, gender differences are evident in the decision to retire, and the idea that retirement proceeds in an orderly stagelike sequence has been abandoned (Sterns & Gray, 1999). Instead, researchers support the idea that people's adjustment to retirement evolves over time as a result of complex interrelations with physical health, financial status, voluntary retirement status, and feelings of personal control (Gall, Evans, & Howard, 1997).

How do most people fare? As long as people have financial security, health, and a supportive network of relatives and friends, they report feeling very good about being retired (Gall et al., 1997; Matthews & Brown, 1987). For men, being in good health, having enough income, and having retired voluntarily are associated with relatively high satisfaction early in retirement; having an internal sense of personal control is correlated with well-being over the long run (Gall et al., 1997). For men, personal priorities are also important. Men who place more emphasis on family roles (e.g., as husband or grandfather) report being happier retirees. Interestingly, women's morale in retirement does not appear to be related to an emphasis on any specific roles (Matthews & Brown, 1987). For both men and women, high personal competence is associated with higher retirement satisfaction, probably because competent people are able to optimize their level of environmental press (as described on pages 579–581).

But what about couples? Just because one or the other partner is satisfied may or may not mean that the couple as a whole is. That's exactly what Smith and Moen (2004) found. The couples most likely to report being satisfied with retirement, individually and jointly, are retired wives and their husbands where wives reported that their husbands were not influential in their retirement decision. Barnes and Parry (2004) report that both gender roles and finances are the most important factors in predicting satisfaction with retirement in their sample in the United Kingdom, with traditional gender roles creating more difficulties for older retired men. Clearly, we need to view satisfaction in retirement as an outcome dependent upon one's gender and one that is experienced at both the individual and couple levels.

One stereotype of retirement is that health begins to decline as soon as people stop working. Research findings do not support this belief. There is no evidence that retirement has any immediate negative effects on health; on the contrary, health affects the decision to retire (Weymouth, 2005). Moreover, well-being typically increases for men during the first year of retirement (Gall et al., 1997).

A second stereotype is that retirement dramatically reduces the number and quality of personal friendships. Again, there is no research support for this belief. In fact, several studies have shown that men like Marcus, from the vignette, are typical; neither the number nor the quality of friendships declines as a result of retiring (Bossé et al., 1993). When friendships change during retirement, it is usually due to other factors, such as very serious health problems, that interfere with people's ability to maintain friendships.

Finally, some people believe that retired people become much less active overall. This stereotype is also not supported by research. Although the number of hours in paid work decreases on average with age, older adults are still engaged for hundreds of hours per year in productive activities such as unpaid volunteer work and helping others (Herzog et al., 1989). We will specifically consider volunteer activities in the next section.

KEEPING BUSY IN RETIREMENT

Retirement is an important life transition, one that is best understood through a life course perspective (see Chapter 1; Moen et al., 2000b; Schlossberg, 2004). This life change means that retirees must look for ways to maintain social integration and being active in various ways.

The past few decades have witnessed the rapid growth of organizations devoted to providing such opportunities to retirees. National groups such as AARP provide the chance to learn, through magazines and pamphlets, about other retirees' activities and about services such as insurance and discounts. Many smaller groups exist at the local community level, including senior centers and clubs. These organizations promote the notion of lifelong learning and help keep older adults cognitively active. Many also offer travel opportunities specifically designed for active older adults.

Healthy, active retired adults also maintain community ties by volunteering (Moen et al., 2000a). Older adults report that they volunteer for many reasons that benefit their well-being (Greenfield & Marks, 2005): to provide service to others, to maintain social interactions and improve their communities, and to keep active. There are many opportunities for retirees to help others, both at the local and national levels. One federal agency, ACTION, administers four programs that have hundreds of local chapters: Foster Grandparents, Senior Companions, the Retired Senior Volunteer Program (RSVP), and the Service Corps of Retired Executives (SCORE). The AmeriCorp program also has many older adult participants. Why do so many people volunteer?

Several factors are responsible (Moen et al., 2000a, 2000b): developing a new aspect of the self, finding a personal sense of purpose, desire to share one's skills and expertise, a redefinition of the nature and merits of volunteer work, a more highly educated and healthy population of older adults, and greatly expanded opportunities for people to become involved in volunteer work that they enjoy. Given the demographic trends of increased numbers and educational levels of older adults (discussed in Chapter 14), even

THINK ABOUT IT

What might the opportunity for more older adults to volunteer for organizations mean politically? Check your answer with research data later in the chapter.

higher rates of volunteerism are expected during the next few decades. Moen and colleagues (2000a) argue that volunteerism offers a way for society to tap into the vast resources that older adults offer.

TEST YOURSELF

1. One useful way to view retirement is as a _____.

2. The most common reason people retire is _____.

3. Overall, most retirees are _____ with retirement.

4. Many retirees keep contacts in their communities by _____.

Using the information from Chapter 12 on occupational development, create a developmental description of occupations that incorporates retirement.

Answers: (1) complex process by which people gradually withdraw from employment, (2) by choice, (3) satisfied, (4) volunteering

---

15.4

FRIENDS AND FAMILY IN LATE LIFE

LEARNING OBJECTIVES

What role do friends and family play in late life?

What are older adults' marriages like?

What is it like to provide basic care for one's partner?

How do people cope with widowhood? How do men and women differ?

What special issues are involved in being a great-grandparent?

Alma was married to Charles for 46 years. Even though he died 20 years ago, Alma still speaks about him as if he had only recently passed away. Alma still gets sad on special dates, such as their anniversary, or Charles's birthday, or the date on which he died. Alma tells everyone that she and Chuck, as she called him, had a wonderful marriage and that she still misses him terribly even after all these years.

TO OLDER ADULTS LIKE ALMA, the most important thing in life is relationships. In this section, we consider many of the relationships older adults have. Whether it is friendship or family ties, having relationships with others is what keeps us connected. Thus, when one's spouse is in need of care, it is not surprising to find wives and husbands devoting themselves to caregiving. Widows like Alma also feel close to departed spouses. For a growing number of older adults, becoming a great-grandparent is an exciting time.

We have seen throughout this text how our lives are shaped and shared by the company of others. *The term __social convoy__ is used to suggest how a group of people journeys with us throughout our lives, providing support in good and bad times.* People form the convoy, and under ideal conditions the convoy provides a protective, secure cushion that permits the person to explore and learn about the world (Antonucci, 2001). Especially for older adults, the social convoy also provides a source of affirmation of who they are and what they mean to others, and leads to better mental health and well-being.

Several studies have shown that the size of the social convoy and the amount of support it provides do not differ across generations. This lack of differences by age strongly supports the conclusion that friends and family are essential aspects of all adults' lives. Social support is especially important in the African American community (Ajrouch,

Antonucci, & Janevic, 2000; Taylor, Hardison, & Chatters, 1996). Although their networks are smaller, they have more family members who have more contact with each other. In general, there are more similarities than differences in the social networks of European Americans, African Americans, Latino Americans, and Asian Americans (Kim & McKenry, 1998).

FRIENDS AND SIBLINGS

By late life, some members of a person's social network have been friends for several decades. Research consistently finds that older adults have the same need for friends as do people in younger generations, and that their life satisfaction is hardly related at all to the number or quality of relationships with younger family members, but it is strongly correlated with the number and quality of their friendships (Rawlins, 2004). Why? As will become clear, friends serve as confidants and sources of support in ways that children and nieces and nephews, for example, typically do not. Both of Charlie Brown's grandmothers in the cartoon are examples of active older adults who like to be with friends.

Friendships

The quality of late-life friendships is particularly important (Rawlins, 2004). Having at least one very close friend or confidant provides a buffer against the losses of roles and status that accompany old age, such as retirement or the death of a loved one, and can increase people's happiness and self-esteem (Rawlins, 2004; Sherman, de Vries, & Lansford, 2000). Patterns of friendship among older adults tend to mirror those in young adulthood described in Chapter 11 (Rawlins, 2004). That is, older women have more numerous and more intimate friendships than older men do. As noted previously, these differences help explain why women are in a better position to deal with the stresses of life. Widows, especially, take advantage of their friendship networks; they are more involved with their friends than are married women, never-married women, or men (Hatch & Bulcroft, 1992).

In general, older adults have fewer relationships in general and develop fewer new relationships than younger or middle-aged adults (Carstensen, 1995). This decline in numbers does not merely reflect the loss of relationships to death or other means. Rather, the changes reflect a more complicated process (Carstensen, 1993, 1995). *This process, termed* **socioemotional selectivity,** *implies that social contact is motivated by many goals, including information seeking, self-concept, and emotional regulation.* Each of these goals is differentially relevant at different times and results in different social behaviors. For example, information seeking tends to lead to meeting more people, whereas emotional regulation results in being very picky in the choice of social partners, with a strong preference for people who are familiar.

With time, older adults begin to lose members of their friendship network, usually through death. Rook (2000) proposes that older adults compensate for this loss by form-

ing new ties, redefining the need for friends, or developing alternative nonsocial activities. Although not always successful, these strategies reflect the need to address an important loss in people's lives.

Perceptions of friendship vary. What it takes for one person to call someone a "friend" may not be what it takes for another. Surprisingly little research has examined the role of people's definitions of friendship, especially in comparing definitions across cultures. Adams and colleagues' (2000) study comparing older adults' definitions of friendship in Greensboro, North Carolina, and Vancouver, British Columbia, Canada is one of the best. They found that psychological and sociocultural forces result in marked differences in how people define friendship. In Vancouver, people based their definitions mostly on the affective (feeling) and cognitive processes of friendship (what they think about relationships), whereas in Greensboro people relied more on behavioral, relational quality (what they actually do for others), and being like themselves (solidarity and homogeneity) aspects. Life-cycle forces also played a role, in that middle-aged and young-old participants in both cities were less likely than middle-old and old-old participants to use relational quality and solidarity and homogeneity as part of their definitions. So although people around the world all have friendships, how they define them differs.

Sibling Relationships

For many older adults, the preference for long-term friendships may explain older adults' desire to keep in touch with their siblings. As we saw in Chapter 11, maintaining connections with a sibling is important for most adults (Connidis, 2001). Five types of relationships among older adult siblings have been identified (Gold, Woodbury, & George, 1990):

- *Intimate sibling relationships*, characterized by high levels of closeness and involvement, high levels of contact, but low levels of envy and resentment.

- *Congenial sibling relationships*, characterized by high levels of closeness and involvement, average levels of contact, and relatively low levels of envy and resentment.

- *Loyal sibling relationships*, characterized by average levels of closeness, involvement, and contact and relatively low levels of envy and resentment.

- *Apathetic sibling relationships*, characterized by low levels on all dimensions.

- *Hostile sibling relationships*, characterized by relatively high levels of involvement and resentment and relatively low levels on all other dimensions.

Note that older adult siblings play an important role in the lives of older adults.

The relative frequencies of these five types of sibling relationships are shown in Figure 15.5. As you can see, loyal and congenial relationships characterize nearly two thirds of all older sibling pairs. In addition, it appears that older African American siblings have apathetic or hostile relationships with their siblings nearly five times less often than older European Americans do (4.5% for African Americans versus 22% for European Americans; Gold, 1990). Sometimes hostile sibling relationships in late life date back to sibling rivalries in childhood and may require considerable effort to heal (Goldenthal, 2002; Levitt, Levitt, & Levitt, 2001).

When different combinations of siblings are considered separately, ties between sisters are typically the strongest, most frequent, and most intimate (Schmeeckle, Giarusso, & Wang, 1998). In contrast, brothers tend to maintain less frequent contact (Connidis,

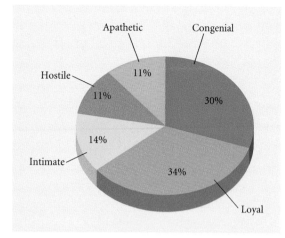

From "Relationship Classification Using Grade of Membership Analysis: A Typology of Sibling Relationships in Later Life," by D. T. Gold, M. A. Woodbury, and L. K. George, 1990. *Journal of Gerontology: Social Sciences, 45,* pp. 43–51. Copyright © 1990 Gerontological Society of America. Reprinted by permission.

■ **Figure 15.5**
Types of sibling relationships. Note that older siblings tend to have loyal or congenial relationships.

2001). Little is known about brother-sister relationships. Even though many older adults end up providing care for or living with one of their siblings, we know virtually nothing about how well this works.

Clearly, there are major gaps in our understanding of sibling relationships. This is truly unfortunate as brothers and sisters play an important and meaningful role throughout life.

MARRIAGE AND GAY AND LESBIAN PARTNERSHIPS

"It's great to be 72 and still married," said Lucia. "Yeah, it's great to have Juan around to share old times with and have him know how I feel even before I tell him." Lucia and Juan are typical of most older married couples. Marital satisfaction improves once the children leave home and remains fairly high in older couples (Connidis, 2001). Whether this is due to renewed commitment to the marriage, the fact that couples who were very unhappy have already broken up, or to cohort effects is unclear (Glenn, 1998).

Older married couples show several specific characteristics (O'Rourke & Cappeliez, 2005). Many older couples show a selective memory regarding the occurrence of negative events and perceptions of their spouse. Like the older couple in the For Better or Worse cartoon, older couples have a reduced potential for marital conflict and greater potential for pleasure, are more likely to be similar in terms of mental and physical

health, and show fewer gender differences in sources of pleasure. In short, most older married couples have developed adaptive ways to avoid conflict and have grown more alike. In general, marital satisfaction among older couples remains high until health problems begin to interfere with the relationship (Connidis, 2001).

Being married in late life has several benefits. A study of 9,333 European Americans, African Americans, and Latino Americans showed that marriage helps people deal better with chronic illness, functional problems, and disabilities (Pienta, Hayward, & Jenkins, 2000). The division of household chores becomes more egalitarian after the husband retires than it was when the husband was employed, irrespective of whether the wife was working outside the home (Kulik, 2001a, 2001b).

Very little research on long-term gay and lesbian partnerships has been conducted. Based on the available data, it appears that long-term relationships between gay and lesbian partners do not differ in quality from long-term heterosexual marriages (Connidis, 2001; O'Brien & Goldberg, 2000). As is true for heterosexual married couples, relationship satisfaction is better when partners communicate well and are basically happy themselves. Some researchers argue that occupying two stigmatizing statuses—being gay or lesbian *and* being old—may make aging especially challenging for these couples (Grossman, 1997). For example, age-related declines in health may force individuals to disclose their sexual orientation much more publicly.

CARING FOR A PARTNER

When couples pledge their love to each other "in sickness and in health," most envision the sickness part to be no worse than an illness lasting a few weeks. That may be the case for many couples, but for some the illness they experience severely tests their pledge. Almost certainly Nancy Reagan did not think that she would need to care for her husband for several years, former U.S. President Ronald Reagan, who developed Alzheimer's disease and died from it in 2004.

Francine and Ron are another such couple. After 42 years of mainly good times together, Ron was diagnosed as having Alzheimer's disease. When first contacted by researchers, Francine had been caring for Ron for 6 years. "At times it's very hard, especially when he looks at me and doesn't have any idea who I am. Imagine, after all these years, not to recognize me. But I love him, and I know that he would do the same for me. But, to be perfectly honest, we're not the same couple we once were. We're just not as close; I guess we really can't be."

Francine and Ron are typical of couples in which one spouse cares for the other. Caring for a chronically ill partner presents different challenges than caring for a chronically ill parent (see Chapter 13). The partner caregiver assumes the new role after decades of shared responsibilities. Often without warning, the division of labor that had worked for years must be readjusted. Such change inevitably puts stress on the relationship (Cavanaugh & Kinney, 1994). This is especially true in cases involving Alzheimer's disease or other dementias because of the cognitive and behavioral consequences of the disease (see Chapter 14), but it is also the case in diseases such as AIDS. Caregiving challenges are felt by partner caregivers in any type of long-term, committed relationship.

Caring for a spouse can be both extremely stressful and highly rewarding.

© Cleo Photography/PhotoEdit

Studies of spousal caregivers of persons with Alzheimer's disease show that marital satisfaction is much lower than for healthy couples (Cavanaugh & Kinney, 1994; Kinney et al., 1993). Spousal caregivers report a loss of companionship and intimacy over the course of caregiving, but also more rewards than adult child caregivers (Raschick & Ingersoll-Dayton, 2004). Marital satisfaction is also an important predictor of spousal caregivers' reports of depressive symptoms; the better the perceived quality of the marriage, the fewer symptoms caregivers report (Kinney et al., 1993). Sadly, caring for a spouse often leads the caregiver to question the meaningfulness of life (Wells & Kendig, 1997).

Most partner caregivers are forced to respond to an environmental challenge that they did not choose—their partner's illness. They adopt the caregiver role out of necessity. Once they adopt the role, caregivers assess their ability to carry out the duties required. Longitudinal research indicates that how caregivers perceive their ability to provide care at the outset of caregiving may be all-important (Kinney & Cavanaugh, 1993). Caregivers who perceive themselves as competent try to rise to the occasion. For example, data indicate that spousal caregivers who perceive themselves as highly competent report fewer and less intense caregiving hassles than spousal caregivers who see themselves as less competent (Kinney & Cavanaugh, 1993). However, spousal caregivers do not always remember their major hassles accurately over time; in one study, caregivers remembered only about two thirds of their major hassles after a one-month delay (Cavanaugh & Kinney, 1998). This finding points out that health care professionals should not rely exclusively on partner caregivers' reports about the caregiving situation in making diagnostic judgments.

The importance of feeling competent as a partner caregiver fits with the docility component of the competence–environmental press model presented earlier in this chapter. Caregivers attempt to balance their perceived competence with the environmental demands of caregiving. Perceived competence allows them to be proactive rather than merely reactive (and docile), which gives them a better chance to optimize their situation.

Even in the best of committed relationships, providing full-time care for a partner is both very stressful and rewarding in terms of the marital relationship (Baek, 2005). Coping with a wife, for example, who may not remember her husband's name, who may act strangely, and who has a chronic and fatal disease presents serious challenges even to the happiest of couples, as depicted in the Doonesbury cartoon. Yet even in that situation, the caregiving husband may experience no change in marital happiness despite the changes in his wife due to the disease.

WIDOWHOOD

Alma, the woman we met in the vignette, still feels the loss of her husband, Chuck. "There are lots of times when I feel him around. We were together for so long that you take it for granted that your husband is just there. And there are times when I just don't want to go on without him. But I suppose I'll get through it."

Traditional marriage vows proclaim that the union will last "'til death do us part." Like Alma and Chuck, virtually all older married couples will see their marriages end be-

cause one partner dies. For most people, the death of a spouse follows a period of care-giving (Martin-Matthews, 1999) and is one of the most traumatic events they will ever experience (Miller, Smerglia, & Bouchet, 2004). Although widowhood may occur at any age, it is much more likely to occur in old age—and to women (Martin-Matthews, 1999). More than half of all women over age 65 are widows, but only 15% of men the same age are widowers. The reasons for this discrepancy are related to biological and so-cial forces: As we saw in Chapter 14, women have longer life expectancies. Also, women typically marry men older than themselves, as discussed in Chapter 11. Consequently, the average married woman can expect to live 10 to 12 years as a widow.

The impact of widowhood goes well beyond the ending of a long-term partnership (Martin-Matthews, 1999; Miller et al., 2004). Widowed people may be left alone by fam-ily and friends who do not know how to deal with a bereaved person (see Chapter 16). As a result, widows and widowers may lose not only a spouse but also those friends and family who feel uncomfortable including a single person rather than a couple in social functions (Felber, 2000). Because women tend to have more friends than men and keep stronger family ties, widows typically get more help than widowers from siblings and friends (Barrett & Lynch, 1999; Martin-Matthews, 2000). But feelings of loss do not dis-sipate quickly, as the case of Alma shows clearly. As we will see in Chapter 16, feeling sad on important dates is a common experience, even many years after a loved one has died.

Men and women react differently to widowhood. In general, those who were most dependent on their spouses during the marriage report the highest increase in self-esteem in widowhood because they have learned to do the tasks formerly done by their spouses (Carr, 2004). Widowers are at higher risk of dying themselves soon after their spouse, either by suicide or natural causes (Osgood, 1992), and are at higher risk for de-pression (Lee et al., 2001). Some people believe that the loss of a wife presents a more serious problem for a man than the loss of a husband for a woman. Perhaps this is be-cause a wife is often a man's only close friend and confidant, or because men are usually unprepared to live out their lives alone (Martin-Matthews, 1999; see Chapter 11). Older men are often ill equipped to handle such routine and necessary tasks as cooking, shop-ping, and keeping house, and they become emotionally isolated from family members.

Although both widows and widowers suffer financial loss, widows often suffer more because survivor's benefits are usually only half of their husband's pensions (Felber, 2000; Martin-Matthews, 1999). For many women, widowhood results in difficult finan-cial circumstances, particularly regarding medical expenses (McGarry & Schoeni, 2005).

An important factor to keep in mind about gender differences in widowhood is that men are usually older than women when they are widowed. To some extent, the diffi-culties reported by widowers may be partly due to this age difference. Regardless of age, men have a clear advantage over women in the opportunity to form new heterosexual relationships, as there are fewer social restrictions on relationships between older men and younger women (Matthews, 1996). However, older widowers are actually less likely to form new, close friendships than are widows. Perhaps this is simply a continuation of men's lifelong tendency to have few close friendships (see Chapter 11).

For many reasons, including the need for companionship and financial security, some widowed people remarry. Widowers are about five times more likely than widows to remarry (Lee, Willetts, & Seccombe, 1998). However, remarriage after being widowed is still less likely than after divorce (Connidis, 2001). Most likely this is because there are objective limitations (decreased mobility, poorer health, poorer finances), absence of incentives common to younger ages (desire for children), and social pressures to pro-tect one's estate (Talbott, 1998).

GREAT-GRANDPARENTHOOD

As discussed in Chapter 13, grandparenting is an important and enjoyable role for many adults. With increasing numbers of people, especially women, living to very old age, more people are experiencing great-grandparenthood. Age at first marriage and age at parenthood also play a critical role; people who reach these milestones at relatively

Becoming a great-grandparent is a meaningful role and a way to ensure the continuity of one's lineage.

younger ages are more likely to become great-grandparents. Most current great-grandparents are women who married relatively young and had children and grandchildren who also married and had children relatively early in adulthood.

Although little research has been conducted on great-grandparents, their investment in their roles as parents, grandparents, and great-grandparents forms a single family identity (Drew & Silverstein, 2005). That is, great-grandparents see a true continuity of the family through the passing on of the genes. However, their sources of satisfaction and meaning apparently differ from those of grandparents (Doka & Mertz, 1988; Wentkowski, 1985). Compared to grandparents, great-grandparents are much more similar as a group in what they derive from the role, largely because they are less involved with the children than grandparents are. Three aspects of great-grandparenthood appear to be most important (Doka & Mertz, 1988).

First, being a great-grandparent provides a sense of personal and family renewal—important components for achieving integrity. Their grandchildren have produced new life, renewing their own excitement for life and reaffirming the continuance of their lineage. Seeing their families stretch across four generations may also provide psychological support, through feelings of symbolic immortality, to help them face death. They take pride and comfort in knowing that their families will live many years beyond their own lifetime.

Second, great-grandchildren provide new diversions in great-grandparents' lives. There are now new people with whom they can share their experiences. Third, becoming a great-grandparent is a major milestone, a mark of longevity that most people never achieve. The sense that one has lived long enough to see the fourth generation is perceived very positively.

As you might expect, people with at least one living grandparent and great-grandparent interact more with their grandparent, who is also perceived as more influential (Roberto & Skoglund, 1996). Unfortunately, some great-grandparents must assume the role of primary caregiver to their great-grandchildren, a role that few great-grandparents are prepared for (Bengtson, Mills, & Parrott, 1995; Burton, 1992). As more people live longer, it will be interesting to see whether the role of great-grandparents changes and becomes more prominent.

TEST YOURSELF

1. The two most common forms of sibling relationships in old age are loyal and _____.

2. In general, marital satisfaction in older couples is high until _____.

3. A key predictor of stress among spousal caregivers is _____.

4. _____ are at a higher risk of dying themselves soon after they lose their spouse.

5. Three aspects of being a great-grandparent that are especially important are personal and family renewal, diversion, and _____.

How do the descriptions of marital satisfaction and spousal caregiving presented here fit with the descriptions of marital satisfaction in Chapter 11 and caring for aging parents in Chapter 13? What similarities and differences are there?

Answers: (1) congenial, (2) health problems arise, (3) marital satisfaction, (4) Widowers, (5) the fact that it is a milestone

15.5

SOCIAL ISSUES AND AGING

Rosa is an 82-year-old woman who still lives in the same neighborhood where she grew up. She has been in relatively good health for most of her life, but in the last year she has needed help with tasks, such as preparing meals and shopping for personal items. Rosa wants very much to continue living in her own home. She dreads being placed in a nursing home, but her family wonders whether that might be the best option.

O UR CONSIDERATION OF LATE LIFE thus far has focused on the experiences of most people. In this final section, we consider people like Rosa, who represent a substantial number, but still a minority of all older adults. Like Rosa, some older adults experience problems completing such common tasks as taking care of themselves. We consider the prevalence and kinds of problems such people face. Although most older adults live in the community, some reside in nursing homes; we consider the kinds of people most likely to live in institutional settings. Unfortunately, some older adults are the victims of abuse or neglect; we will examine some of the key issues relating to how elder abuse happens. Finally, we conclude with an overview of the most important emerging social policy issues.

All of these issues are critical when viewed from Baltes and Smith's (2003) Fourth Age perspective, as described in Chapter 14. We will see that it is the oldest old who make up most of the frail and who live in nursing homes. With the very rapid increase in the number of oldest old on the horizon with the baby boom generation, finding ways to deal with these issues is essential.

FRAIL OLDER ADULTS

In our discussion about aging, to this point we have focused on the majority of older adults who are healthy, cognitively competent, financially secure, and have secure family relationships. Some older adults are not as fortunate. *They are **frail older adults** who have physical disabilities, are very ill, and may have cognitive or psychological disorders.* These frail older adults constitute a minority of the population over age 65, but a proportion that increases with age.

Frail older adults are people whose competence (in terms of the competence–environmental press model presented earlier) is declining. They do not have one specific problem that differentiates them from their active, healthy counterparts but rather tend to have multiple problems (Rockwood et al., 2004).

Assessing everyday competence consists of examining how well people can complete activities of daily living and instrumental activities of daily living (Johnson et al., 2004). *__Activities of daily living (ADLs)__ are basic self-care tasks such as eating, bathing, toileting, walking, or dressing.* A person could be considered frail if he or she needs help with one of these tasks. Other tasks are also considered important for living independently. *These **instrumental activities of daily living (IADLs)** are actions that require some intellectual competence and planning.* Which actions constitute IADLs vary

LEARNING OBJECTIVES

Who are frail older adults? How common is frailty?

Where do older adults live in the community?

Who are the most likely people to live in nursing homes? What are the characteristics of good nursing homes?

How do you know whether an older adult is abused or neglected? Which people are most likely to be abused and to be abusers?

What are the key social policy issues affecting older adults?

Older adults over age 85 are much more likely to be frail and need help doing basic daily tasks.

considerably from one culture to another and factor into cross-cultural differences in conceptions of competence (Sternberg & Grigorenko, 2004). For example, for most older adults in Western cultures, IADLs would include shopping for personal items, paying bills, making telephone calls, taking medications appropriately, and keeping appointments. In other cultures, IADLs might include caring for animal herds, making bread, threshing grain, and tending crops.

Prevalence of Frailty

How common are people like Rosa, the 82-year-old woman in the vignette who still lives in the same neighborhood in which she grew up? As you can see in Figure 15.6, the number of older people needing help with ADLs increases dramatically with age (AgingStats.gov, 2004). Less than 5% of adults aged 65–74 need assistance, whereas 20% of those over age 85 may need help (AgingStats.gov, 2004). Similar results are found for IADLs. As you can also see in the figure, the number of adults requiring assistance with IADLs also increases drastically after age 85 (AgingStats.gov, 2004). The percentage of people needing assistance varies somewhat across ethnic groups, with European Americans over age 65 having the lowest rate (15%), African Americans the highest rate (25%), and Asian Americans (19%) and Latino Americans (21%) in between (Administration on Aging, 2001). Rates for Native Americans were not reported.

In addition to basic assistance with ADLs and IADLs, frail older adults have other needs. Research shows that these individuals are also prone to higher rates of anxiety disorders and depression (Solano, 2001).

Although frailty becomes more likely with increasing age, especially during the last year of life, there are many ways to provide a supportive environment for frail older adults. We have already seen how many family members provide care. Exercise can also help improve the quality of life of some frail older adults (Rockwood et al., 2004; Schechtman & Ory, 2001). Next, we will consider the role that nursing homes play. The key to providing a supportive context for frail older adults is to create an optimal match between the person's competence and the environmental demands.

LIVING IN NURSING HOMES

The last place that Bessie thought she would ever end up was in a bed in a local nursing home. "That's a place where old people go to die," she would tell her friends. "It's not gonna be for me." But here she is. Bessie fell a few weeks ago and broke her hip. Because

Figure 15.6
The number of people needing assistance with ADLs and IADLs increases dramatically in people over age 85.

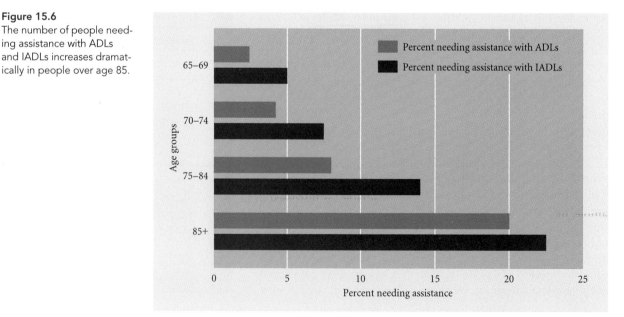

she lives alone, she needs to stay in the nursing home until she recovers. She detests the food; "tasteless" she calls it. Her roommate, Doris, refers to her room as "jail" to her daughter. Doris, age 78, has dementia.

Bessie and Doris are representative of the people who live in nursing homes, some temporarily, some permanently. If given the choice, the vast majority of older adults do not want to live in nursing homes; their families would also prefer some other solution. Sometimes, though, placement in a nursing home is necessary because of the older person's needs or the family's circumstances.

Misconceptions about nursing homes are common. Contrary to what some people believe, only about 5% of older adults live in nursing homes on any given day. However, about 50% of people who live past age 85 will spend at least some time in a long-term care facility (National Academy on an Aging Society, 2003). Thus, over the adult life span the number of people who spend time in a nursing home is rather large.

However, the rate of nursing home residence for people over age 65 has been declining slightly since the mid-1980s (AgingStats.gov, 2004). This decline is larger for people ages 75 to 84 (21%) than for people ages 65 to 74 (14%) and age 85 and over (13%). This decline is most likely due to the large increase in the number of assisted living facilities (AgingStats.gov, 2004). **_Assisted living facilities_** *provide a supportive living arrangement for people who need assistance with ADLs or IADLs but who are not so impaired physically or cognitively that they need 24-hour care.* Estimates are that roughly a quarter of residents of assisted living facilities need assistance with three or more ADLs and about one third have moderate to severe cognitive impairment (AgingStats.gov, 2004).

Governmental regulations in the United States define two primary levels of care in nursing homes (Ebersole et al., 2004). **_Intermediate care_** *consists of 24-hour care necessitating nursing supervision, but usually not at an intense level.* **_Skilled nursing care_** *consists of 24-hour care requiring fairly constant monitoring and provision of medical and other health services, usually by nurses.* Each state has specific regulations concerning each type of care. In actual practice the major differences between the two levels of care are the types and numbers of health care workers on the staff, resulting in a blurred distinction between the two.

Who Lives in Nursing Homes?

Who is the typical resident of a nursing home? She is very old, European American, financially disadvantaged (and eligible for Medicaid), probably widowed or divorced, possibly without living children, and she has lived in the nursing home for more than a year. Major risk factors are (Davis & Lapane, 2004):

- Over age 85
- Female
- Recently admitted to a hospital
- Lives in retirement housing rather than being a homeowner
- Unmarried or lives alone
- Has no children or siblings nearby
- Has cognitive impairment
- Has problems with IADLs

Figure 15.7 shows the average age, gender, and race breakdown of the typical nursing home in the United States. Note that the characteristics of the typical nursing home resident are not similar to the population at large, as discussed in Chapter 1. For example, men are underrepresented in nursing homes, as are minorities. The reasons for the lower rate among minorities are not entirely clear. Also, for financial reasons, poor people in all ethnic groups have less access to health care providers, including nursing homes (Belgrave, Wykle, & Choi, 1993). This may explain why people of color who live in nursing homes tend to be more impaired than European American residents (Davis & Lapane, 2004). With the cost of a typical nursing home $70,000 or more annually per person, depending on the type of facility and location (Payne, 2004), most lower income

■ Figure 15.7
The majority of people in
nursing homes are older
European American women.

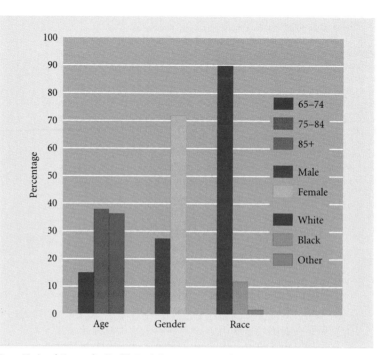

From National Center for Health Statistics, 1997. www.cdc.gov/nchs

people cannot afford such care until they have no other option. Programs such as Medi-care, Medicaid, and private long-term care insurance pay a portion of the cost, but most people face huge expenses. These costs often mean that working poor and middle-income people cannot afford nursing homes.

What are the problems of typical nursing home residents? For the most part, the average nursing home resident is clearly impaired, both mentally and physically. Indeed, the main reason for placing almost 80% of nursing home residents is health. Estimates are that nearly 80% of residents have mobility problems, and more than one third have mobility, eating, and incontinence problems (AgingStats.gov, 2004).

As you may have surmised from the high level of impairment among nursing home residents, frail older people and their relatives do not see nursing homes as an option until other avenues have been explored. This may account for the numbers of truly impaired people who live in nursing homes; the kinds and number of problems make life outside the nursing home very difficult for them and their families and beyond the level of assistance provided by assisted living facilities. For these reasons, the decision to enter a nursing home often is made quickly in reaction to a crisis, such as a person's impending discharge from a hospital or other health emergency (Hooyman & Kiyak, 1999).

What Characterizes a Good Nursing Home?

Nursing homes vary a great deal in the amount and quality of care they provide. One useful way of evaluating them is by applying the competence–environmental press model. When applied to nursing homes, the goal is to find the optimal level of environmental support for people who have relatively low levels of competence.

Selecting a nursing home should be done carefully. The Centers for Medicare and Medicaid Services of the U.S. Department of Health and Human Services provides a detailed guide for choosing a nursing home. Among the most important things to consider are quality of life for residents (e.g., whether residents are well groomed, the food is tasty, and rooms contain comfortable furniture); quality of care (whether staff respond quickly to calls, whether staff and family are involved in care decisions); safety (whether there are enough staff, whether hallways are free of clutter); and other issues (whether there are outdoor areas for residents to use). These aspects of nursing homes reflect those dimensions considered by states in their inspections and licensing process.

Based on the various theories of person-environment interaction discussed earlier in this chapter and in Chapter 1, researchers recommend a "person-centered planning" approach to nursing home policies (Reese, 2001). This approach is based on promoting residents' well-being through increasing their perceived level of personal control and treating them with respect. Taking this approach means such things as residents getting to decorate their own rooms, choosing what they want to eat from a buffet, and deciding whether they want to take a shower or a bath. Such policies are grounded in classic research showing that residents who have higher perceived personal control show significant improvement in well-being and activity level, and actually live longer (Langer & Rodin, 1976; Rodin & Langer, 1977). Nursing homes that use the person-centered planning approach also note major decreases in the need for certain medications (e.g., sleep and anti-anxiety drugs) and soft restraints, as well as substantial declines in the number of residents who are incontinent (Reese, 2001). Feelings of self-efficacy are crucial to doing well and have a profound impact on nursing home residents' functional abilities (Johnson et al., 1998; Reese, 2001).

*Equally important, people interacting with nursing home residents must avoid **patronizing speech,** which is marked by slower speech, exaggerated intonation, higher pitch, increased volume, repetitions, closed-ended questions, and simplified vocabulary and grammar. A related form of demeaning speech, called **infantilization,** involves the use of a person's first name when it is not appropriate, terms of endearment, simplified expressions, short imperatives, assumptions that the resident has no memory, and manipulation to get compliance.* Several studies document that the use of patronizing speech and infantilization results in negative feelings on the part of residents and may lower self-esteem among those who perceive such speech negatively (Ryan et al., 2000; Whitmer & Whitbourne, 1997).

The first time most people visit a nursing home, they are ill-prepared to talk to family members who are frail, have trouble remembering, and cannot get around very well. The hardest part is trying to figure out what to say in order to avoid patronizing speech. However, visiting residents of nursing homes is a way to maintain social contacts and provide a meaningful activity. Even if the person you are visiting is frail or has a sensory impairment or some other type of disability, visits can be uplifting. As noted earlier in the chapter, high-quality social contacts help older adults maintain their life satisfaction. Here are several suggestions for making visits more pleasant (Papalia & Olds, 1995; adapted from Davis, 1985):

■ Concentrate on the older adult's expertise and wisdom, as discussed in Chapter 14, by asking for advice on a life problem that he or she knows a lot about, such as dealing with friends, cooking, or crafts.

■ Allow the older person to exert control over the visit: where to go (even inside the facility), what to wear, what to eat (if choices are possible).

■ Listen attentively, even if the older person is repetitive. Avoid being judgmental, be sympathetic to complaints, and acknowledge feelings.

■ Talk about things the person likes to remember, such as raising children, military service, growing up, work, courtship, and so on.

■ Do a joint activity, such as putting a jigsaw puzzle together, arranging a photograph album, or doing arts and crafts.

Good nursing homes try to make residents feel as much at home as possible and treat each resident with respect.

© Jeff Greenberg/PhotoEdit

- Record your visit on audiotape or videotape. This is valuable for creating a family history that you will be able to keep. The activity may facilitate a life review as well as provide an opportunity for the older person to leave something of value for future generations by describing important personal events and philosophies.
- Bring children when you visit, if possible. Grandchildren are especially important, as most older adults are very happy to include them in conversations. Such visits also give children the opportunity to see their grandparents and learn about the diversity of older adults.
- Stimulate as many senses as possible. Wearing bright clothes, singing songs, reading books, and sharing foods (as long as they have been checked with the staff) help keep residents involved with their environment. Above all, though, hold the resident's hands. There's nothing like a friendly touch.

Always remember that your visits may be the only way that the residents have of maintaining social contacts with friends and family. By following these guidelines, you will be able to avoid difficulties and make your visits more pleasurable.

✳ELDER ABUSE AND NEGLECT

Arletta, an 82-year-old woman in relatively poor health, has been living with her 60-year-old daughter, Sally, for the past 2 years. Recently, neighbors became concerned because they had not seen Arletta very much for several months. When they did, she looked rather worn and extremely thin, and as if she had not bathed in weeks. Finally, the neighbors decided that they should do something, so they called the local office of the department of human services. Upon hearing the details of the situation, a caseworker immediately investigated. The caseworker found that Arletta was severely malnourished, had not bathed in weeks, and appeared disoriented. Based on these findings, the agency concluded that Arletta was a victim of neglect. She was moved to a county nursing home temporarily.

Unfortunately, some older adults who need quality caregiving by family members or in nursing homes do not receive it. In some cases, older adults like Arletta are treated inappropriately. Arletta's case is representative of this sad but increasing problem: elder abuse and neglect. In this section, we consider what elder abuse and neglect are, how often they happen, and what victims and abusers are like.

Defining Elder Abuse and Neglect

Like child abuse (see Chapter 7, pages 279–283) and partner abuse (see Chapter 11, pages 422–425), elder abuse is difficult to define precisely in practice (Wilber & McNeilly, 2001). In general, researchers and public policy advocates describe several different categories of elder abuse (Anetzberger, 2005; Bergeron, 2004):

- *Physical abuse:* the use of physical force that may result in bodily injury, physical pain, or impairment.
- *Sexual abuse:* nonconsensual sexual contact of any kind.
- *Emotional or psychological abuse:* infliction of anguish, pain, or distress.
- *Financial or material exploitation:* the illegal or improper use of an older adult's funds, property, or assets.
- *Abandonment:* the desertion of an older adult by an individual who had physical custody or otherwise had assumed responsibility for providing care for the older adult.
- *Neglect:* refusal or failure to fulfill any part of a person's obligation or duties to an older adult.
- *Self-neglect:* the behaviors of an older person that threaten his or her own health or safety, excluding those conscious and voluntary decisions by a mentally competent and healthy adult.

Part of the problem in agreeing on definitions of elder abuse and neglect is that perceptions differ among ethnic groups. For example, African American, Korean American, and European American older females used different criteria in deciding whether scenarios they read represented abuse (Moon & Williams, 1993). Specifically, older Korean American women were much less likely to judge a particular scenario as abusive and to indicate that help should be sought than women in either of the other two groups. Such ethnic differences may result in conflicts between social service workers using one set of definitions and clients using another in deciding who should receive protective services (Williams & Griffin, 1996).

Prevalence

Only one national study of elder abuse and neglect has ever been conducted in the United States that attempted to estimate the number of victims. Based on the number of cases actually reported to adult protective service agencies in 20 representative counties in 15 states, and an assumption that the number of unreported cases is roughly five times greater, more than 551,000 people over age 60 were abused or neglected in the United States in 1996 (Administration on Aging, 2004). The most common forms are neglect (roughly 60%), physical abuse (16%), and financial or material exploitation (12%). Thus, Arletta's case of neglect would be one of the most common types.

Characteristics of Elder Abuse Victims

Studies of risk factors in elder abuse have produced conflicting results. Some data indicate that women are more likely to be abused than men (Administration on Aging, 2004), whereas other data show no differences in the rates between men and women (Lachs et al., 1997). There is more agreement that people over age 80 are abused two to three times more often that people under age 80 (Administration on Aging, 2004). A 9-year longitudinal study of risk factors identified age, poverty, functional and cognitive impairment, and living with someone as factors that increase the likelihood of abuse or neglect (Lachs et al., 1997).

In roughly 90% of the elder abuse and neglect incidents in which the perpetrator is known, it is a family member, two thirds of whom are either spouses or adult children (Administration on Aging, 2004). People in positions of trust, such as bankers, accountants, attorneys, and clergy, are also in a position to take advantage of an older client (Kapp, 1999; Quinn, 1998). Telemarketing fraud, including fraudulent investment schemes and sweepstakes, against older adults is a growing problem (Gross, 1999; Rabiner, Brown, & O'Keeffe, 2004; Schuett & Burke, 2000). Perpetrators of telemarketing fraud prey on the fears and needs of their targets by focusing on older adults' loneliness, desire to please, need to help, and other weaknesses.

Causes of Elder Abuse

Why elder abuse occurs is a matter of debate (Wilber & McNeilly, 2001). Several explanations have been offered that reflect the multidimensional and multidisciplinary approaches researchers have taken (Harbison, 1999).

One of the most popular theories, which has its roots in the child abuse literature, states that elder abuse occurs when caregivers who are under great stress take out their frustrations on the person requiring care (Quinn & Tomita, 1997). However, research evidence fails to support the idea that caregiver stress alone is the primary cause (Wilber & McNeilly, 2001). Similarly, the theory that patterns of abuse are transmitted across generations, shown to be a factor in other forms of family violence, also has little research support as a major cause of elder abuse (Wilber & McNeilly, 2001).

Research findings support a more complex set of causes. Based on two decades of research, Reis and Nahmiash (1998) showed that characteristics of both the caregiver and the care-recipient must be considered. They found that abuse cases could be discriminated from nonabuse cases up to 84% of the time by considering several things: (a) intrapersonal problems of the caregiver, such as substance abuse, mental disorder, and behavior problems; (b) interpersonal problems of the caregiver, such as family or marital conflict, a poor relationship with the care-recipient, and financial dependence on the care-recipient; and (c) social characteristics of the care-recipient, such as lack of social support and past abuse.

Clearly, elder abuse is an important social problem that has had insufficient attention from researchers and policymakers. Increased educational efforts, better reporting and investigation, more options for placement of victims, and better mental health treatment for victims are all needed for the problem to be adequately addressed (Wilber & McNeilly, 2001).

POLITICS, SOCIAL SECURITY, AND MEDICARE

Without doubt, the 20th century saw a dramatic improvement in the everyday lives of older adults in industrialized countries. The increase in the number of older adults and their gain in political power, coupled with increased numbers of social programs addressing issues specifically involving older adults, created unprecedented gains for the average older person (Crown, 2001). The economic well-being of the majority of older adults has never been better than it is currently; for example, in the 1950s, roughly 35% of older adults were below the federal poverty line compared to about 10% in 2003 (Administration on Aging, 2005; Crown, 2001). But times have changed. Many younger and middle-aged adults are quite skeptical of the long-term viability of these government programs, especially in view of the enormous increase in costs associated with the aging of the baby boom generation (Binstock, 1999). The political climate has also changed, though the seeds were planted two decades earlier.

The Political Landscape

Beginning in the 1970s, older adults began to be portrayed as scapegoats in the political debates concerning government resources. Part of the reason was due to the tremendous growth in the amount and proportion of federal dollars expended on benefits to them, such as through the liberalization of benefits paid from Social Security during the 1970s (Crown, 2001). Older adults were also portrayed as highly politically active, fiscally conservative, and selfish (Fairlie, 1988; Gibbs, 1988; Smith, 1992). The health care reform debate of the early 1990s focused attention on the spiraling costs of care for older adults that were projected to bankrupt the federal budget if left uncontrolled (Binstock, 1999). Consequently, older adults emerged as the source of all the United States' fiscal problems.

It was in this context that the U.S. Congress began making substantive changes in the benefits for older adults on the grounds of intergenerational fairness. The argument was that the United States must treat all generations fairly and cannot provide differential benefits to any one generation (Binstock, 1994). Beginning in 1983, Congress has made several changes in Social Security, Medicare, the Older Americans Act, and other programs and policies. Some of these changes reduced benefits to wealthy older adults, whereas others provided targeted benefits for poor older adults (Binstock, 1999).

The aging of the baby boom generation presents very difficult and expensive problems (Congressional Budget Office, 2005). In fiscal year 2006, federal spending on Social Security, Medicare, and Medicaid alone was over $1.1 trillion, representing 44% of the entire federal budget. As you can see in Figure 15.8, if spending patterns do not change, by 2030 (when most of the baby boomers will have reached old age) expenditures for Social Security and Medicare alone are projected to consume roughly 13% of the Gross Domestic Product (GDP). Without major reforms in these programs, such growth will force extremely difficult choices in how to pay for them.

Clearly, the political and social issues concerning benefits to older adults are quite complex. Spurred by President George W. Bush's proposals for Social Security and Medicare in 2005, the next decade will see increased urgency and action in confronting the issues. There are no easy solutions, and it will be essential to discuss all aspects of the

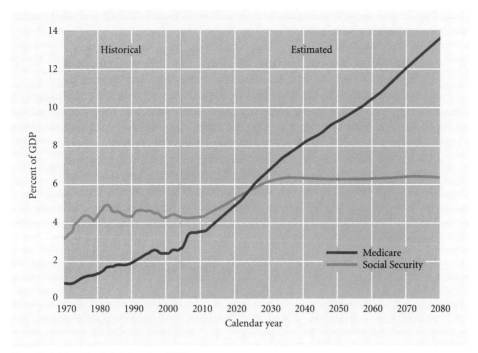

From Social Security Administration, 2005.

Figure 15.8
Social Security and Medicare expenditures as a percentage of Gross Domestic Product in the United States. Note that Medicare expenditures are rising much faster than Social Security.

problem. Let's look more closely at three key issues: political activity, Social Security, and Medicare.

Political Activity

By most measures, adults over age 65 are the most politically active of all age groups. They write more letters to elected representatives, belong to more organizations that lobby for their positions, are better informed about local and national issues, and are generally more knowledgeable about politics (Binstock & Quadagno, 2001).

These activities have created a very powerful and active constituency, one that has increasing influence on legislation. The primary organization representing the interests of older adults is AARP, which is also the largest interest group in the United States. In 2005 membership in AARP exceeded 35 million. Anyone over age 50 is eligible to join for a fee of $12.50 per year. AARP is not alone in organizing older adults in the political arena (Binstock & Quadagno, 2001). In the United States alone more than 100 organizations help shape public policy relating to older adults. Aging-based groups are also active in many countries around the world, including Australia, Canada, Japan, Germany, the United Kingdom, Poland, and Denmark.

Social Security

Social Security had its beginnings in 1935 as an initiative by President Franklin Roosevelt to "frame a law which will give some measure of protection to the average citizen and to his family against the loss of a job and against poverty-ridden old age." Thus Social Security was originally intended to provide a supplement to savings and other means of financial support.

Over the years, revisions to the original law have changed Social Security so that it now represents the primary source of financial support after retirement for most U.S. citizens, and the only source for many (Binstock, 1999; Kingson & Williamson, 2001). Since the 1970s, however, increasing numbers of workers have been included in employer-sponsored pension plans such as 401(k), 403(b), and 457 plans, mutual funds, as well as various types of Individual Retirement Accounts (IRAs) (U.S. Department of Labor, 2005e). This inclusion of various retirement plans, especially savings options, may permit more future retirees to use Social Security as the supplemental financial source it was intended to be.

The primary challenge facing Social Security is the aging of the very large baby boom generation and the much smaller generation that follows them. Because Social Security is funded by payroll taxes, the amount of money each worker must pay depends to a large extent on the ratio of the number of people paying Social Security taxes to the number of people collecting benefits. By 2030 this ratio will drop nearly in half; that is, by the time baby boomers have largely retired, there will be nearly twice as many people collecting Social Security per worker paying into the system as there are today (Social Security Administration, 2005). Various plans have been proposed since the early 1970s to address this issue, and several U.S. presidents have addressed the issue, but Congress has not yet taken the actions necessary to ensure the financial stability of Social Security over the long term (Social Security Administration, 2005). As discussed in the Current Controversies feature, the suggestions for doing this present difficult choices for politicians.

CURRENT CONTROVERSIES

SAVING SOCIAL SECURITY

Few political issues have been around as long and are as politically sensitive as the issues relating to making Social Security fiscally sound for the long term. The basic issues have been well known for decades: the baby boom generation and the following smaller workforce will greatly stretch the current system, and the present method for raising and distributing revenues cannot be sustained (Social Security Administration, 2005).

Because Social Security is based on current workers paying a tax to support current retirees, the looming funding problems depend critically on the worker-retiree ratio. As you can see in Figure 15.9, this ratio has declined precipitously since Social Security began and will continue to do so, placing an increasing financial burden on workers to provide the level of benefits that people have come to expect. Due to this declining ratio, if the current tax rate of 12.4% each on workers and employers is maintained, payments will exceed income from payroll taxes by 2018, will exceed all sources of revenue including interest on the available surplus (the trust fund) by 2028, and will be bankrupt by 2043 (Social Security Administration, 2005).

What steps can be taken to keep Social Security sound in the long term? In 2005 President Bush made a concerted effort to incorporate reports from many special commissions established to study the problem (including one

he set up in 2001), economists, and researchers who have all proposed changes in the current operation of Social Security. Among the changes proposed over the years are these:

• *Privatization:* Various proposals have been made for allowing or requiring workers to invest at least part of their money in personal retirement accounts managed by either the federal

■ **Figure 15.9**
The dramatic decrease in the number of workers paying into the Social Security system per retiree is the main reason Social Security taxes have steadily increased.

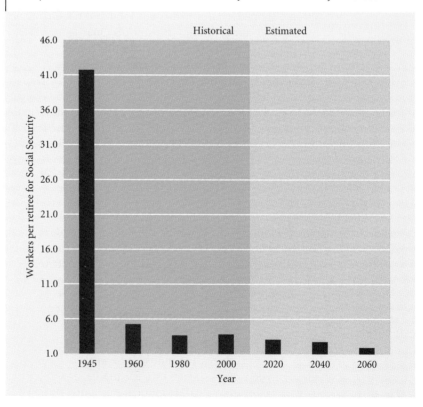

government or private investment companies. A variation would take trust funds and invest them in private-sector equity markets. Another option would be for people to be allowed to create personal accounts with a portion of the funds paid in payroll taxes.

- *Means-test benefits:* This proposal would reduce or eliminate benefits to people with high incomes.
- *Increase the number of years used to compute the benefit:* Currently, benefits are based on one's history of contributions over a 35-year period. This proposal would increase that to 38 or 40 years.
- *Increase the retirement age:* The age of eligibility for full Social Security benefits is increasing slowly from age 65 in 2000 to age 67 in 2027. Various

proposals to speed up the increase, to increase the age to 70, or to connect age at which a person becomes fully eligible to average longevity statistics have been made.

- *Adjust cost of living increases downward:* Some proposals have been made to lower the increases given to beneficiaries as a result of increases in cost of living.
- *Increase the payroll tax rate:* One direct way to address the coming funding shortfall is to increase revenues through a higher tax rate.
- *Increase the earnings cap for payroll tax purposes:* This proposal would either raise or remove the cap on income subject to the Social Security payroll tax ($90,000 in 2005).
- *Make across-the-board reductions in Social Security pension benefits:*

A reduction in benefits of 3 to 5% would resolve most of the funding problem.

None of these proposals has universal support, and many would significantly disadvantage people, especially minorities and older widows, who depend almost entirely on Social Security for their retirement income (Kingson & Williamson, 2001).

Solving the funding problems facing Social Security will become increasingly important in the next few years. The first baby boomers become eligible for reduced retirement benefits in 2008. Given the political difficulties inherent in tackling the issue, and the lack of perfect solutions, it is likely that Social Security will remain a major controversy over the next several years.

Medicare

Nearly 40 million U.S. citizens depend on Medicare for their medical insurance. To be eligible, a person must meet one of the following criteria: be over age 65, be disabled, or have permanent kidney failure. Medicare consists of three parts (Medicare.gov, 2005): Part A, which covers inpatient hospital services, skilled nursing facilities, home health services, and hospice care; Part B, which covers the cost of physician services, outpatient hospital services, medical equipment and supplies, and other health services and supplies; and starting in 2006 Part D, which provides some coverage for prescription medications. Expenses relating to most long-term care needs are funded by Medicaid, another major health care program funded by the U.S. government and aimed at people who are poor. Out-of-pocket expenses associated with co-payments and other charges are often paid by supplemental insurance policies, sometimes referred to as "Medigap" policies (AARP, 2005).

Like Social Security, Medicare is funded by a payroll tax. So the funding problems facing Medicare are very similar to those facing Social Security and are grounded in the aging of the baby boom generation. In addition, Medicare costs have increased dramatically due to more general rapid cost increases in health care; by the mid-1990s, the rate of increase was still more than twice that of inflation (Feder et al., 2001).

Due to these rapid increases and the specter of the baby boom generation, cost containment was a major concern in the 1990s. Indeed, two major policy trends emerged. First, a growing emphasis was placed on managed care through health maintenance organizations (HMOs). But older adults were reluctant to give up their choice of physicians and join HMOs, so they attained declining profit margins (Feder et al., 2001).

Second, home health care has been championed by some as a means to minimize the need for more expensive hospital and long-term care (Kane & Kane, 2001). By enabling people to be cared for in their homes, policymakers and service providers hope to reserve hospitals and nursing homes for those in most need and save money. However, research to date shows that home care is not cheaper (Kane & Kane, 2001).

Taken together, the challenges facing society concerning older adults' financial security and health will continue to be major political issues throughout the first few decades of the 21st century. There are no easy answers, but open discussion of the various arguments will be essential for creating the optimal solution.

TEST YOURSELF

1. Activities of daily living (ADLs) include functioning in the areas of bathing, toileting, walking, dressing, and _____.

2. Most people who live in nursing homes are _____.

3. The group that most often abuses older adults is _____.

4. The two important public policy issues in the United States that are being affected by the aging

baby boom generation are Social Security and _____.

How would the competence–environmental press framework, presented earlier in this chapter, apply specifically to the various types of housing and nursing homes discussed in this section?

Answers: (1) eating, (2) older European American women who are very ill, (3) their adult children, (4) Medicare

Putting It All Together

We are involved in human relationships throughout our lives. In a very real sense, people grow old within the broader social context of their environment and social network.

The match between people's competence and the environmental demands they face sets the stage for how well they adapt. How older people cope with daily life is typically a continuation of the ways they coped throughout their lives. We encountered people who, like Olive, spend time reflecting on their past in order to determine whether their lives have been well spent. We saw that the view of retirement as detrimental to health and as a cause of isolation is wrong; most people are like Marcus, who greatly enjoys retirement. Many older women, like Alma, are widows; such women are especially vulnerable to financial pressures. Also, like Rosa, many people over 80 need assistance with their daily activities.

The general picture of older adults is characterized by continued activity for most. Still, we need to recognize that, especially among the oldest old, physical limitations are an important aspect of living. Although only a very small proportion of older adults are in nursing homes,

many people over 80 need varying degrees of help to continue living independently. The rapid increase in the number of older people that the United States will experience over the next few decades will seriously strain traditional public policies toward older adults.

Combined with Chapter 14, this chapter provides insight into the complexities of old age. So what is known about a person if we know she is 85 years old? Not much more than the fact that she has celebrated 85 birthdays. That's not bad either—it means that if you want to know something more than that, you'll need to get to know her.

We can now take a broader view of the biopsychosocial model as it relates to aging. In this chapter, we focused mainly on how sociocultural forces shape people's lives by setting the context for retirement and interpersonal relationships, as well as setting the agenda for social and public policy issues. How well people are able to face sociocultural forces (as exemplified by environmental press) is a function of their biological and psychological competence. Of course, this function is a dynamic one that changes as people grow older.

Summary

15.1 Theories of Psychosocial Aging

Continuity Theory

◼ Continuity theory is based on the view that people tend to cope with daily life in later adulthood by applying familiar strategies based on past experience to

maintain and preserve both internal and external structures.

Competence and Environmental Press

◼ According to competence–environmental press theory, people's optimal adaptation occurs when there is a balance between their ability to cope and the level of environmental demands placed on them. When balance is not achieved, behavior becomes maladaptive. Several studies indicate that competence–environmental press theory can be applied to a variety of real-world situations.

15.2 Personality, Social Cognition, and Spirituality

Integrity Versus Despair

■ Older adults face the Eriksonian struggle of integrity versus despair, primarily through a life review. Integrity involves accepting one's life for what it is; despair involves bitterness about one's past. People who reach integrity become self-affirming and self-accepting, and they judge their lives to have been worthwhile and good.

Well-Being and Social Cognition

■ Subjective well-being is a positive evaluation of one's life that is associated with positive feelings. In life-span developmental psychology, subjective well-being is usually assessed with measures of life satisfaction, happiness, and self-esteem.

Religiosity and Spiritual Support

■ Older adults use religion and spiritual support more often than any other strategy to help them cope with problems of life. This is especially true for African American women, who are more active in their church groups and attend services more frequently.

15.3 I Used to Work at . . . : Living in Retirement

What Does Being Retired Mean?

■ Retirement is a complex process by which people withdraw from full-time employment. No single definition is adequate for all ethnic groups; self-definition involves several factors, including eligibility for certain social programs.

Why Do People Retire?

■ People generally retire because they choose to, although some people are forced to retire or do so because of serious health problems, such as cardiovascular disease or cancer. However, there are important gender and ethnic differences in why people retire and how they label themselves after retirement. Most of the research is based on European American men from traditional marriages.

Adjustment to Retirement

■ Retirement is an important life transition. Most people are satisfied with retirement. Most retired

people maintain their health, friendship networks, and activity levels, at least in the years immediately following retirement. For men, personal life priorities are all-important; little is known about women's retirement satisfaction. Most retired people stay busy in activities such as volunteer work and helping others.

Keeping Busy in Retirement

■ From a life course perspective, it is important to maintain social integration in retirement. Participation in community organizations and volunteering are primary ways of achieving this.

15.4 Friends and Family in Late Life

Friends and Siblings

■ A person's social convoy is an important source of satisfaction in late life. Patterns of friendships among older adults are very similar to those among young adults, but older adults are more selective. Sibling relationships are especially important in old age. Five types of sibling relationships have been identified: intimate, congenial, loyal, apathetic, and hostile. The loyal and congenial types are the most common. Ties between sisters are the strongest.

Marriage and Gay and Lesbian Partnerships

■ Long-term marriages tend to be happy until one partner develops serious health problems. Older married couples show a lower potential for marital conflict and greater potential for pleasure. Long-term gay and lesbian relationships tend to be very similar in characteristics to long-term heterosexual marriages.

Caring for a Partner

■ Caring for a spouse puts considerable strain on the relationship. The degree of marital satisfaction strongly affects how spousal caregivers perceive stress. Although caught off guard initially, most spousal caregivers are able to provide adequate care. Perceptions of competence among spousal caregivers at the outset of caregiving may be especially important.

Widowhood

■ Widowhood is a difficult transition for most people. Feelings of loneliness are hard to cope with, especially during the first few months following bereavement. Men generally have problems in social relationships and in household tasks; women tend to have more severe financial problems. Some widowed people remarry, partly to solve loneliness and financial problems.

Great-Grandparenthood

■ Becoming a great-grandparent is an important source of personal satisfaction for many older adults. Great-grandparents as a group are more similar to each other than grandparents are. Three aspects of great-grandparenthood are most important: sense of personal and family renewal, new diversions in life, and a major life milestone.

15.5 Social Issues and Aging

Frail Older Adults

■ The number of frail older adults is growing. Frailty is defined in terms of impairment in activities of daily living (basic self-care skills) and instrumental activities of daily living (actions that require intellectual competence or planning). As many as half of the women over age 85 may need assistance with ADLs or IADLs. Supportive environments are useful in optimizing the balance between competence and environmental press.

Living in Nursing Homes

■ Two levels of care are provided in nursing homes: intermediate care and skilled nursing care. Most residents of nursing homes are European American women who are in poor health. Ethnic minority older adults have a lower rate of placement in nursing homes than European Americans. Maintaining a resident's sense of control is an important component of good nursing homes. Communications with residents must avoid patronizing speech and infantilization.

Elder Abuse and Neglect

■ Abuse and neglect of older adults is an increasing problem. However, abuse and neglect are difficult to define precisely. Several categories are used, including physical abuse, sexual abuse, emotional or psychological abuse, financial or material exploitation, abandonment, neglect, and self-neglect. Most perpetrators are family members, usually spouses or adult children of the victims. Research indicates that abuse results from a complex interaction of characteristics of the caregiver and care-recipient.

Politics, Social Security, and Medicare

■ Treating all generations fairly in terms of government programs is a difficult public policy challenge. The U.S. Congress has enacted several changes in social program benefits to older adults to address the changing demographics of the U.S. population.

■ Older adults are the most politically active age group. Numerous organizations are dedicated to furthering issues and positions pertaining to older adults.

■ Although designed as an income supplement, Social Security has become the primary source of retirement income for most U.S. citizens. The aging of the baby boom generation will place considerable stress on the financing of the system.

■ Medicare is the principal health insurance program for adults in the United States over age 65. Cost containment is a major concern, resulting in emphases on health maintenance organizations and home health care.

Key Terms

continuity theory (578)

competence (579)

environmental press (579)

adaptation level (579)

zone of maximum performance potential (579)

zone of maximum comfort (579)

proactivity (580)

docility (580)

integrity versus despair (582)

life review (582)

subjective well-being (583)

spiritual support (586)

bridge job (590)

social convoy (593)

socioemotional selectivity (594)

frail older adults (601)

activities of daily living (ADLs) (601)

instrumental activities of daily living (IADLs) (601)

assisted living facilities (603)

intermediate care (603)

skilled nursing care (603)

patronizing speech (605)

infantilization (605)

Learn More About It

Books

ESTES, C. L. (2001). *Social policy and aging: A critical perspective.* Thousand Oaks, CA: Sage. A good overview of the major social policy issues facing the United States.

KIDDER, T. (1993). *Old friends.* Boston: Houghton Mifflin. This engaging book tells the story of two male residents of a nursing home and how they and others deal with everyday life.

MACE, N. L., & RABINS, P. V. (2001). *The 36-hour day: A family guide to caring for persons with Alzheimer disease, related dementing illnesses, and memory loss in later life* (rev. ed.). Baltimore: Johns Hopkins University Press. This is still the best available overall guide to family caregiving for dementia patients.

MOBERG, D. O. (2001). *Aging and spirituality: Spiritual dimensions of aging theory, research, practice and policy.* Binghamton, NY: Haworth Press. This book examines the role that spirituality plays in many older adults' lives. It also offers research-based strategies for practice.

ROTHMAN, R. (2005). *Early bird: A memoir of premature retirement.* New York: Simon & Schuster. Rodney Rothman was a head writer for David Letterman before retiring at age 25 to a retirement community in Florida. The book describes his experiences with, and the stereotypes of, older adult retirees.

Websites

Visit the Human Development book companion website for all URLs.

■ **The Human Development Book Companion Website**

See the book companion website **http://psychology .wadsworth.com/kail_cavanaugh4e/** for practice quiz questions, Internet links, updates, critical thinking exercises, discussion forums, and more. Also accessible from the Wadsworth Psychology Study Center (http://psychology.wadsworth.com).

■ **ElderWeb**

Information on many psychosocial aspects of aging can be found at ElderWeb. The site includes such topics as health care, living arrangements, spiritual support, financial and legal information, and regional resources.

■ **Centers for Medicare and Medicaid Services**

The Centers for Medicare and Medicaid Services site contains much information both for the general public and for professionals interested in more technical background and data. The consumer information section provides a wealth of basic information about how Medicare and Medicaid work and their basic guidelines. In addition, the website provides a superb publication describing in detail the key factors one should use in choosing a nursing home. The booklet gives step-by-step guidelines for what type of facility to consider, important selection factors, nursing home residents' rights, information to collect, and sources of help and other information.

■ **Social Security Administration**

The official website of the Social Security Administration provides information about Social Security including its history, funding sources, statistics on recipients, and plans for the future.

Life-Span CD-ROM

For more information about the concepts covered in this chapter, go to
Module 6: Late Adulthood

• *Emotional and Social Development*

Thomson NOW!

http://www.thomsonedu.com
Go to this site for the link to ThomsonNOW, your one-stop study shop. Take a pre-test for this chapter, and ThomsonNOW will generate a personalized study plan based on your test results. The study plan will identify the topics you need to review and direct you to online resources to help you master those topics. You can then take a post-test to help you determine the concepts you have mastered and what you still need to work on.

16.1 Definitions and Ethical Issues
Sociocultural Definitions of Death
Legal and Medical Definitions
Ethical Issues

■ CURRENT CONTROVERSIES: The Terri Schiavo Case

16.2 Thinking About Death: Personal Aspects
A Life Course Approach to Dying
Dealing With One's Own Death
Death Anxiety
Creating a Final Scenario
The Hospice Option

■ REAL PEOPLE: APPLYING HUMAN DEVELOPMENT: One Family's Experience With Dying

16.3 Surviving the Loss: The Grieving Process
The Grief Process
Normal Grief Reactions
Coping With Grief

■ SPOTLIGHT ON RESEARCH: Grief Processing and Avoidance in the United States and China

Traumatic Grief Reactions

16.4 Dying and Bereavement Experiences Across the Life Span
Childhood
Adolescence
Adulthood
Late Adulthood

Putting It All Together

Summary

Key Terms

Learn More About It

CHAPTER 16

The Final Passage

Dying and Bereavement

We have a paradoxical relationship with death. Sometimes we are fascinated by it. As tourists, we visit places where famous people died or are buried. We watch as television newscasts show people who have been killed in war. But when it comes to pondering our own death or that of people close to us, we have many problems. As French writer and reformer La Rochefoucauld wrote over 300 years ago, looking into the sun is easier than contemplating our death. When death is personal, we become uneasy. Looking at the sun is hard indeed.

In this chapter we first consider definitional and ethical issues surrounding death. Next, we look specifically at the process of dying. Dealing with grief is important for survivors, so we consider this topic in the third section. Finally, we examine how people view death at different points in the life span.

DEFINITIONS AND ETHICAL ISSUES

LEARNING OBJECTIVES

How is death defined?

What legal and medical criteria are used to determine when death occurs?

What are the ethical dilemmas surrounding euthanasia?

Greta, a college sophomore, was very upset when she learned that her roommate's mother had died suddenly. Her roommate is Jewish, and Greta had no idea what customs would be followed during the funeral. When Greta arrived at her roommate's house, she was surprised to find all of the mirrors in the house covered. Greta realized for the first time that death rituals vary in different religious traditions.

WHEN ONE FIRST THINKS ABOUT IT, death seems a very simple concept to define: It is the point at which a person is no longer alive. Similarly, dying is simply the process of making the transition from being alive to being dead. It all seems clear enough, doesn't it? But death and dying are actually far more complicated concepts.

As we will see, Greta's experience reflects the many cultural and religious differences in the definition of death and the customs surrounding it. The meaning of death depends on the observer's perspective, as well as on the specific medical and biological criteria one uses.

SOCIOCULTURAL DEFINITIONS OF DEATH

What comes to mind when you hear the word *death*? A driver killed in a traffic accident? A transition to an eternal reward? Flags at half-staff? A cemetery? A car battery that doesn't work anymore? Each of these possibilities represents a way in which death can be considered in Western culture (Kalish, 1987; Kastenbaum, 1999; Penson, 2004). All cultures have their own views. Among Melanesians, the term *mate* includes the very sick, the very old, and the dead; the term *toa* refers to all other living people (Counts

The symbols we use when people die, such as certain types of floral arrangements, caskets, and the like, provide insights into how cultures think about death.

© A. Ramey/PhotoEdit

The large international public displays of grief at the death of Pope John Paul II shows that death can bring together people from around the world.

Marco Di Lauro/Getty Images

& Counts, 1985). Other South Pacific cultures believe that the life force leaves the body during sleep or illness; sleep, illness, and death are considered together. Thus people "die" several times before experiencing "final death" (Counts & Counts, 1985). The Kwanga of Papua New Guinea believe that most deaths are caused by sorcery (Brison, 1995).

In Ghana people are said to have a "peaceful" or "good" death if the dying person finished all business and made peace with others before death, which implies being at peace with his or her own death (van der Geest, 2004). A good and peaceful death comes "naturally" after a long and well-spent life. Such a death preferably takes place at home, which is the epitome of peacefulness, surrounded by children and grandchildren. Finally, a good death is a death that is accepted by the relatives.

Mourning rituals and states of bereavement also vary in different cultures (Rosenblatt, 2001). There is great variability across cultures in the meaning of death and whether there are rituals or other behaviors to express grief. Some cultures have formalized periods of time during which certain prayers or rituals are performed. For example, after the death of a close relative, Orthodox Jews recite ritual prayers and cover all the mirrors in the house. The men slash their ties as a symbol of loss. These are the customs that Greta, the college student in the vignette, experienced. Ancestor worship, a deep respectful feeling toward individuals from whom a family is descended or who are important to them, is an important part of customs of death in Japanese culture and of Buddhism in Japan (Klass, 1996b). Some cultures, such as the Toraja of Indonesia, do not encourage people to dwell on the dead or memories of them; nevertheless, they still maintain contact with the deceased through dreams (Hollan, 1995). We must keep in mind that the experiences of our culture or particular group may not generalize to other cultures or groups.

Death can be a truly cross-cultural experience. The international outpouring of grief over the death of Pope John Paul II in 2005 and the thousands killed in the terrorist attacks in the United States in September 2001 drew much attention to the ways in which the deaths of people we do not know personally can still affect us. It is at these times we realize that death happens to us all and that death can simultaneously be personal and public.

Altogether, death can be viewed in at least 10 ways (Kalish, 1987; Kastenbaum, 1985). Look at the list that follows and think about the examples given for these definitions. Then take another moment to think up additional examples of your own.

**DEATH AS AN IMAGE
OR OBJECT**

A flag at half-staff

Sympathy cards

Tombstone

Black crepe paper

Monument or memorial

DEATH AS A STATISTIC

Mortality rates

Number of AIDS patients who die

Murder and suicide rates

Life expectancy tables

DEATH AS AN EVENT

Funeral

Family gathering

Memorial service

Viewing or wake

DEATH AS A STATE OF BEING

Time of waiting

Nothingness

Being happy with God all the time

State of being; pure energy

DEATH AS AN ANALOGY

Dead as a doornail

Dead-letter box

Dead-end street

You're dead meat

In the dead of winter

DEATH AS A MYSTERY

What is it like to die?

Will we meet family?

What happens after death?

Will I learn everything when I die?

DEATH AS A BOUNDARY

How many years do I have left?

What happens to my family?

What do I do now?

You can't come back.

**DEATH AS A THIEF
OF MEANING**

I feel so cheated.

Why should I go on living?

Life doesn't mean much anymore.

I have much left to do.

DEATH AS FEAR AND ANXIETY

Will dying be painful?

I worry about my family.

I'm afraid to die.

Who will care for the kids?

**DEATH AS REWARD
OR PUNISHMENT**

Live long and prosper

The wicked go to hell

Heaven awaits the just

Purgatory prepares you for heaven

The many ways of viewing death can be seen in various customs involving funerals. You may have experienced a range of different types of funeral customs, from very small, private services to very elaborate rituals. Variations in the customs surrounding death are reflected in some of the oldest monuments on earth, such as the pyramids in Egypt, and some of the most beautiful, such as the Taj Mahal in India.

LEGAL AND MEDICAL DEFINITIONS

Sociocultural approaches help us understand the different ways in which people view death. But they do not address a very fundamental question: How do we determine that someone has died? The medical and legal communities have grappled with this question for centuries and continue to do so today. Let's see what the current answers are.

Determining when death occurs has always been subjective. *For hundreds of years, people accepted and applied the criteria that now define* **clinical death**: *lack of heartbeat and respiration. Today, however, the most widely accepted criteria are those that character-ize* **whole-brain death.** In 1981 the President's Commission for the Ethical Study of Problems in Medicine and Biomedical and Behavioral Research established several cri-teria still used today that must be met for the determination of whole-brain death:

1. No spontaneous movement in response to any stimuli

2. No spontaneous respirations for at least one hour

3. Total lack of responsiveness to even the most painful stimuli

4. No eye movements, blinking, or pupil responses

5. No postural activity, swallowing, yawning, or vocalizing

6. No motor reflexes

7. A flat electroencephalogram (EEG) for at least 10 minutes

8. No change in any of these criteria when they are tested again 24 hours later

For a person to be declared dead, all eight criteria must be met. Moreover, other conditions that might mimic death—such as deep coma, hypothermia, or drug overdose—must be ruled out. Finally, according to most hospitals, the lack of brain activity must occur both in the brainstem, which involves vegetative functions such as heartbeat and respiration, and in the cortex, which involves higher processes such as thinking. In the United States all 50 states and the District of Columbia use the whole-brain standard to define death.

*It is possible for a person's cortical functioning to cease while brainstem activity continues; this is a **persistent vegetative state,** from which the person does not recover.* This condition can occur following disruption of the blood flow to the brain, a severe head injury, or a drug overdose. Persistent vegetative state allows for spontaneous heartbeat and respiration, but not for consciousness. The whole-brain standard does not permit a declaration of death for someone who is in a persistent vegetative state. Because of conditions like persistent vegetative state, family members sometimes face difficult ethical decisions concerning care for the individual. These issues are the focus of the next section.

Some philosophers and scientists argue that the whole-brain standard does not go far enough because they define those aspects that make us "human" as functions of the cortex, not the brainstem (e.g., Capron, 2001; Truog, 2004). They advocate a *higher-brain* standard, according to which death is the irreversible cessation of the capacity for consciousness. This standard is often met prior to whole-brain death. Thus, a patient in a permanent coma or persistent vegetative state meets the higher-brain, but not the whole-brain, standard of death.

ETHICAL ISSUES

An ambulance screeches to a halt, and emergency personnel rush a woman into the emergency room. As a result of an accident at a swimming pool, she has no pulse and no respiration. Working rapidly, the trauma team reestablishes a heartbeat through electric shock. A respirator is connected. An EEG and other tests reveal extensive and irreversible brain damage. What should be done?

*This is an example of the kinds of problems faced in the field of **bioethics,** the study of the interface between human values and technological advances in health and life sciences.* Bioethics grew from two bases: respect for individual freedom and the impossibility of establishing any single version of morality by rational argument or common sense. Both of these bases are increasingly based on empirical evidence (Borry, Schotsmans, & Dierickx, 2005). In practice, bioethics emphasizes the minimization of harm over the maximization of good, and the importance of individual choice. That is, bioethics requires people to weigh how much the patient will benefit from a treatment relative to the amount of suffering he or she will endure as a result of the treatment.

*In the arena of death and dying, the most important bioethical issue is **euthanasia**— the practice of ending life for reasons of mercy.* The moral dilemma posed by euthanasia becomes apparent when we try to decide the circumstances under which a person's life should be ended. In our society this dilemma occurs most often when a person is being kept alive by machines or when someone is suffering from a terminal illness.

Active Euthanasia

Euthanasia can be carried out in two different ways: active and passive. *__Active euthanasia__ involves the deliberate ending of someone's life, which may be based on a clear statement of the person's wishes or be a decision made by someone else who has the legal authority to* *do so.* Usually, this involves situations in which people are in a persistent vegetative state or suffer from the end stages of a terminal disease. Examples of active euthanasia would be administering a drug overdose, disconnecting a life-support system, or ending a person's life through so-called mercy killing.

Most Americans favor such actions as disconnecting life support in situations involving patients in a persistent vegetative state, but feelings also run strongly against it for religious or other reasons (Benson, 1999). Similarly, Israelis hold a range of opinions (Leichtentritt & Rettig, 2000), as do Germans (Oehmichen & Meissner, 2000). A Swedish study showed that better education about palliative care (care aimed at pain management) options reduced the number of requests for active euthanasia (Valverius, Nilstun, & Nilsson, 2000). A systematic survey of laypersons and health care professionals in the Netherlands and Belgium found that most laypeople and health care professionals said that they would support euthanasia under certain specific conditions (Teisseyre, Mullet, & Sorum, 2005). Respondents assigned most importance to patients' specific requests for it and supported these requests; they did not view patients' willingness to donate organs as an acceptable reason to request euthanasia.

Dr. Jack Kevorkian's controversial approach to physician-assisted suicide resulted in his conviction for murder.

The most controversial version of active euthanasia involves physician-assisted suicide. Dr. Jack Kevorkian, a physician in Michigan who was convicted of murder in 1999 for assisting in a patient's suicide broadcast on the TV news show *60 Minutes,* is a strong proponent of the right to die who created a suicide machine to help people end their lives. Dr. Kevorkian's actions do not reflect mainstream thought on the subject, but they brought attention to the issue.

Taking one's own life has never been popular in the United States due to religious and other prohibitions. In other cultures, such as Japan, suicide is viewed as an honorable way to die under certain circumstances. Asian Americans have the highest suicide rate in the United States, and their suicide notes are more likely to reveal that they felt they were a burden on their families (Pascual, 2000). Nationwide, about half (45 to 59% depending on the survey) of Americans in most ethnic groups support physician-assisted suicide and the Oregon Death With Dignity law (Benson, 1999; Braun, Tanji, & Heck, 2001), but there is less support among Americans of Filipino and Hawaiian ancestry (Braun et al., 2001).

Several countries—including Switzerland, Belgium, and Colombia—tolerate physician-assisted suicide but do not have official policies about it. In 1984 the Dutch Supreme Court eliminated prosecution of physicians who assist in suicide if five criteria are met:

1. The patient's condition is intolerable with no hope for improvement.
2. No relief is available.
3. The patient is competent.
4. The patient makes a request repeatedly over time.
5. Two physicians must review the case and agree with the patient's request.

The Dutch Parliament approved the policy in April 2001, making the Netherlands the first country to have an official policy legalizing physician-assisted suicide (Deutsch, 2001).

Voters in Oregon passed the Death With Dignity Act in 1994, the first physician-assisted suicide law in the United States. This law makes it legal for people to request a lethal dose of medication if they have a terminal disease and make the request voluntarily. Although the U.S. Supreme Court ruled in two cases in 1997 (*Vacco v. Quill* and *Washington v. Glucksberg*) that there is no right to assisted suicide, the court decided in 1998 not to overturn the Oregon law.

The Oregon law is more restrictive than the law in the Netherlands (Deutsch, 2001). The Oregon law requires that a physician inform the person that he or she is terminally ill and describe alternative options (e.g., hospice care, pain control), and the person must be mentally competent and make two oral requests and a written one, with at least 15 days between each oral request. Such provisions are included to ensure that people making the request fully understand the issues and that the request is not made hastily.

Several studies have examined the impact of the Oregon law. In the first 7 years in which the law was in effect (1997–2004), 208 people took lethal medications (Oregon Department of Human Services, 2005). In a direct comparison between the 69 Kevorkian cases and the first 43 Oregon cases, a key difference emerged: only 25% of the individuals were terminally ill in the Kevorkian cases, whereas all individuals in the Oregon cases were (Roscoe et al., 2001). Other comprehensive reviews of the implementation of the Oregon law conclude that all safeguards appear to be working and that such things as depression, coercion, and misunderstanding of the law are carefully screened (Orentlicher, 2000). Available data also indicate that Oregon's law has psychological benefits for patients, who are comforted by knowing they have this option (Cerminara & Perez, 2000).

There is no question that the debate over physician-assisted suicide has only begun. As the technology to keep people alive continues to improve, the ethical issues about active euthanasia in general and physician-assisted suicide in particular will continue to get more complex.

Passive Euthanasia

A second form of euthanasia, **passive euthanasia,** *involves allowing a person to die by withholding available treatment.* For example, chemotherapy might be withheld from a cancer patient; a surgical procedure might not be performed; or food could be withdrawn. Again, these approaches are controversial. For example, Garrard and Wilkinson (2005) point out that the idea of passive euthanasia was attacked in February 2001 in a particularly clear and explicit way by an "Ethics Task Force" established by the European Association of Palliative Care (EAPC). The EAPC Task Force claims that the expression "passive euthanasia" is a contradiction in terms because any ending of a life is by definition active. Despite these concerns, Garrard and Wilkinson (2005) conclude that there is really no reason to abandon the category provided that it is properly and narrowly understood and provided that "euthanasia reasons" for withdrawing or withholding life-prolonging treatment are carefully distinguished from other reasons, such as family members not wanting to wait to divide the patient's estate.

At a practical level, passive euthanasia can be viewed in at least two ways. On one hand, few would argue with a decision not to treat a newly discovered cancer in a person in the late stages of Alzheimer's disease if treatment would do nothing but prolong and make even more agonizing an already certain death. Indeed, a survey in England revealed that caregivers agreed that treatments could and should be withheld from dementia patients in the case of critical physical conditions (Tadros & Salib, 2001). On the other hand, many people might argue against withholding nourishment from a terminally ill person; indeed, such cases often end up in court. The first high-profile legal case involving passive euthanasia in the United States was brought to the courts in 1990; the U.S. Supreme Court took up the case of Nancy Cruzan, whose family wanted to end her forced feeding. The court ruled that unless clear and incontrovertible evidence is presented that an individual desires to have nourishment stopped, such as through a durable power of attorney or living will, a third party, such as a parent or partner, cannot decide to end it.

To date, the most widely publicized and politicized case of passive euthanasia involved Terri Schiavo, who died in Florida in 2005. This extremely controversial case involving the withdrawal of forced feeding had its origins in a disagreement between Terri's husband Michael, who said that Terri would have wanted to die with dignity and therefore the feeding tube should be removed, and her parents, who argued the oppo-

THINK ABOUT IT

How do sociocultural forces shape attitudes about euthanasia?

site. The debate resulted in government officials, state and federal legislators, and courts getting involved. As discussed in the Current Controversies feature, such cases reveal the difficult legal, medical, and ethical issues as well as the high degree of emotion surrounding the topic of euthanasia and death with dignity.

CURRENT CONTROVERSIES

THE TERRI SCHIAVO CASE

On February 25, 1990, 26-year-old Terri Schiavo collapsed in her home from a possible potassium imbalance caused by an eating disorder, temporarily stopping her heart and cutting off oxygen to her brain. On March 31, 2005, Terri Schiavo died after her feeding tube had been removed 13 days earlier. On these two points everyone connected with Terri's case agreed. But on all other essential aspects of it, Terri's husband Michael and Terri's parents deeply disagreed.

The central point of disagreement was Terri's medical condition. Terri's husband and numerous physicians argued that she was in a persistent vegetative state. Based on this diagnosis, Michael Schiavo requested that Terri's feeding tube be withdrawn and that she be allowed to die with dignity in the way he asserted she would have wanted to.

Terri's parents and some other physicians said she was not in a persistent vegetative state, and that she was capable of recognizing them and others. Based on this diagnosis, their belief that Terri would not want the intervention stopped, and their contention that pas-

sive euthanasia is morally wrong, they fought Michael's attempts to remove the feeding tube.

What made this case especially difficult was that Terri left no written instructions that would have clearly stated her thoughts and intentions on the issue. So the ensuing legal and political debates became based on what various people thought Terri would have wanted, as well as reflecting various aspects of people's positions on personal rights regarding life and death.

The legal and political battles began in 1993, when Terri's parents tried unsuccessfully to have Michael removed as Terri's guardian. But the most heated aspects of the case began in 2000, when a circuit court judge ruled that Terri's feeding tube could be removed based on his belief that she had told Michael that she would not have wanted it. In April 2001 the feeding tube was removed after state courts and the U.S. Supreme Court refused to hear the case. However, the tube was reinserted 2 days later when another judge ordered it. In November 2002 the original circuit court judge ruled that Terri had no hope of recovery and again ordered the tube removed, an order eventually carried out in October 2003. Within a week, however, Florida Governor Jeb Bush signed a bill passed by the Florida legislature requiring that the tube be reinserted. This law was ruled unconstitutional by the Florida Supreme Court in September 2004. In February 2005 the original circuit court judge again ordered

the tube removed. On March 16 to 27, the Florida House introduced and passed a bill that would have required the tube be reinserted, but the Florida Senate defeated a somewhat different version of the bill. On March 19 to 21, bills that would have allowed a federal court to review the case passed in the U.S. House of Representatives and the U.S. Senate, but the two versions could not be reconciled. Over the next 10 days, the Florida Supreme Court, the U.S. district court, and a U.S. circuit court refused to hear the case, as did the U.S. Supreme Court. The original circuit court judge rejected a final attempt by Terri's parents to get the tube reinserted.

As long and complex as the legal and political issues were, the public debate on the case was as well. On the positive side, the legal and political complexities dramatically illustrated the need for people to reflect on end-of-life issues and to make their wishes known to family members and others (e.g., health care providers) in writing. The case also brought to light the high cost of long-term care, the difficulties in actually determining whether someone is in a persistent vegetative state and in turn what that implies about life, the tough moral and ethical issues surrounding the withdrawal of nutrition, and the individual's personal feelings about death.

Should Terri Schiavo's feeding tube have been removed? Every answer to this question stirs strong personal emotions, and this case will remain a watershed event for people on all sides of the debate about dying with dignity. That a state governor, state legislators, national legislators, the U.S. president, other elected and government officials, and numerous judges all became directly involved in the case demonstrates that passive euthanasia generates intense feelings and will remain an extremely controversial issue for years to come.

The legal and political debate over the removal of Terri Schiavo's feeding tube raised people's awareness of the need to make one's wishes about end-of-life issues known in writing.

Making Your Intentions Known

As has been clearly shown, euthanasia raises complex legal, political, and ethical issues. In most jurisdictions, euthanasia is legal only when a person has made known his or her wishes concerning medical intervention. Unfortunately, many people fail to take this step, perhaps because it is difficult to think about such situations or because they do not know the options available to them. But without clear directions, medical personnel may be unable to take a patient's preferences into account.

There are two ways to make one's intentions known: a living will, in which a person simply states his or her wishes about life support and other treatments, and durable power of attorney (Figure 16.1), in which an individual appoints someone to act as his or her agent. A major purpose of both is to make one's wishes known about the use of life support in the event that the person is unconscious or otherwise incapable of expressing them, along with other related end-of-life issues such as organ transplantation and other health care options (Rosenfeld, 2004). A durable power of attorney has an additional advantage: It names an individual who has the legal authority to speak for the

■ **Figure 16.1**
A durable power of attorney, like the one shown here, is a way to make your end-of-life wishes known to others.

California Medical Association
DURABLE POWER OF ATTORNEY FOR HEALTH CARE DECISIONS
(California Probate Code Sections 4600-4753)

WARNING TO PERSON EXECUTING THIS DOCUMENT

This is an important legal document. Before executing this document, you should know these important facts:

This document gives the person you designate as your agent (the attorney-in-fact) the power to make health care decisions for you. Your agent must act consistently with your desires as stated in this document or otherwise made known.

Except as you otherwise specify in this document, this document gives your agent power to consent to your doctor not giving treatment or stopping treatment necessary to keep you alive.

Notwithstanding this document, you have the right to make medical and other health care decisions for yourself so long as you can give informed consent with respect to the particular decision. In addition, no treatment may be given to you over your objection, and health care necessary to keep you alive may not be stopped or withheld if you object at the time.

This document gives your agent authority to consent, to refuse to consent, or to withdraw consent to any care, treatment, service, or procedure to maintain, diagnose, or treat a physical or mental condition. This power is subject to any statement of your desires and any limitations that you include in this document. You may

state in this document any types of treatment that you do not desire. In addition, a court can take away the power of your agent to make health care decisions for you if your agent (1) authorizes anything that is illegal, (2) acts contrary to your known desires or (3) where your desires are not known, does anything that is clearly contrary to your best interests.

This power will exist for an indefinite period of time unless you limit its duration in this document.

You have the right to revoke the authority of your agent by notifying your agent or your treating doctor, hospital, or other health care provider orally or in writing of the revocation.

Your agent has the right to examine your medical records and to consent to their disclosure unless you limit this right in this document.

Unless you otherwise specify in this document, this document gives your agent the power after you die to (1) authorize an autopsy, (2) donate your body or parts thereof for transplant or therapeutic or educational or scientific purposes, and (3) direct the disposition of your remains.

If there is anything in this document that you do not understand, you should ask a lawyer to explain it to you.

1. CREATION OF DURABLE POWER OF ATTORNEY FOR HEALTH CARE

By this document I intend to create a durable power of attorney by appointing the person designated below to make health care decisions for me as allowed by Sections 4600 to 4753, inclusive, of the California Probate Code. This power of attorney shall not be affected by my subsequent incapacity. I hereby revoke any prior durable power of attorney for health care. I am a California resident who is at least 18 years old, of sound mind, and acting of my own free will.

2. APPOINTMENT OF HEALTH CARE AGENT

(Fill in below the name, address and telephone number of the person you wish to make health care decisions for you if you become incapacitated. You should make sure that this person agrees to accept this responsibility. The following may not serve as your agent: (1) your treating health care provider; (2) an operator of a community care facility or residential care facility for the elderly; or (3) an employee of your treating health care provider, a community care facility, or a residential care facility for the elderly, unless that employee is related to you by blood, marriage or adoption, or unless you are also an employee of the same treating provider or facility. If you are a conservatee under the Lanterman-Petris-Short Act (the law governing involuntary commitment to a mental health facility) and you wish to appoint your conservator as your agent, you must consult a lawyer, who must sign and attach a special declaration for this document to be valid.)

I, _____, hereby appoint:
           (insert your name)

Name _____

Address _____

Work Telephone (_____) _____ Home Telephone (_____) _____

as my agent (attorney-in-fact) to make health care decisions for me as authorized in this document. I understand that this power of attorney will be effective for an indefinite period of time unless I revoke it or limit its duration below.

(Optional) This power of attorney shall expire on the following date: _____

© California Medical Association 1996 (revised)

person if necessary. Although there is considerable support for both mechanisms, there are several problems as well. Many people fail to inform their relatives and physicians about their health care decisions. Others do not tell the person named in a durable power of attorney where the document is kept. Obviously, this puts relatives at a serious disadvantage if decisions concerning the use of life-support systems need to be made.

A living will or a durable power of attorney can be the basis for a "Do Not Resuscitate" (DNR) medical order. A DNR order applies only to cardiopulmonary resuscitation should one's heart and breathing stop. In the normal course of events, a medical team will immediately try to restore normal heartbeat and respiration. With a DNR order, this treatment is not done. As with living wills and durable powers of attorney, it is very important to let all appropriate medical personnel know that a DNR order is desired.

TEST YOURSELF

1. The phrase "dead as a doornail" is an example of the sociocultural definition of death as _____.
2. The difference between brain death and a persistent vegetative state is _____.
3. Withholding an antibiotic from a person who dies as a result is an example of _____.

Describe how people at each level of Kohlberg's theory of moral reasoning (described in Chapter 8) would deal with the issue of euthanasia.

Answers: (1) an analogy, (2) the brainstem still functions in a persistent vegetative state, (3) passive euthanasia

---

16.2

THINKING ABOUT DEATH: PERSONAL ASPECTS

LEARNING OBJECTIVES

How do feelings about death change over adulthood?

———

How do people deal with their own death?

———

What is death anxiety, and how do people show it?

———

How do people deal with end-of-life issues and create a final scenario?

———

What is hospice?

Jean is a 72-year-old woman who was diagnosed with advanced colon cancer recently. She has vivid memories of her father dying a long, protracted death in great pain. Jean is very afraid that she will suffer the same fate. She has heard that the hospice in town emphasizes pain management and provides a lot of support for families. Jean wonders whether that is something she should explore in the time she has left.

LIKE JEAN, most people are uncomfortable thinking about their own death, especially if they think it will be unpleasant. As one research participant put it, "You are nuts if you aren't afraid of death" (Kalish & Reynolds, 1976). Still, death is a paradox, as we noted at the beginning of the chapter. That is, we are afraid of or anxious about death, but we are drawn to it, sometimes in very public ways. We examine this paradox at the personal level in this section. Specifically, we focus on two questions: How do people's feelings about death differ with age? What is it about death that we fear or that makes us anxious?

Before proceeding, however, take a few minutes to complete the following exercise.

A SELF-REFLECTIVE EXERCISE ON DEATH

1. In 200 words or less, write your own obituary. Be sure to include your age and cause of death. List your lifetime accomplishments. Don't forget to list your survivors.

2. Think about all the things you will have done that are not listed in your obituary. List some of them.

3. Think of all the friends you will have made and how you will have affected them.

4. Would you make any changes in your obituary now?

A LIFE COURSE APPROACH TO DYING

How do you feel about dying? Do you think people of different ages feel the same way? It probably doesn't surprise you to learn that feelings about dying vary across adulthood. Because young adults are just beginning to pursue the family, career, and personal goals they have set, they tend to be more intense in their feelings toward death. If you were to ask young adults who are at a funeral how they feel about death, they would be likely to report a strong sense that those who die at this point in their lives would be cheated out of their future (Attig, 1996).

Dealing with the death of a friend is often difficult for young adults.

Although not specifically addressed in research, the shift from formal operational thinking to postformal thinking (see Chapter 10) could be important in young adults' contemplation of death. Presumably, this shift in cognitive development is accompanied by a lessening of the feeling of immortality as young adults begin to integrate personal feelings and emotions with their thinking.

Midlife is the time when most people confront the death of their parents. Up until that point, people tend not to think much about their own death; the fact that their parents are still alive buffers them from reality. After all, in the normal course of events, our parents are supposed to die before we do.

Once their parents have died, people realize that they are now the oldest generation of their family—the next in line to die. Reading the obituary pages, they are reminded of this, as the ages of many of the people who have died get closer and closer to their own.

Probably as a result of this growing realization of their own mortality, middle-aged adults' sense of time undergoes a subtle yet profound change. It changes from an emphasis on how long they have already lived to how long they have left to live (Attig, 1996; Neugarten, 1969). This may lead to occupational change or other redirection such as improving relationships that had deteriorated over the years.

In general, older adults are less anxious about death and more accepting of it than any other age group (Kastenbaum, 1999; Keller, Sherry, & Piotrowski, 1984). In part, this results from the achievement of ego integrity, as described in Chapter 15. For many older adults, the joy of living is diminishing (Kalish, 1987). More than any other group, they have experienced loss of family and friends and have come to terms with their own mortality. Older adults have more chronic diseases, which are not likely to go away. They may feel that their most important life tasks have been completed (Kastenbaum, 1999).

Understanding how adults deal with death and their consequent feelings of grief is best approached from the perspective of attachment theory (Field, Gao, & Paderna, 2005; Stroebe, Schut, & Stroebe, 2005). In this view, a person's reactions are a natural consequence of forming attachments and then losing them. We consider adult grief a bit later in the chapter.

DEALING WITH ONE'S OWN DEATH

Thinking about death from an observer's perspective is one thing. Thinking about one's own death, like Jean is doing, is quite another. The reactions people have to their own impending death, long thought to be the purview of religion and philosophy, were not researched until well into the 20th century.

■ **Figure 16.2**
Some fatal diseases, such as lung cancer, have a clear decline phase, whereas others, such as congestive heart failure, do not.

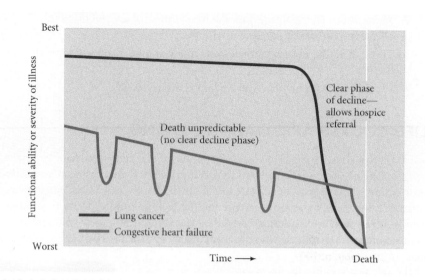

Skolnick, A. A. (1998). MediCaring project to demonstrate and evaluate innovative end-of-life program for chronically ill. *Journal of the American Medical Association, 279*, 1511–1512. Reprinted with permission of American Medical Association.

Many authors have tried to describe the dying process, often using the metaphor of a trajectory that captures both the duration of time between the onset of dying (e.g., from the diagnosis of a fatal disease) and death and the course of the dying process (Wilkinson & Lynn, 2001). These dying trajectories vary a great deal across diseases, as illustrated in Figure 16.2. Some diseases, such as lung cancer, have a clear and rapid period of decline; this "terminal phase" is often used to determine eligibility for certain services (e.g., hospice, discussed later). Other diseases, such as congestive heart failure, have no clear terminal phase; any significant health event could cause death. The two approaches of describing the dying process that we will consider try to account for both types of trajectories.

Kübler-Ross's Theory

Elisabeth Kübler-Ross became interested in the experience of dying when she was an instructor in psychiatry at the University of Chicago in the early 1960s. When she began her investigations into the dying process, such research was controversial; her physician colleagues initially were outraged, and some even denied that their patients were terminally ill. Still, she persisted. More than 200 interviews with terminally ill people convinced her that most people experienced several emotional reactions. Using her experiences, she described five reactions that represented the ways in which people dealt with death: denial, anger, bargaining, depression, and acceptance (Kübler-Ross, 1969). Although they were first presented as a sequence, it was subsequently realized that the emotions can overlap and can be experienced in different order.

When people are told that they have a terminal illness, their first reaction is likely to be shock and disbelief. Denial is a normal part of getting ready to die. Some want to shop around for a more favorable diagnosis, and most feel that a mistake has been made. Others try to find assurance in religion. Eventually, though, reality sets in for most people.

At some point, people express anger as hostility, resentment, and envy toward health care workers, family, and friends. People ask, "Why me?" and

Dr. Elisabeth Kübler-Ross revolutionized the study of death and dying.

express a great deal of frustration. The fact that they are going to die when so many others will live seems so unfair. With time and work, most people confront their anger and resolve it.

In the bargaining phase, people look for a way out. Maybe a deal can be struck with someone, perhaps God, that would allow survival. For example, a woman might promise to be a better mother if only she could live. Or a person sets a timetable: "Just let me live until my daughter graduates from college." Eventually, the person becomes aware that these deals will not work.

When one can no longer deny the illness, perhaps because of surgery or pain, feelings of depression are very common. People report feeling deep loss, sorrow, guilt, and shame over their illness and its consequences. Kübler-Ross believes that allowing people to discuss their feelings with others helps move them to an acceptance of death.

In the acceptance stage, the person accepts the inevitability of death and often seems detached from the world and at peace. "It is as if the pain is gone, the struggle is over, and there comes a time for the 'final rest before the journey' as one patient phrased it" (Kübler-Ross, 1969, p. 100).

Although she believes that these five stages represent the typical range of emotional development in the dying, Kübler-Ross (1974) cautions that not everyone experiences all of them or progresses through them at the same rate or in the same order. Research supports the view that her "stages" should not be viewed as a sequence (Neimeyer, 1997). In fact, we could actually harm dying people by considering these stages as fixed and universal. Individual differences are great, as Kübler-Ross points out. Emotional responses may vary in intensity throughout the dying process. Thus the goal in applying Kübler-Ross's theory to real-world settings would be to help people achieve an appropriate death. An appropriate death is one that meets the needs of the dying person, allowing him or her to work out each problem as it comes.

A Contextual Theory of Dying

One of the difficulties with most theories of dying is a general lack of research evaluating them in a wide variety of contexts (Kastenbaum & Thuell, 1995). By their very nature, stages or sequences imply a particular directionality. Stage theories, in particular, emphasize qualitative differences between the various stages. However, the duration of a particular stage, or a specific phase, varies widely from person to person. Such theories assume some sort of underlying process for moving through the stages or phases but do not clearly state what causes a person to move from one to another.

One reason for these problems is the realization that there is no one right way to die, although there may be better or worse ways of coping (Corr, 1991–1992). A perspective that recognizes this realization would approach the issue from the mindset of the dying person and the issues or tasks he or she must face. Corr identified four dimensions of such tasks: bodily needs, psychological security, interpersonal attachments, and spiritual energy and hope. This holistic approach acknowledges individual differences and rejects broad generalizations. Corr's task work approach also recognizes the importance of the coping efforts of family members, friends, and caregivers as well as those of the dying person.

Kastenbaum and Thuell (1995) argue that what is needed is an even broader, contextual approach that takes a more inclusive view of the dying process. They point out that theories must be able to handle people who have a wide variety of terminal illnesses and be sensitive to dying people's own perspectives and values related to death. The socioenvironmental context within which dying occurs, which often changes over time, must be recognized. For example, a person may begin the dying process living independently but end up in a long-term care facility. Such moves may have profound implications for how the person copes with dying. A contextual approach would provide guidance for health care professionals and families for discussing how to protect the quality of life, provide better care, and prepare caregivers for dealing with the end of life. Such an approach would also provide research questions. For example, how does one's acceptance of dying change across various stages?

Frank discussions of end-of-life issues with patients and their families by health care workers provide a better context for handling these issues.

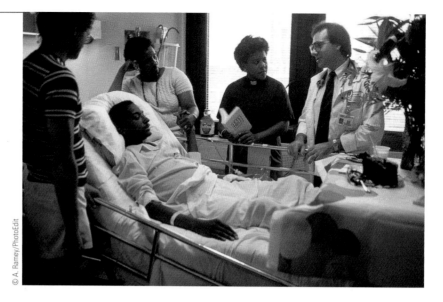

© A. Ramey/PhotoEdit

We do not yet have such a comprehensive theory of dying. But as Kastenbaum and Thuell point out, we can move in that direction by rejecting a reductionistic approach that focuses on set stages for a truly holistic one. One way to accomplish this is to examine people's experiences as a narrative that can be written from many points of view (e.g., the patient, family members, caregivers). What would emerge would be a rich description of a dynamically changing process.

DEATH ANXIETY

We have seen that how people view death varies with age. In the process, we encountered the notion of feeling anxious about death. Death anxiety is tough to pin down; indeed, it is the ethereal nature of death, rather than something about it in particular, that usually makes us feel so uncomfortable. We cannot put our finger on something specific about death that is causing us to feel uneasy. Because of this, we must look for indirect behavioral evidence to document death anxiety. Research findings suggest that death anxiety is a complex, multidimensional construct.

In the late 1990s, researchers began using terror management theory (Pyszczynski, Greenbert, & Solomon, 1997, 1999) as a framework to study death anxiety. *Terror management theory addresses the issue of why people engage in certain behaviors to achieve particular psychological states* (Strachan et al., 2001). The theory proposes that ensuring that one's life continues is the primary motive underlying behavior; all other motives can be traced to this basic one. Additionally, some suggest that older adults present an existential threat for the younger and middle-aged adults because they remind us all that death is inescapable, the body is fallible, and the bases by which we may secure self-esteem (and manage death anxiety) are transitory (Martens, Goldenberg,, & Greenberg, 2005). Thus, death anxiety is a reflection of one's concern over dying, an outcome that would violate the prime motive.

On the basis of several diverse studies using many different measures, researchers conclude that death anxiety consists of several components. Each of these components is most easily described with terms that resemble examples of fear but cannot be tied to anything specific. That is, fear is connected to a specific stimulus (e.g., spiders) but anxiety is nonspecific. Early research indicated that components of death anxiety included pain, body malfunction, humiliation, rejection, nonbeing, punishment, interruption of goals, and negative impact on survivors (Fortner & Neimeyer, 1999). To complicate matters further, any of these components can be assessed at any of three levels: public, private, and nonconscious. That is, what we admit feeling about death in public may differ greatly from what we feel when we are alone with our own thoughts. In short, the measurement of death anxiety is complex, and researchers need to specify which aspects they are assessing.

Much research has been conducted to learn what demographic and personality variables are related to death anxiety. Although the results often are ambiguous, some patterns have emerged. For example, older adults tend to have lower death anxiety than younger adults, perhaps because of their tendency to engage in life review and their higher level of religious motivation (Thorson & Powell, 2000a, 2000b). Lower ego integrity, more physical problems, and more psychological problems are predictive of higher levels of death anxiety in older adults (Fortner & Neimeyer, 1999). Men show greater fear of the unknown than women, who fear the dying process more (Cicirelli, 2001). And few differences have been reported in death anxiety levels across ethnic groups (Cicirelli, 2000).

Strange as it may seem, death anxiety may have a beneficial side. For one thing, being afraid to die means that we often go to great lengths to make sure we stay alive, as argued by terror management theory (Pyszczynski et al., 1997, 1999). Because staying alive helps to ensure the continuation and socialization of the species, fear of death serves as a motivation to have children and raise them properly.

Learning to Deal With Death Anxiety

Although some degree of death anxiety may be appropriate, we must guard against letting it become powerful enough to interfere with our normal daily routines. Several ways exist to help us in this endeavor. Perhaps the one most often used is to live life to the fullest. Kalish (1984, 1987) argues that people who do this enjoy what they have; although they may still fear death and feel cheated, they have few regrets. Adolescents are particularly likely to do this; research shows that teenagers, especially males, engage in risky behavior that is correlated with low death anxiety (Cotter, 2001).

Koestenbaum (1976) proposes several exercises and questions to increase one's death awareness. Some of these are to write your own obituary and plan your own death and funeral services. You can also ask yourself, "What circumstances would help make my death acceptable?" "Is death the sort of thing that could happen to me right now?"

These questions serve as a basis for an increasingly popular way to reduce anxiety: death education. Most death education programs combine factual information about death with issues aimed at reducing anxiety and fear to increase sensitivity to others' feelings. These programs vary widely in orientation; they can include such topics as philosophy, ethics, psychology, drama, religion, medicine, art, and many others. Additionally, they can focus on death, the process of dying, grief and bereavement, or any combination of them. In general, death education programs help primarily by increasing our awareness of the complex emotions felt and expressed by dying people and their families. Research shows that participating in experiential workshops about death significantly lowers death anxiety in younger, middle-aged, and older adults (Abengozar, Bueno, & Vega, 1999).

Engaging in risky, life-threatening behavior is one way that people attempt to overcome death anxiety.

CREATING A FINAL SCENARIO

*When given the chance, many adults would like to discuss a variety of issues, collectively called **end-of-life issues**: management of the final phase of life, after-death disposition of their body and memorial services, and distribution of assets (Kastenbaum, 1999; Kleespies,*

A traditional funeral is one way that people achieve closure with the loss of a loved one.

2004). People want to manage the final part of their lives by thinking through the choices between traditional care (e.g., provided by hospitals and nursing homes) and alternatives (such as hospices, which we discuss in the next section), completing advance directives (e.g., durable power of attorney, living will), resolving key personal relationships, and perhaps choosing the alternative of ending one's life prematurely through euthanasia.

What happens to one's body and how one is memorialized is very important to most people. Is a traditional burial preferred over cremation? A traditional funeral over a memorial service? Such choices often are based in people's religious beliefs and their desire for privacy for their families after they have died.

Making sure that one's estate and personal effects are passed on appropriately often is overlooked. Making a will is especially important in ensuring that one's wishes are carried out. Providing for the informal distribution of personal effects also helps prevent disputes between family members.

Whether people choose to address these issues formally or informally, it is important that they be given the opportunity to do so. In many cases, family members are reluctant to discuss these matters with the dying relative because of their own anxiety about death. *Making such choices known about how they do and do not want their lives to end constitutes a* **final scenario**.

One of the most crucial parts of a final scenario for most people is the process of separation from family and friends (Kastenbaum, 1999). The final days, weeks, and months of life provide opportunities to affirm love, resolve conflicts, and provide peace to dying people. The failure to complete this process often leaves survivors feeling that they did not achieve closure in the relationship, which can result in bitterness toward the deceased.

Health care workers realize the importance of giving dying patients the chance to create a final scenario and recognize the uniqueness of each person's final passage. Any given final scenario reflects the person's personal past, which is the unique combination of the development forces the person experienced. Primary attention is paid to how people's total life experiences have prepared them to face end-of-life issues (Neimeyer, 1997).

One's final scenario helps family and friends interpret one's death, especially when the scenario is constructed jointly, such as between spouses (Byock, 1997; Kastenbaum, 1992). The different perspectives of everyone involved are unlikely to converge without clear communication and discussion. Respecting each person's perspective is key and greatly helps in creating a good final scenario.

Encouraging people to decide for themselves how the end of their lives should be handled has helped people take control of their dying (Wass, 2001). Taking personal control over one's dying process is a trend that is occurring even in cultures like Japan that traditionally defer to physician's opinions (Hayashi et al., 2000). The emergence of final scenarios as an important consideration fits well with the emphasis on addressing pain through palliative care, an approach underlying hospice.

Completing a living will helps communicate your own final scenario.

THE HOSPICE OPTION

As we have seen, most people would like to die at home among family and friends. An important barrier to this choice is the availability of support systems when the person has a terminal disease. In this case

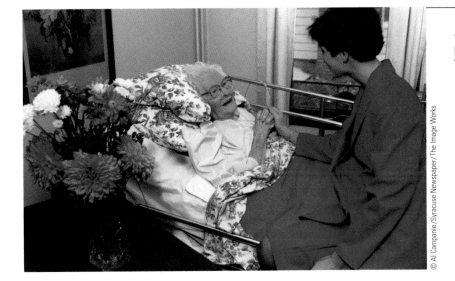

Hospice outpatient health care workers provide help for people with terminal diseases who choose to die at home.

most people believe that they have no choice but to go to a hospital or nursing home. However, another alternative exists. **_Hospice_** *is an approach to assisting dying people that emphasizes pain management, or palliative care, and death with dignity* (Saunders, 1997). The emphasis in a hospice is on the quality of life. This approach grows out of an important distinction between the prolongation of life and the prolongation of death, a distinction that is important to Jean, the woman we met in the vignette. In a hospice the concern is to make the person as peaceful and comfortable as possible, not to delay an inevitable death. Although medical care is available at a hospice, it is aimed primarily at controlling pain and restoring normal functioning. This orientation places hospices between hospitals and one's own home in terms of contexts for dying.

Modern hospices are modeled after St. Christopher's Hospice in England, founded in 1967 by Dr. Cicely Saunders. Hospice services are requested only after the person or physician believes that no treatment or cure is possible, making the hospice program markedly different from hospital or home care. The differences are evident in the principles that underlie hospice care: Clients and their families are viewed as a unit, clients should be kept free of pain, emotional and social impoverishment must be minimal, clients must be encouraged to maintain competencies, conflict resolution and fulfillment of realistic desires must be assisted, clients must be free to begin or end relationships, and staff members must seek to alleviate pain and fear (Saunders, 1997).

Two types of hospices exist: inpatient and outpatient. Inpatient hospices provide all care for clients; outpatient hospices provide services to clients who remain in their own homes. The outpatient variation, in which a hospice nurse visits clients in their home, is becoming increasingly popular, largely because more clients can be served at a lower cost. Having hospice services available to people at home is a viable option for many more people, especially in helping home-based caregivers cope with loss (Grande et al., 2004).

Hospices do not follow a hospital model of care. The role of the staff in a hospice is not so much to treat the client as it is just to be with the client. A client's dignity is always maintained; often more attention is paid to appearance and personal grooming than to medical tests. Hospice staff members also provide a great deal of support to the client's family. The Real People feature provides some insight into one family's experience with a hospice.

REAL PEOPLE: Applying Human Development

ONE FAMILY'S EXPERIENCE WITH DYING

The news from Roseanne's oncologist was predictable, but it still came as a shock to her and her husband, Harry, and two daughters: her cancer had spread and she only had about 3 months to live. At first, the family didn't know what to do. But her oncologist made a suggestion that turned out to be extremely helpful: Roseanne and her family should contact the local hospice for help.

The hospice in Roseanne's city was typical. The nurse who visited the house, along with an entire back-up team, were the most caring people the family had ever met. Far from being in a rush to complete the work-up, the nurse spent a great deal of time asking Roseanne about her pain and how she wanted to manage it, her wishes and desires about her process of dying, and many other

personal topics. This approach made Roseanne and her family feel much at ease. They knew that their feelings mattered and that Roseanne would be cared for well.

As Roseanne's condition deteriorated, the home hospice nurse made sure that her pain medication was adequate to provide physical comfort. Counselors worked with the family to help them discuss their feelings about Roseanne's pending death, and with Roseanne to help her prepare to die. They also explained to the family that should Roseanne die when no one from the hospice was present, to call them first. This would ensure that Roseanne's wishes concerning life support and resuscitation would be honored.

Two and a half months after contacting the hospice, Roseanne died at home, surrounded by her family and the hospice nurse, just as she wanted. Because her pain was well managed, she was comfortable even at the end. Harry's and Roseanne's daughters' grief was made easier through the constant support they received and the counseling they needed.

The hospice staff who worked with Roseanne and her family have the client's physical comfort as their primary goal, followed by supporting the family. The way they helped Roseanne die, and Harry and their daughters to grieve with support, made a very difficult process a bit easier.

Researchers have documented important differences between inpatient hospices and hospitals (Kastenbaum, 1999). Hospice clients are more mobile, less anxious, and less depressed; spouses visit hospice clients more often and participate more in their care; and hospice staff members are perceived as more accessible. In addition, Walsh and Cavanaugh (1984) showed that most hospice clients who were in hospitals before coming to a hospice strongly preferred the care at the hospice. Significant improvements in clients' quality of life have been documented after hospice placement (Cohen et al., 2001).

Although the hospice is a valuable alternative for many people, it may not be appropriate for everyone. Most people who select hospice are suffering from cancer, AIDS, or a progressive neurological condition (most often amyotrophic lateral sclerosis, also known as Lou Gehrig's disease; Kastenbaum, 1999). Other disorders may necessitate treatments or equipment not available at hospices, and some people may find that a hospice does not meet their needs or fit with their personal beliefs. Walsh and Cavanaugh (1984) found that the perceived needs of hospice clients, their families, and the staff did not always coincide. In particular, the staff and family members emphasized pain management, whereas many clients wanted more attention paid to personal issues, such as spirituality and the process of dying. The important point from this study is that the staff and family members may need to ask clients what they need more often rather than making assumptions about what they need.

How do people decide to explore the hospice option? Kastenbaum (1999) lists six key considerations:

- *Is the person completely informed about the nature and prognosis of his or her condition?* Full knowledge and the ability to communicate with health care personnel are essential to understand what hospice has to offer.
- *What options are available at this point in the progress of the person's disease?* Knowing about all available treatment options is critical. Exploring treatment options also requires health care professionals to be aware of the latest approaches and willing to disclose them.
- *What are the person's expectations, fears, and hopes?* Some older adults, like Jean, remember or have heard stories about people who suffered greatly

at the end of their lives. This can produce anxiety about one's own death. Similarly, fears of becoming dependent play an important role in a person's decision making. Discovering and discussing these anxieties helps clarify options.

- *How well do the people in the person's social network communicate with each other?* Talking about death in many families is still taboo (Book, 1996). In others, intergenerational communication is difficult or impossible. Even in families with good communication, the pending death of a loved relative is difficult. As a result, the dying person may have difficulty expressing his or her wishes. The decision to explore the hospice option is best made when it is discussed openly.

- *Are family members available to participate actively in terminal care?* Hospice relies on family members to provide much of the care, which is supplemented by professionals and volunteers. We saw in Chapter 13 that being a primary caregiver can be highly stressful. Having a family member who is willing to accept this responsibility is essential for the hospice option to work.

- *Is a high-quality hospice care program available?* Hospice programs are not uniformly good. As with any health care provider, patients and family members must investigate the quality of local hospice programs before making a choice. The Hospice Foundation of America provides excellent material for evaluating a hospice program (go to the book companion website for the URL for the foundation's home page).

Hospice provides an important end-of-life option for many terminally ill people and their families. Moreover, the supportive follow-up services they provide are often used by surviving family and friends. Most important, the success of the hospice option has had important influences on traditional health care. For example, much discussion occurred in the American Medical Association in 1999 about putting more emphasis on pain management.

Despite the importance of the hospice option for end-of-life decisions, terminally ill older adults cannot benefit from it unless two barriers are overcome (Kastenbaum, 1999): family reluctance to face the reality of terminal illness and participate in the decision-making process; and physician reluctance to approve hospice care for patients until very late in the terminal process, thereby depriving them of the supportive benefits they may have otherwise received.

As the end of life approaches, the most important thing to keep in mind is that the dying person has the right to state-of-the-art approaches to treatment and pain management. Irrespective of the choice of traditional health care or hospice, the wishes of the dying person should be honored, and family members must participate.

[handwritten note in margin: Hospice is not about money]

THINK ABOUT IT

How might the availability of hospices relate to physician-assisted suicide?

TEST YOURSELF

1. _____ are most likely to face the death of their parents.

2. A _____ approach to dying acknowledges individual differences and rejects broad generalizations.

3. The primary framework for studying death anxiety is _____.

4. Making choices known about how people do and do not want their lives to end constitutes a _____.

5. _____ is an approach to assisting dying people that emphasizes pain management, or palliative care, and death with dignity.

Using Erikson's theory as a framework, explain how death anxiety changes from adolescence to late life.

Answers: (1) Middle-aged adults, (2) holistic, (3) terror management theory, (4) final scenario, (5) Hospice

16.3

SURVIVING THE LOSS: THE GRIEVING PROCESS

After 67 years of marriage, Bertha recently lost her husband. At 90, Bertha knew that neither she nor her husband was likely to live much longer, but the death was a shock just the same. Bertha thinks about him much of the time and often finds herself making decisions on the basis of "what John would have done" in the same situation.

EACH OF US SUFFERS MANY LOSSES over a lifetime. Whenever we lose someone close to us through death or other separation, like Bertha we experience bereavement, grief, and mourning. **Bereavement** *is the state or condition caused by loss through death.* **Grief** *is the sorrow, hurt, anger, guilt, confusion, and other feelings that arise after suffering a loss.* **Mourning** *concerns the ways in which we express our grief.* For example, you can tell that people in some cultures are bereaved and in mourning because of the clothing they wear. Mourning is highly influenced by culture. For some, mourning may involve wearing black, attending funerals, and observing an official period of grief; for others, it means drinking, wearing white, and marrying the deceased spouse's sibling. Grief corresponds to the emotional reactions following loss, whereas mourning is the culturally approved behavioral manifestations of those feelings. Even though mourning rituals may be fairly standard within a culture, how people grieve varies, as we see next. We will also see how Bertha's reactions are fairly typical of most people.

In some cultures, wearing certain types of clothing indicates that the person is in a period of mourning the loss of a loved one.

THE GRIEF PROCESS

How do people grieve? What do they experience? Perhaps you already have a good idea about the answers to these questions from your own experience. If so, you already know that the process of grieving is a complicated and personal one. Just as there is no right way to die, there is no right way to grieve. Recognizing that there are plenty of individual differences, we consider these patterns in this section.

The grieving process is often described as reflecting many themes and issues that people confront (Attig, 1996; Stroebe et al., 1996). Like the process of dying, grieving does not have clearly demarcated stages through which we pass in a neat sequence. When someone close to us dies, we must reorganize our lives, establish new patterns of behavior, and redefine relationships with family and friends. Indeed, Attig (1996) considers grief to be the process by which we relearn the world.

Unlike bereavement, over which we have no control, grief is a process that involves choices in coping (Attig, 1996). From this perspective, grief is an active process in which a person must do several things (Worden, 1991):

- *Acknowledge the reality of the loss.* We must overcome the temptation to deny the reality of our loss, fully and openly acknowledge it, and realize that it affects every aspect of our life.
- *Work through the emotional turmoil.* We must find effective ways to confront and express the complete range of emotions we feel after the loss and must not avoid or repress them.
- *Adjust to the environment where the deceased is absent.* We must define new patterns of living that adjust appropriately and meaningfully to the fact that the deceased is not present.

■ *Loosen ties to the deceased.* We must free ourselves from the bonds of the deceased in order to reengage with our social network. This means finding effective ways to say good-bye.

The notion that grief is an active coping process emphasizes that survivors must come to terms with the physical world of things, places, and events, as well as our spiritual place in the world; the interpersonal world of interactions with family and friends, the dead, and, in some cases, God; and aspects of our inner selves and our personal experiences (Attig, 1996). Bertha, the woman in the vignette, is in the middle of this process. Even the matter of deciding what to do with the deceased's personal effects can be part of this active coping process (Attig, 1996).

In considering the grief process, we must avoid making several mistakes. First, grieving is a highly individual experience. The process that works well for one person may not be the best for someone else. Second, we must not underestimate the amount of time people need to deal with the various issues. To a casual observer, it may appear that a survivor is "back to normal" after a few weeks. Actually, it takes much longer to resolve the complex emotional issues that are faced during bereavement (Attig, 1996; Stroebe et al., 1996). Researchers and therapists alike agree that a person needs at least 1 year following the loss to begin recovery, and 2 years is not uncommon. Finally, "recovery" may be a misleading term. It is probably more accurate to say that we learn to live with our loss rather than that we recover from it (Attig, 1996). The impact of the loss of a loved one lasts a very long time, perhaps for the rest of one's life. Recognizing these aspects of grief makes it easier to know what to say and do for bereaved people. Among the most useful things are to simply let the person know that you are sorry for his or her loss, that you are there for support, and mean what you say.

Going through the personal effects of a loved one after he or she has died can be a difficult process for survivors.

Risk Factors in Grief

Bereavement is a life experience that most people have many times, and most people eventually handle it. However, there are some risk factors that may make bereavement much more difficult. Several of the more important are the mode of death, personal factors (e.g., personality, religiosity, age, gender), and interpersonal context (social support, kinship relationship; W. Stroebe & Schut, 2001).

Most people believe that the circumstances or mode of death affects the grief process. A person whose family member was killed in an automobile accident has a different situation to deal with than a person whose family member died after a long period with Alzheimer's disease. It is believed that when death is anticipated, people go through a period of anticipatory grief before the death that supposedly serves to buffer the impact of the loss when it does come, as well as facilitating recovery (Attig, 1996). However, the research evidence for this is mixed. Some studies find that sudden loss increases the likelihood of problems, whereas other studies have found that anticipating the death of someone close produces considerable stress in itself (Attig, 1996; W. Stroebe & Schut, 2001). Other research reveals a more complex outcome. Some caregivers of Alzheimer's patients, for example, show a decline in feelings of anticipatory grief during the middle stages of caregiving, only to have these feelings increase in intensity later (Ponder & Pomeroy, 1996). Other caregivers simply show higher levels of anticipatory grief regardless of other factors (Mcrae, 2005).

The strength of attachment to the deceased person does make a difference. When the deceased person was one with whom the survivor had a strong and close attachment, and the loss was sudden, greater grief is experienced (Wayment & Vierthaler, 2002). However, such secure attachment styles tend to result in less depression after the loss due to less guilt over unresolved issues (because there are fewer of them), things not provided (because more were likely provided), and so on.

Few studies of personal risk factors have been done, and few firm conclusions can be drawn. To date there are no consistent findings regarding personality traits that either help buffer people from the effects of bereavement or exacerbate them (W. Stroebe & Schut, 2001). There is some evidence to suggest that church attendance helps people deal with bereavement 13 to 18 months after the loss (Nolen-Hoeksema & Larson, 1999), but this effect may be due more to the social support such people receive than to religion per se (W. Stroebe & Schut, 2001). There are, however, consistent findings regarding gender. Men have higher mortality rates following bereavement than women, who have higher rates of depression than men, but the reasons for these differences are unclear (W. Stroebe & Schut, 2001). Research also consistently shows that younger people suffer more health consequences following bereavement than do older people, with the impact perhaps being strongest for middle-aged adults (Nolen-Hoeksema & Larson, 1999; W. Stroebe & Schut, 2001).

Two interpersonal risk factors have been examined: lack of social support and kinship. Studies indicate that social support helps buffer the effects of bereavement more for older adults than for middle-aged adults (Stroebe & Schut, 1999; W. Stroebe & Schut, 2001). The type of kinship relationship involved in the loss matters a great deal. Research consistently shows that the loss of a child is the most difficult, followed by loss of a spouse or partner and parent (Leahy, 1993; Nolen-Hoeksema & Larson, 1999).

THINK ABOUT IT

How are risk factors in grief influenced by sociocultural factors?

NORMAL GRIEF REACTIONS

The feelings experienced during grieving are intense, which not only makes it difficult to cope but can also make a person question her or his own reactions. The feelings involved usually include sadness, denial, anger, loneliness, and guilt. A summary of these feelings is presented in the following list (Vickio, Cavanaugh, & Attig, 1990). Take a minute to read through them to see whether they agree with what you expected.

Disbelief	Denial	Shock
Sadness	Anger	Hatred
Guilt	Fear	Anxiety
Confusion	Helplessness	Emptiness
Loneliness	Acceptance	Relief
Happiness	Lack of enthusiasm	Absence of emotion

Many authors refer to the psychological side of coming to terms with bereavement as **grief work.** This notion fits well with the earlier discussion of grief as active coping (Attig, 1996). Even without personal experience of the death of close family members, people recognize the need to give survivors time to deal with their many feelings. One study asked college students to describe the feelings they thought were typically experienced by a person who had lost particular loved ones (such as a parent, child, sibling, or friend). The students were well aware of the need for grief work, recognized the need for at least a year to do it, and were very sensitive to the range of emotions and behaviors demonstrated by the bereaved (Vickio et al., 1990).

Muller (2002) examined people's experience of grief in a detailed interview study and found five themes. *Coping* relates to what people do to deal with their loss in terms of what helps them. *Affect* refers to people's emotional reactions to the death of their loved one; for example, most people have certain topics that serve as emotional triggers for memories of their loved one. *Change* involves the ways in which survivors' lives change as a result of the loss; personal growth (e.g., "I didn't think I could deal with something that painful, but I did.") is a common experience. *Narrative* relates to the stories survivors tell about their deceased loved one, which sometimes includes details about the process of the death. Finally, *relationship* reflects who the deceased person was and the nature of the ties between that person and the survivor. Collectively, these themes indicate that the experience of grief is complex and involves dealing with one's feelings as a survivor as well as memories of the deceased person.

How people show their feelings of grief varies across ethnic groups. For example, Latino American men show more of their grief behaviorally than do European American men (Sera, 2001). Such differences also are found across cultures. For example, in many cultures the bereaved construct a relationship with the person who died, but how this happens differs widely, from "ghosts" to appearances in dreams to connection through prayer (Rosenblatt, 2001).

In the time following the death of a loved one, dates that have personal significance may reintroduce feelings of grief. For example, holidays such as Thanksgiving or birthdays that were spent with the deceased person may be difficult times. The actual anniversary of the death can be especially troublesome. *The term **anniversary reaction** refers to changes in behavior related to feelings of sadness on this date.* Personal experience and research show that recurring feelings of sadness or other examples of the anniversary reaction are very common in normal grief (Attig, 1996; Rosenblatt, 1996).

Grief Over Time

Most research on how people react to the death of a loved one is cross-sectional. However, some work has been done to examine how people continue grieving many years after the loss. Rosenblatt (1996) reported that people still felt the effects of the deaths of family members 50 years after the event. The depth of the emotions over the loss of loved ones never totally went away, as people still cried and felt sad when discussing the loss despite the length of time that had passed.

Norris and Murrell (1987) conducted a longitudinal study of older adults' grief work; three interviews were conducted before the death and one after. Among bereaved families, overall family stress increased before the death and then decreased. The level of stress experienced by these families was highest in the period right around the death. Moreover, bereavement was the only significant predictor of family stress, meaning that the anticipation and experience of bereavement caused stress.

Even more interesting were the findings concerning the relationship between health and stress. As shown in Figure 16.3, bereaved individuals who reported stress before the death were in poorer health before the death than were bereaved persons who were not experiencing stress. However, as shown in Figure 16.4, bereaved individuals reporting prior stress showed a significant drop in physical symptoms 6 months after the death; bereaved persons reporting no prior stress reported a slight increase. The net result was that both groups ended up with about the same level of physical symptoms 6 months after bereavement. These findings also have important implications for interventions.

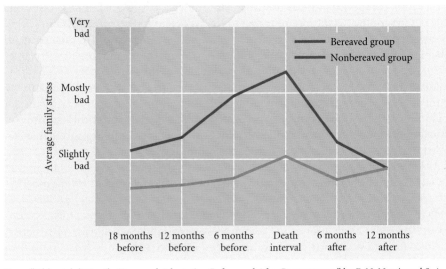

■ Figure 16.3
Family stress is worse in families who have experienced the loss of a loved one; this stress tends to peak around the time of the death.

From "Older Adult Family Stress and Adaptation Before and After Bereavement," by F. N. Norris and S. A. Murrell, 1987, *Journal of Gerontology Social Sciences, 42,* pp. 606–612. Copyright © 1990 Gerontological Society of America. Reprinted with permission.

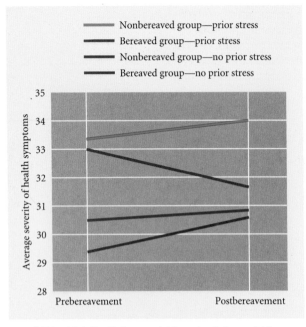

Nonbereaved group—prior stress
Bereaved group—prior stress
Nonbereaved group—no prior stress
Bereaved group—no prior stress

From "Older Adult Family Stress and Adaptation Before and After Bereavement," by F. N. Norris and S. A. Murrell, 1987, *Journal of Gerontology Social Sciences, 42,* pp. 606–612. Copyright © 1990 Gerontological Society of America. Reprinted with permission.

■ **Figure 16.4**
Only those bereaved older adults who reported stress prior to the death of a loved one showed a drop in reported stress after bereavement.

That is, interventions aimed at reducing stress or promoting health may be more effective if performed before the death. In addition, because health problems increased only among those in the bereaved group who felt no stress before the death, it may be that the stress felt before the death is a product of anticipating it. Lundin (1984) also found it to be the case that health problems increased only for those bereaved individuals experiencing sudden death.

Religiosity is thought to provide a support mechanism for people following the loss of a loved one. Research evidence for this belief is mixed. Some studies (e.g., Nelson, 2001) show that religiosity has no effect on the duration of grief. Other research points to a different conclusion. For example, Latino men who practice their religion openly show lower levels of grief than do Latino men who are not openly religious or European American men (Sera, 2001). Bereavement counselors also report better outcomes when religious or spiritual issues are included in the therapeutic process (Golsworthy & Coyle, 2001). Clearly, more and more carefully designed research is needed in order to understand the role that survivors' religious beliefs play in grief.

COPING WITH GRIEF

Thus far, we have considered the behaviors people show when they are dealing with grief. We have also seen that these behaviors change over time. How does this happen? How can we explain the grieving process?

Numerous theories have been proposed to account for the grieving process, such as general life event theories, psychodynamic theories, attachment theories, and cognitive process theories (M. Stroebe & Schut, 2001). All of these approaches to grief are based on more general theories, which results in none of them providing an adequate explanation of the grieving process. Two integrative approaches have been proposed that are specific to the grief process: the four component model and the dual process model of coping with bereavement.

The four component model proposes that understanding grief is based on four things: (1) *the context of the loss,* referring to the risk factors such as whether the death was expected; (2) *continuation of subjective meaning associated with loss,* ranging from evaluations of everyday concerns to major questions about the meaning of life; (3) *changing representations of the lost relationship over time;* and (4) *the role of coping and emotion-regulation processes* that cover all coping strategies used to deal with grief (Bonanno & Kaltman, 1999). The four component model relies heavily on emotion theory, has much in common with the transactional model of stress, and has some empirical support. According to the four component model, dealing with grief is a complex process that can only be understood as a complex outcome that unfolds over time.

An important aspect of this model is that encouraging people to express their grief may actually not be helpful. *An alternative view, called the* **grief work as rumination hypothesis,** *not only rejects the necessity of grief processing for recovery from loss but views extensive grief processing as a form of rumination that may actually increase distress* (Bonanno, Papa, & O'Neill, 2001). One recent prospective study has shown, for instance, that bereaved individuals who were not depressed prior to their spouse's death but then evidenced chronically elevated depression through the first year and a half of bereavement (i.e., a chronic grief pattern) had also tended to report more frequently thinking about and talking about their recent loss at the 6-month point in bereavement (Bonanno, Wortman, & Neese, 2004). Thus, some bereaved individuals engage in minimal grief processing, whereas others are predisposed toward more extensive grief processing. Furthermore, the individuals who engage in minimal grief processing will show a relatively favorable grief outcome, whereas those who are predisposed toward more extensive grief processing will tend toward ruminative preoccupation and, consequently, toward a more prolonged grief course (Bonanno et al., 2001; Nolen-Hoeksema, 2001).

The grief work as rumination hypothesis also views grief avoidance as an independent but maladaptive form of coping with loss. In contrast to the traditional perspective, which equates the absence of grief processing with grief avoidance, the grief work as rumination framework assumes that resilient individuals are able to minimize processing of a loss through relatively automated processes, such as distraction or shifting attention toward more positive emotional experiences (Bonanno et al., 1995). The grief work as rumination framework argues that the deliberate avoidance or suppression of grief represents a less effective form of coping (Wegner & Gold, 1995) that tends to exacerbate rather than minimize the experience of grief (Bonanno et al., 1995; Nolen-Hoeksema, 1998).

The Spotlight on Research feature explores grief work regarding the loss of a spouse and the loss of a child in two cultures, the United States and China. As you read it, pay special attention to the question of whether encouraging people to express and deal with their grief is necessarily a good idea.

SPOTLIGHT ON RESEARCH

GRIEF PROCESSING AND AVOIDANCE IN THE UNITED STATES AND CHINA

Who were the investigators and what was the aim of the study? Bonanno and colleagues (2005) noted that grief following the loss of a loved one often tends to be denied. However, research evidence related to positive benefits of resolving grief is largely lacking. Thus, whether unresolved grief is "bad" remains an open issue. Likewise, cross-cultural evidence is also lacking.

How did the investigators measure the topic of interest? Collaborative meetings between U.S. and Chinese researchers resulted in a 13-item grief processing scale and a 7-item grief avoidance scale, with both English and Mandarin Chinese versions. Self-reported psychological symptoms and physical health were also collected.

Who were the participants in the study? Adults under age 66 who had experienced the loss of either a spouse or child approximately 4 months prior to the start of data collection were asked to participate through solicitation letters. Participants were from either the metropolitan areas of Washington, DC or Nanjing, Jiangsu province in China.

What was the design of the study? Two sets of measures were collected at approximately 4 months and 18 months after the loss.

Were there ethical concerns in the study? Because participation was voluntary, there were no ethical concerns.

What were the results? Consistent with the grief work as rumination view, scores on the two grief measures were uncorrelated. Overall, women tended to show more grief processing than men, and grief processing decreased over time. As you can see in Figure 16.5, Chinese participants reported more

■ **Figure 16.5**
Grief processing and deliberate grief avoidance across time in the People's Republic of China and the United States.

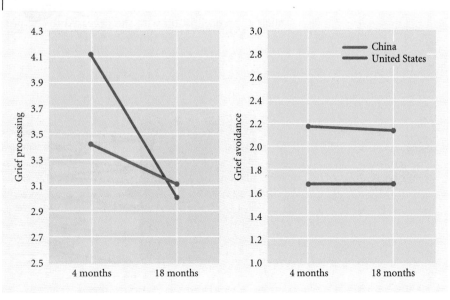

From Bonanno et al., 2005, p. 92.

grief processing and grief avoidance than U.S. participants at the first time of measurement, but differences disappeared by the second measurement for grief processing.

What did the investigators conclude? Based on converging results from the United States and China, the researchers concluded that the data supported the grief work as rumination view. The results support the notion that excessive processing of grief may actually increase a bereaved person's stress and feelings

of discomfort rather than being helpful. These findings contradict the idea that people should be encouraged to work through their grief and that doing so will always be helpful.

What converging evidence would strengthen these conclusions? Although the data were collected in two cities in two countries, additional areas (e.g., rural and urban) and more cross-cultural data would be helpful. Also, the sample was limited to people under age 66, and to those who had recently experi-

enced the loss of either a spouse or child. Older adults and people experiencing different types of loss (parent, partner, sibling, or friend) would provide a richer dataset.

To enhance your understanding of this research, go to http://psychology .wadsworth.com/kail_cavanaugh4e/ to complete critical thinking questions and explore related websites.

The dual process model of coping with bereavement (DPM) integrates existing ideas (M. Stroebe & Schut, 2001). As shown in Figure 16.6, the DPM defines two broad types of stressors. *Loss-oriented stressors* are those having to do with the loss itself, such as the grief work that needs to be done. *Restoration-oriented stressors* are those relating to adapting to the survivor's new life situation, such as building new relationships and finding new activities. The DPM proposes that dealing with these stressors is a dynamic process, as indicated by the lines connecting them in the figure. This is a distinguishing feature of DPM. It shows how bereaved people cycle back and forth between dealing mostly with grief and trying to move on with life. At times the emphasis will be on grief; at other times on moving forward.

The DPM captures well the process that bereaved people themselves report—at times they are nearly overcome with grief, while at other times they handle life well. The DPM also helps us understand how, over time, people come to a balance between the long-term effects of bereavement and the need to live life.

TRAUMATIC GRIEF REACTIONS

Not everyone is able to cope with grief well and begin rebuilding a life. Sometimes the feelings of hurt, loneliness, and guilt are so overwhelming that they become the focus of the survivor's life to such an extent that there is never any closure and the grief continues to interfere indefinitely with one's ability to function. What distinguishes normal from traumatic grief is that traumatic grief involves (a) symptoms of *separation distress* such as preoccupation with the deceased to the point that it interferes with everyday

■ **Figure 16.6**
The dual process model of coping with bereavement shows the relationship between dealing with the stresses of the loss itself (loss-oriented) and moving on with one's life (restoration-oriented).

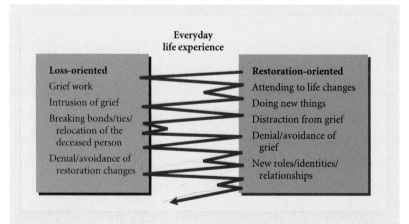

From M. Stroebe and Schut, 2001.

functioning, upsetting memories of the deceased, longing and searching for the deceased, loneliness following the loss, and (b) symptoms of *traumatic distress* such as feeling disbelief about the death, mistrust, anger, and detachment from others as a result of the death, feeling shocked by the death, and the experience of somatic (physical) symptoms of the deceased (Prigerson & Jacobs, 2001).

Two common manifestations of traumatic grief are excessive guilt and self-blame (Anderson, 1997). In some people, guilt results in a disruption of everyday routines and a diminished ability to function. People begin to make judgment errors, may reach a state of agitated depression, may experience problems sleeping or eating, and may have intense recurring thoughts about the deceased person. Many of these individuals either seek professional help voluntarily or are referred by concerned family members or friends.

Identifying traumatic grief is not always easy because cultural variations in the process of grief must be respected (Anderson, 1997). Length of time after the loss is not a good indicator, as grief can still be quite strong 10 years after a loss (Derman, 2000). Prigerson and Jacobs (2001) report that the criteria listed earlier for traumatic grief can be used successfully to differentiate the typical grief of bereaved people, even when they are depressed, from traumatic grief.

TEST YOURSELF

1. Feeling sad on the date when your grandmother died the previous year is an example of an
   _____.

2. Compared to other age groups, _____ show the most negative effects following bereavement.

3. Two common manifestations of traumatic grief are guilt and _____.

If you were to create a brochure listing the five most important things to do and not to do in reacting to someone who just lost a close family member or friend through death, what would you include? Why?

Answers: (1) anniversary reaction, (2) middle-aged adults, (3) self-blame

---

16.4

DYING AND BEREAVEMENT EXPERIENCES ACROSS THE LIFE SPAN

Donna and Carl have a 6-year-old daughter, Jennie, whose grandmother just died. Jennie and her grandmother were very close, as the two saw each other almost every day. Other adults have told her parents not to take Jennie to the funeral. Donna and Carl aren't sure what to do. They wonder whether Jennie will understand what happened to her grandmother, and they worry about how she will react.

LEARNING OBJECTIVES

What do children understand about death? How should adults help them deal with it?

How do adolescents deal with death?

How do adults deal with death? What are the special issues they face concerning the death of a child or parent?

How do older adults face the loss of a child, grandchild, or partner?

COMING TO GRIPS WITH THE REALITY OF DEATH is probably one of the hardest things we have to do in life. American society does not help much either, as it tends to distance itself from death through euphemisms, such as "passed away" or "dearly departed," and by eliminating many rituals from the home (for example, viewings no longer take place there, no more official mourning visits to the bereaved's house, and so on).

These trends make it difficult for people like Donna, Carl, and Jennie to learn about death in its natural context. Dying itself has been moved from the home to hospitals and other institutions such as nursing homes. The closest most people get to death is a quick glance inside a nicely lined casket at a corpse that has been made to look as if the person were still alive.

What do people, especially children like Jennie, understand about death? How do Donna and Carl feel? How do the friends of Jennie's grandmother feel? In this section, we consider how our understanding of death changes throughout the life span.

CHILDHOOD

Parents often take their children to funerals of relatives and close friends. But many adults, like Donna and Carl in the vignette, wonder whether young children really know what death means. Young preschool-age children tend to believe that death is temporary and magical. They think it is something dramatic that comes to get you in the middle of the night like a burglar or a ghost (Dickinson, 1992). Not until 5 to 7 years of age do children realize that death is permanent, that it eventually happens to everyone, and that dead people no longer have any biological functions (Silverman & Nickman, 1996).

Why does this shift occur? There are three major areas of developmental change in children that affect their understanding of death and grief (Oltjenbruns, 2001): cognitive-language ability, psychosocial development, and coping skills. In terms of cognitive-language ability, think back to Chapters 4 and 6, especially to the discussion of Piaget's theory of cognitive development. Take Jennie, the 6-year-old daughter of Donna and Carl in the vignette. Where would she be in Piaget's terms? In this perspective, the ages 5 to 7 include the transition from preoperational to concrete-operational thinking. Concrete-operational thinking permits children to know that death is final and permanent. Therefore, Jennie is likely to understand what happened to her grandmother.

Children's feelings at the loss of a loved one vary according to Erikson's theory of psychosocial development. For example, in the middle childhood stage of initiative versus guilt, the child may feel responsible and guilty for the loved one's death. Sensitivity to these feelings is essential for the child to understand that he or she did not cause the death.

The ability to cope is more limited in children than in adults. Several common manifestations of grief among children are shown in Figure 16.7. Typical reactions in early childhood include regression, guilt for causing the death, denial, displacement, repression, and wishful thinking that the deceased will return. In later childhood, common behaviors include problems at school, anger, and physical ailments. As children mature, they acquire more coping skills that permit a shift to problem-focused coping, which provides a better sense of personal control. Children will often flip between grief and normal activity, a pattern they may learn from adults (Stroebe & Schut, 1999).

Research shows that bereavement per se during childhood typically does not have long-lasting effects, such as depression (Oltjenbruns, 2001). Problems are more likely to occur if the child does not get adequate care following the death. Understanding death can be particularly difficult for children when adults are not open and honest with them, especially about the meaning of death (Buchsbaum, 1996). The use of euphemisms, such as "Grandma has gone away" or "Mommy is only sleeping," is unwise. Young children do not understand the deeper level of meaning in such statements; they are likely to take them literally (Attig, 1996; Silverman & Nickman, 1996).

When explaining death to children, it is best to deal with them on their terms. Keep explanations simple, at a level they can understand. Try to allay their fears and reassure

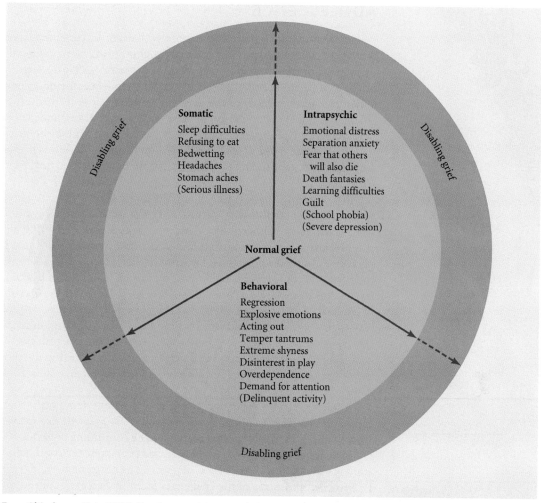

Somatic
Sleep difficulties
Refusing to eat
Bedwetting
Headaches
Stomach aches
(Serious illness)

Intrapsychic
Emotional distress
Separation anxiety
Fear that others
   will also die
Death fantasies
Learning difficulties
Guilt
(School phobia)
(Severe depression)

Normal grief

Behavioral
Regression
Explosive emotions
Acting out
Temper tantrums
Extreme shyness
Disinterest in play
Overdependence
Demand for attention
(Delinquent activity)

Disabling grief

From Oltjenbruns, K. A. (2001). Developmental Context of Childhood Grief and Re-grief Phenomena. *Handbook of Bereavement Research: Consequences, Coping, and Care.* Edited by M. S. Stroebe, R. O. Hansson, W. Stroebe, & H. Schut. Fig. 8.1, p. 177. Copyright © 2001 by the American Psychological Association. Reprinted with permission.

▪ **Figure 16.7**
Children show their grief in many ways, including physiological (somatic), emotional (intrapsychic), and behavioral ones.

them that whatever reaction they have is okay. Providing loving support for the child will maximize the potential for a successful (albeit painful) introduction to one of life's realities. One male college student recalled how, when he was 9, his father helped him deal with his feelings after his grandfather's death:

> The day of my grandfather's death my dad came over to my aunt and uncle's house where my brother and I were staying. He took us into one of the bedrooms and sat us down. He told us Grandaddy Doc had died. He explained to us that it was okay if we needed to cry. He told us that he had cried, and that if we did cry we wouldn't be babies, but would just be men showing our emotions. (Dickinson, 1992, pp. 175–176)

It is important for children to know that it is okay for them to feel sad, to cry, or to show their feelings in whatever way they want. The Family Circus cartoon reflects well that children feel loss and miss the person who died. Reassuring children that it's okay to feel this way helps them deal with their confusion at some adults' explanations of death. Young adults remember feeling uncomfortable as children around dead bodies, often fearing that the deceased person would come after them. Still, researchers believe it is very important for children to attend the funeral of a relative. Even though they tend to remember few details immediately, their overall recovery is enhanced (Silverman & Worden, 1992).

"I wish Granddad could've been at the reunion, too."

ADOLESCENCE

Adolescents are much more experienced with death and grief than many people realize. Surveys of college students indicate that roughly 50% have experienced the loss of a family member or friends in the past 2 years (Wettemann, 1999; Wrenn, 1999). Adolescence is a time of personal and physical change, when one is trying to develop a theory of self. When teenagers experience the death of someone close to them, they may have considerable trouble making sense of the event (Hogan & DeSantis, 1996). The effects of bereavement in adolescence can be quite severe, and unresolved grief has been linked with agitated depression, chronic illness, enduring guilt, low self-esteem, poorer performance in school and on the job, and problems in interpersonal relationships (Balk & Corr, 2001).

In reaction to the loss of a sibling, younger adolescents are particularly reluctant to discuss their grief, mainly because they do not want to appear different from their peers (Fleming & Balmer, 1996). This reluctance leaves them particularly vulnerable to psychosomatic symptoms such as headaches and stomach pains that signal underlying problems. As these adolescents mature, they tend to become more willing to talk, but their peers become less inclined to want to listen (Balk & Corr, 2001). Adolescents often do not demonstrate a clear end point to their grief over the loss of a sibling (Hogan & DeSantis, 1996). For example, bereaved adolescent siblings continue to miss and to love their dead siblings and to anticipate their eventual reunion in the afterlife. However, grief does not interfere with normative developmental processes. Bereaved adolescent siblings experience continued personal growth following the death of a sibling in much the same way as adolescents who did not experience such a loss (Hogan & DeSantis, 1996).

Adolescents who experience the loss of a parent show many similar behaviors to those who have lost a sibling. Tyson-Rawson (1996) reports that female college students whose fathers had died reported maintaining a continuing presence of the deceased parent in their lives. However, few nonbereaved peers were willing to talk with the bereaved students about their experience or even felt comfortable being with them. Wrenn (1999) relates that one of the challenges faced by bereaved college students is learning "how to respond to people who ignore their grief, or who tell them that they need to get on with life, that it's not good for them to continue to grieve" (p. 134). Adolescents who lose a parent also get involved in the family dynamics of reallocating roles within the family, finding a way to refer to the deceased parent, and dealing with different ways of expressing grief among different family members (Tyson-Rawson, 1996).

Little research has examined adolescents' reactions to the death of a friend. Oltjenbruns (1996) reports that grief following the death of a peer is often accompanied by survivor guilt. Such feelings may result in the ending of relationships with other mutual friends and an increase in grief. However, these adolescents also report some positive outcomes, such as gaining a deeper appreciation of life as a result of their friend's death. The complexity of these feelings is a major reason schools offer grief counseling following tragedies at schools.

Adolescents may not always openly express their feelings after the loss of a loved one; sometimes their feelings are manifested through problems at school.

ADULTHOOD

Because young adults are just beginning to pursue the family, career, and personal goals they have set, they tend to be more intense in their feelings toward death. When asked how they feel about death, young adults report a strong sense that those who die at this point in their lives would be cheated out of their future (Attig, 1996).

Experiencing the loss of one's partner in young adulthood can be very traumatic, not only because of the loss itself but also because such loss is unexpected. As Trish Straine, a 32-year-old widow whose husband was killed in the World Trade Center attack, put it, "I suddenly thought, 'I'm a widow.' Then I said to my self, 'A widow? that's an older woman, who's dressed in black. It's certainly not a 32-year-old like me'" (Lieber, 2001). One of the most difficult aspects for young widows and widowers is that they must deal with both their own and their young children's grief and provide the support their children need. But that can be very hard. "Every time I look at my children, I'm reminded of Mark," said Stacey, a 35-year-old widow whose husband died of bone cancer. "And people don't want to hear you say that you don't feel like moving on, even though there is great pressure from them to do that." Stacey is a good example of what research shows: young adult widows report that their level of grief does not typically diminish significantly until 5 to 10 years after the loss, and they maintain strong attachments to their deceased husbands for at least that long (Derman, 2000).

Losing one's spouse in midlife often results in the survivor challenging basic assumptions about self, relationships, and life options (Danforth & Glass, 2001). By the first year anniversary of the loss, the surviving spouse has usually begun transforming his or her perspectives on these issues.

Death of One's Child in Young and Middle Adulthood

Many people believe that the death of one's child is the worst type of loss (Klass, 1996a). Because children are not supposed to die before their parents, it is as if the natural order of things has been violated, shaking parents to their core (Rubin & Malkinson, 2001). Mourning is always intense, and some parents never recover or reconcile themselves to the death of their child (Klass, 1996a). The intensity of feelings is due to the strong parent-child bond that begins before birth and that lasts a lifetime (Bornstein, 1995).

Young parents who lose a child due to Sudden Infant Death Syndrome (SIDS) report high anxiety, a more negative view of the world, and much guilt, resulting in a devastating experience (Rubin & Malkinson, 2001). The most overlooked losses of a child are those that happen through stillbirth, miscarriage, abortion, or neonatal death (Klass, 1996a; McCarthy, 2002; Rubin & Malkinson, 2001). Attachment to the child begins before birth, especially for mothers, so the loss hurts very deeply. Yet parents who experience this type of loss are expected to recover very quickly. The experience of parents in support groups, such as Compassionate Friends, tells a very different story (Klass, 1996a). These parents report a deep sense of loss and hurt, especially when others do not understand their feelings. Worst of all, if societal expectations for quick recovery are not met, the parents may be subjected to unfeeling comments. As one mother notes, parents often just wish somebody would acknowledge the loss (Okonski, 1996).

The loss of a young adult child for a middle-aged parent is experienced differently but is equally devastating (Rubin & Malkinson, 2001). For example, parents who lost sons in wars (Rubin, 1996) and in traffic accidents (Shalev, 1999) still report strong feelings of anxiety, problems in functioning, and difficulties in relationships with both surviving siblings and the deceased as long as 13 years after the loss.

Death of One's Parent

Most parents die after their children are grown. But whenever parental death occurs, it hurts. We lose not only a key relationship but also an important psychological buffer between ourselves and death (Anderson, 1997; Attig, 1996). We, the children, are now next in line. Indeed, the death of a parent often leads the surviving children to redefine the

© David Young-Wolff/PhotoEdit

Becoming a widow as a young adult can be especially traumatic.

For most people, the loss of a child is the most difficult type of loss to understand and deal with.

AP / Wide World Photos

meaning of their relationships with their siblings, children, and other family members (Moss, Moss, & Hansson, 2001).

The death of a parent deprives people of many important things: a source of guidance and advice, a source of love, and a model for their own parenting style (Buchsbaum, 1996). It also cuts off the opportunity to improve aspects of their relationship with the parent. Expressing feelings toward a parent before he or she dies is important.

The loss of a parent is perceived as a very significant one; no matter how old we are, society allows us to grieve for a reasonable length of time. For young adult women transitioning to motherhood, losing their own mother during adolescence raises many feelings, such as deep loss at not being able to share their pregnancies with their mothers and fear of dying young themselves (Franceschi, 2005). Middle-aged women who lose a parent report feeling a complex set of emotions (Westbrook, 2002); they have intense emotional feelings of both loss and freedom, they remember both positive and negative aspects of their parent, and they experience shifts in their own sense of self.

The feelings accompanying the loss of an older parent reflect a sense of letting go, loss of a buffer against death, better acceptance of one's own eventual death, and a sense of relief that the parent's suffering is over (Moss et al., 2001). Whether the adult child now tries to separate from the deceased parent's expectations or finds comfort in the memories, the impact of the loss is great.

LATE ADULTHOOD

In general, older adults are less anxious about death and more accepting of it than any other age group (Kastenbaum, 1999). They may feel that their most important life tasks have been completed (Kastenbaum, 1999).

Death of One's Child or Grandchild in Late Life

Regardless of one's age, the loss of a parent is typically a difficult experience.

Many older adults experience the loss of one or more of their children, who are typically middle-aged or older (Moss & Moss, 1996), and others continue to feel the loss of a child from many years before (Ben-Israel Reuveni, 1999). Older bereaved parents tend to reevaluate their grief as experienced shortly after the loss and years and decades later. Even more than 30 years after the death of a child, older adults still feel a keen sense of loss and have continued difficulty coming to terms with it (Malkinson & Bar-Tur, 2004–2005). The long-lasting effects of the loss of a child are often accompanied by a sense of guilt that the pain affected the parents' relationships with the surviving children.

Clearly, the loss of a child has profound, lifelong effects. The meaning of the loss changes somewhat over time (Neimeyer, Keese, & Fortner, 2000), but the feelings of distress may never go away. Indeed, many parents view the relationship to the deceased child as either the closest or one of the closest relationships they ever had (Ben-Israel Reuveni, 1999).

The loss of a grandchild results in similar feelings: intense emotional upset, survivor guilt, regrets about the relationship with the deceased grandchild, and a need to

© Frank Siteman

restructure relationships with the surviving family. However, bereaved grandparents tend to control and hide their grief behavior in an attempt to shield their child (the bereaved parent) from the level of pain being felt.

Death of One's Partner

Experiencing the loss of one's partner is the type of loss in late life we know most about. The death of a partner differs from other losses. It clearly represents a deep personal loss, especially when the couple has had a long and close relationship (Moss et al., 2001). In a very real way, when our partner dies, a part of ourself dies too.

There is pressure from society to mourn the loss of one's partner for a period of time, and then to "move on" (Jenkins, 2003). Typically, this pressure is manifested if the survivor begins to show interest in finding another partner before an "acceptable" period of mourning has passed. Although Americans no longer specify the length of the period, many feel that about a year is appropriate. The fact that such pressure and negative commentary usually do not accompany other losses is another indication of the seriousness with which most people take the death of a partner.

Older bereaved spouses may grieve for a long time; in one study grief lasted for at least 30 months (Thompson et al., 1991). Given that, you might wonder whether having a supportive social network might help people cope. Research findings on this topic are mixed, however. Some studies find that social support plays a significant role in the outcome of the grieving process. For example, during the first 2 years after the death of a partner, some data show that the quality of the support system rather than simply the number of friends is especially important for the grieving partner. Survivors who have a few friends or relatives with whom they have strong, close relationships are better off than survivors who have many acquaintances (Dimond, Lund, & Caserta, 1987). In contrast, other studies find that having a supportive social network plays little role in helping people cope. For example, Miller, Smerglia, and Bouchet (2004) reported that the type of social support available to a widow had no relation to her adjustment to widowhood. It may be that there is a complex relationship between the bereaved person, whether he or she wants to have contact with others, who in the social network is wanting to provide support, and whether that support is of high quality.

When one's partner dies, how he or she felt about the relationship could play a role in coping with bereavement. One study of spousal bereavement measured how the surviving spouse rated the marriage. Bereaved older widows/widowers rated their relationships at 2, 12, and 30 months after the death of their spouses. Nonbereaved older adults served as a comparison group. The results are summarized in Figure 16.8. Bereaved widows and widowers gave their marriages more positive ratings than nonbereaved older adults. A marriage lost through death left a positive bias in memory. However, bereaved spouses' ratings were related to depression in an interesting way. The more depressed the bereaved spouse, the more positive the marriage's rating. In contrast, depressed nonbereaved spouses gave their marriages negative ratings. This result suggests that depression following bereavement signifies positive aspects of a relationship; whereas depression not connected with bereavement indicates a troubled relationship (Futterman et al., 1990).

Several studies of widows document a tendency for some women to "sanctify" their husbands (Lopata, 1996). Sanctification involves describing deceased husbands in idealized terms, and serves several functions: validating that the widow had a strong marriage, is a good and worthy person, and is capable of rebuilding her life. European American women who view being a wife as above all other roles a woman can perform are somewhat more likely to sanctify their husbands (Lopata, 1996).

Getting older bereaved spouses to talk about their feelings concerning their loss reduces feelings of hopelessness, intrusive thoughts, and obsessive-compulsive behaviors (Segal et al., 1999). Cognitive-behavioral therapy is one especially effective intervention to help bereaved people make sense of the loss and deal with their other feelings and thoughts (Fleming & Robinson, 2001).

Unmarried heterosexual couples and gay and lesbian couples may experience other feelings and reactions in addition to typical feelings of grief. For example, family mem-

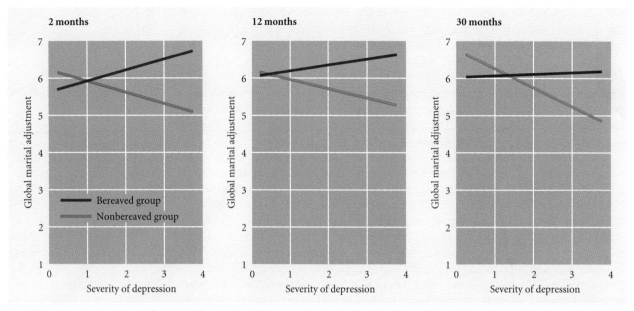

From "Retrospective Assessment of Marital Adjustment and Depression During the First Two Years of Spousal Bereavement," by A. Futterman, D. Gallagher, L. W. Thompson, S. Lovett, and M. Gilewski, 1990. *Psychology and Aging, 5,* 277–283. Copyright © 1990 American Psychological Association. Reprinted with permission of the author.

■ **Figure 16.8**
In general, bereaved spouses rate their marriages more positively than non-bereaved spouses, and they tend to be more positive the more depressed they are after their loss.

bers of the deceased may not make the partner feel welcome at the funeral, making it hard for the partner to bring closure to the relationship. Gays whose partners died of AIDS may experience increased personal concern, such as contracting AIDS themselves, and have difficulty dealing with their feelings (Goodkin et al., 1997).

TEST YOURSELF

1. In general, adults should be _____ when discussing death with children.

2. Adolescents are usually _____ to talk about their grief experiences.

3. The most devastating type of loss for an adult is the loss of a _____.

4. In general, a marriage ended by death is rated _____ than a marriage ended in some other way.

How do the different ways that adults view death relate to the stages of Erikson's theory discussed in Chapters 10, 13, and 15?

Answers: (1) honest, (2) reluctant, (3) child, (4) more positively

Putting It All Together

Thinking about death isn't easy. We aren't taught how to deal with it very well. Like Greta, we encounter different rituals and customs concerning funerals and mourning and we do not fully understand them. You may have been in a situation like that of Donna and Carl, facing the dilemma of whether to bring young children to a funeral.

You may know someone like Betty who has just been diagnosed with a terminal disease, or someone like Bertha who just lost a spouse. Like Clare and Alex, you may have experienced the loss of a close relative or friend.

Death is not as pleasant a topic as children's play or occupational development. It's not something we can go to college to master. What it represents to many people is the end of their existence, and that is a very scary prospect. But because we all share in this fear at some level, each of us is equipped to provide support and comfort for grieving survivors.

Death is the last life-cycle force we encounter, the ultimate triumph of biological forces that limit the length of life. Yet the same psychological and social forces that are so influential throughout life help us deal with death, either our own or someone else's. As we come to the end of our life journey, we understand death through an interaction of psychological forces, such as coping skills and intellectual and emotional understanding of death, and the sociocultural forces expressed in a particular society's traditions and rituals.

Learning about and dealing with death is clearly a developmental process across the life span that fits well in the biopsychosocial framework. Most apparent is that biological forces are essential to understanding death. The very definition of death is based on whether certain biological functions are present; these same definitions create numerous ethical dilemmas that must be dealt with psychologically and socioculturally. Life-cycle forces also play a key role. We have seen that the same concept—death—has varied meanings beyond the mere cessation of life depending on people's age.

How a person's understanding of death develops is also the result of psychological forces. As the ability to think and reflect undergoes fundamental change, the view of death changes from a mostly magical approach to one that can be transcendent and transforming. As we have seen, people who are facing their own imminent death experience certain feelings. Having gained experience through the deaths of friends and relatives, a person's level of comfort with his or her own death may increase. Such personal experience may also come about by sharing rituals, defined through sociocultural forces. People observe how others deal with death and how the culture sets the tone and prescribes behavior for survivors. The combined action of forces also determines how they cope with the grief that accompanies the loss of someone close. Psychologically, confronting grief depends on many things, including the quality of the support system we have.

Thus, just as the beginning of life represents a complex interaction of biological, psychological, sociocultural, and life-cycle factors, so does death. What people believe about what happens after death is also an interaction of these factors. So, as we bring the study of human development to a close, we end where we began—what we experience in our lives cannot be understood if one only uses a single perspective.

Summary

16.1 Definitions and Ethical Issues

Sociocultural Definitions of Death

■ Death is a difficult concept to define precisely. Different cultures have different meanings for death. Among the meanings in Western culture are images, statistics, events, state of being, analogy, mystery, boundary, thief of meaning, basis for anxiety, and reward or punishment.

Legal and Medical Definitions

■ For many centuries, a clinical definition of death was used: the absence of a heartbeat and respiration. Currently, whole-brain death is the most widely used definition. It is based on several highly specific criteria, including brain activity and responses to specific stimuli.

Ethical Issues

■ Two types of euthanasia are distinguished. Active euthanasia consists of deliberately ending someone's life, such as turning off a life-support system. Physician-assisted suicide is a controversial issue and a form of active euthanasia. Passive euthanasia is ending someone's life by withholding some type of intervention or treatment (e.g., by stopping nutrition). It is essential that people make their wishes known, through either a durable power of attorney or a living will.

16.2 Thinking About Death: Personal Aspects

A Life Course Approach to Dying

■ Young adults report a sense of being cheated by death. Cognitive developmental level is important for understanding how young adults view death.

■ Middle-aged adults begin to confront their own mortality and undergo a change in their sense of time lived and time until death.

■ Older adults are more accepting of death.

Dealing With One's Own Death

■ Kübler-Ross's theory includes five stages: denial, anger, bargaining, depression, and acceptance. Some people do not progress through all these stages, and some people move through them at different rates. People may be in more than one stage at a time and do not necessarily go through them in order.

■ A contextual theory of dying emphasizes the tasks a dying person must face. Four dimensions of these tasks have been identified: bodily needs, psychological security, interpersonal attachments, and spiritual energy and hope. A contextual theory would be able to incorporate differences in reasons people die and the places people die.

Death Anxiety

■ Most people exhibit some degree of anxiety about death, even though it is difficult to define and measure. Individual difference variables include gender, religiosity, age, ethnicity, and occupation. Death anxiety may have some benefits.

■ The main ways death anxiety is shown are by avoiding death (e.g., refusing to go to funerals) and deliberately challenging it (e.g., engaging in dangerous sports). Other ways of showing it include changing lifestyles, dreaming and fantasizing, using humor, displacing fears, and becoming a death professional.

■ Several ways to deal with anxiety exist: living life to the fullest, personal reflection, and education. Death education has been shown to be extremely effective.

Creating a Final Scenario

■ Managing the final aspects of life, after-death disposition of the body and memorial services, and distribution of assets are important end-of-life issues. Making choices about what people do and do not want done constitutes making a final scenario.

The Hospice Option

■ The goal of a hospice is to maintain the quality of life and to manage the pain of terminally ill patients. Hospice clients typically have cancer, AIDS, or a progressive neurological disorder. Family members tend to stay involved in the care of hospice clients.

16.3 Surviving the Loss: The Grieving Process

The Grief Process

■ Grief is an active process of coping with loss. Four aspects of grieving must be confronted: the reality of the loss, the emotional turmoil, adjusting to the environment, and loosening the ties with the deceased. When death is expected, survivors go through anticipatory grief; unexpected death is usually more difficult for people to handle.

Normal Grief Reactions

■ Dealing with grief, called *grief work,* usually takes at least 1 to 2 years. Grief is equally intense for both expected and unexpected death, but it may begin before the actual death when the patient has a terminal illness. Normal grief reactions include sorrow, sadness, denial, disbelief, guilt, and anniversary reactions.

■ In terms of dealing with normal grief, middle-aged adults have the most difficult time. Poor copers tend to have low self-esteem before losing a loved one.

Coping With Grief

■ The four component model proposes that the context of the loss, continuation of subjective meaning associated with the loss, changing representations of the lost relationship over time, and the role of coping and emotion-regulation processes describe the grief process.

■ The dual process model of coping with bereavement focuses on loss-oriented stressors and restoration-oriented stressors.

Traumatic Grief Reactions

■ Traumatic grief involves symptoms of separation distress and symptoms of traumatic distress. Excessive guilt and self-blame are common manifestations of traumatic grief.

16.4 Dying and Bereavement Experiences Across the Life Span

Childhood

■ The cognitive and psychosocial developmental levels of children determine their understanding of and ability to cope with death. This is especially evident in the behaviors children use to display their grief.

■ Research indicates that there are few long-lasting effects of bereavement in childhood.

Adolescence

■ Adolescents may have difficulty making sense of death, and they are often severely affected by bereavement. Adolescents may be reluctant to discuss their feelings of loss, and peers often provide little support.

Adulthood

■ Young and middle-aged adults usually have intense feelings about death. Attachment theory provides a useful framework to understand these feelings.

■ Midlife is a time when people usually deal with the death of their parents and confront their own mortality.

■ The death of one's child is especially difficult to cope with.

■ The death of one's parent deprives an adult of many important things, and the feelings accompanying it are often complex.

Late Adulthood

■ Older adults are usually less anxious about death and deal with it better than any other age group.

■ The death of a grandchild can be very traumatic for older adults, and the feelings of loss may never go away.

■ The death of one's partner represents a deep personal loss, especially when the couple had a long and close relationship. Older widowers often have a difficult time coping, whereas older widows often have a difficult time financially.

Key Terms

clinical death (620)

whole-brain death (620)

persistent vegetative state (621)

bioethics (621)

euthanasia (621)

active euthanasia (621)

passive euthanasia (623)

terror management theory (630)

end-of-life issues (631)

final scenario (632)

hospice (633)

bereavement (636)

grief (636)

mourning (636)

grief work (638)

anniversary reaction (639)

grief work as rumination hypothesis (640)

Learn More About It

Readings

JAFFE, C. (1997). *All kinds of love: Experiencing hospice.* Amityville, NY: Baywood. An excellent source of information about the philosophy and role of hospice.

KUNG, H., & JENS, W. (1995). *Dying with dignity: A plea for personal responsibility.* New York: Continuum. A superb, easy-to-read book that discusses death with dignity. This book will make you think.

KUSHNER, H. S. (1981). *When bad things happen to good people.* New York: Schocken. A classic written by a rabbi after the death of his son. This is easy reading but contains very thought-provoking material.

NULAND, S. B. (1994). *How we die: Reflections on life's final chapter.* New York: Knopf. This is a good discussion of the actual things that happen when people die. It is excellent for countering myths about death.

ROSENBLATT, P. C. (2000). *Parent grief: Narratives of loss and relationship.* Philadelphia: Brunner/Mazel. This book is a compilation of interviews of 29 couples who lost at least one child (age newborn to mid-30s). It is an excellent source for understanding the nature of parental grief.

TAYLOR, N. (1993). *A necessary end.* New York: Nan A. Talese. The author tells how he dealt with the death of his parents and found meaning in it.

Websites

Visit the Human Development book companion website for all URLs.

■ **The Human Development Book Companion Website**

See the companion website **http://psychology .wadsworth.com/kail_cavanaugh4e/** for practice quiz questions, Internet links, updates, critical thinking exercises, discussion forums, and more. Also accessible from the Wadsworth Psychology Study Center (http://psychology.wadsworth.com).

■ **Australian Museum DeathOnline**

A general site that provides information about several topics related to death, such as what happens, rituals surrounding death, remembering the dead, and numerous other resources.

■ **State of Oregon Physician-Assisted Suicide Information**

The State of Oregon provides a section on their official state website that has detailed information about the Oregon Death With Dignity law.

■ **National Hospice and Palliative Care Organization**

A resource for detailed information about hospice is the National Hospice and Palliative Care Organization. The site includes general information, providers, conference and educational opportunities, and information about the National Hospice Foundation.

■ **The Compassionate Friends**

The Compassionate Friends is a national organization dedicated to helping parents deal with the grief of the loss of a child. Chapters throughout the United States and Canada are listed on the website.

■ **AARP Resources on Grief and Loss**

AARP maintains a good site with general resources about grief and coping with loss. The site includes information for people of all ages and provides a wealth of information including information about practical matters (e.g., dealing with legal matters) and community support resources.

Thomson™ NOW!

http://www.thomsonedu.com

Go to this site for the link to ThomsonNOW, your one-stop study shop. Take a pre-test for this chapter, and ThomsonNOW will generate a personalized study plan based on your test results. The study plan will identify the topics you need to review and direct you to online resources to help you master those topics. You can then take a post-test to help you determine the concepts you have mastered and what you still need to work on.

Exploring Late Adulthood

Although aging is not without problems, older adults can age successfully by adopting strategies and behaviors for optimal aging.

Development in Late Adulthood

Physical

Average life expectancy has increased steadily over the last few decades. Genes and environment affect longevity.

Biological Theories of Aging	
Wear-and-tear	Aging is caused by the body's systems wearing out.
Cellular	Processes within cells cause buildup of harmful substances or cell deterioration over time.
Metabolic	The body's metabolism—especially related to caloric intake and stress—affects how people age.
Programmed cell death	Aging is genetically programmed.

© Tim Pannell /Corbis

Endurance, vision, and hearing decline in old age. Sense of smell declines after age 70 in many people.

The risk of cardiovascular disease (e.g., heart attack, stroke, hypertension) increases with age. However, risks are affected by lifestyle, and overall death rates from these diseases have declined in recent decades.

Older adults suffer shortness of breath and have increased risk of chronic obstructive pulmonary disorder (COPD). Emphysema and asthma are two common forms of COPD.

Sleep disturbances as well as cancer risk increase with age.

Cognitive

Age differences in attention tasks depend on the level of difficulty. On easy tasks, older and younger adults have few differences; on difficult tasks, younger adults do better.

Older adults' psychomotor speed is slower than younger adults. Practice, task expertise, and being physically fit lessen the amount of slowing.

Working memory typically declines with age. Older adults usually do worse on tests of episodic recall; recognition tasks are less affected by age. Semantic memory and implicit memory are affected little by aging. Memory aids can help older adults compensate.

Contrary to popular belief, wisdom is correlated with life experience, not age. After early middle age, creativity declines with increasing age, but an individual's creative peak varies across disciplines and occupations.

Rates of depression are reduced from young adulthood to old age, and symptoms vary by age. Treatment for older adults includes medication, behavior therapy, and cognitive therapy.

Anxiety disorders increase in older adulthood due to loss of health, relocation stress, isolation, and fear of losing independence. Medication and psychotherapy are effective treatments.

Dementia causes severe cognitive impairment. Alzheimer's disease is the most common form of irreversible dementia and is fatal. Various interventions can improve the patient's quality of life.

© David Young-Wolff /PhotoEdit

© Norbert Schaefer /Corbis

Three Factors That Contribute to Wisdom	
Factor	**Trait**
General personal condition	Mental ability
Specific expertise condition	Practice or mentoring
Facilitative life context	Education or leadership experience

Socioemotional

Erikson proposed that older adults struggle between *integrity versus despair,* primarily through a life review.

Whether older adults achieve subjective well-being depends on hardiness, chronic illness, marital status, social network, and stress.

Older adults use religion and spiritual support more often than any other strategy to cope with problems. Older adults who are committed to their faith have better physical and mental health.

Long-term marriages tend to be happy until one partner develops serious health problems. Caring for a spouse considerably strains the relationship.

Two Theories of Psychosocial Aging	
Continuity Theory	Older adults cope with daily life by applying familiar strategies based on past experience to maintain internal and external structures.
Competence and Environmental Press Theory	Older adults' optimal adaptation is when there is a balance between their ability to cope and the level of environmental demands placed on them.

Older adults' life satisfaction is strongly related to the number and quality of their friendships. Sibling relationships are important in old age.

Richard Koek/Getty Images

Most people retire by choice, although some are forced to because of health problems or job loss. Financial security, good health, and friends are correlated with satisfaction with retirement. Most retirees maintain their health, friendships, and activity levels.

Lawrence M. Sawyer/Getty Images

Abuse and neglect of older adults is an increasing problem. Most perpetrators are family members.

Older adults are the most politically active age group.

Older adults are less anxious about death and deal with it better than any other age group. Kübler-Ross proposes that people deal with their own death in five stages: denial, anger, bargaining, depression, and acceptance.

Dealing with grief can take 1 to 2 years; unexpected death is usually more difficult to handle. Normal grief reactions include sorrow, sadness, denial, disbelief, guilt, and anniversary reactions.

The death of one's partner is a deeply personal loss; the death of a grandchild can be very traumatic for older adults.

Cohen/Ostrow/Getty Images

© Paul Barton/Corbis

Glossary

abusive relationship when one partner in a relationship becomes violent or aggressive toward the other

accommodation according to Piaget, changing existing knowledge based on new knowledge

acquaintance rape see date rape

active euthanasia deliberate ending of someone's life

activities of daily living (ADLs) self-care tasks such as eating, bathing, toileting, walking, or dressing

adaptation level area where environmental press is average for a particular level of competence

addiction physical dependence on a particular substance, such as alcohol

adolescent egocentrism self-absorption that is characteristic of teenagers as they search for identity

adolescent-limited antisocial behavior the behavior of youth who engage in relatively minor criminal acts yet aren't consistently antisocial

aerobic exercise exercise that places a moderate stress on the heart by maintaining a pulse rate between 60 and 90% of the maximum heart rate

age discrimination denying a job or promotion to someone solely on the basis of age

age of viability age at which a fetus can survive because most of its bodily systems function adequately; typically at 7 months after conception

agreeableness dimension of personality associated with being accepting, willing to work with others, and caring

alert inactivity state in which a baby is calm with eyes open and attentive; the baby seems to be deliberately inspecting the environment

alienation when workers feel that what they are doing is meaningless, that their efforts are devalued, or when they do not see the connection between what they do and the final product

alleles variations of genes

altruism prosocial behavior such as helping and sharing in which the individual does not benefit directly from his or her behavior

Alzheimer's disease disease associated with aging characterized by gradual declines in memory, learning, attention, and judgment; confusion as to time and where one is; difficulties in communicating and finding the words one wants to use; declines in personal hygiene and self-care skills; inappropriate social behavior; and changes in personality

amniocentesis prenatal diagnostic technique that involves withdrawing a sample of amniotic fluid through the abdomen using a syringe

amnion inner sac in which the developing child rests

amniotic fluid fluid that surrounds the fetus

amyloid protein that is produced in abnormally high levels in Alzheimer's disease and that may be responsible for the neurofibrillary tangles and neuritic plaques

analytic ability in Sternberg's theory of intelligence, the ability to analyze problems and generate different solutions

animism crediting inanimate objects with life and lifelike properties such as feelings

anniversary reaction changes in behavior related to feelings of sadness on the actual anniversary of a death

anorexia nervosa persistent refusal to eat, accompanied by an irrational fear of being overweight

anxiety disorders problems such as feelings of severe anxiety for no apparent reason, phobias to specific things or places, and obsessive-compulsive disorders in which thoughts or actions are repeatedly performed

appraise to evaluate a situation to determine whether it exceeds a person's resources and is, therefore, stressful

approval-focused orientation behaving as one thinks society expects "good people" to behave

assimilation according to Piaget, taking in information that is compatible with what one already knows

assisted-living facilities a supportive living arrangement for people who need assistance with ADLs or IADLs but who are not so impaired physically or cognitively that they need 24-hour care

assortative mating theory of mating that states that people find partners based on their similarity to each other

attachment enduring social-emotional relationship between infants and their caregivers

attention processes that determine which information will be processed further by an individual

attentional control the abilities to focus, switch, and divide attention

authoritarian parenting parents who show high levels of control and low levels of warmth toward their children

authoritative parenting parents who use a moderate amount of control and are warm and responsive to their children

autobiographical memory memories of the significant events and experiences of one's own life

autosomes first 22 pairs of chromosomes

average children as applied to children's popularity, children who are liked and disliked by classmates, but with relatively little intensity

average life expectancy age at which half of the people born in a particular year will have died

avoidant attachment relationship in which infants turn away from their mothers when they are reunited following a brief separation

axon tubelike structure that emerges from the cell body and transmits information to other neurons

babbling speechlike sounds that consist of vowel-consonant combinations

basal metabolic rate the speed at which the body consumes calories

basic cry cry that starts softly and gradually becomes more intense; often heard when babies are hungry or tired

basic emotions emotions experienced by humankind and that consist of three elements: a subjective feeling, a physiological change, and an overt behavior

battered woman syndrome situation in which a woman believes that she cannot leave an abusive situation

behavior therapy approach to treating depression based on increasing the number of rewards or reinforcements in the environment

behavioral genetics the branch of genetics that studies the inheritance of behavioral and psychological traits

bereavement state or condition caused by loss through death

binge drinking consuming five or more drinks in a row for men or four or more drinks in a row for women within the past 2 weeks

bioethics study of the interface between human values and technological advances in health and life sciences

biological forces all genetic and health-related factors that affect development

biopsychosocial framework view that integrates biological, psychological, sociocultural, and life-cycle forces on development

blended family family consisting of a biological parent, a stepparent, and children

body mass index (BMI) an adjusted ratio of weight to height; used to define overweight

bridge job the job one holds between one's exit from the career job and final retirement

bulimia nervosa disease in which people alternate between binge eating—periods when they eat uncontrollably—and purging through self-induced vomiting or with laxatives

burnout depletion of a person's energy and motivation

cardinality principle counting principle that the last number name denotes the number of objects being counted

career plateauing either a lack of promotional opportunity from the organization or a person's decision not to seek advancement

cell body center of the neuron that keeps the neuron alive

cellular theories theories of aging that focus on processes that occur within individual cells, which cause the buildup of harmful substances over one's lifetime

centrality meaning derived when grandparenting is the most important thing in grandparents' lives

centration according to Piaget, narrowly focused type of thought characteristic of preoperational children

cephalocaudal principle a principle of physical growth that states that structures nearest the head develop first

cerebral cortex wrinkled surface of the brain that regulates many functions that are distinctly human

cerebral vascular accidents see strokes

cesarean section (C-section) surgical removal of infant from the uterus through an incision made in the mother's abdomen

chorionic villus sampling prenatal diagnostic technique that involves taking a sample of tissue from the chorion

chromosomes threadlike structures in the nuclei of cells that contain genetic material

chronic obstructive pulmonary disease (COPD) most common form of incapacitating respiratory disease among older adults; examples are asthma and emphysema

circadian rhythm sleep-wake cycle

classical conditioning a form of learning that involves pairing a neutral stimulus and a response originally produced by another

climacteric loss of ability to bear children, which usually begins in the 40s and is complete by age 50 or 55

clinical death death defined by a lack of heartbeat and respiration

clique small group of friends who are similar in age, sex, and race

cognitive self-regulation skill at identifying goals, selecting effective strategies, and accurate monitoring; a characteristic of successful students

cognitive therapy approach to depression based on the idea that maladaptive beliefs or cognitions about oneself are responsible for depression

cohabitation two or more unrelated adults living together

cohort effects differences between individuals that result from experiences and circumstances unique to a person's particular generation

common couple violence violence that occurs occasionally within a relationship that is instigated by either partner

comparable worth equating pay in occupations that are determined to be equivalent in importance but differ in terms of the gender distribution of the people in them

competence upper limit of a person's ability to function in five domains: physical health, sensory-perceptual skills, motor skills, cognitive skills, and ego strength

comprehension the process of extracting meaning from a sequence of words

cones specialized neurons in the back of the eye that sense color

congenital adrenal hyperplasia (CAH) genetic disorder in which girls are masculinized because the adrenal glands secrete large amounts of androgen during prenatal development

conscientiousness dimension of personality associated with being hard-working, ambitious, energetic, scrupulous, and persevering

constricting actions one partner tries to emerge as the victor by threatening or contradicting the other

continuity theory view that people tend to cope with daily life in late adulthood in essentially the same ways they coped in earlier periods of life

continuity-discontinuity issue issue concerned with whether a developmental phenomenon follows a smooth progression throughout the lifespan or a series of abrupt shifts

controversial children as applied to children's popularity, children who are liked or disliked, intensely, by classmates

conventional level second level of reasoning in Kohlberg's theory, where moral reasoning is based on society's norms

convergent thinking using information to arrive at one standard and correct answer

cooing early vowel-like sounds that babies produce

cooperative play play that is organized around a theme, with each child taking on a different role; begins at about 2 years of age

coping attempts to deal with stress

core knowledge hypothesis infants are born with rudimentary knowledge of the world, which is elaborated based on experiences

corpus callosum thick bundle of neurons that connects the two hemispheres

correlation coefficient statistic that reveals the strength and direction of the relation between two variables

correlational study investigation looking at relations between variables as they exist naturally in the world

counterimitation learning what should not be done by observing the behavior

creative ability in Sternberg's theory of intelligence, the ability to deal adaptively with novel situations and problems

cross-linking theory of aging in which some proteins interact randomly with certain body tissues, such as muscles and arteries

cross-sectional study research design in which people of different ages are compared at one point in time

crowd large group including many cliques that have similar attitudes and values

crowning appearance of the top of the baby's head during labor

crying state in which a baby cries vigorously, usually accompanied by agitated but uncoordinated movement

crystallization first phase in Super's theory of career development, in which adolescents use their emerging identities for ideas about careers

crystallized intelligence knowledge acquired through experience and education in a particular culture

cultural conservator status of grandparents whose grandchildren live with them to learn the native ways

culture-fair intelligence tests intelligence tests devised using items common to many cultures

date (acquaintance) rape when someone is forced to have sexual intercourse with someone she or he knows

deductive reasoning drawing conclusions from facts; characteristic of formal operational thought

dementia family of diseases involving serious impairment of behavioral and cognitive functioning

demographers people who study population trends

dendrite end of the neuron that receives information; it looks like a tree with many branches

deoxyribonucleic acid (DNA) molecule composed of four nucleotide bases that is the biochemical basis of heredity

dependent variable behavior that is observed after other variables are manipulated

depression disorder characterized by pervasive feelings of sadness, irritability, and low self-esteem

differentiation distinguishing and mastering individual motions

direct instruction telling a child what to do, when, and why

disinhibition form of observational learning in which all behaviors like those observed are more likely following observation

disorganized (disoriented) attachment relationship in which infants don't seem to understand what's happening when they are separated and later reunited with their mothers

divergent thinking thinking in novel and unusual directions

dizygotic twins result of the fertilization of two separate eggs by two sperm; also called fraternal twins

docility when people allow the situation to dictate the options they have

dominance hierarchy ordering of individuals within a group in which group members with lower status defer to those with greater status

dominant form of an allele whose chemical instructions are followed

doula person familiar with childbirth who provides emotional and physical support throughout labor and delivery

dream as related to vocational development, a vision of one's career

dynamic systems theory theory that views motor development as involving many distinct skills organized and reorganized over time to meet specific needs

dynamic testing measures learning potential by having a child learn something new in the presence of the examiner and with the examiner's help

dysphoria feeling sad or down; the most prominent symptom of depression

ecological theory view that human development cannot be separated from the environmental contexts in which development occurs

ectoderm outer layer of the embryo that will become the hair, outer layer of skin, and the nervous system

ego resilience powerful personality resource that enables people to handle midlife

egocentrism difficulty in seeing the world from another's point of view; typical of children in the preoperational period

elaboration memory strategy in which information is embellished to make it more memorable

electroencephalogram (EEG) pattern of brain waves recorded from electrodes that are placed on the scalp

embryo term given to the zygote once it is completely embedded in the uterine wall

emotional intelligence ability to use one's own and others' emotions effectively for solving problems and living happily

empathic orientation according to Eisenberg, a level of prosocial reasoning common in some children and many adolescents in which their thinking considers the injured child's perspective and how their own actions would make the child feel

empathy experiencing another person's feelings

enabling actions individuals' actions and remarks that tend to support others and sustain the interaction

encapsulated result of the processes of thinking becoming connected with the products of thinking

endoderm inner layer of the embryo, which will become the lungs and the digestive system

end-of-life issues includes management of the final phase of life, disposition of body and memorial services, and distribution of assets

environmental press number and types of physical, interpersonal, or social demands that environments make on people

epigenetic principle view in Erikson's theory that each psychosocial stage has its own period of importance

episodic memory the general class of memory having to do with the conscious recollection of information from a specific time or event

equilibration according to Piaget, a process by which children reorganize their schemes to return to a state of equilibrium when disequilibrium occurs

ethnic identity feeling of belonging to a specific ethnic group

ethology branch of biology concerned with adaptive behaviors that are characteristic of different species

eugenics effort to improve the human species by letting only people whose characteristics are valued by a society mate and pass along their genes

euthanasia practice of ending a life for reasons of mercy

evolutionary psychology theoretical view that many human behaviors represent successful adaptations to the environment

exchange theory view that marriage is based on each partner contributing something to the relationship that the other would be hard-pressed to provide

exosystem according to Bronfenbrenner, social settings that influence one's development even though one does not experience them firsthand

experiment systematic way of manipulating factors that a researcher thinks cause a particular behavior

explicit memory conscious and intentional recollection of information

expressive style language-learning style that describes children whose vocabularies include many social phrases that are used like one word

extended family family in which grandparents and other relatives live with parents and children

external aids memory aids that rely on environmental resources, such as notebooks or calendars

extraversion dimension of personality in which an individual thrives on social interaction, likes to talk, takes charge easily, readily expresses opinions and feelings, likes to keep busy, has seemingly unending energy, and prefers stimulating and challenging environments

extremely low birth weight newborns who weigh less than 1,000 grams (2 pounds)

familial mental retardation form of mental retardation that does not involve biological damage but represents the low end of the normal distribution of intelligence

familism the idea that the well-being of the family takes precedence over the concerns of individual family members

fast mapping fact that children make connections between new words and referents so quickly that they can't be considering all possible meanings

fetal alcohol syndrome (FAS) disorder affecting babies whose mothers consumed large amounts of alcohol while they were pregnant

fetal medicine field of medicine concerned with treating prenatal problems before birth

fictive grandparenting style that allows adults to fill in for missing or deceased biological grandparents, functionally creating the role of surrogate grandparent

filial obligation sense of responsibility to care for a parent if necessary

final scenario making choices known to others about how a person wants his or her life to end

fine motor skills motor skills associated with grasping, holding, and manipulating objects

fluid intelligence abilities such as thinking in a flexible, adaptive manner, drawing inferences, and understanding relations between concepts

frail older adults older adults who have physical disabilities, are very ill, and may have cognitive or psychological disorders

free radicals chemicals produced randomly during normal cell metabolism that bond easily to other substances inside cells; may cause cellular damage associated with aging

friendship voluntary relationship between two people involving mutual liking

frontal cortex brain region that regulates personality and goal-directed behavior

functional magnetic resonance imaging (fMRI) method of studying brain activity by using magnetic fields to track blood flow in the brain

gender constancy understanding that maleness and femaleness do not change over situations or personal wishes

gender discrimination denying a job to someone solely on the basis of whether the person is a man or a woman

gender identity sense of oneself as male or female

gender labeling young children's understanding that they are either boys or girls and naming themselves accordingly

gender stability understanding in preschool children that boys become men and girls become women

gender stereotype beliefs and images about males and females that are not necessarily true

gender-schema theory theory that states that children first decide whether an object, activity, or behavior is female or male, then use this information to decide whether they should learn more about the object, activity, or behavior

gene group of nucleotide bases that provide a specific set of biochemical instructions

generativity according to Erikson, being productive by helping others to ensure the continuation of society by guiding the next generation

genotype person's hereditary makeup

germ disc small cluster of cells near the center of the zygote that will eventually develop into a baby

glass ceiling level to which women and minorities may rise in a company but beyond which they may not go

grammatical morphemes words or endings of words that make a sentence grammatical

grief sorrow, hurt, anger, guilt, confusion, and other feelings that arise after suffering a loss

grief work psychological side of coming to terms with bereavement

grief work as rumination hypothesis rejects the necessity of grief processing for recovery from loss and views extensive grief processing as a form of rumination that may actually increase distress

habituation becoming unresponsive to a stimulus that is presented repeatedly

hassles day-to-day events that upset and annoy people

hedonistic orientation according to Eisenberg, a level of prosocial reasoning common in preschool and elementary school children in which they emphasize pursuing their own pleasure

hemispheres right and left halves of the cortex

hemorrhage break in any blood vessel that leads to loss of blood

heterocyclic antidepressants (HCAs) type of medication used to treat depression

heterozygous when the alleles differ from each other

high-density lipoproteins (HDLs) lipoproteins that help clear arteries

homogamy similarity of values and interests

homozygous when the chromosomes in a pair are the same

hope according to Erikson, an openness to new experience tempered by wariness that occurs when trust and mistrust are in balance

hormone replacement theory treatment for symptoms accompanying the climacteric in which women take low doses of estrogen and progesterone

hospice movement that provides a supportive environment for dying people by keeping families engaged in caregiving and by providing professional assistance during this very stressful time

hostile aggression unprovoked aggression that seems to have the sole goal of intimidating, harassing, or humiliating another child

human development multidisciplinary scientific study of how people change and how they stay the same

Huntington's disease progressive and fatal type of dementia

hypoxia a birth complication in which umbilical blood flow is disrupted and the infant does not receive adequate oxygen

illusion of invulnerability adolescents' belief that misfortunes cannot happen to them

imaginary audience adolescents' feeling that their behavior is constantly being watched by their peers

imitation (observational learning) learning that happens by watching those around us

immortality through clan meaning derived from grandparenting when grandparents take pride in the fact that they will be followed by not one but two generations

implantation step in which the zygote burrows into the uterine wall and establishes connections with a woman's blood vessels

implementation third phase in Super's theory of career development, in which individuals now enter the workforce

implicit memory effortless recollection of information

implicit stereotyping the automatic and nonconscious activation of strong stereotypes

in vitro fertilization process by which sperm and an egg are mixed in a petri dish to create a zygote, which is then placed in a woman's uterus

incomplete dominance situation in which one allele does not dominate another completely

incontinence loss of bladder or bowel control

independent variable factor that researchers manipulate in an experiment

index offense acts that are illegal regardless of the age of the perpetrator

indulgence meaning derived when grandparents spoil their grandchildren

infant mortality the number of infants out of 1,000 births who die before their first birthday

infant-directed speech way of speaking in which adults speak slowly and with exaggerated changes in pitch and loudness

infantilization way of speaking to a nursing home resident based on using a person's first name when it is not appropriate, terms of endearment, simplified expressions, short imperatives, assumptions that a nursing home resident has no memory, and manipulation to get compliance

information-processing theory view that human cognition consists of mental hardware and software

inhibition as applied to observational learning, a decrease in an entire class of behaviors after children observe another person performing a specific behavior

instrumental activities of daily living (IADLs) acts that require some intellectual competence and planning, such as cooking and doing the laundry

instrumental aggression aggression used to achieve an explicit goal

instrumental orientation characteristic of Kohlberg's Stage 2, in which moral reasoning is based on the aim of looking out for one's own needs

integration linking individual motions into a coherent, coordinated whole

integrity versus despair according to Erikson, a struggle that comes about as older adults try to integrate their lives with a view of their family's and community's futures

intelligence quotient (IQ) mathematical representation of how a person scores on an intelligence test in relation to how other people of the same age score

interindividual variability patterns of change in a domain (e.g., intelligence) are different for different people

intermediate care facility that provides 24-hour care but does not involve intensive skilled nursing

internal aids memory aids that rely on mental processes, such as imagery

internal belief systems what one tells oneself about why certain things are happening

internal working model infant's understanding of how responsive and dependable the mother is; thought to influence close relationships throughout the child's life

interpersonal norms characteristic of Kohlberg's Stage 3, in which moral reasoning is based on winning the approval of others

intersensory redundancy infants' sensory systems are attuned to information presented simultaneously to different sensory modes

intimacy versus isolation according to Erikson, the psychosocial conflict of young adulthood

irregular or rapid-eye-movement (REM) sleep irregular sleep in which an infant's eyes dart rapidly beneath the eyelids while the body is quite active

job satisfaction good feeling that results from a positive appraisal of one's work

joint custody when, following divorce, both parents retain legal custody of their children

juvenile delinquency when adolescents commit illegal acts that are destructive toward themselves or others

kinetic cues cues to depth perception in which motion is used to estimate depth

kinkeepers people who gather their family together for celebrations and keep family members in touch with each other

knowledge-telling strategy writing down information as it is retrieved from memory, a common practice for young writers

knowledge-transforming strategy deciding what information to include and how best to organize it to convey a point

learning disability when a child with normal intelligence has difficulty mastering at least one academic subject

leisure discretionary activity that includes simple relaxation, activities for enjoyment, creative pursuits, and sensual transcendence

life course persistent antisocial behavior antisocial behavior that emerges at an early age and continues throughout life

life course perspective describes the ways in which various generations experience the biological, psychological, and sociocultural forces of development in their respective historical contexts

life review process of reviewing one's life

life story second manifestation of the life-span construct, a personal narrative that organizes past events into a coherent sequence

life-cycle forces differences in how the same event may affect people of different ages

life-span construct unified sense of the past, present, and future that is based on one's experiences and input from others

life-span perspective view that development is determined by many biological, psychological, and social factors and that all parts of the lifespan are interrelated

linear perspective a cue to depth perception based on the fact that parallel lines come together at a single point in the distance

locomote ability to move around in the world

longevity number of years a person will live

longitudinal study research design in which a single cohort is studied over multiple measurements

long-term memory permanent storehouse for memories that has unlimited capacity

low birth weight newborns who weigh less than 2,500 grams (5 pounds)

low-density lipoproteins (LDLs) lipoproteins that cause fatty acids to accumulate in arteries, which impedes the flow of blood

macrosystem according to Bronfenbrenner, the cultural and subcultural settings in which the microsystems, mesosystems, and exosystems are embedded

mad cry more intense version of a basic cry

malnourished being small for one's age because of inadequate nutrition

maximum life expectancy oldest age to which any person lives

menarche onset of menstruation

menopause cessation of menstruation

mental age (MA) in intelligence testing, a measure of children's performance corresponding to the chronological age of those whose performance equals the child's

mental hardware mental and neural structures that are built-in and that allow the mind to operate

mental operations cognitive actions that can be performed on objects or ideas

mental retardation substantially below-average intelligence and problems adapting to an environment that emerge before the age of 18

mental software mental "programs" that are the basis for performing particular tasks

mesoderm middle layer of the embryo; becomes the muscles, bones, and circulatory system

mesosystem according to Bronfenbrenner, the interrelations between different microsystems

meta-analysis tool that allows researchers to synthesize the results of many studies to estimate relations between variables

metabolic theories theories of aging that focus on aspects of the body's metabolism as a reason people age

metabolism energy required for bodily functions

metacognitive knowledge person's knowledge and awareness of cognitive processes

metamemory person's informal understanding of memory; includes the ability to diagnose memory problems accurately and to monitor the effectiveness of memory strategies

microsystem according to Bronfenbrenner, the people and objects that are present in one's immediate environment

midlife crisis time of psychological questioning during which people reevaluate their lives

monoamine oxidase (MAO) inhibitors type of medication used to treat depression

monozygotic twins result when a single fertilized egg splits to form two new individuals; also called identical twins

motion parallax kinetic cue to depth perception based on the fact that nearby moving objects move across our visual field faster than distant objects do

motor skills coordinated movements of the muscles and limbs

mourning culturally approved ways in which people express their grief

multidimensional approaches to intelligence that identify different areas of intellectual abilities

multidirectionality refers to the fact that some aspects of intelligence improve and other aspects decline across adulthood

myelin fatty sheath that wraps around neurons to permit them to transmit information more rapidly

naturalistic observation form of systematic observation in which people are observed as they behave spontaneously in some real-life situation

nature-nurture issue issue concerning the manner in which genetic and environmental factors influence development

needs-oriented orientation according to Eisenberg, a level of prosocial reasoning common in some preschool and many elementary school children in which they are concerned about others' needs and want to help

negative reinforcement trap unwittingly reinforcing a behavior you want to discourage

neglected children as applied to children's popularity, children who are ignored by their classmates, being neither liked nor disliked

neural plate flat group of cells present in prenatal development that becomes the brain and spinal cord

neuritic plaques damaged and dying neurons that collect around a core of protein

neurofibrillary tangles abnormal filaments found in large numbers of neurons in persons with Alzheimer's disease

neuron basic cellular unit of the brain and nervous system that specializes in receiving and transmitting information

neuroplasticity extent to which brain organization is flexible

neuroticism dimension of personality that refers to the extent that individuals tend to be anxious, hostile, self-conscious, depressed, impulsive, and vulnerable

neurotransmitters chemicals released by the terminal buttons that allow neurons to communicate with each other

niche-picking process of deliberately seeking environments that are compatible with one's genetic makeup

night terrors state of partial consciousness associated with panic, rapid breathing, and heavy perspiration; may result from waking rapidly from a deep sleep

nightmares vivid, frightening dreams that occur toward morning and wake the child

nonshared environmental influences forces within a family that make siblings different from one another

nuclear family family consisting of parent(s) and child(ren)

obedience orientation characteristic of Kohlberg's Stage 1, in which moral reasoning is based on the belief that adults know what is right and wrong

object permanence understanding, acquired in infancy, that objects exist independently of oneself

one-to-one principle counting principle that states that there must be one and only one number name for each object counted

openness to experience dimension of personality that displays a vivid imagination and dream life, appreciation of art, and a strong desire to try anything once

operant conditioning view of learning, proposed by B. F. Skinner, that emphasizes reward and punishment

optimal level of development the highest level of information-processing capacity that a person is capable of doing

optimally exercised ability level of performance a normal, healthy adult demonstrates under the best conditions of training or practice

ordinality numbers that differ in magnitude with some values greater than others

organic mental retardation mental retardation that can be traced to a specific biological or physical problem

organization as applied to children's memory, a strategy in which information to be remembered is structured so that related information is placed together

orienting response individual fixes eyes on a strong or unfamiliar stimulus and changes in heart rate and brainwave activity occur

osteoarthritis a bone disease marked by gradual onset and progression of joint pain and disability with minor signs of inflamation

osteoporosis disease in which bones become porous, like honeycombs, and break extremely easily

overextension when children define words more broadly than adults do

overregularization grammatical usage that results from applying rules to words that are exceptions to the rule

pain cry cry that begins with a sudden long burst, followed by a long pause and gasping

parallel play when children play alone but are aware of and interested in what another child is doing

Parkinson's disease common disease among older adults that results in motor problems, including slow walking, difficulty getting into and out of chairs, and hand tremors

passive euthanasia allowing a person to die by withholding an available treatment

patriarchal terrorism systematic violence within a relationship that is directed to a woman from a man

patronizing speech way of speaking to older adults that is marked by slower rate, exaggerated intonation, higher pitch, increased volume, repetitions, closed-end questions, and simplified vocabulary and grammar

perception processes by which the brain receives, selects, modifies, and organizes incoming nerve impulses that are the result of physical stimulation

period of the fetus longest period of prenatal development, extending from the 9th until the 38th week after conception

permissive parenting style of parenting that offers warmth and caring but little parental control over children

persistent vegetative state state in which a person's cortical functioning ceases while brainstem activity continues

personal control beliefs beliefs about the degree to which one's performance in a situation is within one's control

personal fable attitude of many adolescents that their feelings and experiences are unique and have never been experienced by anyone else before

personality-type theory view proposed by Holland that people find their work fulfilling when the important features of a job or profession fit the worker's personality

phenotype physical, behavioral, and psychological features that result from the interaction between one's genes and the environment

phenylketonuria (PKU) inherited disorder in which the infant lacks a liver enzyme

phonemes unique speech sounds that can be used to create words

phonological awareness the ability to hear the distinctive sounds of letters

phonological memory ability to remember speech sounds briefly; an important skill in acquiring vocabulary

pictorial cues cues to depth perception used to convey depth in drawings and paintings

placenta structure through which nutrients and wastes are exchanged between the mother and the developing child

plasticity the fact that abilities can be modified by certain conditions or experiences

polygenic inheritance when phenotypes are the result of the combined activity of many separate genes

popular children children who are liked by many classmates

population broad group of people that is the focus of research

population pyramid graphic technique used by demographers to illustrate population trends

possible selves projecting what we could become, what we would like to become, and what we are afraid of becoming

postconventional level third level of reasoning in Kohlberg's theory, in which morality is based on a personal moral code

postformal thought thought characterized by the realization that the correct answer may vary from situation to situation, that problem solutions must be realistic, that most situations are ambiguous, and that emotion and other subjective factors are an important part of thought

practical ability in Sternberg's theory of intelligence, the ability to know solutions to problems are likely to work

practical intelligence skills and knowledge necessary for people to function in everyday life

preconventional level first level of reasoning in Kohlberg's theory, where moral reasoning is based on external forces

prejudice a view of other people, usually negative, that is based on their membership in a specific group

prenatal development the many changes that turn a fertilized egg into a newborn human

presbycusis loss in the ability to hear high-pitched tones

presbyopia difficulty in seeing close objects clearly, caused by the inability of the lens to focus as the muscles around it stiffen

preterm (premature) babies born before the 36th week after conception

primary mental abilities groups of related intellectual skills, such as spatial skill and mathematical skill

primary sex characteristics physical signs of maturity directly linked to the reproductive organs

private speech comments that are not intended for others but serve the purpose of helping children regulate their behavior

proactivity when people choose new behaviors to meet new desires or needs

processes of thinking information processing, memory, fluid intelligence, products of thinking, products applied to thinking, expertise

programmed cell death theories theories that suggest that aging is genetically programmed

propositions ideas derived by combining words

prosocial behavior any behavior that benefits another person

proximodistal principle principle of physical growth that states that structures nearest the center of the body develop first

psychodynamic theories theories in which human behavior is said to be guided by motives and drives that are internal and often unconscious

psychological forces all internal perceptual, cognitive, emotional, and personality factors that affect development

psychometricians psychologists who specialize in measuring psychological traits such as intelligence and personality

psychomotor speed speed with which a person makes a particular response

psychosocial theory theory proposed by Erikson in which personality development results from the interaction of maturation and societal demands

puberty collection of physical changes that marks the onset of adolescence, such as growth of breasts or testes and the growth spurt

punishment applying an aversive stimulus (e.g., a spanking) or removing an attractive stimulus (e.g., TV viewing)

purpose according to Erikson, balance between individual initiative and the willingness to cooperate with others

reaction range a genotype is manifested in reaction to the environment where development takes place, so a single genotype can lead to a range of phenotypes

"reasonable woman" standard legal criterion for determining whether sexual harassment has occurred; based on whether a reasonable woman would view a behavior as harassing

recessive allele whose instructions are ignored when it is combined with a dominant allele

referential style language-learning style that describes children whose vocabularies are dominated by names of objects, persons, or actions

reflective judgment reasoning about dilemmas that is characterized by the realization that the search for truth is an ongoing, never-ending journey

reflexes unlearned responses triggered by specific stimulation

regular (nonREM) sleep sleep in which heart rate, breathing, and brain activity are steady

reinforcement consequence that increases the likelihood that a behavior will be repeated in the future

reinvolvement with personal past meaning grandparents derive from recalling the relationship they had with their own grandparents

rejected children as applied to children's popularity, children who are disliked by many classmates

relational aggression aggression used to hurt others by undermining their social relationships

reliability as applied to tests, when test scores are consistent from one testing time to another

resistant attachment relationship in which, after a brief separation, infants want to be held but are difficult to console

retinal disparity way to infer depth based on differences in the retinal images in the left and right eyes

returning adult students college students over the age of 25 years

rheumatoid arthritis a more destructive joint disease than osteoarthritis that develops slowly and affects joints, causing stiffness and pain

rites of passage initiation rituals that mark the onset of a new phase of development, such as adulthood

role transitions assuming new responsibilities and duties when a person moves from one phase of development (e.g., adolescence) to another (e.g., adulthood)

sample subset of a population

sandwich generation middle-aged adults between two generations (their parents and children) that put demands and pressures on them

savants individuals with mental retardation who are extremely talented in one domain

scaffolding teaching style in which adults adjust the amount of assistance that they offer, based on the learner's needs

scenario life-span construct that consists of expectations about the future

scheme according to Piaget, a mental structure that organizes information and regulates behavior

secondary mental abilities broad categories of related primary mental abilities

secondary sex characteristics physical signs of maturity not directly linked to reproductive organs

secure attachment relationship in which infants have come to trust and depend on their mothers

selective attention the selection of relevant information for further processing and inhibition of irrelevant information

selective optimization with compensation (SOC) a model of successful adaptation to aging that emphasizes selection of goals, followed by efforts to maintain or enhance those chosen goals

selective serotonin reuptake inhibitors (SSRIs) type of medication used to treat depression that alters the balance of serotonin in the brain

self reports people's answers to questions about the topic of interest

self-efficacy belief that one is capable of performing a certain task

semantic memory the general class of memory concerning the remembering of meanings of words or concepts

sensorimotor period first of Piaget's four stages of cognitive development, which lasts from birth to approximately 2 years

sequential design complex research design consisting of multiple cross-sectional or longitudinal designs

sex chromosomes 23rd pair of chromosomes; these determine the sex of the child

sickle-cell trait disorder in which individuals only show signs of mild anemia when they are seriously deprived of oxygen; occurs in individuals who have one dominant allele for normal blood cells and one recessive sickle-cell allele

simple social play play that begins at about 15 to 18 months; toddlers engage in similar activities as well as talk and smile at each other

skill acquisition the gradual, somewhat haphazard process by which people learn new abilities

skilled nursing care 24-hour care requiring fairly constant monitoring and provision of medical and other health services, usually by nurses

sleeping state in which a baby alternates from being still and breathing regularly to moving gently and breathing irregularly and in which the eyes are closed throughout

sleepwalking sleep disturbance during deep sleep in which children get out of bed and walk about

social clock when adults associate future events with a time or age by which they expect to complete them

social cognitive theory view that thinking, as well as direct reinforcement and punishment, plays an important part in shaping behavior

social contract characteristic of Kohlberg's Stage 5, in which moral reasoning is based on the belief that laws are for the good of all members of society

social convoy group of people who journey together throughout their lives and provide each other support in good and bad times

social referencing behavior in which infants in unfamiliar or ambiguous environments often look at their mother or father, as if searching for cues to help them interpret the situation

social role set of cultural guidelines about how one should behave, especially with other people

social smiles smile that infants produce when they see a human face

social system morality characteristic of Kohlberg's Stage 4, in which moral reasoning is based on maintenance of order in society

socialization teaching children the values, roles, and behaviors of their culture

sociocultural forces all interpersonal, societal, cultural, and ethnic factors that influence development

socioemotional selectivity way of maintaining social contact that is motivated by many goals, including information seeking, self-concept, and emotional regulation

spaced retrieval memory intervention that involves teaching persons with Alzheimer's disease to remember new information by gradually increasing the time between retrieval attempts

specification second phase in Super's theory of career development, in which adolescents learn more about specific lines of work and begin training

spermarche first spontaneous ejaculation of sperm

spina bifida disorder in which the embryo's neural tube does not close properly

spiritual support type of coping in which people seek pastoral care, participate in organized and nonorganized religious activities, and express faith in a God who cares for people

stable-order principle counting principle that states that number names must always be counted in the same order

stagnation according to Erikson, a state in which people are not able to deal with the needs of their children or are unable to provide mentoring to younger adults

status offense an act that is not a crime if it is committed by an adult, such as truancy or running away from home

stem cells unspecialized human or animal cells that can produce mature specialized body cells and at the same time replicate themselves

stereotype threat an evoked fear of being judged in accordance with a negative stereotype about a group to which you belong

stereotypes a special type of social knowledge structure or social belief representing organized prior knowledge about a group of people that affects how we interpret new information

stranger wariness first distinct signs of fear that emerge around 6 months of age when infants become wary in the presence of unfamiliar adults

stress physical and psychological responses to threatening or challenging conditions

stress and coping paradigm dominant framework used to study stress

strokes interruption in the flow of blood in the brain due to a blockage in a cerebral artery

structured observations setting created by a researcher that is particularly likely to elicit the behavior of interest so that it can be observed

subjective well-being a positive evaluation of one's life associated with positive feelings

sudden infant death syndrome (SIDS) situation in which a healthy baby dies suddenly, for no apparent reason

synaptic pruning gradual reduction in the number of synapses, beginning in infancy and continuing until early adolescence

systematic observation involves watching people and carefully recording what they say or do

telegraphic speech speech used by young children that contains only the words that are necessary to get a message across

telomeres tips of the chromosomes, which apparently play a major role in limiting the number of times a cell can divide before dying

temperament consistent style or pattern of behavior

teratogen agent that causes abnormal prenatal development

terminal buttons small knobs at the end of the axon that release neurotransmitters

terror management theory addresses the issue of why people engage in certain behaviors to achieve particular psychological states

tertiary circular reaction according to Piaget, repeating old schemes with new objects

texture gradient perceptual cue to depth based on the fact that the texture of objects changes from coarse but distinct for nearby objects to finer and less distinct for distant objects

theory organized set of ideas that explains development

theory of mind ideas about connections between thoughts, beliefs, intentions, and behavior that create an intuitive understanding of the link between mind and behavior

time-out punishment that involves removing children who are misbehaving from a situation to a quiet, unstimulating environment

toddlers young children who have learned to walk

toddling early, unsteady form of walking done by infants

transient ischemic attacks (TIAs) an interruption of blood flow to the brain that often is an early warning sign of stroke

Type A behavior pattern ongoing displays of intense competitiveness, anger, hostility, restlessness, aggression, and impatience

Type B behavior pattern ongoing displays of noncompetitiveness, calm, lack of aggression, and patience

ultrasound prenatal diagnostic technique that bounces sound waves off the fetus to generate an image of the fetus

umbilical cord structure containing veins and arteries that connects the developing child to the placenta

underextension when children define words more narrowly than adults do

unexercised ability level of performance a person exhibits without practice or training

uninvolved parenting style of parenting that provides neither warmth nor control and that minimizes the amount of time parents spend with children

universal ethical principles characteristic of Kohlberg's Stage 6, in which moral reasoning is based on moral principles that apply to all

universal versus context-specific development issue issue of whether there is one path of development or several

useful life expectancy number of years a person has that are free from debilitating chronic disease and impairment

validity as applied to tests, the extent to which the test measures what it is supposed to measure

valued elder status grandparents derive from being seen as wise

vascular dementia disease caused by numerous small cerebrovascular accidents

vernix substance that protects the fetus's skin during development

very low birth weight newborns who weigh less than 1,500 grams (3 pounds)

vigilance the maintenance of attention over time; also called sustained attention

visual acuity smallest pattern that one can distinguish reliably

visual cliff glass-covered platform that appears to have a "shallow" side and "deep" side; used to study infants' depth perception

visual expansion kinetic cue to depth perception that refers to the fact that as an object moves closer it fills an ever-greater proportion of the retina

vocational maturity degree of congruity between a person's age and occupational behaviors

waking activity state in which a baby's eyes are open but seem unfocused and the arms or legs move in bursts of uncoordinated motion

wear-and-tear theory theory of aging that suggests that the body, much like a machine, gradually deteriorates over time and finally wears out

whole-brain death the most widely used measure to determine death, based on an established set of criteria

will according to Erikson, a young child's understanding that he or she can act on the world intentionally, which occurs when autonomy, shame, and doubt are in balance

word recognition the process of identifying a unique pattern of letters

work-family conflict feeling of being pulled in multiple directions by incompatible demands from one's job and one's family

working memory type of memory in which a small number of items can be stored briefly

zone of maximum comfort in environmental press theory, the area where slight decreases in press allow people to live happily without worrying about environmental demands

zone of maximum performance potential in environmental press theory, the area in which slight increases in press tend to improve performance

zone of proximal development difference between what children can do with assistance and what they can do alone

zygote fertilized egg

References

AARP. (1999a). *AARP/Modern Maturity sexuality survey: Summary of findings.* Retrieved July 3, 2005, from http://www.aarpmagazine.org/lifestyle/relationships/great_sex.html

AARP. (2005). *Supplemental plans (Medigap).* Retrieved August 8, 2005, from http://www.aarp.org/health/medicare/supplemental/

Abengozar, M. C., Bueno, B., & Vega, J. L. (1999). Intervention on attitudes toward death along the lifespan. *Educational Gerontology, 25,* 435–447.

Aberson, C. L., Shoemaker, C., & Tomolillo, C. (2004). The role of interethnic friendships. *Journal of Social Psychology, 144,* 335–347.

Aboud, F. E. (1993). The developmental psychology of racial prejudice. *Transcultural Psychiatric Research Review, 30,* 229–242.

Aboud, F. E. (2003). The formation of in-group favoritism and out-group prejudice in young children: Are they distinct attitudes? *Developmental Psychology, 39,* 48–60.

Abraham, M. (2000). Isolation as a form of marital violence: The South Asian immigrant experience. *Journal of Social Distress and the Homeless, 9,* 221–236.

Abraham, R. (2000). Organizational cynicism: Bases and consequences. *Genetic, Social, and General Psychology Monographs, 126,* 269–292.

Ackerman, B. P. (1993). Children's understanding of the speaker's meaning in referential communication. *Journal of Experimental Child Psychology, 55,* 56–86.

Acock, A. C., & Demo, D. H. (1994). *Family diversity and well-being.* Thousand Oaks, CA: Sage.

Adair, R. H., & Bauchner, H. (1993, April). Sleep problems in childhood. *Current Problems in Pediatrics, 147–170.*

Adams, J. (1999). On neurodevelopmental disorders: Perspectives from neurobehavioral teratology. In H. Tager-Flusberg (Ed.), *Neurodevelopmental disorders* (pp. 451–468). Cambridge, MA: MIT.

Adams, M. J., Treiman, R., & Pressley, M. (1998). Reading, writing, and literacy. In W. Damon (Ed.), *Handbook of child psychology* (Vol. 4). New York: Wiley.

Adams, R. G., Blieszner, R., & de Vries, B. (2000). Definitions of friendship in the third age: Age, gender, and study location effects. *Journal of Aging Studies, 14,* 117–133.

Adams, R. J., & Courage, M. L. (1995). Development of chromatic discrimination in early infancy. *Behavioural Brain Research, 67,* 99–101.

Adler, L. L. (2001). Women and gender roles. In L. L. Adler & U. P. Gielen (Eds.), *Cross-cultural topics on psychology* (2nd ed., pp. 103–114). Westport, CT: Praeger/Greenwood.

Adler, N. (1994). *Adolescent sexual behavior looks irrational—But looks are deceiving.* Washington, DC: Federation of Behavioral, Psychological, and Cognitive Sciences.

Administration on Aging. (2001). *Americans with disabilities: 1997.* Retrieved August 7, 2005, from http://www.aoa.gov/prof/Statistics/disabilities_data/97sipp-disabiliestable.pdf

Administration on Aging. (2004). *Elder abuse is a serious problem.* Retrieved August 8, 2005, from http://www.aoa.gov/press/fact/alpha/fact_elder_abuse.asp

Administration on Aging. (2005). *A profile of older Americans: 2004.* Retrieved August 8, 2005, from http://www.aoa.gov/prof/Statistics/profile/2004/10.asp

Adolph, K. E. (1997). Learning in the development of infant locomotion. *Monographs of the Society for Research in Child Development, 62,* 1–140.

Adolph, K. E. (2000). Specificity of learning: Why infants fall over a veritable cliff. *Psychological Science, 11,* 290–295.

Adolph, K. (2003). Learning to keep balance. In R. V. Kail (Ed.), *Advances in child development and behavior* (Vol. 30). Orlando. FL: Academic Press.

Adolph, K. E., Eppler, M. A., & Gibson, E. J. (1993). Crawling versus walking: Infants' perception of affordances for locomotion over sloping surfaces. *Child Development, 64,* 1158–1174.

Adolph, K. E., Vereijken, B., & Denny, M. A. (1998). Learning to crawl. *Child Development, 69,* 1299–1312.

AgingStats.gov. (2004). *Older Americans 2004: Key indictors of well-being.* Retrieved August 7. 2005, from http://www.agingstats.gov/chartbook2004/default.htm

Aguayo, G. M. (2005). The effect of occupational environment and gender traditionality on self-efficacy for a nontraditional occupation in community college women. *Dissertation Abstracts International: Section B: The Sciences & Engineering, 65(7-B),* 3696.

Ahluwalia, N. (2004). Aging, nutrition and immune function. *Journal of Nutrition, Health & Aging, 8,* 2–6.

Ahrons, C., & Wallisch, L. (1986). The relationship between former spouses. In D. Perlman & S. Duck (Eds.), *Intimate relationships: Development, dynamics, and deterioration* (pp. 269–296). Newbury Park, CA: Sage.

Ainsworth, M. D. S. (1978). The development of infant-mother attachment. In B. M. Caldwell & H. N. Ricciuti (Eds.), *Review of child development research* (Vol. 3). Chicago: University of Chicago Press.

Ainsworth, M. S. (1993). Attachment as related to mother-infant interaction. *Advances in Infancy Research, 8,* 1–50.

Ajrouch, K. J., Antonucci, T. C., & Janevic, M. (2000). Social networks among Blacks and Whites: The interaction between race and age. *Journal of Gerontology: Social Sciences, 56B,* S112–S118.

Akhtar, N., Jipson, J., & Callanan, M. (2001). Learning words through overhearing. *Child Development, 72,* 416–430.

al'Absi, M., Bongard, S., & Lovallo, W. R. (2000). Adrenocorticotropin responses to interpersonal stress: Effects of overt anger expression style and defensiveness. *International Journal of Psychophysiology, 37,* 257–265.

Albeck, S., & Kaydar, D. (2002). Divorced mothers: Their network of friends pre- and post-divorce. *Journal of Divorce and Remarriage, 36,* 111–118.

Albert, M. S., & Killiany, R. J. (2001). Age-related cognitive change and brain-behavior relationships. In J. E. Birren & K. W. Schaie (Eds.), *Handbook of the psychology of aging* (5th ed., pp. 161–185). San Diego, CA: Academic Press.

Alberts, A. E. (2005). Neonatal behavioral assessment scale. In C. B. Fisher & R. M. Lerner (Eds.), *Encyclopedia of applied developmental science* (Vol. 1, pp. 111–115). Thousand Oaks CA: Sage.

Aldwin, C. M., & Gilmer, D. F. (2004). *Health, illness, and optimal aging: Biological and psychosocial perspectives.* Thousand Oaks, CA: Sage.

Alexander, E. N., & Bowen, A. M. (2004). Excessive drinking in college: Behavioral outcome, not binge, as a basis for prevention. *Addictive Behaviors, 29,* 1199–1205.

Allaire J. C., & Marsiske, M. (1999). Everyday cognition: Age and intellectual ability correlates. *Psychology and Aging, 14,* 627–644.

Allen, K. R., & Chin-Sang, V. (1990). A lifetime of work: The context and meanings of leisure for aging Black women. *The Gerontologist, 30,* 734–740.

Allen, T. D. (2001). Family-supportive work environments: The role of organizational perceptions. *Journal of Vocational Behavior, 58,* 414–435.

Alley, J. L. (2004). The potential meaning of the grandparent-grandchild relationship as perceived by young adults: An exploratory study. *Dissertation Abstracts International: Section B: The Sciences & Engineering, 65(3–B),* 1536.

Allgeier, E. R., & Allgeier, A. R. (2000). *Sexual interactions* (5th ed.). Boston: Houghton Mifflin.

Aman, C. J., Roberts, R. J., & Pennington, B. F. (1998). A neuropsychological examination of the underlying deficit in attention deficit hyperactivity disorder: Frontal lobe versus right parietal lobe theories. *Developmental Psychology, 34,* 956–969.

Amato, P. R. (2001). Children of divorce in the 1990s: An update of the Amato and Keith (1991) meta-analysis. *Journal of Family Psychology, 15,* 355–370.

Amato, P. R., & Cheadle, J. (2005). The long reach of divorce: Divorce and child well-being across three generations. *Journal of Marriage & Family, 67,* 191–206.

Amato, P. R., & Fowler, F. (2002). Parenting practices, child adjustment, and family diversity. *Journal of Marriage and the Family, 64,* 703–716.

Amato, P. R., & Keith, B. (1991). Parental divorce and the well-being of children: A meta-analysis. *Psychological Bulletin, 110,* 26–46.

Amato, P. R., & Previti, D. (2003). People's reasons for divorcing: Gender, social class, the life course, and adjustment. *Journal of Family Issues, 24,* 602–626.

American Academy of Pediatrics. (1997). Adolescents and anabolic steroids: A subject review (RE9720). *Pediatrics, 99.*

American Academy of Pediatrics (AAP) Committee on Sports Medicine and Committee on School Health. (1989). Organized athletics for preadolescent children. *Pediatrics, 84,* 583–584.

American Automobile Association. (2005). *AAA Roadwise Review—A tool to help seniors drive safely longer: Overview.* Retrieved July 31, 2005, from http://www.aaasouth.com/acs_news/roadwisereview.asp

American Cancer Society. (2005a). *Quitting smoking.* Retrieved June 7, 2005, from http://www.cancer.org/docroot/PED/content/PED_10_13X_Guide_for_Quitting_Smoking.asp?sitearea=PED

American Cancer Society. (2005b). *Secondhand smoke.* Retrieved June 7, 2005, from http://www.cancer.org/docroot/PED/content/PED_10_2X_Secondhand_Smoke-Clean_Indoor_Air.asp?sitearea=PED

American Cancer Society. (2005c). *Statistics for 2005.* Retrieved July 3, 2005, from http://www.cancer.org/docroot/STT/stt_0.asp

American Cancer Society. (2005d). *Cancer facts and figures, 2005.* Retrieved July 31, 2005, from http://www.cancer.org/downloads/STT/CAFF2005f4PWSecured.pdf

American Heart Association. (2005a). *Cholesterol.* Retrieved June 8, 2005, from http://www.americanheart.org/presenter.jhtml?identifier=4488

American Heart Association. (2005b). *Fat.* Retrieved June 8, 2005, from http://www.americanheart.org/presenter.jhtml?identifier=4582

American Psychiatric Association. (1994). *Diagnostic and statistical manual of mental disorders* (4th ed.). Washington, DC: American Psychiatric Association.

American Psychological Society. (1993, December). Vitality for life. *APS Observer,* 1–24.

Anand, K. J., & Hickey, P. R. (1987). Pain and its effect in the human neonate and fetus. *New England Journal of Medicine, 31,* 1321–1329.

Anastasi, A. (1988). *Psychological testing* (6th ed.). New York: Macmillan.

Ancoli-Israel, S., & Alessi, C. (2005). Sleep and aging. *American Journal of Geriatric Psychiatry, 13,* 341–343.

Andersen, A. M. N., Wohlfahrt, J., Christens, P., Olsen, J., & Melbye, M. (2000). Maternal age and fetal loss: Population based register linkage study. *British Medical Journal, 320,* 1708–1712.

Anderson, C. A., & Bushman, B. J. (2001). Effects of violent video games on aggressive behavior, aggressive cognition, aggressive affect, physiological arousal, and prosocial behavior: A meta-analytic review of the scientific literature. *Psychological Science, 12,* 353–359.

Anderson, D. R., Huston, A. C., Schmitt, K. L., Linebarger, D. L., & Wright, J. C. (2001). Early childhood television viewing and adolescent behavior. *Monographs of the Society for Research in Child Development, 66.*

Anderson, E. R., Greene, S. M., Hetherington, E. M., & Clingempeel, W. G. (1999). The dynamics of parental remarriage: Adolescent, parent, and sibling. In E. M. Hetherington (Ed.), *Coping with divorce, single parenting, and remarriage: A risk and resiliency perspective.* Mahwah, NJ: Erlbaum.

Anderson, E. R., Greene, S. M., Walker, L., Malerba, C., Forgatch, M. S., & DeGarmo, D. S. (2004). Ready to take a chance again: Transitions into dating among divorced parents. *Journal of Divorce & Remarriage, 40,* 61–75.

Anderson, R. N., & Smith, B. L. (2005). Deaths: Leading causes for 2002. *National vital statistics reports* (Vol. 53, No. 17). Hyattsville, MD: National Center for Health Statistics.

Anderson, S. W., Damasio, H., Tranel, D., & Damasio, A. R. (2001). Long-term sequelae of prefrontal cortex damage acquired in early childhood. *Developmental Neuropsychology, 18,* 281–296.

Anderson, W. T. (1997). Dying and death in aging intergenerational families. In T. D. Hargrave & S. M. Hanna (Eds.), *The aging family* (pp. 270–291). New York: Brunner/Mazel.

Anetzberger, G. J. (2005). The reality of elder abuse. *Clinical Gerontologist, 28,* 2–25.

Angel, J. L., Buckley, C. J., & Sakamoto, A. (2001). Duration or disadvantage? Exploring nativity, ethnicity, and health in midlife. *Journal of Gerontology: Social Sciences, 56B,* S275–S284.

Anglin, J. M. (1993). Vocabulary development: A morphological analysis. *Monographs of the Society for Research in Child Development, 58*(10, Serial No. 238).

Anisfeld, M. (1991). Neonatal imitation. *Developmental Review, 11,* 60–97.

Anisfeld, M. (1996). Only tongue protrusion modeling is matched by neonates. *Developmental Review, 16,* 149–161.

Annett, M. (2002). *Handedness and brain asymmetry: The right shift theory.* New York: Psychology Press.

Antonarakis, S. E., & the Down Syndrome Collaborative Group. (1991). Parental origin of the extra chromosome in trisomy 21 as indicated by analysis of DNA polymorphisms. *New England Journal of Medicine, 324,* 872–876.

Antonucci, T. (2001). Social relations: An examination of social networks, social support, and sense of control. In J. E. Birren & K. W. Schaie (Eds.), *Handbook of the psychology of aging* (5th ed., pp. 427–453). San Diego: Academic Press.

Antonucci, T. C., Akiyama, H., & Lansford, J. E. (1998). Negative effects of close social relations. *Family Relations, 47,* 379–384.

Apgar, V. (1953). A proposal for a new method of evaluation of the newborn infant. *Current Researches in Anesthesia and Analgesia, 32,* 260–267.

Apter, T. (2001). *The myth of maturity: What teenagers need from parents to become adults.* New York: Norton.

Aranda, M. P., & Knight, B. G. (1997). The influence of ethnicity and culture on the caregiver stress and coping process: A sociocultural review and analysis. *The Gerontologist, 37,* 342–354.

Araujo, A. B., Mohr, B. A., & McKinlay, J. B. (2004). Changes in sexual function in middle-aged and older men: Longitudinal data from the Massachusetts Aging Study. *Journal of the American Geriatrics Society, 52,* 1502–1509.

Arbona, C. (1990). Career counseling research and Hispanics: A review of the literature. *Counseling Psychologist, 18,* 300–323.

Archer, N., & Bryant, P. (2001). Investigating the role of context in learning to read: A direct test of Goodman's model. *British Journal of Psychology, 92,* 579–591.

Arcus, D., & Kagan, J. (1995). Temperament and craniofacial variation in the first two years. *Child Development, 66,* 1529–1540.

Arellano, L. M. (2001). The psychological experiences of Latina professionals. *Dissertation Abstracts International Section B: The Sciences and Engineering, 62*(1–B), 534.

Arendell, T. (1995). *Fathers and divorce.* Thousand Oaks, CA: Sage.

Arenofsky, J. (1993). Childless and proud of it. *Newsweek,* February 8, p. 12.

Armstrong-Stassen, M., & Templer, A. (2005). Adapting training for older employees: The Canadian response to an aging workforce. *Journal of Management Development, 24,* 57–67.

Arnett, J., & Taber, S. (1994). Adolescence terminable and interminable: When does adolescence end? *Journal of Youth and Adolescence, 23,* 517–537.

Arnold, J. (2004). The congruence problem in John Holland's theory of vocational decisions. *Journal of Occupational and Organizational Psychology, 77,* 95–113.

Arseneault, L., Tremblay, R. E., Boulerice, B., & Saucier, J. F. (2002). Obstetrical complications and violent delinquency: Testing two developmental pathways. *Child Development, 73,* 496–508.

Artazcoz, L., Benach, J., Borrell, C., & Cortès, I. (2004). Unemployment and mental health: Understanding the interactions among gender, family roles, and social class. *American Journal of Public Health, 94,* 82–88.

Aryee, S. (1993). Dual-earner couples in Singapore: An examination of work and nonwork sources of their experienced burnout. *Human Relations, 46,* 1441–1468.

Aryee, S., & Luk, V. (1996). Work and nonwork influences on the career satisfaction of dual-earner couples. *Journal of Vocational Behavior, 49,* 38–52.

Asbury, K., Dunn, J. F., Pike, A., & Plomin, R. (2003). Nonshared environmental influences on individual differences in early behavioral development: A monozygotic twin differences study. *Child Development, 74,* 933–943.

Aseltine, R. H., Jr., & Gore, S. L. (2000). The variable effects of stress on alcohol use from adolescence to early adulthood. *Substance Use and Misuse, 35,* 643–668.

Ashcraft, M. H. (1982). The development of mental arithmetic: A chronometric approach. *Developmental Review, 2,* 212–236.

Ashendorf, L., Constantinou, M., Duff, K., & McCaffrey, R. J. (2005). Performance of community-dwelling adults ages 55 to 75 on the University of Pennsylvania Smell Identification Test: An item analysis. *Applied Neuropsychology, 12,* 24–29.

Asher, S. R., & Paquette, J. A. (2003). Loneliness and peer relations in childhood. *Current Directions in Psychological Science, 12,* 75–78.

Aslin, R. N., Jusczyk, P. W., & Pisoni, D. B. (1998). Speech and auditory processing during infancy: Constraints on and precursors to language. In W. Damon (Ed.), *Handbook of child psychology* (Vol. 2). New York: Wiley.

Aslin, R. N., Saffran, J. R., & Newport, W. L. (1998). Computation of conditional probability statistics by 8-month-old infants. *Psychological Science, 9,* 321–324.

Atchley, R. C. (1989). A continuity theory of normal aging. *The Gerontologist, 29,* 183–190.

Attig, T. (1996). *How we grieve: Relearning the world.* New York: Oxford University Press.

Atwater, E. (1992). *Adolescence.* Englewood Cliffs, NJ: Prentice-Hall.

Au, T. K., & Glusman, M. (1990). The principle of mutual exclusivity in word learning: To honor or not to honor? *Child Development, 61,* 1474–1490.

Aunola, K., Stattin, H., & Nurmi, J.-E. (2000). Parenting styles and adolescents' achievement strategies. *Journal of Adolescence, 23,* 205–222.

Avis, N. E. (1999). Women's health at midlife. In S. L. Willis & J. D. Reid (Eds.), *Life in the middle: Psychological and social development in middle age* (pp. 105–146). San Diego: Academic Press.

Azar, S. T. (2002). Parenting and child maltreatment. In M. Bornstein (Ed.), *Handbook of parenting* (Vol. 4, pp. 361–388). Mahwah NJ: Erlbaum.

Bachman, J. (1983, Summer). Premature affluence: Do high school students earn too much? *Economic Outlook USA,* 64–67.

Bachman, J. G., & Schulenberg, J. (1993). How part-time work intensity relates to drug use, problem behavior, time use, and satisfaction among high school seniors: Are these consequences or merely correlates? *Developmental Psychology, 29,* 229–230.

Bäckman, L., Small, B. J., & Wahlin, Å. (2001). Aging and memory: Cognitive and biological processes. In J. E. Birren & K. W. Schaie (Eds.), *Handbook of the psychology of aging* (5th ed., pp. 349–377). San Diego, CA: Academic Press.

Backscheider, A., G., Shatz, M., & Gelman, S. A. (1993). Preschoolers' ability to distinguish living kinds as a function of regrowth. *Child Development, 64,* 1242–1257.

Baek, J. (2005). Individual variations in family caregiving over the caregiving career. *Dissertation Abstracts International: Section B: The Sciences and Engineering, 65(B),* 3769.

Baer, D. M., & Wolf, M. M. (1968). The reinforcement contingency in preschool and remedial education. In R. D. Hess & R. M Baer (Eds.), *Early education.* Chicago: Aldine.

Bagwell, C. L. (2004). Friendships, peer networks and antisocial behavior. In J. B. Kupersmidt & K. A. Dodge (Eds.), *Children's peer relations* (pp. 37–57). Washington DC: American Psychological Association.

Bagwell, C. L., Bender, S. E., Andreassi, C. L., Kinoshita, T. L., Montarello, S. A., & Muller, J. G. (2005). Friendship quality and perceived relationship changes predict psychosocial adjustment in early adulthood. *Journal of Social & Personal Relationships, 22,* 235–254.

Bagwell, C. L., Newcomb, A. F., & Bukowski, W. M. (1998). Preadolescent friendship and peer rejection as predictors of adult adjustment. *Child Development, 69,* 140–153.

Bahrick, L. E., & Lickliter, R. (2002). Intersensory redundancy guides early perceptual and cognitive development. In R. V. Kail (Ed.), *Advances in child development and behavior* (Vol. 30). Orlando, FL: Academic Press.

Bailey, D. A., & Rasmussen, R. L. (1996). Sport and the child: Physiological and skeletal issues. In F. L. Smoll & R. E. Smith (Eds.), *Children and youth in sport: A biopsychological perspective* (pp. 187–199). Dubuque, IA: Brown & Benchmark.

Bailey, J. M., Bobrow, D., Wolfe, M., & Mikach, S. (1995). Sexual orientation of adult sons of gay fathers. *Developmental Psychology, 31,* 124–129.

Bailey, J., M., Dunne, M. P., & Martin, N. G. (2000). Genetic and environmental influences on sexual orientation and its correlates in an Austrian twin sample. *Journal of Personality and Social Psychology, 78,* 524–436.

Baillargeon, R. (1987). Object permanence in 3½- and 4½-month-old infants. *Developmental Psychology, 23,* 655–664.

Baillargeon, R. (1994). How do infants learn about the physical world? *Current Directions in Psychological Science, 3,* 133–140.

Baillargeon, R. (1998). Infants' understanding of the physical world. *Advances in Psychological Science, 2,* 503–529.

Baillargeon, R. (2004). Infants' reasoning about hidden objects: Evidence for event-general and event-specific expectations. *Developmental Science, 7,* 391–424.

Baker, C. (1993). *Foundations of bilingual education and bilingualism.* Clevedon, England: Multilingual Matters.

Baker, L. (1994). Fostering metacognitive development. In H. W. Reese (Ed.), *Advances in child development and behavior* (Vol. 25). San Diego: Academic Press.

Baker, L., & Brown, A. L. (1984). Metacognitive skills and reading. In P. D. Pearson (Ed.), *Handbook of reading research* (Part 2). New York: Longman.

Bakermans-Kranenburg, M., van IJzendoorn, M. H., & Juffer, F. (2003). Less is more: Meta-analyses of sensitivity and attachment interventions in early childhood. *Psychological Bulletin, 129,* 195–215.

Balk, D. E., & Corr, C. A. (2001). Bereavement during adolescence: A review of research. In M. S. Stroebe, R. O. Hansson, W. Stroebe, & H. Schut (Eds.), *Handbook of bereavement research: Consequences, coping, and care* (pp. 169–197). Washington, DC: American Psychological Association.

Ball, K. (1997). Enhancing mobility in the elderly: Attentional interventions for driving. In S. M. C. Dollinger & L. F. Dilalla (Eds.), *Assessment and intervention issues across in the lifespan* (pp. 267–292). Mahwah, NJ: Erlbaum.

Ball, K., & Owsley, C. (1993). The Useful Field of View Test: A new technique for evaluating age-related declines in visual function. *Journal of the American Optometric Association, 64,* 71–79.

Ball, K., Owsley, C., Sloane, M. E., Roenker, D. L., & Bruni, J. R. (1993). Visual attention problems as a predictor of vehicle accidents among older drivers. *Investigative Ophthalmology and Visual Science, 34*(11), 3110–3123.

Baltes, B. B., & Heydens-Gahir, H. A. (2003). Reduction of work-family conflict through the use of selection, optimization, and compensation behaviors. *Journal of Applied Psychology, 88,* 1005–1018.

Baltes, M. M., & Carstensen, L. L. (1999). Social-psychological theories and their applications to aging: From individual to collective. In V. L. Bengtson & K. W. Schaie (Eds.), *Handbook of theories of aging* (pp. 209–226). New York: Springer.

Baltes, P. B. (1987). Theoretical propositions of life-span developmental psychology: On the dynamics between growth and decline. *Developmental Psychology, 23,* 611–626.

Baltes, P. B. (1993). The aging mind: Potential and limits. *The Gerontologist, 33,* 580–594.

Baltes, P. B. (1997). On the incomplete architecture of human ontogeny: Selection, optimization, and compensation as foundation of developmental theory. *American Psychologist, 52,* 366–380.

Baltes, P. B., Lindenberger, U., & Staudinger, U. M. (1998). Life-span theory in developmental psychology. In R. M. Lerner (Ed.), *Handbook of child psychology, Vol. 1. Theoretical models of human development* (5th ed., pp. 1029–1143). New York: Wiley.

Baltes, P. B., & Smith, J. (2003). New frontiers in the future of aging: From successful aging of the young old to the dilemmas of the fourth age. *Gerontology, 49,* 123–135.

Baltes, P. B., & Staudinger, U. M. (1993). The search for a psychology of wisdom. *Current Directions in Psychological Science, 2,* 75–80.

Baltes, P. B., & Staudinger, U. M. (2000). Wisdom: A meta-heuristic (pragmatic) to orchestrate mind and virtue toward excellence. *American Psychologist, 55,* 122–136.

Baltes, P. B., Staudinger, U. M., & Lindenberger, U. (1999). Lifespan psychology: Theory and application to intellectual functioning. *Annual Review of Psychology, 50,* 471–507.

Bandura, A. (1977). *Social learning theory.* Englewood Cliffs, NJ: Prentice-Hall.

Bandura, A. (1986). *Social foundations of thought and action: A social-cognitive theory.* Englewood Cliffs, NJ: Prentice-Hall.

Bandura A., & Bussey, K. (2004). On broadening the cognitive, motivational, and sociocultural scope of theorizing about gender development and functioning: Comment on Martin, Ruble, and Szkrybalo (2002). *Psychological Bulletin, 130,* 691–701.

Banger, M. (2003). Affective syndrome during perimenopause. *Maturitas, 41* (Suppl. I), S13–S18.

Banks-Wallace, J., & Parks, L. (2004). It's all sacred: African American women's perspectives on spirituality. *Issues in Mental Health Nursing, 25,* 25–45.

Barber, B. K., & Olsen, J. A. (1997). Socialization in context: Connection, regulation, and autonomy in the family, school, and neighborhood, and with peers. *Journal of Adolescent Research, 12,* 287–315.

Barenboim, C. (1981). The development of person perception in childhood and adolescence: From behavioral comparisons to psychological constructs to psychological comparisons. *Child Development, 52,* 129–144.

Bargh, J. A., Chaiken, S., Raymond, P., & Hymes, C. (1996). The automatic evaluation effect: Unconditional automatic attitude activation with a pronunciation task. *Journal of Experimental Psychology, 32,* 104–128.

Barinaga, M. (1997). Researchers find signals that guide young brain neurons. *Science, 278,* 385–386.

Barkley, R. A. (1990). Attention deficit disorders: History, definition, and diagnosis. In M. Lewis & S. M. Miller (Eds.), *Handbook of developmental psychopathology.* New York: Plenum.

Barkley, R. A. (1994). Impaired delayed responding: A unified theory of attention-deficit hyperactivity disorder. In R. A. Barkley (Ed.), *Disruptive behavior disorders in childhood.* New York: Plenum.

Barkley, R. A. (1996). Attention-deficit hyperactivity disorder. In E. J. Mash & R. A. Barkley (Eds.), *Child psychopathology.* New York: Guilford Press.

Barnes, A. (Ed.). (2005). *The handbook of women, psychology, and the law.* New York: Wiley.

Barnes, H., & Parry, J. (2004). Renegotiating identity and relationships: Men and women's adjustments to retirement. *Ageing and Society, 24,* 213–233.

Barr, R., & Hayne, H. (1999). Developmental changes in imitation from television during infancy. *Child Development, 70,* 1067–1081.

Barrett, A. E., & Lynch, S. M. (1999). Caregiving networks of elderly persons: Variation by marital status. *The Gerontologist, 39,* 695–704.

Barton, M. E., & Tomasello, M. (1991). Joint attention and conversation in mother-infant-sibling triads. *Child Development, 62,* 517–529.

Bartsch, K., & Wellman, H. M. (1995). *Children talk about the mind.* New York: Oxford University Press.

Baskett, L. M. (1985). Sibling status effects: Adult expectations. *Developmental Psychology, 21,* 441–445.

Basso, K. H. (1970). *The Cibecue Apache.* New York: Holt, Rinehart, & Winston.

Bates, E., Benigni, L., Bretherton, I., Camaioni, L., & Volterra, V. (1979). *The emergence of symbols: Cognition and communication in infancy.* New York: Academic Press.

Bates, E., Bretherton, I., & Snyder, L. (1988). *From first words to grammar: Individual differences and dissociable mechanisms.* New York: Cambridge University Press.

Bates, J. E., Pettit, G. S., Dodge, K. A., & Ridge, B. (1998). Interaction of temperamental resistance to control and restrictive parenting in the development of externalizing behavior. *Developmental Psychology, 34,* 982–995.

Bauer, J., & McAdams, D. P. (2004). Growth goals, maturity, and well-being. *Developmental Psychology, 40,* 114–127.

Bauer, J., McAdams, D. P., & Sakaeda, A. R. (2005). Interpreting the good life: Growth memories in the lives of mature, happy people. *Journal of Personality & Social Psychology, 88,* 203–217.

Bauer, P. J. (2004). Getting explicit memory off the ground: Steps toward construction of a neuro-developmental account of changes in the first two years of life. *Developmental Review, 24,* 347–373.

Bauer, P. J., Burch, M. M., & Kleinknecht, E. F. (2003). Developments in early recall memory: Normative trends and individual differences. In R. V. Kail (Ed), *Advances in child development and behavior* (Vol. 30). San Diego: Academic Press.

Baugh, S. G., Lankau, M. J., & Scandura, T. A. (1996). An investment of the effects of protégé gender on responses to mentoring. *Journal of Vocational Behavior, 49,* 309–323.

Baumeister, A. A., & Baumeister, A. A. (1995). Mental retardation. In M. Hersen & R. T. Ammerman (Eds.), *Advanced abnormal child psychology.* Hillsdale, NJ: Erlbaum.

Baumrind, D. (1975). Early socialization and the discipline controversy. Morristown, NJ: General Learning Press.

Baumrind, D. (1991). Parenting styles and adolescent development. In R. M. Lerner, A. C. Petersen, & J. Brooks-Gunn (Eds.), *Encyclopedia of adolescence.* New York: Garland.

Bauserman, R. (2002). Child adjustment in joint-custody versus sole-custody arrangements: A meta-analytic review. *Journal of Family Psychology, 16,* 91–102.

Bayley, N. (1969). *Bayley Scales of Infant Development.* New York: Psychological Corporation.

Beal, C. R. (1996). The role of comprehension monitoring in children's revision. *Educational Psychology Review, 8,* 219–238.

Beal, C. R., & Belgrad, S. L. (1990). The development of message evaluation skills in young children. *Child Development, 61,* 705–712.

Beck, A. T. (1967). *Depression: Clinical, experimental, and theoretical aspects.* New York: Harper & Row.

Beck, A. T., Rush, J., Shaw, B., & Emery, G. (1979). *Cognitive therapy of depression.* New York: Guilford Press.

Beck, J. G., & Averill, P. M. (2004). Older adults. In R. G. Heimberg, C. L. Turk, & D. S. Mennin (Eds.), *Generalized anxiety disorder: Advances in research and practice* (pp. 409–433). New York: Guilford Press.

Becker, B. J. (1986). Influence again: An examination of reviews and studies of gender differences in social influence. In J. S. Hyde & M. C. Linn (Eds.), *The psychology of gender differences. Advances through meta-analysis.* Baltimore, MD: Johns Hopkins University Press.

Becker, B. J. (2003). Introduction to the special section on metric in meta-analysis. *Psychological Methods, 8,* 403–405.

Behnke, M., & Eyler, F. D. (1993). The consequences of prenatal substance use for the developing fetus, newborn, and young child. *International Journal of the Addictions, 28,* 1341–1391.

Behrend, D. A., Rosengren, K. S., & Perlmutter, M. S. (1992). The relation between private speech and parental interactive style. In R. M. Diaz & L. E. Berk (Eds.), *Private speech: From social interaction to self-regulation* (pp. 85–100). Hillsdale, NJ: Erlbaum.

Belgrave, L. L., Wykle, M. L., & Choi, J. M. (1993). Health, double jeopardy, and culture: The use of institutionalization by African-Americans. *The Gerontologist, 33*, 379–385.

Beller, M., & Gafni, N. (1996). The 1991 international assessment of educational progress in mathematics and sciences: The gender differences perspective. *Journal of Educational Psychology, 88*, 365–377.

Belsky, J., Fish, M., & Isabella, R. A. (1991). Continuity and discontinuity in infant negative and positive emotionality: Family antecedents and attachment consequences. *Developmental Psychology, 27*, 421–431.

Belsky, J., Steinberg, L., & Draper, P. (1991). Childhood experience, interpersonal development, and reproductive strategy: An evolutionary theory of socialization. *Child Development, 62*, 647–670.

Belsky, J., Woodworth, S., & Crnic, K. (1996). Trouble in the second year: Three questions about family interaction. *Child Development, 67*, 556–578.

Bem, D. J. (1996). Exotic becomes erotic: A developmental theory of sexual orientation. *Psychological Review, 103*, 320–335.

Benenson, J. F., & Christakos, A. (2003). The greater fragility of females' versus males' closest same-sex friendships. *Child Development, 74*, 1123–1129.

Bengtson, V. L., Mills, T. L., & Parrott, T. M. (1995). Ageing in the United States at the end of the century. *Korea Journal of Population and Development, 24*, 215–244.

Ben-Israel Reuveni, O. (1999). *The effects of time on the adjustment of war bereaved parents: Functioning, relationship and marital adjustment.* Unpublished master's thesis, University of Haifa.

Bennett, K. M. (2005). Psychological wellbeing in later life: The longitudinal effects of marriage, widowhood and marital status change. *International Journal of Geriatric Psychiatry, 20*, 280–284.

Benokraitis, N. V. (1999). *Marriages and families: Changes, choices, and constraints.* Upper Saddle River, NJ: Prentice-Hall.

Benokraitis, N. (2005). *Marriages and families: Changes, choices, and constraints* (5th ed.). Upper Saddle River, NJ: Prentice Hall.

Benson, J. M. (1999). The polls-trends: End of life issues. *Public Opinion Quarterly, 63*, 263–277.

Benton, S. L., Corkill, A. J., Sharp, J. M., Downey, R. G., et al. (1995). Knowledge, interest, and narrative writing. *Journal of Educational Psychology, 87*, 66–79.

Berdahl, J. L., Magley, V. J., & Waldo, C. R. (1996). The sexual harassment of men? *Psychology of Women Quarterly, 20*, 527–547.

Berdes, C., & Zych, A. A. (2000). Subjective quality of life of Polish, Polish-immigrant, and Polish-American elderly. *International Journal of Aging and Human Development, 50*, 385–395.

Bereiter, C., & Scardamalia, M. (1987). *The psychology of written composition.* Hillsdale NJ: Erlbaum.

Berenbaum, S. A., & Snyder, E. (1995). Early hormonal influences on childhood sex-typed activity and playmate preferences: Implications for the development of sexual orientation. *Developmental Psychology, 31*, 31–42.

Berenbaum, S. A., Duck, S. C., & Bryk, K. (2000). Behavioral effects of prenatal vs. postnatal androgen excess in children with 21-hydroxylase-deficient congenital adrenal hyperplasia. *Journal of Clinical Endocrinology and Metabolism, 85*, 727–733.

Bergeron, L. R. (2004). Elder abuse: Clinical assessment and obligation to report. In K. A. Kendall-Tackett (Ed.), *Health consequences of abuse in the family: A clinical guide for evidence-based practice* (pp. 109–128). Washington, DC: American Psychological Association.

Berk, L. E. (1992). Children's private speech: An overview of theory and the status of research. In R. M. Diaz & L. E. Berk (Eds.), *Private speech: From social interaction to selfregulation.* Hillsdale, NJ: Erlbaum.

Berk, L. E. (1994). Vygotsky's theory: The importance of make believe play. *Young Children, 50*, 30–38.

Berko, J. (1958). The child's learning of English morphology. *Word, 14*, 150–177.

Berkowitz, M. W., & Gibbs, J. C. (1985). The process of moral conflict resolution and moral development. In M. W. Berkowitz (Ed.), *Peer conflict and psychological growth* (pp. 71–84). San Francisco: Jossey-Bass.

Berliner, A. J. (2000). Re-visiting Erikson's developmental model: The impact of identity crisis resolution on intimacy motive, generativity formation, and psychological adaptation in never-married, middle-aged adults. *Dissertation Abstracts International: Section B: The Sciences and Engineering, 61*, 560.

Berman, D., & Trickett, E. J. (2001). Cultural transitions in first-generation immigrants: Acculturation of Soviet Jewish refugee adolescents and parents. *Journal of Cross-Cultural Psychology, 32*, 456–477.

Berman, J. M. (2004). Industry output and employment projects to 2012. *Monthly Labor Review, 127*, 58–79.

Berndt, T. J., & Keefe, K. (1995). Friends' influence on adolescents' adjustment to school. *Child Development, 66*, 1312–1329.

Berndt, T. J., & Murphy, L. M. (2002). Influences of friends and friendships: Myths, truths, and research recommendations. *Advances in Child Development and Behavior, 30*, 275–310.

Berndt, T. J., & Perry, T. B. (1990). Distinctive features and effects of adolescent friendships. In R. Montemeyer, G. R. Adams, & T. P. Gullotta, (Eds.), *From childhood to adolescence: A transition period?* London: Sage.

Bertenthal, B. H., & Clifton, R. K. (1998). Perception and action. In W. Damon (Ed.), *Handbook of child psychology* (Vol. 2). New York: Wiley.

Berthier, N. E. (1996). Learning to reach: A mathematical model. *Developmental Psychology, 32*, 811–823.

Besharov, D. J., & Gardiner, K. N. (1997). Trends in teen sexual behavior. *Children and Youth Services Review, 19*, 341–367.

Best, C. T. (1995). Learning to perceive the sound pattern of English. In C. Rovee-Collier (Ed.), *Advances in infancy research.* Norwood NJ: Ablex.

Best, D. L. (2001). Gender concepts: Convergence in cross-cultural research and methodologies. *Cross-Cultural Research: The Journal of Comparative Social Science, 35*, 23–43.

Best, D. L., & Williams, J. E. (1993). A cross-cultural viewpoint. In A. E. Beall & R. J. Sternberg (Eds.), *The psychology of gender* (pp. 215–250). New York: Guilford.

Best, D. L., Williams, J. E., Cloud, J. M., Davis, S. W., Robertson, L. S., Edwards, J. R., Giles, H., & Fowles, J. (1977). Development of sex-trait stereotypes among young children in the United States, England, and Ireland. *Child Development, 48*, 1375–1384.

Betz, N. E., Harmon, L. W., & Borgen, F. H. (1996). The relationships of self-efficacy for the Holland themes to gender, occupational group membership, and vocational interests. *Journal of Counseling Psychology, 43*, 90–98.

Bhatt, R. S., Bertin, E., Hayden, A., & Reed, A. (2005). Face processing in infancy: Developmental changes in the use of different kinds of relational information. *Child Development, 76,* 169–181.

Bialystok, E. (1988). Levels of bilingualism and levels of linguistic awareness. *Developmental Psychology, 24,* 560–567.

Bigler, R. S., Jones, L. C., & Lobliner, D. B. (1997). Social categorization and the formation of intergroup attitudes in children. *Child Development, 68,* 530–543.

Bigler, R., Brown, C. S., & Markell, M. (2001). When groups are not created equal: Effects of group status on the formation of intergroup attitudes in children. *Child Development, 72,* 1151–1162.

Bingenheimer, J. B., Brennan, R. T., & Earls, F. J. (2005). Firearm violence exposure and serious violent behavior. *Science, 308,* 1323–1326.

Binstock, R. H. (1994). Changing criteria in old-age programs: The introduction of economic status and need for services. *The Gerontologist, 34,* 726–730.

Binstock, R. H. (1999). Public policy issues. In J. C. Cavanaugh & S. K. Whitbourne (Eds.), *Gerontology: Interdisciplinary perspectives* (pp. 414–447). New York: Oxford University Press.

Binstock, R. H., & Quadagno, J. (2001). Aging and politics. In R. H. Binstock & L. K. George (Eds.), *Handbook of aging and the social sciences* (5th ed., pp. 333–351). San Diego, CA: Academic Press.

Birch, L. L. (1991). Obesity and eating disorders: A developmental perspective. *Bulletin of the Psychonomic Society, 29,* 265–272.

Birch, L. L., & Fisher, J. A. (1995). Appetite and eating behavior in children. *Pediatric Clinics of North America, 42,* 931–953.

Birch, S. A. J., & Bloom, P. (2002). Preschoolers are sensitive to the speaker's knowledge when learning proper names. *Child Development, 73,* 434–444.

Bird, D. J. (2001). The influences and impact of burnout on occupational therapists. *Dissertation Abstracts International Section B: The Sciences and Engineering, 62(1–B),* 204.

Bishop, J. B. (2000). An environmental approach to combat binge drinking on college campuses. *Journal of College Student Psychotherapy, 15,* 15–30.

Bjorklund, D. F., & Pellegrini, A. D. (2000). Child development and evolutionary psychology. *Child Development, 71,* 1687–1708.

Bjorklund, D. F., Yunger, J. L., & Pellegrini, A. D. (2002). The evolution of parenting and evolutionary approaches to childrearing. In M. H. Bornstein (Ed.), *Handbook of parenting, Vol. 2: Biology and ecology of parenting* (pp. 3–30). Mahwah, NJ: Erlbaum.

Black, S. A., Markides, K. S., & Miller, T. Q. (1998). Correlates of depressive symptomatology among older community-dwelling Mexican Americans: The Hispanic EPESE. *Journal of Gerontology: Social Sciences, 53B,* S198–S208.

Black-Gutman, D., & Hickson, F. (1996). The relationship between racial attitudes and social-cognitive development in children: An Australian study. *Developmental Psychology, 32,* 448–456.

Blake, J., O'Rourke, P., & Borzellino, G. (1994). Form and function in the development of pointing and reaching gestures. *Infant Behavior & Development, 17,* 195–203.

Blake-Beard, S. D. (2001). Taking a hard look at formal mentoring programs: A consideration of potential challenges facing women. *Journal of Management Development, 20,* 331–345.

Blanchard-Fields, F. (1986). Reasoning on social dilemmas varying in emotional saliency: An adult developmental study. *Psychology and Aging, 1,* 325–333.

Blanchard-Fields, F. (1996). Causal attributions across the adult lifespan: The influence of social schemas, life context, and domain specificity. *Applied Cognitive Psychology, 10* (Spec. Issue), 5137–5146.

Blanchard-Fields, F. (1999). Social schematicity and causal attributions. In T. M. Hess & F. Blanchard-Fields (Eds.), *Social cognition and aging* (pp. 219–236). San Diego: Academic Press.

Blanchard-Fields, F., Baldi, R. A., & Constantin, L. P. (2004). *Interrole conflict across the adult life-span: The role of parenting stage, career stages and quality of experiences.* Unpublished manuscript.

Blanchard-Fields, F., Chen, Y., & Norris, L. (1997). Everyday problem solving across the adult lifespan: Influence of domain specificity and cognitive appraisal. *Psychology and Aging, 12,* 684–693.

Blanchard-Fields, F., & Hertzog, C. (2000). Age differences in schematicity. In U. von Hecker, S. Dutke, & G. Sedek (Eds.), *Processes of generative mental representation and psychological adaptation.* Dordrecht, The Netherlands: Kluwer.

Blanchard-Fields, F., Janke, H. C., & Camp, C. J. (1995). Age differences in problem-solving style: The role of emotional salience. *Psychology and Aging, 10,* 173–180.

Blazer, D. G. (2000). Spirituality, aging, and depression. In J. A. Thorson (Ed.), *Perspectives on spiritual well-being and aging* (pp. 161–169). Springfield, IL: Charles C. Thomas.

Bloom, L., Margulis, C., Tinker, E., & Fujita, N. (1996). Early conversations and word learning: Contributions from child and adult. *Child Development, 67,* 3154–3175.

Bloom, L., & Tinker, E. (2001). The intentionality model and language acquisition. *Monographs of the Society for Research in Child Development, 66* (Serial No. 267).

Bluck, S. (2003). Autobiographical memory: Exploring its functions in everyday life. *Memory, 11,* 113–123.

Bluck, S., & Habermas, T. (2000). The life story schema. *Motivation and Emotion, 24,* 121–147.

Bogaert, A. F. (2003). Number of older brothers and sexual orientation: New tests and the attraction/behavior distinction in two national probability samples. *Journal of Personality and Social Psychology, 84,* 644–652.

Bogatz, G. A., & Ball, S. (1972). The second year of "Sesame Street": A continuing evaluation. Princeton, NJ: Educational Testing Service.

Boivin, M., Vitaro, F., & Gagnon, C. (1992). A reassessment of the self-perception profile for children: Factor structure, reliability, and convergent validity of a French version among second through sixth grade children. *International Journal of Behavioral Development, 15,* 275–290.

Bolger, K. E., & Patterson, C. J. (2001). Developmental pathways from child maltreatment to peer rejection. *Child Development, 72,* 549–568.

Bollmer, J. M., Milich, R., Harris, M. J., & Maras, M. A. (2005). A friend in need: The role of friendship quality as a protective factor in peer victimization and bullying. *Journal of Interpersonal Violence, 20,* 701–712.

Bonanno, G., & Kaltman, S. (1999). Toward an integrative perspective on bereavement. *Psychological Bulletin, 125,* 760–776.

Bonanno, G. A., Keltner, D., Holen, A., & Horowitz, M. J. (1995). When avoiding unpleasant emotions might not be such a bad thing: Verbal-autonomic response dissociation and midlife conjugal bereavement. *Journal of Personality and Social Psychology, 69,* 975–989.

Bonanno, G. A., Papa, A., Lalande, K., Zhang, N., & Noll, J. G. (2005). Grief processing and deliberate grief avoidance: A prospective comparison of bereaved spouses and parents in the United States and the People's Republic of China. *Journal of Consulting and Clinical Psychology, 73,* 86–98.

Bonanno, G. A., Papa, A., & O'Neill, K. (2001). Loss and human resilience. *Applied and Preventive Psychology, 10,* 193–206.

Bonanno, G. A., Wortman, C. B., & Neese, R. M. (2004). Prospective patterns of resilience and maladjustment during widowhood. *Psychology and Aging, 19,* 260–271.

Bond, T. G. (1995). Piaget and measurement II: Empirical validation of the Piagetian model. *Archives de Psychologie, 63,* 155–185.

Bonomo, Y. A., Bowes, G., Coffey, C., Carlin, J. B., & Patton, G. C. (2004). Teenage drinking and the onset of alcohol dependence: A cohort study over seven years. *Addiction, 99,* 1520–1528.

Book, P. L. (1996). How does the family narrative influence the individual's ability to communicate about death? *Omega, Journal of Death and Dying, 33,* 323–342.

Boone, R. T., & Cunningham, J. G. (1998). Children's decoding of emotion in expressive body movement: The development of cue attention. *Developmental Psychology, 34,* 1007–1016.

Booth, J. R., Perfetti, C. A., & MacWhinney, B. (1999). Quick, automatic, and general activation of orthographic and phonological representations in young readers. *Developmental Psychology, 35,* 3–19.

Bornstein, M. C. (Ed.). (1995). *Handbook of parenting* (Vols. 1–3). Mahweh, NJ: Erlbaum.

Bornstein, M. H., & Arterberry, M. E. (2003). Recognition, discrimination, and categorization of smiling by 5-month-old infants. *Developmental Science, 6,* 585–599.

Bornstein, M. H., Haynes, O. M., O'Reilly, A. W., & Painter, K. M. (1996). Solitary and collaborative pretense play in early childhood: Sources of individual variation in the development of representational competence. *Child Development, 67,* 2910–2929.

Borry, P., Schotsmans, P., & Dierickx, K. (2005). The birth of the empirical turn in bioethics. *Bioethics, 19,* 49–71.

Bossé, R., Aldwin, C. M., Levenson, M. R., Spiro, A. I., & Mroczek, D. K. (1993). Change in social support after retirement: Longitudinal findings from the Normative Aging Study. *Journal of Gerontology: Psychological Sciences, 48,* P210–P217.

Bouchard, T. J., Jr. (1997). The genetics of personality. In K. Blum & E. P. Noble (Eds.), *Handbook of psychiatric genetics* (pp. 273–296). Boca Raton, FL: CRC Press.

Bouchard, T. J., & McGue, M. (1981). Familial studies of intelligence: A review. *Science, 212,* 1055–1059.

Bowlby, J. (1969). *Attachment and loss* (Vol. 1). New York: Basic Books.

Bowlby, J. (1991). Ethological light on psychoanalytical problems. In P. Bateson et al. (Eds.), *The development and integration of behaviour: Essays in honour of Robert Hinde.* Cambridge, England: Cambridge University Press.

Bowles, S. (2003, July 18–20). More older drivers in car accidents. *USA Today,* p. 1.

Bozikas, V., Kioseoglou, V., Palialia, M., Nimatoudis, I., Iakovides, A., Karavatos, A., & Kaprinis, G. (2000). Burnout among hospital workers and community-based mental health staff. *Psychiatriki, 11,* 204–211.

Bradley, R. H., Caldwell, B. M., Rock, S. L., Ramey, C. T., Barnard, K. E., Gray, C., et al. (1989). Home environment and cognitive development in the first 3 years of life: A collaborative study involving six sites and three ethnic groups in North America. *Developmental Psychology, 25,* 217–235.

Brady, J. E., Newcomb, A. F., & Hartup, W. W. (1983). Context and companion's behavior as determinants of cooperation and competition in school-age children. *Journal of Experimental Child Psychology, 36,* 396–412.

Braet, C., Mervielde, I., & Vandereycken, W. (1997). Psychological aspects of childhood obesity: A controlled study in a clinical and nonclinical sample. *Journal of Pediatric Psychology, 22,* 59–71.

Braine, M. D. S. (1976). Children's first word combinations. *Monographs of the Society for Research in Child Development, 41* (Serial No. 164).

Braine, M. D. S. (1992). What sort of innate structure is needed to "bootstrap" into syntax? *Cognition, 45,* 77–100.

Brainerd, C. J. (1996). Piaget: A centennial celebration. *Psychological Science, 7,* 191–203.

Brandtstädter, J. (1989). Personal self-regulation of development: Cross-sequential analyses of development-related control beliefs and emotions. *Developmental Psychology, 25,* 96–108.

Brandtstädter, J. (1999). Sources of resilience in the aging self. In T. M. Hess & F. Blanchard-Fields (Eds.), *Social cognition and aging* (pp. 123–141). San Diego: Academic Press.

Brandtstädter, J., & Greve, W. (1994). The aging self: Stabilizing and protective processes. *Developmental Review, 14,* 52–80.

Braun, K. L., Tanji, V. M., & Heck, R. (2001). Support for physician-assisted suicide: Exploring the impact of ethnicity and attitudes toward planning for death. *The Gerontologist, 41,* 51–60.

Braungart, J. M., Plomin, R., DeFries, J. C., & Fulker, D. W. (1992). Genetic influence on tester-rated infant temperament as assessed by Bayley's Infant Behavior Record: Nonadoptive and adoptive siblings and twins. *Developmental Psychology, 28,* 40–47.

Bray, J. H. (1999). From marriage to remarriage and beyond: Findings from the Developmental Issues in Stepfamilies Research Project. In E. M. Hetherington (Ed.), *Coping with divorce, single parenting, and remarriage: A risk and resilience perspective* (pp. 295–319). Mahwah NJ: Erlbaum.

Brazelton, T. B., & Nugent, J. K. (1995). Neonatal behavioral assessment scale (3rd ed). London: MacKeith.

Brazelton, T. B., Nugent, J. K., & Lester, B. M. (1987). Neonatal behavioral assessment scale. In J. D. Osofsky (Ed.), *Handbook of infant development* (2nd ed). New York: Wiley.

Brennan, P. A., Grekin, E. R., Mortensen, E. L., & Mednick, S. A. (2002). Relationship of maternal smoking during pregnancy with criminal arrest and hospitalization for substance abuse in male and female adult offspring. *American Journal of Psychiatry, 159,* 48–54.

Bridges, C. R. (1996). The characteristics of career achievement perceived by African American college administrators. *Journal of Black Studies, 26,* 748–767.

Brioni, J. D., & Decker, M. W. (Eds.). (1997). *Pharmacological treatment of Alzheimer's disease.* New York: Wiley.

Brison, K. J. (1995). You will never forget: Narrative, bereavement, and worldview among Kwanga women. *Ethos, 23,* 474–488.

Brissette, I., Scheier, M. F., & Carver, C. S. (2002). The role of optimism in social network development, coping, and psychological adjustment during a life transition. *Journal of Personality and Social Psychology, 82,* 102–111.

Brissett-Chapman, S., & Issacs-Shockley, M. (1997). *Children in social peril: A community vision for preserving family care of African American children and youths.* Washington, DC: Child Welfare League of America, Inc.

Brockington, I. (1996). *Motherhood and mental health.* Oxford, England: Oxford University Press.

Brodie, D. (1999). *Untying the knot: Ex-husbands, ex-wives, and other experts on the passage of divorce.* New York: St. Martin's Griffin.

Brody, G. H. (1998). Sibling relationship quality: Its causes and consequences. *Annual Review of Psychology, 49,* 1–24.

Brody, G. H., & Ge, X. (2001). Linking parenting processes and self-regulation to psychological functioning and alcohol use during early adolescence. *Journal of Family Psychology, 15,* 82–94.

Brody, G. H., Kim, S., Murry, V. M., & Brown, A. C. (2003). Longitudinal direct and indirect pathways linking older sibling competence to the development of younger sibling competence. *Developmental Psychology, 39,* 618–628.

Brody, G. H., Stoneman, A., & McCoy, J. K. (1994). Forecasting sibling relationships in early adolescence from child temperaments and family processes in middle childhood. *Child Development, 65,* 771–784.

Brodzinsky, D. M., & Pinderhughes, E. (2002). Parenting and child development in adoptive families. In M. H. Bornstein (Ed.), *Handbook of parenting, Vol. 1: Children and parenting* (pp. 279–311). Mahwah, NJ: Erlbaum.

Brodzinsky, D. M., & Rightmyer, J. (1980). Individual differences in children's humor development. In P. McGhee & A. Chapman (Eds.), *Children's humour.* Chichester, UK: Wiley.

Broman, C. L. (1988). Household work and family life satisfaction of Blacks. *Journal of Marriage and the Family, 50,* 743–748.

Bronfenbrenner, U. (1979). Contexts of child rearing: Problems and prospects. *American Psychologist, 34,* 844–850.

Bronfenbrenner, U. (1989). Ecological systems theory. In R. Vasta (Ed.), *Annals of child development: Vol. 6. Theories of child development: Revised formulations and current issues.* Greenwich, CT: JAI Press.

Bronfenbrenner, U. (1995). Developmental ecology through space and time: A future perspective. In P. Moen, G. H. Elder Jr., & K. Luscher (Eds.), *Examining lives in context: Perspectives on the ecology of human development.* Washington, DC: American Psychological Association.

Bronfenbrenner, U., & Morris, P. A. (1998). The ecology of developmental processes. In W. Damon & R. M. Lerner (Eds.), *Handbook of Child psychology: Vol. 1. Theoretical modes of human development* (5th ed., pp. 993–1028). New York: Wiley.

Bronfenbrenner, U., & Morris, P. (2006). The ecology of developmental processes. In W. Damon & R. M. Lerner (Eds.), *Handbook of child psychology* (6th ed). New York: Wiley.

Brooks-Gunn, J., Klebanov, P. K., & Duncan, G. J. (1996). Ethnic differences in children's intelligence test scores: Role of economic deprivation, home environment, and maternal characteristics. *Child Development, 67,* 396–408.

Brooks-Gunn, J., & Paikoff, R. (1993). "Sex is a gamble, kissing is a game": Adolescent sexuality, contraception, and sexuality. In S. P. Millstein, A. C. Petersen, & E. O. Nightingale, (Eds.), *Promoting the health behavior of adolescents.* New York: Oxford University Press.

Brooks-Gunn, J., & Ruble, D. N. (1982). The development of menstrual-related beliefs and behaviors during early adolescence. *Child Development, 53,* 1567–1577.

Brougham, R. R., & Walsh, D. A. (2005). Goal expectations as predictors of retirement intentions. *International Journal of Aging and Human Development, 61,* 141–160.

Brown, B. B., & Lohr, M. J. (1987). Peer-group affiliation and adolescent self-esteem: An integration of ego-identity and symbolic-interaction theories. *Journal of Personality and Social Psychology, 52,* 47–55.

Brown, B. B., Lohr, M. J., & McClenahan, E. L. (1986). Early adolescents' perceptions of peer pressure. *Journal of Early Adolescence, 6,* 139–154.

Brown, B. B., Mounts, N., Lamborn, S. D., & Steinberg, L. (1993). Parenting practices and peer group affiliation in adolescence. *Developmental Psychology, 64,* 467–482.

Brown, B. B., & Theobald, W. (1999). How peers matter: A research synthesis of peer influences on adolescent pregnancy. In P. Bearman, H. Bruckner, B. B. Brown, W. Theobald, & S. Philliber (Eds.), *Peer potential: Making the most of how teens influence each other.* Washington DC: National Campaign to Prevent Teen Pregnancy.

Brown, C. S., & Bigler, R. S. (2002). Effects of minority status in the classroom on children's intergroup attitudes. *Journal of Experimental Child Psychology, 83,* 77–110.

Brown, J. R., & Dunn, J. (1992). Talk with your mother or your sibling? Developmental changes in early family conversations about feelings. *Child Development, 63,* 336–349.

Brown, J. R., & Dunn, J. (1996). Continuities in emotion understanding from three to six years. *Child Development, 67,* 789–802.

Brown, J. V., Bakeman, R., Coles, C. D., Platzman, K. A., & Lynch, M. E. (2004). Prenatal cocaine exposure: A comparison of 2-year-old children in parental and nonparental care. *Child Development, 75,* 1282–1295.

Brown, R., Pressley, M., Van Meter, P., & Schuder, T. (1996). A quasi-experimental validation of transactional strategies instruction with low-achieving second-grade readers. *Journal of Educational Psychology, 88,* 18–37.

Bryce, J. (2001). The technological transformation of leisure. *Social Science Computer Review, 19,* 7–16.

Buchanan, C. M., Eccles, J. S., & Becker, J. B. (1992). Are adolescents the victims of raging hormones? Evidence for activational effects of hormones on moods and behavior at adolescence. *Psychological Bulletin, 111,* 62–107.

Buchanan, C. M., & Heiges, K. L. (2001). When conflict continues after the marriage ends: Effects of postdivorce conflict on children. In J. Grych & F. D. Fincham (Eds.), *Interparental conflict and child development* (pp. 337–362). New York: Cambridge University Press.

Buchanan, C. M., Maccoby, E. E., & Dornbusch, S. M. (1996). *Adolescents after divorce.* Cambridge MA: Harvard University Press.

Buchholz, M., Karl, H. W., Pomietto, M., & Lynn, A. (1998). Pain scores in infants: A modified infant pain scale versus visual analogue. *Journal of Pain & Symptom Management, 15,* 117–124.

Buchsbaum, B. C. (1996). Remembering a parent who has died: A developmental perspective. In D. Klass, P. R. Silverman, & S. L. Nickman (Eds.), *Continuing bonds: New understandings of grief* (pp. 113–124). Washington, DC: Taylor & Francis.

Buckle, L., Gallup, G. G., Jr., & Rodd, Z. A. (1996). Marriage as a reproductive contract: Patterns of marriage, divorce, and remarriage. *Ethology and Sociobiology, 17,* 363–377.

Bugental, D. B., & Happaney, K. (2004). Predicting infant maltreatment in low-income families: The interactive effects of maternal attributions and child status at birth. *Developmental Psychology, 40,* 234–243.

Buhrmester, D., & Furman, W. (1990). Perceptions of sibling relationships during middle childhood and adolescence. *Child Development, 61,* 1387–1398.

Bullock, K. (2004). The changing role of grandparents in rural families: The results of an exploratory study in southeastern North Carolina. *Families in Society, 85,* 45–54.

Bullock, M., & Lutkenhaus, P. (1990). Who am I? The development of self-understanding in toddlers. *Merrill-Palmer Quarterly, 36,* 217–238.

Bumpass, L. L., & Aquilino, W. S. (1995). *A social map of midlife: Family and work over the middle years.* Madison: University of Wisconsin-Madison, Center for Demography and Ecology.

Bunce, D. (2001). The locus of age x health-related physical fitness interactions in serial choice responding as a function of task complexity: Central processing or motor function? *Experimental Aging Research, 27,* 103–122.

Burchinal, M. R., Roberts, J. E., Riggins, R., Zeisel, S. A., Neebe, E., & Bryant, D. (2000). Relating quality of center-based child care to early cognitive and language development longitudinally. *Child Development, 71,* 338–357.

Bureau of Labor Statistics. (2005). *Work activity of high school students: Data from the National Longitudinal Study of Youth.* Retrieved September 29, 2005, from http://www.bls.gov/news.release/pdf/nlsyth.pdf

Burgess, D., & Borgida, E. (1997). Sexual harassment: An experimental test of sex-role spillover theory. *Personality and Social Psychology Bulletin, 23,* 63–75.

Burke, R. J. (1991a). Organizational treatment of minority managers and professionals: Costs to the majority? *Psychological Reports, 68,* 439–449.

Burke, R. J. (1991b). Work experiences of minority managers and professionals: Individual and organizational costs of perceived bias. *Psychological Reports, 69,* 1011–1023.

Burnette, D. (1999). Social relationships of Latino grandparent caregivers: A role theory perspective. *The Gerontologist, 39,* 49–58.

Burton, L. M. (1992). Black grandparents rearing children of drug-addicted parents: Stressors, outcomes, and social service needs. *The Gerontologist, 32,* 744–751.

Buss, D. M., Abbott, M., Angeleitner, A., Asherian, A., Biaggio, A., Blanco Villasenor, et al. (1990). International preferences in selecting mates: A study of 37 cultures. *Journal of Cross-Cultural Psychology, 21,* 5–47.

Buss, K. A., & Goldsmith, H. H. (1998). Fear and anger regulation in infancy: Effects on the temporal dynamics of affective expression. *Child Development, 69,* 359–374.

Buss, K. A., & Kiel, E. J. (2004). Comparison of sadness, anger, and fear facial expressions when toddlers look at their mothers. *Child Development, 75,* 1761–1773.

Bylsma, F. W., Ostendorf, C. A., & Hofer, P. J. (2002). Challenges in providing neuropsychological and psychological services in Guam and the Commonwealth of the Northern Marianas Islands (CNMI). In F. R. Ferraro (Ed.), *Minority and cross-cultural aspects of neuropsychological assessment: Studies on neuropsychology, development, and cognition* (pp. 145–157). Bristol, PA: Swets & Zeitlinger.

Byock, I. (1997). *Dying well.* New York: Riverhead.

Byrne, B. M., & Gavin, D. A. W. (1996). The Shavelson model revisited: Testing for the structure of academic self-concept across pre-, early, and late adolescents. *Journal of Educational Psychology, 88,* 215–228.

Cain, K. (1999). Ways of reading: How knowledge and use of strategies are related to reading comprehension. *British Journal of Developmental Psychology, 17,* 293–312.

Calasanti, T. M. (1996). Gender and life satisfaction in retirement: An assessment of the male model. *Journal of Gerontology: Social Sciences, 51B,* S18–S29.

Callahan, C. M. (2000). Intelligence and giftedness. In R. J. Sternberg (Ed.), *Handbook of intelligence* (pp. 159–175). Cambridge, UK: Cambridge University Press.

Callanan, M. A., & Sabbagh, M. A. (2004). Multiple labels for objects in conversations with young children: Parents' language and children's developing expectations about word meanings. *Developmental Psychology, 40,* 746–763.

Calvert, S. L., & Kotler, J. A. (2003). Lessons from children's television: The impact of the Children's Television Act on children's learning. *Journal of Applied Developmental Psychology, 24,* 275–335.

Camlibel, A. R. (2000). Affectivity and attachment: A comparison of binge drinking and non-binge drinking first-year college students. *Dissertation Abstracts International: Section B: The Sciences and Engineering, 60,* 5757.

Camp, C. J. (1999a). Memory interventions for normal and pathological older adults. In R. Schulz, M. P. Lawton, & G. Maddox (Eds.), *Annual review of gerontology and geriatrics* (Vol. 18, pp. 155–189). New York: Springer.

Camp, C. J. (Ed.). (1999b). *Montessori-based activities for persons with dementia: Volume 1.* Beachwood, OH: Menorah Park Press.

Camp, C. J. (2001). From efficacy to effectiveness to diffusion: Making the transitions in dementia intervention research. *Neuropsychological Rehabilitation, 11,* 495–517.

Camp, C. J., Foss, J. W., Stevens, A. B., Reichard, C. C., McKitrick, L. A., & O'Hanlon, A. M. (1993). Memory training in normal and demented elderly populations: The E-I-E-I-O model. *Experimental Aging Research, 19,* 277–290.

Camp, C. J., Judge, K. S., Bye, C. A., Fox, K. M., Bowden, J., Bell, M., et al. (1997). An intergenerational program for persons with dementia using Montessori methods. *The Gerontologist, 37,* 688–692.

Camp, C. J., & McKitrick, L. A. (1991). Memory interventions in Alzheimer-type dementia populations: Methodological and theoretical issues. In R. L. West & J. D. Sinnott (Eds.), *Everyday memory and aging: Current research and methodology* (pp. 155–172). New York: Springer-Verlag.

Camp, C. J., & Skrajner, M. J. (2005). Resident-assisted Montessori programming (RAMP): Training persons with dementia to serve as group activity leaders. *The Gerontologist, 44,* 426–431.

Campagne, A., Pebayle, T., & Muzet, A. (2004). Correlation between driving errors and vigilance level: Influence of the driver's age. *Physiology and Behavior, 80,* 515–524.

Campbell, F. A., Pungello, E. P., Miller-Johnson, S., Burchinal, M., & Ramey, C. T. (2001). The development of cognitive and academic abilities: Growth curves from an early childhood educational experiment. *Developmental Psychology, 37,* 231–242.

Campbell, F. A., & Ramey, C. T. (1994). Effects of early intervention on intellectual and academic achievement: A follow-up study of children from low-income families. *Child Development, 65,* 684–698.

Campbell, R., & Sais, E. (1995). Accelerated metalinguistic (phonological) awareness in bilingual children. *British Journal of Developmental Psychology, 13,* 61–68.

Campbell, S. B. (2000). Developmental perspectives on attention deficit disorder. In A. Sameroff, M. Lewis, & S. Miller (Eds.), *Handbook of child psychopathology* (2nd ed., pp 383–401). New York: Plenum.

Campbell, S. B., Cohn, J. F., Flanagan, C., Popper, S., & Meyers, T. (1992). Course and correlates of postpartum depression during the transition to parenthood. *Development and Psychopathology, 4,* 29–47.

Campos, J. J., Hiatt, S., Ramsay, D., Henderson, C., & Svejda, M. (1978). The emergence of fear on the visual cliff. In M. Lewis & L. Rosenblum (Eds.), *The origins of affect.* New York: Plenum.

Camras, L. A., Oster, H., Campos, J., Campos, R., Ujiie, T., Miyake, K., et al. (1998). Production of emotional facial expressions in European, American, Japanese, and Chinese infants. *Developmental Psychology, 34,* 616–628.

Canfield, R. L., & Smith, E. G. (1996). Number-based expectations and sequential enumeration by 5-month-old infants. *Developmental Psychology, 32,* 269–279.

Cannon, T. D., Rosso, I. M., Hollister, J. M., Bearden, C. E., Sanchez, L. E., & Hadley, T. (2000). A prospective cohort study of genetic and perinatal influences in the etiology of schizophrenia. *Schizophrenia Bulletin, 26,* 351–366.

Capron A. M. (2001). Brain death: Well settled yet still unresolved. *New England Journal of Medicine, 344,* 1244–1246.

Capuzzi, D., & Gross, D. R. (2004). Counseling suicidal adolescents. In D. Capuzzi (Ed.), *Suicide across the lifespan: Implications for counselors* (pp. 235–270). Alexandria, VA: American Counseling Association.

Carey, S. (1992). Becoming a face expert. In V. Bruce, A. Cowey, A. W. Ellis, & D. I. Perrett (Eds.), *Processing the facial image.* Oxford: Clarendon Press.

Carey, S., & Spelke, E. S. (1994). Domain-specific knowledge and conceptual change. In L. A. Hirschfeld & S. A. Gelman (Eds.), *Mapping the mind* (pp. 169–200). Cambridge, UK: Cambridge University Press.

Carlo, G., Koller, S. H., Eisenberg, N., Da Silva, M. S., & Frohlich, C. B. (1996). A cross-national study on the relations among prosocial moral reasoning, gender role orientations, and prosocial behaviors. *Developmental Psychology, 32,* 231–240.

Carlson, C. L., Pelham, W. E., Milich, R., & Dixon, J. (1992). Single and combined effects of methylphenidate and behavior therapy on the classroom performance of children with attention-deficit hyperactivity disorder. *Journal of Abnormal Child Psychology, 20,* 213–232.

Carlson, E. A. (1998). A prospective longitudinal study of attachment disorganization/disorientation. *Child Development, 69,* 1107–1128.

Carlson Jones, D. (2004). Body image among adolescent girls and boys: A longitudinal study. *Developmental Psychology, 40,* 823–835.

Carnelley, K., & Ruscher, J. B. (2000). Adult attachment and exploratory behavior in leisure. *Journal of social Behavior and Personality, 15,* 153–165.

Carpenter, P. A., & Daneman, M. (1981). Lexical retrieval and error recovery in reading: A model based on eye fixations. *Journal of Verbal Learning and Verbal Behavior, 20,* 137–160.

Carr, D. (2004). Gender, preloss marital dependence, and older adults' adjustment to widowhood. *Journal of Marriage and the Family, 66,* 220–235.

Carrere, S., & Gottman, J. M. (1999). Predicting the future of marriages. In E. M. Hetherington (Ed.), *Coping with divorce, single parenting, and remarriage: A risk and resiliency perspective.* Mahwah, NJ: Erlbaum.

Carroll, J. B. (1993). *Human cognitive abilities: A survey of factor-analytic studies.* New York: Cambridge University Press.

Carroll, J. L., & Loughlin, G. M. (1994). Sudden infant death syndrome. In F. A. Oski, C. D. DeAngelis, R. D. Feigin, J. A. McMillan, & J. B. Warshaw (Eds.), *Principles and practice of pediatrics.* Philadelphia: Lippincott.

Carstensen, L. L. (1993). Motivation for social contact across the lifespan: A theory of socioemotional selectivity. In J. E. Jacobs (Ed.), *Nebraska symposium on motivation: Vol. 40. Developmental perspectives on motivation* (pp. 209–254). Lincoln: University of Nebraska Press.

Carstensen, L. L. (1995). Evidence for a life-span theory of socioemotional selectivity. *Current Directions in Psychological Science, 4,* 151–156.

Carstensen, L. L., & Freund, A. M. (1994). The resilience of the aging self. *Developmental Review, 14,* 81–92.

Carstensen, L. L., Graff, J., Levenson, R. W., & Gottmann, J. M. (1996). Affect in intimate relationships: The developmental course of marriage. In C. Magai & S. H. McFadden (Eds.), *Handbook of emotion, adult development, and aging* (pp. 227–247). San Diego, CA: Academic Press.

Carver, K., Joyner, K., & Udry, J. R. (2003). National estimates of adolescent romantic relationships. In P. Florsheim (Ed.), *Adolescent romantic relations and sexual behavior: Theory, research, and practical implications* (pp. 23–56). Mahwah, NJ: Erlbaum.

Carver, P. R., Egan, S. K., & Perry, D. G. (2004). Children who question their heterosexuality. *Developmental Psychology, 40,* 43–53.

Casaer, P. (1993). Old and new facts about perinatal brain development. *Journal of Child Psychology and Psychiatry, 34,* 101–109.

Cascio, W. F. (1995). Whither industrial and organizational psychology in a changing world of work? *American Psychologist, 50,* 928–939.

Caselli, M. C., Bates. E., Casadio, P., Fenson, J., Fenson, L., Sanderl, L., & Weir, J. (1995). Cross-linguistic lexical development. *Cognitive Development, 10,* 159–199.

Casey, B. J., Tottenham, N., Liston, C., & Durston, S. (2005). Imaging the developing brain: What have we learned about cognitive development? *Trends in Cognitive Sciences, 9,* 104–110.

Casey, M. B. (1996). Understanding individual differences in spatial ability within females: A nature/nurture interactionist framework. *Developmental Review, 16,* 241–260.

Casper, W. J. (2000). The effects of work-life benefits and perceived organizational support on organizational attractiveness and employment desirability. *Dissertation Abstract International Section B: The Sciences and Engineering, 61(5–B),* 2803.

Caspi, A. (1998). Personality development across the life course. In N. Eisenberg (Ed.), *Handbook of child psychology, Vol. 3: Social, emotional, and personality development* (5th ed., pp. 311–388). New York: Wiley.

Castro, I. L. (1997). Worth more than we earn: Fair pay as a step toward gender equity. *National Forum, 77(2),* 17–21.

Castro, W. (2000). The assessment of practical intelligence in a multicultural context. *Dissertation Abstracts International Section A: Humanities and Social Sciences, 60(10–A),* 3638.

Cattell, R. B. (1965). *The scientific analysis of personality.* Baltimore: Penguin.

Cavanaugh, J. C. (1996). Memory self-efficacy as a key to understanding cognitive aging. In F. Blanchard-Fields & T. M. Hess (Eds.), *Perspectives on cognitive changes in adulthood and aging* (pp. 488–507) New York: McGraw-Hill.

Cavanaugh, J. C. (1999). Caregiving to adults: A life event challenge. In I. H. Nordhus, G. R. VandenBos, S. Berg, & P. Fromholt (Eds.), *Clinical geropsychology* (pp. 131–135). Washington, DC: American Psychological Association.

Cavanaugh, J. C. (2000). Metamemory from a social-cognitive perspective. In D. Park & N. Schwarz (Eds.), *Cognitive aging: A primer* (pp. 115–130). Philadelphia: Psychology Press.

Cavanaugh, J. C., Feldman, J. M., & Hertzog, C. (1998). Metamemory as social cognition: A reconceptualization of what memory questionnaires assess. *Review of General Psychology, 2,* 48–65.

Cavanaugh, J. C., & Kinney, J. M. (1994, July). *Marital satisfaction as an important contextual factor in spousal caregiving.* Paper presented at the 7th International Conference on Personal Relationships, Groningen, The Netherlands.

Cavanaugh, J. C., & Kinney, J. M. (1998). Accuracy of caregivers' recollections of caregiving hassles. *Journal of Gerontology: Psychological Sciences, 53B,* P40–P42.

Cavanaugh, J. C., & Nocera, R. (1994). Cognitive aspects and interventions in Alzheimer's disease. In J. D. Sinnott (Ed.), *Interdisciplinary handbook of adult lifespan learning* (pp. 389–407). New York: Greenwood Press.

Ceballo, R., Lansford, J. E., Abbey, A., & Stewart, A. J. (2004). Gaining a child: Comparing the experiences of biological parents, adoptive parents, and stepparents. *Family Relations: Interdisciplinary Journal of Applied Family Studies, 53,* 38–48.

Ceci, S. J., & Bruck, M. (1995). *Jeopardy in the courtroom: A scientific analysis of children's testimony.* Washington, DC: American Psychological Association.

Ceci, S. J., & Bruck, M. (1998). Children's testimony: Applied and basic issues. In W. Damon (Ed.), *Handbook of child psychology* (Vol. 4). New York: Wiley.

Centers for Disease Control and Prevention. (2001). *Exposure to environmental tobacco smoke and nicotine levels—Fact sheet.* Retrieved June 18, 2005, from http://www.cdc.gov/tobacco/research_data/environmental/factsheet_ets.htm

Centers for Disease Control and Prevention. (2004a). *BMI—Body Mass Index: BMI for adults: What does this all mean?* Retrieved June 18, 2005, from http://www.cdc.gov/nccdphp/dnpa/bmi/bmi-means.htm

Centers for Disease Control and Prevention. (2004b). *HIV/AIDS Surveillance Report, 2003* (Vol.15). Atlanta: Author.

Centers for Disease Control and Prevention. (2005). *Sexually transmitted diseases.* Retrieved October 24, 2005, from http://www.cdc.gov/std/

Cerminara, K. L., & Perez, A. (2000). Therapeutic death: A look at Oregon's law. *Psychology, Public Policy, and Law, 6,* 503–525.

Cervantes, C. A., & Callanan, M. A. (1998). Labels and explanations in mother-child emotion talk: Age and gender differentiation. *Developmental Psychology, 34,* 88–98.

Champion, H. L., Foley, K. L., DuRant, R. H., Hensberry, R., Altman, D., & Wolfson, M. (2004). Adolescent sexual victimization, use of alcohol and other substances, and other health risk behaviors. *Journal of Adolescent Health, 35,* 321–328.

Chan, A. Y., & Smith, K. R. (1995). Perceptions of marital stability of Black–White intermarriages. In C. K. Jacobson (Ed.), *American families: Issues in race and ethnicity* (pp. 369–386). New York: Garland.

Chandler, M., & Moran, T. (1990). Psychopathy and moral development: A comparative study of delinquent and nondelinquent youth. *Development and Psychopathology, 2,* 227–246.

Chanquoy, L. (2001). How to make it easier for children to revise their writing: A study of text revision from 3rd to 5th grades. *British Journal of Educational Psychology, 71,* 15–41.

Chao, G. T. (1997). Mentoring phases and outcomes. *Journal of Vocational Behavior, 51,* 15–28.

Chao, R. K. (2001). Extending research on the consequences of parenting style for Chinese Americans and European Americans. *Child Development, 72,* 1832–1843.

Chapman, P. D. (1988). *Schools as sorters: Lewis M. Terman, applied psychology, and the intelligence testing movement, 1890–1930.* New York: New York University Press.

Charles, S. T. (1998). Genetic and environmental influences on osteoarthritis. *Dissertation Abstracts International: Section B: The Sciences and Engineering, 58(11B),* 6272.

Charness, N., & Bosman, E. A. (1990). Expertise and aging: Life in the lab. In T. M. Hess (Ed.), *Aging and cognition: Knowledge organization and utilization* (pp. 343–385). Amsterdam, The Netherlands: North-Holland.

Chassin, L., Pitts, S. C., & Prost, J. (2002). Binge drinking trajectories from adolescence to emerging adulthood in a high-risk sample: Predictors and substance abuse outcomes. *Journal of Consulting and Clinical Psychology, 70,* 67–78.

Chassin, L., Ritter, J., Trim, R. S., & King, K. M. (2003). Adolescent substance use disorders. In E. J. Mash & R. A. Barkely (Eds.), *Child psychopathology* (2nd ed.), New York: Guilford Press.

Chasteen, A. L. (1994). "The world around me": The environment and single women. *Sex Roles, 31,* 309–328.

Chavous, T. M., Bernat, D. H., Schmeelk-Cone, K., Caldwell, C. H., Kohn-Wood, L., & Zimmerman, M. A. (2003). Racial identity and academic attainment among African

American adolescents. *Child Development, 74,* 1076–1090.

Chen, X., Rubin, K. H., & Li, Z. (1995). Social functioning and adjustment in Chinese children. *Developmental Psychology, 31,* 531–539.

Chen, X., Unger, J. B., Palmer, P., Weiner, M. D., Johnson, C. A., Wong, M. M., & Austin, G. (2002). Prior cigarette smoking initiation predicting current alcohol use: Evidence for a gateway drug effect among California adolescents from eleven ethnic groups. *Addictive Behaviors, 27,* 799–817.

Chen, Z. X., Aryee, S., & Lee, C. (2005). Test of a mediation model of perceived organizational support. *Journal of Vocational Behavior, 66,* 457–470.

Cherlin, A. J., & Furstenberg, F. F., Jr. (1986). *The new American grandparent: A place in the family, a life apart.* New York: Basic Books.

Cherlin, A. J., & Furstenberg, F. F., Jr. (1994). Stepfamilies in the United States: A reconsideration. *Annual Review of Sociology, 20,* 359–381.

Chetro-Szivos, J. (2001). Exploring the meaning of work: A CMM analysis of the grammar of working Acadian-Americans. *Dissertation Abstracts International Section A: Humanities and Social Sciences, 62*(1–A), 14.

Children's Defense Fund. (1996). *The state of America's children yearbook, 1996.* Washington, DC: Author.

Children's Defense Fund. (2001). *The state of America's children.* Washington, DC: Author.

Chilman, C. S. (1983). *Adolescent sexuality in a changing American society* (2nd ed.). New York: Wiley.

Chinen, A. B. (1989). *In the ever after.* Willmette, IL: Chiron.

Chipperfield, J. G., Campbell, D. W., & Perry, R. P. (2004). Stability in perceived control: Implications for health among very old community-dwelling adults. *Journal of Aging and Health, 16,* 116–147.

Chiu, W. C. K., Chan, A. W., Snape, E., & Redman, T. (2001). Age stereotypes and discriminatory attitudes towards older workers: An East-West comparison. *Human Relations, 54,* 629–661.

Chomitz, V. R., Cheung, L. W. Y., & Lieberman, E. (1995). The role of lifestyle in preventing low birth weight. *The Future of Children, 5,* 121–138.

Chomsky, N. (1957). *Syntactic structures.* The Hague: Mouton.

Chomsky, N. (1995). *The minimalist program.* Cambridge: MIT Press.

Chorpita, B. F., & Barlow, D. H. (1998). The development of anxiety: The role of control in the early environment. *Psychological Bulletin, 124,* 3–21.

Chou, K-L., & Chi, I. (2005). Prevalence and correlates of depression in Chinese oldest-old. *International Journal of Geriatric Psychiatry, 20,* 41–50.

Christensen, A. (1990). Gender and social structure in the demand/withdrawal pattern of marital conflict. *Journal of Personality and Social Psychology, 59,* 73–81.

Christensen, A., & Heavey, C. L. (1999). Intervention for couples. *Annual Review of Psychology, 50,* 165–190.

Cicchetti, D., & Toth, S. L. (2006). Developmental psychopathology and preventive intervention. In W. Damon & R. M. Lerner (Eds.), *Handbook of child psychology* (Vol. 4). New York: Wiley.

Cicirelli, V. G. (2000). Older adults' ethnicity, fear of death, and end-of-life decisions. In A. Tomer (Ed.), *Death attitudes and the older adult: Theories, concepts, and applications* (pp. 175–191). Philadelphia: Brunner-Routledge.

Cicirelli, V. G. (2001). Personal meaning of death in older adults and young adults in relation to their fears of death. *Death Studies, 25,* 663–683.

Cicirelli, V. G. (2004). God as the ultimate attachment figure for older adults. *Attachment and Human Development, 6,* 371–388.

Cillessen, A. H. N., & Rose, A. (2005). Understanding popularity in the peer system. *Current Directions in Psychological Science, 14,* 102–105.

Cipani, E. (1991). Educational classification and placement. In J. L. Matson & J. A. Mulick (Eds.), *Handbook of mental retardation* (2nd ed.). New York: Pergamon Press.

Clarke-Anderson, P. (2005). Minorities' attainability to leadership positions in business settings: A study of self-efficacy and leadership aspirations. *Dissertation Abstracts International Section A: Humanities & Social Sciences, 65*(9–A), 3456.

Clarke-Stewart, K. A., & Bretano, C. (2005). *Till divorce do us part.* New Haven CT: Yale University Press.

Clements, M., & Markman, H. J. (1996). The transition to parenthood: Is having children hazardous to marriage? In N. Vanzetti & S. Duck (Eds.), *A lifetime of relationships* (pp. 290–310). Pacific Grove, CA: Brooks/Cole.

Clifton, R., Perris, E., & Bullinger, A. (1991). Infants' perception of auditory space. *Developmental Psychology, 27,* 187–197.

Cnattingius, S. (2004). The epidemiology of smoking during pregnancy: Smoking prevalence, maternal characteristics, and pregnancy outcomes. *Nicotine & Tobacco Research, 6,* S125–S140.

Cohen, G. D. (1990). Psychopathology and mental health in the mature and elderly adult. In J. E. Birren & K. W. Schaie (Eds.), *Handbook of the psychology of aging* (3rd ed., pp. 359–371). San Diego, CA: Academic Press.

Cohen, R. R., Boston, P., Mount, B. M., & Porterfield, P. (2001). Changes in quality of life following admission to palliative care units. *Palliative Medicine, 15,* 363–371.

Cohen, S., Lichtenstein, E., Prochaska, J. O., Rossi, J. S., Gutz, E. R., Carr, C. R., et al. (1989). Debunking myths about selfquitting: Evidence from 10 prospective studies of persons who attempt to quit smoking by themselves. *American Psychologist, 44,* 1355–1365.

Cohen, S., & Williamson, G. M. (1991). Stress and infectious disease in humans. *Psychological Bulletin, 109,* 5–24.

Coie, J. D., & Dodge, K. A. (1998). Aggression and antisocial behavior. In W. Damon (Ed.), *Handbook of child psychology* (Vol. 3., pp. 779–862). New York: Wiley.

Coie, J. D., Dodge, K. A., Terry, R., & Wright, V. (1991). The role of aggression in peer relations: An analysis of aggression episodes in boys' play groups. *Child Development, 62,* 812–826.

Colby, A., Kohlberg, L., Gibbs, J., & Lieberman, M. (1983). A longitudinal study of moral judgment. *Monographs of the Society for Research in Child Development, 48* (Serial #200).

Cole, D. A., & Jordan, A. E. (1995). Competence and memory: Integrating psychosocial and cognitive correlates of child depression. *Child Development, 66,* 459–473.

Cole, M. L. (2000). The experience of never-married women in their thirties who desire marriage and children. *Dissertation Abstracts International Section A: Humanities and Social Sciences, 60*(9–A), 3526.

Cole, P. M., Bruschi, C. J., & Tamang, B. L. (2002). Cultural differences in children's emotional reactions to difficult situations. *Child Development, 73,* 983–996.

Coleman, M., & Ganong, L. H. (1990). Remarriage and step-family research in the 1980s: Increased interest in an old family form. *Journal of Marriage and the Family, 52,* 925–940.

Collaer, M. L., & Hines, M. (1995). Human behavioral sex differences: A role for gonadal hormones during early development? *Psychological Bulletin, 118,* 55–107.

Collins, N. L., & Read, S. J. (1990). Adult attachment, working models, and relationship quality in dating couples. *Journal of Personality and Social Psychology, 58,* 644–663.

Collins, W. A. (2003). More than myth: The developmental significance of romantic relationships during adolescence. *Journal of Research on Adolescence, 13,* 1–24.

Coltheart, M., Curtis, B., Atkins, P., & Haller, M. (1993). Models of reading aloud: Dual-route and parallel-distributed-processing approaches. *Psychological Review, 100,* 589–608.

Colwell, M. J., Mize, J., Pettit, G. S., & Laird, R. D. (2002). Contextual determinants of mothers' interventions in young children's peer interactions. *Developmental Psychology, 38,* 492–502.

Congressional Budget Office. (2005). *CBO's current budget projections.* Retrieved August 8, 2005, from http://www.cbo.gov/showdoc.cfm?index=1944&sequence=0#table6

Connell, C. M., & Gibson, G. D. (1997). Racial, ethnic, and cultural differences in dementia caregiving: Review and analysis. *The Gerontologist, 37,* 355–364.

Connelly, R., Degraff, D. S., & Willis, R. A. (2004). The value of employer-sponsored child care to employees. *Industrial Relations: A Journal of Economy & Society, 43,* 759–792.

Connidis, I. A. (2001). *Family ties and aging.* Thousand Oaks, CA: Sage.

Conway, M. A., & Pleydell-Pearce, C. W. (2000). The construction of autobiographical memories in the self-memory system. *Psychological Review, 107,* 261–288.

Cooke, R. (2005, January 18). On the eve of medical history: Experts say gene therapy had learned its lessons and is poised for a breakthrough. *Newsday,* p. B10.

Cooney, T. M., & Uhlenberg, P. (1990). The role of divorce in men's relations with their adult children after mid-life. *Journal of Marriage and the Family, 52,* 677–688.

Cooney, T. M., Pedersen, F. A., Indelicato, S., & Palkovitz, R. (1993). Timing of fatherhood: Is "on time" optimal? *Journal of Marriage and the Family, 55,* 205–215.

Cooney, T. M., Smyer, M. A., Hagestad, G. O., & Klock, R. (1986). Parental divorce in young adulthood: Some preliminary findings. *American Journal of Orthopsychiatry, 56,* 470–477.

Cooper, C. L., & Quick, J. C. (2003). The stress and loneliness of success. *Counselling Psychology Quarterly, 16,* 1–7.

Coopersmith, S. (1967). *The antecedents of self-esteem.* San Francisco: W. H. Freeman.

Coplan, R. J., Prakash, K., O'Neil, K., & Armer, M. (2004). Do you "want" to play? Distinguishing between shyness and social disinterest in early childhood. *Developmental Psychology, 40,* 244–258.

Copper, R. L., Goldenberg, R. L., Das, A., Elder, N., Swain, M., Norman, G., et al. (1996). The preterm prediction study: Maternal stress is associated with spontaneous preterm birth at less than thirty-five weeks' gestation. National Institute of Child Health and Human Development Maternal-Fetal Medicine Units Network. *American Journal of Obstetrics & Gynecology, 175,* 1286–1292.

Cornelius, M., Taylor, P., Geva, D., & Day, N. (1995). Prenatal tobacco exposure and marijuana use among adolescents: Effects on offpsring gestational age, growth, and morphology. *Pediatrics, 95,* 738–743.

Cornwell, K. S., Harris, L. J., & Fitzgerald, H. E. (1991). Task effects in the development of hand preference in 9-, 13-, and 20-month-old infant girls. *Developmental Neuropsychology, 7,* 19–34.

Corr, C. A. (1991–1992). A task-based approach to coping with dying. *Omega: Journal of Death and Dying, 24,* 81–94.

Cosentino, S. A., Jefferson, A. L., Carey, M., Price, C. C., Davis-Garrett, K., Swenson, R., & Libon, D. J. (2004). The clinical diagnosis of vascular dementia: A comparison among four classification systems and a proposal for a new paradigm. *Clinical Neuropsychologist, 18,* 6–21.

Costa, P. T., Jr., & McCrae, R. R. (1988). Personality in adulthood: A six-year longitudinal study of self-reports and spouse ratings on the NEO Personality Inventory. *Journal of Personality and Social Psychology, 54,* 853–863.

Costa, P. T., Jr., & McCrae, R. R. (1997). Longitudinal stability of adult personality. In R. Hogan, J. Johnson, & S. Briggs (Eds.), *Handbook of personality psychology* (pp. 269–292). San Diego: Academic Press.

Costa, P. T., Jr., McCrae, R. R., & Arenberg, D. (1980). Enduring dispositions in adult males. *Journal of Personality and Social Psychology, 38,* 793–800.

Costa, P. T., Jr., McCrae, R. R., & Holland, J. L. (1984). Personality and vocational interests in an adult sample. *Journal of Applied Psychology, 42,* 390–400.

Costin, S. E., & Jones, D. C. (1992). Friendship as a facilitator of emotional responsiveness and prosocial interventions among young children. *Developmental Psychology, 28,* 941–947.

Coté, S., Zoccolillo, M., Tremblay, R. E., Nagin, D., & Vitaro, F. (2001). Predicting girls' conduct disorder in adolescence from childhood trajectories of disruptive behaviors. *Journal of the American Academy of Child and Adolescent Psychiatry, 40,* 678–684.

Cotter, R. P. (2001). High-risk behaviors in adolescence and their relationship to death anxiety and death personification. *Dissertation Abstracts International Section B: The Sciences and Engineering, 61*(8-B), 4446.

Cotton, S., Anthill, J. K., & Cunningham, J. D. (1989). The work motivations of mothers with preschool children. *Journal of Family Issues, 10,* 189–210.

Coulton, C. J., Korbin, J. E., & Su, M. (1999). Neighborhoods and child maltreatment: A mutli-level study. *Child Abuse and Neglect, 23,* 1019–1040.

Coulton, C. J., Korbin, J. E., Su, M., & Chow, J. (1995). Community level factors and child maltreatment rates. *Child Development, 66,* 1262–1276.

Counts, D., & Counts, D. (Eds.). (1985). *Aging and its transformations: Moving toward death in Pacific societies.* Lanham, MD: University Press of America.

Courage, M. L., & Howe, M. L. (2004). Advances in early memory development research: Insights about the dark side of the moon. *Developmental Review, 24,* 6–32.

Cousins, R., Mackay, C. J., Clarke, S. D., Kelly, C., Kelly, P. J., & McCaig, R. H. (2004). "Management standards" and work-related stress in the UK: Practical development. *Work & Stress, 18,* 113–136.

Cox, C. B. (2000). Why grandchildren are going to and staying at grandmother's house and what happens when they get there. In C. B. Cox (Ed.), *To grandmother's house we go and stay: Perspectives on custodial grandparents* (pp. 3–19). New York: Springer.

Cox, M. J., Owen, M. T., Henderson, V. K., & Margand, N. A. (1992). Prediction of infant-father and infant-mother attachment. *Developmental Psychology, 28,* 474–483.

Cox, M. J., Paley, B., & Harter, K. (2001). Interparental conflict and parent-child relationships. In J. H. Grych & F. D. Fincham (Eds.), *Interparental conflict and child development* (pp. 249–272). New York: Cambridge University Press.

Craig, K. D., Whitfield, M. F., Grunau, R. V. E., Linton, J., & Hadjistavropoulos, H. D. (1993). Pain in the preterm neonate: Behavioural and physiological indices. *Pain, 52,* 238–299.

Creed, P. A., Bloxsome, T. D., & Johnston, K. (2001). Self-esteem and self-efficacy outcomes for unemployed individuals attending occupational skills training programs. *Community, Work and Family, 4,* 285–303.

Crick, N. R., Casas, J. F., & Nelson, D. A. (2002). Toward a more comprehensive understanding of peer maltreatment: Studies of relational victimization. *Current Directions in Psychological Science, 11,* 98–101.

Crick, N. R., & Dodge, K. A. (1994). A review and reformulation of social information-processing mechanisms in children's social adjustment. *Psychological Bulletin, 115,* 74–101.

Crick, N. R., & Grotpeter, J. K, (1995). Relational aggression, gender, and social-psychological adjustment. *Child Development, 66,* 710–722.

Crick, N. R., Ostrov, J. M., Appleyard, K., Jansen, E. A., & Casas, J. F. (2004). Relational aggression in early childhood: "You can't come to my birthday party unless." In M. Puttalaz & K. L. Bierman (Eds.), *Aggression, antisocial behavior, and violence among girls* (pp. 71–89). New York: Guilford.

Crispi, E. L., Schiaffino, K., & Berman, W. H. (1997). The contribution of attachment to burden in adult children of institutionalized parents with dementia. *The Gerontologist, 37,* 52–60.

Crohan, S. E. (1996). Marital quality and conflict across the transition to parenthood in African American and white couples. *Journal of Marriage and the Family, 58,* 933–944.

Cross, S., & Markus, H. (1991). Possible selves across the lifespan. *Human Development, 34,* 230–255.

Crowder, R. G., & Wagner, R. K. (1992). *The psychology of reading: An introduction* (2nd ed.). New York: Oxford University Press.

Crown, W. (2001). Economic status of the elderly. In R. H. Binstock & L. K. George (Eds.), *Handbook of aging and the social sciences* (5th ed., pp. 352–368). San Diego, CA: Academic Press.

Csikszentmihalyi, M., & Larson, R. (1984). *Being adolescent: Conflict and growth in the teenage years.* New York: Basic Books.

Cuddy, A. J. C., & Fiske, S. T. (2002). Doddering but dear: Process, content, and function in stereotyping of older persons. In T. D. Nelson (Ed.), *Ageism: Stereotyping and prejudice against older persons* (pp. 3–26). Cambridge, MA: MIT Press.

Cuellar, I., Nyberg, B., Maldonado, R. E., & Roberts, R. E. (1997). Ethnic identity and acculturation in a young adult Mexican-origin population. *Journal of Community Psychology, 25,* 535–549.

Cunningham, A. E., Perry, K. E., Stanovich, K. E., & Share, D. L. (2002). Orthographic learning during reading: Examining the role of self-teaching. *Journal of Experimental Child Psychology.*

Curcio, C. A., Buell, S. J., & Coleman, P. D. (1982). Morphology of the aging central nervous system: Not all downhill. In J. A. Mortimer, F. J. Pirozzola, & G. I. Maletta (Eds.), *Advances in neurogerontology: Vol. 3. The aging motor system* (pp. 7–35). New York: Praeger.

Curran, P. J., Stice, E., & Chassin, L. (1997). The relation between adolescent alcohol use and peer alcohol use: A longitudinal random coefficients model. *Journal of Consulting and Clinical Psychology, 65,* 130–140.

Curtain, S. C., & Park, M. M. (1999). Trends in the attendant, place, and timing of births and in the use of obstetric interventions: United States, 1989–1997. *National Vital Statistics Report, 47,* 1–12.

Cutler, S. J., & Hendricks, J. (1990). Leisure and time use across the life course. In R. H. Binstock & L. K. George (Eds.), *Handbook of aging and the social sciences* (3rd ed., pp. 169–185). San Diego, CA: Academic Press.

Cutrona, C. E. (1996). *Social support in couples.* Thousand Oaks, CA: Sage.

Daley, T. C., Whaley, S. E., Sigman, M. D., Espinosa, M. P., & Neumann, C. (2003). IQ on the rise: The Flynn effect in rural Kenyan children. *Psychological Science, 14,* 215–219.

Dalton, S. T. (1992). Lived experience of never-married women. *Issues in Mental Health Nursing, 13,* 69–80.

Daly, M., & Wilson, M. (1996). Violence against stepchildren. *Current Directions in Psychological Science, 5,* 77–81.

Damon, W., & Hart, D. (1988). *Self-understanding in childhood and adolescence.* New York: Cambridge University Press.

Danforth, M. M., & Glass, J. C., Jr. (2001). Listen to my words, give meaning to my sorrow: A study in cognitive constructs in middle-age bereaved widows. *Death Studies, 25,* 513–529.

Dannemiller, J. L. (1998). Color constancy and color vision during infancy: Methodological and empirical issues. In V. Walsh & J. Kulikowski (Eds.), *Perceptual constancy: Why things look as they do.* New York: Cambridge University Press.

D'Augelli, A. R. (1996). Lesbian, gay, and bisexual development during adolescence and young adulthood. In R. P. Cabaj & T. S. Stein (Eds.), *Textbook of homosexuality and mental health.* Washington, DC: American Psychiatric Press.

D'Augelli, A. (2002). Mental health problems among lesbian, gay, and bisexual youths ages 14 to 21. *Clinical Child Psychology and Psychiatry, 7,* 433–456.

Davidson, F. H., & Davidson, M. M. (1994). *Changing childhood prejudice: The caring work of the schools.* Westport, CT: Bergin & Garvey/Greenwood.

Davies, L. (2000). *Transitions and singlehood: The forgotten life course.* Unpublished manuscript.

Davies, L. (2003). Singlehood: Transitions within a gendered world. *Canadian Journal on Aging, 22,* 343–352.

Davies, P. T., & Cummings, E. M. (1998). Exploring children's emotional security as a mediator of the link between marital relations and child adjustment. *Child Development, 69,* 124–139.

Davies, P. T., Cummings, E. M., & Winter, M. A. (in press). Pathways between profiles of family functioning, child security in the interparental subsystem, and child psychological problems. *Development and Psychopathology.*

Davis, B. L., MacNeilage, P. F., Matyear, C. L., & Powell, J. K. (2000). Prosodic correlates of stress in babbling: An acoustical study. *Child Development, 71,* 1258–1270.

Davis, B. W. (1985). *Visits to remember: A handbook for visitors of nursing home residents.* University Park: Pennsylvania State University Cooperative Extension Service.

Davis, J. A., & Lapane, K. L. (2004). Do characteristics associated with nursing home residents vary by race/ethnicity? *Journal of Health Care for the Poor and Underserved, 15,* 251–266.

Davis, M., McKay, M., & Eshelman, E. R. (2000). *The relaxation and stress reduction workbook.* Oakland, CA: New Harbinger.

Dawson, G., Ashman, S. B., Panagiotides, H., Hessl, D., Self, J., Yamada, E., & Embry, L. (2003). Preschool outcomes of children of depressed mothers: Role of maternal behavior, contextual risk, and children' brain activity. *Child Development, 74,* 1158–1175.

Day, J. D., Engelhardt, S. E., Maxwell, S. E., & Bolig, E. E. (1997). Comparison of static and dynamic assessment procedures and their relation to independent performance. *Journal of Educational Psychology, 89,* 358–368.

Day, S. X., Rounds, J., & Swaney, K. (1998). The structure of vocational interests for diverse racial-ethnic groups. *Psychological Science, 9,* 40–44.

De Andrade, C. E. (2000). Becoming the wise woman: A study of women's journeys through midlife transformation. *Dissertation Abstracts International Section B: The Sciences and Engineering, 61*(2–B), 1109.

De Beni, R., & Palladino, P. (2000). Intrusion errors in working memory tasks: Are they related to reading comprehension ability? *Learning & Individual Differences, 12,* 131–143.

de St. Aubin, E., & McAdams, D. P. (1995). The relations of generative concern and generative action to personality traits, satisfaction/happiness with life, and ego development. *Journal of Adult Development, 2,* 99–112.

De Vries, B. (1996). The understanding of friendship: An adult life course perspective. In C. Magai & S. H. McFadden (Eds.), *Handbook of emotion, adult development, and aging.* San Diego, CA: Academic Press.

De Witt, P. M. (1994). The second time around. *American Demographics* [reprint packet], 14–16.

De Wolff, M. S., & van IJzendoorn, M. H. (1997). Sensitivity and attachment: A meta-analysis on parental antecedents of infant attachment. *Child Development, 68,* 571–591.

DeAngelis, T. (1997). Menopause symptoms vary among ethnic groups. *APA Monitor, 28*(11), 16–17.

DeCasper, A. J., & Spence M. J. (1986). Prenatal maternal speech influences newborn's perception of speech sounds. *Infant Behavior and Development, 9,* 133–150.

Dekovic, M., & Janssens, J. M. (1992). Parents' child-rearing style and child's sociometric status. *Developmental Psychology, 28,* 925–932.

del Pinal, J., & Singer, A. (1997). Generations of diversity: Latinos in the United States. *Population Bulletin, 52,* whole issue.

Delaney, C. (2000). Making babies in a Turkish village. In J. S. DeLoache & A. Gottlieb (Eds.), *A world of babies: Imagined childcare guides for seven societies.* New York: Cambridge University Press.

Dellas, M., & Jernigan, L. P. (1990). Affective personality characteristics associated with undergraduate ego identity formation. *Journal of Adolescent Research, 5,* 306–324.

DeLoache, J. S. (1995). Early understanding and use of models: The model model. *Current Directions in Psychological Science, 4,* 109–113.

DeLoache, J. S. (2000). Dual representation and young children's use of scale models. *Child Development, 71,* 329–338.

DeLoache, J. S., Miller, K. F., & Rosengren, K. S. (1997). The credible shrinking room: Very young children's performance with symbolic and nonsymbolic relations. *Psychological Science, 8,* 308–313.

DeMaris, A., & Rao, K. V. (1992). Premarital cohabitation and subsequent marital stability in the United States: A reassessment. *Journal of Marriage and the Family, 54,* 178–190.

Dendinger, V. M., Adams, G. A., & Jacobson, J. D. (2005). Reasons for working and their relationship to retirement attitudes, job satisfaction and occupational self-efficacy of bridge employees. *International Journal of Aging and Human Development, 61,* 21–35.

Denney, N. W. (1982). Aging and cognitive changes. In B. B. Wolman (Ed.), *Handbook of developmental psychology* (pp. 807–827). Englewood Cliffs, NJ: Prentice-Hall.

Denney, N. W. (1989). Everyday problem solving: Methodological issues, research findings, and a model. In L. W. Poon, D. C. Rubin, & B. A. Wilson (Eds.), *Everyday cognition in adulthood and late life* (pp. 330–351). Cambridge, UK: Cambridge University Press.

Denney, N. W. (1990). Adult age differences in traditional and practical problem solving. In E. A. Lovelace (Ed.), *Aging and cognition: Mental processes, self-awareness, and interventions* (pp. 329–349). Amsterdam, The Netherlands: North-Holland.

Denney, N. W., Pearce, K. A., & Palmer, A. M. (1982). A developmental study of adults' performance on traditional and practical problem-solving tasks. *Experimental Aging Research, 8,* 115–118.

Derman, D. S. (2000). Grief and attachment in young widowhood. *Dissertation Abstracts International Section A: Humanities and Social Sciences, 60*(7-A), 2383.

Detterman, D. K., Gabriel, L. T., & Ruthsatz, J. M. (2000). Intelligence and giftedness. In R. J. Sternberg (Ed.), *Handbook of intelligence* (pp. 141–158). Cambridge, UK: Cambridge University Press.

Deutsch, A. (2001, April 11). Dutch parliament OKs strict euthanasia bill. *Wilmington (NC) Morning Star,* p. 2A.

Devine, M. A., & Lashua, B. (2002). Constructing social acceptance in inclusive leisure contexts: The role of individuals with disabilities. *Therapeutic Recreation Journal, 36,* 65–83.

Devine, P. G. (1989). Stereotypes and prejudice: Their automatic and controlled components. *Journal of Personality and Social Psychology, 56,* 5–18.

Diamond, A., Prevor, M. B., Callender, G., & Druin, D. P. (1997). Prefontal cortex deficits in children treated early and continuously for PKU. *Monographs of the Society for Research in Child Development, 62* (4, Serial No. 252).

Dick, D. M., & Rose, R. J. (2002). Behavior genetics: What's new? What's next? *Current Directions in Psychological Science, 11,* 70–74.

Dick, D. M., Rose, R. J., Viken, R. J., & Kaprio, J. (2000). Pubertal timing and substance abuse: Associations between and within families across late adolescence. *Developmental Psychology, 36,* 180–189.

Dickens, W. T., & Flynn, J. R. (2001). Heritability estimates versus large environmental effects: The IQ paradox resolved. *Psychological Review, 108,* 346–369.

Dickinson, G. E. (1992). First childhood death experiences. *Omega, 25,* 169–182.

Dick-Read, G. (1959). *Childbirth without fear.* New York: Harper and Brothers.

Diehl, M. (1998). Everyday competence in later life: Current status and future directions. *The Gerontologist, 4,* 422–433.

Diehl, M., Marsiske, M., Horgas, A. L., Rosenberg, A., Saczynski, J. S., & Willis, S. L. (2005). The Revised Observed Tasks of Daily Living: A performance-based assessment of everyday problem solving in older adults. *Journal of Applied Gerontology, 24,* 211–230.

Diesendruck, G., Markson, L., Akhtar, N., & Reudor, A. (2004). Two-year-olds' sensitivity to speakers' intent: An alternative account of Samuelson and Smith. *Developmental Science, 7,* 33–41.

DiGrande, L., Perrier, M. P., Lauro, M. G., & Contu, P. (2000). Alcohol correlates of binge drinking among university students on the Island of Sardinia. *Substance Use and Misuse, 35,* 1471–1483.

Dimond, M., Lund, D. A., & Caserta, M. S. (1987). The role of social support in the first two years of bereavement in an elderly sample. *The Gerontologist, 27,* 599–604.

Dionne, G., Dale, P. S., Boivin, M., & Plomin, R. (2003). Genetic evidence for bidirectional effects of early lexical and grammatical development. *Child Development, 74,* 394–412.

Dionne, G., Tremblay, R., Bolvin, M., Laplante, D., & Perusse, D. (2003). Physical aggression and expressive vocabulary in 19-month-old twins. *Developmental Psychology, 39,* 261–273.

DiPietro, J. A. (2004). The role of prenatal maternal stress in child development. *Current Directions in Child Development, 13,* 71–74.

DiPietro, J. A., Caulfield, L., Costigan, K. A., Merialdi, M., Nguyen, R. H. N., Zavaleta, N., & Gurewitsch, E. D. (2004). Fetal neurobehavioral development: A tale of two cities. *Developmental Psychology, 40,* 445–456.

DiPietro, J. A., Hodgson, D. M., Costigan, K. A., & Johnson, T. R. B. (1996). Fetal antecedents of infant temperament. *Child Development, 67,* 2568–2583.

Dishion, T. J., Poulin, F., & Burraston, B. (2001). Peer group dynamics associated with iatrogenic effects in group interventions with high-risk young adolescents. In D. W. Nangle & C. A. Erdley (Eds.), *The role of friendship in psychological adjustment* (pp. 79–92). San Francisco: Jossey-Bass.

Dixon, R. A., & Hultsch, D. F. (1999). Intelligence and cognitive potential in late life. In J. C. Cavanaugh & S. K. Whitbourne (Eds.), *Gerontology: An interdisciplinary perspective.* New York: Oxford University Press.

Dixon, R. A., Kramer, D. A., & Baltes, P. B. (1985). Intelligence: A life-span developmental perspective. In B. B. Wolman (Ed.), *Handbook of intelligence: Theories, measurements, and application* (pp. 301–350). New York: Wiley.

Dockrell, J., & McShane, J. (1993). *Children's learning difficulties: A cognitive approach.* Cambridge, UK: Blackwell.

Dodge, K. A., & Rabiner, D. L. (2004). Returning to roots: On social information processing and moral development. *Child Development, 75,* 1003–1008.

Dohanich, G. (2003). Ovarian steroids and cognitive function. *Current Directions in Psychological Science, 12,* 57–61.

Doka, K. J., & Mertz, M. E. (1988). The meaning and significance of great-grandparenthood. *The Gerontologist, 28,* 192–197.

Domino, G. (1992). Cooperation and competition in Chinese and American children. *Journal of Cross Cultural Psychology, 23,* 456–467.

Donatelle, R. J., & Davis, L. G. (1997). *Health: The basics* (2nd ed.). Englewood Cliffs, NJ: Prentice-Hall.

Dorgan, J. F., Stanczyk, F. A., Longcope, C., Stephenson, H. E., Jr., Chang, L., Miller, R., et al. (1997). Relationship of serum dehydroepiandrosterone (DHEA), DHEA sulfate, and 5-androstene-3 beta, 17 beta-diol to risk of breast cancer in postmenopausal women. *Cancer Epidemiology, Biomarkers and Prevention, 6,* 177–181.

Dorton, H. E., Jr. (2001). Job exit and the meaning of work in declining industries: Comparing retirement, displacement by retirement, and displacement by layoff at Weirton Steel Corporation. *Dissertation Abstracts International Section A: Humanities and Social Sciences, 61*(12–A), 4952.

Dougherty, D. D., Rauch, S. L., & Rosenbaum, J. F. (2004). *Essentials of neuroimaging for clinical practice.* Washington, DC: American Psychiatric Publishing.

Draghi-Lorenz, R., Reddy, V., & Costall, A. (2001). Rethinking the development of "nonbasic" emotions: A critical review of existing theories. *Developmental Review, 21,* 263–304.

Drew, L. M., & Silverstein, M. (2005). Inter-generational role investments of great-grandparents: Consequences for psychological well-being. *Ageing and Society. 24,* 95–111.

Duncan, C., & Loretto, W. (2004). Never the right age? Gender and age-based discrimination in employment. *Gender, Work & Organization, 11,* 95–115.

Dunham, P. J., Dunham, F., & Curwin, A. (1993). Joint-attentional states and lexical acquisition at 18 months. *Developmental Psychology, 29,* 827–831.

Dunn, J. (2002). Sibling relationships. In P. K. Smith & C. H. Hart (Eds.), *Handbook of childhood social development* (pp. 223–237). Malden, MA: Blackwell.

Dunn, J., Brown, J. R., & Maguire, M. (1995). The development of children's moral sensibility: Individual differences and emotion understanding. *Developmental Psychology, 31,* 649–659.

Dunn, J., & Davies, L. (2001). Sibling relationships and interpersonal conflict. In J. Grych & F. D. Fincham (Eds.), *Interparental conflict and child development* (pp. 273–290). New York: Cambridge University Press.

Dunn, J., & Kendrick, C. (1981). Social behavior of young siblings in the family context: Differences between same-sex and different-sex dyads. *Child Development, 52,* 1265–1273.

Dunn, J., O'Connor, T. G., & Cheng, H. (2005). Children's responses to conflict between their different parents: Mothers, stepfathers, nonresident fathers, and nonresident stepmothers. *Journal of Clinical Child and Adolescent Psychology, 34,* 223–234.

Dunn, J., Slomkowski, C., & Beardsall, L. (1994). Sibling relationships from the preschool period through middle childhood and early adolescence. *Developmental Psychology, 30,* 315–324.

Dunson, D. B., Colombo, B., & Baird, D. D. (2002). Changes in age in the level and duration of fertility in the menstrual cycle. *Human Reproduction, 17,* 1399–1403.

Durik, A., Hyde, J. S., & Clark, R. (2000). Sequelae of cesarean and vaginal deliveries: Psychosocial outcomes for mothers and infants. *Developmental Psychology, 36,* 251–260.

Dyk, P. H., & Adams, G. R. (1990). Identity and intimacy: An initial investigation of three theoretical models using cross-lag panel correlations. *Journal of Youth and Adolescence, 19,* 91–110.

Eagly, A. H., Karau, S. J., & Makhijani, M. G. (1995). Gender and the effectiveness of leaders: A meta-analysis. *Psychological Bulletin, 117,* 125–145.

Easterbrook, M. A., Kisilevsky, B. S., Hains, S. M. J., & Muir, D. W. (1999). Faceness or complexity: Evidence from newborn visual tracking of facelike stimuli. *Infant Behavior & Development, 22,* 17–35.

Eaton, J., & Salari, S. (2005). Environments for lifelong learning in senior centers. *Educational Gerontology, 31,* 461–480.

Eaton, W. O., & Enns, L. R. (1986). Sex differences in human motor activity level. *Psychological Bulletin, 100,* 19–28.

Ebberwein, C. A. (2001). Adaptability and the characteristics necessary for managing adult career transition: A qualitative investigation. *Dissertation Abstracts International section B: The Sciences and Engineering, 62*(1–B), 545.

Ebersole, P., Hess, P., & Luggen, A. S. (2004). *Toward healthy aging* (6th ed.). St. Louis: Mosby.

Eddleston, K. A., Baldridge, D. C., & Veiga, J. F. (2004). Toward modeling the predictors of managerial career success: Does gender matter? *Journal of Managerial Psychology, 19,* 360–385.

Eddy, J. M., Reid, J. B; Stoolmiller, M.. & Fetrow, R. A. (2003). Outcomes during middle school for an elementary school-based preventive intervention for conduct problems: Follow-up results from a randomized trial. *Behavior Therapy, 34,* 535–552.

Edelstein, B., & Kalish, K. (1999). Clinical assessment of older adults. In J. C. Cavanaugh & S. K. Whitbourne (Eds.), *Gerontology: An interdisciplinary perspective* (pp. 269–304). New York: Oxford University Press.

Editorial Board. (1996). Definition of mental retardation. In J. W. Jacobson & J. A. Mulick (Eds.), *Manual of diagnosis and professional practice in mental retardation.* Washington, DC: American Psychological Association.

Edwards, C. A. (1994). Leadership in groups of school-age girls. *Developmental Psychology, 30,* 920–927.

Edwards, J. D., Vance, D. E., Wadley, V. G., Cissell, G. M., Roenker, D. L., & Ball, K. K. (2005). Reliability and validity of useful field of view test scores as administered by personal computer. *Journal of Clinical & Experimental Neuropsychology, 27,* 529–543.

Egan, S. K., & Perry, D. G. (1998). Does low self-regard invite victimization? *Developmental Psychology, 34,* 299–309.

Eisenberg, N. (1982). The development of reasoning regarding prosocial behavior. In N. Eisenberg (Ed.), *The development of prosocial behavior.* New York: Academic Press.

Eisenberg, N. (1986). *Altruistic emotion, cognition, and behavior.* Hillsdale, NJ: Erlbaum.

Eisenberg, N. (2000). Emotion, regulation, and moral development. *Annual Review of Psychology, 51,* 665–697.

Eisenberg, N., Carlo, G., Murphy, B., & Van Court, P. (1995). Prosocial development in late adolescence: A longitudinal study. *Child Development, 66,* 1179–1197.

Eisenberg, N., Cumberland, A., Spinrad, T. L., Fabes, R. A., Shepard, S. A., Reiser, M., et al. (2001). The relations of regulation and emotionality to children's externalizing and internalizing problem behavior. *Child Development, 72,* 1112–1134.

Eisenberg, N., & Fabes, R. A. (1998). Prosocial development. In W. Damon (Ed.), *Handbook of child psychology* (Vol. 3, pp. 701–778). New York: Wiley.

Eisenberg, N., Fabes, R. A., & Spinrad, T. (2006). Prosocial development. In W. Damon & R. M. Lerner (Eds.), *Handbook of child psychology* (Vol. 3, 6th ed.). New York: Wiley.

Eisenberg, N., & Morris, A. S. (2002). Children's emotion-related regulation. *Advances in Child Development and Behavior, 30,* 189–229.

Eisenberg, N., Sadovsky, A., Spinrad, T. L., Fabes, R. A., Losoya, S. H., Valienta, C. et al. (2005). The relations of problem behavior status to children's negative emotionality, effortful control, and impulsivity: Concurrent relations and prediction of change. *Developmental Psychology, 41,* 193–211.

Eisenberg, N., & Shell, R. (1986). Prosocial moral judgment and behavior in children: The mediating role of cost. *Personality and Social Psychology Bulletin, 12,* 426–433.

Eizenman, D. R., & Bertenthal, B. I. (1998). Infants' perception of object unity in translating and rotating displays. *Developmental Psychology, 34,* 426–434.

Elder, G. H., Jr., & Pavalko, E. K. (1993). Work careers in men's later years: Transitions, trajectories, and historical change. *Journal of Gerontology: Social Sciences, 48,* S180–S191.

Elkind, D. (1978). *The child's reality: Three developmental themes.* Hillsdale, NJ: Erlbaum.

Elkind, D., & Bowen, R. (1979). Imaginary audience behavior in children and adolescents. *Developmental Psychology, 15,* 38–44.

Ellen, T. R. (2000). The expression of generativity and the relationship among generativity, life satisfaction, and self-esteem in Black American males between ages 37 and 55. *Dissertation Abstracts International section A: Humanities and Social Sciences, 60*(8–A), 3136.

Ellis, B. J. (2004). Timing of pubertal maturation in girls: An integrated life history approach. *Psychological Bulletin, 130,* 920–958.

Ellis, B. J., Bates, J. E., Dodge, K. A., Fergusson, D. M., Horwood, L. J., Pettit, G. S., & Woodward, L. (2003). Does father absence place daughters at special risk for early sexual activity and teenage pregnancy? *Child Development, 74,* 801–821.

Ellis, B. J., & Garber, J. (2000). Psychosocial antecedents of variation in girls' pubertal timing: Maternal depression, stepfather presence, and marital and family stress. *Child Development, 71,* 485–501.

Ellis, B. J., McFadyen-Ketchum, S., Dodge, K. A., Pettit, G. S., & Bates, J. E. (1999). Quality of early family relationships and individual differences in the timing of pubertal maturation in girls: A longitudinal test of an evolutionary model. *Journal of Personality and Social Psychology, 77,* 387–401.

Ellison, C. G. (1990). Family ties, friendships, and subjective well-being among Black Americans. *Journal of Marriage and the Family, 52,* 298–310.

Emick, M. A., & Hayslip, B., Jr. (1999). Custodial grandparenting: Stresses, coping skills, and relationships with grandchildren. *International Journal of Aging and Human Development, 48,* 35–61.

Engle, E., Miguel, R., Steelman, L., & McDaniel, M. A. (1994, April). *The relationship between age and work needs: A comprehensive research integration.* Paper presented at the annual meeting of the Society for Industrial and Organizational Psychology, Nashville, TN.

Enright, R. D., Gassin, E. A., & Wu, C. (1992). Forgiveness: A developmental view. *Journal of Moral Education, 21,* 99–114.

Epstein, L. H., & Cluss, P. A. (1986). Behavioral genetics of childhood obesity. *Behavior Therapy, 17,* 324–334.

Epstein, L. H., Valoski, A. M., Vara, L. S., McCurley, J., et al. (1995). Effects of decreasing sedentary behavior and increasing activity on weight change in obese children. *Health Psychology, 14,* 109–108.

Erel, O., & Burman, B. (1995). Interrelatedness of marital relations and parent-child relations: A meta-analytic review. *Psychological Bulletin, 118,* 108–132.

Erel, O., Margolin, G., & John, R. S. (1998). Observed sibling interaction: Links with the marital and the mother-child relationship. *Developmental Psychology, 34,* 288–298.

Erera-Weatherley, P. I. (1996). On becoming a stepparent: Factors associated with the adoption of alternative stepparenting styles. *Journal of Divorce and Remarriage, 25,* 155–174.

Ericsson, K. A., & Smith, J. (Eds.). (1991). *Toward a general theory of expertise: Prospects and limits.* New York: Cambridge University Press.

Erikson, E. H. (1968). *Identity: Youth and crisis.* New York: Norton.

Erikson, E. H. (1982). *The life cycle completed: Review.* New York: Norton.

Erikson, E. H., Erikson, J. M., & Kivnick, H. Q. (1986). *Vital involvement in old age.* New York: Norton.

Ernst, M., Moolchan, E. T., & Robinson, M. L. (2001). Behavioral and neural consequences of prenatal exposure to nicotine. *Journal of the American Academy of Child & Adolescent Psychiatry, 40,* 630–641.

Eskritt, M., & Lee, K. (2002). Remember when you last saw that card?: Children's production of external symbols as a memory aid. *Developmental Psychology, 38,* 254–266.

Etaugh, C., & Liss, M. B. (1992). Home, school, and playroom: Training grounds for adult gender roles. *Sex Roles, 26,* 129–147.

Etzioni, A. (1997, August 13). Marriage with no easy outs. *New York Times,* A23.

Evans, M., Platt, L., & De La Cruz, F. (Eds.). (2001). *Fetal therapy.* New York: Parthenon.

Eyer, D. E. (1992). *Mother-infant bonding: A scientific fiction.* New Haven, CT: Yale University Press.

Eyler, A. E., Wilcox, S., Matson-Koffman, D., Evenson, K. R., Sanderson, B., Thompson, J., Wilbur, J., & Rohm-Young, D. (2002). Correlates of physical activity among women from diverse racial/ethnic groups. *Journal of Women's Health and Gender Based Medicine, 11,* 239–253.

Faber, A. J. (2004). Examining remarried couples through a bowenian family systems lens. *Journal of Divorce & Remarriage, 40,* 121–133.

Fabes, R. A., Eisenberg, N., Jones, S., Smith, M., Guthrie, I., Poulin, R., et al. (1999). Regulation, emotionality, and preschoolers' socially competent peer interactions. *Child Development, 70,* 432–442.

Fagot, B. I. (1985). Changes in thinking about early sex role development. *Developmental Review, 5,* 83–98.

Fairlie, H. (1988). Talkin' bout my generation. *New Republic, 198,* 19–22.

Falbo, T., & Polit, E. F. (1986). Quantitative review of the only child literature: Research evidence and theory development. *Psychological Bulletin, 100,* 176–186.

Farver, J. M., & Shin, Y. L. (1997). Social pretend play in Korean- and Anglo-American preschoolers. *Child Development, 68,* 544–556.

Fasig, L. G. (2000). Toddlers' understanding of ownership: Implications for self-concept development. *Social Development, 9,* 370–382.

Faulkner, R. A., Davey, M., & Davey, A. (2005). Gender-related predictors of change in marital satisfaction and marital conflict. *American Journal of Family Therapy, 33,* 61–83.

Feder, J., Komisar, H. L., & Niefeld, M. (2001). The financing and organization of health care. In R. H. Binstock & L. K. George (Eds.), *Handbook of aging and the social sciences* (5th ed., pp. 387–405). San Diego, CA: Academic Press.

Federal Interagency Forum on Child and Family Statistics. (2005). *America's Children: Key National Indicators of Well-Being, 2005.* Federal Interagency Forum on Child and Family Statistics, Washington, DC: U.S. Government Printing Office.

Fehr, B. (1996). *Friendship processes.* Thousand Oaks, CA: Sage.

Feigenson, L., Carey, S., & Hauser, M. (2002). The representations underlying infants' choice of more: Object files versus analog magnitudes. *Psychological Science, 13,* 150–156.

Feinberg, M. E., McHale, S. M., Crouter, A. C., & Cumsille, P. (2003). Sibling differentiation: Sibling and parent relationships trajectories in adolescence. *Child Development, 74,* 1261–1274.

Felber, M. (2000). *Finding your way after your spouse dies.* Notre Dame, IN: Ave Maria Press.

Feldhusen, J. F. (1996). Motivating academically able youth with enriched and accelerated learning experiences. In C. P. Benbow & D. J. Lubinski (Eds.), *Intellectual talent: Psychometric and social issues.* Baltimore, MD: Johns Hopkins Press.

Feldman, D. H., & Goldsmith, L. T. (1991). *Nature's gambit.* New York: Teachers College Press.

Feminist Majority Foundation. (2005). *Domestic violence facts.* Retrieved June 12, 2005, from http://www.feminist.org/other/dv/dvfact.html

Fenson, L., Dale, P. S., Reznick, J. S., Bates, E., Thal, D. J., & Pethick, S. J. (1994). Variability in early communicative development. *Monographs of the Society for Research in Child Development, 59* (5, Serial No. 242).

Fergusson, D. M., Horwood, L. J., & Shannon, F. T. (1987). Breastfeeding and subsequent social adjustment in six- to eight-year-old children. *Journal of Child Psychology and Psychiatry and Allied Disciplines, 28,* 379–386.

Fergusson, D. M., & Woodward, L. J. (2000). Teenage pregnancy and female educational underachievement: A prospective study of a New Zealand birth cohort. *Journal of Marriage & the Family, 62,* 147–161.

Ferreol-Barbey, M., Piolat, A., & Roussey, J. (2000). Text recomposition by eleven-year-old children: Effects of text length, level of reading comprehension, and mastery of prototypical schema. *Archives de Psychologie, 68,* 213–232.

Field, N. P., Gao, B., & Paderna, L. (2005). Continuing bonds in bereavement: An attachment theory based perspective. *Death Studies, 29,* 277–299.

Field, T., Hernandez-Reif, M., & Freedman, J. (2004). Stimulation programs for preterm infants. *Social Policy Report, 18,* No. 1.

Field, T. M. (1990). *Infancy.* Cambridge, MA: Harvard University Press.

Field, T. M., & Widmayer, S. M. (1982). Motherhood. In B. J. Wolman (Ed.), *Handbook of developmental psychology* (pp. 681–701). Englewood Cliffs, NJ: Prentice-Hall.

Fife, J. E. (2005). The relationship between religious commitment, self identification, and life satisfaction among African Americans and European Americans. *Dissertation Abstracts International: Section B: The Sciences & Engineering, 65*(7-B), 3704.

Filanosky, C. A., Jr. (2004). The nature of continuing bonds with the deceased and their effect on bereavement outcome. *Dissertation Abstracts International: Section B: The Sciences & Engineering. 65*(2-B), 1027.

Finch, C. E., & Seeman, T. E. (1999). Stress theories of aging. In V. L. Bengtson & K. W. Schaie (Eds.), *Handbook of theories of aging* (pp. 81–97). New York: Springer.

Fincham, F. D. (2003). Marital conflict: Correlates, structure, and context. *Current Directions in Psychological Science, 12,* 23–27.

Finchum, T., & Weber, J. A. (2000). Applying continuity theory to elder adult friendships. *Journal of Aging and Identity, 5,* 159–168.

Finckh, U., von der Kammer, H., Velden, J., Michel, T., Andersen, B., Deng, A., et al. (2000). Genetic association of a cystatin C gene polumorphism with late-onset Alzheimer disease. *Archives of Neurology, 57,* 1579–1583.

Fingerman, K. L. (1996). Sources of tension in the aging mother and adult daughter relationship. *Psychology and Aging, 11,* 591–606.

Finkler, K. (2004). Traditional healers in Mexico: The effectiveness of spiritual practices. In U. P. Gielen, J. M. Fish, & J. G. Draguns (Eds.), *Handbook of culture, therapy, and healing* (pp. 161–174). Mahwah, NJ: Erlbaum.

Finley, G. E. (1999). Children of adoptive families. In W. K. Silverman & T. H. Ollendick (Eds.), *Developmental issues in the clinical treatment of children* (pp. 358–370). Boston: Allyn and Bacon.

Fisch, S., & McCann, S. K. (1993). Making broadcast television participative: Eliciting mathematical behavior through Square One TV. *Educational Technology Research and Development, 41,* 103–109.

Fischer, M., Barkley, R. A., Fletcher, K. E., & Smallish, L. (1993). The adolescent outcome of hyperactive children: Predictors of psychiatric, academic, social, and emotional adjustment. *Journal of the American Academy of Child and Adolescent Psychiatry, 32,* 324–332.

Fischoff, B., & Quadrel, M. J. (1995). Adolescent alcohol decisions. In G. M. Boyd, J. Howard, & R. A. Zucker (Eds.), *Alcohol problems among adolescents: Current directions in prevention research.* Hillsdale NJ: Erlbaum.

Fisher, C. (1996). Structural limits on verb mapping: The role of analogy in children's interpretations of sentences. *Cognitive Psychology, 31,* 41–81.

Fisher, H. E. (1994). The nature of romantic love. *Journal of NIH Research, 6*(4), 59–64.

Fiske, S. (1993). Social cognition and social perception. *Annual Review of Psychology, 50,* 229–238.

Fitzgerald, H. E. (2005). Alcoholism prevention programs for children. In C. B. Fisher & R. M. Lerner (Eds.), *Encyclopedia of applied developmental science* (Vol. 1, pp. 73–76). Thousand Oaks CA: Sage.

Fitzgerald, H. E., & Brackbill, Y. (1976). Classical conditioning in infancy: Development and constraints. *Psychological Bulletin, 83,* 353–375.

Fitzgerald, J. (1987). Research on revision in writing. *Review of Educational Research, 57,* 481–506.

Fitzgerald, J. M. (1999). Autobiographical memory and social cognition: Development of the remembered self in adulthood. In T. M. Hess & F. Blanchard-Fields (Eds.), *Social cognition and aging* (pp. 143–171). San Diego: Academic Press.

Fitzgerald, L., Hulin, C. L., Dragow, F., Gelfand, M., & Magley, V. J. (1997). Antecedents and consequences of sexual harassment in organizations: A test of an integrated model. *Journal of Applied Psychology, 82,* 578–589.

Flaks, D. K., Filcher, I., Masterpasqua, F., & Joseph, G. (1995). Lesbians choosing motherhood: A comparative study of lesbian and heterosexual parents and their children. *Developmental Psychology, 31,* 105–114.

Flavell, J. H. (1985). *Cognitive development* (2nd ed.). Englewood Cliffs, NJ: Prentice-Hall.

Flavell, J. H. (1996). Piaget's legacy. *Psychological Science, 7,* 200–203.

Flavell, J. H. (1999). Cognitive development: Children's knowledge about the mind. *Annual Review of Psychology, 50,* 21–45.

Flavell, J. H. (2000). Development of children's knowledge about the mental world. *International Journal of Behavioral Development, 24,* 15–23.

Fleischman, D. A., & Gabrieli, J. D. E. (1998). Repetition priming in normal aging and Alzheimer's disease: A review of findings and theories. *Psychology and Aging, 13,* 88–119.

Fleming, S. J., & Balmer, L. E. (1996). Bereavement in adolescence. In C. A. Coor & D. E. Balk (Eds.), *Handbook of adolescent death and bereavement* (pp. 139–154). New York: Springer.

Fleming, S., & Robinson, P. (2001). Grief and cognitive-behavioral therapy: The reconstruction of meaning. In M. S. Stroebe, R. O. Hansson, W. Stroebe, & H. Schut (Eds.), *Handbook of bereavement research: Consequences, coping, and care* (pp. 647–669). Washington, DC: American Psychological Association.

Flynn, J. R. (1998). IQ gains over time: Toward finding the causes. In U. Neisser (Ed.), *The rising curve: Long-term gains in IQ and related measures* (pp. 25–66). Washington, DC: American Psychological Association.

Flynn, J. R. (1999). Searching for justice: The discovery of IQ gains over time. *American Psychologist, 54,* 5–20.

Foley, D., Ancoli-Israel, S., Britz, P., & Walsh, J. (2004) Sleep disturbances and chronic disease in older adults: Results of the 2003 National Sleep Foundation Sleep in America Survey. *Journal of Psychosomatic Research, 56,* 497–502.

Fonzi, A., Schneider, B. H., Tani, F., & Tomada, G. (1997). Predicting children's friendship status from their dynamic interaction in structured situations of potential conflict. *Child Development, 68,* 496–506.

Forbes, K. (2005). A multi-disciplinary approach to diagnosis and assessment in early-onset dementia. *Cortex, 41,* 90–95.

Foreyt, J. P., & Goodrick, G. K. (1995). Obesity. In R. T. Ammerman & M. Hersen (Eds.), *Handbook of child behavior therapy in the psychiatric setting.* New York: Wiley.

Fortner, B. V., & Neimeyer, R. A. (1999). Death anxiety in older adults: A quantitative review. *Death Studies, 23,* 387–411.

Foshee, V. A., Benefield, T. S., Ennett, S. T., Bauman, K. E., & Suchindran, S. (2004). Longitudinal predictors of serious physical and sexual dating violence victimization during adolescence. *Preventive Medicine, 39,* 1007–1016.

Foshee, V. A., & Langwick, S. (2004). *Safe dates: An adolescent dating abuse prevention curriculum.* Center City, MN: Hazelden Publishing and Educational Services.

Foshee, V. A., Linder, F., MacDougall, J. E., & Bangdiwala, S. (2001). Gender differences in the longitudinal predictors of adolescent dating violence. *Preventive Medicine, 32,* 128–141.

Foster, E. (2005). Juvenile justice, racial differences. In C. B. Fisher & R. M. Lerner (Eds.), *Encyclopedia of applied developmental science* (Vol. 1, pp. 620–622). Thousand Oaks CA: Sage.

Foster, S. H. (1986). Learning discourse topic management in the preschool years. *Journal of Child Language, 13,* 231–250.

Fouad, N. A., & Mohler, C. J. (2004). Cultural validity of Holland's theory and the Strong Interest Inventory for five racial/ethnic groups. *Journal of Career Assessment, 12,* 423–439.

Fox, N. A. (1991). If it's not left, it's right. *American Psychologist, 46,* 863–872.

Fozard, J. L., & Gordon-Salant, S. (2001). Changes in vision and hearing with aging. In J. E. Birren & K. W. Schaie (Eds.), *Handbook of the psychology of aging* (5th ed., pp. 241–266). San Diego, CA: Academic Press.

Fraley, R. C., & Roberts, B. W. (2005). Patterns of continuity: A dynamic model for conceptualizing the stability of individual differences in psychological constructs across the life course. *Psychological Review. 112,* 60–74.

Franceschi, K. A. (2005). The experience of the transition to motherhood in women who have suffered maternal loss in adolescence. *Dissertation Abstracts International: Section B: The Sciences and Engineering, 65*(8-B), 4282.

Frank, D. A., Augustyn, M., Knight, W. G., Pell, T., & Zuckerman, B. (2001). Growth, development, and behavior in early childhood following prenatal cocaine exposure: A systematic review. *Journal of the American Medical Association, 285,* 1613–1625.

Franklin, A., Pilling, M., & Davies, I. (2005). The nature of infant color categorization: Evidence from eye movements on a target detection task. *Journal of Experimental Child Psychology, 91,* 227–248.

Frazier, L. D., Hooker, K., Johnson, P. M., & Kaus, C. R. (2000). Continuity and change in possible selves in later life: A 5-year longitudinal study. *Basic and Applied Social Psychology, 22,* 237–243.

Frazier, L. D., Johnson, P. M., Gonzalez, G. K., & Kafka, C. L. (2002) Psychosocial influences on possible selves: A comparison of three cohorts of older adults. *International Journal of Behavioral Development, 26,* 308–317.

Fredricks, J. A., & Eccles, J. S. (2005). Family socialization, gender, and sport motivation and involvement. *Journal of Sport and Exercise Psychology, 27,* 3–31.

Frerichs, F., & Naegele, G. (1997). Discrimination of older workers in Germany: Obstacles and options for the integration into employment. *Journal of Aging and Social Policy, 9,* 89–101.

Fretz, B. R. (2001). Coping with licensing, credentialing, and lifelong learning. In S. Walfish & A. K. Hess (Eds.), *Succeeding in graduate school: The career guide for psychology students* (pp. 353–367). Mahwah, NJ: Erlbaum.

Freund, A. (2005). Commitment and job satisfaction as predictors of turnover intentions among welfare workers. *Administration in Social Work, 29,* 5–21.

Freund, B., Gravenstein, S., Ferris, R., Burke, B. L., & Shaheen, E. (2005). Drawing clocks and driving cars: Use of brief tests of cognition to screen driving competency in older adults. *Journal of General Internal Medicine, 20,* 240–244.

Fried, P. A., O'Connell, C. M., & Watkinson, B. (1992). 60- and 72-month follow-up of children prenatally exposed to marijuana, cigarettes, and alcohol: Cognitive and language assessment. *Journal of Developmental & Behavioral Pediatrics, 13,* 383–391.

Friedman, J. M., & Polifka, J. E. (1996). *The effects of drugs on the fetus and nursing infant: A handbook for health care professionals.* Baltimore: Johns Hopkins University Press.

Friedman, M., & Rosenman, R. H. (1974). *Type A behavior and your heart.* New York: Random House.

Froman, L. (1994). Adult learning in the workplace. In J. D. Sinnott (Ed.), *Interdisciplinary handbook of adult lifespan learning* (pp. 203–217). Westport, CT: Greenwood Press.

Frye, D. (1993). Causes and precursors of children's theories of mind. In D. F. Hay & A. Angold (Eds.), *Precursors and causes in development and psychopathology.* Chichester, UK: Wiley.

Fu, S.-Y., Anderson, D., & Courtney, M. (2003). Cross-cultural menopausal experience: Comparison of Australian and Taiwanese women. *Nursing & Health Sciences, 5,* 77–84.

Fujita, F., & Diener, E. (2005). Life satisfaction set point: Stability and change. *Journal of Personality and Social Psychology, 88,* 158–164.

Fuller-Thompson, E., Hayslip, B., Jr., & Patrick, J. H. (2005). Introduction to the special issue: Diversity among grandparent caregivers. *International Journal of Aging and Human Development, 60,* 269–272.

Furman, W. (1995). Parenting siblings. In M. H. Bornstein (Ed.), *Handbook of parenting* (Vol. 1). Mahwah, NJ: Erlbaum.

Futterman, A., Gallagher, D., Thompson, L. W., Lovett, S., & Gilewski, M. (1990). Retrospective assessment of marital adjustment and depression during the first two years of spousal bereavement. *Psychology and Aging, 5,* 277–283.

Gaddis, A., & Brooks-Gunn, J. (1985). The male experience of pubertal change. *Journal of Youth and Adolescence, 14,* 61–69.

Gagliardi, A. (2005). Postpartum depression. In C. B. Fisher & R. M. Lerner (Eds.), *Encyclopedia of applied developmental science* (Vol. 2, pp. 867–870). Thousand Oaks CA: Sage.

Gailey, C. W. (1987). Evolutionary perspectives in gender hierarchy. In B. B. Hess & M. M. Feree (Eds.), *Analyzing gender: A handbook of social science research* (pp. 32–67). Thousand Oaks, CA: Sage.

Galinsky, E., Bond, J. T., & Friedman, D. E. (1996). The role of employers in addressing the needs of employed parents. *Journal of Social Issues, 52,* 111–136.

Gall, T. L., Evans, D. R., & Howard, J. (1997). The retirement adjustment process: Changes in the well-being of male retirees across time. *Journal of Gerontology: Psychological Sciences, 52B,* P110–P117.

Gallagher, M. (1996). Re-creating marriage. In D. Popenoe, J. B. Elshtain, & D. Blankenhorn (Eds.), *Promises to keep: Decline and renewal of marriage in America* (pp. 233–246). Lanham, MD: Rowman & Littlefield.

Gallagher, R., Bruzzese, J.-M., & McCann-Doyle, S. (2005). Cigarette smoking in adolescents. In C. B. Fisher & R. M. Lerner (Eds.), *Encyclopedia of applied developmental science* (Vol. 1, pp. 254–256). Thousand Oaks CA: Sage.

Galler, J. R., & Ramsey, F. (1989). A follow-up study of the influence of early malnutrition on development: Behavior at home and at school. *Journal of the American Academy of Child and Adolescent Psychiatry, 28,* 254–261.

Galler, J. R., Ramsey, F., & Forde, V. (1986). A follow-up study of the influence of early malnutrition on subsequent development: IV. Intellectual performance during adolescence. *Nutrition and Behavior, 3,* 211–222.

Gangestad, S. W., & Thornhill, R. (1997). Human sexual selection and developmental stability. In J. A. Simpson & D. T. Kenrick (Eds.), *Evolutionary social psychology* (pp. 169–196). Mahwah, NJ: Erlbaum.

Ganong, L. M., & Coleman, M. (1994). *Remarried family relationships.* Thousand Oaks, CA: Sage.

Gardner, H. (1983). *Frames of mind: The theory of multiple intelligences.* New York: Basic Books.

Gardner, H. (1993). *Multiple intelligences: The theory in practice.* New York: Basic Books.

Gardner, H. (1995). Reflections on multiple intelligences: Myths and messages. *Phi Delta Kappan, 77,* 200–203, 206–209.

Gardner, H. (1999). *Intelligence reframed: Multiple intelligences for the 21st century.* New York: Basic Books.

Gardner, H. (2002). *MI millennium: Multiple intelligences for the new millennium* [video recording]. Los Angeles: Into the Classroom Media.

Garner, P. W., Jones, D. C., & Palmer, D. J. (1994). Social cognitive correlates of preschool children's sibling caregiving behavior. *Developmental Psychology, 30,* 905–911.

Garrard, E., & Wilkinson, S. (2005). Passive euthanasia. *Journal of Medical Ethics, 31,* 64–68.

Garrod, A., & Larimore, C. (Eds.). (1997). *First person, first peoples: Native American college graduates tell their life stories.* Ithaca, NY: Cornell University Press.

Garvey, C., & Berninger, G. (1981). Timing and turn taking in children's conversations. *Discourse Processes, 4,* 27–59.

Gathercole, S. E., Willis, C. S., Emslie, H., & Baddeley, A. D. (1992). Phonological memory and vocabulary development during the early school years: A longitudinal study. *Developmental Psychology, 28,* 887–898.

Gatz, M. (2000). Variations on depression in later life. In S. H. Qualls & N. Abeles (Eds.), *Psychology and the aging revolution* (pp. 239–254). Washington, DC: American Psychological Association.

Gatz, M., Pedersen, N. L., Berg, S., Johansson, B., Johansson, K., Mortimer, J. A., et al. (1997). Heritability for Alzheimer's disease: The study of dementia in Swedish twins. *Journal of Gerontology: Medical Sciences, 52A,* M117–M125.

Gatz, M., & Smyer, M. A. (2001). Mental health and aging at the outset of the twenty-first century. In J. E. Birren & K. W. Schaie (Eds.), *Handbook of the psychology of aging* (5th ed., pp. 523–544). San Diego, CA: Academic Press.

Gaulin, S. J. C., & McBurney, D. H. (2001). *Psychology: An evolutionary approach.* Upper Saddle River, NJ: Prentice-Hall.

Gavin, L. A., & Furman, W. (1996). Adolescent girls' relationships with mothers and best friends. *Child Development, 67,* 375–386.

Gaylord, S. A., & Zung, W. W. K. (1987). Affective disorders among the aging. In L. L. Carstensen & B. A. Edelstein (Eds.), *Handbook of clinical gerontology* (pp. 76–95). New York: Pergamon Press.

Gazelle, H., & Ladd, G. W. (2003). Anxious solitude and peer exclusion: A diathesis-stress model of internalizing trajectories in childhood. *Child Development, 74,* 257–278.

Ge, X., Brody, G. H., Conger, R. D., Simons, R. L., & Murry, V. M. (2002). Contextual amplication of pubertal transition effects on deviant peer affiliation and externalizing behavior among African American children. *Developmental Psychology, 38,* 45–54.

Ge, X., Conger, R. D., & Elder, G. H. (2001). Pubertal transition, stressful life events, and the emergence of gender differences in adolescent depressive symptoms. *Developmental Psychology, 37,* 404–417.

Ge, X., Kim, I. J., Brody, G. H., Conger, R. D., Simons, R. L., Gibbons, F. X., & Cutrona, C. E. (2003). It's about timing and change: Pubertal transition effects on symptoms of major depression among African American youths. *Developmental Psychology, 39,* 430–439.

Geary, D. C. (2002). Sexual selection and human life history. In R. V. Kail (Ed.), *Advances in child development and behavior* (Vol. 30, pp. 41–102). San Diego, CA: Academic Press.

Geary, D. C., Byrd-Craven, J., Hoard, M. K., Vigil, J., & Numtee, C. (2003). Evolution and development of boys' social behavior. *Developmental Review, 23,* 444–470.

Gelman, R., & Meck, E. (1986). The notion of principle: The case of counting. In J. Hiebert (Ed.), *Conceptual and procedural knowledge: The case of mathematics.* Hillside, NJ: Lawrence Erlbaum.

Gelman, S. A., Coley, J. D., Rosengren, K. S., Hartman, E., & Pappas, A. (1998). Beyond labeling: The role of maternal input in the acquisition of richly structured categories. *Monographs of the Society for Research in Child Development, 63* (Serial No. 253).

Gelman, S. A., & Gottfried, G. M. (1996). Children's casual explanations of animate and inanimate motion. *Child Development, 67,* 1970–1987.

Gelman, S. A., Taylor, M. G., & Nguyen, S. P. (2004). Mother-child conversations about gender. *Monographs of the Society for Research in Child Development, 69* (Serial No. 275).

Gershkoff-Stowe, L., & Smith, L. B. (2004). Shape and the first hundred nouns. *Child Development, 75,* 1098–1114.

Giarusso, R., Feng, D., Silverstein, M., & Marenco, A. (2000). Primary and secondary stressors of grandparents raising grandchildren: Evidence from a national survey. *Journal of Mental Health and Aging, 6,* 291–310.

Gibbs, J. C., Clark, P. M., Joseph, J. A., Green, J. L., Goodrick, T. S., & Makowski, D. (1986). Relations between moral judgment, moral courage, and field independence. *Child Development, 57,* 185–193.

Gibbs, N. R. (1988). Grays on the go. *Time, 131*(8), 66–75.

Giberson, P. K., & Weinberg, J. (1992). Fetal alcohol syndrome and functioning of the immune system. *Alcohol Health and Research World, 16,* 29–38.

Gibran, K. (1923). *The prophet.* New York: Knopf.

Gibson, E. J., Riccio, G., Schmuckler, M. A., Stoffregen, T. A., Rosenberg, D., & Taormina, J. (1987). Detection of the traversability of surfaces by crawling and walking infants. *Journal of Experimental Psychology: Human Perception & Performance, 13,* 533–544.

Gibson, E. J., & Walk, R. D. (1960). The visual cliff. *Scientific American, 202,* 64–71.

Gibson, R. C. (1986). *Blacks in an aging society.* New York: Carnegie.

Gibson, R. C. (1987). Reconceptualizing retirement for Black Americans. *The Gerontologist, 27,* 691–698.

Gibson, R. C. (1991). The subjective retirement of Black Americans. *Journal of Gerontology: Social Sciences, 46,* S204–S209.

Gignac, M. A. M., Kelloway, E. K., & Gottlieb, B. H. (1996). The impact of caregiving on employment: A mediational model of work-family conflict. *Canadian Journal on Aging, 15,* 525–542.

Giles, J. W., & Heyman, G. D. (2005). Young children's beliefs about the relationship between gender and aggressive behavior. *Child Development, 76,* 107–121.

Gilligan, C. (1982). *In a different voice: Psychological theory and women's development.* Cambridge, MA: Harvard University Press.

Gilligan, C., & Attanucci, J. (1988). Two moral orientations: Gender differences and similarities. *Merrill-Palmer Quarterly, 34,* 223–237.

Gilmore, D. (1990). *Manhood in the making: Cultural components of masculinity.* New Haven, CT: Yale University Press.

Ginn, J., & Arber, S. (1996). Gender, age, and attitudes toward retirement in midlife. *Aging and Society, 16,* 27–55.

Gjerdingen, D., McGovern, P., Bekker, M., Lundberg, U., & Willemsen, T. (2000). Women's work roles and their impact on health, well-being and career: Comparisons between the United States, Sweden, and The Netherlands. *Women and Health, 31,* 1–20.

Glamser, F., & Hayslip, B., Jr. (1985). The impact of retirement on participation in leisure activities. *Therapeutic Recreation Journal, 19,* 28–38.

Glenn, N. D. (1998). The course of marital success and failure in five American 10-year marriage cohorts. *Journal of Marriage and the Family, 60,* 569–576.

Glick, P. C. (1989). The family life cycle and social change. *Family Relations, 38,* 123–129.

Glick, P. C., & Lin, S. (1986). Recent changes in divorce and remarriage. *Journal of Marriage and the Family, 48,* 737–747.

Glickman, H. M. (2001). The relationship between person-organization value congruence and global job satisfaction. *Dissertation Abstracts International Section B: The Sciences and Engineering, 61*(12–B), 6745.

Global Youth Tobacco Survey Collaborative Group. (2002). Tobacco use among youth: A cross-country comparison. *Tobacco Control, 11,* 252–270.

Go, C. G., Brustrom, J. E., Lynch, M. F., & Aldwin, C. M. (1995). Ethnic trends in survival curves and mortality. *The Gerontologist, 35,* 318–326.

Goeke-Morey, M. C., Cummings, E. M., Harold, G. T., & Shelton, K. H. (2003). Categories and continua of destructive and constructive conflict tactics from the perspective of U.S. and Welsh children. *Journal of Family Psychology, 17,* 327–338.

Goff, S. J., Fick, D. S., & Opplinger, R. A. (1997). The moderating effect of spouse support on the relation between serious leisure and spouses' perceived leisure-family conflict. *Journal of Leisure Research, 29,* 47–60.

Golby, A., Silverberg, G., Race, E., Gabrieli, S., O'Shea, J., Knierim, K., et al. (2005). Memory encoding in Alzheimer's disease: An fMRI study of explicit and implicit memory. *Brain, 128,* 773–787.

Gold, D. T. (1990). Late-life sibling relationships: Does race affect typological distribution? *The Gerontologist, 30,* 741–748.

Gold, D. T., Woodbury, M. A., & George, L. K. (1990). Relationship classification using grade of membership analysis: A typology of sibling relationships in later life. *Journal of Gerontology: Social Sciences, 45,* S43–S51.

Goldenberg, R. L., & Klerman, L. V. (1995). Adolescent pregnancy—another look. *New England Journal of Medicine, 332,* 1161–1162.

Goldenthal, P. (2002). *Why can't we get along? Healing adult sibling relationships.* New York: Wiley.

Goldfield, B. A., & Reznick, J. S. (1990). Early lexical acquisition: Rate, content, and the vocabulary spurt. *Journal of Child Language, 17,* 171–184.

Goldman, L. S., Genel, M., Bezman, R. J., & Slanetz, P. J. (1998). Diagnosis and treatment of attention-deficit/hyperactivity disorder in children and adolescents. *Journal of the American Medical Association, 279,* 1100–1107.

Goldsmith, H. H., Buss, K. A., & Lemery, K. S. (1997). Toddler and childhood temperament: Expanded content, stronger genetic evidence, new evidence for the importance of environment. *Developmental Psychology, 33,* 891–905.

Goldsmith, H. H., & Harman, C. (1994). Temperament and attachment: Individuals and relationships. *Current Directions in Psychological Science, 3,* 53–57.

Goleman, D. (1995). *Emotional intelligence: Why it can matter more than IQ.* New York: Bantam.

Golinkoff, R. M. (1993). When is communication a "meeting of minds"? *Journal of Child Language, 20,* 199–207.

Golombok, S., MacCallum, F., & Goodman, E. (2001). The "test-tube" generation: Parent-child relationships and the psychological well-being of in vitro fertilization children at adolescence. *Child Development, 72,* 599–608.

Golombok, S., Murray, C., Jadva, V., MacCallum, F., & Lycett, E. (2004). Families created through surrogacy arrangements: Parent-child relationships in the first year of life. *Developmental Psychology, 40,* 400–411.

Golombok, S., & Tasker, F. (1996). Do parents influence the sexual orientation of their children? Findings from a longitudinal study of lesbian families. *Developmental Psychology, 32,* 3–11.

Golsworthy, R., & Coyle, A. (2001). Practitioners' accounts of religious and spiritual dimension in bereavement therapy. *Counselling Psychology Quarterly, 14,* 183–202.

Gomez, T. R. A. (2000). College undergraduate binge drinking: A reconceptualization of the problem and an examination of socialization contexts. *Dissertation Abstracts International: Section A: Humanities and Social Sciences, 60,* 4621.

Gonzales, P., Guzmán, J. C., Partelow, L., Pahlke, E., Jocelyn, L., Kastberg, D., & Williams, T. (2004). *Highlights From the Trends in International Mathematics and Science Study (TIMSS) 2003.* U.S. Department of Education, National

Center for Education Statistics. Washington, DC: U.S. Government Printing Office.

Gonzalez, H. M., Haan, M. N., & Hinton, L. (2001). Acculturation and the prevalence of depression in older Mexican Americans: Baseline results of the Sacramento Area Latino Study on Aging. *Journal of the American Geriatrics Society, 49,* 948–953.

Good, T. L., & Brophy, J. E. (1994). *Looking in classrooms* (6th ed.). New York: HarperCollins.

Goodkin, K., Burkhalter, J. E., Blaney, N. T., Leeds, B., Tuttle, R. S., & Feaster, D. J. (1997). A research derived bereavement support group technique for the HIV-1 infected. *Omega: Journal of Death and Dying, 34,* 279–300.

Goodman, G. S., Emery, R. E., & Haugaard, J. J. (1998). Developmental psychology and law: Divorce, child maltreatment, foster care, and adoption. In W. Damon (Ed.), *Handbook of child psychology* (Vol. 4). New York: Wiley.

Goodnow, J. J. (1992). *Parental belief systems: The psychological consequences for children.* Hillsdale, NJ: Erlbaum.

Goodwyn, S. W., & Acredolo, L. P. (1993). Symbolic gesture versus word: Is there a modality advantage for onset of symbol use? *Child Development, 64,* 688–701.

Gordon, B. N., Baker-Ward, L., & Ornstein, P. A. (2001). Children's testimony: A review of research on memory for past experiences. *Clinical Child & Family Psychology Review, 4,* 157–181.

Gordon, C. P. (1996). Adolescent decision making: A broadly based theory and its application to the prevention of early pregnancy. *Adolescence, 31,* 561–584.

Gordon, R. A., Chase-Lansale, P. L., & Brooks-Gunn, J. (2004). Extended households and the life course of young mothers: Understanding the associations using a sample of mothers with premature, low birth weight babies. *Child Development, 75,* 1013–1038.

Gottesman, I. R., & Hanson, D. R. (2005). Human development: Biological and genetic processes. *Annual Review of Psychology, 56,* 263–286.

Gottfredson, L. S. (1997). Why *g* matters: The complexity of everyday life. *Intelligence, 24,* 79–132.

Gottlieb, G. (2000). Environmental and behavioral influences on gene activity. *Current Directions in Psychological Science, 9,* 93–97.

Gottlieb, L. N., & Mendelson, M. J. (1990). Parental support and firstborn girls' adaptation to the birth of a sibling. *Journal of Applied Developmental Psychology, 11,* 29–48.

Gottman, J. M. (1986). The world of coordinated play: Same- and cross-sex friendships in children. In J. M. Gottman & J. G. Parker (Eds.), *Conversations of friends.* New York: Cambridge University Press.

Gottman, J. M., Katz, L. F., & Hooven, C. (1996). Parental meta-emotion philosophy and the emotional life of families: Theoretical models and preliminary data. *Journal of Family Psychology, 10,* 243–268.

Gottman, J. M., & Levenson, R. W. (2000). The timing of divorce: Predicting when a couple will divorce over a 14-year period. *Journal of Marriage and the Family, 62,* 737–745.

Goubet, N., & Clifton, R. K. (1998). Object and event representation in 6½-month-old infants. *Developmental Psychology, 34,* 63–76.

Goubet, N., Clifton, R. K., & Shah, B. (2001). Learning about pain in preterm newborns. *Journal of Developmental and Behavioral Pediatrics, 22,* 418–424.

Gould, R. L. (1978). *Transformation: Growth and change in adult life.* New York: Simon & Schuster.

Gould, S. J. (1999). A critique of Heckhausen and Schulz's (1995) life-span theory of control from a cross-cultural perspective. *Psychological Review, 106,* 597–604.

Govier, E., & Salisbury, G. (2000). Age-related sex differences in performance on a side-naming spatial task. *Psychology, Evolution, & Gender, 2,* 209–222.

Graesser, A. C., Singer, M., & Trabasso, T. (1994). Constructing inferences during narrative text comprehension. *Psychological Review, 101,* 371–395.

Graham, S., Harris, K. R., & Fink, B. (2000). Is handwriting causally related to learning to write? Treatment of handwriting problems in beginning writers. *Journal of Educational Psychology, 92,* 620–633.

Graham, S., & Juvonen, J. (1998). Self-blame and peer victimization in middle school: An attributional analysis. *Developmental Psychology, 34,* 587–599.

Graham-Bermann, S. A., & Brescoll, V. (2000). Gender, power, and violence: Assessing the family stereotypes of the children of batterers. *Journal of Family Psychology, 14,* 600–612.

Graham-Kevan, N., & Archer, J. (2003). Intimate terrorism and common couple violence: A test of Johnson's predictions in four British Samples. *Journal of Interpersonal Violence, 18,* 1247–1270.

Grande, G. E., Farquhar, M. C., Barclay, S. I. G., & Todd, C. J. (2004). Caregiver bereavement outcome: Relationship with hospice at home, satisfaction with care, and home death. *Journal of Palliative Care, 20,* 69–77.

Grandey, A. A. (2001). Family friendly policies: Organizational justice perceptions of need-based allocations. In R. Cropanzano (Ed.), *Justice in the workplace: From theory to practice* (pp. 145–173). Mahwah, NJ: Erlbaum.

Grantham-McGregor, S., Ani, C., & Fernald, L. (2001). The role of nutrition in intellectual development. In R. J. Sternberg & E. L. Grigorenko (Eds.), *Environmental effects on cognitive abilities* (pp. 119–155). Mahwah, NJ: Erlbaum.

Graves, R., & Landis, T. (1990). Asymmetry in mouth opening during different speech tasks. *International Journal of Psychology, 25,* 179–189.

Greenberg, M. T., & Crnic, K. A. (1988). Longitudinal predictors of developmental status and social interaction in premature and full-term infants at age two. *Child Development, 59,* 554–570.

Greenberger, E., O'Neil, R., & Nagel, S. K. (1994). Linking workplace and homeplace: Relations between the nature of adults' work and their parenting behaviors. *Developmental Psychology, 30,* 990–1002.

Greenfield, E. A., & Marks, N. F. (2005). Formal volunteering as a protective factor for older adults' psychological well-being. *Journals of Gerontology: Social Sciences, 59,* S258–S264.

Greenfield, P. M. (1998). The cultural evolution of IQ. In U. Neisser (Ed.), *The rising curve: Long-term gains in IQ and related measures* (pp. 81–123). Washington, DC: American Psychological Association.

Greenhaus, J. H., Parasuraman, S., & Wormley, W. M. (1990). Effects of race on organizational experiences, job performance evaluations, and career outcomes. *Academy of Management Journal, 33,* 64–86.

Greenwald, A. G., McGhee, D. E., & Schwaartz, J. L. K. (1998). Measuring individual differences in implicit cognition: The implicit association test. *Journal of Personality and Social Psychology, 74,* 1464–1480.

Grice, H. P. (1975). Logic and conversation. In P. Cole & J. Morgan (Eds.), *Speech acts: Syntax and semantics.* (Vol. 3, pp. 41–58). New York: Academic Press.

Grigorenko, E. L., Jarvin, L., & Sternberg, R. J. (2002). School-based tests of the triarchic theory of intelligence: Three settings, three samples, three syllabi. *Contemporary Educational Psychology, 27,* 167–208.

Grigorenko, E. L., Meier, E., Lipka, J., Mohatt, G., Yanez, E., & Sternberg, R. J. (2004). Academic and practical intelligence: A case study of the Yup'ik in Alaska. *Learning & Individual Differences, 14,* 183–207.

Grigorenko, E. L., & Sternberg, R. J. (1998). Dynamic testing. *Psychological Bulletin, 124,* 75–111.

Grigorenko, E. L., & Sternberg, R. J. (2001). Analytical, creative, and practical intelligence as predictors of self-reported adaptive functioning: A case study in Russia. *Intelligence, 29,* 57–73.

Grob, A., Little, T. D., & Wanner, B. (1999). Control judgements across the lifespan. *International Journal of Behavioral Decisions, 23,* 833–854.

Groen, G. J., & Resnick, L. B. (1977). Can preschool children invent addition algorithms? *Journal of Educational Psychology, 69,* 645–652.

Gross, E. A. (1999). *Telemarketing fraud.* Unpublished doctoral dissertation, Department of Educational Counseling, University of Southern California, Los Angeles.

Grossman, A. H. (1997). The virtual and actual identities of older lesbians and gay men. In M. Duberman (Ed.), *A queer world: The Center for Lesbian and Gay Studies reader* (pp. 615–626). New York: New York University Press.

Grusec, J. E., Goodnow, J. J., & Cohen, L. (1996). Household work and the development of concern for others. *Developmental Psychology, 32,* 999–1007.

Guelzow, M. G., Bird, G. W., & Koball, E. H. (1991). An exploratory path analysis of the stress process for dual-career men and women. *Journal of Marriage and the Family, 53,* 151–164.

Guillemin, J. (1993). Cesarean birth: Social and political aspects. In B. K. Rothman (Ed.), *Encyclopedia of childbearing.* Phoenix AZ: Oryx Press.

Gunnar, M. R., Bruce, J., & Grotevant, H. D. (2000). International adoption of institutionally reared children: Research and policy. *Development and Psychopathology, 12,* 677–693.

Gurucharri, C., & Selman, F. L. (1982). The development of interpersonal understanding during childhood, preadolescence, and adolescence: A longitudinal follow-up study. *Child Development, 53,* 924–927.

Gutmann, D. L. (1987). *Reclaimed powers: Toward a new psychology of men and women in later life.* New York: Basic Books.

Gutmann, D. L. (1994). *Reclaimed powers: Men and women in later life.* Evanston, IL: Northwestern University Press.

Guttmacher, A. F., & Kaiser, I. H. (1986). *Pregnancy, birth, and family planning.* New York: New American Library.

Hagestad, G. O., & Dannefer, D. (2001). Concepts and theories of aging: Beyond microfication in social science approaches. In R. H. Binstock & L. K. George (Eds.), *Handbook of aging and the social sciences* (5th ed., pp. 3–21). San Diego: Academic Press.

Hagestad, G. O., & Neugarten, B. L. (1985). Age and the life course. In R. H. Binstock & E. Shanas (Eds.), *Handbook of aging and the social sciences* (2nd ed., pp. 35–61). New York: Van Nostrand Reinhold.

Hairston, R. E. (2001). Predicting marital satisfaction among African American couples. *Dissertation Abstracts International Section B: The Sciences and Engineering, 61*(10–B), 5564.

Hall, D. G., Lee, S. C., & Belanger, J. (2001). Young children's use of syntactic cues to learn proper names and count nouns. *Developmental Psychology, 37,* 298–307.

Hall, D. R., & Zhao, J. Z. (1995). Cohabitation and divorce in Canada: Testing the selectivity hypothesis. *Journal of Marriage and the Family, 57,* 421–427.

Hall, J. A., & Halberstadt, A. G. (1981). Sex roles and nonverbal communication skills. *Sex Roles, 7,* 273–287.

Hallinan, M. T., & Teixeira, R. A. (1987). Opportunities and constraints: Black-White differences in the formation of interracial friendships. *Child Development, 58,* 1358–1371.

Halpern, D. F. (2004). A cognitive-process taxonomy for sex differences in cognitive abilities. *Current Directions in Psychological Science, 13,* 135–139.

Halpern L. F., MacLean, W. E., & Baumeister, A. A. (1995). Infant sleep-wake characteristics: Relation to neurological status and the prediction of developmental outcome. *Developmental Review, 15,* 255–291.

Hamilton, C. E. (2000). Continuity and discontinuity of attachment from infancy through adolescence. *Child Development, 71,* 690–694.

Hamm, J. V. (2000). Do birds of a feather flock together? The variable bases for African American, Asian American, and European American adolescents' selection of similar friends. *Developmental Psychology, 36,* 209–219.

Hammer, L. B., Neal, M. B., Newsom, J. T., Brockwood, K. J., & Colton, C. L. (2005). A longitudinal study of the effects of dual-earner couples' utilization of family-friendly workplace supports on work and family outcomes. *Journal of Applied Psychology, 90,* 799–810.

Hamon, R. R., & Blieszner, R. (1990). Filial responsibility expectations among adult child–older parent pairs. *Journal of Gerontology: Psychological Sciences, 45,* P110–P112.

Hanaoka, H., & Okamura, H. (2004). Study on effects of life review activities on the quality of life of the elderly: A randomized controlled trial. *Psychotherapy and Psychosomatics, 73,* 302–311.

Hance, V. M. (2000). An existential perspective describing undergraduate students' ideas about meaning in work: A q-method study. *Dissertation Abstracts International Section A: Humanities and Social Sciences, 61*(3–A), 878.

Hannon, E. E., & Trehub, S. E. (2005). Metrical categories in infancy and adulthood. *Psychological Science, 16,* 48–55.

Hanson, D. J. (2005). *Alcoholic beverage consumption in the U.S.: Patterns and trends.* Retrieved June 7, 2005, from http://www2.potsdam.edu/hansondj/Controversies/1116895242.html

Harbison, J. (1999). Models of intervention for "elder abuse and neglect": A Canadian perspective on ageism, participation, and empowerment. *Journal of Elder Abuse and Neglect, 10,* 1–17.

Hareven, T. K. (1995). Introduction: Aging and generational relations over the life course. In T. K. Hareven (Ed.), *Aging and generational relations over the life course: A historical and cross-cultural perspective* (pp. 1–12). Berlin: de Gruyter.

Hareven, T. K. (2002). *The silk weavers of Kyoto: Family and work in a changing traditional industry.* Berkeley, CA: University of California Press.

Hareven, T. K., & Adams, K. (1996). The generation in the middle: Cohort comparisons in assistance to aging parents in an American community. In T. K. Hareven (Ed.), *Aging and generational relations: Life course and cross-cultural perspectives* (pp. 3–29). New York: Aldine de Gruyter.

Harringer, C. (1994). Adults in college. In J. D. Sinnott (Ed.), *Interdisciplinary handbook of adult lifespan learning* (pp. 171–185). Westport, CT: Greenwood Press.

Harrington, D., Bean, N., Pintello, D., & Mathews, D. (2001). Job satisfaction and burnout: Predictors of intentions to leave a job in a military setting. *Administration in Social Work, 25,* 1–16.

Harris, B., Lovett, L., Newcombe, R. G., Read, G. F., Walker, R., & Riad-Fahmy, D. (1994). Maternity blues and major endocrine changes: Cardiff puerperal mood and hormone study II. *British Medical Journal, 308,* 949–953.

Harris, P. L., Brown, E., Marriot, C., Whithall, S., & Harmer, S. (1991). Monsters, ghosts, and witches: Testing the limits of the fantasy-reality distinction in young children. *British Journal of Developmental Psychology, 9,* 105–123.

Harris, P. L., & Kavanaugh, R. D. (1993). Young children's understanding of pretense. *Monographs of the Society for Research in Child Development, 58* (Serial No. 231).

Harrist, A. W., Zaia, A. F., Bates, J. E., Dodge, K. A., & Pettit, G. S. (1997). Subtypes of social withdrawal in early childhood: Sociometric status and social-cognitive differences across four years. *Child Development, 68,* 278–294.

Hart, C. H., Yang, C., Nelson, L. J., Robinson, C. C., Olsen, J. A. & Nelson, D. A. (2000). Peer acceptance in early childhood and subtypes of socially withdrawn behavior in China, Russia, and the United States. *International Journal of Behavioral Development, 24,* 73–81.

Hart, D. A. (1992). *Becoming men: The development of aspirations, values, and adaptational styles.* New York: Plenum.

Hart, H. M., McAdams, D. P., Hirsch, B. J., & Bauer, J. J. (2001). Generativity and social involvement among African Americans and White adults. *Journal of Research in Personality, 35,* 208–230.

Harter, S. (1990). Self and identity development. In S. S. Feldman & G. R. Elliott (Eds.), *At the threshold: The developing adolescent.* Cambridge, MA: Harvard University Press.

Harter, S. (1994). Developmental changes in self-understanding across the 5 to 7 shift. In A. Sameroff & M. M. Haith (Eds.), *Reason and responsibility: The passage through childhood.* Chicago: University of Chicago Press.

Harter, S. (1999). *The construction of the self: A developmental perspective.* New York: Guilford.

Harter, S. (2005). Self-concepts and self-esteem, children and adolescents. In C. B. Fisher & R. M. Lerner (Eds.), *Encyclopedia of applied developmental science* (Vol. 2., pp. 972–977). Thousand Oaks CA: Sage.

Harter, S. (2006). The self. In W. Damon & R. M. Lerner (Eds.), *Handbook of child psychology* (Vol. 3, 6th ed.). New York: Wiley.

Harter, S., Waters, P., & Whitesell, N. R. (1998). Relational self-worth: Differences in perceived worth as a person across interpersonal contexts among adolescents. *Child Development, 69,* 756–766.

Harter, S., Whitesell, N. R., & Kowalski, P. S. (1992). Individual differences in the effects of educational transitions on young adolescents' perceptions of competence and motivational orientation. *American Educational Research Journal, 29,* 777–807.

Hartman, P. S. (2001). Women developing wisdom: Antecedents and correlates in a longitudinal sample. *Dissertation Abstracts International Section B: The Sciences and Engineering, 62*(1–B), 591.

Hartup, W. W. (1983). Peer relations. In P. H. Mussen (Ed.), *Handbook of child psychology* (Vol. 4). New York: Wiley.

Hartup, W. W. (1992). Friendships and their developmental significance. In H. McGurk (Ed.), *Contemporary issues in childhood social development.* London: Routledge.

Hartup, W. W., & Stevens, N. (1999). Friendships and adaptation across the lifespan. *Current Directions in Psychological Science, 8,* 76–79.

Haselager, G. J. T., Hartup, W. W., van Lieshout, C. F. M., & Riksen-Walraven, J. M. A. (1998). Similarities between friends and nonfriends in middle childhood. *Child Development, 69,* 1198–1208.

Haslam, C., & Lawrence, W. (2004). Health-related behavior and beliefs of pregnant smokers. *Health Psychology, 23,* 486–491.

Hastings, P. D., & Rubin, K. H. (1999). Predicting mothers' beliefs about preschool-aged children's social behavior: Evidence for maternal attitudes moderating child effects. *Child Development, 70,* 722–741.

Hatch, L. R., & Bulcroft, C. (1992). Contact with friends in later life: Disentangling the effects of gender and marital stability. *Journal of Marriage and the Family, 54,* 222–232.

Haviland, J. M., & Lelwica, M. (1987). The induced affect response: 10-week-old infants' responses to three emotion expressions. *Developmental Psychology, 23,* 97–104.

Hawkins, A. J., Nock, S. L., Wilson, J. C., Sanchez, L., & Wright, J. D. (2002). Attitudes about covenant marriage and divorce: Policy implications from a three-state comparison. *Family Relations, 51,* 166–175.

Hawley, P. H. (1999). The ontogenesis of social dominance: A strategy-based evolutionary perspective. *Developmental Review, 19,* 7–132.

Haworth, J., & Lewis, S. (2005). Work, leisure and well-being. *British Journal of Guidance & Counselling, 33,* 67–78.

Hay, D. F., Pawlby, S., Angold, A., Harold, G. T., & Sharp, D. (2003). Pathways to violence in the children of mothers who were depressed postpartum. *Developmental Psychology, 39,* 1083–1094.

Hayashi, M., Hasui, C., Kitamura, F., Murakami, M., Takeuchi, M., Katoh, H., & Kitamura, T. (2000). Respecting autonomy in difficult medical settings: A questionnaire study in Japan. *Ethics and Behavior, 10,* 51–63.

Hayflick, L. (1996). *How and why we age* (2nd ed.). New York: Ballantine.

Hayflick, L. (1998). How and why we age. *Experimental Gerontology, 33,* 639–653.

Hayslip, B., Jr., & Goldberg-Glen, R. (2000). *Grandparents raising grandchildren: theoretical, empirical, and clinical perspectives.* New York: Springer.

Hayslip, B., Jr., Henderson, C. E., & Shore, R. J. (2003). The structure of grandparental role meaning. *Journal of Adult Development, 10,* 1–11.

Hayslip, B., Jr., Shore, R. J., Hendereson, C. E., & Lambert, P. L. (1998). Custodial grandparenting and the impact of grandchildren with problems on role satisfaction and role meaning. *Journal of Gerontology: Social Sciences, 53B,* S164–S173.

Hazan, C., & Shaver, P. (1987). Romantic love conceptualized as an attachment process. *Journal of Personality and Social Psychology, 52,* 511–524.

Hazan, C., & Shaver, P. (1990). Love and work: An attachment-theoretical perspective. *Journal of Personality and Social Psychology, 59,* 270–280.

Heckhausen, J., & Schulz, R. (1999). Selectivity in lifespan development: Biological and societal canalizations and individuals developmental goals. In J. Brandtstädter, B. M. Lerner, et al. (Eds.), *Action and self development: Theory and research through the lifespan* (pp. 67–130). Thousand Oaks, CA: Sage.

Heidrich, S. M., & Denney, N. W. (1994). Does social problem solving differ from other types of problem solving during the adult years? *Experimental Aging Research, 20,* 105–126.

Heilman, M. E., Wallen, A. S., Fuchs, D., & Tamkins, M. M. (2004). Penalties for success: Reactions to women who succeed at male gender-typed tasks. *Journal of Applied Psychology, 89,* 416–427.

Heimann, B., & Pittenger, K. K. S. (1996). The impact of formal mentorship on socialization and commitment of newcomers. *Journal of Managerial Issues, 8,* 108–117.

Helpguide.org. (2005). *Adult day care centers: A guide to options and selecting the best center for your needs.* Retrieved July 3, 2005, from http://www.helpguide.org/elder/adult _day_care_centers.htm

Henderson, B. N., Davison, K. P., Pennebaker, J. W., Gatchel, R. J., & Baum, A. (2002). Disease disclosure patterns among breast cancer patients. *Psychology and Health, 17,* 51–62.

Henderson, K. A. (1990). The meaning of leisure for women: An integrative review of the research. *Journal of Leisure Research, 22,* 228–243.

Henderson, S., & Gilding, M. (2004). "I've never clicked this much with anyone in my life": Trust and hyperpersonal communication in online friendships. *New Media & Society, 6,* 487–506.

Henderson, V. W. (1997). Estrogen, cognition, and a woman's risk of Alzheimer's disease. *American Journal of Medicine, 103*(3A), 11S–18S.

Henretta, J. C. (1997). Changing perspectives on retirement. *Journal of Gerontology: Social Sciences, 52B,* S1–S3.

Henretta, J. C. (2001). Work and retirement. In R. H. Binstock & L. K. George (Eds.), *Handbook of aging and the social sciences* (pp. 255–271). San Diego, CA: Academic Press.

Henretta, J. C., Chan, C. G., & O'Rand, A. M. (1992). Retirement reason versus retirement process: Examining the reasons for retirement typology. *Journal of Gerontology: Social Sciences, 47,* S1–S7.

Herman, M. (2004). Forced to choose: Some determinants of racial identification in multiracial adolescents. *Child Development, 75,* 730–748.

Herrera, N. C., Zajonc, R. B., Wieczorkowska, G., & Cichomski, B. (2003). Beliefs about birth rank and their reflection in reality. *Journal of Personality and Social Psychology, 85,* 142–150.

Herrnstein, R. J., & Murray, C. (1994). *The bell curve: Intelligence and class structure in American life.* New York: Free Press.

Hertenstein, M. J., & Campos, J. J. (2004). The retention effects of an adult's emotional displays on infant behavior. *Child Development, 75,* 595–613.

Hertz, R. (1997). A typology of approaches to child care: The centerpiece of organizing family life for dual-earner couples. *Journal of Family Issues, 18,* 355–385.

Hertzog, C., & Dunlosky, J. (2004). Aging, metacognition, and cognitive control. In B. H. Ross (Ed.), *The psychology of learning and motivation: Advances in research and theory* (Vol. 45, pp. 215–251). San Diego, CA: Elsevier Academic Press.

Hertzog, C., & Hultsch, D. F. (2000). Metacognition in adulthood and old age. In F. I. M. Craik & T. A. Salthouse (Eds.), *The handbook of aging and cognition* (2nd ed., pp. 417–466). Mahwah, NJ: Erlbaum.

Herzog, A. R., Kahn, R. L., Morgan, J. N., Jackson, J. S., & Antonucci, T. C. (1989). Age differences in productive activities. *Journal of Gerontology: Social Sciences, 44,* S129–S138.

Hespos, S. J., & Baillargeon, R. (2001a). Infants' knowledge about occlusion and containment events: A surprising discrepancy. *Psychological Science, 121,* 141–147.

Hespos, S. J., & Baillargeon, R. (2001b). Reasoning about containment events in very young infants. *Cognition, 78,* 207–245.

Hess, U., & Kirouac, G. (2000). Emotion expression in groups. In M. Lewis & J. Haviland-Jones (Eds.), *Handbook of emotions* (2nd ed., pp. 368–381). New York: Guilford Press.

Hetherington, E. M., Bridges, M., & Insabella, G. M. (1998). Five perspectives on the association between divorce and remarriage and children's adjustment. *American Psychologist, 53,* 167–184.

Hetherington, E. M., & Kelly, J. (2002). *For better or for worse: Divorce reconsidered.* New York: W. W. Norton.

Hetherington, S. E. (1990). A controlled study of the effect of prepared childbirth classes on obstetric outcomes. *Birth, 17,* 86–90.

Heyman, G. D., & Gelman, S. A. (1999). The use of trait labels in making psychological inferences. *Child Development, 70,* 604–619.

Higgins, A. (1991). The Just Community approach to moral education: Evolution of the idea and recent findings. In W. M. Kurtines & J. L. Gewirtz (Eds.), *Handbook of moral behavior and development* (Vol. 3). Hillsdale, NJ: Erlbaum.

Hill, J. L., Brooks-Gunn, J., & Waldfogel, J. (2003). Sustained effects of high participation in an early intervention for low-birth-weight premature infants. *Developmental Psychology, 39,* 730–744.

Himsel, A. J., Hart, H., Diamond, A., & McAdams, D. P. (1997). Personality characteristics of highly generative adults as assessed in Q-sort ratings of life stories. *Journal of Adult Development, 4,* 149–161.

Hobdy, J. (2000). The role of individuation processes in the launching of children into adulthood. *Dissertation Abstracts International Section B: The Sciences and Engineering, 60*(9–B), 4929.

Hodges, E. V. E., Boivin, M., Vitaro, F., & Bukowski, W. M. (1999). The power of friendship: Protection against an escalating cycle of peer victimization. *Developmental Psychology, 35,* 94–101.

Hoff, E. (2003). The specificity of environmental influence: Socioeconomic status affects early vocabulary development via maternal speech. *Child Development, 74,* 1368–1378.

Hoff, E. (2005). *Language development* (3rd ed.). Belmont, CA: Thomson Wadsworth.

Hoff, E., & Naigles, L. (2002). How children use input to acquire a lexicon. *Child Development, 73,* 418–433.

Hoff-Ginsberg, E. (1997). *Language development.* Pacific Grove, CA: Brooks/Cole.

Hoff-Ginsberg, E., & Tardif, T. (1995). Socioeconomic status and parenting. In M. H. Bornstein (Ed.), *Handbook of parenting* (Vol. 2, pp. 161–188). Mahwah, NJ: Erlbaum.

Hoffman, M. L. (1988). Moral development. In M. H. Bornstein and M. E. Lamb (Eds.), *Developmental psychology: An advanced textbook* (2nd ed.). Hillsdale, NJ: Erlbaum.

Hoffman, M. L. (1994). Discipline and internalization. *Developmental Psychology, 30,* 26–28.

Hoffman, M. L. (2000). *Empathy and moral development: Implications for caring and justice.* Cambridge, UK: Cambridge University Press.

Hogan, D. P., & Astone, N. M. (1986). The transition to adulthood. *Annual Review of Sociology, 12,* 109–130.

Hogan, N., & DeSantis, L. (1996). Basic constructs of a theory of adolescent sibling bereavement. In D. Klass, P. R. Silverman, & S. L. Nickman (Eds.), *Continuing bonds: New understandings of grief* (pp. 235–254). Washington, DC: Taylor & Francis.

Hogge, W. A. (1990). Teratology. In I. R. Merkatz & J. E. Thompson (Eds.), *New perspectives on prenatal care.* New York: Elsevier.

Hoier, S. (2003). Father absence and age at menarche: A test of four evolutionary models. *Human Nature, 14,* 209–233.

Holden, G. W., & Miller, P. C. (1999). Enduring and different: A meta-analysis of the similarity in parents' child rearing. *Psychological Bulletin, 125,* 223–254.

Hollan, D. (1995). To the afterworld and back: Mourning and dreams of the dead among the Toranja. *Ethos, 23,* 424–436.

Holland, J. L. (1985). *Making vocational choices: A theory of vocational personalities and work environments* (2nd ed.). Englewood Cliffs, NJ: Prentice-Hall.

Holland, J. L. (1987). Current status of Holland's theory of careers: Another perspective. *Career Development Quarterly, 36,* 24–30.

Holland, J. L. (1996). Exploring careers with a typology: What we have learned and some new directions. *American Psychologist, 51,* 397–406.

Holland, J. L. (1997). *Making vocational choices: A theory of vocational personalities and work environments* (3rd ed.). Baltimore: Johns Hopkins University Press.

Hollich, G. J., Hirsh-Pasek, K., & Golinkoff, R. M. (2000). Breaking the language barrier: An emergentist coalition model for the origins of word learning. *Monographs of the Society for Research in Child Development, 65* (Serial No. 262).

Hollon, S. D., Thase, M. E., & Markowitz, J. C. (2002). Treatment and prevention of depression. *Psychological Science in the Public Interest, 3,* 39–77.

Holowka, S., & Petitto, L. A. (2002). Left hemisphere cerebral specialization for babies while babbling. *Science, 297,* 1515.

Hom, P. W., & Kinicki, A. J. (2001). Toward a greater understanding of how dissatisfaction drives employee turnover. *Academy of Management Journal, 44,* 975–987.

Honda-Howard, M., & Homma, M. (2001). Job satisfaction of Japanese career women and its influence on turnover intention. *Asian Journal of Social Psychology, 4,* 23–38.

Hood, B., Carey, S., & Prasada, S. (2000). Predicting the outcomes of physical events: Two-year-olds fail to reveal knowledge of solidity and support. *Child Development, 71,* 1540–1554.

Hooker, K. (1999). Possible selves in adulthood. In T. M. Hess & F. Blanchard-Fields (Eds.), *Social cognition and aging* (pp. 97–122). San Diego, CA: Academic Press.

Hooker, K. (2002). New directions for research in personality and aging: A comprehensive model for linking levels, structures, and processes. *Journal of Research in Personality, 36,* 318–334.

Hooker, K., Fiese, B. H., Jenkins, L., Morfei, M. Z., & Schwagler, J. (1996). Possible selves among parents of infants and pre-schoolers. *Developmental Psychology, 32,* 542–550.

Hooker, K., & Kaus, C. R. (1994). Health-related possible selves in young and mid-adulthood. *Psychology and Aging, 9,* 126–133.

Hooyman, N., & Kiyak, H. A. (1999). *Social gerontology: A multidisciplinary perspective* (5th ed.). Boston: Allyn & Bacon.

Horn, J. L. (1982). The aging of human abilities. In B. B. Wolman (Ed.), *Handbook of developmental psychology* (pp. 847–870). Englewood Cliffs, NJ: Prentice-Hall.

Horn, J. L., & Hofer, S. M. (1992). Major abilities and development in the adult period. In R. J. Sternberg & C. A. Berg (Eds.), *Intellectual development* (pp. 44–99). Cambridge, UK: Cambridge University Press.

Houston, D. M., & Jusczyk, P. W. (2003). Infants' long-term memory for the sound patterns of words and voices. *Journal of Experimental Psychology: Human Perception and Performance, 29,* 1143–1154.

Hovey, J. D., & Magana, C. (2000). Acculturative stress, anxiety, and depression among Mexican farmworkers in the Midwest United States. *Journal of Immigrant Health, 2,* 119–131.

Howe, N., Petrakos, H., & Rinaldi, C. M. (1998). "All the sheeps are dead. He murdered them": Sibling pretense, negotiation, internal state language, and relationship quality. *Child Development, 69,* 182–191.

Howe, N., & Ross, H. S. (1990). Socialization perspective taking and the sibling relationship. *Developmental Psychology, 26,* 160–165.

Howes, C., & Matheson, C. C. (1992). Sequences in the development of competent play with peers: Social and social pretend play. *Developmental Psychology, 28,* 961–974.

Howes, C., Unger, O., & Seidner, L. B. (1990). Social pretend play in toddlers: Parallels with social play and with solitary pretend. *Child Development, 60,* 77–84.

Hoyer, W. J., & Rybash, J. M. (1994). Characterizing adult cognitive development. *Journal of Adult Development, 1,* 7–12.

Hubbard, F. O. A., & van IJzendoorn, M. H. (1991). Maternal unresponsiveness and infant crying across the first 9 months: A naturalistic longitudinal study. *Infant Behavior and Development, 14,* 299–312.

Huesmann, L. R., & Miller, L. S. (1994). Long-term effects of repeated exposure to media violence in childhood. In L. R. Huesmann (Ed.), *Aggressive behavior: Current perspectives.* New York: Plenum.

Huizink, A., Robles de Medina, P., Mulder, E., Visser, G., & Buitelaar, J. (2002). Psychological measures of prenatal stress as predictors of infant temperament. Journal *of the American Academy of Child and Adolescent Psychiatry, 41,* 1078–1085.

Hummert, M. L., Garstka, T. A., O'Brien, L. T., Greenwald, A. G., & Mellott, D. S. (2002). Using the implicit association test to measure age differences in implicit social cognitions. *Psychology and Aging, 17,* 482–495.

Huston, A. C., Watkins, B. A., & Kunkel, D. (1989). Public policy and children's television. *American Psychologist, 44,* 424–433.

Huston, A. C., & Wright, J. C. (1998). Mass media and children's development. In W. Damon (Ed.), *Handbook of child psychology* (Vol. 4). New York: Wiley.

Huston, M., & Schwartz, P. (1995). The relationships of lesbians and of gay men. In J. T. Wood & S. Duck (Eds.), *Understudied relationships: Off the beaten track* (pp. 89–121). Thousand Oaks, CA: Sage.

Huston, T. L., Caughlin, J. P., Houts, R. M., Smith, S. E., & George, L. J. (2001). The connubial crucible: Newlywed years as predictors of marital delight, distress, and divorce. *Journal of Personality and Social Psychology, 80,* 237–252.

Huth-Bocks, A. C., Levendosky, A. A., Bogat, G. A., & von Eye, A. (2004). The impact of maternal characteristics and contextual variables on infant-mother attachment. *Child Development, 75,* 480–496.

Huttenlocher, J., Haight, W., Bryk, A., Seltzer, M., & Lyons, T. (1991). Early vocabulary growth: Relation to language input and gender. *Developmental Psychology, 27,* 236–248.

Huyck, M. H. (1999). Gender roles and gender identity in midlife. In S. Willis & J. D. Reid (Eds.), *Life in the middle* (pp. 209–233). San Diego: Academic Press.

Hyde, J. S., Krajnik, M., & Skuldt-Niederberger, K. (1991). Androgyny across the lifespan: A replication and longitudinal follow-up. *Developmental Psychology, 27,* 516–519.

Hymel, S., Vaillancourt, T., McDougall, P., & Renshaw, P. D. (2004). Peer acceptance and rejection in childhood. In P. K. Smith & C. H. Hart (Eds.), *Blackwell handbook of childhood social development* (pp. 265–284). Malden, MA: Blackwell.

Ilies, R., Hauserman, N., Schwochau, S., & Stibal, J. (2003). Reported incidence rates of work-related sexual harassment in the United States: Using meta-analysis to explain reported rate disparities. *Personnel Psychology, 56,* 607–631.

Ingoldsby, E. M., Shaw, D. S., Owens, E. B., & Winslow, E. B. (1999). A longitudinal study of interparental conflict, emotional and behavioral reactivity, and preschoolers' adjustment problems among low-income families. *Journal of Abnormal Child Psychology, 27,* 343–356.

Inhelder, B., & Piaget, J. (1958). *The growth of logical thinking from childhood to adolescence.* New York: Basic Books.

Institute of Medicine. (1990). *Nutrition during pregnancy.* Washington, DC: National Academy Press.

Isaksen, J. (2000). Constructing meaning despite drudgery of repetitive work. *Journal of Humanistic Psychology, 40,* 84–107.

Isley, S. L., O'Neil, R., Clatfelter, D., Parke, R. D. (1999). Parent and child expressed affect and children's social competence: Modeling direct and indirect pathways. *Developmental Psychology, 35,* 547–560.

Israel, A. C., Guile, C. A., Baker, J. E., & Silverman, W. K. (1994). An evaluation of enhanced self-regulation training in the treatment of childhood obesity. *Journal of Pediatric Psychology, 19,* 737–749.

Ivancevich, J. M., & Matteson, M. T. (1988). Type A behavior and the healthy individual. *British Journal of Medical Psychology, 61,* 37–56.

Iverson, J. M., & Goldin-Meadow, S. (2005). Gesture paves the way for language development. *Psychological Science, 16,* 367–371.

Ivory, B. T. (2004). A phenomenological inquiry into the spiritual qualities and transformational themes associated with a self-styled rite of passage into adulthood. *Dissertation Abstracts International Section A: Humanities & Social Sciences, 65*(2–A), 429.

Ivy, D. K., & Hamlet, S. (1996). College students and sexual dynamics: Two studies of peer sexual harassment. *Communication Education, 45,* 149–166.

Iwasaki, Y., & Mannell, R. C. (2000). Hierarchical dimensions of leisure-stress coping. *Leisure Sciences, 22,* 163–181.

Izard, C. E. (1991). *The psychology of emotions.* New York: Plenum.

Izard, C. E., Fantauzzo, C. A., Castle, J. M., Haynes, O. M., Rayias, M. F., & Putnam, P. H. (1995). The ontogeny and significance of infants' facial expressions in the first 9 months of life. *Developmental Psychology, 31,* 997–1013.

Jaccard, J., Blanton, H., & Dodge, T. (2005). Peer influences on risk behavior: An analysis of the effects of a close friend. *Developmental Psychology, 41,* 135–147.

Jackson, B., Taylor, J., & Pyngolil, M. (1991). How age conditions the relationship between climacteric status and health symptoms in African American women. *Research in Nursing and Health, 14,* 1–9.

Jackson, J. S., & Gibson, R. C. (1985). Work and retirement among the Black elderly. In Z. Blau (Ed.), *Current perspectives on aging and the life cycle* (pp. 193–222). Greenwich, CT: JAI.

Jacobi, C., Hayward, C., de Zwaan, M., Kraemer, H. C., & Agras, W. S. (2004). Coming to terms with risk factors for eating disorders: Application of risk terminology and suggestions for a general taxonomy. *Psychological Bulletin, 130,* 19–65.

Jacobs, J. A., & Gerson, K. (2001). Overworked individuals or overworked families? Explaining trends in work, leisure, and family time. *Work and Occupations, 28,* 40–63.

Jacobs, J. E., & Eccles, J. S. (1992). The impact of mothers' gender-role stereotypic beliefs on mothers' and children's ability perceptions. *Journal of Personality and Social Psychology, 63,* 932–944.

Jacobs-Lawson, J. M., Hershey, D. A., & Neukam, K. A. (2004). Gender differences in factors that influence time spent planning for retirement. *Journal of Women and Aging, 16,* 55–69.

Jacobson, J. L., Jacobson, S. W., & Humphrey, H. E. B. (1990). Effects of in utero exposure to polychlorinated biphenyls and related contaminants on cognitive functioning in young children. *The Journal of Pediatrics, 116,* 38–45.

Jacobson, S. W., & Jacobson, J. L. (2000). Teratogenic insult and neurobehavioral function in infancy and childhood. In C. A. Nelson (Ed.), *The Minnesota symposium on child psychology, Vol. 31: The effects of early adversity on neurobehavioral development* (pp. 61–112). Mahwah, NJ: Erlbaum.

Jaffee, S., & Hyde, J. S. (2000). Gender differences in moral orientation: A meta-analysis. *Psychological Bulletin, 126,* 703–726.

James, W. (1890). *The principles of psychology.* New York: Holt.

Janoff-Bulman, R., & Berger, A. R. (2000). The other side of trauma: Toward a psychology of appreciation. In J. H.

Harvey & E. D. Miller (Eds.), *Loss and trauma: General and close relationship perspectives* (pp. 29–44). Philadelphia: Brunner-Routledge.

Jarrett, R. L. (1995). Growing up poor: The experiences of socially mobile youth in low-income African American neighborhoods. *Journal of Adolescent Research, 10,* 111–135.

Jaswal, V. K. (2004). Don't believe everything you hear: Preschoolers' sensitivity to speaker intent in category induction. *Child Development, 76,* 1871–1885.

Jenkins, C. L. (1997). Women, work, and caregiving: How do these roles affect women's well-being? *Journal of Women and Aging, 9,* 27–45.

Jenkins, C. L. (Ed.). (2003). *Widows and divorcees in later life: On their own again.* Binghamton, NY: Haworth Press.

Jensen, P. S., Hinshaw, S. P., Swanson, J. M., Greenhill, L. L., Conners, C. K., & Arnold, L. E., et al. (2001). Findings from the NIMH Multimodal Treatment Study of ADHD (MTA): Implications and applications for primary care providers. *Journal of Developmental and Behavioral Pediatrics, 22,* 60–73.

Jiao, S., Ji, G., & Jing, Q. (1996). Cognitive development of Chinese urban only children and children with siblings. *Child Development, 67,* 387–395.

Jiao, Z. (1999, April). *Which students keep old friends and which become new friends across school transition?* Paper presented at the 1999 meeting of the Society for Research in Child Development, Albuquerque, New Mexico.

Johanson, R. B., Rice, C., Coyle, M., Arthur, J., Anyanwu, L., Ibrahim, J., et al. (1993). A randomized prospective study comparing the new vacuum extractor policy with forceps delivery. *British Journal of Obstetrics and Gynecology, 100,* 524–530.

Johansson, B., Whitfield, K., Pedersen, N. L., Hofer, S. M., Ahern, F., & McClearn, G. E. (1999). Origins of individual differences in episodic memory in the oldest-old: A population-based study of identical and same-sex fraternal twins aged 80 and older. *Journal of Gerontology: Psychological Sciences, 54B,* P173–P179.

Johnson, B. D., Stone, G. L., Altmaier, E. M., & Berdahl, L. D. (1998). The relationship of demographic factors, locus of control and self-efficacy to successful nursing home adjustment. *The Gerontologist, 38,* 209–216.

Johnson, D. L. (2000). The Black corporate experience: Perceptions of the impact of skin color and gender on Black professionals success. *Dissertation Abstracts International Section B: The Sciences and Engineering, 60*(8–B), 4282.

Johnson, J. G., Cohen, P., Smailes, E. M., Kasen, S., & Brook, J. S. (2002). Television viewing and aggressive behavior during adolescence and adulthood. *Science, 295,* 2468–2471.

Johnson, M. H. (2000). Functional brain development in infants: Elements of an interactive specialization framework. *Child Development, 71,* 75–81.

Johnson, M. P. (1995). Patriarchal terrorism and common couple violence: Two forms of violence against women. *Journal of Marriage and the Family, 57,* 283–294.

Johnson, M. P. (2001). Conflict and control: Symmetry and asymmetry in domestic violence. In A. Booth, A. C. Crouter, & M. Clements (Eds.), *Couples in conflict* (pp. 95–104). Mahwah, NJ: Erlbaum.

Johnson, M. P., & Ferraro, K. J. (2000). Research on domestic violence in the 1990s: Making distinctions. *Journal of Marriage and the Family, 62,* 948–963.

Johnson, N., Barion, A., Rademaker, A., Rehkemper, G., & Weintraub, S. (2004). The Activities of Daily Living Questionnaire: A validation study in patients with dementia. *Alzheimer Disease and Associated Disorders, 18,* 223–230.

Johnson, S. P. (2001). Visual development in human infants: Binding features, surfaces, and objects. *Visual Cognition, 8,* 565–578.

Johnson, S. P., & Aslin, R. N. (1995). Perception of object unity in 2-month-old infants. *Developmental Psychology, 31,* 739–745.

Johnson, W., & Krueger, R. F. (2005). Predictors of physical health: Toward an integrated model of genetic and environmental antecedents. *Journals of Gerontology: Psychological Sciences & Social Sciences, 60B,* 42–52.

Johnson-Laird, P. N. (1988). *The computer and the mind: An introduction to cognitive science.* London, UK: Fontana.

Johnston, L. D., O'Malley, P. M., Bachman, J. G., & Schulenberg, J. E. (2004, December 21). *Overall teen drug use continues gradual decline; but use of inhalants rises.* Ann Arbor, MI: University of Michigan News and Information Services. Retrieved September 27, 2005, from www.monitoringthefuture.org

Joltin, A., Camp, C. J., & McMahon, C. M. (2003). Spaced-retrieval over the telephone: An intervention for persons with dementia. *Clinical Psychologist, 7,* 50–55.

Jones, C. J., & Meredith, W. (1996). Patterns of personality change across the lifespan. *Psychology and Aging, 11,* 57–65.

Jones, D., & Christensen, C. A. (1999). Relationship between automaticity in handwriting and students' ability to generate written text. *Journal of Educational Psychology, 91,* 44–49.

Jones, D. C., Abbey, B. B., & Cumberland, A. (1998). The development of display rule knowledge: Linkages with family expressiveness and social competence. *Child Development, 69,* 1209–1222.

Jones, F. L. (1996). Convergence and divergence in ethnic divorce patterns: A research note. *Journal of Marriage and the Family, 58,* 213–218.

Joseph, R. (2000). Fetal brain behavior and cognitive development. *Developmental Review, 20,* 81–98.

Joyner, K., & Udry, J. R. (2000). You don't bring me anything but down: Adolescent romance and depression. *Journal of Health and Social Behavior, 41,* 369–391.

Jung, C. (1933). *Modern man in search of a soul* (W. S. Dell & C. F. Baynes, Trans.). New York: Harcourt, Brace, & World.

Jung, C. G. (1960/1933). The stages of life. In G. Adler, M. Fordham, & H. Read (Eds.), *The collected works of C. J. Jung: Vol. 8. The structure and dynamics of the psyche.* London, UK: Routledge & Kegan Paul.

Jusczyk, P. W. (1995). Language acquisition: Speech sounds and phonological development. In J. L. Miller & P. D. Eimas (Eds.), *Handbook of perception and cognition: Vol. 11. Speech, language, and communication.* Orlando, FL: Academic Press.

Jusczyk, P. W. (2002). How infants adapt speech-processing capacities to native-language structure. *Current Directions in Psychological Science, 11,* 15–18.

Kagan, J. (1989). Temperamental contributions to social behavior. *American Psychologist, 44,* 668–674.

Kagan, J., Arcus, D., Snidman, N., Feng, W. Y., Hendler, J., & Greene, S. (1994). Reactivity in infants: A cross-national comparison. *Developmental Psychology, 30,* 342–345.

Kagan, J., & Moss, H. A. (1962). *Birth to maturity: A study in psychological development.* New York: John Wiley.

Kager, M. B. (2000). Factors that affect hiring: A study of age discrimination and hiring. *Dissertation Abstracts International Section A: Humanities and Social Sciences, 60*(11–A), 4201.

Kaijura, H., Cowart B. J., & Beauchamp, G. K. (1992). Early developmental change in bitter taste responses in human infants. *Developmental Psychobiology, 25,* 375–386.

Kail, R. (1990). *The development of memory in children* (3rd ed.). New York: Freeman.

Kail, R. (2004). Cognitive development includes global and domain-specific processes. *Merrill-Palmer Quarterly, 50,* 445–455.

Kail, R., & Bisanz, J. (1992). The information-processing perspective on cognitive development in childhood and adolescence. In R. J. Sternberg & C. A. Berg (Eds.), *Intellectual development.* New York: Cambridge University Press.

Kail, R. V., & Salthouse, T. A. (1994). Processing speed as a mental capacity. *Acta Psychologica, 86,* 199–225.

Kalish, R. A. (1984). *Death, grief, and caring relationships* (2nd ed.). Pacific Grove, CA: Brooks/Cole.

Kalish, R. A. (1987). Death and dying. In P. Silverman (Ed.), *The elderly as modern pioneers* (pp. 320–334). Bloomington: Indiana University Press.

Kalish, R. A., & Reynolds, D. (1976). *Death and ethnicity: A psychocultural study.* Los Angeles: University of Southern California Press.

Kalmijn, M., & Flap, H. (2001). Assortative meeting and mating: Unintended consequences of organized settings for partner choices. *Social Forces, 79,* 1289–1312.

Kamerman, S. B. (1993). International perspectives on child care policies and programs. *Pediatrics, 91,* 248–252.

Kandel, E., & Mednick, S. A. (1991). Perinatal complications predict violent offending. *Criminology, 29,* 519–529.

Kane, R. L., & Kane, R. A. (2001). Emerging issues in chronic care. In R. H. Binstock & L. K. George (Eds.), *Handbook of aging and the social sciences* (5th ed., pp. 406–425). San Diego, CA: Academic Press.

Kanekar, S., Kolsawalla, M. B., & Nazareth, T. (1989). Occupational prestige as a function of occupant's gender. *Journal of Applied Social Psychology, 19,* 681–688.

Kann L., Collins, J. L., Pateman, B. C., Small, M. L., Ross, J. G., & Kolbe L. J. (1995). The School Health Policies and Programs Study (SHPPS): Rationale for a nationwide status report on school health programs. *Journal of School Health, 65,* 291–294.

Kaplan, P. S., Goldstein, M. H., Huckeby, E. R., & Cooper, R. P. (1995). Habituation, sensitization, and infants' responses to motherese speech. *Developmental Psychobiology, 28,* 45–57.

Kapp, M. B. (1999). *Geriatrics and the law: Patient rights and professional responsibilities* (3rd ed.). New York: Springer.

Karney, B. R., & Bradbury, T. N. (1995). The longitudinal course of marital quality and stability: A review of theory, method, and research. *Psychological Bulletin, 118,* 3–34.

Karniol, R. (1989). The role of manual manipulative states in the infant's acquisition of perceived control over objects. *Developmental Review, 9,* 205–233.

Kaslow, F. W., Hansson, K., & Lundblad, A. (1994). Long-term marriages in Sweden: And some comparisons with similar couples in the United States. *Contemporary Family Therapy, 16,* 521–537.

Kastenbaum, R. (1985). Dying and death: A life-span approach. In J. E. Birren & K. W. Schaie (Eds.), *Handbook of the psychology of aging* (2nd ed., pp. 619–643). New York: Van Nostrand Reinhold.

Kastenbaum, R. (1992). *The psychology of death* (Rev. ed.). New York: Springer.

Kastenbaum, R. (1999). Dying and bereavement. In J. C. Cavanaugh & S. K. Whitbourne (Eds.), *Gerontology: An interdisciplinary perspective.* New York: Oxford University Press.

Kastenbaum, R., & Thuell, S. (1995). Cookies baking, coffee brewing: Toward a contextual theory of dying. *Omega, 31,* 175–187.

Katz, L. F., & Woodin, E. M. (2002). Hostility, hostile detachment, and conflict engagement in marriages: Effects on child and family functioning. *Child Development, 73,* 636–652.

Katz, P., Machtigall, R., & Showstack, J. (2002). The economic impact of the assisted reproductive technologies. *Nature Medicine, 8,* S29–S32.

Keane, S. P., Brown, K. P., & Crenshaw, T. M. (1990). Children's intention-cue detection as a function of maternal social behavior: Pathways to social rejection. *Developmental Psychology, 26,* 1004–1009.

Keiley, M. K., Bates, J. F., Dodge, K. A., & Pettit, G. (2000). A cross-domain growth analysis: Externalizing and internalizing behaviors during 8 years of childhood. *Journal of Abnormal Child Psychology, 28,* 161–179.

Keith, J. (1990). Age in social and cultural context: Anthropological perspectives. In R. H. Binstock & L. K. George (Eds.), *Handbook of aging and the social sciences* (3rd ed., pp. 91–111). San Diego, CA: Academic Press.

Keller, H. (1965). *Helen Keller: The story of my life.* New York: Airmont.

Keller, H. H. (2004). Nutrition and health-related quality of life in frail older adults. *Journal of Nutrition, Health, and Aging, 8,* 245–252.

Keller, J. W., Sherry, D., & Piotrowski, C. (1984). Perspectives on death: A developmental study. *Journal of Psychology, 116,* 137–142.

Keller, M., Edelstein, W., Schmid, S., Fang, F., & Fang, G. (1998). Reasoning about responsibilities and obligations in close relationships: A comparison across two cultures. *Developmental Psychology, 34,* 731–741.

Kellman, P. J., & Banks, M. S. (1998). Infant visual perception. In W. Damon (Ed.), *Handbook of child psychology* (Vol. 2). New York: Wiley.

Kemeny, M. E. (2003). The psychobiology of stress. *Current Directions in Psychological Science, 12,* 124–129.

Kennedy, G. E. (1991). Grandchildren's reasons for closeness with grandparents. *Journal of Social Behavior and Personality, 6,* 697–712.

Kenrick, D. T. (1987). Gender, genes, and the social environment. In P. C. Shaver & C. Hendrick (Eds.), *Review of Personality and Social Psychology: Vol. 7. Sex and gender* (pp. 14–43). Newbury Park, CA: Sage.

Keyes, C. L., & Ryff, C. D. (1998). Generativity in adult lives: Social structural contours and quality of life consequences. In D. McAdams & E. de St. Aubin (Eds.), *Generativity and adult development: Perspectives on caring for and contributing to the next generation* (pp. 227–263). Washington, DC: American Psychological Association.

Keyes, C. M., & Ryff, C. D. (1999). Psychological well-being in midlife. In S. Willis & J. D. Reid (Eds.), *Life in the middle* (pp. 161–181). San Diego: Academic Press.

Kilgore, K., Snyder, J., & Lentz, C. (2000). The contribution of parental discipline, parental monitoring, and school risk to early-onset conduct problems in African American boys and girls. *Developmental Psychology, 36*, 835–845.

Killen, M., & McGlothlin, H. (2005). Prejudice in childhood. In C. B. Fisher & R. M. Lerner (Eds.), *Encyclopedia of applied developmental science* (Vol. 2., pp. 870–872). Thousand Oaks CA: Sage.

Kim, H. K., & McKenry, P. C. (1998). Social networks and support: A comparison of African Americans, Asian Americans, Caucasians, and Hispanics. *Journal of Comparative Family Studies, 29*, 313–334.

Kim, S. S. (2000). Gradual return to work: The antecedents and consequences of switching to part-time work after first childbirth. *Dissertation Abstract International Section A: Humanities and Social Sciences, 61*(3–A), 1182.

Kim, S., & Feldman, D. C. (2000). Working in retirement: The antecedents of bridge employment and its consequences for quality of life in retirement. *Academy of Management Journal, 43*, 1195–1210.

Kim, Y. H., & Goetz, E. T. (1994). Context effects on word recognition and reading comprehension of good and poor readers: A test of the interactive compensatory hypothesis. *Reading Research Quarterly, 29*, 178–188.

Kimball, M. M. (1986). Television and sex-role attitudes. In T. M. Williams (Ed.), *The impact of television* (pp. 265–301). New York: Academic Press.

King, P. M., & Kitchener, K. S. (1994). *Developing reflective judgment: Understanding and promoting intellectual growth and critical thinking in adolescents and adults.* San Francisco: Jossey-Bass.

King, P. M., & Kitchener, K. S. (2004). Reflective judgment: Theory and research on the development of epistemic assumptions through adulthood. *Educational Psychologist, 39*, 5–18.

King, V., Elder, G. H., & Whitbeck, L. B. (1997). Religious involvement among rural youth: An ecological and life-course perspective. *Journal of Research on Adolescence, 7*, 431–456.

King, V., & Scott, M. E. (2005). A comparison of cohabiting relationships among older and younger adults. *Journal of Marriage & Family, 67*, 271–285.

Kingson, E. R., & Williamson, J. B. (2001). Economic security policies. In R. H. Binstock & L. K. George (Eds.), *Handbook of aging and the social sciences* (5th ed., pp. 369–386). San Diego, CA: Academic Press.

Kinney, J. M., & Cavanaugh, J. C. (1993, November). *Until death do us part: Striving to find meaning while caring for a spouse with dementia.* Paper presented at the annual meeting of the Gerontological Society of America, New Orleans.

Kinney, J. M., Haff, M., Isacson, A., Nocera, R., Cavanaugh, J. C., & Dunn, N. J. (1993, November). *Marital satisfaction and caregiving hassles among caregivers to spouses with dementia.* Paper presented at the annual meeting of the Gerontological Society of America, New Orleans.

Kinney, J. M., Ishler, K. J., Pargament, K. I., & Cavanaugh, J. C. (2003). Coping with the uncontrollable: The use of general and religious coping by caregivers to spouses with dementia. *Journal of Religious Gerontology, 14*, 171–188.

Kirby, D. (2001). *Emerging answers: Research findings on programs to reduce teen pregnancy* [summary]. Washington, DC: National Campaign to Prevent Teen Pregnancy.

Kirby, D. (2002). *Do abstinence-only programs delay the initiation of sex among young people and reduce teen pregnancy?* Washington, DC: National Campaign to Prevent Teen Pregnancy.

Kirby, P. G., Biever, J. L., Martinez, I. G., & Gómez, J. P. (2004). Adults returning to school: The impact on family and work. *Journal of Psychology: Interdisciplinary & Applied, 138*, 65–76.

Kirby, S. E., Coleman, P. G., & Daley, D. (2004). Spirituality and well-being in frail and nonfrail older adults. *Journal of Gerontology: Psychological Sciences, 59*, P123–P129.

Kitchener, K. S., & Fischer, K. W. (1990). A skill approach to the development of reflective thinking. In D. Kuhn (Ed.), *Contributions to human development: Developmental perspectives on teaching and learning* (Vol. 21, pp. 48–62). Basel, Switzerland: Karger.

Kitchener, K. S., & King, P. M. (1989). The reflective judgment model: Ten years of research. In M. L. Commons, C. Armon, L. Kohlberg, F. A. Richards, T. A. Grotzer, & J. D. Sinnott (Eds.), *Adult development: Vol. 2. Models and methods in the study of adolescent and adult thought* (pp. 63–78). New York: Praeger.

Kittrell, D. (1998). A comparison of the evolution of men's and women's dreams in Daniel Levinson's theory of adult development. *Journal of Adult Development, 5*, 105–115.

Kivett, V. R. (1991). Centrality of the grandfather role among older rural Black and White men. *Journal of Gerontology: Social Sciences, 46*, S250–S258.

Kivnick, H. Q. (1982). *The meaning of grandparenthood.* Ann Arbor, MI: UMI Research.

Kivnick, H. Q. (1985). Grandparenthood and mental health: Meaning, behavior, and satisfaction. In V. L. Bengtson & J. F. Robertson (Eds.), *Grandparenthood* (pp. 151–158). Beverly Hills, CA: Sage.

Klaczynski, P. A. (2004). A dual-process model of adolescent development: Implications for decision making, reasoning, and identity. In R. Kail (Ed.), *Advances in Child Development and Behavior* (Vol 32, pp. 73–123).San Diego, CA: Elsevier.

Klaczynski, P. A., & Narasimham, G. (1998). Development of scientific reasoning biases: Cognitive versus ego-protective explanations. *Developmental Psychology, 34*, 175–187.

Klass, D. (1996a). The deceased child in the psychic and social worlds of bereaved parents during the resolution of grief. In D. Klass, P. R. Silverman, & S. L. Nickman (Eds.), *Continuing bonds: New understandings of grief* (pp. 199–215). Washington, DC: Taylor & Francis.

Klass, D. (1996b). Grief in Eastern culture: Japanese ancestor worship. In D. Klass, P. R. Silverman, & S. L. Nickman (Eds.), *Continuing bonds: New understandings of grief* (pp. 59–70). Washington, DC: Taylor & Francis.

Klaus, M., & Kennell, H. H. (1976). *Mother-infant bonding.* St. Louis: Mosby.

Kleespies, P. M. (2004). *Life and death decisions: Psychological and ethical considerations in end-of-life care.* Washington, DC: American Psychological Association.

Kleiber, D. A., Hutchinson, S. L., & Williams, R. (2002). Leisure as a resource in transcending negative life events: Self-protection, self-restoration, and personal transformation. *Leisure Sciences, 24*, 219–235.

Klohnen, E. C., Vandewater, E. A., & Young, A. (1996). Negotiating the middle years: Ego-resiliency and successful midlife adjustment in women. *Psychology and Aging, 11*, 431–442.

Knapp, D. E., & Kustis, G. A. (2000). Same-sex sexual harassment: A legal assessment with implications for organizational policy. *Employee Responsibilities and Rights Journal, 12,* 105–119.

Knapp, M. L., & Taylor, E. H. (1994). Commitment and its communication in romantic relationships. In A. L. Weber & J. H. Harvey (Eds.), *Perspectives on close relationships* (pp. 153–175). Boston: Allyn & Bacon.

Knowles, M. S., Swanson, R. A., & Holton, E. F. (2005). *The adult learner: The Definitive Classic in Adult Education and Human Resource Development.* New York: Elsevier.

Knox, D., Custis, L. L., & Zusman, M. E. (2000). Abuse in dating relationships among college students. *College Student Journal, 34,* 505–508.

Kobak, R. (1994). Adult attachment: A personality or relationship construct? *Psychological Inquiry, 5,* 42–44.

Kobus, K. (2003). Peers and adolescent smoking. *Addiction, 98,* 37–55.

Kochanska, G. (1997). Mutually responsive orientation between mothers and their young children: Implications for early socialization. *Child Development, 68,* 94–112.

Kochanska, G., Gross, J. N., Lin, M., & Nichols, K. E. (2002). Guilt in young children: Development, determinants, and relations with a broader system of standards. *Child Development, 73,* 461–482.

Kochenderfer, B. J., & Ladd, G. W. (1996). Peer victimization: Cause or consequence of school maladjustment? *Child Development, 67,* 1305–1317.

Kochenderfer-Ladd, B., & Wardrop, J. L. (2001). Chronicity and instability of children's peer victimization experiences as predictors of loneliness and social satisfaction trajectories. *Child Development, 72,* 134–151.

Koenig, H. G. (1999). *The healing power of faith: Science explores medicine's last great frontier.* New York: Simon & Schuster.

Koestenbaum, P. (1976). *Is there an answer to death?* Englewood Cliffs, NJ: Prentice-Hall.

Kogan, N. (1983). Stylistic variation in childhood and adolescence: Creativity, metaphor, and cognitive style. In P. H. Mussen (Ed.), *Handbook of child psychology* (Vol. 3, pp. 630–706). New York: Wiley.

Kohlberg, L. (1966). A cognitive-developmental analysis of children's sex-role concepts and attitudes. In. E. E. Maccoby (Ed.), *The development of sex differences.* Stanford: Stanford University Press.

Kohlberg, L. (1969). Stage and sequence: The cognitive-developmental approach to socialization. In D. Goslin (Ed.), *Handbook of socialization theory and research* (pp. 347–480). Chicago: Rand McNally.

Kohlberg, L., & Ullian, D. Z. (1974). Stages in the development of psychosexual concepts and attitudes. In R. C. Friedman, R. M. Richart, & R. L. Van Wiele (Eds.), *Sex differences in behavior.* New York: Wiley.

Kolata, G. (1990, February 6). Rush is on to capitalize on test for gene causing cystic fibrosis. *New York Times,* p. C3.

Kolb, B. (1989). Brain development, plasticity, and behavior. *American Psychologist, 44,* 1203–1212.

Kolberg, K. J. S. (1999). Environmental influences on prenatal development and health. In T. L. Whitman & T. V. Merluzzi (Eds.), *Life-span perspectives on health and illness* (pp. 87–103). Mahwah, NJ: Erlbaum.

Kornhaber, A. (1985). Grandparenthood and the "new social contract." In V. L. Bengtson & J. F. Robertson (Eds.), *Grandparenthood* (pp. 159–172). Newbury Park, CA: Sage.

Kotovsky, L., & Baillargeon, R. (1998).The development of calibration-based reasoning about collision events in young infants. *Cognition, 67,* 311–351.

Kovacs, D. M., Parker, J. G., & Hoffman, L. W. (1996). Behavioral, affective, and social correlates of involvement in cross-sex friendship in elementary school. *Child Development, 67,* 2269–2286.

Kowal, A., & Kramer, L. (1997). Children's understanding of parental differential treatment. *Child Development, 68,* 113–126.

Kram, K. E. (1985). *Mentoring at work: Developmental relationships in organizational life.* Glenview, IL: Scott, Foresman.

Kramer, A. F., Hahn, S., McAuley, E., Cohen, N. J., Banich, M. T., Harrison, C., et al. (2001). Exercise, aging, and cognition: Healthy body, healthy mind? In W. A. Rogers & A. D. Fisk (Eds.), *Human factors interventions for the health care of older adults* (pp. 91–120). Mahwah, NJ: Erlbaum.

Kramer, D. A. (1989). A developmental framework for understanding conflict resolution processes. In J. D. Sinnott (Ed.), *Everyday problem solving: Theory and applications* (pp. 138–152). New York: Praeger.

Kramer, D. A. (1990). Conceptualizing wisdom: The primacy of affect-cognition relations. In R. J. Sternberg (Ed.), *Wisdom: Its nature, origins, and development* (pp. 279–313). Cambridge, UK: Cambridge University Press.

Kramer, D. A., Angiuld, N., Crisafi, L., & Levine, C. (1991, August). *Cognitive processes in real-life conflict resolution.* Paper presented at the annual meeting of the American Psychological Association, San Francisco.

Kramer, D. A., & Kahlbaugh, P. E. (1994). Memory for a dialectical and nondialectical prose passage in younger and older adults. *Journal of Adult Development, 1,* 13–26.

Krause, N. (1991). Stress and inoculation from close ties in later life. *Journal of Gerontology: Social Sciences, 46,* S183–S194.

Krause, N. (1995). Religiosity and self-esteem among older adults. *Journal of Gerontology: Psychological Sciences, 50B,* P236–P246.

Krause, N. (2001). Social support. In R. H. Binstock & L. K. George (Eds.), *Handbook of aging and the social sciences* (pp. 273–294). San Diego, CA: Academic Press.

Krause, N., Morgan, D., Chatters, L., & Meltzer, T. (2000). Using focus groups to explore the nature of prayer in late life. *Journal of Aging Studies, 14,* 191–212.

Krebs, D., & Gillmore, J. (1982). The relationship among the first stages of cognitive development, role-taking abilities, and moral development. *Child Development, 53,* 877–886.

Krispin, O., Sternberg, K. J., & Lamb, M. E. (1992). The dimensions of peer evaluation in Israel: A cross-cultural perspective. *International Journal of Behavioral Development, 15,* 299–314.

Kroger, J. (2005). Identity statuses. In C. B. Fisher & R. M. Lerner (Eds.), *Encyclopedia of applied developmental science* (Vol. 1, pp. 567–568). Thousand Oaks CA: Sage.

Kroger, J., & Green, K. E. (1996). Events associated with identity status change. *Journal of Adolescence, 19,* 477–490.

Kübler-Ross, E. (1969). *On death and dying.* New York: Macmillan.

Kübler-Ross, E. (1974). *Questions and answers on death and dying.* New York: Macmillan.

Kuhl, P. K., Andruski, J. E., Chistovich, I. A., Chistovich, L. A., Kozhevnikova, E. V., Ryskina, V. L., et al. (1997). Cross-language analysis of phonetic units in language addressed to infants. *Science, 277*, 684–686.

Kuhn, D. (2000). Metacognitive development. *Current Directions in Psychological Science, 9*, 178–181.

Kulik, L. (2001a). Impact of length of unemployment and age on jobless men and women: A comparative analysis. *Journal of Employment Counseling, 38*, 15–27.

Kulik, L. (2001b). The impact of men's and women's retirement on marital relations: A comparative analysis. *Journal of Women and Aging, 13*, 21–37.

Kulik, L. (2001c). Marital relationships in late adulthood: Synchronous versus asynchronous couples. *International Journal of Aging and Human Development, 52*, 323–339.

Kulwicki, A. D. (2002). The practice of honor crimes: A glimpse of domestic violence in the Arab world. *Issues in Mental Health Nursing, 23*, 77–87.

Kumar, R., O'Malley, P. M., Johnston, L. D., Schulenberg, J. E., & Bachman, J. G. (2002). Effects of school-level norms on student substance use. *Prevention Science, 3*, 105–124.

Kunzig, R. (1998). Climbing through the brain. *Discover, 19*, 60–69.

Kurdek, L. A. (1991a). Predictors of increases in marital distress in newlywed couples: A 3-year prospective longitudinal study. *Developmental Psychology, 27*, 627–636.

Kurdek, L. A. (1991b). The relations between reported well-being and divorce history, availability of a proximate adult, and gender. *Journal of Marriage and the Family, 53*, 71–78.

Kurdek, L. A. (1995a). Developmental changes in relationship quality in gay male and lesbian cohabiting couples. *Developmental Psychology, 31*, 86–94.

Kurdek, L. A. (1995b). Lesbian and gay couples. In A. R. D'Augelli & C. J. Patterson (Eds.), *Lesbian, gay, and bisexual identities over the lifespan* (pp. 243–261). New York: Oxford University Press.

Kurup, R. K., & Kurup, P. A. (2003). Hypothalamic digoxin, hemispheric dominance, and neurobiology of love and affection. *International Journal of Neuroscience, 113*, 721–729.

Kurz, D. (1995). *For richer, for poorer: Mothers confront divorce.* Philadelphia: Women's Studies Program, University of Pennsylvania.

Labouvie-Vief, G. (1997). Cognitive–emotional integration in adulthood. In K. W. Schaie & M. P. Lawton (Eds.), *Annual review of gerontology and geriatrics* (Vol. 17, pp. 206–237). New York: Springer.

Labouvie-Vief, G. (2005). Self-with-other representations and the organization of the self. *Journal of Research in Personality, 39*, 185–205.

Labouvie-Vief, G., & Diehl, M. (1999). Self and personality development. In J. C. Cavanaugh & S. K. Whitbourne (Eds.), *Gerontology: Interdisciplinary perspectives* (pp. 238–268). New York: Oxford University Press.

Labouvie-Vief, G., & Diehl, M. (2000). Cognitive complexity and cognitive-affective integration: Related or separate domains of adult development? *Psychology and Aging, 15*, 490–504.

Lachman, M. E. (1985). Personal efficacy in middle and old age: Differential and normative patterns of change. In G. H. Elder Jr. (Ed.), *Life-course dynamics: Trajectories and transitions, 1968–1980* (pp. 188–213). Ithaca, NY: Cornell University Press.

Lachs, M. S., Williams, C., O'Brien, S., Hurst, L., & Horwitz, R. (1997). Risk factors for reported elder abuse and neglect: A nine-year observational cohort study. *The Gerontologist, 37*, 469–474.

LaCroix, A. Z., Lang, J., Scherr, P., Wallace, R. B., Cornoni-Huntley, J., Berkman, L., et al. (1991). Smoking and mortality among older men and women in three communities. *New England Journal of Medicine, 324*, 1619–1625.

Ladd, G. W. (1998). Peer relationships and social competence during early and middle childhood. *Annual Review of Psychology, 50*, 333–359.

Ladd, G. W. (2003). Probing the adaptive significance of children's behavior and relationships in the school context: A child by environment perspective. In R. V. Kail (Ed.), *Advances in child development and behavior* (Vol. 31). San Diego, CA: Academic Press.

Ladd, G. W., & Ladd, B. K. (1998). Parenting behaviors and parent-child relationships: Correlates of peer victimization in kindergarten? *Developmental Psychology, 34*, 1450–1458.

Ladd, G. W., & Le Sieur, K. D. (1995). Parents and children's peer relationships. In M. H. Bornstein (Ed.), *Handbook of parenting, Vol. 4. Applied and practical parenting* (pp. 377–410). Mahwah, NJ: Erlbaum.

Lagattuta, K. H., & Wellman, H. M. (2002). Differences in early parent-child conversations about negative versus positive emotions: Implications for the development of psychological understanding. *Developmental Psychology, 38*, 564–580.

LaGreca, A. M. (1993). Social skills training with children: Where do we go from here? *Journal of Clinical Child Psychology, 22*, 288–298.

Lakshmanan, I. A. R. (1997, September 22). Marriage? Think logic, not love. *Baltimore Sun*, p. A2.

Lalumière, M. L., Blanchard, R., & Zucker, K. J. (2000). Sexual orientation and handedness in men and women: A meta-analysis. *Psychological Bulletin, 126*, 575–592.

Lamanna, M. A., & Riedmann, A. (2003). *Marriages and families: Making choices in a diverse society* (8th ed.). Belmont, CA: Wadsworth.

Lamaze, F. (1958). *Painless childbirth.* London: Burke.

Lamb, M. E. (1999). Nonparental child care. In M. E. Lamb (Ed.), *Parenting and child development in "nontraditional" families.* Mahwah, NJ: Erlbaum.

Lamb, M. E., Sternberg, K. J., & Esplin, P. W. (2000). Effects of age and delay on the amount of information provided by alleged sex abuse victims in investigative interviews. *Child Development, 71*, 1586–1596.

Lambert, S. (2005). Gay and lesbian families: What we know and where to go from here. *Family Journal: Counseling & Therapy for Couples & Families, 13*, 43–51.

Lampinen, J. M., & Smith, V. L. (1995). The incredible (and sometimes incredulous) child witness: Child eyewitnesses' sensitivity to source credibility cues. *Journal of Applied Psychology, 80*, 621–627.

Lampman, C., & Dowling-Guyer, S. (1995). Attitudes toward voluntary and involuntary childlessness. *Basic and Applied Social Psychology, 17*, 213–222.

Landreck, B. F., Wallace, D. D., & Neuberger, J. S. (2000). Smoking survey at a midwestern U.S. medical center. *Preventive Medicine, 31*, 271–278.

Lang, F. R., & Heckhausen, J. (2001). Perceived control over development and subjective well-being: Differential benefits across adulthood. *Journal of Personality and Social Psychology, 81,* 509–523.

Lang, J. C., & Lee, C. H. (2005). Identity accumulation, others' acceptance, job-search self-efficacy, and stress. *Journal of Organizational Behavior, 26,* 293–312.

Langer, E. J., & Rodin, J. (1976). The effects of choice and enhanced personal responsibility for the aged: A field experiment in an institutional setting. *Journal of Personality and Social Psychology, 34,* 191–198.

Langlois, J. H., & Downs, A. C. (1980). Mothers, fathers, and peers as socialization agents of sex-typed play behaviors in young children. *Child Development, 51,* 1237–1247.

Lanza, E. (1992). Can bilingual two-year-olds code-switch? *Journal of Child Language, 19,* 633–658.

Larson, R. W. (1997). The emergence of solitude as a constructive domain of experience in early adolescence. *Child Development, 68,* 80–93.

Larson, R. W. (2000). Toward a psychology of positive youth development. *American Psychologist, 55,* 170–183.

Larson, R. W., Gillman, S. A., & Richards, M. H. (1997). Divergent experiences of family leisure: Fathers, mothers, and young adolescents. *Journal of Leisure Research, 29,* 78–97.

Larson, R. W., Raffaelli, M., Richards, M. H., Ham, M., & Jewell, L. (1990). Ecology of depression in late childhood and early adolescence: A profile of daily states and activities. *Journal of Abnormal Psychology, 99,* 92–102.

Laungani, P. (2001). The influence of culture on stress: India and England. In L. L. Adler & U. P. Gielen (Eds.), *Cross-cultural topics in psychology* (2nd ed., pp. 149–169). Westport, CT: Praeger.

Laursen, B., & Collins, W. A. (1994). Interpersonal conflict during adolescence. *Psychological Bulletin, 115,* 197–209.

Lawton, M. P. (1982). Competence, environmental press, and the adaptation of old people. In M. P. Lawton, P. G. Windley, & T. O. Byerts (Eds.), *Aging and the environment: Theoretical approaches* (pp. 33–59). New York: Springer-Verlag.

Lawton, M. P. (1989). Environmental proactivity in older people. In V. L. Bengtson & K. W. Schaie (Eds.), *The course of later life: Research and reflections* (pp. 15–23). New York: Springer.

Lawton, M. P., & Nahemow, L. (1973). Ecology of the aging process. In C. Eisdorfer & M. P. Lawton (Eds.), *The psychology of adult development and aging* (pp. 619–674). Washington, DC: American Psychological Association.

Lazarus, R. S., & Folkman, S. (1984). *Stress, appraisal, and coping.* New York: Springer.

Leach, P. (1991). *Your baby and child: From birth to age five* (2nd ed.). New York: Knopf.

Leahy, J. M. (1993). A comparison of depression in women bereaved of a spouse, a child, or a parent. *Omega, 26,* 207–217.

Leana, C. R., & Feldman, D. C. (1992). *Coping with job loss.* New York: Lexington Books.

Leaper, C., & Smith, T. E. (2004). A meta-analytic review of gender variations in children's language use: Talkativeness, affiliative speech, and assertive speech. *Developmental Psychology, 40,* 993–1027.

Lecanuet, J. P., Granier-Deferre, C., & Busnel, M. C. (1995). Human fetal auditory perception. In J. P. Lecanuet, W. P. Fifer, N. A. Krasnegor, & W. P. Smotherman (Eds.), *Fetal development: A psychobiological perspective.* Hillsdale, NJ: Erlbaum.

Ledebt, A. (2000). Changes in arm posture during the early acquisition of walking. *Infant Behavior and Development, 23,* 79–89.

Ledebt, A., van Wieringen, P. C. W., & Saveslsbergh, G. J. P. (2004). Functional significance of foot rotation in early walking. *Infant Behavior and Development, 27,* 163–172.

LeDoux, J. E., & Gorman, J. M. (2001). A call to action: Overcoming anxiety through active coping. *American Journal of Psychiatry, 158,* 1953–1955.

Lee, G. R., Demaris, A., Bavin, S., & Sullivan, R. (2001). Gender differences in the depressive effect of widowhood in later life. *Journal of Gerontology: Social Sciences, 56B,* S56–S61.

Lee, G. R., Seccombe, K., & Shehan, C. L. (1991). Marital status and personal happiness: An analysis of trend data. *Journal of Marriage and the Family, 53,* 839–844.

Lee, G. R., Willetts, M. C., & Seccombe, K. (1998). Widowhood and depression: Gender differences. *Research on Aging, 20,* 611–630.

Lee, J. W., & Guerrero, L. K. (2001). Types of touch in cross-sex relationships between coworkers: Perceptions of relational and emotional messages, inappropriateness, and sexual harassment. *Journal of Applied Communication Research, 29,* 197–220.

Lee, K. T., Mattson, S. N., & Riley, E. P. (2004). Classifying children with heavy prenatal alcohol exposure using measures of attention. *Journal of the International Neuropsychological Society, 10,* 271–277.

Lee, P. C. B. (2003). Going beyond career plateau: Using professional plateau to account for work outcomes. *Journal of Management Development, 22,* 538–551.

Leichtentritt, R. D., & Rettig, K. D. (2000). Elderly Israelis and their family members' meanings towards euthanasia. *Families, Systems, and Health, 18,* 61–78.

Leman, P. J. Ahmed, S., & Ozarow, L. (2005). Gender, gender relations, and the social dynamics of children's conversations. *Developmental Psychology, 41,* 64–74.

LeMare, L. J., & Rubin, K. H. (1987). Perspective taking and peer interaction: Structural and developmental analyses. *Child Development, 58,* 306–315.

Lemery, K. S., Goldsmith, H. H., Klinnert, M. D., & Mrazek, D. A. (1999). Developmental models of infant and childhood temerament. *Developmental Psychology, 35,* 189–204.

Lemieux, R., & Hale, J. L. (2002). Cross-sectional analysis of intimacy, passion, and commitment: Testing the assumptions of the triangular theory of love. *Psychological Reports, 90,* 1009–1014.

Lemire, L., Saba, T., & Gagnon, Y. C. (1999). Managing career plateauing in the Quebec public sector. *Public Personnel Management, 28,* 375–391.

Lengua, L. J., Sandler, I. N., West, S. G., Wolchik, S. A., & Curran, P. J. (1999). Emotionality and self-regulation, threat appraisal, and coping in children of divorce. *Development & Psychopathology, 11,* 15–37.

Leon, G. R., Gillum, B., Gillum, R., & Gouze, M. (1979). Personality stability and change over a 30-year period: Middle to old age. *Journal of Consulting and Clinical Psychology, 47,* 517–524.

Leon, K. (2003). Risk and protective factors in young children's adjustment to parental divorce: A review of the research. *Family Relations, 52,* 258–270.

Lepper, M. R., & Gurtner, J. (1989). Children and computers. *American Psychologist, 44,* 170–178.

Lerner, R. M. (2002). *Concepts and theories of human development.* Mahwah, NJ: Erlbaum.

Leventhal, H., Rabin, C., Leventhal, E. A., & Burns, E. (2002). Health risk behaviors and aging. In J. E. Birren & K. W. Schaie (Eds.), *Handbook of the psychology of aging* (5th ed., pp. 186–214. San Diego, CA: Academic Press.

Levin, J. S., Taylor, R. J., & Chatters, L. M. (1994). Race and gender differences in religiosity among older adults: Findings from four national surveys. *Journal of Gerontology: Social Sciences, 49,* S137–S145.

Levine, L. E. (1983). *Mine:* Self-definition in 2-year-old boys. *Developmental Psychology, 19,* 544–549.

Levinger, G. (1980). Toward the analysis of close relationships. *Journal of Experimental Social Psychology, 16,* 510–544.

Levinger, G. (1983). Development and change. In H. H. Kelley, E. Berscheid, A. Christensen, J. H. Harvey, T. L. Hutson, G. Levinger, E. McClintock, L. A. Peplau, & D. R. Peterson (Eds.), *Close relationships* (pp. 315–359). New York: Freeman.

Levinson, D. J., Darrow, C., Kline, E., Levinson, M., & McKee, B. (1978). *The seasons of a man's life.* New York: Knopf.

Levinson, D., & Levinson, J. D. (1996). *The seasons of a woman's life.* New York: Knopf.

Levitt, A. G., & Utman, J. A. (1992). From babbling towards the sound systems of English and French: A longitudinal two-case study. *Journal of Child Language, 19,* 19–49.

Levitt, J. M., Levitt, M., & Levitt, J. (2001). *Sibling revelry: 8 steps to successful adult sibling relationships.* New York: Dell.

Levitt, M. J., Guacci-Franco, N., & Levitt, J. L. (1993). Convoys of social support in childhood and early adolescence: Structure and function. *Developmental Psychology, 29,* 811–818.

Levy, B. R. (2003). Mind matters: Cognitive and physical effects of aging self-stereotypes. *Journal of Gerontology: Psychological Sciences, 58B,* P103–P211.

Levy, G. D., Taylor, M. G., & Gelman, S. A. (1995). Traditional and evaluative aspects of flexibility in gender roles, social conventions, moral rules, and physical laws. *Child Development, 66,* 515–531.

Levy, J. (1976). A review of evidence for a genetic component in the determination of handedness. *Behavior Genetics, 6,* 429–453.

Lewinsohn, P. M. (1975). The behavioral study and treatment of depression. In M. Hersen, R. M. Eisler, & P. M. Miller (Eds.), *Progress in behavior modification* (Vol. 1, pp. 19–64). New York: Academic Press.

Lewinsohn, P. M., & Gotlib, I. H. (1995). Behavioral theory and treatment of depression. In E. E. Beckham & W. R. Leber (Eds.), *Handbook of depression* (2nd ed.). New York: Guilford Press.

Lewis, K. G., & Moon, S. (1997). Always single and single again women: A qualitative study. *Journal of Marital and Family Therapy, 23,* 115–134.

Lewis, M. (2000). The emergence of human emotions. In M. Lewis & J. Haviland-Jones (Eds.), *Handbook of emotions* (2nd ed., pp. 265–280). New York: Guilford Press.

Lewis, M., & Brooks-Gunn, J. (1979). *Social cognition and the acquisition of self.* New York: Plenum.

Lewis, M., & Ramsay, D. (2004). Development of self-recognition, personal prounoun use, and pretend play during the second year. *Child Development, 75,* 1821–1831.

Lewis, M., Ramsay, D. S., & Kawakami, K. (1993). Differences between Japanese infants and Caucasian American infants in behavioral and cortisol response to inoculation. *Child Development, 64,* 1722–1731.

Lewis, M. D., Koroshegyi, C., Douglas, L., & Kampe, K. (1997). Age-specific associations between emotional responses to separation and cognitive performance in infancy. *Developmental Psychology, 33,* 32–42.

Lewis, M. I. (1995). Sexuality. In W. B. Abrams, M. H. Beers, & R. Berkow (Eds.), *The Merck manual of geriatrics* (2nd ed., pp. 827–838). Whitehouse Station, NJ: Merck Research Laboratories.

Lewis, R. A., & Lin, L-W. (1996). Adults and their midlife parents. In N. Vanzetti & S. Duck (Eds.), *A lifetime of relationships* (pp. 364–382). Pacific Grove, CA: Brooks/Cole.

Lewkowicz, D. J. (2000a). The development of intersensory perception: An epigenetic systems/limitations view. *Psychological Bulletin, 126,* 281–308.

Lewkowicz, D. J. (2000b). Infants' perception of the audible, visible, and bimodal attributes of multimodal syllables. *Child Development, 71,* 1241–1257.

Lewontin, R. (1976). Race and intelligence. In N. J. Block & G. Dworkin (Eds.), *The IQ controversy* (pp. 78–92). New York: Pantheon.

Li, F., Fisher, K. J., Harmer, P., & McAuley, E. (2005). Falls self-efficacy as a mediator of fear of falling in an exercise intervention for older adults. *Journals of Gerontology: Psychological Sciences & Social Sciences, 60B,* P34–P40.

Liben, L. S., & Bigler, R. S. (2002). The developmental course of gender differentiation. *Monographs of the Society for Research in Child Development, 67* (Serial No. 269).

Liben, L. S., Bigler, R. S., & Krogh, H. R. (2001). Pink and blue collar jobs: Children's judgments of job status and job aspirations in relation to sex of worker. *Journal of Experimental Child Psychology, 79,* 346–363.

Lieber, J. (2001, October 10). Widows of towers disaster cope, but with quiet fury. *USA Today,* A1–A2.

Lieberman, M., Doyle, A., & Markiewicz, D. (1999). Developmental patterns in security of attachment to mother and father in late childhood and early adolescence: Associations with peer relations. *Child Development, 70,* 202–213.

Liebert, R. M., Sprafkin, J. N., & Poulos, R. W. (1975). Selling cooperation to children. In W. S. Hale (Ed.), *Proceedings of the 20th annual conference of the Advertising Research Foundation* (pp. 54–57). New York: Advertising Research Foundation.

Liebowitz, M. (1983). *The chemistry of love.* Boston: Little, Brown.

Lim, S., & Cortina, L. M. (2005). Interpersonal mistreatment in the workplace: The interface and impact of general incivility and sexual harassment. *Journal of Applied Psychology, 90,* 483–496.

Lin, C. C., & Fu, V. R. (1990). A comparison of childrearing practices among Chinese, immigrant Chinese, and Caucasian-American parents. *Child Development, 61,* 429–433.

Lindlaw, S. (1997, April 25). Ethical issues surround oldest new mom. *News Journal* (Wilmington, DE), p. A13.

Linn, S. (2004). *Consuming kids: The hostile takeover of childhood.* New York: New Press.

Linn, S. (2005). The commercialization of childhood. In S. Oldman (Ed.), *Childhood lost: How American culture is failing our kids* (pp. 107–122). Westport CT: Praeger.

Lipsitt, L. P. (1990). Learning and memory in infants. *Merrill-Palmer Quarterly, 36,* 53–66.

Lips-Wiersma, M. S. (2003). Making conscious choices in doing research on workplace spirituality: Utilizing the "holistic development model" to articulate values, assumptions and dogmas of the knower. *Journal of Organizational Change Management, 16,* 2003, 406–425.

Liu, H.-M., Kuhl, P. K., & Tsao, F.-M. (2003). An association between mothers' speech clarity and infants' speech discrimination skills. *Developmental Science, 6,* F1–F10.

Livesley, W. J., & Bromley, D. B. (1973). *Person perception in childhood and adolescence.* New York: Wiley.

Lock, M. (1991). Contested meanings of the menopause. *The Lancet, 337,* 1270–1272.

Loehlin, J. C. (2000). Group differences in intelligence. In R. J. Sternberg (Ed.), *Handbook of intelligence* (pp. 176–193). New York: Cambridge University Press.

Logan, R. D. (1986). A reconceptualization of Erikson's theory: The repetition of existential and instrumental themes. *Human Development, 29,* 125–136.

Lopata, H. Z. (1996). Widowhood and husband sanctification. In D. Klass, P. R. Silverman, & S. L. Nickman (Eds.), *Continuing bonds: New understandings of grief* (pp. 149–162). Washington, DC: Taylor & Francis.

Lord, S. E., Eccles, J. S., & McCarthy, K. A. (1994). Surviving the junior high transition: Family processes and self-perception as protective and risk factors. *Journal of Early Adolescence, 14,* 162–199.

Lourenco, O. M. (1993). Toward a Piagetian explanation of the development of prosocial behaviour in children: The force of negational thinking. *British Journal of Developmental Psychology, 11,* 91–106.

Lovoy, L. (2001). A historical survey of the glass ceiling and the double bind faced by women in the workplace: Options for avoidance. *Law and Psychology Review, 25,* 179–203.

Lozoff, B., Klein, N. K., Nelson, E. C., McClish, D. K., Manuel, M., & Chacon, M. E. (1998). Behavior of infants with iron-deficiency anemia. *Child Development, 69,* 24–36.

Lozoff, B., Wolf, A. W., & Davis, N. S. (1985). Sleep problems seen in pediatric practice. *Pediatrics, 75,* 477–483.

Lucas, J. L. (2000). Mentoring as a manifestation of generativity among university faculty. *Dissertation Abstracts International Section A: Humanities and Social Sciences, 61*(3–A), 881.

Luecke-Aleksa, D., Anderson, D. R., Collins, P. A., & Schmitt, K. L. (1995). Gender constancy and television viewing. *Developmental Psychology, 31,* 773–780.

Lueptow, L. B., Garovich-Szabo, L., & Lueptow, M. B. (2001). Social change and the persistence of sex typing: 1974–1997. *Social Forces, 80,* 1–36.

Lundin, T. (1984). Morbidity following sudden and unexpected bereavement. *British Journal of Psychiatry, 144,* 84–88.

Lung, F.-W., Fan, P.-L.; Chen, N. C., & Shu, B.-C. (2005). Telomeric length varies with age and polymorphisms of the MAOA gene promoter in peripheral blood cells obtained from a community in Taiwan. *Psychiatric Genetics, 15,* 31–35.

Luo, T. Y. (1996). Sexual harassment in the Chinese workplace: Attitudes toward and experiences of sexual harassment among workers in Taiwan. *Violence Against Women, 2,* 284–301.

Luthar, S. S., Zigler, E., & Goldstein, D. (1992). Psychosocial adjustment among intellectually gifted adolescents: The role of cognitive-developmental and experiential factors. *Journal of Child Psychology and Psychiatry and Allied Disciplines, 33,* 361–373.

Lutz, S. E., & Ruble, D. N. (1995). Children and gender prejudice: Context, motivation, and the development of gender conception. In R. Vasta (Ed.), *Annals of child development* (Vol. 10, pp. 131–166). London: Jessica Kingsley.

Lyness, K. S., & Thompson, D. E. (1997). Above the glass ceiling? A comparison of matched samples of female and male executives. *Journal of Applied Psychology, 82,* 359–375.

Lynsky, M. T., & Fergusson, D. M. (1997). Factors protecting against the development of adjustment difficulties in young adults exposed to childhood sexual abuse. *Child Abuse and Neglect, 21,* 1177–1190.

Lyon, G. R. (1996). Learning disabilities. In E. J. Mash & R. A. Barkley (Eds.), *Child psychopathology.* New York: Guilford Press.

Lytton, H. (2000). Toward a model of family-environmental and child-biological influences on development. *Developmental Review, 20,* 150–179.

Lytton, H., & Romney, D. M. (1991). Parents' differential socialization of boys and girls: A meta-analysis. *Psychological Bulletin, 109,* 267–296.

Maccoby, E. E. (1984). Socialization and developmental change. *Child Development, 55,* 317–328.

Maccoby, E. E. (1990). Gender and relationships: A developmental account. *American Psychologist, 45,* 513–520.

Maccoby, E. E. (1998). *The two sexes: Growing up apart, coming together.* Cambridge, MA: Belknap Press.

Maccoby, E. E., Buchanon, C. M., Mnookin, R. H., & Dornbusch, S. M. (1993). Postdivorce roles of mothers and fathers in the lives of their children. *Journal of Family Psychology, 7,* 24–38.

Maccoby, E. E., & Jacklin, C. N. (1974). *The psychology of sex differences.* Stanford, CA: Stanford University Press.

MacDermid, S. M., De Haan, L. G., & Heilbrun, G. (1996). Generativity in multiple roles. *Journal of Adult Development, 3,* 145–158.

Mackay, C. J., Cousins, R., Kelly, P. J., Lee, S., & McCaig, R. H. (2004). "Management Standards" and work-related stress in the UK: Policy background and science. *Work & Stress, 18,* 91–112.

Mackey, R. A., Diemer, M. A., & O'Brien, B. A. (2004). Relational factors in understanding satisfaction in the lasting relationships of same-sex and heterosexual couples. *Journal of Homosexuality, 47,* 111–136.

MacWhinney, B. (1998). Models of the emergence of language. *Annual Review of Psychology, 49,* 199–227.

Madden, D. J. (2001). Speed and timing of behavioral processes. In J. E. Birren & K. W. Schaie (Eds.), *Handbook of the psychology of aging* (5th ed., pp. 288–312). San Diego, CA: Academic Press.

Magai, C. (2001). Emotions over the lifespan. In J. E. Birren & K. W. Schaie (Eds.), *Handbook of the psychology of aging* (5th ed., pp. 399–426). San Diego: Academic Press.

Maiden, R. J., Peterson, S. A., Caya, M., & Hayslip, B. (2003). Personality changes in the old-old: A longitudinal study. *Journal of Adult Development, 10,* 31–39.

Main, M. (1996). Introduction to the special section on attachment and psychopathology: 2. Overview of the field of attachment. *Journal of Consulting and Clinical Psychology, 64,* 237–243.

Main, M., & Cassidy, J. (1988). Categories of response to reunion with the parent at age 6: Predictable from infant attachment classifications and stable over a 1-month-period. *Developmental Psychology, 24,* 415–426.

Malach-Pines, A. (2005). The Burnout Measure, Short Version. *International Journal of Stress Management, 12,* 78–88.

Malina, R. M., & Bouchard, C. (1991). *Growth, maturation, and physical activity.* Champaign, IL: Human Kinetics Academic.

Malinosky-Rummell, R., & Hansen, D. J. (1993). Long-term consequences of childhood physical abuse. *Psychological Bulletin, 114,* 68–79.

Malkinson, R., & Bar-Tur, L. (2004–2005). Long term bereavement processes of older parents: The three phases of grief. *Omega: Journal of Death and Dying, 50*(2), 103–129.

Mandel, D. R., Jusczyk, P. W., & Pisoni, D. B. (1995). Infants' recognition of the sound patterns of their own names. *Psychological Science, 6,* 314–317.

Mange, A. P., & Mange, E. J. (1990). *Genetics: Human aspects* (2nd ed.). Sunderland, MA: Sinhauer Associates.

Mangelsdorf, S., Gunnar, M., Kestenbaum, R., Lang, S., & Andreas, D. (1990). Infant proneness-to-distress temperament, maternal personality, and mother-infant attachment: Associations and goodness of fit. *Child Development, 61,* 820–831.

Mangelsdorf, S. C. (1992). Developmental changes in infant-stranger interaction. *Infant Behavior and Development, 15,* 191–208.

Mangelsdorf, S. C., Shapiro, J. R., & Marzolf, D. (1995). Developmental and temperamental differences in emotional regulation in infancy. *Child Development, 66,* 1817–1828.

Mantler, J., Matejicek, A., Matheson, K., & Anisman, H. (2005). Coping with employment uncertainty: A comparison of employed and unemployed workers. *Journal of Occupational Health Psychology, 10,* 200–209.

Maratsos, M. (1998). The acquisition of grammar. In W. Damon (Ed.), *Handbook of child psychology* (Vol. 2). New York: Wiley.

Marcia, J. E. (1980). Identity in adolescence. In J. Adelson (Ed.), *Handbook of adolescent psychology.* New York: Wiley.

Marcia, J. E. (1991). Identity and self-development. In R. M. Lerner, A. C. Petersen, & J. Brooks-Gunn (Eds.), *Encyclopedia of adolescence* (Vol. 1). New York: Garland.

Marcovitch, S., & Zelazo, P. D. (1999). The A-not-B error: Results from a logistic meta-analysis. *Child Development, 70,* 1297–1313.

Marcus, G. F., Pinker, S., Ullman, M., Hollander, M., Rosen, T. J., & Xu, F. (1992). Overregularization in language acquisition. *Monographs of the Society for Research in Child Development, 58*(4, Serial No. 228).

Marcussen, K. A. (2001). Marital status and psychological well-being: A comparison of married and cohabiting individuals. *Dissertation Abstracts International Section A: Humanities and Social Sciences, 61*(8–A), 3372.

Markovits, H., Benenson, J., & Dolensky, E. (2001). Evidence that children and adolescents have internal models of peer interactions that are gender differentiated. *Child Development, 72,* 879–886.

Markovits, H., & Vachon, R. (1989). Reasoning with contrary-to-fact propositions. *Journal of Experimental Child Psychology, 47,* 398–412.

Markus, H., & Nurius, P. (1986). Possible selves. *American Psychologist, 41,* 954–969.

Marsh, H. W. (1991). Employment during high school: Character building or a subversion of academic goals? *Sociology of Education, 64,* 172–189.

Marsh, H. W., & Yeung, A. S. (1997). Causal effects of academic self-concept on academic achievement: Structural equation models of longitudinal data. *Journal of Educational Psychology, 89,* 41–54.

Marshall, E. O. (2001). The influence of marital satisfaction on the cognitive component of subjective well-being among the elderly. *Dissertation Abstracts International Secton B: The Sciences and Engineering, 61B*(7-B), 3850.

Marsiglio, W. (1993). Attitudes toward homosexual activity and gays as friends: A national survey of heterosexual 15- to 19-year-old males. *Journal of Sex Research, 30,* 12–17.

Marteau, T. M., Roberts, S., LaRusse, S., & Green, R. C. (2005). Predictive genetic testing for Alzheimer's disease: Impact upon risk perception. *Risk Analysis, 25,* 397–404.

Martens, A., Goldenberg, J. L., & Greenberg, J. (2005). A terror management perspective on ageism. *Journal of Social Issues, 61,* 223–239.

Martin, C. L., Eisenbud, L., & Rose, H. (1995). Children's gender-based reasoning about toys. *Child Development, 66,* 1453–1471.

Martin, C. L., Fabes, R. A., Evans, S. M., & Wyman, H. (1999). Social cognition on the playground: Children's beliefs about playing with girls versus boys and their relations to sex segregated play. *Journal of Social and Personal Relationships, 16,* 751–772.

Martin, C. L., & Halverson, C. F. (1987). The roles of cognition in sex roles and sex typing. In D. B. Carter (Ed.), *Current conceptions of sex roles and sex typing: Theory and research.* New York: Praeger.

Martin, C. L., & Little, J. K. (1990). The relation of gender understandings to children's sex-typed preferences and gender stereotypes. *Child Development, 61,* 1427–1439.

Martin, C. L., & Ruble, D. (2004). Children's search for gender cues: Cognitive perspectives on gender development. *Current Directions in Psychological Science, 13,* 67–70.

Martin, G. M. (1998). Toward a genetic analysis of unusually successful neural aging. In E. Wang & D. Snyder (Eds.), *Handbook of the aging brain* (pp. 125–142). San Diego: Academic Press.

Martin J. A., Hamilton, B. E., Sutton, P. D., et al. (2005). Births: Final data for 2003. *National vital statistics reports, 54*(2). Hyattsville, MD: National Center for Health Statistics.

Martin, J. A., Hamilton, B. E., Ventura, S. J., Menacker, F., & Park, M. M. (2002). Births: Final data for 2000. *National Vital Statistics Reports, 50,* 1–5.

Martin, J. L., & Ross, H. S. (2005). Sibling aggression: Sex differences and parents' reactions. *International Journal of Behavioral Development, 29,* 129–138.

Martin, M., Grünendahl, M., & Martin, P. (2001). Age differences in stress, social resources, and well-being in middle and older age. *Journal of Gerontology: Psychological Sciences, 56B,* P214–P222.

Martin, M., Long, M. V., & Poon, L. W. (2003). Age changes and differences in personality traits and states of the old and very old. *Journal of Gerontology: Psychological Sciences, 57B,* 144–152.

Martin-Matthews, A. (1999). Widowhood: Dominant renditions, changing demographics, and variable meaning. In S. M. Neysmith (Ed.), *Critical issues for future social work practice with aging persons* (pp. 27–46). New York: Columbia University Press.

Martin-Matthews, A. (2000). Change and diversity in aging families and intergenerational relations. In N. Mandell & A. Duffy (Eds.), *Canadian families: Diversity, conflict, and change* (2nd ed., pp. 323–359). Toronto: Harcourt Brace.

Masheter, C. (1997). Healthy and unhealthy friendship and hostility between ex-spouses. *Journal of Marriage and the Family, 59*, 463–475.

Masunaga, H., & Horn, J. (2001). Expertise and age-related changes in components of intelligence. *Psychology and Aging, 16*, 293–311.

Masur, E. F. (1995). Infants' early verbal imitation and their later lexical development. *Merrill-Palmer Quarterly, 41*, 286–306.

Matthews, A. M., & Brown, K. H. (1987). Retirement as a critical life event: The differential experiences of men and women. *Research on Aging, 9*, 548–571.

Matthews, R., & Matthews, A. M. (1986). Infertility and involuntary childlessness: The transition to nonparenthood. *Journal of Marriage and the Family, 48*, 641–649.

Matthews, S. H. (1996). Friendships in old age. In N. Vanzetti & S. Duck (Eds.), *A lifetime of relationships* (pp. 406–430). Pacific Grove, CA: Brooks/Cole.

Mattys, S. L., & Jusczyk, P. W. (2001). Phonotactic cues for segmentation of fluent speech by infants. *Cognition, 78*, 91–121.

Mattys, S. L., Jusczyk, P. W., Luce, P. A., & Morgan, J. L. (1999). Phonotactic and prosodic effects on word segmentation in infants. *Cognitive Psychology, 38*, 465–494.

Matud, M. P. (2004). Gender differences in stress and coping styles. *Personality & Individual Differences, 37*, 1401–1415.

Maughan, A., & Cicchetti, D. (2002). Impact of child maltreatment and interadult violence on children's emotion regulation abilities and socioemotional adjustment. *Child Development, 73*, 1525–1542.

Maume, D. J., Jr. (2004). Is the glass ceiling a unique form of inequality? Evidence from a random-effects model of managerial attainment. *Work & Occupations, 31*, 250–274.

Mayer, J. D., Caruso, D. R., & Salovey, P. (1999). Emotional intelligence meets traditional standards for an intelligence. *Intelligence, 27*, 267–298.

Mayer, J. D., Salovey, P., & Caruso, D. R. (2000). Selecting a measure of emotional intelligence: The case for ability scales. In R. Bar-On & J. D. A. Parker (Eds.), *Handbook of emotional intelligence* (pp. 320–342). San Francisco: Jossey-Bass.

Maynard, A. E. (2002). Cultural teaching: the development of teaching skills in Maya sibling interactions. *Child Development, 73*, 969–982.

Mayo Clinic. (2003a). *Exercise: What's it all about?* Retrieved July 4, 2005, from http://www.mayoclinic.com/invoke.cfm?objectid=2F776F30-10D2-49FC-BA32D2D61AD736E1

Mayo Clinic. (2003b). *Menopause: Complications.* Retrieved July 3, 2005, from http://www.mayoclinic.com/invoke.cfm?objectid=FDA7CB3A-4F3C-4FDB-9FDD926923BCDCB9&dsection=7

Mayo Clinic. (2004). *Perimenopause.* Retrieved July 3, 2005, from http://www.mayoclinic.com/invoke.cfm?objectid=AD5A5A12-B388-40F4-B8073113B0A8BF4E

Mayo Clinic. (2005a). *Alcoholism.* Retrieved June 7, 2005, from http://www.mayoclinic.com/invoke.cfm?retryCount=1&id=DS00340

Mayo Clinic. (2005b). *Food and nutrition center.* Retrieved June 7, 2005, from http://www.mayoclinic.com/findinformation/conditioncenters/centers.cfm?retryCount=1&objectid=000851DA-6222-1B37-8D7E80C8D77A0000

Mazur, E., Wolchik, S. A., Virdin, L., Sandler, I. N., & West, S. G. (1999). Cognitive moderators of children's adjustment to stressful divorce events: The role of negative cognitive errors and positive illusions. *Child Development, 70*, 231–245.

McAdams, D. P. (1992). The five-factor model in personality: A critical appraisal. *Journal of Personality, 60*, 329–361.

McAdams, D. P. (1994). Can personality change? Levels of stability and growth in personality across the lifespan. In T. F. Heatherton & J. L. Weinberger (Eds.), *Can personality change?* (pp. 299–313). Washington, DC: American Psychological Association.

McAdams, D. P. (1995). What do we know when we know a person? *Journal of Personality, 63*, 365–396.

McAdams, D. P. (1996). Personality, modernity and the storied self: A contemporary framework for studying persons. *Psychological Inquiry, 4*, 295–321.

McAdams, D. P. (1999). Personal narratives and the life story. In L. Pervin & O. John (Eds.), *Handbook of personality: Theory and research* (2nd ed., pp. 478–500). New York: Guildford Press.

McAdams, D. P. (2001a). Generativity at midlife. In M. E. Lachman (Ed.), *Handbook of midlife development* (pp. 395–443). New York: Wiley.

McAdams, D. P. (2001b). The psychology of life stories. *Review of General Psychology, 5*, 100–122.

McAdams, D. P., de St. Aubin, E., & Logan, R. (1993). Generativity in young, midlife, and older adults. *Psychology and Aging, 8*, 221–230.

McAdams, D. P., Hart, H. M., & Maruna, S. (1998). The anatomy of generativity, In D. P. McAdams & E. de St. Aubin (Eds.), *Generativity and adult development: How and why do we care for the next generation* (pp. 7–43). Washington, DC: American Psychological Association.

McBride-Chang, C., & Kail, R. V. (2002). Cross-cultural similarities in the predictors of reading acquisition. *Child Development.*

McCall, R. B. (1979). *Infants.* Cambridge, MA: Harvard University Press.

McCarthy, M. R. (2002). Gender differences in reactions to perinatal loss: A qualitative study of couples. *Dissertation Abstracts International Section B: The Sciences and Engineering, 62*(8B), 3809.

McCarty, M. E., & Ashmead, D. H. (1999). Visual control of reaching and grasping in infants. *Developmental Psychology, 35*, 620–631.

McCarty, M. E., Clifton, R. K., Ashmead, D. H., Lee, P., & Goubet, N. (2001). How infants use vision for grasping objects. *Child Development, 72*, 973–987.

McClure, E. B. (2000). A meta-analytic review of sex differences in facial expression processing and their development in infants, children, and adolescents. *Psychological Bulletin, 126*, 424–453.

McConatha, J. T., Stoller, P., & Oboudiat, F. (2001). Reflections of older Iranian women: Adapting to life in the United States. *Journal of Aging Studies, 15,* 369–381.

McCormick, C. (2000, August 26). Twin miracles: Mashpee mother has groundbreaking surgery to save her two fetuses. *Cape Code Times.* Retrieved May 10, 2002, from http://www.capecodonline.com/cctimes/archives/2000/aug/26/twinmiracles26.htm

McCormick, C. B., & Pressley, M. (1997). *Educational psychology.* New York: Longman.

McCrae, R. R. (2002). The maturation of personality psychology: Adult personality development and psychological well-being. *Journal of Research in Personality, 36,* 307–317.

McCrae, R. R., & Costa, P. T. (1994). The stability of personality: Observation and evaluations. *Current Directions in Psychological Sciences, 3,* 173–175.

McCutchen, D., Covill, A., Hoyne, S. H, & Mildes, K. (1994). Individual differences in writing: Implications of translating fluency. *Journal of Educational Psychology. 86,* 256–266.

McCutchen, D., Francis, M., & Kerr, S. (1997). Revising for meaning: Effects of knowledge and strategy. *Journal of Educational Psychology, 89,* 667–676.

McDowd, J. M., & Shaw, R. J. (2000). Attention and aging: A functional perspective. In F. I. M. Craik & T. A. Salthouse (Eds.), *The handbook of aging and cognition* (2nd ed., pp. 221–292). Mahwah, NJ: Erlbaum.

McEwen, B. S. (1998). Protective and damaging effects of stress mediators. *New England Journal of Medicine, 338,* 171–179.

McFadden, S. H. (1996). Religion, spirituality, and aging. In J. E. Birren & K. W. Schaie (Eds.), *Handbook of the psychology of aging* (4th ed., pp. 162–177). San Diego, CA: Academic Press.

McGarry, K., & Schoeni, R. F. (2005). Widow(er) poverty and out-of-pocket medical expenditures near the end of life. *Journal of Gerontology: Social Sciences, 60,* S160–S168.

McGee, R., Williams, S., & Feehan, M. (1992). Attention deficit disorder and age of onset of problem behaviors. *Journal of Abnormal Child Psychology, 20,* 487–502.

McGhee, P. E. (1976). Children's appreciation of humor: A test of the cognitive congruency principle. *Child Development, 47,* 420–426.

McGraw, M. B. (1935). *Growth: A study of Johnny and Jimmy.* East Norwalk, CT: Appleton-Century-Crofts.

McGuire, L. C., & Cavanaugh, J. C. (1992, April). *Objective measures versus spouses' perceptions of cognitive status in dementia patients.* Paper presented at the biennial Cognitive Aging Conference, Atlanta.

McGuire, L. C., & Codding, R. (1998, August). *Improving older adults' memory for medical information: The efficacy of note taking and elder speak.* Paper presented at the annual meeting of the American Psychological Association, San Francisco.

McHale, J. P., Laurette, A., Talbot, J., & Pourquette, C. (2002). Retrospect and prospect in the psychological study of coparenting and family group process. In J. P. McHale & W. Grolnick (Eds.), *Retrospect and prospect in the psychological study of families* (pp. 127–165). Mahwah NJ: Erlbaum.

McHale, S. M., Kim, J-Y., Whiteman, S., & Crouter, A. C. (2004). Links between sex-typed time use in middle childhood and gender development in early adolescence. *Developmental Psychology, 40,* 868–881.

McKee-Ryan, F., Song, Z., Wanberg, C. R., & Kinicki, A. J. (2005). Psychological and physical well-being during unemployment: A meta-analytic study. *Journal of Applied Psychology, 90,* 53–76.

McKenna, P., Jefferies, L., Dobson, A., & Frude, N. (2004). The use of a cognitive battery to predict who will fail an on-road driving test. *British Journal of Clinical Psychology, 43,* 325–336.

McKown, C., & Weinstein, R. S. (2003). The development and consequences of stereotype consciousness in middle childhood. *Child Development, 74,* 498–515.

McKusick, V. A. (1995). *Mendelian inheritance in man: Catalogs of autosomal dominant, autosomal recessive, and X-linked phenotypes* (10th ed.). Baltimore: Johns Hopkins University Press.

McLanahan, S. (1999). Father absence and the welfare of children. In E. M. Hetherington (Ed.), *Coping with divorce, single parenting, and remarriage: A risk and resilience perspective* (pp. 117–145). Mahwah NJ: Erlbaum.

McLaughlin, D. K., Stokes, C. S., & Nonoyama, A. (2001). Residence and income inequality: Effects on mortality among U.S. counties. *Rural Sociology, 66,* 579–598.

McLellan, J. A., & Youniss, J. (2003). Two systems of youth service: Determinants of voluntary and required youth community service. *Journal of Youth and Adolescence, 32,* 47–58.

McManus, I. C., Sik, G., Cole, D. R., Kloss, J., Mellon, A. F., & Wong, J. (1988). The development of handedness in children. *British Journal of Developmental Psychology, 6,* 257–273.

Mcrae, P. J. (2005). Multigenerational caregiving and dementia: The phenomenological experience of daughters-in-law. *Dissertation Abstracts International: Section B: The Sciences and Engineering, 65*(7-B), 3716.

McRae, S. (1997). Cohabitation: A trial run for marriage? *Sexual and Marital Therapy, 12,* 259–273.

Medicare.gov. (2005). *Medicare and you 2005.* Retrieved August 8, 2005, from http://www.medicare.gov/publications/pubs/pdf/10050.pdf

Mehta, K. K. (1997). The impact of religious beliefs and practices on aging: A cross-cultural comparison. *Journal of Aging Studies, 11,* 101–114.

Meltzoff, A. N. (1995). Understanding the intentions of others: Re-enactment of intended acts by 18-month-old children. *Developmental Psychology, 31,* 838–850.

Meltzoff, A. N., & Moore, M. K. (1989). Imitation in newborn infants: Exploring the range of gestures imitated and the underlying mechanisms. *Developmental Psychology, 25,* 954–962.

Meltzoff, A. N., & Moore, M. K. (1994). Imitation, memory, and the representation of persons. *Infant Behavior and Development, 17,* 83–99.

Mennella, J. A., & Beauchamp, G. K. (1996). The human infant's response to vanilla flavors in mother's milk and formula. *Infant Behavior and Development, 19,* 13–19.

Mennella, J., & Beauchamp, G. K. (1997). The ontogeny of human flavor perception. In G. K. Beauchamp & L. Bartoshuk (Eds.), *Tasting and smelling. Handbook of perception and cognition.* San Diego, CA: Academic Press.

Mennella, J. A., Jagnow, C. P., & Beauchamp, G. K. (2001). Prenatal and postnatal flavor learning by human infants. *Pediatrics, 107,* e88.

Mera, S. L. (1998). The role of telomeres in ageing and cancer. *British Journal of Biomedical Science, 55*, 221–225.

Merat, N., Anttila, V., & Luoma, J. (2005). Comparing the driving performance of average and older drivers: The effect of surrogate in-vehicle information systems. *Transportation Research Part F: Traffic Psychology and Behaviour, 8*, 147–166.

Mervis, C. B., & Johnson, K. E. (1991). Acquisition of the plural morpheme: A case study. *Developmental Psychology, 27*, 222–235.

Messinger, D. S. (2002). Positive and negative: Infant facial expressions and emotions. *Current Directions in Psychological Science, 11*, 1–6.

Michael, R. T., Gagnon, J. H., Lauman, E. O., & Kolata, G. (1994). *Sex in America: A definitive survey.* Boston: Little, Brown.

Milberger, S., Biederman, J., Faraone, S. V., Guite, J., & Tsuang, M. T. (1997). Pregnancy, delivery and infancy complication, and attention deficit hyperactivity disorder: Issues of gene-environment interaction. *Biological Psychiatry, 41*, 65–75.

Milford, M. (1997, November 9). Making a tough transition. *Sunday News Journal* (Wilmington, DE), pp. G1, G6.

Miller, B. C., Benson, B., & Galbraith, K. A. (2001). Family relationships and adolescent pregnancy risk: A research synthesis. *Developmental Review, 21*, 1–38.

Miller, B. C., Fan, X., Christensen, M., Grotevant, H. D., & van Dulmen, M. (2000). Comparisons of adopted and nonadopted adolescents in a large, nationally representative sample. *Child Development, 71*, 1458–1473.

Miller, J. G., & Bersoff, D. M. (1992). Culture and moral judgment: How are conflicts between justice and interpersonal responsibilities resolved? *Journal of Personality and Social Psychology, 62*, 541–554.

Miller, K. F., Smith, C. M., Zhu, J., & Zhang, H. (1995). Preschool origins of cross-national differences in mathematical competence: The role of number-naming systems. *Psychological Science, 6*, 56–60.

Miller, L. K. (1999). The savant syndrome: Intellectual impairment and exceptional skill. *Psychological Bulletin, 125*, 31–46.

Miller, N. B., Smerglia, V. L., & Bouchet, N. (2004). Women's adjustment to widowhood: Does social support matter? *Journal of Women and Aging, 16*, 149–167.

Miller, P. A., Eisenberg, N., Fabes, R. A., & Shell, R. (1996). Relations of moral reasoning and vicarious emotion to young children's prosocial behavior toward peers and adults. *Developmental Psychology, 32*, 210–219.

Miller, P. M., Danaher, D. L., & Forbes, D. (1986). Sex-related strategies of coping with interpersonal conflict in children aged five to seven. *Developmental Psychology, 22*, 543–548.

Miller, R. B., Hemesath, K., & Nelson, B. (1997). Marriage in middle and later life. In T. D. Hargrave & S. M. Hanna (Eds.), *The aging family: New visions in theory, practice, and reality* (pp. 178–198). New York: Brunner/Mazel.

Mindell, J. A., & Cashman, L. (1995). Sleep disorders. In A. R. Eisen, C. A. Kearney, & C. E. Schaefer (Eds.), *Clinical handbook of anxiety disorders in children and adolescents.* Northvale, NJ: Aronson.

Ministry of Internal Affairs and Communications. (2005). *Statistical handbook of Japan 2004.* Retrieved July 16, 2005, from http://www.stat.go.jp/english/data/handbook/c02cont.htm#cha2_2

Mirabella, R. L. (2001). Determinants of job satisfaction in psychologists. *Dissertation Abstracts International Section B: The Sciences and Engineering, 61*(12–B), 6714.

Mischel, W. (1970). Sex-typing and socialization. In P. H. Mussen (Ed.), *Carmichaels' manual of child psychology* (Vol. 2). New York: Wiley.

Mischel, W., & Shoda, Y. (1995). A cognitive–affective system theory of personality: Reconceptualizing situations, dispositions, dynamics, and invariance in personality structure. *Psychological Review, 102*, 246–268.

Missildine, W., Feldstein, G., Punzalan, J. C., & Parsons, J. T. (2005). S/he loves me, s/he loves me not: Questioning heterosexist assumptions of gender differences for romantic and sexually motivated behaviors. *Sexual Addiction & Compulsivity, 12*, 65–74.

Mitchell, C. V. (2000). Managing gender expectations: A competency model for women in leadership. *Dissertation Abstracts International Section B: The Sciences and Engineering, 61*(3–B), 1682.

Mitchell, L. M., & Messner, L. (2003–2004). Relative child care: Supporting the providers. *Journal of Research in Childhood Education, 18*, 105–113.

Miura, I. T., Kim, C. C., Chang, C. M., & Okamoto, Y. (1988). Effects of language characteristics on children's cognitive representation of number: Cross-national comparisons. *Child Development, 59*, 1445–1450.

Mix, K. S., Huttenlocher, J., & Levine, S. C. (2002). Multiple cues for quantification in infancy: Is number one of them? *Psychological Bulletin, 128*, 278–294.

Mize, J., & Ladd, G. W. (1990). A cognitive social-learning approach to social skill training with low-status preschool children. *Developmental Psychology, 26*, 388–397.

Mize, J., & Pettit, G. S. (1997). Mothers' social coaching, mother-child relationship style, and children's peer competence: Is the medium the message? *Child Development, 68*, 312–332.

Mize, J., Pettit, G. S., & Brown, E. G. (1995). Mothers' supervision of their children's peer play: Relations with beliefs, perceptions, and knowledge. *Developmental Psychology, 31*, 311–321.

Mizes, J., Scott, P., & Tonya, M. (1995). Eating disorders. In M. Hersen & R. T. Ammerman (Eds.), *Handbook of prevention and treatment with children and adolescents: Intervention in the real world context.* New York: Wiley.

Moats, L. C., & Lyon, G. R. (1993). Learning disabilities in the United States: Advocacy, science, and the future of the field. *Journal of Learning Disabilities, 26*, 282–294.

Mobily, K. E., Lemke, J. H., & Gisin, G. J. (1991). The idea of leisure repertoire. *Journal of Applied Gerontology, 10*, 208–223.

Modelska, K., Litwack, S., Ewing, S. K., & Yaffe, K. (2004). Endogenous estrogen levels affect sexual function in elderly post-menopausal women. *Maturitas, 49*, 124–133.

Moen, P. (1999). *The Cornell couples and careers study.* Ithaca, NY: Cornell University.

Moen, P, Fields, V., Meador, R., & Rosenblatt, H. (2000a). Fostering integration: A case study of the Cornell Retirees Volunteering in service (CRVIS) program. In K. Pillemer & Moen, P. (Eds.), *Social integration in the second half of life* (pp. 247–264). Baltimore: Johns Hopkins University Press.

Moen, P, Fields, V., Quick, H.. E., & Hofmeister, H. (2000b). A life course approach to retirement and social integration. In K. Pillemer & Moen, P. (Eds.), *Social integration in the second half of life* (pp. 75–107). Baltimore: Johns Hopkins University Press.

Moffitt, T. E. (1993). Adolescence-limited and life-course-persistent antisocial behavior: A developmental taxonomy. *Psychological Review, 100,* 674–701.

Moffitt, T. E., Caspi, A., Belsky, J., & Silva, P. A. (1992). Childhood experience and the onset of menarche: A test of a sociobiological model. *Child Development, 63,* 47–58.

Moffitt, T. E., Caspi, A., Harrington, H., & Milne, B. J. (2002). Males on the life-course-persistent and adolescence-limited antisocial pathways: Follow-up at age 26 years. *Development and Psychopathology, 14,* 179–207.

Mohlman, J., de Jesus, M., Gorenstein, E. E., Kleber, M., Gorman, J. M., & Papp, L. A. (2004). Distinguishing generalized anxiety disorder, panic disorder, and mixed anxiety states in older treatment-seeking adults. *Journal of Anxiety Disorders, 18,* 275–290.

Molfese, D. L., & Burger-Judisch, L. M. (1991). Dynamic temporal-spatial allocation of resources in the human brain: An alternative to the static view of hemisphere differences. In F. L. Ketterle (Ed.), *Cerebral laterality: Theory and research. The Toledo symposium.* Hillsdale, NJ: Erlbaum.

Moller, L. C., Hymel, S., & Rubin, K. H. (1992). Sex typing in play and popularity in middle childhood. *Sex Roles, 26,* 331–353.

Monczunski, J. (1991). That incurable disease. *Notre Dame Magazine, 20*(1), 37.

Mondloch, C. J., Lewis, T. L., Budreau, D. R., Maurer, D., Dannemiller, J. L., Stephens, B. R., & Kleiner-Gathercoal, K. A. (1999). Face perception during infancy. *Psychological Science, 10,* 419–422.

Monk, C., Fifer, W. P., Myers, M. M., Sloan, R. P., Trien, L., & Hurtado, A. (2000). Maternal stress responses and anxiety during pregnancy: Effects on fetal heart rate. *Developmental Psychobiology, 36,* 67–77.

Montague, D. P., & Walker-Andrews, A. S. (2001). Peekaboo: A new look at infants' perception of emotion expressions. *Developmental Psychology, 37,* 826–838.

Montgomery, M. J. (2005). Psychosocial intimacy and identity: From early adolescence to emerging adulthood. *Journal of Adolescent Research, 20,* 346–374.

Moon, A., & Williams, O. (1993). Perceptions of elder abuse and help-seeking patterns among African-American, Caucasian American, and Korean-American elderly women. *The Gerontologist, 33,* 386–395.

Moore, K. D. (2005). Using place rules and affect to understand environmental fit: A theoretical exploration. *Environment and Behavior, 37,* 330–363.

Moore, K. L., & Persaud, T. V. N. (1993). *Before we are born* (4th ed.). Philadelphia: W. B. Saunders.

Moore, M. R., & Brooks-Gunn, J. (2002). Adolescent parenthood. In M. H. Bornstein (Ed.), *Handbook of parenting: Vol. 3: Being and becoming a parent* (2nd ed., pp. 173–214). Mahwah, NJ: Erlbaum.

Morahan-Martin, J., & Schumacher, P. (2003). Loneliness and social uses of the Internet. *Computers in Human Behavior, 19,* 659–671.

Morfei, M. Z., Hooker, K., Fiese, B. H., & Cordeiro, A. M. (2001). Continuity and change in parenting possible selves: A longitudinal follow-up. *Basic & Applied Social Psychology, 23,* 217–223.

Morgan, B., & Gibson, K. R. (1991). Nutritional and environmental interactions in brain development. In K. R. Gibson and A. C. Peterson (Eds.), *Brain maturation and cognitive development: Comparative and crosscultural perspectives.* New York: Aldine De Gruyter.

Morgane, P. J., Austin-Lafrance, R., Bronzino, J. D., Tonkiss, J., Diaz-Cintra, S., Cintra, L., et al. (1993). Prenatal malnutrition and development of the brain. *Neuroscience and Biobehavioral Reviews, 17,* 91–128.

Morioka, K. (1998). Comment 1: Toward a paradigm shift in family sociology. *Japanese Journal of Family Sociology, 10,* 139–144.

Morris, S. C., Taplin, J. E., & Gelman, S. A. (2000). Vitalism in naïve biological thinking. *Developmental Psychology, 36,* 582–595.

Morrongiello, B. A., Fenwick, K. D., & Chance, G. (1990). Sound localization acuity in very young infants: An observer-based testing procedure. *Developmental Psychology, 26,* 75–84.

Morrow, D. G., Hier, C. M., Menard, W. E., & Von Leirer, O. (1998). Icons improve older and younger adults' comprehension of medication information. *Journal of Gerontology: Psychological Sciences, 53B,* P240–P254.

Mortimer, J. T., Finch, M. D., Rye, S., Shanahan, M. J., & Call, K. T. (1996). The effects of work intensity on adolescent mental health, achievement, and behavioral adjustment: New evidence from a prospective study. *Child Development, 67,* 1243–1261.

Mortimer, J. T., Harley, C., & Staff, J. (2002). The quality of work and youth mental health. *Work & Occupations, 29,* 166–197.

Mortimer, J. T., & Staff, J. (2004). Early work as a source of developmental discontinuity during the transition to adulthood. Development and Psychopathology, 16, 1047–1070.

Morton, J., & Johnson, M. H. (1991). CONSPEC and CONLERN: A two-process theory of infant face recognition. *Psychological Review, 98,* 164–181.

Moses, L. J., Baldwin, D. A., Rosicky, J. G., & Tidball, G. (2001). Evidence for referential understanding in the emotions domain at twelve and eighteen months. *Child Development, 72,* 718–735.

Moshman, D. (1998). Cognitive development beyond childhood. In W. Damon (Ed.), *Handbook of child psychology* (5th ed.). New York: Wiley.

Moss, E., Rousseau, D., Parent, S., St-Laurent, D., & Saintonge, J. (1998). Correlates of attachment at school age: Maternal reported stress, mother-child interaction, and behavior problems. *Child Development, 69,* 1390–1405.

Moss, M. S., & Moss, S. Z. (1996). Remarriage of widowed persons: A triadic relationship. In D. Klass, P. R. Silverman, & S. L. Nickman (Eds.), *Continuing bonds: New understandings of grief* (pp. 163–178). Washington, DC: Taylor & Francis.

Moss, M. S., Moss, S. Z., & Hansson, R. O. (2001). Bereavement and old age. In M. S. Stroebe, R. O. Hansson, W. Stroebe, & H. Schut (Eds.), *Handbook of bereavement research: Consequences, coping, and care* (pp. 241–260). Washington, DC: American Psychological Association.

Mounts, N. S., & Steinberg, L. (1995). An ecological analysis of peer influence on adolescent grade point average and drug use. *Developmental Psychology, 31,* 915–922.

Mugadza, T. (2005). Discrimination against women in the world of human rights: The case of women in southern Africa. In A. Barnes (Ed.). *The handbook of women, psychology, and the law* (pp. 354–365). New York: Wiley.

Muller, E. D. (2002). The experience of grief after bereavement: A phenomenological investigation. *Dissertation*

Abstracts International Section B: The Sciences and Engineering, 62(8B), 3810.

Mumme, D. L., Fernald, A., & Herrera, C. (1996). Infants' responses to facial and vocal emotional signals in a social referencing paradigm. *Child Development, 67,* 3219–3237.

Munakata, Y., McClelland, J. L., Johnson, M., H., & Siegler, R. S. (1997). Rethinking infant knowledge: Toward an adaptive process account of successes and failures in object permanence tasks. *Psychological Review, 104,* 686–713.

Murphy, N., & Messer, D. (2000). Differential benefits from scaffolding and children working alone. *Educational Psychology, 20,* 17–31.

Murrell, A. J., Frieze, I. H., & Frost, J. L. (1991). Aspiring to careers in male- and female-dominated professions: A study of black and white college women. *Psychology of Women Quarterly, 15,* 103–126.

Murstein, B. I. (1987). A clarification and extension of the SVR theory of dyadic pairing. *Journal of Marriage and the Family, 49,* 929–933.

Musil, C. M., & Standing, T. (2005). Grandmothers' diaries: A glimpse at daily lives. *International Journal of Aging and Human Development, 60,* 317–329.

Mustanski, B. S., Viken, R. J., Kaprio, J., Pulkkinen, L., & Rose, R. J. (2004). Genetic and environmental influences on pubertal development: Longitudinal data from Finnish twins at ages 11 and 14. *Developmental Psychology, 40,* 1188–1198.

Mutchler, J. E., Burr, J. A., Pienta, A. M., & Massagli, M. P. (1997). Pathways to labor force exit: Work transitions and work instability. *Journal of Gerontology: Social Sciences, 52B,* S4–S12.

Muter, V., Hulme, C., Snowling, M. J., & Stevenson, J. (2004). Phonemes, rimes, vocabulary, and grammatical skills as foundations of early reading development: Evidence from a longitudinal study. *Developmental Psychology, 40,* 665–681.

Myers, E. G., & Cavanaugh, J. C. (1995). Filial anxiety in mothers and daughters: Cross-validation of the Filial Anxiety Scale. *Journal of Adult Development, 2,* 137–145.

Myskow, L. (2002). Perimenopausal issues in sexuality. *Sexual & Relationship Therapy, 17,* 253–260.

Nadig, A. S., & Sedivy, J. C. (2002). Evidence of perspective-taking constraints in children's on-line reference resolution. *Psychological Science, 13,* 329–336.

Nahemow, L. (2000). The ecological theory of aging: Powell Lawton's legacy. In R. L. Rubinstein & M. Moss (Eds.), *The many dimensions of aging* (pp. 22–40). New York: Springer.

Naigles, L. G., & Gelman, S. A. (1995). Overextensions in comprehension and production revisited: Preferential-looking in a study of dog, cat, and cow. *Journal of Child Language, 22,* 19–46.

Náñez, J., Sr., & Yonas, A. (1994). Effects of luminance and texture motion on infant defensive reactions to optical collision. *Infant Behavior and Development, 17,* 165–174.

Nation, K., Adams, J. W., Bowyer-Crane, C. A., & Snowling, M. J. (1999). Working memory deficits in poor comprehenders reflect underlying language impairments. *Journal of Experimental Child Psychology, 73,* 139–158.

National Academy on an Aging Society. (2000). *Caregiving.* Washington, DC: Author.

National Academy on an Aging Society. (2003). *The state of aging and health in America.* Retrieved August 7, 2005, from http://www.agingsociety.org/agingsociety/pdf/state_of_aging_report.pdf

National Cancer Institute. (2002). *Tamoxifen: Questions and answers.* Retrieved November 16, 2003, from http://cis.nci.nih.gov/fact/7_16.htm

National Cancer Institute. (2005). *Tobacco statistics snapshot.* Retrieved June 7, 2005, from http://www.cancer.gov/cancertopics/tobacco/statisticssnapshot

National Center for Health Statistics. (1999). *Vital statistics of the United States, 1993: Volume 1 Natality* (Center for Disease Control Publication No. PHS 99–1100). Hyattsville, MD: Centers for Disease Controls.

National Center for Health Statistics. (2004a). *Health, United States, 2004: With chartbook on trends in the health of Americans.* Retrieved July 17, 2005, from http://www.cdc.gov/nchs/data/hus/hus04.pdf

National Center for Health Statistics. (2004b). *Older Americans 2004: Key indicators of well-being.* Retrieved July 17, 2005, from http://www.agingstats.gov/chartbook2004/default.htm

National Center for Injury Prevention and Control. (2005). *Sexual violence: Fact sheet.* Retrieved September 28, 2005, from http://www.cdc.gov/ncipc/factsheets/svfacts.htm

National Federation of State High School Associations. (2004). *NFHS participation survey, 2003–2004.* Indianapolis, IN: Author.

National Heart, Lung, and Blood Institute. (2003). *Facts about postmenopausal hormone therapy.* Retrieved July 3, 2005, from http://www.nhlbi.nih.gov/health/women/pht_facts.htm

National High Blood Pressure Education Program Working Group on Hypertension Control in Children and Adolescents. (1996). Update on the 1987 task force report on high blood pressure in children and adolescents: A working group report from the National High Blood Pressure Education Program. *Pediatrics, 98,* 649–658.

National Highway Transportation Safety Administration. (2003). *Older population.* Retrieved July 31, 2005, from http://www-nrd.nhtsa.dot.gov/pdf/nrd-30/NCSA/TSF2003/809766.pdf

National Institute of Arthritis, Musculoskeletal and Skin Diseases. (2002). *Handout on health: Osteoarthritis.* Retrieved July 3, 2005, from http://www.niams.nih.gov/hi/topics/arthritis/oahandout.htm

National Institute of Arthritis, Musculoskeletal and Skin Diseases. (2004). *Handout on health: Rheumatoid arthritis.* Retrieved July 3, 2005, from http://www.niams.nih.gov/hi/topics/arthritis/rahandout.htm

National Institute of Arthritis, Musculoskeletal and Skin Diseases. (2005). *Osteoporosis: Peak bone mass in women.* Retrieved July 3, 2005, from http://www.niams.nih.gov/bone/hi/bone_mass.htm

National Institute of Neurological Disorders and Stroke. (2005). *NINDS deep brain stimulation for Parkinson's disease information page.* Retrieved July 17, 2005, from http://www.ninds.nih.gov/disorders/deep_brain_stimulation/deep_brain_stimulation.htm

National Institute on Alcohol Abuse and Alcoholism. (1998). *Frequently asked questions about alcohol abuse and alcoholism.* Retrieved June 18, 2005, from http://www.niaaa.nih.gov/faq/faq.htm

National Institutes of Health. (2000a). *Osteoporosis Prevention, Diagnosis, and Therapy: Consensus Statement.* Retrieved July 3, 2005, from http://consensus.nih.gov/cons/111/111_statement.htm

National Institutes of Health. (2000b). *To reduce SIDS risk, doctor's advice most important in choice of placing infants to sleep on their backs.* Washington, DC: Author.

National Research Council. (1989). *Recommended dietary allowances* (10th ed.). Washington, DC: National Academy Press.

Neff, L. A., & Karney, B. R. (2005). To know you is to love you: The implications of global adoration and specific accuracy for marital relationships. *Journal of Personality & Social Psychology, 88,* 480–497.

Neft, N., & Levine, A. D. (1997). *Where women stand: An international report on the status of women in over 140 countries, 1997–1998.* New York: Random House.

Neimeyer, R. (1997). Knowledge at the margins. *The Forum Newsletter* (Association for Death Education and Counseling), *23*(2), 2, 10.

Neimeyer, R. Keese, B. V., & Fortner, M. (2000). Commemoration and bereavement: Cultural aspects of collective myth and the creation of national identity. In R. Malkinson, S. Rubin, & E. Witztum (Eds.), *Traumatic and nontraumatic loss and bereavement: Clinical theory and practice* (pp. 295–320). Madison, CT: Psychosocial Press/International Universities Press.

Neisser, U., Boodoo, G., Bouchard, T. J., Boykin, A. W., Brody, N., Ceci, S. J., et al. (1996). Intelligence: Knowns and unknowns. *American Psychologist, 51,* 77–101.

Nell, V. (2002). Why young men drive dangerously: Implications for injury prevention. *Current Directions in Psychological Science, 11,* 75–79.

Nelson, C. A. (1999). Neural plasticity and human development. *Current Directions in Psychological Science, 8,* 42–45.

Nelson, C. H. (2001). Determinants of grief duration: An exploratory model and multivariate analysis. *Dissertation Abstracts International Section A: Humanities and Social Sciences, 61*(12A), 4963.

Nelson, K. (1973). Structure and strategy in learning to talk. *Monographs of the Society for Research in Child Development, 38* (Serial No. 149).

Nelson, K. (1993). Explaining the emergence of autobiographical memory in early childhood. A. F. Collins & S. E. Gathercole (Eds.), *Theories of memory.* Hove, UK: Erlbaum.

Nelson, K. (2001). Language and the self: From the "Experiencing I" to the "Continuing Me." In C. Moore & K. Lemmon (Eds.), *The self in time: Developmental perspectives* (pp. 15–33). Mahwah, NJ: Erlbaum.

Nelson, K., & Fivush, R. (2004). The emergence of autobiographical memory: A social cultural developmental theory. *Psychological Review, 111,* 486–511.

Nelson, L. J., Badger, S., & Wu, B. (2004). The influence of culture in emerging adulthood: Perspectives of Chinese college students. *International Journal of Behavioral Development, 28,* 26–36.

Nelson, M. A. (1996). Protective equipment. In O. Bar-Or (Ed.), *The child and adolescent athlete.* Oxford, UK: Blackwell.

Nesdale, D., & Flesser, D. (2001). Social identity and the development of children's group attitudes. *Child Development, 72,* 506–517.

Nesdale, D., Maass, A., Durkin, K., & Griffiths, J. (2005). Group norms, threat, and children's ethnic racial prejudice. *Child Development, 76,* 652–663.

Neugarten, B. L. (1969). Continuities and discontinuities of psychological issues into adult life. *Human Development, 12,* 121–130.

Neugarten, B. L., & Weinstein, K. K. (1964). The changing American grandparent. *Journal of Marriage and the Family, 26,* 299–304.

Newcomb, A. F., & Bagwell, C. L. (1995). Children's friendship relations: A meta-analytic review. *Psychological Bulletin, 117,* 306–347.

Newman, B. S, & Muzzonigro, P. G. (1993). The effects of traditional family values on the coming out process of gay male adolescents. *Adolescence, 28,* 213–226.

Newport, E. L. (1991). Contrasting conceptions of the critical period for language. In S. Carey & R. Gelman (Eds.), *The epigenesis of mind: Essays on biology and cognition* (pp. 111–130). Hillsdale, NJ: Erlbaum.

Newsom, J. T. (1999). Another side to caregiving: Negative reactions to being helped. *Current Directions in Psychological Science, 8,* 183–187.

NICHD. (2004). *The NICHD community connection.* Washington, DC: Author.

NICHD Early Child Care Research Network. (1997). The effects of infant child care on infant-mother attachment security: Results of the NICHD Study of Early Child Care. *Child Development, 68,* 860–879.

NICHD Early Child Care Research Network. (2001). Childcare and family predictors of preschool attachment and stability from infancy. *Developmental Psychology, 37,* 847–862.

Nistor, G. I., Totoiu, M. O., Haque, N., Carpenter, M. K., & Keirstead, H. S. (2005). Human embryonic stem cells differentiate into oligodendrocytes in high purity and myelinate after spinal cord transplantation. *Glia, 49,* 385–396.

Nolen-Hoeksema, S. (1998). The other end of the continuum: The costs of rumination. *Psychological Inquiry, 9,* 216–219.

Nolen-Hoeksema, S. (2001). Ruminative coping and adjustment to bereavement. In M. S. Stroebe, R. O. Hansson, W. Stroebe, & H. Schut (Eds.), *Handbook of bereavement research* (pp. 545–562). Washington, DC: American Psychological Association.

Nolen-Hoeksema, S., & Larson, J. (1999). *Coping with loss.* Mahwah, NJ: Erlbaum.

Noller, P., & Fitzpatrick, M. A. (1993). *Communication in family relationships.* Upper Saddle River, NJ: Prentice-Hall.

Noonan, D. (2005, June 6). A little bit louder, please. *Newsweek.* Retrieved July 17, 2005, from http://www.msnbc.msn.com/id/8017906/site/newsweek/

Norlander, B. & Eckhardt, C. (2005). Anger, hostility, and male perpetrators of intimate partner violence: A meta-analytic review. *Clinical Psychology Review, 25,* 119–152.

Norris, F. N., & Murrell, S. A. (1987). Older adult family stress and adaptation before and after bereavement. *Journal of Gerontology, 42,* 606–612.

Notarius, C. I. (1996). Marriage: Will I be happy or will I be sad? In N. Vanzetti & S. Duck (Eds.), *A lifetime of relationships* (pp. 265–289). Pacific Grove, CA: Brooks/Cole.

Nurmi, J., Poole, M. E., & Kalakoski, V. (1996). Age differences in adolescent identity exploration and commitment in urban and rural environments. *Journal of Adolescence, 19,* 443–452.

O'Brien, C.-A., & Goldberg, A. (2000). Lesbians and gay men inside and outside families. In N. Mandell & A. Duffy (Eds.), *Canadian families: Diversity, conflict, and change* (2nd ed., pp. 115–145). Toronto, Canada: Harcourt Brace.

O'Conner, T., Heron, J., Golding, J., Beveridge, M., & Glover, V. (2002). Maternal antenatal anxiety and children's behavioural/emotional problems at 4 years. *British Journal of Psychiatry, 180,* 502–508.

O'Leary, K. D. (1993). Through a psychological lens: Personality traits, personality disorders, and levels of violence. In R. J. Gelles & D. R. Loseke (Eds.), *Current controversies on family violence* (pp. 7–30). Newbury Park, CA: Sage.

O'Neill, D. K. (1996). Two-year-old children's sensitivity to a parent's knowledge state when making requests. *Child Development, 67,* 659–677.

O'Rand, A. M., & Campbell, R. T. (1999). On reestablishing the phenomenon and specifying ignorance: Theory development and research design in aging. In V. L. Bengtson & K. W. Schaie (Eds.), *Handbook of theories of aging* (pp. 59–78). New York: Springer.

O'Rourke, N., & Cappeliez, P. (2005). Marital satisfaction and self-deception: Reconstruction of relationship histories among older adults. *Social Behavior and Personality, 33,* 273–282.

Oburu, P. O., & Palmérus, K. (2005). Stress related factors among primary and part-time caregiving grandmothers of Kenyan grandchildren. *International Journal of Aging and Human Development, 60,* 273–282.

Oehmichen, M., & Meissner, C. (2000). Life shortening and physician assistance in dying: Euthanasia from the viewpoint of German legal medicine. *Gerontology, 46,* 212–218.

Offer, D., Ostrov, E., Howard, K. I., & Atkinson, R. (1988). *The teenage world: Adolescents' self-image in ten countries.* New York: Plenum.

Ogletree, R. J. (1993). Sexual coercion experience and help-seeking behavior of college women. *Journal of American College Health, 41,* 149–153.

Okagaki, L., & Sternberg, R. J. (1993). Parental beliefs and children's school performance. *Child Development, 64,* 36–56.

Okie, S. (2000, April 12). Over the tiniest patients, big ethical questions: Fetal surgery's growing reach raises issues of need and risks. *Washington Post,* pp. A1, A16.

Okonski, B. (1996, May 6). Just say something. *Newsweek,* p. 14.

Oliner, S. P., & Oliner, P. M. (1988). *The altruistic personality: Rescuers of Jews in Nazi Europe.* New York: Free Press.

Olsen, O. (1997). Meta-analysis of the safety of home birth. *Birth—Issues in Perinatal Care, 24,* 4–13.

Olshansky, S. J., Hayflick, L., & Perls, T. (2004a). Anti-aging medicine: The hype and the reality—Part I. *Journal of Gerontology: Biological Sciences, 59A,* 513–514.

Olshansky, S. J., Hayflick, L., & Perls, T. (2004b). Anti-aging medicine: The hype and the reality—Part II. *Journal of Gerontology: Biological Sciences, 59A,* 649–651.

Olson, D. H., & McCubbin, H. (1983). *Families: What makes them work.* Newbury Park, CA: Sage.

Olson, L. N. (2000). Power, control, and communication: An analysis of aggressive, violent, and abusive couples. *Dissertation Abstracts International Section A: Humanities and Social Sciences, 61*(2-A), 427.

Olson, S. L., Bates, J. E., Sandy, J. M., & Lanthier, R. (2000). Early developmental precursors of externalizing behavior in middle childhood and adolescence. *Journal of Abnormal Child Psychology, 28,* 119–133.

Olson, S. L., Sameroff, A. J., Kerr, David C. R., Lopez, N. L., & Wellman, H. M. (2005). Developmental foundations of externalizing problems in young children: The role of effortful control. *Development and Psychopathology, 17,* 25–45.

Oltjenbruns, K. A. (1996). Death of a friend during adolescence: Issues and impacts. In C. A. Coor & D. E. Balk (Eds.), *Handbook of adolescent death and bereavement* (pp. 196–215). New York: Springer.

Oltjenbruns, K. A. (2001). Developmental context of childhood: Grief and regrief phenomena. In M. S. Stroebe, R. O. Hansson, W. Stroebe, & H. Schut (Eds.), *Handbook of bereavement research: Consequences, coping, and care* (pp. 169–197). Washington, DC: American Psychological Association.

Olweus, D. (1978). *Aggression in the schools: Bullies and whipping boys.* Washington, DC: Hemisphere.

Olweus, D. (1994). Bullying at school: Basic facts and effects of school based intervention program. *Journal of Child Psychology and Psychiatry, 35,* 1171–1190.

Olweus, D., Mattson, A., Schalling, D., & Low, H. (1988). Circulating testosterone levels and aggression in adolescent males: A causal analysis. *Psychosomatic Medicine, 50,* 261–272.

Opfer, J. E., & Siegler, R. S. (2004).Revisiting preschoolers' living things concept: A microgenetic analysis of conceptual change in basic biology. *Cognitive Psychology, 49,* 301–332.

Oregon Department of Human Services. (2005). *Seventh annual report on Oregon's Death with Dignity Act.* Retrieved August 27, 2005, from http://egov.oregon.gov/DHS/ph/pas/docs/year7.pdf

Orentlicher, D. (2000). The implementation of Oregon's Death with Dignity Act: Reassuring, but more data are needed. *Psychology, Public Policy, and Law, 6,* 489–502.

Orlick, T., Zhou, Q. Y., & Partington, J. (1990). Co-operation and conflict within Chinese and Canadian kindergarten settings. *Canadian Journal of Behavioural Science, 22,* 20–25.

Osgood, D. W., Ruth, G., Eccles, J. S., Jacobs, J. E., & Barber, B. L. (2005). Six paths to adulthood: Fast starters, parents without careers, educated partners, educated singles, working singles, and slow starters. In R. A. Settersten, Jr., F. F. Furstenberg, Jr., & R. G. Rumbaut (Eds.), *On the frontier of adulthood: Theory, research, and public policy* (pp. 320–355). Chicago: University of Chicago Press.

Osgood, N. J. (1992). *Suicide in later life.* Lexington, MA: Lexington Books.

Oygard, L., & Hardeng, S. (2001). Divorce support groups: How do group characteristics influence adjustment to divorce? *Social Work with Groups, 24,* 69–87.

Ozawa, M. N., & Yoon, H. S. (2002). The economic benefit of remarriage: Gender and class income. *Journal of Divorce and Remarriage, 36,* 21–39.

Paarlberg, K. M., Vingerhoets, A. J. J. M., Passchier, J., Dekker, G. A., et al. (1995). Psychosocial factors and pregnancy outcome: A review with emphasis on methodological issues. *Journal of Psychosomatic Research, 39,* 563–595.

Pacy, B. (1993, Spring). Plunged into flux. *Notre Dame Magazine, 22,* 34–38.

Papalia, D. E., & Olds, S. W. (1995). *Human development* (6th ed.). New York: McGraw-Hill.

Parasuraman, R. (1998). The attentive brain: Issues and prospects. In R. Parasuraman (Ed.), *The attentive brain* (pp. 3–15). Cambridge, MA: MIT Press.

Parault, S. J., & Schwanenflugel, P. J. (2000). The development of conceptual categories of attention during the elementary school years. *Journal of Experimental Child Psychology, 75,* 245–262.

Parazzini, F., Luchini, L., La Vecchia, C., & Crosignani, P. G. (1993). Video display terminal use during pregnancy and reproductive outcome—a meta-analysis. *Journal of Epidemiology and Community Health, 47,* 265–268.

Pargament, K. I. (1997). *The psychology of religion and coping: Theory, research, and practice.* New York: Guilford.

Park, D. C., Morrell, R. W., & Shifrin, K. (Eds.). (1999). *Processing of medical information in aging patients: Cognitive and human factors perspectives.* Mahwah, NJ: Erlbaum.

Park, D. C., Smith, A. D., Lautenschlager, G., Earles, J. L., Frieski, D., Zwahr, M., & Gaines, C. L. (1996). Mediators of long-term memory performance across the lifespan. *Psychology and Aging, 11,* 621–637.

Parke, R. D. (2002). Fathers and families. In M. H. Bornstein (Ed.), *Handbook of parenting, Vol. 3: Being and becoming a parent* (pp. 27–73). Mahwah, NJ: Erlbaum.

Parke, R. D. (1977). Punishment in children: Effects, side effects and alternative strategies. In H. L. Hom, Jr. & A. Robinson (Eds.), *Psychological processes in early education.* New York: Academic Press.

Parke, R. D., & Bahvnagri, N. P. (1989). Parents as managers of children's peer relationships. In D. Belle (Ed.), *Children's social networks and social supports.* New York: Wiley.

Parke, R. D., & Buriel, R. (1998). Socialization in the family: Ethnic and ecological perspectives. In W. Damon (Ed.), *Handbook of child psychology* (Vol. 3). New York: Wiley.

Parker, J. G., & Seal, J. (1996). Forming, losing, renewing, and replacing friendships: Applying temporal parameters to the assessment of children's friendship experiences. *Child Development, 67,* 2248–2268.

Parker, R. A., & Aldwin, C. M. (1997). Do aspects of gender identity change from early to middle adulthood? Disentangling age, cohort, and period effects. In M. E. Lachman & J. B. James (Eds.), *Multiple paths of midlife development* (pp. 67–107). Chicago: University of Chicago Press.

Parkinson's Disease Foundation. (2005). *Treatments.* Retrieved July 17, 2005, from http://www.pdf.org/AboutPD/med_treatment.cfm

Parmet, S., Lynm, C., & Glass, R. M. (2003). Chronic obstructive pulmonary disease. *JAMA, 290,* 2362.

Parritz, R. H. (1996). A descriptive analysis of toddler coping in challenging circumstances. *Infant Behavior and Development, 19,* 171–180.

Parten, M. (1932). Social participation among preschool children. *Journal of Abnormal and Social Psychology, 27,* 243–269.

Pascalis, O., de Hann, M., & Nelson, C. A. (2002). Is face processing species-specific during the first year of life? *Science, 296,* 1321–1323.

Pascual, C. (2000, October 3). Asians have highest elderly suicide rate. *Wilmington (NC) Morning Star,* p. 5D.

Pasupathi, M. (2001). The social construction of the personal past and its implications for adult development. *Psychological Bulletin, 127,* 651–672.

Pasupathi, M., & Carstensen, L. L. (2003). Age and emotional experience during mutual reminiscing. *Psychology and Aging, 18,* 430–442.

Patterson, C. J. (1992). Children of lesbian and gay parents. *Child Development, 63,* 1025–1042.

Patterson, G. R. (1980). Mothers: The unacknowledged victims. *Monographs of the Society for Research in Child Development, 45*(5, Serial No. 186).

Patterson, G. R. (1995). Coercion as a basis for early age of onset for arrest. In J. McCord (Ed.), *Coercion and punishment in long-term perspectives.* New York: Cambridge University Press.

Patterson, M., & Werker, J. F. (2003). Two-month-old infants match phonetic information in lips and voice. *Developmental Science, 6,* 191–196.

Patterson, S. J., Sochting, I., & Marcia, J. E. (1992). The inner space and beyond: Women and identity. In G. R. Adams, T. P. Gullotta, & R. Montemayor (Eds.), *Adolescent identity formation: Vol. 4. Advances in adolescent development.* Newbury Park, CA: Sage.

Pavalko, E. K., & Artis, J. E. (1997). Women's caregiving and paid work: Causal relationships in late midlife. *Journals of Gerontology: Social Sciences, 52B,* S170–S179.

Payne, J. W. (2004, October 5). Nursing home costs. *Washington Post.* Retrieved August 7, 2005, from http://www.washingtonpost.com/wp-dyn/articles/A7280-2004Oct4.html

Pearlin, L. I., Mullan, J. T., Semple, S. J., & Skaff, M. M. (1990). Caregiving and the stress process: An overview of concepts and their measures. *The Gerontologist, 30,* 583–594.

Pearson, J. D., Morrell, C. H., Brant, L. J., Landis, P. K., & Fleg, J. L. (1997). Age-associated changes in blood pressure in a longitudinal study of healthy men and women. *Journal of Gerontology: Medical Sciences, 52A,* M177–M183.

Pelphrey, K. A., Reznick, J. S., Davis Goldman, B., Sasson, N., Morrow, J., Donahoe, A., & Hodgson, K. (2004). Development of visuospatial memory in the second half of the first year. *Developmental Psychology, 40,* 836–851.

Penha-Lopes, V. (1995). "Make room for daddy": Patterns of family involvement among contemporary African American men. In C. K. Jacobson (Ed.), *American families: Issues in race and ethnicity* (pp. 179–199). New York: Garland.

Pennebaker, J. W., & Graybeal, A. (2001). Patterns of natural language use: Disclosure, personality, and social integration. *Current Directions in Psychological Science, 10,* 90–93.

Pennington, B. F., Groisser, D., & Welsh, M. C. (1993). Contrasting cognitive deficits in attention deficit hyperactivity disorder versus reading disability. *Developmental Psychology, 29,* 511–523.

Pennington, B. F., Willcutt, E., & Rhee, S. H. (2005). Analyzing comorbidity. In R. V. Kail (Ed.), *Advances in child development and behavior* (Vol. 33, pp. 263–304). San Diego, CA: Elsevier.

Penson, R. T. (2004). Bereavement across cultures. In R. J. Moore & D. Spiegel (Eds.), *Cancer, culture, and communication* (pp. 241–279). New York: Kluwer Academic/Plenum.

Peplau, L., & Gordon, S. L. (1985). Women and men in love: Sex differences in close heterosexual relationships. In V. O'Leary, R. K. Unger, & B. S. Wallston (Eds.), *Women, gender, and social psychology* (pp. 257–292). Hillsdale, NJ: Erlbaum.

Perfetti, C. A., & Curtis, M. E. (1986). Reading. In R. F. Dillon & R. J. Sternberg (Eds.), *Cognition and instruction.* Orlando, FL: Academic Press.

Perls, T., & Terry, D. (2003). Genetics of exceptional longevity. *Experimental Gerontology, 38,* 725–730.

Perry, W. I. (1970). *Forms of intellectual and ethical development in the college years.* New York: Holt, Rinehart & Winston.

Peters, A. M. (1995). Strategies in the acquisition of syntax. In P. Fletcher & B. MacWhinney (Eds.), *The handbook of child language* (pp. 462–483). Oxford, UK: Blackwell.

Peters, R. (2004). Racism and hypertension among African Americans. *Western Journal of Nursing Research. 26,* 612–631.

Peterson, B. E., & Klohnen, E. C. (1995). Realization of generativity in two samples of women at midlife. *Psychology and Aging, 10,* 20–29.

Peterson, C. (1996). *The psychology of abnormality.* Fort Worth, TX: Harcourt Brace.

Peterson, L. (1983). Role of donor competence, donor age, and peer presence on helping in an emergency. *Developmental Psychology, 19,* 873–880.

Petrie, R. H. (1991). Intrapartum fetal evaluation. In S. G. Gabbe, J. R. Niebyl, & J. L. Simpson (Eds.), *Obstetrics: Normal & problem pregnancies* (2nd ed.). New York: Churchill Livingstone.

Pettit, G. S., Bates, J. E., & Dodge, K. A. (1997). Supportive parenting, ecological context, and children's adjustment: A seven-year longitudinal study. *Child Development, 68,* 908–923.

Pettit, G. S., Laird, R. D., Dodge, K. A., Bates, J. E., & Criss, M. N. (2001). Antecedents and behavior problem outcomes of parental monitoring and psychological control in early adolescence. *Child Development, 72,* 283–598.

Phelps, J. A., Davis, J. O., & Schartz, K. M. (1997). Nature, nurture, and twin research strategies. *Current Directions in Psychological Science, 6,* 117–121.

Phelps, R. E., & Constantine, M. G. (2001). Hitting the roof: The impact of the glass-ceiling effect on the career development of African Americans. In W. B. Walsh, R. P. Bingham, et al. (Eds.), *Career counseling for African Americans* (pp. 161–175). Mahwah, NJ: Erlbaum.

Phinney, J. (1989). Stage of ethnic identity in minority group adolescents. *Journal of Early Adolescence, 9,* 34–49.

Phinney, J. (1990). Ethnic identity in adolescents and adults. *Psychological Bulletin, 108,* 499–514.

Phinney, J. S. (2005). Ethnic identity development in minority adolescents. In C. B. Fisher & R. M. Lerner (Eds.), *Encyclopedia of applied developmental science* (Vol. 1, pp. 420–423). Thousand Oaks CA: Sage.

Phinney, J. S., & Chavira, V. (1992). Ethnic identity and self-esteem: An exploratory longitudinal study. Journal of *Adolescence, 15,* 271–281.

Phinney, J. S., Ong, A., & Madden, T. (2000). Cultural values and intergenerational value discrepancies in immigrant and non-immigrant families. *Child Development, 71,* 528–539.

Piaget, J. (1929). *The child's conception of the world.* New York: Harcourt, Brace.

Piaget, J. (1951). *Plays, dreams, and imitation in childhood.* New York: Norton.

Piaget, J. (1952). *The origins of intelligence in children.* New York: International Universities Press.

Piaget, J. (1954). *The construction of reality in the child.* New York: Basic Books.

Piaget, J., & Inhelder, B. (1956). *The child's conception of space.* Boston: Routledge & Kegan Paul.

Piccininni, M., Di Carlo, A., Baldereschi, M., Zaccara, G., & Inzitari, D. (2005). Behavioral and psychological symptoms in Alzheimer's disease: Frequency and relationship with duration and severity of the disease. *Dementia and Geriatric Cognitive Disorders, 19,* 276–281.

Pickard, M., Bates, L., Dorian, M., Greig, H., & Saint, D. (2000). Alcohol and drug use in second-year medical students at the University of Leeds. *Medical Education, 34,* 148–150.

Picot, S. J., Debanne, S. M., Namazi, K. H., & Wykle, M. L. (1997). Religiosity and perceived rewards of black and white caregivers. *The Gerontologist, 37,* 89–101.

Pienta, A. M., Hayward, M. D., & Jenkins, K. R. (2000). Health consequences of marriage for the retirement years. *Journal of Family Issues, 21,* 559–586.

Pierce, C. A., & Aguinis, H. (1997). Bridging the gap between romantic relationships and sexual harassment in organizations. *Journal of Organizational Behavior, 18,* 197–200.

Pierce, S. H., & Lange, G. (2000). Relationships among metamemory, motivation, and memory performance in young school-age children. *British Journal of Developmental Psychology, 18,* 121–135.

Pincus, T., Callahan, L. F., & Burkhauser, R. V. (1987). Most chronic diseases are reported more frequently by individuals with fewer than 12 years of formal education in the age 18–64 United States population. *Journal of Chronic Diseases, 40,* 865–874.

Pinquart, M. (2005). Self-concept. In C. B. Fisher & R. M. Lerner (Eds.), *Encyclopedia of applied developmental science* (Vol. 2., pp. 971–972). Thousand Oaks CA: Sage.

Pinquart, M., & Sörensen, S. (2001). Gender differences in self-concept and psychological well-being in old age: A meta-analysis. *Journal of Gerontology: Psychological Sciences, 56B,* P195–P213.

Piscione, D. P. (2004). *The many faces of 21st century working women: A report to the Women's Bureau of the U.S. Department of Labor.* Retrieved July 2, 2005, from http://www.choose2lead.org/Publications/Many%20Faces%20of%2021st%20Century%20Working%20Women.pdf

Pleck, J. H. (1997). Paternal involvement: Levels, sources, and consequences. In M. E. Lamb (Ed.), *The role of the father in child development* (pp. 66–103). New York: Wiley.

Plomin, R. (1990). *Nature and nurture.* Pacific Grove, CA: Brooks/Cole.

Plomin, R., & Crabbe, J. (2000). DNA. *Psychological Bulletin, 126,* 806–828.

Plomin, R., Fulker, D. W., Corley, R., & DeFries, J. C. (1997). Nature, nurture, and cognitive development from 1 to 16 years: A parent-offspring adoption study. *Psychological Science, 8,* 442–447.

Plomin, R., & Petrill, S. A. (1997). Genetics and intelligence: What's new? *Intelligence, 24,* 53–77.

Plomin, R., & Spinath, F. (2004). Intelligence: Genes, genetics, and genomics. *Journal of Personality and Social Psychology, 86,* 112–129.

Plumert, J. M., & Nichols-Whitehead, P. (1996). Parental scaffolding of young children's spatial communication. *Developmental Psychology, 32,* 523–532.

Plunkett, K. (1996). *Connectionism and development: Neural networks and the study of change.* New York: Oxford University Press.

Pollitt, E. (1994). Poverty and child development: Relevance of research in developing countries to the United States. *Child Development, 65,* 283–295.

Pollitt, E. (1995). Does breakfast make a difference in school? *Journal of the American Dietetic Association, 95,* 1134–1139.

Ponde, M. P., & Santana, V. S. (2000). Participation in leisure activities: Is it a protective factor for women's mental health? *Journal of Leisure Research, 32,* 457–472.

Ponder, R. J., & Pomeroy, E. C. (1996). The grief of caregivers: How pervasive is it? *Journal of Gerontological Social Work, 27,* 3–21.

Poole, D. A., & Lindsay, D. S. (1995). Interviewing preschoolers: Effects of nonsuggestive techniques, parental coaching, and leading questions on reports of nonexperienced events. *Journal of Experimental Child Psychology, 60,* 129–154.

Porter, R. H., & Winberg, J. (1999). Unique salience of maternal breast odors for newborn infants. *Neuroscience & Biobehavioral Reviews, 23,* 439–449.

Poulin-Dubois, D., & Forbes, J. N. (2002). Toddlers' attention to intentions-in-action in learning novel action words. *Developmental Psychology, 38,* 104–114.

Poulson, C. L., Kymissis, E., Reeve, K. F., Andreatos, M., & Reeve, L. (1991). Generalized vocal imitation in infants. *Journal of Experimental Child Psychology, 51,* 267–279.

Power, F. C., Higgins, A., & Kohlberg, L. (1989). *Lawrence Kohlberg's approach to moral education.* New York: Columbia University Press.

Powlishta, K., Serbin, L. A., Doyle, A., & White, D. R. (1994). Gender, ethnic, and body type biases: The generality of prejudice in childhood. *Developmental Psychology, 30,* 526–536.

Pozzi, S., Healy, L., & Hoyles, C. (1993). Learning and interaction in groups with computers: When do ability and gender matter? *Social Development, 2,* 222–241.

Pratt, M. W., Danso, H. A., Arnold, M. L., Norris, J. E., & Filyer, R. (2001). Adult generativity and the socialization of adolescents: Relations to mothers' and fathers' parenting beliefs, styles, and practices. *Journal of Personality, 69,* 89–120.

President's Council on Physical Fitness and Sports. (2004). Physical activity for children: Current patterns and guidelines. *Research digest.* Series 5, No. 2.

Prigerson, H. G., & Jacobs, S. C. (2001). Traumatic grief as a distinct disorder: A rationale, consensus criteria, and a preliminary empirical test. In M. S. Stroebe, R. O. Hansson, W. Stroebe, & H. Schut (Eds.), *Handbook of bereavement research: Consequences, coping, and care* (pp. 613–637). Washington, DC: American Psychological Association.

Principe, G. F., & Ceci, S. J. (2002). I saw it with my own ears: The effects of peer conversations on preschoolers' reports of nonexperienced events. *Journal of Experimental Child Psychology, 83,* 1–25.

Prinstein, M. J., & Cillessen, A. H. N. (2003). Forms and functions of adolescent peer aggression associated with high levels of peer status. *Merrill Palmer Quarterly, 49,* 310–342.

Probert, B. (2005). "I just couldn't fit it in": Gender and unequal outcomes in academic careers. *Gender, Work & Organization, 12,* 50–72.

Project Zero. (1999). *Project SUMIT: Schools Using Multiple Intelligence Theory.* Retrieved from http://pzweb.harvard.edu/SUMIT/OUTCOMES.HTM.

Pruchno, R. (1999). Raising grandchildren: The experiences of Black and White grandmothers. *The Gerontologist, 39,* 209–221.

Pruett, M. K., Insabella, G. M., & Gustafson, K. (2005). The collaborative divorce project: A court-based intervention for separating parents with young children. *Family Court Review, 43,* 38–51.

Pryor, J. B., Desouza, E. R., Fitness, J., & Hutz, C. (1997). Gender differences in the interpretation of social-sexual behavior: A cross-cultural perspective on sexual harassment. *Journal of Cross Cultural Psychology, 28,* 509–534.

Puhl, R. M., & Brownell, K. D. (2005). Bulimia nervosa. In C. B. Fisher & R. M. Lerner (Eds.), *Encyclopedia of applied developmental science* (Vol. 1, pp. 192–195). Thousand Oaks CA: Sage.

Pyszczynski, T., Greenberg, J., & Solomon, S. (1997). Why do we need what we need? A terror management perspective on the roots of human social motivation. *Psychological Inquiry, 8,* 1–20.

Pyszczynski, T., Greenberg, J., & Solomon, S. (1999). A dual-process model of defense against conscious and unconscious death-related thoughts: An extension of terror management theory. *Psychological Review, 106,* 835–845.

Qualls, S. H. (1999). Mental health and mental disorders in older adults. In J. C. Cavanaugh & S. K. Whitbourne (Eds.), *Gerontology: An interdisciplinary perspective* (pp. 305–328). New York: Oxford University Press.

Quillian, L., & Campbell, M. E. (2003). Beyond Black and White: The present and future of multiracial friendship segregation. *American Sociological Review, 68,* 540–566.

Quinn, J. F. (1999). *Retirement patterns and bridge jobs in the 1990s* (Issue Brief 206). Washington, DC: Employee Benefit Research Institute.

Quinn, M. J. (1998). Undue influence: An emotional con game. *Aging Today, 9,* 11.

Quinn, M. J., & Tomita, S. K. (1997). *Elder abuse and neglect: Causes, diagnosis, and intervention strategies* (2nd ed.). New York: Springer.

Rabiner, D. J., Brown, D., & O'Keeffe, J. (2004). Financial exploitation of older persons: Policy issues and recommendations for addressing them. *Journal of Elder Abuse and Neglect, 16,* 65–84.

Radford, A. (1995). Phrase structure and functional categories. In P. Fletcher & B. MacWhinney (Eds.), *The handbook of child language* (pp. 483–507). Oxford, UK: Blackwell.

Raeburn, P. (1995, November 7). Genetic trait may delay Alzheimer's. *News Journal (Wilmington, DE),* p. A3.

Ragins, B. R., Cotton, J. L., & Miller, J. S. (2000). Marginal mentoring: The effects of type of mentor, quality of relationship, and program design on work and career attitudes. *Academy of Management Journal, 43,* 117–1194.

Ragland, O. R., & Brand, R. J. (1988). Type A behavior and mortality from coronary heart disease. *New England Journal of Medicine, 318,* 65–69.

Ragozin, A. S., Basham, R. B., Crnic, K. A., Greenberg, M. T., & Robinson, N. M. (1982). Effects of maternal age on parenting role. *Developmental Psychology, 18,* 627–634.

Raine, A., Moffitt, T. E., Caspi, A., Loeber, R., Stouthamer-Loeber, M., & Lynam, D. (2005). Neurocognitive impairments in boys on the life-course persistent antisocial path. *Journal of Abnormal Psychology, 114,* 38–49.

Rakic, P. (1995). Corticogenesis in human and nonhuman primates. In M. S. Gazzaniga (Ed.), *The cognitive neurosciences.* Cambridge, MA: MIT Press.

Rakison, D. H., & Hahn, E. R. (2004). The mechanisms of early categorization and induction: Smart or dumb infants? *Advances in child development and behavior, 32,* 281–322.

Rakison, D. H., & Poulin-Dubois, D. (2001). Developmental origin of the animate-inanimate distinction. *Psychological Bulletin, 127,* 209–228.

Raley, G. (1999). No good choices: Teenage childbearing, concentrated poverty, and welfare reform. In S. Coontz (Ed.), *American families: A multicultural reader* (pp. 258–272). New York: Routledge.

Raman, L., & Gelman, S. A. (2005). Children's understanding of the transmission of genetic disorders and contagious illnesses. *Developmental Psychology, 41,* 171–182.

Ramey, C. T., & Campbell, F. A. (1991). Poverty, early childhood education, and academic competence: The Abecedarian experiment. In A. Huston (Ed.), *Children reared in poverty.* New York: Cambridge University Press.

Ramey, C. T., & Ramey, S. L. (1990). Intensive educational intervention for children of poverty. *Intelligence, 14,* 1–9.

Ransjoe-Arvidson, A. B., Matthiesen, A. S., Lilja, G., Nissen, E., Widstroem, A. M., & Uvnaes-Moberg, K. (2001). Maternal analgesia during labor disturbs newborn behavior: Effects on breastfeeding, temperature, and crying. *Birth-Issues in Perinatal Care, 28,* 5–12.

Ranwez, S., Leidig, T., & Crampes, M. (2000). Formalization to improve lifelong learning. *Journal of Interactive Learning Research, 11,* 389–409.

Rapaport, J. L., & Ismond, D. R. (1990). *DSM-III-R training guide for diagnosis of childhood disorders.* New York: Brunner/Mazel.

Rape, Abuse, and Incest National Network (RAINN). (2005). *The facts about rape.* Retrieved June 12, 2005, from http://www.rainn.org/statistics.html

Rapoport, R., & Rapoport, R. N. (1975). *Leisure and the family life cycle.* London, UK: Routledge & Kegan Paul.

Rappaport, L. (1993). The treatment of nocturnal enuresis—where are we now? *Pediatrics, 92,* 465–466.

Rapport, M. D. (1995). Attention-deficit hyperactivity disorder. In M. Hersen & R. T. Ammerman (Eds.), *Advanced abnormal child psychology.* Hillsdale, NJ: Erlbaum.

Raschick, M., & Ingersoll-Dayton, B. (2004). The costs and rewards of caregiving among aging spouses and adult children. *Family Relations: Interdisciplinary Journal of Applied Family Studies, 53,* 317–325.

Rathunde, K. R., & Csikszentmihalyi, M. (1993). Undivided interest and the growth of talent: A longitudinal study of adolescents. *Journal of Youth and Adolescence, 22,* 385–405.

Rawlins, W. K. (1992). *Friendship matters.* Hawthorne, NY: Aldine de Gruyter.

Rawlins, W. K. (2004). Friendships in later life. In J. F. Nussbaum & J. Coupland (Eds.), *Handbook of communication and aging research* (2nd ed., pp. 273–299). Mahwah, NJ: Erlbaum.

Rayner, K., Foorman, B. R., Perfetti, C. A. Pesetsky, D., & Seidenberg, M. S. (2001). How psychological science informs the teaching of reading. *Psychological Science in the Public Interest, 2,* 31–75.

Read, J. P., Wood, M. D., Davidoff, O. J., McLacken, J., & Campbell, J. F. (2002). Making the transition from high school to college: The role of alcohol-related social influence factors in students' drinking. *Substance Abuse, 23,* 53–65.

Reese, D. (2001). Putting the resident first. *Contemporary Long Term Care* (May), 24–28.

Reese, E., & Cox, A. (1999). Quality of adult book reading affects children's emergent literacy. *Developmental Psychology, 35,* 20–28.

Reich, P. A. (1986). *Language development.* Englewood Cliffs, NJ: Prentice-Hall.

Reid, D. H., Wilson, P. G., & Faw, G. D. (1991). Teaching self-help skills. In J. L. Matson & J. A. Mulick (Eds.), *Handbook of mental retardation* (2nd ed.). New York: Pergamon Press.

Reid, J., & Hardy, M. (1999). Multiple roles and well-being among midlife women: Testing role strain and role enhancement theories. *Journal of Gerontology: Social Sciences, 54B,* S329–S338.

Reid, M., Miller, W., & Kerr, B. (2004). Sex-based glass ceilings in U.S. state-level bureaucracies, 1987–1997. *Administration & Society, 36,* 377–405.

Reifman, A., & Watson, W. K. (2004). Binge drinking during the first semester of college: Continuation and desistance from high school patterns. *Journal of American College Health, 52,* 73–81.

Reimer, M. S. (1996). "Sinking into the ground": The development and consequences of shame in adolescence. *Developmental Review, 16,* 321–363.

Reinhoudt, C. J. (2005). Factors related to aging well: The influence of optimism, hardiness and spiritual well-being on the physical health functioning of older adults. *Dissertation Abstracts International: Section B: The Sciences & Engineering.* 65(7-B), 3762.

Reis, M., & Nahmiash, D. (1998). Validation of the Indicators of Abuse (IOA) screen. *The Gerontologist, 38,* 471–480.

Repacholi, B. M. (1998). Infants' use of attentional cues to identify the referent of another person's emotional expression. *Developmental Psychology, 34,* 1017–1025.

Reubens, B., Harrison, J., & Kupp, K. (1981). *The youth labor force, 1945–1995: A cross-national analysis.* Totowa, NJ: Allanheld, Osmun.

Reynolds, A. J., & Robertson, D. L. (2003). School-based early intervention and later child maltreatment in the Chicago Longitudinal Study. *Child Development, 74,* 3–26.

Reynolds, A. J., & Temple, J. A. (1998). Extended early childhood intervention and school achievement: Age thirteen findings from the Chicago longitudinal study. *Child Development, 69,* 231–246.

Ricciardelli, L. A., & McCabe, M. P. (2004). A biopsychosocial model of disordered eating and the pursuit of muscularity in adolescent boys. *Psychological Bulletin, 130,* 179–205.

Ricciuti, H. N. (1993). Nutrition and mental development. *Current Directions in Psychological Science, 2,* 43–46.

Rice, M. L., Huston, A. C., Truglio, R., & Wright, J. (1990). Words from "Sesame Street": Learning vocabulary while viewing. *Developmental Psychology, 26,* 421–428.

Rice, S. G. (1993). Injury rates among high school athletes 1979–1992. Unpublished raw data.

Rich, C. L., Sherman, M., & Fowler, R. C. (1990, Winter). San Diego suicide study: The adolescents. *Adolescence,* pp. 855–865.

Richters, J. E., Arnold, L. E., Jensen, P. S., Abikoff, H., Conners, C. K., & Greenhill, L. L., et al. (1995). NIMH collaborative multisite multimodal treatment study of children with ADHD: I. Background and rationale. *Journal of the American Academy of Child and Adolescent Psychiatry, 34,* 987–1000.

Ridings, C., & Gefen, D. (2004). Virtual community attraction: Why people hang out online. *Journal of Computer-Mediated Communication, 10,* http://www.ascusc.org/jcmc/vol10/issue1/ridings_gefen.html.

Riggs, D. S., & O'Leary, K. D. (1992). *Violence between dating partners: Background and situational correlates of courtship aggression.* Unpublished manuscript, State University of New York, Stony Brook.

Riley, K. P., Snowden, D. A., Saunders, A. M., Roses, A. D., Mortimer, J. A., & Nanayakkara, N. (2000). Cognitive function and apolipoprotein E in very old adults: Findings from the nun study. *Journal of Gerontology: Social Sciences, 55B,* S69–S75.

Riley, L. D., & Bowen, C. (2005). The sandwich generation: Challenges and coping strategies of multigenerational family. *Counseling & Therapy for Couples & Families, 13,* 52–58.

Riley, M. W. (1979). Introduction. In M. W. Riley (Ed.), *Aging from birth to death: Interdisciplinary perspectives* (pp. 3–14). Boulder, CO: Westview Press.

Rindfuss, R. R., Cooksey, E. C., & Sutterlin, R. L. (1999). Young adult occupational achievement: Early expectations versus behavioral reality. *Work and Organizations, 26,* 220–263.

Ritchie, K.L. (1999). Maternal behaviors and cognitions during discipline episodes: A comparison of power bouts and single acts of noncompliance. *Developmental Psychology, 35,* 580–589.

Rivara, F. P., & Grossman, D.C. (1996). Prevention of traumatic deaths to children in the United States: How far have we come and where do we need to go? *Pediatrics, 97,* 791–798.

Robbins, A., & Wilner, A. (2001). *Quarterlife crisis: The unique challenges of life in your twenties.* New York: Putnam.

Roberto, K. A., & Skoglund, R. R. (1996). Interactions with grandparents and great-grandparents: A comparison of activities, influences, and relationships. *International Journal of Aging and Human Development, 43,* 107–117.

Roberts, D. F., Foehr, U. G., & Rideout, V. (2005). *Generation M: Media in the lives of 8–18 year olds.* Menlo Park CA: Henry J. Kaiser Family Foundation.

Roberts, J. D. (1980). *Roots of a Black future: Family and church.* Philadelphia: Westminster.

Roberts, J. E., Burchinal, M., & Durham, M. (1999). Parents' report of vocabulary and grammatical development of African American preschoolers: Child and environmental associations. *Child Development, 70,* 92–106.

Roberts, R. E., Phinney, J. S., Masse, L. C., Chen, Y. R., Roberts, C. R., & Romero, A. (1999). The structure of ethnic identity of young adolescents from diverse ethnocultural groups. *Journal of Early Adolescence, 19,* 301–322.

Robinson, A., & Clinkenbeard, P. R. (1998). Giftedness: An exceptionality examined. *Annual Review of Psychology, 49,* 117–139.

Robinson, J. M., Johnson, A. L., Benton, S. L., Janey, B.A., Cabral, J., & Woodford, J.A. (2002). What's in a picture? Comparing gender constructs of younger and older adults. *Journal of Men's Studies, 11,* 1–27.

Rockwood, K., Howlett, S. E., MacKnight, C., Beattie, B. L., Bergman, H., Hébert, R., et al. (2004). Prevalence, attributes, and outcomes of fitness and frailty in community-dwelling older adults: Report from the Canadian study of health and aging. *Journal of Gerontology: Biological Sciences and Medical Sciences, 59,* 1310–1317.

Rodin, J., & Langer, E. J. (1977). Long-term effects of a control relevant intervention with the institutionalized aged. *Journal of Personality and Social Psychology, 35,* 897–902.

Roffwarg, H. P., Muzio, J. N., & Dement, W. C. (1966). Ontogenetic development of the human sleep-dream cycle. *Science, 152,* 604–619.

Rogers, S. J., & Amato, P. R. (1997). Is marital quality declining? The evidence from two generations. *Social Forces, 75,* 1089–1100.

Rogers, W. A., & Fisk, A. D. (2001). Understanding the role of attention in cognitive aging research. In J. E. Birren & K. W. Schaie (Eds.), *Handbook of the psychology of aging* (5th ed., pp. 267–287). San Diego, CA: Academic Press.

Rogoff, B., Mistry, J., Goncu, A., & Mosier, C. (1993). Guided participation in cultural activity by toddlers and caregivers. *Monographs of the Society for Research in Child Development, 58* (Serial No. 236).

Rogosch, F. A., Cicchetti, D., Shields, A., & Toth, S. L. (1995). Parenting dysfunction in child maltreatment. In M. H. Bornstein (Ed.), *Handbook of parenting* (Vol. 4). Mahwah NJ: Erlbaum.

Rokach, R., Cohen, O., & Dreman, S. (2004). Triggers and fuses in late divorce: The role of short term crises vs. ongoing frustration on marital break-up. *Journal of Divorce & Remarriage, 40,* 41–60.

Rook, K. S. (2000). The evolution of social relationships in later adulthood. In S. H. Qualls & N. Abeles (Eds.), *Psychology and the aging revolution* (pp. 173–191). Washington, DC: American Psychological Association.

Roscoe, L., A., Malphurs, J. E., Dragovic, L. J., & Cohen, D. (2001). A comparison of characteristics of Kevorkian euthanasia cases and physician-assisted suicides in Oregon. *The Gerontologist, 41,* 439–446.

Rose, A. J., & Asher, S. R. (1999). Children's goals and strategies in response to conflicts within a friendship. *Developmental Psychology, 35,* 69–79.

Rose, A. J., Swenson, L. P., & Waller, E. M. (2004). Overt and relational aggression and perceived popularity: Developmental differences in concurrent and prospective relations. *Developmental Psychology, 40,* 378–387.

Rose, S., & Zand, D. (2000). Lesbian dating and courtship from young adulthood to midlife. *Journal of Gay and Lesbian Social Services, 11,* 77–104.

Rosenberg, E. B. (1992). *The adoption life cycle.* Lexington, MA: Lexington Books.

Rosenberg, J. (1993). Just the two of us. In L. Abraham, L. Green, M. Krance, J. Rosenberg, J. Somerville, & C. Stoner (Eds.), *Reinventing love: Six women talk about lust, sex, and romance* (pp. 301–307). New York: Plume.

Rosenberg, L., Palmer, J. R., & Shapiro, S. (1990). Decline in the risk of myocardial infarction among women who stop smoking. *New England Journal of Medicine, 322,* 213–217.

Rosenberg, S. D., Rosenberg, H. J., & Farrell, M. P. (1999). Midlife crisis revisited. In S. L. Willis & J. D. Reid (Eds.), *Life in the middle: Psychological and social development in middle age* (pp. 47–70). San Diego: Academic Press.

Rosenblatt, P. C. (1996). Grief that does not end. In D. Klass, P. R. Silverman, & S. L. Nickman (Eds.), *Continuing bonds: New understandings of grief* (pp. 45–58). Washington, DC: Taylor & Francis.

Rosenblatt, P. C. (2001). A social constructivist perspective on cultural differences in grief. In M. S. Stroebe, R. O. Hansson, W. Stroebe, & H. Schut (Eds.), *Handbook of bereavement research: Consequences, coping, and care* (pp. 285–300). Washington, DC: American Psychological Association.

Rosenfeld, B. (2004). Do not resuscitate orders, living wills, and surrogate decision making. In B. Rosenfeld (Ed.), *Assisted suicide and the right to die: The interface of social science, public policy, and medical ethics* (pp. 41–59). Washington, DC: American Psychological Association.

Rosengren, K. S., Gelman, S. A., Kalish, C., & McCormick, M. (1991) As time goes by: Children's early understanding of growth in animals. *Child Development, 62,* 1302–1320.

Rosenthal, D. A., & Feldman, S. S. (1992). The relationship between parenting behaviour and ethnic identity in Chinese-American and Chinese-Australian adolescents. *International Journal of Psychology, 27,* 19–31.

Rosenthal, R., & Vandell, D. L. (1996). Quality of care at school-aged child-care programs: Regulatable features, observed experiences, child perspectives, and parent perspectives. *Child Development, 67,* 2434–2445.

Ross, C. E. (1995). Reconceptualizing marital status as a continuum of social attachment. *Journal of Marriage and the Family, 57,* 129–140.

Rostenstein, D., & Oster, H. (1997). Differential facial responses to four basic tastes in newborns. In P. Ekman & E. L. Rosenberg (Eds), *What the face reveals: Basic and applied studies of spontaneous expression using the Facial Action Coding System (FACS). Series in affective science.* New York: Oxford University Press.

Rothbart, M. K., & Bates, J. E. (1998). Temperament. In N. Eisenberg (Ed.), *Handbook of child psychology, Vol. 3: Social, emotional, and personality development* (5th ed., pp. 105–176). New York: Wiley.

Rothbart, M. K., & Rueda, M. R. (2005). The development of effortful control. In U. Mayr, E. Awh, & S. W. Keele (Eds.), *Developing individuality in the human brain: A tribute to Michael I. Posner* (pp. 167–188). Washington DC: American Psychological Association.

Rothbaum, F., Weisz, J., Pott, M., Miyake, K., & Morelli, G. (2000). Attachment and culture: Security in the United States and Japan. *American Psychologist, 55,* 1093–1104.

Rotherman-Borus, M. J., & Langabeer, K. A. (2001). Developmental trajectories of gay, lesbian, and bisexual youths. In A. R. D'Augelli & C. Patterson (Eds.), *Lesbian, gay, and bisexual identities among youth: Psychological perspectives* (pp. 97–128). New York: Oxford University Press.

Rotondo, D. M., & Perrewe, P. L. (2000). Coping with a career plateau: An empirical examination of what works and what doesn't. *Journal of Applied Social Psychology, 30,* 2622–2646.

Rotundo, M., Nguyen, D. H., & Sackett, P. R. (2001). A meta-analytic review of gender differences in perceptions of sexual harassment. *Journal of Applied Psychology, 86,* 914–922.

Rovee-Collier, C. (1987). Learning and memory in infancy. In J. D. Osofsky (Ed.), *Handbook of infant development* (2nd ed.). New York: Wiley.

Rovee-Collier, C. (1997). Dissociations in infant memory: Rethinking the development of implicit and explicit memory. *Psychological Review, 104,* 467–498.

Rovee-Collier, C. (1999). The development of infant memory. *Current Directions in Psychological Science, 8,* 80–85.

Rowe, J. W., & Kahn, R. I. (1998). *Successful aging.* New York: Pantheon.

Rowe, M. M., & Sherlock, H. (2005). Stress and verbal abuse in nursing: Do burned out nurses eat their young? *Journal of Nursing Management, 13,* 242–248.

Roxburgh, S. (1997). The effect of children on the mental health of women in the paid labor force. *Journal of Family Issues, 18,* 270–289.

Rubin, D. C. (Ed.). (1996). *Remembering our past: Studies in autobiographical memory.* Cambridge, UK: Cambridge University Press.

Rubin, D. C., Rahhal, T., & Poon, L. W. (1998). Things learned in early adulthood are remembered best: Effects of a major transition on memory. *Memory and Cognition, 26,* 3–19.

Rubin, K. H., Bukowski, W., & Parker, J. G. (1998). Peer interactions, relationships, and groups. In W. Damon (Ed.), *Handbook of child psychology* (Vol. 3). New York: Wiley.

Rubin, K. H., Bukowski, W., & Parker, J. (2006). Peer interaction and social competence. In W. Damon & R. M. Lerner (Eds.), *Handbook of child psychology: Vol. 3* (6th ed.). New York: Wiley.

Rubin, K. H., Burgess, K. B., & Hastings, P. D. (2002). Stability and social-behavioral consequences of toddlers' inhibited temperament and parenting behaviors. *Child Development, 73,* 483–495.

Rubin, K. H., Stewart, S., & Chen, X. (1995). Parents of aggressive and withdrawn children. In M. Bornstein (Ed.), *Handbook of parenting* (Vol. 1). Hillsdale, NJ: Erlbaum.

Rubin, S. S., & Malkinson, R. (2001). Parental response to child loss across the life cycle: Clinical and research perspectives. In M. S. Stroebe, R. O. Hansson, W. Stroebe, & H. Schut (Eds.), *Handbook of bereavement research: Consequences, coping, and care* (pp. 169–197). Washington, DC: American Psychological Association.

Ruff, H. A., Capozzoli, M., & Weissberg, R. (1998). Age, individuality, and context as factors in sustained visual attention during the preschool years. *Developmental Psychology, 34,* 454–464.

Ruffman, T., Perner, J., Naito, M., Parkin, L., & Clements, W. A. (1998). Older (but not younger) siblings facilitate false belief understanding. *Developmental Psychology, 34,* 161–174.

Rushton, J. P., & Bons, T. A. (2005). Mate choice and friendship in twins. *Psychological Science, 16,* 555–559.

Russell, J. A., & Paris, F. A. (1994). Do children acquire concepts for complex emotions abruptly? *International Journal of Behavioral Development, 17,* 349–365.

Rutland, A., Cameron, L., Milne, A., & McGregor, P. (2005). Social norms and self-presentation. Children's implicit and explicit intergroup attitudes. *Child Development, 76,* 451–466.

Rwampororo, R. K. (2001). Social support: Its mediation of gendered patterns in work-family stress and health for dual-earner couples. *Dissertation Abstract International Section A: Humanities and Social Sciences, 61*(9-A), 3792.

Ryan, E. B., Kennaley, D. E., Pratt, M. W., & Shumovich, M. A. (2000). Evaluations by staff, residents, and community seniors of patronizing speech in the nursing home: Impact of passive, assertive, or humorous responses. *Psychology and Aging, 15,* 272–285.

Rybash, J. M., Hoyer, W. J., & Roodin, P. A. (1986). *Adult cognition and aging.* New York: Pergamon Press.

Rye, M. S., Folck, C. D., Heim, T. A., Olszewski, B. T., & Traina, E. (2004). Forgiveness of an ex-spouse: How does it relate to mental health following a divorce? *Journal of Divorce & Remarriage, 41,* 31–51.

Ryff, C. D. (1991). Possible selves in adulthood and old age: A tale of shifting horizons. *Psychology and Aging, 6,* 286–295.

Rylands, K., & Rickwood, D. J. (2001). Ego integrity versus despair: The effect of "accepting the past" on depression in older women. *International Journal of Aging and Human Development, 53,* 75–89.

Rymer, R. (1993). *Genie.* New York: HarperCollins.

Sacco, W. P., & Beck, A. T. (1995). *Cognitive theory and therapy.* In E. E. Beckham & W. R. Leber (Eds.), *Handbook of depression* (2nd ed.). New York: Guilford Press.

Saffran, J. R., Aslin, R. N., & Newport, E. L. (1996). Statistical learning by 8-month-old infants. *Science, 274,* 1926–1928.

Sagi, A., Koren-Karie, N., Gini, M., Ziv, Y., & Joels, T. (2002). Shedding further light on the effects of various types and quality of early child care on infant-mother attachment relationship: The Haifa study of early child care. *Child Development, 73,* 1166–1186.

Sagi, A., van IJzendoorn, M. H., Aviezer, O., Donnell, F., & Mayseless, O. (1994). Sleeping out of home in a kibbutz communal arrangement: It makes a difference for infant-mother attachment. *Child Development, 65,* 992–1004.

Saginak, K. A., & Saginak, M. A. (2005). Balancing work and family: Equity, gender, and marital satisfaction. *Family Journal: Counseling & Therapy for Couples & Families, 13,* 162–166.

Sakraida, T. J. (2005). Divorce transition differences of midlife women. *Issues in Mental Health Nursing, 26,* 225–249.

Salomone, P. R. (1996). Tracing Super's theory of vocational development: A 40-year retrospective. *Journal of Career Development, 22,* 167–184.

Salthouse, T. A. (1984). Effects of age and skill in typing. *Journal of Experimental Psychology: General, 113,* 345–371.

Salthouse, T. A. (2000). Steps toward the explanation of adult age differences in cognition. In T. Perfect & E. Maylor (Eds.), *Theoretical debate in cognitive aging* (pp.19–49). Oxford, UK: Oxford University Press.

Sanders, M. R., Montgomery, D. T., & Brechman-Toussaint, M. L. (2000). The mass media and the prevention of child behavior problems: The evaluation of a television series to promote positive outcome for parents and their children. *Journal of Child Psychology & Psychiatry & Allied Disciplines, 41,* 939–948.

Sandler, I. N., Tein, J., Mehta, P., Wolchik, S., & Ayers, T. (2000). Coping efficacy and psychological problems of children of divorce. *Child Development, 71,* 1099–1118.

Sangrador, J. L., & Yela, C. (2000). "What is beautiful is loved": Physical attractiveness in love relationships in a representative sample. *Social Behavior and Personality, 28,* 207–218.

Sanson, A., Prior, M., Smart, D., & Oberklaid, F. (1993). Gender differences in aggression in childhood: Implications for a peaceful world. *Australian Psychologist, 28,* 86–92.

Sargeant, M. (2004). Mandatory retirement age and age discrimination. *Employee Relations, 26,* 151–166.

Satariano, W. A., MacLeod, K. E., Cohn, T. E., & Ragland, D. R. (2004). Problems with vision associated with limitations or avoidance of driving in older populations. *Journal of Gerontology: Social Sciences, 59B,* S281–S286.

Saunders, S. (1997). Hospices worldwide: A mission statement. In C. Saunders & R. Kastenbaum (Eds.), *Hospice care on the international scene* (pp. 3–12). New York: Springer.

Savage-Rumbaugh, E. S., Murphy, J., Sevcik, R. A., Brakke, K. E., Williams, S. L., & Rumbaugh, D. M. (1993). Language comprehension in ape and child. *Monographs of the Society for Research in Child Development, 58*(34, Serial No. 233).

Saxe, G. B. (1988a). Candy selling and math learning. *Educational Researcher, 17,* 14–21.

Saxe, G. B. (1988b). The mathematics of child street vendors. *Child Development, 59,* 1415–1425.

Saxon, S. V., & Etten, M. J. (1994). *Physical changes and aging* (3rd ed.). New York: Tiresias.

Sbraga, T. P., & O'Donohue, W. (2000). Sexual harassment. *Annual Review of Sex Research, 11,* 258–285.

Scandura, T. A., & Williams, E. A. (2004). Mentoring and transformational leadership: The role of supervisory career mentoring. *Journal of Vocational Behavior, 65,* 448–468.

Scarr, S. (1992). Developmental theories for the 1990s: Development and individual differences. *Child Development, 63,* 1–19.

Scarr, S., & McCartney, K. (1983). How people make their own environments: A theory of genotype environment effects. *Child Development, 54,* 424–435.

Schaal, B., Marlier, L., & Soussignan, R. (1998). Olfactory function in the human fetus: Evidence from selective neonatal responsiveness to the odor of amniotic fluid. *Behavioral Neuroscience, 112,* 1438–1449.

Schaie, K. W. (1994). The course of adult intellectual development. *American Psychologist, 49,* 304–313.

Schaie, K. W. (1995). *Intellectual development in adulthood: The Seattle longitudinal study.* New York: Cambridge University Press.

Schaie, K. W., Maitland, S. B., Willis, S. L., & Intrieri, R. L. (1998). Longitudinal invariance of adult psychometric ability factor structures across seven years. *Psychology and Aging, 13,* 8–20.

Schaie, K. W., & Willis, S. L. (1995). Perceived family environment across generations. In V. L. Bengston & K. W. Schaie (Eds.), *Adult intergenerational relations: Effects of societal change* (pp. 174–226). New York: Springer.

Schapira, A. H. V., & Olanow, C. W. (2004). Neuroprotection in Parkinson disease: Mysteries, myths, and misconceptions. *JAMA, 291,* 358–364.

Schechtman, K. B., & Ory, M. G. (2001). the effects of exercise on the quality of life of frail older adults: A preplanned meta-analysis of the FICSIT trials. *Annals of Behavioral Medicine, 23,* 186–197.

Schlegel, A., & Barry, H. (1991). *Adolescence: An anthropological inquiry.* New York: Free Press.

Schlossberg, N. K. (2004). *Retire smart, retire happy: Finding your true path in life.* Washington, DC: American Psychological Association.

Schmeeckle, M., Giarusso, R., & Wang, Q. (1998, November). *When being a brother or sister is important to one's identity: Life stage and gender differences.* Paper presented at the annual meeting of the Gerontological Society, Philadelphia.

Schmidt, F. L., & Hunter, J. E. (1998). The validity and utility of selection methods in personnel psychology: Practical and theoretical implications of 85 years of research findings. *Psychological Bulletin, 124,* 262–274.

Schmiege, C. J., Richards, L. N., & Zvonkovic, A. M. (2001). Remarriage: For love or money? *Journal of Divorce and Remarriage, 36,* 123–140.

Schmitt, D. P., Alcalay, L., Allensworth, M., Allik, J., Ault, L., Austers, I., et al. (2004). Patterns and universals of adult romantic attachment across 62 cultural regions: Are models of self and of other pancultural constructs? *Journal of Cross-Cultural Psychology, 35,* 367–402.

Schmitt, F. A., & Estus, S. (2004). Alzheimer's disease genetic susceptibility and causality: What is ApoE's impact? *Neurobiology of Aging, 25,* 661–662.

Schmitz-Scherzer, R., & Thomae, H. (1983). Constancy and change of behavior in old age: Findings from the Bonn Longitudinal Study on Aging. In K. W. Schaie (Ed.), *Longitudinal studies of adult psychological development* (pp. 191–221). New York: Guilford.

Schneider, B. H., Atkinson, L., & Tardif, C. (2001). Child-parent attachment and children's peer relations: A quantitative review. *Developmental Psychology, 37,* 86–100.

Schneider, K. T., Swan, S., & Fitzgerald, L. F. (1997). Job-related and psychological effects of sexual harassment in the workplace: Empirical evidence from two organizations. *Journal of Applied Psychology, 82,* 401–415.

Schneider, M. L., Roughton, E. C., Koehler, A. J., & Lubach, G. R. (1999). Growth and development following prenatal stress exposure in primates: An examination of ontogenetic vulnerability. *Child Development, 70,* 253–274.

Schneider, M. L., Roughton, E. C., & Lubach, G. R. (1997). Moderate alcohol consumption and psychological stress during pregnancy induce attention and neuromotor impairments in primate infants. *Child Development, 68,* 747–759.

Schneider, W., & Bjorklund, D. F. (1998). Memory. In W. Damon (Ed.), *Handbook of child psychology, Volume 2.* New York: Wiley.

Schneider, W., & Pressley, M. (1997). *Memory development between 2 and 20* (2nd ed.). Mahwah, NJ: Erlbaum.

Schnorr, T. M., Grajewski, B. A., Hornung, R. W., Thun, M. J., Egeland, G. M., Murray, W. E., et al. (1991). Video display terminals and the risk of spontaneous abortion. *The New England Journal of Medicine, 324,* 727–733.

Schoenborn, C. A., & Adams, P. F. (2001). *Alcohol use among adults: United States 1997–1998.* Retrieved June 18, 2005, from http://www.cdc.gov/nchs/data/ad/ad324.pdf

Schoon, I. (2001). Teenage job aspirations and career attainment in adulthood: A 17-year follow-up study of teenagers who aspired to become scientists, health professionals, or engineers. *International Journal of Behavioral Development, 25,* 124–132

Schuett, A., & Burke, W. J. (2000). *The hazards of participating in sweepstakes games by the elderly.* Unpublished manuscript.

Schulz, R., & Heckhausen, J. (1999). Aging, culture, and control: Setting a new research agenda. *Journal of Gerontology: Psychological Sciences, 54B,* P139–P145.

Schwartz, D., Chang, L., & Farver, J. M. (2001). Correlates of victimization in Chinese children's peer groups. *Developmental Psychology, 37,* 520–532.

Schwartz, D., Dodge, K. A., Pettit, G. S., & Bates, J. E. (1997). The early socialization of aggressive victims of bullying. *Child Development, 68,* 665–675.

Scott, W. A., Scott, R., & McCabe, M. (1991). Family relationships and children's personality: A cross-cultural, cross-source comparison. *British Journal of Social Psychology, 30,* 1–20.

Scozzaro, P. P., & Subich, L. M. (1990). Gender and occupational sex-type differences in job outcome factor perceptions. *Journal of Vocational Behavior, 36,* 109–119.

Segal, D. L., Bogaards, J. A., Becker, L. A., & Chatman, C. (1999). Effects of emotional expression on adjustment to spousal loss among older adults. *Journal of Mental Health and Aging, 5,* 297–310.

Segrin, C., Taylor, M. E., & Altman, J. (2005). Social cognitive mediators and relational outcomes associated with parental divorce. *Journal of Social and Personal Relationships, 22,* 361–377.

Seidenberg, M. S., & McClelland, J. L. (1989). A distributed, developmental model of word recognition and naming. *Psychological Review, 96,* 523–568.

Seidman, S. M. (2003). The aging male: Androgens, erectile dysfunction, and depression. *Journal of Clinical Psychology, 64,* 31–37.

Seifer, R., Schiller, M., Sameroff, A. J., Resnick, S., & Riordan, K. (1996). Attachment, maternal sensitivity, and infant temperament during the first year of life. *Developmental Psychology, 32,* 12–25.

Selman, R. L. (1980). *The growth of interpersonal understanding: Developmental and clinical analyses.* New York: Academic Press.

Selman, R. L. (1981). The child as a friendship philosopher: A case study in the growth of interpersonal understanding. In S. R. Asher & J. M. Gottman (Eds.), *The development of children's friendships.* Cambridge, UK: Cambridge University Press.

Selman, R. L., & Byrne, D. F. (1974). A structural-developmental analysis of levels of role-taking in middle childhood. *Child Development, 45,* 803–806.

Seltzer, J. A. (1991). Relationships between fathers and children who live apart: The father's role after separation. *Journal of Marriage and the Family, 53,* 79–102.

Sénéchal, M., & LeFevre, J. (2002). Parental involvement in the development of children's reading skill: A five-year longitudinal study. *Child Development, 73,* 445–460.

Sénéchal, M., Thomas, E., & Monker, J. (1995). Individual differences in 4-year-old children's acquisition of vocabulary during storybook reading. *Journal of Educational Psychology, 87,* 218–229.

Sera, E. J. (2001). Men and spousal bereavement: A cross-cultural study of majority-culture and Hispanic men and the role of religiosity and acculturation on grief. *Dissertation Abstracts International Section B: The Sciences and Engineering, 61*(11-B), 6149.

Serbin, L., & Karp, J. (2003). Intergenerational studies of parenting and the transfer of risk from parent to child. *Current Directions in Psychological Science, 12,* 138–142.

Serbin, L. A., Poulin-Dubois, D., Colburne, K A., Sen, M. G., & Eichstedt, J. A. (2001). Gender stereotyping in infancy: Visual preferences for and knowledge of gender-stereotyped toys in the second year. *International Journal of Behavioral Development, 25,* 7–15.

Serbin, L. A., Powlishta, K. K., & Gulko, J. (1993). The development of sex typing in middle childhood. *Monographs of the Society for Research in Child Development, 58* (Serial No. 232).

Serdula, M. K., Ivery, D., Coates, R. J., Freedman, D. S., Williamson, D. F., & Byers, T. (1993). Do obese children become obese adults? A review of the literature. *Preventive Medicine, 22,* 167–177.

Servin, A., Nordenstroem, A., Larsson, A., & Bohlin, G. (2003). Prenatal androgens and gender-typed behavior: A study of girls with mild and severe forms of congenital adrenal hyperplasia. *Developmental Psychology, 39,* 440–450.

Seyfarth, R., & Cheney, D. (1996). Inside the mind of a monkey. In M. Bekoff & D. Jamieson (Eds.), *Readings in animal cognition.* Cambridge, MA: MIT Press.

Shaiko, R. G. (1996). Female participation in public interest nonprofit governance: Yet another glass ceiling? *Nonprofit and Voluntary Sector Quarterly, 25,* 302–320.

Shainess, N. (1984). *Sweet suffering: Woman as victim.* Indianapolis, IN: Bobbs-Merrill.

Shalev, R. (1999). *Comparison of war-bereaved and motor vehicle accident-bereaved parents.* Unpublished master's thesis, University of Haifa.

Shanahan, M. J., Elder, G. H., Burchinal, M., & Conger, R. D. (1996a). Adolescent earnings and relationships with parents: The work-family nexus in urban and rural ecologies. In J. T. Mortimer & M. D. Finch (Eds.), *Adolescents, work, and family: An intergenerational developmental analysis.* Thousand Oaks CA: Sage.

Shanahan, M. J., Elder, G. H., Burchinal, M., & Conger, R. D. (1996b). Adolescent paid labor and relationships with parents: Early work-family linkages. *Child Development, 67,* 2183–2200.

Share, D. L. (1999). Phonological recoding and orthographic learning: A direct test of the self-teaching hypothesis. *Journal of Experimental Child Psychology, 72,* 95–129.

Sharpe, R. M., & Skakkebaek, N. E. (1993). Are oestrogens involved in falling sperm counts and disorders of the male reproductive tract? *Lancet, 341,* 1392–1395.

Shaw, D. S., Winslow, E. B., & Flanagan, C. (1999). A prospective study of the effects of marital status and family relations on young children's adjustment among African American and European American families. *Child Development, 70,* 742–755.

Shaw, G. M., Schaffer, D., Velie, E. M., Morland, K., & Harris, J. A. (1995). Periconceptional vitamin use, dietary folate, and the occurrence of neural tube defects. *Epidemiology, 6,* 219–226.

Shebilske, L. J. (2000). Affective quality, leisure time, and marital satisfaction: A 13-year longitudinal study. *Dissertaion Abstracts International Section A: Humanities and Social Sciences, 60*(9-A), 3545.

Shelov, S. P. (1993). *Caring for your baby and young child: Birth to age 5.* New York: Bantam Books.

Shelton, B. A., & John, D. (1993). Ethnicity, race, and difference: A comparison of White, Black, and Hispanic men's household labor time. In J. C. Hood (Ed.), *Men, work, and family* (pp. 131–150). Newbury Park, CA: Sage.

Sher, T. G. (1996). Courtship and marriage: Choosing a primary relationship. In N. Vanzetti & S. Duck (Eds.), *A lifetime of relationships* (pp. 243–264). Pacific Grove, CA: Brooks/Cole.

Sherman, A. M., de Vries, B., & Lansford, J. E. (2000). Friendship in childhood and adulthood: Lessons across the lifespan. *International Journal of Aging and Human Development, 51,* 31–51.

Sherman, D. K., Iacono, W. G., & McGue, M. K. (1997). Attention-deficit hyperactivity disorder dimensions: A twin study of inattention and impulsivity-hyperactivity. *Journal of the American Academy of Child and Adolescent Psychiatry, 36,* 745–753.

Shi, R., & Werker, J. F. (2001). Six-month old infants' preference for lexical words. *Psychological Science, 12,* 70–75.

Shirley, M. M. (1931). *The first two years: A study of twenty-five babies: Vol. 1. Postural and locomotor development.* Westport, CT: Greenwood Press.

Shirom, A., & Mazeh, T. (1988). Periodicity in seniority-job satisfaction relationship. *Journal of Vocational Behavior, 33,* 38–49.

Shiwach, R. (1994). Psychopathology in Huntington's disease patients. *Acta Psychiatrica Scandinavica, 90,* 241–246.

Shonk, S. M., & Cicchetti, D. (2001). Maltreatment, competency deficits, and risk for academic and behavioral maladjustment. *Developmental Psychology, 37,* 3–17.

Shulman, S., & Kipnis, O. (2001). Adolescent romantic relationships: A look from the future. *Journal of Adolescence, 24,* 337–351.

Shuter-Dyson, R. (1982). Musical ability. In D. Deutsch (Ed.), *The psychology of music.* New York: Academic Press.

Shwe, H. I., & Markman, E. M. (1997). Young children's appreciation of the mental impact of their communicative signals. *Developmental Psychology, 33,* 630–636.

Sicotte, N. L., Woods, R. P., & Mazziotta, J. C. (1999). Handedness in twins: A meta-analysis. *Laterality: Asymmetries of Body, Brain, and Cognition, 4,* 265–286.

Siddiqui, A. (1995). Object size as a determinant of grasping in infancy. *Journal of Genetic Psychology, 156,* 345–358.

Sidebotham, P., Heron, J., & The ALSPAC Study Team. (2003). Child maltreatment in the "children of the nineties": The role of the child. *Child Abuse and Neglect, 27,* 337–352.

Siegler, I. C., George, L. K., & Okun, M. A. (1979). A cross-sequential analysis of adult personality. *Developmental Psychology, 15,* 350–351.

Siegler, R. S. (1981). Developmental sequences within and between concepts. *Monographs of the Society for Research in Child Development, 46* (Serial No. 189).

Siegler, R. S. (1986). Unities in strategy choices across domains. In M. Perlmutter (Ed.), *Minnesota symposia on child development* (Vol. 19). Hillsdale, NJ: Erlbaum.

Siegler, R. S. (1988). Strategy choice procedures and the development of multiplication skill. *Journal of Experimental Psychology: General, 117,* 258–278.

Siegler, R. S., & Alibali, M. W. (2005). *Children's thinking* (4th ed). Upper Saddle River, NJ: Prentice-Hall.

Siegler, R. S., & Jenkins, E. (1989). *How children discover new strategies.* Hillsdale, NJ: Erlbaum.

Siegler, R. S., & Robinson, M. (1982). The development of numerical understandings. In H. W. Reese and L. P. Lipsitt (Eds.), *Advances in child development and behavior* (Vol. 16). New York: Academic Press.

Siegler, R. S., & Shrager, J. (1984). Strategy choices in addition and subtraction: How do children know what to do? In C. Sophian (Ed.), *Origins of cognitive skills.* Hillsdale, NJ: Erlbaum.

Signorielli, N., & Lears, M. (1992). Children, television, and conceptions about chores: Attitudes and behaviors. *Sex Roles, 27,* 157–170.

Silk, J. S., Morris, A. S., Kanaya, T., & Steinberg, L. D. (2003). Psychological control and autonomy granting: Opposite ends of a continuum or distinct constructs? *Journal of Research on Adolescence, 13,* 113–128.

Silverman, P. R., & Nickman, S. L. (1996). Children's construction of their dead parents. In D. Klass, P. R. Silverman, & S. L. Nickman (Eds.), *Continuing bonds: New understandings of grief* (pp. 73–86). Washington, DC: Taylor & Francis.

Silverman, P. R., & Worden, J. W. (1992). Children's understanding of funeral ritual. *Omega, 25,* 319–331.

Silverman, W. K., La Greca, A. M., & Wasserstein, S. (1995). What do children worry about? Worries and their relations to anxiety. *Child Development, 66,* 671–686.

Silverstein, J. S. (2001). Connections and disconnections: Towards an understanding of reasons mid-career professional women leave large corporations. *Dissertation Abstracts International Section B: The Sciences and Engineering, 62*(1-B), 581.

Simmons, R., & Blyth, D. (1987). *Moving into adolescence.* New York: Aldine de Gruyter.

Simons, D. J., & Keil, F. C. (1995). An abstract to concrete shift in the development of biological thought: The insides story. *Cognition, 56,* 129–163.

Simons-Morton, B., Haynie, D. L., Crump, A. D. Eitel, P., & Saylor, K. E. (2001). Peer and parent influences on smoking and drinking among early adolescents. *Health Education and Behavior, 28,* 95–107.

Simonton, D. K. (1997). Creative productivity: A predictive and explanatory model of career trajectories and landmarks. *Psychological Review, 104,* 66–89.

Simpson, E. L. (1974). Moral development research: A case study of scientific cultural bias. *Human Development, 17,* 81–106.

Simpson, J. M. (2001). Infant stress and sleep deprivation as an aetiological basis for the sudden infant death syndrome. *Early Human Development, 61,* 1–43.

Singer, J. D., Fuller, B., Keiley, M. K., & Wolf, A. (1998). Early child-care selection: Variation by geographic location, maternal characteristics, and family structure. *Developmental Psychology, 34,* 1129–1144.

Singer, L. T., Arendt, R., Minnes, S., Farkas, K., Salvator, A., Kirchner, H. L., & Kliegman, R. (2002). Cognitive and motor outcomes of cocaine-exposed infants. *Journal of the American Medical Association, 287,* 1952–1960.

Sinnott, J. D. (Ed.). (1994a). *Interdisciplinary handbook of adult lifespan learning.* Westport, CT: Greenwood Press.

Sinnott, J. D. (1994b). New science models for teaching adults: Teaching as a dialogue with reality. In J. D. Sinnott (Ed.), *Interdisciplinary handbook of adult lifespan learning* (pp. 90–104). Westport, CT: Greenwood Press.

Sinnott, J. D. (1994c). The relationship of postformal thought, adult learning, and lifespan development. In J. D. Sinnott (Ed.), *Interdisciplinary handbook of adult lifespan learning* (pp. 105–119). Westport, CT: Greenwood Press.

Sinnott, J. D. (1998). *The development of logic in adulthood: Postformal thought and its applications.* New York: Plenum.

Sinnott, J. D., & Shifren, K. (2001). Gender and aging: Gender differences and gender roles. In J. E. Birren & K. W. Schaie's (Eds.) *Handbook of the psychology of aging.* (5th ed., pp. 454–476). San Diego, CA: Academic Press.

Siu, O-L., Spector, P. E., Cooper, C. L., & Donald, I. (2001). Age differences in coping and locus of control: A study of managerial stress in Hong Kong. *Psychology and Aging, 16,* 707–710.

Skinner, B. F. (1957). *Verbal behavior.* New York: Appleton-Century-Crofts.

Skinner, E. A. (1985). Determinants of mother-sensitive and contingent-responsive behavior: The role of childbearing

beliefs and socioeconomic status. In I. E. Sigel (Ed.), *Parental belief systems: The psychological consequences for children* (pp. 51–82). Hillsdale NJ: Erlbaum.

Slobin, D. I. (1985). Cross-linguistic evidence for the language-making capacity. In D. I. Slobin (Ed.), *The cross-linguistic study of language acquisition: Vol. 2: Theoretical issues.* Hillsdale, NJ: Erlbaum.

Small, B. J., Hertzog, C., Hultsch, D. F., & Dixon, R. A. (2003). Stability and change in adult personality over 6 years: Findings from the Victoria longitudinal study. *Journal of Gerontology: Psychological Sciences, 58B,* P166–P176.

Smith, C. J., Beltran, A., Butts, D. M., & Kingson, E. R. (2000). Grandparents raising grandchildren: Emerging program and policy issues for the 21st century. *Journal of Gerontological Social Work, 34,* 81–94.

Smith, D. B., & Moen, P. (2004). Retirement satisfaction for retirees and their spouses: Do gender and the retirement decision-making process matter? *Journal of Family Issues, 25,* 262–285.

Smith, E. R., & Mackie, D. M. (2000). *Social psychology* (2nd ed.). Philadelphia: Psychology Press.

Smith, J., & Freund, A.M. (2002). The dynamics of possible selves in old age. *Journal of Journal of Gerontology: Psychological Sciences, 57B,* P492–P500.

Smith, L. (1992). The tyranny of America's old. *Fortune, 125*(1), 68–72.

Smith, L. B. (2000). How to learn words: An associative crane. In R. Golinkoff & K. Hirsch-Pasek (Eds.), *Breaking the word learning barrier* (pp. 51–80). Oxford, UK: Oxford University Press.

Smith, L. B., Thelen, E., Titzer, R., & McLin, D. (1999). Knowing in the context of acting: The task dynamics of the A-not-B error. *Psychological Review, 106,* 235–260.

Smith, L. L. (2001). On the relationship between goals and possible selves. *Dissertation Abstracts International: Section B: The Sciences and Engineering, 61,* 4465.

Smith, R. E., & Smoll, F. L. (1996). The coach as the focus of research and intervention in youth sports. In F. L. Smoll & R. E. Smith (Eds.), *Children and youth in sport: A biopsychological perspective* (pp. 125–141). Dubuque, IA: Brown & Benchmark.

Smith, R. E., & Smoll, F. L. (1997). Coaching the coaches: Youth sports as a scientific and applied behavioral setting. *Current Directions in Psychological Science, 6,* 16–21.

Smith, W. J., Howard, J. T., & Harrington, K. V. (2005). Essential formal mentor characteristics and functions in governmental and non-governmental organizations from the program administrator's and the mentor's perspective. *Public Personnel Management, 34,* 31–58.

Smoll, F. L., & Schutz, R. W. (1990). Quantifying gender differences in physical performance: A developmental perspective. *Developmental Psychology, 26,* 360–369.

Smoll, F. L., Smith, R. E., Barnett, N. P., & Everett, J. J. (1993). Enhancement of children's self-esteem through social support training for youth sport coaches. *Journal of Applied Psychology, 78,* 602–610.

Snedeker, B. (1982). *Hard knocks: Preparing youth for work.* Baltimore, MD: Johns Hopkins University Press.

Snow, C. W. (1998). *Infant development* (2nd ed.). Upper Saddle River, NJ: Prentice-Hall.

Snow, M. E., Jacklin, C. N., & Maccoby, E. E. (1983). Sex-of-child differences in father-child interaction at one year of age. *Child Development, 54,* 227–232.

Social Security Administration. (2005). *A summary of the 2005 annual reports.* Retrieved August 8, 2005, from http://www.ssa.gov/OACT/TRSUM/trsummary.html

Soederberg Miller, L. M., & Lachman, M. (1999, August). *Stress reactivity and cognitive performance in adulthood.* Paper presented at the annual meeting of the American Psychological Association, Boston.

Solano, N. H. (2001). Anxiety, depression, and older veterans: Implications for functional status. *Dissertation Abstract International Section B: The Sciences and Engineering, 61*(7-B), 3862.

Sommerville, J. A., & Woodward, A. L. (2005). Pulling out the intentional structure of action: The relation between action processing and action production in infancy. *Cognition, 95,* 1–30.

Sousa, P., Altran, S., & Medin, D. (2002). Essentialism and folkbiology: Further evidence from Brazil. *Journal of Cognition and Culture, 2,* 195–223.

Spearman, C. (1904). "General intelligence" objectively determined and measured. *American Journal of Psychology, 15,* 201–293.

Spelke, E. S. (1994). Initial knowledge: Six suggestions. *Cognition, 50,* 431–445.

Spencer, W. D., Steele, C. M., & Quinn, D. M. (1999). Stereotype threat and women's math performance. *Journal of Experimental Social Psychology, 35,* 4–28.

Spetner, N. B., & Olsho, L. W. (1990). Auditory frequency resolution in human infancy. *Child Development, 61,* 632–652.

Springer, K., & Keil, F. C. (1991). Early differentiation of causal mechanisms appropriate to biological and non-biological kinds. *Child Development, 62,* 767–781.

Srivastava, S., John, O. P., Gosling, S. D., & Potter, J. (2003). Development of personality in early and middle adulthood: Set like plaster or persistent change? *Journal of Personality and Social Psychology, 84,* 1041–1053.

Sroufe, L. A., & Waters, E. (1976). The ontogenesis of smiling and laughter: A perspective on the organization of development in infancy. *Psychological Review, 83,* 173–189.

St. George, I. M., Williams, S., & Silva, P. A. (1994). Body size and the menarche: The Dunedin study. *Journal of Adolescent Health, 15,* 573–576.

St. James-Roberts, I., & Plewis, I. (1996). Individual differences, daily fluctuations, and developmental changes in amounts of infant waking, fussing, crying, feeding, and sleeping. *Child Development, 67,* 2527–2450.

Staff, J., & Uggen, C. (2003). The fruits of good work: Early work experiences and adolescent deviance. *Journal of Research in Crime and Delinquency, 40,* 263–290.

Stafford, L., Kline, S. L., & Rankin, C. T. (2004). Married individuals, cohabiters, and cohabiters who marry: A longitudinal study of relational and individual well-being. *Journal of Social & Personal Relationships, 21,* 231–248.

Stanford, E. P., Happersett, C. J., Morton, D. J., Molgaard, C. A., & Peddecord, K. M. (1991). Early retirement and functional impairment from a multi-ethnic perspective. *Research on Aging, 13,* 5–38.

Stark, E. (1992, May). *From dependency to empowerment: Framing and reframing the battered woman.* Paper presented at the Second Annual Conference: Domestic Violence: The Family/Community Connection, State University of New York Division of Nursing, Stony Brook.

Starko, A. J. (1988). Effects of the Revolving Door Identification Model on creative productivity and self-efficacy. *Gifted Child Quarterly, 32,* 291–297.

Stauss, J. H. (1995). Reframing and refocusing American Indian family strengths. In C. K. Jacobson (Ed.), *American families: Issues in race and ethnicity* (pp. 105–118). New York: Garland.

Steele, C. M. (1997). A threat in the air: How stereotypes shape intellectual identity and performance. *American Psychologist, 52,* 613–629.

Steele, C. M., & Aronson, J. (1995). Stereotype threat and the intellectual test performance of African Americans. *Journal of Personality and Social Psychology, 69,* 797–811.

Steelman, J. D. (1994). Revision strategies employed by middle level students using computers. *Journal of Educational Computing Research, 11,* 141–152.

Steen, T. A., & Peterson, C. (2000, August). *Predicting young adults' return to the nest.* Paper presented at the annual meeting of the American Psychological Association, Washington, DC.

Stein, J. H., & Reiser, L. W. (1994). A study of White middle-class adolescent boys' responses to "semenarche" (the first ejacualtion). *Journal of Youth and Adolescence, 23,* 373–384.

Steinbart, E. J., Smith, C. O., Poorkaj, P., & Bird, T. D. (2001). Impact of DNA testing for early-onset familial Alzheimer disease and frontotemporal dementia. *Archives of Neurology, 58,* 1828–1831.

Steinberg, L. (1990). Autonomy, conflict, and harmony in the family relationship. In S. S. Feldman & G. R. Elliott (Eds.), *At the threshold: The developing adolescent.* Cambridge, MA: Harvard University Press.

Steinberg, L. D. (1999). *Adolescence* (5th ed.). Boston, MA: McGraw-Hill.

Steinberg, L., & Dornbusch, S. M. (1991). Negative correlates of part-time employment during adolescence: Replication and elaboration. *Developmental Psychology, 27,* 304–313.

Steinberg, L., Fegley, S., & Dornbusch, S. M. (1993). Negative impact of part-time work on adolescent adjustment: Evidence from a longitudinal study. *Developmental Psychology, 29,* 171–180.

Steinberg, L., Grisso, T., Woolard, J., Cauffman, E., Scott, E., Graham, S., Lexcen, F., Reppucci, N., & Schwartz, R. (2003). Juveniles' competence to stand trial as adults. *SRCD Policy Report, 17*(4).

Steiner, J. E., Glaser, D., Hawilo, M. E., & Berridge, K. C. (2001). Comparative expression of hedonic impact: Affective reactions to taste by human infants and other primates. *Neuroscience & Biobehavioral Reviews, 25,* 53–74.

Stephens, M. A. P., & Clark, S. L. (1996). Interpersonal relationships in multi-generational families. In N. Vanzetti & S. Duck (Eds.), *A lifetime of relationships* (pp. 431–454). Pacific Grove, CA: Brooks/Cole.

Stephens, M. A. P., & Franks, M. M. (1999). Intergenerational relationships in later-life families: Adult daughters and sons as caregivers to aging parents. In J. C. Cavanaugh & S. K. Whitbourne (Eds.), *Gerontology: An interdisciplinary perspective* (pp. 329–354). New York: Oxford University Press.

Stephens, M. A. P., & Townsend, A. L. (1997). Stress of parent care: Positive and negative effects of women's other roles. *Psychology and Aging, 12,* 376–386.

Stephens, M. A. P., Townsend, A. L., Martire, L. M., & Druley, J. A. (2001). Balancing parent care with other roles: Interrole conflict of adult daughter caregivers. *Journal of Gerontology: Psychological Sciences, 56B,* P24–P34.

Stern, M., & Karraker, K. H. (1989). Sex stereotyping of infants: A review of gender labeling studies. *Sex Roles, 20,* 501–522.

Sternberg, C. R., & Campos, J. (1990). The development of anger expressions in infancy. In N. Stein, B. Leventhal, & T. Trabasso (Eds.), *Psychological and biological approaches to emotion.* Hillsdale, NJ: Erlbaum.

Sternberg, R. (2003). Issues in the theory and measurement of successful intelligence: A reply to Brody. *Intelligence, 31,* 331–337.

Sternberg, R. J. (1985). *Beyond IQ: A triarchic theory of human intelligence.* Cambridge, UK: Cambridge University Press.

Sternberg, R. J. (1986). A triangular theory of love. *Psychological Review, 93,* 119–135.

Sternberg, R. J. (1999). The theory of successful intelligence. *Review of General Psychology, 3,* 292–316.

Sternberg, R. J. (2002). Successful intelligence: A new approach to leadership. In R. E. Riggio & S. E. Murphy (Eds.), *Multiple intelligences and leadership* (pp. 9–28). Mahwah, NJ: Erlbaum.

Sternberg, R. J., & Grigorenko, E. L. (2000). Practical intelligence and its development. In R. Bar-On & D. A. Parker (Eds.), *The handbook of emotional intelligence: Theory, development, assessment, and application at home, school, and in the workplace* (pp. 215–243). San Francisco: Jossey-Bass.

Sternberg, R. J., & Grigorenko, E. L. (2002). *Dynamic testing: The nature and measurement of learning potential.* New York: Cambridge University Press.

Sternberg, R. J., & Grigorenko, E. L. (Eds.). (2004). *Culture and competence: Contexts of life success.* Washington, DC: American Psychological Association.

Sternberg, R. J., & Kaufman, J. C. (1998). Human abilities. *Annual Review of Psychology, 49,* 479–502.

Sternberg, R. J., & Lubart, T. I. (2001). Wisdom and creativity. In J. E. Birren & K. W. Schaie (Eds.), *Handbook of the psychology of aging* (5th ed., pp. 500–522). San Diego, CA: Academic Press.

Sterns, A. A., Marsh, B. A., & McDaniel, M. A. (1994). *Age and job satisfaction; A comprehensive review and meta-analysis.* Unpublished manuscript, University of Akron.

Sterns, H. L., & Gray, J. H. (1999). Work, leisure, and retirement. In J. C. Cavanaugh & S. K. Whitbourne (Eds.), *Gerontology: Interdisciplinary perspectives.* New York: Oxford University Press.

Stevenson, H. W., & Lee, S. (1990). Contexts of achievement. *Monographs of the Society for Research in Child Development, 55* (Serial No. 221).

Stevenson, H. W., & Stigler, J. W. (1992). *The learning gap.* New York: Summit Books.

Steward, R. J., & Krieshok, T. S. (1991). A cross-cultural study of vocational identity: Does a college education mean the same for all persisters? *Journal of College Student Development, 32,* 562–563.

Stewart, L., & Pascual-Leone, J. (1992). Mental capacity constraints and the development of moral reasoning. *Journal of Experimental Child Psychology, 54,* 251–287.

Stewart R. B., Mobley, L. A., Van Tuyl, S. S., & Salvador, W. A. (1987). The firstborns' adjustment to the birth of a sibling: A longitudinal assessment. *Child Development, 58,* 341–355.

Stice, E., Presnell, K., & Bearman, S. K. (2001). Relation of early menarche to depession, eating disorders, substance abuse, and comorbid psychopathology among adolescent girls. *Developmental Psychology, 37,* 608–619.

Stice, E., & Shaw, H. (2004). Eating disorder prevention programs: A meta-analytic review. *Psychological Bulletin, 130,* 206–227.

Stier, H., & Lewin-Epstein, N. (2000). Women's part-time employment and gender inequality in the family. *Journal of Family Issues, 21,* 390–410.

Stifter, C. A., & Fox, N. A. (1990). Infant reactivity: Physiological correlates of newborn and 5-month temperament. *Developmental Psychology, 26,* 582–588.

Stiles, J. (2001). Neural plasticity and cognitive development. *Developmental Neuropsychology, 18,* 237–272.

Stiles, J., Reilly, J., Paul, B., & Moses, P. (2005). Cognitive development following early brain injury: Evidence for neural adaptation. *Trends in Cognitive Sciences, 9,* 136–143.

Stine-Morrow, E. A. L., & Soederberg Miller, L. M. (1999). Basic cognitive processes. In J. C. Cavanaugh & S. K. Whitbourne (Eds.), *Gerontology: An interdisciplinary perspective.* New York: Oxford University Press.

Stoolmiller, M. (2001). Synergistic interaction of child manageability problems and parent-discipline tactics in predicting future growth in externalizing behavior for boys. *Developmental Psychology, 37,* 814–825.

Stoolmiller, M., Eddy, J. M., & Reid, J. B. (2000). Detecting and describing preventive intervention effects in a universal school-based randomized trial targeting delinquent and violent behavior. *Journal of Consulting and Clinical Psychology, 68,* 296–306.

Strachan, E., Pyszczynski, T., Greenberg, J., & Solomon, S. (2001). Coping with the inevitability of death: Terror management and mismanagement. In C. R. Snyder (Ed.), *Coping with stress: Effective people and processes* (pp. 114–136). New York: Oxford University Press.

Strano, D. A., Cuomo, M. J., & Venable, R. H. (2004). Predictors of undergraduate student binge drinking. *Journal of College Counseling, 7,* 50–63.

Strauss-Blasche, G., Ekmekcioglu, C., & Marktl, W. (2002). Moderating effects of vacation on reactions to work and domestic stress. *Leisure Sciences, 24,* 237–249.

Strayer, J., & Roberts, W. (2004). Children's anger, emotional expressiveness, and empathy: Relations with parents' empathy, emotional expressiveness, and parenting practices. *Social Development, 13,* 229–254.

Streissguth, A. P., Barr, H. M., Sampson, P. D., & Bookstein, F. L. (1994). Prenatal alcohol and offspring development: The first fourteen years. *Drugs & Alcohol Dependence, 36,* 89–99.

Stroebe, M. S., Gergen, M., Gergen, K., & Stroebe, W. (1996). Broken hearts or broken bonds? In D. Klass, P. R. Silverman, & S. L. Nickman (Eds.), *Continuing bonds: New understandings of grief* (pp. 31–44). Washington, DC: Taylor & Francis.

Stroebe, M. S., & Schut, H. (1999). The dual process model of bereavement: Rationale and description. *Death Studies, 23,* 197–224.

Stroebe, M. S., & Schut, H. (2001). Models of coping with bereavement: A review. In M. S. Stroebe, R. O. Hansson, W. Stroebe, & H. Schut (Eds.), *Handbook of bereavement research: Consequences, coping, and care* (pp. 375–403). Washington, DC: American Psychological Association.

Stroebe, M., Schut, H., & Stroebe, W. (2005). Attachment in coping with bereavement: A theoretical integration. *Review of General Psychology, 9,* 48–66.

Stroebe, W., & Schut, H. (2001). Risk factors in bereavement outcome: A methodological and empirical review. In

M. S. Stroebe, R. O. Hansson, W. Stroebe, & H. Schut (Eds.), *Handbook of bereavement research: Consequences, coping, and care* (pp. 349–371). Washington, DC: American Psychological Association.

Strough, J., & Berg, C. A. (2000). Goals as a mediator of gender differences in high-affiliation dyadic conversations. *Developmental Psychology, 36,* 117–125.

Stuckey, J. C. (2001). Blessed assurance: The role of religion and spirituality in Alzheimer's disease caregiving and other significant life events. *Journal of Aging Studies, 15,* 69–84.

Stunkard, A. J., Sorensen, T. I. A., Hanis, C., Teasdale, T. W., Chakraborty, R, Schull, W. J., & Schulsinger, F. (1986). An adoption study of human obesity. *New England Journal of Medicine, 314,* 193–198.

Sullivan, L. W. (1987). The risks of the sickle-cell trait: Caution and common sense. *New England Journal of Medicine, 317,* 830–831.

Sullivan, S. A., & Birch, L. L. (1990). Pass the sugar, pass the salt: Experience dictates preference. *Developmental Psychology, 26,* 546–551.

Sulloway, F. J. (1995). Birth order and evolutionary psychology: A meta-analytic overview. *Psychological Inquiry, 6,* 75–80.

Summerville, M. B., Kaslow, N. J., & Doepke, K. J. (1996). Psychopathology and cognitive and family functioning in suicidal African-American adolescents. *Current Directions in Psychological Science, 5,* 7–11.

Sundet, J. M., Barlaug, D. G., & Torjussen, T. M. (2004). The end of the Flynn effect? A study of secular trends in mean intelligence scores of Norwegian conscripts during half a century. *Intelligence, 32,* 349–362.

Super, C. M. (1981). Cross-cultural research on infancy. In H. C. Triandis and A. Heron (Eds.), *Handbook of cross-cultural psychology, Vol. 4: Developmental psychology.* Boston: Allyn & Bacon.

Super, C. M., Herrera, M. G., & Mora, J. O. (1990). Long-term effects of food supplementation and psychosocial intervention on the physical growth of Colombian infants at risk of malnutrition. *Child Development, 61,* 29–49.

Super, D. E. (1957). *The psychology of careers.* New York: Harper & Row.

Super, D. E. (1976). *Career education and the meanings of work.* Washington, DC: U. S. Offices of Education.

Super, D. E. (1980). A lifespan, life space approach to career development. *Journal of Vocational Behavior, 16,* 282–298.

Surgeon General. (2001). *Women and smoking: A report of the Surgeon General 2001.* Retrieved January 10, 2005, from http://www.cdc.gov/tobacco/sgr_forwomen.htm

Suzuki, L., & Aronson, J. (2005). The cultural malleability of intelligence and its impact on the racial/ethnic hierarchy. *Psychology, Public Policy, and Law, 11,* 320–327.

Suzuki, Y., Yamamoto, S., Umegaki, H., Onishi, J., Mogi, N., Fujishiro, H., & Iguchi, A. (2004). Smell identification test as an indicator for cognitive impairment in Alzheimer's disease. *International Journal of Geriatric Psychiatry, 19,* 727–733.

Sykes, D. H., Hoy, E. A., Bill, J. M., McClure, B. G., et al. (1997). Behavioral adjustment in school of very low birthweight children. *Journal of Child Psychology and Psychiatry and Allied Disciplines, 38,* 315–325.

Taaffe, D. R., Jin, I. H., Vu, T. H., Hoffman, A. R., & Marcus, R. (1996). Lack of effect of recombinant human growth hormone (GH) on muscle morphology and GH-insulin-like growth factor expression in resistance-trained elderly men. *Journal of Clinical Endocrinology and Metabolism, 81,* 421–425.

Tadros, G., & Salib, E. (2001). Carer's views on passive euthanasia. *International Journal of Geriatric Psychiatry, 16,* 230–231.

Talaga, J. A., & Beehr, T. A. (1995). Are there gender differences in predicting retirement decisions? *Journal of Applied Psychology, 80,* 16–28.

Talbott, M. M. (1998). Older widows' attitudes towards men and remarriage. *Journal of Aging Studies, 12,* 429–449.

Tamis-LeMonda, C. S., & Bornstein, M. H. (1996). Variation in children's exploratory, nonsymbolic, and symbolic play: An explanatory multidimensional framework. In C. Rovee-Collier & L. P. Lipsitt (Eds.), *Advances in infancy research* (Vol. 10). Norwood, NJ: Ablex.

Tamis-Lemonda, C. S., & Bornstein, M. H. (2002). Maternal responsiveness and early language acquisition. In R. V. Kail & H. W. Reese (Eds.), *Advances in child development and behavior* (Vol. 29, pp. 90–127). San Diego, CA: Academic Press.

Tang, T. L. P., & McCollum, S. L. (1996). Sexual harassment in the workplace. *Public Personnel Management, 25,* 53–58.

Tanner, J. M. (1970). Physical growth. In P. H. Mussen (Ed.), *Carmichael's manual of child psychology* (3rd ed.). New York: Wiley.

Tanner, J. M. (1990). *Fetus into man: Physical growth from conception to maturity* (2nd ed.). Cambridge, MA: Harvard University Press.

Taub, G. E., Hayes, B. G., Cunningham, W. R., & Sivo, S. A. (2001). Relative roles of cognitive ability and practical intelligence in the prediction of success. *Psychological Reports, 88,* 931–942.

Taylor, J. L., O'Hara, R., Mumenthaler, M. S., Rosen, A. C., & Yesavage, Jerome A. (2005). Cognitive ability, expertise, and age differences in following air-traffic control instructions. *Psychology and Aging, 20,* 117–133.

Taylor, M., Carlson, S. M., Maring, B. L., Gerow, L., & Charley, C. M. (2004). The characteristics and correlates of fantasy in school-age children: Imaginary companions, impersonation, and social understanding. *Developmental Psychology, 40,* 1173–1187.

Taylor, M., Cartwright, B. S., & Carlson, S. M. (1993). A developmental investigation of children's imaginary companions. *Developmental Psychology, 29,* 276–285.

Taylor, R. J., Hardison, C. B., & Chatters, L. M. (1996). Kin and nonkin as sources of informal assistance. In H. W. Neighbors & J. S. Jackson (Eds.), *Mental health in Black America* (pp. 130–145). Thousand Oaks, CA: Sage.

Teichman, Y. (2001). The development of Israeli children's images of Jews and Arabs and their expression in human figure drawings. *Developmental Psychology, 37,* 749–761.

Teisseyre, N., Mullet, E., & Sorum, P. C. (2005). Under what conditions is euthanasia acceptable to lay people and health professionals? *Social Science and Medicine, 60,* 357–368.

Tenenbaum, H. R., & Leaper, C. (2002). Are parents' gender schemas related to their children's gender-related cognitions? A meta-analysis. *Developmental Psychology, 38,* 615–630.

Terkel, S. (1974). *Working*. New York: Pantheon Books.

Terman, M. (1994). Light therapy. In M. H. Kryger, T. Roth, & W. C. Dement (Eds.), *Principles and practice of sleep medicine* (2nd ed., pp. 1012–1029). Philadelphia: Saunders.

Tesch-Römer, C. (1997). Psychological effects of hearing aid use in older adults. *Journal of Gerontology: Psychological Sciences, 52B*, P127–P138.

Teti, D. M. (2005). Intervention for premature infants. In C. B. Fisher & R. M. Lerner (Eds.), *Encyclopedia of applied developmental science* (Vol. 1, pp. 582–586). Thousand Oaks CA: Sage.

Thelen, E., & Smith, L. B. (1998). Dynamic systems theories. In W. Damon (Ed.), *Handbook of Child Psychology* (Vol. 1). New York: Wiley.

Thelen, E., & Ulrich, B. D. (1991). Hidden skills. *Monographs of the Society for Research in Child Development, 56* (Serial No. 223).

Thelen, E., Ulrich, B. D., & Jensen, J. L. (1989). The developmental origins of locomotion. In M. H. Woollacott and A. Shumway-Cook (Eds.), *Development of posture and gait across the lifespan.* Columbia, SC: University of South Carolina Press.

Thiessen, E. D., & Saffran, J. R. (2003). When cues collide: Use of stress and statistical cues to word boundaries by 7- to 9-month-old infants. *Developmental Psychology, 39,* 706–716.

Thomas, A., Chess, S., & Birch, H. G. (1968). *Temperament and behavior disorders in children.* New York: New York University Press.

Thomas, D. A. (1990). The impact of race on managers' experiences of developmental relationships (mentoring and sponsorship): An intra-organizational study. *Journal of Organizational Behavior, 11,* 479–492.

Thomas, J. W., Bol, L., Warkentin, R. W., Wilson, M., Strage, A., & Rohwer, W. D. (1993). Interrelationships among students' study activities, self-concept of academic ability, and achievement as a function of characteristics of high-school biology courses. *Applied Cognitive Psychology, 7,* 499–532.

Thomas, N. G., & Berk, L. E. (1981). Effects of school environments on the development of young children's creativity. *Child Development, 52,* 1152–1162.

Thompson, L. W., Gallagher-Thompson, D., Futterman, A., Gilewski, M. J., & Peterson, J. (1991). The effects of late-life spousal bereavement over a 30-month interval. *Psychology and Aging, 6,* 434–441.

Thompson, R. A. (1998). Early socio-personality development. In N. Eisenberg (Ed.), *Handbook of child psychology, Vol. 3: Social, emotional, and personality development* (5th ed., pp. 25–104). New York: Wiley.

Thompson, R. A. (2000). The legacy of early attachments. *Child Development, 71,* 145–152.

Thompson, R. A., Laible, D. J., & Ontai, L. L. (2003). Early understandings of emotion, morality, and self: Developing a working model. *Advances in Child Development and Behavior, 31,* 137–172.

Thompson, R. A., & Limber, S. (1991). "Social anxiety" in infancy: Stranger wariness and separation distress. In H. Leitenberg (Ed.), *Handbook of social and evaluation anxiety.* New York: Plenum.

Thomson, E., & Colella, U. (1992). Cohabitation and marital stability: Quality or commitment? *Journal of Marriage and the Family, 54,* 259–267.

Thorne, A. (2000). Personal memory telling and personality development. *Personality and Social Psychology Review, 4,* 45–56.

Thorson, J. A., & Powell, F. C. (2000a). Death anxiety in younger and older adults. In A. Tomer (Ed.), *Death attitudes and the older adult: Theories, concepts, and applications* (pp. 123–136). Philadelphia: Brunner-Routledge.

Thorson, J. A., & Powell, F. C. (2000b). Developmental aspects of death anxiety and religion. In J. A. Thorson (Ed.), *Perspectives on spiritual well-being and aging* (pp. 142–158). Springfield, IL: Charles C. Thomas.

Thurstone, L. L., & Thurstone, T. G. (1941). Factorial studies of intelligence. *Psychometric Monograph,* No. 2.

Tiffany, D. W., & Tiffany, P. G. (1996). Control across the lifespan: A model for understanding self-direction. *Journal of Adult Development, 3,* 93–108.

Timiras, P. (2002). *Physiological bases of aging and geriatrics* (3rd ed.). Boca Raton, FL: CRC Press.

Tincoff, R., & Jusczyk, P. W. (1999). Some beginnings of word comprehension in 6-month-olds. *Psychological Science, 10,* 172–175.

Tolan, P. H., Gorman-Smith, D., & Henry, D. B. (2003). The developmental ecology of urban males' youth violence. *Developmental Psychology, 39,* 274–291.

Tolmacz, R., Goldzweig, G., & Guttman, R. (2004). Attachment styles and the ideal image of a mate. *European Psychologist, 9,* 87–95.

Torgesen, J. K. (2004). Learning disabilities: An historical and conceptual overview. In B. Y. L. Wong (Ed.), *Learning about learning disabilities* (3rd ed., pp. 3–40). San Diego: Elsevier Academic Press.

Trainor, L. J., Austin, C. M., & Desjardins, R. N. (2000). Is infant-directed speech prosody a result of the vocal expression of emotion? *Psychological Science, 11,* 188–195.

Trainor, L. J., & Heinmiller, B. M. (1998). The development of evaluative responses to music: Infants prefer to listen to consonance over dissonance. *Infant Behavior and Development, 21,* 77–88.

Trainor, L. J., Wu, L., & Tsang, C. D. (2004). Long-term memory for music: Infants remember tempo and timbre. *Developmental Science, 7,* 289–296.

Treiman, R., & Kessler, B. (2003). The role of letter names in the acquisition of literacy. *Advances in Child Development and Behavior, 31,* 105–135.

Tremblay, R. E., Schall, B., Boulerice, B., Arsonault, L., Soussignan, R. G., & Paquette, D. (1998). Testosterone, physical aggression, and dominance and physical development in adolescence. *International Journal of Behavioral Development, 22,* 753–777.

Troll, L. E., & Fingerman, K. L. (1996). Connections between parents and their adult children. In C. Magai & S. H. McFadden (Eds.), *Handbook of emotion, adult development, and aging* (pp. 185–205). San Diego, CA: Academic Press.

Trost, S. G., Pate, R. R., Sallis, J. F., Freedson, P. S., Taylor, W. C., Dowda, M., et al. (2002). Age and gender differences in objectively measured physical activity in youth. *Medicine and Science in Sports and Exercise, 34,* 350–355.

Trujillo, K. M., Walsh, D. M., & Brougham, R. R. (1991, June). *Age differences in exercise motivation.* Paper presented at the annual meeting of the American Psychological Society, Washington, DC.

Truog, R. D. (2004). *Brain death: At once "well settled" and "persistently unresolved."* Retrieved August 27, 2005, from http://www.ama-assn.org/ama/pub/category/12715.html

Tsao, T.-C. (2004). New models for future retirement: A study of college/university-linked retirement communities. *Dissertation Abstracts International Section A: Humanities and Social Sciences, 64*(10-A), 3511.

Turati, C. (2004). Why faces are not special to newborns: An alternative account of the face preference. *Current Directions in Psychological Science, 13*, 5–8.

Turiel, E. (2006). The development of morality. In W. Damon & R. M. Lerner (Eds.), *Handbook of child psychology* (Vol. 3, 6th ed.). New York: Wiley.

Turiel, E., & Neff, K. (2000). Religion, culture, and beliefs about reality in moral reasoning. In K. S. Rosengren, C. N. Johnson, & P. L. Harris (Eds.), *Imagining the impossible: Magical, scientific, and religious thinking in children* (pp. 269–304). New York: Cambridge University Press.

Turkheimer, E., & Waldron, M. (2000). Nonshared environment: A theoretical, methodological, and quantitative review. *Psychological Bulletin, 126*, 78–108.

Turley, R. N. L. (2003). Are children of young mothers disadvantaged because of their mother's age or family background? *Child Development, 74*, 465–474.

Twenge, J. M., & Campbell, W. K. (2001). Age and birth cohort differences in self-esteem: A cross-temporal meta-analysis. *Personality & Social Psychology Review, 5*, 321–344.

Tyson-Rawson, K. J. (1996). Adolescent responses to the death of a parent. In C. A. Coor & D. E. Balk (Eds.), *Handbook of adolescent death and bereavement* (pp. 155–172). New York: Springer.

Ucello, C. E. (1998). *Factors influencing retirement: Their implications for raising retirement age.* Washington, DC: Washington Public Policy Institute.

Umbel, V. M., Pearson, B. Z., Fernandez, M. C., & Oller, D. K. (1992). Measuring bilingual children's receptive vocabularies. *Child Development, 63*, 1012–1020.

Underlid, K. (2005). Poverty and experiences of social devaluation: A qualitative interview study of 25 long-standing recipients of social security payments. *Scandinavian Journal of Psychology, 46*, 273–283.

UNICEF. (2004). *The state of the world's children 2005.* New York: Author.

United Nations. (2002). *Demographic yearbook, 2002.* Retrieved June 12, 2005, from http://unstats.un.org/unsd/demographic/products/dyb/dyb2.htm

Upchurch, S., & Mueller, W. H. (2005). Spiritual influences on ability to engage in self-care activities among older African Americans. *International Journal of Aging and Human Development, 60*, 77–94.

Updegraff, K. A., Thayer, S. M., Whiteman, S. D., Denning D. J., & McHale, S. M. (2005). Aggression in adolescents' sibling relationships: Links to sibling and parent-adolescent relationship quality. *Family Relations: Interdisciplinary Journal of Applied Family Studies, 54*, 373–385.

Urberg, K. A., Degirmencioglu, S. M., & Pilgrim, C. (1997). Close friend and group influence on adolescent cigarette smoking and alcohol use. *Developmental Psychology, 33*, 834–844.

U.S. Census Bureau. (1995). *Statistical abstract of the United States* (115th ed.). Washington, DC: Government Printing Office.

U.S. Census Bureau. (2000). *Statistical abstract of the United States.* Washington, DC: Government Printing Office.

U.S. Census Bureau. (2003). *Married-couple and unmarried-partner households: 2000.* Retrieved June 12, 2005, from http://www.census.gov/prod/2003pubs/censr-5.pdf

U.S. Census Bureau. (2005a). *Facts for Features: Mother's Day, 2005.* Retrieved March 29, 2005, from http://www.census.gov/Press-Release/www/releases/archives/facts_for_features_special_editions/004109.html

U.S. Census Bureau. (2005b). *Statistical abstract of the United States 2004–2005.* Washington, DC: Government Printing Office.

U.S. Department of Agriculture. (2005a). *Dietary guidelines for Americans, 2005.* Retrieved June 8, 2005, from http://www.health.gov/dietaryguidelines/dga2005/document/

U.S. Department of Agriculture. (2005b). *Expenditures on children by families, 2004.* Retrieved June 12, 2005, from http://www.cnpp.usda.gov/Crc/crc2004.pdf

U.S. Department of Health and Human Services. (1997). *Vital statistics of the United States, 1994: Vol. 2. Mortality* (Part A). Hyattsville, MD: U.S. Public Health Service.

U.S. Department of Health and Human Services. (2000). *Reducing tobacco us: A report of the surgeon general—Executive summary.* Atlanta, GA: U.S. Department of Health and Human Services, Centers for Disease Control and Prevention, National Center for Chronic Disease Prevention and Health Promotion, Office on Smoking and Health.

U.S. Department of Health and Human Services. (2001). *The Surgeon General's call to action to prevent and decrease overweight and obesity.* Rockville MD: Author.

U.S. Department of Health and Human Services. (2004a). *2002 assisted reproductive technology success rates.* Washington, DC: Author.

U.S. Department of Health and Human Services. (2004b). Youth risk behavior surveilliance. *Morbidity and Mortality Weekly Report, 53* (No. SS-2). Atlanta GA: Centers for Disease Control and Prevention.

U.S. Department of Health and Human Services. (2005). *Child maltreatment 2004: Summary of key findings.* Washington DC: National Clearinghouse on Child Abuse and Neglect Information.

U.S. Department of Justice. (2001). *A guide to disability rights laws.* Retrieved June 18, 2005, from http://www.usdoj.gov/crt/ada/cguide.pdf

U.S. Department of Labor. (2000). *Report on the youth labor force.* Washington DC: Author.

U.S. Department of Labor. (2004, October). *Monthly Labor Review.* Retrieved July 2, 2005, from http://www.bls.gov/opub/ted/2004/oct/wk4/art01.htm

U.S. Department of Labor. (2005a). *Current population survey.* Retrieved July 3, 2005, from http://www.bls.gov/cps/

U.S. Department of Labor. (2005b). *Employment characteristics of families in 2004.* Retrieved July 3, 2005, from http://www.bls.gov/news.release/pdf/famee.pdf

U.S. Department of Labor. (2005c). *Nontraditional occupations for women, 2004.* Retrieved July 2, 2005, from http://www.dol.gov/wb/factsheets/nontra2004.htm

U.S. Department of Labor. (2005d). *Women in the labor force 2004.* Retrieved July 2, 2005, from http://www.dol.gov/wb/factsheets/Qf-laborforce-04.htm

U.S. Department of Labor. (2005e). *Retirement plans, benefits, and savings.* Retrieved August 8, 2005, from http://www.dol.gov/dol/topic/retirement/index.htm

U.S. Department of State. (2002). *Country reports on human rights practices, 2001.* Retrieved from http://www.state.gov/g/drl/rls/hrrpt/2001/

Usita, P. M., & Blieszner, R. (2002). Immigrant family strengths: Meeting communication challenges. *Journal of Family Issues, 23,* 266–286.

Vacca v. Quill 521 US 793 (1997).

Vaillant, G. E. (1977). *Adaptation to life.* Boston: Little, Brown.

Valkenburg, P. M., & van der Voort, T. H. A. (1994). Influence of TV on daydreaming and creative imagination: A review of research. *Psychological Bulletin, 116,* 316–339.

Valkenburg, P. M., & van der Voort, T. H. A. (1995). The influence of television on children's daydreaming styles: A 1-year-panel study. *Communication Research, 22,* 267–287.

Valois, R. F., Dunham, A. C. A., Jackson, K. L., Waller, J. (1999). Association between employment and substance abuse behaviors among public high school adolescents. *Journal of Adolescent Health, 25,* 256–263.

Valverius, E., Nilstun, T., & Nilsson, B. (2000). Palliative care, assisted suicide and euthanasia: Nationwide questionnaire to Swedish physicians. *Palliative Medicine, 14,* 141–148.

van den Boom, D. C. (1994). The influence of temperament and mothering on attachment and exploration: An experimental manipulation of sensitive responsiveness among lower-class mothers with irritable infants. *Child Development, 65,* 1457–1477.

van den Boom, D. C. (1995). Do first-year intervention effects endure? Follow-up during toddlerhood of a sample of Dutch irritable infants. *Child Development, 66,* 1798–1816.

van der Geest, S. (2004). Dying peacefully: Considering good death and bad death in Kwahu-Tafo, Ghana. *Social Science and Medicine, 58,* 899–911.

van der Mark, I. L., van IJzendoorn, M. H., & Bakermans-Kranenburg, M. J. (2002). Development of empathy in girls during the second year of life: Associations with parenting, attachment, and temperament. *Social Development, 11,* 451–468.

van Dierendonck, D., Garssen, B., & Visser, A. (2005). Burnout prevention through personal growth. *International Journal of Stress Management, 12,* 62–77.

Van Hof, P., van der Kamp, J., & Savelsbergh, G. J. P. (2002). The relation of unimanual and bimanual reaching to crossing the midline. *Child Development, 73,* 1352–1362.

Van IJzendoorn, M. H., Vereijken, C. M. J. L., Bakermans-Kranenburg, M. J., & Riksen-Walraven, J. (2004). Assessing attachment security with the Attachment Q Sort: Meta-analytic evidence for the validity of the observer AQS. *Child Development, 75,* 1188–1213.

van Solinge, H., & Henkens, K. (2005). Couples' adjustment to retirement: A multi-actor panel study. *Journal of Gerontology: Social Sciences, 60,* S11–S20.

Vandello, J. A. (2000). Domestic violence in cultural context: Male honor, female fidelity, and loyalty. *Dissertation Abstracts International: Section B: The Sciences and Engineering, 61*(5-B), 2821.

Vander Wal, J. S., & Thelen, M. H. (2000). Eating and body image concerns among obese and average-weight children. *Additive Behaviors, 25,* 775–778.

Vazsonyi, A. T., Hibbert, J. R., & Snider, J. B. (2003). Exotic enterprise no more? Adolescent reports of family and parenting practices from youth in four countries. *Journal of Research on Adolescence, 13,* 129–160.

Ventura, S. J., Martin, J. A., Hartin, A., Taffell, S. M., Mathews, T. J., & Clarke, S. C. (1994). Advance report of final natality statistics, 1992. *National Center for Health Statistics, Monthly Vital Statistics Report, 43.*

Verhaeghen, P., & Salthouse, T. A. (1997). Meta-analysis of age–cognition relations in adulthood: Establishment of linear and non-linear age effects and structural models. *Psychological Bulletin, 122,* 231–249.

Verma, I. M. (1990). Gene therapy. *Scientific American, 263,* 68–84.

Vicary, J. R., & Karshin, C. M. (2002). College alcohol abuse: A review of the problems, issues, and prevention approaches. *Journal of Primary Prevention, 22,* 299–331.

Vickio, C. J., Cavanaugh, J. C., & Attig, T. (1990). Perceptions of grief among university students. *Death Studies, 14,* 231–240.

Viinamaki, H., Koskela, K., & Niskanen, L. (1996). Rapidly declining mental well-being during unemployment. *European Journal of Psychiatry, 10,* 215–221.

Villa, R. F., & Jaime, A. (1993). *La fé de la gente.* In M. Sotomayor & A. Garcia (Eds.), *Elderly Latinos: Issues and solutions for the 21st century.* Washington, DC: National Hispanic Council on Aging.

Vinters, H. V. (2001). Aging and the human nervous system. In J. E. Birren & K. W. Schaie (Eds.), *Handbook of the psychology of aging* (5th ed., pp. 135–160). San Diego, CA: Academic Press.

Visher, E. B., Visher, J. S., & Pasley, K. (2003). Remarriage families and stepparenting. In F. Walsh (Ed.), *Normal family processes* (pp. 153–175). New York: Guilford.

Vitaro, F., Tremblay, R. E., Kerr, M., Pagani, L., & Bukowski, W. M. (1997). Disruptiveness, friends' characteristics, and delinquency in early adolescence: A test of two competing models of development. *Child Development, 68,* 676–689.

Vitulano, L. A. (2005). Delinquency. In C. B. Fisher & R. M. Lerner (Eds.), *Encyclopedia of applied developmental science* (Vol. 1, pp. 327–328). Thousand Oaks CA: Sage.

Voisin, T., Reynish, E., Portet, F., Feldman, H., & Vellas, B. (2005). What are the treatment options for patients with severe Alzheimer's disease? *CNS Drugs, 18,* 575–583.

Volling, B. L., & Belsky, J. (1992). The contribution of mother-child and father-child relationships to the quality of sibling interaction: A longitudinal study. *Child Development, 63,* 1209–1222.

Vorhees, C. V., & Mollnow, E. (1987). Behavior teratogenesis: Long-term influences on behavior. In J. D. Osofsky (Ed.), *Handbook of infant development* (2nd ed.). New York: Wiley.

Voyer, D., Voyer, S., & Bryden, M. P. (1995). Magnitude of sex differences in spatial abilities: A meta-analysis and consideration of critical variables. *Psychological Bulletin, 117,* 250–270.

Vygotsky, L. S. (1986). *Thought and language* (A. Kozulin, Trans.). Cambridge, MA: MIT Press. (Original work published in 1934)

Wachs, T. D. (1983). The use and abuse of environment in behavior-genetic research. *Child Development, 54,* 396–407.

Wachs, T. D., & Bates, J. E. (2001). Temperament. In G. Bremner & A. Fogel (Eds.), *Blackwell handbook of infant development* (pp. 465–501). Malden, MA: Blackwell.

Wadlington, W. (2005). Family law in America. *Family Court Review, 43,* 178–179.

Wagner, R. K., Torgesen, J. K., Rashotte, C. A., Hecht, S. A., Barker, T. A., Burgess, S. R., et al. (1999). Changing relations between phonological processing abilities and word-level reading as children develop from beginning to skilled readers: A 5-year longitudinal study. *Developmental Psychology, 33*, 468–479.

Wahl, H.-W. (2001). Environmental influences on aging and behavior. In J. E. Birren & K. W. Schaie (Eds.), *Handbook of the psychology of aging* (5th ed., pp. 215–237). San Diego, CA: Academic Press.

Walberg, H. J. (1995). General practices. In G. Cawelti (Ed.), *Handbook of research on improving student achievement*. Arlington VA: Educational Research Service.

Waldrop, D. P., & Weber, J. A. (2001). From grandparent to caregiver: The stress and satisfaction of raising grandchildren. *Families in Society, 82*, 461–472.

Walker, L. E. A. (1984). *The battered woman syndrome.* New York: Springer.

Walker, L. J. (1980). Cognitive and perspective-taking prerequisites for moral development. *Child Development, 51*, 131–139.

Walker, L. J., Hennig, K. H., & Krettenauer, T. (2000). Parent and peer contexts for children's moral reasoning development. *Child Development, 71*, 1033–1048.

Walker, L. J., & Taylor, J. H. (1991). Family interactions and the development of moral reasoning. *Child Development, 62*, 264–283.

Wall, S., & Arden, H. (1990). *Wisdomkeepers: Meetings with Native American spiritual elders.* Hillsboro, OR: Beyond Words.

Wallace, J. E. (2001). The benefits of mentoring for female lawyers. *Journal of Vocational Behavior, 58*, 366–391.

Wallace, J. I., & Schwartz, R. S. (1994). Involuntary weight loss in the elderly. In R. R. Watson (Ed.), *Handbook of nutrition in the aged* (pp. 99–111). Boca Raton, FL: CRC Press.

Wallerstein, J. S., & Lewis, J. M. (2004). The unexpected legacy of divorce: Report of a 25-year study. *Psychoanalytic Psychology, 21*, 353–370.

Walsh, E. K., & Cavanaugh, J. C. (1984, November). *Does hospice meet the needs of dying clients?* Paper presented at the annual meeting of the Gerontological Society of America, San Antonio.

Walther, A. N. (1991). *Divorce hangover.* New York: Pocket Books.

Wang, S. S., & Brownell, K. D. (2005). Anorexia nervosa. In C. B. Fisher & R. M. Lerner (Eds.), *Encyclopedia of applied developmental science* (Vol. 1, pp. 83–85). Thousand Oaks CA: Sage.

Ward, R., Logan, J., & Spitze, G. (1992). The influence of parent and child needs on coresidence in middle and later life. *Journal of Marriage and the Family, 54*, 209–221.

Ward, S. L., & Overton, W. F. (1990). Semantic familiarity, relevance, and the development of deductive reasoning. *Developmental Psychology, 26*, 288–493.

Warr, P., Butcher, V., & Robertson, I. (2004). Activity and psychological well-being in older people. *Aging and Mental Health, 8*, 172–183.

Washington v. Glucksberg 521 US 702 (1997).

Washko, M. (2001). *An examination of generativity: Past, present, and future research directions.* Unpublished master's thesis, University of Delaware.

Wass, H. (2001). Past, present, and future of dying. *Illness, Crisis, and Loss, 9*, 90–110.

Waters, E., & Cummings, E. M. (2000). A secure base from which to explore close relationships. *Child Development, 71*, 164–172.

Waters, E., Merrick, S., Treboux, D., Crowell, J., & Albersheim, L. (2000). Attachment security in infancy and early adulthood. *Child Development, 71*, 684–689.

Waters, H. F. (1993, July 12). Networks under the gun. *Newsweek,* pp. 64–66.

Waters, H. S. (1980). "Class news": A single-subject longitudinal study of prose production and schema formation during childhood. *Journal of Verbal Learning and Verbal Behavior, 19*, 152–167.

Waters, L., & Moore, K. A. (2001). Coping with economic deprivation during unemployment. *Journal of Economic Psychology, 22*, 461–482.

Watson, J. A., & Koblinsky, S. A. (1997). Strengths and needs of working-class African-American and Anglo-American grandparents. *International Journal of Aging and Human Development, 44*, 149–165.

Watson, J. B. (1925). *Behaviorism.* New York: Norton.

Wayment, H. A., & Vierthaler, J. (2002). Attachment style and bereavement reactions. *Journal of Loss and Trauma, 7*, 129–149.

Webb, S. J., Monk, C. S., & Nelson, C. A. (2001). Mechanisms of postnatal neurobiological development: Implications for human development. *Developmental Neuropsychology, 19*, 147–171.

Webber, L. S., Wattigney, W. A., Srinivasan, S. R., & Berenson, G. S. (1995). Obesity studies in Bogalusa. American Journal of Medical Science, 310, S53–S61.

WebMD. (2004). *Stress management: Effects of stress.* Online document available at the website http://my.webmd.com/hw/emotional_wellness/ta4209.asp (accessed July 4, 2005).

Wechsler, D. (1991). *Manual for the Wechsler Intelligence Test for Children–III.* New York: The Psychological Corporation.

Wechsler, H., Davenport, A., Dowdall, G., Moeykens, B., & Castillo, S. (1994). Health and behavioral consequences of binge drinking in college. *Journal of the American Medical Association, 272*, 1672–1677.

Wechsler, H., Dowdall, G. W., Davenport, A., & Castillo, S. (1995). Correlates of college student binge drinking. *American Journal of Public Health, 85*, 921–926.

Wechsler, H., Lee, J. E., Kuo, M., Seibrung, M., Nelson, T. F., & Lee, H. (2002). Trends in college binge drinking during a period of increased prevention efforts. *Journal of American College Health, 2002*, 203–217.

Wechsler, H., Seibring, M., Liu, C., & Ahl, M. (2004). Colleges respond to student binge drinking: Reducing student demand or limiting access. *Journal of American College Health, 52*, 159–168.

Wegman, M. E. (1994). Annual summary of vital statistics—1993. *Pediatrics, 95*, 792–803.

Wegner, D. M., & Gold, D. G. (1995). Fanning old flames: Emotional and cognitive effects of suppressing thoughts of a past relationship. *Journal of Personality and Social Psychology, 68*, 782–792.

Weibel-Orlando, J. (1990). Grandparenting styles: Native American perspectives. In J. Sokolovsky (Ed.), *The cultural context of aging* (pp. 109–125). New York: Bergin & Garvey.

Weichold, K., & Silbereisen, R. K. (2005). Puberty. In C. B. Fisher & R. M. Lerner (Eds.), *Encyclopedia of applied de-*

velopmental science (Vol. 2, pp. 893–898). Thousand Oaks CA: Sage.

Weinberg, M. K., & Tronick, E. Z. (1994). Beyond the face: An empirical study of infant affective configurations of facial, vocal, gestural, and regulatory behaviors. *Child Development, 65,* 1503–1515.

Weinberg, M. K., Tronick, E. Z., Cohn, J. F., & Olson, K. L. (1999). Gender differences in emotional expressivity and self-regulation during early infancy. *Developmental Psychology, 35,* 175–188.

Weishaus, S., & Field, D. (1988). A half century of marriage: Continuity or change? *Journal of Marriage and the Family, 50,* 763–774.

Weisner, T. S., & Wilson-Mitchell, J. E. (1990). Nonconventional family lifestyles and sex typing in six-year-olds. *Child Development, 61,* 1915–1933.

Weissman, M. D., & Kalish, C. W. (1999). The inheritance of desired characteristics: Children's view of the role of intention in parent-offspring resemblance. *Journal of Experimental Child Psychology, 73,* 245–265.

Welle, S., Thompson, C., Statt, M., & McHenry, B. (1996). Growth hormone increases muscle mass and strength but does not rejuvenate myofibrillar protein synthesis in healthy subjects over 60 years old. *Journal of Clinical Endocrinology and Metabolism, 81,* 3239–3243.

Wellman, H. M. (1993). Early understanding of mind: The normal case. In S. Baron-Cohen, H. Tager-Flusberg, & D. J. Cohen (Eds.), *Understanding other minds: Perspectives from autism.* Oxford, UK: Oxford University Press.

Wellman, H. M. (2002). Understanding the psychological world: Developing a theory of mind. In U. Goswami (Ed.), *Blackwell handbook of childhood cognitive development* (pp. 167–187). Malden, MA: Blackwell.

Wellman, H. M., Cross, D., & Bartsch, K. (1986). Infant search and object permanence: A meta-analysis of the A not B error. *Monographs of the Society for Research in Child Development, 51* (Serial No. 214).

Wellman, H. M., Cross, D., & Watson, J. (2001). Meta-analysis of theory-of-mind development: The truth about false belief. *Child Development, 72,* 655–684.

Wellman, H. M., & Gelman, S. A. (1998). Knowledge acquisition in foundational domains. In W. Damon (Ed.), *Handbook of child psychology* (Vol. 2). New York: Wiley.

Wells, Y. D., & Kendig, H. L. (1997). Health and well-being of spouse caregivers and the widowed. *The Gerontologist, 37,* 666–674.

Wentkowski, G. (1985). Older women's perceptions of great-grandparenthood: A research note. *The Gerontologist, 25,* 593–596.

Wentworth, N., Benson, J. B., & Haith, M. M. (2000). The development of infants' reaches for stationary and moving targets. *Child Development, 71,* 576–601.

Werker, J. F., & Tees, R. C. (1999). Influences on infant speech processing: Toward a new synthesis. *Annual Review of Psychology, 50,* 509–535.

Werner, E. (1994). Overcoming the odds. *Journal of Developmental and Behavioral Pediatrics, 15,* 131–136.

Werner, E. E. (1989). Children of Garden Island. *Scientific American, 260,* 106–111.

Werner, E. E. (1995). Resilience in development. *Current Directions in Psychological Science, 4,* 81–85.

Werner, E. E., & Smith, R. S. (1992). *Overcoming the odds: High risk children from birth to adulthood.* Ithaca, NY: Cornell University Press.

Werner, H. (1948). *Comparative psychology of mental development.* Chicago: Follet.

Wertsch, J. V., & Tulviste, P. (1992). L. S. Vygotsky and contemporary developmental psychology. *Developmental Psychology, 28,* 548–557.

West, R. L., & Yassuda, M. S. (2004). Aging and memory control beliefs: Performance in relation to goal setting and memory self-evaluation. *Journal of Gerontology: Psychological Sciences, 59,* P56–P65.

Westbrook, L. A. (2002). The experience of mid-life women in the years after the deaths of their parents. *Dissertation Abstracts International Section A: Humanities and Social Sciences, 62*(8-A), 2884.

Wethington, E. (2000). Expecting stress: Americans and the "midlife crisis." *Motivation and Emotion, 24,* 85–103.

Wettemann, B. A. (1999). *Bereavement and college students.* Unpublished manuscript, Oklahoma State University, Stillwater.

Weymouth, P. L. (2005). A longitudinal look at the predictors of four types of retirement. *Dissertation Abstracts International: Section B: The Sciences & Engineering. 65*(7-B), 3760.

Whalley, L. J., Fox, H. C., Deary, I. J., & Starr, J. M. (2005). Childhood IQ, smoking, and cognitive change from age 11 to 64 years. *Addictive Behaviors, 30,* 77–88.

Whitbourne, S. K. (1986). *The me I know: A study of adult identity.* New York: Springer-Verlag.

Whitbourne, S. K. (1987). Personality development in adulthood and old age: Relationships among identity style, health, and well-being. In K. W. Schaie (Ed.), *Annual review of gerontology and geriatrics* (Vol. 7, pp. 189–216). New York: Springer.

Whitbourne, S. K. (1996). *The aging individual.* New York: Springer.

Whitbourne, S. K. (1999). Physical changes. In J. C. Cavanaugh & S. K. Whitbourne (Eds.), *Gerontology: An interdisciplinary perspective* (pp. 91–122). New York: Oxford University Press.

Whitbourne, S. K. (2000). *Psychopathology in later adulthood.* New York: Wiley.

White, L., & Gilbreth, J. G. (2001). When children have two fathers: Effects of relationships with stepfathers and noncustodial fathers on adolescent outcomes. *Journal of Marriage and the Family, 63,* 155–167.

Whitehead, J. R., & Corbin, C. B. (1997). Self-esteem in children and youth: The role of sport and physical education. In K. R. Fox, et al (Eds.), *The physical self: From motivation to well-being.* Champaign, IL: Human Kinetics.

Whitehurst, G. J., & Vasta, R. (1975). Is language acquired through imitation? *Journal of Psycholinguistic Research, 4,* 37–59.

Whitehurst, G. J., & Vasta, R. (1977). *Child behavior.* Boston: Houghton Mifflin.

Whiting, B. B., & Edwards, P. E. (1988). *Children of different worlds.* Cambridge MA: Harvard University Press.

Whiting, J. W. M., & Child, I. L. (1953). *Child training and personality: A cross-cultural study.* New Haven: Yale University Press.

Whitmer, R. A., & Whitbourne, S. K. (1997). Evaluation of infantilizing speech in a rehabilitation setting: Relation to age. *International Journal of Aging and Human Development, 44,* 129–136.

Whitney, E. N., & Hamilton, E. M. N. (1987). *Understanding nutrition* (4th ed). St. Paul, MN: West.

Wickrama, K. A. S., Lorenz, F. O., Conger, R. D., & Elder, G. H., Jr. (1997). Marital quality and physical illness: A latent growth curve analysis. *Journal of Marriage and the Family, 59,* 143–155.

Wicks-Nelson, R., & Israel, A. C. (2006). *Behavior disorders of childhood* (6th ed.). Upper Saddle River, NJ: Prentice-Hall.

Wiegers, T. A., van der Zee, J., & Keirse, M. J. (1998). Maternity care in The Netherlands: The changing home birth rate. *Birth, 25,* 190–197.

Wiener, R. L., Hurt, L., Russell, B., Mannen, K., & Gasper, C. (1997). Perceptions of sexual harassment: The effects of gender, legal standard, and ambivalent sexism. *Law and Human Behavior, 21,* 71–93.

Wilber, K. H., & McNeilly, D. P. (2001). Elder abuse and victimization. In J. E. Birren & K. W. Schaie (Eds.), *Handbook of the psychology of aging* (5th ed., pp. 569–591). San Diego, CA: Academic Press.

Wilkinson, A. M., & Lynn, J. (2001). The end of life. In R. H. Binstock & L. K. George (Eds.), *Handbook of aging and the social sciences* (5th ed., pp. 444–461). San Diego: Academic Press.

Wille, S. (1994). Primary nocturnal enuresis in children. *Scandinavian Journal of Urology and Nephrology, 156* (Suppl. 156), 6–23.

Williams, J. M. (1997). *Style: Ten lessons in clarity and grace* (5th ed.). New York: Longman.

Williams, O. J., & Griffin, L. W. (1996). Elderly maltreatment and cultural diversity: When laws are not enough. *Journal of Multicultural Social Work, 4,* 1–13.

Willinger, M. (1995). Sleep position and sudden infant death syndrome. *Journal of the American Medical Association, 273,* 818–819.

Wilson, E. O. (1975). *Sociobiology: The new synthesis.* Cambridge MA: Harvard University Press.

Wilson, G. T., Heffernan, K., & Black, C. M. D. (1996). Eating disorders. In E. J. Marsh & R. A. Barkley (Eds.), *Child psychopathology.* New York: Guilford.

Wilson, R. D. (2000). Amniocentesis and chorionic villus sampling. *Current Opinion in Obstetrics & Gynecology, 12,* 81–86.

Wilson, R. S. (1983). The Louisville Twin Study: Developmental synchronies in behavior. *Child Development, 54,* 298–316.

Wilson, R. S., Gilley, D. W., Bennett, D. A., Beckett, L. A., & Evans, D. A. (2000). Person-specific paths of cognitive decline in Alzheimer's disease and their relation to age. *Psychology and Aging, 15,* 18–28.

Winblad, B., Brodaty, H., Gauthier, S., Morris, J. C., Orgogozo, J. M., Rockwood, K., et al. (2001). Pharmacotherapy of Alzheimer's disease: Is there a need to redefine treatment success? *International Journal of Geriatric Psychiatry, 16,* 653–666.

Winer, G. A., Craig, R. K., & Weinbaum, E. (1992). Adults' failure on misleading weight-conservation tests: A developmental analysis. *Developmental Psychology, 28,* 109–120.

Winner, E. (2000). Giftedness: Current theory and research. *Current Directions in Psychological Science, 9,* 153–156.

Winner, K. (1996). *Divorced from justice: The abuse of women and children by divorce lawyers and judges.* New York: Regan Books.

Wise, B. W., Ring, J., & Olson, R. K. (1999). Training phonological awareness with and without explicit attention to articulation. *Journal of Experimental Child Psychology, 72,* 271–304.

Wolfe, D. A. (1985). Child-abusive parents: An empirical review and analysis. *Psychological Bulletin, 97,* 462–482.

Wolfe, R., Morrow, J., & Fredrickson, B. L. (1996). Mood disorders in older adults. In L. L. Carstensen, B. A. Edelstein, & L. Dornbrand (Eds.), *The practical handbook of clinical gerontology* (pp. 274–303). Thousand Oaks, CA: Sage.

Wolff, P. H. (1987). *The development of behavioral states and the expression of emotions in early infancy.* Chicago: University of Chicago Press.

Wolfson, A. R., & Carskadon, M. A. (1998). Sleep schedules and daytime functioning in adolescents. *Child Development, 69,* 875–887.

Wolraich, M. L., Lindgren, S. D., Stumbo, P. J., Stegink, L. D., Appelbaum, M. I., & Kiritsy, M. C. (1994). Effects of diets high in sucrose or aspartame on the behavior and cognitive performance of children. *New England Journal of Medicine, 330,* 301–307.

Woodruff-Pak, D., & Papka, M. (1999). Theories of neuropsychology and aging. In V. L. Bengtson & K. W. Schaie (Eds.), *Handbook of theories of aging* (pp. 113–132). New York: Springer.

Woodward, A. L., & Markman, E. M. (1998). Early word learning. In W. Damon (Ed.), *Handbook of child psychology* (Vol. 2). New York: Wiley.

Woollacott, M. H., Shumway-Cook, A., & Williams, H. (1989). The development of balance and locomotion in children. In M. H. Woollacott, & A. Shumway-Cook (Eds.), *Development of posture and gait across the lifespan.* Columbia, SC: University of South Carolina Press.

Worden, W. (1991). *Grief counseling and grief therapy: A handbook for the mental health practitioner* (2nd ed.). New York: Springer.

Worobey, J. (2005). Effects of malnutrition. In C. B. Fisher & R. M. Lerner (Eds.), *Encyclopedia of applied developmental science* (Vol. 2, pp. 673–676). Thousand Oaks CA: Sage.

Wrenn, R. L. (1999). The grieving college student. In J. D. Davidson & K. J. Doka (Eds.), *Living with grief: At work, at school, at worship* (pp. 131–141). Levittown, PA: Brunner/Mazel.

Wu, Z. (1994). Remarriage in Canada: A social exchange perspective. *Journal of Divorce and Remarriage, 21,* 191–224.

Wu, Z., & Schimmele, C. M. (2005). Repartnering after first union disruption. *Journal of Marriage & Family, 67,* 27–36.

WuDunn, S. (1997, September 2). The face of the future in Japan. *New York Times,* pp. D1, D14.

Wynn, K. (1992). Addition and subtraction by human infants. *Nature, 358,* 749–750.

Wynn, K. (1996). Infants' individuation and enumeration of actions. *Psychological Science, 7,* 164–169.

Xiaohe, X., & Whyte, M. K. (1990). Love matches and arranged marriages: A Chinese replication. *Journal of Marriage and the Family, 52,* 709–722.

Xu, X., Ji, J., & Tung, Y. Y. (2000). Social and political assortative mating in urban China. *Journal of Family Issues, 21,* 47–77.

Xu, X., Zhu, F., O'Campo, P., Koenig, M. A., Mock, V., & Campbell, J. (2005). Prevalence of and risk factors for intimate partner violence in China. *American Journal of Public Health, 95,* 78–85.

Yang, B., Ollendick, T. H., Dong, Q., Xia, Y., & Lin, L. (1995). Only children and children with siblings in the People's Republic of China: Levels of fear, anxiety, and depression. *Child Development, 66,* 1301–1311.

Yang, N., Chen, C. C., Choi, J., & Zou, Y. (2000). Sources of work-family conflict: A Sino-U.S. comparison of the effects of work and family. *Academy of Management Journal, 43,* 113–123.

Yang, Q., Rasmussen, S. A., & Friedman, J. M. (2002). Mortality associated with Down's syndrome in the USA from 1983 to 1997: A population-based study. *The Lancet, 359,* 1019–1025.

Yates, M., & Youniss, J. (1996). Community service and political-moral identity in adolescents. *Journal of Research on Adolescence, 6,* 271–284.

Yeung, W. J., Sandberg, J. F., Davis-Kean, P. E., & Hofferth, S. L. (2001). Children's time with fathers in intact families. *Journal of Marriage and Family, 63,* 136–154.

Yick, A. G. (2000). Domestic violence beliefs and attitudes in the Chinese American community. *Journal of Social Service Research, 27,* 29–51.

Yonas, A., & Owsley, C. (1987). Development of visual space perception. In P. Salapatek and L. Cohen (Eds.), *Handbook of infant perception* (Vol. 2). Orlando, FL: Academic Press.

Youngblade, L. M., & Dunn, J. (1995). Individual differences in young children's pretend play with mother and sibling: Links to relationships and understanding of other people's feelings and beliefs. *Child Development, 66,* 1472–1492.

Youngjohn, J. R., & Crook, T. H., III. (1996). Dementia. In L. L. Carstensen, B. Edelstein, & L. Dornbrand (Eds.), *The practical handbook of clinical gerontology* (pp. 239–254). Thousand Oaks, CA: Sage.

Yu, Y. (1995). Patterns of work and family: An analysis of the Chinese American family since the 1920s. In C. K. Jacobson (Ed.), *American families: Issues in race and ethnicity* (pp. 131–144). New York: Garland.

Yuill, N., & Pearson, A. (1998). The development of bases for trait attribution: Children's understanding of traits as causal mechanisms based on desire. *Developmental Psychology, 34,* 574–586.

Zacks, R. T., Hasher, L., & Li, K. Z. H. (2000). Human memory. In F. I. M. Craik & T. A. Salthouse (Eds.), *Handbook of aging and cognition* (2nd ed.). Mahwah, NJ: Erlbaum.

Zafarullah, H. (2000). Through the brick wall and the glass ceiling: Women in the civil service in Bangladesh. *Gender, Work and Organization, 7,* 197–209.

Zahn-Waxler, C., Friedman, R. J., Cole, P. M., Mizuta, I., & Hiruma, N. (1996). Japanese and United States preschool children's responses to conflict and distress. *Child Development, 67,* 2462–2477.

Zahn-Waxler, C., Radke-Yarrow, M., Wagner, E., & Chapman, M. (1992). Development of concern for others. *Developmental Psychology, 28,* 126–136.

Zappert, L. T. (1996). Psychological aspects of sexual harassment in the academic workplace: Considerations for fo-rensic psychologists. *American Journal of Forensic Psychology, 14,* 5–17.

Zaslow, M. J., & Hayes, C. D. (1986). Sex differences in children's responses to psychosocial stress: Toward a cross-context analysis. In M. E. Lamb, A. L. Brown, & B. Rogoff (Eds.), *Advances in developmental psychology* (Vol. 4). Hillsdale, NJ: Erlbaum.

Zelazo, N. A., Zelazo, P. R., Cohen, K. M., & Zelazo, P. D. (1993). Specificity of practice effects on elementary neuromotor patterns. *Developmental Psychology, 29,* 686–691.

Zelazo, P. R. (1993). The development of walking: New findings and old assumptions. *Journal of Motor Behavior, 15,* 99–137.

Zhang, F., & Labouvie-Vief, G. (2004). Stability and fluctuation in adult attachment style over a 6-year period. *Attachment & Human Development, 6,* 419–437.

Zhou, Q., Eisenberg, N., Losoya, S. H., Fabes, R. A., Reiser, M., Guthrie, I. K., Murphy, B. C., Cumberland, A. J., & Shepard, S. A. (2002). The relations of parental warmth and positive expressiveness to children's empathy-related responding and social functioning: A longitudinal study. *Child Development, 73,* 893–915.

Ziemelis, A., Bucknam, R. B., & Elfessi, A. M. (2002). Prevention efforts underlying decreases in binge drinking at institutions of higher education. *Journal of American College Health, 50,* 238–252.

Zigler, E., & Finn-Stevenson, M. (1992). Applied developmental psychology. In M. H. Bornstein & M. E. Lamb (Eds.), *Developmental psychology: An advanced textbook.* Hillsdale, NJ: Erlbaum.

Zimiles, H., & Lee, V. E. (1991). Adolescent family structure and educational progress. *Developmental Psychology, 27,* 314–320.

Zimmer-Gembeck, M. J., Seibenbruner, J., & Collins, W. A. (2001). Diverse aspects of dating: Associations with psychosocial functioning from early to middle adolescence. *Journal of Adolescence, 24,* 313–336.

Zimmerman, B. J. (2001). Theories of self-regulated learning and academic achievement: An overview and analysis. In B. J. Zimmerman & D. H. Schunk (Eds.), *Self-regulated learning and academic achievement: Theoretical perspectives* (2nd ed., pp. 1–37). Mahwah, NJ: Erlbaum.

Zmuda, J. M., Cauley, J. A., Kriska, A., Glynn, N. W., Gutai, J. P., & Kuller, L. H. (1997). Longitudinal relation between endogenous testosterone and cardiovascular disease risk factors in middle-aged men: A 13-year follow-up of former Multiple Risk Factors Intervention Trial participants. *American Journal of Epidemiology, 146,* 609–617.

Zsembik, B. A., & Singer, A. (1990). The problem of defining retirement among minorities: The Mexican Americans. *The Gerontologist, 30,* 749–757.

Zukow-Goldring, P. (2002). Sibling caregiving. In M. H. Bornstein (Ed.), *Handbook of parenting: Vol. 3. Status and social conditions of parenting* (2nd ed., pp. 253–286). Mahwah, NJ: Erlbaum.

Name Index

A

Abbey, B. B., 191
Abengozar, M. C., 631
Aberson, C. L., 417
Aboud, F. E., 300
Abraham, M., 424
Abraham, R., 460
Ackerman, B. P., 171
Acock, A. C., 433, 448
Acredolo, L. P., 162
Adair, R. H., 92
Adams, G. A., 590
Adams, G. R., 382
Adams, J., 71
Adams, K., 517, 520
Adams, M. J., 225, 247
Adams, P. F., 386
Adams, R. G., 595
Adams, R. J., 115
Adler, N., 350
Adolph, K. E., 107, 108
Aguayo, G. M., 463
Aguinis, H., 468
Ahluwalia, N., 553
Ahmed, S., 196
Ahrons, C., 445
Ainsworth, M. D. S., 181
Ajrouch, K. J., 593–94
Akhtar, N., 163
Akiyama, H., 418
al'Absi, M., 390
Albeck, S., 444
Albert, M. S., 547
Alberts, A. E., 90
Albom, M., 575
Aldwin, C. M., 491, 493, 494, 501, 515
Alessi, C., 553
Alexander, E. N., 387
Alfred, H., 84
Ali, Muhammad, 549
Alibali, M. W., 142, 175, 222, 247
Allaire, J. C., 505
Allen, K. R., 448, 482
Allen, T. D., 477
Alley, J. L., 524
Allgeier, A. R., 353
Allgeier, E. R., 353
Altran, S., 145
Aman, C. J., 243
Amato, P. R., 268, 276, 277, 434, 441, 443
Anand, K. J., 113
Anastasi, A., 236
Ancoli-Israel, S., 553
Andersen, A. M. N., 65
Anderson, C. A., 293
Anderson, D., 494
Anderson, D. R., 295, 296
Anderson, E. R., 279, 438
Anderson, R. N., 364
Anderson, S. W., 103
Anderson, W. T., 643, 647
Anetzberger, G. J., 606
Angel, J. L., 554
Anglin, J. M., 160
Ani, C., 99–100
Anisfeld, M., 149

Annett, M., 111
Anthill, J. K., 476
Antonarakis, S. E., 50
Antonucci, T., 408, 409, 593
Antonucci, T. C., 418, 593–94
Anttila, V., 557
Apgar, V., 89
Apter, T., 382
Aquilino, W. S., 516
Aranda, M. P., 522
Araujo, A. B., 498
Arber, S., 470
Arbona, C., 465
Archer, J., 424
Archer, N., 246
Arcus, D., 94
Arden, H., 587
Arellano, L. M., 501
Arendell, T., 444
Arenofsky, J., 436
Armstrong-Stassen, M., 472, 473
Arnett, J., 382
Arnold, C., 336
Arnold, J., 357
Aronson, J., 237, 402
Arp, C. S., 528
Arp, D. H., 528
Arseneault, L., 79
Artazcoz, L., 474
Arterberry, M. E., 190
Artis, J. E., 520, 522
Aryee, S., 460, 477, 479, 481
Asbury, K., 200
Ashcraft, M. H., 249
Ashendorf, L., 552
Asher, S. R., 285, 289
Ashmead, D. H., 109
Aslin, R. N., 113, 117, 158, 159
Astone, N. M., 379
Atchley, R. C., 578, 579
Atkinson, L., 183
Attanucci, J., 331
Attig, T., 627, 636, 637, 638, 639, 644, 646, 647
Atwater, E., 364
Au, T. K., 163
Aunola, K., 268
Austin, C. M., 159
Averill, P. M., 567
Avis, N. E., 494, 497
Azar, S. T., 281

B

Bachman, J., 359
Bachman, J. G., 359
Bäckman, L., 559
Backscheider, A. G., 146
Badger, S., 379
Baek, J., 520, 522, 598
Baer, D. M., 14
Bagwell, C. L., 284, 285, 289, 416
Bahrick, L. E., 121
Bahvnagri, N. P., 197
Bailey, D. A., 258
Bailey, J. M., 351, 439
Baillargeon, R., 142–43, 144
Baker, C., 165
Baker, L., 247, 248

Bakermans-Kranenburg, M., 184
Bakermans-Kranenburg, M. J., 198
Baker-Ward, L., 151
Baldi, R. A., 480
Baldridge, D. C., 457
Balk, D. E., 646
Ball, K., 557
Ball, S., 295
Balmer, L. E., 646
Baltes, B. B., 21
Baltes, P. B., 12, 20–21, 40, 392, 506–7, 543, 563, 601
Bandura, A., 12, 15, 204–5, 292
Banger, M., 495
Banks, M. S., 115, 116, 117
Banks-Wallace, J., 587
Barber, B. K., 268
Barenboim, C., 297
Bargh, J. A., 401
Barinaga, M., 104
Barkley, R. A., 242, 243, 262
Barlaug, D. G., 234
Barlow, D. H., 189
Barnes, A., 466
Barnes, H., 592
Barr, R., 149
Barrett, A. E., 599
Barry, H., 379
Barton, M. E., 170
Bartsch, K., 124, 125, 142
Bar-Tur, L., 648
Baskett, L. M., 276
Basso, K. H., 312
Bates, E., 165, 170
Bates, J. E., 93, 94, 267, 273
Bauchner, H., 92
Bauer, J., 405, 406
Bauer, P. J., 149, 150
Baugh, S. G., 457
Baumeister, A. A., 91, 239, 240
Baumrind, D., 268
Bauserman, R., 277
Beal, C. R., 171, 248
Beardsall, L., 274
Bearman, S. K., 314
Beauchamp, G. K., 62, 112
Beavers, T., 552
Beck, A. T., 364, 566, 567
Beck, J. G., 567
Becker, B. J., 34, 203
Becker, J. B., 313
Beehr, T. A., 591
Beers, M. H., 575
Behnke, M., 66
Behrend, D. A., 156
Belanger, J., 164
Belgrad, S. L., 171
Belgrave, L. L., 603
Beller, M., 203
Belsky, J., 94, 273, 275, 311
Bem, D. J., 351
Benenson, J., 284
Benenson, J. F., 284
Bengtson, V. L., 448, 600
Ben-Israel Reuveni, O., 648
Bennett, K. M., 434
Bennett, N., 370

Benokraitis, N., 426, 428, 430, 435, 436, 437, 442, 444
Benokraitis, N. V., 431
Benson, B., 349
Benson, J. B., 110
Benson, J. M., 622
Benton, S. L., 247, 515
Berdahl, J. L., 468
Berdes, C., 554
Bereiter, C., 248
Berenbaum, S. A., 207–8
Berg, C. A., 203
Berger, A. R., 483
Bergeron, L. R., 606
Berk, L. E., 156, 194, 239
Berko, J., 167
Berkowitz, M. W., 333
Berliner, A. J., 382
Berman, D., 344
Berman, J. M., 354
Berman, W. H., 522
Berndt, T. J., 284, 285
Berninger, G., 170
Bersoff, D. M., 330
Bertenthal, B. H., 107, 109
Bertenthal, B. I., 117
Berthier, N. E., 109
Besharov, D. J., 349
Best, C. T., 158
Best, D. L., 202, 203, 515
Betz, N. E., 454
Bhatt, R. S., 118
Bialystok, E., 165
Bigler, R., 301
Bigler, R. S., 203, 206, 300, 301
Binet, Alfred, 230
Bingenheimer, J. B., 366
Binstock, R. H., 608, 609
Birch, H. G., 93
Birch, L. L., 98, 99, 317
Birch, S. A. J., 163
Bird, D. J., 460
Bird, G. W., 480
Bisanz, J., 147
Bishop, J. B., 386
Bjorklund, D. F., 179, 266, 323
Black, C. M. D., 317
Black, S. A., 565
Black-Gutman, D., 300, 301
Blake, J., 170
Blanchard, R., 351
Blanchard-Fields, F., 400, 402, 403, 480, 505
Blanton, H., 286
Blazer, D. G., 586
Blieszner, R., 522, 554
Bloom, L., 164, 169, 170
Bloom, P., 163
Bloxsome, T. D., 474
Bluck, S., 406
Blumberg, S. L., 528
Blyth, D., 315
Bogaert, A. F., 351
Bogatz, G. A., 295
Boivin, M., 345
Bolger, K. E., 281
Bolles, M. E., 486
Bolles, R. N., 486

Bollmer, J. M., 291
Bolton, M. K., 486
Bonanno, G., 640
Bonanno, G. A., 640, 641
Bond, J. T., 477
Bond, T. G., 221
Bongard, S., 390
Bonomo, Y. A., 361
Bons, T. A., 284
Boone, R. T., 191
Booth, J. R., 246
Borgen, F. H., 454
Borgida, E., 463
Bornstein, M. C., 647
Bornstein, M. H., 165, 190, 196
Borry, P., 621
Borzellino, G., 170
Bosman, E. A., 507
Bossé, R., 592
Bouchard, C., 310
Bouchard, T. J., Jr., 546
Bouchet, N., 599, 649
Bowen, A. M., 387
Bowen, C., 518
Bowen, R., 342
Bowlby, J., 180
Bowles, S., 557
Bozikas, V., 460
Brackbill, Y., 148
Bradbury, T. N., 433
Bradley, R. H., 234
Brady, J. E., 197
Braet, C., 316
Braine, M. D. S., 167, 169
Brainerd, C. J., 140
Brand, R. J., 500
Brandtstädter, J., 408, 409, 585
Braun, K. L., 622
Braungart, J. M., 55
Bray, J. H., 279
Brazelton, T. B., 76, 89
Brechman-Toussaint, M. L., 295
Brennan, P. A., 66
Brennan, R. T., 366
Brescoll, V., 366
Bretano, C., 279
Bretherton, I., 165
Bridges, C. R., 466
Bridges, M., 279
Brioni, J. D., 571
Brison, K. J., 619
Brissett-Chapman, S., 437
Brissette, I., 416
Brizzee, H. R., 552
Brockington, I., 77, 78
Brodie, D., 443
Brody, G. H., 273, 275
Brodzinsky, D. M., 221, 275, 276
Broman, C. L., 479
Bromley, D. B., 297–98
Bronfenbrenner, U., 12, 18–19, 235, 266
Brooks-Gunn, J., 65, 80, 123, 235, 312, 349, 437
Brophy, J. E., 252, 253, 254
Brougham, R. R., 502, 590
Brown, A. L., 248
Brown, B. B., 287, 288, 349
Brown, C. S., 301
Brown, D., 607
Brown, E. G., 196
Brown, J. R., 191, 274
Brown, J. V., 71
Brown, K. H., 591
Brown, K. P., 290

Brown, Louise, 57
Brown, R., 225, 247
Brownell, K. D., 317, 318
Bruce, J., 275, 276
Bruck, M., 151, 152
Bruschi, C. J., 190
Bruzzese, J.-M., 362–63
Bryant, P., 246
Bryce, J., 482
Bryden, M. P., 203
Bryk, K., 207–8
Buchanan, C. M., 277, 279, 313
Buchholz, M., 113
Buchsbaum, B. C., 644, 648
Buckle, L., 446
Buckley, C. J., 554
Buell, S. J., 546
Bueno, B., 631
Bugental, D. B., 281
Buhrmester, D., 275
Bukowski, W., 287, 289
Bukowski, W. M., 285
Bulcroft, C., 594
Bullinger, A., 114
Bullock, K., 525
Bullock, M., 123
Bumpass, L. L., 516
Bunce, D., 556
Burch, M. M., 149
Burchinal, M., 166
Burchinal, M. R., 185
Burger-Judisch, L. M., 104
Burgess, D., 463
Burgess, K. B., 95
Buriel, R., 267, 269
Burke, R. J., 465
Burke, W. J., 607
Burkhauser, R. V., 390
Burman, B., 278
Burnette, D., 524
Burraston, B., 285
Burton, L. M., 600
Bush, George W., 36, 408, 608
Bush, Jeb, 624
Bushman, B. J., 293
Busnel, M. C., 62
Buss, D. M., 420
Buss, K. A., 94, 191, 192
Bussey, K., 205
Butcher, V., 483
Bylsma, F. W., 554
Byock, I., 632
Byrne, B. M., 345
Byrne, D. F., 299

C

Cain, D., 336
Cain, K., 247
Calasanti, T. M., 590
Callahan, C. M., 238
Callahan, L. F., 390
Callanan, M., 163
Callanan, M. A., 162, 191
Calvert, S. L., 295
Camp, C. J., 505, 561, 571, 572
Campagne, A., 557
Campbell, D. W., 585–86
Campbell, F. A., 78, 234
Campbell, M. E., 284
Campbell, R., 165
Campbell, R. T., 22
Campbell, S. B., 365
Campbell, W. K., 345
Campos, J., 188
Campos, J. J., 116, 191

Camras, L. A., 189
Canfield, R. L., 152
Cannon, T. D., 79
Cantor, J., 305
Capozzoli, M., 148
Cappeliez, P., 596
Capron, A. M., 621
Capuzzi, D., 365
Carey, S., 118, 144
Carlo, G., 330
Carlson, C. L., 243
Carlson, E. A., 183
Carlson, S. M., 195
Carlson Jones, D., 312
Carnelley, K., 483
Carpenter, P. A., 247
Carr, D., 599
Carrere, S., 273
Carroll, J. B., 227
Carroll, J. L., 92
Carskadon, M. A., 346
Carstensen, L. L., 406, 433, 585, 594
Cartwright, B. S., 195
Caruso, D. R., 228
Carver, C. S., 416
Carver, K., 348
Carver, P. R., 351
Casaer, P., 101
Casas, J. F., 291
Cascio, W. F., 455
Caselli, M. C., 160
Caserta, M. S., 649
Casey, B. J., 103
Casey, M. B., 204
Cashman, L., 92
Casper, W. J., 478
Caspi, A., 93
Cassidy, J., 181
Castro, I. L., 467
Castro, W., 506
Cattell, R. B., 226
Cavanaugh, J. C., 520, 522, 559, 560, 569, 597, 598, 634
Ceballo, R., 438
Ceci, S. J., 151, 152
Cerminara, K. L., 623
Cervantes, C. A., 191
Champion, H. L., 352
Chan, A. Y., 438
Chance, G., 114
Chandler, M., 330
Chang, L., 291
Chanquoy, L., 248
Chao, G. T., 457
Chao, R. K., 268
Chapman, P. D., 230, 231
Charles, S. T., 545
Charness, N., 507
Chase-Lansdale, P. L., 65
Chassin, L., 285, 388
Chasteen, A. L., 427
Chatters, L. M., 587, 594
Chavira, V., 344
Chavous, T. M., 344
Cheadle, J., 443
Chen, X., 289, 290, 362
Chen, Y., 505
Chen, Z. X., 460
Cheney, D., 169
Cheng, H., 279
Cherlin, A. J., 439, 523
Chess, S., 93
Chetro-Szivos, J., 452
Cheung, L. W. Y., 79

Chi, I., 565
Child, I. L., 268
Chilman, C. S., 310
Chinen, A. B., 563
Chin-Sang, V., 482
Chipperfield, J. G., 585–86
Chiu, W. C. K., 470
Choi, J. M., 603
Chomitz, V. R., 79
Chomsky, N., 168
Chorpita, B. F., 189
Chou, K-L., 565
Christakos, A., 284
Christensen, A., 273, 442
Christensen, C. A., 248
Cicchetti, D., 279, 280, 281, 282
Cicirelli, V. G., 586, 631
Cillessen, A. H. N., 289
Cipani, E., 239
Clark, R., 79
Clark, S. L., 523
Clarke-Anderson, P., 465
Clarke-Stewart, K. A., 279
Clements, M., 433
Clifton, R., 114
Clifton, R. K., 107, 109, 113, 142
Clinkenbeard, P. R., 238
Clinton, Bill, 454, 468, 550
Cluss, P. A., 317
Cnattingius, S., 66
Codding, R., 561
Cohen, L., 201
Cohen, O., 434
Cohen, R. R., 634
Cohen, S., 64, 385
Coie, J. D., 290
Colby, A., 329, 336
Cole, D. A., 363
Cole, M. L., 426
Cole, P. M., 190
Colella, U., 428
Coleman, M., 446
Coleman, P. D., 546
Coleman, P. G., 586
Collaer, M. L., 207
Collins, N. L., 419
Collins, W. A., 346, 348
Coltheart, M., 245
Colwell, M. J., 196
Conger, R. D., 314
Connell, C. M., 522
Connelly, R., 477
Connidis, I. A., 427, 434, 436, 519, 595–96, 597, 599
Constantin, L. P., 480
Constantine, M. G., 467
Conway, M. A., 150
Cooke, R., 74
Cooksey, E. C., 456
Cooney, T. M., 436, 445
Coontz, S., 448
Cooper, C. L., 498
Cooper, K., 336
Coopersmith, S., 346
Coplan, R. J., 195
Copper, R. L., 64
Corbin, C. B., 319
Cornelius, M., 66
Cornwell, K. S., 111
Corr, C. A., 629, 646
Cortina, L. M., 468, 469
Cosentino, S. A., 548
Costa, P. T., 511, 515
Costa, P. T., Jr., 510, 511, 516
Costall, A., 187

Costin, S. E., 199
Coté, S., 290
Cotter, R. P., 631
Cotton, J. L., 457
Cotton, S., 476
Coulton, C. J., 280
Counts, D., 618–19
Courage, M. L., 115, 149
Courtney, M., 494
Cousins, R., 501
Cowart, B. J., 112
Cox, A., 166
Cox, C. B., 525
Cox, M. J., 183, 266, 272
Coyle, A., 640
Crabbe, J., 53
Craig, K. D., 113
Craig, R. K., 142
Crampes, M., 508
Creed, P. A., 474
Crenshaw, T. M., 290
Crick, N. R., 204, 290, 291, 366
Crispi, E. L., 522
Crnic, K., 273
Crnic, K. A., 79
Crohan, S. E., 433
Crook, T. H., III., 568
Cross, D., 124, 142
Cross, S., 407, 408
Crowder, R. G., 246
Crown, W., 608
Cruzan, Nancy, 623
Csikszentmihalyi, M., 238, 313, 314
Cuddy, A. J. C., 401
Cuellar, I., 344
Cumberland, A., 191
Cummings, E. M., 182, 271, 277–78
Cunningham, A. E., 246
Cunningham, J. D., 476
Cunningham, J. G., 191
Cuomo, M. J., 387
Curcio, C. A., 546
Curran, P. J., 285
Curtain, S. C., 77
Curtis, M. E., 246
Curwin, A., 166
Custis, L. L., 425
Cutler, S. J., 483
Cutrona, C. E., 418

D

Daley, D., 586
Daley, T. C., 234
Dalla Corta, Rosanno, 495–96
Dalton, S. T., 426
Daly, M., 281
Damon, W., 21, 123, 336
Danaher, D. L., 203
Daneman, M., 247
Danforth, M. M., 647
Dannefer, D., 22
Dannemiller, J. L., 115
D'Augelli, A., 351, 352
Davey, A., 433
Davey, J. D., 412
Davey, M., 433
Davidson, F. H., 301
Davidson, M. M., 301
Davies, I., 115
Davies, L., 279, 426, 427
Davies, P. T., 271, 277–78
Davis, B. L., 160
Davis, B. W., 605

Davis, J. A., 603
Davis, J. O., 53
Davis, L. G., 434
Davis, M., 500
Davis, N. S., 91
Dawson, G., 78
Day, J. D., 232
Day, S. X., 356
De Andrade, C. E., 563
DeAngelis, T., 497
De Beni, R., 247
DeCasper, A. J., 62
Decker, M. W., 571
Degirmencioglu, S. M., 288
Degraff, D. S., 477
De Haan, L. G., 514
de Haan, M., 120
Dekovic, M., 290
De La Cruz, F., 73
Delaney, C., 90
Delany, Elizabeth (Bessie), 23, 40
Delany, Sarah (Sadie), 23, 40
Dellas, M., 341
DeLoache, J. S., 135, 139–40
del Pinal, J., 437
DeMaris, A., 428
Dement, W. C., 91
Demo, D. H., 433
Dendinger, V. M., 590
Denney, N. W., 503, 504, 505
Derman, D. S., 643, 647
DeSalle, R., 84
DeSantis, L., 646
Desjardins, R. N., 159
de St. Aubin, E., 514, 528
Detterman, D. K., 239
Deutsch, A., 623
Devine, M. A., 484
Devine, P. G., 401
De Vries, B., 416, 417
de Vries, B., 416, 594
De Witt, P. M., 446
De Wolff, M. S., 183
Diamond, A., 50
Dick, D. M., 53, 313–14
Dickens, W. T., 234
Dickinson, G. E., 644, 645
Dick-Read, G., 76
Diehl, M., 399, 503, 505, 506, 516
Diemer, M. A., 429
Diener, E., 31, 32
Dierickx, K., 621
Diesendruck, G., 163
DiGrande, L., 387
Dilworth-Anderson, P., 448
Dimond, M., 649
Dionne, G., 365
DiPietro, J. A., 62, 64, 95
Dishion, T. J., 285
Dixon, R. A., 507, 562, 563
Dockrell, J., 240
Dodge, K. A., 267, 290, 366
Dodge, T., 286
Doepke, K. J., 364
Dohanich, G., 496
Doka, K. J., 600
Dolensky, E., 284
Domino, G., 197
Donatelle, R. J., 434
Dorgan, J. F., 494
Dornbusch, S. M., 279, 358, 359
Dorton, H. E., Jr., 452
Dowling-Guyer, S., 436
Downs, A. C., 205
Doyle, A., 183

Draghi-Lorenz, R., 187
Draper, P., 311
Dreman, S., 434
Drew, L. M., 600
Duck, S. C., 207–8
Duncan, C., 469
Duncan, G. J., 235, 437
Dunham, F., 166
Dunham, P. J., 166
Dunlosky, J., 559, 560
Dunn, J., 191, 194, 274, 275, 279, 305
Dunne, M. P., 351
Dunson, D. B., 65
Durham, M., 166
Durik, A., 79
Dyk, P. H., 382

E

Eagly, A. H., 203
Earls, F. J., 366
Easterbrook, M. A., 118
Eaton, J., 508
Eaton, W. O., 203
Ebberwein, C. A., 474, 475
Ebersole, P., 386, 390, 492, 493, 498, 569, 603
Eccles, J. S., 205–6, 258, 313, 346
Eckhardt, C., 423
Eddleston, K. A., 457
Eddy, J. M., 367
Edelstein, B., 560, 566
Edison, Thomas, 562
Edwards, C. A., 287
Edwards, J. D., 557
Edwards, P. E., 203
Egan, S. K., 291, 351
Eisenberg, N., 192, 198, 200, 332, 333
Eisenbud, L., 207
Eizenman, D. R., 117
Ekmekcioglu, C., 484
Elder, G. H., 314, 340
Elder, G. H., Jr., 588
Elkind, D., 342
Ellen, T. R., 514
Ellington, Duke, 562
Ellis, B. J., 54, 311
Emery, R. E., 277
Emick, M. A., 525
Engle, E., 459
Enns, L. R., 203
Enright, R. D., 434
Eppler, M. A., 108
Epstein, L. H., 317
Erel, O., 275, 278
Erera-Weatherley, P. I., 439
Ericsson, K. A., 507
Erikson, E. H., 10, 11–13, 178–79, 182, 340, 405, 422, 431, 457, 513–14, 516, 582
Erikson, J. M., 582
Ernst, M., 66
Eshelman, E. R., 500
Eskritt, M., 223
Esplin, P. W., 151
Estes, C. P., 528, 614
Estus, S., 569, 570
Etaugh, C., 203
Etten, M. J., 498
Etzioni, A., 443
Evans, D. R., 591–92
Evans, M., 73
Eyer, D. E., 77
Eyler, A. E., 482

Eyler, F. D., 66

F

Faber, A. J., 442
Fabes, R. A., 195, 198, 200, 205
Fagot, B. I., 206
Fairlie, H., 608
Falbo, T., 276
Farrell, M. P., 516
Farver, J. M., 194, 291
Fasig, L. G., 123
Faulkner, R. A., 433
Faw, G. D., 240
Feder, J., 611
Feehan, M., 242
Fegley, S., 358
Fehr, B., 417, 418
Feinberg, M. E., 275
Felber, M., 599
Feldhusen, J. F., 238
Feldman, D. C., 473, 474, 579, 590
Feldman, D. H., 238
Feldman, J. M., 560
Feldman, S. S., 344
Fenson, L., 160, 162, 165
Fenwick, K. D., 114
Fergusson, D. M., 65, 98, 282
Fernald, A., 190
Fernald, L., 99–100
Ferraro, K. J., 424
Ferreol-Barbey, M., 247
Fick, D. S., 484
Field, D., 434
Field, N. P., 627
Field, T., 79
Field, T. M., 170, 181
Fife, J. E., 587
Filanosky, C. A., Jr., 579
Finch, C. E., 545
Fincham, F. D., 441
Finchum, T., 579
Finckh, U., 570
Fingerman, K. L., 519, 521
Fink, B., 248
Finkler, K., 587
Finley, G. E., 275
Finn-Stevenson, M., 236
Fisch, S., 295
Fischer, K. W., 398–99
Fischer, M., 243
Fischoff, B., 321
Fish, M., 94
Fisher, C., 164
Fisher, H. E., 422
Fisher, J. A., 99
Fisk, A. D., 555, 556
Fiske, E. B., 262
Fiske, S., 400
Fiske, S. T., 401
Fitzgerald, H. E., 111, 148, 361
Fitzgerald, J., 248
Fitzgerald, J. M., 559
Fitzgerald, L., 469
Fitzgerald, L. F., 468
Fitzpatrick, M. A., 433
Fivush, R., 150
Flaks, D. K., 439, 440
Flanagan, C., 278
Flap, H., 419
Flavell, J. H., 140, 175, 221, 224, 262
Fleischman, D. A., 559
Fleming, S., 649
Fleming, S. J., 646
Flesser, D., 301

Flynn, J. R., 234
Foehr, U. G., 292
Foley, D., 553
Folkman, S., 499
Fonzi, A., 285
Forbes, D., 203
Forbes, J. N., 163
Forbes, K., 569
Ford, Cheryl, 384
Forde, V., 99
Foreyt, J. P., 317
Fortner, B. V., 630, 631
Fortner, M., 648
Foshee, V. A., 352–53
Foster, E., 365
Foster, S. H., 170
Fouad, N. A., 453
Fowler, F., 268
Fowler, R. C., 364
Fox, Michael J., 549
Fox, N. A., 95, 188
Fozard, J. L., 384, 549, 550, 551
Fraley, R. C., 405
Franceschi, K. A., 648
Francis, M., 248
Frank, D. A., 71
Franklin, A., 115
Franks, M. M., 520, 522
Frazier, L. D., 407
Fredricks, J. A., 258
Fredrickson, B. L., 565
Freedman, J., 79
Frerichs, F., 470
Fretz, B. R., 508
Freud, Sigmund, 11
Freund, A., 460, 557
Freund, A. M., 408, 585
Fried, P. A., 66
Friedman, D. E., 477
Friedman, J. M., 50, 66
Friedman, M., 500
Frieze, I. H., 465
Froman, L., 472
Frost, J. L., 465
Frye, D., 124
Fu, S.-Y., 494
Fu, V. R., 269
Fujita, F., 31, 32
Fuller-Thompson, E., 525
Furman, W., 275, 276, 285
Furstenberg, F. F., Jr., 439, 523
Futterman, A., 649, 650

G
Gabriel, L. T., 239
Gabrieli, J. D. E., 559
Gaddis, A., 312
Gafni, N., 203
Gagliardi, A., 78
Gagnon, C., 345
Gagnon, Y. C., 472
Gailey, C. W., 515
Galbraith, K. A., 349
Galinsky, E., 477
Gall, T. L., 591–92
Gallagher, R., 362–63
Galler, J. R., 99
Gallo, D. R., 370
Gallup, G. G., Jr., 446
Gangestad, S. W., 118
Ganong, L. H., 446
Ganong, L. M., 446
Gao, B., 627
Garber, J., 311
Gardere, J., 305

Gardiner, H. W., 40–41
Gardiner, K. N., 349
Gardner, H., 227–29, 262, 263
Garner, P. W., 274
Garovich-Szabo, L., 202
Garrard, E., 623
Garrod, A., 437
Garssen, B., 461
Garvey, C., 170
Gassin, E. A., 434
Gathercole, S. E., 165
Gatz, M., 565, 566, 568, 569, 570, 586
Gaulin, S. J. C., 179
Gavin, D. A. W., 345
Gavin, L. A., 285
Gaylord, S. A., 566
Gazelle, H., 195
Ge, X., 273, 314, 315
Geary, D. C., 179, 196, 207
Gefen, D., 417
Gelman, R., 153
Gelman, S. A., 144, 145, 146, 165, 203, 298
George, L. K., 511, 595, 596
Gershkoff-Stowe, L., 164
Gerson, K., 480
Giarusso, R., 417, 525, 595
Gibbs, J. C., 330, 333
Gibbs, N. R., 608
Giberson, P. K., 71
Gibran, K., 418, 452
Gibson, E. J., 108, 115
Gibson, G. D., 522
Gibson, K. R., 100
Gibson, R. C., 589, 591
Gignac, M. A. M., 477
Gilbreth, J. G., 279
Giles, J. W., 203
Gilligan, C., 331
Gillman, S. A., 483
Gillmore, J., 300
Gillum, B., 511
Gillum, R., 511
Gilmer, D. F., 491, 493, 494, 501
Gilmore, D., 379
Ginn, J., 470
Ginsburg, Ruth Bader, 466
Gisin, G. J., 482
Gjerdingen, D., 479
Glamser, F., 482
Glass, J. C., Jr., 647
Glass, R. M., 549
Glenn, N. D., 596
Glick, P. C., 278
Glickman, H. M., 459
Glusman, M., 163
Go, C. G., 541
Goeke-Morey, M. C., 272
Goethe, Wolfgang, 562
Goetz, E. T., 246
Goff, S. J., 484
Golby, A., 568, 569
Gold, D. G., 641
Gold, D. T., 595, 596
Goldberg, A., 597
Goldberg-Glen, R., 525
Goldenberg, J. L., 630
Goldenberg, R. L., 65
Goldenthal, P., 595
Goldfield, B. A., 165
Goldman, L. S., 243
Goldsmith, H. H., 94, 184, 191
Goldsmith, L. T., 238

Goldstein, D., 238
Goldzweig, G., 419
Goleman, D., 228
Golinkoff, R. M., 162, 170, 175
Golombok, S., 58, 351
Golsworthy, R., 640
Gomez, T. R. A., 386
Gonzales, P., 250
Gonzalez, H. M., 554, 565
Good, T. L., 252, 253, 254
Goodkin, K., 650
Goodman, E., 58
Goodman, G. S., 277
Goodnow, J. J., 201, 268
Goodrick, G. K., 317
Goodwyn, S. W., 162
Gordon, B. N., 151, 152
Gordon, C. P., 350
Gordon, R. A., 65
Gordon, S. L., 433
Gordon-Salant, S., 384, 549, 550, 551
Gorman, J. M., 501
Gorman-Smith, D., 366
Gosling, S. D., 512–13
Gotlib, I. H., 364
Gottesman, I. R., 54
Gottfredson, L. S., 231–32
Gottfried, G. M., 145
Gottlieb, B. H., 477
Gottlieb, G., 54
Gottlieb, L. N., 274
Gottman, J. M., 194, 269, 273, 442
Goubet, N., 113, 142
Gould, R. L., 516
Gould, S. J., 585
Gouze, M., 511
Govier, E., 203
Graesser, A. C., 247
Graham, S., 248, 291
Graham-Bermann, S. A., 366
Graham-Kevan, N., 424
Grande, G. E., 633
Grandey, A. A., 477
Granier-Deferre, C., 62
Grantham-McGregor, S., 99–100
Graves, R., 160
Gray, J. H., 457, 588, 589, 590–91
Graybeal, A., 501
Green, K. E., 341
Greenberg, J., 630–31
Greenberg, M. T., 79
Greenberger, E., 269
Greenfield, E. A., 592
Greenfield, P. M., 234
Greenhaus, J. H., 465
Greenwald, A. G., 401
Greve, W., 585
Grice, H. P., 169
Griffin, L. W., 607
Grigorenko, E. L., 229, 232, 503, 506, 602
Grob, A., 585
Groen, G. J., 249
Groisser, D., 242
Gross, D. R., 365
Gross, E. A., 607
Grossman, A. H., 597
Grossman, D.C., 320
Grotevant, H. D., 275, 276
Grotpeter, J. K., 204
Grünendahl, M., 583
Grusec, J. E., 201
Guacci-Franco, N., 284
Guelzow, M. G., 480

Guerrero, L. K., 469
Guillemin, J., 79
Gulko, J., 203–4
Gunnar, M. R., 275, 276
Gurtner, J., 253
Gurucharri, C., 300
Gustafson, K., 445
Gutmann, D. L., 515
Guttmacher, A. F., 64
Guttman, R., 419

H
Haan, M. N., 554
Habermas, T., 406
Hagestad, G. O., 22, 405
Hahn, E. R., 145
Hairston, R. E., 434
Haith, M. M., 110
Halberstadt, A. G., 204
Hale, J. L., 418
Hall, D. G., 164
Hall, D. R., 428
Hall, J. A., 204
Hallinan, M. T., 284
Halpern, D. F., 203
Halpern, L. F., 91
Halverson, C. F., 206, 207
Hamilton, C. E., 182
Hamilton, E. M. N., 63
Hamlet, S., 468
Hamm, J. V., 284
Hammer, L. B., 357
Hamon, R. R., 522
Hanaoka, H., 582
Hance, V. M., 453
Hannon, E. E., 113
Hansen, D. J., 282
Hanson, D. J., 386
Hanson, D. R., 54
Hansson, K., 428
Hansson, R. O., 648
Happaney, K., 281
Harbison, J., 607
Hardeng, S., 444
Hardison, C. B., 594
Hardy, M., 480
Hareven, T. K., 22, 517, 520
Harley, C., 359
Harman, C., 184
Harmon, L. W., 454
Harringer, C., 380
Harrington, D., 460
Harrington, K. V., 457
Harris, B., 78
Harris, K. R., 248
Harris, L. J., 111
Harris, P. L., 124, 194
Harrison, J., 358
Harrist, A. W., 195
Hart, C. H., 289
Hart, D., 123
Hart, D. A., 382
Hart, H. M., 514
Harter, K., 272
Harter, S., 123, 343, 345, 346, 348
Hartman, P. S., 563
Hartup, W. W., 193, 197, 285
Haselager, G. J. T., 284
Hasher, L., 558
Haslam, C., 71
Hastings, P. D., 95, 273
Hatch, L. R., 594
Haugaard, J. J., 277
Haviland, J. M., 190
Hawkins, A. J., 443

Hawley, P. H., 287
Haworth, J., 471
Hay, D. F., 78
Hayashi, M., 632
Hayes, C. D., 203
Hayflick, L., 540, 541, 542, 544, 545
Hayne, H., 149
Hayslip, B., Jr., 482, 524, 525
Hayward, M. D., 597
Hazan, C., 419
Healy, L., 253
Heavey, C. L., 273
Heck, R., 622
Heckhausen, J., 409, 585
Heffernan, K., 317
Heidrich, S. M., 505
Heiges, K. L., 277
Heilbrun, G., 514
Heilman, M. E., 463
Heimann, B., 456
Heinmiller, B. M., 113
Hemesath, K., 432
Henderson, B. N., 417, 501
Henderson, C. E., 524
Henderson, K. A., 482
Henderson, V. W., 568
Hendricks, J., 483
Henkens, K., 591
Hennig, K. H., 333
Henretta, J. C., 589
Henry, D. B., 366
Herman, M., 345
Hernandez-Reif, M., 79
Herrera, C., 190
Herrera, M. G., 100
Herrera, N. C., 276
Herrnstein, R. J., 236
Hershey, D. A., 591
Hertenstein, M. J., 191
Hertz, R., 476
Hertzog, C., 402, 559, 560
Herzog, A. R., 592
Hespos, S. J., 144
Hess, P., 386, 492, 493
Hess, U., 189
Hetherington, E. M., 279, 305
Hetherington, S. E., 76
Heydens-Gahir, H. A., 21
Heyman, G. D., 203, 298
Hibbert, J. R., 272
Hickey, P. R., 113
Hickson, F., 300, 301
Higgins, A., 333, 334
Hill, Anita, 468
Hill, J. L., 80
Himsel, A. J., 514
Hines, M., 207
Hinton, L., 554
Hirsh-Pasek, K., 162, 175
Hobdy, J., 519
Hocker, K., 407
Hodges, E. V. E., 285
Hofer, P. J., 554
Hofer, S. M., 395, 396, 506
Hoff, E., 160, 163, 164, 165, 170
Hoff-Ginsberg, E., 160, 269
Hoffman, L. W., 285
Hoffman, M. L., 198, 334
Hogan, D. P., 379
Hogan, N., 646
Hogge, W. A., 69
Hoier, S., 311
Holden, G. W., 267
Hollan, D., 619

Holland, J. L., 356, 357, 453–54, 459
Hollich, G. J., 162
Hollon, S. D., 364
Holton, E. F., 508
Hom, P. W., 458
Homma, M., 481
Honda-Howard, M., 481
Hood, B., 144
Hooker, K., 407
Hooven, C., 269
Hooyman, N., 604
Horn, J., 507
Horn, J. L., 392, 394, 395, 396, 506
Horwood, L. J., 98
Houston, D. M., 159
Hovey, J. D., 501
Howard, J., 591–92
Howard, J. T., 457
Howe, M. L., 149
Howe, N., 194, 274
Howes, C., 193
Hoyer, W. J., 507, 508
Hoyles, C., 253
Hubbard, F. O. A., 91
Huesmann, L. R., 293
Hugo, Victor, 326
Huizink, A., 64
Hultsch, D. F., 560, 562, 563
Hummert, M. L., 401, 402
Humphrey, H. E. B., 69
Hunter, J. E., 231–32
Huston, A. C., 292, 293, 294, 295, 296
Huston, M., 430
Huston, T. L., 433
Hutchinson, S. L., 483
Huth-Bocks, A. C., 183
Huttenlocher, J., 153, 166
Huyck, M. H., 515
Hyde, J. S., 79, 331–32, 515
Hymel, S., 196, 289

I

Iacono, W. G., 243
Ilies, R., 468
Ingersoll-Dayton, B., 597
Ingoldsby, E. M., 366
Inhelder, B., 221
Insabella, G. M., 279, 445
Isabella, R. A., 94
Isaksen, J., 452
Isley, S. L., 196
Ismond, D. R., 242
Israel, A. C., 203, 242, 282, 317, 363, 367
Issacs-Shockley, M., 437
Ivancevich, J. M., 501
Iverson, J. M., 162
Ivory, B. T., 379
Ivy, D. K., 468
Iwasaki, Y., 483
Izard, C. E., 187, 188

J

Jablow, M. M., 336
Jaccard, J., 286
Jacklin, C. N., 203, 205
Jackson, B., 494
Jackson, J. S., 591
Jacobi, C., 318
Jacobs, J. A., 480
Jacobs, J. E., 205–6
Jacobs, S. C., 643
Jacobs-Lawson, J. M., 591

Jacobson, J. D., 590
Jacobson, J. L., 66, 68, 69
Jacobson, S. W., 66, 68, 69
Jaffee, C., 653
Jaffee, S., 331–32
Jagnow, C. P., 62
Jaime, A., 587
James, W., 582
Janevic, M., 593–94
Janke, H. C., 505
Janoff-Bulman, R., 483
Janssens, J. M., 290
Jarrett, R. L., 437
Jarvin, L., 229
Jaswal, V. K., 163
Jefferson, Thomas, 328
Jenkins, C. L., 476, 477, 649
Jenkins, E., 249
Jenkins, K. R., 597
Jens, W., 653
Jensen, J. L., 107
Jensen, P. S., 243
Jernigan, L. P., 341
Ji, G., 276
Ji, J., 422
Jiao, S., 276
Jiao, Z., 284
Jing, Q., 276
Jipson, J., 163
Johanson, R. B., 76
Johansson, B., 546
John, D., 479
John, O. P., 512–13
John, R. S., 275
John Paul II, Pope, 549, 619
Johnson, A. L., 515
Johnson, B. D., 605
Johnson, D. L., 105, 467
Johnson, J. G., 293
Johnson, K. E., 168
Johnson, M. H., 118
Johnson, M. P., 424
Johnson, N., 362, 601
Johnson, S. P., 117, 118
Johnson, W., 540
Johnson-Laird, P. N., 558
Johnston, K., 474
Johnston, L. D., 360
Jones, C. J., 512
Jones, D., 248
Jones, D. C., 191, 199, 274
Jones, F. L., 441
Jones, L. C., 300
Jones, T. V., 575
Jordan, A. E., 363
Joseph, R., 62
Joyner, K., 348
Juffer, F., 184
Jung, C. G., 515, 516, 582
Jusczyk, P. W., 113, 158, 159
Juvonen, J., 291

K

Kagan, J., 94, 95
Kager, M. B., 470
Kahlbaugh, P. E., 399
Kahn, R. I., 388
Kaijura, H., 112
Kail, Ben, 55, 88, 90
Kail, Laura, 99
Kail, Matt, 55
Kail, R., 147, 175, 221, 224, 322
Kail, R. V., 245, 556
Kaiser, I. H., 64
Kalakoski, V., 340

Kalish, C. W., 145
Kalish, K., 560, 566
Kalish, R. A., 618, 619, 626, 627, 631
Kalmijn, M., 419
Kaltman, S., 640
Kamerman, S. B., 80
Kandel, E., 79
Kane, R. A., 611
Kane, R. L., 611
Kanekar, S., 463
Kann, L., 318
Kaplan, P. S., 159
Kaplan, S., 528
Kapp, M. B., 607
Karau, S. J., 203
Karney, B. R., 433
Karniol, R., 110
Karp, J., 281
Karraker, K. H., 202
Karshin, C. M., 387
Kaslow, F. W., 428
Kaslow, N. J., 364
Kastenbaum, R., 618, 619, 627, 629, 631, 632, 634–35, 648
Katz, L. F., 269, 272, 278
Katz, P., 58
Kaufman, J. C., 226, 230
Kaus, C. R., 407
Kavanaugh, R. D., 194
Kawakami, K., 94
Kaydar, D., 444
Keane, S. P., 290
Keefe, K., 285
Keese, B. V., 648
Keil, F. C., 145, 146
Keiley, M. K., 366
Keirse, M. J., 77
Keirstead, Hans, 37
Keith, B., 277
Keith, J., 380
Keller, H. H., 553
Keller, Helen, 161–62
Keller, J. W., 627
Keller, M., 330
Kellman, P. J., 115, 116, 117
Kelloway, E. K., 477
Kelly, J., 305
Kemeny, M. E., 500
Kendig, H. L., 598
Kendrick, C., 275
Kennedy, G. E., 524
Kennell, H. H., 77
Kenrick, D. T., 208
Kerr, B., 466–67
Kerr, S., 248
Kessler, B., 245
Kevorkian, Jack, 622
Keyes, C. L., 408
Kidder, T., 614
Kiel, E. J., 192
Kilgore, K., 267
Killen, M., 301
Killiany, R. J., 547
Kim, S., 579, 590
Kim, S. S., 476
Kim, Y. H., 246
Kimball, M. M., 293
King, Martin Luther, Jr., 200, 587
King, Martin Luther, Sr., 200
King, P. M., 380, 381, 397, 398, 399
King, V., 340, 428
Kingson, E. R., 609, 611
Kinicki, A. J., 458

Kinney, J. M., 499, 586, 597, 598
Kipnis, O., 348
Kirby, D., 349, 350, 351
Kirby, P. G., 380
Kirby, S. E., 586
Kirouac, G., 189
Kitchener, K. S., 380, 381, 397, 398–99
Kivnick, H. Q., 524, 582
Kiyak, H. A., 604
Klaczynski, P. A., 222, 324–25
Klass, D., 619, 647
Klaus, M., 77
Klebanov, P. K., 235, 437
Kleespies, P. M., 631–32
Kleiber, D. A., 483
Klein, D. M., 448
Kleinknecht, E. F., 149
Klerman, L. V., 65
Kline, S. L., 428
Klohnen, E. C., 514, 517
Klopp, Claire B., 18
Knapp, D. E., 468
Knapp, M. L., 434
Knight, B. G., 522
Knowles, M. S., 508
Knox, D., 425
Kobak, R., 419
Koball, E. H., 480
Koblinsky, S. A., 524
Kobus, K., 362
Kochanska, G., 189, 273
Kochenderfer, B. J., 291
Kochenderfer-Ladd, B., 291
Koenig, H. G., 586
Koestenbaum, P., 631
Kogan, N., 238
Kohlberg, L., 12, 16, 17, 206, 326–30, 333
Kolata, G., 390
Kolb, B., 101
Kolberg, K. J. S., 66
Kolsawalla, M. B., 463
Korbin, J. E., 280
Kornhaber, A., 524
Koskela, K., 474
Kosmitzki, C., 40–41
Kotler, J. A., 295
Kotovsky, L., 144
Kotre, J., 575
Kovacs, D. M., 285
Kowal, A., 275
Kowalski, P. S., 345
Krajnik, M., 515
Krakow, J. B., 18
Kram, K. E., 457
Kramer, A. F., 399, 556
Kramer, D. A., 399, 507, 563
Kramer, L., 275
Krause, N., 501, 583, 586
Krebs, D., 300
Krettenauer, T., 333
Krieshok, T. S., 465
Krispin, O., 289
Kroger, J., 341, 370
Krogh, H. R., 203
Krueger, R. F., 540
Kübler-Ross, E., 628–29
Kuhl, P. K., 160
Kuhn, D., 224
Kulik, L., 474, 475, 597
Kulwicki, A. D., 425
Kumar, R., 362
Kung, H., 653
Kunkel, D., 294

Kunzig, R., 104
Kupp, K., 358
Kurdek, L. A., 429, 433, 443
Kurup, P. A., 422
Kurup, R. K., 422
Kushner, H. S., 653
Kustis, G. A., 468
Kwan, Michelle, 307

L
Labouvie-Vief, G., 399, 400, 516
Lachman, M., 408, 585
Lachman, M. E., 409
Lachs, M. S., 607
LaCroix, A. Z., 386
Ladd, B. K., 291
Ladd, G. W., 195, 196, 285, 289, 290, 291
Lagattuta, K. H., 191
La Greca, A. M., 189
LaGreca, A. M., 290
Laible, D. J., 191
Lakshmanan, I. A. R., 422
Lalumière, M. L., 351
Lamanna, M. A., 426, 427, 433, 434, 437, 438, 443, 444, 446
Lamaze, F., 76
Lamb, M. E., 151, 175, 185, 289
Lambert, S., 439
Lampinen, J. M., 151
Lampman, C., 436
Landis, T., 160
Landreck, B. F., 385
Lang, F. R., 409
Lang, J. C., 453
Langabeer, K. A., 351
Lange, G., 224
Langer, E. J., 580, 605
Langlois, J. H., 205
Langwick, S., 353
Lankau, M. J., 457
Lansford, J. E., 416, 418, 594
Lanza, E., 165
Lao Tzu, 562
Lapane, K. L., 603
Larimore, C., 437
Larson, J., 638
Larson, R., 313, 314
Larson, R. W., 319, 346, 363, 483
Lashua, B., 484
Laungani, P., 499
Laursen, B., 346
Lawrence, W., 71
Lawton, M. P., 12, 19, 579, 580
Lazarus, R. S., 499
Leach, P., 99
Leahy, J. M., 638
Leana, C. R., 473, 474
Leaper, C., 203, 205
Lears, M., 294
Lecanuet, J. P., 62
Ledebt, A., 109
LeDoux, J. E., 501
Lee, C., 460
Lee, C. H., 453
Lee, G. R., 443, 599
Lee, J. W., 469
Lee, K., 223
Lee, K. T., 66
Lee, P. C. B., 472
Lee, S., 250, 251
Lee, S. C., 164
Lee, V. E., 277
LeFevre, J., 245
Leichtentritt, R. D., 622

Leidig, T., 508
Lelwica, M., 190
Leman, P. J., 196
LeMare, L. J., 220, 300
Lemery, K. S., 94, 95
Lemieux, R., 418
Lemire, L., 472
Lemire, R. J., 102
Lemke, J. H., 482
Lengua, L. J., 278
Lentz, C., 267
Leon, G. R., 511
Leon, K., 277
Lepper, M. R., 253
Lerner, R. M., 11, 41
LeSieur, K. D., 196
Lester, B. M., 76
Levenson, R. W., 442
Levin, J. S., 587
Levine, A., 370
Levine, A. D., 428, 429
Levine, L. E., 123
Levine, S. C., 153
Levinger, G., 416
Levinson, D., 455, 516
Levinson, D. J., 455–56, 516
Levinson, J. D., 455, 516
Levitt, A. G., 160
Levitt, J., 595
Levitt, J. L., 284
Levitt, J. M., 595
Levitt, M., 595
Levitt, M. J., 284
Levy, B. R., 402
Levy, G. D., 203, 205
Levy, J., 111
Lewin-Epstein, N., 479
Lewinsohn, P. M., 364, 566
Lewis, J. M., 445
Lewis, K. G., 426
Lewis, M., 94, 123, 188, 189
Lewis, M. D., 180
Lewis, M. I., 497
Lewis, R. A., 519
Lewis, S., 471
Lewkowicz, D. J., 121, 189
Lewontin, R., 235
Li, F., 552
Li, K. Z. H., 558
Li, Z., 289
Liben, L. S., 203, 206
Lickliter, R., 121
Lieber, J., 647
Lieberman, E., 79
Lieberman, M., 183, 196
Liebert, R. M., 197
Liebowitz, M., 422
Lim, S., 468, 469
Limber, S., 189
Lin, C. C., 269
Lin, L-W., 519
Lin, S., 278
Lindenberger, U., 20–21, 506–7
Lindlaw, S., 496
Lindsay, D. S., 151
Linn, S., 294
Lipsitt, L. P., 148
Lips-Wiersma, M. S., 453
Liss, M. B., 203
Little, J. K., 206
Little, T. D., 585
Liu, H.-M., 160
Livesley, W. J., 297–98
Lobliner, D. B., 300
Lock, M., 494

Locke, John, 14
Loehlin, J. C., 235
Logan, J., 519
Logan, R. D., 13
Lohr, M. J., 287, 288
Long, M. V., 511
Lopata, H. Z., 649
Lord, S. E., 346
Loretto, W., 469
Loughlin, G. M., 92
Lourenco, O. M., 197
Lovallo, W. R., 390
Lovoy, L., 466, 467
Lozoff, B., 91, 99
Lubart, T. I., 562, 563
Lucas, J. L., 514
Luecke-Aleksa, D., 207
Lueptow, L. B., 202
Luggen, A. S., 386, 493
Luk, V., 477, 479
Lund, D. A., 649
Lundblad, A., 428
Lundin, T., 640
Lung, F.-W., 545
Luoma, J., 557
Lupetow, M. B., 202
Luthar, S. S., 238
Lütkenhaus, P., 123
Lutz, S. E., 202
Lynch, S. M., 599
Lyness, K. S., 467
Lynm, C., 549
Lynn, J., 628
Lynsky, M. T., 282
Lyon, G. R., 241, 242
Lytton, H., 56, 205

M
MacCallum, F., 58
Maccoby, E. E., 195, 203, 205, 272, 279
MacDermid, S. M., 514
Mace, N. L., 615
Mackay, C. J., 501
Mackey, R. A., 429
Mackie, D. M., 202
Maclean, W. E., 91
MacWhinney, B., 169, 246
Madden, D. J., 556
Madden, T., 344
Magai, C., 400
Magana, C., 501
Magley, V. J., 468
Maguire, M., 191
Maiden, R. J., 512
Main, M., 181, 419
Makhijani, M. G., 203
Malach-Pines, A., 460
Malina, R. M., 310
Malinosky-Rummell, R., 282
Malkinson, R., 647, 648
Mandel, D. R., 113
Mange, A. P., 50
Mange, E. J., 50
Mangelsdorf, S., 184
Mangelsdorf, S. C., 188, 189
Mannell, R. C., 483
Mantler, J., 473
Maratsos, M., 169
Marcia, J. E., 340, 342, 382
Marcovitch, S., 142
Marcus, G. F., 168
Marcussen, K. A., 428
Margolin, G., 275
Markell, M., 301

Markides, K. S., 565
Markiewicz, D., 183
Markman, E. M., 160, 164, 171
Markman, H. J., 433, 528
Markovits, H., 222, 284
Markowitz, J. C., 364
Marks, N. F., 592
Marktl, W., 484
Markus, H., 406, 407, 408
Marlier, L., 112
Marsh, B. A., 459
Marsh, H. W., 345, 359
Marshall, E. O., 583
Marsiglio, W., 351
Marsiske, M., 505
Marteau, T. M., 571
Martens, A., 630
Martin, C. L., 195, 205, 206, 207
Martin, Casey, 381
Martin, G. M., 545–46
Martin, J. A., 65, 349
Martin, J. L., 204, 205
Martin, M., 511, 583
Martin, N. G., 351
Martin, P., 583
Martin-Matthews, A., 599
Martz, S. H., 575
Maruna, S., 514
Marzolf, D., 188
Masheter, C., 444
Masunaga, H., 507
Masur, E. F., 166
Matheson, C. C., 193
Matteson, M. T., 501
Matthews, A. M., 433, 591
Matthews, R., 433
Matthews, S. H., 599
Mattson, S. N., 66
Mattys, S. L., 159
Matud, M. P., 498
Maughan, A., 282
Maume, D. J., Jr., 463, 466–67
Mayer, J. D., 228
Maynard, A. E., 274
Mazeh, T., 459
Mazur, E., 278
Mazziotta, J. C., 111
McAdams, D. P., 405, 406, 514, 528
McBride-Chang, C., 245, 262
McBurney, D. H., 179
McCabe, M., 346
McCabe, M. P., 318
McCall, R. B., 96
McCann, S. K., 295
McCann-Doyle, S., 362–63
McCarthy, K. A., 346
McCarthy, M. R., 647
McCartney, K., 55
McCarty, M. E., 109, 110
McClelland, J. L., 246
McClenahan, E. L., 288
McClure, E. B., 34, 204
McCollum, S. L., 468
McConatha, J. T., 554
McCormick, C., 74
McCormick, C. B., 224
McCoy, J. K., 275
McCrae, R. R., 510, 511, 515, 516
McCubbin, H., 433
McCutchen, D., 248
McDaniel, M. A., 459
McDowd, J. M., 555
McEwen, B. S., 499

McFadden, S. H., 586
McGarry, K., 599
McGee, R., 242
McGhee, D. E., 401
McGhee, P. E., 220, 221
McGlothlin, H., 301
McGraw, M. B., 107
McGue, M. K., 243
McGuire, L. C., 561, 569
McHale, J. P., 272
McHale, S. M., 195
McKay, M., 500
McKee-Ryan, F., 473, 474
McKenna, P., 557
McKinlay, J. B., 498
McKitrick, L. A., 571
McKown, C., 300
McKusick, V. A., 49
McLanahan, S., 277
McLaughlin, D. K., 390
McLellan, J. A., 201
McLoyd, V. C., 41
McManus, I. C., 111
McNeilly, D. P., 606, 607, 608
Mcrae, P. J., 637
McRae, S., 428
McShane, J., 240
Meck, E., 153
Medart, P., 552
Medin, D., 145
Mednick, S. A., 79
Mehta, K. K., 586
Meissner, C., 622
Meltzoff, A. N., 124, 149
Mendel, Gregor, 562
Mendelson, M. J., 274
Mennella, J., 112
Mennella, J. A., 62
Mera, S. L., 545
Merat, N., 557
Meredith, W., 512
Mertz, M. E., 600
Mervielde, I., 316
Mervis, C. B., 168
Messer, D., 156
Messner, L., 476
Michael, R. T., 494
Milberger, S., 243
Milford, M., 476
Miller, B. C., 275, 349
Miller, J. G., 330
Miller, J. S., 457
Miller, K. F., 139–40
Miller, L. K., 228
Miller, L. S., 293
Miller, N. B., 599, 649
Miller, P. A., 333
Miller, P. C., 267
Miller, P. H., 175, 262
Miller, P. M., 203
Miller, Paul, 198
Miller, R. B., 432, 434
Miller, S. A., 175, 262
Miller, T. Q., 565
Miller, W., 466–67
Mills, T. L., 600
Mindell, J. A., 92
Mirabella, R. L., 459
Mischel, W., 205, 403
Missildine, W., 430
Mitchell, C. V., 466
Mitchell, L. M., 476
Mix, K. S., 153
Mize, J., 196, 269, 290
Mizes, J., 317

Moats, L. C., 242
Moberg, D. O., 615
Mobily, K. E., 482
Modelska, K., 497
Moen, P., 477, 478, 592, 593
Moffitt, T. E., 311, 365
Mohler, C. J., 453
Mohlman, J., 567
Mohr, B. A., 498
Molfese, D. L., 104
Moller, L. C., 196
Mollnow, E., 69
Monczunski, J., 545
Mondloch, C. J., 118
Monk, C., 64
Monk, C. S., 103
Monker, J., 166
Montague, D. P., 190
Montgomery, D. T., 295
Montgomery, M. J., 382
Moolchan, E. T., 66
Moon, A., 607
Moon, S., 426
Moore, K. A., 474
Moore, K. D., 580
Moore, K. L., 51, 61
Moore, M. K., 149
Moore, M. R., 65
Mora, J. O., 100
Morahan-Martin, J., 417
Moran, T., 330
Morfei, M. Z., 407, 408
Morgan, B., 100
Morgane, P. J., 99
Morioka, K., 520
Morrell, R. W., 561
Morris, A. S., 192
Morris, P., 266
Morris, P. A., 235
Morris, S. C., 146
Morrongiello, B. A., 114
Morrow, D. G., 561
Morrow, J., 565
Mortimer, J. T., 358, 359
Morton, J., 118
Moses, L. J., 190
Moshman, D., 222
Moss, E., 183
Moss, H. A., 95
Moss, M. S., 648, 649
Moss, S. Z., 648
Mounts, N. S., 288
Mozart, W. A., 238
Mueller, W. H., 586
Mugadza, T., 467
Muller, E. D., 638
Mullet, E., 622
Mumme, D. L., 190
Munakata, Y., 142
Murphy, L. M., 284, 285
Murphy, N., 156
Murray, C., 236
Murrell, A. J., 465
Murrell, S. A., 639
Murstein, B. I., 419
Mustanski, B. S., 310
Mutchler, J. E., 589
Muter, V., 245
Mutter, J. D., 40–41
Muzet, A., 557
Muzio, J. N., 91
Muzzonigro, P. G., 351
Myers, E. G., 520
Myskow, L., 494

N

Nachtigall, R., 58
Nadig, A. S., 171
Naegele, G., 470
Nagel, S. K., 269
Nahemow, L., 12, 19, 579, 580
Nahmiash, D., 607
Naigles, L., 164, 165
Naigles, L. G., 165
Nánez, J., Sr., 116
Narasimham, G., 324–25
Nation, K., 247
Nazareth, T., 463
Neese, R. M., 640
Neff, K., 330
Neff, L. A., 433
Neft, N., 428, 429
Neimeyer, R., 629, 632, 648
Neimeyer, R. A., 630, 631
Neisser, U., 231, 235
Nell, V., 320
Nelson, B., 432
Nelson, C. A., 103, 104, 120
Nelson, C. H., 640
Nelson, D. A., 291
Nelson, K., 123, 150, 160, 165
Nelson, L. J., 379
Nelson, M. A., 319
Nesdale, D., 300, 301
Nesselroade, J. R., 40
Neuberger, J. S., 385
Neugarten, B. L., 405, 523, 627
Neukam, K. A., 591
Newcomb, A. F., 197, 284, 285
Newman, B. S., 351
Newport, E. L., 159, 169
Newsom, J. T., 522, 523
Nguyen, D. H., 469
Nguyen, S. P., 203
Nichols-Whitehead, P., 156
Nickman, S. L., 644
Nilsson, B., 622
Nilsson, L., 84
Nilstun, T., 622
Niskanen, L., 474
Nistor, G. I., 37
Nocera, R., 569
Nolen-Hoeksema, S., 638, 641
Noller, P., 433
Nonoyama, A., 390
Noonan, D., 551
Norlander, B., 423
Norris, F. N., 639
Norris, L., 505
Notarius, C. I., 434
Nugent, J. K., 76, 89
Nuland, S. B., 653
Nurius, P., 406, 407
Nurmi, J., 340
Nurmi, J.-E., 268

O

Oboudiat, F., 554
O'Brien, B. A., 429
O'Brien, C.-A., 597
Oburu, P. O., 525
O'Connell, C. M., 66
O'Conner, T., 64
O'Connor, Sandra Day, 466
O'Connor, T. G., 279
O'Donohue, W., 468, 469, 486
Oehmichen, M., 622
Offer, D., 346
Ogletree, R. J., 352
Okagaki, L., 268

Okamura, H., 582
O'Keeffe, J., 607
Okie, S., 74
Okonski, B., 647
Okun, M. A., 511
Olanow, C. W., 549
Olds, S. W., 605
O'Leary, K. D., 423–24
Oliner, P. M., 200
Oliner, S. P., 200
Olsen, J. A., 268
Olsen, O., 77
Olshansky, S. J., 545
Olsho, L. W., 114
Olson, D. H., 433
Olson, L. N., 424
Olson, R. K., 241
Olson, S. L., 192, 365
Oltjenbruns, K. A., 644, 645, 646
Olweus, D., 291, 365
O'Neal, Shaquille, 15
O'Neil, R., 269
O'Neill, D. K., 171
O'Neill, K., 640
Ong, A., 344
Ontai, L. L., 191
Opfer, J. E., 146
Opplinger, R. A., 484
O'Rand, A. M., 22
Ordy, H. M., 552
Orentlicher, D., 623
Orlick, T., 197
Ornstein, P. A., 151
O'Rourke, N., 596
O'Rourke, P., 170
Ory, M. G., 602
Osgood, D. W., 519
Osgood, N. J., 599
Ostendorf, C. A., 554
Oster, H., 112
Overton, W. F., 222
Owsley, C., 557
Oygard, L., 444
Ozarow, L., 196
Ozawa, M. N., 446

P
Paarlberg, K. M., 64
Pacy, B., 368
Paderna, L., 627
Paikoff, R., 349
Paley, B., 266, 272
Palladino, P., 247
Palmer, A. M., 503
Palmer, D. J., 274
Palmer, J. R., 386
Palmérus, K., 525
Papa, A., 640
Papalia, D. E., 605
Papka, M., 546
Paquette, J. A., 289
Parasuraman, R., 555
Parasuraman, S., 465
Parault, S. J., 224
Pargament, K. I., 586
Paris, F. A., 191
Park, D. C., 556, 561
Park, M. M., 77
Parke, R. D., 181, 197, 267, 269, 270
Parker, J., 289
Parker, J. G., 285, 287
Parker, R. A., 515
Parks, L., 587

Parmet, S., 549
Parritz, R. H., 191
Parrott, T. M., 600
Parry, J., 592
Parten, M., 193
Partington, J., 197
Pascalis, O., 120
Pascual, C., 622
Pascual-Leone, J., 329
Pasley, K., 279
Pasupathi, M., 406
Patrick, J. H., 525
Patterson, C. J., 281, 351, 439
Patterson, G. R., 270, 366
Patterson, M., 158
Patterson, S. J., 382
Pavalko, E. K., 520, 522, 588
Pavlov, Ivan, 148
Payne, J. W., 603
Pearce, K. A., 503
Pearlin, L. I., 521
Pearson, A., 298
Pearson, J. D., 547
Pebayle, T., 557
Peck, Kathy, 550–51
Pellegrini, A. D., 179, 266
Pelphrey, K. A., 149
Penha-Lopes, V., 437
Pennebaker, J. W., 501
Pennington, B. F., 242, 243
Penson, R. T., 618
Peplau, L., 433
Perez, A., 623
Perfetti, C. A., 246
Perlmutter, M. S., 156
Perls, T., 540, 542, 545
Perrewe, P. L., 472
Perris, E., 114
Perry, D. G., 291, 351
Perry, R. P., 585–86
Perry, T. B., 284
Perry, W. I., 380, 397
Persaud, T. V. N., 51, 61
Peters, A. M., 167
Peters, R., 390
Peterson, B. E., 514
Peterson, C., 363, 519
Peterson, L., 199
Petrakos, H., 194
Petrill, S. A., 232
Pettit, G. S., 196, 267, 269, 366
Phelps, J. A., 53
Phelps, R. E., 467
Phinney, J., 343, 344
Phinney, J. S., 343, 344
Piaget, J., 221
Piaget, Jean, 12, 15–16, 17, 132–46, 220–23
Piccininni, M., 568, 569
Pickard, M., 387
Picot, S. J., 587
Pienta, A. M., 597
Pierce, C. A., 468
Pierce, S. H., 224
Pilgrim, C., 288
Pilling, M., 115
Pincus, T., 390
Pinderhughes, E., 275, 276
Pinquart, M., 123, 583
Piolat, A., 247
Piotrowski, C., 627
Piscione, D. P., 463, 464
Pisoni, D. B., 113, 158
Pittenger, K. K. S., 456
Pitts, S. C., 388

Platt, L., 73
Pleck, J. H., 437
Plewis, I., 90, 91
Pleydell-Pearce, C. W., 150
Plomin, R., 53, 55, 84, 96, 232, 233
Plumert, J. M., 156
Plunkett, K., 147
Polifka, J. E., 66
Polit, E. F., 276
Polkovitz, R. J., 486
Pollitt, E., 99, 257
Pomeroy, E. C., 637
Ponde, M. P., 483
Ponder, R. J., 637
Poole, D. A., 151, 175
Poole, M. E., 340
Poon, L. W., 511, 559
Porter, R. H., 112
Potter, J., 512–13
Poulin, F., 285
Poulin-Dubois, D., 145, 163
Poulos, R. W., 197
Poulson, C. L., 160
Powell, F. C., 631
Power, F. C., 333, 334
Powlishta, K., 300
Powlishta, K. K., 203–4
Pozzi, S., 253
Prather, E., 448
Prather, H., 448
Pratt, M. W., 514
Presnell, K., 314
Pressley, M., 224, 225, 323–24
Previti, D., 441
Prigerson, H. G., 643
Principe, G. F., 151
Prinstein, M. J., 289
Probert, B., 463
Prosada, S., 144
Prost, J., 388
Pruchno, R., 525
Pruett, M. K., 445
Pryor, J. B., 468
Puhl, R. M., 318
Pyngolil, M., 494
Pyszczynski, T., 630–31

Q
Quadagno, J., 609
Quadrel, M. J., 321
Qualls, S. H., 565, 566, 569
Quick, J. C., 498
Quillian, L., 284
Quinn, D. M., 402
Quinn, J. F., 590
Quinn, M. J., 607

R
Rabiner, D. J., 607
Rabiner, D. L., 366
Rabins, P. V., 615
Radford, A., 167
Ragins, B. R., 457
Ragland, O. R., 500
Ragozin, A. S., 436
Rahhal, T., 559
Raine, A., 290
Rakic, P., 101
Rakison, D. H., 145
Raman, L., 146
Ramey, C. T., 234
Ramey, S. L., 234
Ramsay, D., 123
Ramsay, D. S., 94

Ramsey, F., 99
Rankin, C. T., 428
Ransjoe-Arvidson, A. B., 76
Ranwez, S., 508
Rao, K. V., 428
Rapaport, J. L., 242
Rapoport, R., 482
Rapoport, R. N., 482
Rappaport, L., 92
Rapport, M. D., 242, 243
Raschick, M., 597
Rasmussen, R. L., 258
Rasmussen, S. A., 50
Rathunde, K. R., 238
Rawlins, W. K., 418, 594
Rayner, K., 245
Read, J. P., 386, 387
Read, S. J., 419
Reagan, Nancy, 597
Reagan, Ronald, 597
Reddy, V., 187
Reese, D., 605
Reese, E., 166
Reese, H. W., 40
Reich, P. A., 162
Reid, D. H., 240
Reid, J., 480
Reid, J. B., 367
Reid, M., 466–67
Reifman, A., 387
Reimer, M. S., 189
Reinhoudt, C. J., 586
Reis, M., 607
Reiser, L. W., 312
Reno, Janet, 549
Repacholi, B. M., 190
Resnick, L. B., 249
Rettig, K. D., 622
Reubens, B., 358
Reynolds, A. J., 234, 282
Reynolds, D., 626
Reznick, J. S., 165
Rhee, S. H., 243
Ricciardelli, L. A., 318
Ricciuti, H. N., 100
Rice, Jerry, 384
Rice, M. L., 167
Rice, S. G., 319
Rich, C. L., 364
Richards, L. N., 446
Richards, M. H., 483
Richters, J. E., 243
Rickwood, D. J., 582
Rideout, V., 292
Ridings, C., 417
Ridley, M., 84
Riedmann, A., 426, 427, 433, 434, 437, 438, 443, 444, 446
Riggs, D. S., 423
Rightmyer, J., 221
Riley, E. P., 66
Riley, K. P., 570
Riley, L. D., 518
Riley, M. W., 20
Rinaldi, C. M., 194
Rindfuss, R. R., 456
Ring, J., 241
Ritchie, K.L., 266
Rivara, F. P., 320
Rivera, Diego, 562
Robbins, A., 382, 412
Roberto, K. A., 600
Roberts, B. W., 405
Roberts, D. F., 292
Roberts, J. D., 587

Roberts, J. E., 166
Roberts, R. E., 344
Roberts, R. J., 243
Roberts, W., 198
Robertson, D. L., 282
Robertson, I., 483
Robinson, A., 238
Robinson, J. M., 515
Robinson, M., 153
Robinson, M. L., 66
Robinson, P., 649
Rockwood, K., 601, 602
Rodd, Z. A., 446
Rodin, J., 580, 605
Roffwarg, H. P., 91
Rogers, S. J., 434
Rogers, W. A., 555, 556
Rogers, Will, 177
Rogoff, B., 156
Rogosch, F. A., 281
Rokach, R., 434
Romney, D. M., 205
Roodin, P. A., 507
Rook, K. S., 594
Roosevelt, Franklin, 609
Roscoe, L. A., 623
Rose, A., 289
Rose, A. J., 285, 289
Rose, H., 207
Rose, R. J., 53
Rose, S., 416
Rosenberg, E. B., 439
Rosenberg, H. J., 516
Rosenberg, J., 434
Rosenberg, L., 386
Rosenberg, S. D., 516
Rosenblatt, P. C., 619, 639, 653
Rosenfeld, B., 625
Rosengren, K. S., 139–40, 145, 156
Rosenman, R. H., 500
Rosenthal, D. A., 344
Rosenthal, R., 185
Ross, C. E., 444
Ross, H. S., 204, 205, 274
Rostenstein, D., 112
Rothbart, M. K., 93, 191
Rothbaum, F., 181
Rotherman-Borus, M. J., 351
Rothman, R., 615
Rotondo, D. M., 472
Rotundo, M., 469
Rounds, J., 356
Roussey, J., 247
Rovee-Collier, C., 148, 149
Rowe, J. W., 388
Rowe, M. M., 461
Roxburgh, S., 477
Rozakis, L., 336
Rubin, D. C., 559
Rubin, K. H., 95, 196, 220, 273, 287, 289, 290, 300
Rubin, S. S., 647
Ruble, D., 206, 207
Ruble, D. N., 202, 312
Rueda, M. R., 191
Ruff, H. A., 148
Ruffman, T., 125
Ruscher, J. B., 483
Rushton, J. P., 284
Russell, J. A., 191
Ruthsatz, J. M., 239
Rutland, A., 301
Rwampororo, R. K., 477
Ryan, E. B., 605
Ryan, Nolan, 384

Rybash, J. M., 507, 508
Rye, M. S., 444
Ryff, C. D., 408
Rylands, K., 582
Rymer, R., 169

S

Saba, T., 472
Sabbagh, M. A., 162
Sacco, W. P., 364
Sackett, P. R., 469
Saffran, J. R., 159
Sagi, A., 184
Saginak, K. A., 478, 479, 480, 481
Saginak, M. A., 478, 479, 480, 481
Sais, E., 165
Sakaeda, A. R., 405, 406
Sakamoto, A., 554
Sakraida, T. J., 444
Salapatek, Philip, 119
Salari, S., 508
Salib, E., 623
Salieri, A., 238
Salisbury, G., 203
Salomone, P. R., 455
Salovey, P., 228
Salthouse, T. A., 556, 558, 559
Sanders, M. R., 295
Sangrador, J. L., 420
Sanson, A., 204
Santana, V. S., 483
Sargeant, M., 590
Satariano, W. A., 557
Saunders, Cicely, 633
Saunders, S., 633
Savage-Rumbaugh, E. S., 169
Savelsbergh, G. J. P., 109, 110
Saxon, S. V., 498
Sbraga, T. P., 468, 469, 486
Scandura, T. A., 457
Scardamalia, M., 248
Scarr, S., 55
Schaal, B., 112
Schaie, K. W., 392, 393, 394, 412, 511
Schapira, A. H. V., 549
Schartz, K. M., 53
Schechtman, K. B., 602
Scheier, M. F., 416
Schiaffino, K., 522
Schiavo, Terri, 623–24
Schimmele, C. M., 446
Schindler, Oskar, 328–29
Schlegel, A., 379
Schlossberg, N. K., 589, 590, 591, 592
Schmeeckle, M., 417, 595
Schmidt, F. L., 231–32
Schmiege, C. J., 446
Schmitt, D. P., 420–21
Schmitt, F. A., 569, 570
Schmitz-Scherzer, R., 511
Schneider, B. H., 183
Schneider, K. T., 468
Schneider, M. L., 64
Schneider, W., 323–24
Schnorr, T. M., 68
Schoenborn, C. A., 386
Schoeni, R. F., 599
Schoon, I., 455
Schotsmans, P., 621
Schuett, A., 607
Schulenberg, J., 359
Schulz, R., 409, 585
Schumacher, P., 417

Schut, H., 627, 637, 638, 640, 641, 642, 644
Schutz, R. W., 258, 309
Schwaartz, J. L. K., 401
Schwanenflugel, P. J., 224
Schwartz, D., 291
Schwartz, P., 430
Schwartz, R. S., 553
Schwarzenegger, Arnold, 37
Scott, M. E., 428
Scott, P., 317
Scott, R., 346
Scott, W. A., 346
Scozzaro, P. P., 463
Seal, J., 285
Seccombe, K., 443, 599
Sedivy, J. C., 171
Seeman, T. E., 545
Segal, D. L., 649
Seibenbruner, J., 348
Seidenberg, M. S., 246
Seidman, S. M., 497
Seidner, L. B., 193
Seifer, R., 184
Selman, F. L., 300
Selman, R. L., 298–300
Seltzer, J. A., 445
Sénéchal, M., 166, 245
Sera, E. J., 639, 640
Serbin, L., 281
Serbin, L. A., 203–4
Serdula, M. K., 316
Servin, A., 207–8
Seyfarth, R., 169
Shah, B., 113
Shaiko, R. G., 467
Shainess, N., 463
Shalev, R., 647
Shanahan, M. J., 359
Shannon, F. T., 98
Shapiro, J. R., 188
Shapiro, S., 386
Share, D. L., 246
Sharpe, R. M., 71
Shatz, M., 146
Shaver, P., 419
Shaw, D. S., 278
Shaw, G. M., 63
Shaw, H., 318
Shaw, R. J., 555
Shebilske, L. J., 484
Shehan, C. L., 443
Shell, R., 200
Shelov, S. P., 98
Shelton, B. A., 479
Sher, T. G., 419
Sherlock, H., 461
Sherman, A. M., 416, 417, 594
Sherman, D. K., 243
Sherman, M., 364
Sherry, D., 627
Shi, R., 159
Shifren, K., 515
Shifrin, K., 561
Shin, Y. L., 194
Shirom, A., 459
Shiwach, R., 50
Shoda, Y., 403
Shoemaker, C., 417
Shonk, S. M., 282
Shore, R. J., 524
Showstack, J., 58
Shrager, J., 249
Shulman, S., 348
Shumway-Cook, A., 107

Shuter-Dyson, R., 228
Shwe, H. I., 171
Sicotte, N. L., 111
Siddiqui, A., 109–10
Sidebotham, P., 281
Siegler, I. C., 511
Siegler, R. S., 142, 143, 146, 153, 175, 222, 246, 247, 249
Signorielli, N., 294
Silbereisen, R. K., 310, 314, 315
Silk, J. S., 268
Silva, P. A., 311
Silverman, P. R., 644, 645
Silverman, W. K., 189
Silverstein, J. S., 464
Silverstein, M., 600
Simmons, R., 315
Simon, Theophile, 230
Simons, D. J., 145
Simons-Morton, B., 361
Simonton, D. K., 562, 563
Simpson, E. L., 330
Simpson, J. M., 92
Singer, A., 437, 590
Singer, J. D., 184
Singer, L. T., 71
Singer, M., 247
Sinnott, J. D., 396, 397, 399, 412, 473, 515
Siu, O-L., 501
Skakkebaek, N. E., 71
Skinner, B. F., 12, 14, 15, 168
Skinner, E. A., 269
Skoglund, R. R., 600
Skolnick, A. A., 628
Skrajner, M. J., 571, 572
Skuldt-Niederberger, K., 515
Slap, G. A., 336
Slobin, D. I., 168
Slomkowski, C., 274
Small, B. J., 512, 559
Smerglia, V. L., 599, 649
Smith, B. L., 364
Smith, C. J., 525
Smith, D. B., 592
Smith, E. G., 152
Smith, E. R., 202
Smith, J., 20, 408, 507, 543, 601
Smith, K. R., 438
Smith, L., 608
Smith, L. B., 107, 142, 164
Smith, L. L., 380, 382
Smith, R. E., 258
Smith, R. S., 80
Smith, T. E., 203
Smith, V. L., 151
Smith, W. J., 457
Smoll, F. L., 258, 309
Smyer, M. A., 568, 569, 586
Snedeker, B., 358
Snider, J. B., 272
Snow, C. W., 90, 114
Snow, M. E., 205
Snyder, E., 207
Snyder, J., 267
Snyder, L., 165
Sochting, I., 382
Soederberg Miller, L. M., 408, 555, 556, 585
Solano, N. H., 602
Solomon, S., 630–31
Sommerville, J. A., 124
Sörensen, S., 583
Sorum, P. C., 622
Sousa, P., 145

Soussignan, R., 112
Spearman, C., 226
Spears, Britney, 383
Spelke, E. S., 144
Spence, M. J., 62
Spencer, W. D., 402
Spetner, N. B., 114
Spielberg, Steven, 328
Spinath, F., 55
Spinrad, T., 198
Spitze, G., 519
Sprafkin, J. N., 197
Springer, K., 145, 146
Srivastava, S., 512–13
St. George, I. M., 311
St. James-Roberts, I., 90, 91
Staff, J., 358, 359
Stafford, L., 428
Stanford, E. P., 590
Stanley, S. M., 528
Staples, R., 448
Stark, E., 423
Starko, A. J., 239
Stattin, H., 268
Staudinger, U. M., 20–21, 506–7, 563
Stauss, J. H., 437
Steele, C. M., 237, 402
Steelman, J. D., 253
Steen, T. A., 519
Stein, J. H., 312
Steinbart, E. J., 570
Steinberg, K. J., 151
Steinberg, L., 288, 311, 346, 347, 358, 359, 368
Steinberg, L. D., 311, 312, 321, 349, 370
Steiner, J. E., 112
Stephens, M. A. P., 520, 522, 523
Stern, M., 202
Sternberg, C. R., 188
Sternberg, K. J., 289
Sternberg, R. J., 226, 229–30, 232, 268, 392, 418, 503, 506, 562, 563, 602
Sterns, A. A., 459
Sterns, H. L., 457, 588, 589, 590–91
Stevens, N., 285
Stevenson, H. W., 190, 250, 251, 252, 253, 254
Steward, R. J., 465
Stewart, L., 329
Stewart, R. B., 274
Stewart, S., 290
Stice, E., 285, 314, 318
Stier, H., 479
Stifter, C. A., 95
Stigler, J. W., 190, 251, 252, 253, 254
Stiles, J., 104
Stine-Morrow, E. A. L., 555, 556
Stokes, C. S., 390
Stoller, P., 554
Stoneman, A., 275
Stoolmiller, M., 273, 367
Strachan, E., 630
Straine, Trish, 647
Strano, D. A., 387
Strauss-Blasche, G., 484
Strayer, J., 198
Streissguth, A. P., 67
Stroebe, M., 627
Stroebe, M. S., 636, 637, 638, 640, 641, 642, 644

Stroebe, W., 627, 637, 638
Strough, J., 203
Stunkard, A. J., 316
Su, M., 280
Subich, L. M., 463
Sullivan, L. W., 49
Sullivan, S. A., 98
Sulloway, F. J., 276
Summerville, M. B., 364
Sundet, J. M., 234
Super, C. M., 100
Super, D. E., 355, 356, 454–55
Sutterlin, R. L., 456
Suzuki, L., 237
Suzuki, Y., 552
Swan, S., 468
Swaney, K., 356
Swanson, R. A., 508
Swenson, L. P., 289
Sykes, D. H., 79

T

Taaffe, D. R., 494
Taber, S., 382
Tadros, G., 623
Talaga, J. A., 591
Talbott, M. M., 599
Tamang, B. L., 190
Tamis-LeMonda, C. S., 196
Tamis-Lemonda, C. S., 165
Tan, A., 528
Tang, T. L. P., 468
Tanji, V. M., 622
Tannen, D., 448
Tanner, J. M., 309
Taplin, J. E., 146
Tardif, C., 183
Tardif, T., 269
Tasker, F., 351
Taub, G. E., 503
Taylor, E. H., 434
Taylor, J., 494
Taylor, J. H., 329, 334
Taylor, J. L., 507
Taylor, M., 194, 195
Taylor, M. G., 203
Taylor, N., 653
Taylor, R. J., 587, 594
Tees, R. C., 158
Teichman, Y., 301
Teisseyre, N., 622
Teixeira, R. A., 284
Temple, J. A., 234
Templer, A., 472, 473
Tenenbaum, H. R., 205
Terkel, S., 452, 459
Terman, Lewis, 230–31
Terman, M., 553
Terry, D., 540, 542, 545
Teti, D. M., 79
Thase, M. E., 364
Thelen, E., 107
Thelen, M. H., 312
Theobald, W., 349
Thiessen, E. D., 159
Thomae, H., 511
Thomas, A., 93
Thomas, Clarence, 468
Thomas, D. A., 466
Thomas, E., 166
Thomas, J. W., 324
Thomas, N. G., 239
Thompson, D. E., 467
Thompson, L. W., 649
Thompson, R. A., 183, 189, 191

Thomson, E., 428
Thoreau, Henry David, 200
Thorne, A., 406
Thornhill, R., 118
Thorson, J. A., 631
Thuell, S., 629
Thurstone, L. L., 226–27
Thurstone, T. G., 226–27
Tiffany, D. W., 409
Tiffany, P. G., 409
Timiras, P., 544, 545
Tincoff, R., 159
Tinker, E., 164, 169
Tolan, P. H., 366
Tolmacz, R., 419
Tomasello, M., 170
Tomita, S. K., 607
Tomolillo, C., 417
Tonya, M., 317
Torgesen, J. K., 240
Torjussen, T. M., 234
Toth, S. L., 279, 280, 281
Townsend, A. L., 522
Trabasso, T., 247
Trainor, L. J., 113, 159
Trehub, S. E., 113
Treiman, R., 225, 245
Tremblay, R. E., 365
Trickett, E. J., 344
Troll, L. E., 519
Trost, S. G., 258
Trujillo, K. M., 502
Truog, R. D., 621
Tronick, E. Z., 188
Trost, S. G., 258
Tsang, C. D., 113
Tsao, F.-M., 160
Tsao, T.-C., 588
Tulviste, P., 155
Tung, Y. Y., 422
Turati, C., 118
Turiel, E., 330, 332
Turkheimer, E., 56
Turley, R. N. L., 65
Twenge, J. M., 345
Tyson-Rawson, K. J., 646

U

Ucello, C. E., 590
Udry, J. R., 348
Uggen, C., 358
Uhlenberg, P., 445
Ullian, D. Z., 206
Ulrich, B. D., 107
Umbel, V. M., 165
Underlid, K., 390
Unger, O., 193
Upchurch, S., 586
Updegraff, K. A., 275
Urberg, K. A., 288
Usita, P. M., 554
Utman, J. A., 160

V

Vachon, R., 222
Vaillant, G. E., 516
Valkenburg, P. M., 296
Valois, R. F., 358
Valverius, E., 622
Vandell, D. L., 185
Vandello, J. A., 424
van den Boom, D. C., 184
Vandereycken, W., 316
van der Geest, S., 619
van der Kamp, J., 110
van der Mark, I. L., 198

van der Voort, T. H. A., 296
Vander Wal, J. S., 312
van der Zee, J., 77
Vandewater, E. A., 517
van Dierendonck, D., 461
van Hof, P., 110
van IJzendoorn, M. H., 91, 182, 183, 184, 198
van Solinge, H., 591
van Wieringen, P. C. W., 109
Vasta, R., 168, 271
Vazsonyi, A. T., 272
Vega, J. L., 631
Veiga, J. F., 457
Venable, R. H., 387
Ventura, S. J., 79
Vereijken, B., 108
Verhaeghen, P., 559
Verma, I. M., 74
Vicary, J. R., 387
Vierthaler, J., 637
Viinamaki, H., 474
Villa, R. F., 587
Vinters, H. V., 546, 547
Visher, E. B., 279
Visher, J. S., 279
Visser, A., 461
Vitaro, F., 288, 345
Vitulano, L. A., 365
Voisin, T., 571
Volling, B. L., 275
Vorhees, C. V., 69
Voyer, D., 203
Voyer, S., 203
Vygotsky, L. S., 12, 17, 154–56

W

Wachs, T. D., 54, 94
Wadlington, W., 444
Wagner, R. K., 245, 246
Wahl, H.-W., 579
Wahlin, Å., 559
Walberg, H. J., 252, 253, 254
Waldfogel, J., 80
Waldo, C. R., 468
Waldron, M., 56
Waldrop, D. P., 525
Walk, R. D., 115
Walker, L. E. A., 422
Walker, L. J., 329, 333, 334
Walker-Andrews, A. S., 190
Wall, S., 587
Wallace, D. D., 385
Wallace, J. E., 457
Wallace, J. I., 553
Waller, E. M., 289
Wallerstein, J. S., 445
Wallisch, L., 445
Walsh, D., 370
Walsh, D. A., 590
Walsh, D. M., 502
Walsh, E. K., 634
Walther, A. N., 443
Wang, Q., 417, 595
Wang, S. S., 317, 318
Wanner, B., 585
Ward, R., 519
Ward, S. L., 222
Wardrop, J. L., 291
Warr, P., 483
Washko, M., 514
Wass, H., 632
Wasserstein, S., 189
Waters, E., 182
Waters, H. F., 292

Waters, H. S., 248
Waters, L., 474
Waters, P., 345
Watkins, B. A., 294
Watkinson, B., 66
Watson, J., 124
Watson, J. A., 524
Watson, J. B., 266
Watson, John, 12, 14
Watson, W. K., 387
Wayment, H. A., 637
Webb, S. J., 103, 105
Webber, L. S., 256
Weber, J. A., 525, 579
Wechsler, D., 231
Wechsler, H., 386, 387
Wegman, M. E., 92
Wegner, D. M., 641
Weibel-Orlando, J., 525
Weichold, K., 310, 314, 315
Weinbaum, E., 142
Weinberg, J., 71
Weinberg, M. K., 188, 204
Weinstein, K. K., 523
Weinstein, R. S., 300
Weishaus, S., 434
Weisner, T. S., 208
Weissberg, R., 148
Weissman, M. D., 145
Welle, S., 494
Wellman, H. M., 124, 125, 142,
    144, 145, 191
Wells, Y. D., 598
Welsh, M. C., 242
Wentkowski, G., 600
Wentworth, N., 110
Werker, J. F., 158, 159
Werner, E. E., 80
Werner, H., 108
Wertsch, J. V., 155
West, R. L., 585
Westbrook, L. A., 648
Westheimer, R., 528
Wethington, E., 516
Wettemann, B. A., 646
Weymouth, P. L., 592

Whalley, L. J., 385
Whitbeck, L. B., 340
Whitbourne, S. K., 384, 427, 497,
    498, 545, 546, 547, 549, 550,
    551, 552, 565, 566, 569, 575,
    605
White, L., 279
Whitehead, J. R., 319
Whitehurst, G. J., 168, 271
Whitesell, N. R., 345
Whiting, B. B., 203
Whiting, J. W. M., 268
Whitmer, R. A., 605
Whitney, E. N., 63
Whyte, M. K., 348
Wickrama, K. A. S., 434
Wicks-Nelson, R., 203, 242, 282,
    363, 367
Widmayer, S. M., 170
Wiegers, T. A., 77
Wiener, R. L., 469
Wilber, K. H., 606, 607, 608
Wilkinson, A. M., 628
Wilkinson, S., 623
Willcutt, E., 243
Willetts, M. C., 599
Williams, E. A., 457
Williams, H., 107
Williams, J. E., 515
Williams, J. M., 247, 248
Williams, O., 607
Williams, O. J., 607
Williams, R., 483
Williams, S., 242, 311
Williamson, G. M., 64
Williamson, J. B., 609, 611
Willinger, M., 93
Willis, R. A., 477
Willis, S. L., 511
Wilner, A., 382, 412
Wilson, E. O., 198
Wilson, G. T., 317
Wilson, M., 281
Wilson, P. G., 240
Wilson, R. D., 73
Wilson, R. S., 232, 568

Wilson-Mitchell, J. E., 208
Winblad, B., 571
Winburg, J., 112
Winer, G. A., 142
Winner, E., 238
Winner, K., 444
Winslow, E. B., 278
Winter, M. A., 271
Wise, B. W., 241
Wolf, A. W., 91
Wolf, M. M., 14
Wolfe, D. A., 280
Wolfe, R., 565, 566
Wolff, P. H., 90
Wolfson, A. R., 346
Wolraich, M. L., 243
Woodbury, M. A., 595, 596
Woodin, E. M., 272, 278
Woodruff-Pak, D., 546
Woods, R. P., 111
Woodward, A. L., 124, 160, 164
Woodward, L. J., 65
Woodworth, S., 273
Woollacott, M. H., 107
Worden, J. W., 645
Worden, W., 636
Wormley, W. M., 465
Worobey, J., 100
Wortman, C. B., 640
Wrenn, R. L., 646
Wright, J. C., 292, 293, 295, 296
Wu, B., 379
Wu, C., 434
Wu, L., 113
Wu, Z., 446
WuDunn, S., 539
Wykle, M. L., 603
Wynn, K., 152–53

X

Xiaohe, X., 348
Xu, X., 422, 425

Y

Yang, B., 276
Yang, N., 481

Yang, Q., 50
Yassuda, M. S., 585
Yates, M., 340
Yela, C., 420
Yeung, A. S., 345
Yeung, W. J., 180
Yick, A. G., 424
Yonas, A., 116
Yoon, H. S., 446
Young, A., 517
Youngblade, L. M., 194
Youngjohn, J. R., 568
Youniss, J., 201, 340
Yu, Y., 437
Yuill, N., 298
Yunger, J. L., 266

Z

Zacks, R. T., 558, 559
Zafarullah, H., 467
Zahn-Waxler, C., 190, 198
Zal, H. M., 528
Zand, D., 416
Zappert, L. T., 468
Zaslow, M. J., 203
Zelazo, N. A., 88, 108
Zelazo, P. D., 142
Zhang, F., 399
Zhao, J. Z., 428
Zhou, Q., 267
Zhou, Q. Y., 197
Zigler, E., 236, 238
Zimiles, H., 277
Zimmer-Gembeck, M. J., 348
Zimmerman, B. J., 224
Zmuda, J. M., 500
Zsembik, B. A., 590
Zucker, K. J., 351
Zukow-Goldring, P., 274
Zung, W. W. K., 566
Zusman, M. E., 425
Zvonkovic, A. M., 446
Zych, A. A., 554

Subject Index

A

AAMR (American Association on Mental Retardation), 239–40
AARP (American Association of Retired People), 609
AARP Resources on Grief and Loss (website), 654
abandonment of elders, 606
ABCDE model, 416
abnormal chromosomes, 50–51
absolutist thinking, 399
abuse and neglect of older adults, 606–8
abuse of children, 151, 279–82
abusive relationships, 422–23
academic self-concepts, 345
academic skills, 244–55. See also education
  effectiveness of schools and teachers, 252–54
  math skills, 249–50
  reading, 244–47
  in U.S. vs. other countries, 249–52
  writing, 247–49
accommodation, 133
accommodative activities, 585–86
achievement identity status, 341–42
acquaintance rape, 352–53
acquired immunodeficiency syndrome (AIDS), 67, 349
active euthanasia, 621–23
activities of daily living (ADLs), 601
activity level as dimension of temperament, 94
ADA (Americans with Disabilities Act), 380–81
adaptation level, 579
addiction to alcohol, 388
ADHD (attention-deficit hyperactivity disorder), 242–43
ADLs (activities of daily living), 601
Administration on Aging, 575
adolescent egocentrism, 342–43
adolescent-limited antisocial behavior, 365
adolescents
  ADHD and, 243
  cognitive development, 221–25
  death, causes of, 320–21
  death and bereavement, reaction to, 646
  defined, 3
  delinquency, 365–68
  depression in, 363–64
  divorce and, 279
  drinking and smoking by, 360–63
  health issues, 315–21
  identity formation, 340–43
  moral reasoning, 326–34
  peer relationships, 283–91
  pregnant teenagers, 64–65
  puberty, 308–15
  romantic relationships and sexuality, 348–54
  self-esteem in, 345–46
  sexual activity, 286
  storm and stress myth, 345–46
  suicide by, 364–65
  work and, 354–59
adopted children, 275–76, 439
adoption studies, 53, 233
adulthood. See also middle-age adults; older adults; work; young adults
  cognitive development, 381–82, 391–404, 555–64

death and bereavement, experience of, 646–48
divorce and remarriage, 276–79, 440–46
family life cycle, 435–40
health, 384–90
intelligence in, 392–96
lifestyles, 425–35
personality development, 404–10, 510–17, 582–88
physical development, 384
postformal thought and reflective judgment, 396–400
relationships, 416–25. See also family relationships; parenting
stereotypes and social beliefs in, 400–404
transition to, 378–83
advertising, 294–95
aerobic exercise, 501–2
affect, positive and negative, 94
affluence, misleading, 359
African Americans
  caregiving stress and, 522
  death, causes of, 320
  death rates, 385
  divorce rate, 441
  frail older adults, 602
  household division of labor and, 479
  life expectancy of, 390
  menopause and, 495
  occupational development and, 465
  older adults among, 538
  parenting by, 437
  prenatal care and, 65
  problematic terminology, 9
  religion and, 586, 587
  retirement and, 590, 591
  SIDS and, 93
  singlehood among, 426
  stereotype threat and intelligence tests, 235, 236–37, 402
  suicide rates, 364
age, mental, 230
age and parenting, 272–73
aged, the. See older adults
age discrimination, 469–70
age of pregnant women, 64–65
age of variability, 61
aggression
  abusive relationships, 422–25
  bullying, 290–91
  gender differences, 204
  television and, 292–93
aggressive children, 289, 290–91
aging, theories of, 544–46
aging stereotyping, 401–2, 559–60
agreeableness, 511
AIDS (acquired immunodeficiency syndrome), 67, 349
alcohol
  binge drinking, 386–87
  peer pressure and, 288
  prenatal development and, 66–67
  teenage drinking, 360–61
  young adults and, 386–88
alcoholism, 388
alert inactivity state, 90
alienation, 459–60
alleles, 48

allergies and infants, 98
altruism, 197–201
Alzheimer's Association, 575
Alzheimer's disease, 548, 567–72, 597
American Association of Retired People (AARP), 609
American Association on Mental Retardation (AAMR), 239–40
American Bar Association Section on Family Law, 449
American Heart Association, 412
American Psychological Association, 41, 575
American Sign Language Browser, 175
American Speech-Language-Hearing Association, 175
Americans with Disabilities Act (ADA), 380–81
amniocentesis, 72–73
amnion, 59–60
amniotic fluid, 59, 60
amyloid, 569
anabolic steroids, 319–20
analytic ability, 229
androgen, 207–8, 310
anesthesia and childbirth, 76
anger, 188, 190
Anglo Americans. See European Americans
animism, 136
anniversary reaction, 639
anorexia nervosa, 317–18
Anorexia Nervosa and Related Eating Disorders, Inc., 336
antidepressants, 566, 571
antioxidants, 545
antisocial behavior and delinquency, 365
anxiety about death, 630–31
anxiety disorders, 567
Apache, 312
apathetic sibling relationships, 595
Apgar scores, 89
appearance as reality, 138–40, 141
appraisal of a situation, and stress, 499
approval-focused orientation, 332
arthritis, 494
artistic personality type, 357
Asian Americans
  abusive relationships and, 424
  children's play among, 194
  dating patterns, 348
  death, causes of, 320
  death rates, 385
  elder abuse and, 607
  frail older adults, 602
  intelligence tests and, 236
  older adults among, 538
  parenting, 437
  problematic terminology, 9
  suicide rates, 364
aspirin, 66
assimilation, 132–33
assimilative activities, 585–86
assisted living facilities, 603
assortative mating, 419
attachment
  defined, 180
  falling in love and, 419, 422
  forms of, 181–82
  grief and, 637

attachment (*continued*)
  growth of, 179–83
  quality of, 183–84, 195–96
Attachment Q-Set, 182
attachment styles in love relationships, 419, 421
attention
  in infants and preschoolers, 147–48
  joint attention in language learning, 162–64
  in older adults, 555–56
attentional control, 555–56
attention-deficit hyperactivity disorder (ADHD), 242–43
attraction, 422
audience, imaginary, 342–43
Australian Museum DeathOnline (website), 653
authoritarian parenting, 268
authoritative parenting, 268
autobiographical memory, 150–52, 406, 559
autonomy vs. shame and doubt, 179
autosomes, 46
average children (in popularity), 289
average life expectancy, 539–40
avoidant attachment, 182
awareness of self, 122–26
axons, 100, 101

B

babbling, 160
babies. *See* infants; newborns
Babinksi reflex, 88, 89
baby boom generation, 608, 610
balance, 107, 552–53
Baltimore Longitudinal Study of Aging, 511
basal metabolic rate, 316–17
basic cries, 90
basic emotions, 187, 188–89
basic trust vs. mistrust, 178–79
battered woman syndrome, 422
bedwetting, 92
behavioral genetics, 51–53
behaviorism, 14, 168
behavior therapy, 566–67
beliefs, 124–25, 324–25. *See also* stereotypes
bereavement. *See* grief, mourning, and bereavement
Big Five personality traits, 511–13
bilingualism, 165
binge drinking, 386–87
bioethics, 621
biological forces, 7, 8
biology, naive theories of, 145–46
biopsychosocial framework, 7–10, 275
biracial children, 437–38
birth. *See* labor and delivery
birth order, 276
birth weight, low, 79–80
blended families, 278–79, 438–39
blink reflex, 88, 89
blood clots, 497
BMI (body mass index), 316, 389
bodily-kinesthetic intelligence, 227–28
body image, 312
body mass index (BMI), 316, 389
bone growth, in puberty, 309
bone mass, loss of, 491–94
bottle-feeding, 98
boys vs. girls. *See* gender differences
brain and nervous system
  changes in older adulthood, 546–47
  development of, 101–5
  injuries to the brain, 103, 104
  measures of brain activity, 27, 547
  neuroplasticity, 104–5
  organization of the brain, 100–101

"Brain Briefings" (Society for Neuroscience), 129
breast cancer, 497
breast-feeding, 97–98
bridge jobs, 590
Bronfenbrenner's theory, 18–19
bulimia nervosa, 317–18
bullying, 290–91
burnout, 460–61

C

caffeine, 66
CAH (congenital adrenal hyperplasia), 207–8
calcium intake, 493
cancer, 497, 553–54
cardinality principle, 153
cardiovascular disease
  hormone replacement and, 497
  nutrition and, 388–89
  in older adults, 547
  stress and, 500–501
cardiovascular system and aging, 547–49
career development, 354–58. *See also* work
career plateauing, 472
caregiving
  for aging parents, 520–23
  day care and attachment, 184–86
  dependent care dilemma, 476–78
  nursing homes, 602–6
  for spouse or partner, 597–98
caring, ethic of, 331–32
Carolina Abecedarian Project, 234
cataracts, 550
cell body, 100, 101
cellular theories of aging, 544–45
Centers for Disease Control and Prevention, 370, 412
Centers for Medicare and Medicaid Services, 615
centrality, 524
centration, 137–38, 141
cephalocaudal principle, 60, 97
cephalopelvic disproportion, 78
cerebral cortex, 61, 100–101
cerebral vascular incidents (strokes), 497, 547–48
cesarean section (C-section), 79
chastity and mate selection, 420
child abuse, 151, 279–82
childbirth. *See* labor and delivery
child care. *See* caregiving
chlamydia, 350
cholesterol, 389
chorionic villus sampling, 73
chromosomes, 46–49, 50–51, 545
chronic obstructive pulmonary disease (COPD), 549
cigarette smoking
  by adolescents, 361–63
  prenatal development and, 66
  quitting, 385–86
  SIDS and, 92
  by young adults, 385–86
circadian rhythm, 553
classical conditioning, 148
climacteric, 494–96
clinical death, 620
cliques, 287
coaches, code for, 259
coach role of parents, 196
cocaine, 66, 71
cochlear implants, 551
cognitive development. *See also* intelligence; language skills; memory; Piaget's theory

absolutist, relativistic, and dialectical thinking, 399
adolescents, 221–23, 322–25
creativity and wisdom, 561–64
delinquency and, 366
emotion and logic, integration of, 399–400
encapsulation and expertise, 507–8
in infants, 132–46
information processing, 147–54, 322–25, 555–58
learning and conditioning, 148–49
lifelong learning, 508–9
make-believe play and, 194
metacognitive knowledge, 224–25
in middle age, 503–9
naive theories, 144–46
number skills, 152–54
in older adulthood, 555–64
postformal thought, 396–400
preoperational thinking, 135–40, 141
reflective judgment model, 397–99
schemes, assimilation, and accommodation, 132–33
school-age children, 220–25
self-regulation, 156
Selman's theory of perspective-taking, 298–300
sensorimotor thinking, 134–35
social beliefs and stereotypes, 400–404
television and, 166–67, 295
Vygotsky's theory, 154–56
in young adulthood, 381–82, 391–404
cognitive-developmental theory, 12, 15–17, 169. *See also* social cognitive theory
cognitive self-regulation, 224–25
cognitive therapy, 567
cohabitation, 427–29
cohort effects, 32–33
Collaborative Divorce Project, 445
college, 380–81, 386–87
Colorado Adoption Project, 233
colorectal cancer, 497
color perception in infants, 115
commercials, 294–95
common couple violence, 424
communication of research results, 35–36
companions, imaginary, 194–95
comparable worth, 467
The Compassionate Friends, 654
compensation, in SOC model, 22
competence, 199, 579
competence–environmental press theory, 19, 579–81
complex emotions, 189
comprehension, reading, 245, 246–47
computers in the classroom, 253
conception, 57–58
concrete-operational period, 16, 220–21, 222
conditioning, 14, 148–49
cones, 115
conflict between parents, 271–72, 276–78. *See also* divorce
congenial sibling relationships, 595
congenital adrenal hyperplasia (CAH), 207–8
conscientiousness, 511
consent, informed, 35
conservation problems, 137–38, 142
constricting actions, 195–96
consumer behavior, 294–95
context-specific vs. universal development, 6
contextual theory of dying, 629–30
continuing education, 508–9
continuity-discontinuity issue, 6
continuity theory, 578–79

contraception, 349–51
control beliefs, personal, 408–9, 585–86
controversial children, 289
conventional level of moral reasoning, 327
conventional personality type, 357
convergent thinking, 238
cooing, 160
cooperative play, 193, 197
coordination of locomotor skills, 108–9
COPD (chronic obstructive pulmonary disease), 549
coping, 499
core knowledge hypothesis, 144
corpus callosum, 100–101
correlational studies, 28–29, 33
correlation coefficients, 28–29
cortex, 100–101
cortisol, 27
counterimitation, 270
counting skills, 153–54
countries, differences between. *See* culture and international differences
covenant marriage, 443
creative ability, 229, 562–63
creative children, 238–39
crime, 365–68
cross-linking, 545
cross-sectional studies, 32–33
crowds, 287
crowning, 75
crying, 90–91
crystallization, 355, 356
crystallized intelligence, 395–96
C-section (cesarean section), 79
cultural conservators, 525
culture and international differences. *See also* ethnicity
    abusive relationships, 424–25
    adolescent conflict, 346
    adulthood, transition to, 379–80
    bilingualism, 165
    child abuse, 280–81
    counting skills, 153–54
    dating patterns, 348
    death, concepts of, 618–19
    demographics of aging, 539
    education, 249–52
    emotional expression, 189–90
    euthanasia, 622
    grieving, 641–42
    household division of labor, 479
    intelligence, 230, 235–37
    locomotor skills, 108–9
    longevity, 542–43
    mate preferences, 420, 422
    menopause, 495
    moral reasoning, 330–31
    parenting styles, 268–69
    personal control beliefs, 585–86
    play, 194, 195, 197
    popularity, 289
    puberty, 311, 312
    scaffolding, 156
    self-esteem, 501
    sociocultural forces, 8–9
    work, gender differences in, 463
    work-family conflict, 480–81
culture-fair intelligence tests, 236
custody, joint, 277
cytomegalovirus, 67

D

date rape, 352–53
dating. *See* love relationships
day care. *See* caregiving

death and dying. *See also* grief, mourning, and bereavement
    anxiety about, 630–31
    causes of, in adolescents, 320–21
    contextual theory of, 629–30
    dealing with one's own death, 627–30
    definitions of, 618–21
    end-of-life issues and final scenarios, 631–32
    ethics and euthanasia, 621–26
    hospice, 632–35
    infant mortality, 80–81
    Kübler-Ross's theory on, 628–29
    life-course approach to, 627
    life-span experiences of, 643–50
    self-reflective exercise on, 626–27
    suicide, 364–65
    widowhood, 598–99, 647
DeathOnline (Australian Museum website), 653
Death With Dignity Act (1994, Oregon), 622–23
deceleration stage of work development, 455
deductive reasoning, 222
delinquency, 365–68
dementia, 548, 567–72
demographers, 536
demographics of aging, 536–39
dendrites, 100, 101, 546
deoxyribonucleid acid (DNA), 47–48
dependent care. *See* caregiving
dependent variables, 30
depression
    in adolescents, 363–65
    causes of, 566
    diagnosis of, 565–66
    in older adults, 565–67
    older immigrants and, 554
    postpartum, 77–78
    treatment of, 566–67
depth perception, 115–16
descriptions of others, 297–98
DES (diethylstilbestrol), 71
designs for research, general, 28–30
developmental theories, 11–24
    cognitive-developmental theory, 15–17
    comparison of perspectives, 12
    defined, 11
    ecological theory, 18–19
    learning theory, 14–15
    life-span and life course perspective, 19–23
    psychodynamic theories, 11–14
diabetic retinopathy, 550
dialectical thinking, 399
diet. *See* eating; nutrition
diethylstilbestrol (DES), 71
dieting, 317
differentiation, 108
diffusion identity status, 341
direct instruction, 269
direction of a relation, 29
disabilities, 380–81
disciplinary practices and altruism, 200
discrimination, 466–67, 469–70. *See also* stereotypes
discussion and moral reasoning, 333–34
disease. *See* illness and disease
disinhibition, 270
disorders, genetic, 49–51
disorganized (disoriented) attachment, 182
distress, fearful vs. irritated, 93–94
divergent thinking, 238
Division 20, Adult Development and Aging (American Psychological Association), 575
division of labor and household chores, 478–79

divorce
    adult children, effects on, 445–46
    children, effects on, 276–78, 444–45
    reasons for, 441–43
    and single parenthood, 438
divorce hangover, 443
dizygotic twins, 53
DNA (deoxyribonucleid acid), 47–48
DNR (Do Not Resuscitate) order, 626
docility, 580
domestic abuse, 422–25
dominance hierarchy, 287
dominant alleles, 48, 49, 50
Do Not Resuscitate (DNR) order, 626
doulas, 76
Down syndrome, 50, 239
Down Syndrome website, 85
DPM (dual process model), 642
dream formation and work expectations, 456
drinking. *See* alcohol
driving by older adults, 557–58
"dropouts" in experimental research, 32
drugs, 66–71, 243
dual process model (DPM), 642
durable power of attorney, 625–26
dynamic systems theory, 107
dynamic testing, 232
dysphoria, 565

E

EAPC (European Association of Palliative Care), 623
early childhood. *See* toddlers; preschoolers
eating, 9, 110. *See also* nutrition
eating disorders, 317–18
ecological theory, 12, 18–19
ectoderm, 59
education. *See also* learning
    cognitive growth, practices to promote, 140–42
    college, 380–81
    computers in the classroom, 253
    health and, 390
    lifelong learning, 508–9
    math skills, 249–50
    moral reasoning, promotion of, 333–34
    part-time employment and, 358–59
    reading, 244–47
    scaffolding, 155–56
    school-based influences on achievement, 252–53
    teacher-based influences on achievement, 253–54
    in U.S. vs. other countries, 249–52
    writing, 247–49
    zone of proximal development and, 155
EEG (electroencephalogram), 103–4
EEOC (U.S. Equal Employment Opportunity Commission), 486
egocentrism
    in adolescents, 342–43
    in preschool children, 135–36, 141
    in school-age children, 220
ego resilience, 516–17
E-I-E-I-O framework, 561, 571
elaboration memory strategy, 223
ElderWeb, 615
elective selection, 22
electroencephalogram (EEG), 103–4
embryo, period of the, 59–60, 70. *See also* prenatal development
embryonic stem cells, 37
emergencies and structured observation, 25
emotional abuse, 606
emotional intelligence, 228

emotions
  basic, 187, 188–89
  complex, 189
  cultural differences in expression of, 189–90
  divorce and, 442
  gender and sensitivity to, 204
  judging from photographs, 26, 38
  logic, integration with, 399–400
  measuring in infants, 187–88
  recognition in others, 190–91
  regulation of, 191–92
empathic orientation, 332
empathy, 198–99
emphysema, 549
empty nest, 434, 518–19
enabling actions, 195
encapsulation, 507–8
endoderm, 59
end-of-life issues, 631–32
English language, 153–54, 159, 160
enterprising personality type, 357
environmental hazards and prenatal development, 67–69
environmental press, 19, 579–81
environmental stimulation and brain development, 105
environment and genetics, 54–56
environment vs. genetics. *See* nature-nurture issue
epigenetic principle, 13
episodic memory, 558–59
equilibration, 133–34
Erikson's theory
  identity formation, 340
  infancy and early childhood, 178–79
  middle-age adulthood, 513–14
  older adulthood, 582
  psychosocial theory, 11–13
  stages in, 13
  young adulthood, 382
establishment stage of work development, 455
estrogen, 310, 496–97
ethical issues in death and dying, 621–26
ethical reasoning. *See* moral reasoning
ethics of research, 34–35
ethnic identity, 343–45
ethnicity. *See also* culture and international differences
  biracial children, 437–38
  caregiver stress and, 522
  divorce rate and, 441
  elder abuse and, 607
  frail older adults and, 602
  friendship and, 284
  grandparenthood and, 524–25
  grief and, 639
  health and life expectancy differences, 385, 390
  household division of labor and, 479
  intelligence tests and, 230, 235–37
  longevity and, 541
  occupational development and, 465–66
  older adults and, 538–39
  parenting and, 437–38
  physical development and, 256
  problematic terminology, 9
  retirement and, 590, 591
  self-esteem and, 501
  singlehood and, 426
  suicide rates by, 364
  unemployment and, 475
eugenics, 58
European Americans
  abusive relationships and, 424
  caregiving stress and, 522

children's play among, 194
dating patterns, 348
death, causes of, 320
death rates, 385
divorce rate, 441
emotional expression, 189–90
frail older adults, 602
grief and, 639, 640
household division of labor and, 479
intelligence tests and, 235–36
menopause and, 495
nursing homes and, 603
occupational development and, 465
older adults among, 538
problematic terminology, 9
religion and, 587
retirement and, 590
singlehood among, 426
suicide rates, 364
unemployment and, 475
European Association of Palliative Care (EAPC), 623
euthanasia, 621–26
evolutionary psychology, 179–80
exchange theory, 431–32
exercise. *See* physical fitness
existential intelligence, 227–28
exosystems, 18–19
expectations, occupational, 455–56
experiment, defined, 30
experimental studies, 30, 33
expertise, 507–8
explicit memory, 558, 561
exploration of the environment, 134
expressive style, 166
external memory aids, 561
extremely low birth weight, 79
extroversion and introversion, 51–52, 510
eye, aging and, 549–50

F

face recognition, 118–21
falls by older adults, 552–53
false-belief tasks, 124–25
false memories, 151–52
familial mental retardation, 239
familism, 437
Family Caregiver Alliance, 529
family relationships, 266–83. *See also* love relationships; parenting
  adjustment to parenthood, 77–78
  adolescence, myth of conflict in, 346–47
  adopted children, 275–76, 439
  birth order, impact of, 276
  blended families, 278–79, 438–39
  caregiving for aging parents, 520–23
  child abuse and, 279–82
  conflict in, 271–72. *See also* divorce
  death of a family member, 598–99, 646–49
  decision to have children, 435–36
  delinquency and, 366
  divorce and remarriage, 276–79
  grandparents and grandchildren, 523–25
  great-grandparenthood, 599–600
  marriage satisfaction and parenthood, 433
  of middle-age adults, 517–26
  nuclear and extended families, 435
  parental role, 436–37
  reciprocal influences, 272–74
  siblings, 274–75
  single parents, 438
  systems view of, 266–67
Family Violence Prevention Fund, 449
FAS (fetal alcohol syndrome), 66–67
fast food, 316

fast mapping, 162–65
father-infant relationships, 180–81
fathering. *See* parenting
fear
  death, anxiety about, 630–31
  emergence of, 188–89
  expression of, 188
  make-believe play and, 194
  in preschoolers, 189
fearful distress, 93
feedback, 270–71
Fels Longitudinal Project, 95
fertilization, 57–58
fetal alcohol syndrome (FAS), 66–67
fetal medicine, 73–74
fetus, period of the, 61–62, 70. *See also* prenatal development
fictive grandparenting, 525
filial obligation, 520
final scenarios, 632
financial or material exploitation of elders, 606
fine motor skills, 106
finger foods, 110
five-factor model of personality stability, 510–13
fluid intelligence, 395–96
fMRI (functional magnetic resonance imaging), 103, 104, 547
folic acid, 63
foreclosure identity status, 341
formal-operational period, 16, 221–22, 396–97
formula, 98
foster parents, 439
four component model of grief, 640–42
Fourth Age, 543
frail older adults, 601–2
fraud against older adults, 606, 607
free radicals, 545
friends, imaginary, 194–95
friendships
  with adult children, 518–19
  in adulthood, 416–18
  in childhood and adolescence, 283–86
  in older adulthood, 594–95
frontal cortex, 101
functional imaging of the brain, 547
functional magnetic resonance imaging (fMRI), 103, 104, 547

G

gay and lesbian people
  adolescents, 351–52
  adult relationships, 429–30
  death of a partner, 649–50
  as parents, 439–40
  partnerships in older adulthood, 596–97
gender constancy, 206
gender differences
  in divorce and remarriage, 444, 446
  friendships and, 284–85, 417–18
  in health of young adults, 385, 390
  in longevity, 541–42
  in occupation, 453–54, 462–63
  in play, 195–96
  in responses to puberty, 312
  in retirement, 590–91
  singlehood and, 427
  social roles, 203–4
  in widowhood, 599
gender discrimination, 466–67
gender identity, 206–7, 515–16
gender labeling, 206
gender roles
  biological influences, 207–8
  evolution of, 208

in intellectual and psychosocial arenas, 203–4
stereotypes, 202–3
typing, 204–7
gender-schema theory, 206–7
gender stability, 206
gender stereotypes, 202–3, 293–94
gene, defined, 47–48
generativity, 513–15
genetic counseling, 72
genetic engineering, 74
genetics and heredity, 46–56
Alzheimer's disease and, 569–71
behavioral genetics, 51–53
chromosomes, 46–49
delinquency and, 365–66
disorders, genetic, 49–51
environmental influences, 54–56
intelligence and, 232–35
longevity and, 540
obesity and, 316
and puberty, timing of, 310–11
temperament and, 94
genital herpes, 67, 350
genital human papilloma virus (HPV), 350
genotype, 48
German measles (rubella), 67, 71
germ disc, 58
gerontology, 543. See also older adults
gestures, 135, 162
gifted children, 238–39
Girl Scouts, 287
girls vs. boys. See gender differences
glass ceiling, 466–67
glaucoma, 550
God, belief in, 586
gonorrhea, 350
grammatical development, 167–69
grammatical morphemes, 167
grandchild, death of, 648–49
grandparenthood, 523–25
grasping, 109–11
gravity, 144–45
great-grandparenthood, 599–600
grief, mourning, and bereavement
adolescent experiences of, 646
childhood experiences of, 644–45
cultural differences in, 619
definitions, 636
dual process model (DPM), 642
four component model, 640–42
friend, loss of, 646
grief work, 638–40
grieving process, 636–38
late adulthood experiences of, 648–50
parent, loss of, 646, 647–48, 649–50
partner, loss of, 598–99, 647
risk factors in grief, 637–38
sibling, loss of, 646
traumatic grief, 642–43
young and middle adulthood experiences of, 646–48
grief work, 638–40
grief work as rumination hypothesis, 640–41
group dynamics, 286–88
growth, in naive theories of biology, 145
growth, physical. See also physical development
in infancy and early childhood, 96–100
in middle childhood, 256–57
pubertal, 308–10
in young adulthood, 384
Guilford-Zimmerman Temperament Survey (GZTS), 511

GZTS (Guilford-Zimmerman Temperament Survey), 511

H

habituation, 147–48
hand coordination, 109–11
handedness, 111
harassment, sexual, 468–69
hardware, mental, 17, 147
hassles, 499
Hayflick limit, 545
HCAs (heterocyclic antidepressants), 566
HDLs (high-density lipoproteins), 389
headphones and exercise, 551
Head Start, 234
healing, in naive biology, 146
health. See also illness and disease; physical development
in adolescence, 315–21
in young adulthood, 384–90
in middle age, 491–501
in older adulthood, 553–54
stress and, 498–501
hearing, sense of, 113–14
hearing aids, 551
hearing loss, 550–52
heart disease. See cardiovascular disease
height percentiles, 96–97
Helpguide.com, 529
helping behaviors, 197–201, 295
helplessness, learned, 363
hemispheres of the brain, 100–101
hemorrhages, 548
hepatitis B, 350
heredity. See genetics and heredity
heroin, 66
herpes, genital, 67, 350
heterocyclic antidepressants (HCAs), 566
heterozygous alleles, 48
hierarchical theory of intelligence, 227
high-density lipoproteins (HDLs), 389
Hindu religion, 330–31
hip fractures, 497
Hispanic Americans. See Latino Americans
historical context, in life-span perspective, 20–21
HIV (human immunodeficiency virus), 349, 350
Holocaust Memorial Museum, United States, 336
homogamy, 431–32
homozygous alleles, 48
hope, 179
hormone replacement therapy (HRT), 496–97
hospice, 632–35
hostile aggression, 290
hostile sibling relationships, 595
household chores and division of labor, 478–79
HPV (genital human papilloma virus), 350
HRT (hormone replacement therapy), 496–97
human development, defined, 1
Human Development and Family Science Extension (Ohio State University), 129
Human Genome Project, 85, 540
human growth hormone, 494
human immunodeficiency virus (HIV), 349, 350
Huntington's Disease, 50
hypoxia, 79

I

IADLs (instrumental activities of daily living), 601–2

identity
in adolescence, 340–43
ethnic, 343–45
gender, 206–7, 515–16
life-span constructs, 405
Marcia's theory of identity statuses, 340–42
McAdams' life-story model, 405–6
possible selves, 406–8
work and, 340, 453, 465
in young-adulthood, 404–10
illness and disease. See also AIDS (acquired immunodeficiency syndrome)
aging and, 547–49
Alzheimer's disease, 548, 567–72, 597
arthritis, 494
cancer, 497, 553–54
cardiovascular disease, 388–89, 497, 500–501, 547–48
child abuse and, 281
eyes diseases and degeneration, 550
hormone replacement and, 497
Huntington's Disease, 50
in naive biology, 146
osteoporosis, 492–94
Parkinson's disease, 549
prenatal development and, 67
respiratory disease, 549
sexually transmitted diseases (STDs), 349, 350
illusion of invulnerability, 342–43
imaginary audience, 342–43
imaginary companions, 194–95
imitation (observational learning), 14–15, 149, 269–70
immigrant status and health in older adults, 554
immortality through clan, 524
implantation, 58–59
implementation, 356, 454
Implicit Aptitudes Test, 402
implicit memory, 558, 561
implicit stereotyping, 401–2
impulsivity and ADHD, 242
inattention and ADHD, 242
income. See socioeconomic status
incomplete dominance, 49
incontinence, 568
independent variables, 30
index offenses, 365
Indians. See Native Americans
indulgence, 524
infant-directed speech, 159–60
infantilization, 605
infant mortality, 80–81
infants
attachment, 179–86
attention in, 147–48
brain development, 102–3
day care, 184–86
defined, 3
emotional development, 187–91
fine motor skills, 109–10
growth of, 96
information processing, 147–53
language skills, 158–60, 171
learning and conditioning, 148–49
locomotor skills and walking, 106–9
memory in, 149–50
naive theories of, 145–46
number skills, 152–53
in Piaget's theory, 132–33, 134–35
play of, 193
self-concept, 123
sense of hearing, 113–14
sense of smell, taste, and touch, 112–13

infants (*continued*)
  siblings and, 274
  trust vs. mistrust, 178–79
  visual perception, 114–21
influence, social, 203
information processing, 147–54
  in adolescents, 322–25
  in older adults, 555–58
  psychomotor speed, 556–58
information-processing theory, 16–17, 227–29
informed consent, 35
inheritance, in naive biology, 145
inhibition, 94, 270
initiative vs. guilt, 179
inner speech, 156
insecurity, occupational, 473
Institute on Race, Health Care, and the Law, 412
instrumental activities of daily living (IADLs), 601–2
instrumental aggression, 290
instrumental orientation, 327
integration, 108
integrity vs. despair, 582
intelligence, 226–37
  in adulthood, 392–96, 503–7
  Carroll's hierarchical theory of, 227
  correlation studies and, 29
  ethnicity and socioeconomic status, impact of, 230, 235–37
  fluid vs. crystallized, 395–96
  Gardner's theory of multiple intelligences, 227–29
  genetics and, 54
  gifted and creative children, 238–39
  heredity and environmental factors, 232–35
  learning disabilities, 240–42
  mental retardation, 239–40
  multidimensional, 392
  practical, 503–7
  primary mental abilities, 392–94
  secondary mental abilities, 394–96
  Sternberg's theory of successful intelligence, 229–30
  testing and measurement, 226–27, 230–36
intelligence quotient (IQ), 230–35, 239–40
intentionality, awareness of, 123–24
interindividual variability in intelligence, 392
intermediate care, 603
internal belief systems, 566
internal memory aids, 561
internal parts, in naive biology, 145
internal working model, 183
international comparisons. *See* culture and international differences
interpersonal intelligence, 227–28
interpersonal norms, 327
intersensory redundancy, 121
intimacy and friendship, 284
intimacy vs. isolation stage, 382
intimate sibling relationships, 595
intrapersonal intelligence, 227–28
introversion and extroversion, 51–52
investigative personality type, 357
in vitro fertilization, 57–58, 495–96
invulnerability, illusion of, 342–43
IQ (intelligence quotient), 230–35, 239–40
irregular (REM) sleep, 91
irritated distress, 93–94
isolation, social, 280

J

Japanese students, 251–52
Jean Piaget Society, 175
job satisfaction, 457–59

joint attention, 162–64
joint custody, 277
joints, 494
jokes, 220–21
journals, scientific, 35–36
Judeo-Christian tradition, 330
juvenile delinquents, 365–68

K

Kidshealth (website), 129
Kids Nutrition (website), 129
kinetic cues to depth, 116
kinkeeper role, 517–18
Klinefelter's syndrome, 51
knowledge-telling strategy, 248
knowledge-transforming strategy, 248
Kohlberg's theory of moral reasoning, 16, 326–30

L

labor and delivery, 75–81
  adjustment to parenthood, 77–78
  birth complications, 78–80
  infant mortality, 80–81
  natural approaches, 76–77
  stages of labor, 75–76
language skills, 157–72
  autobiographical memory and, 150–51
  babbling and cooing, 160
  conservation problems and, 142
  effective communication, 169–71
  encouraging, 166–67
  fast mapping, 162–65
  first words, 161
  gender differences, 203
  grammatical development, 167–69
  impact of exposure to language, 158
  individual differences, 165–66
  milestones in, 171
  perception of speech, 158–60
  private speech, 156
  reading disabilities, 241–42
  words as symbols, 161–62
Latino Americans
  abusive relationships and, 424
  caregiving stress and, 522
  dating patterns, 348
  death, causes of, 320
  death rates, 385
  family patterns, 437
  frail older adults, 602
  grief and, 639, 640
  household division of labor and, 479
  intelligence tests and, 236
  occupational development and, 465
  older adults among, 538
  religion and, 587
  retirement and, 590
  singlehood among, 426
  suicide rates, 364
  variations among, 9
LDLs (low-density lipoproteins), 389
lead, 68
learned helplessness, 363
learning. *See also* cognitive development; education
  classical and operant conditioning, 148–49
  observational (imitation), 14–15, 149, 269–70
learning disabilities, 240–42
learning theory, 12, 14–15
left handedness, 111
leisure, 481–84
Les Misérables (Hugo), 326–27
life-course persistent antisocial behavior, 365

life course perspective, 12, 627
life-cycle forces, 7, 10
life expectancy. *See* longevity
lifelong learning, 508–9
life review, 582
life satisfaction, 31–32
life-span constructs, 405
life-span perspective, 12, 20–22, 583
life transitions, 23, 516–17
LIFT (Linking the Interests of Families and Teachers), 367
linear perspective, 116, 117
linguistic intelligence, 227–28
linguistic theory
  on grammar acquisition, 168–69
Linking the Interests of Families and Teachers (LIFT), 367
liquid quantity, conservation of, 138, 142
listening and communication, 171
Living to 100 Life Expectancy Calculator, 543
living wills, 625–26
locomotor skills, 106–9, 143
logical-mathematical intelligence, 227–28
logic and emotion, integration of, 399–400
longevity, 539–40
  African Americans, life expectancy of, 390
  estimation of, 543
  genetic and environmental factors in, 540–41
  types of life expectancy, 539–40
longitudinal studies, 31–32, 33
long-term memory, 223
loss-based selection, 22
love relationships. *See also* marriage
  abusive relationships, 422–23
  of adolescents, 348
  of adults, 418–22
  cohabitation, 427–29
  death of a partner, 598–99, 647, 649–50
  gay and lesbian, 429–30
  lifestyles, 425–35
  mate selection and coupling behavior, 418–22
  single parents and, 438
  social rules on, 403–4
low birth weight, 79–80
low-density lipoproteins (LDLs), 389
loyal sibling relationships, 595
loyalty and friendship, 284

M

macrosystems, 18–19
macular degeneration, 550
mad cries, 90, 91
magnetic resonance imaging (MRI), 103, 104, 547, 548
maintenance stage of work development, 455
make-believe, 193–95
malnutrition, 99–100
MA (mental age), 230
MAO (monoamine oxidase) inhibitors, 566
marijuana, 66
marriage, 430–34. *See also* divorce
  beliefs about, 431
  covenant marriage, 443
  in older adulthood, 596–97
  remarriage, 278–79, 446
  satisfaction in, 432–34, 597
  social rules of, 403–4
  success factors, 430–32
married singles, 434
math skills
  counting skills in preschoolers, 153–54
  gender differences, 203
  infant number skills, 152–53

overview, 249
story problems, structuring of, 155
and universal vs. context-specific development, 6
in U.S. vs. other countries, 249–50
mating. *See* love relationships
maximum life expectancy, 540
Mayo Clinic and WebMD, 529
measurement in human development research, 25–28, 38
mediator role of parents, 196
Medicare, 611
MedlinePlus, 305
memory
  adolescents, 322–23
  autobiographical, 150–52, 406, 559
  explicit, implicit, episodic, and semantic, 558–59
  infants and preschoolers, 149–52
  long-term, 223
  metacognition, 224–25
  normal and abnormal changes in, 560–61
  older adults, 558–61
  phonological, 165
  reading skills and, 247
  remediation of problems with, 561
  school-age children and adolescents, 223–25
  working memory, 223, 247, 322, 558
memory, autobiographical, 150–52
menarche, 310, 312
menopause, 494–97
menstruation, 54, 310, 312
mental age (MA), 230
mental hardware and software, 17, 147
mental health. *See also* self-esteem
  anxiety disorders, 567
  dementia, 548, 567–72
  depression, 363–65, 565–67
  in older adults, 564–72
  part-time employment and, 358–59
  stress and, 501
mental operations, 220
mental retardation, 239–40
mentors, 456–57, 465–66
mercury, 68
mesoderm, 59
mesosystems, 18–19
meta-analysis, 34
metabolic theories of aging, 545
metabolism, 316–17, 388
metacognitive knowledge, 224–25, 323–24
metamemory, 224
Mexican Americans. *See* Latino Americans
microsystems, 18–19
middle-age adults
  care for aging parents by, 520–23
  cognitive development, 503–9
  death, experience of, 647
  death, feelings towards, 627
  defined, 3
  divorce among, 444
  family dynamics, 517–26
  gender-role identity convergence, 515–16
  grandparenthood, 523–25
  leisure activities, 483
  personality development in, 510–17
  physical changes and health, 490–502
middle childhood. *See* school-age children
midlife crisis, 516–17
mind, theory of, 123–26
mirrors, 123
modeling
  of altruism, 200
  by parents, 269–70
models, scale, 138–40

monoamine oxidase (MAO) inhibitors, 566
monozygotic twins, 53
Monster.com, 486
mood, 199–200, 312–13, 314
moral reasoning, 326–34
  cultural differences in, 330–31
  Eisenberg's levels of prosocial reasoning, 332–33
  Gilligan's ethic of caring, 331–32
  Kohlberg's theory of, 16, 326–30
  promotion of, 333–34
moratorium identity status, 341
Moro reflex, 89
morphemes, grammatical, 167
motherese, 159
motion and perception, 116, 117
motion parallax, 116
motor skills
  fine motor skills, 109–11
  gender differences in, 257–58
  in infancy and early childhood, 105–11
  locomotion, 106–9
mourning, defined, 636. *See also* grief, mourning, and bereavement
movement in naive biology, 145
MRI (magnetic resonance imaging), 103, 104, 547, 548
MTA (Multimodal Treatment Study of Children with ADHD), 243
multidimensional intelligence, 392
multidirectionality, 20, 23, 392
Multimodal Treatment Study of Children with ADHD (MTA), 243
multiple causation, 21
multiple intelligences, 227–29
muscle growth, in puberty, 309
music, 113
musical intelligence, 227–28
myelin, 101–2

N

naive theories, 144–46
naming errors, 164–65
National Association for Gifted Children, 263
National Coalition Building Institute, 305
National Council on Family Relations, 449
National Hospice and Palliative Care Organization, 653
National Institute of Child Health and Human Development (NICHD), 184–85
National Institute on Aging, 575
National Institute on Alcohol and Alcoholism, 412
National Institutes of Health, 41, 371
National Youth Violence Prevention Resource Center, 305
Native Americans
  family values, 437
  frail older adults, 602
  older adults among, 538
  religion and, 587
  suicide rates, 364
naturalistic intelligence, 227–28
naturalistic observation, 25, 27
nature-nurture issue, 5. *See also* culture and international differences; ethnicity; genetics and heredity
  brain development, 104–5
  handedness, 111
  heredity-environment interactions, 54–56
  intelligence, 232–35
  life expectancy and, 540–41
  obesity, 316–17
  puberty onset, 310–11
  temperament, 94

NBAS (Neonatal Behavioral Assessment Scale), 89–90
needs-oriented orientation, 332
negative affect, 94
negative reinforcement trap, 270
neglected children, 289
neglected elders, 606–8
Neonatal Behavioral Assessment Scale (NBAS), 89–90
nervous system. *See* brain and nervous system
neural plate, 101
neuritic plaques, 547
neurofibrillary tangles, 546
neurons, 100, 101–2
neuroplasticity, 104–5
neuroticism, 510
neurotransmitters, 100, 547
newborns
  assessment of, 89–90
  defined, 3
  imitation by, 149
  labor and delivery, 75–81
  language skills, 158, 160
  low birth weight, 79–80
  in Piaget's theory, 134
  preterm or premature babies, 79
  reflexes, 88, 89
  sense of smell, taste, and touch, 112–13
  siblings of, 274
  states of, 90–91
  temperament, 93–95
New York Longitudinal Study, 93
New York Online Access to Health (NOAH), 84
NICHD (National Institute of Child Health and Human Development), 184–85
niche-picking, 55
nicotine, 66
nightmares, 92
night terrors, 92
NOAH (New York Online Access to Health), 84
nonREM (regular) sleep, 91
nonshared environmental influences, 56
norepinephrine, 363
number skills, in infants, 152–53. *See also* math skills
nursery school, 184–86
nursing homes, 602–6
nurture. *See* nature-nurture issue
nutrition. *See also* eating
  adolescents and, 316–18
  caloric requirements, 316
  cardiovascular disease and, 388–89
  eating disorders, 317–18
  growth and, 97–100, 256–57
  malnutrition, 99–100
  obesity, 316–17
  in older adulthood, 553
  picky eaters, 98–99
  prenatal risk factors, 63–64
  USDA dietary guidelines, 388
  of young adults, 388–89

O

obedience orientation, 327
obesity, 316–17, 389
object perception, 116–21
object permanence, 134–35, 142–43
observational learning (imitation), 14–15, 149, 269–70
observation (systematic, naturalistic, and structured), 25
occupation. *See* work

ODTL (Revised Observed Tasks of Daily Living), 506
off-time hypothesis, 315
older adults
    abuse and neglect of, 606–8
    brain, changes in, 546–47
    caregiving for, 520–23
    cognitive processes, 555–64
    creativity and wisdom, 561–64
    death, feelings towards, 627
    demeaning speech toward, 605
    demographics of aging, 536–39
    driving by, 557–58
    falls by, 552–53
    frail, 601–2
    friendships and sibling relationships, 594–96
    great-grandparenthood, 599–600
    immigrants as, 554
    information processing, 555–58
    longevity, 539–40
    marriage and partnerships, 596–97
    Medicare and, 611
    memory and, 558–61
    mental health of, 564–72
    in nursing homes, 602–6
    politics and, 608–9
    psychosocial aging, 578–81
    religiosity and spiritual support, 586–87
    retirement, 588–93
    social security and, 609–11
    social support, importance of, 593–94
    theories of aging, 544–46
    Third Age vs. Fourth Age, 543
    widowhood, 598–99
    young-old vs. old-old, 3
old-old adults, 3
one-to-one principle, 153
online friendships, 417
only children, 276
openness to experience, 511
operant conditioning, 14, 148–49
operational thought, concrete vs. formal, 16, 220–22
optimal level of development, 399
optimally exercised ability, 504–5
optimization, in SOC model, 22
ordinality, 153
Oregon Social Learning Center, 367, 371
organic mental retardation, 239
organization memory strategy, 223
orienting response, 147–48
osteoarthritis, 494
osteoporosis, 492–94
overactivity and ADHD, 242
overextension, 164–65
overregularizations, 168

P

pain cries, 90
pain perception, 113
palmar reflex, 89
parallel play, 193
parenting. *See also* family relationships
    adolescent storm and stress, myth of, 345–46
    adoptive parents, 439
    altruism, fostering, 200–201
    delinquency and, 366, 367
    direct instruction, 269
    ethnic diversity and, 437–38
    feedback, 270–71
    by gays and lesbians, 439–40
    gender typing and, 205
    general dimensions of, 267
    by grandparents, 525

language skills, encouraging, 166–67
    marital system and, 271–72
    middle-age adults and, 518–19
    modeling, 269–70
    play and, 196–97
    role of, 436–37
    self-esteem and, 346
    stepparents, 278–79, 438–39
    styles of, 268–69
    teenage drinking and, 361
    teen smoking and, 362
Parkinson's disease, 549
passive euthanasia, 623–24
passive victims, 291
paternal investment theory, 311
patriarchal terrorism, 424
patronizing speech, 605
PCBs, 68–69, 71
peer pressure
    gender roles and, 205
    group norms, 288
    teenage drinking and, 361
    teen smoking and, 362
peer relationships, 283–91
    friendships, 283–86, 416–18
    groups, 286–88
    popularity and rejection, 288–90
    self-esteem and, 346
perception, defined, 112
perceptual cues in walking, 108
perceptual development in infants, 112–22
    color, 115
    hearing, 113–14
    integration of sensory information, 121
    objects and faces, 116–21
    smell, taste, and touch, 112–13
    visual acuity, 114–15
perimenopause, 495
permissive parenting, 268
persistence, 94
persistent vegetative state, 621
personal control beliefs, 408–9, 585–86
personal fable, 342–43
personality development. *See also* identity
    five-factor model and stability, 510–13
    integrity vs. despair, 582
    life-span constructs, 405
    McAdams' life-story model, 405–6
    in middle age, 510–17
    in older adulthood, 582–88
    possible selves, 406–8
    young adult identity and, 404–10
personality-type theory, 356–58, 453–54
perspective-taking, 298–300
phenotype, behavioral, 51–53
phenotypes, 48, 49. *See also* genetics and heredity
phenylketonuria (PKU), 50, 54, 74
phonemes, 158
phonological awareness, 241, 245
phonological memory, 165
photographs, judging emotion from, 26, 38
physical abuse, 606
physical development. *See also* nutrition
    brain and nervous system, 100–105
    growth of the body, 96–100, 256–57, 384
    in infancy and early childhood, 96–105
    middle-age changes and health, 490–502
    motor skills, 105–11, 257–58
    physical fitness, 258
    puberty, 308–15
    school-age children, 255–59
    sports participation, 258–59
    young adults, 384–91

physical fitness
    in adolescents, 318–20
    aerobic exercise, 501–2
    headphones and exercise, dangers of, 551
    in middle-age adults, 501–2
    in school-age children, 258
physics, naive theories of, 144–45
physiological measures, 27
Piaget's theory, 15–16
    concrete-operational period, 16, 220–21, 222
    equilibration, 133
    evaluation of, 140–44, 222–23
    formal-operational period, 16, 221–22
    infancy and early childhood, 132–46
    naive theories, 144
    preoperational period, 16, 135–40, 141
    schemes, assimilation, and accommodation, 132–33
    school-age children and adolescence, 220–23
    sensorimotor period, 16, 134–35
    stages of development, 16, 133–34
picky eaters, 98–99
pictorial cues to depth, 116
pituitary gland, 310
PKU (phenylketonuria), 50, 54, 74
placenta, 59
plasticity
    of the brain, 104–5
    in intellectual abilities, 392
    in life-span perspective, 20
play, 193–97
politics and older adults, 608–9
polygenic inheritance, 52
popular children, 288–89
population pyramid, 536–37
populations, 28
positive affect, 94
possible selves, 406–8
postconventional level of moral reasoning, 327–28
postformal thought, 396–400, 505
postpartum depression, 77–78
posture, 107
poverty. *See* socioeconomic status
practical ability, 229
practical intelligence, 503–7
preattachment, 180
preconventional level of moral reasoning, 327
preeclampsia, 78
pregnancy, teenage, 349–51
pregnancy and development. *See* prenatal development
prejudice, 300–302
prenatal development, 57–74
    brain structures, 101–2
    defined, 57
    diagnosis and treatment, 72–74
    embryo, 59–60
    fetus, 61–62
    labor and delivery, 75–81
    risk factors, general, 63–65
    sense of hearing in fetus, 113
    teratogens (drugs, diseases, and hazards), 65–72
    zygote, 57–59
preoperational period, 16, 135–40, 141, 298
presbycusis, 551
presbyopia, 550
preschoolers
    attention in, 148
    autobiographical memory, 150–52
    autonomy vs. shame and doubt, 179
    defined, 3
    emotional development, 189, 191

empathy and altruism in, 198–201
fine motor development, 110–11
gender and, 203, 205–6
handedness in, 111
information processing, 148–54
initiative vs. guilt, 179
language skills, 167–71
locomotor development, 109
moral reasoning of, 332
naive theories of, 145–46
peer relationships, 283–84
in Piaget's theory, 132
picky eaters, 98–99
play of, 193–97
self-concept, 123
sleep routines, 91–92
theory of mind and false-belief tasks, 124–25
President's Council on Physical Fitness and
    Sports, 336
preterm or premature babies, 79
primary control, 409, 585–86
primary mental abilities, 392–94
primary sex characteristics, 309–10
private speech, 156
proactivity, 580
processes of thinking, 507–8
processing speed, 322–23, 556–58
products of thinking, 507–8
progesterone, 496–97
programmed cell death theories, 545
prolapsed umbilical cord, 78
Prophet, The (Gibran), 418, 452
propositions, 246
prosocial behavior, 197–98, 295
prosocial reasoning, 332–33
prostate gland, 497
proximal development, zone of, 155
proximodistal principle, 60
psychodynamic theories, 11–14
psychological abuse, 606
psychological forces, 7, 8
psychometricians, 226
psychomotor speed, 556–58
psychosocial aging, 578–81
psychosocial theory. *See* Erikson's theory
psychotherapy, 566–67
puberty, 308–15
punishment, 14, 270–71, 280
purpose, 179

Q

quantity, conservation of, 137–38, 142

R

race, 284, 437–38. *See also* ethnicity
racial stereotypes and prejudice, 300–301
racism, stress from, 390
rape, 352–53
rapid-eye movement (REM) sleep, 91
Raven's Progressive Matrices, 236
reaching, 109–11
reaction range, 54
reaction times, 556–58
reading disabilities, 241–42
reading skills, 244–47
realistic personality type, 357
reality shock, 456
reality vs. appearance, 138–40, 141
reasonable woman standard, 469
reasoning, deductive, 222. *See also* cognitive
    development
recessive alleles, 48, 50
reciprocal influences in parenting, 272–74
reciprocal relationships and attachment, 180

referential style, 165–66
reflective judgment, 397–99
reflexes of newborns, 88, 89
regular (nonREM) sleep, 91
reinforcement, 14, 270
reinvolvement with personal past, 524
rejected children, 289–90
relational aggression, 204
Relationship Questionnaire (RQ), 420–21
relationships. *See* family relationships; friend-
    ships; love relationships; peer relationships
relativistic thinking, 399
reliability, 27
religiosity, 586–87, 640
remarriage, 278–79, 446
REM (rapid-eye movement) sleep, 91
representative sampling, 28
research, developmental, 24–38
    communication of, 35–36
    correlational studies, 28–39, 33
    cross-sectional studies, 32–33
    designs for studying, 30–34
    ethical, 34–35
    experimental studies, 30, 33
    integration of findings, 34
    longitudinal studies, 31–32, 33
    measurement, 25–28, 38
    sequential studies, 33–34
    social policy application, 36–37
    stem cell research, 37
resistant attachment, 182
respiratory disease, 549
responsibility feelings and altruism, 199
retinal disease, 550
retinal disparity, 116
retirement, 588–93
retirement stage, 455
retraining of workers, 472–73
retrieval, spaces, 571
returning adult students, 380–81
Revised Observed Tasks of Daily Living
    (ODTL), 506
revision, as writing skill, 248–49
rheumatoid arthritis, 494
right handedness, 111
risk-taking, 320–21, 631
rites of passage, 379–80
roles, social, 202
role transitions, 379
romantic relationships. *See* love relationships
Roosevelt High School, Detroit, 252
rooting reflex, 88, 89
rubella (German measles), 67, 71
rumination, grief work as, 640–41
running, 109

S

sadness, development of, 188
sample, defined, 28
sampling, 26, 27, 28
sandwich generation, 518
SAT (Scholastic Aptitude Test), 381
savants, 228
scaffolding, 155–56, 196
scale models, 138–40
scenarios, 405
schemes, 132–33
Schindler's List (film), 328–29
Scholastic Aptitude Test (SAT), 381
school-age children. *See also* parenting
    academics and schooling. *See* education
    cognitive development, 220–21, 223–25
    death and bereavement, reaction to, 644–45
    defined, 3

emotional development, 189
family relationships and, 266–83
gender and, 203
intelligence and aptitudes, 226–37
moral reasoning of, 332, 333–34
peer relationships, 283–91
physical development, 255–59
prejudice in, 300–302
self-esteem in, 345
special children and special needs, 238–44
television and, 292–96
understanding others, 296–302
Seattle Longitudinal Study, 393–94
secondary control, 409, 585–86
secondary mental abilities, 394–96
secondary sex characteristics, 309–10
secure attachment, 181, 183–84, 195–96, 637
selective attention, 555
selective estrogen receptor modulators
    (SERMs), 497
selective optimization with compensation
    (SOC) model, 21–22
selective serotonin reuptake inhibitors (SSRIs),
    566
self-awareness and self-concept
    in adulthood, 405–9
    autobiographical memory and, 150–51, 406
    in infancy and early childhood, 122–26
    occupational development and, 455
    possible selves, 406–8
self-efficacy, 15, 453
self-esteem, 345–46, 501
self-neglect, 606
self-reflective perspective-taking, 299
self-regulation, 156, 224–25
self reports, 26, 27
semantic memory, 558–59
sensorimotor period, 16, 134–35
sentence cues to word meaning, 164
sequential design, 33–34
SERMs (selective estrogen receptor modula-
    tors), 497
serotonin, 363
Sesame Street, 166–67, 295
sex characteristics, primary and secondary,
    309–10
sex chromosomes, 46–47, 51
sex differences. *See* gender differences
sexual abuse, 282, 606
sexual behavior and activity
    in adolescence, 348–51
    friends, influence of, 286
    in middle age, 495, 498
sexual coercion, 352–53
sexual harassment, 468–69
sexually transmitted diseases (STDs), 349, 350
sexual maturation, 309–10
sexual orientation, 351–52
shrinking machine experiment, 139–40
shyness, 94
siblings. *See also* twins
    death of a sibling, 646
    and environment vs. heredity, 55–56
    as friends, 417
    in older adulthood, 595–96
    relationships among, 274–75
sickle-cell trait, 46, 48–49
SIDS (sudden infant death syndrome), 92–93
simple social play, 193
singlehood, 426–27
single-parent families, 277
single parents, 438
Skeptic magazine, 263
skill acquisition, 399

skilled nursing care, 603
sleeping
    disturbances, 92
    of newborns and children, 91–93
    in older adulthood, 553
    SIDS and, 92–93
smell, sense of, 112, 552
smiles, social, 188
smoking. *See* cigarette smoking
social beliefs, 402–4. *See also* stereotypes
social clocks, 405
social cognitive theory, 15, 204–5, 403–4
social contract, 327–28
social convoy, 593
social influence, gender differences in, 203
social-informational perspective-taking, 299
social-interaction theory, 169
socialization, 265
social learning theory, 14–15. *See also* social
    cognitive theory
social personality type, 357
social policy and research results, 36–37
social referencing, 190
social resources and well-being, 584
social roles, 202
social rules, 403–4
social security, 609–11
Social Security Administration, 615
social smiles, 188
social system morality, 327
societal perspective-taking, 299
Society for Neuroscience "Brain Briefings,"
    129
sociocultural forces, 7, 8–9
socioeconomic status
    child abuse and, 280, 282
    delinquency and, 366
    health differences according to, 390
    intelligence tests and, 235–37
    longevity and, 541
    parenting styles and, 268–69
socioemotional development. *See also* love
        relationships; personality development
    attachment, 179–86
    emotions, 187–92
    in Erikson's theory, 178–79
    family relationships, 266–83
    peer relationships, 283–91
    play, 193–97
    prejudice, 300–302
    prosocial behavior and altruism, 197–201
    religiosity and spiritual support, 586–87
    subjective well-being, 583–86
    television and, 292–96
    understanding others, 296–302
socioemotional selectivity, 594
SOC (selective optimization with compensa-
        tion) model, 21–22
software, mental, 17, 147
solitary play, 195
sound perception, 113–14
source-monitoring skills, 151–52
spaced retrieval, 571
spatial ability, gender differences in, 203
spatial intelligence, 227–28
special children and special needs
    attention-deficit hyperactivity disorder
        (ADHD), 242–43
    gifted and creative children, 238–39
    learning disabilities, 240–42
    mental retardation, 239–40
specification, 355, 356
speech. *See* language skills
spermarche, 310, 312
spina bifida, 63–64, 73–74

spiritual support, 586–87
sports participation, 258–59, 319–20
stable-order principle, 153
stagnation, 514
Stanford-Binet test, 230–31
State of Oregon Physician-Assisted Suicide
        Information, 653
status offenses, 365
STDs (sexually transmitted diseases), 349, 350
stem cells, 37
stepparents and stepchildren, 278–79, 438–39
stepping, 107–8
stepping reflex, 88, 89
stereotypes
    of aging, 401–2, 559–60, 561–64
    defined, 401
    gender, 202–3, 515–16
    implicit stereotyping, 401–2
    as knowledge structures, 400–402
    prejudice and, 300–301
    of retirement, 592
    television and, 293–94
stereotype threat, 236–37, 402
steroids, anabolic, 319–20
stimulant drugs, 243
story problems, 155
stranger wariness, 188–89
Strange Situation, 181–82
strength of a relation, 29
stress
    burnout from, 460–61
    caregiving and, 521–22
    dynamics of, 498–500
    grief stressors, 642
    in middle age, 498–501
    as prenatal risk factor, 64
    puberty and, 311
    subjective well being and, 583–85
    teenage drinking and, 361
stress and coping paradigm, 498–99
strokes, 497, 547–48
Strong Interest Inventory (SII), 357
structural imaging of the brain, 547
structured observation, 25, 27
subjective well-being, 583–86
sucking reflex, 88, 89
sudden infant death syndrome (SIDS), 92–93
suicide, 364–65
symbols, words as, 161–62
symbol use, 135
synaptic pruning, 102–3
syphilis, 67, 350
systematic observation, 25, 27
systems approach, 18–19, 266–67

T

Taiwanese students, 250–52
tasks, sampling behavior with, 26, 27
taste, sense of, 112
teaching practices. *See* education
teenagers. *See* adolescents
telegraphic speech, 167
telemarketing fraud, 607
television
    aggression and, 292–93
    consumer behavior and, 294–95
    criticisms of, 296
    gender identity and, 207
    language growth and, 166–67
    prosocial behavior and, 295
    stereotypes and, 293–94
telomeres, 545
temperament, 93–95, 184, 273
teratogens, 65–72
terminal buttons, 100, 101

terrorism, patriarchal, 424
terror management theory, 630
testimony by children, 151–52
testing for intelligence, 230–35
testosterone, 497–98
test-wise participants, 32
texture gradient, 116, 117
thalidomide, 65–66
theory, defined, 11. *See also* developmental
        theories
theory of mind, 123–26
thinking, development of. *See* cognitive
        development
Third Age, 543
third-person perspective-taking, 299
three-mountain problem, 136
thresholders, 382
TIAs (transient ischemic attacks), 548
time-outs, 271
timing, in life course perspective, 22
Today's Parent (website), 305
toddlers. *See also* infants; language skills
    aggression in, 290
    altruism in, 198
    autonomy vs. shame and doubt, 179
    classical conditioning and, 148
    day care, 184–86
    defined, 3
    emotional development, 189, 191–92
    handedness in, 111
    memory in, 149–50
    naive theories of, 145–46
    preoperational thinking, 135–40
    self-concept, 123
    siblings and, 274
    sleep of, 91
    symbol use, 135
    theory of mind, 124
    walking by, 107–9
toddling, 107
Total Baby Care (website), 129
touch, sense of, 113
transient ischemic attacks (TIAs), 548
traumatic grief, 642–43
treadmills, 107–8
trust vs. mistrust, 178–79
Turner's syndrome, 51
turnover and job satisfaction, 458–59
turn-taking, conversational, 170
Twenty-First Century Teachers initiative, 263
twins
    handedness and, 111
    intelligence and, 232–33
    monogyzotic vs. dizygotic, 53
    and pubertal timing, 310
Type A behavior pattern, 500–501
Type B behavior pattern, 500–501

U

UFOV (useful field of view), 557
ultrasound, 72
umbilical cord, 59–60
umbilical cord, prolapsed, 78
underextension, 164
undifferentiated perspective-taking, 299
unemployment, 473–75
unexercised ability, 504–5
uninvolved parenting, 268
universal ethical principles, 328
universal vs. context-specific development
        issue, 6–7
U.S. Department of Labor, 486
U.S. Equal Employment Opportunity Commis-
        sion (EEOC), 486
USDA dietary guidelines, 388

useful field of view (UFOV), 557
useful life expectancy, 540

V

vacation, 484
validity, 27
valued elders, 524
variability, age of, 61
vascular dementia, 548
vegetative state, persistent, 621
verbal ability. *See* language skills
vernix, 61, 88
very low birth weight, 79
victimized children, 290–91
vigilance, 555
violence, 292–93, 422–25. *See also* aggression
vision and aging, 549–50
visual acuity, 114–15, 550
visual cliffs, 115–16
visual expansion, 116
visual perception, 114–21
vital signs of newborns, 89
vitamin D, 493
vocational maturity, 454–55
volunteerism, 592–93
Vygotsky's theory, 17, 154–56

W

waking activity state, 90
walking, 107–9
wear-and-tear theory, 544
WebMD, 529
Wechsler Intelligence Scale for Children III
    (WISC-III), 231
weight
    low birth weight, 79–80
    obesity and body-mass index, 316–17, 389
weight percentiles, 96–97

well-being, subjective, 583–86
whole-brain death, 620–21
widowhood, 598–99, 647
will, 179
WISC-III (Wechsler Intelligence Scale for Children III), 231
wisdom, 563–64
withdrawal reflex, 88, 89
women and men. *See* gender differences
women and work
    dependent care dilemma, 476–77
    household chores and, 478–79
    mentor relationships, 457
    occupational development, 463–65
    occupational selection, 463
word recognition, 245–46
work, 450–81
    adolescents and, 354–59
    age discrimination, 469–70
    alienation and burnout, 459–61
    career development, 354–58
    family and, 475–81
    gender bias and the glass ceiling, 466–67
    gender differences, 453–54, 462–65
    Holland's personality-type theory and, 356–58, 453–54
    job satisfaction, 457–59
    leisure and vacation, 481–84
    meaning derived from, 452–53
    mentor relationships, 456–57, 465–66
    occupational development, 454–57, 463–66
    part-time employment, 358–59
    retirement, 588–93
    sexual harassment, 468–69
    stress from, 501
    transitions, occupational, 470–73
    unemployment, 473–75
work-family conflict, 479–81

working memory, 223, 247, 322, 558
Working (Terkel), 452
writing skills, 247–49

X

X-rays, 68
XXX complement, 51
XYY complement, 51

Y

young adults. *See also* adulthood; love relationships; work
    alcohol and, 386–88
    cognitive development, 381–82
    college, 380–81
    death, feelings towards, 627
    death of a partner, 647
    defined, 3
    friendships of, 416–17
    growth, strength, and physical function, 384
    health of, 384–90
    leisure activities, 482
    moving back home, 519
    nutrition and, 388–89
    parents, relationship with, 58–519
    personality and identity in, 404–10
    physical development, 384–91
    smoking by, 385–86
    transition to adulthood, 378–83
young-old adults, 3. *See also* older adults

Z

zone of maximum comfort, 579
zone of maximum performance potential, 579
zone of proximal development, 155
zygote, period of the, 57–59, 70, 101